W9-APG-016

The Editor

SUSAN MCREYNOLDS ODDO is Associate Professor and Chair of the Department of Slavic Languages and Literatures at Northwestern University. She is the author of *Redemption and the Merchant God: Dostoevsky's Economy of Salvation and Antisemitism.* Her articles have appeared in *Philosophy and Literature, Partisan Review, Dostoevsky Studies, Slavic and East European Journal,* and *Literary Imagination.*

W. W. NORTON & COMPANY, INC.
Also Publishes

ENGLISH RENAISSANCE DRAMA: A NORTON ANTHOLOGY
edited by David Bevington et al.

THE NORTON ANTHOLOGY OF AFRICAN AMERICAN LITERATURE
edited by Henry Louis Gates Jr. and Nellie Y. McKay et al.

THE NORTON ANTHOLOGY OF AMERICAN LITERATURE
edited by Nina Baym et al.

THE NORTON ANTHOLOGY OF CHILDREN'S LITERATURE
edited by Jack Zipes et al.

THE NORTON ANTHOLOGY OF DRAMA
edited by J. Ellen Gainor, Stanton B. Garner Jr., and Martin Puchner

THE NORTON ANTHOLOGY OF ENGLISH LITERATURE
edited by M. H. Abrams and Stephen Greenblatt et al.

THE NORTON ANTHOLOGY OF LITERATURE BY WOMEN
edited by Sandra M. Gilbert and Susan Gubar

THE NORTON ANTHOLOGY OF MODERN AND CONTEMPORARY POETRY
edited by Jahan Ramazani, Richard Ellmann, and Robert O'Clair

THE NORTON ANTHOLOGY OF POETRY
edited by Margaret Ferguson, Mary Jo Salter, and Jon Stallworthy

THE NORTON ANTHOLOGY OF SHORT FICTION
edited by R. V. Cassill and Richard Bausch

THE NORTON ANTHOLOGY OF THEORY AND CRITICISM
edited by Vincent B. Leitch et al.

THE NORTON ANTHOLOGY OF WORLD LITERATURE
edited by Sarah Lawall et al.

THE NORTON FACSIMILE OF THE FIRST FOLIO OF SHAKESPEARE
prepared by Charlton Hinman

THE NORTON INTRODUCTION TO LITERATURE
edited by Alison Booth and Kelly J. Mays

THE NORTON READER
edited by Linda H. Peterson and John C. Brereton

THE NORTON SAMPLER
edited by Thomas Cooley

THE NORTON SHAKESPEARE, BASED ON THE OXFORD EDITION
edited by Stephen Greenblatt et al.

For a complete list of Norton Critical Editions, visit
www.wwnorton.com/college/English/nce_home.htm

A NORTON CRITICAL EDITION

Fyodor Dostoevsky

THE BROTHERS KARAMAZOV

A REVISED TRANSLATION

CONTEXTS

CRITICISM

SECOND EDITION

Edited by
SUSAN McREYNOLDS ODDO
NORTHWESTERN UNIVERSITY

Translated by
CONSTANCE GARNETT

Revised by
RALPH E. MATLAW
and
SUSAN McREYNOLDS ODDO

W · W · NORTON & COMPANY · *New York* · *London*

W. W. Norton & Company has been independent since its founding in 1923, when William Warder Norton and Mary D. Herter Norton first published lectures delivered at the People's Institute, the adult education division of New York City's Cooper Union. The firm soon expanded its program beyond the Institute, publishing books by celebrated academics from America and abroad. By midcentury, the two major pillars of Norton's publishing program—trade books and college texts—were firmly established. In the 1950s, the Norton family transferred control of the company to its employees, and today—with a staff of four hundred and a comparable number of trade, college, and professional titles published each year—W. W. Norton & Company stands as the largest and oldest publishing house owned wholly by its employees.

Copyright © 2011 by W. W. Norton & Company, Inc.

All rights reserved.
Printed in the United States of America.
First Edition.

The text of this book is composed in Fairfield Medium
with the display set in Bernhard Modern.
Book design by Antonina Krass.
Composition by Westchester Book Group.
Manufacturing by the Courier Companies—Westford division.
Production manager: Eric Pier-Hocking.

Library of Congress Cataloging-in-Publication Data

Dostoyevsky, Fyodor, 1821–1881.
 [Brat'ia Karamazovy. English]
 The Brothers Karamazov : a revised translation, contexts, criticism / Fyodor Dostoevsky ; edited by Susan McReynolds Oddo ; translated by Constance Garnett ; revised by Ralph E. Matlaw and Susan McReynolds Oddo. — 2nd ed.
   p. cm. — (A Norton critical edition)
 Includes bibliographical references.
 ISBN 978-0-393-92633-0 (pbk.)
 1. Fathers and sons—Fiction. 2. Brothers—Fiction. 3. Russia—Social life and customs—19th century—Fiction. 4. Dostoyevsky, Fyodor, 1821–1881. Brat'ia Karamazovy. I. Oddo, Susan McReynolds. II. Garnett, Constance, 1861–1946. III. Matlaw, Ralph E. IV. Title.
 PG3326.B7 2011
 891.73'3—dc22

                                                                    2011004106

W. W. Norton & Company, Inc., 500 Fifth Avenue, New York, N.Y. 10110-0017
www.wwnorton.com
W. W. Norton & Company Ltd., Castle House, 75/76 Wells Street, London W1T 3QT

1 2 3 4 5 6 7 8 9 0

Contents

Introduction

Dostoevsky's final novel caused a sensation when it began appearing as serial installments in the journal *The Russian Messenger* in January 1879. "*The Brothers Karamazov* is producing a furor—in the palace, with the public, and at public readings, which, by the way, you will see in the newspapers," he noted proudly.[1] Many of its original Russian readers experienced the novel as a call to action. When Dostoevsky read from "The Grand Inquisitor" at a benefit for students of Saint Petersburg University, he elicited such a fevered response from the audience that the government placed the chapter under a ban, forbidding any future public readings. Describing the urge for personal, social, and political renewal the novel inspired, one reader wrote:

> After the Karamazovs (and while reading it), several times I looked around in horror and was amazed that everything went on as before, that the world did not shift on its axis. . . . [T]his is something to such a degree prophetic, fiery, apocalyptic, that it seemed impossible to remain in the same place where we were yesterday, to have the same feelings that we had, to think of anything other than the terrible day of judgment.

"Dostoevsky," this reader concluded, "was indeed our social conscience!" (15:512).

The regime eyed *The Brothers Karamazov* warily, but the rest of literate Russia, including members of the Tsar's family, embraced it with fervor. Father Zosima was welcomed into the Winter Palace. At the request of Tsarevna Marya Fyodorovna, wife of the future Alexander III, Dostoevsky was invited to a small gathering in Grand Duke Konstantin's chambers in May 1880. Dostoevsky read passages from the life of Zosima before members of the ruling family; according to Konstantin, the Tsarevna had tears in her eyes (30.1:343–44).

These were the striking features of the novel's first reception: readers perceived it as a cataclysmic *event*, an eruption of something extraordinary into everyday life. The novel enjoyed broadly inclusive appeal, and many believed that it had something intensely vital and personal to say to each reader. "I cannot find words equal to my feeling of gratitude for the pleasure I experienced and the benefit my soul received," one reader wrote Dostoevsky in December 1880; "I would very much like to repeat my words of gratitude personally" (15:500). "Thanks to *The Brothers Karamazov*, it's possible to remake oneself and become better," another reader confided to her diary in November 1879 (15:495).

---

1. Unless otherwise noted, quotations from Dostoevsky's works are my translations from the *Polnoe sobranie sochinenii v tridtsati tomakh*, ed. G. M. Fridlender, et al. (Leningrad: Nauka, 1972–90). Quotation at 30.1:57. Hereafter referred to as *Pss*.

The text we know as *The Brothers Karamazov* resulted from Dostoevsky's decision to fuse his plans for two novels, works he intended to call *Atheism* and *The Life of a Great Sinner*. Elements of their prospective hero—a Russian who goes on a quest to recover his lost Christian faith—were eventually distributed among Dmitri, Ivan, and Alyosha Karamazov. Discussing his plans for *The Life of a Great Sinner* in 1870, Dostoevsky wrote: "The main question, which will run through all the parts—is the very one I have struggled with consciously and unconsciously all my life—the existence of God" (654). The fundamental outline of this "main question" posed in *The Brothers Karamazov*—whether or not God exists, and if so, why he permits innocent suffering—remains accessible, thanks to Dostoevsky's remarkable artistic strategy. The novel does not try to bring us to a decision "pro or contra," for Ivan's rebellion against God's creation or Zosima's affirmation of faith, through logical argumentation; instead, the prosecution and defense of God proceed poetically and pictorially.

"It is an enraptured and poetic chapter," Dostoevsky wrote regarding part of "The Russian Monk"; "it is not a sermon but rather a story" (661, 660). Robin Feuer Miller studies the "complexity of form" distinguishing "The Russian Monk," its narrative complexity and subtle realization of the novel's epigraph of the seed; these features of Zosima's life story, she argues, subtly defuse the power of Ivan's rebellion.[2] Despite his protestation that he has a "Euclidean" or logical mind, Ivan, like his creator Dostoevsky, harnesses the power of story and emotion. Ivan does not bring gentle Alyosha—or the reader—to the point of wanting to shoot the murderer of a little boy through rational argument; he accomplishes this through graphic images and gripping stories of children hounded, beaten, and killed.

We fall under the spell of Zosima's almost incantatory language, are entranced by the story of his elder brother Markel, and find ourselves arrested by the image of the wise old man praying before the setting sun. But we also share Ivan's indignation as he recounts the tale of Richard, whose life was taken away twice—once, symbolically, by the biological parents who gave him away as chattel to some shepherds, and then by his social family, his fellow citizens of Geneva, who chop off his head in brotherly fashion. We reel from the vision of the naked, terrified little boy ripped apart by hunting dogs before his mother's eyes. Dostoevsky presents us with contrasting images of equal power that sear themselves on our memory.

Whose fate transfixes us, whose image lasts longer: the bloody, mangled body of the little boy, or the beatific old man blessing the setting sun? What sounds resound in our memory: the ecstatic cheers of the schoolboys gathered around Alyosha, or the whimpers of the anguished little girl locked away in a cold dark privy? Dostoevsky is indeed engaging "not in communication but in manipulation," as Robert Belknap writes, but he manipulates us towards two irreconcilable states of mind with equal passion (770). *The Brothers Karamazov* compels many Dostoevsky specialists to conclude that the contest between joyful faith and tormented doubt remains inconclusive. "Both extremes," Malcolm Jones writes of this contest in Dostoevsky's life, "persisted to the end."[3]

---

2. See pp. 743 ff. of this Norton Critical Edition.
3. Malcolm Jones, "Modelling the Religious Dimension of Dostoevsky's Fictional World," in *New Zealand Slavonic Journal* 37 (2003): 41–53; quotation at p. 48.

The Brothers Karamazov doesn't provoke furor at public gatherings or elicit government decrees anymore, but it retains the power to move us. We respond to Zosima's last words, even though our translation is but a faint echo of the original, and despite our ignorance of his prototypes, figures from the Russian spiritual tradition such as Tikhon Zadonsky and the monk Parfeny. For twenty-first-century readers, the novel may be most immediately accessible as a stirring plot, on what Horst-Jürgen Gerigk calls the realist level of reading. We become engrossed in the crises of three interesting young men; entangled in a complicated web of erotic intrigues; and gripped by a court drama centered on the fate of a loathsome old man, with whom we, as readers attached to the three brothers, are intimately and uncomfortably connected. Dostoevsky confronts us with some of our deepest fears and most disturbing taboos: the death of children, feelings of aggression against our own family, and the experience of obsessive desire. These dimensions of the novel still generate raw emotional power.

Crucial dimensions of the novel remain hidden from us without expert assistance, however. "I wrote this book for *a few* (*dlya nemnogikh*) and consider it the culminating point of my work," Dostoevsky wrote in 1879 (30.1:105). This edition enables twenty-first-century English-speaking readers to join *the few* by reconstructing the novel's original contexts. Relevant information about Dostoevsky, nineteenth-century Russia, and the Christian tradition renders the novel more intelligible to those without prior knowledge of the author and the cultural and religious traditions that profoundly shaped his art. All aspects of Christian belief and practice, not just those unique to nineteenth-century Russian Orthodoxy, have been annotated.

Not surprisingly, the music of the original Russian requires the most reconstructive labor. Zosima's last words, Nathan Rosen explains, are "a mosaic of old Russian literary style": a tapestry woven from Biblical texts, the writings of Church figures such as Isaac the Syrian, and Dostoevsky's recollections of his visit to the Optyna Pustyn' monastery (p. 729). For Dostoevsky and his contemporaries, Rosen argues, the elder's words tapped into a deep well of communal memory; the process of choosing between Ivan and Zosima would have been influenced by this richly layered quality of Zosima's speech.

The novel is composed of complex speech zones, some difficult to render into English. Smerdyakov and Snegiryov use speech forms that signal servility, but their linguistic cues resist facile translation. Church Slavonic, the liturgical language of the Russian Orthodox Church, permeates the conversation of Zosima, the other monks, and, in parodied form, Fyodor Pavlovich. Rakitin's desperate desire to appear emancipated from all vestiges of traditional authority results in a crude pseudoscientific lingo, which manages to be both swaggering and cringing. The language of the unnamed narrator-chronicler captures the quality of conversational speech or inner monologue; it features the run-on sentences, repetitions, and inept or inaccurate turns of phrase that mark our conversation and thoughts, but that look odd when written down. Not everything can be entirely conveyed in translation, but the essays by Matlaw and Rosen alert readers to what they are missing, and suggest ways of appreciating recalcitrant passages.

The linguistic barrier is only the first hurdle with which today's Western reader must contend. *The Brothers Karamazov* asks to be opened up to a whole world of literary, cultural, and biographical allusions. This novel, which explores the role of memory for individuals and communities, is itself a tissue of memories, a fabric spun of threads of other texts. Its richly layered quality has inspired scholars to approach it as "a veritable cornucopia of direct and indirect quotations from other texts, both sacred and secular, ranging from the Bible to Voltaire, from Pushkin to popular songs."[4] Dostoevsky had encyclopedic ambitions for *The Brothers Karamazov*. "Before I can start on it," he wrote, "I have to read practically a whole library of atheists, Catholics, and Orthodox" (653). The modern reader, who may not be in a position to acquire Dostoevsky's vast learning, will benefit from the extensive annotations provided here.

The twenty-first century reader's path to *The Brothers Karamazov* is rendered even more daunting by the extent to which it is saturated not just with wide-ranging allusions to the Western tradition, but also with references to Dostoevsky's contemporary Russian environment and his other writings. Some of the most important memories reverberating through *The Brothers Karamazov* are of other works by Dostoevsky. One of the most important texts for this novel is his *Diary of a Writer*, the one-man monthly journal dedicated to often polemical reflections about the people and events making news in his time.[5] Many of the topical references the reader encounters in *The Brothers Karamazov* are drawn from the *Diary*, which Dostoevsky published in 1873, 1876–77, 1880, and 1881.[6] We encounter the novel as a discrete, independent text, but Dostoevsky's original readers experienced it as a serialized work sandwiched between issues of the *Diary*. William Mills Todd's essay (689) introduces modern readers to the significance of serialization for understanding Dostoevsky's art.

Discussing his philosophy of art in April 1876, Dostoevsky asserted that a writer must describe reality "down to the most trivial exactitude (historical and contemporary)" (29.2:77). He regarded the *Diary* as a laboratory for exploring the topical dilemmas he would address in *The Brothers Karamazov* as well. Both works are preoccupied with the state of the Russian family, fatherhood, child abuse, the role of the environment in character development, and the complexity of guilt and crime. The astounding quantity of cross-references invites us to ponder the relationship between these intimately linked texts; by alerting readers to the existence of these parallels, the annotations provided here open vistas onto additional layers of depth and complexity in the novel.

Dostoevsky took his role as Russia's "social conscience" seriously. He regarded *The Brothers Karamazov*, like the more overtly topical and tendentious *Diary*, as a work of political import. Zosima's faith, Dostoevsky believed, offered a solution to social as well as individual dilemmas. If I succeed with the character Zosima, he explained to his editor Nikolay Lyubimov in June 1879, "I'll accomplish something good: I'll force them

---

4. Diane Oenning Thompson, The Brothers Karamazov *and the Poetics of Memory* (Cambridge: Cambridge UP, 1991), 15.
5. All quotations from the *Diary of a Writer* are from Fyodor Dostoevsky, *A Writer's Diary*, trans. and annotated by Kenneth Lantz, with an introductory study by Gary Saul Morson (Evanston: Northwestern UP, 1994).
6. Only one issue of the *Diary* appeared in 1880; the January 1881 issue was Dostoevsky's last publication before his death at the end of that month.

to realize that a pure, ideal Christian is not something abstract, but graphically real, possible, standing before our eyes, and that Christianity is the only refuge from all its ills for the Russian land."[7] Ivan's atheism, like Zosima's faith, has political ramifications. "These convictions," Dostoevsky writes to Lyubimov regarding Ivan's views,

> are precisely that which I recognize as the synthesis of contemporary Russian anarchism. The refutation not of God, but of the meaning of His creation. All socialism comes from and began with the refutation of the meaning of historical reality and arrived at a program of destruction and anarchism (659).

Attacks on biological, divine, and political father figures, the novel suggests, are inextricable. Critics have long recognized that Ivan's resentment of a biological father such as Fyodor Pavlovich and his rebellion against the heavenly father blend together. "The image of the father," Harold Bloom writes, "is ultimately also the image of the Czar and God."[8] The revolutionary energy simmering within Smerdyakov, who claims inspiration from Ivan, threatens more than the life of Fyodor Pavlovich—it also poses a threat to the authority of the *Tsar'-batyushka*, or Tsar-father, as he was called by the Russian people.

The essays and annotations provided here reveal the extent to which the novel's spiritual dramas are intertwined with political dilemmas of the Russian 1860s and 70s. Knowledge of the novel's complex engagement of contemporary events provides crucial support for reaching informed judgments about *The Brothers Karamazov*. The reader who knows that Dostoevsky was a passionate reader of newspapers, considered his journalistic writings as important as his novels, and saturated *The Brothers Karamazov* with references to the contemporary press, especially his own *Diary of a Writer*, will be in a unique position to assess the crucial chapters "The Brothers Get Acquainted" and "Rebellion."

Ivan's indictment of God, just as much as Zosima's defense, tapped into a deep well of shared experience: his speech in these chapters is a mosaic of excerpts from the press, something that was a point of pride for Dostoevsky. Responding to accusations that Ivan's accounts of child abuse strained credulity, Dostoevsky protested to Lyubimov: "Everything my hero says in the text I sent you is based in reality. All the anecdotes about children took place, existed, were published in the press, and I can cite the places, I invented nothing" (659). Ivan's rebellion acquired immeasurable power for Dostoevsky's original audience through this blurring of fiction and reality.

Belknap's study of Rakitin, Kolya Krasotkin, and the schoolboys exemplifies how an informed reader can make sense of the cultural allusions permeating the novel. It's worth noting which passages and characters require the most glossing: Alyosha's passages require very little, whereas the conversations of Kolya and Ivan's devil, for example, call for extensive annotation. Kolya and the devil are examples of what Miller calls "second-tier

---

7. Dostoevsky was in close correspondence with Lyubimov (1830–1897), an editor at *The Russian Messenger*, during composition of the novel.
8. *Fyodor Dostoevsky's* The Brothers Karamazov, ed. and with an introduction by Harold Bloom (New York: Chelsea House, 1988), 3.

characters representing aspects or potentials of the main character."[9] Significant aspects of Ivan, Belknap demonstrates, are mirrored in Kolya and Rakitin; these second-tier characters are in turn associated with negative cultural prototypes that were familiar to Dostoevsky's readers.

Any determination about Ivan and his rebellion that fails to take these complex associations into account is based on incomplete evidence. Dostoevsky, like Dmitri's defense attorney Fetyukovich, reminds us that arguments cut both ways (in Russian one speaks of a stick with two ends). The aura of contemporary culture enhances Ivan's status—the fact that his evidence against God's creation consists largely of real child abuse cases familiar to the public gives weight to his condemnation. Yet his association with well-known public figures whose ethical standards seemed questionable to Dostoevsky and many others also undermines the status of his complaint.

The references to Biblical and sacred texts, extensively annotated here, may pose the greatest interpretive challenges, with an extraordinary diversity of opinion among experts regarding their significance. According to one school of thought, the relationship between the novel and the Biblical and sacred models it invokes is one of reflection or amplification: *The Brothers Karamazov* refers to passages from the Bible or Church Fathers in order to illustrate and expand on them, to provide these passages or teachings with the color and vitality of literary embodiment. The essay by Vetlovskaya (677), for example, argues that Dostoevsky drew on the hagiographical tradition of Saint Alexey to create Alyosha Karamazov. Through Alyosha, Vetlovskaya suggests, Dostoevsky brought aspects of an ancient sacred tradition to life.

Dostoevsky would have approved of this approach to his novel. He had pedagogical intentions for *The Brothers Karamazov*—he hoped that the invocation of figures such as Alexey and Tikhon would educate Russians about their native spiritual tradition. He modestly claimed that he was transmitting existing truth, rather than creating something new: "Perhaps I will create a grandiose, *positive*, holy figure," he wrote regarding the character who became Zosima. "Actually I won't create anything, I will merely present the real Tikhon" (654). When an anonymous mother sought his advice on how to raise her son, Dostoevsky responded: "Acquaint him with the Gospels, teach him to believe in God strictly according to the law. This is a sine qua non, otherwise he won't be a good person" (30.1:17). Responding to another correspondent who bemoaned a loss of faith, Dostoevsky advised: "Wouldn't it be best for you to read more carefully the whole of Apostle Paul? Much is said there specifically about faith, and it is not possible to say it better" (30.1:10).

The author's self-understanding may not be the best guide for interpreting the novel's relationship to religious tradition, however. It may not be possible to say it better than the Bible, but Dostoevsky was clearly compelled to say it differently. If there was anyone who didn't believe "strictly according to the law," it was Fyodor Dostoevsky and his Father Zosima, a fact that was not lost on many of Dostoevsky's contemporaries. Those who felt entitled to speak for the Russian Orthodox Church criticized core elements of Zosima's teachings—the emphasis on joy and this world, for example—as deviating from true Christian doctrine. When a charac-

9. Robin Feuer Miller, *The Brothers Karamazov: Worlds of the Novel* (New Haven: Yale UP, 2008), 49.

ter like Fyodor Pavlovich quotes sacred texts, it's obvious that he willfully misunderstands the essence of the original, resulting in blasphemy. Zosima, on the other hand, reveres sacred texts and tradition; yet he, too, is capable of unconsciously challenging their authority in his own way.

Responding to Zosima's complexity, some scholars maintain that the spiritual core of *The Brothers Karamazov* diverges radically from the religious tradition Dostoevsky inherited. These scholars point out that Zosima blatantly flouts Christian doctrine on key points such as suicide, and that he quotes Biblical passages selectively, sometimes altering their original meanings. Zosima's enthusiasm for the Book of Job, for example, is based on a highly reductive reading. "He leaves much out," Rosen observes of Zosima's version, and "what is left out is revealing: . . . Job's integrity and independence, his intellectual and spiritual energy," resulting in a rendition that is "carefully pruned of Job's defiance and intellectual challenge of God" (728). Some scholars maintain that the forms of spirituality embodied by Zosima and Alyosha were derived from diverse sources, such as Western Romanticism and Idealism; in their opinion, the traces left by these traditions predominate over the Christian elements.[1] Roger Anderson argues (733) that Zosima's beliefs contain significant elements of Slavic paganism, and owe more to mythic consciousness than Christian theology.

Readers have always sought Dostoevsky in *The Brothers Karamazov*. "I put much of myself and what is mine into it," he wrote of this novel (30.1:214). Ivan was modeled on many contemporary figures, but the most significant source for this character was probably Dostoevsky himself, as Miller points out: "Dostoevsky's hero, like all the Karamazovs, without exception, is also profoundly autobiographical."[2] This edition supplies readers with relevant biographical information that suggests intriguing parallels linking Dostoevsky with his characters. One of the most obvious points of similarity between Dostoevsky and Ivan is their preoccupation with children. Dostoevsky's concern for children—his own, those he encountered on the street, those he read about in newspaper accounts of crimes committed by and against children, those whose fates he followed at sensational trials—stands at the center of his spiritual biography and writings.

A specific type of child occupies center stage in this novel: the dead child. Dostoevsky and his wife Anna Grigoryevna were familiar with the loss of children. Their first child, a daughter named Sofya, died in infancy in 1868; their second son, Alexey, died in May 1878, when Dostoevsky was in the early stages of work on *The Brothers Karamazov*. Alexey Dostoevsky, like the little boy bemoaned by the peasant mother in the chapter "Peasant Women Who Have Faith," died three months before his third birthday—"three years all but three months," wails that inconsolable parent (47). "The outpouring of grief for a dead, injured, or suffering child constitutes the fundamental groundswell to this novel," Miller writes; "Dostoevsky instilled in *The Brothers Karamazov* his own grief and love for his dead child, Alexey."[3] Devastated by his son's death, Dostoevsky sought solace from a visit to Optyna Pustyn', where he encountered the elder Amvrosy, a prototype for Father Zosima.

1. See for example Steven Cassedy, *Dostoevsky's Religion* (Stanford: Stanford UP, 2005).
2. Miller, *Worlds of the Novel*, 55.
3. Ibid. p. 39.

The novel is unquestionably imbued with Dostoevsky's parental grief, but this mourning is counterbalanced by a fervent belief in—or is it insistence on?—resurrection. Throughout his life, Dostoevsky asserted that belief in immortality was a cornerstone of Christian faith. In his attempts to convince himself and others, he sometimes pursued an interesting line of argument, the essence of which is suggested by characters in the novel and outlined in one of his letters included here (656). In this letter, written during the early stages of work on *The Brothers Karamazov,* Dostoevsky deduces proof of immortality through the following argument: the law of self-preservation or self-interest (egoism) obtains on earth, but human beings sense the existence of another realm, where this law is nullified. "Man strives on earth toward an ideal that is *contrary* to his nature," he had written in his 1864 notebooks (20:175). The fact that we sense the possibility of transcending this law and yearn to do so is evidence that we do not belong entirely to the earth or fall exclusively under its jurisdiction. According to Dostoevsky, the desire to transcend the self—the desire to accede to a law higher than that of self-preservation—proves that we are not doomed to the death sentence decreed on earth.

One key aspect of Dostoevsky's belief in immortality, which he imputes to Alyosha Karamazov, might be overlooked or misunderstood without annotation. You have done half the work toward being saved, Alyosha tells Ivan, because you love life; now you must complete the second half: you must "raise up your dead, who perhaps have not died at all" (200). This enigmatic comment invites close scrutiny. According to Alyosha, Ivan cannot be saved until he adopts a certain relationship to the resurrection of his forefathers—he, Ivan, must take responsibility for their resurrection and raise them up. In a letter of March 1878, Dostoevsky asserted that the living must bring about the resurrection of their forebears: we have "the duty of resurrecting ancestors who lived before," he claimed. It would be a mistake to conceive of this resurrection "intellectually, allegorically," he cautioned, and insisted that

> the resurrection will be real, personal (*real'noe, lichnoe*), that the abyss separating us from the souls of our ancestors will be filled in, . . . and they will be resurrected not only in our consciousness, not allegorically, but actually (*deistvitel'no*), individually (*lichno*), materially in bodies (*real'no v telakh*) (30.1:14–15).

Alyosha's seemingly offhand comment sheds light on an essential quality of Dostoevsky's faith. Dostoevsky consistently defended the miraculous within Christianity, rebutting any claims that Christian faith could be a matter of morals or ethics, shorn of belief in the divinity of Christ or personal resurrection.[4]

Dostoevsky's voice resounds throughout this deeply autobiographical novel, but other voices speak as well. One of Dostoevsky's most famous readers, the Russian philosopher and literary critic Mikhail Bakhtin (1895–1975), characterized Dostoevsky as a profoundly dialogical writer who orchestrated open conversations among different viewpoints in his

---

4. Dostoevsky's fervent belief in literal resurrection has many points in common with the views of his contemporary, the philosopher Nikolay Fyodorov (1828–1903). One of Fyodorov's followers sent Dostoevsky selections from his writings in 1876 and 1877; Dostoevsky composed the letter cited here as a response to that material.

novels. Bakhtin's contention that Dostoevsky's novels are polyphonic or multi-voiced has had a considerable impact on our understanding of Dostoevsky, and serious engagement with *The Brothers Karamazov* must grapple with Bakhtin's legacy. Ulrich Schmid's essay (776) suggests that we can enrich our appreciation of the polyphonic quality of Dostoevsky's novels by realizing that what appears to be dialogue or debate among different ideological viewpoints, represented by different characters, may in fact be a form of monologue. The Karamazov brothers, Schmid argues, function as components of "complex consciousnesses," and the dialogue among them can be most accurately understood as a form of monologue carried out by elements of a higher order consciousness.

Two of the most important characters, Ivan and Alyosha, are authors themselves, and their texts—*The Grand Inquisitor* and *Notes of the Life in God of the Deceased Hieromonk, the Elder Zosima, Taken from His Own Words by Alexey Fyodorovich Karamazov*—form the core of the novel. Dostoevsky stressed Alyosha's independence as a writer. "There is introduced into the novel as it were a foreign document (the notes of Alexey Karamazov)," he explained to Lyubimov in August 1879, "and this document is copied down by Alexey Karamazov in his own way" (30.1:103). Dostoevsky cedes some of the most important passages in *The Brothers Karamazov* to other authors with distinct voices.

One task of this edition is to orchestrate a dialogue among readers. The critical essays were selected not only because they shed light on important dimensions of the novel, but also because their juxtaposition vividly illustrates the multiplicity of perspectives *The Brothers Karamazov* continues to inspire. "Where we are involved with Dostoevsky versus Dostoevsky," Robert Louis Jackson writes, "—and that is almost always the case in his major novels—there is not likely to be an answer, or voice, that definitively drowns out the other contending voices."[5] When a novel as complex as *The Brothers Karamazov* is under consideration, these essays demonstrate, no single voice can have the last word. The dialogical quality of Dostoevsky's writing produces dialogue among his readers.

The variety of informed responses this text can support is exemplified here by the varied appraisals of Smerdyakov and the contest between Ivan and Zosima. Scholars agree that *The Brothers Karamazov* represents a powerful investigation into the sources of human behavior, exploring what drives some individuals to transgress the most sacred bonds and what holds others back. The essays by Belknap, Gerigk, Golstein, and Kantor offer very different assessments of each brother's role in the violence. Like Miller, Rosen focuses on properties of the text that sway the reader toward agreement with Zosima, arguing that the artistic picture crafted by Zosima wins the debate with Ivan about God. Morson, on the other hand, declares that Ivan definitively repudiates both God (as defended by Zosima), and Christ (as defended by Alyosha), but argues that the novel shifts the locus of debate, from an argument about the Father and Son to a victory for the Holy Spirit.

For all its complexity, there is no question that *The Brothers Karamazov* ends with joy. The rapturous hope that rings through the final scene can be

---

5. Robert Louis Jackson, "Alyosha's Speech at the Stone," in *A New Word on* The Brothers Karamazov, ed. Robert Louis Jackson (Evanston: Northwestern UP, 2004), 234.

found in Dostoevsky's correspondence from this period as well. "There's no doubt that new people are coming (and will soon arrive), so there is no cause for grieving and lamenting. Let us be worthy to recognize and meet them," he exhorts a correspondent in a letter from March 1878 (30.1:19). The conclusion of *The Brothers Karamazov* brings us to ecstatic heights, but it also leaves us with the question: how do we make ourselves worthy to meet these new people, the newly articulate and charismatic Alyosha and the beaming boys gathered around him? As he was composing the novel, Dostoevsky wrote in his notebooks "we are all, to the last man, Fyodor Pavlovichs" (667). How, we must ask ourselves when the rapture subsides, will we transcend our inner Fyodor Pavlovich and be worthy to partake of the joy the novel promises?

"Every day and every hour, every minute, walk around yourself and watch yourself, and see that your image is a seemly one," Zosima commands the monks (275). The essence of *The Brothers Karamazov* is strict and demanding, calling for constant self-scrutiny and self-control. Regarding the "loving humility" Zosima urges, Caryl Emerson writes: "there is nothing passive or easy about this humility, Zosima reminds us. It is extremely hard work."[6] In *The Brothers Karamazov*, all are called upon to manifest the reality of goodness, which must emerge from our daily myriad interactions. When "the heavens give no pledge," as Ivan says, quoting Schiller, the existence of goodness is always at stake and dependent on each of us. Anyone in a position to influence others—and that, according to this novel, is all of us, at all times in our daily lives—must constantly model good behavior.

This emphasis on practicing or exemplifying goodness, rather than asserting that one is good or demanding respect, has interesting implications for the novel's approach to biological parents and the divine father, whose goodness Ivan calls into question. Parents especially, Dostoevsky cautions, flout this injunction at their own risk. Before he composed the tragic story of Fyodor Pavlovich, Dostoevsky admonished a real parent with the dangerous possibility that her child could cease to love her. "Imagine that your child . . . comes to you . . . and asks you or his father such a question: 'Why should I love you and why should this be my duty?'" Dostoevsky warns the mother to whom he recommended the Bible (657) that she must constantly model good conduct, acting so that the question never arises for her child: "Be good, and let your child understand that you are good (himself, without hints) . . . And for this he will remember your image with great respect his whole life" (657). The decision to love is a choice. Any attempt to demand love or deference as parental privileges, Dostoevsky explains to a real parent while composing *The Brothers Karamazov*, is doomed to failure.

In his retelling of the Book of Job, Zosima overlooks Job's challenge to God, but he also omits God's reaction to Job's rebellion. As Rosen points out, Zosima neglects to mention the "power of coercion" God exercises in the Bible. No voice from the whirlwind asserts its authority in *The Brothers Karamazov*; assertion and coercion are emphatically rejected as the bases for relations between the divine father and his children as well as

---

6. Caryl Emerson, "Zosima's 'Mysterious Visitor': Again Bakhtin on Dostoevsky, and Dostoevsky on Heaven and Hell," in Jackson, *A New Word on* The Brothers Karamazov, 155–79; quotation at p. 157.

between biological parents and children.[7] In the absence of divine authority, an absence or vacuum implied by Zosima's decision to pass over in silence the coercive power present in the Book of Job, authority is transferred to human beings. The power of the Biblical creator or an authority figure such as the Grand Inquisitor is transformed into individual responsibility, into what Miller calls "a radically egalitarian responsibility of each for all and all for each."[8]

Dostoevsky sensed what this novel would mean for his legacy, and suffered while writing it. "It's necessary to finish it well, to polish it like a jewel, but it's a difficult and risky thing, it depletes my strength," he wrote his wife in August 1879. "But it's also fateful: it must establish my name, otherwise there is no hope" (30.1:109). After completing *The Brothers Karamazov*, he confessed:

> in some difficult moments of inner accounting I often realize with pain that I literally have not expressed a twentieth of what I wanted, and perhaps could express. At these times the only thing that saves me is the hope that God will someday send enough inspiration and strength so that I will express myself fully, in a word, that I will speak out everything that is contained in my heart and fantasy . . . I feel that there is more hidden in me than I have been able to express till now as a writer (30.1:148).

Despite more than one hundred years of engagement with *The Brothers Karamazov*, we still have not apprehended everything it has to offer. This volume seeks to inspire new generations to mine its depths and equips them with the tools to do so.

Acknowledgments

I am grateful to many individuals for their help in the preparation of this new edition. Katherine Bowers, Tatiana Filimonova, Lisa Yountchi, and Natalie Zelensky assisted with the translation and footnotes. Robin Feuer Miller, Gary Saul Morson, and William Mills Todd III have provided incalculable inspiration in all things Dostoevskian. Carol Bemis, Rivka Genesen, Ben Reynolds, and Eric Pier-Hocking have expertly and patiently guided it through to completion.

7. For more on the theological significance of the novel's rejection of coercion, see Paul Contino: "one of the key thematic affirmations of *The Brothers Karamazov* is the sacred dignity of human freedom. Dostoevsky's respect for his character's freedom is analogous to divine respect for human freedom" in Paul J. Contino, "Incarnational Realism and the Case for Casuistry: Dmitry Karamazov's Escape." In *Dostoevsky's Brothers Karamazov: Art, Creativity, and Spirituality*. Eds. Predrag Cicovacki and Maria Granik. Heidelberg, Germany: Universitätsverlag Winter, 2010. Quotation at p. 145.
8. Ibid. p. 76.

Names in *The Brothers Karamazov*

Russians have three names: a first, or given name; a patronymic; and a last, or family name. Patronymics are derived from the first name of the father and are modified according to gender. A son acquires his father's first name with the ending -ovich / -evich; a daughter acquires her father's name with the ending -ovna / -evna. For example, the Karamazov brothers each have a first name—Dmitri, Ivan, and Alexey—and all receive the patronymic Fyodorovich from their father, Fyodor. He in turn received the patronymic Pavlovich from his father, whose first name must have been Pavel (Russian for Paul). If there were a Karamazov sister, her patronymic would be Fyodorovna. Family names, like patronymics, are declined according to gender. Liza Khokhlakova's deceased father would have used the name Khokhlakov (without the feminine ending); a Karamazov sister would bear the name Karamazova.

Character Names

Karamazov
Kará is the Turkish root for *black*. The Russian root *maz'* signifies tar or grease; *mazat'* means to smear, coat, paint, or soil. The name Karamazov thus means roughly "black smear." It may also evoke the Russian word *chernomazyi* (swarthy). The Russian root for *black* is *chern*, so Ilyusha's mother is translating from Turkish to Russian when she calls Alyosha "Chernomazov" (see p. 175).

Fyodor Pavlovich Karamazov
Fyodor is the Russian form of Theodore (derived from Greek meaning "gift of God").

Dmitri Fyodorovich Karamazov (*Mitya, Mitka, Mitenka*)
The name Dmitri is derived from the ancient Greek goddess of agriculture, Demeter. Dmitri is a popular Russian name, associated with saints worshipped in the Eastern Orthodox Church and with many figures from Russian history.

Ivan Fyodorovich Karamazov (*Vanya, Vanka, Vanechka*)
Ivan is the Russian form of John.

Alexey Fyodorovich Karamazov (*Alyosha, Alyoshka, Alyoshechka, Lyosha, Lyoshechka*)
Alexey is the name of one of the most beloved saints in the Russian Orthodox Church. (see p. 48.)

Pavel Fyodorovich Smerdyakov
Smerd has several meanings in Russian: a bad smell, a man of low origins, a slave or serf. *Smerdet'* means to stink.

Sophya Ivanovna
Sophya means divine wisdom in Greek. It can also be pronounced Sophya, with end stress; this sounds more sophisticated to Russian ears and is closer to the Greek pronunciation.

Agrafena Alexandrova Svetlova (*Grushenka, Grusha*)
Svet is Russian for light, bright; *grusha* means pear.

Katerina Ivanovna Verkhovtseva (*Katya, Katenka*)
Verkh means upper, supreme, proud in Russian; *verkhovnyi* means supreme.

Liza Khokhlakova (*Lise*)
Khokhol means the crest of a bird or a topknot in Russian. Lise is the French form of Liza; upper-class Russians like the Khokhlakovs often spoke French at home and adopted French versions of their names.

Mikhail Rakitin (*Misha*)
Rakitnik means broom bush in Russian.

Ilyusha Snegiryov (*Ilyushechka*)
Ilyusha and Ilyushecka are nicknames for Il'ya (Russian for Elias or Elijah). *Sneg* means snow in Russian; *snegir'* means bullfinch.

Herzenstube
Pronounced "Gertsenshtube" in Russian. *Herz* is heart in German; *Stube* is room or chamber.

Fetyukovich
The name implies *blockhead* in Russian.

Zosima
Pronounced "Zasima" in Russian. A great elder and ascetic, Zosimas of Palestine (c. 460–560; also spelled Zosimus or Zosima) is recognized as a saint in Eastern Orthodox Christianity. While fasting and praying in the desert in preparation for Lent, he encountered St. Mary of Egypt (see p. 254).

Kolya Krasotkin
Kolya is the short form of Nikolai (Nicholas). Krasota means *beauty* in Russian.

Grigory Vasil'yevich Kutuzov
The name Grigory (Russian for Gregory) is derived from Greek meaning watchful or awake. Russian readers would associate the name Kutuzov with Field Marshal Mikhail Kutuzov (1745–1813), the military hero whose tactics contributed to Russia's defeat of Napoleon in 1812.

Martha Ignat' yevna Kutuzova
Her name may allude to the Martha in the Gospels: see John 11.1–28. (All references to the Bible are to the King James Version.)

Maximov

Pyotr Alexandrovich Miüsov

Perkhotin

Nicknames

Russian is rich in nicknames and diminutives. Papa and mama, for example, yield a variety of forms, such as *papenka/mamenka* and *papasha/mamasha*. The longer the nickname, the more intimate and affectionate it is: for example, Mitenka and Ilyushechka are more diminutive and intimate than Mitya and Ilyusha.

Place Names

Chermashnya
Stems from the Slavonic word for vermillion or red. Dostoevsky's father bought a village named Chermashnya in 1832.

Mokroe
Means wet in Russian.

Sukhoi Posyolok
Means dry hamlet in Russian.

Skotoprigon'evsk
Based on the word *skotoprigonka* (stockyard) derived from *skot*, Russian for cattle or livestock.

The Karamazov Family Tree

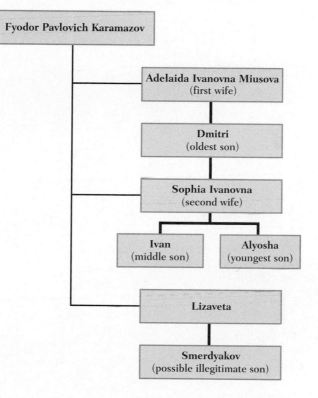

The Text of
THE BROTHERS
KARAMAZOV

Dedicated to
*Anna Grigoryevna Dostoevskaya**

*"Verily, verily, I say unto you, except a corn of wheat fall into the ground
and die, it abideth alone: but if it die, it bringeth forth much fruit."*
John 12.24

*Dostoevsky's second wife, born Snitkina (1846–1918).

Contents of *The Brothers Karamazov*

PART FOUR

From the Author

In beginning the life story[1] of my hero, Alexey Fyodorovich Karamazov, I find myself in somewhat of a quandary. Namely: although I call Alexey Fyodorovich my hero, still I myself know that he is by no means a great man, and hence I foresee such unavoidable questions as these: What is so remarkable about your Alexey Fyodorovich, that you have chosen him as your hero? What has he done? What is he known for, and by whom? Why should I, the reader, waste time learning the facts of his life?

The last question is the most fateful, for to it I can only answer: "Perhaps you will see for yourself from the novel." Well, suppose you read the novel, and fail to see, and so do not agree that my Alexey Fyodorovich is remarkable? I say this because unhappily I foresee it. For me he is remarkable, but I doubt strongly whether I shall succeed in proving this to the reader. The thing is, perhaps, that he is a protagonist, but a vague and undefined protagonist. And, in truth, in times such as ours it would be strange to require clarity of people. One thing, I dare say, is fairly certain: this man is odd, even eccentric. But oddness and eccentricity interfere rather than help, especially when everyone is trying to put the particulars together and to find some sort of common meaning in the general confusion. In most cases the eccentric is a particularity, a separate element. Isn't that so?

Now if you do not agree with this last thesis and answer, "Not so," or "It isn't always so," then I might perhaps become encouraged about the significance of my hero, Alexey Fyodorovich. For not only is an eccentric "not always" a particularity and a separate element, but, on the contrary, it happens sometimes that such a person, I dare say, carries within himself the very heart of the whole, and the rest of the men of his epoch have for some reason been temporarily torn from it, as if by a gust of wind . . .

Still, I should not have plunged into these quite uninteresting and confused explanations and should have begun quite simply, without introduction: If they like it, they will read it; but the trouble is that I have two novels and only one life story. The main novel is the second—it is the action of my hero in our day, at the very present time.[2] The first novel takes place thirteen years ago, and it is hardly even a novel, but only one moment in my hero's early youth.[3] I cannot do without this first novel, because much in the second novel would be unintelligible without it. But in this way my original difficulty is rendered still more complicated: if I, that is, the biographer himself, find that even one novel might perhaps be

---

1. "Life story" is translated from *zhizneopisanie*, a term that refers to highly stylized hagiographies of Russian Orthodox saints. For the impact of Russian Orthodox hagiography on the composition of *The Brothers Karamazov*, see Vetlovskaya, "Alyosha Karamazov and the Hagiographic Hero" (p. 677).
2. According to Dostoevsky's second wife, Anna Grigoryevna, he planned to write a sequel to *The Brothers Karamazov*. The projected sequel is referred to here as "the main novel," with the existing novel a prequel to what Dostoevsky intended to be the main work. How Dostoevsky's plans for a second novel might have influenced composition of *The Brothers Karamazov* is discussed in Vetlovskaya. For a hypothetical reconstruction of Dostoevsky's plans for the second novel, see James Rice, "Dostoevsky's Endgame: The Projected Sequel to *The Brothers Karamazov*" in *Russian History / Histoire Russe* 33, No. 1 (Spring 2006): 46–62.
3. *The Brothers Karamazov* was first published as a series of installments in the journal *The Russian Messenger* (*Russkii vestnik*) from January 1879 to November 1880. The events described here, "thirteen years ago," would thus have taken place in 1866. The significance of serialization for composition of the novel is discussed in Todd, "*The Brothers Karamazov* and the Poetics of Serial Publication," p. 689.

superfluous for such a modest and undefined hero, then how can I appear with two, and how on my part can I justify such presumption?

Finding myself lost in the solution of these questions, I decide to bypass them with no solution at all. Of course, the astute reader has long since guessed that from the very first I was leading up to this, and was annoyed with me for wasting fruitless words and precious time. To this, I shall answer explicitly: I was spending fruitless words and precious time, first, out of courtesy, and second, out of shrewdness: "Still," the reader might say, "he has forewarned us of something." Indeed, I am actually glad that my novel has of itself split into two narratives, "with essential unity of the whole": having become acquainted with the first tale, the reader will then decide for himself whether it is worth his while to attempt the second. Of course, no one is bound by anything—he can abandon the book at the second page of the first story, and never open it again. But then, you know, there are those considerate readers who absolutely must read to the end, so as not to be mistaken in their impartial judgment; such, for example, are all the Russian critics. It is before this type of person that my heart somehow becomes lighter: despite all their careful exactness and conscientiousness, I nevertheless give them a perfectly legitimate pretext to abandon the story at the novel's first episode. Well, there is the whole foreword. I completely agree that it is superfluous, but since it has already been written, let it stand.

And now to business.

Part One

Book One

THE HISTORY OF A CERTAIN LITTLE FAMILY

Chapter I

Fyodor Pavlovich Karamazov

Alexey Fyodorovich Karamazov was the third son of Fyodor Pavlovich Karamazov, a landowner well known in our district in his own day (and still remembered among us) owing to his tragic and obscure death, which happened exactly thirteen years ago and which I shall describe in its proper place.[1] For the present I will only say that this "landowner" (for so we used to call him, although he hardly lived on his own estate at all) was a strange type, yet one pretty frequently to be met with, precisely the type of person who is not only trashy and depraved, but also without any sense—but he was one of those senseless people, however, who know how to take care of their little worldly business quite well, and, apparently, nothing else. Fyodor Pavlovich, for instance, began with next to nothing, he was a very small landowner, he ran to dine at other men's tables, and fastened on to them as a sponger, yet at his death it appeared that he had a hundred thousand rubles in hard cash.[2] At the same time he was all his life one of the most senseless madcaps in our whole district. I repeat: it was not stupidity; the majority of these madcaps are shrewd and intelligent enough—but just senselessness, and a special, national form of it.

He was married twice and had three sons: the eldest, Dmitri, by his first wife, and the other two, Ivan and Alexey, by his second. Fyodor Pavlovich's first wife belonged to a fairly rich and distinguished noble family, also landowners in our district, the Miüsovs. How it came to pass that an heiress, who was also a beauty, and moreover one of those lively, intelligent girls not at all uncommon in this generation, but sometimes also to be found in the last, could have married such an insignificant "puny fellow," as everyone called him, I won't attempt to explain. But I knew a

1. Before 1861, Russian society was divided into hereditary classes: the nobility (also referred to as landowners), merchants, clergy, and peasants or serfs. Members of the nobility such as Fyodor Pavlovich enjoyed many social and economic privileges, such as the right to own estates; until the Emancipation of 1861, they also had the right to own serfs.
2. The basic units of Russian currency are the ruble and kopeck. One ruble is worth 100 kopecks. It is difficult to calculate the purchasing power of specific sums of money in nineteenth-century Russia, but Dostoevsky's novels provide some clues. In *Crime and Punishment* (1866), Marmeladov is able to support a wife and three children on a salary of twenty-three rubles per month; a 3,000-ruble inheritance from Martha Petrovna Svidrigailova enables Raskolnikov's sister Dunya to make a new start in life for herself, her mother, and her fiancé Razumikhin. Fyodor Pavlovich's capital of 100,000 rubles was thus a colossal sum.

young lady, still of the "romantic" generation before the last,[3] who after some years of enigmatic love for a gentleman, whom she might quite easily have married at any moment, invented insuperable obstacles to their union, and ended by throwing herself one stormy night into a rather deep and rapid river from a high bank, almost a precipice, and so perished, entirely to satisfy her own caprice, and to be like Shakespeare's Ophelia, and indeed, if this precipice, a chosen and favorite spot of hers, had been less picturesque, if there had been a prosaic flat bank in its place, most likely the suicide would never have taken place.[4] This is a true fact, and one must assume that in our Russian life, in the last two or three generations, there have been not a few such facts or ones similar to it. In the same way the act of Adelaïda Ivanovna Miüsova was no doubt an echo of foreign ideas and was also due to the irritation caused by lack of mental freedom.[5] She, perhaps, wanted to assert feminine independence, to go against social conventions, against the despotism of her family and birth, and an obliging imagination persuaded her, if only briefly, that Fyodor Pavlovich, in spite of his rank as a sponger, nevertheless was one of the boldest and most ironical people of that epoch that was transitional to everything better, when he was actually just an evil buffoon, and nothing more. There was also piquancy, in that the affair began with elopement, which greatly flattered Adelaïda Ivanovna. Fyodor Pavlovich's social position made him quite ready for any such enterprises at the time, for he passionately desired to make a career one way or another; to attach himself to a good family and get a dowry was very alluring. As for mutual love, it did not, it seems, exist at all—not on the bride's part, nor on his, even despite the beauty of Adelaïda Ivanovna. This was, perhaps, a unique case of the kind in the life of Fyodor Pavlovich, who was a most sensuous person all his life, ready to run after any skirt, if it gave him any encouragement. She seems to have been the only woman who made no particular impression on him, sensually speaking.

Adelaïda Ivanovna, immediately after the elopement, instantly realized that she simply despised her husband, and nothing more. Accordingly, the consequences of the marriage revealed themselves extraordinarily quickly. Although the family actually accepted the event pretty quickly, and apportioned the runaway her dowry, the spouses began to lead a most disorderly life and there were everlasting scenes between them. It was said that the young wife showed incomparably more nobility and loftiness than Fyodor Pavlovich, who, as is now known, got hold of all her money, some twenty-five thousand rubles, as soon as she received it, so that those thousands were lost to her for ever. The little village and the rather fine town house which formed part of her dowry he did his utmost for a long time to transfer to his name, by means of some deed of conveyance, and he probably would have succeeded simply due to the contempt and disgust, so to say, that he constantly aroused in his spouse with his shameless

3. Romanticism was a nineteenth-century artistic and cultural movement that valorized passionate emotion, connection to nature, and national identity. In Russia the romantic generation usually refers to the generation of the 1840s.
4. Ophelia, a character in Shakespeare's tragedy *Hamlet* (c. 1603), drowns herself partly because of her unhappy love for the title character. Dostoevsky owned a complete edition of Shakespeare's dramatic works in Russian translation.
5. This line includes a slightly altered phrase from the poem "Do Not Believe in Yourself" (*Ne ver' sebe*, 1839) by the Russian Romantic poet and novelist Mikhail Lermontov (1814–1841).

extortions and entreaties, simply from her emotional exhaustion, just to be rid of him. But, fortunately, Adelaïda Ivanovna's family intervened and put a stop to the swindling. It is known for a fact that frequent fights took place between the husband and wife, but according to legend it was not Fyodor Pavlovich who did the beating, but Adelaïda Ivanovna, a hot-tempered, bold, dark-browed, impatient woman, possessed of remarkable physical strength. Finally she left the house and ran away from Fyodor Pavlovich with a destitute seminarian,[6] leaving three-year-old Mitya on her husband's hands. Fyodor Pavlovich immediately introduced a regular harem into the house and abandoned himself to orgies of drunkenness, and in the intermissions he would drive all over the province, complaining tearfully to each and all of Adelaïda Ivanovna's having left him, going into details too disgraceful for a husband to mention in regard to his own married life. Most of all, it seemed pleasant and even flattering to him to play the ridiculous role of the injured husband and to recount the details of his insult even with relish and embellishments. "One would think that you'd got a promotion, Fyodor Pavlovich, you seem so pleased in spite of your sorrow," scoffers said to him. Many even added that he was glad to appear once more in the role of buffoon, and that it was simply to make it funnier that he pretended to be unaware of his ludicrous position. But who knows, maybe it was just naïve of him. At last he succeeded in finding the trail of the runaway. The poor woman turned out to be in Petersburg, where she had gone with her seminarian, and where she had thrown herself into a life of complete emancipation. Fyodor Pavlovich at once began bustling about and making preparations to go to Petersburg—for what reason, he himself could not have said. He would perhaps have really gone; but having determined to do so he felt at once entitled to fortify himself for the journey by throwing himself into another bout of reckless drinking. And just at that time his wife's family received the news of her death in Petersburg. She somehow suddenly died, somewhere in a garret, according to one story—of typhus; or according to another version—of starvation. Fyodor Pavlovich was drunk when he heard of his wife's death; they say that he ran out into the street and began shouting with joy, raising his hands to Heaven: "Lord, now lettest Thou Thy servant depart in peace,"[7] but according to others he wept without restraint like a little child, so much so, they say, that it was pitiful to look at him, in spite of the repulsion he inspired. It is quite possible that both versions were true, that is, that he rejoiced at his release, and at the same time wept for her who released him—both at the same time. In most cases, people, even the wicked, are much more naïve and simple-hearted than we suppose. And we ourselves are, too.

---

6. Seminarians, or divinity students, attended theological seminaries that prepared them to serve as clergy in the Orthodox Church. Dostoevsky's readers would have assumed that a seminarian was poor and uncouth and espoused a materialistic worldview. Many seminarians abandoned their religious studies and became involved in revolutionary activities.
7. According to the Gospel of Luke, it was prophesied to Simeon of Jerusalem that he would not die before seeing Christ. When the baby Jesus was carried into the temple, Simeon took him in his arms and said "Lord, now lettest thou thy servant depart in peace, according to thy word" (Luke 2.29). This passage from Luke forms the basis of a prayer, the Song of Simeon, in the Orthodox liturgy.

Chapter II

He Gets Rid of His Eldest Son

Of course, you can imagine what kind of father such a man would be and how he would raise his children. His behavior as a father was exactly what might be expected, that is, he wholly and utterly abandoned his child by Adelaïda Ivanovna, not from malice towards him or because of any wounded matrimonial feelings, but simply because he completely forgot him. While he was wearying everyone with his tears and complaints, and turning his house into a sink of debauchery, a faithful servant of the family, Grigory, took the three-year-old Mitya into his care, and if he hadn't looked after him, then, perhaps, there would have been no one even to change the child's little shirt.

It happened moreover that the child's relations on his mother's side also seemed to forget about him at first. His grandfather, that is Mr. Miüsov himself, Adelaïda Ivanovna's father, was then no longer living; his widowed spouse, Mitya's grandmother, had moved to Moscow, and was seriously ill, while the sisters were married, so that Mitya remained for almost a whole year in old Grigory's charge and lived with him in the servant's cottage. Even if his papasha had remembered him, however (he could not, indeed, have been altogether unaware of his existence), he himself would have sent him back to the cottage, as the child would only have been in the way of his debaucheries. But it so happened that a cousin of the late Adelaïda Ivanovna returned from Paris, Pyotr Alexandrovich Miüsov, who afterwards lived abroad for many years, but at that time he was still quite a young man, distinguished among the Miüsovs, enlightened, a man of the capitals and foreign lands, moreover a lifelong European, and toward the end of his life a liberal of the forties and fifties.[8] In the course of his career he had come into contact with many of the most Liberal men of his epoch, both in Russia and abroad. He had known Proudhon and Bakunin personally, and, when he was already near the end of his journeys, he especially liked to recall and describe the three days of the February 1848 revolution in Paris, hinting that he himself had almost been a participant on the barricades.[9] This was one of the most comforting recollections of his youth. He had an independent property of about a thousand souls, to reckon in the old style.[1] His splendid estate lay on the outskirts of our little town

8. Imperial Russia had two capital cities, Moscow and Saint Petersburg. Nineteenth-century Russian liberals sought the adoption of certain features of Western government, such as a constitution and the separation of church and state. Association with the capitals, life abroad, enlightenment, and liberalism identifies Miüsov as a privileged, educated Russian noble.
9. A socialist and one of the founders of anarchism, the French political philosopher and economist Pierre-Joseph Proudhon (1809–1865) was well-known in Russia. Mikhail Bakunin (1814–1876) was a Russian revolutionary and anarchist who spent much of his life in Western Europe. While living in Geneva, Dostoevsky attended the 1867 Congress of the League of Peace and Freedom, where Bakunin spoke. Dostoevsky expressed extremely critical views of the Congress in an 1867 letter to his niece Sophya Ivanova (Pss 28.2:224). His attitude towards Bakuninites is discussed in Kantor, "Pavel Smerdyakov and Ivan Karamazov: The Problem of Temptation" (see p. 696). The Paris Revolution of February 1848 refers to the overthrow of King Louis-Philippe I of France. Some Russian émigrés took part in the street battles, and liberal "men of the forties" such as Miüsov regarded participation in the barricades as a mark of distinction.
1. Before the emancipation of the serfs in 1861, the value of an estate was calculated by the number of adult male serfs, referred to as "souls," living on it. An estate of one thousand souls was a sizable property.

and bordered on the lands of our famous monastery,[2] with which Pyotr Alexandrovich began an endless lawsuit, almost as soon as he came into his inheritance, concerning the rights of fishing in the river or woodcutting in the forest, I don't know exactly which, he even considered it his civic and enlightened duty to begin a court case against the "clericals."[3] Hearing all about Adelaïda Ivanovna, whom he, of course, remembered, and in whom he had at one time been interested, and learning of the existence of Mitya, he intervened, in spite of all his youthful indignation and contempt for Fyodor Pavlovich. He made Fyodor Pavlovich's acquaintance for the first time. He declared to him straight off that he wished to undertake the child's education. Long afterwards he used to recount, as a characteristic trait of the man, that when he began to speak to Fyodor Pavlovich about Mitya, for some time he looked completely uncomprehending, as though he had no idea what child they were talking about, and even as though he seemed surprised that he had a young son somewhere in the house. If there may have been some exaggeration in Pyotr Alexandrovich's story, still there must have been something resembling the truth. But Fyodor Pavlovich really was all his life fond of acting, of suddenly playing an unexpected part in front of you, and, most importantly, sometimes without any motive for doing so, even to his own direct disadvantage, as, for instance, in the present case. This trait, however, is characteristic of a very great number of people, and even some very intelligent ones, not like Fyodor Pavlovich. Pyotr Alexandrovich carried the business through vigorously and was even appointed (along with Fyodor Pavlovich) joint guardian of the child, who had a small property, a house and land, left him by his mother. Mitya did in fact pass into the keeping of his mother's cousin, but the latter had no family of his own, and, having arranged and secured the revenues of his estates, he was in a hurry to return to Paris for a long time, and so entrusted the child to one of his own mother's cousins, a Moscow lady. It so happened that, having settled in Paris, he too forgot about the child, especially with the advent of that February Revolution, which so struck his imagination and which he could not forget for the rest of his life. The Moscow lady died, and Mitya passed into the care of one of her married daughters. It seems he changed his home a fourth time later on. I won't enlarge upon that now, as I shall have much to tell later of Fyodor Pavlovich's firstborn, and must confine myself now to the most essential facts about him, without which I could not even begin my novel.

In the first place, this Dmitri Fyodorovich was the only one of Fyodor Pavlovich's three sons who grew up in the belief that he had some property, and that he would be independent on coming of age. His boyhood and youth passed in a disorderly way: he did not finish his studies at the gymnasium,[4] then he ended up in a military school, then he served in the Caucasus, was promoted, fought a duel, was demoted to the ranks, was promoted again, led a wild life, and spent a comparatively large amount of money. He did not begin to receive any income from Fyodor Pavlovich

---

2. Monasteries are religious institutions run by groups of men who have left secular life in order to pursue a spiritual calling. Monastic life is typically based on celibacy and prayer.
3. Miüsov uses the term *klerikaly*, based on the French term *clericals*. This word sounds foreign in Russian and is not typically used to describe Russian Orthodox clergy.
4. The Russian gymnasium was similar to the French *lycée* or German *Gymnasium*; it provided high-school age students a humanities-based education in preparation for university study.

until he came of age, and until then got into debt. He saw and got to know his father, Fyodor Pavlovich, for the first time on coming of age, when he visited our neighborhood with the purpose of settling with him about his property. It seems he did not like his parent even then; he did not stay long with him and left quickly, having succeeded only in obtaining a sum of money and entering into an agreement for future payments from the estate—of which (a fact worthy of note) he was able to learn neither the revenues nor the value from Fyodor Pavlovich at that time. Fyodor Pavlovich noticed for the first time then (this too should be remembered) that Mitya had a false and exaggerated idea of his property. Fyodor Pavlovich was very satisfied with this, having his own plans. He simply concluded that the young man was frivolous, unruly, with violent passions, impatient, and dissipated, and that if he could obtain ready money he would be satisfied, although only, of course, for a short time. So Fyodor Pavlovich began to take advantage of this fact, sending him from time to time small doles, installments, and in the end it so happened that when, four years later, Mitya lost patience and appeared in our little town for a second time, in order to completely finalize affairs with his parent, it suddenly turned out, to his great surprise, that he had nothing, that it was even difficult to get an account, that he had received the whole value of his property in sums of money from Fyodor Pavlovich and was perhaps even in debt to him; that by various agreements into which he had of his own desire entered at previous dates, he had no right to expect anything more, and so on, and so on. The young man was struck, suspected deceit, cheating, was almost beside himself and seemed to lose his mind. And this very circumstance led to the catastrophe, the account of which forms the subject of my first introductory novel, or rather the external side of it. But, before I pass to that novel, I must say a little of Fyodor Pavlovich's other two sons, Mitya's brothers, and of their origin.

Chapter III

The Second Marriage and Second Children

Fyodor Pavlovich, having gotten rid of four-year-old Mitya, very quickly married a second time. This second marriage lasted eight years. He took this second wife, Sofya Ivanovna, also a very young girl, from another province, where he had gone upon some small piece of business in the company of some little Yid.[5] Though Fyodor Pavlovich caroused, drank, and went on debauches, he never neglected investing his capital and always managed his business affairs very successfully, though, of course, always unscrupulously. Sofya Ivanovna was a "little orphan," left in childhood without relations, the daughter of some obscure deacon, growing up in the wealthy home of her benefactress, educator, and tormentor, an aristocratic

---

5. Like English, Russian has two terms that indicate Jewish identity: *evrei* (Jew) is neutral; *zhid* (Yid) is a slur, and was so in Dostoevsky's time as well. Extremely negative views of Jews can be found in Dostoevsky's personal correspondence. His most extensive writing on the subject of Jews and Russians can be found in chapter 2 of the March 1877 issue of his *Diary*, including the section "The Jewish Question."

old woman, the widow of General Vorokhov.[6] I do not know the details, but I have only heard that the orphan girl, a mild, meek, and gentle creature, was once taken down from a noose which she had hung from a nail in the storeroom—it was that difficult for her to bear the capriciousness and eternal nagging of this old woman, who was apparently not evil but had simply become the most insufferable tyrant from idleness. Fyodor Pavlovich offered his hand, inquiries were made about him and he was kicked out, but again, as in his first marriage, he proposed an elopement to the little orphan. It is very, very possible that she would not have married him for anything if she had known a little more about him in time. But she lived in another province; besides, what could a little girl of sixteen know about it, except that she would be better at the bottom of the river than remaining with her benefactress. So the poor child exchanged a benefactress for a benefactor. Fyodor Pavlovich did not get a penny this time, for the general's widow was furious, gave them nothing and, on top of it all, cursed them both; but he had not counted on getting anything this time, he was enticed simply by the remarkable beauty of the innocent girl, and, mainly, by her innocent look, which struck him, a sensualist who until this time had been a depraved connoisseur of exclusively coarse feminine beauty. "Those innocent eyes slit my soul like a razor," he used to say afterwards, with his loathsome snigger. In a man so depraved this, of course, could only be sensual attraction. As he had gotten no reward, Fyodor Pavlovich did not stand on ceremony with his spouse, and took advantage of the fact that she was, so to speak, "guilty" before him and that he had practically "taken her from the noose," he took advantage, moreover, of her phenomenal humility and meekness, to trample even on the most ordinary decencies of marriage. In his home, in his wife's presence, loose women would gather, and orgies took place. As a characteristic trait, I may report that Grigory, the gloomy, stupid, obstinate, argumentative servant, who had hated his first mistress, Adelaïda Ivanovna, this time took the side of his new mistress, defending her and abusing Fyodor Pavlovich in a manner little befitting a servant, and once even broke up the orgy and drove all the disorderly women out of the house. Later something occurred with this unhappy young woman, who had been terrorized since childhood, that was like some kind of nervous feminine illness, most often encountered among the peasants in the village women, who are called "shriekers" because of this illness.[7] From this illness, with its terrible hysterical fits, the sick woman at times even lost her reason. Yet she bore Fyodor Pavlovich two sons, Ivan and Alexey, the first in the first year of marriage, and the second three years later. When she died, the little boy Alexey was in his fourth year, and, strange as it seems, I know that he remembered his mother all his life—as if in a dream, of course. At her death almost exactly the same thing happened to the two little boys as to their elder brother, Mitya: they were completely forgotten and abandoned by their father and fell to that same Grigory and landed in his cottage. And in that cottage they were found by the tyrannical old general's widow, their mother's benefactress and educator. She was still alive and in

6. A deacon belonged to the lower ranks of the clergy. Sofya Ivanovna has a lower social rank than either her benefactress or a landowner such as Fyodor Pavlovich.
7. Hysterical illness, often perceived as demonic possession, was sometimes diagnosed in Russian peasant women, especially after childbirth.

all that time, all those eight years, had not been able to forget the insult done to her. For all those eight years, she had been getting the most precise information, underhandedly, as to her "Sophie's" manner of life, and, hearing how sick she was and what disorder surrounded her, she pronounced aloud two or three times to her lady spongers: "It serves her right, God has sent it to her for her ingratitude."

Exactly three months after Sofya Ivanovna's death the general's widow suddenly appeared in our town in person and went straight to Fyodor Pavlovich's house. She spent only half an hour in town, but she did a great deal. It was evening. Fyodor Pavlovich, whom she had not seen for those eight years, was a little drunk when he came out to her. The story is that she instantly, without any explanation, as soon as she saw him, gave him two good resounding slaps and jerked him three times up and down by a tuft of hair, then, without adding a word, went straight to the cottage for the two boys. Seeing at first glance that they were unwashed and in dirty linen, she promptly gave Grigory a slap and announced to him that she would take both children home with her, then she led them out as they were, wrapped them in a plaid blanket, put them in the carriage and drove off to her own town. Grigory accepted the blow like a devoted slave,[8] without a word, and when he escorted the old lady to her carriage he made her a low bow and pronounced impressively that "God would repay her for the orphans." "You are a blockhead all the same," the old lady shouted to him as she drove away. Fyodor Pavlovich, thinking it over, decided that it was a good thing and in his formal agreement regarding his children's upbringing by the general's widow he did not object to a single point. As for the slaps he had received, he himself drove all over the town telling the story.

It so happened that the old lady died soon after this, but she left the boys in her will a thousand rubles each "for their instruction, and so that all this money be spent only on them, with the condition that it be so portioned out as to last till they are twenty-one, for such a handout is more than enough for such children, and if anyone wants to, then let him open his own purse, etc., etc." I did not read the will myself, but I heard there was in fact something strange of the sort, and very distinctively expressed. The old woman's principal heir, however, turned out to be an honest man, the provincial Marshall of the Nobility[9] of that province, Yefim Petrovich Polyonov. Writing to Fyodor Pavlovich and instantly guessing that it was impossible to drag anything out of him for the education of his own children (although he never directly refused, but always procrastinated in such cases, sometimes even pouring out sentimentalities), he took a personal interest in the orphans and came to especially love the younger of them, Alexey, so that he even grew up in his family for a long while. I ask the reader to note this at the very beginning. And if the young people were indebted to anyone for their education and upbringing for their whole lives, it was to this Yefim Petrovich, a most generous and humane person, one of those who are seldom found. He kept the thousand rubles left to

---

8. The word *rab* (slave) was sometimes applied to serfs before the Emancipation. Because the event described here took place before 1861, Grigory was Fyodor Pavlovich's legal property at the time.

9. Russian noblemen enjoyed a degree of self-government, meeting every three years to elect local officials. The largely ceremonial position of Marshall of the Nobility (*gubernskii predvoditel' dvorianstva*), which entailed expensive social obligations, was the highest elected office in the Russian provinces before 1861.

each boy by the general's widow intact, so that by the time they came of age it had grown to two thousand rubles for each by the accumulation of interest, and he educated them both at his own expense, and certainly spent far more than a thousand rubles upon each of them. I won't enter into a detailed account of their boyhood and youth for the time being, but will mention only a few of the most important circumstances. Of the elder, Ivan, I will report only that he grew into a somewhat morose and reserved, though far from timid, boy, who, it seems, at ten years old had already realized that they were growing up in someone else's family and on other people's charity, and that their father was a man of whom it was disgraceful to speak, etc., etc. This boy very early, almost in his infancy (so they say at least), began to show some sort of brilliant and unusual aptitude for learning. I don't know precisely why, but it somehow happened that he left the family of Yefim Petrovich when he was hardly thirteen, entering one of the Moscow gymnasiums and boarding with some experienced and then famous pedagog, an old friend of Yefim Petrovich's from childhood. Ivan himself used to say afterwards that it was all due, so to speak, to the "ardor for good works" of Yefim Petrovich, who was captivated by the idea that the boy's genius should be trained by a teacher of genius. But neither Yefim Petrovich nor this teacher of genius was living when the young man finished at the gymnasium and entered the university. Since Yefim Petrovich had not managed things well and the receipt of the children's own money left by the tyrannical old general's widow, which had grown with interest from one to two thousand rubles each, was delayed due to various completely unavoidable formalities in Russia, the young man was in great straits for the first two years at the university, since he was forced this whole time to feed and support himself and to study at the same time. It must be noted that he did not even attempt to write to his father at that time—perhaps from pride, from contempt for him, or perhaps from his cool common sense, which told him that from such a papenka he would not get any real assistance. However that may have been, the young man was by no means at a loss and succeeded in getting work, at first twenty-kopeck lessons and afterward running around to newspaper publishers and submitting little ten-line articles on street incidents, signed "Eyewitness." These little articles, they say, were always so interestingly and piquantly done that they quickly became popular, and even in this alone the young man showed his practical and intellectual superiority over that numerous, eternally needy and unhappy part of our student youth of both sexes, which typically hangs around the doors of various newspapers and journals in the capitals, unable to think up anything better than the eternal repetition of one and the same request for French translations or copying.[1] Having once got in touch with the editors, Ivan Fyodorovich always kept up his connection with them, and in his last years at the university he published brilliant reviews of books upon various special subjects, so that he became well-known in literary circles. But he only very recently suddenly succeeded in attracting the attention of a far wider circle of readers, so that a great many people noticed and remembered him. This was rather a curious incident. When

1. Copying and translating documents from French were common forms of temporary work, frequently sought by students.

he had just left the university and was preparing to go abroad upon his two thousand rubles, Ivan Fyodorovich suddenly published in one of the more important journals a strange article, one that attracted the attention even of non-experts, and, most importantly, on a subject, it seems, completely unfamiliar to him, as he graduated in the natural sciences. The article dealt with the question that was being raised everywhere at the time about ecclesiastical courts.[2] Considering several opinions already given on the question, he also expressed his own personal view. The main thing was the tone and the remarkably unexpected conclusion. And yet many from the church decidedly considered him one of their own. But suddenly alongside them not only secularists but even atheists began to applaud from their side. Finally some clever people decided that the whole article was nothing more than an impudent farce and mockery. I mention this incident particularly because this article in time penetrated into the famous monastery in our neighborhood where they were particularly interested in the newly arisen question of the ecclesiastical courts—it penetrated and produced complete bewilderment. Learning the author's name, they were also interested in the fact that he was a native of the town and the son of "that very same Fyodor Pavlovich." And at that very same time the author himself suddenly appeared among us.

Why Ivan Fyodorovich came to us then—I remember that even at that time I asked myself this question with almost some kind of uneasiness. This so fateful arrival, which served as the start of so many consequences, remained for a long time afterward, almost always, something unclear for me. In general, it was strange that a young man who was so learned, so proud and seemingly cautious, should suddenly appear in such a disorderly house, before such a father, who had ignored him all his life, who didn't know or remember him, and who, although he would never, of course, have given him money for anything or under any circumstances if his son had asked for it, nevertheless his whole life feared that his sons Ivan and Alexey would also come someday and ask for money. And here the young man settles in the house of such a father, lives with him for a month, then another, and they are on the best possible terms. This last fact especially amazed not only me, but many others as well. Pyotr Alexandrovich Miüsov, about whom I have already spoken, a distant relative of Fyodor Pavlovich's through his first wife, happened to be among us again at that time, on his nearby estate, visiting from Paris, where he had already permanently settled. I remember that it was precisely he who was more amazed than anyone when he made the acquaintance of the young man, who interested him extremely, and with whom he sometimes, not without an inner pang, had intellectual altercations. "He is proud," he used to say about him, "he will never be in want of money; he has money enough to go abroad even now—what does he want here? It's clear to

2. Ecclesiastical courts, governed by the church rather than the state, tried transgressions that violated church law but did not necessarily break any laws of the Russian state. These courts were scrutinized when the Russian government undertook a review of the judicial system in the early 1860s. Reforms passed in 1864 transformed the Russian justice system, introducing public hearings, trial by jury, the principle of the equality of all parties involved in criminal trials, and the institution of professional advocates, or lawyers. Following the reforms several government committees formed to examine the role of the ecclesiastical courts, and lively debate on the subject continued well into the 1870s. Dostoevsky was extremely interested in the new legal system and analyzed it extensively in his *Diary*; see for example the chapters "Environment" (1873) and "Lies Are Indispensable for Truth" (October 1877, chapter 2, number 3).

everyone that he hasn't come for money, because his father would never give him any. He doesn't like wine or dissipation, and yet his father can't do without him, they get on so well together!" That was the truth; the young man even had an unmistakable influence over his father; the latter almost began to seemingly obey him at times, although he was extremely and even spitefully perverse sometimes; he actually began to behave himself more decently at times . . .

It became clear only later that Ivan Fyodorovich had come partly at the request of and on behalf of his older brother, Dmitri Fyodorovich, whom he met and saw for the first time in his life also at almost that very same time, on this very visit, but with whom, however, he had entered into correspondence regarding one important matter more concerning Dmitri Fyodorovich, before his arrival from Moscow. What that business was the reader will learn fully in due time in detail. Yet even then, when I already knew of this special circumstance, Ivan Fyodorovich still seemed to me an enigmatic figure, and his arrival among us inexplicable.

I may add that Ivan Fyodorovich appeared at the time in the guise of a conciliator and mediator between his father and his elder brother Dmitri Fyodorovich, who was in open quarrel with his father and even planning to bring formal action against him.

This little family, I repeat, now came together for the first time, and some of its members saw each other for the first time in their lives. Only the younger brother, Alexey Fyodorovich, had already been among us for about a year, having been the first of all the brothers to arrive. It is about this Alexey that I find it most difficult to speak in the introduction to my story, before bringing him on the scene in the novel. But it is necessary to write an introduction about him as well, if only to explain in advance one very strange fact, namely: I am forced to present my future hero to the reader from the first scene of his novel in the cassock of a novice.[3] Yes, he had been living in our monastery for about a year at that time, and, it seemed, was preparing to shut himself up there for the rest of his life.

Chapter IV

The Third Son, Alyosha

He was only twenty at the time (his brother Ivan was in his twenty-fourth year at the time, while their elder brother Dmitri was twenty-seven). First of all, I declare that this young man, Alyosha, was not a fanatic, and, in my opinion, at least, was not even a mystic at all. I will say my full opinion in advance: he was simply an early lover of humanity, and if he set out on the monastic path, it was only because at that time it alone struck him and presented him, so to speak, with the ideal way out for his soul struggling from the darkness of worldly wickedness to the light of love. And this path struck him only because he met on it at that time an extraordinary, in his opinion, being—our celebrated monastery elder Zosima, to whom he became attached with all the warm first love of his insatiable heart.

3. A novice is an individual seeking membership in a religious community who has not yet taken vows.

However, I do not dispute that he was already very strange even at that time, and had been so even from the cradle. By the way, I have already mentioned about him, that although he lost his mother in his fourth year, he remembered her all his life, her face, her caresses, "as though she stood living before me." Such memories may persist (and everyone knows this) from an even earlier age, even from two years old, but only appearing throughout one's whole life like spots of light out of darkness, like a corner torn out of a huge picture, which has all faded and disappeared except for that one little corner. That is exactly how it was with him: he remembered one evening, in the summer, quiet, an open window, the slanting rays of the setting sun (those slanting rays he remembered most vividly of all), an icon in the corner of the room, in front of it a lighted lamp, and in front of the icon, on her knees sobbing as if in hysterics, with cries and shrieks, his mother, snatching him up in both arms, hugging him close until it hurt and praying for him to the Mother of God, holding him out from her embraces in both arms to the icon as though to put him under the Mother of God's protection . . . and suddenly a nurse runs in and grabs him from her in terror.[4] That was the picture! And Alyosha remembered his mother's face at that minute: he used to say that it was frenzied, but beautiful, as far as he could remember. But he rarely cared to entrust this memory to anyone. In his childhood and youth he was by no means expansive and even talked very little, but not from mistrust, not from shyness or sullen unsociability, even quite the contrary, from something else, from some kind of inner preoccupation as it were, entirely personal, not concerning anyone else, but so important to him, that because of it he as it were forgot about others. But he loved people: he, it seems, lived his whole life completely trusting in people, yet no one ever considered him to be a simpleton or naïve person. There was something about him which said and made one feel at once (and it was so all his life afterwards) that he did not want to be a judge of people, that he would never take judgment upon himself and would never condemn anyone for anything. It even seemed that he accepted everything, not condemning at all, although often grieving bitterly. Even more, in this sense he went so far that no one could surprise or frighten him, and this even in his earliest youth. Coming at twenty to his father's house, that den of filthy debauchery, he, chaste and pure, simply withdrew in silence when to look on was unbearable, but without the slightest sign of contempt or condemnation of anyone. His father, who had once been a sponger and so was sensitive and ready to take offense, met him mistrustfully and gloomily at first ("He keeps too quiet," he would say, "and reasons too much"), soon ended up, however, embracing and kissing him terribly often, after not more than two weeks, to be sure with drunken tears, with tipsy sentimentality, but it was evident that he came to love him sincerely and deeply, as it had never, of course, been possible for someone like him to love anyone . . .

And everyone indeed loved this young man wherever he went, and it was so from his earliest childhood. When he entered the household of his

---

4. The Russian word for "icon" is *obraz* (image). Typically painted on flat wood panels, most icons portray Mary, Jesus, or angels; some are decorated with elaborate frames and jewels. Icons are central to Russian Orthodox faith and worship; in the nineteenth century, most houses would have had an icon corner, where icons were displayed and candles kept burning. As Jesus' mother, Mary is often referred to as the Mother of God.

benefactor and guardian, Yefim Petrovich Polyonov, he gained the hearts of all the family, so that they looked on him quite as it were as their own child. Yet he entered the house at such a tender age that he could not have acted from design nor artfulness in winning affection. So that the gift of making himself loved directly and unconsciously was inherent in him, in his very nature so to speak. It was the same at school, though he seemed to be just one of those children who are distrusted, sometimes ridiculed, and even hated by their schoolmates. He was dreamy, for instance, and rather solitary. From his earliest childhood he was fond of going off to a corner to read, and yet his schoolmates liked him so much that he could definitely be called the general favorite the whole time he was in school. He was seldom playful, even seldom merry, but anyone could see at the first glance that this was not at all from any kind of sullenness in him, that, on the contrary, he was bright and good-tempered. He never tried to show off among his schoolmates. Perhaps because of this, he was never afraid of anyone, yet the boys immediately understood that he was not proud of his fearlessness and seemed to be unaware that he was bold and courageous. He never remembered an insult. It would happen that an hour after the insult he would address the insulter or answer some question with as trustful and candid an expression as though nothing had happened between them. And it was not that he seemed to have forgotten or intentionally forgiven the insult, but simply that he did not regard it as an insult, and this completely conquered and captivated the boys. He had just one characteristic which awoke in all his schoolmates from the bottom class to the top a desire to tease him, not from malice but because it amused them. This characteristic was a wild fanatical modesty and chastity. He could not bear to hear certain words and certain conversations about women. These "certain" words and conversations, unfortunately, are impossible to eradicate in schools. Boys pure in mind and heart, practically still children, very often like to talk in school among themselves, and even aloud, of such things, pictures, and images of which even soldiers would sometimes hesitate to speak, more than that, much that soldiers have no knowledge or conception of is familiar to quite young children of our intellectual and higher classes. There is as yet no moral depravity, perhaps, no real corrupt inner cynicism, but there is the appearance of it, and this is often looked upon among them as something refined, subtle, daring, and worthy of imitation. Seeing that "Alyoshka Karamazov" put his fingers in his ears when they talked about "that," they used to intentionally crowd around him sometimes, pull his hands away, and shout nastiness into both ears, while he struggled, slipped to the floor, lay there, tried to hide himself, and all this without uttering one word of abuse, enduring their insults in silence. In the end, however, they left him alone and gave up taunting him with being a "regular girl," and what's more they looked upon him in this respect with compassion. Incidentally, he was always one of the best in the class but was never first.

When Yefim Petrovich died, Alyosha had two more years to complete at the provincial gymnasium. Yefim Petrovich's inconsolable widow went almost immediately after his death for a long visit to Italy with her whole family, which consisted only of persons of the female sex. Alyosha went to live in the house of two distant relations of Yefim Petrovich, ladies whom he had never seen before, but on what terms he lived with them he did not know himself. It was a characteristic, even very characteristic, trait of his that he never cared at whose expense he was living. In that respect he was the complete opposite of his elder brother Ivan Fyodorovich, who struggled with poverty for his first two years in the university, fed himself by his own labor, and had from childhood bitterly sensed that he was living on the bread of others at his benefactor's. But this strange trait in Alyosha's character should not, it seems, be criticized too severely, for at the slightest acquaintance with him anyone would have perceived that Alyosha was one of those youths, almost of the type of holy fool,[5] who, if they were suddenly to come into possession of a large fortune, would not hesitate to give it away for the asking, either for a good deed or perhaps to a clever swindler. And in general he seemed not to know the value of money at all, not, of course, in a literal sense. When he was given pocket money, which he himself never asked for, he was either terribly careless of it so that it was gone in a moment or he kept it for weeks on end, not knowing what to do with it. Pyotr Alexandrovich Miüsov, a man very sensitive regarding money and bourgeois honesty, later pronounced the following aphorism, after getting to know Alyosha: "Here is perhaps the one man in the world whom you might leave alone without a penny, in the center of a strange city of a million inhabitants, and he would not perish, he would not die of cold and hunger, for he would be fed and sheltered at once; and if he were not, he would find a shelter for himself, and it would cost him no effort or humiliation, and to shelter him would be no burden, but, on the contrary, would probably be looked on as a pleasure."

He did not finish his studies at the gymnasium; he still had an entire year left when he suddenly announced to his ladies that he was going to his father's on a certain business which had come into his head. They were sorry and didn't want to let him go. The trip was very inexpensive, and the ladies would not let him pawn his watch, a parting present from his benefactor's family when they went abroad, but provided him liberally with means and even fitted him out with new clothes and linen. He, however, returned half the money they gave him, announcing that he intended to go third class.[6] On his arrival in our little town he made no answer to his parent's first inquiries—Why had he come before completing his studies?—and seemed, so they say, unusually thoughtful. It soon became apparent that he was looking for his mother's grave. He practically acknowledged at the time that he had come for that reason only. But it can hardly have been the whole reason for his coming. It is more probable that he himself did not understand and could not have explained what had suddenly arisen in his soul, and drawn him irresistibly into a new, unknown but inevitable path. Fyodor Pavlovich could not show him where he had buried his second wife, for he had never visited her grave since he had thrown earth upon her coffin, and in the course of years had entirely forgotten where she was buried . . .

5. Russian culture has traditionally venerated "holy fools," individuals who exhibit unconventional behavior that is interpreted as evidence of God's favor. Extreme asceticism, nakedness, truth-telling, and silence are among the traits that can characterize holy fools, who are typically cared for by the community. The tradition ultimately derives from reference to "the poor in spirit" in Matthew 5.3: "Blessed are the poor in spirit: for theirs is the kingdom of heaven."
6. The cheapest seats on the train, considered inappropriate for someone of Alyosha's social rank.

A word about Fyodor Pavlovich. For a long time before then he had not been living in our town. Three or four years after his second wife's death he had gone to the south of Russia and finally turned up in Odessa,[7] where he spent several years. At first he became acquainted with, in his own words, "a lot of Yids, Yiddels, Yidkins, and Yidlets," and he finally ended up being received not only by Yids, but even "by Jews as well." It may be presumed that in this period of his life he developed a particular faculty for making and hoarding money. He finally returned to our town only three years before Alyosha's arrival. His former acquaintances found him looking terribly aged, although he was by no means an old man. He behaved not exactly with more dignity, but with more effrontery. There appeared, for example, an insolent need in the former buffoon—to make others into buffoons. He loved to be depraved with the female sex not as before, but in a somehow even more revolting way. In a short time he opened a great number of new taverns in the district. It was evident that he had perhaps a hundred thousand rubles or not much less. Many of the inhabitants of the town and district were soon in his debt and, of course, had given good security. Most recently he became somehow bloated, seemed somehow more irresponsible, more uneven, had even sunk into a sort of incoherence; he used to begin one thing and finish with another, was somehow letting himself go altogether and was more and more frequently drunk, and, if it had not been for the same servant Grigory, who by that time had aged considerably too, and used to look after him sometimes almost like a tutor, Fyodor Pavlovich might have gotten into terrible scrapes. Alyosha's arrival seemed to affect even his moral side, as though something had awakened in this prematurely old man which had long been dead in his soul: "Do you know," he used often to say, looking at Alyosha, "that you look like her, the shrieker?" That was what he used to call his dead wife, Alyosha's mother. The lackey Grigory finally pointed out the "shrieker's" grave to Alyosha. He took him to our town cemetery and showed him in a remote corner a cast-iron tombstone, cheap but decently kept, on which were even inscribed the name, rank, and age of the deceased and the date of her death, and below there was even something like a four-line verse, such as are commonly used on old-fashioned middle-class tombs. Amazingly, this tombstone turned out to be Grigory's doing. He had put it up on the poor "shrieker's" grave at his own expense, after Fyodor Pavlovich, whom he had often pestered about the grave, had gone to Odessa, abandoning the grave and all his memories. Alyosha showed no particular emotion at his mother's grave; he only listened to Grigory's reasoned and solemn account of the erection of the tomb, stood with bowed head and walked away, without uttering a word. After that, perhaps the whole year, he did not visit the cemetery again. But this little episode had its effect on Fyodor Pavlovich, and a very original one. He suddenly took a thousand rubles to our monastery to pay for requiems for the soul of his wife; but not for the second, not for Alyosha's mother, not the "shrieker," but for the first, Adelaïda Ivanovna, who used to thrash him. In the evening of the same day he got drunk and abused the monks to Alyosha. He himself was

---

7. The city of Odessa, located on the Black Sea in present-day Ukraine, was one of the Russian Empire's most important ports, famous for its ethnically diverse population and large Jewish community.

far from being religious; he had probably never put a five-kopeck candle in front of an icon. Strange impulses of sudden feeling and sudden thought happen with such subjects.

I have mentioned already that he had become very bloated. His physiognomy at this time presented acute testimony about the characteristics and essence of his whole past life. Besides the long and fleshy bags under his little, always insolent, suspicious, and ironical eyes, besides the multitude of deep wrinkles in his small but fat little face, a large Adam's apple hung below his sharp chin, like a great, fleshy goiter, which gave him a peculiar, repulsive, sensual appearance. Add to that a long rapacious mouth with puffy lips, between which could be seen little stumps of black decayed teeth. He slobbered every time he began to speak. He himself liked to make fun of his own face, although, it seems, he was satisfied with it. He used particularly to point to his nose, which was not very large, but very delicate and conspicuously aquiline: "A regular Roman nose," he used to say, "with my Adam's apple I have the authentic physiognomy of an ancient Roman patrician of the decadent period."[8] He seemed proud of it.

Not long after visiting his mother's grave Alyosha suddenly announced that he wanted to enter the monastery, and that the monks were willing to receive him as a novice. He explained that this was his strong desire, and that he was solemnly asking his consent as his father. The old man knew that the elder Zosima, who was living in the monastery hermitage, had made a special impression upon his "gentle boy."

"That elder is the most honest monk among them, of course," he observed, after listening in thoughtful silence to Alyosha, and seeming scarcely surprised at his request. "Hmm! . . . So that's where you want to go, my gentle boy?" He was half drunk, and suddenly he grinned his slow half-drunken grin, which was not without a certain cunning and tipsy slyness. "H'm! . . . I had a presentiment that you would end in something like this, would you believe it? You were making straight for it. Well, to be sure you have your own two thousand, that's a dowry for you, and I'll never desert you, my angel, and I'll pay what's wanted for you there, if they ask for it. But, of course, if they don't ask, why should we impose ourselves? What do you say? You know, you spend money like a canary, two grains a week. Hmmm . . . You know, near one monastery there's a little village outside the town, and this is known to everyone there, that only 'monastery wives' live in it, that's how they call them there, thirty women, I think . . . I was there, and, you know, it's interesting, in its own way of course, as variety. The only trouble with it is this terrible Russianism, there are no French women at all, but there could be, they have the means. If they get to hear of it they'll come along. Well, there's nothing of that sort here, no 'monks' wives,' and two hundred monks. They're honest. They keep the fasts.[9] I admit it. . . . Hmm. So you want to be a monk? And do you know I'm sorry

8. Ancient Roman society was divided into patricians and plebeians. Nineteenth-century Russians such as Fyodor Pavlovich often used *patrician* as a synonym for *upper-class*. The Roman Empire experienced a protracted period of decline known as the decadent period that ended with its destruction by invading Germanic tribes. For discussion of this reference to Rome see Vetlovskaya, "Alyosha Karamazov," p. 677.
9. The Orthodox Church prescribes regular periods of fasting throughout the year, including extended periods during Lent (see p. 88) and Christmas; all Wednesdays and Fridays; and, in some monasteries, all Mondays. A fast can entail abstaining from all food, or from certain foods such as meat, dairy products, oil, and wine.

to lose you, Alyosha; would you believe it, I've really grown fond of you? Well, it's a good opportunity. You'll pray for us sinners; we have sinned too much here. I've always been thinking: who will pray for me? Is there such a man on earth? My dear boy, I'm awfully stupid about that, you perhaps wouldn't believe it? Awfully. You see, however stupid I am about it, I keep thinking, I keep thinking—from time to time, of course, not all the while. It's impossible, I think, for the devils to forget to drag me down to hell with their hooks when I die.[1] Then I wonder—hooks? Where would they get them? What of? Iron hooks? Where do they forge them? Have they a foundry there of some sort? The monks in the monastery probably believe that there's a ceiling in hell, for instance. Now I'm ready to believe in hell, but without a ceiling. It makes it more refined, more enlightened, more Lutheran, that is.[2] And, after all, what does it matter whether it has a ceiling or hasn't? But, do you know, there's a damnable question involved in it? If there's no ceiling there can be no hooks, and if there are no hooks it all breaks down, which is unlikely again, for then there would be none to drag me down to hell, and if they don't drag me down what justice is there in the world? *Il faudrait les inventer*,[3] those hooks, on purpose for me alone, for if you only knew, Alyosha, what a shameless person I am!

"But there are no hooks there," said Alyosha, looking gently and seriously at his father.

"Yes, yes, only the shadows of hooks. I know, I know. That's how a Frenchman described hell. *'J'ai vu l'ombre d'un cocher qui avec l'ombre d'une brosse frottait l'ombre d'une carosse.'*[4] How do you know there are no hooks, darling? When you've lived with the monks you'll sing a different tune. But go and get at the truth there, and then come and tell me. Anyway it's easier going to the other world if one knows what there is there. Besides, it will be more seemly for you with the monks than here with me, with a drunken old man and young harlots . . . though you're like an angel, nothing touches you. And I daresay nothing will touch you there. That's why I let you go, because I hope for that. You've got all your wits about you. You will burn and you will burn out, you will be healed and come back again. And I will wait for you. I feel that you're the only one in the world who has not condemned me. My dear boy, I feel it, you know. I can't help feeling it."

And he even began blubbering. He was sentimental. He was wicked and sentimental.

1. The image of devils dragging the soul down to hell with hooks is depicted on some Russian icons and is described in spiritual verses based on the Gospel story of the rich and poor Lazarus. See Luke 16.19–31.
2. Some of Dostoevsky's Russian contemporaries viewed Lutheranism as a rational religion, more compatible with modernity than Russian Orthodoxy. For Dostoevsky's views on the appeal of Protestantism for some Russians, see his *Diary*, January 1877, chapter 1, number 2: "Mirages. Stundism and the Radstockists."
3. "They would have to be invented" (French). A paraphrase of a well-known saying of the French Enlightenment philosopher Voltaire (1694–1778), who said: "If God did not exist, he would have to be invented." Dostoevsky read Voltaire's writings in 1868–69 while living in Western Europe.
4. "I saw the shade of a coachman, who scrubbed the shade of a coach with the shade of a brush" (French). From *Eneïde travesti*, a 1648 parody of Virgil's *Aeneid* (first century B.C.E.) by Charles Perrault (1628–1703), the author of fairy tales such as *Little Red Riding Hood* and *Cinderella*.

Chapter V

Elders

Some of my readers may imagine that my young man was a sickly, ecstatic, poorly developed creature, a pale, thin, consumptive dreamer. On the contrary, Alyosha was at this time a well-grown, red-cheeked, clear-eyed lad of nineteen, radiant with health. He was very handsome, too, graceful, moderately tall, with dark brown hair, a regular, rather long, oval-shaped face, and wide-set dark gray, shining eyes; he was very thoughtful, and apparently very serene. I shall be told, perhaps, that red cheeks are not incompatible with fanaticism and mysticism; but I fancy that Alyosha was more of a realist than any one. Oh, no doubt, in the monastery he fully believed in miracles, but, to my thinking, miracles are never a stumbling block to the realist. It is not miracles that dispose realists to belief. The genuine realist, if he is an unbeliever, will always find strength and ability to disbelieve in the miraculous, and if he is confronted with a miracle as an irrefutable fact he would rather disbelieve his own senses than admit the fact. Even if he admits it, he admits it as a fact of nature till then unrecognized by him. Faith does not, in the realist, spring from the miracle but the miracle from faith. If the realist once believes, then he is bound by his very realism to admit the miraculous also. The Apostle Thomas[5] said that he would not believe till he saw, but when he did see he said, "My Lord and my God!" Was it the miracle that forced him to believe? Most likely not, but he believed solely because he desired to believe and possibly he fully believed in his secret heart even when he said, "I shall not believe except I see."

Some will say, perhaps, that Alyosha was stupid, undeveloped, had not finished his studies, and so on. That he did not finish his studies is true, but to say that he was stupid or dull would be a great injustice. I'll simply repeat what I have said above. He entered upon this path only because, at that time, it alone struck his imagination and presented itself to him as offering an ideal means of escape for his soul from darkness to light. Add to that that he was to some extent a youth of our last epoch—that is, honest in nature, desiring the truth, seeking for it and believing in it, and seeking to serve it at once with all the strength of his soul, seeking for immediate action, and ready to sacrifice everything, life itself, for it. Though these young men unfortunately fail to understand that the sacrifice of life is, perhaps, the easiest of all sacrifices, and that to sacrifice, for instance, five or six years of their seething youth to hard and tedious study, if only to multiply tenfold their powers of serving the truth and the cause they have set before them as their goal—such a sacrifice is utterly beyond the strength of many of them. The path Alyosha chose was a path going in the opposite direction, but he chose it with the same thirst for swift achievement. As soon as he reflected seriously he was convinced of the existence of God and immortality, and at once he instinctively said to

---

5. The term *apostle*, derived from a Greek word originally meaning *messenger*, refers to the twelve men Jesus chose to accompany him and assist in his mission. Thomas, one of the twelve, declared that he would not believe in the resurrection until he saw Christ risen from the dead (John 20.19–29)

himself: "I want to live for immortality, and I will accept no compromise." In the same way, if he had decided that God and immortality did not exist, he would at once have become an atheist and a socialist (for socialism is not merely the labor question or the so-called fourth estate,[6] it is before all things the atheistic question, the question of the form taken by atheism today, the question of the tower of Babel[7] built without God, not to mount to Heaven from earth but to set up Heaven on earth). Alyosha even found it strange and impossible to go on living as before. It is written: "Give all that thou hast to the poor and follow Me, if thou wouldst be perfect."[8] Alyosha said to himself: "I can't give two rubles instead of 'all,' and only go to mass instead of 'following Him.'" From the memories of his childhood, perhaps something remained about our monastery, to which his mother may have taken him to mass. Perhaps the slanting rays of the setting sun before the icon, to which his poor shrieker-mother had held him up, also acted upon his imagination. Brooding on these things he may have come to us perhaps only to see whether here he could sacrifice all or only "two rubles," and in the monastery he met this elder . . .

This elder, as I have already explained, was the elder Zosima. I must digress to explain what an "elder" is in Russian monasteries, and I am sorry that I do not feel very sure and competent to do so.[9] I will try, however, to give a superficial account of it in a few words. Authorities on the subject assert that the institution of "elders" is of recent date, not more than a hundred years old in our monasteries, though in the orthodox East, especially in Sinai and Athos, it has existed over a thousand years.[1] It is maintained that it existed in ancient times in Russia also, but through the calamities which overtook Russia—the Tartars, civil war, the interruption of relations with the East after the destruction of Constantinople[2]—this institution fell into oblivion. It was revived among us towards the end of last century by one of the great ascetics (that is what they call him), Païssy

6. The term *fourth estate* is used generally to refer to the press, but it has also been used to indicate the proletariat, or mob; Dostoevsky appears to be using the term in this latter meaning. Dostoevsky was deeply opposed to socialism and discusses it extensively throughout his *Diary of a Writer*, where he condemns it as "the acme of egoism, the acme of inhumanity, the acme of economic bungling and disorder, the acme of slander on human nature, the acme of destruction of every human freedom" (January 1877, p. 831).
7. In Genesis 11.1–9, the descendents of Noah, who all spoke a common language, tried to build a tower that would reach the heavens. To stop this, God caused them to speak different languages, making it impossible for them to understand each other and complete the tower.
8. In the Gospels of Matthew (19.21) and Mark (10.21), Jesus tells a wealthy young man to sell all his possessions and follow him.
9. In the Russian Orthodox tradition, an elder is a venerated adviser and teacher, a charismatic spiritual guide. The title of elder does not represent an official position or office in the Orthodox Church, but reflects the esteem in which the individual is held.
1. The "orthodox East" refers to countries where Orthodox Christianity, as opposed to Roman Catholicism or Protestantism, is the predominant religion. The Sinai Peninsula, part of Israel, was a center of early Christian monastic life. Mount Athos is a semiautonomous monastic republic within Greece, on a peninsula in the Aegean Sea. There are twenty monasteries in the republic of Athos; only Eastern Orthodox males over eighteen years of age are allowed to live there, and women are prohibited from visiting.
2. The Tartars were a nomadic people from inner Asia. They first defeated Russian princes in battle in 1223 and then ruled large territories of present-day Russia until the sixteenth century. Most Russians associate the period of Tartar dominance with extreme cruelty and oppression. Also known as the Great Feudal War (1425–53), the civil war was a period of internecine violence, when Russian princes struggled against each other for the title Grand Prince of Moscow. Constantinople, the capital of the Byzantine Empire, was the center of Eastern Orthodox Christianity from 330 c.e. until it was conquered by the Ottoman Empire in 1453. The takeover by the Moslem Ottoman Turks weakened traditional religious and cultural ties between Byzantium and Russia, and further isolated Russia from Europe.

Velichkovsky,[3] and his disciples, but to this day, even after a century, it exists in only a few monasteries, and has sometimes been almost persecuted as an innovation in Russia. It flourished especially in the celebrated Kozel'skaia Optina Monastery.[4] When and by whom it was introduced into our monastery I cannot say. There had already been three such elders and Zosima was the last of them. But he was almost dying of weakness and disease, and they had no one to take his place. The question was an important one for our monastery, for it had not been distinguished by anything in particular till then: it had neither relics of saints, nor wonderworking icons, nor even glorious traditions connected with our history, it had no historical exploits or services to the Fatherland. It had flourished and been glorious all over Russia through its elders, to see and hear whom pilgrims had flocked for thousands of miles from all parts. What was such an elder? An elder was one who took your soul, your will, into his soul and his will. When you choose an elder, you renounce your own will and yield it to him in complete submission, complete self-abnegation. This ordeal, this terrible school of abnegation, is undertaken voluntarily, in the hope of self-conquest, of self-mastery, in order, after such a long ordeal, to attain perfect freedom, that is, from self; to escape the lot of those who have lived their whole life without finding their true selves in themselves. This institution of elders is not founded on theory, but was established in the East from the practice of a thousand years. The obligations due to an elder are not the ordinary "obedience" which has always existed in our Russian monasteries. The obligation involves confession to the elder by all who have submitted themselves to him, and to the indissoluble bond between him and them. The story is told, for instance, that in the early days of Christianity one such novice, failing to fulfill some command laid upon him by his elder, left his monastery in Syria and went to Egypt.[5] There, after great exploits he was found worthy at last to suffer torture and a martyr's death for the faith. When the Church was burying his body, already regarding him as a saint, suddenly, at the deacon's exhortation, "Depart all ye unbaptized," the coffin containing the martyr's body left its place and was cast forth from the church, and this took place three times. And only at last they learned that this martyr had broken his vow of obedience and left his elder, and, therefore, could not be forgiven without the elder's absolution in spite of his great deeds. Only after this could the funeral take place. This, of course, is only an old legend, but here is a recent instance:[6] One of our contemporary monks was seeking salvation

3. Born Pyotr Velichovsky (1722–1794), the Orthodox monk Païssy initiated a religious revival that greatly influenced Dostoevsky. Under Païssy's supervision, the writings of the Church Fathers were translated into Slavonic, the language used in Russian Orthodox worship. He emphasized the importance of continual prayer and obedience to an elder, and was canonized by the Russian Orthodox Church after his death.

4. One of the spiritual centers of Russia, Kozel'skaia Optina monastery (*Optina pustyn'*) played a significant role in the composition of *The Brothers Karamazov*. Dostoevsky visited the monastery in June 1878, soon after his second son Alexey died (in May) and right before beginning composition of the novel. While staying at the monastery he met with the elder Amvrosy, one inspiration for the character of Zosima.

5. This story can be found in the *Prologue*, or Saints' Calendar, in the entry for October 15. The *Prologue* is a medieval text in which lives of the saints are arranged in calendar order, that is, the order in which their feast days occur.

6. The following vignette was probably inspired by *The Tale of Wanderings and Travels through Russia, Moldavia, Turkey, and the Holy Land by Parfeny, a Monk Tonsured at Holy Mount Athos*. This account by Parfeny (Pyotr Ageev, 1807–1878) was widely known in Dostoevsky's time, and he drew on it for many of the details of monastic life and elders that appear in the novel.

on Athos, and suddenly his elder commanded him to leave Athos, which he loved to the depth of his soul as a sacred place, as a quiet refuge, and to go first to Jerusalem in homage to the holy places, and then back to Russia, to the north, to Siberia: "Your place is there, and not here." The monk, overwhelmed with sorrow, went to the Ecumenical Patriarch at Constantinople[7] and besought him to release him from his obedience. But the Patriarch replied that not only was he unable to release him, but there was not and could not be on earth a power which could release him except the elder who had himself laid that duty upon him. In this way the elders are endowed in certain cases with unbounded and inexplicable authority. That is why in many of our monasteries the institution was at first resisted almost to persecution. In the meantime the elders immediately began to be highly esteemed among the people. Masses of the ignorant people as well as men of distinction flocked, for instance, to the elders of our monastery to confess their doubts, their sins, and their sufferings, and to ask for counsel and admonition. Seeing this, the opponents of the elders declared, among other objections, that the sacrament of confession was being arbitrarily and frivolously degraded, though the continual opening of the heart to the elder by the monk or the layman had nothing of the character of the sacrament.[8] In the end, however, the institution of elders has been retained and is becoming established in Russian monasteries. It is true, perhaps, that this instrument which had stood the test of a thousand years for the moral regeneration of a man from slavery to freedom and to moral perfectibility may be a two-edged weapon, and it may lead some not to humility and complete self-control but to the most Satanic pride, that is, to bondage and not to freedom.

The elder Zosima was sixty-five,[9] came of a family of landowners, and at some point in early youth had been in the army and served in the Caucasus as an officer. He had, no doubt, impressed Alyosha by some peculiar quality of his soul. Alyosha lived in the cell of the elder, who was very fond of him and let him wait upon him. It must be noted that Alyosha, who lived in the monastery at that time, was bound by no obligation and could go where he pleased and be absent for whole days. Though he wore the monastic dress it was voluntarily, not to be different from others. No doubt he liked to do so. Possibly his youthful imagination was deeply stirred by the power and fame of his elder. It was said that so many people had for years past come to confess their sins to Father Zosima and to entreat him for words of advice and healing, that he had taken into his heart so many disclosures, afflictions, admissions, that Father Zosima had acquired the

7. The Ecumenical Patriarch of Constantinople, or Archbishop of Constantinople, is the highest figure in Eastern Orthodoxy. He does not exercise control over the autocephalous (independent) churches of Eastern Orthodoxy, such as the Russian Orthodox Church, but may be consulted to resolve disputes, and he frequently represents the Eastern Churches in communications with other religions.
8. A Christian sacrament, referred to as a "mystery" (tainstvo) in Russian Orthodoxy, is a religious rite which manifests divine grace; confession is one of the most commonly administered sacraments.
9. Dostoevsky drew on the life stories of several historical elders for the portrait of Father Zosima: Amvrosy (1812–1891) of Optyna Pustyn', Zosima of Tobolsk (1767–1835), and Tikhon of Zadonsk (1724–1783). Dostoevsky discusses Tikhon of Zadonsk in "On Love of the People. An Essential Contract with the People" in his Diary, February 1876, chapter 1, number 2. For analysis of Father Zosima's relationship to the tradition of elders, see Roger B. Anderson, "Mythical Implications of Father Zosima's Religious Teachings," p. 733.

keenest intuition[1] and could tell from an unknown face what a newcomer wanted, and what was the suffering on his conscience. He sometimes astounded and almost alarmed his visitors by his knowledge of their secrets before they had spoken a word. Alyosha almost always noticed that many, almost all, went in to the elder for the first time with apprehension and uneasiness, but almost always came out with bright and happy faces, and the gloomiest face turned into a happy one. Alyosha was particularly struck by the fact that Father Zosima was not at all stern. On the contrary, he was always almost gay. The monks used to say that he was more drawn to those who were more sinful, and the greater the sinner the more he loved him. There were, no doubt, up to the end of his life, among the monks some who hated and envied him, but they were few in number and they were silent, though among them were some of great dignity in the monastery, one, for instance, of the older monks distinguished for his strict keeping of fasts and vows of silence. But the vast majority were on Father Zosima's side and very many of them loved him with all their hearts, warmly and sincerely; some were almost fanatically attached to him. These said outright, though not quite aloud, that he was a saint, that there could be no doubt of it, and, seeing that his end was near, they anticipated miracles and great glory to the monastery in the immediate future from the deceased.[2] Alyosha had unquestioning faith in the miraculous power of the elder, just as he had unquestioning faith in the story of the coffin that flew out of the church. He saw many who came with sick children or adult relatives and besought the elder to lay hands on them and to pray over them, return shortly after—some the next day—and, falling in tears at the elder's feet, thank him for healing their sick. Whether they had really been healed or were simply better in the natural course of the disease was a question which did not exist for Alyosha, for he fully believed in the spiritual power of his teacher and rejoiced in his fame, in his glory, as though it were his own triumph. His heart throbbed, and he beamed, as it were, all over when the elder came out to the gates of the hermitage into the waiting crowd of pilgrims of the humbler class who had flocked from all parts of Russia on purpose to see the elder and obtain his blessing. They fell down before him, wept, kissed his feet, kissed the earth on which he stood, and wailed, while the women held up their children to him and brought him the sick shriekers. The elder spoke to them, read a brief prayer over them, blessed them, and dismissed them. Of late he had become so weak through attacks of illness that he was sometimes unable to leave his cell, and the pilgrims waited for him to come out for several days. Alyosha did not wonder why they loved him so, why they fell down before him and wept with emotion merely at seeing his face. Oh! he understood very well that for the humble soul of the Russian common people, worn out by grief and toil, and still more by the everlasting injustice and everlasting sin, their own and the world's, it was the greatest need and comfort to find someone or something holy to fall down before and worship. "Among us there is sin, injustice, and temptation, but yet, somewhere on earth there is someone holy and exalted.

---

1. The gift of spiritual intuition (Russian *prozorlivost'*) is frequently ascribed to holy men in the religious literature of Russian Orthodoxy. The elder Amvrosy of Optyna Pustyn', one of the prototypes for Father Zosima, was said to be endowed with this gift.
2. The hagiographical literature of Russian Orthodoxy includes many accounts of miracles worked by the remains of deceased saints.

He has the truth; he knows the truth; so it is not dead upon the earth; so it will come one day to us, too, and rule over all the earth according to the promise." Alyosha knew that this was just how the people felt and even reasoned. He understood it, but that the elder Zosima was the saint and custodian of God's truth—of that he had no more doubt than the weeping peasants and the sick women who held out their children to the elder. The conviction that after his death the elder would bring extraordinary glory to the monastery was even stronger in Alyosha than in anyone there, and of late a kind of deep flame of inner ecstasy burnt more and more strongly in his heart. He was not at all troubled at this elder's standing as a solitary example before him. "No matter. He is holy. He carries in his heart the secret of renewal for all: that power which will, at last, establish truth on the earth, and all men will be holy and love one another, and there will be no more rich nor poor, no exalted nor humbled, but all will be as the children of God, and the true Kingdom of Christ will come." That was the dream in Alyosha's heart. The arrival of his two brothers, whom he had not known till then at all, seemed to make a great impression on Alyosha. He more quickly made friends with his brother Dmitri Fyodorovich, although he arrived later, than with his other (full) brother Ivan Fyodorovich. He was extremely interested in his brother Ivan, but when the latter had been two months in the town, though they had met fairly often, they were still not intimate. Alyosha was naturally silent, and he seemed to be expecting something, ashamed about something, while his brother Ivan, though Alyosha noticed at first that he looked long and curiously at him, seemed soon to have left off thinking of him. Alyosha noticed it with some embarrassment. He ascribed his brother's indifference at first to the disparity in their ages and particularly in their education. But he also wondered whether the absence of curiosity and sympathy in Ivan might be due to some other cause entirely unknown to him. He kept fancying that Ivan was absorbed in something—something inward and important—that he was striving towards some goal, perhaps very hard to attain, and that that was the only reason why he had no thought for him. Alyosha wondered, too, whether there was not some contempt on the part of the learned atheist for him—a foolish novice. He knew for certain that his brother was an atheist. He could not take offense at this contempt, if it existed; yet, with an uneasy embarrassment which he did not himself understand, he waited for his brother to come nearer to him. His brother Dmitri Fyodorovich used to speak of Ivan with the deepest respect and with a peculiar earnestness. From him Alyosha learned all the details of the important affair which had of late formed such a close and remarkable bond between the two elder brothers. Dmitri's enthusiastic references to Ivan were the more striking in Alyosha's eyes since Dmitri was, compared with Ivan, almost uneducated, and the two brothers were such a contrast in personality and character that it would be difficult to find two men more unlike.

It was at this time that the meeting, or rather family gathering, of the members of this inharmonious family took place in the cell of the elder who had such an extraordinary influence on Alyosha. The pretext for this gathering, in reality, was a false one. It was at this time that the discord between Dmitri Fyodorovich and his father seemed at its acutest stage and their relations had become insufferably strained. Fyodor Pavlovich seems to have been the first to suggest, apparently in jest, that they should all meet in Father Zosima's cell, and that, without appealing to his direct intervention, they might more decently come to an understanding under the conciliating influence of the elder's presence. Dmitri Fyodorovich, who had never seen the elder, naturally supposed that his father was trying to intimidate him, but, as he secretly blamed himself for his outbursts of temper with his father on several recent occasions, he accepted the challenge. It must be noted that he was not, like Ivan Fyodorovich, staying with his father, but living apart at the other end of the town. It happened that Pyotr Alexandrovich Miüsov, who was staying in the district at the time, caught eagerly at the idea. A Liberal of the forties and fifties, a freethinker and atheist, he, from boredom perhaps, or perhaps for a frivolous diversion, took part in this affair extremely enthusiastically. He was suddenly seized with the desire to see the monastery and the "holy man." As his lawsuit with the monastery about boundaries, woodcutting rights, river fishing, and so on still dragged on, he made it the pretext for seeing the Superior, in order to attempt to settle it amicably. A visitor coming with such laudable intentions might be received with more attention and consideration than if he came from simple curiosity. Influences from within the monastery were brought to bear on the elder, who of late had scarcely left his cell, and had been forced by illness to deny even his ordinary visitors. In the end he consented to see them, and the day was fixed.

"Who has made me a judge over them?" was all he said, smilingly, to Alyosha.[3]

Alyosha was much perturbed when he heard of the proposed visit. Of all the wrangling, quarrelsome party, his brother Dmitri was the only one who could regard the interview seriously; all the others would come from frivolous motives, perhaps insulting to the elder—Alyosha was well aware of that. His brother Ivan and Miüsov would come from curiosity, perhaps of the coarsest kind, while his father might be contemplating some piece of acting and buffoonery. Oh, though he said nothing, Alyosha thoroughly understood his father. The boy, I repeat, was far from being so simple as everyone thought him. He awaited the day with a heavy heart. No doubt he was always secretly pondering in his heart how the family discord could be ended. But his chief anxiety concerned the elder. He trembled for him, for his glory, and dreaded any affront to him, especially the refined, courteous irony of Miüsov and the supercilious half-utterances of the highly educated Ivan. That is how he imagined all that. He even wanted to risk warning the elder, telling him something about them, but, on second thought, said nothing. He only sent word the day before, through a friend, to his brother Dmitri, that he loved him and expected him to keep his promise. Dmitri wondered, for he could not remember what he had promised, but he answered by letter that he would do his utmost not to let himself be provoked "by vileness," but that, although he had a deep respect for the elder and for his brother Ivan, he was convinced that the meeting was either a trap for him or an unworthy farce. "Nevertheless I would rather bite out my tongue than be lacking in respect to the sainted man whom you reverence so highly," he concluded his little letter. Alyosha was not greatly encouraged by it.

3. According to the Gospel of Luke (12.13–14), a man asked Jesus to intercede with his brother on his behalf, saying, "Master, speak to my brother, that he divide the inheritance with me," to which Jesus replied, "Man, who made me a judge or a divider over you?"

Book Two

AN INAPPROPRIATE GATHERING

Chapter I

They Arrive at the Monastery

The day was splendid, warm, and bright. It was the end of August. The interview with the elder had been fixed for half-past eleven in the morning, immediately after late mass. Our visitors did not take part in the service, but arrived just as it was over. First an elegant open carriage, drawn by two valuable horses, drove up with Miüsov and a distant relative of his, a very young man of twenty, called Pyotr Fomich Kalganov. This young man was preparing to enter the university. Miüsov, with whom he was staying for the time, was trying to persuade him to go abroad to the university of Zurich or Jena. The young man was still undecided. He was thoughtful and absentminded. He was nice-looking, strongly built, and rather tall. There was a strange fixity in his gaze at times. Like all very absentminded people he would sometimes stare at a person for some time without seeing him. He was silent and rather awkward, but sometimes, when he was alone with anyone he became talkative and effusive, and would laugh at anything or nothing. But his animation vanished as quickly as it appeared. He was always well and even elegantly dressed; he already had some independent fortune and expectations of much more. He was a friend of Alyosha's.

In an ancient, jolting, but roomy hired carriage, with a pair of old pinkish-gray horses, a long way behind Miüsov's carriage, came Fyodor Pavlovich, with his son Ivan Fyodorovich. Dmitri Fyodorovich was late, though he had been informed of the time the evening before. The visitors left their carriage at the hotel, outside the precincts, and went to the gates of the monastery on foot. Except Fyodor Pavlovich, none of the party had ever seen the monastery, and Miüsov had probably not even been to church for thirty years. He looked about him with some curiosity, together with assumed ease. But, except the church and the domestic buildings, though these too were ordinary enough, there was nothing of interest to his observant mind in the interior of the monastery. The last of the worshippers were coming out of the church, bareheaded and crossing themselves. Among the humbler people were a few of higher rank—two or three ladies and a very old general. They were all staying at the hotel. Our visitors were at once surrounded by beggars, but none of them gave them anything. Only Petrusha Kalganov took a ten-kopeck piece out of his purse, and, nervous and embarrassed—God knows why—hurriedly shoved it at an old woman, quickly saying: "Divide it equally." None of his companions made any remark upon it, so that he had no reason to be embarrassed; but, perceiving this, he was even more overcome.

It was strange, however; they really should have been expected, and, perhaps, even with some respect: one of them had recently made a donation of a thousand rubles, while another was the wealthiest landowner, and, so to say, most cultured man, upon whom all in the monastery were in a sense dependent, as a decision of the lawsuit might at any moment put their fishing rights in his hands. Yet no official personage met them.

Miüsov looked absentmindedly at the tombstones round the church, and was on the point of saying that the dead buried here must have paid a pretty penny for the right of lying in this "holy place," but refrained. His liberal irony was rapidly changing almost into anger.

"Who the devil is there to ask in this imbecile place? We must find out, for time is passing," he observed suddenly, as though speaking to himself.

All at once there came up a bald-headed, elderly man with ingratiating little eyes, wearing a broad summer overcoat. Lifting his hat, he introduced himself with a honeyed lisp as Maximov, a landowner of Tula. He at once entered into our visitors' difficulty.

"The Elder Zosima lives in the hermitage, shut tight in the hermitage, four hundred paces from the monastery, through the woods, through the woods . . ."

"I know it's the other side of the woods," observed Fyodor Pavlovich, "but we don't remember the way, it is a long time since we've been here."

"This way, through this gate, and straight through the woods . . . the woods. Come with me, won't you? I'll show you. I have to go . . . I am going myself. This way, this way."

They came out of the gate and turned towards the woods. Maximov, a man of sixty, ran rather than walked, turning sideways to stare at them all, with an incredible degree of nervous curiosity. His eyes seemed to start out of his head.

"You see, we have come to the elder upon business of our own," observed Miüsov severely. "We, so to speak, have been granted an audience by 'that personage,' and although we are grateful to you for showing us the way, we cannot ask you to go in with us."

"I've been there, been there, I've already been; *un chevalier parfait*,"[1] and the landowner snapped his fingers in the air.

"Who is a *chevalier*?" asked Miüsov.

"The elder, the splendid elder, the elder . . . the honor and glory of the monastery. Zosima. Such an elder . . ."

But his incoherent talk was cut short by a very pale, wan-looking little monk of medium height, wearing a monk's cap, who overtook them. Fyodor Pavlovich and Miüsov stopped. The monk, with an extremely courteous, profound bow, announced:

"The Father Superior invites all of you gentlemen to dine with him after your visit to the hermitage. At one o'clock, not later. And you also," he added, addressing Maximov.

"That I certainly will, without fail," cried Fyodor Pavlovich, hugely delighted at the invitation. "And, believe me, we've all given our word to

---

1. "A perfect cavalier" (French).

behave properly here. . . . And you, Pyotr Alexandrovich, will you go, too?"

"Yes, of course. What have I come for but to study all the customs here? The only obstacle to me is your company. . . ."

"Yes, Dmitri Fyodorovich does not exist yet."

"Yes, and it would be an excellent thing if he failed to appear, do you think I like all this business, and in your company, too? So we will come to dinner. Thank the Father Superior," he said to the monk.

"No, it is my duty now to conduct you to the elder," answered the monk.

"If so I'll go straight to the Father Superior—to the Father Superior," babbled the landowner.

"The Father Superior is engaged just now, however, as you please—" the monk said hesitatingly.

"A most impertinent little old man!" Miüsov observed aloud, when the landowner Maximov ran back to the monastery.

"He's like von Sohn,"[2] Fyodor Pavlovich said suddenly.

"Is that all you can think of? . . . In what way is he like von Sohn? Have you ever seen von Sohn?"

"I've seen his portrait. It's not the features, but something indefinable. He's a second von Sohn. I can always tell from the physiognomy."

"Ah, I dare say you are a connoisseur in that. But, look here, Fyodor Pavlovich, you said just now that we had given our word to behave properly, remember it. I tell you, control yourself. But if you begin to act like a buffoon, I don't intend to be associated with you here. . . . You see what a man he is"—he turned to the monk—"I'm afraid to go among decent people with him." A fine smile, not without a certain slyness, came on to the pale, bloodless lips of the monk, but he made no reply, and was evidently silent from a sense of his own dignity. Miüsov frowned more than ever.

"Oh, devil take them all! An outer show elaborated through centuries, and nothing but charlatanism and nonsense underneath," flashed through Miüsov's mind.

"Here's the hermitage, we've arrived!" cried Fyodor Pavlovich. "The gates are shut."

And he repeatedly made the sign of the cross to the saints painted above and on the sides of the gates.

"When in Rome, do as the Romans do. Here in this hermitage there are twenty-five holy men being saved, they look at one another, and eat cabbage. And not one woman goes in at this gate, that's what is especially remarkable. And that really is so. But I did hear that the elder receives ladies," he remarked suddenly to the monk.

"Women of the people are here too now, lying near the portico there waiting. For ladies of higher rank two rooms have been built adjoining the portico, but outside the precincts—you can see the windows—and the elder goes out to them by an inner passage when he is well enough. They are always outside the precincts. There is a Kharkov[3] lady, Madame Khokhlakova, waiting there now with her debilitated daughter. Probably

---

2. Von Sohn was the victim in a notorious 1870 murder case. After being killed in a Saint Petersburg brothel, his corpse was stuffed into a box and mailed to Moscow.
3. Kharkhov (Ukrainian Kharkiv) is a city and administrative region in northwest Ukraine.

he has promised to come out to her, though of late he has become so debilitated that he has hardly shown himself even to the people."

"So then there are little loopholes, after all, to creep out of the hermitage to the ladies. Don't suppose, holy father, that I mean anything, I'm just saying. Do you know, on Athos, have you heard, that not only are the visits of women not allowed, but no women at all are allowed or even any creatures of the female sex, no hens, turkey hens, cows . . ."

"Fyodor Pavlovich, I will go back and leave you here, and they'll throw you out when I'm gone, I warn you."

"But how am I interfering with you, Pyotr Alexandrovich. Look," he cried suddenly, stepping within the precincts, "what a vale of roses they live in!"

Indeed, though there were no roses now, there were many rare and beautiful autumn flowers growing wherever there was space for them. A skillful hand evidently tended them. There were flowerbeds round the church, and between the tombs. The little house with the elder's cell, wooden, one-storied, with a porch in front, was also surrounded by flowers.

"And was it like this in the time of the last elder, Varsonofy? He didn't care for such elegance, they say, he used to jump up and thrash even ladies with a stick," observed Fyodor Pavlovich, as he went up the steps.[4]

"The elder Varsonofy did sometimes seem somehow like a holy fool, but a great deal that's told is nonsense. He never thrashed anyone with a stick," answered the little monk. "Now, gentlemen, if you will wait a minute I will announce you."

"Fyodor Pavlovich, for the last time, your compact, do you hear? Behave yourself or I'll pay you back for it," Miüsov had time to mutter again.

"I can't think why you are so agitated," Fyodor Pavlovich observed sarcastically. "Are you uneasy about your sins? They say he can tell by one's eyes what one has come about. And what a lot you think of their opinion, you, a Parisian, and such a progressive gentleman, I'm even surprised at you!"

But Miüsov had no time to reply to this sarcasm, they were asked to come in. He walked in somewhat irritated . . .

"Now, I know myself, I am annoyed, I will lose my temper and begin to quarrel—and lower myself and my ideas," flashed through his mind.

Chapter II

The Old Buffoon

They entered the room almost at the same moment as the elder, who immediately appeared from his bedroom on their arrival. There were already in the cell, awaiting the elder, two hieromonks of the hermitage.[5] One—the Father Librarian, and the other—Father Païssy, a sick man, although not old, but, as they said of him, very learned. In addition, standing in the corner (and he remained standing the whole time), was a young fellow who looked to be about twenty-two years old, in an ordinary frock

---

4. This anecdote derives from *The Tale of Wanderings and Travels.*
5. A hieromonk is a monk who is also a priest, or a priest who has also been tonsured as a monk.

coat,[6] a seminarian and future theologian, who was for some reason under the patronage of the monastery and brothers. He was quite tall, with a fresh face, broad cheekbones, and intelligent and attentive narrow brown eyes. His expression was one of unquestioning, but self-respecting, reverence. Being in a subordinate and dependent position, and so not on an equal level with the guests, he did not greet them with a bow.

Father Zosima came out accompanied by a novice and Alyosha. The two hieromonks rose and greeted him with a very deep bow, touching the ground with their fingers; then they crossed themselves and kissed his hand. Blessing them, the elder replied with as deep a bow to them, touching the ground with his fingers, and asked each for his blessing. The whole ceremony was performed very seriously, not at all like some everyday ritual, and almost with some feeling. To Miüsov, however, it all seemed done with intentional impressiveness. He stood in front of the other visitors. He ought—and he had even reflected upon it the evening before—despite whatever ideas he held, solely from simple courtesy (since it was the custom here), to have gone up to receive the elder's blessing, even if he did not kiss his hand. But, when he saw all this bowing and kissing of the hieromonks, he instantly changed his mind: With dignified gravity he made a rather deep, conventional bow, and moved away to a chair. Fyodor Pavlovich did the same, exactly imitating Miüsov this time like an ape. Ivan Fyodorovich bowed with great dignity and courtesy, but he too kept his hands at his sides, while Kalganov was so flustered that he did not bow at all. The elder let fall the hand raised to bless them, and bowing to them again, asked them all to sit down. The blood rushed to Alyosha's cheeks; he was ashamed. His forebodings were coming true.

The elder sat down on a very old-fashioned little mahogany sofa, covered with leather, and he sat his visitors, except for the two hieromonks, in a row along the opposite wall on four mahogany chairs, covered with very worn black leather. The hieromonks sat one at the door and the other at the window. The seminarian, Alyosha, and the novice remained standing. The cell was not very large and had a somewhat faded look. The objects and furniture were coarse, poor, and only the most necessary. There were two pots of flowers in the window, and many icons in the corner—one of them of the Mother of God, of very large size and painted, probably, long before the Schism.[7] Before it burned a little lamp. Near it were two other icons in shining settings, and near them carved cherubim, porcelain eggs, a Catholic cross of ivory with a Mater Dolorosa[8] embracing it and several foreign engravings from the great Italian artists of past centuries. Next to these elegant and expensive engravings were several of the most common

6. In other words, he is wearing neither the clothing of any religious ordination nor the uniforms students often wore in nineteenth-century Russia.
7. The Schism (Russian *Raskol*) was a reaction against reforms implemented in 1653 by Patriarch Nikon (1605–1681; Patriarch 1652–58). As Patriarch, or highest authority in the Russian Orthodox Church, Nikon mandated certain changes in ritual, such as making the sign of the cross with three fingers instead of two, and correcting Russian translations of divine service books against Greek versions. Those who objected to the reforms were anathematized as heretics and often brutally persecuted. Known as Old Believers, many fled to border regions such as Siberia.
8. In Christian iconography, *Mater Dolorosa* (Latin for "sorrowful mother") refers to images of Mary, the mother of Jesus, as she witnesses his crucifixion. For discussion of why this preeminently Roman Catholic image appears in Zosima's cell, see the complete version of Vetlovskaya, "Alyosha Karamazov and the Hagiographic Hero" (an excerpt from which is included in this Norton Critical Edition, p. 677).

Russian prints of saints, martyrs, prelates,[9] and so on, such as are sold for a few kopecks at all the fairs. There were portraits of Russian bishops, past and present, but on other walls. Miüsov glanced at all this "conventionalism" and fixed an intent gaze on the elder. He respected his gaze, he had this weakness, which was in any case excusable in him, taking into consideration that he was already fifty years old—an age at which an intelligent established man of the world always becomes more respectful of himself, sometimes even against his will.

From the first moment he did not like the elder. There was, indeed, something in the elder's face which many people besides Miüsov might not have liked. This was a short bent little man with very weak legs, only sixty-five years old, but illness made him look at least ten years older. His whole face, which by the way was quite withered, was covered with little wrinkles, especially around his eyes. His eyes were small, light-colored, quick and shining, like two shining points. He had a sprinkling of gray hair left around his temples, his pointed little beard was small and scanty, and his lips, which smiled frequently, were as thin as two threads. His nose was not long, but sharp, like a bird's beak.

"To all appearances a malicious and pettily arrogant little soul," flashed through Miüsov's head. He felt altogether dissatisfied with himself.

A cheap little clock on the wall struck twelve hurriedly, and served to begin the conversation.

"Precisely to our time," cried Fyodor Pavlovich, "but no sign of my son, Dmitri Fyodorovich. I apologize for him, sacred elder!" (Alyosha shuddered all over at "sacred elder.") "I am always punctual myself, minute for minute, remembering that punctuality is the courtesy of kings . . ."[1]

"But you are not a king, anyway," Miüsov muttered, losing his self-restraint at once.

"Yes, that's true, I'm not a king. And, just imagine, Pyotr Alexandrovich, I even knew it myself, by God! I always say the wrong thing! Your reverence!" he cried with sudden pathos, "you behold before you a buffoon, a real buffoon! I introduce myself as such. It's an old habit, alas! And if I sometimes talk nonsense out of place it's with an object, with the object of amusing people and making myself agreeable. One must be agreeable, mustn't one? I was seven years ago in a little town where I had business, and I made friends with some merchants there. We went to the captain of police because we had to see him about something, and to ask him to dine with us. He was a tall, fat, fair, sulky man, the most dangerous type in such cases. It's their liver. I went straight up to him, and with the ease of a man of the world, you know, 'Mr. Ispravnik,' said I, 'be our Napravnik.'[2] 'What do you mean by Napravnik?' said he. I see, at the first half-second, that it had misfired, he stands there so glum, stubborn: 'I wanted to make a joke,' said I, 'for the general diversion, as Mr. Napravnik is our well-known Russian orchestra conductor and what we need for the harmony of our undertaking is someone of that sort.' And I explained my comparison very reasonably, didn't I? 'Excuse me,' said he, 'I am an Ispravnik, and I do

9. Prelates are high-ranking members of the clergy.
1. A well-known saying of King Louis XVIII of France (1755–1824; ruled 1814–24).
2. E. F. Napravnik (1839–1916) conducted at the Mariinsky Opera in Saint Petersburg. The Russian word *napravnik* suggests "conductor" or "director," whereas *ispravnik* suggests "rectifier" or "corrector."

not allow puns to be made on my calling.' He turned and walked away. I followed him, shouting, 'Yes, yes, you are an Ispravnik, not a Napravnik.' 'No,' he said, 'since you called me a Napravnik I am one.' And would you believe it, it ruined our business! And I'm always like that, always like that. Always injuring myself with my politeness. Once, many years ago, I said to an influential person: 'Your wife is a ticklish woman,' in an honorable sense, of the moral qualities, so to speak. But he asked me, 'Why, have you tickled her?' I thought I'd be polite, so I couldn't help saying 'Yes,' and he gave me a fine tickling on the spot. Only that happened long ago, so I'm not ashamed to tell the story. I'm always injuring myself like that."

"You're doing it now," muttered Miüsov, with disgust.

The elder scrutinized them both in silence.

"Am I? Imagine, I knew it, Pyotr Alexandrovich, and I even, you know, had a feeling that I was doing it, as soon as I started speaking, and you know, I even had a feeling that you would be the first to point it out to me. The minute I see my joke isn't coming off, your reverence, both my cheeks feel as though they were drawn down to the lower jaw and there is almost a spasm in them. That's been so since I was young, when I had to make jokes for my living in noblemen's families. I am an inveterate buffoon from birth, reverend father, just like a holy fool; I don't deny that there may be an unclean spirit in me, not a very high-caliber one, by the way, a more important one would have chosen different quarters, but not yours, Pyotr Alexandrovich, you are also not very grand quarters. But I do believe, I believe in God. I only began to have doubts lately, but I am sitting now and waiting for words of wisdom. I'm like the philosopher, Diderot,[3] your reverence. Did you ever hear, most Holy Father, how Diderot went to see the Metropolitan Platon, in the time of the Empress Catherine?[4] He went in and said straight out, 'There is no God.' To which the great Bishop lifted up his finger and answered, 'The fool has said in his heart there is no God.'[5] And he fell down at his feet on the spot. 'I believe,' he cried, 'and will be christened.'[6] And so he was. Princess Dashkova was his godmother, and Potyomkin his godfather."[7]

"Fyodor Pavlovich, this is unbearable! You know you're telling lies and that that stupid anecdote isn't true. Why are you playing the fool?" cried Miüsov in a shaking voice, losing all control of himself.

"I have had a feeling all my life that it wasn't true!" Fyodor Pavlovich cried with conviction. "But I'll tell you the whole truth, gentlemen: great elder! Forgive me, that last thing, about Diderot's baptism, I composed

---

3. Denis Diderot (1713–1784), French Enlightenment philosopher. Diderot received financial assistance from Catherine the Great and visited Russia from November 1773 through March 1774. Dostoevsky read Diderot's writings intensively in 1868–69 while living in Western Europe.

4. Born Pyotr Levshin, Platon (1737–1812) served as Metropolitan or Head Bishop of Moscow 1775–1812. Known for his sermons and writings, Platon did in fact meet with Diderot, although the event is distorted here by Fyodor Pavlovich. Catherine II (Catherine the Great, 1729–1796), Empress of Russia (reigned 1762–96).

5. "The fool hath said in his heart, There is no God" (Psalms 14.1 and 53.1).

6. The hagiographical literature of Russian Orthodoxy includes dramatic accounts of the effect of Christian miracles on pagans. Fyodor Pavlovich places the ecstatic exclamation of a pagan moved to convert to Christianity in the mouth of Diderot, an impassioned critic of religion.

7. Yekaterina Vorontsova-Dashkova (1743–1810) played an important role at the court of Catherine the Great and in the Russian enlightenment. A friend of Diderot and Voltaire, she served as the first president of the Russian Academy, part of the Saint Petersburg Academy of Arts and Sciences. Grigory Potyomkin (1739–1791) was a leading Russian statesman, a favorite advisor and lover of Catherine the Great.

myself just now, this very minute, while I was telling it to you, it never occurred to me before. I made it up for piquancy. I play the fool, Pyotr Alexandrovich, to make myself agreeable. Though I really don't know myself, sometimes, what I do it for. And as for Diderot, I heard as far as 'the fool hath said in his heart' twenty times from the gentry around here when I was young and living with them; I also heard it from your aunt, Pyotr Alexandrovich, Martha Fominishna, by the way. They all believe to this day that the infidel Diderot came to dispute about God with the Metropolitan Platon. . . ."

Miüsov got up, not only losing his patience but even somehow forgetting himself. He was furious and realized that this made him ridiculous. What was taking place in the cell was really incredible. For forty or fifty years past, from the times of former elders, no visitors had entered that cell without feelings of the profoundest veneration. Almost everyone admitted to the cell felt that a great favor was being shown him. Many remained kneeling during the whole visit. Of those visitors, many had been men of high rank and learning, even some freethinkers, attracted by curiosity, or for other reasons, but all without exception had shown the profoundest reverence and delicacy, for here there was no question of money, but only on the one side love and kindness, and on the other repentance and the desire to resolve some difficult question of the soul or difficult moment in the life of the heart. So that the buffoonery shown by Fyodor Pavlovich, the lack of reverence for the place he was in, amazed and bewildered the spectators, or at least some of them. The hieromonks, with unchanged countenances, waited, with earnest attention, to hear what the elder would say, but seemed on the point of standing up, like Miüsov. Alyosha stood, with hanging head, on the verge of tears. What seemed to him strangest of all was that his brother Ivan Fyodorovich, on whom alone he had rested his hopes, and who alone had such influence on his father that he could have stopped him, sat now quite unmoved, with downcast eyes, apparently even waiting with some kind of curious interest to see how it would end, as though he himself were a complete stranger there. At Rakitin (the seminarian), whom he knew well and was almost close with, Alyosha could not even look: he knew his thoughts (although Alyosha alone in the whole monastery knew them).

"Forgive me," began Miüsov, addressing the elder, "for perhaps I seem to be taking part in this unworthy foolery. I made a mistake in believing that even a man like Fyodor Pavlovich would understand what was due on a visit to so honored a personage. I did not suppose I should have to apologize simply for having come with him. . . ."

Pyotr Alexandrovich could say no more and, becoming completely flustered, was about to leave the room.

"Don't worry, I beg you." The elder suddenly got onto his feeble legs and, taking Pyotr Alexandrovich by both hands, made him sit down again. "I beg you not to disturb yourself. I particularly beg you to be my guest." And with a bow he went back and sat down again on his little sofa.

"Great elder, speak, do I annoy you by my vivacity?" Fyodor Pavlovich cried suddenly, clutching the arms of his chair in both hands, as though ready to leap up from it if the answer was unfavorable.

"I earnestly beg you, too, not to worry yourself, and don't be uncomfortable," the elder said impressively. "Don't be uncomfortable, make yourself quite at home. And, above all, do not be so ashamed of yourself, for that is at the root of it all."

"Quite at home? To be my natural self? Oh, that is much too much, but I am deeply moved and accept it! Do you know, blessed father, you'd better not invite me to be my natural self. Don't risk it. . . . I will not go so far as that myself. I warn you for your own sake. Well, the rest is still plunged in the mists of uncertainty, though there are people who'd be pleased to describe me for you. I mean that for you, Pyotr Alexandrovich, but as for you, holy being, let me tell you: I am brimming over with ecstasy!"

He got up, and throwing up his hands, declaimed, "Blessed be the womb that carried thee, and the paps that gave thee suck[8]—the paps especially. When you said just now, 'Don't be so ashamed of yourself for that is at the root of it all,' you pierced right through me by that remark, and read me to the core. Indeed, I always feel when I meet people that I am lower than all, and that they all take me for a buffoon. So I say, 'Let me really play the buffoon. I am not afraid of your opinion, for you are every one of you worse than I am.' That is why I am a buffoon. It is from shame, great elder, from shame; it's simply over-sensitiveness that makes me rowdy. If I had only been sure that everyone would accept me as the kindest and wisest of men, oh, Lord, what a good man I should have been then! Teacher!" he fell suddenly on his knees, "what must I do to gain eternal life?"[9] It was difficult even now to decide: was he joking or was he really moved?

The elder, lifting his eyes, looked at him, and said with a smile:

"You have known for a long time what you must do, you have sense enough: don't give way to drunkenness and incontinence of speech; don't give way to sensual lust; and, above all, to the love of money. And close your taverns. If you can't close all, at least two or three. And, above all—don't lie."

"You mean about Diderot?"

"No, not about Diderot. Above all, don't lie to yourself. The man who lies to himself and listens to his own lie comes to such a pass that he cannot distinguish the truth within him, or around him, and so loses all respect for himself and for others. And having no respect he ceases to love, and in order to occupy and distract himself without love he gives way to passions and coarse pleasures, and sinks to bestiality in his vices, all from continual lying to other men and to himself. The man who lies to himself can be more easily offended than anyone. You know it is sometimes very pleasant to take offense, isn't it? A man may know that nobody has insulted him, but that he has invented the insult for himself, has lied and exaggerated to make it picturesque, has caught at a word and made a mountain out of a molehill—he knows that himself, yet he will be the first to take offense, and will revel in his resentment till he feels great pleasure in it, and so pass to genuine vindictiveness. But get up, sit down, I beg you. All this, too, is deceitful posturing . . ."

"Blessed man! Give me your hand to kiss." Fyodor Pavlovich skipped up, and imprinted a rapid kiss on the elder's thin hand. "It is, it is pleasant to take offense. You said that so well, as I never heard it before. Yes, I have

---

8. In Luke 11.27, a woman cries to Jesus, "Blessed is the womb that bore thee, and the paps which thou has sucked."
9. See Luke 10.25: "a certain lawyer stood up, and tempted him, saying, Master, what shall I do to inherit eternal life?" Matthew 19.16 and Mark 10.17 also provide similar accounts.

been all my life taking offense, to please myself, taking offense on aesthetic grounds, for it is not so much pleasant as beautiful sometimes to be
insulted—that you had forgotten, great elder, it is beautiful! I shall make
a note of that. But I have been lying, lying positively my whole life long,
every day and hour of it. Truly I am a lie and the father of lies! But probably I am not the father of lies, I am getting the texts mixed up, but just the
son of lies, and that will be enough.[1] Only . . . my angel . . . I may sometimes talk about Diderot! Diderot will do no harm, though sometimes a
word will do harm. Great elder, by the way, I was forgetting, though I had
been meaning for the last two years to come here on purpose to ask and to
find out something. Only do tell Pyotr Alexandrovich not to interrupt me.
Here is my question: Is it true, great father, that the story is told somewhere in the *Lives of the Saints*[2] of some holy miracle worker martyred for
his faith who, when his head was cut off at last, stood up, picked up his
head, and walked a long way, carrying it in his hands 'courteously kissing
it.' Is that true or not, honored fathers?"

"No, it is not true," said the elder.

"There is nothing of the kind in all the *Lives of the Saints*. What saint do
you say the story is told of?" asked the hieromonk, the Father Librarian.

"I do not know what saint. I do not know, and can't tell. I was deceived.
I was told the story. I heard it, and do you know who told it? Pyotr Alexandrovich Miüsov here, who was so angry just now about Diderot, it was
he who told the story."

"I never told it to you, I never speak to you at all."

"It is true you did not tell me, but you told it to company when I was
present, it was three years ago. I mentioned it because by that ridiculous
story you shook my faith, Pyotr Alexandrovich. You knew nothing of it,
but I went home with my faith shaken, and I have been getting more and
more shaken ever since. Yes, Pyotr Alexandrovich, you were the cause of
a great fall! That was not a Diderot!"

Fyodor Pavlovich got excited and pathetic, though it was perfectly clear
to everyone by now that he was playing a part again. Yet Miüsov was
stung by his words.

"What nonsense, and it is all nonsense," he muttered. "I may really have
told it, sometime or other . . . but not to you. I was told it myself. I heard it
in Paris from a Frenchman, who told me it was read at our mass from the
Lives of the Saints . . . he was a very learned man who had made a special
study of Russian statistics . . . he lived a long time in Russia. . . . I have not
read the *Lives of the Saints* myself . . . and I am not going to read them . . .
all sorts of things are said at dinner . . . we were dining then."

"Yes, you were dining then, and so I lost my faith!" said Fyodor Pavlovich, mimicking him.

---

1. "The father of lies" refers to the devil. In John 8.33–44, Jesus debates the issue of paternity
with a group of men in the temple. As Jews, the men claim Abraham as their father, to which
Jesus responds: "Ye are of your father the devil, and the lusts of your father ye will do. He was
a murderer from the beginning, and abode not in the truth, because there is no truth in him.
When he speaketh a lie, he speaketh of his own: for he is a liar, and the father of it."
2. A collection of brief biographies of saints recognized by the Russian Orthodox Church.
Intended for daily devotional reading, *Lives of the Saints* (Russian *Cheti Minei*) was popular in
nineteenth-century Russia. The legend Fyodor Pavlovich recounts is from the life of St. Denis
of Paris, patron saint of France. Denis is a Catholic saint not recognized by the Orthodox
Church, and his story would not have been included in the *Lives*. Voltaire and Diderot ridiculed this legendary episode from the life of Denis.

"What do I care about your faith?" Miüsov almost shouted, but he suddenly checked himself, and said with contempt: "You defile everything you touch."

The elder suddenly rose from his seat. "Excuse me, gentlemen, for leaving you a few minutes," he said, addressing all his guests. "I have visitors awaiting me who arrived before you. But don't you tell lies all the same," he added, turning to Fyodor Pavlovich with a cheerful face.

He went out of the cell, and Alyosha and the novice flew to escort him down the steps. Alyosha was breathless, he was glad to leave, but he was glad, too, that the elder was cheerful and not offended. Father Zosima was going towards the portico to bless the people waiting for him there. But Fyodor Pavlovich persisted in stopping him at the door of the cell.

"Most blessed man!" he cried, with feeling. "Allow me to kiss your hand once more. Yes, with you I could still talk, I could still get on. Do you think I always lie and play the fool like this? Believe me, I have been acting like this all the time on purpose to try you. I have been testing you all the time to see whether I could get on with you. Is there room for my humility beside your pride? I am ready to give you a testimonial that one can get on with you! But now, I'll be quiet; I will keep quiet all the time. I'll sit in a chair and hold my tongue. Now it is for you to speak, Pyotr Alexandrovich. You are the principal person left now . . . for ten minutes."

Chapter III

Peasant Women Who Have Faith

Near the wooden portico below, built onto the outer wall of the precinct, there was a crowd of about twenty peasant women. They had been told that the elder was at last coming out, and they had gathered together in anticipation. The Khokhlakovs, who were landowners, were also awaiting the elder and had come out onto the portico, but in a separate area set aside for women of rank. There were two of them: mother and daughter. Madame Khokhlakova, the mother, a wealthy lady and always tastefully dressed, was still fairly young and quite attractive, slightly pale, with very lively and almost completely black eyes. She was not more than thirty-three, and had been five years a widow. Her daughter, a girl of fourteen, suffered paralysis in her legs. The poor girl had not been able to walk for the last six months, and was wheeled about in a long reclining chair. She had a charming little face, rather thin from illness, but full of gaiety. There was a gleam of mischief in her big dark eyes with their long lashes. Her mother had been intending to take her abroad ever since the spring, but they had been detained all summer by business connected with their estate. They had been staying a week in our town, where they had come more for purposes of business than devotion, but had visited the elder once already, three days before. Though they knew that the elder scarcely saw anyone, they had now suddenly turned up again, and urgently entreated "the happiness of beholding once again the great healer."

In anticipation of the elder's entrance, the mamma was sitting on a chair by the side of her daughter's invalid carriage, and two paces from her stood an old monk, not one of our monastery, but a visitor from an obscure monastery in the far north. He too sought the elder's blessing. But Father Zosima, on entering the portico, went first straight to the common people who were crowded at the foot of the three steps that led up into the portico. Father Zosima stood on the top step, put on his stole,[3] and began blessing the women who thronged about him. One possessed woman was led up to him by both hands. As soon as she caught sight of the elder she began shrieking and writhing as though in the pains of childbirth. Laying the stole on her forehead, he read a short prayer over her, and she was at once soothed and quieted. I do not know how it may be now, but in my childhood I often happened to see and hear these "possessed" women in the villages and monasteries. They used to be brought to mass; they would squeal or bark like a dog so that they were heard all over the church. But when the sacrament[4] was carried in and they were led up to it, at once the "possession" ceased, and the sick women were always soothed for a time. I was greatly impressed and amazed at this as a child; but then I heard from country neighbors and from my town teachers that the whole illness was simulated to avoid work, and that it could always be cured by suitable severity; various anecdotes were told to confirm this. But later on I learned with astonishment from medical specialists that there is no pretense about it, that it is a terrible illness to which women are subject, especially prevalent among us in Russia, and that it is due to the hard lot of the peasant women, a disease arising from exhausting toil too soon after hard, abnormal labor in child birth, unassisted by medical help; and, moreover, from the hopeless misery, from beatings, and so on, which some women were not able to endure like others. The strange and instant healing of the frantic and struggling woman as soon as she was led up to the holy sacrament, which had been explained to me as pretense and even trickery on the part of the "clericals," arose probably in the most natural manner, and both the women who supported her and, most importantly, the invalid herself fully believed as a truth beyond question that the evil spirit in possession of her could not hold out if the sick woman were brought to the sacrament and made to bow down before it. And so, with a nervous and psychically deranged woman, a sort of convulsion of the whole organism always took place (and was bound to take place) at the moment of bowing down to the sacrament, aroused by the expectation of the miracle of healing and the implicit belief that it would come to pass. And it did come to pass, though only for a moment. It was exactly the same now as soon as the elder covered the sick woman with the stole.

Many of the women crowding towards him were moved to tears of emotional ecstasy by the effect of the moment; some strove to kiss at least the hem of his garment, others cried out in singsong voices. He blessed them all and talked with some of them. The "possessed" woman he knew already. She came from a village only four miles from the monastery, and had been brought to him before.

"But here is one from afar!" He pointed to a woman by no means old but very thin and wasted, with a face not merely sunburned but almost

<hr />

3. A liturgical vestment worn by clergy of many Christian denominations, consisting of an embroidered band or strip of cloth worn over the shoulders.
4. The sacrament referred to here is the bread and wine of communion.

blackened by exposure. She was kneeling and gazing with a fixed stare at the elder; there was something almost frenzied in her eyes.

"From afar off, Father, from afar off! From two hundred miles from here. From afar off, Father, from afar off!" the woman began in a singsong voice, swaying her head from side to side with her cheek resting in her hand. She spoke as if she were lamenting. There is silent and long-suffering grief to be met with in the common people; it withdraws into itself and is silent. But there is also grief that breaks out: it bursts into tears and from that moment finds vent in lamentation. This is particularly common with women. But it is no lighter a grief than the silent. Lamentations comfort only by lacerating the heart still more. Such grief does not even want consolation, it feeds on the sense of its unquenchableness. Lamentation is simply the need to constantly irritate the wound.

"You are of the tradesman class?"[5] said Father Zosima, looking curiously at her.

"Townfolk we are, Father, townfolk. Yet we are peasants though we live in the town. I have come to see you, oh Father! We heard of you, Father, we heard of you. I have buried my little son, and I have come on a pilgrimage. I have been in three monasteries, but they told me, 'Go, Nastasya, go to them'—that is to you, my dear. I have come; I was yesterday at the service, and today I have come to you."

"What are you weeping for?"

"It's my little son I'm grieving for, Father, he was three years old, three years all but three months. I grieve for my little boy, Father, for my little boy. He was the last little son left, we had four, my Nikitushka and I, and now we've no children, our little children didn't stay with us, they didn't stay. I buried the first three without grieving overmuch, but now I have buried the last and I can't forget him. It's as though he's always standing before me, he doesn't go away. He has withered my heart. I look at his little clothes, his little shirt, his little boots, and I wail. I lay out all that is left of him, all his little things, I look at them and wail. I say to Nikitushka, my husband, let me go on a pilgrimage, master. He is a coachman. We're not poor people, Father, not poor; he drives our own horse. It's all our own, the horse and the carriage. And what good is it all to us now? My Nikitushka has begun drinking while I am away, he's sure to, it used to be so before: as soon as I turn my back he gives way to it. But now I don't think about him. It's three months since I left home. I've forgotten, I've forgotten everything, and I don't want to remember; and what would I do with him now? I've finished with him, I've finished, I've finished with them all. And I don't want to look upon my house and my things, I don't want to see anything at all!"

"Listen, mother," said the elder. "Once in olden times a holy saint saw in the Temple a mother like you weeping for her little one, her only one, whom God had taken. 'Knowest thou not,' said the saint to her, 'how bold these little ones are before the throne of God? Verily there are none bolder than they in the Kingdom of Heaven. "Thou didst give us life, oh Lord," they say, "and scarcely had we looked upon it when Thou didst take it back again." And so boldly they ask and ask again that God gives them at once the rank

5. Zosima asks the pilgrim if she belongs to the *meshchanstvo*, the lowest ranks of the urban merchant class; she responds that she and her husband are peasants who live in town and operate their own business. It was not uncommon for peasants to live in urban areas and pursue nonagricultural livelihoods.

of angels. Therefore,' said the saint, 'thou too, oh mother, rejoice and weep not, for thy little one is with the Lord in the fellowship of the angels.' That's what the saint said to the weeping mother of old.[6] He was a great saint and he could not have spoken falsely. Therefore you too, mother, know that your little one is surely before the throne of God, is rejoicing and happy, and praying to God for you, and therefore weep, but rejoice."

The woman listened to him, looking down with her cheek in her hand. She sighed deeply.

"My Nikitushka tried to comfort me with the same words as you. 'Foolish one,' he said, 'why weep? Our son is no doubt singing with the angels before God.' He says that to me, but he weeps himself. I see that he cries like me. 'I know, Nikitushka,' said I, 'where could he be if not with the Lord God, only he is not here with us now, Nikitushka, he isn't beside us, sitting here as before!' And if only I could look upon him one little time, if only I could peep at him one little time, without going up to him, without speaking, if I could be hidden in a corner and only see him for one little minute, hear him playing in the yard, calling in his little voice, 'Mommy, where are you?' If only I could hear him pattering with his little feet, pat pat about the room just once, only once, for so often, so often I remember how he used to run to me and shout and laugh, if only I could hear his little feet I should know him! But he's gone, Father, he's gone, and I shall never hear him again! His little sash is here, but not him, and I shall never see or hear him now! . . ."

She drew out of her bosom her boy's little embroidered sash, and as soon as she looked at it she began shaking with sobs, hiding her eyes with her fingers through which the tears flowed, suddenly bursting in a stream.

"It is 'Rachel of old,'" said the elder, "'weeping for her children, and will not be comforted because they are not,' and such is the lot set on earth for you mothers.[7] And do not be comforted, you should not be comforted, do not be comforted but weep, only each time you weep, remember unwaveringly that your little son—he is one of God's angels—he looks down on you from there and sees you, and rejoices at your tears, and points them out to the Lord God.[8] And for a long time you will have this great mother's weeping, but in the end it will turn into quiet joy for you,[9] and your bitter tears will be only tears of quiet tenderness and the heart's purification, which saves from sin. And I shall pray for the peace of your child's soul. What was his name?"

"Alexey, Father."

"A sweet name. After Alexey, the man of God?"[1]

---

6. Zosima freely paraphrases from the "Tale of the Blessed Father Daniel about Andronicus and His Wife," found in the *Prologue* (see p. 30).
7. Zosima quotes the Bible: "A voice was heard in Ramah, lamentation, and bitter weeping; Rahel weeping for her children refused to be comforted for her children, because they were not" (Jeremiah 31.15). According to Matthew 2.16, King Herod ordered all male children two years and under in Bethlehem to be killed, thereby fulfilling Jeremiah's prophecy.
8. In Matthew 18.10, Jesus tells his disciples, "Take heed that ye despise not one of these little ones, for I say unto you, That in heaven their angels do always behold the face of my Father which is in heaven."
9. Zosima paraphrases passages from the Bible. In Jeremiah 31.13, the Lord says "Then shall the virgin rejoice in the dance, both young men and old together: for I will turn their mourning into joy, and will comfort them, and make them rejoice from their sorrow." In John 16.20, Jesus tells his disciples "ye shall be sorrowful, but your sorrow shall be turned into joy."
1. In the early fifth century, Alexius (the name means *defender* or *helper*), the son of a wealthy Roman official, sought to devote himself to God rather than enter a marriage arranged by his parents. With his fiancée's cooperation, Alexius disguised himself as a beggar and escaped

"The man of God, Father, the man of God, Alexey, the man of God."

"What a saint he was! I will remember him, mother, and your grief in my prayers, and I will pray for your husband's health. It is a sin for you to leave him. Go to your husband and take care of him. Your little one will see from heaven that you have forsaken his father, and will weep over you. Why do you trouble his happiness? He is living, for the soul lives forever, and though he is not in the house, he is near you, unseen. How can he go into the house when you say that the house is hateful to you? To whom is he to go if he finds you, his mother and father, not together? You dream of him now, and you are agonized, but then he will send you gentle dreams. Go to your husband, mother; go this very day."

"I will go, Father, at your word, I will go. You've gone straight to my heart. My Nikitushka, my Nikitushka, you are waiting for me, my dear," the woman began in a singsong voice; but the elder had already turned away to a very old woman, dressed like a dweller in the town, not like a pilgrim. Her eyes showed that she had come with an object, and in order to say something. She said she was the widow of a noncommissioned officer, and lived close by in the town. Her son Vasenka was in the commissariat service, and had gone to Irkutsk[2] in Siberia. He had written twice from there, but now a year had passed since he had written. She did inquire about him, but she did not know the proper place to inquire.

"Only the other day Stepanida Il'inishna Bedryagina—she's a rich merchant's wife—said to me, 'You go, Prokhorovna, and put your son's name down for prayer in the church, and pray for the peace of his soul as though he were dead. His soul will be troubled,' she said, 'and he will write you a letter.' And Stepanida Il'inishna told me it was a certain thing which had been many times tried. Only I am in doubt. . . . Oh, you light of ours, is it true or false, and would it be right?"

"Don't think of it. It's shameful to ask the question. How is it possible to pray for the peace of a living soul? And his own mother too! It's a great sin, akin to sorcery. Only for your ignorance it is forgiven you. Better pray to the Queen of Heaven,[3] our swift intercessor and helper, for his good health, and that she may forgive you for your error. And another thing I will tell you, Prokhorovna: either he will soon come back to you, your son, or he will be sure to send a letter. Go, and henceforward be in peace. Your son is alive, I tell you."

"Dear Father, God reward you, our benefactor, who prays for all of us and for our sins . . ."

But the elder had already noticed in the crowd two glowing eyes fixed upon him by an exhausted, consumptive-looking, though young peasant woman. She looked at him in silence, her eyes were asking him for something, but she seemed afraid to approach.

"What is it, my dear?"

---

his parents' house on his wedding day. After years living a monastic life in Syria, he returned to his parents' house in Rome, once again dressed as a beggar. His parents did not recognize him but were kind to the poor and allowed him to live in a corner under the stairs. For seventeen years he lived this way, praying and teaching children. When he died, a note revealing his true identity was discovered on his body. The significance of the name Alexey is discussed in Vetlovskaya, "Alyosha Karamazov and the Hagiographic Hero," p. 677.

2. A major administrative center of Siberia, approximately 3,000 miles east of Moscow.
3. Queen of Heaven is one of the names sometimes given to Mary, the mother of Jesus.

"Absolve my soul, Father," she articulated softly and unhurriedly, sank on her knees and bowed down at his feet. "I have sinned, Father. I am afraid of my sin."

The elder sat down on the lower step. The woman crept closer to him, still on her knees.

"I am a widow these three years," she began in a half-whisper, with a sort of shudder. "I had a hard life with my husband. He was an old man. He used to beat me cruelly. He lay ill; I thought, looking at him, if he were to get well, if he were to get up again, what then? And then the thought came to me—" ,

"Wait," said the elder, and he put his ear close to her lips. The woman went on in a low whisper, so that it was almost impossible to catch anything. She had soon done.

"Three years ago?" asked the elder.

"Three years. At first I didn't think about it, but now I've begun to be ill, and the grief never leaves me."

"Have you come from far?"

"Over three hundred miles away."

"Have you told it in confession?"

"I have confessed it. Twice I have confessed it."

"Have you been admitted to Communion?"

"Yes. I am afraid; I am afraid to die."

"Fear nothing and never be afraid, and don't be depressed. If only your penitence fail not—God will forgive all. There is no sin and there can be no sin on all the earth, which the Lord will not forgive to the truly repentant.[4] Man cannot commit a sin so great as to exhaust the infinite love of God. Can there be a sin which could exceed the love of God? Think only of repentance, continual repentance, but banish fear altogether. Believe that God loves you as you cannot conceive, that He loves you with your sin, in your sin. It has been said of old that over one repentant sinner there is more joy in heaven than over ten righteous men.[5] Go, and be not afraid. Be not bitter against men, be not angry if you are wronged. Forgive the dead man in your heart what wrong he did you, be reconciled with him in truth. If you are penitent, you love. And if you love you are of God. With love all things are bought, all things are saved. If I, a sinner, even as you are, am tender with you and have pity on you, how much more will God. Love is such a priceless treasure that you can buy the whole world with it, and redeem not only your own, but the sins of others as well. Go, and be not afraid."

He signed her three times with the cross, took from his own neck a little icon and put it upon her. She bowed down to the earth without speaking. He got up and looked cheerfully at a healthy peasant woman with a tiny baby in her arms.

---

4. Zosima paraphrases words of Isaac the Syrian (died ca. 700 A.D.), who said "there is no unforgivable sin except the sin of the unrepentant." (This is also an echo of Matthew 12.31: "All manner of sin and blasphemy shall be forgiven unto men.") Also known as Isaac of Ninevah and Isaac Cyrus, the hermit monk Isaac was renowned as an ascetic who emphasized virtues such as humility, love, and self-denial, and he is recognized as a saint by the Eastern Orthodox Church. Dostoevsky owned an 1858 edition of Isaac's writings and sayings.

5. Zosima refers to Luke 15.7, in which Jesus tells the scribes and Pharisees, "joy shall be in heaven over one sinner that repenteth, more than over ninety and nine just persons, which need no repentance."

"From Vyshegorye, dear."

"Four miles you have dragged yourself with the baby. What do you want?"

"I've come to look at you. I have been to you before—or have you forgotten? You've no great memory if you've forgotten me. They told us you were ill. Thinks I, I'll go and see him for myself. Now I see you, and you're not ill. You'll live another twenty years. God bless you! There are plenty to pray for you; how should you be ill?"

"I thank you for all, daughter."

"By the way, I have a thing to ask, not a great one. Here are sixty kopecks. Give them, dear Father, to someone poorer than me. I thought as I came along, better give through him. He'll know whom to give to."

"Thanks, my dear, thanks! You are a good woman. I love you. I will do so certainly. Is that your little girl in your arms?"

"My little girl, Father, Lizaveta."

"May the Lord bless you both, you and your babe Lizaveta! You have gladdened my heart, mother. Farewell, dear children, farewell, dear ones."

He blessed them all and bowed low to them.

Chapter IV

A Lady of Little Faith

The visiting lady landowner, looking on the scene of his conversation with the peasants and his blessing them, shed silent tears and wiped them away with her handkerchief. She was a sentimental society lady of genuinely good disposition in many respects. When the elder went up to her at last she met him ecstatically:

"I have borne so much, so much, looking on at this touching scene . . ." She could not go on for emotion. "Oh, I understand the people's love for you, I love the people myself, I want to love them, and who could help loving them, our splendid Russian people, so simple in their greatness!"

"How is your daughter's health? You wanted to talk to me again?"

"Oh, I have been urgently begging for it, I have prayed for it, I was ready to fall on my knees and kneel for three days at your windows until you let me in. We have come, great healer, to express our ecstatic gratitude. You have healed my Liza,[6] healed her completely, and how? By praying over her last Thursday and laying your hands upon her. We have hastened here to kiss those hands, to pour out our feelings and our homage!"

"What do you mean by healed? Isn't she still lying down in her chair?"

"But her night fevers have stopped completely, for two days now, ever since Thursday," said the lady with nervous haste. "And that's not all: her legs are stronger. This morning she got up well, she had slept all night, look at her rosy cheeks, her bright eyes. She used to be always crying, but now she laughs and is gay and happy. Today she demanded that we put her on her feet, and she stood up for a whole minute, without any

---

6. In the original Russian text, Madame Khokhlakova's daughter's name is sometimes spelled *Liza* (in Cyrillic letters) and sometimes *Lise* (in Roman letters). Use of French words and names carries a negative connotation in Dostoevsky's writings; it signifies the split between the educated upper class, who were conversant in French, and the Russian common people.

support. She wagers that in two weeks she'll be dancing a quadrille.[7] I've called in the local doctor, Herzenstube. He shrugged his shoulders and said, 'I am amazed; I can make nothing of it.' And would you have us not come here to disturb you, not fly here to thank you? Lise, thank him—thank him!"

Lise's pretty little laughing face became suddenly serious, she rose in her chair as far as she could and, looking at the elder, clasped her hands before him, but could not restrain herself and broke into laughter . . .

"It's at him, at him," she said, pointing to Alyosha, with childish vexation at herself for not being able to repress her mirth. If anyone had looked at Alyosha standing a step behind the elder, he could have caught a quick flush crimsoning his cheeks in an instant. His eyes shone and he looked down.

"She has a message for you, Alexey Fyodorovich . . . how are you?" the mamma went on, holding out her exquisitely gloved hand to Alyosha. The elder turned round and all at once looked attentively at Alyosha. The latter went nearer to Liza and, smiling in a strange and awkward way, held out his hand to her too. Lise assumed an important air.

"Katerina Ivanovna has sent you this through me." She handed him a little note. "She especially asks you to go and see her soon, soon and that you will not fail her, but will be sure to come."

"She asks me to go and see her? Me? What for?" Alyosha muttered in great astonishment. His face suddenly looked anxious.

"Oh, it's all to do with Dmitri Fyodorovich and . . . all these recent events," the mamma explained hurriedly. "Katerina Ivanovna has made a certain decision . . . but for this it is necessary for her to see you. . . . Why? Of course, I can't say, but she wants to see you at once. And you will go to her, of course, it is even a Christian duty."

"I have only seen her once," Alyosha continued with the same perplexity.

"Oh, she is such a lofty, incomparable being! If only for her suffering . . . Think what she has gone through, what she is enduring now, think what awaits her . . . It's all terrible, terrible!"

"Very well, I will come," Alyosha decided, after rapidly scanning the brief, enigmatic note, which consisted of an urgent entreaty that he would come, without any sort of explanation.

"Oh, how sweet and magnificent that would be of you," cried Lise with sudden animation. "And I just said to mamma: he won't go for anything, he's saving his soul. How splendid you are! I've always thought you were splendid, how glad I am to tell you so!"

"Lise!" said her mother significantly, though she smiled after she had said it.

"You have quite forgotten us, Alexey Fyodorovich," she said; "you never come to see us. Yet Lise has told me twice that she is never happy except with you." Alyosha raised his downcast eyes and again flushed, and again smiled without knowing why. But the elder was no longer watching him. He had begun talking to a monk who, as mentioned before, had been

---

7. The quadrille, a dance performed by couples in a square formation, became extremely popular among the European upper classes in the nineteenth century.

awaiting his entrance by Lise's chair. He was evidently a monk of the humblest, that is of the peasant, class, of a narrow unshakable outlook, but a true believer, and, in his own way, a stubborn one. He announced that he had come from the far north, from Obdorsk, from Saint Sylvester, and was a member of a poor monastery, consisting of only nine monks. The elder gave him his blessing and invited him to come to his cell whenever he liked.

"How can you presume to do such deeds?" the monk asked suddenly, pointing solemnly and significantly at Lise. He was hinting at her "healing."

"It's too early, of course, to speak of that. Relief is not complete cure, and may proceed from different causes. But if there has been any healing, it is by no power but God's will. It's all from God. Visit me, Father," he added to the monk. "It's not often I can see visitors. I am ill, and I know that my days are numbered."

"Oh, no, no! God will not take you from us. You will live a long, long time yet," cried the mamma. "And in what way are you ill? You look so well, so gay and happy."

"I am extraordinarily better today. But I know that it's only for a moment. I understand my disease now thoroughly. If I seem so happy to you, you could never say anything that would please me so much. For men are made for happiness, and anyone who is completely happy has a right to say to himself, 'I am doing God's will on earth.' All the righteous, all the saints, all the holy martyrs were happy."

"Oh, how you speak! What bold and lofty words!" cried the mamma. "You seem to pierce with your words. And yet—happiness, happiness—where is it? Who can say of himself that he is happy? Oh, since you have been so good as to let us see you once more today, let me tell you what I could not utter last time, what I dared not say, all I am suffering and have been for so long, for so long! I am suffering, forgive me, I am suffering . . ." And in some kind of rush of fervent feeling she clasped her hands before him.

"From what specially?"

"I suffer . . . from lack of faith."

"Lack of faith in God?"

"Oh, no, no, I don't dare to even think of that. But the future life—it is such an enigma! And no one, no one can solve it! Listen, you are a healer, you are deeply versed in the human soul, and of course I dare not expect you to believe me entirely, but I assure you on my word of honor that I am not speaking lightly now. The thought of the life beyond the grave distracts me to anguish, to terror and to fear . . . and I don't know whom to turn to, and have not dared to all my life . . . and now I am so bold as to turn to you. Oh, God, what will you think of me now!" She clasped her hands.

"Don't distress yourself about my opinion of you," said the elder. "I fully believe in the sincerity of your suffering."

"Oh, how thankful I am to you! You see, I shut my eyes and ask myself: if everyone has faith, where did it come from? And then they do say that it all comes from terror at the menacing phenomena of nature, and that none of it's real. And I say to myself, 'What if I've been believing all my life, and when I come to die, there's nothing but the "burdocks growing

on my grave,"[8] as I read in one author. It's awful! How, how can I get back
my faith? But I only believed when I was a little child, mechanically,
without thinking of anything. How, how is one to prove it? I have come
now to lay my soul before you and to ask you about it. If I let this chance
slip, no one all my life will answer me. How can I prove it? How can I
convince myself? Oh, how unhappy I am! I stand and look about me and
see that scarcely anyone else cares; no one troubles his head about it now,
and I'm the only one who can't stand it. It's deadly, deadly!"

"No doubt, deadly. But there's no proving it, though you can be convinced of it."

"How?"

"By the experience of active love. Strive to love your neighbor actively
and indefatigably. Insofar as you advance in love you will grow surer of the
reality of God and of the immortality of your soul. If you attain to perfect
self-forgetfulness in the love of your neighbor, then you will believe without doubt, and no doubt can possibly enter your soul. This has been tried.
This is certain."

"In active love? There's another question—and such a question! You
see, I so love humanity that—would you believe it?—I often dream of for-
saking all that I have, leaving Lise, and becoming a sister of mercy. I close
my eyes and think and dream, and at that moment I feel full of strength
to overcome all obstacles. No wounds, no festering sores could at that
moment frighten me. I would bind them up and wash them with my own
hands. I would nurse the afflicted. I would be ready to kiss such wounds."

"It is much, and well that your mind is full of such dreams and not
others. Sometime, unawares, you may do a good deed in reality."

"Yes, but could I endure such a life for long?" the lady went on fervently,
almost frantically. "That's the chief question! That's my most agonizing
of questions. I shut my eyes and ask myself: Would you persevere long on
that path? And if the patient whose wounds you are washing did not meet
you with gratitude, but worried you with his whims, without valuing or
remarking your charitable services, began abusing you and rudely commanding you, and complaining to the superior authorities of you (which
often happens when people are in great suffering)—what then? Will your
love continue, or not? And imagine, I understood with a shudder: if there
is anything that could immediately cool my 'active love for humanity,' it's
ingratitude. In a word, I work for pay, and demand my payment at once,
that is, praise for myself and love paid for with love. Otherwise I'm incapable of loving anyone!"

She was in a very paroxysm of self-castigation, and, concluding, she
looked with defiant resolution at the elder.

"It's just the same story a doctor once told me," observed the elder.
"He was a man getting on in years, and undoubtedly intelligent. He spoke
as frankly as you, though in jest, in bitter jest. 'I love humanity,' he said,
'but I wonder at myself. The more I love humanity in general, the less
I love man in particular, that is, separately, as single individuals. In my
dreams,' he said, 'I have often come to making enthusiastic schemes for

---

8. Khokhlakova quotes Evgeny Bazarov, the main character from the 1862 novel *Fathers and
Children* by Ivan Turgenev (1818–1883). Bazarov espouses a radical version of materialism that
denies human life any spiritual dimension, including the existence of a soul or possibility of
life after death. The portrait of Bazarov sparked a great deal of controversy in Russia.

the service of humanity, and perhaps I might actually have faced crucifixion if it had been suddenly necessary; and yet I am incapable of living in the same room with anyone for two days together, as I know by experience. As soon as anyone is near me, his personality disturbs my self-esteem and restricts my freedom. In twenty-four hours I can begin to hate even the best of men: one because he's too long over his dinner; another because he has a cold and keeps on blowing his nose. I become hostile to people the moment they come close to me. But it has always happened that the more I detest men individually the more ardent becomes my love for humanity.'"

"But what's to be done?[9] What can one do in such a case? Must one despair?"

"No, it is enough that you are distressed at it. Do what you can, and it will be reckoned unto you.[1] Much is done already in you since you can so deeply and sincerely know yourself. If you have been talking to me so sincerely, simply to gain approbation for your frankness, as you did from me just now, then of course you will not attain to anything in the achievement of real love; it will all get no further than dreams, and your whole life will slip away like a phantom. In that case you will naturally cease to think of the future life too, and will of yourself grow calmer after a fashion in the end."

"You have crushed me! Only now, as you speak, I understand that I was really only seeking your approbation for my sincerity when I told you I could not endure ingratitude. You have revealed me to myself. You have seen through me and explained me to myself!"

"Are you speaking the truth? Well, now, after such an admission, I believe that you are sincere and good at heart. If you do not attain happiness, always remember that you are on the right road, and try not to leave it. Above all, avoid falsehood, every kind of falsehood, especially falseness to yourself. Watch over your own deceitfulness and look into it every hour, every minute. Avoid being scornful, both to others and to yourself. What seems to you bad within you will grow purer from the very fact of your observing it in yourself. Avoid fear, too, though fear is only the consequence of every sort of falsehood. Never be frightened at your own faintheartedness in attaining love. Don't be frightened overmuch even at your evil actions. I am sorry I can say nothing more consoling to you, for love in action is a harsh and dreadful thing compared with love in dreams. Love in dreams is greedy for immediate action, rapidly performed and in the sight of all. Men will even give their lives if only the ordeal does not last long but is soon over, with all looking on and applauding as though on the stage. But active love is labor and fortitude, and for some people too, perhaps, a complete science. But I predict that just when you see with horror that in spite of all your efforts you are getting further from your goal

---

9. Khokhlakova's question refers to the title of one of the most influential works of nineteenth-century Russian literature, Nikolay Chernyshevsky's 1862 novel *What Is to Be Done?* Dostoevsky was deeply opposed to the philosophies of materialism and rational egoism advanced by this novel. Chernyshevsky (1828–1889), the son of a priest, was one of Russia's leading philosophers and social theorists of the 1860s. Dostoevsky discusses his relationship with Chernyshevsky in the *Diary of a Writer*: "One can have a good deal of respect for a man even when one has radically different opinions from him" (153). See "Something Personal" (1873), chapter 4.

1. This language has Biblical resonance; see for example Romans 4.3: "Abraham believed God, and it was counted unto him for righteousness."

instead of nearer to it—at that very moment I predict that you will reach it and behold clearly the miraculous power of the Lord who has been all the time loving and mysteriously guiding you. Forgive me for not being able to stay longer with you. They are waiting for me. Good-bye."

The lady was weeping.

"Lise, Lise! Bless her—bless her!" she cried, starting up suddenly.

"She does not deserve to be loved. I have seen her naughtiness all along," the elder said jestingly. "Why have you been laughing at Alexey?"

Lise had in fact been occupied in mocking him all the time. She had noticed before that Alyosha was shy and tried not to look at her, and she found this extremely amusing. She waited intently to catch his eye. Alyosha, unable to endure her persistent stare, was irresistibly and suddenly drawn to glance at her, and at once she smiled triumphantly in his face. Alyosha was even more disconcerted and vexed. At last he turned away from her altogether and hid behind the elder's back. After a few minutes, drawn by the same irresistible force, he turned again to see whether he was being looked at or not, and found Lise almost hanging out of her chair to peep sideways at him, eagerly waiting for him to look. Catching his eye, she laughed so that the elder could not help saying, "Why do you make fun of him like that, naughty girl?"

Lise suddenly and quite unexpectedly blushed. Her eyes flashed and her face became terribly serious. She began speaking quickly and nervously, with a resentful, heated complaint:

"Why has he forgotten everything, then? He used to carry me about when I was little. We used to play together. He used to come to teach me to read, do you know? Two years ago, when he went away, he said that he would never forget me, that we were friends forever, forever, forever! And now he's afraid of me all at once. Am I going to eat him? Why doesn't he want to come near me? Why doesn't he talk? Why won't he come and see us? It's not that you won't let him: we know that he goes everywhere. It's not good manners for me to invite him, he ought to have thought of it first, if he hasn't forgotten me. No, now he's saving his soul! Why have you put that long gown on him? If he runs he'll fall."

And suddenly, no longer able to contain herself, she hid her face in her hand and went off into irresistible, prolonged, nervous, inaudible laughter. The elder listened to her with a smile, and blessed her tenderly. As she kissed his hand she suddenly pressed it to her eyes and began crying.

"Don't be angry with me. I'm silly and good for nothing . . . and perhaps Alyosha's right, quite right, in not wanting to come and see such a ridiculous girl."

"I will certainly send him," said the elder.

Chapter V

So Be It! So Be It!

The elder's absence from his cell had lasted for about twenty-five minutes. It was more than half-past twelve, but Dmitri Fyodorovich, on whose account they had all met there, had still not appeared. But he seemed almost to be forgotten, and when the elder entered the cell again, he found his guests engaged in eager conversation. Ivan Fyodorovich and the two hieromonks took the leading share in it. Miüsov, too, was trying to take a part, and apparently very eagerly, in the conversation. But he was unsuccessful in this also. He was evidently in the background, and his remarks were treated with neglect, so that this new circumstance only increased his irritability. He had had intellectual encounters with Ivan Fyodorovich before and he could not endure a certain carelessness Ivan showed him. "Hitherto at least I have stood in the front ranks of all that is progressive in Europe, and here the new generation positively ignores us," he thought. Fyodor Pavlovich, who had given his word to sit still and be quiet, had actually been quiet for some time, but he watched his neighbor Miüsov with an ironical little smile, obviously enjoying his irritation. He had been waiting for some time to pay back some old scores, and now he could not let the opportunity slip. Finally unable to hold out any longer, he bent over his neighbor's shoulder and began teasing him again in a whisper:

"Why didn't you go away just now, after the 'courteously kissing'? Why did you consent to remain in such unseemly company? It was because you felt insulted and injured, and you remained to vindicate your self by showing off your intelligence. Now you won't go till you've displayed your intellect to them."

"You again? . . . On the contrary, I'll leave right now."

"You'll be the last, the last of all to go!" Fyodor Pavlovich delivered him another thrust. This was almost at the moment of the elder's return.

The discussion died down for a moment, but the elder, seating himself in his former place, looked at them all as though cordially inviting them to go on. Alyosha, who knew every expression of his face, saw that he was fearfully exhausted and making a great effort. Of late he had been liable to fainting fits from exhaustion. His face had the pallor that was common before such attacks, and his lips were white. But he evidently did not want to break up the gathering. He seemed to have some special object of his own in keeping them. What object? Alyosha watched him intently.

"We are discussing this gentleman's most interesting article," said hieromonk Iosif, the librarian, addressing the elder, and indicating Ivan Fyodorovich. "He brings forward much that is new, but I think the argument cuts both ways. It is an article written in answer to a book by an ecclesiastical authority on the question of the ecclesiastical court, and the scope of its jurisdiction."[2]

"I'm sorry I have not read your article, but I've heard of it," said the elder, looking keenly and intently at Ivan Fyodorovich.

"He takes up a most interesting position," continued the Father Librarian. "As far as Church jurisdiction is concerned he is apparently quite opposed to the separation of Church from State."

"That's interesting. But in what sense?" the elder asked Ivan Fyodorovich.

The latter, at last, answered him, not condescendingly, as Alyosha had feared, but with modesty and reserve, with evident goodwill and apparently without the slightest ulterior purpose.

---

2. The prototype for the book Father Iosif refers to was an 1875 essay by Saint Petersburg University professor M. I. Gorchakov, "Toward a Scientific Formulation of Ecclesiastic-Judiciary Law." Dostoevsky had a copy of this essay in his library.

"I start from the position that this merging of elements, that is, of the essential principles of Church and State taken separately, will, of course, go on for ever, in spite of the fact that it is impossible, and can never lead to any consistent or even normal results, for there is falsity at the very foundation of it. Compromise between the Church and State in such questions as, for instance, jurisdiction, is, to my thinking, impossible in any real sense. My clerical opponent maintained that the Church holds a precise and defined position in the State. I maintain, on the contrary, that the Church ought to include the whole State, and not simply to occupy a corner in it, and if this is, for some reason, impossible at present, then it ought, in reality, to be set up as the direct and chief aim of the future development of Christian society."[3]

"Perfectly true!" firmly and nervously blurted out Father Païssy, the silent and learned hieromonk.

"The purest Ultramontanism!"[4] cried Miüsov impatiently, crossing and recrossing his legs.

"Oh, well, we have no mountains," cried Father Iosif, and turning to the elder he continued, "observe the answer he makes to the following 'fundamental and essential' propositions of his opponent, who is, you must note, an ecclesiastic. First, that 'no social organization can or ought to arrogate to itself power to dispose of the civic and political rights of its members.' Secondly, that 'criminal and civil jurisdiction ought not to belong to the Church, and is inconsistent with its nature, both as a divine institution and as an organization of men for religious purposes,' and, finally, in the third place, 'the Church is a kingdom not of this world.'"[5]

"A most unworthy play on words for an ecclesiastic!" Father Païssy could not refrain from breaking in again. "I have read the book which you have answered," he added, addressing Ivan Fyodorovich, "and was astounded at the words 'the Church is a kingdom not of this world.' If it is not of this world, then it cannot exist on earth at all. In the Gospel, the words 'not of this world' are not used in that sense. To play with such words is indefensible. Our Lord Jesus Christ came to set up the Church upon earth. The Kingdom of Heaven, of course, is not of this world, but in Heaven; but it is entered only through the Church which has been founded and established upon earth. And so a frivolous play upon words in such a connection is unpardonable and improper. The Church is, in truth, a kingdom and ordained to rule, and in the end must undoubtedly become the kingdom ruling over all the earth. For that we have the divine promise."[6]

He ceased speaking suddenly, as though restraining himself. After listening attentively and respectfully Ivan Fyodorovich went on, addressing the elder with perfect composure and as before with ready cordiality:

"The whole point of my article lies in the fact that during the first three centuries of Christianity, Christianity appeared on earth only as the Church and was nothing but the Church. When the pagan Roman Empire desired to become Christian, it inevitably happened that, by becoming Christian,

---

3. Dostoevsky discusses the relationship between secular, "civic" spheres and religion in "Two Halves," *Diary of a Writer*, August 1880, chapter 3, number 3.
4. The term Ultramontanism, derived from the Latin *ultra montis* (beyond the mountains), refers to a movement that arose in the fifteenth century to assert the Pope's authority in secular politics. It spread again in the nineteenth century as a reaction against revolutionary movements in Europe.
5. During his interrogation by Pilate, Jesus says, "My kingdom is not of this world" (John 18.36).
6. Father Païssy refers to Daniel 2.44 and Revelation 20.4.

it included the Church but remained a pagan State in very many of its departments.[7] In reality this was bound to happen. But in Rome, as in a State, too much of the pagan civilization and culture has been retained, as, for example, in the very objects and fundamental principles of the State. The Christian Church entering into the State could, of course, surrender no part of its fundamental principles—the rock on which it stands—and could pursue no other aims than those which have been ordained and revealed by God Himself, among them that of transforming the whole world and, therefore, the ancient pagan State itself, into the Church. In that way (that is, with a view to the future) it is not the Church that should seek a definite position in the State, like 'every social organization' or as 'an organization of men for religious purposes' (as my opponent calls the Church) but, on the contrary, every earthly State should be, in the end, completely transformed into the Church and should become nothing else but a Church, rejecting every purpose incongruous with the aims of the Church. All this will not degrade it in any way or take from its honor and glory as a great State, nor from the glory of its rulers, but will only turn it from a false, still pagan, and mistaken path to the true and rightful path, which alone leads to the eternal goal. This is why the author of the book *On the Foundations of Church Jurisdiction* would have judged correctly if, in seeking and laying down those foundations, he had looked upon them as only a temporary compromise inevitable in our sinful and imperfect days. But as soon as the author ventures to declare that the foundations which he predicates now, part of which Father Iosif just enumerated, are the permanent, essential, and eternal foundations, he is going directly against the Church and its sacred, eternal, and unwavering mission. That is my whole article, a full synopsis."

"That is, in brief," Father Païssy began again, laying stress on each word, "according to certain theories only too clearly formulated in the nineteenth century, the Church ought to be reborn into the State, as though this would be an advance from a lower to a higher form, so as to disappear into it, making way for science, for the spirit of the age, and civilization. And if the Church resists and is unwilling, some corner will be set apart for her in the State, and even that under control—and this will be so everywhere in all modern European countries. But Russian hopes and conceptions demand not that the Church should pass as from a lower into a higher type into the State, but, on the contrary, that the State should end by being worthy to become only the Church and nothing else. So be it! So be it!"

"Well, sir, I confess you've reassured me somewhat," Miüsov said smiling, again crossing his legs. "So far as I understand then, the realization of such an ideal is infinitely remote, at the second coming of Christ.[8] That's as you like. It's a beautiful utopian dream of the abolition of war, diplomacy, banks, and so on. Something even resembling socialism. But I thought that it was all meant seriously, and that the Church might be *now* going to try criminals, and sentence them to beating, prison, and even death."

---

7. Emperor Constantine I (272–337, reigned 306 until his death) made Christianity the official religion of the Roman Empire. He was canonized by the Russian Orthodox Church.
8. The Christian Bible prophesies that Jesus will return to earth at the end of time.

"But if there were none but the ecclesiastical court, the Church would not even now sentence a criminal to prison or to death. Crime and the way of regarding it would inevitably change, not all at once of course, but fairly soon," Ivan Fyodorovich replied calmly, without flinching.

"Are you serious?" Miüsov looked intently at him.

"If everything became the Church, the Church would exclude all the criminal and disobedient, and would not cut off their heads," Ivan Fyodorovich went on. "I ask you, what would become of the excluded? He would be cut off then not only from men, as now, but from Christ. By his crime he would have transgressed not only against men but against the Church of Christ. This is so even now, of course, strictly speaking, but it is not clearly enunciated, and very, very often the criminal of today compromises with his conscience: 'I steal,' he says, 'but I don't go against the Church. I'm not an enemy of Christ.' That's what the criminal of today is continually saying to himself, but when the Church takes the place of the State it will be difficult for him, in opposition to the Church all over the world, to say: 'All men are mistaken, all in error, all mankind are the false Church. I, a thief and murderer, am the only true Christian Church.' It will be very difficult to say this to himself; it requires a rare combination of unusual circumstances. Now, on the other side, take the Church's own view of crime: is it not bound to change from the present, almost pagan attitude, and to transform itself from a mechanical cutting off of its tainted member as is now done for the preservation of society, into completely and honestly adopting the idea of the regeneration of the man, of his resurrection and salvation . . ."

"What do you mean? I fail to understand again," Miüsov interrupted. "Some sort of dream again. Something shapeless and even incomprehensible. What is excommunication? What sort of exclusion? I suspect you are simply amusing yourself, Ivan Fyodorovich."

"Yes, but you know, in reality it is so now," said the elder suddenly, and all turned to him at once. "If it were not for the Church of Christ there would be nothing to restrain the criminal from evildoing, no real chastisement for it afterwards; none, that is, but the mechanical chastisement spoken of just now, which in the majority of cases only embitters the heart; and not the real chastisement, the only effectual one, the only deterrent and softening one, which lies in the recognition of sin by one's own conscience."

"How is that, may one inquire?" asked Miüsov, with lively curiosity.

"Why," began the elder, "all these sentences to exile with hard labor, and formerly with flogging also, reform no one, and what's more, deter hardly a single criminal, and the number of crimes does not diminish but is continually on the increase. You must admit that. Consequently the security of society is not protected, for, although the harmful member is mechanically cut off and sent far away out of sight, another criminal always comes to take his place at once, and often two of them. If anything does preserve society, even in our time, and does regenerate and transform the criminal, it is only the law of Christ speaking in his conscience. It is only by recognizing his wrongdoing as a son of a Christian society—that is, of the Church—that he recognizes his sin against society—that is, against the Church. So that it is only against the Church, and not against the State, that the criminal of today can recognize that he has sinned. If society, as a Church, had jurisdiction then it would know whom to bring back from exclusion and to reunite to itself. Now the Church having no real jurisdiction, but only the power of moral condemnation, withdraws of her own accord from chastising the criminal actively. She does not excommunicate him but simply persists in fatherly exhortation of him. What is more, the Church even tries to preserve all Christian communion with the criminal. She admits him to church services, to the holy sacrament, gives him alms, and treats him more as a captive than as a convict. And what would become of the criminal, O Lord, if even the Christian society— that is, the Church—were to reject him even as the civil law rejects him and cuts him off? What would become of him if the Church chastised him with her excommunication as the direct consequence of the secular law? There could be no more terrible despair, at least for a Russian criminal, for Russian criminals still have faith. Though, who knows, perhaps then a fearful thing would happen, perhaps the despairing heart of the criminal would lose its faith and then what would become of him? But the Church, like a tender, loving mother, holds aloof from active chastisement herself, as the sinner is too severely punished already by the civil law, and there must be at least some one to have pity on him. The Church holds aloof, above all, because her judgment is the only one that contains the truth, and therefore cannot practically and morally be united to any other judgment even as a temporary compromise. She can enter into no compact about that. The foreign criminal, they say, rarely repents, for the very doctrines of today confirm him in the idea that his crime is not a crime, but only a reaction against an unjustly oppressive force. Society cuts him off completely by a force that triumphs over him mechanically and (so at least they say of themselves in Europe) accompanies this exclusion with hatred, forgetfulness, and the most profound indifference as to the ultimate fate of the erring brother. In this way, it all takes place without the compassionate intervention of the Church, for in many cases there are no churches there at all, for though ecclesiastics and splendid church buildings remain, the churches themselves have long ago striven to pass from the lower form, as Church, into the higher form, as State, and to disappear in it completely. So it seems at least in Lutheran countries. As for Rome, it was proclaimed a State instead of a Church a thousand years ago.[9] And so the criminal is no longer conscious of being a member of the Church and sinks into despair. If he returns to society, often it is with such hatred that society itself cuts him off. You can judge for yourself how it must end. In many cases it would seem to be the same with us, but the difference is that besides the established law courts we have the Church too, which always keeps up relations with the criminal as a dear and still precious son. And besides that, there is still preserved, though only in thought, the judgment of the Church, which though no longer existing in practice is still living as a dream for the future, and is, no doubt, instinctively recognized by the criminal in his soul. What was said here just now is true too, that is, that if the jurisdiction of the Church were introduced in practice in its full force, that is, if the whole of the society were changed into the Church, not only would the judgment of the Church have influence on the reformation of the criminal such as it never has now, but possibly also

9. The Vatican is the last modern consolidation of the Papal States that were founded in 756.

the crimes themselves would be incredibly diminished. And there can be no doubt that the Church would look upon the criminal and the crime of the future in many cases quite differently and would succeed in restoring the excluded, in restraining those who plan evil, and in regenerating the fallen. It is true," said Father Zosima with a smile, "the Christian society now is not ready and is only resting on some seven righteous men,[1] but as they are never lacking, it will continue still unshaken in expectation of its complete transformation from a society almost heathen in character into a single universal and all-powerful Church. So be it, so be it! even though at the end of the ages,[2] for it is ordained to come to pass! And there is no need to be troubled about times and seasons, for the secret of the times and seasons is in the wisdom of God, in His foresight, and His love.[3] And what in human reckoning seems still afar off, may by the Divine ordinance be close at hand, on the eve of its appearance. And so be it, so be it!"

"So be it, so be it!" Father Païssy repeated austerely and reverently.

"Strange, strange in the highest degree!" Miüsov pronounced, not so much with heat as with latent indignation.

"What strikes you as so strange?" Father Iosif inquired cautiously.

"But, really, what is this?" cried Miüsov, suddenly breaking out, "the State is eliminated and the Church is raised to the position of the State! It's not simply Ultramontanism, it's arch-Ultramontanism! It's beyond the dreams of Pope Gregory the Seventh!"[4]

"You completely misunderstand it!" said Father Païssy sternly. "Understand the Church is not to be transformed into the State. That is Rome and its dream. That is the third temptation of the devil![5] On the contrary, the State is transformed into the Church, will ascend and become a Church over the whole world—which is the complete opposite of Ultramontanism and Rome, and your interpretation, and is only the glorious mission ordained for orthodoxy. This star will arise in the east."[6]

Miüsov was significantly silent. His whole figure expressed extraordinary personal dignity. A supercilious and condescending smile played on his lips. Alyosha watched it all with a throbbing heart. The whole conversation stirred him to his very core. He glanced by chance at Rakitin, who was standing immovable in his place by the door listening and watching intently though with downcast eyes. But from the color in his cheeks

---

1. This may be a reference to the "seven men of honest report" discussed in Acts 6.3. It may also refer to speculation regarding the number of reliable followers of socialism in Chernyshevsky's *What Is to be Done?* See note 9 on p. 55.

2. The phrase "at the end of the ages" is found in the Russian text of 1 Corinthians 10.11.

3. Zosima paraphrases several Biblical passages. In Acts 1.7, Jesus tells the apostles, "It is not for you to know the times or the seasons, which the Father hath put in his own power." See also Matthew 24.33, Mark 13.29, and 1 Thessalonians 5.1.

4. Pope Gregory VII (c. 1029–1085; served 1073 until his death) attempted sweeping reforms of the Catholic Church, aimed at asserting papal supremacy over secular authority. Dostoevsky discusses Roman Catholicism extensively in the *Diary*, where he writes, "Roman Catholicism (and this is all too clear) needs not Christ but universal dominion . . ." (1014). See for example May and June 1877, chapter 3, number 3, "Both Angry and Strong."

5. According to the Christian Gospel, Jesus spent forty days and nights fasting and praying in the desert, during which time the devil subjected him to three temptations. For the third temptation, the devil attempted to seduce Jesus with the lure of worldly power: "The devil taketh him up into an exceeding high mountain, and sheweth him all the kingdoms of the world, and the glory of them; And saith unto him, All these things will I give thee, if thou wilt fall down and worship me" (Matthew 4.8–9).

6. See Matthew 2.2.

Alyosha guessed that Rakitin was probably no less excited than himself, and he knew what caused his excitement.

"Allow me to tell you one little anecdote, gentlemen," Miüsov said impressively, with a peculiarly majestic air. "Some years ago, soon after the coup d'état of December,[7] I happened to be calling in Paris on an extremely influential personage in the Government, and I met a very interesting man in his house. This individual was not precisely a detective but was a sort of superintendent of a whole regiment of political detectives—a rather powerful position in its own way. I was prompted by curiosity to seize the opportunity of conversation with him. And as he had not come as a visitor but as a subordinate official bringing a special report, and as he saw the reception given me by his chief, he deigned to speak with some openness, to a certain extent only, of course. He was rather courteous than open, as Frenchmen know how to be courteous, especially to a foreigner. But I thoroughly understood him. The subject was the socialist revolutionaries who were at that time persecuted. Skipping the gist of the conversation, I will quote only one most curious remark suddenly dropped by this person. 'We are not particularly afraid,' said he, 'of all these socialists, anarchists, atheists, and revolutionists; we keep watch on them and know all their goings on. But there are a few peculiar men among them who believe in God and are Christians, but at the same time are socialists. Those are the people we are most afraid of. They are dreadful people! The socialist who is a Christian is more to be dreaded than a socialist who is an atheist.' The words struck me at the time, and now they have suddenly come back to me here, gentlemen."

"You apply them to us, and look upon us as socialists?" Father Païssy asked directly, without beating about the bush. But before Pyotr Alexandrovich could think what to answer, the door opened, and the guest so long expected, Dmitri Fyodorovich, came in. They had, in fact, given up expecting him, and his sudden appearance caused some surprise for a moment.

Chapter VI

Why Is Such a Man Alive!

Dmitri Fyodorovich, a young man of twenty-eight, of medium height and agreeable countenance, looked much older than his years. He was muscular, and showed signs of considerable physical strength, yet there was something sickly in his face. It was rather thin, his cheeks were hollow, and there was an unhealthy sallowness in their color. His rather large, prominent dark eyes had an expression of firm determination, and yet there was a vague look in them, too. Even when he was excited and talking irritably, his eyes somehow did not follow his mood, but betrayed something else, sometimes quite incongruous with what was passing. "It's hard to tell what he's thinking," those who talked to him sometimes

---

7. Louis-Napoléon Bonaparte (1808–1873), a nephew of Napoléon I, was elected President of France following the 1848 Revolution. He overthrew the government in 1851 and ruled as Napoléon III until 1870.

declared. People who saw something pensive and sullen in his eyes were startled by his sudden laugh, which bore witness to cheerful and playful thoughts at the very time when his eyes were so gloomy. Moreover, a certain sickliness in his face was easy to understand at this moment. Everyone knew or had heard of the extremely restless and "dissipated" life which he had been leading of late, as well as of the violent anger to which he had been roused in his quarrels with his father about the disputed money. There were several stories current in the town about it. It is true that he was irascible by nature, "of an unstable and unbalanced mind," as our justice of the peace, Semyon Ivanovich Kachalnikov, characteristically described him at one gathering. He was stylishly and irreproachably dressed in a carefully buttoned frock coat. He wore black gloves and carried a top hat. Having only lately left the army, he still had a moustache and for the time being shaved his beard. His dark brown hair was cropped short, and combed forward on his temples. He had the long determined stride of a military man. He stood still for a moment on the threshold, and glancing at the whole party went straight up to the elder, guessing him to be their host. He made him a low bow, and asked his blessing. Father Zosima, rising in his chair, blessed him. Dmitri Fyodorovich kissed his hand respectfully, and with intense feeling, almost anger, he said:

"Be so generous as to forgive me for having kept you waiting so long, but Smerdyakov, the servant sent me by my father, in reply to my insistent inquiries, told me twice over in the most assured tone that the appointment was for one. Now I suddenly find out . . ."

"Don't worry," interrupted the elder. "It's nothing, you are a little late, it doesn't matter . . ."

"I'm extremely obliged to you, and expected no less from your goodness." Saying this abruptly Dmitri Fyodorovich bowed once more. Then, turning suddenly towards his father, he made him, too, a similarly low and respectful bow. He had evidently considered it beforehand, and made this bow in all seriousness, thinking it his duty to show his respect and good intentions. Although Fyodor Pavlovich was taken unaware, he was equal to the occasion. In response to Dmitri Fyodorovich's bow he jumped up from his chair and made his son a bow as low in return. His face was suddenly solemn and impressive, which gave him a positively malignant look. Dmitri Fyodorovich bowed generally to all present, and without a word walked to the window with his long, resolute stride, sat down on the only empty chair, near Father Païssy, and, bending forward, prepared to listen to the conversation he had interrupted.

Dmitri Fyodorovich's entrance had taken no more than two minutes, and the conversation was resumed. But this time Pyotr Alexandrovich thought it unnecessary to reply to Father Païssy's persistent and almost irritable question.

"Allow me to withdraw from this discussion," he observed with a certain well-bred nonchalance. "It's a subtle question, too. Here Ivan Fyodorovich is smiling at us. He must have something interesting to say about that also. Ask him."

"Nothing special, except one little remark," Ivan Fyodorovich replied at once. "European Liberalism in general, and even our Russian liberal dilettantes have for a long time mixed up the final results of socialism with those of Christianity. This wild conclusion is, of course, a characteristic feature. But it's not only Liberals and dilettantes who mix up socialism and Christianity, but, in many cases, it appears, the police—the foreign police, of course—do the same. Your Paris anecdote is rather to the point, Pyotr Alexandrovich."

"I again ask your permission to drop this subject altogether," Miüsov repeated. "I will tell you instead, gentlemen, another most interesting and characteristic anecdote of Ivan Fyodorovich himself. Only five days ago, in a gathering here, principally of ladies, he solemnly declared in argument that there was nothing in the whole world to make men love their neighbors. That there was no law of nature that man should love mankind, and that, if there had been any love on earth hitherto, it was not owing to a natural law, but simply because men have believed in their immortality. Ivan Fyodorovich added in parenthesis that the whole natural law lies in that faith, and that if you were to destroy in mankind the belief in immortality, not only love but every living force maintaining the life of the world would at once be dried up. Moreover, nothing then would be immoral, everything would be permitted,[8] even cannibalism. That's not all. He ended by asserting that for every individual, like ourselves, who does not believe in God or immortality, the moral law of nature must immediately be changed into the exact contrary of the former religious law, and that egoism, even unto crime, must become not only lawful but even recognized as the inevitable, the most rational, even honorable outcome of his position.[9] From this paradox, gentlemen, you can judge of the rest of our eccentric and paradoxical friend Ivan Fyodorovich's theories."

"Excuse me," Dmitri Fyodorovich unexpectedly cried suddenly, "If I've heard correctly: 'crime must not only be permitted but even recognized as the inevitable and the most rational outcome of his position for every atheist!' Is that so or not?"

"Exactly that," said Father Païssy.

"I'll remember it."

Having uttered these words Dmitri Fyodorovich ceased speaking as suddenly as he had begun. Everyone looked at him with curiosity.

"Is that really your conviction as to the consequences of the disappearance of the faith in immortality?" the elder asked Ivan Fyodorovich suddenly.

"Yes. That was my contention. There is no virtue if there is no immortality."

"You are blessed in believing that, or else most unhappy!"

"Why unhappy?" Ivan Fyodorovich asked smiling.

"Because, in all probability you don't believe yourself in the immortality of your soul, nor in what you have written yourself in your article on Church jurisdiction."

"Perhaps you are right! . . . But I wasn't altogether joking," Ivan Fyodorovich suddenly and strangely confessed, flushing quickly.

"You were not altogether joking, that's true. This idea is still unresolved in your heart and torments it. But the martyr likes sometimes to divert himself with his despair, as if from despair itself. Meanwhile, in your

---

8. See 1 Corinthians 6.12: "All things are lawful unto me."
9. Dostoevsky explicates a similar view of the relationship between morality and belief in immortality in an 1878 letter to a correspondent. See p. 656.

despair, you, too, divert yourself with magazine articles, and discussions in society, though you don't believe your own arguments, and with an aching heart mock at them inwardly. . . . That question is not solved in you, and it is your great grief, for it demands an answer . . ."

"But can it be answered by me? Answered in the affirmative?" Ivan Fyodorovich went on asking strangely, still looking at the elder with the same inexplicable smile.

"If it can't be decided in the affirmative, it will never be decided in the negative, you yourself know that that is the peculiarity of your heart; and all its torment is due to it. But thank the Creator who gave you a lofty heart, capable of such suffering, 'of thinking and seeking higher things, for our dwelling is in the heavens.'[1] God grant that your heart will attain the answer on earth, and may God bless your path!"

The elder raised his hand and would have made the sign of the cross over Ivan Fyodorovich from where he stood. But the latter rose from his seat, went up to him, received his blessing, kissed his hand, and went back to his place in silence. His face looked firm and earnest. This action and all the preceding conversation, which was so surprising from Ivan Fyodorovich, impressed everyone by its strangeness and a certain solemnity, so that all were silent for a moment, and there was a look almost of fear in Alyosha's face. But Miüsov suddenly shrugged his shoulders, and at the same moment Fyodor Pavlovich jumped up from his seat.

"Most pious and holy elder!" he cried, pointing to Ivan Fyodorovich, "that is my son, flesh of my flesh, the dearest of my flesh! He is my most dutiful Karl Moor, so to speak, while this son who has just come in, Dmitri Fyodorovich, against whom I am seeking justice from you, is the undutiful Franz Moor—they are both out of Schiller's *Robbers*, and so I am the *regierender* Graf von Moor![2] Judge and save us! We need not only your prayers but your prophecies."

"Speak without foolery, and don't begin by insulting the members of your family," answered the elder, in a faint, exhausted voice. He was obviously getting more and more fatigued, and his strength was failing.

"An unseemly farce which I foresaw when I came here!" cried Dmitri Fyodorovich indignantly. He too leaped up. "Forgive it, reverend Father," he added, addressing the elder. "I am not an educated man, and I don't even know how to address you properly, but you have been deceived and you have been too good-natured in letting us meet here. All my father wants is a scandal, why he wants it—only he can tell. He always has some motive. But I believe I know why . . ."

"They all blame me, all of them!" cried Fyodor Pavlovich in his turn. "Pyotr Alexandrovich here blames me too. You have been blaming me, Pyotr Alexandrovich, you have!" he turned suddenly to Miüsov, although

---

1. Zosima paraphrases Colossians 3.1–2: "If ye then be risen with Christ, seek those things which are above, where Christ sitteth on the right hand of God. Set your affection on things above, not on things on the earth." See also Philippians 3.18–20.
2. "The reigning Count Moor" (German). *Die Räuber* (The Robbers, 1781) was one of the most popular plays of Friedrich Schiller (1759–1805), German poet, essayist, and playwright. Dostoevsky and his brother Mikhail (d. 1864) translated it into Russian in 1844 (published 1857). Fyodor Pavlovich is mistaken: in the play it is Franz, not Karl, who betrays his father and brother. Schiller's works exerted an enormous influence on Dostoevsky's spiritual and artistic development. Dostoevsky later recounted seeing a performance of *The Robbers* when he was ten years old, and claimed that it had an enormous impact on him: "the tremendous impression I carried away from it then acted very richly on my spiritual side" (August 1880 Letter to N. L. Ozmidov, 30.1: 212).

the latter was not dreaming of interrupting him. "They all accuse me of having hidden the children's money in my boots, and cheated them, but isn't there a court of law? There they will reckon out for you, Dmitri Fyodorovich, from your notes, your letters, and your agreements, how much money you had, how much you have spent, and how much you have left. Why does Pyotr Alexandrovich refuse to pass judgment? Dmitri Fyodorovich is not a stranger to him. Because they are all against me, while Dmitri Fyodorovich is in debt to me, and not a little, but some thousands, of which I have documentary proof. The whole town shakes and echoes with his debaucheries. And where he was stationed before, he several times spent a thousand or two for the seduction of some respectable girls; we know all about that, Dmitri Fyodorovich, sir, in its most secret details. I'll prove it, sir . . . Would you believe it, holy Father, he has captivated the heart of the most honorable of young ladies of good family and fortune, daughter of a gallant colonel, formerly his superior officer, who had received many honors and had the Anna Order [3] on his breast. He compromised the girl by his promise of marriage, now she is an orphan and here; she is betrothed to him, yet before her very eyes he is dancing attendance on a certain local seductress. And although this seductress has lived in, so to speak, civil marriage with a respectable man, yet she is of an independent character, an unapproachable fortress for everybody, just like a legal wife—for she is virtuous, yes, holy Fathers, she is virtuous. Dmitri Fyodorovich wants to open this fortress with a golden key, and that's why he is insolent to me now, trying to get money from me, though he had wasted thousands on this enchantress already. He's continually borrowing money for the purpose. From whom do you think? Shall I say, Mitya?"

"Be silent!" cried Dmitri Fyodorovich, "wait till I'm gone. Don't dare in my presence to dirty the good name of the noblest girl . . . That you even dare to speak about her is a disgrace . . . I won't permit it!"

He was breathless.

"Mitya! Mitya!" cried Fyodor Pavlovich hysterically, squeezing out a tear. "And is your father's blessing nothing to you? If I curse you, what then?"

"Shameless pretender!" roared Dmitri Fyodorovich furiously.

"He says that to his father! his father! What would he be with others? Gentlemen, just imagine: there's a poor but honorable man living here, burdened with a numerous family, a captain who got into trouble and was discharged from the army, but not publicly, not by court-martial, with no slur on his honor. And three weeks ago, our Dmitri Fyodorovich seized him by the beard in a tavern, dragged him out into the street by that very beard, and beat him publicly, and all because he is an agent in a little business of mine."

"It's all a lie! Outwardly it's the truth, but inwardly, a lie!" Dmitri Fyodorovich was trembling with rage. "Father, I don't justify my action. Yes, I confess it publicly, I behaved like a brute to that captain, and I regret it now, and I'm disgusted with myself for my brutal rage. But this captain, this agent of yours, went to that lady whom you call an enchantress, and suggested to her from you, that she should take IOUs of mine which were in your possession, and should sue me for the money so as to get me into

---

3. The Order of St. Anna was awarded for distinguished service in the civil service, or valor and outstanding achievement in the military. This was not an especially high decoration.

prison by means of them, if I persisted in claiming an account from you of my property. Now you reproach me for having a weakness for that lady when you yourself incited her to captivate me! She told me so to my face. She told me the story and laughed at you! You wanted to put me in prison because you are jealous of me with her, because you'd begun to force your attentions upon her; and I know all about that, too; she laughed at you for that as well—you hear—she laughed at you as she described it. So here you have this man, holy men, this father who reproaches his profligate son! Gentlemen witnesses, forgive my anger, but I foresaw that this crafty old man had only brought you together to create a scandal. I had come to forgive him if he held out his hand; to forgive him, and ask forgiveness! But as he has just this minute insulted not only me, but an honorable young lady for whom I feel such reverence that I dare not take her name in vain, I have made up my mind to reveal his game publicly, though he is my father! . . ."

He could not go on. His eyes were glittering and he breathed with difficulty. But everyone in the cell was stirred. All except Father Zosima got up from their seats anxiously. The hieromonks looked severe but waited for guidance from the elder. He sat still, pale, not from excitement but from the weakness of illness. An imploring smile played on his lips; from time to time he raised his hand, as though to check the storm, and, of course, a gesture from him would have been enough to end the scene; but he seemed to be waiting for something and watched them intently as though trying to make out something which was not perfectly clear to him. At last Pyotr Alexandrovich felt completely humiliated and disgraced.

"We are all to blame for this scandalous scene!" he said hotly. "But I did not foresee it when I came, though I knew with whom I had to deal . . . This must be stopped at once! Believe me, your reverence, I had no precise knowledge of the details that have just come to light, I was unwilling to believe them, and I learn for the first time. . . . A father is jealous of his son's relations with a woman of loose behavior and intrigues with the creature to get his son into prison . . . This is the company in which I have been forced to be present . . . I was deceived. I declare to you all that I was as much deceived as anyone . . ."

"Dmitri Fyodorovich!" yelled Fyodor Pavlovich suddenly, in an unnatural voice, "if you were not my son I would challenge you this instant to a duel . . . with pistols, at three paces . . . across a handkerchief!"[4] he ended, stamping with both feet.

With old liars who have been acting all their lives there are moments when they enter so completely into their part that they tremble or shed tears of emotion in earnest, although at that very moment, or a second later, they are able to whisper to themselves, "You know you are lying, you shameless old sinner! You're acting now, in spite of your 'holy' wrath and your 'holy' moment of wrath."

Dmitri Fyodorovich frowned painfully, and looked with unutterable contempt at his father.

4. Fyodor Pavlovich parodies a scene from Schiller's romantic tragedy *Kabale und Liebe* (*Intrigues and Love*, 1784), in which an idealistic young man and an old profligate both seek the love of young Luise. In Act IV, scene 3, the young hero Ferdinand challenges his rival to a duel. Here Fyodor Pavlovich plays the role of Ferdinand, and places Dmitri in the role of the old man seeking to corrupt Luise.

"I thought . . . I thought," he said, in a soft and, as it were, controlled voice, "that I was coming to my native place with the angel of my heart, my betrothed, to cherish his old age, and I find nothing but a depraved sensualist, a despicable clown!"

"A duel!" yelled the old wretch again, breathless and spluttering at each syllable. "And you, Pyotr Alexandrovich Miüsov, let me tell you, sir, that there has never been in all your family a loftier, and more honest—you hear—more honest woman than this 'creature,' as you have dared to call her! And you, Dmitri Fyodorovich, have abandoned your betrothed for that 'creature,' so you must yourself have thought that your betrothed couldn't hold a candle to her. That's the woman called a 'creature'!"

"Shameful!" broke suddenly from Father Iosif.

"Shameful and disgraceful!" Kalganov, flushing crimson, cried in his adolescent voice, trembling with agitation. He had been silent till that moment.

"Why is such a man alive!" Dmitri Fyodorovich growled in a hollow voice, beside himself with rage, hunching up his shoulders till he looked almost deformed. "Tell me, can he be allowed to go on defiling the earth?" He looked round at everyone and pointed at the old man. He spoke evenly and deliberately.

"Listen, listen, monks, to the parricide," cried Fyodor Pavlovich, rushing up to Father Iosif. "That's the answer to your 'shameful!' What is shameful? That 'creature,' that 'woman of loose behavior' is perhaps holier than you are yourselves, you monks who are seeking salvation! She fell perhaps in her youth, ruined by her environment.[5] But she loved much, and Christ himself forgave the woman 'who loved much.'"[6]

"It was not for such love Christ forgave her," broke impatiently from the gentle Father Iosif.

"Yes, it was for such, monks, it was! You save your souls here, eating cabbage, and think you are the righteous! You eat a gudgeon a day, and you think you bribe God with gudgeon!"[7]

"This is unendurable!" was heard on all sides in the cell.

But this unseemly scene was cut short in a most unexpected way. The elder rose suddenly from his seat. Almost distracted with anxiety for the elder and everyone else, Alyosha succeeded, however, in supporting him by the arm. The elder moved towards Dmitri Fyodorovich and reaching him sank on his knees before him. Alyosha thought that he had fallen from weakness, but this was not so. The elder distinctly and deliberately bowed down at Dmitri Fyodorovich's feet till his forehead touched the floor. Alyosha was so astounded that he failed to assist him when he got up again. There was a faint smile on his lips.

"Good-bye! Forgive me, all of you!" he said, bowing on all sides to his guests.

---

5. The Russian original is *zaedennaia sredoi*, literally "eaten up by the environment." The notion of the environment's all-important impact on a person's character was a commonplace among Russian radicals in Dostoevsky's time. Dostoevsky was an outspoken critic of environmental determinism; see for example the chapter "Environment" in his 1873 *Diary*.
6. According to Luke 7.46–47, a sinful woman washed and kissed Jesus' feet, weeping tears of love. When questioned as to why he allowed such a sinner near him, Jesus responded "Her sins, which are many, are forgiven; for she loved much."
7. A gudgeon is a small freshwater fish.

Dmitri Fyodorovich stood for a few moments in amazement. Bowing down to him—what did it mean? Suddenly he cried aloud: "Oh God!" hid his face in his hands, and rushed out of the room. All the guests flocked out after him, in their confusion not saying good-bye, or bowing to their host. Only the hieromonks went up to him again for a blessing.

"What did it mean, falling at his feet like that? Was it some kind of emblem?" said Fyodor Pavlovich, suddenly quieted and trying to reopen conversation without venturing to address anybody in particular. They were all passing out of the precincts of the hermitage at the moment.

"I can't answer for a madhouse and for madmen," Miüsov answered at once ill-humoredly, "but I will spare myself your company, Fyodor Pavlovich, and, trust me, forever. Where's that monk?"

"That monk," that is, the monk who had invited them to dine with the Superior, did not keep them waiting. He met them as soon as they came down the steps from the elder's cell, as though he had been waiting for them all the time.

"Reverend Father, kindly do me a favor. Convey my deepest respect to the Father Superior, apologize for me, personally, Miüsov, to his reverence, telling him that I deeply regret that owing to unforeseen circumstances I am unable to have the honor of being present at his table, despite my most sincere desire to do so," Pyotr Alexandrovich said irritably to the monk.

"And that unforeseen circumstance, of course, is me," Fyodor Pavlovich cut in immediately. "Do you hear, Father; Pyotr Alexandrovich doesn't want to remain in my company or else he'd come at once. And you shall go, Pyotr Alexandrovich, pray go to the Father Superior and good appetite to you! I will decline, and not you. Home, home, I'll eat at home, I don't feel equal to it here, Pyotr Alexandrovich, my amiable relative."

"I am not your relative and never have been, you contemptible man!"

"I said it on purpose to make you mad, because you always disclaim the relationship, though you really are a relation in spite of your shuffling. I'll prove it by the church calendar.[8] As for you, Ivan Fyodorovich, stay if you like. I'll send the horses for you later. Propriety requires you to go to the Father Superior, Pyotr Alexandrovich, to apologize for the disturbance we've been making. . . ."

"Is it true that you are going home? Aren't you lying?"

"Pyotr Alexandrovich! How could I dare after what's happened! Forgive me, gentlemen, I was carried away! And upset besides! And, indeed, I am ashamed. Gentlemen, one man has the heart of Alexander the Great[9] and another the heart of the little dog Fido. Mine is that of the little dog Fido. I am abashed! After such an escapade how can I go to dinner, to gobble up the monastery's sauces. I am ashamed, I can't. You must excuse me!"

"The devil only knows, what if he deceives us," thought Miüsov, still hesitating, and watching the retreating buffoon with distrustful eyes. The latter turned round, and noticing that Miüsov was watching him, waved him a kiss.

---

8. The Orthodox Church calendar designates church holidays, periods of fasting, and saints' days dedicated to celebrating the memory of specific saints. Kinship cannot be established by the Church calendar.
9. Alexander the Great (356–323 B.C.E.), King of Macedonia 336–323 B.C.E., conquered much of the world of Classical antiquity, spreading Greek culture throughout Egypt and Persia and as far as India.

"Well, are you coming to the Superior?" Miüsov asked Ivan Fyodorovich abruptly.

"Why not? I was especially invited by the Superior yesterday."

"Unfortunately I feel myself almost compelled to go to this confounded dinner," said Miüsov with the same bitter irritability, regardless of the fact that the little monk was listening. "We ought, at least, to apologize for the disturbance, and explain that it was not our doing. What do you think?"

"Yes, we must explain that it wasn't us. Besides, father won't be there," observed Ivan Fyodorovich.

"Well, I should hope not! Curse this dinner!"

They all walked on, however. The little monk listened in silence. On the road through the woods he made one observation however—that the Father Superior had been waiting a long time, and that they were more than half an hour late. He received no answer. Miüsov looked with hatred at Ivan Fyodorovich.

"Here he is, going to the dinner as though nothing had happened!" he thought. "A brazen face, and the conscience of a Karamazov!"

Chapter VII

A Seminarian-Careerist

Alyosha brought his elder to his little bedroom and seated him on his bed. It was a little room furnished with the bare necessities. There was a narrow iron bedstead, with a strip of felt for a mattress. In the corner, under the icons, was a lectern with a cross and the Gospel lying on it. The elder sank exhausted on the bed; his eyes glittered and he breathed hard. After he sat down, he looked intently at Alyosha, as though considering something.

"Go, my dear boy, go. Porfiry is enough for me. Make haste, you are needed there, go and wait at the Father Superior's table."

"Give me your blessing to stay here," Alyosha entreated with a pleading voice.

"You are more needed there. There is no peace there. You will serve, and be of use. If evil spirits rise up, repeat a prayer. And know, my little son" (the elder liked to call him that), "that this is not the place for you in the future. Remember that, young man. As soon as it is God's will to call me, leave the monastery. Go away for good."

Alyosha started.

"What is it? This is not your place for the time. I bless you for great service in the world. Yours will be a long pilgrimage. And you will have to take a wife, too, you will have to. You will have to bear all before you come back. There will be much to do. But I don't doubt of you, and so I send you forth. Christ is with you. Do not abandon Him and He will not abandon you. You will see great sorrow, and in that sorrow you will be happy. Here is a commandment for you: seek happiness in sorrow. Work, work unceasingly. Remember my words henceforth, for although I shall talk with you again, not only my days but my hours are numbered."

Alyosha's face again betrayed strong emotion. The corners of his mouth quivered.

"What is it again?" the elder asked, smiling gently. "The worldly may follow their dead with tears, but here we rejoice over the father who is departing. We rejoice and pray for him. Leave me, I must pray. Go, and make haste. Be near your brothers. And not near one only, but near both."

The elder raised his hand to bless him. Alyosha could make no protest, though he had a great longing to remain. He longed, moreover, to ask the significance of his bowing to his brother Dmitri, the question was on the tip of his tongue, but he dared not ask it. He knew that the elder would have explained it unasked if he had thought fit. But evidently it was not his will. That bow had made a terrible impression on Alyosha; he believed blindly that there was a secret meaning in it. Secret, and perhaps awful. As he hastened out of the hermitage precincts to reach the monastery in time for the Father Superior's dinner (of course only to serve at the table), he felt a sudden pang at his heart, and stopped short. He seemed to hear again the elder's words, foretelling his approaching end. What he had foretold so exactly must infallibly come to pass. Alyosha believed that implicitly. But how could he be left without him, how could he live without seeing and hearing him? And where should he go? He had told him not to weep, and to leave the monastery, good God! It was long since Alyosha had known such anguish. He hurried through the woods that divided the monastery from the hermitage, and unable to bear the burden of his thoughts, he gazed at the ancient pines beside the path. He had not far to go, no more than five hundred paces; he expected to meet no one at that hour, but suddenly at the first turn of the path he noticed Rakitin. He was waiting for someone.

"Are you waiting for me?" asked Alyosha, overtaking him.

"Yes, you in particular," grinned Rakitin. "You are hurrying to the Father Superior, I know; he has a banquet. There's not been such a banquet since the Superior entertained the Bishop and General Pakhatov, do you remember? I won't be there, but you go and hand the sauces. Tell me one thing, Alexey, what's the meaning of that dream?[1] That's what I want to ask you."

"What dream?"

"That bowing to your brother, Dmitri Fyodorovich. He even hit his forehead to the ground!"

"You mean Father Zosima?"

"Yes, Father Zosima."

"His forehead?"

"Ah, an irreverent expression! Well, what of it? Anyway, what does that dream mean?"

"I don't know what it means, Misha."

"I knew he wouldn't explain it to you! There's nothing very deep about it, of course, only the usual holy nonsense.[2] But there was an object in the performance. All the pious people in the town will talk about it and

---

1. Rakitin paraphrases a line from the poem "Zhenikh" ("The Bridegroom," 1825) by Alexander Pushkin. This became a common expression in the 1860s and 1870s, used frequently by the novelist and satirist Mikhail Saltykov-Shchedrin (1826–1889). Saltykov-Shchedrin, a frequent contributor to the radical "thick" journals Notes of the Fatherland and The Contemporary, was one of Dostoevsky's bitterest ideological rivals. See p. 76.
   Alexander Sergeevich Pushkin (1799–1837), poet, novelist, dramatist, and essayist, considered by many in Dostoevsky's time and today to be Russia's foremost man of letters. Dostoevsky professed admiration for Pushkin above all other artists.
2. "Holy nonsense" (Russian blagoglUposti) was a phrase coined by Saltykov-Shchedrin.

spread the story through the province, wondering what it meant. To my thinking the old man really has a keen nose: he sniffed a crime. Your house stinks of it."

"What crime?"

Rakitin evidently had something he was eager to speak of.

"It'll be in your nice little family, this crime. Between your brothers and your rich little father. So Father Zosima hit his forehead to the ground to be ready for what may turn up. If something happens later on, it'll be: 'Ah, the holy man foresaw it, prophesied it!' though it's a poor sort of prophecy, hitting the ground like that. 'Ah, but it was an emblem,' they'll say, 'an allegory,' and the devil knows what all! It'll be remembered to his glory: 'He predicted the crime and marked the criminal!' That's always the way with these holy fools: they cross themselves in front of a tavern and cast stones at the temple. Just like your elder: he takes a stick to a just man and falls at the feet of a murderer."

"What crime? What murderer? What do you mean?"

Alyosha stopped dead. Rakitin stopped, too.

"What murderer? As though you didn't know! I'll bet you've thought of it before. That's interesting, too, by the way. Listen, Alyosha, you always speak the truth, though you're always between two stools.[3] Have you thought of it or not? Answer."

"I have," answered Alyosha in a low voice. Even Rakitin was taken aback.

"What? Is it possible that even you have thought about it?" he cried.

"I . . . It's not exactly that I thought it," muttered Alyosha, "but when you began speaking so strangely just now, it seemed to me I had thought of it myself."

"You see (and how well you expressed it), you see? Looking at your papasha and your brother Mitenka today you thought of a crime? Then I'm not mistaken?"

"But wait, wait a minute," Alyosha broke in uneasily, "What has led you to see all this? Why does it interest you so much, that's the first question."

"Two questions, disconnected, but natural. I'll deal with them separately. What led me to see it? I wouldn't have seen it, if I hadn't suddenly understood your brother Dmitri Fyodorovich, seen right into the very heart of him all at once. I caught the whole man from one trait. These very honest but passionate people have a line which mustn't be crossed. If it is—if it is, he'd run at your papenka with a knife. But your papenka's a drunken and abandoned old sinner, who can never draw the line—if they both let themselves go, they'll both come to a catastrophe."

"No, Misha, no. If that's all, you've reassured me! It won't come to that."

"But why are you trembling? Let me tell you; he may be honest—your Mitenka (he is stupid, but honest) but he's—a sensualist. That's the very definition and inner essence of him. It's your father who has handed his base sensuality on to him. Do you know, I simply wonder at you, Alyosha: how is it you're a virgin? You're a Karamazov too, you know! In your family sensuality is carried to a disease. But now, these three sensualists are

<hr />

3. Saltykov-Shchedrin used the expression "between two stools" to criticize Dostoevsky's positions on sociopolitical issues in the early 1860s.

watching one another, with their knives in their belts. The three of them
are knocking their heads together, and you may be the fourth."

"You are mistaken about that woman. Dmitri—despises her," said Alyosha, with a sort of shudder.

"Grushenka? No, brother, he doesn't despise her. Since he has openly
abandoned his betrothed for her, he doesn't despise her. There's something here, my dear boy, that you don't understand yet. A man will fall
in love with some beauty, with a woman's body, or even with a part of a
woman's body (a sensualist can understand that) and he'll abandon his
own children for her, sell his father and mother, and his country, Russia,
too. If he's honest, he'll steal; if he's humane, he'll murder; if he's faithful, he'll betray. Pushkin, the poet of women's feet,[4] sung of their feet in
his verse. Others don't sing their praises, but they can't look at feet without a thrill—and it's not only feet. Contempt's no help here, brother, even
if he did despise Grushenka. Even if he does, he can't tear himself away."

"I understand that," Alyosha jerked out suddenly.

"Really? Well, I daresay you do understand, since you blurt it out at the
first word," said Rakitin, malignantly. "That escaped you unawares, and
the admission is the more precious. So it's a familiar subject; you've thought
about it already, about sensuality, I mean! Oh, you virgin! You're a quiet
one, Alyosha, you're a saint, I know, but the devil only knows what you've
thought about, and what you know already! A virgin, but you've already
been down into the depths. . . . I've been watching you a long time. You're
a Karamazov yourself; you're a thorough Karamazov—no doubt birth and
selection mean something. You're a sensualist from your father, a holy fool
from your mother. Why do you tremble? Is it true, then? Do you know
what: Grushenka has been asking me: 'bring him (you, that is), and I'll
pull his cassock off.' She's really been asking: 'bring him, bring him!' Just
think: why are you so interesting to her? Do you know, she's an extraordinary woman, too!"

"Thank her and say I'm not coming," said Alyosha, with a strained smile.
"Finish what you were saying, Michael. I'll tell you my idea after."

"There's nothing to finish. It's all clear. It's the same old tune, brother.
If even you are a sensualist at heart what of your brother, Ivan, your full
brother? He's a Karamazov, too. What is at the root of all you Karamazovs
is that you're all sensualists, money grubbers, and holy fools! Your brother
Ivan writes theological articles in jest, for some idiotic, unknown motive
of his own, though he's an atheist, and he admits that vileness himself—
that's your brother Ivan. Moreover, he is trying to get Mitya's betrothed for
himself, and I fancy he'll succeed, too. And what's more it's with Mitenka's
consent. For Mitenka will surrender his betrothed to him to be rid of her,
and escape to Grushenka. And he's ready to do that in spite of all his nobility and disinterestedness. Observe that. Those are the most fatal people!
Who the devil can make you out? He recognizes his vileness and goes
on with it! Let me tell you, too, the old man, your father, is standing in
Mitenka's way now. He has suddenly gone crazy over Grushenka. His
mouth waters at the sight of her. It's simply on her account he made that
scene in the cell just now, simply because Miüsov called her an 'abandoned creature.' He's worse than a tomcat in love. At first she was only

---

4. Pushkin writes of feet in a number of works, including his verse novel *Eugene Onegin* (1833).

employed by him in connection with his taverns and in some other shady business, but now he has suddenly realized all she is and has gone wild about her. He keeps pestering her with his offers, not honorable ones, of course. And they'll come into collision, the precious papenka and son, on that path. But Grushenka favors neither of them, she's still playing with them, and teasing them both, considering which she can get most out of. For though she could filch a lot of money from the papasha he wouldn't marry her, and maybe he'll turn stingy in the end, and keep his purse shut. That's where Mitenka's value comes in, he has no money, but he's capable of marrying her. Yes, sir, capable of marrying! Abandon his betrothed, a rare beauty, Katerina Ivanovna, who's rich, and the daughter of a colonel, and marry Grushenka, who has been the mistress of a dissolute old merchant, Samsonov, a coarse, uneducated, provincial mayor. Some murderous conflict may well come to pass from all this, and that's what your brother Ivan is waiting for. It would suit him down to the ground. He'll carry off Katerina Ivanovna, for whom he is languishing, and pocket her dowry of sixty thousand. That's very alluring to start with, for a man of no consequence and a beggar. And, take note, he won't be wronging Mitya, but doing him the greatest service. For I know as a fact that Mitya only last week, when he was with some gypsy girls drunk in a tavern, cried out aloud that he was unworthy of his betrothed, Katya, but that his brother Ivan, he was the man who deserved her. And Katerina Ivanovna will not in the end refuse such a fascinating man as Ivan Fyodorovich. She's hesitating between the two of them already. And how has that Ivan won you all, so that you all worship him? He is laughing at you, and enjoying himself at your expense."

"How do you know? How can you speak so confidently?" Alyosha asked sharply, frowning.

"Why do you ask, and are frightened at my answer? It shows that you know I'm speaking the truth."

"You don't like Ivan. Ivan wouldn't be tempted by money."

"Really? And the beauty of Katerina Ivanovna? It's not only the money, though a fortune of sixty thousand is an attraction."

"Ivan aims higher than that. He wouldn't be seduced by thousands. Ivan is not seeking money or comfort. He is seeking suffering, perhaps."

"What wild dream now? Oh, you—aristocrats!"

"Ah, Misha, he has a stormy spirit. His mind is in bondage. He is haunted by a great, unsolved doubt. He is one of those who don't want millions, but an answer to their questions."

"That's plagiarism, Alyoshka. You're paraphrasing your elder. Ah, Ivan has posed a riddle for you!" cried Rakitin, with undisguised malice. His face even changed, and his lips twitched. "And the riddle's a stupid one. It is no good guessing it. Rack your brains—you'll understand it. His article is absurd and ridiculous. And did you hear his stupid theory just now: if there's no immortality of the soul, then there's no virtue, and everything is permitted. (And by the way, do you remember how your brother Mitenka cried out: 'I will remember!') An attractive theory for scoundrels! . . . I'm being abusive, that's stupid. . . . Not for scoundrels, but for pedantic poseurs, 'haunted by profound, unsolved doubts.' He's showing off, and what it all comes to is, 'on the one hand we cannot but admit' and 'on the other it must be confessed!' His whole theory is vileness! Humanity will find in itself the power to live for virtue even without believing in immortality! It will find it in love for liberty, for equality, for fraternity."

Rakitin could hardly restrain himself in his heat, but, suddenly, as though remembering something, he stopped short.

"Well, that's enough," he said, with a still more crooked smile. "Why are you laughing? Do you think I'm a vulgar fool?"

"No, I never dreamed of thinking you a vulgar fool. You are clever but . . . never mind, I was silly to smile. I understand your getting hot about it, Misha. I guess from your excitement that you are not indifferent to Katerina Ivanovna yourself, I've suspected that for a long time, brother, that's why you don't like my brother Ivan. Are you jealous of him?"

"And jealous of her money, too? Won't you add that?"

"No, I won't say anything about money, I am not going to insult you."

"I believe it, since you say so, but devil take you, and your brother Ivan with you! Don't you understand that one might very well dislike him, apart from Katerina Ivanovna? And why the devil should I like him! He condescends to abuse me, you know. Why haven't I a right to abuse him?"

"I never heard of his saying anything about you, good or bad. He doesn't speak of you at all."

"But I heard that the day before yesterday at Katerina Ivanovna's he was abusing me for all he was worth—you see what an interest he takes in your humble servant. And which is the jealous one after that, brother, I can't say! He was so good as to express the opinion that, if I don't go in for the career of an archimandrite[5] in the very near future and don't become a monk, I will most certainly go to Petersburg and join some thick journal,[6] most certainly in the criticism section, I will write for ten years and in the end take over the journal. Then I will again publish it, most certainly with a liberal and atheistic tendency, with a socialist tinge, with a little gloss of socialism, but keeping a sharp lookout all the time, that is, essentially, playing both sides and pulling the wool over the fools' eyes. The point of my career, according to your brother's interpretation, is in the fact that the tinge of socialism will not prevent me from putting aside the subscription money into an account and investing it under the guidance of some little Yid, until I build myself a great house in Petersburg and move the publishing offices to it, and rent out the upper stories to lodgers. He has even chosen the place for it, near the New Stone bridge across the Neva, which they say is to be built in Petersburg to connect Liteiny Prospect with the Vyborg side . . ."[7]

"Ah, Misha, that's just what will really happen, every word of it!" cried Alyosha, unable to restrain himself and laughing cheerfully.

"And you are embarking on sarcasm, too, Alexey Fyodorovich."

"No, no, I'm joking, forgive me. I've something quite different in my mind. But, excuse me, who can have told you all this? You can't have been at Katerina Ivanovna's yourself when he was talking about you?"

---

5. The abbot or head abbot of an important monastery.

6. Thick journals (tol'stye zhurnaly) were the primary forum of public opinion in Dostoevsky's Russia. Steered by editorial boards with distinct ideological agendas, thick journals published material ranging from fiction (both original Russian compositions and translations from Europe) to essays on politics, society, and economics.

7. The fictional biography Ivan projects for Rakitin includes elements from the life of Dostoevsky's contemporary Grigory Eliseev (1821–1891), a divinity school graduate and journalist. For discussion of Eliseev as a prototype for Rakitin, see Belknap, "The Rhetoric of an Ideological Novel," p. 770.

"I wasn't there, but Dmitri Fyodorovich was; and I heard him tell it with my own ears; if you want to know, he didn't tell me, but I overheard him, unintentionally, of course, for I was sitting in Grushenka's bedroom and I couldn't go away because Dmitri Fyodorovich was in the next room."

"Oh yes, I'd forgotten she was a relation of yours."

"A relation? That Grushenka a relation of mine?" cried Rakitin, turning crimson. "Are you mad? You're out of your mind."

"Why, isn't she a relation of yours? That's what I heard."

"Where can you have heard it? You Karamazovs brag of being an ancient, noble family, though your father used to run about playing the buffoon at other men's tables, and was only admitted to the kitchen as a favor. I may be only a priest's son, and dirt in the eyes of noblemen like you, but don't insult me so lightly and wantonly.[8] I have a sense of honor, too, Alexey Fyodorovich, I couldn't be a relation of Grushenka, a common harlot. I beg you to understand that, sir!"

Rakitin was intensely irritated.

"Forgive me, for goodness' sake, I had no idea . . . besides . . . how can you call her a harlot? Is she really . . . that sort of woman?" Alyosha flushed suddenly. "I tell you again, I heard that she was a relation of yours. You often go to see her, and you told me yourself you're not her lover. I never dreamed that you of all people had such contempt for her! Does she really deserve it?"

"If I visit her, I may have reasons of my own for doing so, that's not your business. But as for relationship, your brother, or even your father is more likely to make her yours, than mine. Well, here we are. You'd better go to the kitchen. Hey! what's wrong, what is it? Are we late? They have finished dinner so soon? Have the Karamazovs been making trouble again? No doubt they have. Here's your father and Ivan Fyodorovich after him. They've broken out from the Father Superior's. Father Isidor's shouting out something after them from the steps. And your father's shouting and waving his arms, he must be swearing. Bah, and Miüsov drove away in his carriage, you see, he's going. And there's Maximov the landowner—there must have been a scandal; that means there wasn't any dinner! Maybe they were beating the Father Superior? Or maybe they were beaten? It would serve them right!"

There was reason for Rakitin's exclamations. There had indeed been a scandal, unheard of and unexpected. It all happened "by inspiration."

Chapter VIII

Scandal

Miüsov and Ivan Fyodorovich were already entering the Father Superior's rooms when a certain process, delicate in its own way, quickly took place within Pyotr Alexandrovich, a sincerely decent and delicate person: he was ashamed of losing his temper. He felt that, essentially, he ought to have disdained that despicable wretch, Fyodor Pavlovich, too much to have been upset by him in Father Zosima's cell, and so to have forgotten

8. Rakitin's defensiveness of his origins illustrates the low esteem in which clergy were held.

himself. "The monks were not to blame, in any case," he suddenly decided, on the Father's porch, "and if they're decent people here (and the Father Superior, Nikolay, it seems, is a nobleman), then why not be pleasant, friendly, and courteous with them? I won't argue, I'll fall in with everything, I'll win them by politeness, and . . . and finally prove to them that I have nothing in common with that Aesop, that buffoon, that Pierrot,[9] and have merely been taken in by this affair, just as they have."

The contested woodcutting in the forest and the fishing (where it all was, he himself did not know) he decided to relinquish to them for good, at once, this very day, all the more so that it was all was worth very little, and stop all of his legal proceedings against the monastery.

These good intentions were strengthened when he entered the Father Superior's dining room. Strictly speaking, it was not a dining room, for the Father Superior had only two rooms altogether; they were, however, much larger and more comfortable than Father Zosima's. But there was no great luxury about the furnishing of these rooms either: the furniture was of mahogany, covered with leather, in the old-fashioned style of the 1820s; the floor was not even stained; but everything was shining with cleanliness, and there were many choice flowers in the windows; the main luxury at the moment was, naturally, the luxuriously set table, here too, by the way, comparatively speaking: the cloth was clean, the service shone; there were three kinds of well-baked bread, two bottles of wine, two of excellent mead, and a large glass jug of kvass[1]—both the latter made in the monastery, and famous in the neighborhood. There was no vodka at all. Rakitin recounted afterwards that there were five dishes: fish soup made of sterlets, served with little fish patties; then boiled fish somehow very excellently and specially prepared; then salmon cutlets, ices and compote, and finally, blancmange.[2] Rakitin sniffed out all this, for he could not resist peeping into the kitchen, where he already had connections. He had connections everywhere and got information about everything. He had a restless and envious heart. He was well aware of his own considerable abilities, but nervously exaggerated them in his self-conceit. He knew he would play a prominent part of some sort, but Alyosha, who was attached to him, was distressed to see that his friend Rakitin was dishonorable, and quite unconscious of being so himself, considering, on the contrary, that because he would not steal money left on the table he was a man of the highest integrity. Neither Alyosha nor anyone else could have influenced him in that.

Rakitin was a person of too little consequence to be invited to the dinner, to which Father Iosif, Father Païssy, and one other hieromonk were invited. They were already waiting when Miüsov, Kalganov, and Ivan Fyodorovich arrived. The other guest, the landowner Maximov, stood a little aside, waiting also. The Father Superior stepped into the middle of the room to receive his guests. He was a tall, thin, but still vigorous old man, with black hair streaked with grey, and a long, grave, ascetic face. He bowed to his guests in silence, but this time they approached to receive

9. Aesop (620–560 B.C.), who lived in various Greek cities, was the author of popular fables still widely read today. Pierrot is a clown, a stock character in Commedia dell'Arte and pantomime theater.
1. An alcoholic beverage made from fermented bread, kvass was a favorite drink of Russian peasants.
2. A sweet dish made with milk or cream, chilled and set in molds.

his blessing. Miüsov even risked kissing his hand, but the Father Superior somehow drew it back in time and the kiss did not take place. But Ivan Fyodorovich and Kalganov went through the ceremony in the most simple-hearted and complete manner, kissing his hand as peasants do.

"We must apologize most fervently, your reverence," began Pyotr Alexandrovich, grinning affably, and speaking in a dignified and respectful tone, "for having come alone, without our companion whom you invited, Fyodor Pavlovich; he felt obliged to decline the honor of your hospitality, and not without reason. In the reverend Father Zosima's cell he was carried away by the unhappy dissension with his son, and let fall words which were quite out of keeping . . . in fact, quite unseemly . . . as"—he glanced at the hieromonks—"your reverence is, no doubt, already aware. And therefore, recognizing his blame and sincerely repenting, he felt ashamed and, unable to overcome this, asked us, myself and his son Ivan Fyodorovich, to convey to you his sincere apology, distress, and contrition . . . In brief, he hopes and desires to make amends later, but now, he asks your blessing, and begs you to forget what has taken place . . ."

Miüsov fell silent. As he uttered the last word of his tirade, he completely recovered his self-complacency, and all traces of his former irritation disappeared. He fully and sincerely loved humanity again. The Father Superior listened to him with dignity, and, with a slight bend of the head replied:

"I am sincerely sorry for his absence. Perhaps at our table he might have learned to love us, and we him. Pray be seated, gentlemen."

He stood before the icon, and began to say grace, aloud. All bent their heads reverently, and the landowner Maximov even leaned especially forward and clasped his hands before him with peculiar fervor.

And it was at this very moment that Fyodor Pavlovich played his last prank. It must be noted that he really had meant to go home, and really had felt the impossibility of going to dine with the Father Superior as though nothing had happened, after his disgraceful behavior in the elder's cell. Not that he felt so very much ashamed or blamed himself; maybe even quite the opposite. But still he felt it would be unseemly to go to dinner. Yet his creaking carriage had hardly been brought to the steps of the hotel, and he had hardly got into it, when he suddenly stopped short. He remembered his own words at the elder's: "I always feel when I meet people that I am lower than all, and that they all take me for a buffoon; so I say let me play the buffoon, for you are, every one of you, stupider and lower than I." He longed to take revenge on everyone for his own unseemliness. He suddenly recalled how he had once in the past been asked, "Why do you hate so and so, so much?" And he had answered them, in a fit of his buffoonish shamelessness: "I'll tell you why: he never did me any harm, it's true, but I played a dirty trick on him, and as soon as I did it, I immediately began to hate him for it." Remembering that now, he smiled quietly and malignantly in a moment of reflection. His eyes gleamed, and his lips even quivered. "Well, since I have begun, I may as well go on," he decided suddenly. His predominant sensation at that moment might be expressed in the following words, "Well, there is no rehabilitating myself now, so I'll spit all over them shamelessly: 'I'm not ashamed before you,' I'll show them, and that's that!" He told the coachman to wait, while with rapid steps he returned to the monastery and straight to the Father Superior's. He had no clear idea what he would do, but he knew that he could not control himself, and that a touch might drive him to the utmost limits of obscenity, but only to obscenity, to nothing criminal, nothing for which he could be legally punished. In the last resort, he could always restrain himself, and had indeed marveled at himself sometimes on that score. He appeared in the Father Superior's dining room, at exactly the moment when the prayer was over, and all were moving to the table. Standing in the doorway, he scanned the company, and laughing his prolonged, impudent, malicious chuckle, looked them all boldly in the face. "They thought I had gone, and here I am again," he cried to the whole room.

For one moment everyone stared at him without a word; and at once everyone felt that something revolting, unseemly, undoubtedly scandalous, was about to happen. Pyotr Alexandrovich passed immediately from the most benevolent frame of mind to the most savage. All the feelings that had subsided and died down in his heart revived instantly.

"No! this I cannot endure!" he cried. "I absolutely cannot! and . . . I certainly cannot!"

The blood rushed to his head. He positively stammered; but he was beyond thinking of style, and he seized his hat.

"What is it he cannot?" cried Fyodor Pavlovich, "that he absolutely cannot and certainly cannot? Your reverence, am I to come in or not? Will you receive me as your guest?"

"You are welcome with all my heart," answered the Superior. "Gentlemen!" he added, "I venture to beg you most earnestly to lay aside your dissensions, and to be united in love and family harmony—with prayer to the Lord at our humble table."

"No, no, it is impossible!" cried Pyotr Alexandrovich, as if not himself.

"Well, if it is impossible for Pyotr Alexandrovich, it is impossible for me, and I won't stay. That is why I came. I will be with Pyotr Alexandrovich everywhere now: If you go away, Pyotr Alexandrovich, I will go away too, if you remain, I will remain. You stung him by what you said about family harmony, Father Superior, he does not admit he is my relation! That's right, isn't it, von Sohn? Here's von Sohn. Greetings, von Sohn."

"You . . . do you mean me?" muttered the landowner Maximov, puzzled.

"Of course I mean you," cried Fyodor Pavlovich, "Who else? The Father Superior could not be von Sohn."

"But I am not von Sohn either. I am Maximov."

"No, you are von Sohn. Your reverence, do you know what this Sohn means? It was a famous murder case. He was killed in a house of harlotry. I believe that is what such places are called among you—he was killed and robbed, and in spite of his venerable age, he was nailed up in a box and sent from Petersburg to Moscow in the luggage van, and while they were nailing him up, the harlots sang songs and played the harp, that is to say, the piano.[3] So this is that very von Sohn. He has risen from the dead, hasn't he, von Sohn?"

"What is happening? What's this?" voices were heard in the group of hieromonks.

"Let's go," cried Pyotr Alexandrovich, addressing Kalganov.

---

3. Fyodor Pavlovich's description of the murder uses words and imagery similar to those found in Biblical passages describing the dance of Herod's stepdaughter.

"No, excuse me," Fyodor Pavlovich broke in shrilly, taking another step into the room. "Allow me to finish. There in the cell you blamed me for behaving disrespectfully just because I spoke of eating gudgeon. Pyotr Alexandrovich Miüsov, my relation, prefers to have *plus de noblesse que de sincerité* in his words, but I prefer in mine *plus de sincerité que de noblesse*,[4] and—damn the noblesse! That's right, isn't it, von Sohn? Allow me, Father Superior, though I am a buffoon and play the buffoon, yet I am a knight of honor, and I want to speak my mind. Yes, I am a knight of honor, while in Pyotr Alexandrovich there is wounded vanity and nothing else. I came here perhaps to have a look and speak my mind. My son, Alexey, is here, being saved. I am his father; I care for his welfare, and it is my duty to care. While I've been playing the fool, I have been listening and having a look on the sly; and now I want to give you the last act of the performance. You know how things are with us? As a thing falls, so it lies. As a thing once has fallen, so it must lie for ever. Not a bit of it! I want to get up again. Holy Father, I am indignant with you. Confession is a great sacrament, before which I am ready to bow down reverently; but there in the cell, they all kneel down and confess aloud. Can it be right to confess aloud? It was ordained by the holy fathers to confess in secret: then only your confession will be a mystery, and so it was of old.[5] But how can I explain to him before everyone that I did this and that . . . Well, you know, this and that, you understand? Sometimes it would be improper to talk about it. There would be a scandal! No, fathers, one might be carried along with you to the flagellants,[6] I daresay . . . I will write to the Synod[7] at the first opportunity, and take my son Alexey home . . ."

A nota bene here. Fyodor Pavlovich knew where to look for the weak spot. There had been at one time malicious rumors which had even reached the Archbishop (not only regarding our monastery, but in others where the institution of elders existed) that too much respect was paid to the elders, even to the detriment of the authority of the Superior, that, by the way, the elders abused the sacrament of confession and so on and so on. Absurd charges which had died away of themselves everywhere. But the stupid devil which had caught Fyodor Pavlovich and was bearing him on the current of his own nerves into lower and lower depths of ignominy prompted him with this old slander. Fyodor Pavlovich did not understand a word of it, and he could not even put it sensibly, for on this occasion no one had been kneeling and confessing aloud in the elder's cell, so that he could not have seen anything of the kind. He was only speaking from confused memory of old slanders. But as soon as he had uttered his foolish tirade, he felt he had been talking absurd nonsense, and at once longed to prove to his audience and above all to himself, that he had not been talking nonsense. And, though he knew perfectly well that with each word he

4. "More nobility than sincerity" and "more sincerity than nobility" (French).
5. Confession was public for the first centuries of Christianity, so Fyodor Pavlovich has it wrong: private confession is the more recent innovation.
6. Russian flagellants (*khlysty*) were a mystical sect that broke off from the Orthodox Church in the seventeenth century. *Khlysty* sought to purge the individual of evil by reaching ecstatic states in their rituals.
7. Founded by Peter the Great in 1721, the Synod was the highest organ of the Russian Orthodox Church, comprised of lay and ecclesiastical officials who reported to a procurator appointed by the Emperor.

would be adding more and more absurdity, he could not restrain himself, and plunged forward blindly.

"What vileness!" cried Pyotr Alexandrovich.

"Pardon me," said the Father Superior suddenly. "It was said of old, 'Many have begun to speak against me and have uttered evil sayings about me. And hearing it I have said to myself: it is the correction of the Lord and He has sent it to heal my vain soul.' And so we humbly thank you, honored guest!" and he made Fyodor Pavlovich a low bow.

"Tut-tut-tut—sanctimoniousness and old phrases! Old phrases and old gestures! The old lies and formal prostrations! We know all about these bows! 'A kiss on the lips and a dagger in the heart,' as in Schiller's *Robbers*.[8] I don't like falsehood, fathers, I want the truth! But the truth is not to be found in eating gudgeon and that I proclaim aloud! Father monks, why do you fast? Why do you expect reward in heaven for that? Why, for reward like that I will come and fast too! No, saintly monk, you try being virtuous in the world, do good to society, without shutting yourself up in a monastery at other people's expense, and without expecting a reward up aloft for it—you'll find that a bit harder. I can talk sense, too, Father Superior. What have they got here?" He went up to the table. "Old port wine, médoc from the Eliseyev Brothers.[9] So that's the kind of fathers you are! That is something beyond gudgeon. Look at the bottles the fathers have brought out, he! he! he! And who has provided it all? The Russian peasant, the laborer, brings here the kopeck earned by his calloused hand, wringing it from his family and the tax gatherer![1] You bleed the people, you know, holy fathers!"

"This is unworthy on your part," said Father Iosif. Father Païssy kept obstinately silent. Miüsov rushed from the room, and Kalganov after him.

"Well, Father, I will follow Pyotr Alexandrovich! I won't come to see you again, you can beg me on your knees, I won't come. I sent you a thousand rubles, and so you pricked up your ears again, ha ha ha! No, I won't add anymore. I am taking my revenge for my lost youth, for all the humiliation I endured!" He thumped the table with his fist in a paroxysm of simulated feeling. "This monastery has played a great part in my life! It has cost me many bitter tears! You used to set my wife, the shrieker, against me. You cursed me at seven councils,[2] you spread stories about me all over the place! Enough, fathers, this is a liberal age, an age of steamers and railways. Neither a thousand, nor a hundred rubles, no, nor a hundred kopecks will you get out of me!"

Once again a nota bene. Our monastery never had played any great part in his life, and he never had shed a bitter tear because of it. But he was so carried away by his simulated emotion, that for one moment he almost believed it himself. He was so touched he almost wept. But at that

---

8. *The Robbers*, Act I, scene 2.
9. The Eliseev brothers owned the fanciest food stores in nineteenth-century Moscow and Saint Petersburg.
1. The term *tax gatherer* translates *nuzhd gosudarstvennykh*, literally needs of the state.
2. In the early centuries of Christianity, church leaders gathered in councils to decide questions of dogma. At almost every council, some views and the people who held them were condemned as heretical. The Russian Orthodox Church recognizes only the first seven councils, held before the East-West Schism of 1054, when Christianity split into Eastern Orthodoxy and Roman Catholicism.

very instant, he felt that it was time to draw back. The Father Superior bowed his head at his malicious lie, and again spoke impressively.

"It is written again, 'Bear circumspectly and gladly dishonor that cometh upon thee by no act of thine own, be not confounded and hate not him who hath dishonored thee.'[3] And so will we."

"Tut-tut-tut! Bethinking thyself! And the rest of the rigmarole! Bethink yourselves, fathers, I will go. But I will take my son, Alexey, away from here forever, on my parental authority. Ivan Fyodorovich, my most dutiful son, permit me to order you to follow me. Von Sohn, what have you to stay for? Come and see me now in the town. It is fun at my place. It is only one short mile. Instead of lenten oil, I will give you sucking pig and kasha. We will have dinner with some brandy and then liqueur; I have cloudberry wine. Hey, von Sohn, don't miss your chance!" He went out, shouting and gesticulating.

It was at that moment Rakitin saw him and pointed him out to Alyosha.

"Alexey!" his father shouted, from far off, catching sight of him. "You come home to me today, for good, and bring your pillow and mattress, and leave no trace behind."

Alyosha stood rooted to the spot, watching the scene in silence. Meanwhile, Fyodor Pavlovich had got into the carriage, and Ivan Fyodorovich was about to follow him in grim silence without even turning to say good-bye to Alyosha. But at this point another almost incredible scene of grotesque buffoonery gave the finishing touch to the episode. The landowner Maximov suddenly appeared by the side of the carriage. He ran up, panting, afraid of being too late, Rakitin and Alyosha saw him running. He was in such a hurry that in his impatience he put his foot on the step on which Ivan Fyodorovich's left foot was still resting, and clutching the carriage he kept trying to jump in.

"I am going with you!" he kept shouting, laughing a thin mirthful laugh with a look of reckless glee in his face. "Take me, too!"

"Didn't I say he was von Sohn!" cried Fyodor Pavlovich, ecstatically. "It is von Sohn himself, risen from the dead! Why, how did you tear yourself away? What did you vonsohn there, and how could you get away from the dinner? You must be a brazen-faced fellow! I am that myself, but I am surprised at you, brother! Jump in, jump in quickly! Let him in, Vanya, it will be fun. He can lie somewhere at our feet. Will you lie at our feet, von Sohn? Or perch on the box with the coachman? Jump onto the box, von Sohn!"

But Ivan Fyodorovich, who had by now taken his seat, without a word gave Maximov a violent shove in the breast and sent him flying. It was quite by chance he did not fall.

"Drive on!" Ivan Fyodorovich shouted angrily to the coachman.

"What are you doing, what are you doing?" Why did you do that?" Fyodor Pavlovich protested. But the carriage had already driven away. Ivan Fyodorovich made no reply.

"Well, you are a fellow!" Fyodor Pavlovich said again after a pause of two minutes, looking askance at his son. "Why, it was you got up all this monastery business. You urged it, you approved of it, why are you angry now?"

---

3. This may be a quotation from the writings of one of the Fathers of the Church.

"You've talked enough drivel, give it a little rest now," Ivan Fyodorovich snapped sullenly.

Fyodor Pavlovich was silent again for two minutes.

"A drop of brandy would be nice now," he observed sententiously, but Ivan Fyodorovich made no response.

"You shall have some, too, when we get home."

Ivan Fyodorovich was silent.

Fyodor Pavlovich was silent again for two minutes.

"But I shall take Alyoshka away from the monastery just the same, no matter how unpleasant that will be for you, most respectful Karl von Moor."

Ivan Fyodorovich shrugged his shoulders contemptuously, and turning away stared at the road. And they did not speak again all the way home.

Book Three

SENSUALISTS

Chapter I

In the Servants' Quarters

Fyodor Pavlovich's house was far from being in the center of town, but it was not quite outside it. It was rather dilapidated, but had a pleasant exterior: a one-story house with a mezzanine painted gray and a red iron roof. It might still last many years, and was roomy and snug. There were all sorts of unexpected little cupboards and closets and staircases. There were rats in it, but Fyodor Pavlovich did not altogether dislike them. "One doesn't feel so solitary when one's left alone in the evening," he used to say. And indeed, it was his habit to send the servants away to the lodge for the night and to lock himself up alone. The lodge was a roomy and solid building in the yard. Fyodor Pavlovich used to have the cooking done there, although there was a kitchen in the house; he did not like the smell of cooking, and, winter and summer alike, the dishes were carried in across the courtyard. The house was built for a large family; there was room for five times as many, with their servants. But at the time of our story there was no one living in the house but Fyodor Pavlovich and his son Ivan Fyodorovich. And in the lodge there were only three servants: old Grigory, and his old wife Martha, and the servant Smerdyakov, still a young man. We must say a bit more about these three auxiliary figures. Of old Grigory Vasilyevich Kutuzov, by the way, we have already said enough. This was a firm and determined man who blindly and obstinately pursued his point, if once he had been brought by any reasons (and they were often very illogical ones) to believe that it was immutably right. Generally speaking, he was honest and incorruptible. His wife, Martha Ignatyevna, had obeyed her husband's will implicitly all her life, yet she had pestered him terribly, for example, immediately after the emancipation of the serfs.[1] She was set on leaving Fyodor Pavlovich and opening a little shop in Moscow (they had a bit of money saved up). But Grigory decided then, once for all, that the woman's talking nonsense, "for every woman is dishonest," and that they ought not to leave their old master, whatever he might be, for "that was now their duty."

"Do you understand what duty is?" he asked Martha Ignatyevna.

---

1. The serfs were emancipated by decree of Tsar Alexander II (1818–1881; reigned 1855–81) on February 19, 1861. According to the time frame established by the narrator in "From the Author," this would have been about six years before the events of the novel.

"I understand what duty means, Grigory Vasilyevich, but why it's our duty to stay here I never shall understand," Martha Ignatyevna answered firmly.

"Well, don't understand then. But so it shall be. And in the future you hold your tongue."

And so it was: they did not go away, and Fyodor Pavlovich promised them a small salary, and paid it regularly. Grigory knew, too, that he had an indisputable influence over his master. He felt it, and it was true: Fyodor Pavlovich, an obstinate and cunning buffoon, who had a very firm character "in certain things in life," as he himself put it, was, to his own surprise, even a rather weak character in certain other "things in life." And he himself knew which ones, knew and feared a great deal. In certain things in life one has to keep a sharp lookout, and in such cases it is difficult without a trustworthy man, and Grigory was a most trustworthy man. Many times in the course of his life Fyodor Pavlovich had only just escaped being beaten, and beaten badly, through Grigory's intervention, although on each occasion the old servant gave him a good lecture. But it wasn't only beatings that Fyodor Pavlovich was afraid of: there were higher occasions, and even very subtle and complicated ones, when Fyodor Pavlovich himself would not have been able, perhaps, to explain this remarkable need for a faithful and close man, which he sometimes suddenly and unaccountably all in a moment began to feel within himself. These were almost morbid occurrences: corrupt and often cruel in his lust, like a noxious insect, Fyodor Pavlovich suddenly felt within himself at other times, in drunken moments, spiritual fear and moral trembling, almost, so to say, even physically resounding in his soul. "My soul simply quakes in my throat at those times," he would say sometimes. At such moments he liked to feel that there was near at hand, in the lodge if not in the room, a strong, faithful man, virtuous and completely unlike himself, who had seen all his debauchery and knew all his secrets, but was ready in his devotion to overlook all that, not to oppose him, above all, not to reproach him or threaten him with anything, either in this world or in the next, and, in case of need, to defend him—from whom? From somebody unknown, but terrible and dangerous. What he needed was to feel that there was *another* man, an old and tried friend, that he might call him in his sick moments merely to look at his face, or, perhaps, exchange some quite irrelevant words with him. And if the old servant were not angry, he felt comforted, and if he were angry, he was more dejected. It happened even (very rarely however) that Fyodor Pavlovich went at night to the lodge to wake Grigory and fetch him for a moment. When the old man came, Fyodor Pavlovich would begin talking about the most trivial matters, and would soon let him go again, sometimes even with a little joke or jest, and after he had gone, Fyodor Pavlovich would get into bed with a curse and sleep the sleep of the just. Something of the same sort had happened to Fyodor Pavlovich on Alyosha's arrival. Alyosha "pierced his heart" by "living with him, seeing everything and judging nothing." Moreover, Alyosha brought with him something his father had never known before: a complete absence of contempt for him and an invariable kindness, a perfectly natural unaffected devotion to the old man who deserved it so little. All this was a complete surprise to the old profligate, who had dropped all family ties. It was a new and surprising experience for him, who had till then loved nothing but "evil." When Alyosha had left him, he confessed to himself that he had understood something he had not till then been willing to understand.

I mentioned already at the beginning of my story that Grigory had detested Adelaïda Ivanovna, the first wife of Fyodor Pavlovich and the mother of Dmitri Fyodorovich, and that he had, on the contrary, protected Sofya Ivanovna, the poor "shrieker," against his master and anyone who chanced to speak ill or lightly of her. His sympathy for the unhappy wife had become something sacred to him, so that even twenty years after, he could not bear a slighting allusion to her from anyone, and would at once check the offender. Externally, Grigory was cold, dignified and taciturn, and spoke, weighing his words, without frivolity. It was impossible to tell at first sight whether he loved his meek, obedient wife; but he really did love her, and she, of course, knew it. Martha Ignatyevna was by no means stupid, but, indeed, was possibly smarter than her husband, or, at least, more prudent than he in worldly affairs, and yet she had given in to him in everything without question or complaint ever since her marriage, and respected him for his spiritual superiority. It was remarkable how little they spoke to one another in the course of their lives, and only of the most necessary daily affairs. The grave and dignified Grigory thought over all his cares and duties alone, so that Martha Ignatyevna had long grown used to knowing that he did not need her advice. She felt that her husband respected her silence, and took it as a sign of her good sense. He had never beaten her but once, and then only slightly. Once during the year after Fyodor Pavlovich's marriage with Adelaïda Ivanovna, the village girls and women—at that time serfs—were called together before the house to sing and dance. They were beginning "In the Green Meadows," when Martha, at that time a young woman, skipped forward and danced "the Russian Dance," not in the village fashion, as the peasant women did, but as she had danced it when she was a servant in the service of the rich Miüsov family, in their private theater, where the actors were taught to dance by a dancing master from Moscow.[2] Grigory saw how his wife danced, and, an hour later, at home in their cottage he gave her a lesson, pulling her hair a little. But there it ended: the beating was never repeated, and Martha Ignatyevna gave up dancing.

God did not give them children, there was one little baby, but it died. Grigory was fond of children, didn't hide it, that is, he was not ashamed of showing it. When Adelaïda Ivanovna had run away, Grigory took Dmitri Fyodorovich, then a child of three, combed his hair and even washed him in a tub with his own hands, and looked after him for almost a year. Afterwards he had looked after Ivan Fyodorovich and Alyosha, for which the general's widow had rewarded him with a slap in the face; but I have already related all that. The only happiness his own child had brought him had been in the anticipation of its birth, when Martha Ignatyevna had been pregnant. When it was born, he was overwhelmed with grief and horror. The fact is that the baby was born with six fingers. Grigory was so crushed by this, that he was not only silent till the day of the christening,

---

2. "In the Green Meadows" is a Russian folksong in which a young girl implores her father to give her in marriage to a man her same age, not someone significantly older or younger. Wealthy landowners sometimes provided talented serfs with training and assembled entire orchestras, theaters, and ballet troupes on their estates.

but kept away in the garden. It was spring, and he spent three days digging the kitchen garden. The third day was fixed for christening the boy; meantime Grigory had reached a conclusion. Going into the cottage where the clergy were assembled and the visitors had arrived, including Fyodor Pavlovich, who had appeared personally to be godfather, he suddenly announced that the baby "ought not to be christened at all." He announced this quietly, briefly, forcing out his words and gazing with dull intentness at the priest, and did not elaborate further.

"Why not?" asked the priest with good-humored surprise.

"Because . . . it's a dragon . . ." muttered Grigory.

"A dragon, what dragon?"

Grigory did not speak for some time. "A confusion of nature has occurred," he muttered vaguely, but firmly, and obviously unwilling to say more.[3]

They laughed, and of course christened the poor little baby. Grigory prayed earnestly at the font, but his opinion of the newborn child remained unchanged. Yet he did not interfere in any way. As long as the sickly infant lived he scarcely looked at it, tried indeed not to notice it, and for the most part kept out of the cottage. But when the little boy died of thrush[4] two weeks later, he himself laid the child in its little coffin, looked at it in profound grief, and when they were filling up the shallow little grave he fell on his knees and bowed down to the earth. He did not for years afterwards mention his child, nor did Martha speak of her baby before him, and when she did happen to speak to someone about her "little one," she spoke in a whisper, even if Grigory Vasilyevich were not present. Martha observed that, from the day of the burial, he devoted himself to "religion," and took to reading the *Lives of the Saints*, for the most part sitting alone and in silence, and always putting on his big, round, silver-rimmed spectacles. He rarely read aloud, only perhaps in Lent.[5] He was fond of the book of Job, and had somehow got hold of a copy of the sayings and sermons of "the Godfearing Father Isaac the Syrian,"[6] which he read persistently for years together, understanding very little of it, but perhaps prizing and loving it the more for that. Of late he had begun to listen to the doctrines of the sect of Flagellants settled in the neighborhood. He was evidently shaken by them, but judged it unfitting to go over to the new faith. His habit of theological reading gave him an expression of still greater gravity.

He was perhaps inclined to mysticism. And the birth of his six-fingered baby, and its death, had, as though by special design, been accompanied by another strange and marvelous event, which, as he said later, had left a "stamp" upon his soul. It happened that, on the very night after the burial of his child, Martha was awakened by the wail of a newborn baby. She was frightened and woke up her husband. He listened and said he thought it was more like someone groaning, "it might be a woman." He got up and dressed. It was a rather warm night in May. As he went down the steps, he

3. According to Russian folk belief, a physical deformity such as a sixth finger could indicate the presence of an evil spirit.
4. A fungal infection.
5. Great Lent is the most significant period of fasting prescribed by the Orthodox Church, beginning on Monday seven weeks before Easter Sunday and lasting forty contiguous days until the Friday before Holy Week (the week before Easter). It is a period of prayer, penitence, fasting, and self-denial.
6. For Isaac the Syrian, see p. 50.

distinctly heard groans coming from the garden. But the gate from the yard into the garden was locked at night, and there was no other way of entering it, for it was enclosed all round by a strong, high fence. Going back into the house, Grigory lighted a lantern, took the garden key, and taking no notice of the hysterical fears of his wife, who was still persuaded that she heard a child crying, and that it was her own baby crying and calling for her, went into the garden in silence. There he heard at once that the groans came from the bathhouse that stood near the garden gate, and that they were groans of a woman. Opening the door of the bathhouse, he saw a sight which petrified him. A local girl, a holy fool who wandered about the streets and was known to the whole town by the nickname of Lizaveta Smerdyaschaya (Stinking Lizaveta), had got into the bathhouse and had just given birth to a baby. She lay dying with the baby beside her. She said nothing, for she had never been able to speak. But all this should be explained separately.

Chapter II

Stinking Lizaveta

There was one circumstance which struck Grigory particularly, and confirmed a very unpleasant and revolting suspicion. This Lizaveta was a dwarfish creature, "not five foot within a wee bit," as many of the pious old women said pathetically about her, after her death. She was twenty years old. Her broad, healthy, red face had a look of blank idiocy and the fixed stare in her eyes was unpleasant, in spite of their meek expression. She wandered about, summer and winter alike, barefooted, wearing nothing but a hempen smock. Her coarse, almost black hair curled like lamb's wool, and formed a sort of huge cap on her head. It was always crusted with mud, and had leaves, bits of sticks, and shavings clinging to it, as she always slept on the ground and in the dirt. Her father, a homeless, sickly drunkard, called Ilya, had lost everything and lived many years as a workman with some well-to-do tradespeople. Her mother had long been dead. Eternally ill and spiteful, Ilya used to beat Lizaveta inhumanly whenever she returned to him. But she rarely did so, for everyone in the town was ready to look after her as one of God's holy fools. Ilya's employers, and Ilya himself, and many others in the town, especially of the tradespeople, tried to clothe her better, and always rigged her out with boots and a sheepskin coat for the winter. But, although she allowed them to dress her up without resisting, she usually went away, preferably to the cathedral porch, and taking off all that had been given her—kerchief, sheepskin, skirt or boots—she left them there and walked away barefoot in her smock as before. It happened on one occasion that a new governor of the province, making a tour of inspection in our little town, saw Lizaveta, and was wounded in his noblest feelings, and though he understood that she was a "holy fool," as had been reported to him, he pronounced that for a young woman of twenty to wander about in nothing but a smock was a breach of the proprieties, and must not occur again. But the governor went his way, and Lizaveta was left as she was. At last her father died, which made her even more acceptable in the eyes of the religious persons of the town, as an orphan. In fact, everyone seemed to like her; even the boys did not tease her, and the boys of our town, especially the schoolboys, are a mischievous lot. She would walk into strange houses, and no one drove her away. Everyone was kind to her and gave her something. If she were given a kopeck, she would take it, and at once drop it in the poor box of the church or prison. If she were given a roll or bun in the market, she would hand it to the first child she met. Sometimes she would stop one of the richest ladies in the town and give it to her, and the lady would be pleased to take it. She herself never tasted anything but black bread and water. If she went into an expensive shop, where there were expensive goods or money lying about, no one kept watch on her, for they knew that if she saw thousands of rubles overlooked by them, she would not have touched a kopeck. She scarcely ever went to church. She slept either in the church porch or climbed over a wattle-fence (there are many wattle-fences instead of regular fences in our town to this very day) into a kitchen garden. She used at least once a week to turn up "at home," that is at the house of her father's former employers, and in the winter went there every night, and slept either in the passage or the cowshed. People were amazed that she could stand such a life, but she was accustomed to it, and, although she was so tiny, she was of a robust constitution. Some of the townspeople declared that she did all this only from pride, but that is hardly credible. She could hardly speak, and only from time to time uttered an inarticulate grunt—how could she have been proud? It happened one clear, warm, moonlit night in September (many years ago) that a band of five or six of our gentlemen, drunken revelers, were returning from the club at a very late hour, according to our provincial notions. They passed through the "backway," which led between the back gardens of the houses, with wattle-fences on either side. This way leads out onto the bridge over the long, stinking pool which we were accustomed to call a river. Among the nettles and burdocks under the hurdle our revelers saw Lizaveta asleep. They stopped to look at her, laughing, and began jesting with unbridled licentiousness. It suddenly occurred to one young gentleman to pose a completely eccentric question on an impossible topic: whether any one could possibly look upon such an animal as a woman, and so forth. . . . They all pronounced with lofty repugnance that it was impossible. But Fyodor Pavlovich, who was among them, sprang forward at once and declared that it was by no means impossible, and that, indeed, there was a certain piquancy about it, and so on. . . . It is true that at that time he was overdoing his part as a buffoon. He liked to put himself forward and entertain the company, ostensibly on equal terms, of course, though in reality he was on a servile footing with them. It was just at the time when he had received the news of his first wife's death in Petersburg, and, with crepe upon his hat,[7] was drinking and behaving so shamelessly that even the most reckless among us were shocked at the sight of him. The revelers, of course, laughed at this unexpected opinion; and one of them even began challenging him to act upon it. The others repelled the idea even more emphatically, although still with the utmost hilarity, and at last they went on their way. Later on, Fyodor Pavlovich swore that he had gone with them; perhaps it was so, no one knows for certain, and no one ever knew,

---

7. To indicate that he is in mourning.

but five or six months later, all the town was talking, with intense and sincere indignation, of Lizaveta's pregnancy, and asking and trying to find out: whose sin, who was the offender? Then suddenly a terrible rumor was all over the town that this miscreant was no other than Fyodor Pavlovich. Who set the rumor going? Of that drunken band five had left the town and the only one still among us was an elderly and much respected civil councilor,[8] the father of grownup daughters, who could hardly have spread the tale, even if there had been any foundation for it. But rumor pointed straight at Fyodor Pavlovich, and persisted in pointing at him. Of course this was no great grievance to him: he would not have troubled to contradict a set of tradespeople. In those days he was proud, and did not condescend to talk except in his own circle of the officials and nobles, whom he entertained so well. This time Grigory energetically and with all his strength stood up for his master and not only defended him against all this slander, but even got into quarrels and altercations in his defense and brought many people around to his side. "She herself, the low woman, is to blame," he asserted, and the offender was none other than "Karp with the screw" (that was what they called one terrible criminal who was then well known in town, who had just escaped from the provincial prison and was living secretly in our town). This conjecture sounded plausible, for it was remembered that Karp had been in the neighborhood just at that time in the autumn, and had robbed three people. But this affair and all the talk about it did not estrange popular sympathy from the poor idiot. She was better looked after than ever. A well-to-do merchant's widow named Kondratyev arranged to take her into her house at the end of April, meaning not to let her go out until after the confinement. They kept a constant watch over her, but in spite of their vigilance she escaped on the very last day, and made her way into Fyodor Pavlovich's garden. How, in her condition, she managed to climb over the high, strong fence remained a mystery. Some maintained that she must have been lifted over by somebody; others hinted at something more uncanny. The most likely explanation is that it happened naturally—that Lizaveta, accustomed to clambering over hurdles to sleep in gardens, had somehow managed to climb Fyodor Pavlovich's fence, in spite of her condition, and had leaped down, injuring herself. Grigory rushed to Martha and sent her to Lizaveta, while he ran to fetch an old midwife who lived close by. They saved the baby, but Lizaveta died at dawn. Grigory took the baby, brought it home, and making his wife sit down, put it on her lap, right to her chest. "A child of God—an orphan is akin to all," he said, "and to us above others. Our little lost one has sent us this, who has come from the devil's son and a holy innocent. Nurse him and weep no more." So Martha brought up the little child. He was christened Pavel, to which people were not slow in adding Fyodorovich. Fyodor Pavlovich did not object to any of this, and thought it amusing, though he persisted vigorously in denying it all. The townspeople were pleased at his adopting the foundling. Later on, Fyodor Pavlovich invented

8. A civil or state councilor (*statskii sovetnik*) was the fifth rank on the Table of Ranks. Implemented by Peter the Great in 1722, the Table of Ranks listed all civil government, military, and court positions in the Russian empire on a scale from one to fourteen, one being the highest. A civil servant of the fourteenth grade or rank was automatically ennobled, but could not pass his status to his descendants; promotion to the eighth rank conferred hereditary nobility and the right to own land with serfs. The Table remained in effect until the Russian Revolution in 1917.

a surname for the child, calling him Smerdyakov, after his mother's nickname. So this Smerdyakov became Fyodor Pavlovich's second servant, and was living in the lodge with the old man Grigory and the old woman Martha at the time our story begins. He was employed as cook. I ought to say something about him in particular, but I am ashamed of keeping my readers' attention so long occupied with these ordinary lackeys,[9] and so I will go back to my story, hoping to say more of Smerdyakov in the course of it.

Chapter III

The Confession of an Ardent Heart.—In Verse

Alyosha remained irresolute for some time after hearing the command his father shouted to him from the carriage. But in spite of his uneasiness he did not stand still. That was not his way. He went at once to the kitchen to find out what his papasha had been doing above. Then he set off, trusting that on the way he would find some answer to the doubt tormenting him. I hasten to add that his father's shouts, commanding him to return home "with his mattress and pillow," did not frighten him in the least. He understood perfectly that those peremptory shouts were merely "a flourish," even so to say for the beauty of it—in the same way a tradesman in our town who was celebrating his name day[1] with a party of friends, getting angry at being refused more vodka, smashed up his own crockery and furniture and tore his own and his wife's clothes, and finally broke his windows, all likewise for the beauty of it; the same sort of thing, of course, had happened now with his papasha. The next day, of course, when he was sober, he regretted the broken cups and saucers. Alyosha knew that the old man would let him go back to the monastery the next day, possibly even that evening. Moreover he was fully persuaded that his father might hurt anyone else, but would not hurt him. Alyosha was certain that no one in the whole world ever would want to hurt him, and, what is more, he knew that no one could hurt him. This was for him an axiom, assumed once for all without question, and he went his way without hesitation, relying on it.

But at that moment some other fear was stirring in him, of a completely different sort, and it was all the more tormenting that he himself could not define it, namely, fear of a woman, and namely, of Katerina Ivanovna, who had so urgently entreated him, in a note handed to him by Madame Khokhlakova, to come see her about something. This request and the necessity of going had at once aroused an uneasy feeling in his heart, and this feeling had grown more and more painful all the morning in spite of all the scenes and events at the hermitage and at the Father Superior's. He was not uneasy because he did not know what she would speak of and what he must answer. And he was not afraid of her simply as a woman. Though he knew little of women, he had spent his life, from

---

9. Like English, Russian distinguishes between a servant (*sluga*) and a lackey (*lakei*). The significance of Smerdyakov's status as a lackey is elucidated in Kantor, "Pavel Smerdyakov and Ivan Karamazov: The Problem of Temptation," p. 696.
1. Orthodox Russians celebrate the feast days (days on which saints are commemorated by the Church) of the saints for whom they are named.

early childhood till he entered the monastery, entirely with women. He was afraid of that woman, Katerina Ivanovna. He had been afraid of her from the first time he saw her. He had only seen her two or three times, and had only chanced to say a few words to her. He thought of her as a beautiful, proud, imperious girl. It was not her beauty which troubled him, but something else. And the vagueness of his apprehension increased the apprehension itself. The girl's aims were of the noblest, he knew that. She was trying to save his brother Dmitri simply through generosity, though he had already behaved badly to her. Yet, although Alyosha recognized and did justice to all these fine and generous sentiments, a shiver began to run down his back as soon as he drew near her house.

He reflected that he would not find Ivan Fyodorovich, who was so intimate a friend, with her, for Ivan was certainly now with his father. Dmitri he was even more certain not to find there, and he had a foreboding of the reason. And so his conversation would be with her alone. He had a great longing to run and see his brother Dmitri before that fateful interview. Without showing him the letter, he could talk to him about it. But Dmitri lived a long way off, and he was sure to be away from home too. Standing still for a minute, he reached a final decision. Crossing himself with a rapid and accustomed gesture, and at once smiling, he turned resolutely in the direction of his terrible lady.

He knew her house. If he went by Main Street and then across the marketplace, it was a long way round. Though our town is small, it is scattered, and the houses are far apart. And meanwhile his father was expecting him, and perhaps had not yet forgotten his command. He might be unreasonable, and so he had to make haste to get there and back. So he decided to take a short cut by the back-way, for he knew every inch of the ground. This meant skirting fences, climbing over wattle-fences, and crossing other people's backyards, where everyone he met knew him and greeted him. In this way he could reach Main Street in half the time.

He had to pass the garden ajoining his father's and belonging to a little tumbledown house with four windows. The owner of this house, as Alyosha knew, was a bedridden old woman, living with her daughter, who had been a genteel maidservant in generals' families in Petersburg. Now she had been at home a year, looking after her sick mother. She always dressed up in fine clothes, though her old mother and she had sunk into such poverty that they went every day to Fyodor Pavlovich's kitchen for soup and bread, which Martha gave readily. Yet, though the young woman came up for soup, she had never sold any of her dresses, and one of these even had a long train—a fact which Alyosha had learned quite accidentally, of course, from Rakitin, who always knew everything that was going on in the town. He had forgotten it as soon as he heard it, but now, on reaching the garden, he remembered the dress with the train, raised his head, which had been bowed in thought, and came upon something quite unexpected.

Over the hurdle in the garden, his brother Dmitri Fyodorovich, mounted on something, was leaning forward, gesticulating violently, beckoning to him, obviously afraid to utter a word for fear of being overheard. Alyosha ran up to the hurdle.

"It's a good thing you looked up. I was nearly going to shout to you," Dmitri Fyodorovich said in a joyful, hurried whisper. "Climb in here quickly! How splendid that you've come! I was just thinking of you!"

Alyosha was delighted too, but he did not know how to get over the hurdle. But "Mitya" put his powerful hand under his elbow to help him jump. Tucking up his cassock, Alyosha leaped over the hurdle with the agility of a bare-legged street urchin.

"Well done! Now come along," said Mitya in an enthusiastic whisper.

"Where?" whispered Alyosha, looking about him and finding himself in a deserted garden with no one near but themselves. The garden was small, but the house was at least fifty paces away.

"There's no one here. Why do you whisper?" asked Alyosha.

"Why do I whisper? Devil take it!" cried Dmitri Fyodorovich at the top of his voice. "You see what silly tricks nature plays on one. I am here in secret, and I am guarding a secret. I'll explain later on, but, knowing it's a secret, I suddenly began to speak secretly and to whisper like a fool, when there's no need. Let us go! Over there! Till then be quiet. I want to kiss you!

> Glory to God in the world,
> Glory to God in me . . .[2]

I was just repeating that, sitting here, before you came."

The garden was about three acres in extent, and planted with trees only along the fence at the four sides. There were apple trees, maples, limes and birch trees. The middle of the garden was an empty grass space, from which several hundredweight of hay were carried in the summer. The garden was let out for a few rubles for the summer. There were also plantations of raspberries and currants and gooseberries laid out along the sides; a kitchen garden had been planted lately near the house.

Dmitri Fyodorovich led his brother to the most secluded corner of the garden. There, in a thicket of lime trees and old bushes of black currant, elder, snowball tree, and lilac, there stood a tumble-down green gazebo, blackened with age. Its walls were of latticework, but there was still a roof which could give shelter. God knows when this gazebo was built, there was a tradition that it had been put up some fifty years before by some former owner of the house, Alexander Karlovich von Schmidt, a retired colonel. It was all in decay, the floor was rotting, the planks were loose, the woodwork smelled musty. In the gazebo there was a green wooden table fixed in the ground, and round it were some green benches upon which it was still possible to sit. Alyosha had at once observed his brother's exhilarated condition, and on entering the arbor he saw half a bottle of brandy and a wineglass on the table.

"That's brandy," Mitya laughed. "I see your look: 'He's drinking again!' Don't believe in a phantom.

> Don't believe the worthless, lying crowd,
> And lay aside thy doubts.[3]

I'm not drinking, I'm only 'indulging,' as that pig, your Rakitin, says. He'll be a civil councilor one day, but he'll always talk about 'indulging.' Sit down. I could take you in my arms, Alyosha, and press you to my bosom

---

2. Dmitri's words may be a paraphrase of Luke 2.14: "Glory to God in the highest, and on earth peace, good will toward men."

3. From the 1846 poem by Nikolay Nekrasov (1821–1878) "When from the Gloom of Corruption" (*Kogda iz mraka zabluzhdeniia*, 1846), in which an intellectual helps a prostitute find redemption. This poem is the epigraph to Part II of Dostoevsky's *Notes from Underground* (1864), and Dostoevsky read it aloud as part of a public event in 1880.

till I crush you, for in the whole world—in reality—in re-al-i-ty—(can you take it in?) I love no one but you!"

He uttered the last words in a sort of exaltation.

"No one but you and one 'low woman' I have fallen in love with, to my ruin. But being in love doesn't mean loving. You may be in love with a woman and yet hate her. Remember that! I can talk about it gaily still. Sit down here by the table and I'll sit beside you and look at you, and go on talking. You shall keep quiet and I'll go on talking, for the time has come. But on reflection, you know, I'd better speak quietly, for here—here—you can never tell what ears are listening. I will explain everything, as they say, 'the story will be continued.' Why have I been longing for you? Why have I been thirsting for you all these days, and just now? (It's five days since I've cast anchor here.) Because it's only to you I can tell everything; because I must, because I need you, because tomorrow I shall fly from the clouds, because tomorrow life will end and begin. Have you ever felt, have you ever dreamt of falling down a precipice into a pit? That's just how I'm falling, but not in a dream. And I'm not afraid, and don't you be afraid. At least, I am afraid, but I enjoy it. It's not enjoyment though, but ecstasy. Damn it all, whatever it is! A strong spirit, a weak spirit, a womanish spirit—whatever it is! Let us praise nature: you see what sunshine, how clear the sky is, the leaves are all green, it's still summer; three o'clock in the afternoon and the stillness! Where were you going?"

"I was going to father's, but I meant to go to Katerina Ivanovna's first."

"To her, and to father! Oo! What a coincidence! Why was I waiting for you? Hungering and thirsting for you in every cranny of my soul and even in my ribs? Why, to send you to father from me and to her, Katerina Ivanovna, so as to have done with her and with father. To send an angel. I might have sent anyone, but I had to send an angel. And here you are on your way to see father and her."

"Did you really mean to send me?" cried Alyosha with a distressed expression.

"Wait! You knew it! And I see you understand it all at once. But be quiet, be quiet for a time. Don't be sorry, and don't cry."

Dmitri Fyodorovich stood up, thought a moment, and put his finger to his forehead.

"She's asked you, written to you a letter or something, that's why you're going to her? You wouldn't be going except for that?"

"Here is her note." Alyosha took it out of his pocket. Mitya looked through it quickly.

"And you were going the back-way! Oh, gods, I thank you for sending him by the back-way, and he came to me like the golden fish to the silly old fisherman in the fairy tale![4] Listen, Alyosha, listen, brother! Now I mean to tell you everything, for I must tell someone. An angel in heaven I've told already; but I want to tell an angel on earth. You are an angel on earth. You will hear and judge and forgive. And that's what I need, that someone above me should forgive. Listen! If two people break away from everything on earth and fly off into the unknown, or at least one of them, and before flying off or going to ruin he comes to someone else and says,

---

4. Pushkin's fable in verse "The Tale of the Fisherman and the Fish" (1833) tells of a poor fisherman who catches a magic fish in his net.

'Do this for me'—some favor never asked before that could only be asked on one's deathbed—would that other refuse, if he were a friend or a brother?"

"I will do it, but tell me what it is, and quickly," said Alyosha.

"Quickly . . . Hmm! . . . Don't be in a hurry, Alyosha, you hurry and worry yourself. There's no need to hurry now. Now the world has taken a new turning. Ah, Alyosha, what a pity you can't understand ecstasy. But what am I saying to him? As though you didn't understand it. What an ass I am, what am I saying: 'Be noble, oh, man!' Whose verse is that?"[5]

Alyosha made up his mind to wait. He felt that, perhaps, indeed, his work lay here. Mitya sank into thought for a moment, with his elbow on the table and his head in his hand. Both were silent.

"Lyosha," said Mitya, "you're the only one who won't laugh. I should like to begin—my confession—with Schiller's 'Ode to Joy,' *An die Freude!*[6] I don't know German, I only know it's called that. Don't think I'm talking nonsense because I'm drunk. I'm not a bit drunk. Brandy's all very well, but I need two bottles to make me drunk:

> Silenus with his rosy phiz
> Upon his stumbling ass.[7]

But I've not drunk a quarter of a bottle, and I'm not Silenus. I'm not Silenus, though I am strong,[8] for I've made a decision once for all. Forgive me the pun; you'll have to forgive me a lot more than puns today. Don't be uneasy. I'm not spinning it out. I'm talking sense, and I'll come to the point in a minute. I won't keep you in suspense. Wait, how does it go?"

He raised his head, thought a minute, and began with enthusiasm:

> Wild and fearful in his cavern
> Hid the naked troglodyte,
> And the homeless nomad wandered
> Laying waste the fertile plain.
> Menacing with spear and arrow
> In the woods the hunter strayed. . . .
> Woe to all poor wretches stranded
> On those cruel and hostile shores!
>
> From the peak of high Olympus
> Came the mother Ceres[9] down,
>
> Seeking in those savage regions
> Her lost daughter Proserpine.
> But the Goddess found no refuge,
> Found no kindly welcome there,
> And no temple bearing witness

5. Johann Wolfgang von Goethe (1749–1832), "Das Göttliche" ("The Divine," 1783). Dostoevsky possessed a complete edition of Goethe's works in Russian translation.
6. Written in 1785, Schiller's poem celebrates joy and the brotherhood of mankind.
7. From the 1842 poem "Bas-relief" by Dostoevsky's friend, the poet and literary critic Apollon Maykov (1821–1897). Silenus was the oldest satyr, the companion of Bacchus. Maykov's poetry was published in Dostoevsky's journals *Time* and *Epoch*.
8. The Russian word *silen* (strong) allows Dmitri to make this pun on Silenus.
9. The Roman goddess of agriculture.

> To the worship of the gods.
> From the fields and from the vineyards
> Came no fruits to deck the feasts,
> Only flesh of blood-stained victims
> Smouldered on the altar-fires,
> And where'er the grieving goddess
> Turns her melancholy gaze,
> Man in deepest degradation
> Ceres beholds everywhere.[1]

Mitya broke into sobs and seized Alyosha's hand.

"My dear, my dear, in degradation, in degradation now, too. There's a terrible amount of suffering for man on earth, a terrible lot of trouble. Don't think I'm only a brute in an officer's uniform, who drinks vodka and leads a dissolute life. I hardly think of anything but of that degraded man—if only I'm not lying. I pray God I'm not lying now and showing off. I think about that man because I am that man myself.

> Would he purge his soul from vileness
> And attain to light and worth,
> He must turn and cling forever
> To his ancient Mother Earth.[2]

But the difficulty is how am I to cling forever to Mother Earth. I don't kiss her. I don't cleave her bosom.[3] Am I to become a peasant or a shepherd? I go on and I don't know whether I'm going to shame or to light and joy. That's the trouble, for everything in the world is a riddle! And whenever I've happened to sink into the vilest degradation (and it's always been happening) I always read that poem about Ceres and man. Has it reformed me? Never! For I'm a Karamazov. For when I do leap into the abyss, I go headlong with my heels up, and am pleased to be falling in that degrading attitude, and consider it something beautiful. And in the very depths of that degradation I suddenly begin a hymn of praise. Let me be accursed. Let me be vile and base, only let me kiss the hem of the veil in which my God is shrouded.[4] Though I may be following the devil, I am Thy son, O Lord, and I love Thee, and I feel the joy without which the world cannot stand.

> Joy everlasting fostereth
> The soul of God's creation,
> Her secret force of ferment fires
> The cup of life with flame.
> Enticed each blade towards the light
> And solar systems evolved
> From chaos and dark night,
> Filling the realms of boundless space
> Beyond the stargazer's sight.

---

1. Dmitri quotes Schiller's 1798 poem "The Eleusinian Festival," stanzas 2–4.
2. "The Eleusinian festival," stanza 7.
3. This image may be taken from the 1866 poem "Spring Has Come" by the Romantic poet Afanasy Fet (1820–1892).
4. This image is found in Goethe's poem "Grenzen der Menschheit" ("The Limits of Mankind," 1778–81), translated by Fet in 1878. Dostoevsky owned a copy of Fet's Goethe translations.

> At bounteous nature's breast,
> All things that breathe drink Joy,
> All creatures, all nations,
> She draws in her wake.
> Her gifts to man are friends in need,
> The wreath, the foaming must,
> To angels—vision of God's throne,
> To insects—sensual lust.[5]

But enough poetry! I am in tears; let me cry. It may be foolishness that everyone would laugh at. But you won't laugh. Your eyes are shining, too. Enough poetry. I want to tell you now about the insects to whom God gave 'sensual lust.'

> To insects—sensual lust.

I am that insect, brother, and it is said of me especially. All we Karamazovs are such insects, and, angel as you are, that insect lives in you, too, and will stir up a tempest in your blood. Tempests, because sensual lust is a tempest—worse than a tempest! Beauty is a terrible and awful thing! It is terrible because it has not been defined and is undefinable, for God sets us nothing but riddles. Here the two shores of the river meet and all contradictions stand side by side. I am not a cultivated man, brother, but I've thought a lot about this. It's terrible what mysteries there are! Too many riddles weigh men down on earth. We must solve them as we can, and try to keep a dry skin in the water. Beauty! I can't endure the thought that a man of lofty mind and heart begins with the ideal of the Madonna and ends with the ideal of Sodom.[6] What's still more awful is that a man with the ideal of Sodom in his soul does not renounce the ideal of the Madonna, and his heart may be on fire with that ideal, genuinely on fire, just as in his days of youth and innocence. Yes, man is broad, too broad, indeed. I'd have him narrower. The devil only knows what to make of it! What to the mind is shameful is beauty and nothing else to the heart. Is there beauty in Sodom? Believe me, that for the immense mass of mankind beauty is found in Sodom. Did you know that secret? The awful thing is that beauty is mysterious as well as terrible. God and the devil are fighting there and the battlefield is the heart of man. But a man always talks of his own ache. Listen, now to come to facts."

---

5. Dmitri quotes stanzas 4 and 3 of Schiller's "Ode to Joy."
6. The Madonna is Mary, the mother of Jesus; for Christians, she represents purity, beauty, and sanctity. In the Bible, the ancient town of Sodom is invoked to signify sinfulness, especially sexual excess and deviation, which provokes God's wrath. "Even as Sodom and Gomorra, and the cities about them in like manner, giving themselves over to fornication, and going after strange flesh, are set forth for an example, suffering the vengeance of eternal fire" (Jude 1.7). See also Genesis 13.13 and 19.1–25, and Ezekiel 16:46–50.

Chapter IV

The Confession of an Ardent Heart.—In Anecdote

"I was leading a wild life then. Father said just now that I spent several thousand rubles in seducing young girls. That's a swinish phantom, and there was nothing of the sort. And if there was, I didn't need money simply for *that*. With me money is an accessory, the overflow of my heart, the framework. Today she would be my lady, tomorrow a wench out of the streets in her place. I entertained them both. I threw away money by the handful on music, rioting, and gypsies. Sometimes I gave it to the ladies, too, for they'll take it greedily, that must be admitted, and be pleased and thankful for it. Ladies used to be fond of me: not all of them, but it happened, it happened. But I always liked side paths, little dark back alleys behind the main road—there one finds adventures and surprises, and precious metal in the dirt. I am speaking figuratively, brother. In the town I was in, there were no such back alleys in the literal sense, but morally there were. If you were like me, you'd know what that means. I loved vice, I loved the ignominy of vice. I loved cruelty; am I not a bug, am I not a noxious insect? In fact a Karamazov! Once we went, a whole lot of us, for a picnic, in seven sleighs. It was dark, it was winter, and I began squeezing a girl's hand, and forced her to kiss me. She was the daughter of an official, sweet, gentle, submissive. She allowed me, she allowed me much in the dark. She thought, poor thing, that I should come next day to make her an offer (I was looked upon as a good match, too). But I didn't say a word to her for five months. I used to see her in a corner at dances (we were always having dances), her eyes watching me. I saw how they glowed with fire—a fire of gentle indignation. This game only tickled that insect lust I cherished in my soul. Five months later she married an official and left the town, still angry, and still, perhaps, in love with me. Now they live happily. Observe that I told no one. I didn't boast of it. Though I'm full of low desires, and love what's low, I'm not dishonorable. You're blushing; your eyes flashed. Enough of this filth with you. And all this was nothing much—wayside blossoms à la Paul de Kock[7]—though the cruel insect had already grown strong in my soul. I've a perfect album of reminiscences, brother. God bless them, the darlings. I always tried to break it off without quarreling. And I never gave them away. I never bragged of one of them. But that's enough. You can't suppose I brought you here simply to talk of such nonsense. No, I'm going to tell you something more curious; and don't be surprised that I'm glad to tell you, instead of being ashamed."

"You say that because I blushed," Alyosha said suddenly. "I wasn't blushing at what you were saying or at what you've done. I blushed because I am the same as you are."

"You? Come, that's going a little too far."

"No, it's not too far," said Alyosha warmly (obviously the idea was not a new one). "The ladder's the same. I'm at the bottom step, and you're above,

---

7. Charles Paul de Kock, popular French writer (1793–1871) whose novels portraying Parisian life were viewed in some circles as immoral.

somewhere about the thirteenth. That's how I see it. But it's all the same. Absolutely the same in kind. Anyone on the bottom step is bound to go up to the top one."

"Then one ought not to step on at all."

"Anyone who can help it had better not."

"But can you?"

"I think not."

"Hush, Alyosha, hush, darling! I could kiss your hand, you touch me so. That rogue Grushenka has an eye for men. She told me once that she'd devour you one day. There, there, I won't! From this field of corruption fouled by flies, let's pass to my tragedy, also befouled by flies, that is by every sort of vileness. Although the old man told lies about my seducing innocence, there really was something of the sort in my tragedy, though it was only once, and then it did not come off. The old man who has reproached me with what never happened does not even know of this fact; I never told anyone about it. You're the first, except Ivan, of course— Ivan knows everything. He knew about it long before you. But Ivan's a tomb."

"Ivan's a tomb?"

"Yes."

Alyosha listened with great attention.

"I was lieutenant in a line regiment, but still I was under supervision, like a kind of exile. Yet I was awfully well received in the little town. I spent money right and left. I was thought to be rich; I thought so myself. But I must have pleased them in other ways as well. Although they shook their heads over me, they liked me. My colonel, who was an old man, took a sudden dislike to me. He was always down upon me, but I had powerful friends, and, moreover, all the town was on my side, so he couldn't do me much harm. I was at fault myself for refusing to treat him with proper respect. I was proud. This obstinate fellow, who was really a very good sort, kind-hearted and hospitable, had had two wives, both now dead. His first wife, who was from some kind of humble family, left a daughter as unpretentious as herself. She was a young woman of twenty-four when I was there, and was living with her father and an aunt, her mother's sister. The aunt was simple and illiterate; the niece, the older daughter of the colonel, was simple but lively. I like to say nice things about people. I never knew a woman of more charming character than Agatha—fancy, her name was Agatha Ivanovna! And she wasn't bad looking either, in the Russian style: tall, stout, with a full figure, and beautiful eyes, though a rather coarse face. She had not married, although she had had two suitors. She refused them, but was as cheerful as ever. I was intimate with her, not in 'that' way, it was pure friendship. I have often been friendly with women quite innocently. I used to talk to her with shocking frankness, and she only laughed. Many women like such freedom, and she was a virgin too, which made it very amusing. Another thing, one could never think of her as a young lady. She and her aunt lived in her father's house with a sort of voluntary humility, not putting themselves on an equality with other people. She was a general favorite, and of use to everyone, for she was a clever dressmaker. She had a talent for it. She gave her services freely without asking for payment, but if anyone offered her payment, she didn't refuse. The colonel, of course, was a very different matter. He was one of the chief personages in the district. He kept open house, entertained the whole town, gave suppers and dances. At the time I arrived and joined the battalion, all the town was talking of the expected return of the colonel's second daughter, a great beauty, who had just left a fashionable school in the capital. This second daughter was Katerina Ivanovna, and she was the child of the second wife, who belonged to a distinguished general's family; although, as I learned on good authority, she too brought the colonel no money. She had connections, and that was all. There may have been expectations, but they had come to nothing. And yet, when the young lady came from boarding school on a visit, not to settle in, the whole town revived. Our most distinguished ladies—two Excellencies[8] and a colonel's wife—and all the rest following their lead, at once took her up and gave entertainments in her honor. She was the belle of the balls and picnics, and they got up charades in aid of distressed governesses. I took no notice, I went on as wildly as before, and one of my exploits at the time set all the town talking. I saw her eyes taking my measure one evening at the battery commander's, but I didn't go up to her, as though I disdained her acquaintance. I did go up and speak to her at an evening party not long after. She scarcely looked at me, and compressed her lips scornfully. 'Wait a bit. I'll have my revenge,' thought I. I behaved like a boor on many occasions at that time, and I was conscious of it myself. What made it worse was that I felt that 'Katenka' was not an innocent boarding-school miss, but a person of character, proud and really virtuous; above all, she had education and intellect, and I had neither. You think I meant to propose? No, I simply wanted to revenge myself, because I was such a hero and she didn't seem to feel it. Meanwhile, I spent my time in drink and riot, till the lieutenant colonel put me under arrest for three days. Just at that time father sent me six thousand rubles in return for my sending him a deed giving up all claims upon him—settling our accounts, so to speak, and saying that I wouldn't expect anything more. I didn't understand a word of it at the time. Until I came here, Alyosha, till the last few days, indeed, perhaps even now, I haven't been able to make head or tail of my money affairs with father. But never mind that, we'll talk of it later. Just as I received the money, I got a letter from a friend telling me something that interested me immensely. The authorities, I learned, were dissatisfied with our lieutenant colonel. He was suspected of irregularities; in fact, his enemies were preparing a surprise for him. And then the commander of the division arrived, and kicked up a hell of a row. Shortly afterwards he was ordered to retire. I won't tell you how it all happened. He had enemies certainly. Suddenly there was a marked coolness in the town towards him and all his family. His friends all turned their backs on him. Then I took my first step. I met Agatha Ivanovna, with whom I'd always kept up a friendship, and said, 'Do you know there's a deficit of forty-five hundred rubles of government money in your papasha's accounts?' 'What do you mean? What makes you say so? The general was here not long ago, and everything was all right.' 'Then it was, but now it isn't.' She was terribly scared. 'Don't frighten me!' she said. 'Who told you so?' 'Don't be uneasy,' I said, 'I won't tell anyone. You know I'm as silent as the tomb. I only

---

8. *Excellency* was the official title of address for officials of the third and fourth grades in the Table of Ranks.

wanted, in view of "possibilities," to add, that when they demand that forty-five hundred rubles from your papasha, and he can't produce it, he'll be tried, and made to serve as a common soldier in his old age, unless you like to send me your young lady secretly. I've just had money paid me. I'll give her four thousand, if you like, and keep the secret religiously.' 'Ah, you scoundrel!' that's what she said. 'You wicked scoundrel! How dare you!' She went away furiously indignant, while I shouted after her once more that the secret would be kept sacred. Those two simple women, Agatha and her aunt, I may as well say at once, behaved like perfect angels all through this business. They genuinely adored their sister, the proud one, Katya, thought her far above them, and waited on her, hand and foot. But Agatha told her of our conversation. I found that out afterwards. She didn't keep it back, and of course that was all I wanted.

"Suddenly the new major arrived to take command of the battalion. The old lieutenant colonel was taken ill at once, couldn't leave his room for two days, and didn't hand over the government money. Dr. Kravchenko declared that he really was ill. But I knew for a fact, and had known for a long time, that for the last four years the money had never been in his hands except when the Commander made his visits of inspection. He used to lend it to a trustworthy person, a merchant of our town called Trifonov, an old widower, with a big beard and gold-rimmed spectacles. He used to go to the fair, do a profitable business with the money, and return the whole sum to the colonel, bringing with it a present from the fair, as well as interest on the loan. But this time (I heard all about it quite by chance from Trifonov's son and heir, a driveling youth and one of the most vicious in the world)—this time, I say, Trifonov brought nothing back from the fair. The lieutenant colonel flew to him. 'I've never received any money from you, and couldn't possibly have received any.' That was all the answer he got. So now our lieutenant colonel is confined to the house, with a towel round his head, while they're all three busy putting ice on it. All at once an orderly arrives on the scene with the book and the order to 'hand over the battalion money immediately, within two hours.' He signed the book (I saw the signature in the book afterwards), stood up, saying he would put on his uniform, ran to his bedroom, loaded his double-barreled gun, took the boot off his right foot, fixed the gun against his chest, and began feeling for the trigger with his foot. But Agatha, remembering what I had told her, had her suspicions. She stole up and peeped into the room just in time. She rushed in, flung herself upon him from behind, threw her arms round him, and the gun went off, hit the ceiling, but hurt no one. The others ran in, took away the gun, and held him by the arms. I heard all about this afterwards in detail. I was at home, it was getting dusk, and I was just preparing to go out. I had dressed, brushed my hair, scented my handkerchief, and taken up my cap, when suddenly the door opened, and facing me in the room stood Katerina Ivanovna.

"It's strange how things happen sometimes. No one had seen her in the street, so that no one knew of it in the town. I lodged with two decrepit old ladies, who looked after me. They were most obliging old things, ready to do anything for me, and at my request were as silent afterwards as two cast-iron posts. Of course I grasped the position at once. She walked in and looked straight at me, her dark eyes determined, even defiant, but on her lips and round her mouth I saw uncertainty.

"'My sister told me,' she began, 'that you would give me four thousand rubles if I came to you for it—myself. I have come . . . give me the money!'

"She couldn't keep it up. She was breathless, frightened, her voice failed her, and the corners of her mouth and the lines round it quivered. Alyoshka, are you listening, or are you asleep?"

"Mitya, I know you will tell the whole truth," said Alyosha in agitation.

"I am telling it. If I tell the whole truth just as it happened I shan't spare myself. My first idea was a—Karamazov one. Once I was bitten by a spider, brother, and laid up a fortnight with fever from it. Well, I felt a spider biting at my heart then—a noxious insect, you understand? I looked her up and down. You've seen her? She's a beauty. But she was beautiful in another way then. At that moment she was beautiful because she was noble, and I was a scoundrel; she in all the grandeur of her generosity and sacrifice for her father, and I—a bug! And, bug and scoundrel as I was, she was *completely* at my mercy, body and soul. She was hemmed in. I tell you frankly, that thought, that venomous thought, so possessed my heart that it almost swooned with suspense. It seemed as if there could be no resisting it; as though I should act like a bug, like a venomous spider, without a spark of pity. I could scarcely breathe. Understand, I should have gone next day to ask for her hand, so that it might end honorably, so to speak, and that nobody would or could know. For though I'm a man of base desires, I'm honest. And at that very second some voice seemed to whisper in my ear, 'But when you come tomorrow to make your proposal, that girl won't even see you; she'll order her coachman to kick you out of the yard. "Publish it through all the town," she would say, "I'm not afraid of you."' I looked at the young lady, my voice had not deceived me. That is how it would be, not a doubt of it. I could see from her face now that I should be turned out of the house. My spite was roused. I longed to play her the nastiest swinish cad's trick: to look at her with a sneer, and on the spot where she stood before me to stun her with a tone of voice that only a shopman could use.

"'Four thousand! What do you mean? I was joking. You've been counting your chickens too easily, madam. Two hundred, if you like, with all my heart. But four thousand is not a sum to throw away on such frivolity. You've put yourself out to no purpose.'

"I should have lost the game, of course. She'd have run away. But it would have been an infernal revenge. It would have been worth it all. I'd have howled with regret all the rest of my life, only to have played that trick. Would you believe it, it has never happened to me with any other woman, not one, to look at her at such a moment with hatred. But, on my oath, I looked at that one for three seconds, or five perhaps, with fearful hatred—that hate which is only a hairsbreadth from love, from the maddest love!

"I went to the window, put my forehead against the frozen pane, and I remember the ice burned my forehead like fire. I did not keep her long, don't be afraid. I turned round, went up to the table, opened the drawer and took out a banknote for five thousand rubles (it was lying in a French dictionary). Then I showed it to her in silence, folded it, handed it to her, opened the door into the passage, and, stepping back, made her a deep bow, a most respectful, a most impressive bow, believe me! She shuddered all over, gazed at me for a second, turned horribly pale—white as a sheet, in fact—and all at once, not impetuously but softly, gently, bowed down to my feet—not a boarding-school curtsey, but a Russian bow, with her forehead to the floor. She jumped up and ran away. I was wearing my sword. I drew it and nearly stabbed myself with it on the spot; why, I don't know. It would have been frightfully stupid, of course. I suppose it was from delight. Can you understand that one might kill oneself from delight? But I didn't stab myself. I only kissed my sword and put it back in the scabbard—which there was no need to have told you, by the way. And I fancy that in telling you about my inner conflict I have laid it on rather thick to glorify myself. But let it pass, and to hell with all who pry into the human heart! Well, so much for that 'adventure' with Katerina Ivanovna. So now brother Ivan knows of it, and you—no one else."

Dmitri Fyodorovich got up, took a step or two in his excitement, pulled out his handkerchief and mopped his forehead, then sat down again, not in the same place as before, but on the opposite side, so that Alyosha had to turn quite round to face him.

Chapter V

The Confession of an Ardent Heart.—"Heels Up"

"Now," said Alyosha, "I understand the first half of this business."

"You understand the first half: That half is a drama, and it was played out there. The second half is a tragedy, and it is being acted here."

"And I understand nothing of that second half so far," said Alyosha.

"And I? Do you suppose I understand it?"

"Wait, Dmitri. There's one main word here. Tell me: you were betrothed, you are betrothed still?"

"We weren't betrothed at once, not for three months after that had happened. The next day I told myself that the incident was closed, concluded, that there would be no continuation. It seemed to me caddish to make her an offer. On her side she gave no sign of life for the six weeks that she remained in the town; except, indeed, for one action. The day after her visit the maidservant slipped round with an envelope addressed to me. I tore it open; it contained the change out of the banknote. Only forty-five hundred was needed, but there was a fee of two hundred and something on changing it. She only sent me about two hundred sixty rubles, I don't remember exactly, but not a note, not a word of explanation. I searched the packet for a pencil mark—n-nothing! Well, I spent the rest of the money on such an orgy that the new major was obliged to reprimand me. Well, the lieutenant colonel produced the battalion money, to the astonishment of everyone, for nobody believed that he had the money untouched. He'd no sooner paid it than he fell ill, took to his bed, and, three weeks later, softening of the brain set in, and he died five days afterwards. He was buried with military honors, for he had not had time to receive his discharge. Ten days after his funeral, Katerina Ivanovna, with her aunt and sister, went to Moscow. And, behold, on the very day they went away (I hadn't seen them, didn't see them off) I received a tiny note, a sheet of thin blue paper, and on it only one line in pencil: 'I will write to you. Wait. K.' And that was all.

"I'll explain the rest to you now in two words. In Moscow their fortunes changed with the swiftness of lightning and the unexpectedness of an Arabian fairy tale. That general's widow, their nearest relation, suddenly loses the two nieces who were her heiresses and next of kin—both die in the same week of smallpox. The old lady, prostrated with grief, welcomed Katya as her own daughter, as a star of salvation, clutched at her, altered her will in Katya's favor, but that concerned the future, and in the meantime she gave her, for present use, eighty thousand rubles, as a dowry, to do what she liked with. She was an hysterical woman, I saw something of her in Moscow, later. Well, suddenly I received by post forty-five hundred rubles; I was speechless with surprise, as you may suppose. Three days later came the promised letter. I have it with me now, it is always with me, and I will die with it—do you want me to show you? You must read it: she offers to be my bride, offers herself to me, 'I love you madly,' she says, 'even if you don't love me—never mind, just be my husband. Don't be afraid—I won't hamper you in any way, I will be your furniture, I will be the carpet on which you walk . . . I want to love you forever, I want to save you from yourself . . .' Alyosha, I am not even worthy to repeat those lines in my vulgar words and in my vulgar tone, my constantly vulgar tone, from which I could never cure myself! That letter stabs me even now, and is it easy for me now, is it easy for me today? I wrote her an answer at once (it was impossible for me to go to Moscow). I wrote it with tears; one thing I shall be ashamed of forever: I referred to her being rich and having a dowry while I was only an impoverished boor—I mentioned money! I ought to have borne it in silence, but it slipped from my pen. Then I wrote at once to Ivan, and told him all I could about it in a letter of six pages, and sent him to her. Why do you look like that, why are you staring at me? Yes, Ivan fell in love with her, he's in love with her still, I know that, I did a stupid thing, in the world's opinion, but perhaps that one stupid thing may save us all now! Oo! Don't you see what a lot she thinks of Ivan, how she respects him? When she compares us, do you suppose she can love a man like me, especially after all that has happened here?"

"But I'm convinced that she does love a man like you, and not a man like him."

"She loves her own virtue, not me." The words suddenly broke involuntarily, and almost malignantly, from Dmitri. He laughed, but a minute later his eyes flashed, he flushed crimson and struck the table violently with his fist.

"I swear, Alyosha," he cried, with intense and genuine anger at himself; "you may not believe me, but as God is holy, and as Christ is God, I swear that though I smiled at her lofty sentiments just now, I know that I am a million times baser in soul than she, and that these lofty sentiments of hers are as sincere as a heavenly angel's! That's the tragedy of it, that I know that for certain. What if anyone does show off a bit? Don't I show off? And yet I'm sincere, I'm sincere. As for Ivan, I can understand how he must be cursing nature now—with his intellect, too! To see the preference given—to whom, to what? To a monster who, though he is betrothed and all eyes are fixed on him, can't restrain his debaucheries—and before the very eyes of his betrothed! And a man like me is preferred, while he is rejected. And why? Because a girl wants to sacrifice her life and destiny out of gratitude! It's ridiculous! I've never said a word of this to Ivan, Ivan, of course, has never said a half word to me, not the slightest hint; but destiny will be fulfilled, and the worthy man will stand his ground, while the unworthy man will hide himself in his back alley forever—in his filthy back alley, in his own beloved back alley, and there, in filth and stench, he will perish of his own free will and with pleasure. I've been talking foolishly, all my words are worn out, I use them at random, but it will be as I have said. I will drown in the back alley, and she will marry Ivan."

"Brother, wait," Alyosha interrupted again with great anxiety. "There's one thing you haven't made clear to me yet: you are still betrothed, you are still betrothed all the same? How can you break off the engagement if she, your betrothed, doesn't want to?"

"I am betrothed, formally and solemnly betrothed, it was all done on my arrival in Moscow, with great ceremony, with icons, all in fine style. The general's wife blessed us, and—would you believe it?—congratulated Katya: 'You've made a good choice,' she said, 'I see right through him.' And, would you believe it, she didn't like Ivan, and hardly greeted him. I had a lot of talks with Katya in Moscow. I told her about myself, honorably, exactly, sincerely. She listened to everything.

> There was sweet confusion,
> There were tender words.[9]

Though there were proud words, too. She wrung out of me a mighty promise to reform. I gave my promise. And now . . ."

"What?"

"Why, I called to you and dragged you out here today, this very day—remember it—to send you—this very day again—to Katerina Ivanovna, and . . ."

"What?"

"To tell her that I will never come to see her again. Say 'He bows to you.'"[1]

"But is that possible?"

"That's just the reason I'm sending you, in my place, because it's impossible, for how could I tell her myself?"

"And where are you going?"

"To the back alley."

"To Grushenka then!" Alyosha exclaimed mournfully, clasping his hands. "Can Rakitin really have told the truth? I thought that you had just visited her, and that was all."

"Can a betrothed man pay such visits? Is such a thing possible and with such a betrothed, and before the eyes of all the world? Confound it, I have some honor! As soon as I began visiting Grushenka, I ceased to be betrothed, and to be an honest man. I understand that. Why do you look at me? You see, I went in the first place to beat her. I had heard, and I know for a fact now, that that captain, father's agent, had given Grushenka an IOU of mine for her to sue me for payment, so as to put an end to me. They wanted to scare me. I went to beat her. I had had a glimpse of her before. She isn't striking. I knew about her old merchant, who's lying ill now, paralyzed; but he's leaving her a decent little sum. I knew,

---

9. These lines have not been identified.
1. The Russian word *klaniat'sia* means to send greetings, to give one's regards to, and to bow.

too, that she likes money, that she hoarded it, and lent it at a wicked rate of interest, that she's a merciless cheat and rogue. I went to beat her, and with her I stayed. The storm broke, the plague struck, I'm plague-stricken still, and I know that everything is over, that there will never be anything more for me. The cycle of the ages is accomplished. That's my position. And though I'm a beggar, as fate would have it, I had three thousand just then in my pocket.[2] I drove with Grushenka to Mokroe, a place fifteen miles from here. I got gypsies there and champagne and made all the peasants there drunk on it, and all the women and girls. I sent the thousands flying. In three days' time I was stripped bare, but a hero. Do you suppose the hero had gained his end? Not a sign of it from her. I tell you that rogue, Grushenka, has a supple curve all over her body. You can see it in her little foot, even in her little toe. I saw it, and kissed it, but that was all I swear! 'I'll marry you if you like,' she said, 'you're a beggar you know. Say that you won't beat me, and will let me do anything I choose, and perhaps I will marry you,' she laughed. And she's laughing still!"

Dmitri Fyodorovich leaped up almost in a sort of fury, he suddenly seemed as though he were drunk. His eyes became suddenly bloodshot.

"And do you really mean to marry her?"

"At once, if she will, and if she won't, I will stay all the same; I'll be the porter at her gate. You, you, Alyosha . . ." He suddenly stopped short before him, and taking him by the shoulders suddenly began shaking him violently, "Do you know, you innocent boy, that this is all delirium, senseless delirium, for there's a tragedy here! Let me tell you, Alexey, that I may be a low man, with low and degraded passions, but a thief and a pickpocket Dmitri Karamazov never can be. Well, then, let me tell you that I am a thief and a pickpocket! That very morning, just before I went to beat Grushenka, Katerina Ivanovna sent for me, and in strict secrecy, so that no one would know (why I don't know, I suppose she had some reason) asked me to go to the chief town of the province and to send by mail three thousand rubles to Agatha Ivanovna in Moscow, so that nothing should be known of it in the town here. So I had that three thousand rubles in my pocket when I went to see Grushenka, and it was that money we spent at Mokroe. Afterwards I pretended I had been to the town, but did not show her the post office receipt. I said I had sent the money and would bring the receipt, and so far I haven't brought it, I've forgotten it. Now what do you think—you'll go to her today and say, 'He bows to you,' and she'll ask you, 'What about the money?' You might still have said to her, 'He's a degraded sensualist, and a low creature, with uncontrolled passions. He didn't send your money then, but wasted it, because, like an animal, he couldn't control himself.' But still you might have added, 'He isn't a thief though. Here is your three thousand; he sends it back. Send it yourself to Agatha Ivanovna. But he told me to say "he bows to you."' But, as it is, she will ask, 'But where is the money?'"

"Mitya, you are unhappy, yes! But not as unhappy as you think. Don't kill yourself with worry, don't kill yourself!"

2. Three thousand rubles—the amount Dmitri owes Katerina Ivanovna, and which he feels entitled to from his father—would have been enough to provide some financial security. For more on the value of nineteenth-century Russian currency, see p. 11.

"What, do you suppose I'd shoot myself because I can't get three thousand to pay back? That's just it, I won't shoot myself. I don't have the strength now, afterwards, perhaps, but now I'm going to Grushenka . . . I don't care what happens."

"And what then?"

"I'll be her husband if she deigns to have me, and when a lover comes, I'll go into the next room. I'll clean her friends' galoshes, heat up their samovar, run their errands."

"Katerina Ivanovna will understand it all," Alyosha suddenly said solemnly. "She'll understand the whole depth of this sorrow and will forgive. She has a lofty mind, and no one could be more unhappy than you. She'll see that for herself."

"She won't forgive everything," said Mitya, with a grin. "There's something in it, brother, that no woman could forgive. Do you know what would be the best thing to do?"

"What?"

"Pay back the three thousand."

"Where can we get it from? Listen, I have two thousand, Ivan will give you another thousand, that makes three, take it and pay it back."

"And when would you get it, your three thousand? You're not of age, besides, and you must—you absolutely must—bow me out to her today, with the money or without it, for I can't drag on any longer, things have come to such a point. Tomorrow is too late. I will send you to father."

"To father?"

"Yes, to father first. Ask him for three thousand."

"But, Mitya, he won't give it."

"As though he would! I know he won't. Do you know the meaning of despair, Alexey?"

"I do."

"Listen: legally he owes me nothing. I've taken it all from him, everything, I know that. But morally he owes me something, doesn't he? You know he started with twenty-eight thousand of my mother's money and made a hundred thousand with it. Let him give me back only three out of the twenty-eight thousand, and he'll draw my soul out of hell,[3] and it will be reckoned unto him! For that three thousand—I give you my solemn word—I'll make an end of everything, and he won't hear anything more of me at all. For the last time I give him the chance to be a father. Tell him God Himself sends him this chance."

"Mitya, he won't give it for anything."

"I know he won't, I know it perfectly well. Now, especially. That's not all. I know something more. Now, only a few days ago, perhaps only yesterday he found out for the first time *in earnest* (underline *in earnest*) that Grushenka is really perhaps not joking, and really means to marry me. He knows her nature, he knows the cat. And do you suppose he's going to give me money to help to bring that about when he's crazy about her himself? And that's not all, either. I can tell you more than that. I know that for the last five days he has had three thousand drawn out of the bank, changed into notes of a hundred rubles, packed into a large envelope, sealed with five seals, and tied across with a red ribbon. You see how well

---

3. Refers to Jonah 2.6.

I know all about it! On the envelope is written: 'To my angel, Grushenka, if she comes to me.' He scrawled it himself in silence and in secret, and no one knows that the money's there except the lackey, Smerdyakov, whom he trusts like himself. So now he has been expecting Grushenka for the last three or four days; he hopes she'll come for the money. He has sent her word of it, and she has sent him word that perhaps she'll come. And if she does go to the old man, can I marry her after that? You understand now why I'm here in secret and what I'm on the watch for?"

"For her?"

"Yes, for her. Thomas has a room in the house of these sluts here. Thomas comes from our parts; he was a soldier in our regiment. He does jobs for them. He's watchman at night and goes grouse shooting in the daytime; and that's how he lives. I've established myself in his room. Neither he nor the women of the house know the secret—that is, that I am on the watch here."

"No one but Smerdyakov knows, then?"

"No one else. He will let me know if she goes to the old man."

"It was he who told you about the money, then?"

"Yes. It's top secret. Even Ivan doesn't know about the money, or about anything. The old man is sending Ivan to Chermashnya[4] on a two or three days' journey. A purchaser has turned up for the copse: he'll give eight thousand for the timber. So the old man keeps asking Ivan to help him by going to arrange it. It will take him two or three days. That's what the old man wants, so that Grushenka can come while he's away."

"Then he's expecting Grushenka today?"

"No, she won't come today; there are signs. She's certain not to come!" cried Mitya suddenly. "Smerdyakov thinks so, too. Father's drinking now. He's sitting at a table with brother Ivan. Go to him, Alexey, and ask for the three thousand."

"Mitya, dear, what's the matter with you?" cried Alyosha, jumping up from his place, and looking keenly at Dmitri Fyodorovich's frenzied face. For one moment the thought struck him that Dmitri Fyodorovich had gone insane.

"What is it? I'm not insane," said Dmitri Fyodorovich, looking intently and even somehow earnestly at him. "No fear. I am sending you to father, and I know what I'm saying. I believe in miracles."

"In miracles?"

"In a miracle of Divine Providence. God knows my heart. He sees my despair. He sees the whole picture. Surely He won't let something awful happen. Alyosha, I believe in miracles. Go!"

"I am going. Tell me, will you wait for me here?"

"Yes. I know it will take some time. You can't just go at him point blank. He's drunk now. I'll wait three hours—four, five, six, seven. Only remember you must go to Katerina Ivanovna today, if it has to be at midnight, *with the money or without the money*, and say, 'He bows to you.' I want you to say that verse to her: 'He bows to you.'"

"Mitya! And what if Grushenka comes today—if not today, tomorrow, or the next day?"

"Grushenka? I shall see her. I shall rush out and prevent it."

---

4. Dostoevsky's father bought a village named Chermashnya in 1832.

"And if——?"

"If there's an if, it will be murder. I couldn't endure it."

"Who will be murdered?"

"The old man. I won't kill her."

"Brother, what are you saying!"

"Oh, I don't know. . . . I don't know . . . Perhaps I won't kill him, and perhaps I will. I'm afraid that he will suddenly become so loathsome to me with his face at that moment. I hate his ugly throat, his nose, his eyes, his shameless snigger. I feel a physical repulsion. That's what I'm afraid of. And I won't be able to contain myself . . ."

"I'll go, Mitya. I believe that God will order things for the best, that nothing awful may happen."

"And I will sit and wait for the miracle. And if it doesn't come to pass . . ."

Alyosha went towards his father's house in deep thought.

Chapter VI

Smerdyakov

He did in fact find his father still at the table. The table was laid, as usual, in the drawing room, although there was an actual dining room in the house. The drawing room was the largest room in the house, and furnished with old-fashioned ostentation. The furniture was white and very old, upholstered in old, red, silky material. In the spaces between the windows there were mirrors with old-fashioned, elaborately carved frames, also white with gold. On the walls, covered with white paper, which was torn in many places, there hung two large portraits—one of some prince who had been governor of the district thirty years before, and the other of some bishop, also long since dead. In the corner opposite the door there were several icons, before which a lamp was lighted at nightfall . . . not so much for devotional purposes as to light the room. Fyodor Pavlovich used to go to bed very late, at three or four o'clock in the morning, and would wander about the room at night or sit in an armchair, thinking. This had become a habit with him. He often slept completely alone in the house, sending his servants to the lodge; but usually Smerdyakov remained, sleeping on a bench in the hall. When Alyosha came in, dinner was over, but coffee and preserves had been served. Fyodor Pavlovich liked sweet things with brandy after dinner. Ivan Fyodorovich was also at table, sipping coffee. The servants, Grigory and Smerdyakov, were standing by. Both the gentlemen and the servants seemed in singularly good spirits. Fyodor Pavlovich was roaring with laughter. Before he entered the room, Alyosha heard the shrill laugh he knew so well, and could tell from the sound of it that his father had only reached the good-humored stage, and was far from being completely drunk.

"Here he is! Here he is!" Fyodor Pavlovich suddenly howled, highly delighted at seeing Alyosha. "Join us. Sit down. Coffee is a lenten dish, but it's hot and good. I don't offer you brandy, you're keeping the fast.[5] But would you like some, would you? No; I'd better give you some of our

5. Alyosha is observing the fasts prescribed for Lent.

liqueur, its famous! Smerdyakov, go to the cupboard, the second shelf on the right. Here are the keys. Look sharp!"

Alyosha began refusing the liqueur.

"Never mind. If you won't have it, we will," said Fyodor Pavlovich, beaming. "But wait—have you eaten?"

"Yes," answered Alyosha, who had in truth only eaten a piece of bread and drunk a glass of kvass in the Father Superior's kitchen. "Though I would have some hot coffee with pleasure."

"Bravo, my darling! He'll have some coffee. Does it need to be warmed up? No, it's boiling. It's splendid coffee: Smerdyakov's making. My Smerdyakov's an artist at coffee and at fish patties, and at fish soup, too. You must come one day and have some fish soup. Let me know beforehand. . . . But, wait; didn't I tell you this morning to come home with your mattress and pillow and all? Have you brought your mattress? He, he, he!"

"No, I haven't," said Alyosha, smiling, too.

"Ah, but you were frightened, you were frightened this morning, weren't you? There, my darling, I couldn't do anything to upset you. Do you know, Ivan, I can't resist the way he looks one straight in the face and laughs? My whole insides begin to laugh when I look at him. I'm so fond of him. Alyosha, let me give you my blessing—a father's blessing."

Alyosha rose, but Fyodor Pavlovich had already changed his mind.

"No, no," he said, "I'll just make the sign of the cross over you, for now. Sit still. Now we've a treat for you, in your own line, too. It'll make you laugh. Balaam's ass[6] has begun talking to us here—and how he talks! How he talks!"

Balaam's ass, it appeared, was the lackey, Smerdyakov. He was still a young man of about twenty-four, remarkably unsociable and taciturn. Not that he was shy or bashful. On the contrary, he was conceited and seemed to despise everybody. But we must pause to say a few words about him, and it must be done now. He was brought up by Grigory and Martha, but the boy grew up "with no sense of gratitude," as Grigory expressed it; he was an unsociable boy, and seemed to look at the world mistrustfully. In his childhood he was very fond of hanging cats, and burying them with great ceremony. He used to dress up in a sheet as though it were a surplice, and sing, and wave some object over the dead cat as though it were a censer. All this he did on the sly, with the greatest secrecy. Grigory caught him once at this diversion and gave him a sound beating. He shrank into a corner and sulked there for a week. "He doesn't love us, the monster," Grigory used to say to Martha Ignatyevna, "and he doesn't love anyone. Are you a human being?" he would suddenly turn to him directly. "You're not a human being, you grew from the mildew in the bathhouse,[7] that's who you are." Smerdyakov, it appeared afterwards, could never forgive him those words. Grigory taught him to read and write, and when he was twelve years old, began

6. In Numbers 22.21–34, an ass carrying its master sees that their path is blocked by an angel wielding a sword and refuses to advance. Balaam, the master, cannot see the angel, and beats the animal cruelly until the angel bestows it with the gift of speech. The ass then reproaches Balaam, who finally sees the angel and realizes his mistake. For analysis of this passage and its significance for the novel, see Golstein, "Accidental Families and Surrogate Fathers," p. 756; and Kantor, "Pavel Smerdyakov and Ivan Karamazov: The Problem of Temptation," p. 696.

7. Literally, "you sprang from the bathhouse slime," a proverbial expression used as an insult, roughly meaning "you came from nowhere." Dostoevsky heard this expression in Siberian prison camp and recorded it in his notebooks.

teaching him the Scriptures. But this teaching came to nothing. At the second or third lesson the boy suddenly grinned.

"What's that for?" asked Grigory, looking at him threateningly from under his spectacles.

"Oh, nothing. God created light on the first day, and the sun, moon, and stars on the fourth day. Where did the light come from on the first day?"[8] Grigory was thunderstruck. The boy looked sarcastically at his teacher. There was even something positively condescending in his expression. Grigory could not restrain himself. "I'll show you where!" he cried, and gave the boy a violent slap on the cheek. The boy took the slap without a word, but withdrew into his corner again for some days. A week later he had his first attack of the disease to which he was subject all the rest of his life—epilepsy. When Fyodor Pavlovich heard of it, his attitude to the boy seemed to change at once. Till then he had taken no notice of him, though he never scolded him, and always gave him a kopeck when he met him. Sometimes, when he was in good humor, he would send the boy something sweet from his table. But as soon as he heard of his illness, he showed an active interest in him, sent for a doctor, and tried remedies, but the disease turned out to be incurable. The fits occurred, on an average, once a month, but at various intervals. The fits varied, too, in violence: some were light and some were very severe. Fyodor Pavlovich strictly forbade Grigory to use corporal punishment on the boy, and began allowing him to come upstairs to him. He forbade him to be taught anything whatever for a time, too. One day when the boy was about fifteen, Fyodor Pavlovich noticed him lingering by the bookcase, and reading the titles through the glass. Fyodor Pavlovich had a fair number of books—over a hundred—but no one ever saw him reading. He at once gave Smerdyakov the key of the bookcase. "Come, read. You shall be my librarian. You'll be better sitting reading than hanging about the courtyard. Come, read this," and Fyodor Pavlovich gave him *Evenings on a Farm near Dikanka*.[9]

The boy read it, but didn't like it. He did not smile once, and finished it frowning.

"What? Isn't it funny?" asked Fyodor Pavlovich.

Smerdyakov was silent.

"Answer, fool."

"It's all untrue," mumbled the boy, with a grin.

"Then go to the devil, you have the soul of a lackey. Wait, here's Smaragdov's *Universal History*.[1] That's all true, read that."

But Smerdyakov did not get through ten pages of Smaragdov, he found it boring. So the bookcase was closed again. Shortly afterwards Martha and Grigory reported to Fyodor Pavlovich that Smerdyakov was gradually beginning to show an extraordinary fastidiousness. He would sit before his soup, take up his spoon and look into the soup, bend over it, examine it, take a spoonful and hold it to the light.

"What is it? A cockroach?" Grigory would ask.

"A fly, perhaps," observed Martha.

---

8. Smerdyakov is questioning the story of creation told in Genesis 1.
9. A collection of short stories by Nikolay Gogol (1809–1852), first published 1831–32.
1. *A Brief Universal History for Primary Schools*, a textbook by S. N. Smaragdov (1805–1871), was first published in 1845 and went through many editions.

The squeamish youth never answered, but he did the same with his bread, his meat, and everything he ate. He would hold a piece on his fork to the light, scrutinize it microscopically, and only after long deliberation decide to put it in his mouth. "Ach! What fine gentleman's airs!" Grigory muttered, looking at him. When Fyodor Pavlovich heard of this new quality in Smerdyakov he immediately decided to make him his cook, and sent him to Moscow to be trained. He spent some years there and came back remarkably changed in appearance. He suddenly became somehow extremely old, even wrinkled disproportionately to his age, turned sallow, and began to look like a eunuch. In character he seemed almost exactly the same as before he went away: he was just as unsociable, and showed not the slightest inclination for any companionship. In Moscow too, it was later reported, he had always been silent. Moscow itself had little interest for him; he saw very little there, and took scarcely any notice of anything. He went once to the theater, but returned silent and displeased with it. On the other hand, he came back to us from Moscow well dressed, in a clean coat and clean linen. He invariably brushed his clothes most scrupulously twice a day, and was very fond of cleaning his smart calf boots with a special English polish, so that they shone like mirrors. He turned out a first-rate cook. Fyodor Pavlovich paid him a salary, almost the whole of which Smerdyakov spent on clothes, pomade, perfumes, and such things. But he seemed to have as much contempt for the female sex as for men; he was aloof, almost unapproachable, with them. Fyodor Pavlovich began to regard him rather differently. His fits were becoming more frequent, and on the days he was ill Martha cooked, which did not suit Fyodor Pavlovich at all.

"Why are your fits getting worse?" asked Fyodor Pavlovich, looking askance at his new cook. "Why don't you marry someone, do you want a wife?"

But Smerdyakov just turned pale with anger at these words, and didn't reply. Fyodor Pavlovich would walk away, waving his hand. The main thing was that he had absolute confidence in his honesty. It happened once, when Fyodor Pavlovich was drunk, that he dropped in the muddy court-yard three hundred-ruble notes which he had only just received. He only missed them the next day, and was just hastening to search his pockets when he saw the notes lying on the table. Where had they come from? Smerdyakov had picked them up and brought them in the day before. "Well, my lad, I've never met anyone like you," Fyodor Pavlovich snapped out, and gave him ten rubles. We may add that he not only believed in his honesty, but had, for some reason, a liking for him, although the young man looked as morosely at him as at everyone and was always silent. He rarely spoke. If it had occurred to any one to wonder at the time what the young man was interested in, and what was in his mind, it would have been impossible to tell by looking at him. Yet he used sometimes to stop suddenly in the house, or even in the yard or street, and would stand still for ten minutes, lost in thought. A physiognomist studying his face would have said that there was no thought in it, no reflection, but only a sort of contemplation. There is a remarkable picture by the painter Kramskoy,[2] called

---

2. Ivan Kramskoy (1837–1887), well-known Russian painter of the Wanderers school (*Peredvizh-niki*), famous for his portraits. Dostoevsky and Kramskoy were personally acquainted. The painting "Contemplation" was first exhibited in 1878.

"Contemplation." There is a forest in winter, and on a roadway through the forest, in absolute solitude, stands a wandering peasant in a torn caftan and bark shoes. He stands, as it were, lost in thought. Yet he is not thinking; he is "contemplating." If any one touched him he would start and look at one as though awakening and bewildered. It's true he would come to himself immediately; but if he were asked what he had been thinking about, he would remember nothing. Yet probably he has hidden within himself, the impression which had dominated him during the period of contemplation. Those impressions are dear to him and no doubt he hoards them imperceptibly, and even unconsciously. How and why, of course, he does not know either. He may suddenly, after hoarding impressions for many years, abandon everything and go off to Jerusalem on a pilgrimage for his soul's salvation, or perhaps he will suddenly set fire to his native village, and perhaps do both. There are a good many "contemplatives" among the peasantry. Well, Smerdyakov was probably one of them, and he probably was greedily hoarding up his impressions, hardly knowing why.

Chapter VII

The Controversy[3]

But Balaam's ass had suddenly spoken. The subject was a strange one. Grigory had gone in the morning to make purchases, and had heard from the shopkeeper Lukyanov the story of a Russian soldier which had appeared in the newspaper of that day.[4] This soldier had been taken prisoner in some remote part of Asia, and was threatened with an immediate agonizing death if he did not renounce Christianity and follow Islam. He refused to deny his faith, and was tortured, flayed alive, and died, praising and glorifying Christ. Grigory had related the story at table. Fyodor Pavlovich always liked, over the dessert after dinner, to laugh and talk, if only with Grigory. This afternoon he was in a particularly good-humored and expansive mood. Sipping his brandy and listening to the reported news, he observed that they ought to make a saint of a soldier like that, and to take his flayed skin to some monastery. "That would make the people flock, and bring the money in." Grigory frowned, seeing that Fyodor Pavlovich was by no means touched, but, as was his habit, was beginning to scoff. At that moment, Smerdyakov, who was standing by the door, smiled. Smerdyakov often waited at table towards the end of dinner, and since Ivan's arrival in our town he had done so every day.

"What are you grinning at?" asked Fyodor Pavlovich, catching the smile instantly, and knowing that it referred to Grigory.

"Well, my opinion is, sir," Smerdyakov began suddenly and unexpectedly in a loud voice, "that if that laudable soldier's exploit was so very great, sir, there would have been, to my thinking, no sin in it if he had on such an emergency renounced, so to speak, the name of Christ and his own

---

3. Dostoevsky's title for this chapter, "Controverza," sounds foreign in Russian.
4. The following anecdote is based on the case of Foma Danilov, whom Dostoevsky described as "the emblem of Russia." See "Foma Danilov, A Russian Hero Tortured to Death" in the January 1877 issue of Dostoevsky's *Diary* (quote at p. 822).

christening, to save by that same his life, for good deeds, by which, in the course of years, to redeem his cowardice."

"How could it not be a sin? You're talking nonsense. For that you'll go straight to hell and be roasted there like mutton," put in Fyodor Pavlovich.

It was at this point that Alyosha came in, and Fyodor Pavlovich, as we have seen, was highly delighted at his appearance.

"We're on your subject, your subject!" he chuckled gleefully, making Alyosha sit down to listen.

"As for mutton, that's not so, sir, and there'll be nothing there for this, and there shouldn't be either, sir, if it's according to justice," Smerdyakov maintained stoutly.

"How do you mean 'according to justice'?" Fyodor Pavlovich cried still more gaily, nudging Alyosha with his knee.

"He's a scoundrel, that's what he is!" burst from Grigory. He looked Smerdyakov wrathfully right in the eyes.

"As for being a scoundrel, wait a little, Grigory Vasilyevich," answered Smerdyakov with perfect composure. "You'd better consider yourself that, once I am taken prisoner by the enemies of the Christian race, and they demand from me to curse the name of God and renounce my holy christening, I am fully entitled to act by my own reason, since there would be no sin in it."

"You've said that before, don't waste words, but prove it!" cried Fyodor Pavlovich.

"Soup maker!" muttered Grigory contemptuously.

"As for being a soup maker, wait a bit, too, and consider for yourself, Grigory Vasilyevich, without abusing me. For as soon as I say to those tormentors: 'no, I'm not a Christian, and I curse my true God,' then at once, by God's high judgment, I become immediately and specially anathema[5] accursed, and I am cut off from the Holy Church, exactly as though I were a heathen, so that at that very instant, not only when I say it aloud, but when I think of saying it, before a quarter of a second has passed, I am cut off. Is that so or not, Grigory Vasilyevich?"

He addressed Grigory with obvious satisfaction, though he was really answering Fyodor Pavlovich's questions, and was well aware of it, and intentionally pretending that Grigory had asked the questions.

"Ivan!" cried Fyodor Pavlovich suddenly, "give me your ear. He set all this up for you, he wants you to praise him. Praise him."

Ivan Fyodorovich listened with perfect seriousness to his papasha's rapturous communication.

"Wait, Smerdyakov, be quiet a minute," cried Fyodor Pavlovich once more. "Ivan, your ear again."

Ivan Fyodorovich bent down again with a most serious expression.

"I love you as I do Alyosha. Don't think I don't love you. Some brandy?"

"Yes." "But you're rather drunk yourself," thought Ivan Fyodorovich, looking intently at his father. He was watching Smerdyakov with great curiosity.

"You're anathema accursed, as it is," Grigory suddenly burst out, "and how dare you argue, you scoundrel, after that, if . . ."

---

5. In modern usage, anathema is used primarily to designate something or someone cursed or excommunicated, or something or someone intensely disliked.

"Don't scold him, Grigory, don't scold him!" Fyodor Pavlovich cut him short.

"You should wait, Grigory Vasilyevich, if only a short time, and listen, for I haven't finished all I had to say. For at the very moment I become accursed, sir, at that same highest moment, sir, I become exactly like a heathen, and my christening is taken off me and becomes of no avail. Isn't that so, sir?"

"Make haste and finish, my boy," Fyodor Pavlovich urged him, sipping from his wineglass with relish.

"And if I've ceased to be a Christian, then I told no lie to the tormentors when they asked whether I was a Christian or not a Christian, seeing I had already been relieved by God Himself of my Christianity by reason of the thought alone, before I had time to utter a word to the tormentors. And if I have already been discharged, in what manner and with what sort of justice can I be held responsible as a Christian in the other world for having denied Christ, when, through the very thought alone, before denying Him I had been relieved from my christening? If I'm no longer a Christian, then I can't renounce Christ, for I've nothing then to renounce. Who will hold a heathen Tatar responsible, Grigory Vasilyevich, even in heaven, for not having been born a Christian? And who would punish him for that, considering that you can't take two skins off one ox? For God Almighty Himself, even if He did make the Tatar responsible, when he dies would give him the smallest possible punishment, I imagine (since he must be punished), judging that he is not to blame if he has come into the world an unclean heathen, from heathen parents. The Lord God can't take a Tatar by force and say he was a Christian? That would mean that the Almighty would tell a real untruth. And can the Lord of Heaven and Earth tell a lie, even in one word, sir?"

Grigory was thunderstruck and looked at the orator, his eyes nearly starting out of his head. Though he did not clearly understand what was said, he suddenly caught something in this rigmarole, and stood, looking like a man who has just hit his head against a wall. Fyodor Pavlovich emptied his glass and went off into his shrill laugh.

"Alyoshka, Alyoshka! What do you say to that! Ah, you casuist![6] He must have been with the Jesuits[7] somewhere, Ivan. Oh, you stinking Jesuit, who taught you? But you're lying, you casuist, lying, lying, lying. Don't cry, Grigory, we'll reduce him to smoke and ashes in a moment. Tell me this, oh, ass; you may be right before your tormentors, but you have renounced your faith all the same in your own heart, and you say yourself that in that very hour you became anathema accursed, and once you're anathema they won't pat you on the head for it in hell. What do you say to that, my fine Jesuit?"[8]

---

6. Someone who engages in casuistry (from Latin *cāsus*, case), case-based reasoning about moral matters, as opposed to principle-based reasoning. A casuist begins with the specific case at hand rather than with an absolute principle. Casuistry has acquired a pejorative meaning as false reasoning about moral matters, and *casuist* is typically used to designate someone whose reasoning is overly subtle and specious.

7. The Jesuits are a Catholic order founded by St. Ignatius of Loyola (1491–1556) and approved by Pope Paul III in 1540. The Jesuit order was associated with casuistry.

8. "My fine Jesuit" is an inexact quotation from Pushkin's poem "The Tale of Tsar Saltan" (1831), which contains the phrase "my fine prince."

"There is no doubt, sir, that I have renounced it in my own heart, but there was no special sin in that, sir. Or if there was sin, it was the most ordinary, sir."

"How's that the most ordinary, sir!"

"You lie, accursed one!" hissed Grigory.

"Consider yourself, Grigory Vasilyevich," Smerdyakov went on, staid and unruffled, conscious of his triumph, but, as it were, generous to the vanquished foe. "Consider yourself, Grigory Vasilyevich; it is said in the Scripture that if you have faith, even as a mustard seed, and bid a mountain move into the sea, it will move without the least delay at your bidding.[9] Well, Grigory Vasilyevich, if I'm without faith and you have so great a faith that you are continually swearing at me, you try yourself telling this mountain, not to move into the sea for that's a long way off, sir, but even to our stinking little river which runs at the bottom of the garden. You'll see for yourself, sir, that it won't budge, but will remain just where it is however much you shout at it, and that shows, Grigory Vasilyevich, that you haven't faith in the proper manner, and only abuse others about it. Again, taking into consideration that no one in our day, not only you, sir, but actually no one, from the highest person to the lowest peasant, sir, can shove mountains into the sea—except perhaps some one man in the world, or, at most, two, and they most likely are saving their souls in secret somewhere in the Egyptian desert, so you wouldn't find them—if so it be, sir, if all the rest have no faith, will God curse all the rest? that is, the population of the whole earth, except a couple of hermits in the desert, and in His well-known mercy will He not forgive one of them? And so I'm persuaded that though I may once have doubted I shall be forgiven if I shed tears of repentance."

"Wait!" shrieked Fyodor Pavlovich, in an apotheosis of delight. "So you do suppose there are two who can move mountains? Ivan, make a note of it, write it down: The whole Russian man speaks here!"

"You're quite right in saying it's characteristic of the people's faith," Ivan Fyodorovich assented, with an approving smile.

"You agree! Then it must be so, if you agree! It's true, isn't it, Alyoshka? That's the Russian faith all over, isn't it?"

"No, Smerdyakov's faith is not Russian at all," said Alyosha firmly and gravely.

"I'm not talking about his faith, I mean those two in the desert, only that idea: Surely that's Russian, isn't it Russian?"

"Yes, that's purely Russian," said Alyosha smiling.

"Your words are worth a gold piece, ass, and I'll send it to you today, but as for the rest you still lie, lie, lie; let me tell you, fool, that we here are all of little faith, only from carelessness, because we don't have time; first of all, things are too much for us, and, in the second place, the Lord God has given us so little time, only twenty-four hours in the day, so that there's not even time to sleep enough, much less to repent of one's sins. Whereas you have denied your faith to your tormentors when you had

9. Smerdyakov refers to a well-known passage from the Synoptic Gospels. When his disciples ask Jesus why they were unable to heal a child, Jesus rebukes them, saying "Because of your unbelief: for verily I say unto you, If ye have faith as a grain of mustard seed, ye shall say unto this mountain, Remove hence to yonder place; and it shall remove; and nothing shall be impossible unto you" (Matthew 17.20). See also Matthew 21.21, Mark 11.23, and Luke 17.6.

nothing else to think about, and when it was precisely time to show your faith! So I consider, brother, that it constitutes a sin."

"Constitute a sin it may, but consider yourself, Grigory Vasilyevich, that it only extenuates it, if it does constitute. If I had believed then in very truth, as I ought to have believed, then it really would have been sinful if I had not faced tortures for my faith, and had gone over to the pagan Mohammedan faith. But, of course, it wouldn't have come to torture then, because I should only have had to say at that instant to the mountain 'move and crush the tormentor,' and it would have moved and at the very instant have crushed him like a cockroach, and I should have walked away as though nothing had happened, praising and glorifying God. But, suppose at that very moment I had tried all that, and cried to that mountain, 'Crush these tormentors,' and it hadn't crushed them, how could I have helped doubting, pray, at such a time, and at such a dread hour of mortal terror? And apart from that, I should know already that I could not attain to the fullness of the Kingdom of Heaven (for since the mountain had not moved at my word, they could not think very much of my faith up aloft, and there could be no very great reward awaiting me in the world to come). So why should I let them flay the skin off me as well, and to no good purpose? For, even though they had flayed my skin half off my back, even then the mountain would not have moved at my word or at my cry. And at such a moment not only doubt might come over one but one might lose one's reason from fear, so that one would not be able to think at all. And, therefore, how should I be particularly to blame if not seeing my advantage or reward there or here, I should, at least, save my skin? And so trusting fully in the grace of the Lord I should cherish the hope that I might be altogether forgiven, sir . . ."

Chapter VIII

Over the Brandy

The argument was over, but strange to say, Fyodor Pavlovich, who had been having such a good time, suddenly began frowning. He frowned and gulped brandy, and it was already a glass too much.

"Get along with you, Jesuits!" he cried to the servants. "Go away, Smerdyakov. I'll send you the gold piece I promised you today, but be off! Don't cry, Grigory, go to Martha, she'll comfort you and put you to bed. The rascals won't let us sit in peace after dinner," he suddenly snapped peevishly, as the servants promptly withdrew at his word. "Smerdyakov always pokes himself in now after dinner, it's you he's so interested in, what have you done to fascinate him?" he added to Ivan Fyodorovich.

"Nothing whatever," he answered. "He's taken to respecting me; he's a lackey and a mean soul. A prime candidate, however, when the time comes."

"Prime?"

"There will be others and better ones. But there will be some like him as well. His kind will come first, and better ones after."

"And when will the time come?"

"The rocket will go off and fizzle out, perhaps. The peasants are not very fond of listening to these soup makers, so far."

"Ah, brother, but a Balaam's ass like that thinks and thinks, and the devil knows where he gets to."

"He's storing up ideas," said Ivan, smiling.

"You see, I know he can't bear me, nor anyone else, even you, though it seems to you 'he's taken to respecting you.' Worse still with Alyoshka, he despises Alyoshka. But he doesn't steal, that's one thing, and he's not a gossip, he holds his tongue, and doesn't wash our dirty linen in public, he makes splendid fish patties too, but, devil take him, is he worth talking about so much?"

"Of course he isn't."

"And as for the ideas he may be hatching, the Russian peasant, generally speaking, needs thrashing. That I've always maintained. Our peasants are swindlers, and don't deserve to be pitied, and it's a good thing they're still flogged sometimes. The strength of the Russian land is in birches.[1] If they cut down the forests, it will be the downfall of the Russian land. I stand up for the intelligent people. We've stopped thrashing the peasants, we've grown so intelligent, but they go on thrashing themselves. And a good thing too. 'For with what measure ye mete it shall be measured to you again,'[2] or how does it go? Anyhow, it will be measured. But Russia's all swinishness. My dear, if you only knew how I hate Russia. . . . That is, not Russia, but all this vice! But maybe I mean Russia. *Tout cela c'est de la cochonnerie.*[3] . . . Do you know what I like? I like wit."

"You've had another glass. That's enough."

"Wait a bit. I'll have one more, and then another, and then I'll stop. No, wait, you interrupted me. At Mokroe I was talking to an old man, and he told me: 'There's nothing we like so much as sentencing girls to be thrashed, and we always give the lads the job of thrashing them.[4] And the girl he has thrashed today, the young man will ask in marriage tomorrow. So it quite suits the girls, too,' he said. There's a set of Marquis de Sades[5] for you! But it's clever, anyway. Shall we go over and have a look at it, eh? Alyoshka, are you blushing? Don't be bashful, child. I'm sorry I didn't stay to dinner at the Superior's and tell the monks about the girls at Mokroe. Alyoshka, don't be angry that I offended your Superior this morning. I lost my temper. If there is a God, if He exists, then, of course, I'm to blame, and I shall have to answer for it. But if there isn't a God at all, what do they deserve, your fathers? It's not enough to cut their heads off, for they keep back progress. Would you believe it, Ivan, that that tears at my feelings? No, you don't believe it as I see from your eyes. You believe what people say, that I'm nothing but a buffoon. Alyosha, do you believe that I'm more than just a buffoon?"

---

1. Birch branches were used as instruments for corporal punishment in Tsarist Russia. The Judicial Reform Act of 1864 placed some limitations on corporal punishment.
2. Fyodor Pavlovich quotes from a passage found in the synoptic Gospels. In Matthew 7.1–2, Jesus tells the people "Judge not, that ye be not judged. For with what judgment ye judge, ye shall be judged; and with what measure ye mete, it shall be measured to you again." See also Mark 4.24 and Luke 6.37–38.
3. "That's all swinishness" (French).
4. After the Emancipation of 1861, peasants elected local courts that had the power to impose corporal punishment.
5. Count (Marquis) Donatien de Sade (1740–1814), French aristocrat, writer, and thinker, author of works such as *Philosophy in the Bedroom* (1795) which describe sex and cruelty.

"I believe that you are more than just a buffoon."

"And I believe you do, and that you speak the truth. You look sincere and you speak sincerely. But not Ivan. Ivan's supercilious. . . . I'd make an end of your monks, though, all the same. I'd take all that mystic stuff and suppress it, once for all, all over Russia, so as to bring all the fools to reason. And the gold and the silver that would flow into the mint!"

"But why suppress it?" asked Ivan.

"That Truth may prevail. That's why."

"Well, if Truth were to prevail, you know, you'd be the first to be robbed and then . . . suppressed."

"Bah! Actually, perhaps you are right. Ah, I'm an ass!" burst out Fyodor Pavlovich suddenly, striking himself lightly on the forehead. "Well, your little monastery may stand then, Alyoshka, if that's how it is. And we intelligent people will sit snug and enjoy our brandy. You know, Ivan, it must have been so ordained by the Almighty Himself. Ivan, speak, is there a God or not? Stay, speak the truth, speak seriously! Why are you laughing again?"

"I'm laughing that you should have made a clever remark just now about Smerdyakov's belief in the existence of two saints who could move mountains."

"Why, am I like him now, then?"

"Very much."

"Well, that shows I'm a Russian, too, and I have a Russian trait, and you may be caught on the same trait, though you are a philosopher. Shall I catch you? What do you bet that I'll catch you tomorrow. Speak, all the same, is there a God, or not? Only, be serious! I need you to be serious now."

"No, there is no God."

"Alyoshka, is there a God?"

"There is."

"Ivan, and is there immortality of some sort, just a little, just a tiny bit?"

"There is no immortality either."

"None at all?"

"None at all."

"There's absolute nothingness then? Perhaps there is just something? Anything is better than nothing!"

"Absolute nothingness."

"Alyoshka, is there immortality?"

"There is."

"God and immortality?"

"God and immortality. In God is immortality."

"Hmm! It's more likely Ivan's right. Good Lord, to think what faith, what force of all kinds, man has lavished for nothing, on that dream, and for how many thousand years! Who is it laughing at man? Ivan? For the last time, once for all: is there a God or not? I ask for the last time!"

"And for the last time there is not."

"Who is laughing at people, Ivan?"

"It must be the devil," said Ivan Fyodorovich, smiling.

"And does the devil exist?"

"No, there's no devil either."

"It's a pity. Devil take it, what wouldn't I do to the man who first invented God! Hanging on a bitter aspen tree would be too good for him."[6]

"There would have been no civilization if they hadn't invented God."

"Wouldn't there have been? Without God?"

"No. And there would have been no brandy, either. But I must take your brandy away from you, anyway."

"Stop, stop, stop, dear boy, one more little glass. I've hurt Alyosha's feelings. You're not angry with me, Alexey? My dear little Alexeychik, my Alexeychik!"

"No, I am not angry. I know your thoughts. Your heart is better than your head."

"My heart better than my head, is it? Oh, Lord, and that from you? Ivan, do you love Alyoshka?"

"Yes."

"You must love him" (Fyodor Pavlovich was by this time very drunk). "Listen, Alyosha, I was rude to your elder this morning. But I was excited. But there's wit in that elder, don't you think, Ivan?"

"There may very well be."

"There is, there is. Il y a du Piron là dedans.[7] He's a Jesuit, a Russian one, that is. As he's an honorable person there's a hidden indignation boiling within him at having to pretend and affect holiness."

"But, of course, he believes in God."

"Not a bit of it. Didn't you know? Why, he tells everyone so, himself. That is, not everyone, but all the clever people who come to him. He said straight out to Governor Schultz not long ago: 'Credo,[8] but I don't know in what.'"

"Really?"

"He really did. But I respect him. There's something of Mephistopheles about him, or rather of The Hero of Our Time. . . . Arbenin, or what's his name?[9] . . . You see, he's a sensualist; he's such a sensualist that I should be afraid for my daughter or my wife if she went to confess to him. You know, when he begins telling stories. . . . The year before last he invited us to tea, tea with liqueur (the ladies send him liqueur) and began telling us about old times till we nearly split our sides. . . . Especially how he once cured a paralyzed woman. 'If my legs were not bad I know a dance I could dance you,' he said. What do you say to that? 'I've pulled off plenty of tricks in my time,' said he. He got sixty thousand out of the merchant Demidov."

"What, he stole it?"

"He brought him the money as a man he could trust, saying, 'Take care of it for me, friend, there'll be a police search at my place tomorrow.' And he kept it. 'You have given it to the Church,' he declared. I said to him: 'You're a scoundrel,' I said. 'No,' said he, 'I'm not a scoundrel, but I'm broad-natured.' But that wasn't he, that was someone else. I've muddled

6. According to legend, Judas Iscariot, the apostle who betrayed Christ and so set in motion the chain of events leading to the crucifixion, hung himself on such a tree.
7. "There's something of Piron in him" (French). Alexis Piron (1689–1773) French wit, poet, and dramatist, some of whose writings were considered risqué.
8. "I believe" (Latin). Usually refers to the statement of belief found in the Christian liturgical rite.
9. Fyodor Pavlovich names several demonic or tormented characters from literature. Mephistopheles is the devil in Goethe's Faust (Part One published 1808; Part Two published posthumously in 1832). Dostoevsky was rereading Faust in Russian translation during composition of The Brothers Karamazov. The main character of A Hero of Our Time (1841), a novel by Lermontov, is Pechorin; Arbenin is the rake in Lermontov's play Masquerade (written 1835).

him with someone else . . . without noticing it. Come, another glass and that's enough; take away the bottle, Ivan. I've been telling lies, why didn't you stop me, Ivan, and tell me I was lying?"

"I knew you'd stop yourself."

"That's a lie, you did it from spite, from simple spite against me. You despise me. You have come to me and despised me in my own house."

"Well, I'm going away. The brandy is getting to you."

"I've begged you for Christ's sake to go to Chermashnya for a day or two, and you don't go."

"I'll go tomorrow if you're so set upon it."

"You won't go. You want to keep an eye on me. That's what you want, you wicked soul. That's why you won't go."

The old man persisted. He had reached that point of drunkenness when some drunks, who until then have been peaceful, suddenly want to get angry and make a show of themselves.

"Why are you looking at me? Why do you look like that? Your eyes look at me and say, 'You ugly drunkard.' Your eyes are mistrustful, they're contemptuous. . . . You've come here with some design. Alyoshka, here, looks at me and his eyes shine. Alyosha doesn't despise me. Alexey, don't love Ivan. . . ."

"Don't be angry with my brother. Leave off attacking him," Alyosha suddenly said emphatically.

"Oh, all right. Ugh, my head aches. Take away the brandy, Ivan. It's the third time I've told you." He mused, and suddenly a slow, cunning grin spread over his face. "Don't be angry with a feeble old man, Ivan. I know you don't love me, but don't be angry all the same. You've nothing to love me for. You go to Chermashnya. I'll come to you myself and bring you a present. I'll show you a little wench there. I've had my eye on her a long time. She's still running about barefoot. Don't be afraid of barefooted wenches—don't despise them—they're pearls!"

And he kissed his hand with a smack.

"For me," he suddenly revived at once, seeming to grow sober the instant he touched on his favorite topic. "For me . . . Ah, you boys! You children, little sucking pigs, for me . . . even my whole life there has never been an ugly woman, that's been my rule! Can you understand that? How could you understand it? You've milk in your veins, not blood, you're not hatched yet! My rule has been that you can always find something devilishly interesting in every woman that you wouldn't find in any other. Only, one must know how to find it, there's the rule! That's a talent! For me there are no ugly women. The very fact that she is a woman is half the battle . . . but how could you understand that! Even in *vieilles filles*,[1] even in them you may discover something that makes you simply wonder that men have been such fools as to let them grow old without noticing them! Barefooted girls or unattractive ones, you must take by surprise. Didn't you know that? You must astound them till they're fascinated, upset, ashamed that such a gentleman should fall in love with such a little sloven. It's a jolly good thing that there always are and will be masters and slaves in the world, so there always will be a little maid-of-all-work and her master, and you know, that's all that's needed for happiness. Stay . . . listen, Alyoshka,

1. Old maids (French).

I always used to surprise your mother, but in a different way. I paid no attention to her at all, but all at once, when the minute came, I'd be all devotion to her, crawl on my knees, kiss her feet, and I always, always—I remember it as though it were today—reduced her to that tinkling, quiet, nervous, queer little laugh. It was peculiar to her. I knew her attacks always used to begin like that, the next day she would begin shrieking hysterically, and that this little laugh was not a sign of delight, but it made a very good counterfeit. That's the great thing, to know how to take everyone. Once Belyavsky—a handsome fellow, and rich—he used to like to come here and hang about her—suddenly gave me a slap in the face in her presence. And she—such a mild sheep—why, I thought she would have knocked me down for that blow, how she attacked me! 'You're beaten, beaten now,' she said, 'You've taken a blow from him. You have been trying to sell me to him,' she said. . . . 'And how dared he strike you in my presence. And don't dare come near me again, never, never! Run at once, challenge him to a duel' . . . I took her to the monastery then to humble her. The holy Fathers brought her back around. But I swear, by God, Alyosha, I never insulted my poor little shrieker! Only once, perhaps, in the first year: then she was very fond of praying, she used to keep the feasts of Our Lady[2] particularly and used to turn me out of her room then. I'll knock that mysticism out of her, thought I! 'Here,' said I, 'you see your icon, here it is, here I take it down. You believe it's miraculous, but here, I'll spit on it directly and nothing will happen to me for it!' . . . When she saw it, good Lord! I thought she would kill me. But she only jumped up, wrung her hands, then suddenly hid her face in them, began trembling all over and fell on the floor . . . fell all of a heap. Alyosha, Alyosha! What's the matter, what's the matter?"

The old man jumped up in alarm. From the time he had begun speaking about his mother, a change had gradually come over Alyosha's face. He flushed crimson, his eyes glowed, his lips quivered. The drunken old sot had gone spluttering on, noticing nothing, till the moment when something very strange happened to Alyosha. Precisely what he was describing in "the shrieker" was suddenly repeated with Alyosha. He jumped up from the table exactly as his mother was said to have done, wrung his hands, then hid his face in them, and fell back in his chair, shaking all over in an hysterical paroxysm of sudden violent, silent weeping. His extraordinary resemblance to his mother particularly struck the old man.

"Ivan, Ivan! Water, quickly! It's like her, exactly as she used to be then, his mother. Spurt some water on him from your mouth, that's what I used to do to her. He's upset about his mother, his mother," he muttered to Ivan.

"But she was my mother, too, I believe, his mother, was she not?" said Ivan, with uncontrolled anger and contempt. The old man shrank before his flashing eyes. But something very strange had happened, though only for a second; it seemed really to have escaped the old man's mind that Alyosha's mother actually was the mother of Ivan too . . .

"Your mother?" he muttered, not understanding. "What do you mean? What mother are you talking about? Was she? . . . Why, damn it! of course she was yours too! Damn it! My mind has never been so darkened before. Excuse me, why, I was thinking Ivan . . . He, he, he!" He stopped. A broad,

2. Holidays celebrated in honor of the Virgin Mary.

drunken, half senseless grin overspread his face. And suddenly at that moment a fearful noise and clamor was heard in the hall, there were violent shouts, the door was flung open, and Dmitri Fyodorovich burst into the room. The old man rushed to Ivan in terror.

"He'll kill me! He'll kill me! Don't let him get me, don't let him!" he screamed, clinging to the skirt of Ivan's coat.

Chapter IX

Sensualists

Grigory and Smerdyakov ran into the room after Dmitri Fyodorovich. They had been struggling with him in the hall, refusing to admit him (acting on instructions given them by Fyodor Pavlovich some days before). Taking advantage of the fact that Dmitri Fyodorovich stopped a moment on entering the room to look about him, Grigory ran round the table, closed the double doors on the opposite side of the room leading to the inner rooms, and stood before the closed doors, stretching wide his arms, prepared to defend the entrance, so to speak, with the last drop of his blood. Seeing this, Dmitri uttered a scream rather than a shout and rushed at Grigory.

"Then she's there! She's hidden there! Out of the way, scoundrel!" He tried to pull Grigory away, but the old servant pushed him back. Beside himself with fury, Dmitri struck out, and hit Grigory with all his might. The old man fell like a log, and Dmitri, leaping over him, broke through the door. Smerdyakov remained pale and trembling at the other end of the room, huddling close to Fyodor Pavlovich.

"She's here," shouted Dmitri Fyodorovich. "I saw her turn towards the house just now, but I couldn't catch her. Where is she? Where is she?"

That shout, "She's here!" produced an indescribable effect on Fyodor Pavlovich. All his terror left him.

"Hold him! Hold him!" he cried, and dashed after Dmitri Fyodorovich. Meanwhile Grigory had got up from the floor, but still seemed stunned. Ivan Fyodorovich and Alyosha ran after their father. In the third room something was heard to fall on the floor with a ringing crash: it was a large glass vase—not an expensive one—on a marble pedestal which Dmitri Fyodorovich had upset as he ran past it.

"At him!" shouted the old man. "Help!"

Ivan Fyodorovich and Alyosha caught the old man and forcibly brought him back.

"Why do you run after him? He'll murder you outright!" Ivan Fyodorovich cried wrathfully at his father.

"Vanechka, Lyoshechka! She must be here. Grushenka's here. He said he saw her himself, running by."

He was choking. He was not expecting Grushenka at the time, and the sudden news that she was here made him beside himself. He was trembling all over. He seemed frantic.

"But you've seen for yourself that she hasn't come!" cried Ivan.

"But maybe she came through that other entrance?"

"You know that entrance is locked, and you have the key . . ."

Dmitri suddenly reappeared in the drawing room. He had, of course, found the other entrance locked, and the key actually was in Fyodor Pavlovich's pocket. The windows of all the rooms were also closed so Grushenka could not have come in anywhere nor have darted out from anywhere.

"Hold him!" shrieked Fyodor Pavlovich, as soon as he saw Dmitri again. "He's been stealing money in my bedroom!" And tearing himself from Ivan he rushed again at Dmitri. But Dmitri raised both hands and suddenly clutched the old man by the two tufts of hair that remained on his temples, tugged at them, and flung him with a crash on the floor. He kicked him two or three times with his heel in the face. The old man moaned shrilly. Ivan Fyodorovich, though not so strong as Dmitri, threw his arms round him, and with all his might pulled him away. Alyosha helped him with his meager strength, holding his brother in front.

"Madman! You've killed him!" cried Ivan.

"Serves him right!" shouted Dmitri breathlessly. "If I haven't killed him, I'll come again and kill him. You can't protect him!"

"Dmitri! Go away at once!" cried Alyosha commandingly.

"Alexey! You tell me. It's only you I can believe: was she here just now, or not? I saw her myself; I saw how she slipped by the fence from the lane in this direction. I shouted, she ran away . . ."

"I swear to you, she hasn't been here, and no one expected her at all!"

"But I saw her. . . . So she must . . . I'll find out at once where she is. . . . Goodbye, Alexey! Not a word to Aesop about the money now. But go to Katerina Ivanovna at once and be sure to say, 'He bid me to bow to you, bid me to bow, bow! Expressly bows and bows out!' Describe the scene to her."

Meanwhile Ivan and Grigory had raised the old man and seated him in an armchair. His face was covered with blood, but he was conscious and listened greedily to Dmitri's cries. He still fancied that Grushenka really was somewhere in the house. Dmitri Fyodorovich looked at him with hatred as he went out.

"I don't repent shedding your blood!" he cried. "Beware, old man, beware of your dream, for I have my dream, too! I curse you, and disown you altogether . . ."

He ran out of the room.

"She's here. She must be here. Smerdyakov, Smerdyakov," the old man wheezed, scarcely audibly, beckoning to him with his finger.

"No, she's not here, you crazy old man!" Ivan shouted at him angrily. "Here, he's fainting! Water, a towel! get going, Smerdyakov!"

Smerdyakov ran for water. At last they got the old man undressed, and put him to bed. They wrapped a wet towel round his head. Exhausted by the brandy, by his violent emotion, and the blows he had received, he shut his eyes and fell asleep as soon as his head touched the pillow. Ivan Fyodorovich and Alyosha went back to the drawing room. Smerdyakov removed the fragments of the broken vase, while Grigory stood by the table looking gloomily at the floor.

"Shouldn't you put a wet bandage on your head and go to bed, too?" Alyosha said to him. "We'll look after him. My brother gave you a terrible blow . . . on the head."

"He dared me!" Grigory articulated gloomily and distinctly.

"He's 'dared' his father, not only you," observed Ivan Fyodorovich, twisting his mouth.

"I used to wash him in his tub . . . He's dared me," repeated Grigory. ·

"Devil take it, if I hadn't pulled him away perhaps he'd have murdered him. It wouldn't take much to do for Aesop, would it?" whispered Ivan Fyodorovich to Alyosha.

"God forbid!" cried Alyosha.

"Why should He forbid?" Ivan went on in the same whisper, malignantly twisting his face. "One viper will devour the other, and serve them both right, too!"

Alyosha shuddered.

"Of course I won't let him be murdered as I didn't just now. Stay here, Alyosha, I'll walk a bit in the yard; my head's begun to ache."

Alyosha went to his father's bedroom and sat by his bedside behind the screen for about an hour. The old man suddenly opened his eyes and gazed for a long while at Alyosha, evidently remembering and meditating. All at once his face betrayed extraordinary excitement.

"Alyosha," he whispered apprehensively, "where's Ivan?"

"In the yard. He's got a headache. He's guarding us."

"Give me that mirror. It stands over there. Give it to me."

Alyosha gave him a little round folding mirror which stood on the chest of drawers. The old man looked at himself in it; his nose was considerably swollen, and on the left side of his forehead there was a rather large crimson bruise.

"What does Ivan say? Alyosha, my dear, my only son, I'm afraid of Ivan. I'm more afraid of Ivan than the other. You're the only one I'm not afraid of. . . ."

"Don't be afraid of Ivan either. He is angry, but he'll defend you."

"Alyosha, and what of the other? He's run to Grushenka. My angel, tell me the truth, was she here just now or not?"

"No one has seen her. It was a mistake. She has not been here."

"You know Mitka wants to marry her, to marry her!"

"She won't marry him."

"She won't, she won't, she won't, she won't, she won't marry him for anything!"

The old man fairly fluttered with joy, as though nothing more comforting could have been said to him. In his delight he seized Alyosha's hand and pressed it warmly to his heart. Tears glittered in his eyes.

"That little icon of the Mother of God of which I was telling you just now," he said. "Take it home and keep it for yourself. And I'll let you go back to the monastery. . . . I was joking this morning, don't be angry with me. My head aches, Alyosha. . . . Alyosha, comfort my heart. Be an angel and tell me the truth!"

"You're still asking whether she has been here or not?" Alyosha said sorrowfully.

"No, no, no, I believe you, I'll tell you what it is: you go to Grushenka yourself, or see her somehow; make haste and ask her; see for yourself, which she means to choose, him or me? Eh? What? Can you?"

"If I see her I'll ask her," Alyosha muttered embarrassed.

"No, she won't tell you," the old man interrupted, "she's a rogue. She'll begin kissing you and say that it's you she wants. She's deceitful, she's shameless, a hussy, no, you mustn't go to her, you mustn't!"

"No, father, and it wouldn't be suitable, it wouldn't be right at all."

"Where was he sending you just now? He shouted 'Go' as he ran away."

"To Katerina Ivanovna."

"For money? To ask her for money?"

"No, not for money."

"He has no money; not a drop. I'll settle down for the night, and think things over, and you can go. Perhaps you'll meet her. . . . Only be sure to come to me tomorrow in the morning; be sure to. I have a little word to say to you tomorrow; will you come?"

"I'll come."

"When you come, pretend you've come of your own accord to ask after me. Don't tell any one I told you to. Don't say a word to Ivan."

"Very well."

"Good-bye, my angel, you stood up for me, just now, I shall never forget it. I have a little word to say to you tomorrow—but I must think about it."

"And how do you feel now?"

"I shall get up tomorrow and go out, perfectly well, perfectly well, perfectly well!"

Crossing the yard Alyosha found his brother Ivan sitting on the bench at the gateway: he was sitting writing something in pencil in his notebook. Alyosha told Ivan that their father had woken up, was conscious, and had let him go back to sleep at the monastery.

"Alyosha, I would be very glad to meet you tomorrow morning," said Ivan cordially, standing up. His cordiality was a complete surprise to Alyosha.

"I shall be at the Khokhlakovs' tomorrow," answered Alyosha, "I may be at Katerina Ivanovna's, too, if I don't find her now."

"But you're going to her now, anyway? For that 'bows and bows out,'" said Ivan smiling. Alyosha was disconcerted.

"I think I quite understand his exclamations just now, and part of what went before. Dmitri has asked you to go to her and say that he—well, in fact—bows out?"

"Brother! How will all this horror end between father and Dmitri?" exclaimed Alyosha.

"One can't tell for certain. Perhaps in nothing: it may all fizzle out. That woman is a beast. In any case we must keep the old man indoors and not let Dmitri in the house."

"Brother, let me ask one thing more: does any man have the right to look at other people and decide who of them is worthy of living, and who is more unworthy?"

"Why bring in the question of worth? The matter is most often decided in people's hearts not at all on the basis of worth, but on other, much more natural grounds. And as for rights, who has not the right to wish?"

"Not for another man's death?"

"What even if for another man's death? Why lie to oneself, when all people live this way and perhaps cannot live any other way? Are you referring to what I said just now—that 'the two vipers will devour each other'?

In that case let me ask you, do you think me like Dmitri capable of shedding Aesop's blood, murdering him, eh?"

"What are you saying, Ivan? Such an idea never crossed my mind. I don't think Dmitri is capable of it, either."

"Thanks, if only for that," smiled Ivan. "Be sure, I shall always defend him. But in my wishes I reserve myself full latitude in this case. Goodbye till tomorrow. Don't condemn me, and don't look on me as a villain," he added with a smile.

They shook hands warmly as they had never done before. Alyosha felt that his brother had taken the first step towards him, and that he had certainly done this with some definite motive.

Chapter X

Both Together

Alyosha left his father's house feeling even more exhausted and dejected in spirit than when he had entered it. His mind too seemed shattered and unhinged, while he felt that he was afraid to put together the disjointed fragments and form a general idea from all the agonizing and conflicting experiences of the day. He felt something bordering upon despair, which he had never known till then. Towering like a mountain above all the rest stood the fatal insoluble question: How would things end between his father and his brother Dmitri with this terrible woman? Now he had himself been a witness of it, he had been present and seen them face to face. Yet only his brother Dmitri could be made unhappy, terribly, completely unhappy: there was trouble awaiting him. It appeared too that there were other people concerned, far more so than Alyosha could have supposed before. There was something positively mysterious in it, too. His brother Ivan had made a step towards him, which was what Alyosha had been long desiring. Yet now he felt for some reason that he was frightened at it. And these women? Strange to say, earlier he had set out for Katerina Ivanovna's in the greatest embarrassment; now he felt nothing of the kind. On the contrary, he was hastening there as though expecting to find guidance from her. Yet to give her this message was obviously more difficult than before. The matter of the three thousand was decided irrevocably, and Dmitri, feeling himself dishonored and losing his last hope, might sink to any depth. He had, moreover, told him to describe to Katerina Ivanovna the scene which had just taken place with his father.

It was by now seven o'clock, and it was getting dark as Alyosha entered the very spacious and convenient house on Main Street occupied by Katerina Ivanovna. Alyosha knew that she lived with two aunts. One of them, a woman of little education, was that aunt of her half-sister Agatha Ivanovna who had looked after her in her father's house when she came from boarding school. The other aunt was a Moscow lady of style and consequence, though in straitened circumstances. It was said that they both gave way in everything to Katerina Ivanovna, and that she only kept them with her as chaperones. Katerina Ivanovna herself gave way to no one but her benefactress, the general's widow, who had been kept by illness in

Moscow, and to whom she was obliged to write twice a week a full account of all her doings.

When Alyosha entered the hall and asked the maid who opened the door to him to take his name up, it was evident that they were already aware of his arrival. Possibly he had been noticed from the window. At least, Alyosha heard a noise, caught the sound of flying footsteps and rustling skirts. Two or three women perhaps had run out of the room. Alyosha thought it strange that his arrival should cause such excitement. He was conducted however to the drawing room at once. It was a large room, elegantly and amply furnished, not at all in provincial style. There were many sofas, lounges, settees, big and little tables. There were pictures on the walls, vases and lamps on the tables, masses of flowers, and even an aquarium in the window. It was twilight and rather dark. Alyosha made out a silk mantle thrown down on the sofa, where people had evidently just been sitting; and on a table in front of the sofa were two unfinished cups of chocolate, cakes, a crystal dish with Malaga raisins, and another with sweets. Alyosha saw that he had interrupted visitors, and frowned. But at that instant the portière was raised, and with rapid, hurrying footsteps Katerina Ivanovna came in, holding out both hands to Alyosha with a radiant smile of delight. At the same instant a servant brought in two lighted candles and set them on the table.

"Thank God, at last you have come too! All day I've been praying to God for no one but you! Sit down."

Alyosha had been struck by Katerina Ivanovna's beauty when, three weeks before, his brother Dmitri had first brought him, at Katerina Ivanovna's special request, to be introduced to her. There had been no conversation between them at that interview, however. Supposing Alyosha to be very shy, Katerina Ivanovna had talked all the time to Dmitri Fyodorovich to spare him. Alyosha had been silent, but he had seen a great deal very clearly. He was struck by the imperiousness, proud ease, and self-confidence, of the haughty girl. And all that was certain, Alyosha felt that he was not exaggerating it. He thought her great glowing black eyes were very fine, especially with her pale, even rather sallow, longish face. But in those eyes and in the lines of her exquisite lips there was something with which his brother might well be passionately in love, but which perhaps could not be loved for long. He expressed this thought almost plainly to Dmitri when, after the visit, his brother besought and insisted that he should not conceal his impressions on seeing his betrothed.

"You'll be happy with her, but perhaps—not tranquilly happy."

"Quite so, brother. Such people remain always the same. They don't yield to fate. So you think I won't love her forever."

"No, perhaps you will love her forever, but perhaps you won't always be happy with her . . ."

Alyosha had given his opinion at the time, blushing, and angry with himself for having yielded to his brother's entreaties and put such "foolish" ideas into words. For his opinion had struck him as awfully foolish immediately after he had uttered it. He felt ashamed too of having given so confident an opinion about a woman. It was with the more amazement that he felt now, at the first glance at Katerina Ivanovna as she ran in to him, that he had perhaps been utterly mistaken. This time her face was beaming with spontaneous good-natured kindliness, and direct warm-hearted sincerity.

The "pride and haughtiness," which had struck Alyosha so much before, was only betrayed now in a frank, generous energy and a sort of clear strong faith in herself. Alyosha realized at the first glance, at the first word, that all the tragedy of her position in relation to the man she loved so dearly was no secret to her; that she perhaps already knew everything, positively everything. And yet, in spite of that, there was such brightness in her face, such faith in the future. Alyosha felt at once that he had gravely wronged her in his thoughts. He was conquered and captivated immediately. Besides all this, he noticed at her first words that she was very excited, an excitement perhaps quite exceptional and almost approaching ecstasy.

"I was so eager to see you, because I can learn from you the whole truth—from you and no one else."

"I have come . . ." muttered Alyosha confusedly, "I . . . he sent me."

"Ah, he sent you, I foresaw that. Now I know everything, everything!" cried Katerina Ivanovna, her eyes flashing. "Wait a moment, Alexey Fyodorovich, I'll tell you why I've been so longing to see you. You see, I know perhaps far more than you do yourself, and there's no need for you to tell me anything. I'll tell you what I want from you. I want to know your own last impression of him. I want you to tell me most directly, plainly, coarsely even (oh, as coarsely as you like!), what you thought of him just now and of his position after your meeting with him today. That will perhaps be better than if I had a personal explanation with him, as he does not want to come to me. Do you understand what I want from you? Now, tell me simply, tell me every word of the message he sent you with (I knew he would send you)."

"He told me to bow to you—and to say that he would never come again—but to bow to you."

"To bow? Was that what he said—his own expression?"

"Yes."

"Accidentally perhaps he made a mistake in the word, perhaps he did not use the right word?"

"No; he told me precisely to repeat that word, 'bows.' He begged me two or three times not to forget to say so."

Katerina Ivanovna flushed hotly.

"Help me now, Alexey Fyodorovich, now I really need your help: I'll tell you what I think, and you must simply say whether it's right or not. Listen, if he had said to bow to me in passing, without insisting on your repeating the words, without emphasizing them, that would be the end of everything! But if he particularly insisted on those words, if he particularly told you not to forget to repeat that *bow* to me, then perhaps he was excited, beside himself? He had made his decision and was frightened at it! He wasn't walking away from me with a resolute step, but leaping headlong. The emphasis on that phrase may have been simply bravado . . ."

"Yes, yes!" cried Alyosha warmly. "I believe that is it."

"And, if so, he's not altogether lost. He is only in despair, but now I can still save him. Wait! Did he not tell you anything about money—about three thousand rubles?"

"He not only spoke about it, but that, perhaps, is crushing him more than anything. He said he had lost his honor and that nothing matters now," Alyosha answered warmly, feeling with all his heart that hope was flowing into his heart and believing that there really might be a way of escape and salvation for his brother. "But do you really know about the money?" he added, and suddenly broke off.

"I've known about it a long time and for certain. I telegraphed to Moscow to inquire, and heard long ago that the money had not arrived. He hadn't sent the money, but I said nothing. Last week I learnt that he was still in need of money. My only object in all this was that he should know to whom to turn, and who was his true friend. No, he won't recognize that I am his truest friend; he won't know me, and looks on me merely as a woman. I've been tormented all week, trying to think how to prevent him from being ashamed to face me because he spent that three thousand. Let him feel ashamed of himself, let him be ashamed of other people's knowing, but not of my knowing. He can tell God everything without shame. Why is it he still does not understand how much I am ready to bear for his sake? Why, why doesn't he know me? How dare he not know me after all that has happened? I want to save him forever. Let him forget me as his betrothed. And here he fears that he is dishonored in my eyes. Why, he wasn't afraid to be open with you, Alexey Fyodorovich. How is it that I don't deserve the same?"

The last words she uttered in tears. Tears gushed from her eyes.

"I must tell you," Alyosha began, his voice trembling too, "what happened just now between him and my father." And he described the whole scene, how Dmitri had sent him to get the money, how he had broken in, knocked his father down, and after that had again specially and emphatically begged him to "bow to her and bow out." "He went to that woman," Alyosha added softly.

"And do you suppose that I can't put up with that woman? Does he think I can't? But he won't marry her," she suddenly laughed nervously. "Could such a passion burn forever in a Karamazov? It's passion, not love. He won't marry her because she won't marry him . . ." Again Katerina Ivanovna suddenly laughed strangely.

"He may marry her," said Alyosha mournfully, looking down.

"He won't marry her, I tell you. That girl is an angel, do you know that? Do you know that?" Katerina Ivanovna exclaimed suddenly with extraordinary warmth. "She is one of the most fantastic of fantastic creations. I know how bewitching she is, but I know too that she is kind, firm and noble. Why do you look at me like that, Alexey Fyodorovich? Perhaps you are wondering at my words, perhaps you don't believe me? Agrafena Alexandrovna, my angel!" she cried suddenly to someone, peeping into the next room, "come in to us. This is a friend. This is Alyosha. He knows all about our affairs. Show yourself to him."

"I've only been waiting behind the curtain for you to call me," said a soft, one might even say sugary, feminine voice.

The portière was raised, and . . . Grushenka herself, smiling and beaming, came up to the table. Something inside Alyosha seemed to flinch. He fixed his eyes on her and could not take them off. Here she was, that awful woman, the "beast," as his brother Ivan had called her half an hour before. And yet one would have thought the being standing before him most simple and ordinary, a good-natured, kind woman, handsome certainly, but so like other handsome "ordinary" women! It is true she was very, very good looking with that Russian beauty so passionately loved by many men. She was a rather tall woman, though a little shorter than Katerina Ivanovna, who was exceptionally tall. She had a full figure, with soft, as it were, noiseless, movements, softened to a peculiar over-sweetness, like her voice. She moved, not like Katerina Ivanovna, with a vigorous, bold step, but noiselessly. Her feet made absolutely no sound on the floor. She sank softly into a low chair, softly rustling her sumptuous black silk dress, and delicately nestling her milk-white neck and broad shoulders in a costly black cashmere shawl. She was twenty-two years old, and her face looked exactly that age. She was very white in the face, with a pale pink tint on her cheeks. The modeling of her face might be said to be too broad, and the lower jaw was set a trifle forward. Her upper lip was thin, but the slightly prominent lower lip was at least twice as full, and looked swollen somehow. But her magnificent, abundant dark brown hair, her sable-colored eyebrows and charming gray-blue eyes with their long lashes would have made the most indifferent person, meeting her casually in a crowd in the street, stop at the sight of her face and remember it long after. What struck Alyosha most in that face was its expression of childlike good nature. There was a childlike look in her eyes, a look of childish delight. She came up to the table, beaming with delight and seeming to expect something with childish, impatient, and confiding curiosity. The light in her eyes gladdened the soul—Alyosha felt that. There was something else in her which he could not understand, or would not have been able to define, and which yet perhaps unconsciously affected him. It was that softness, that delicacy of her bodily movements, that catlike noiselessness. Yet it was a vigorous, ample body. Under the shawl could be seen full broad shoulders, a high, still quite girlish bosom. Her figure suggested the lines of the Venus de Milo, though already in somewhat exaggerated proportions. That could be divined. Connoisseurs of Russian beauty could have foretold with certainty that this fresh, still youthful, beauty would lose its harmony by the age of thirty, would "spread"; that the face would become puffy, and that wrinkles would very soon appear upon her forehead and round the eyes; the complexion would grow coarse and red perhaps—in fact, that it was the beauty of the moment, the fleeting beauty which is so often met with in Russian women. Alyosha, of course, did not think of this; but though he was fascinated, yet he wondered with an unpleasant sensation, and as it were regretfully, why she drawled in that way and could not speak naturally. She did so evidently feeling there was a charm in the exaggerated, honeyed modulation of the syllables. It was, of course, only a bad habit of bad taste that showed poor education and a false idea of good manners. And yet this intonation and manner of speaking impressed Alyosha as almost incredibly incongruous with the childishly simple and happy expression of her face, the soft, babyish joy in her eyes! Katerina Ivanovna at once made her sit down in an armchair facing Alyosha, and ecstatically kissed her several times on her smiling lips. She seemed to be quite in love with her.

"This is the first time we've met, Alexey Fyodorovich," she said rapturously. "I wanted to know her, to see her. I wanted to go to her, but I'd no sooner expressed the wish than she came to me. I knew we should settle everything together—everything! My heart told me so—I was begged not to take the step, but I foresaw it would be a way out of the difficulty, and I was not mistaken. Grushenka has explained everything to me, told me all she means to do. She flew here like an angel of goodness and brought us peace and joy."

"You did not disdain me, sweet, excellent young lady," drawled Grushenka in her singsong voice, still with the same charming smile of delight.

"Don't dare to speak to me like that, you sorceress, you witch! Disdain you! Here I must kiss your lower lip once more. It looks as though it were swollen, and now it will be more so, and more and more. . . . Look how she laughs, Alexey Fyodorovich! It does one's heart good to see the angel . . ."

Alyosha flushed, and faint, imperceptible shivers kept running down him.

"You make so much of me, dear young lady, and perhaps I am not at all worthy of your kindness."

"Not worthy! She's not worthy of it!" Katerina Ivanovna cried again with the same warmth. "You know, Alexey Fyodorovich, we're fanciful, we're self-willed, but proudest of the proud in our little heart. We're noble, we're generous, Alexey Fyodorovich, let me tell you. We have only been unfortunate. We were too ready to make every sacrifice for an unworthy, perhaps, or fickle man. There was one man—one, an officer too, we loved him, we sacrificed everything to him. That was long ago, five years ago, and he has forgotten us, he has married. Now he is a widower, he has written, he is coming here, and do you know, we've loved him, none but him, all this time, and we've loved him all our life! He will come, and Grushenka will be happy again. For the last five years she's been wretched. But who can reproach her, who can boast of her favor? Only that bedridden old merchant, but he is more like our father, our friend, our protector. He found us then in despair, in agony, deserted by the man we loved. She was ready to drown herself then, but the old merchant saved her—saved her!"

"You defend me very kindly, dear young lady, you are in a great hurry about everything," Grushenka drawled again.

"Defend you? Is it for me to defend you, should I dare to defend you? Grushenka, angel, give me your hand. Look at that plump, soft, charming little hand, Alexey Fyodorovich; do you see it, it has brought me happiness and has resurrected me, and I'm going to kiss it, outside and inside, here, here, and here!" And three times she kissed the certainly charming, though rather fat, hand of Grushenka in a sort of rapture. She held out her hand with a charming musical, nervous little laugh, watched the "sweet young lady," and obviously liked having her hand kissed.

"Perhaps there's rather too much ecstasy," thought Alyosha. He blushed. He felt a peculiar uneasiness at heart the whole time.

"You won't make me blush, dear young lady, kissing my hand like this before Alexey Fyodorovich."

"Do you think I meant to make you blush?" said Katerina Ivanovna, somewhat surprised. "Ah, my dear, how little you understand me!"

"Yes, and you too perhaps quite misunderstand me, dear young lady, maybe I'm not so good as I seem to you. I have a bad heart, I am willful. I fascinated poor Dmitri Fyodorovich that day simply for fun."

"But now you'll save him. You've given me your word. You'll explain it all to him. You'll break it to him that you have long loved another man, who is now offering you his hand . . ."

"Oh, no, I didn't give you my word to do that. It was you kept talking about that, but I didn't give you my word."

"Then I didn't quite understand you," said Katerina Ivanovna slowly, turning a little pale. "You promised . . ."

"Oh no, angel lady, I've promised nothing." Grushenka interrupted softly and evenly, still with the same cheerful and innocent expression. "You see at once, dear young lady, what a willful wretch I am compared with you. If I want to do a thing I do it. I may have made you some promise just now. But now again I'm thinking: I may take to Mitya again. I liked him very much once—liked him for almost a whole hour. Now maybe I shall go and tell him to stay with me from this day forward. You see, I'm so changeable."

"Just now you said . . . something quite different . . ." Katerina Ivanovna whispered faintly.

"Ah, just now! But, you know, I'm such a soft-hearted, silly creature. Only think what he's gone through on my account! What if when I go home I feel sorry for him? What then?"

"I never expected . . ."

"Ah, young lady, how good and generous you are compared with me. Now perhaps you'll stop loving such a fool as me, now you know my character. Give me your sweet little hand, angel lady," she said tenderly, and with a sort of reverence took Katerina Ivanovna's hand.

"Here, dear young lady, I'll take your hand and kiss it as you did mine. You kissed mine three times, but I ought to kiss yours three hundred times to be even with you. Well, but let that pass. And then it shall be as God wills. Perhaps I shall be your slave entirely and want to do your bidding like a slave. Let it be as God wills, without any agreements and promises. What a sweet hand, what a sweet hand you have, what a hand! You sweet young lady, you incredible beauty!"

She slowly raised the hand, to her lips, with the strange object indeed of "being even" with her in kisses. Katerina Ivanovna did not take her hand away. She listened with timid hope to the last words, though Grushenka's promise to do her bidding like a slave was very strangely expressed. She looked intently into her eyes; she still saw in those eyes the same simple-hearted, confiding expression, the same bright gaiety. "She's perhaps too naïve," thought Katerina Ivanovna, with a gleam of hope. Grushenka meanwhile seemed enthusiastic over the "sweet hand." She raised it deliberately to her lips. But she held it for two or three moments near her lips, as though reconsidering something.

"Do you know, angel lady," she suddenly drawled in an even more soft and sugary voice, "do you know, after all, I think I won't kiss your hand?" And she laughed a little merry laugh.

"As you please. . . . What's the matter with you?" said Katerina Ivanovna, starting suddenly.

"So that you may be left to remember that you kissed my hand, but I didn't kiss yours." There was a sudden gleam in her eyes. She looked with awful intentness at Katerina Ivanovna.

"Insolent!" cried Katerina Ivanovna, as though suddenly grasping something. She flushed all over and leaped up from her seat. Grushenka too got up, but without haste.

"So I shall tell Mitya how you kissed my hand, but I didn't kiss yours at all. And how he will laugh!"

"Slut! Go away!"

"Ah, for shame, young lady! Ah, for shame! That's unbecoming for you, dear young lady, a word like that."

"Go away! You creature for sale!" screamed Katerina Ivanovna. Every feature was working in her utterly distorted face.

"For sale indeed. You used to visit gentlemen in the dusk for money once, you brought your beauty for sale, you see, I know."

Katerina Ivanovna shrieked, and would have rushed at her, but Alyosha held her with all his strength.

"Not a step, not a word! Don't speak, don't answer her. She'll go away—she'll go at once."

At that instant Katerina Ivanovna's two aunts ran in at her cry, and with them a maidservant. All hurried to her.

"I will go away," said Grushenka, taking up her mantle from the sofa. "Alyosha, darling, see me home!"

"Go away—go away, make haste!" cried Alyosha, clasping his hands imploringly.

"Dear little Alyoshenka, see me home! I've got a pretty little story to tell you on the way. I got up this scene for your benefit, Alyoshenka. See me home, dear, you'll be glad of it afterwards."

Alyosha turned away, wringing his hands. Grushenka ran out of the house, laughing musically.

Katerina Ivanovna went into a fit of hysterics. She sobbed, and was shaken with convulsions. Everyone fussed round her.

"I warned you," said the elder of her aunts. "I tried to prevent your doing this. You're too impulsive. How could you do such a thing? You don't know these creatures, and they say she's worse than any of them. You are too self-willed."

"She's a tiger!" yelled Katerina Ivanovna. "Why did you hold me, Alexey Fyodorovich! I'd have beaten her—beaten her!"

She could not control herself before Alyosha; perhaps she did not care to, indeed.

"She ought to be flogged in public on a scaffold!"

Alyosha withdrew towards the door.

"But, my God!" cried Katerina Ivanovna, clasping her hands. "He! He! He could be so dishonorable, so inhuman! Why, he told that creature what happened on that fatal, accursed day! 'You brought your beauty for sale, dear young lady.' She knows it! Your brother's a scoundrel, Alexey Fyodorovich."

Alyosha wanted to say something, but he couldn't find a word. His heart ached.

"Go away, Alexey Fyodorovich! It's shameful, it's awful for me! Tomorrow, I beg you on my knees, come tomorrow. Don't condemn me. Forgive me. I don't know what I shall do with myself now!"

Alyosha walked out into the street reeling. He could have wept as she did. Suddenly he was overtaken by the maid.

"The young lady forgot to give you this letter from Madame Khokhlakova; it's been left with us since dinnertime."

Alyosha took the little pink envelope mechanically and put it, almost unconsciously, into his pocket.

Chapter XI

One More Ruined Reputation

It was not much more than half a mile from the town to the monastery. Alyosha walked quickly along the road, at that hour deserted. It was almost night, and too dark to see anything clearly thirty paces ahead. There was a crossroad half way. A figure came into sight under a solitary willow at the crossroad. As soon as Alyosha reached the crossroad the figure moved out and rushed at him, shouting savagely:

"Your money or your life!"

"So it's you, Mitya," cried Alyosha, in surprise, violently startled however.

"Ha, ha, ha! You didn't expect me? I wondered where to wait for you. By her house? There are three ways from it, and I might have missed you. At last I thought of waiting here, for you had to pass here, there's no other way to the monastery. Come, tell me the truth. Crush me like a cockroach. But what's the matter?"

"Nothing, brother . . . it's the fright you gave me. Oh, Dmitri! Father's blood just now . . ." Alyosha began to cry, he had been on the verge of tears for a long time, and now something seemed to snap in his soul. "You almost killed him . . . cursed him . . . and now . . . here . . . you're making jokes . . . Your money or your life!"

"Well, what of that? It's not seemly—is that it? Not suitable in my position?"

"No . . . I only . . ."

"Wait. Look at the night: You see what a gloomy night, what clouds, what a wind has risen! I hid here under the willow waiting for you. And as God's above, I suddenly thought, why go on in misery any longer, what is there to wait for? Here I have a willow, a handkerchief, a shirt, I can twist them into a rope in a minute, and suspenders besides, and why go on burdening the earth, dishonoring it with my vile presence. And then I heard you coming—Heavens, it was as though something flew down to me suddenly. So there is a man, then, whom I love. Here he is, that little man,[3] my dear little brother, whom I love more than anyone in the world, the only one I love in the world. And I loved you so much, so much at that moment that I thought, 'I'll fall on his neck at once.' Then a stupid idea struck me, to have a joke with you and scare you. I shouted, like a fool, 'your money!' Forgive my foolery—it was only nonsense, and there's nothing unseemly in my soul. . . . Damn it all, tell me what's happened. What did she say? Strike me, crush me, don't spare me! Was she furious?"

"No, not that. . . . There was nothing like that, Mitya. There . . . I found them both there."

"Both? Whom?"

"Grushenka at Katerina Ivanovna's."

Dmitri Fyodorovich was struck dumb.

"Impossible!" he cried. "You're raving! Grushenka with her?"

---

3. The narrator has described Alyosha as tall. "Little man" is an epithet for Saint Alexey in folk legends.

Alyosha described all that had happened from the moment he went into Katerina Ivanovna's. He was ten minutes telling his story. He can't be said to have told it fluently and consecutively, but he seemed to make it clear, not omitting any word or action of significance, and vividly describing, often in one word, his own sensations. His brother Dmitri listened in silence, gazing at him with a terrible fixed stare, but it was clear to Alyosha that he understood it all, and had grasped every point. But as the story went on, his face became not merely gloomy, but menacing. He scowled, he clenched his teeth, and his fixed stare became still more rigid, more concentrated, more terrible, when suddenly, with incredible rapidity, his wrathful, savage face changed, his tightly compressed lips parted, and Dmitri Fyodorovich broke into uncontrolled, spontaneous laughter. He literally shook with laughter, for a long time he could not speak.

"So she wouldn't kiss her hand! So she didn't kiss it; so she ran away!" he kept exclaiming with some kind of hysterical delight; insolent delight it might have been called, if this delight had not been so spontaneous. "So the other one cried that she's a tiger! And a tiger she is! And that she ought to be on the scaffold? Yes, yes, she should, should, I myself think so, she should have been a long time ago! It's like this, brother, let her be punished, but I must get better first. I understand the queen of impudence. That's her all over! You saw her all over in that hand-kissing, the infernal woman! She's the queen of all infernal women you can imagine in the world! She's magnificent in her own line! So she ran home? I'll go—ah— I'll run to her! Alyosha, don't blame me, I agree that throttling is too good for her . . ."

"But Katerina Ivanovna!" exclaimed Alyosha sorrowfully.

"I see her, too, I see right through her, as I've never done before! It's a regular discovery of the four continents of the world, that is, of the five! What a thing to do! That's just like Katenka, the young lady from the Institute, who was not afraid to face a coarse, unmannerly officer and risk a deadly insult on a generous impulse to save her father! But the pride, the recklessness, the defiance of fate, the unbounded defiance! You say that aunt tried to stop her? That aunt, you know, is overbearing, herself. She's the sister of the general's widow in Moscow, and even more stuck-up than she. But her husband was caught stealing government money. He lost everything, his estate and all, and the proud wife had to lower her colors, and hasn't raised them since. So she tried to prevent Katya, but she wouldn't listen to her! She thinks she can overcome everything, that everything will give way to her. She thought she could bewitch Grushenka if she liked, and she believed it herself; she plays a part to herself, and whose fault is it? Do you think she kissed Grushenka's hand first, on purpose, with a motive? No, she really was fascinated by Grushenka, that's to say, not by Grushenka, but by her own dream, her own delusion—because it was *her* dream, *her* delusion! Alyosha, darling, how did you escape from them, those women? Did you pick up your cassock and run? Ha, ha, ha!"

"Brother, you don't seem to have noticed how you've insulted Katerina Ivanovna by telling Grushenka about that day, and she flung it in her face just now that she had 'gone to gentlemen in secret to sell her beauty!' Brother, what could be worse than that insult?" What worried Alyosha more than anything was that his brother appeared pleased at Katerina Ivanovna's humiliation, though, of course, it could not be so.

"Bah!" Dmitri Fyodorovich frowned fiercely, and struck his forehead with his hand. He only now realized it, though Alyosha had just told him of the insult, and Katerina Ivanovna's cry: "Your brother is a scoundrel!"

"Yes, perhaps, I really did tell Grushenka about that 'fatal day,' as Katya calls it. Yes, I did tell her, I remember! It was that time at Mokroe. I was drunk, the gypsies were singing. . . . But I was sobbing. I was sobbing then, kneeling and praying to Katya's image,[4] and Grushenka understood it. She understood it all then. I remember, she cried herself. . . . Damn it all! But it's bound to be so now. . . . Then she cried, but now 'the dagger in the heart'! That's how women are."

He looked down and sank into thought.

"Yes, I am a scoundrel, a thorough scoundrel!" he said suddenly, in a gloomy voice. "It doesn't matter whether I cried or not, I'm a scoundrel! Tell her I accept the name, if that's any comfort. Come, that's enough. Good-bye. It's no use talking! It's not amusing. You go your way and I mine. And I don't want to see you again except as a last resource. Good-bye, Alexey!" He warmly pressed Alyosha's hand, and still looking down, without raising his head, as though tearing himself away, turned rapidly towards the town. Alyosha looked after him, unable to believe he would go away so abruptly.

"Wait, Alexey, one more admission to you alone!" cried Dmitri Fyodorovich, suddenly turning back. "Look at me. Look at me well. You see here, here—there's terrible disgrace in store for me." (As he said "here," Dmitri Fyodorovich struck his chest with his fist with a strange air, as though the dishonor lay precisely on his chest, in some spot, in a pocket, perhaps, or hanging round his neck.) "You know me now, a scoundrel, an avowed scoundrel, but let me tell you that I've never done anything before and never shall again, anything that can compare in baseness with the dishonor which I bear now at this very minute on my breast, here, here, which will come to pass, though I'm perfectly free to stop it. I can stop it or carry it through, note that. Well, let me tell you, I shall carry it through. I shall not stop it. I told you everything just now, but I didn't tell you this, because even I am not brazen enough for it. I can still stop; if I do, I can give back the full half of my lost honor tomorrow. But I won't stop. I will carry out my base plan, and you can bear witness that I told you so beforehand. Darkness and destruction! No need to explain. You'll find out in due time. The filthy back alley and the infernal woman. Good-bye. Don't pray for me, I'm not worth it. And there's no need, no need at all . . . I don't need it! Away!"

And he suddenly retreated, this time finally. Alyosha went toward the monastery. "What, why will I never see him again, what is he saying?" he wondered wildly. "Tomorrow I will be sure to see him and find him, I will make a point of finding him, what is he talking about?"

He went around the monastery and passed through the pine woods straight to the hermitage. The door was opened to him, though no one was admitted at that hour. There was a tremor in his heart as he went into Father Zosima's cell. "Why, why, had he gone forth? Why had he sent

---

4. The term "image" is used here to translate the Russian word *obraz*, which means both "image" and "icon" in the specifically religious sense.

him into the world? Here was peace. Here was holiness. But there there was confusion, there was gloom in which one lost one's way and went astray at once. . . ."

In the cell he found the novice Porfiry and Father Païssy, who came every hour to inquire after Father Zosima. Alyosha learned with alarm that he was getting worse and worse. Even his usual discourse with the brothers could not take place that day. As a rule every evening after service the monks flocked into Father Zosima's cell, and all confessed aloud their sins of the day, their sinful thoughts and temptations, even their disputes, if there had been any. Some confessed kneeling. The elder absolved, reconciled, exhorted, imposed penance, blessed, and dismissed them. It was against this general "confession" that the opponents of "elders" protested, maintaining that it was a profanation of the sacrament of confession, almost a sacrilege, though this was quite a different thing. They even represented to the diocesan authorities that such confessions attained no good object, but actually to a large extent led to sin and temptation. Many of the brothers disliked going to the elder, and went against their own will because everyone went, and for fear they should be accused of pride and rebellious ideas. People said that some of the monks agreed beforehand, saying, "I'll confess I lost my temper with you this morning, and you confirm it," simply in order to have something to say. Alyosha knew that this actually happened sometimes. He knew, too, that there were among the monks some who deeply resented the fact that letters from relations were habitually taken to the elder, to be opened and read by him before those to whom they were addressed.

It was assumed, of course, that all this was done freely, and in good faith, by way of voluntary submission and salutary guidance. But, in fact, there was sometimes no little insincerity, and much that was false and strained in this practice. Yet the older and more experienced of the monks adhered to their opinion, arguing that "for those who have come within these walls sincerely seeking salvation, such obedience and sacrifice will certainly be salutary and of great benefit; those, on the other hand, who find it irksome, and repine, are no true monks, and have made a mistake in entering the monastery—their proper place is in the world. Even in the temple one cannot be safe from sin and the devil. So it was no good taking it too much into account."

"He is weaker, a drowsiness has come over him," Father Païssy whispered to Alyosha, as he blessed him. "It's difficult to rouse him. And he must not be roused. He woke up for five minutes, sent his blessing to the brothers, and begged their prayers for him at night. He intends to take the sacrament again in the morning. He remembered you, Alexey. He asked whether you had gone away, and was told that you were in the town. 'I blessed him for that work,' he said, 'his place is there, not here, for awhile.' Those were his words about you. He remembered you lovingly, with anxiety; do you understand how he honored you? But how is it that he has decided that you shall spend some time in the world? He must have foreseen something in your destiny! Understand, Alexey, that if you return to the world, it must be to do the duty laid upon you by your elder, and not for frivolous vanity and worldly pleasures."

Father Païssy went out. Alyosha had no doubt that Father Zosima was dying, though he might live another day or two. Alyosha firmly and

ardently resolved that in spite of his promises to his father, the Khokhlakovs, and Katerina Ivanovna, he would not leave the monastery next day,
but would remain with his elder to the end. His heart glowed with love,
and he reproached himself bitterly for having been able for one instant
to forget him whom he had left in the monastery on his deathbed, and
whom he honored above everyone in the world. He went into Father
Zosima's bedroom, knelt down, and bowed to the ground before the elder,
who slept quietly without stirring, with regular, hardly audible breathing
and a peaceful face.

Alyosha returned to the other room, where Father Zosima had received
his guests in the morning. Taking off only his boots, he lay down on the
hard, narrow, leather sofa, which he had long used as a bed, bringing
nothing but a pillow. The mattress, about which his father had shouted to
him that morning, he had long forgotten to lay on. He took off his cassock, which he used as a blanket. But before going to bed, he fell on his
knees and prayed a long time. In his fervent prayer he did not beseech
God to lighten his darkness but only thirsted for the joyous emotion which
always visited his soul after the praise and adoration of which his evening
prayer usually consisted. That joy always brought him light untroubled
sleep. As he was praying, he suddenly felt in his pocket the little pink note
the servant had handed him as he left Katerina Ivanovna's. He was disturbed, but finished his prayer. Then, after some hesitation, he opened the
envelope. In it was a letter to him, signed by Lise, the young daughter of
Madame Khokhlakova, who had laughed at him before the elder in the
morning.[5]

"Alexey Fyodorovich," she wrote, "I am writing to you without anyone's
knowledge, even mamma's, and I know how wrong it is. But I cannot live
without telling you the feeling that has sprung up in my heart, and this
no one but us two must know for a time. But how am I to say what I want
so much to tell you? Paper, they say, does not blush, but I assure you it's
not true and that it's blushing just as I am now, all over. Dear Alyosha, I
love you, I've loved you from my childhood, since our Moscow days, when
you were very different from what you are now, and I shall love you all my
life. My heart has chosen you, to unite our lives, and pass them together
till our old age. Of course, on condition that you will leave the monastery.
As for our age we will wait for the time fixed by the law. By that time I
shall certainly be quite strong, I shall be walking and dancing. There can
be no doubt of that.

"You see how I've thought of everything. There's only one thing I can't
imagine: what you'll think of me when you read this? I'm always laughing
and being naughty. I made you angry this morning, but I assure you before
I took up my pen, I prayed before the image of the Mother of God, and
now I'm praying, and almost crying.

"My secret is in your hands. When you come tomorrow, I don't know
how I shall look at you. Ah, Alexey Fyodorovich, what if I can't restrain
myself like a silly and laugh when I look at you as I did today? You'll think
I'm a nasty girl making fun of you, and you won't believe my letter. And so

---

5. Liza's letter to Alyosha has a clear literary prototype: it strongly resembles a letter written by
the young country girl Tatiana to Onegin, a much more sophisticated city man, in Pushkin's
Eugene Onegin.

I beg you, dear one, if you've any pity for me, when you come tomorrow, don't look me straight in the face, for if I meet your eyes, it will be sure to make me laugh, especially, as you'll be in that long gown. I feel cold all over when I think of it, so when you come, don't look at me at all for a time, look at mamma or at the window. . . .

"Here I've written you a love letter. Oh, dear, what have I done? Alyosha, don't despise me, and if I've done something very horrid and wounded you, forgive me. Now the secret of my reputation, ruined perhaps forever, is in your hands.

"I shall certainly cry today. Good-bye till our meeting, our *awful* meeting.—LISE

"P.S.—Alyosha! You must, must, must come!—LISE."

Alyosha read the note in amazement, read it through twice, thought a little, and suddenly laughed a soft, sweet laugh. He started; that laugh seemed to him sinful. But a minute later he laughed again just as softly and happily. He slowly replaced the note in the little envelope, crossed himself and lay down. The agitation in his soul suddenly passed. "God have mercy upon all of them, have all these unhappy and turbulent souls in Thy keeping, and set them in the right path. All ways are Thine. Save them according to Thy wisdom. Thou art love. Thou wilt send joy to all!" Alyosha murmured, crossing himself, and falling into peaceful sleep.

Part Two

Book Four

LACERATIONS

Chapter I

Father Ferapont

Alyosha was roused early, before daybreak. Father Zosima woke up feeling very weak, though he wanted to get out of bed and sit up in a chair. His mind was quite clear; his face looked very tired, yet bright and almost joyful. It wore an expression of gaiety, kindness and cordiality. "Maybe I shall not live through the coming day," he said to Alyosha. Then he desired to confess and take the communion at once. He always confessed to Father Païssy. After the two sacraments, the service of extreme unction followed.[1] The hieromonks assembled and the cell was gradually filled up by the inmates of the hermitage. Meantime it was daylight. People began coming from the monastery. After the service was over the elder desired to kiss and take leave of everyone. As the cell was so small the earlier visitors withdrew to make room for others. Alyosha stood beside the elder, who was seated again in his armchair. He talked as much as he could. Though his voice was weak, it was fairly steady. "I've been teaching you so many years, and therefore I've been talking aloud so many years, that I've got into the habit of talking, and so much so that it's almost more difficult for me to hold my tongue than to talk, even now, in spite of my weakness, dear fathers and brothers," he jested, looking with emotion at the group round him. Alyosha remembered afterwards something of what he said to them. But though he spoke out distinctly and his voice was fairly steady, his speech was somewhat disconnected. He spoke of many things, he seemed anxious before the moment of death to say everything he had not said in his life, and not simply for the sake of instructing them, but as though thirsting to share with all men and all creation his joy and ecstasy, and once more in his life to open his whole heart . . .

"Love one another, Fathers," said Father Zosima, as far as Alyosha could remember afterwards. "Love God's people. Because we have come here and shut ourselves within these walls, we are no holier than those that are outside, but on the contrary, from the very fact of coming here, each of us has confessed to himself that he is worse than others, than all men on earth. . . . And the longer the monk lives in his seclusion, the more keenly he must recognize that. Else he would have had no reason to come here.

---

1. Extreme unction, one of the seven Christian sacraments, is healing in which specific parts of the body are anointed with oil; also called Last Rites and the Anointing of the Sick.

When he realizes that he is not only worse than others, but that he is responsible to all men for all and everything, for all human sins, general and individual, only then the aim of our seclusion is attained. For know, dear ones, that every one of us is undoubtedly responsible for all men and everything on earth, not merely through the general sinfulness of creation, but each one personally for all mankind and every individual man. This knowledge is the crown of life for the monk and for every man. For monks are not a special sort of men, but only what all men ought to be. Only through that knowledge, our heart grows soft with infinite, universal, inexhaustible love. Then every one of you will have the power to win over the whole world by love and to wash away the sins of the world with your tears. . . . Each of you keep watch over your heart and confess your sins to yourself unceasingly. Be not afraid of your sins, even when perceiving them, if only there be penitence, but make no conditions with God. Again I say, be not proud. Be proud neither to the little nor to the great. Hate not those who reject you, who insult you, who abuse and slander you. Hate not the atheists, the teachers of evil, the materialists—and I mean not only the good ones—for there are many good ones among them, especially in our day—hate not even the wicked ones. Remember them in your prayers thus: Save, O Lord, all those who have none to pray for them, save too all those who will not pray. And add: it is not in pride that I make this prayer, O Lord, for I am lower than all men. . . . Love God's people, let not strangers draw away the flock, for if you slumber in your slothfulness and disdainful pride, or worse still, in covetousness, they will come from all sides and draw away your flock. Expound the Gospel to the people unceasingly . . . be not extortionate. . . . Do not love gold and silver, do not hoard them. . . . Have faith. Cling to the banner and raise it on high."

The elder spoke, however, more disconnectedly than has been set forth here or as recorded later by Alyosha. Sometimes he broke off altogether, as though to take breath and recover his strength, but he was in a sort of ecstasy. They heard him with emotion, though many wondered at his words and found them obscure. . . . Afterwards all remembered those words. When Alyosha happened for a moment to leave the cell, he was struck by the general excitement and suspense in the monks who were crowding about it. This anticipation showed itself in some by anxiety, in others by devout solemnity. All were expecting that something great would happen immediately after the elder's death. Their suspense was, from one point of view, almost frivolous, but even the most austere of the monks were affected by it. Father Païssy's face looked the gravest of all. Alyosha was secetly summoned by a monk to see Rakitin, who had arrived from town with a singular letter for him from Madame Khokhlakova. In it she informed Alyosha of a strange and very opportune incident. It appeared that among the women who had come on the previous day to receive Father Zosima's blessing, there had been an old woman from the town, a sergeant's widow, called Prokhorovna. She had inquired whether she might pray for the rest of the soul of her son, Vasenka, who had gone to Irkutsk, and had sent her no news for over a year. To which Father Zosima had answered sternly, forbidding her to do so, and saying that to pray for the living as though they were dead was a kind of sorcery. He afterwards forgave her on account of her ignorance, and added "as though reading the book of the future" (this was Madame Khokhlakova's expression) words of comfort: "that her son Vasya was certainly alive and he would either come himself very shortly or send a letter, and that she was to go home and expect him." And "would you believe it," exclaimed Madame Khokhlakova enthusiastically, "the prophecy has been fulfilled literally indeed, and more than that." Scarcely had the old woman reached home when they gave her a letter from Siberia which had been awaiting her. But that was not all; in the letter written on the road from Ekaterinburg,[2] Vasya informed his mother that he was returning to Russia with an official, and that three weeks after her receiving the letter he hoped "to embrace his mother." Madame Khokhlakova warmly entreated Alyosha to report this new "miracle of prediction" to the Superior and all the brotherhood: "All, all, ought to know of it!" she exclaimed in conclusion. The letter had been written in haste, the excitement of the writer was apparent in every line of it. But Alyosha had no need to tell the monks, for all knew of it already. Rakitin had commissioned the monk who brought his message "to inform most respectfully his reverence Father Païssy, that he, Rakitin, has a matter to speak of with him, of such gravity that he dare not defer it for a moment, and humbly begs forgiveness for his presumption." As the monk had given the message to Father Païssy before that to Alyosha, the latter found after reading the letter that there was nothing left for him to do but to hand it to Father Païssy in confirmation of the story. And even that austere and cautious man, though he frowned as he read the news of the "miracle," could not completely restrain some inner emotion. His eyes gleamed, and a grave and solemn smile suddenly came into his lips.

"Shall we not behold greater things?" suddenly broke from him.

"We shall behold greater things, greater things yet!" the monks around repeated, but Father Païssy, frowning again, begged all of them at least for a time not to speak of the matter "till it be more fully confirmed, seeing there is so much credulity among those of this world, and indeed this might well have chanced naturally," he added, prudently, as it were to satisfy his conscience, though scarcely believing his own disavowal, a fact his listeners very clearly perceived. Within the hour the "miracle" was of course known to the whole monastery, and many visitors who had come for the mass. No one seemed more impressed by it than the little monk who had come the day before "from St. Sylvester," from the little monastery of Obdorsk in the far north. It was he who had been standing near Madame Khokhlakova the previous day and had asked Father Zosima earnestly, referring to the "healing" of the lady's daughter, "How can you presume to do such things?"

The thing was, he was now somewhat puzzled, and almost did not know whom to believe. The evening before he had visited Father Ferapont in his cell apart, behind the apiary, and had been greatly impressed and overawed by the visit. This Father Ferapont was that aged monk so devout in fasting and observing silence who had been mentioned already, as an opponent of Father Zosima's, and, really, the whole institution of elders, which he regarded as a pernicious and frivolous innovation. This opponent was extremely dangerous, although from his practice of silence

2. A city in western Siberia, now called Sverdlovsk.

he scarcely spoke a word to anyone. What made him dangerous was, mainly, that many brothers fully shared his feeling, and many of the visitors looked upon him as a great saint and ascetic, although they had no doubt that he was a holy fool. But it was the holy foolishness that attracted them. Father Ferapont never went to see the elder. Though he lived in the hermitage they did not bother him about keeping its regulations, and this too because he behaved like a holy fool. He was seventy-five or more, and he lived in a corner beyond the apiary in an old decaying wooden cell which had been built long ago for another great ascetic, Father Iona, who had lived to be a hundred and five, and of whose saintly doings many curious stories were still extant in the monastery and the neighborhood. Father Ferapont had succeeded in getting himself installed in this same solitary cell seven years previously. It was simply a peasant's hut, though it looked like a chapel, for it contained an extraordinary number of icons with lamps perpetually burning before them—which men brought to the monastery as offerings to God. Father Ferapont had been appointed, as it were, to look after them and keep the lamps burning. It was said (and indeed it was true) that he ate only two pounds of bread in three days. The beekeeper, who lived close by the apiary, used to bring him the bread every three days, and even to this man who waited upon him, Father Ferapont rarely uttered a word. The four pounds of bread, together with the sacrament bread, regularly sent him on Sundays after the late mass by the Father Superior, made up his weekly rations. The water in his jug was changed every day. He rarely appeared at mass. Visitors who came to do him homage saw him sometimes kneeling all day long at prayer without looking round. If he addressed them, he was brief, abrupt, strange, and almost always rude. On very rare occasions, however, he would talk to visitors, but for the most part he would utter some one strange saying which was a complete riddle, and no entreaties would induce him to pronounce a word in explanation. He was not a priest, but a simple monk. There was a strange belief, chiefly however among the most ignorant, that Father Ferapont had communication with heavenly spirits and would only converse with them, and so was silent with men. The little monk from Obdorsk, having been directed to the apiary by the beekeeper, who was also a very silent and surly monk, went to the corner where Father Ferapont's cell stood. "Maybe he will speak as you are a stranger and maybe you'll get nothing out of him," the beekeeper had warned him. The monk, as he related afterwards, approached in the utmost apprehension. It was rather late in the evening. Father Ferapont was sitting at the door of his cell on a low bench. A huge old elm was lightly rustling overhead. There was an evening freshness in the air. The monk from Obdorsk bowed down before the saint and asked his blessing.

"Do you want me to bow down to you, monk?" said Father Ferapont. "Get up."

The little monk got up.

"Blessing, be blessed! Sit beside me. Where have you come from?"

What most struck the poor little monk was the fact that in spite of his strict fasting and great age, Father Ferapont still appeared to be a vigorous old man. He was tall, held himself erect, and had a thin but fresh and healthy face. There was no doubt he still had considerable strength. He was of athletic build. In spite of his great age he was not even quite gray, and still had very thick hair and a full beard, both of which had once been black. His eyes were gray, large and luminous, but strikingly prominent. He spoke with a broad accent. He was dressed in a long reddish coat of coarse convict cloth (as it used to be called) and had a stout rope round his waist. His throat and chest were bare. Beneath his coat, his shirt of the coarsest linen showed almost black with dirt, not having been changed for months. They said that he wore irons weighing thirty pounds under his coat.[3] His stockingless feet were thrust in old shoes almost dropping to pieces.

"From the little Obdorsk monastery, from St. Sylvester," the little monk answered humbly, while his keen and inquisitive, but rather frightened little eyes kept watch on the hermit.

"I have been at your Sylvester's. I used to stay there. Is Sylvester well?"

The little monk hesitated.

"You are a senseless lot! How do you keep the fasts?"

"Our dietary is according to the ancient conventional rules: During Lent there are no meals provided for Monday, Wednesday, and Friday. For Tuesday and Thursday we have white bread, stewed fruit with honey, wild berries, or salt cabbage and oatmeal gruel. On Saturday white cabbage soup, noodles with peas, kasha, all with hemp oil. On weekdays we have dried fish and kasha with the cabbage soup. From Monday till Saturday evening, six whole days in Holy Week,[4] nothing is cooked, and we have only bread and water, and that sparingly; if possible not taking food every day, just the same as is ordered for first week in Lent. On Great and Holy Friday[5] nothing is eaten. In the same way on Holy Saturday we have to fast till three o'clock, and then take a little bread and water and drink a single cup of wine. On Great and Holy Thursday[6] we drink wine and have something cooked without oil or not cooked at all. Inasmuch as the Laodicean council[7] lays down for Holy Thursday: 'it is unseemly by remitting the fast on the Holy Thursday to dishonor the whole of Lent!' This is how we keep the fast. But what is that compared with you, holy Father," added the monk, growing more confident, "for all the year round, even at Easter, you take nothing but bread and water, and what we should eat in two days lasts you full seven. It's truly marvelous—your great abstinence."

"And mushrooms?" asked Father Ferapont, suddenly.

"Mushrooms?" repeated the surprised little monk.

"Yes. I can give up their bread, not needing it at all, and go away into the forest and live there on the mushrooms or the berries, but they can't give up their bread here, wherefore they are in bondage to the devil. Nowadays the unclean deny that there is need of such fasting. Haughty and unclean is their judgment."

"Och, true," sighed the little monk.

"And have you seen devils among them?" asked Father Ferapont.

"Among them? Among whom?" asked the little monk, timidly.

3. This means of self-mortification was not unusual among ascetics in Dostoevsky's time.
4. Holy Week, the week before Easter, is a time of prayer and fasting.
5. Great and Holy Friday (known as Good Friday in Western Christian denominations), the Friday before Easter, commemorates Christ's crucifixion.
6. Great and Holy Thursday, also known as Maundy Thursday, the Thursday before Easter, commemorates the last supper of Christ with his apostles.
7. A fourth-century Church council held in the Roman city of Laodicea, located in present-day Turkey.

"I went to the Father Superior on Trinity Sunday[8] last year, I haven't
been since. I saw a devil sitting on one man's chest hiding under his cassock, only his horns poked out; another had one peeping out of his pocket
with such sharp eyes, he was afraid of me; another settled in the unclean
belly of one, right in the guts, another was hanging round a man's neck,
and he was carrying him about without seeing him."

"You—can see spirits?" the little monk inquired.

"I tell you I can see, I can see through them. When I was coming out
from the Superior's I saw one hiding from me behind the door, and a big
one, a yard and a half or more high, with a thick long gray tail, and the tip
of his tail was in the crack of the door and I was quick and slammed the
door, pinching his tail in it. He squealed and began to struggle, and I
made the sign of the cross over him three times. And he died on the spot
like a crushed spider. He must have rotted there in the corner and be
stinking, but they don't see, they don't smell it. It's a year since I have been
there. I reveal it to you, as you are a stranger."

"Your words are terrible! But, holy and blessed Father," said the little
monk, growing bolder and bolder, "is it true, as they noise abroad even to
distant lands about you, that you are in continual communication with
the Holy Ghost?"[9]

"He does fly down at times."

"How does he fly down? In what form?"

"As a bird."

"The Holy Ghost in the form of a Dove?"

"There's the Holy Ghost and there's the Holy Spirit. The Holy Spirit
can appear as other birds—sometimes as a swallow, sometimes a gold-
finch and sometimes as a blue tit."

"How do you know him from an ordinary tit?"

"He speaks."

"How does he speak, in what language?"

"Human language."

"And what does he tell you?"

"Why, today he told me that a fool would visit me and would ask me
unseemly questions. You want to know too much, monk."

"Terrible are your words, most holy and blessed Father," the little monk
shook his head. But there was a doubtful look in his frightened little eyes.

"Do you see this tree?" asked Father Ferapont, after a pause.

"I do, blessed Father."

"You think it's an elm, but for me it has another shape."

"What sort of shape?" inquired the little monk, after a pause of vain
expectation.

"It happens at night. You see those two branches? In the night it is
Christ holding out His arms to me and seeking me with those arms, I see
it clearly and tremble. It's terrible, terrible!"

"What is there terrible if it's Christ Himself?"

8. In Russian Orthodox practice, Trinity Sunday is the Sunday of Pentecost. Falling fifty days
after Easter, Trinity Sunday commemorates the doctrine of the Trinity and the descent of the
Holy Spirit on the apostles. See also p. 000.
9. The Holy Ghost, also referred to as the Holy Spirit, is the third person of the Christian Trinity,
along with the Father and Son. The Holy Ghost at times takes the form of a dove in the Gospels.
See Matthew 3.16, Mark 1.10, Luke 3.22, and John 1.32. For a discussion of pneumatology (the
study of the Holy Ghost) and its significance for the novel, see Morson, p. 785.

"Why, He'll snatch me up and carry me away."

"Alive?"

"In the spirit and glory of Elijah,[1] haven't you heard? He will take me in His arms and bear me away."

Though the little Obdorsk monk returned to the cell he was sharing with one of the brothers, in considerable perplexity of mind, he still cherished at heart a greater reverence for Father Ferapont than for Father Zosima. The little monk from Obdorsk was strongly in favor of fasting, and it was not strange that one who kept so rigid a fast as Father Ferapont should "see marvels." His words, of course, were somehow absurd, but God only knew what was contained in them, those words, and even worse words and acts happen with all those who are holy fools for Christ's sake. The pinching of the devil's tail he was ready and eager to believe, and not only in the figurative sense. Besides he had, before visiting the monastery, a strong prejudice against the institution of "elders," which he only knew of by hearsay and believed to be a pernicious innovation. Before he had been long at the monastery, he had detected the secret murmurings of some shallow brothers who disliked the institution. He was, besides, a meddlesome, inquisitive man, who poked his nose into everything. This was why the news of the fresh "miracle" performed by Father Zosima reduced him to extreme perplexity. Alyosha remembered afterwards how their inquisitive guest from Obdorsk had been continually flitting to and fro from one group to another, listening and asking questions among the monks who were crowding within and without the elder's cell. But he did not pay much attention to him at the time, and only recollected it afterwards. He had no thought to spare for it indeed, for when Father Zosima, feeling tired again, had gone back to bed, he thought of Aloysha as he was closing his eyes, and sent for him. Alyosha ran at once. There was no one else in the cell but Father Païssy, Father Iosif, and the novice Porfiry. The elder, opening his weary eyes and looking intently at Alyosha, asked him suddenly:

"Are your people expecting you, my son?"

Alyosha hesitated.

"Don't they need you? Didn't you promise someone yesterday to see them today?"

"I did promise . . . to my father . . . my brothers . . . others too."

"You see, you must go. Don't grieve. Be sure I shall not die without your being by to hear my last word. To you I will say that word, my son, it will be my last gift to you. To you, dear son, because you love me. But now go to keep your promise."

Alyosha immediately obeyed, though it was hard to go. But the promise that he should hear his last word on earth, that it should be the last gift to him, Alyosha, sent a thrill of rapture through his soul. He made haste that he might finish what he had to do in the town and return quickly. Father Païssy, too, uttered some words of exhortation which moved and surprised him greatly. He spoke as they left the cell together.

"Remember, young man, unceasingly," Father Païssy began, without preface, "that the science of this world, which has become a great power, has, especially in the last century, analyzed everything divine handed down to us in the holy books. After this cruel analysis the learned of this

1. Elijah was a ninth century B.C.E. Jewish prophet. See Luke 1.17.

world have nothing left of all that was sacred of old. But they have only analyzed the parts and overlooked the whole, and indeed their blindness is marvelous. Yet the whole still stands steadfast before their eyes, and the gates of hell shall not prevail against it.[2] Has it not lasted nineteen centuries, is it not still a living, a moving power in the individual soul and in the masses of people? It is still as strong and living even in the souls of atheists, who have destroyed everything! For even those who have renounced Christianity and attack it, in their inmost being still follow the Christian idea, for hitherto neither their subtlety nor the ardor of their hearts has been able to create a higher ideal of man and of virtue than the ideal given by Christ of old. When it has been attempted, the results have been only abominations. Remember this especially, young man, since you are being sent into the world by your departing elder. Maybe, remembering this great day, you will not forget my words, uttered from the heart for your guidance, seeing you are young, and the temptations of the world are great and beyond your strength to endure. Well, now go, my orphan."

With these words Father Païssy blessed him. As Alyosha left the monastery and thought them over, he suddenly realized that he had met a new and unexpected friend, a warmly loving teacher, in this austere monk who had hitherto treated him sternly. It was as though Father Zosima had bequeathed him to him at his death, and "perhaps that's just what had passed between them," Alyosha thought suddenly. The philosophic reflections he had just heard so unexpectedly testified to the warmth of Father Païssy's heart. He was in haste to arm the boy's mind for conflict with temptation and to guard the young soul left in his charge with the strongest defense he could imagine.

Chapter II

At His Father's

Before anything else, Alyosha went to his father. As he approached he remembered that his father had insisted the day before that he should come without his brother Ivan seeing him. "Why so?" Alyosha wondered suddenly. "Even if my father has something to say to me alone, why should I go in unseen? Most likely in his excitement yesterday he meant to say something different," he decided. Yet he was very glad when Martha Ignatyevna, who opened the garden gate to him (Grigory, it appeared, was ill in bed in the lodge), told him in answer to his question that Ivan Fyodorovich had gone out two hours ago.

"And my father?"

"He is up, taking his coffee," Martha answered somewhat drily.

Alyosha went in. The old man was sitting alone at the table, wearing slippers and a little old overcoat, and was amusing himself by looking through some accounts, rather inattentively however. He was quite alone in the house (Smerdyakov too had gone out to buy things for dinner). Though he had got up early and was trying to put a bold face on it, he

---

2. Father Païssy quotes Jesus' words to Peter from Matthew 16.18: "I say also unto thee, That thou art Peter, and upon this rock I will build my church; and the gates of hell shall not prevail against it."

looked tired and weak. His forehead, upon which huge purple bruises had come out during the night, was bandaged with a red handkerchief; his nose too had swollen terribly in the night, and some smaller bruises covered it in patches, decidedly giving his whole face a peculiarly spiteful and irritable look. The old man was aware of this, and turned a hostile glance on Alyosha as he came in.

"The coffee is cold," he cried sharply; "I won't offer you any. I've ordered nothing but a Lenten fish soup today, and I don't invite anyone to share it. Why have you come?"

"To find out how you are feeling," said Alyosha.

"Yes. And besides, I told you to come yesterday. It's all nonsense. You need not have troubled. But I knew you'd come poking in directly."

He said this with the most hostile feeling. At the same time he got up and looked anxiously in the mirror (perhaps for the fortieth time that morning) at his nose. He began, too, binding his red handkerchief more becomingly on his forehead.

"Red's better. It's just like the hospital in a white one," he observed sententiously. "Well, how are things over there? How is your elder?"

"He is very bad; he may die today," answered Alyosha. But his father had not even listened, and had forgotten his own question at once.

"Ivan's gone out," he said suddenly. "He is doing his utmost to carry off Mitka's betrothed. That's what he is staying here for," he added maliciously, and, twisting his mouth, looked at Alyosha.

"Surely he did not tell you so himself?" asked Alyosha.

"Yes, he did, long ago. Would you believe it, he told me three weeks ago? You don't suppose he too came to murder me, do you? He must have had some object in coming."

"What do you mean? Why do you say such things?" said Alyosha, terribly troubled.

"He doesn't ask for money, it's true, but yet he won't get a bit from me. I intend living as long as possible, you may as well know, my dear Alexey Fyodorovich, and so I need every kopeck, and the longer I live, the more I shall need it," he continued, pacing from one corner of the room to the other, keeping his hands in the pockets of his loose greasy overcoat made of yellow cotton material. "I can still pass for a man at fifty-five, but I want to pass for one for another twenty years. As I get older, you know, I won't be a pretty object, they won't come to me of their own accord, so I will need my money. So I am saving up more and more, simply for myself, my dear son Alexey Fyodorovich. You may as well know. For I mean to go on in my sins to the end, let me tell you. For sin is sweet; all abuse it, but all men live in it, only others do it on the sly, and I openly. And so all the other sinners fall upon me for being so simple. And I don't want to go to your paradise, Alexey Fyodorovich, let that be known to you; it's not even the proper place for a gentleman, your paradise, even if it exists. I believe that I fall asleep and don't wake up again, and that's all, you can pray for my soul if you like, and if you don't want to, don't, devil take you! That's my philosophy. Ivan talked well here yesterday, though we were all drunk. Ivan is a conceited coxcomb, but he has no particular learning . . . nor education either. He sits silent and smiles at one without speaking—that's what pulls him through."

Alyosha listened to him in silence.

"Why won't he talk to me? If he does speak, he gives himself airs. Your Ivan is a scoundrel! And I'll marry Grushka in a minute if I want to. For if you've money, Alexey Fyodorovich, you have only to want a thing and you can have it. That's what Ivan is afraid of, he is on the watch to prevent my getting married and that's why he is egging on Mitka to marry Grushka himself. He hopes to keep me from Grushka by that (as though I should leave him my money if I don't marry her!). Besides if Mitka marries Grushka, Ivan will carry off his rich betrothed, that's what he's reckoning on! He's a scoundrel, your Ivan!"

"How cross you are. It's because of yesterday; you had better lie down," said Alyosha.

"There, you say that," the old man observed suddenly, as though it had struck him for the first time, "and I am not angry with you, but if Ivan said it, I would be angry with him. It is only with you I have good moments, otherwise I am a wicked man."

"You are not wicked, but twisted," said Alyosha with a smile.

"Listen, I meant this morning to get that ruffian Mitya locked up and I don't know now what I shall decide about it. Of course in these fashionable days fathers and mothers are looked upon as a prejudice, but even now the law does not allow you to drag your old father about by the hair, to kick him in the face in his own house, and brag of murdering him outright—all in the presence of witnesses. If I liked, I could crush him and could have him locked up at once for what he did yesterday."

"Then you don't mean to take proceedings?"

"Ivan has dissuaded me. I don't care about Ivan, but there's another thing . . ."

And bending down to Alyosha, he went on in a confidential half-whisper.

"If I send the scoundrel to prison, she'll hear of it and run to see him at once. But if she hears today that he has beaten me, a weak old man, within an inch of my life, she may give him up and come to me. . . . That's the kind of character we're endowed with—everything by contraries. I know her through and through! Won't you have a drop of brandy? Take some cold coffee and I'll pour a quarter of a glass of brandy into it, it's delicious, my boy."

"No, thank you. I'll take that roll with me if I may," said Alyosha, and taking a three-kopeck French roll he put it in the pocket of his cassock. "And you'd better not have brandy, either," he suggested apprehensively, looking into the old man's face.

"You are quite right, it irritates my nerves instead of soothing them. Only one little glass. I'll get it out of the cupboard." He unlocked the cupboard, poured out a glass, drank it, then locked the cupboard and put the key back in his pocket.

"That's enough. One glass won't kill me."

"You see you are in a better humor now," said Alyosha smiling.

"Um! I love you even without the brandy, but with scoundrels I am a scoundrel. Vanka is not going to Chermashnya—why is that? He wants to spy: will I give much to Grushenka if she comes? They are all scoundrels! But I don't recognize Ivan at all. Where does he come from? He is not one of us in soul. As though I'd leave him anything? I won't leave a will at all, you may as well know. And I'll crush Mitya like a cockroach. I squash cockroaches at night with my slipper: they squelch when you tread on them. And your Mitka will squelch too. *Your* Mitka, for you love him. Yes, you love him and I am not afraid of your loving him. But if Ivan loved him I would be afraid for myself at his loving him. But Ivan loves nobody, Ivan is not one of us, people like Ivan are not our sort, my boy, they are like a cloud of dust. When the wind blows, the dust will be gone.[3] . . . I had a silly idea in my head when I told you to come today; I wanted to find out from you about Mitka. If I were to hand him over a thousand or maybe two now, would the beggarly wretch agree to take himself off altogether for five years or, better still, thirty-five, and without Grushka, and give her up once for all, eh?"

"I . . . I'll ask him . . ." muttered Alyosha. "If you would give him three thousand, perhaps he . . ."

"You're lying! You needn't ask him now, no need! I've changed my mind. It was a nonsensical idea of mine. I won't give him anything, not a bit, I want my money myself," cried the old man, waving his hand. "I'll crush him like a cockroach without it. Don't say anything to him or else he will begin hoping. There's nothing for you to do here, either, you needn't stay. Is that betrothed of his, Katerina Ivanovna, whom he has kept so carefully hidden from me all this time, going to marry him or not? You went to see her yesterday, I believe?"

"Nothing will induce her to abandon him."

"There you see how dearly these tender young ladies love a rake and a scoundrel. They are trash I tell you, those pale young ladies, very different from . . . Ah, if I had his youth and the looks I had then (for I was better-looking than he at twenty-eight) I'd have been a conquering hero just as he is. He is a low cad! But he will not have Grushenka, sir, anyway, he will not, sir . . . I'll throw him in the mud!"

His anger had returned with the last words.

"You can go, there's nothing for you to do here today," he snapped sharply.

Alyosha went up to say good-bye to him, and kissed him on the shoulder.

"What's that for?" the old man was a little surprised. "We will see each other again, or do you think we won't?"

"Not at all, I didn't mean anything."

"Nor did I, I did not mean anything," said the old man, looking at him. "Listen, listen," he shouted after him, "make haste and come again and I'll have a fish soup for you, a fine one, not like today. Be sure to come! Come tomorrow, do you hear, tomorrow!"

And as soon as Alyosha had gone out of the door, he went to the cupboard again and poured out another half glass.

"I won't have more!" he muttered, clearing his throat, and again he locked the cupboard and put the key in his pocket. Then he went into his bedroom, lay down on the bed, exhausted, and in one minute he was asleep.

---

3. Fyodor Pavlovich paraphrases Psalm 1.4: "the ungodly . . . are like the chaff which the wind driveth away."

Chapter III

He Gets Involved with Schoolboys

"Thank goodness he did not ask me about Grushenka," thought Alyosha, as he left his father's house and turned towards Madame Khokhlakova's, "or I might have to tell him of my meeting with Grushenka yesterday." Alyosha felt painfully that since yesterday both combatants had renewed their energies, and that their hearts had grown hard again: "Father is spiteful and angry, he's made some plan and will stick to it; and what about Dmitri? He too will be harder than yesterday, he too must be spiteful and angry, and he too, no doubt, has made some plan . . . Oh, I must succeed in finding him today, whatever happens."

But Alyosha didn't have a chance to think for long: an incident occurred on the road, which, though apparently of little consequence, made a great impression on him. Just after he had crossed the square and turned the corner coming out into Mikhailovsky Street, which is divided by a small ditch from Main Street (our whole town is intersected by ditches), he saw at the bridge a group of schoolboys, all young children, between the ages of nine and twelve, no older. They were going home from school, some with their bags on their shoulders, others with leather satchels slung across them, some in short jackets, others in little overcoats. Some even had those high boots with creases round the ankles, such as little boys spoiled by rich fathers love to wear. The whole group was talking eagerly about something, apparently holding a council. Alyosha had never from his Moscow days been able to pass children without taking notice of them, and although he was particularly fond of children of three or thereabout, he liked schoolboys of ten and eleven too. And so, anxious as he was today, he wanted at once to turn aside to talk to them. He looked into their excited rosy faces, and noticed at once that all the boys had stones in their hands. Beyond the ditch some thirty paces away, there was another schoolboy standing by a fence. He too had a satchel at his side. He was about ten years old, no older, if anything, younger, pale, delicate-looking and with sparkling black eyes. He kept an attentive and anxious watch on the other six, obviously his schoolfellows with whom he had just come out of school, but with whom he had evidently had a feud. Alyosha went up and addressing a fair, curly-headed, rosy boy in a black jacket observed:

"When I used to wear a satchel like yours, I always used to carry it on my left side, so as to have my right hand free, but you've got yours on your right side. So it will be awkward for you to get at it."

Alyosha began without any premeditated cunning right with this practical remark, which, incidentally, is the only way for an adult to begin if he needs to enter right into the confidence of a child, and especially with a group of children. One must begin in a serious businesslike way so as to be on a perfectly equal footing. Alyosha understood it by instinct.

"But he is left-handed," another, a fine healthy-looking boy of eleven, answered promptly. All the others stared at Alyosha.

"He even throws stones with his left hand," observed a third. At that instant a stone flew into the group, but only just grazed the left-handed boy, though it was well and vigorously thrown by the boy standing on the other side of the ditch.

"Give it to him, hit him back, Smurov!" they all shouted. But Smurov (the left-handed boy) needed no telling, and immediately gave payback: he threw a stone, but it missed the boy and hit the ground. The boy on the other side of the ditch, the pocket of whose coat was, at thirty paces, visibly bulging with stones, flung another stone at the group; this time it flew straight at Alyosha and hit him painfully on the shoulder.

"He aimed it at you, he meant it for you. You are Karamazov, Karamazov?" the boys shouted laughing, "Come, all throw at him at once!"

And six stones flew at the boy. One struck the boy on the head and he fell down, but at once leaped up and began ferociously returning their fire. Both sides threw stones incessantly. Many of the group had their pockets full too.

"What are you doing! Aren't you ashamed, gentlemen! Six against one, why, you'll kill him!" cried Alyosha.

He ran forward and met the flying stones to screen the solitary boy. Three or four ceased throwing for a minute.

"He began first!" cried a boy in a red shirt in an angry childish voice. "He is a scoundrel, he stabbed Krasotkin in class the other day with a penknife. It bled. Krasotkin wouldn't tell tales, but he must be thrashed."

"But what for? I suppose you tease him."

"There, he sent a stone in your back again, he knows you," cried the children. "It's you he is throwing at now, not us. Come, all of you, at him again, don't miss, Smurov!"

And again a fire of stones, and a very vicious one, began. The boy on the other side of the ditch was hit in the chest; he screamed, began to cry and ran away uphill towards Mikhailovsky Street. They all shouted: "Aha, quitter, he is running away. Wisp of tow!"

"You don't know what a beast he is, Karamazov, killing is too good for him," said the boy in the jacket, with flashing eyes. He seemed to be the eldest.

"What's wrong with him?" asked Alyosha. "Is he a tattletale or what?"

The boys looked at one another as though derisively.

"Are you going that way, to Mikhailovsky?" the same boy went on. "Catch up with him. . . . You see he's stopped again, he is waiting and looking at you."

"He is looking at you," the other boys chimed in.

"You ask him, does he like a disheveled bathhouse wisp of tow. Do you hear, ask him that!"

There was a general burst of laughter. Alyosha looked at them, and they at him.

"Don't go near him, he'll hurt you," cried Smurov in a warning voice.

"I won't ask him about the wisp of tow, for I expect you tease him with that question somehow. But I'll find out from him why you hate him so."

"Find out then, find out," cried the boys, laughing.

Alyosha crossed the bridge and walked uphill by the fence, straight towards the boy.

"You'd better look out," the boys called after him; "he won't be afraid of you. He will stab you in a minute, on the sly . . . just like he did to Krasotkin."

The boy waited for him without budging. Coming up to him, Alyosha saw facing him a child no older than nine. He was an undersized weakly boy with a thin long pale face, with large dark eyes that gazed at him vindictively. He was dressed in a rather shabby old overcoat, which he had monstrously outgrown. His bare arms stuck out beyond his sleeves. There was a large patch on the right knee of his trousers, and in his right boot just at the toe there was a big hole in the leather, carefully blackened with ink. Both pockets of his overcoat were weighed down with stones. Alyosha stopped two steps in front of him, looking inquiringly at him. The boy, seeing at once from Alyosha's eyes that he wouldn't beat him, became less defiant, and addressed him first.

"I am alone, and there are six of them. I'll beat them all, alone!" he said suddenly, with flashing eyes.

"I think one of the stones must have hurt you badly," observed Alyosha.

"But I hit Smurov on the head!" cried the boy.

"They told me that you know me, and that you threw a stone at me on purpose," said Alyosha.

The boy looked darkly at him.

"I don't know you. Do you know me?" Alyosha continued.

"Let me alone!" the boy cried irritably, but he did not move, as though he were expecting something, and again there was a vindictive light in his eyes.

"Very well, I am going," said Alyosha; "only I don't know you and I don't tease you. They told me how they tease you, but I don't want to tease you. Good-bye!"

"Friar, friar, pants on fire!" cried the boy, following Alyosha with the same vindictive and defiant expression, and he threw himself into an attitude of defense, feeling sure that now Alyosha would fall upon him; but Alyosha turned, looked at him, and walked away. He had not gone three steps before the biggest stone the boy had in his pocket hit him a painful blow in the back.

"So you'll hit a man from behind? They tell the truth, then, when they say that you attack on the sly?" said Alyosha, turning round again. This time the boy threw a stone savagely right into Alyosha's face; but Alyosha just had time to guard himself, and the stone struck him on the elbow.

"Aren't you ashamed! What have I done to you?" he cried.

The boy waited in silent defiance, certain that now Alyosha would attack him. Seeing that even now he would not, his rage was like a little wild beast's; he flew at Alyosha himself, and before Alyosha had time to move, the spiteful child had seized his left hand with both of his and bit his middle finger. He fixed his teeth in it and it was ten seconds before he let go. Alyosha cried out with pain and pulled his finger away with all his might. The child let go at last and retreated to his former distance. Alyosha's finger had been badly bitten to the bone, close to the nail; it began to bleed. Alyosha took out his handkerchief and bound it tightly round his injured hand. He was a full minute bandaging it. The boy stood waiting all the time. At last Alyosha raised his gentle eyes and looked at him.

"Very well," he said, "you see how badly you've bitten me. That's enough, isn't it? Now tell me, what have I done to you?"

The boy stared in amazement.

"Though I don't know you and it's the first time I've seen you," Alyosha went on with the same serenity, "yet I must have done something to you—you wouldn't have hurt me like this for nothing. So what have I done? How have I wronged you, tell me?"

Instead of answering, the boy broke into a loud tearful wail and ran away. Alyosha walked slowly after him towards Mikhailovsky Street, and for a long time he saw the child running in the distance as fast as ever, not turning his head, and no doubt still keeping up his tearful wail. He made up his mind to find him out as soon as he had time, and to solve this mystery. Just now he had not the time.

Chapter IV

At the Khokhlakovs'

Alyosha soon reached Madame Khokhlakova's house, a handsome stone house of two stories, one of the finest in our town. Though Madame Khokhlakova spent most of her time in another province where she had an estate, or in Moscow, where she had a house of her own, yet she had a house in our town, too, inherited from her forefathers. The estate in our district was the largest of her three estates, yet she had been very little in our province before this time. She ran out to Alyosha in the hall.

"Did you get my letter about the new miracle?" She spoke rapidly and nervously.

"Yes, I got it."

"Did you show it to everyone? He restored the son to his mother!"

"He will die today," said Alyosha.

"I have heard, I know, oh, how I long to talk to you, to you, or someone, about all this! No, to you, to you! And how sorry I am I can't see him! The whole town is in excitement, they are all suspense. But now—do you know Katerina Ivanovna is here now?"

"Ah, that's lucky!" cried Alyosha. "Then I shall see her here. She told me yesterday to be sure to come and see her today."

"I know, I know all. I've heard exactly what happened yesterday—and the atrocious behavior of that—creature. *C'est tragique*,[4] and if I'd been in her place I don't know what I would have done. And your brother Dmitri Fyodorovich, what do you think of him?—my goodness! Alexey Fyodorovich, I am forgetting, imagine: your brother is in there with her, not that dreadful brother who was so shocking yesterday, but the other, Ivan Fyodorovich, he is sitting with her talking; they are having a solemn conversation. If you could only imagine what's passing between them now—it's awful, I tell you it's lacerating, it's like some incredible tale of horror. They are ruining their lives for no reason anyone can see. They both recognize it and revel in it. I've been watching for you! I've been thirsting for you! It's too much for me, that's the worst of it. I'll tell you all about it presently, but now I must speak of something else, the most important thing—I had quite forgotten what's most important. Tell me, why has Lise been in hysterics? As soon as she heard you were here, she began to be hysterical!"

4. "It's tragic" (French).

"*Maman*, it's you who are hysterical now, not I." Lise's little voice suddenly caroled through a tiny crack of the door at the side. Her voice sounded as though she wanted to laugh, but was doing her utmost to control it. Alyosha at once noticed the crack, and no doubt Lise was peeping through it from her chair, but that he could not see.

"And no wonder, Lise, no wonder . . . your caprices will make me hysterical too. But she is so ill, Alexey Fyodorovich, she has been so ill all night, feverish and moaning! I could hardly wait for the morning and for Herzenstube to come. He says that he can make nothing of it, that we must wait. Herzenstube always comes and says that he can make nothing of it. As soon as you approached the house, she screamed, fell into hysterics, and insisted on being wheeled back into this room here."

"Mamma, I didn't know he had come. It wasn't on his account I wanted to be wheeled into this room."

"That's not true, Lise, Yulia ran to tell you that Alexey Fyodorovich was coming. She was on the lookout for you."

"My darling mamma, it's not at all clever of you. But if you want to make up for it and say something very clever, dear mamma, you'd better tell our honored visitor, Alexey Fyodorovich, that he has shown his want of wit by venturing to us after what happened yesterday and although everyone is laughing at him."

"Lise, you go too far. I declare I shall have to be severe. Who laughs at him? I am so glad he has come, I need him, I can't do without him. Oh, Alexey Fyodorovich, I am exceedingly unhappy!"

"But what's the matter with you, mamma, darling?"

"Ah, your caprices, Lise, your fidgetiness, your illness, that awful night of fever, that awful and everlasting Herzenstube, everlasting, everlasting, that's the worst of it! Everything, in fact, everything. . . . And, finally, even that miracle, too! Oh, how it has upset me, how it has shattered me, that miracle, dear Alexey Fyodorovich! And that tragedy in the drawing room, it's more than I can bear, I warn you. I can't bear it. A comedy, perhaps, not a tragedy. Tell me, will Father Zosima live till tomorrow, will he? Oh, my God! What is happening to me? Every minute I close my eyes and see that it's all nonsense, all nonsense."

"I should be very grateful," Alyosha interrupted suddenly, "if you could give me a clean rag to bind up my finger with. I have hurt it, and it's very painful."

Alyosha unbound his bitten finger. The handkerchief was soaked with blood. Madame Khokhlakova screamed and shut her eyes.

"Good heavens, what a wound, how awful!"

But as soon as Lise saw Alyosha's finger through the crack, she flung the door wide open.

"Come, come here," she cried, imperiously. "No nonsense now! Good heavens, why did you stand there saying nothing about it all this time? He might have bled to death, mamma! How did you do it? Water, water! You must wash it first of all, simply hold it in cold water to stop the pain, and keep it there, keep it there. . . . Make haste, mamma, some water in a basin. But do make haste," she finished nervously. She was quite frightened at the sight of Alyosha's wound.

"Shouldn't we send for Herzenstube?" cried Madame Khokhlakova.

"Mamma, you'll be the death of me. Your Herzenstube will come and say that he can make nothing of it! Water, water! Mamma, for goodness' sake go yourself and hurry Yulia, she is such a slowpoke and never can come quickly! Make haste, mamma, or I shall die."

"Why, it's nothing much," cried Alyosha, frightened by their fright.

Yulia ran in with water and Alyosha put his finger in it.

"Some lint, mamma, for mercy's sake, bring some lint and that muddy caustic lotion for wounds, what's it called? We have some, we have some, we have some. You know where the bottle is, mamma; it's in your bedroom in the right-hand cupboard, there's a big bottle of it there with the lint."

"I'll bring everything in a minute, Lise, only don't scream and don't fuss. You see how bravely Alexey Fyodorovich bears it. Where did you get such a dreadful wound, Alexey Fyodorovich?"

Madame Khokhlakova hastened away. This was all Lise was waiting for.

"First of all, answer the question, where did you get hurt like this?" she asked Alyosha, quickly. "And then I'll talk to you about something quite different. Well?"

Instinctively feeling that the time of her mother's absence was precious for her, Alyosha hastened to tell her of his enigmatic meeting with the schoolboys in the fewest words possible. Lise clasped her hands at his story.

"How can you, and in that dress too, associate with schoolboys!" she cried angrily, as though she had a right to control him. "You are nothing but a boy yourself if you can do that, a perfect boy! But you must find out for me about that horrid boy and tell me all about it, for there's some mystery in it. Now for the second thing, but first a question: does the pain prevent you, Alexey Fyodorovich, talking about utterly unimportant things, but talking sensibly?"

"Of course not, and I don't feel much pain now."

"That's because your finger is in the water. It must be changed at once for it will get warm in a minute. Yulia, bring some ice from the cellar and another basin of water. Now she is gone, I can speak; will you give me the letter I sent you yesterday, dear Alexey Fyodorovich—be quick for mamma will be back in a minute and I don't want . . ."

"I don't have the letter with me."

"That's not true, you have. I knew you would say that. You've got it in that pocket. I've been regretting that joke all night. Give me back the letter at once, give it to me!"

"I've left it at home."

"But you can't consider me as a young girl, as a little, little girl, after my letter with such a silly joke! I ask your forgiveness for that silly joke, but you must bring me the letter, if you really haven't got it—bring it today, you must, you must!"

"Today, I can't possibly, for I am going back to the monastery and I won't come and see you for the next two days—three or four perhaps—for Father Zosima——"

"Four days, what nonsense! Listen. Did you laugh at me very much?"

"I didn't laugh at all."

"Why not?"

"Because I believed all you said."

"You are insulting me!"

"Not at all. As soon as I read it, I thought that all that would come to pass, for as soon as Father Zosima dies, I am to leave the monastery. Then I shall go back and finish my studies, and when you reach the legal age we will be married. I will love you. Though I haven't had time to think about it, I believe I couldn't find a better wife than you, and Father Zosima tells me I must marry."

"But I am a freak, wheeled about in a chair!" laughed Liza, flushing crimson.

"I'll wheel you about myself, but I'm sure you'll get well by then."

"But you are crazy," said Liza, nervously, "to make all this nonsense out of a joke! Here's mamma, just in time, perhaps. Mamma, how slow you always are, how can you take so long! And here's Yulia with the ice."

"Oh, Lise, don't scream, above all things don't scream. That scream drives me . . . How can I help it when you put the lint in another place. I've been hunting and hunting—I suspect you did it on purpose."

"But I couldn't tell that he would come with a bitten finger, or else perhaps I might have done it on purpose. Angel mamma, you begin to say really witty things."

"Never mind my being witty, but I must say you show nice feeling for Alexey Fyodorovich's sufferings. Oh, my dear Alexey Fyodorovich, what's killing me is no one thing in particular, not Herzenstube, but everything together, that's what is too much for me."

"That's enough, mamma, enough about Herzenstube," Liza laughed gaily. "Make haste with the lint and the lotion, mamma. That's simply Goulard's water, Alexey Fyodorovich, I remember the name now, but it's a splendid lotion. Would you believe it, mamma, on the way here he had a fight with the boys in the street, and it was a boy bit his finger, isn't he himself little, a little man, and is he fit to be married after that? Because, just imagine, he wants to be married, mama. Just imagine him married, wouldn't it be funny, wouldn't it be awful?"

And Lise kept laughing her thin hysterical giggle, looking slyly at Alyosha.

"But why married, Lise? What makes you talk of such a thing? It's quite out of place—and perhaps the boy was rabid."

"Why, mamma! As though there were rabid boys!"

"Why not, Lise, as though I had said something stupid. Your boy might have been bitten by a mad dog and he would become mad and bite anyone near him. How well she has bandaged it, Alexey Fyodorovich, I couldn't have done it. Do you still feel the pain?"

"It's nothing much now."

"You don't feel afraid of water?" asked Lise.

"Come, that's enough, Lise, perhaps I really was rather too quick talking of the boy being rabid, and you pounced upon it at once. Katerina Ivanovna has only just heard that you are here, Alexey Fyodorovich, she simply rushed at me, she's dying to see you, dying!"

"Ach, mamma, go to them yourself. He can't go just now, he is in too much pain."

"Not at all, I can go quite well," said Alyosha.

"What! You are going away? Is that what you say?"

"Well, when I've seen them, I'll come back here and we can talk as much as you like. But I should like to see Katerina Ivanovna at once, for I am very anxious to be back at the monastery as soon as I can."

"Mamma, take him away quickly. Alexey Fyodorovich, don't trouble to come and see me afterwards, but go straight back to your monastery and good riddance. I want to sleep, I didn't sleep all night."

"Ah, Lise, you are only making fun, but how I wish you would sleep!" cried Madame Khokhlakova.

"I don't know what I've done. . . . I'll stay another three minutes, five if you like," muttered Alyosha.

"Even five! Do take him away quickly, mamma, he is a monster."

"Lise, you've gone mad. Let us go, Alexey Fyodorovich, she is too capricious today. I am afraid to cross her. Oh, the trouble one has with nervous girls! Perhaps she really will be able to sleep after seeing you. How quickly you have made her sleepy, and how fortunate it is."

"Ah, mamma, how sweetly you talk. I must kiss you for it, mamma."

"And I kiss you too, Lise. Listen, Alexey Fyodorovich," Madame Khokhlakova began mysteriously and importantly, speaking in a rapid whisper. "I don't want to suggest anything, I don't want to lift the veil, you will see for yourself what's going on, it's horrible, it's the most fantastic comedy: She loves your brother, Ivan Fyodorovich, and she is doing her utmost to persuade herself she loves your brother, Dmitri Fyodorovich. It's horrible! I'll go in with you, and if they don't turn me out, I'll stay to the end."

Chapter V

A Laceration in the Drawing Room

But in the drawing room the conversation was coming to an end. Katerina Ivanovna was greatly excited, though she looked resolute. At the moment Alyosha and Madame Khokhlakova entered, Ivan Fyodorovich was standing up to take leave. His face was rather pale, and Alyosha looked at him anxiously. The thing was that for Alyosha one of his doubts was now being solved, a troubling enigma that had been tormenting him for some time. During the preceding month it had been several times suggested to him that his brother Ivan was in love with Katerina Ivanovna, and, what was more, that he meant "to carry her off" from Mitya. Until quite lately the idea seemed to Alyosha monstrous, though it worried him extremely. He loved both his brothers, and dreaded such rivalry between them. Meantime, Dmitri Fyodorovich had said outright on the previous day that he was glad that his brother Ivan was his rival, and that it was a great assistance to him, Dmitri. In what way did it assist him? To marry Grushenka? But that Alyosha considered the worst thing possible. Besides all this, Alyosha had till the evening before implicitly believed that Katerina Ivanovna had a steadfast and passionate love for his brother Dmitri; but he had only believed it till the evening before. On top of that, it seemed to him that she was incapable of loving a man like Ivan, and that she did love his brother Dmitri, and loved him just as he was, in spite of all the strangeness of such a love. But during yesterday's scene with Grushenka another idea had struck him. The word "lacerating," which Madame

Khokhlakova had just uttered, almost made him start, because half waking up towards daybreak that night he had cried out: "Laceration, laceration," probably applying it to his dream. He had been dreaming all night of the previous day's scene at Katerina Ivanovna's. Now Alyosha was impressed by Madame Khokhlakova's blunt and persistent assertion that Katerina Ivanovna was in love with his brother Ivan, and only deceived herself through some sort of pose, from "laceration," and tortured herself by her pretended love for Dmitri from some fancied duty of gratitude. "Yes," he thought, "perhaps the whole truth lies in those words." But in that case what was his brother Ivan's position? Alyosha felt instinctively that a character like Katerina Ivanovna's must dominate, and she could only dominate someone like Dmitri, and never a man like Ivan. For Dmitri might at last submit to her domination "to his own happiness" (which was what Alyosha would have desired), but Ivan—no, Ivan could not submit to her, and such submission would not give him happiness. Alyosha could not help believing that of Ivan. And now all these doubts and reflections flitted and flashed through his mind as he entered the drawing room. Another idea, too, suddenly and irresistibly flashed through his mind: "What if she loved neither of them—neither Ivan nor Dmitri?" I must note that Alyosha felt as it were ashamed of his own thoughts and blamed himself when they kept recurring to him during the last month. "What do I know about love and women and how can I decide such questions?" he thought reproachfully, after such doubts and surmises. And yet it was impossible not to think about it. He felt instinctively, for example, that this rivalry was of immense importance in his brothers' lives and that a great deal depended upon it. "One viper will devour the other," his brother Ivan had pronounced the day before, speaking irritably of his father and his brother Dmitri. So Ivan looked upon his brother Dmitri as a viper, and perhaps had long done so? Was it perhaps since he had known Katerina Ivanovna? That phrase had, of course, escaped Ivan unintentionally yesterday, but that only made it more important. If he felt like that, what chance was there of peace? Were there not, on the contrary, new grounds for hatred and hostility in their family? And, most importantly, with which of them was Alyosha to sympathize? And what was he to wish for each of them? He loved them both, but what could he desire for each in the midst of these conflicting interests? He might get quite lost in this tangle, and Alyosha's heart could not endure uncertainty, because his love was always of an active character. He was incapable of passive love. If he loved anyone, he set to work at once to help him. And to do so it was necessary to set a goal; he must know for certain what was best for each, and having ascertained this it was natural for him to help them both. But instead of a definite aim, he found nothing but uncertainty and tangles on all sides. "Laceration" was said just now. But what could he understand even in this laceration? He didn't even understand the first word in this tangle!

Seeing Alyosha, Katerina Ivanovna said quickly and joyfully to Ivan Fyodorovich, who had already got up to go, "A minute! Stay another minute. I want to hear the opinion of this person here whom I trust with my whole being. Katerina Osipovna, don't you leave either," she added, turning to Madame Khokhlakova. She sat Alyosha down beside her, and Madame Khokhlakova sat opposite, by Ivan Fyodorovich.

"You are all my friends here, all I have in the world, my dear friends," she began warmly, in a voice which quivered with genuine tears of suffering, and Alyosha's heart warmed to her at once. "You, Alexey Fyodorovich, were witness yesterday to that abominable scene, and saw what I was like. You did not see it, Ivan Fyodorovich, he did. What he thought of me yesterday I don't know. I only know one thing, that if it were repeated today, this minute, I would express the same feelings again as yesterday—the same feelings, the same words, the same actions. You remember my actions, Alexey Fyodorovich; you checked me in one of them" . . . (as she said that, she flushed and her eyes shone). "I must tell you, Alexey Fyodorovich, that I can't reconcile myself to anything. Listen, Alexey Fyodorovich, I don't even know whether I still love *him*. I feel *pity* for him, and that is a poor sign of love. If I loved him, if I still loved him, perhaps I wouldn't be sorry for him now, but, on the contrary, would hate him . . ."

Her voice quivered, and tears glittered on her eyelashes. Alyosha shuddered inwardly. "That girl is truthful and sincere," he thought, and . . . and she does not love Dmitri any more."

"That's true! true!" Madame Khokhlakova started to cry out.

"Wait, Katerina Osipovna, dear. I haven't told you the chief, the final decision I came to during the night. I feel that perhaps my decision is a terrible one—for me, but I foresee that nothing will induce me to change it—nothing. It will be so all my life. My dear, kind, ever-faithful and generous adviser, the one friend I have in the world, Ivan Fyodorovich, and with his deep insight into the heart, approves and commends my decision. He knows it."

"Yes, I approve of it," Ivan Fyodorovich assented, in a subdued but firm voice.

"But I should like Alyosha, too (Ah! Alexey Fyodorovich, forgive my calling you simply Alyosha), I should like Alexey Fyodorovich, too, to tell me before my two friends whether I am right. I feel instinctively that you, Alyosha, my dear brother (for you are a dear brother to me)," she said again ecstatically, taking his cold hand in her hot one, "I foresee that your decision, your approval, will bring me peace, in spite of all my sufferings, for, after your words, I shall be calm and submit—I foresee it!"

"I don't know what you are asking me," said Alyosha, flushing. "I only know that I love you and at this moment wish for your happiness more than my own! . . . But I know nothing about such affairs," he suddenly added hurriedly for some reason . . .

"In such affairs, Alexey Fyodorovich, in such affairs, the chief thing is honor and duty and something higher—I don't know what—but higher perhaps even than duty. I am conscious of this irresistible feeling in my heart, and it compels me irresistibly. But it may all be put in two words. I've already decided, even if he marries that—creature," she began solemnly, "whom I never, never can forgive, *even then I will not abandon him.* Henceforward I will never, never abandon him!" she cried, with an outburst of a sort of pale, tormented ecstasy. "Not that I would run after him continually, get in his way and worry him. Oh, no! I will go away to another town—where you like—but I will watch over him all my life—I will watch over him all my life unceasingly. When he becomes unhappy with that woman, and that is bound to happen quite soon, let him come to me and he will find a friend, a sister. . . . Only a sister, of course, and so forever; but he will learn at least that that sister is really his sister, who loves him and has sacrificed all her life to him. I will gain my point. I will insist on his knowing me and confiding entirely in me, without reserve," she cried, in a sort of frenzy. "I will be a god to whom he can pray—and that, at least, he owes me for his treachery and for what I suffered yesterday through him. And let him see that all my life I will be true to him and the promise I gave him, in spite of his being untrue and betraying me. I will—I will become nothing but a means for his happiness, or—how shall I say?—an instrument, a machine for his happiness, and that for my whole life, my whole life, and that he may see that all his life! That's my decision. Ivan Fyodorovich fully approves me."

She was breathless. She had perhaps intended to express her idea with more dignity, art and naturalness, but her speech was too hurried and crude. It was full of youthful unrestraint, it betrayed that she was still smarting from yesterday's insult, and that her pride craved satisfaction. She felt this herself. Her face suddenly darkened, an ugly look came into her eyes. Alyosha at once saw it and felt a pang of sympathy. His brother Ivan made it worse by adding:

"I've only expressed my own view," he said. "From anyone else, this would have been affected and overstrained, but from you—no. Any other woman would have been wrong, but you are right. I don't know how to explain it, but I see that you are absolutely genuine and that's why you are right."

"But that's only for the moment . . . And what is this moment? Nothing but yesterday's insult—that's what this moment means!" Madame Khokhlakova obviously had not intended to interfere, but she could not refrain from this very just comment.

"Quite so, quite so," interrupted Ivan, with peculiar eagerness, obviously annoyed at being interrupted, "in anyone else this moment would be only due to yesterday's impression and would be only a moment. But with Katerina Ivanovna's character, that moment will last all her life. What for anyone else would be only a promise is for her an everlasting, burdensome, grim perhaps, but unflagging duty. And she will be sustained by the feeling of this duty being fulfilled. Your life, Katerina Ivanovna, will henceforth be spent in painful brooding over your own feelings, your own heroism, and your own grief; but in the end that suffering will be softened and will pass into sweet contemplation of the fulfillment of a bold and proud design. Yes, proud it certainly is, and desperate in any case, but a triumph for you. And the consciousness of it will at last be a source of complete satisfaction and will make you reconciled to everything else."

This was decidedly said with some malice and obviously on purpose, and even, perhaps, with no desire to conceal that he spoke ironically and on purpose.

"Oh, dear, how wrong it all is!" Madame Khokhlakova cried again.

"Alexey Fyodorovich, you speak! I want dreadfully to know what you will say!" cried Katerina Ivanovna, and burst into tears. Alyosha got up from the sofa.

"It's nothing, nothing!" she went on through her tears. "I'm upset, I didn't sleep last night. But by the side of two such friends as you and your brother I still feel strong—for I know—you two will never desert me."

"Unfortunately, I am obliged to return to Moscow—perhaps tomorrow—and to leave you for a long time—And, unfortunately, it's unavoidable," Ivan Fyodorovich said suddenly.

"Tomorrow—to Moscow!" her face was suddenly contorted; "but—but, dear me, how fortunate!" she cried in a voice suddenly changed. In one instant there was no trace left of her tears. She underwent an instantaneous transformation, which amazed Alyosha. Instead of a poor, insulted girl, weeping in a sort of laceration, he saw a woman completely self-possessed and even exceedingly pleased, as though something agreeable had just happened.

"Oh, not fortunate that I am losing you, of course not," she corrected herself suddenly, with a charming society smile. "Such a friend as you are could not suppose that. I am only too unhappy at losing you." She rushed impulsively at Ivan Fyodorovich and seizing both his hands, pressed them warmly. "But what is fortunate is that you will be able in Moscow to see auntie and Agatha and to tell them all the horror of my present position. You can speak with complete frankness to Agatha, but spare dear auntie. You will know how to do that. You can't think how wretched I was yesterday and this morning, wondering how I could write them that dreadful letter—for one can never tell such things in a letter. . . . Now it will be easy for me to write, for you will see them and explain everything. Oh, how glad I am! But I am only glad of that, believe me. Of course, no one can take your place. . . . I will run at once to write the letter," she finished suddenly, and took a step as though to go out of the room.

"And what about Alyosha? Alexey Fyodorovich and his opinion, which you were so desperately anxious to hear?" cried Madame Khokhlakova. There was a sarcastic, angry note in her voice.

"I had not forgotten that," cried Katerina Ivanovna, coming to a sudden standstill, "and why are you so antagonistic at such a moment, Katerina Osipovna?" she added, with hot and bitter reproachfulness. "What I said, I repeat. I must have his opinion. More than that, I must have his decision! As he says, so it shall be. You see how anxious I am for your words, Alexey Fyodorovich. . . . But what's the matter?"

"I couldn't have believed it. I can't understand it!" Alyosha cried suddenly in distress.

"What? what?"

"He is going to Moscow, and you cry out that you are glad. You cried it out on purpose! And you begin explaining that you are not glad of that but sorry to be—losing a friend. But that was acting, too—you were playing a part—as in a theater!"

"In a theater? What? What do you mean?" exclaimed Katerina Ivanovna, profoundly astonished, flushing crimson, and frowning.

"Though you assure him you are sorry to lose a friend in him, you persist in telling him to his face that it's fortunate he is going," said Alyosha breathlessly. He was standing at the table and did not sit down.

"What are you talking about? I don't understand."

"I don't understand myself. . . . I seemed to see in a flash . . . I know I am not saying it properly but I'll say it all the same," Alyosha went on in the same shaking and broken voice. "What I see is that perhaps you don't love my brother Dmitri at all . . . and never have, from the beginning. . . . And Dmitri, too, perhaps, has never loved you . . . and only esteems you. . . . I really don't know how I dare to say all this, but somebody must tell the truth . . . for nobody here will tell the truth."

"What truth?" cried Katerina Ivanovna, and there was an hysterical ring in her voice.

"I'll tell you," Alyosha went on with desperate haste, as though he were jumping from the top of a house. "Call Dmitri at once—I will fetch him—and let him come here and take your hand and take my brother Ivan's and join your hands. For you're torturing Ivan, simply because you love him—and torturing him, because you love Dmitri through 'laceration'—with an unreal love—because you've persuaded yourself."

Alyosha broke off and was silent.

"You . . . you . . . you are a little holy fool—that's what you are!" Katerina Ivanovna snapped. Her face was white and her lips were moving with anger. Ivan Fyodorovich suddenly laughed and got up. His hat was in his hand.

"You are mistaken, my good Alyosha," he said, with an expression Alyosha had never seen in his face before—an expression of youthful sincerity and strong, irresistibly frank feeling. "Katerina Ivanovna has never loved me! She has known all the time that I loved her—though I never said a word of my love to her—she knew, but she didn't love me. I have never been her friend either, not for one moment; she is too proud to need my friendship. She kept me at her side as a means of revenge. She revenged with me and on me all the insults which she has been continually receiving from Dmitri ever since their first meeting. For even that first meeting has rankled in her heart as an insult—that's what her heart is like! She has talked to me of nothing but her love for him. I am going now; but, believe me, Katerina Ivanovna, you really love only him. And the more he insults you, the more you love him—that's your 'laceration.' You love him just as he is; you love him for insulting you. If he reformed, you'd give him up at once and cease to love him. But you need him so as to contemplate continually your heroic fidelity and to reproach him for infidelity. And it all comes from your pride. Oh, there's a great deal of humiliation and self-abasement about it, but it all comes from pride. . . . I am too young and I've loved you too much. I know that I ought not to say this, that it would be more dignified on my part simply to leave you, and it would be less offensive for you. But I am going far away, and shall never come back. . . . It is forever. I don't want to sit beside a laceration. . . . But I no longer know how to speak. I've said everything. . . . Good-bye, Katerina Ivanovna; you can't be angry with me, for I am a hundred times more severely punished than you, if only by the fact that I shall never see you again. Good-bye. I don't need your hand. You have tortured me too deliberately for me to be able to forgive you at this moment. I shall forgive you later, but now I don't want your hand. 'Den Dank, Dame, begehr ich nicht,'[5] he added, with a forced smile, showing completely unexpectedly, however, that he, too, could read Schiller, and read him till he knew him by heart—which Alyosha would never have believed. He went out of the room without saying good-bye even to his hostess, Madame Khokhlakova. Alyosha clasped his hands.

---

5. "The reward, my lady, I do not desire" (German). From Schiller's poem "Der Handschuh" ("The Glove," 1797), which was included in Dostoevsky's volume of Schiller in Russian translation.

"Ivan!" he cried desperately after him. "Come back, Ivan! No, no, nothing will induce him to come back now!" he cried again, regretfully realizing it; "but it's my fault, my fault. I began it! Ivan spoke angrily, wrongly. Unjustly and angrily," Alyosha kept exclaiming frantically.

Katerina Ivanovna went suddenly into the next room.

"You have done no harm. You behaved beautifully, like an angel," Madame Khokhlakova whispered rapidly and ecstatically to the sorrowful Alyosha. "I will do my utmost to prevent Ivan Fyodorovich from going."

Her face beamed with delight, to the great distress of Alyosha, but Katerina Ivanovna suddenly returned. She had two hundred-ruble bills in her hand.

"I have a great favor to ask of you, Alexey Fyodorovich," she began, addressing Alyosha with an apparently calm and even voice, as though nothing had happened. "A week—yes, I think it was a week ago—Dmitri Fyodorovich was guilty of a hasty and unjust action—a very ugly action. There is a low tavern here and in it he met that discharged officer, that captain, whom your father used to employ in some business. Dmitri Fyodorovich somehow lost his temper with this captain, seized him by the beard and dragged him out into the street and for some distance along it, in that insulting fashion. And I am told that his son, a boy, quite a child, who is at the school here, saw it and ran beside them crying and begging for his father, appealing to everyone to defend him, while everyone laughed. You must forgive me, Alexey Fyodorovich, I cannot think without indignation of that disgraceful action of *his* . . . one of those actions of which only Dmitri Fyodorovich would be capable in his anger . . . and in his passions! I can't describe it even. . . . I can't find my words. I've made inquiries about his victim, and find he is quite a poor man. His name is Snegiryov. He did something wrong in the army and was discharged. I can't tell you what. And now he has sunk into terrible destitution, with his family—an unhappy family of sick children, and, I believe, an insane wife. He has been living here a long time; he used to work as a copying clerk, but now he is getting nothing. I thought if you . . . that is, I thought . . . I don't know. I am so confused. You see, I wanted to ask you, my dear Alexey Fyodorovich, to go to him, to find some excuse to go to them—I mean to that captain—oh, goodness, how badly I explain it!—and delicately, carefully, as only you know how to"—Alyosha blushed—"manage to give him this assistance, these two hundred rubles. He will be sure to take it. . . . I mean, persuade him to take it. . . . Or, rather, what do I mean? You see it's not by way of compensation to prevent him from taking proceedings (for I believe he meant to), but simply a token of sympathy, of a desire to assist him from me, Dmitri Fyodorovich's betrothed, not from himself. . . . But you know. . . . I would go myself, but you'll know how to do it ever so much better. He lives on Lake Street, in the house of a woman called Kalmykova. . . . For God's sake, Alexey Fyodorovich, do it for me, and now . . . now I am rather . . . tired. Good-bye!"

She turned so quickly and disappeared behind the portière that Alyosha had not time to utter a word, though he wanted to speak. He longed to beg her pardon, to blame himself, to say something, for his heart was full and he could not bear to go out of the room without it. But Madame Khokhlakova took him by the hand and drew him along with her. In the hall she stopped him again as before.

"She is proud, she is struggling with herself; but kind, charming, generous," she exclaimed, in a half-whisper. "Oh, how I love her, especially sometimes, and how glad I am again of everything! Dear Alexey Fyodorovich, you didn't know, but I must tell you, that we all, all—both her aunts, I and all of us, Lise, even—have been hoping and praying for nothing for the last month but that she may give up your favorite Dmitri Fyodorovich, who takes no notice of her and does not love her, and may marry Ivan Fyodorovich—such an excellent and cultivated young man, who loves her more than anything in the world. We are in a regular plot to bring it about, and I am even staying on here perhaps on that account."

"But she has been crying—she has been wounded again," cried Alyosha.

"Don't trust a woman's tears, Alexey Fyodorovich. I am never for the women in such cases, I am always for the men."

"Mamma, you are spoiling and ruining him," Lise's little voice cried from behind the door.

"No, it was all my fault. I am horribly to blame!" Alyosha repeated unconsoled, hiding his face in his hands in an agony of remorse for his indiscretion.

"Quite the contrary; you behaved like an angel, like an angel. I am ready to say so a thousand times over,"

"Mamma, how has he behaved like an angel?" Lise's voice was heard again.

"I somehow fancied all at once," Alyosha went on as though he had not heard Liza, "that she loved Ivan, and so I said that stupid thing. . . . What will happen now?"

"To whom, to whom?" cried Lise. "Mamma, you really want to be the death of me. I ask you and you don't answer."

At the moment the maid ran in.

"Katerina Ivanovna is ill. . . . She is crying, struggling . . . hysterics."

"What is the matter?" cried Lise, in a tone of real anxiety. "Mamma, I shall be having hysterics, and not she!"

"Lise, for mercy's sake, don't scream, don't persecute me. At your age one can't know everything that grown-up people know. I'll come and tell you everything you ought to know. Oh, mercy on us! I am coming, I am coming. . . . Hysterics are a good sign, Alexey Fyodorovich; it's an excellent thing that she is hysterical. That's just as it ought to be. In such cases I am always against the women, against all these feminine tears and hysterics. Run and say, Yulia, that I'll fly to her. As for Ivan Fyodorovich's going away like that, it's her own fault. But he won't go away. Lise, for mercy's sake, don't scream! Oh, yes; you are not screaming. It's I am screaming. Forgive your mamma; but I am delighted, delighted, delighted! Did you notice, Alexey Fyodorovich, how young, how young Ivan Fyodorovich was just now when he went out, when he said all that and went out? I thought he was so learned, such an academician, and all of a sudden he behaved so warmly, openly, and youthfully, with such youthful inexperience and it was all so fine, like you. . . . And the way he repeated that German verse, it was just like you! But I must fly, I must fly! Alexey Fyodorovich, make haste to carry out her commission, and then make haste back. Lise, do you want anything now? For mercy's sake, don't keep Alexey Fyodorovich a minute. He will come back to you at once."

Madame Khokhlakova at last ran off. Before leaving, Alyosha would have opened the door to see Lise.

"On no account," cried Lise. "On no account now! Speak through the door. How have you come to be an angel? That's the only thing I want to know."

"For an awful piece of stupidity, Lise! Good-bye."

"Don't dare to go away like that!" Lise was beginning.

"Lise, I have a real grief! I'll be back directly, but I have a great, great grief!"

And he ran out of the room.

Chapter VI

A Laceration in a Cottage

He certainly was really grieved in a way he had seldom been before. He had rushed in and meddled, and in what? In a love affair! "But what do I know about it? What can I tell about such things?" he repeated to himself for the hundredth time, flushing crimson. "Oh, being ashamed would be nothing; shame is only the punishment I deserve. The trouble is I shall certainly have caused more unhappiness. . . . And Father Zosima sent me to reconcile and bring them together. Is that the way to bring them together?" Then he suddenly remembered how he had tried to join their hands, and he felt fearfully ashamed again. "Though I acted quite sincerely, I must be more sensible in the future," he concluded suddenly, and did not even smile at his conclusion.

Katerina Ivanovna's commission took him to Lake Street, and his brother Dmitri lived close by, in a turning out of Lake Street. Alyosha decided to go to him in any case before going to the captain, though he had a presentiment that he would not find his brother. He suspected that he would intentionally keep out of his way now, but he must find him anyhow. Time was passing: the thought of his dying elder had not left Alyosha for one minute from the time he set off from the monastery.

There was one point which interested him particularly about Katerina Ivanovna's commission; when she had mentioned the captain's son, the little schoolboy who had run beside his father crying, the idea had at once struck Alyosha that this must be the schoolboy who had bitten his finger when he, Alyosha, asked him what he had done to hurt him. Now Alyosha felt practically certain of this, though he could not have said why. Thinking of another subject was a relief, and he resolved to think no more about the "mischief" he had done, and not to torture himself with remorse, but to do what he had to do, let come what would. At that thought he was completely comforted. Turning onto the street where his brother Dmitri lodged, he felt hungry, and taking out of his pocket the roll he had brought from his father's, he ate it. It made him feel stronger.

Dmitri was not at home. The people of the house, an old cabinetmaker, his son, and his old wife, looked with positive suspicion at Alyosha. "He hasn't slept here for the last three nights. Maybe he has gone away," the old man said in answer to Alyosha's persistent inquiries. Alyosha saw that he was answering in accordance with instructions. When he asked whether he were not at Grushenka's or in hiding at Thomas's (Alyosha spoke so freely on purpose), all three looked at him in alarm. "They are fond of him, they are doing their best for him," thought Alyosha. "That's good."

At last he found Mrs. Kalmykova's house on Lake Street. It was a decrepit little house, sunk on one side, with three windows looking into the street, and with a muddy yard, in the middle of which stood a solitary cow. He crossed the yard and found the door opening into the hall. On the left of the hall lived the old woman of the house with her old daughter. Both seemed to be deaf. In answer to his repeated inquiry for the captain, one of them at last understood that he was asking for their lodgers, and pointed across the hall at a door to the living room. The captain's lodging actually turned out to be just a simple peasant's cottage. Alyosha had his hand on the iron latch to open the door, when he was struck by the strange hush within. Yet he knew from Katerina Ivanovna's words that the man had a family. "Either they are all asleep or perhaps they have heard me coming and are waiting for me to open the door. I'd better knock first," and he knocked. An answer came, but not at once, after an interval of perhaps ten seconds.

"Who's there?" shouted someone in a loud and very angry voice.

Then Alyosha opened the door and crossed the threshold. He found himself in a hut. Though it was large, it was cluttered up with domestic belongings of all sorts, and there were several people in it. On the left was a large Russian stove.[6] From the stove to the window on the left was a string running across the room, and on it rags were hanging. There was a bedstead against the wall on each side, right and left, covered with knitted quilts. On the one on the left was a pyramid of four print-covered pillows, each smaller than the one beneath. On the other there was only one very small pillow. The opposite corner was screened off by a curtain or a sheet hung on a string. Behind this curtain could be seen a bed made up on a bench and a chair set against it. The rough square table of plain wood had been moved from the foreroom to the middle window. The three windows, which consisted each of four tiny greenish mildewy panes, gave little light, and were closed shut, so that the room was not very light and rather stuffy. On the table was a frying pan with the remains of some fried eggs, a half-eaten piece of bread, and a small bottle with a few drops of vodka remaining on the bottom.

A woman of genteel appearance, wearing a cotton gown, was sitting on a chair by the bed on the left. Her face was thin and yellow, and her sunken cheeks betrayed at the first glance that she was ill. But what struck Alyosha most was the expression in the poor woman's eyes—a look of surprised inquiry and yet of haughty pride. And while he was talking to her husband, her big brown eyes moved from one speaker to the other with the same haughty and questioning expression. Beside her at the window stood a young girl, rather plain, with scanty reddish hair, poorly but very neatly dressed. She looked disdainfully at Alyosha as he came in. Beside the other bed was sitting another female figure. She was a very sad sight, a young girl of about twenty, but hunchback and crippled "with withered legs," as Alyosha was told afterwards. Her crutches stood close by in the corner, between

---

6. The Russian stove, really a large furnace or heater, was used for cooking and heating, or even sitting and sleeping on built-in benches.

the bed and the wall. The strikingly beautiful and gentle eyes of this poor girl looked with mild serenity at Alyosha. A man of forty-five was sitting at the table, finishing the fried eggs. He was spare, small and weakly built. He had reddish hair and a scanty light-colored beard, very much like a wisp of tow (this comparison and the phrase "a wisp of tow" flashed at once into Alyosha's mind for some reason; he remembered it afterwards). It was obviously this gentleman who had shouted to him, as there was no other man in the room. But when Alyosha went in, he leaped up from the bench on which he was sitting, and, hastily wiping his mouth with a ragged napkin, darted up to Alyosha.

"It's a monk come to beg for the monastery. A nice place to come to!" the girl standing in the left corner said aloud. The man spun round instantly towards her and answered her in an excited and breaking voice.

"No, ma'am, Barbara Nikolavna, that's not it, ma'am, you are wrong, ma'am. Allow me to ask in turn, sir," he suddenly turned again to Alyosha, "what has brought you, sir, to—our retreat?"

Alyosha looked attentively at him. It was the first time he had seen him. There was something angular, flurried and irritable about him. Though he had obviously just been drinking, he was not drunk. There was extraordinary impudence in his expression, and yet, strange to say, at the same time there was fear. He looked like a man who had long been kept in subjection and had submitted to it, and now had suddenly turned and was trying to assert himself. Or, better still, like a man who wants dreadfully to hit you but is horribly afraid you will hit him. In his words and in the intonation of his shrill voice there was a sort of crazy humor, at times spiteful and at times cringing, and continually shifting from one tone to another. The question about "our retreat" he had asked as it were quivering all over, rolling his eyes, and skipping up so close to Alyosha that he instinctively drew back a step. He was dressed in a very shabby dark cotton coat, patched and spotted. He wore checked trousers of an extremely light color, long out of fashion, and of very thin material. They were so crumpled and so short that he looked as though he had grown out of them like a little boy.

"I am Alexey Karamazov," Alyosha began in reply.

"I quite understand that, sir," the gentleman snapped out at once to assure him that he knew who he was already. "I, sir, in turn am Captain Snegiryov, sir, but I am still desirous to know precisely what has led you, sir——"

"Oh, I've come for nothing special. I wanted to have a word with you— if only you allow me."

"In that case, here is a chair, sir; kindly be seated, sir. That's what they used to say in the old comedies, 'kindly be seated,'" and with a rapid gesture he seized an empty chair (it was a rough wooden chair, not upholstered) and set it for him almost in the middle of the room; then, taking another similar chair for himself, he sat down facing Alyosha, so close to him that their knees almost touched.

"Nikolay Ilyich Snegiryov, sir, formerly a captain in the Russian infantry, sir, put to shame for his vices, but still a captain. Though I should say Captain Yessirov rather than Snegiryov; for the last half of my life I've learned to say 'sir.' It's a word you use when you've come down in the world."

"That's very true," smiled Alyosha. "But is it used involuntarily or on purpose?"

"As God's above, it's involuntary, and I didn't use it before! I didn't use the word 'sir' all my life, but as soon as I sank into low water I began to say 'sir.' It's the work of a higher power. I see you are interested in contemporary questions, but how can I have excited your curiosity, living as I do in surroundings impossible for the exercise of hospitality?"

"I've come—about that business."

"About what business?" the captain interrupted impatiently.

"About your meeting with my brother Dmitri Fyodorovich," Alyosha blurted out awkwardly.

"What meeting, sir? You don't mean that meeting, sir? About my wisp of tow, then, my bathhouse wisp of tow?" He moved closer so that his knees positively knocked against Alyosha. His lips were strangely compressed like a thread.

"What wisp of tow?" muttered Alyosha.

"He is come to complain of me, papa!" cried a voice familiar to Alyosha—the voice of the schoolboy—from behind the curtain. "I bit his finger just now." The curtain was pulled, and Alyosha saw his assailant lying on a little bed made up on the bench and the chair in the corner under the icons. The boy lay covered by his coat and an old wadded quilt. He was evidently unwell, and, judging by his glittering eyes, he was in a fever. He looked at Alyosha without fear, as though he felt he was at home and could not be touched.

"What! Did he bite your finger?" The captain jumped up from his chair. "Was it your finger he bit, sir?"

"Yes. He was throwing stones with other schoolboys. There were six of them against him alone, I went up to him, and he threw a stone at me and then another at my head. I asked him what I had done to him. And then he rushed at me and bit my finger badly, I don't know why."

"I'll thrash him, sir, at once—this minute!" The captain jumped up from his seat.

"But I am not complaining at all, I am simply telling you . . . I don't want him to be thrashed. Besides, he seems to be ill."

"And do you suppose I'd thrash him, sir? That I'd take my Ilyushechka and thrash him before you for your satisfaction? Would you like it done at once, sir?" said the captain, suddenly turning to Alyosha, as though he were going to attack him. "I am sorry about your little finger sir; but instead of thrashing Ilyushechka, would you like me to chop off my four fingers with this knife here before your eyes to satisfy your just wrath? I should think four fingers would be enough to satisfy your thirst for vengeance, sir. You won't ask for the fifth one too?" He stopped short with a catch in his throat. Every feature in his face was twitching and working; he looked extremely defiant. He was in a sort of frenzy.

"I think I understand it all now," said Alyosha gently and sorrowfully, still keeping his seat. "So your boy is a good boy, he loves his father, and he attacked me as the brother of your assailant. . . . Now I understand it," he repeated thoughtfully. "But my brother Dmitri Fyodorovich regrets his action, I know that, and if only it is possible for him to come to you, or better still, to meet you in that same place, he will ask your forgiveness before everyone—if you wish it."

"After pulling out my beard, you mean, he will ask my forgiveness? And he thinks that will be a satisfactory finish, does he, sir?"

"Oh, no! On the contrary, he will do anything you like and in any way you like."

"So if I were to ask his highness to go down on his knees, sir, before me in that very tavern—'The Metropolis' it's called—or in the marketplace, he would do it?"

"Yes, he would even go down on his knees."

"You've pierced me to the heart, sir. Touched me to tears and pierced me to the heart, sir! I am only too sensible of your brother's generosity. Allow me to introduce my family, my two daughters and my son—my litter, sir. If I die, who will care for them, and while I live who but they will care for a wretch like me? That's a great thing the Lord has ordained for every man of my sort, sir. For there must be someone able to love even a man like me, sir."

"Ah, that's perfectly true!" exclaimed Alyosha.

"Oh, do stop playing the fool! Some fool comes in, and you put us to shame!" cried the girl by the window, suddenly turning to her father with a disdainful and contemptuous air.

"Wait a little, Barbara Nikolavna! Permit me to maintain the tenor," cried her father, speaking peremptorily but looking at her quite approvingly. "That's her character, sir," he said, addressing Alyosha again.

> And in all nature there was nothing
> He wished to bless[7]

or rather in the feminine: that she wished to bless. But now, sir, let me present you to my wife, Arina Petrovna. She is crippled, she is forty-three; she can move, but very little. She is of humble origin. Arina Petrovna, compose your countenance. This is Alexey Fyodorovich Karamazov. Get up, Alexey Fyodorovich." He took him by the hand and with unexpected force pulled him up. "You must stand up to be introduced to a lady, sir. It's not the Karamazov, mamma, who . . . hmm . . . etcetera, but his brother, radiant with modest virtues. Come Arina Petrovna, come, mamma, but first permit me to kiss your hand."

And he kissed his wife's hand respectfully and even tenderly. The girl at the window turned her back indignantly on the scene; an expression of extraordinary cordiality came over the haughtily inquiring face of the woman.

"Hello! Sit down, Mr. Chernomazov,"[8] she said.

"Karamazov, mamma, Karamazov (we are of humble origin, sir)," he whispered again.

"Well, Karamazov, or whatever it is, but I always think of Chernomazov. . . . Sit down. Why has he pulled you up? He calls me crippled but I am not, only my legs are swollen like barrels, and I am shriveled up myself. Once I used to be so fat, but now it's as though I had swallowed a needle."

"We are of humble origin, sir, humble origin, sir," the captain muttered again.

7. From Pushkin's poem "The Demon" (1823).
8. Arina Petrovna uses the Russian root for black, *chern*, instead of the Turkish term *kara*. See p. xix.

"Oh, papa, papa!" the hunchback girl, who had till then been silent on her chair, said suddenly, and she hid her eyes in her handkerchief.

"Buffoon!" blurted out the girl at the window.

"Have you heard our news?" said the mother, pointing at her daughters. "It's like clouds coming over; the clouds pass and we have music again. When we were with the army, we used to have many such guests. I don't mean to make any comparisons; everyone to his taste. The deacon's wife used to come then and say, 'Alexandr Alexandrovich is a man of the noblest heart, but Nastasya Petrovna,' she would say, 'is of the brood of hell.' 'Well,' I said, 'that's a matter of taste; but you are a little spitfire.' 'And you want keeping in your place,' says she. 'You black sword,' said I, 'who asked you to teach me?' 'But my breath,' says she, 'is clean, and yours is unclean.' 'You ask all the officers whether my breath is unclean.' And ever since then I had it in my mind. Not long ago I was sitting here as I am now, when I saw that very general come in who came here for Easter, and I asked him: 'Your Excellency,' said I, 'can a lady's breath be unpleasant?' 'Yes,' he answered; 'you ought to open a window or open the door, for the air is not fresh here.' And they all go on like that! And what is my breath to them? The dead smell worse still! 'I won't spoil the air,' said I, 'I'll order some slippers and go away.' My darlings, don't blame your own mother! Nikolay Ilyich, how is it I can't please you? There's only Ilyushechka who comes home from school and loves me. Yesterday he brought me an apple. Forgive, my dears, forgive your own mother, my darlings forgive me, I am so lonely, why has my breath become unpleasant to you?"

And the poor woman suddenly broke into sobs, and tears streamed down her cheeks. The captain rushed up to her.

"Mamma, mamma, my dear, stop! You are not lonely. Everyone loves you, everyone adores you." He began kissing both her hands again and tenderly stroking her face; taking the dinner napkin, he began wiping away her tears. Alyosha fancied that he too had tears in his eyes. "There, sir, you see, sir, you hear?" he turned with a sort of fury to Alyosha, pointing to the poor imbecile.

"I see and hear," muttered Alyosha.

"Papa, papa!" How can you—with him! Let him alone!" cried the boy suddenly, sitting up in his bed and gazing at his father with glowing eyes.

"That's enough of your clowning, showing off your silly antics which never lead to anything!" shouted Barabara Nikolaevna, even stamping her foot with passion.

"Your anger is quite just this time, Barbara Nikolavna, and I'll make haste to satisfy you. Come, put on your cap, Alexey Fyodorovich, and I'll put on mine. We will go out. I have a word to say to you in earnest, sir, but not within these walls. This girl sitting here is my daughter Nina Nikolaevna, sir. I forgot to introduce her to you, sir. She is a heavenly angel incarnate . . . who has flown down to us mortals, . . . if you can understand . . ."

"There he is shaking all over, as though he is in convulsions!" Barbara Nikolaevna went on indignantly.

"And she there stamping her foot at me and calling me a fool just now, she is a heavenly angel incarnate too, and she has good reason to call me so. Come along, Alexey Fyodorovich, we must make an end, sir."

And, snatching Alyosha's hand, he drew him out of the room into the street.

Chapter VII

And in the Fresh Air

"The air is fresh, sir, but in my mansion it is not so in any sense of the word. Let us walk slowly, my good sir. I should be glad of your kind interest."

"I too have something important to say to you," observed Alyosha, "only I don't know how to begin."

"To be sure you must have business with me, sir. You would never have come to see me without some object. Unless you come simply to complain of the boy, and that's hardly likely, sir. And, by the way, about the boy, sir: I could not explain to you in there, but here I will describe that scene to you. My tow was thicker a week ago—I mean my beard, sir. That's the nickname they give to my beard, the schoolboys most of all. Well, your brother Dmitri Fyodorovich was pulling me by my beard, I'd done nothing, he was in a towering rage and happened to come upon me. He dragged me out of the tavern into the marketplace; at that moment the boys were coming out of school, and with them Ilyusha. As soon as he saw me in such a state, sir, he rushed up to me. 'Papa,' he cried, 'papa!' He caught hold of me, hugged me, tried to pull me away, crying to my assailant, 'Let go, let go, it's my papa, forgive him!—yes, he actually cried 'forgive him.' He clutched at that hand, that very hand, in his little hands and kissed it, sir. . . . I remember his little face at that moment. I haven't forgotten it, sir, and I never shall!"

"I swear," cried Alyosha, "that my brother will express his most deep and sincere regret, even if he has to go down on his knees in that same marketplace. . . . I'll make him or he is no brother of mine!"

"Aha, then it's only a draft project! And it does not come from him but simply from the generosity of your own warm heart, sir. You should have said so, sir. No, in that case allow me to tell you of your brother's highly chivalrous soldierly generosity, for he did give expression to it at the time, sir. He stopped dragging me by my beard and released me: 'You are an officer,' he said, 'and I am an officer, if you can find a decent man to be your second send me your challenge. I will give you satisfaction, though you are a scoundrel.' That's what he said, sir. A chivalrous spirit indeed! I retired with Ilyusha, and this genealogical family picture is imprinted forever on Ilyusha's soul. No, it's not for us to claim the privileges of noblemen. Judge for yourself, sir. You've just been in our mansion, sir, what did you see there? Three ladies, one a cripple and weak-minded, another a cripple and hunchback and the third not crippled but far too clever. She is a student, sir, dying to get back to Petersburg, to work for the emancipation of the Russian woman on the banks of the Neva. I won't speak of Ilyusha, sir, he is only nine. I am alone in the world, and if I die, what will become of all of them, I simply ask you that, sir. And if I challenge him and he kills me on the spot, what then? What will become of them? And worse still, if he doesn't kill me but only cripples me: I couldn't work, but

I should still be a mouth to feed. Who would feed it and who would feed them all? Must I take Ilyusha from school and send him to beg in the streets? That's what it means for me to challenge him to a duel, sir. It's silly talk, sir, and nothing else, sir."

"He will beg your forgiveness, he will bow down at your feet in the middle of the marketplace," cried Alyosha again, with glowing eyes.

"I did think of prosecuting him," the captain went on, "but look in our code, could I get much compensation for a personal injury? And then Agrafena Alexandrovna[9] sent for me and shouted at me: 'Don't dare to dream of it! If you proceed against him, I'll publish it to all the world that he beat you for your dishonesty, and then you will be prosecuted.' I call God to witness, sir, whose was the dishonesty and by whose commands I acted, wasn't it by her own and Fyodor Pavlovich's? 'And what's more,' she went on, 'I'll dismiss you for good and you'll never earn another penny from me. I'll speak to my merchant too'—that's what she calls her old man—'and he will dismiss you!' And if he dismisses me, what can I earn then from anyone? Those two are all I have to look to, for your Fyodor Pavlovich has not only stopped employing me, for another reason, sir, but he means to make use of papers I've signed to go to law against me. And so I kept quiet, sir, and you have seen our retreat. But now let me ask you: did Ilyusha hurt your finger much? I didn't like to go into it in our mansion before him."

"Yes, very much, and he was in a great fury. He was avenging you on me as a Karamazov, I see that now. But if only you had seen how he was throwing stones at his schoolfellows! It's very dangerous. They might kill him. They are children and stupid. A stone may be thrown and break somebody's head."

"That's just what has happened, sir. He has been bruised by a stone today. Not on the head but on the chest, sir, just above the heart. He came home crying and groaning and now he is ill."

"And you know he attacks them first. He is bitter against them on your account. They say he stabbed a boy called Krasotkin with a penknife not long ago."

"I've heard about that too, it's dangerous, sir. Krasotkin is an official here, we may hear more about it, sir."

"I would advise you," Alyosha went on warmly, "not to send him to school at all for a time till he is calmer . . . and his anger is passed."

"Anger!" the captain repeated, "that's just what it is, sir. He is a little being, sir, but it's a mighty anger. You don't know all, sir. Permit me to explain that story to you in detail. Since that incident all the boys have been teasing him about the 'wisp of tow.' Schoolboys are a merciless race, individually they are angels of God, but together, especially in schools, they are often merciless. Their teasing has stirred up a gallant spirit in Ilyusha. An ordinary boy, a weak son, would have submitted, have felt ashamed of his father, sir, but he stood up for his father against them all. For his father and for truth and justice, sir. For what he suffered when he kissed your brother's hand and cried to him 'forgive papochka, forgive papochka,'—that only God knows—and I, sir, his father. For our children— that is, not your children, but ours—the children of the poor gentlemen

9. Grushenka's full first name and patronymic.

looked down upon by everyone—know what justice means, sir, even at the age of nine. How should the rich know? They don't explore such depths once in their lives. But at that moment in the square when he kissed his hand, at that moment my Ilyushka went through the whole truth, sir. That truth entered into him and crushed him forever, sir," the captain said hotly again with a sort of frenzy, and he struck his right fist against his left palm as though he wanted to show how "the truth" crushed Ilyusha. "That very day, sir, he fell ill with fever and was delirious all night. All that day he hardly said a word to me, sir, but I noticed he kept watching me from the corner, though he turned to the window and pretended to be learning his lessons. But I could see his mind was not on his lessons. The next day I got drunk to forget my troubles, sinful man as I am, sir, and I don't remember much. Mamma began crying, too—I am very fond of mamma, sir—well, I spent my last penny drowning my troubles. Don't despise me for that, sir, in Russia men who drink are the best. The best men among us are the greatest drunkards. I lay down and I don't remember about Ilyusha, though all that day the boys had been jeering at him at school, sir, 'Wisp of tow,' they shouted, 'your father was pulled out of the tavern by his wisp of tow, you ran by and begged forgiveness.' On the third day when he·came back from school, I saw he looked pale and wretched. 'What is it?' I asked. He wouldn't answer. Well, there's no talking in our mansion without mamma and the girls taking part in it. What's more the girls had heard about it the very first day. Barbara Nikolavna had begun snarling. 'You fools and buffoons, can you ever do anything rational?' 'Quite so,' I said, 'can we ever do anything rational?' For the time I turned it off like that, sir. So in the evening I took the boy out for a walk, for you must know we go for a walk every evening, always the same way, along which we are going now—from our gate to that great stone which lies alone in the road under the hurdle, which marks the beginning of the town pasture. A beautiful and lonely spot, sir. Ilyusha and I walked along hand in hand as usual. He has a little hand, his fingers are thin and cold—he suffers with his chest, you know. 'Papa,' said he, 'papa!' 'Well?' said I. I saw his eyes flashing. 'Papa, how he treated you then!' 'It can't be helped, Ilyusha,' I said. 'Don't forgive him, papa, don't forgive him! At school they say that he has paid you ten rubles for it.' 'No, Ilyusha,' said I, 'I would not take money from him for anything.' Then he began trembling all over, took my hand in both his and kissed it again. 'Papa,' he said, 'papa, challenge him to a duel, at school they say you are a coward and won't challenge him, and that you'll accept ten rubles from him.' 'I can't challenge him to a duel, Ilyusha,' I answered. And I told briefly what I've just told you. He listened. 'Papa,' he said, 'anyway don't forgive it. When I grow up I'll call him out myself and kill him.' His eyes shone and glowed. And of course I am his father, and I had to put in a word: 'It's a sin to kill,' I said, 'even in a duel.' 'Papa,' he said, 'when I grow up, I'll knock him down, knock the sword out of his hand, I'll fall on him, wave my sword over him and say: "I could kill you, but I forgive you, so there!"' You see what the workings of his little mind have been during these two days; he must have been planning that vengeance all day, and raving about it at night, sir. But he began to come home from school badly beaten, I found out about it the day before yesterday, and you are right, sir. I won't send him to that school any more. I heard that he was standing up against all the class alone and defying them all, that his heart was full of resentment, of bitterness—I was alarmed about him. We went for another walk. 'Papa,' he asked, 'are the rich people stronger than any one else on earth?' 'Yes, Ilyusha,' I said, 'there are no people on earth stronger than the rich.' 'Papa,' he said, 'I will get rich, I will become an officer and conquer everybody. The Tsar will reward me, I will come back here and then no one will dare.' . . . Then he was silent and his lips still kept trembling, 'Papa,' he said, 'what a horrid town this is.' 'Yes, Ilyushechka,' I said, 'it isn't a very nice town.' 'Papa,' let us move into another town, a nice one,' he said, 'where people don't know about us.' 'We will move, we will, Ilyusha,' said I, 'only I must save up for it.' I was glad to be able to turn his mind from painful thoughts, and we began to dream of how we would move to another town, how we would buy a horse and cart. 'We will put mamma and your sisters inside, we will cover them up and we'll walk, you shall have a lift now and then, and I'll walk beside, for we must take care of our horse, we can't all ride. That's how we'll go.' He was enchanted at that, most of all at the thought of having a horse and driving him. For of course a Russian boy is born among horses. We chattered a long while. Thank God, I thought, I have diverted his mind and comforted him. That was the day before yesterday, in the evening, but last night everything was changed. He had gone to school in the morning, he came back depressed, terribly depressed. In the evening I took him by the hand and we went for a walk; he would not talk. There was a wind blowing and no sun, and a feeling of autumn; twilight was coming on. We walked along, both of us depressed. 'Well, my boy,' said I, 'how about our setting off on our travels?' I thought I might bring him back to our talk of the day before. He didn't answer, but I felt his fingers trembling in my hand. Ah, I thought, it's a bad job; there's something new. We had reached the stone where we are now. I sat down on the stone. And in the air there were lots of kites flapping and whirling. There were as many as thirty in sight. Of course, it's just the season for the kites, sir. 'Look, Ilyusha,' said I, 'it's time we got out our last year's kite again. I'll mend it, where have you put it away?' My boy made no answer. He looked away and turned sideways to me. And then a gust of wind blew up the sand. He suddenly fell on me, threw both his little arms round my neck and held me tight. You know, when children are silent and proud, and try to keep back their tears when they are in great trouble and suddenly break down, their tears fall in streams, sir. With those warm streams of tears, sir, he suddenly wetted my face. He sobbed and shook as though he were in convulsions, and squeezed me up against him as I sat on the stone. 'Papochka,' he kept crying, 'Papochka, darling papochka, how he humiliated you!' And I sobbed too, sir. We sat shaking in each other's arms. 'Papochka,' he said, 'papochka.' 'Ilyusha,' I said to him, 'Ilyusha darling.' No one saw us then, sir. God alone saw us, I hope he will enter it on my service record, sir. You must thank your brother, sir, Alexey Fyodorovich. No, sir, I won't thrash my boy for your satisfaction, sir."

He had gone back to his original tone of spiteful buffoonery. Alyosha felt though that he trusted him, and that if there had been someone else in his, Alyosha's place, the man would not have spoken so openly and would not have told what he had just told. This encouraged Alyosha, whose soul was trembling on the verge of tears.

"Ah, how I would like to make friends with your boy!" he cried, "If you could arrange it——"

"Certainly, sir," muttered the captain.

"But now listen to something quite different!" Alyosha went on. "I have a message for you. That same brother of mine, Dmitri, has insulted his betrothed, too, a noble-hearted girl of whom you have probably heard. I have a right to tell you of her wrong; I ought to do so, in fact, for hearing of the insult done to you and learning all about your unfortunate position, she commissioned me at once—just now—to bring you this help from her— but only from her alone, not from Dmitri, who has abandoned her. Nor from me, his brother, nor from anyone else, but from her, only from her! She entreats you to accept her help. . . . You have both been insulted by the same man. She thought of you only when she had just received a similar insult from him—similar in its cruelty, I mean. She comes like a sister to help a brother in misfortune. . . . She told me to persuade you to take these two hundred rubles from her, as from a sister, knowing that you are in such need. No one will know of it, it can give rise to no unjust slander. There are the two hundred rubles, and I swear you must take them unless—unless all men are to be enemies on earth! But there are brothers even on earth. . . . You have a generous heart . . . you must see that, you must."

And Alyosha held out two new rainbow-colored hundred-ruble bills. They were both standing at the time by the great stone close to the fence, and there was no one near. The bills seemed to produce a tremendous impression on the captain. He started, but at first only from astonishment. Such an outcome of their conversation was the last thing he expected. Nothing could have been further from his dreams than help from any one—and such a sum! He took the bills, and for a minute he was almost unable to answer, quite a new expression came into his face.

"That for me? So much money—two hundred rubles! Good heavens! Why, I haven't seen so much money for the last four years! Mercy on us! And she says she is a sister . . . And is that the truth?"

"I swear that all I told you is the truth," cried Alyosha. The captain flushed red.

"Listen, sir, my dear, listen, sir, if I take it, won't I be behaving like a scoundrel? In your eyes, Alexey Fyodorovich, won't I be a scoundrel? No, Alexey Fyodorovich, listen, sir, listen," he hurried, touching Alyosha with both his hands. "You are persuading me to take it, saying that it's a sister sends it, but inwardly, in your heart won't you feel contempt for me if I take it, sir, eh?"

"No, no, on my salvation I swear I won't! And no one will ever know but me—I, you and she, and one other lady, her great friend."

"Never mind the lady! Listen, Alexey Fyodorovich, at a moment like this you must listen, sir, for you can't understand what these two hundred rubles mean to me now." The poor fellow went on rising gradually into a sort of incoherent, almost wild enthusiasm. He was thrown off his balance and talked extremely fast, as though afraid he would not be allowed to say all he had to say.

"Besides its being honestly acquired from a 'sister,' so highly respected and revered, do you know that now I can look after mamma and Nina, my hunchback angel daughter? Doctor Herzenstube came to me in the kindness of his heart and was examining them both for a whole hour. 'I can make nothing of it,' said he, but he prescribed a mineral water which is kept at a chemist's here. He said it would be sure to do her good, and he ordered baths, too, with some medicine in them. The mineral water costs thirty kopecks, and she'd need to drink forty bottles perhaps; so I took the prescription and laid it on the shelf under the icons, and there it lies. And he ordered hot baths for Nina with something dissolved in them, morning and evening. But how can we carry out such a cure in our mansion, sir, without servants, without help, without a bath, and without water? Nina is rheumatic all over, I don't think I told you that. All her right side aches at night, she is in agony, and, would you believe it, the angel bears it without groaning for fear of waking us. We eat what we can get, and she'll only take the leavings, what you'd scarcely give to a dog. 'I am not worth it, I am taking it from you, I am a burden on you,' that's what her angel eyes try to express. We wait on her, but she doesn't like it. 'I am a useless cripple, no good to anyone.' As though she were not worth it, sir, when she is the saving of all of us with her angelic sweetness. Without her, without her gentle word it would be hell among us! She softens even Barbara. And don't judge Barbara Nikolavna harshly either, she is an angel too, she, too, has suffered wrong. She came to us for the summer, and she brought six-teen rubles she had earned by lessons and saved up, to go back with to Petersburg in September, that is now. But we took her money and lived on it, so now she has nothing to go back with, sir. Though indeed she couldn't go back, for she has to work for us like a slave. She is like an overdriven horse with all of us on her back. She waits on us all, mends and washes, sweeps the floor, puts mamma to bed. And mamma is capricious and tear-ful and insane, sir! And now I can get a servant, sir, with this money, you understand, Alexey Fyodorovich, I can get medicines for the dear beings, I can send my student to Petersburg, sir, I can buy beef, I can feed them properly. Good Lord, but it's a dream!"

Alyosha was delighted that he had brought him such happiness and that the poor fellow had consented to be made happy.

"Wait, Alexey Fyodorovich, wait," the captain began to talk with fren-zied rapidity carried away by a new daydream. "Do you know that Ilyusha and I will perhaps really carry out our dream. We will buy a horse and cart, a black horse, he insists on its being black, and we will set off as we pretended the other day. I have an old friend, a lawyer in K——[1] province, sir, and I heard through a trustworthy man that if I were to go he'd give me a place as clerk in his office, so, who knows, maybe he would. So I'd just put mamma and Nina in the cart, and Ilyushechka could drive, and I'd walk, I'd walk. . . . Why, if I only succeed in getting one debt paid that's owing me, I would have perhaps enough for that too!"

"There would be enough!" cried Alyosha. "Katerina Ivanovna will send you as much more as you need, and you know, I have money too, take what you want, as you would from a brother, from a friend, you can give it back later. . . . (You'll get rich, you'll get rich!) And you know you couldn't have a better idea than to move to another province! It would be the saving of you, especially of your boy—and you ought to go quickly, before the winter, before the cold. You must write to us when you are there, and we will always be brothers. . . . No, it's not a dream!"

---

1. Using letters to designate place names was a common practice in nineteenth-century fiction writing.

Alyosha could have hugged him, he was so pleased. But glancing at him he stopped short. The man was standing with his neck outstretched and his lips protruding, with a pale and frenzied face. His lips were moving as though trying to articulate something; no sound came, but still his lips moved. It was uncanny.

"What is it?" asked Alyosha, startled.

"Alexey Fyodorovich . . . I . . . you," muttered the captain, faltering, looking at him with a strange, wild, fixed stare, and an air of desperate resolution. At the same time there was a sort of grin on his lips. "I, sir . . . you, sir . . . wouldn't you like me to show you a little trick I know, sir?" he murmured, suddenly, in a firm rapid whisper, his voice no longer faltering.

"What trick?"

"A pretty trick," whispered the captain. His mouth was twisted on the left side, his left eye was screwed up. He still stared at Alyosha.

"What is the matter, what trick?" Alyosha cried, now thoroughly alarmed.

"Why, look," squealed the captain suddenly, and showing him the two bills, which he had been holding by one corner between his thumb and forefinger during the conversation, he crumpled them up savagely and squeezed them tight in his right hand.

"Do you see, sir, do you see, sir?" he shrieked, pale and infuriated. And suddenly flinging up his hand, he threw the crumpled bills on the sand. "Do you see, sir?" he shrieked again, pointing to them. "Look there!"

And with wild fury he began trampling them under his heel, gasping and exclaiming as he did so:

"So much for your money, sir! So much for your money, sir! So much for your money, sir! So much for your money, sir!"

Suddenly he darted back and drew himself up before Alyosha, and his whole figure expressed unutterable pride.

"Tell those who sent you that the wisp of tow does not sell his honor, sir," he cried, raising his arm in the air. Then he turned quickly and began to run; but he had not run five steps before he turned completely round and kissed his hand to Alyosha. He ran another five paces and then turned round for the last time. This time his face was not contorted with laughter, but quivering all over with tears. In a tearful, faltering, sobbing voice he cried:

"What should I say to my boy if I took money from you for our shame?"

And then he ran on without turning. Alyosha looked after him, inexpressibly grieved. Oh, he saw that till the very last moment the man had not known he would crumple up and fling away the bills. He did not turn back. Alyosha knew he would not. He would not follow him and call him back, he knew why. When he was out of sight, Alyosha picked up the two bills. They were very much crushed and crumpled, and had been pressed into the sand, but were uninjured and even rustled like new ones when Alyosha unfolded them and smoothed them out. After smoothing them out, he folded them up, put them in his pocket and went to Katerina Ivanovna to report on the success of her commission.

Book Five

PRO AND CONTRA

Chapter I

An Engagement

Madame Khokhlakova was again the first to meet Alyosha. She was flustered; something important had happened. Katerina Ivanovna's hysterics had ended in a fainting fit, and then "a terrible, awful weakness had followed, she lay with her eyes turned up and was delirious. Now she was in a fever. They had sent for Herzenstube; they had sent for the aunts. The aunts were already here, but Herzenstube had not yet come. They were all sitting in her room, waiting. She was unconscious now, and what if it turned to brain fever!"

Madame Khokhlakova looked gravely alarmed. "This is serious, serious," she added at every word, as though nothing that had happened to her before had been serious. Alyosha listened with distress, and was beginning to describe his adventures, but she interrupted him at the first words: she had no time to listen, she begged him to sit with Lise and wait for her there.

"Lise," she whispered almost in his ear, "Lise has greatly surprised me just now, my dearest Alexey Fyodorovich. She touched me, too, and so my heart forgives her everything. Imagine, as soon as you had gone, she began to be truly remorseful for having laughed at you today and yesterday, though she was not laughing at you, but only joking. But she was seriously sorry for it, almost ready to cry, so that I was quite surprised. She has never been really sorry for laughing at me, but has only made a joke of it. And you know she laughs at me all the time. But this time she was in earnest. She thinks a great deal of your opinion, Alexey Fyodorovich, and don't take offense or be wounded by her if you can help it. I am never hard upon her, for she's such a clever little thing—would you believe it? She said just now that you were a friend of her childhood, 'the greatest friend of her childhood'—just think of that—'greatest friend'—and what about me? She has very strong feelings and memories, and, what's more, she uses these phrases, most unexpected words, which come out all of a sudden when you least expect them. She spoke lately about a pine tree, for instance: there used to be a pine tree standing in our garden in her early childhood. Very likely it's standing there still; so there's no need to speak in the past tense. Pine trees are not like people, Alexey Fyodorovich, they don't change quickly. 'Mamma,' she said, 'I remember this pine tree and pine for it,' that is, pine tree and pine for it, she must have expressed it differently because there is something wrong there, 'pine' is a stupid word, only she said something so original about it that I can't repeat it. Besides, I've forgotten it. Well, good-bye! I am so worried I feel I shall go out of my mind. Ah! Alexey Fyodorovich, I've been out of my mind twice in my life. Go to Lise, cheer her up, as you always can so charmingly. Lise," she cried, going to her door, "here I've brought you Alexey Fyodorovich, whom you insulted so. He is not at all angry, I assure you; on the contrary, he is surprised that you could suppose so."

"*Merci, maman.* Come in, Alexey Fyodorovich."

Alyosha went in. Lise looked rather embarrassed, and at once flushed crimson. She was evidently ashamed of something, and, as people always do in such cases, she began immediately talking of other things, as though they were of absorbing interest to her at the moment.

"Mamma has just told me all about the two hundred rubles, Alexey Fyodorovich, and your taking them to that poor officer . . . and she told me all the awful story of how he had been insulted . . . and you know, although mamma muddles things . . . she always rushes from one thing to another . . . I cried when I heard. Well, did you give him the money and how is that poor man getting on?"

"The fact is I didn't give it to him, and it's a long story," answered Alyosha, as though he, too, could think of nothing but his regret at having failed, yet Lise saw perfectly well that he, too, looked away, and that he, too, was trying to talk of other things. Alyosha sat down to the table and began to tell his story, but at the first words he lost his embarrassment and gained the whole of Lise's attention as well. He spoke with deep feeling, under the influence of the strong impression he had just received, and he succeeded in telling his story well and circumstantially. In the old days in Moscow he had been fond of coming to Lise and describing to her what had just happened to him, and what he had read, or what he remembered of his childhood. Sometimes they had made daydreams and woven whole romances together—generally cheerful and amusing ones. Now they both felt suddenly transported to the old days in Moscow, two years before. Lise was extremely touched by his story. Alyosha described "Ilyushechka" with warm feeling. When he finished describing how the luckless man trampled on the money, Lise could not help clasping her hands and crying out:

"So you didn't give him the money, so you let him run away! Oh, dear, you ought to have run after him . . ."

"No, Lise; it's better I didn't run after him," said Alyosha, getting up from his chair and walking thoughtfully across the room.

"How so? How is it better? Now they are without food and their case is hopeless!"

"Not hopeless, for the two hundred rubles will still come to them. He'll take the money tomorrow. Tomorrow he will be sure to take it," said Alyosha, pacing up and down, pondering. "You see, Lise," he went on, stopping suddenly before her, "I made one blunder, but that, even that, is all for the best."

"What blunder, and why is it for the best?"

"I'll tell you. He is a man of weak and timorous character; he has suffered so much and is very good-natured. I keep wondering why he took offense so suddenly, for I assure you, up to the last minute, he did not know that he was going to trample on the bills. And I think now that there was a great deal to offend him . . . and it could not have been otherwise in his position. . . . To begin with, he was offended at having been so glad of the money in my presence and not having concealed it from me. If he had been pleased, but not so much; if he had not shown it; if he had begun affecting scruples and difficulties, as other people do when they take money, he might still endure to take it. But he was too genuinely delighted, and that was mortifying. Ah, Lise, he is a good and truthful man—that's the worst of the whole business. All the while he talked, his voice was so weak, so broken, he talked so fast, so fast, he kept laughing such a laugh, or perhaps he was crying—yes, I am sure he was crying, he was so delighted—and he talked about his daughters—and about the situation he could get in another town. . . . And when he had poured out his heart, he felt ashamed at having shown me his inmost soul like that. So he began to hate me at once. He is one of those awfully sensitive poor people. What had made him feel most ashamed was that he had given in too soon and accepted me as a friend, you see. At first he almost flew at me and tried to intimidate me, but as soon as he saw the money he had begun embracing me; he kept touching me with his hands. This must have been how he came to feel it all so humiliating, and then I made that blunder, a very important one. I suddenly said to him that if he had not money enough to move to another town, we would give it to him, and, indeed, I myself would give him as much as he wanted out of my own money. That struck him all at once. Why, he thought, did I put myself forward to help him? You know, Lise, it's awfully hard for a man who has been injured, when other people look at him as though they were his benefactors. . . . I've heard that; Father Zosima told me so. I don't know how to put it, but I have often seen it myself. And I feel like that myself, too. And the worst of it was that though he did not know, up to the very last minute, that he would trample on the bills, he had a kind of presentiment of it, I am sure of that. That's just what made him so ecstatic, that he had that presentiment. . . . And though it's so dreadful, it's all for the best. In fact, I believe nothing better could have happened."

"Why, why could nothing better have happened?" cried Lise, looking with great surprise at Alyosha.

"Because if he had taken the money, in an hour after getting home, he would be crying with mortification, that's just what would have happened. And most likely he would have come to me early tomorrow, and perhaps have flung the bills at me and trampled upon them as he did just now. But now he has gone home awfully proud and triumphant, though he knows he has 'ruined himself.' So now nothing could be easier than to make him accept the two hundred rubles by tomorrow, for he has already vindicated his honor, tossed away the money, and trampled it under foot. . . . He couldn't know when he did it that I would bring it to him again tomorrow, and yet he is in terrible need of that money. Though he is proud of himself now, yet even today he'll be thinking what a help he has lost. He will think of it more than ever at night, will dream of it, and by tomorrow morning he may be ready to run to me to ask forgiveness. It's just then that I'll appear. 'Here, you are a proud man,' I shall say: 'you have shown it; but now take the money and forgive us!' And then he will take it!"

Alyosha was carried away with joy as he uttered the last words. "And then he will take it!" Lise clapped her hands.

"Ah, that's true! I suddenly understand that perfectly now! Ah, Alyosha, how do you know all this? So young and yet he knows what's in the heart. . . . I should never have worked it out . . ."

"The main thing now is to persuade him that he is on an equal footing with us, in spite of his taking money from us," Alyosha went on in his excitement, "and not only on an equal, but even on a higher footing . . ."

"'On a higher footing' is splendid, Alexey Fyodorovich; but go on, go on!"

"You mean there isn't such an expression as 'on a higher footing'; but that doesn't matter because . . ."

"Oh, no, no, of course it doesn't matter. Forgive me, Alyosha, dear. . . . You know, I scarcely respected you till now . . . that is I respected you but on an equal footing; but now I shall begin to respect you on a higher footing. Don't be angry, dear, at my joking," she put in at once, with strong feeling. "I am absurd and small, but you, you . . . Listen, Alexey Fyodorovich. Isn't there in all our analysis—I mean your analysis . . . no, better call it ours . . . aren't we showing contempt for him, for that poor man—in analyzing his soul like this, as it were, from above, eh? In deciding so certainly that he will take the money?"

"No, Lise, it's not contempt," Alyosha answered, as though he had prepared himself for the question. "I was thinking of that on the way here. How can it be contempt when we are all like him, when we are all just the same as he is? For you know we are just the same, no better. If we are better, we should have been just the same in his place. . . . I don't know about you, Lise, but I consider that I have a sordid soul in many ways, and his soul is not sordid; on the contrary, full of fine feeling. . . . No, Lise, I have no contempt for him. Do you know, Lise, my elder told me once to care for most people exactly as one would for children, and for some of them as one would for the sick in hospitals."

"Ah, Alexey Fyodorovich, dear, let us care for people as we would for the sick!"

"Let us, Lise; I am ready. Though I am not altogether ready in myself. I am sometimes very impatient and at other times I don't see things. It's different with you."

"Ah, I don't believe it! Alexey Fyodorovich, how happy I am."

"I am so glad you say so, Lise."

"Alexey Fyodorovich, you are wonderfully good, but you are sometimes sort of pedantic. . . . And yet you are not a bit pedantic really. Go to the door, open it gently, and see whether mamma is listening," said Lise, in a nervous, hurried whisper.

Alyosha went, opened the door, and reported that no one was listening.

"Come here, Alexey Fyodorovich," Lise went on, flushing redder and redder. "Give me your hand—that's right. I have to make a great confession, I didn't write to you yesterday in joke, but in earnest," and she hid her eyes with her hand. It was evident that she was greatly ashamed of the confession.

Suddenly she snatched his hand and impulsively kissed it three times.

"Ah, Lise, what a good thing!" cried Alyosha joyfully. "You know, I was perfectly sure you were in earnest."

"Sure? Upon my word!" she put aside his hand, but did not leave go of it, blushing hotly, and laughing a little happy laugh. "I kiss his hand and he says, 'What a good thing.'"

But her reproach was undeserved; Alyosha, too, was greatly overcome.

"I should like to please you always, Lise, but I don't know how to do it," he muttered, blushing too.

"Alyosha, dear, you are cold and rude. Do you see? He has chosen me as his wife and is quite settled about it. He is sure I was in earnest. What a thing to say! Why, that's impertinence—that's what it is."

"Why, was it wrong of me to feel sure?" Alyosha asked, laughing suddenly.

"Ah, Alyosha, on the contrary, it was delightfully right," cried Lise, looking tenderly and happily at him. Alyosha stood still, holding her hand in his. Suddenly he stooped down and kissed her right on her little lips.

"Oh, what are you doing?" cried Lise. Alyosha was terribly abashed.

"Oh, forgive me if I shouldn't. . . . Perhaps I'm awfully stupid. . . . You said I was cold, so I kissed you. . . . But I see it was stupid."

Lise laughed, and hid her face in her hands. "And in that dress!" she ejaculated in the midst of her mirth. But she suddenly ceased laughing and became serious, almost stern.

"Alyosha, we must put off kissing. We are not ready for that yet, and we shall have a long time to wait," she ended suddenly. "Tell me rather why you who are so clever, so intellectual, so observant, choose a little fool, an invalid like me? Ah, Alyosha, I am awfully happy for I don't deserve you a bit."

"You do, Lise. I shall be leaving the monastery altogether in a few days. If I go into the world, I must marry. I know that. *He* told me to marry, too. Whom could I marry better than you—and who would have me except you? I have been thinking it over. In the first place, you've known me since childhood and you've a great many qualities I haven't. You are more light-hearted than I am; above all, you are more innocent than I am. I have been brought into contact with many, many things already. . . . Ah, you don't know, but I, too, am a Karamazov. What does it matter if you do laugh and make jokes, and at me, too? Go on laughing. I am so glad you do. You laugh like a little child, but you think like a martyr."

"Like a martyr? How?"

"Yes, Lise, your question just now: whether we weren't showing contempt for that poor man by dissecting his soul—that was the question of a sufferer. . . . You see, I don't know how to express it, but anyone who thinks of such questions is capable of suffering. Sitting in your invalid chair you must have thought over many things already."

"Alyosha, give me your hand. Why are you taking it away?" murmured Lise in a failing voice, weak with happiness. "Listen, Alyosha. What will you wear when you come out of the monastery? What sort of suit? Don't laugh, don't be angry, it's very, very important to me."

"I haven't thought about the suit, Lise; but I'll wear whatever you like."

"I should like you to have a dark blue velvet coat, a white piqué waistcoat, and a soft gray felt hat. . . . Tell me, did you believe that I didn't care for you when I said I didn't mean what I wrote?"

"No, I didn't believe it."

"Oh, you insupportable person, you are incorrigible."

"You see, I knew that you—seemed to care for me, but I pretended to believe that you didn't care for me to make it—easier for you."

"That makes it worse! Worse and better than all! Alyosha, I love you terribly. Just before you came this morning, I tried my fortune. I decided I would ask you for my letter, and if you brought it out calmly and gave it to me (as might have been expected from you) it would mean that you did not love me at all, that you felt nothing, and were simply a stupid boy, good for nothing, and that I am ruined. But you left the letter at home and that cheered me. You left it behind on purpose, so as not to give it back, because you knew I would ask for it? That was it, wasn't it?"

"Ah, Lise, it was not so a bit. The letter is with me now, and it was this morning, in this pocket. Here it is."

Alyosha pulled the letter out laughing, and showed it to her at a distance.

"But I am not going to give it to you. Look at it from here."

"Why, then you told a lie? You, a monk, told a lie!"

"I told a lie if you like," Alyosha laughed, too. "I told a lie so as not to give you back the letter. It's very precious to me," he added suddenly, with strong feeling, and again he flushed. "It always will be, and I won't give it up to anyone!"

Lise looked at him joyfully. "Alyosha," she murmured again, "look at the door. Isn't mamma listening?"

"Very well, Lise, I'll look; but wouldn't it be better not to look? Why suspect your mother of such meanness?"

"What meanness? As for her spying on her daughter, it's her right, it's not meanness!" cried Lise, firing up. "You may be sure, Alexey Fyodorovich, that when I am a mother, if I have a daughter like myself I shall certainly spy on her!"

"Really, Lise? That's not right."

"Oh, my goodness! What has meanness to do with it? If she were listening to some ordinary worldly conversation, it would be meanness, but when her own daughter is shut up with a young man . . . Listen, Alyosha, do you know I shall spy upon you as soon as we are married, and let me tell you I shall open all your letters and read them, so you may as well be prepared."

"Yes, of course, if so—" muttered Alyosha, "only it's not right."

"Ah, how contemptuous! Alyosha, dear, we don't quarrel the very first day. I'd better tell you the whole truth. Of course, it's very wrong to spy on people, and, of course, I am not right and you are, only I shall spy on you all the same."

"Do, then; you won't find out anything," laughed Alyosha.

"And Alyosha, will you give in to me? We must decide that too."

"I shall be delighted to, Lise, and certain to, only not in the most important things. Even if you don't agree with me, I shall do my duty in the most important things."

"That's right; but let me tell you I am ready to give in to you not only in the most important matters, but in everything. And I am ready to vow to do so now—in everything, and for all my life!" cried Lise fervently, "and I'll do it gladly, gladly! What's more I'll swear never to spy on you, never once, never to read one of your letters. For you are right and I am not. And though I shall be awfully tempted to spy, I know that I won't do it since you consider it dishonorable. You are my conscience now. . . . Listen, Alexey Fyodorovich, why have you been so sad lately—both yesterday and today? I know you have a lot of anxiety and trouble, but I see you have some special grief besides, some secret one, perhaps?"

"Yes, Lise, I have a secret one, too," answered Alyosha mournfully. "I see you love me, since you guessed that."

"What grief? What about? Can you tell me?" asked Lise with timid entreaty.

"I'll tell you later, Lise—afterwards," said Alyosha, confused. "Now you wouldn't understand it perhaps—and perhaps I couldn't explain it."

"I know your brothers and your father are worrying you, too?"

"Yes, my brothers too," murmured Alyosha, pondering.

"I don't like your brother Ivan Fyodorovich, Alyosha," said Lise suddenly.

He noticed this remark with some surprise, but did not answer it.

"My brothers are destroying themselves," he went on, "my father, too. And they are destroying others with them. It's 'the earthly force of the Karamazovs,' as Father Païssy said the other day, a crude, unbridled, earthly force. Does the spirit of God move above that force? Even that I don't know. I only know that I, too, am a Karamazov. . . . Me a monk, a monk! Am I a monk, Lise? You said just now that I was."

"Yes, I did."

"And perhaps I don't even believe in God."

"You don't believe? What is the matter?" said Lise quietly and gently. But Alyosha did not answer. There was something too mysterious, too subjective in these last words of his, perhaps obscure to himself, but yet torturing him.

"And now on the top of it all, my friend, the best man in the world is going, is leaving the earth. If you knew, Lise, if you knew how bound up in soul I am with him! And then I shall be left alone. . . . I shall come to you, Lise. . . . For the future we will be together."

"Yes, together, together! Henceforward we shall be always together, all our lives! Listen, kiss me, I permit you to."

Alyosha kissed her.

"Well, now go. Christ be with you!" and she made the sign of the cross over him. "Make haste back to *him* while he is alive. I see I've kept you cruelly. I'll pray today for him and you. Alyosha, we shall be happy! Shall we be happy, shall we?"

"I believe we shall, Lise."

Alyosha thought it better not to go in to Madame Khokhlakova and was going out of the house without saying good-bye to her. But no sooner had he opened the door than he found Madame Khokhlakova standing before him. From the first word Alyosha guessed that she had been waiting on purpose to meet him.

"Alexey Fyodorovich, this is awful. This is all childish nonsense and ridiculous. I trust you won't dream . . . It's foolishness, foolishness, nothing but foolishness!" she said, attacking him at once.

"Only don't tell her that," said Alyosha, "or she will be upset, and that's bad for her now."

"Sensible advice from a sensible young man. Am I to understand that you only agreed with her from compassion for her invalid state, because you didn't want to irritate her by contradiction?"

"Oh, no, not at all. I was quite serious in what I said," Alyosha declared stoutly.

"To be serious about it is impossible, unthinkable, and in the first place I shall never be at home to you again, and I shall take her away, you may be sure of that."

"But why?" asked Alyosha. "It's all so far off. We may have to wait another year and a half."

"Ah, Alexey Fyodorovich, that's true, of course, and you'll have time to quarrel and separate a thousand times in a year and a half. But I am so unhappy, so unhappy! Though it's such nonsense, it's a great blow to me. I feel like Famusov in the last scene of *Woe from Wit*.[1] You are Chatsky and she is Sofya, and, only fancy, I've run down to meet you on the stairs, and in the play the fatal scene takes place on the staircase. I heard it all; I almost dropped. So this is the explanation of her dreadful night and her hysterics of late! It means love to the daughter but death to the mother. I might as well be in my grave at once. And a more serious matter still, what is this letter she has written? Show it me at once, at once!"

"No, there's no need. Tell me, how is Katerina Ivanovna now? I must know."

"She still lies in delirium; she has not regained consciousness. Her aunts are here; but they do nothing but sigh and give themselves airs. Herzenstube came, and he was so alarmed that I didn't know what to do for him. I nearly sent for a doctor to look after him. He was driven home in my carriage. And on top of it all, you and this letter! It's true nothing can happen for a year and half. In the name of all that's holy, in the name of your dying elder, show me that letter, Alexey Fyodorovich. I'm her mother. Hold it in your hand, if you like, and I will read it so."

"No, I won't show it to you, Katerina Osipovna. Even if she sanctioned it, I wouldn't. I am coming tomorrow, and if you like, we can talk over many things, but now good-bye!"

And Alyosha ran downstairs and into the street.

Chapter II

Smerdyakov with a Guitar

He had no time to lose indeed. Even while he was saying good-bye to Lise, the thought had struck him that he must attempt some stratagem to find his brother Dmitri, who was evidently keeping out of his way. It was getting late, nearly three o'clock. Alyosha's whole soul turned to the monastery, to his dying elder, but the necessity of seeing Dmitri outweighed everything. The conviction that a great inevitable catastrophe was about to happen grew stronger in Alyosha's mind with every hour. What that catastrophe was, and what he would say at that moment to his brother, he could perhaps not have said definitely. "Even if my benefactor must die without me, anyway I won't have to reproach myself all my life with the thought that I might have saved something and did not, but passed by

---

1. Famusov, Chatsky, and Sofya are the main characters of the play *Gore ot uma* (*Woe from Wit*, 1823) by Alexander Griboyedov (1795–1829).

and hastened home. If I do as I intend, I shall be acting according to his great word . . ."

His plan was to catch his brother Dmitri unawares, to climb over the fence, as he had the day before, get into the garden and sit in the gazebo. If Dmitri were not there, thought Alyosha, he would not announce himself to Thomas or the women of the house, but would remain hidden in the gazebo, even if he had to wait there till evening. If, as before, Dmitri were lying in wait for Grushenka to come, he would be very likely to come to the gazebo. Alyosha did not, however, give much thought to the details of his plan, but resolved to act upon it, even if it meant not getting back to the monastery that day.

Everything happened without hindrance; he climbed over the hurdle almost in the same spot as the day before, and stole into the gazebo unseen. He did not want to be noticed. The women of the house and Thomas too, if he were here, might be loyal to his brother and obey his instructions, and so refuse to let Alyosha come into the garden, or might warn Dmitri that he was being sought and inquired for. There was no one in the gazebo. Alyosha sat down and began to wait. He looked round the gazebo, which somehow struck him as a great deal more ancient than before. Though the day was just as fine as yesterday, it seemed a wretched little place this time. There was a circle on the table, left no doubt from the glass of brandy having been spilt the day before. Foolish and irrelevant ideas strayed about his mind, as they always do in a time of tedious waiting. He wondered, for instance, why he had sat down precisely in the same place as before, why not in the other seat. At last he felt very depressed—depressed by suspense and uncertainty. But he had not sat there more than a quarter of an hour, when he suddenly heard the strumming of a guitar somewhere quite close. People were sitting, or had only just sat down, somewhere in the bushes not more than twenty paces away. Alyosha suddenly recollected that on coming out of the gazebo the day before, he had caught a glimpse of an old green low garden seat among the bushes on the left, by the fence. The people must be sitting on it now. Who were they? A young man's voice suddenly began singing in a sugary falsetto, accompanying himself on the guitar:

> With invincible force
> I am bound to my dear.
> Oh, Lord, have mercy
> On her and on me!
> On her and on me!
> On her and on me![2]

The voice ceased. It was a lackey's tenor and a lackey's song. Another voice, a woman's, suddenly asked insinuatingly and bashfully, though with mincing affectation:

"Why haven't you been to see us for so long, Pavel Fyodorovich? Why do you always look down upon us?"

"Not at all, ma'am," answered a man's voice politely, but with emphatic dignity. It was clear that the man had the best of the position, and that

---

2. In a letter to Lyubimov of May 10, 1879, Dostoevsky claimed that he heard this song forty years earlier in Moscow, where it was popular among petty merchants and lackeys.

the woman was making advances. "I believe the man must be Smerdyakov," thought Alyosha, "from his voice. And the lady must be the daughter of the house here, who has come from Moscow, the one who wears
the dress with a train and goes to Martha for soup."

"I am awfully fond of verses of all kinds, if they rhyme," the woman's
voice continued. "Why don't you go on?"

The man sang again:

> What do I care for royal wealth
> If but my dear one be in health?
> Lord have mercy
> On her and on me!
> On her and on me!
> On her and on me!

"It was even better last time," observed the woman's voice. "You sang 'If
my darling be in health'; it sounded more tender. I suppose you've forgotten today."

"Poetry is rubbish, ma'am!" said Smerdyakov curtly.

"Oh, no! I am very fond of poetry."

"So far as it's poetry, it's essential rubbish, ma'am. Consider yourself,
who ever talks in rhyme? And if we were all to talk in rhyme, even though
it were decreed by government, we shouldn't say much, ma'am, should
we? Poetry is no good, Marya Kondratyevna."

"How clever you are! How is it you've gone so deep into everything?" The
woman's voice was more and more insinuating.

"I could have done better than that, ma'am. I could have known more
than that, if it had not been for my destiny from my childhood up. I would
have shot a man in a duel if he called me names because I am descended
from the stinking one and have no father. And they used to throw it in my
teeth in Moscow. It had reached them from here, thanks to Grigory Vasilyevich, ma'am. Grigory Vasilyevich blames me for rebelling against my
birth, 'You rent her womb,'[3] he says, but I would have sanctioned their killing me before I was born that I might not have come into the world at all,
ma'am. They used to say in the market, and your mamma too, with great
lack of delicacy, set off telling me that her hair was like a mat on her head,
and that she was short of five foot by 'a wee bit.' Why talk of 'a wee bit'
while she might have said 'a little bit,' like everyone else? She wanted to
make it touching, like a peasant's tear, ma'am, so to speak, a regular peasant's feeling. Can a Russian peasant be said to feel, in comparison with an
educated man? He can't be said to have feeling at all, in his ignorance.
From my childhood up when I hear 'a wee bit,' I am ready to burst with
rage. I hate all Russia, Marya Kondratyevna."

"If you'd been a cadet in the army, or a young hussar,[4] you wouldn't have
talked like that, but would have drawn your saber to defend all Russia."

"I don't want to be a hussar, Marya Kondratyevna, and, what's more, I
should like to abolish all soldiers."

---

3. Grigory's language recalls several Biblical passages: "Sanctify unto me all the firstborn, whatsoever openeth the womb" (Exodus 13.2); "All that openeth the matrix is mine" (Exodus 34.19);
see also Exodus 13.12.
4. Hussars were cavalry units known for their colorful uniforms; they had a reputation for being
dashing, brave, and unruly.

"And when an enemy comes, who is going to defend us?"

"There's no need of defense. In 1812 there was a great invasion of Russia by Napoleon, first Emperor of the French, father of the present one,[5] and it would have been a good thing if they had conquered us. A clever nation would have conquered a very stupid one and annexed it, ma'am. We should have had quite different institutions, ma'am."

"Are they so much better in their own country than we are? I wouldn't change a dandy I know of for three young Englishmen," observed Marya Kondratyevna tenderly, doubtless accompanying her words with a most languishing glance.

"That's as one prefers, ma'am."

"But you are just like a foreigner—just like a most gentlemanly foreigner. I tell you that, though it makes me bashful."

"If you care to know, the folks there and ours here are just alike in their vice. They are swindlers, ma'am, only there the scoundrel wears polished boots and here he stinks in filth and sees no harm in it. The Russian people want thrashing, ma'am, as Fyodor Pavlovich said very truly yesterday, though he is mad, and all his children."

"You said yourself you had such a respect for Ivan Fyodorovich."

"But he said I was a stinking lackey. He thinks that I might revolt. He is mistaken there. If I had a certain sum in my pocket, I would have left here long ago. Dmitri Fyodorovich is lower than any lackey in his behavior, in his mind, and in his poverty, ma'am. He doesn't know how to do anything, and yet he is respected by everyone. I may be only a soup maker, but with luck I could open a café restaurant on the Petrovka, in Moscow, for my cookery is something special, and there's no one in Moscow, except the foreigners, whose cookery is anything special. Dmitri Fyodorovich is a beggar, but if he were to challenge the son of the first count in the country, he'd fight him, ma'am. Though in what way is he better than I am? For he is ever so much stupider than I am. Look at the money he has wasted without any need!"

"It must be lovely, a duel," Marya Kondratyevna observed suddenly.

"How so, ma'am?"

"It must be so dreadful and so brave, especially when young officers with pistols in their hands pop at one another for the sake of some lady. A perfect picture! Ah, if only girls were allowed to look on, I'd give anything to see one!"

"It's all very well when you are firing at someone, but when he is firing straight in your mug, you must feel pretty silly. You'd be glad to run away, Marya Kondratyevna."

"You don't mean you would run away?"

But Smerdyakov did not deign to reply. After a moment's silence the guitar sounded again, and he sang again in the same falsetto:

> Whatever you may say,
> I shall go far away.
> Life will be bright and gay

---

5. Napoléon Bonaparte invaded Russia in 1812. Although he commanded an army almost twice the strength of the Russian forces, Napoléon was defeated when the Russians cut his supply lines and set fire to Moscow, thus denying his forces provisions and forcing their retreat. Smerdyakov is mistaken: Napoléon III was Bonaparte's nephew, not his son.

In the city far away.
I shall not grieve,
I shall not grieve at all,
I don't intend to grieve at all.

Then something unexpected happened. Alyosha suddenly sneezed. They were silent. Alyosha got up and walked towards them. He found Smerdyakov dressed up and wearing polished boots, his hair pomaded, and perhaps curled. The guitar lay on the garden seat. His companion was the daughter of the house, wearing a light blue dress with a train two yards long. She was young and would not have been bad-looking, but that her face was so round and terribly freckled.

"Will my brother Dmitri soon be back?" asked Alyosha with as much composure as he could.

Smerdyakov got up slowly; Marya Kondratyevna rose too.

"How am I to know about Dmitri Fyodorovich? It's not as if I were his keeper," answered Smerdyakov quietly, distinctly, and superciliously.[6]

"But I simply asked whether you do know?" Alyosha explained.

"I know nothing of his whereabouts and don't want to, sir."

"But my brother told me that you let him know all that goes on in the house, and promised to let him know when Agrafena Alexandrovna comes."

Smerdyakov turned a deliberate, unmoved glance upon him.

"And how did you get in this time, since the gate was bolted an hour ago?" he asked, looking at Alyosha.

"I came in from the back alley, over the fence, and went straight to the gazebo. I hope you'll forgive me," he added, addressing Marya Kondratyevna. "I was in a hurry to find my brother."

"Ach, as though we could take it amiss in you!" drawled Marya Kondratyevna, flattered by Alyosha's apology. "For Dmitri Fyodorovich often goes to the gazebo in that way. We don't know he is here and he is sitting in the gazebo."

"I am very anxious to find him or to learn from you where he is now. Believe me, it's on business of great importance to him."

"He never tells us," lisped Marya Kondratyevna.

"Though I used to come here as a friend," Smerdyakov began again, "Dmitri Fyodorovich has pestered me in a merciless way even here by his incessant questions about the master. 'What news?' he'll ask. 'What's going on in there now? Who's coming and going?' and can't I tell him something more. Twice already he's threatened me with death."

"With death?" Alyosha exclaimed in surprise.

"Do you suppose he'd think much of that, with his temper, which you had a chance of observing yourself yesterday? He says if I let Agrafena Alexandrovna in and she passes the night there, I'll be the first to suffer for it. I am terribly afraid of him, sir, and if I were not even more afraid of doing so, I ought to let the police know. God only knows what he might not do, sir!"

"His honor said to him the other day, 'I'll pound you in a mortar!'" added Marya Kondratyevna.

---

6. Smerdyakov paraphrases words spoken by Cain to God in the Book of Genesis. Cain, one of the two sons of Adam and Eve, killed his brother Abel out of jealousy. When God asked him "Where is Abel thy brother?", Cain replied "I know not: Am I my brother's keeper?" (Genesis 4.9).

"Oh, if it's pounding in a mortar, it may be only talk," observed Alyosha. "If I could meet him, I might speak to him about that too."

"Well, the only thing I can tell you is this," said Smerdyakov, as though thinking better of it; "I am here as an old friend and neighbor, and it would be odd if I didn't come. On the other hand, Ivan Fyodorovich sent me first thing this morning to your brother's lodging on Lake Street, without a letter, sir, but with a message to Dmitri Fyodorovich to go to dine with him at the restaurant here, in the marketplace. I went, sir, but didn't find Dmitri Fyodorovich at home, though it was eight o'clock. 'He's been here, but he is quite gone,' those were the very words of his landlady. It's as though there was an understanding between them, sir. Perhaps at this moment he is in the restaurant with Ivan Fyodorovich, for Ivan Fyodorovich has not been home to dinner and Fyodor Pavlovich dined alone an hour ago, and has gone to lie down. But I beg you most particularly not to speak of me and of what I have told you, for he'd kill me for nothing at all, sir."

"Brother Ivan invited Dmitri to the restaurant today?" repeated Alyosha quicky.

"Just so, sir."

"The Metropolis tavern in the marketplace?"

"The very same, sir."

"That's quite likely," cried Alyosha, much excited. "Thank you, Smerdyakov; that's important. I'll go there at once."

"Don't betray me, sir," Smerdyakov called after him.

"Oh, no, I'll go to the tavern as though by chance. Don't be anxious."

"But wait a minute, I'll open the gate to you," cried Marya Kondratyevna.

"No; it's a short cut, I'll get over the fence again."

What he had heard threw Alyosha into great agitation. He ran to the tavern. It was impossible for him to go into the tavern in his monastic dress, but he could inquire at the entrance for his brothers and call them down. But just as he reached the tavern, a window was flung open, and his brother Ivan called down to him from it.

"Alyosha, can you come up here to me now or not? I would be awfully grateful."

"To be sure I can, only I don't quite know whether in this dress . . ."

"But I am in a room apart. Come up the steps; I'll run down to meet you."

A minute later Alyosha was sitting beside his brother. Ivan was alone, dining.

Chapter III

The Brothers Get Acquainted

Ivan was not, however, in a separate room, but only in a place shut off by a screen, so that it was unseen by other people in the room. It was the first room from the entrance with a buffet along the wall. Waiters were continually darting to and fro in it. The only customer in the room was an old retired military man drinking tea in a corner. But there was the usual bustle going on in the other rooms of the tavern; there were shouts for the waiters, the sound of bottles being opened, the click of billiard balls, the drone of the organ. Alyosha knew that Ivan did not usually visit this tavern and disliked taverns in general. So he must have come here, he reflected, simply to meet his brother Dmitri by arrangement. Yet Dmitri was not there.

"Shall I order you fish soup, or anything? You don't live by tea alone, I suppose," cried Ivan, apparently delighted at having got hold of Alyosha. He had finished dinner and was drinking tea.

"Let me have fish soup, and tea afterwards; I am hungry," said Alyosha gaily.

"And cherry jam? They have it here. You remember how you used to love cherry jam at the Polyonovs' when you were little?"

"You remember that? Let me have jam too; I like it still."

Ivan called for the waiter and ordered fish soup, jam and tea.

"I remember everything, Alyosha; I remember you till you were eleven, I was nearly fifteen. There's such a difference between fifteen and eleven that brothers are never friends at those ages. I don't know whether I was fond of you even. When I went away to Moscow for the first few years I never thought of you at all. Then, when you came to Moscow yourself, we only met once somewhere, I believe. And now I've been here more than three months, and so far we have scarcely said a word to each other. Tomorrow I am going away, and I was just thinking as I sat here how I could see you to say good-bye and just then you passed."

"So you wished very much to see me?"

"Very, I want to get to know you once for all, and I want you to know me. And then to say good-bye. In my opinion it's always best to get to know people just before leaving them. I've noticed how you've been looking at me these three months. There has been a continual look of expectation in your eyes, and I can't endure that. That's how it is I've kept away from you. But in the end I have learned to respect you. The little man stands firm, I thought. Though I am laughing, I am serious. You do stand firm, don't you? I like people who are firm like that whatever it is they stand by, even if they are such little fellows as you. Your expectant eyes ceased to annoy me; on the contrary, I came to love them in the end, those expectant eyes . . . You seem to love me for some reason, Alyosha?"

"I do love you, Ivan. Brother Dmitri says of you—Ivan is a tomb! I say of you, Ivan is a riddle. You are a riddle to me even now. But I understand something in you, and I did not understand it till this morning."

"What's that?" laughed Ivan.

"You won't be angry?" Alyosha laughed too.

"Well?"

"That you are just as young as other young men of twenty-three, that you are just a young and fresh and nice boy, green in fact! Now, have I insulted you dreadfully?"

"On the contrary, I am struck by a coincidence!" cried Ivan, warmly and good-humoredly. "Would you believe it that ever since that scene with her, I have thought of nothing else but my youthful greenness, and just as though you guessed that, you begin about it. Do you know I've been sitting here thinking to myself: that if I didn't believe in life, if I lost faith in the woman I love, lost faith in the order of things, were convinced in fact that

everything is a disorderly, damned, and perhaps devil-ridden chaos, if I
were struck by every horror of man's disillusionment—still I should want
to live and, having once tasted of the cup, I would not turn away from it
till I had drained it! At thirty, though, I shall be sure to fling down the
cup,[7] even if I've not emptied it, and turn away—where I don't know. But
till I am thirty, I know that my youth will triumph over everything—every
disillusionment, every disgust with life. I've asked myself many times: is
there in the world any despair that would overcome this frantic and perhaps
obscene thirst for life in me, and I've come to the conclusion that there
isn't, that is till I am thirty, and then I shall lose it of myself, so it seems to
me. Some driveling consumptive moralists—and poets especially—often
call that thirst for life base. It's a feature of the Karamazovs it's true, that
thirst for life regardless of everything; you have it no doubt too, but why is
it base? The centripetal force on our planet is still fearfully strong, Alyosha. I have a longing for life, and I go on living in spite of logic. Though I
may not believe in the order of the universe, yet I love the sticky little
leaves as they open in spring.[8] I love the blue sky, I love some people,
whom one loves you know sometimes without knowing why. I love some
great deeds done by men, though I've long ceased perhaps to have faith in
them, yet from old habit one's heart prizes them. Here they have brought
the soup for you, eat it, it will do you good. It's first-rate soup, they know
how to make it here. I want to travel in Europe, Alyosha, I will set off from
here. And yet I know that I am only going to a graveyard, but it's a most
precious graveyard, that's what it is![9] Precious are the dead that lie there,
every stone over them speaks of such burning life in the past, of such passionate faith in their work, their truth, their struggle and their science,
that I know I shall fall on the ground and kiss those stones and weep over
them; though I'm convinced in my heart that it's long been nothing but a
graveyard. And I shall not weep from despair, but simply because I shall
be happy in my tears, I shall steep my soul in my emotion. I love the sticky
leaves in spring, the blue sky—that's all it is. It's not a matter of intellect
or logic, it's loving with one's inside, with one's guts. One loves the first
strength of one's youth . . . Do you understand anything of my tirade,
Alyosha?" Ivan laughed suddenly.

"I understand too well, Ivan: One longs to love with one's inside, with
one's guts. You said that so well and I am awfully glad that you have such
a longing for life," cried Alyosha. "I think every one should love life above
everything in the world."

"Love life more than the meaning of it?"

"Certainly, love it, regardless of logic as you say, it must be regardless
of logic, and it's only then one will understand the meaning of it. I have
thought so a long time. Half your work has been done and has been

<hr/>

7. These images of tasting from and flinging the cup have rich and complex precedents. For
Christian readers, the most obvious source would be Matthew 26.39. Possible secular sources
include Goethe's *Faust* Part I, 11.2759–82.
8. The expression "sticky little leaves" occurs in Pushkin's poem "Chill Winds Still Blow" (1828).
9. Dostoevsky probably drew the notion of Europe as a graveyard from the writings of Alexander
Herzen (1812–1879). A Russian populist and moderate socialist who spent much of his life in
European exile, Herzen was a leading figure in circles opposed to the Tsarist regime. The idea
that Western European culture was past its prime was a commonplace among many Russian
intellectuals in Dostoevsky's time.

acquired, Ivan, you love life, now you've only to try to do the second half and you are saved."

"You are trying to save me, but perhaps I am not lost! And what does your second half mean?"

"Why, one has to raise up your dead, who perhaps have not died after all.[1] Come, let me have tea. I am so glad of our talk, Ivan."

"I see you are feeling inspired. I am awfully fond of such *professions de foi*[2] from such . . . novices. You are a steadfast person, Alexey. Is it true that you mean to leave the monastery?"

"Yes, my elder sends me out into the world."

"We shall see each other then in the world. We shall meet before I am thirty, when I shall begin to turn aside from the cup. Father doesn't want to turn aside from his cup till he is seventy, he dreams of hanging on to eighty in fact, so he says. He means it only too seriously, though he is a buffoon. He stands on a firm rock, too, he stands on his sensuality—though after we are thirty, indeed, there may be nothing else to stand on. . . . But to hang on to seventy is nasty, better only to thirty; one might retain 'a shadow of nobility'[3] by deceiving oneself. Have you seen Dmitri today?"

"No, but I saw Smerdyakov," and Alyosha rapidly, though minutely, described his meeting with Smerdyakov. Ivan began listening anxiously and questioned him.

"But he begged me not to tell brother Dmitri that he had told me about him," added Alyosha. Ivan frowned and pondered.

"Are you frowning on Smerdyakov's account?" asked Alyosha.

"Yes, on his account. Devil take him, I certainly did want to see Dmitri, but now there's no need," said Ivan reluctantly.

"But are you really going so soon, brother?"

"Yes."

"What of Dmitri and father? how will it end?" asked Alyosha anxiously.

"You are always harping upon it! What have I to do with it? Am I my brother Dmitri's keeper?"[4] Ivan snapped irritably, but then he suddenly smiled bitterly. "Cain's answer to God, about his murdered brother, wasn't it? Perhaps that's what you're thinking at this moment? Well, damn it all, I can't stay here to be their keeper, can I? I've finished what I had to do, and I am going. Do you imagine I am jealous of Dmitri, that I've been trying to steal his beautiful Katerina Ivanovna for the last three months? Oh, hell, I had business of my own. I finished it. I am going. I finished it just now, you were witness."

"At Katerina Ivanovna's?"

"Yes, and I've released myself once for all. And after all, what have I to do with Dmitri? Dmitri has nothing to do with it. I had my own business to settle with Katerina Ivanovna. You know, on the contrary, that Dmitri behaved as though there was an understanding between us. I didn't ask him to do it, but he solemnly handed her over to me and gave us his blessing. It's all too funny. Ah, Alyosha, if you only knew how light my heart is

---

1. This seemingly casual remark alludes to Dostoevsky's passionate belief in resurrection. In his notebooks for *The Brothers Karamazov*, Dostoevsky wrote, "*The resurrection of our ancestors depends on us*" (15:204). See p. xiv.
2. "Professions of faith" (French).
3. Inexact quotation from Pushkin's 1825 epigram "Skazali raz tsariu" ("A King was told").
4. Ivan paraphrases Cain's words to God.

now! Would you believe it, I sat here eating my dinner and almost ordered champagne to celebrate my first hour of freedom. Whew! It's been going on nearly six months, and all at once I've thrown it off. I could never have guessed even yesterday, how easy it would be to put an end to it if I wanted."

"You are speaking of your love, Ivan?"

"Of my love, if you like. I fell in love with the young lady, with the girl from the Institute, I tormented myself over her and she tormented me. I sat watching over her . . . and all at once it's collapsed! I spoke this morning with inspiration, but I went away and roared with laughter. Would you believe it? Yes, it's the literal truth."

"You seem very merry about it now," observed Alyosha, looking into his face, which had suddenly grown brighter.

"But how could I tell that I didn't care for her a bit! He-he! It appears after all I didn't. And yet how she attracted me! How attractive she was just now when I made my speech! And do you know she attracts me awfully even now, yet how easy it is to leave her. Do you think I am boasting?"

"No, only perhaps it wasn't love."

"Alyoshka," laughed Ivan, "don't make reflections about love, it's unseemly for you. How you rushed into the discussion this morning! I've forgotten to kiss you for it. . . . But how she tormented me! It certainly was sitting by a 'laceration.' Ah, she knew how I loved her! She loved me and not Dmitri," Ivan insisted gaily. "Her feeling for Dmitri was simply a laceration. All I told her just now was perfectly true, but the worst of it is, it may take her fifteen or twenty years to find out that she doesn't care for Dmitri, and loves me whom she torments, and perhaps she may never find it out at all, in spite of her lesson today. Well, it's better so; I can simply go away for good. By the way, how is she now? What happened after I departed?"

Alyosha told him she had been hysterical, and that she was now, he heard, unconscious and delirious.

"And Khokhlakova isn't lying?"

"It doesn't seem like it."

"I must find out. Nobody ever dies of hysterics though. They don't matter. God sent woman hysterics with love. I won't go to her at all. Why push myself forward again?"

"But you told her that she had never cared for you."

"I did that on purpose. Alyoshka, I'll order some champagne, we'll drink to my freedom. Ah, if only you knew how glad I am!"

"No, brother, we had better not drink," said Alyosha suddenly. "Besides I feel somehow depressed."

"Yes, you've been depressed a long time, I've noticed it."

"Have you settled to go tomorrow morning then?"

"Morning? I didn't say I would go in the morning. . . . But perhaps it may be the morning. Would you believe it, I dined here today only to avoid dining with the old man, I loathe him so. I should have left long ago, so far as he is concerned. You and I still have God knows how much time before I go. A whole eternity of time, immortality!"

"If you are going away tomorrow, what eternity?"

"But what does it matter to us?" laughed Ivan. "We've time enough for our talk, for what brought us here. Why do you look so surprised? Answer: why have we met here? To talk of my love for Katerina Ivanovna? of the old man and Dmitri? of foreign travel? of the fatal position of Russia? of the Emperor Napoleon? Is that it?"

"No."

"Then you know what for. It's different for other people; but we in our green youth have to settle the eternal questions first of all. That's what we care about. The young in Russia talk of nothing but the eternal questions now. Just when the old folks are all taken up with practical questions. Why have you been looking at me in expectation for the last three months? To ask me 'what do you believe, or don't you believe at all?'[5] That's what your eyes have been meaning for these three months, haven't they?"

"Perhaps so," smiled Alyosha. "You are not laughing at me, now, Ivan?"

"Me laughing? I don't want to wound my little brother who has been watching me with such expectation for three months. Alyosha, look straight at me: Of course I am just such a little boy as you are, only not a novice. And what have Russian boys been doing up till now, some of them, I mean? In this stinking tavern, for instance, here, they meet and sit down in a corner. They've never met in their lives before and, when they go out of the tavern, they won't meet again for forty years. And what do they talk about in that momentary halt in the tavern? Of the eternal questions, of the existence of God and immortality. And those who do not believe in God talk of socialism or anarchism, of the transformation of all humanity on a new pattern, so that the same devil comes of it, they're the same questions turned inside out. And masses, masses of the most original Russian boys do nothing but talk of the eternal questions! Isn't it so?"

"Yes, for real Russians the questions of God's existence and of immortality, or, as you say, the same question turned inside out, come first and foremost, of course, and so they should," said Alyosha, still watching his brother with the same gentle and inquiring smile.

"Well, Alyosha, it's sometimes very unwise to be a Russian at all, but anything stupider than the way Russian boys spend their time one can hardly imagine. But there's one Russian boy called Alyosha I am awfully fond of."

"How nicely you put that in!" Alyosha laughed suddenly.

"Well, tell me where to begin, give your orders. The existence of God, eh?"

"Begin where you like, even 'turned inside out.' You declared yesterday at father's that there was no God." Alyosha looked searchingly at his brother.

"I said that yesterday at dinner at the old man's on purpose to tease you and I saw your eyes glow. But now I don't have anything against discussing it with you, and I say so very seriously. I want to be friends with you, Alyosha, for I have no friends and want to try it. Well, imagine, perhaps I too accept God," laughed Ivan, "that's a surprise for you, isn't it?"

"Yes, of course, if you are not joking now."

"Joking? I was told at the elder's yesterday that I was joking. You know, dear boy, there was an old sinner in the eighteenth century who declared that, if there were no God, he would have to be invented. *S'il n'existait pas Dieu, il faudrait l'inventer.*[6] And man has actually invented

<hr />

5. Ivan quotes a formulaic question posed to Orthodox bishops on their investiture.
6. See note 3 on p. 27.

God.[7] And what's strange, what would be marvelous, is not that God should really exist; the marvel is that such an idea, the idea of the necessity of God, could enter the head of such a savage, vicious beast as man. So holy it is, so touching, so wise and so great a credit it does to man. As for me, I've long resolved not to think whether man created God or God man. And I won't go through all the axioms laid down by Russian boys on that subject, all derived from European hypotheses; for what's a hypothesis there, is an axiom with the Russian boy, and not only with the boys but with their professors too, for our Russian professors are often just the same boys themselves. And so I omit all the hypotheses. For what are we aiming at now? I am trying to explain as quickly as possible my essential nature, that is what manner of man I am, what I believe in, and for what I hope, that's it, isn't it? And therefore I tell you that I accept God outright and simply. But you must note this: if God exists and if He really did create the world, then, as we all know, He created it according to the geometry of Euclid and the human mind with the conception of only three dimensions in space. Yet there have been and still are geometricians and philosophers, and even some of the most distinguished, who doubt whether the whole universe, or to speak more widely the whole of being, was only created in Euclid's geometry; they even dare to dream that two parallel lines, which according to Euclid can never meet on earth, may meet somewhere in infinity.[8] I have come to the conclusion that, since I can't understand even that, I can't expect to understand about God. I acknowledge humbly that I have no faculty for settling such questions, I have a Euclidean earthly mind, and how could I solve problems that are not of this world? And I advise you never to think about it either, my dear Alyosha, especially about God, whether He exists or not. All such questions are utterly inappropriate for a mind created with an idea of only three dimensions. And so I accept God and am glad to, and what's more I accept His wisdom and His purpose, which are entirely unknown to us, I believe in the underlying order and the meaning of life, I believe in the eternal harmony in which they say we shall one day be blended, I believe in the Word to Which the universe is striving, and Which Itself was 'with God,' and Which Itself is God and so on, and so on, to infinity.[9] There are all sorts of phrases for it. I seem to be on the right path, don't I? Yet would you believe it, in the final result I don't accept this world of God's, and, although I know it exists, I don't accept it at all. It's not that I don't accept God, you must understand, it's the world created by Him I don't and cannot accept. Let me make it plain: I believe like a child that suffering will be healed and smoothed over, that all the insulting absurdity of human contradictions will vanish like a pitiful mirage, like the despicable fabrication of the impotent and infinitely small Euclidian mind of man, puny as an atom, that, finally, in the world's finale, at the moment of eternal harmony, something so precious will occur and be revealed that it will suffice for all hearts, for the comforting of all resentments, for the redemption of

7. The anthropological basis of faith in God is one of the primary ideas advanced by the German philosopher Ludwig Feuerbach (1804–1872) in *The Essence of Christianity* (1841). Feuerbach's ideas were extremely influential in Russia.
8. The Russian mathematician Nikolay Lobachevsky (1792–1856) published a treatise on non-Euclidean geometry in 1826.
9. Ivan paraphrases John 1.1, which refers to Jesus as the Word: "In the beginning was the Word, and the Word was with God, and the Word was God."

all the crimes of humanity, of all the blood they've shed, that it will make it not only possible to forgive but to justify all that has happened with men—let this, let all this come true and be revealed, but I don't accept it and don't want to accept it! Let the parallel lines even meet and I see it myself: I'll see it and say that they met, but still I won't accept it. That's my essence, Alyosha, that's my thesis. I say it to you seriously. I began our talk as stupidly as I could on purpose, but I've led up to my confession, for that's all you want. You didn't want to hear about God, but only to know what the brother you love lives by. And so I've told you."

Ivan concluded his long tirade suddenly with a sort of special and unexpected feeling.

"And why did you begin 'as stupidly as you could'?" asked Alyosha, looking pensively at him.

"To begin with, for the sake of Russianism: Russian conversations on such subjects are always carried on inconceivably stupidly. And secondly, besides, the stupider, the closer to the point. The stupider, the clearer. Stupidity is brief and artless, while intelligence wriggles and hides itself. Intelligence is a scoundrel, but stupidity is honest and straightforward. I've led the conversation to my despair, and the more stupidly I have presented it, the better for me."

"Will you explain why you don't accept the world?" said Alyosha.

"Of course I'll explain, it's not a secret, that's what I've been leading up to. My dear little brother, I don't want to corrupt you or to turn you from your stronghold, perhaps I want to be healed by you." Ivan smiled suddenly quite like a little gentle boy. Alyosha had never seen such a smile on his face before.

Chapter IV

Rebellion

"I must admit one thing to you," Ivan began: "I could never understand how one can love one's neighbors. It's just one's neighbors, to my mind, that one can't love, though one might love those at a distance. I once read somewhere, sometime of "John the Merciful,"[1] a saint, that when a hungry, frozen beggar came to him, and asked him to warm him up, he took him into his bed, held him in his arms, and began breathing into his mouth, which was putrid and loathsome from some awful disease. I am convinced that he did that from the laceration of falsity, for the sake of the love imposed by duty, as a penance laid on him. For anyone to love a man, he must be hidden, for as soon as he shows his face, love is gone."

"Father Zosima has talked of that more than once," observed Alyosha; "he, too, said that the face of a man often hinders many people not prac-

---

1. Turgenev published a Russian translation of *The Legend of Saint Julian the Hospitaller* (1876) by the French author Gustave Flaubert (1821–1880) in the journal *Messenger of Europe* in 1877. In Flaubert's story, Julian is a parricide who attempts to atone for his sin. He eventually encounters a loathsome beggar whom he feeds and warms; the beggar turns out to be Christ and carries Julian to heaven. Ivan changes the name from Julian to *Ioann*—that is, John (Russian *Ivan*), thus linking this figure to Ivan himself and confusing him with Saint John the Merciful, Patriarch of Alexandria 606–616, who was famous for his generosity to the poor.

tised in love, from loving him. But yet there's a great deal of love in mankind, and almost Christ-like love. I know that myself, Ivan."

"Well, I know nothing of it so far, and can't understand it, and the innumerable mass of mankind are with me there. The question is, whether that's due to men's bad qualities or whether it's inherent in their nature. To my thinking, Christ-like love for men is a miracle impossible on earth. True, He was God. But we are not gods. Suppose that I, for example, can suffer deeply, but another will never be able to know how much I suffer, because he is another and not I, and besides a man seldom agrees to recognize someone else as a sufferer (as though that were some kind of distinction). Why won't he admit it, do you think? Because, for example, I smell bad, because I have a stupid face, because I once stepped on his foot. Besides, there is suffering and suffering—humiliating suffering, which humiliates me, hunger for example, a benefactor will allow me, but slightly higher suffering, for an idea for example, no, that he allows only in rare cases, because he, for example, looks at me and suddenly sees that my face isn't at all the kind he imagines someone who suffers for such an idea, for example, should have. And so he deprives me instantly of his favor, and not at all from badness of heart. Beggars, especially genteel beggars, should never show themselves, but should ask for charity through the newspapers. It's possible to love one's neighbor abstractly and sometimes even from a distance, but almost never up close. If it were all like it is on stage, in the ballet, where the beggars when they appear come in wearing silken rags and tattered lace, dancing gracefully, then it would be possible to like looking at them. Look at them, but still not love them. But enough of that. I simply wanted to show you my point of view. I wanted to talk about the suffering of humanity in general, but better let us stay with the suffering of children. That reduces the scope of my argument by ten times, but still it's better just about children. That's less advantageous for me, of course. But, in the first place, it's possible to love children even up close, even dirty ones, even ugly ones (though it seems to me that children are never ugly). In the second place I won't speak about adults because, aside from the fact that they are disgusting and don't deserve love, they also have retribution: they ate the apple and knew good and evil and became 'like gods.' And they continue eating it now.[2] But little children haven't eaten anything and so far aren't guilty of anything. Do you love children, Alyosha? I know you do, and will understand why I want to speak only of them. If they too suffer terribly on earth, then it is, of course, for their fathers, they are punished for their fathers, who ate the apple—but that is reasoning from another world, it is incomprehensible to the human heart here on earth.[3] It is impossible that an innocent one should suffer for another, and what an innocent one! You may be surprised at me, Alyosha, I love little children terribly too. And observe, cruel people, the violent, rapacious, the Karamazovs, sometimes love children very much. Children, while they are still children, up to seven years for example, are terribly remote from grown-up people: as if they were different beings from a

---

2. According to Genesis 3.5, God commanded Adam and Eve not to eat from the tree of knowledge of good and evil; when they ate the fruit against God's command, they were cursed and banished from the Garden of Eden.
3. According to Christian doctrine, every human being shares in the original sin committed by Adam and Eve—eating from the tree of knowledge against God's command—and suffers for it.

different nature. I knew a criminal in prison who had, in the course of his career as a burglar, murdered whole families, including several children.[4] But when he was in prison, he had a strange affection for them. He spent all his time at his window, watching the children playing in the prison yard. He trained one little boy to come up to his window and made great friends with him. . . . You don't know why I am telling you all this, Alyosha? I somehow have a headache and feel sad."

"You look strange as you speak," Alyosha noticed with uneasiness, "and you seem to be in some kind of madness."

"By the way, a Bulgarian I met recently in Moscow," continued Ivan Fyodorovich as though not listening to his brother, "told me how the Turks and Circassians[5] there, in Bulgaria, are committing atrocities everywhere, fearing an uprising of the Slavs[6]—they burn, kill, rape women and children, nail prisoners to fences by the ears and leave them that way until morning, and in the morning they hang them—and so on, it's impossible to imagine it all. People talk sometimes of 'bestial' cruelty, but that's a great injustice and insult to the beast; a beast can never be so cruel as a man, so artistically, so artfully cruel. The tiger only tears and gnaws, that's all he can do. He would never think of nailing people by the ears, even if he were able to do it. These Turks, among other things, also took pleasure in torturing children, starting with cutting them from their mothers' womb with a dagger, to throwing infants up in the air and catching them on the point of a bayonet before the mothers' eyes. Doing it before the mothers' eyes comprised the main delight. But here is a picture that interested me very much. Imagine: a nursing infant in the arms of its trembling mother, surrounded by invading Turks. They've thought up an amusing trick: they fondle the infant, laugh to make it laugh, and they succeed, the infant laughs. At that moment a Turk aims a pistol at the baby, four inches from its face. The little boy laughs gleefully, stretches out his little hands for the pistol, and suddenly the artist pulls the trigger right in his face and shatters his little head . . . Artistic, isn't it? By the way, Turks, they say, are very fond of sweets."

"Brother, what are you driving at?" asked Alyosha.

"I think if the devil doesn't exist, but man has created him, he has created him in his own image and likeness."

"Just as he did God, then?" observed Alyosha.

"It's wonderful how you can turn words, as Polonius says in *Hamlet*,"[7] laughed Ivan. "You turn my words against me. Well, I am glad. Yours must be a fine God, if man created Him in His image and likeness. You asked

---

4. There is no indication that Ivan was ever in prison or visited one. This anecdote resembles Dostoevsky's reminiscences in *Notes from the House of the Dead* (1862) about the prisoners he met while serving time in the Siberian labor camp at Omsk from 1850 to 1854.

5. Moslem peoples who originated in the northern Caucasus. Their century-long war against the encroachment of the Russian Empire ended in 1864, when Circassian resistance was crushed and many fled to the Ottoman Empire. Circassian regiments in the Ottoman military were notorious for their cruelty in the suppression of Christian Slavic uprisings in the Balkans in the 1870s.

6. The Christian Slavs of Herzegovina rebelled against the Ottoman Empire in 1875. Serbia and Montenegro supported their revolt and declared war against the Ottoman Turks in 1876. Popular opinion in Russia supported the Slavs, and grassroots support of their cause frequently expressed itself in the form of subscriptions or fundraisers. Russia declared war in April 1877, opening the Russo-Turkish War (1877–78). Dostoevsky discusses the Slavic uprisings and Russo-Turkish War extensively in his *Diary*; see for example July/August 1876, chapter 4, number 5, "An Odd Summer for Russia," and April 1877, chapter 1.

7. Ivan refers to the conclusion of *Hamlet* I.iii.

just now what I was driving at. You see, I am an amateur and collector of certain little facts, and, would you believe, I even copy little anecdotes of a certain sort from newspapers and stories, from wherever, and I've already got a fine collection. The Turks, of course, have gone into it, but they are foreigners. I have specimens from home that are even better than the Turks. You know we prefer beating—rods and scourges[8]—that's our national institution: nailing ears is unthinkable for us, for we are, after all, Europeans, but the rod and the scourge we have always with us and they cannot be taken from us. Abroad they apparently don't beat at all anymore, their morals have either become purified or they've passed laws so that one man doesn't dare whip another, but they've rewarded themselves with something else that is also as purely national as what we have, and so national that it would seem to be impossible for us, although, by the way, it seems that it is catching on here, especially since the time of the religious movement in our high society.[9] I have a charming pamphlet, translated from the French, describing how, quite recently, five years ago, a murderer, Richard, was executed—a young man, of twenty-three, I believe, who repented and was converted to the Christian faith at the very scaffold.[1] This Richard was an illegitimate child who was *given* as a child of six by his parents to some shepherds on the Swiss mountains. They brought him up to work for them. He grew up like a little wild beast among them. The shepherds taught him nothing, and scarcely fed or clothed him, but sent him out at age seven to herd the flock in cold and wet, and no one hesitated or scrupled to treat him so. Quite the contrary, they thought they had every right, for Richard had been given to them as a thing, and they did not even see the necessity of feeding him. Richard himself describes how in those years, like the Prodigal Son in the Gospel,[2] he longed to eat of the mash given to the pigs, which were fattened for sale, but they wouldn't even give him that, and beat him when he stole from the pigs, and that was how he spent all his childhood and his youth, till he grew up and was strong enough to go away and be a thief. The savage began to earn his living as a day laborer in Geneva, he drank what he earned, he lived like a monster and finished by killing and robbing an old man. He was caught, tried, and condemned to death. They do not sentimentalize there. And in prison he was immediately surrounded by pastors, members of Christian brotherhoods, philanthropic ladies, and the like. They taught him to read and write in prison, and expounded the Gospel to him. They exhorted him, worked upon him, drummed at him incessantly, till at last he solemnly confessed his crime. He was converted, he wrote to the court himself that he was a monster, but that in the end God had sent him light and shown grace. All Geneva was in excitement about him, all philanthropic and religious Geneva. All the

---

8. Common instruments of corporal punishment.
9. Ivan anachronistically refers to several phenomena of the 1870s. Signs of a religious revival in that decade included a fascination with spiritualism and public lectures on religion called "Lectures on Godmanhood" given by his friend, the young philosopher and Moscow University professor Vladimir Solovyov (1853–1900). Ivan may also be referring to the popularity of the missionary Granville Waldegrave, 3rd Lord Radstock (1833–1913), who addressed audiences in Saint Petersburg in 1874 and 1876.
1. Dostoevsky owned a copy of an anonymous brochure, translated into Russian from French and published in Saint Petersburg in 1877, called "The Conversion and Death of Ludwig Friedrich Richard, Executed in Geneva June 11 1850." Ivan changes the story slightly: Richard (1807–1850) was forty-three, not twenty-three, at the time of his execution.
2. The parable is found in Luke 15.11–32.

aristocratic and well-bred society of the town rushed to the prison; they kiss Richard and embrace him; 'You are our brother, you have found grace.' And Richard does nothing but weep with emotion, 'Yes, I've found grace! All my youth and childhood I was glad of pigs' food, but now even I have found grace, I am dying in the Lord!' 'Yes, yes, Richard, die in the Lord, you have shed blood and must die in the Lord. Though it's not your fault that you knew not the Lord, when you coveted the pigs' food and were beaten for stealing it (which was very wrong of you, for stealing is forbidden); but you've shed blood and you must die.' And so the last day comes. Limp Richard cries and does nothing but repeat every minute 'This is my best day, I am going to the Lord!' 'Yes,' cry the pastors, judges and philanthropic ladies, 'this is your happiest day, for you are going to the Lord!' It's all moving, in carriages and on foot, toward the scaffold behind the cart of shame bearing Richard. They reach the scaffold: 'Die, brother,' they cry to Richard, 'die in the Lord, for grace has come upon you!' And so, covered with his brothers' kisses, Richard is dragged on to the scaffold, and led to the guillotine. And they chopped off his head in brotherly fashion, because he had found grace. Yes, that's characteristic. That pamphlet is translated into Russian by some Russian philanthropists of aristocratic rank and evangelical aspirations, and has been distributed gratis for the enlightenment of the people. The thing about Richard is good because it's national. Though to us it's absurd to cut off a man's head,[3] because he has become our brother and has found grace, still, I repeat, we have our own speciality, which is all but worse. We have our historical, immediate, close pleasure in the torture of beating. There are lines in Nekrasov describing how a peasant lashes a horse on the eyes, 'on its meek eyes,' everyone has seen it, it's Russianism.[4] He describes how a feeble little horse has foundered under too heavy a load and cannot move. The peasant beats it, beats it savagely, beats it at last not knowing what he is doing in the intoxication of cruelty, thrashes it mercilessly over and over again: No matter how weak you are, pull, die, but pull! The little nag strains, and he begins lashing her, the defenseless one, on her weeping, 'meek eyes.' Beside herself she tugs and draws the load, trembling all over, not breathing, moving sideways somehow with some kind of skipping movement, somehow unnaturally and shamefully—it's awful in Nekrasov. But that's only a horse, and God himself gave us horses for beating. So the Tartars have taught us, and they left us the knout as a remembrance of it. But people can be beaten too. And so a well-educated, cultured man and his lady beat their own daughter, an infant of seven, with birch rods—I have it written down exactly. The papenka is glad that the birch is covered with twigs, 'It will sting more,' he says, and begins 'stinging' his own daughter. I know for a fact that there are beaters who get worked up to sensuality, literally sensuality, at every stroke, more and more with every blow, progressively. They beat for one minute, they beat, finally, for five minutes, they beat for ten minutes, longer, more, more often, more savagely. The child cries, the child, finally, cannot cry,

3. Ivan may be referring to the absence of capital punishment in Russia. Capital punishment was theoretically abolished by Empress Elizabeth Petrovna in 1754. Despite the official ban, however, capital punishment continued in the form of harsh corporal punishment that resulted in death. The legal reforms of the 1860s made it illegal to cause death through the infliction of excessive corporal punishment.
4. Ivan refers to Nekrasov's poem "Till Twilight" ("Do sumerek," 1859). This poem may have influenced composition of the horse-beating scene in Crime and Punishment as well.

she gasps 'papa, papa, papochka!' By some diabolically improper accident the case comes to court. The Russian people have long called a lawyer a 'hired conscience.' The lawyer shouts in his client's defense. 'It's such a simple thing,' he says, 'an everyday domestic case, a father beats his daughter, and, to the shame of our times, the matter is brought to court!' The jury, convinced by him, retires and delivers an acquittal.[5] The public roars with delight that the tormentor is acquitted. Ahh, it's a pity I wasn't there, I would have bellowed out the suggestion that they establish a scholarship in honor of the torturer! . . . Charming little pictures. But I have even better things about little children, I've collected a great, great deal about Russian children, Alyosha.[6] A father and mother, 'most worthy and respectable people, of good education and breeding,' hated their little five-year-old girl. You see, I *positively* maintain again that there is a peculiar characteristic in much of humanity—this love of torturing children, but only children. To all other types of humanity these same torturers behave even mildly and benevolently, like educated and humane European people, but they very much love to torment children, they even love children themselves in that sense. It's precisely the defenselessness of these creations that seduces the tormentors, the angelic trustfulness of the little child, who has nowhere to go and no one to go to—that is what enflames the vile blood of the torturer. In every man, of course, a beast lies hidden, a beast of rage, a beast of sensual inflammation from the screams of the tortured victim, a beast without restraint, let off the chain, a beast of diseases acquired through debauchery, gout, kidney disease, and so on. These educated parents subjected this poor five-year-old girl to every possible torture. They beat, thrashed, kicked her, not knowing why themselves, turning her whole body into bruises; finally they reached the highest refinement: in the cold, in the frost, they shut her up all night in the outhouse, because she wouldn't ask to be taken out at night (as though a five-year-old child, sleeping its angelic sound sleep, could be taught to ask)—for that they smeared her whole face with her excrement and made her eat that excrement, and it was her mother, her mother who made her! And that mother could sleep at night, hearing the groans of that poor little child, locked up in that vile place! Can you understand that a little being, who still can't even comprehend what is being done to her, in a vile place, in the dark and cold, beats herself with her tiny little fist on her strained little chest and cries her bloody, unresentful, meek little tears to 'dear God' to protect her—can you understand that nonsense, my friend and my brother, my pious and humble novice, do you understand why this nonsense is necessary and created? Without it, they say, man could not have existed on earth, for he would not have known good and evil. Why should he know that diabolical good and evil, when it costs so much? The whole world of knowledge is not worth the little tears of that little child to 'dear God.' I'm not talking about the suffering of

5. Ivan's account is loosely based on the case of Stanislav Kronenberg (the name appeared in the press as Kroneberg), who was tried for child abuse in January 1876. Dostoevsky attended the trial and recounted his impressions in "Apropos of the Kroneberg Case," *Diary* February 1876, chapter 2, number 1 (see p. 649).
6. These accounts are based on real cases of child abuse that occurred in Russia in the 1870s and were reported in the press. Dostoevsky followed child abuse cases with intense interest and reported his impressions in the *Diary*. See for example July/August 1877, chapter 1, numbers 3–4, "The Case of the Dzhunkovsky Parents and Their Children" and "An Imaginary Speech by the Presiding Judge."

grownups, they ate the apple and can go to the devil, and let the devil take them all, but these little ones, these little ones! I'm tormenting you, Alyoshka, you don't seem to be yourself. I'll stop if you like.

"Never mind. I want to suffer too," muttered Alyosha.

"One picture, just one more, because it's so curious, so characteristic, and above all I just read it in one of the collections of our antiquities, in *The Archive*, in *The Past*,[7] I'll have to check, I've even forgotten where I read it. It was in the darkest days of serfdom at the beginning of the century, and long live the Liberator of the People![8] There was in those days a general of aristocratic connections, the owner of great estates, one of those men (true, even then, it seems, they were very few) who, when retiring from the service into a life of leisure, are convinced that they've earned the power of life and death over their subjects. There were such men then. So our general, settled on his property of two thousand souls, lives in pomp, and domineers over his poor neighbors as though they were spongers and buffoons. He has kennels of hundreds of hounds and nearly a hundred dog-handlers—all mounted, and in uniform. One day a serf boy, a little boy, only eight years old, somehow, playing, threw a stone and hurt the paw of the general's favorite hound. 'Why is my favorite dog lame?' They report to him, here, they say, this boy threw a stone at her and hurt her paw. 'So it was you'—the general looks him up and down—'take him!' They took him, took him from his mother, he sat all night in the lockup, in the morning as soon as it was light the general comes out in full pomp for the hunt, mounts his horse, around him are the spongers, dogs, dog-handlers, and huntsmen, all on horseback. The serfs are gathered for their edification, and in front of them all is the mother of the guilty little boy. The little boy is brought from the lockup. It's a gloomy, cold, foggy day, splendid for hunting. The general orders the little boy to be undressed, the little child is stripped naked, he shivers, he has lost his senses from fear, he doesn't dare to make a peep . . . 'Sic him' commands the general. 'Run, run,' shout the handlers at him, the little boy runs . . . 'At him!' yells the general and sets the whole pack of hounds on him. He hunted him down before the mother's eyes, and the hounds tore the child to pieces! The general, it seems, was afterwards declared incompetent to administer his estates. Well . . . what should be done about him? Shoot him? Shoot him for the satisfaction of our moral feelings? Speak, Alyoshka!"

"Shoot him!" Alyosha said softly, lifting his gaze to his brother with a somehow pale, twisted smile.

"Bravo!" Ivan cried out in some kind of ecstasy. "If even you say so, it means . . . You're a fine monk![9] So that's the kind of little devil that is sitting in your heart, Alyoshka Karamazov!"

"What I said was absurd, but . . ."

---

7. *The Russian Archive* was a monthly magazine published 1863–1917; *The Russian Past* (*Russkaya starina*) was a monthly magazine published 1870–1918. The story of the serf boy attacked by his master's hunting dogs was published in *The Russian Messenger*—the same magazine where *The Brothers Karamazov* was first published in serial form—in 1877 (it had been published previously in *The Bell* in 1860). Dostoevsky discusses Ivan's use of journalistic anecdotes, and the case of the serf boy killed by dogs, in letter 782.
8. See note 1 on p. 85.
9. Ivan calls Alyosha a *skhimnik*, a monk who follows the most stringent, severe monastic rules. Alyosha has not been tonsured and is not yet a monk of any kind.

"That's just the point, that 'but' . . ." cried Ivan. "Let me tell you, novice, that the absurd is only too necessary on earth. The world stands on absurdities, and perhaps nothing would have come to pass in it without them. We know what we know!"

"What do you know?"

"I understand nothing," Ivan went on, as though in delirium, "and I don't want to understand anything now. I want to stick to the fact. I made up my mind long ago not to understand. If I try to understand anything, I will betray the fact, and I have decided to stick to the fact."

"Why are you testing me?" Alyosha cried out in a laceration of grief. "Will you finally tell me?"

"Of course, I will; that's what I've been leading up to. You are dear to me, I don't want to let you go, and I won't give you up to your Zosima."

Ivan was silent for a minute, his face became suddenly very sad. "Listen: I took the case of children only to make my case clearer. Of the other tears of humanity with which the earth is soaked from its crust to its center, I will say nothing, I have narrowed my subject on purpose. I am a bug, and I recognize in all humility that I cannot understand why the world is arranged as it is. Men are themselves to blame, I suppose; they were given paradise, they wanted freedom, and stole fire from heaven, though they knew they would become unhappy,[1] so there is no need to pity them. Oh, with my pitiful, earthly, Euclidian understanding, all I know is that there is suffering and that there are none guilty, that cause follows effect, simply and directly, that everything flows and finds its level—but that's only Euclidian nonsense, I know that, and I can't consent to live by it! What is it to me that none are guilty and I know it—I need retribution, otherwise I will destroy myself. And not retribution somewhere and sometime in eternity, but here, on earth, so that I see it myself. I have believed, and I want to see it myself, and if at that hour I will already be dead, then let them resurrect me, because if it all happens without me, then it will be too unfair. Surely I haven't suffered simply that I, my crimes and my sufferings, may manure the soil of the future harmony for somebody else. I want to see with my own eyes the hind lie down with the lion and the victim rise up and embrace his murderer.[2] I want to be there when everyone suddenly understands what it has all been for. All the religions of the world are built on this longing, and I am a believer. But then there are the children, and what am I to do about them? That's a question I can't answer. For the hundredth time I repeat, there are numbers of questions, but I've only taken the children, because here what I need to say is irresistibly clear. Listen: if everyone must suffer in order to buy eternal harmony with suffering, what do children have to do with it, tell me, please? It's utterly incomprehensible, why should they suffer too, and buy harmony with suffering? Why should they also furnish material to enrich the soil

1. Ivan combines themes from the Christian Bible and Greek mythology. The idea that humanity is to blame for its sufferings because it wanted freedom refers to Adam and Eve's disobedience (eating from the tree of knowledge of good and evil) and fall from God's grace, and the subsequent sinful condition which, according to Christian teaching, characterizes all human beings. According to Greek myth, the Titan Prometheus stole fire from heaven and gave it to humanity, for which he was punished by Zeus, the king of the gods.
2. Ivan refers to the prophecy of Isaiah: "The wolf also shall dwell with the lamb, and the leopard shall lie down with the kid; and the calf and the young lion and the fatling together; and a little child shall lead them" (11.6).

for the harmony of the future? I understand harmony in sin among people, and I understand solidarity in retribution, but children have no solidarity in sin, and if the truth really is that they are in solidarity with their fathers in all their fathers' evil doings, then that, of course, is a truth not of this world and is incomprehensible to me.[3] Some joker will say, perhaps, that the child would have grown up and have sinned, but he didn't grow up, he was torn to pieces by the dogs, at eight years old. Oh, Alyosha, I am not blaspheming! I understand, of course, what an upheaval of the universe it will be, when everything in heaven and earth blends in one hymn of praise and everything that lives and has lived cries aloud: 'Thou art just, O Lord, for Thy ways are revealed.'[4] When the mother embraces the torturer who threw her child to the dogs, and all three cry aloud with tears, 'Thou art just, O Lord!' then, of course, the crown of knowledge will come and everything will be explained. But what pulls me up here is that I can't accept that harmony. And while I am on earth, I hasten to take my own measures. You see, Alyosha, perhaps it really may happen that if I live to that moment, or rise again to see it, I, too, perhaps, may cry aloud with the rest, looking at the mother embracing the child's torturer, 'Thou art just, O Lord!' but I don't want to cry aloud then. While there is still time, I hasten to protect myself, and so I renounce the higher harmony altogether. It's not worth one little tear of even just that one tormented child who beat herself on the chest and prayed in that stinking outhouse to 'dear God' with her unredeemed tears. It's not worth it, because those tears remain unredeemed. They must be redeemed, or there can be no harmony. But how, how will you redeem them? Is it possible? By their being avenged? But what do I care about revenge, what do I care about hell for the tormentors, what is hell going to fix here, if these children have already been tormented? And what kind of harmony is it, if there's hell: I want to forgive and want to embrace, I don't want anyone to suffer anymore. And if the sufferings of children go into the replenishment of that sum of suffering that is needed for purchasing truth, then I declare ahead of time that all of truth is not worth such a price. I do not want, finally, the mother to embrace the tormentor who threw her son to the dogs! She dare not forgive him! If she wants, let her forgive him for herself, let her forgive the tormentor for her own immeasurable maternal suffering; but she does not have the right to forgive the sufferings of her child who was torn to pieces, she dare not forgive the tormentor even if the child himself were to forgive him! But if that's the way it is, if they dare not forgive, then where is the harmony? Is there in the whole world a being who could forgive and had the right to forgive? I don't want harmony, for the love of humanity I don't want it. I would rather remain with unavenged suffering. I'd rather remain with my unavenged suffering and unquenched indignation, *even if I am wrong*. Besides, they have put too high a price on harmony, we can't afford to pay so much for admission. And so I hasten to return my entrance ticket.[5] And if I am an honest man I am obligated to return it as soon as

3. By asserting that children have no solidarity in their fathers' sin, Ivan once again addresses and rejects the Christian doctrine of original sin.
4. Ivan paraphrases a sentiment found in the Book of Revelation: "Great and marvellous are thy works, Lord God Almighty; just and true are thy ways, thou King of saints" (15.3). See also Revelation 19.1–2.
5. Ivan's desire to return his ticket has at least two significant sources. Zhukovsky's translation of Schiller's 1784 poem "Resignation" contains the lines "The entrance letter to an earthly para-

possible. It's not God that I don't accept, Alyosha, only I most respectfully return to him the ticket."

"That's rebellion," murmured Alyosha, looking down.

"Rebellion? I wouldn't want such a word from you," said Ivan earnestly. "One can hardly live in rebellion, and I want to live. Tell me straight out, I call on you—answer: imagine that you yourself are building the edifice of human destiny with the goal of making people happy in the end, giving them peace and rest at last, but for that it was necessary and unavoidable to torture just one tiny little creation, that same little child who was beating herself on the chest with her little fist, and found this edifice on her unavenged tears, would you agree to be the architect under such conditions, tell me and don't lie!"

"No, I would not agree," said Alyosha softly.

"And can you admit the idea that the people for whom you are building it would agree to accept their happiness on the unjustified blood of a tortured little one, and, having accepted it, would remain happy forever?"

"No, I can't admit it. Brother," said Alyosha suddenly, with flashing eyes, "you said just now, is there a being in the whole world who would have the right to forgive and could forgive? But there is a Being and He can forgive everything, all *and for all*, because He gave His innocent blood for all and everything. You have forgotten Him, and on Him is built the edifice, and it is to Him they cry aloud, 'Thou art just, O Lord, for Thy ways are revealed!'"

"Ah! the One without sin and His blood! No, I have not forgotten Him; on the contrary I've been wondering all the time how it was you did not bring Him in before, for usually all arguments on your side put Him in the foreground. Do you know, Alyosha—don't laugh! I composed a poem about a year ago.[6] If you can waste another ten minutes on me, I'll tell it to you."

"You wrote a poem?"

"Oh, no, I didn't write it," laughed Ivan, "and I've never written two lines of poetry in my life. But I composed up this poem in prose and I remembered it. I was carried away when I composed it. You will be my first reader—that is, listener. Why should an author forego even one listener?" smiled Ivan. "Shall I tell it to you?"

"I am all attention," said Alyosha.

"My poem is called 'The Grand Inquisitor'; it's a ridiculous thing, but I want to tell it to you."

Chapter V

The Grand Inquisitor

"But even this must have a preface—that is, a literary preface, bah!" laughed Ivan, "and what sort of writer am I! You see, my action takes place

---

dise / I return to Thee unopened" (lines 3–4, stanza iii). In 1841 the literary and social critic Vissarion Belinsky penned a passionate rejection of Hegel's teleological vision of history, probably the most important source for Ivan's stance in general and this line in particular. Dostoevsky discusses his relationship with Belinsky in his *Diary* (1873), "Old People," chapter 2. See p. 649.

6. The Russian term *poema* can be applied to various forms of writing. Dostoevsky's novella *The Double* (1846), for example, carried the subtitle *A Petersburg Poem* (*Peterburgskaya poema*).

in the sixteenth century, and at that time—you should probably already know that from school—at that time it was customary in poetry to bring heavenly powers down to earth. I won't even mention Dante. In France, clerks, as well as the monks in the monasteries, used to give regular performances in which the Madonna, the saints, the angels, Christ, and God Himself were brought on the stage. At that time it was all done very simpleheartedly. In Victor Hugo's *Notre Dame de Paris*[7] an edifying and gratuitous spectacle was provided for the people in the town hall of Paris in the reign of Louis XI, in honor of the birth of the dauphin,[8] called *Le bon jugement de la très sainte et gracieuse Vierge Marie*,[9] in which she appears herself on the stage and pronounces her *bon jugement*. With us in Moscow, in pre-Petrine antiquity, similar dramatic performances, from the Old Testament especially, were also performed at times; but, besides dramatic performances, many tales and 'verses' circulated around the world, in which saints, angels, and all the powers of heaven took part as necessary. In our monasteries the monks were occupied translating, copying, and even composing such poems—and think when—under the Tatars. There is, for instance, one such little monastery poem (of course, from the Greek), 'The Wanderings of the Mother of God through Hell,'[1] with descriptions as bold as Dante's. The Mother of God visits hell, and the archangel Michael leads her through 'the torments.' She sees the sinners and their punishment. There she sees among others one most entertaining set of sinners in a burning lake: some of them sink to the bottom of the lake so that they can't swim out, and 'these God forgets'—an expression of extraordinary depth and force. And so the Mother of God, shocked and weeping, falls before the throne of God and begs for mercy for all in hell, for all she has seen there, indiscriminately. Her conversation with God is immensely interesting. She beseeches Him, she will not desist, and when God points to the hands and feet of her Son, nailed to the Cross, and asks: 'How can I forgive His tormentors?' she bids all the saints, all the martyrs, all the angels and archangels to fall down with her and pray for mercy on all without distinction. It ends by her winning from God a respite of suffering every year from Great Friday[2] till Trinity day, and the sinners in hell at once thank the Lord and cry out to him: 'Thou art just, O Lord, in this judgment.' Well, my little poem would have been just like that if it had appeared at that time. He comes on the scene in my poem; true, He says nothing in the poem, only appears and passes on. Fifteen centuries have passed since He promised to come in His glory, fifteen centuries since His prophet wrote, 'Behold, I come quickly.'[3] 'Of that day and that hour knoweth no man, neither the Son, but the Father,'[4] as He Himself predicted on earth. But humanity awaits him with the same faith and with the same

7. Dostoevsky greatly admired the French novelist Victor Hugo (1802–1885). He published a Russian translation of Hugo's novel *Notre-Dame de Paris* (known in English translation as *The Hunchback of Notre-Dame*, 1831) in his journal *Time* in 1862.
8. Heir to the French throne.
9. "The compassionate judgment of the very holy and gracious Virgin Mary" (French).
1. A twelfth-century apocryphal tale, translated from a Byzantine source.
2. In Eastern Christianity, Great Friday is the equivalent of Good Friday, the day on which Jesus was crucified.
3. The prophet is John, and the words "Behold, I come quickly" appear in Revelation 3.11 and 22.7.
4. Jesus tells his disciples, "Heaven and earth shall pass away . . . But of that day and that hour knoweth no man, no, not the angels which are in heaven, neither the Son, but the Father" (Mark 13.31–32). See also Matthew 24.36.

love. Oh, with greater faith, for it is fifteen centuries since man has ceased
to see signs from Heaven.

> Have faith in the heart's prompting
> For the heavens give no pledge.[5]

There was nothing left but faith in what the heart prompts. It is true
there were many miracles in those days. There were saints who performed miraculous cures; some holy people, according to their biographies, were visited by the Queen of Heaven herself. But the devil does not
slumber, and doubts were already arising among men of the truth of
these miracles. And just then there appeared in the north of Germany a
terrible new heresy.[6] A huge star 'burning as it were a lamp' (that is, to a
church) 'fell on the sources of the waters and they were made bitter.'[7]
These heretics began blasphemously denying miracles. But those who
remained faithful were all the more ardent in their faith. The tears of
humanity rose up to Him as before, awaited His coming, loved Him,
hoped for him, yearned to suffer and die for Him as before. And so many
ages mankind had prayed with faith and fervor, 'O Lord our God, hasten
Thy coming,'[8] so many ages called upon Him, that in His infinite mercy
He deigned to come down to His servants. Before that day He had come
down, too, He had visited some holy men, martyrs and hermits, as is
written in their 'Lives.' Among us, Tyutchev, with absolute faith in the
truth of his words, bore witness that

> Burdened with bearing the cross,
> The Heavenly King in slave's form
> Went throughout all of you, you,
> Native land, with his blessings.[9]

And that certainly was so, I assure you. And behold, He deigned to appear
for a moment to the people, to the tortured, suffering people, reeking
foully of sin, but loving Him like children. My story is laid in Spain, in
Seville, in the most terrible time of the Inquisition,[1] when fires were
lighted every day to the glory of God, and

> In the splendid *auto da fé*
> The wicked heretics were burnt.[2]

---

5. From Schiller's poem "Longing" ("Sehnsucht," 1801).
6. Protestantism. The heretics referred to in the next line are Protestants.
7. Ivan paraphrases Revelation 8.10–11: "there fell a great star from heaven, burning as it were a
   lamp, and it fell upon the third part of the rivers, and upon the fountains of waters; And the
   name of the star is called Wormwood; and the third part of the waters became wormwood; and
   many men died of the waters, because they were made bitter."
8. "O Lord our God, hasten Thy coming" is a deformation of the language in the original Biblical
   passage, Psalms 117.27. Ivan transforms a statement in the past tense into a command: "Богъ—
   господь, и явися намъ" translates roughly as "God is the Lord, who has appeared to us" (this
   would be и явился нам in modern Russian). The King James version reads "God is the Lord,
   which hath shewed us light." The passage was part of the Orthodox liturgy and so familiar to
   most Russians.
9. From the poem "These Poor Villages" ("Eti bednye selen'ia," 1855) by the Russian Romantic
   poet Fyodor Tyutchev (1803–1873).
1. The Spanish Inquisition was instituted in 1478 by King Ferdinand and Queen Isabella of
   Spain; it persecuted those suspected of failing to adhere to Catholicism, primarily Jews, Muslims, and, to a lesser extent, Protestants. In an auto de fe ("act of faith" in medieval Spanish;
   the Portuguese spelling *auto da fé* is sometimes found in English language texts), those
   accused of heresy were burned alive.
2. From the poem "Corialanus" (1834) by Alexander Polezhaev (1804/5–1838).

Oh, of course, this was not the coming in which He will appear according to His promise at the end of time in all His heavenly glory, and which will be sudden 'as lightning flashing from east to west.'[3] No, He visited His children only for a moment, and there where the flames were crackling round the heretics. In His infinite mercy He came once more among men in that human shape in which He walked among men for three years fifteen centuries ago. He came down to the 'hot pavement' of the southern town in which on the day before almost a hundred heretics had, *ad majorem gloriam Dei*, been burned by the cardinal, the Grand Inquisitor, in 'a magnificent *auto da fé*,' in the presence of the king, the court, the knights, the cardinals, the most charming ladies of the court, and the whole population of Seville.[4]

"He came softly, unobserved, and yet, strange to say, everyone recognized Him. That might be one of the best passages in the poem. I mean, why they recognized Him. The people are irresistibly drawn to Him, they surround Him, they flock about Him, follow Him. He moves silently in their midst with a gentle smile of infinite compassion. The sun of love burns in His heart.[5] Light, Enlightenment, and Power shine from His eyes, and their radiance, shed on the people, stirs their hearts with responsive love. He holds out His hands to them, blesses them, and a healing power comes from contact with Him, even with His garments.[6] An old man in the crowd, blind from childhood, cries out, 'O Lord, heal me and I shall see Thee!' and, as it were, scales fall from his eyes and the blind man sees Him.[7] The crowd weeps and kisses the earth under His feet. Children throw flowers before Him, sing, and cry 'Hosannah.'[8] 'It is He— it is He!' all repeat. 'It must be He, it can be no one but Him!' He stops at the steps of the Seville cathedral at the moment when the weeping mourners are bringing in a little open white coffin. In it lies a child of seven, the only daughter of a prominent citizen. The dead child lies hidden in flowers. 'He will raise your child,' the crowd shouts to the weeping mother. The priest, coming to meet the coffin, looks perplexed, and frowns, but the mother of the dead child throws herself at His feet with a wail. 'If it is Thou, raise my child!' she cries, holding out her hands to Him. The procession halts, the coffin is laid on the steps at His feet. He looks with compassion, and His lips once more softly pronounce, 'Maiden, arise!' and the maiden arises.[9] The little girl sits up in the coffin and looks

---

3. Matthew 24.27 describes the Second Coming of Christ: "For as the lightning cometh out of the east, and shineth even unto the west; so shall also the coming of the Son of man be." See also Luke 17.24.

4. "Hot pavement" and "magnificent *auto da fé*" are quotations from Polezhaev's poem. The Latin phrase *ad majorem gloriam Dei* (for the greater glory of God) is the motto of the Jesuit order.

5. The expression "the sun of love burns in His heart" may be an echo of Heine's poem "Peace" ("Frieden," 1826), published in Russian translation in 1872. Heinrich Heine (1797–1856), German poet and essayist noted for irony.

6. The Synoptic Gospels describe the healing power of Jesus' clothing. "A woman having an issue of blood twelve years, which had spent all her living upon physicians, neither could be healed of any, Came behind him, and touched the border of his garment: and immediately her issue of blood stanched" (Luke 8.43–44.) See also Matthew 9.20–22 and Mark 5.25–34.

7. This encounter between Christ and the blind man is based on Mark 8.22–25.

8. Ivan's description of the crowd's reaction to Jesus evokes several Gospel passages. According to John 12.13, they "went forth to meet him, and cried, Hosanna: Blessed is the King of Israel that cometh in the name of the Lord." See also Matthew 21.8–9 and Mark 11.8–10.

9. The Synoptic Gospels describe an encounter between Jesus and the despairing parents of a dead child: Jesus assures them that the child is not dead but merely sleeping, tells the girl to arise, and she gets up. See Matthew 9.23–25, Mark 5.40–42, and Luke 8.52–55.

round, smiling with wide-open wondering eyes, holding a bunch of white roses they had put in her hand.

"There are cries, sobs, confusion among the people, and at that moment the cardinal himself, the Grand Inquisitor, passes by the cathedral. He is an old man, almost ninety, tall and erect, with a withered face and sunken eyes, in which there is still a gleam of light, like a fiery spark. He is not dressed in his gorgeous cardinal's robes, as he was the day before, when he was burning the enemies of the Roman Church—at that moment he was wearing his coarse, old, monk's cassock. At a distance behind him come his gloomy assistants and slaves and the 'holy guard.' He stops at the sight of the crowd and watches it from a distance. He sees everything; he sees them set the coffin down at His feet, sees the child rise up, and his face darkens. He knits his thick gray brows and his eyes gleam with a sinister fire. He holds out his finger and bids the guards take Him. And such is his power, so completely are the people cowed into submission and trembling obedience to him, that the crowd immediately make way for the guards, and in the midst of deathlike silence they lay hands on Him and lead Him away. The crowd instantly bows down to the earth, like one man, before the old inquisitor. He blesses the people in silence and passes on. The guards lead their prisoner to the close, gloomy vaulted prison in the ancient palace of the Holy Inquisition and shut Him in it. The day passes and is followed by the dark, burning 'breathless' night of Seville. The air is 'fragrant with laurel and lemon.'[1] In the pitch darkness the iron door of the prison is suddenly opened and the Grand Inquisitor himself comes in with a light in his hand. He is alone, the door closes at once behind him. He stands in the doorway and for a long time, for a minute or two, gazes into His face. At last he goes up slowly, sets the light on the table and speaks.

"'Is it Thou? Thou?'[2] but receiving no answer, he adds at once, 'Don't answer, be silent. What canst Thou say, indeed? I know too well what Thou wouldst say. And Thou hast no right to add anything to what Thou hadst said of old. Why, then, art Thou come to hinder us? For Thou hast come to hinder us, and Thou knowest that. But dost Thou know what will be tomorrow? I know not who Thou art and care not to know whether it is Thou or only a semblance of Him, but tomorrow I shall condemn Thee and burn Thee at the stake as the worst of heretics. And the very people who have today kissed Thy feet, tomorrow at the faintest sign from me will rush to heap up the embers of Thy fire. Knowest Thou that? Yes, maybe Thou knowest it,' he added with thoughtful penetration, never for a moment taking his eyes off his prisoner."

"I don't quite understand, Ivan. What does it mean?" Alyosha, who had been listening in silence, said with a smile. "Is it simply a wild fantasy, or a mistake on the part of the old man—some impossible *qui pro quo*?"[3]

"Take it as the last," said Ivan, laughing, "if you are so corrupted by modern realism and can't stand anything fantastic. If you like it to be a case of *qui pro quo*, let it be so. It is true," he went on, laughing, "the old

1. A phrase from the play "The Stone Guest" (*Kamenny gost'*, 1836) by Pushkin.
2. Russian has two forms for the second person, the polite *vy* and familiar *ty* (corresponding to the Spanish *usted* and *tu* or French *vous* and *tu*). Throughout this chapter, the Grand Inquisitor addresses Christ with *ty*, the second person familiar form, which in Russian does not convey the archaic tone of the English *thou*.
3. "One for the other" (Latin), a case of mistaken identity.

man was ninety, and he might well be crazy over his set idea. He might have been struck by the appearance of the prisoner. It might, in fact, be simply his ravings, the delusion of an old man of ninety, approaching his death, overexcited by the *auto da fé* of a hundred heretics the day before. But does it matter to us after all whether it was a *qui pro quo* or a wild fantasy? All that matters is that the old man should speak out, should speak openly of what he has thought in silence for ninety years."

"And the prisoner too is silent? Does He look at him and not say a word?"

"That's inevitable in any case," Ivan laughed again. "The old man has told Him He hasn't the right to add anything to what He has said of old. One may say it is the most fundamental feature of Roman Catholicism, in my opinion at least. 'All has been given by Thee to the Pope,' they say, 'and all, therefore, is still in the Pope's hands, and there is no need for Thee to come now at all. Thou must not meddle for the time, at least.' That's how they speak and write too—the Jesuits, at any rate. I have read it myself in the works of their theologians. 'Hast Thou the right to reveal to us one of the mysteries of that world from which Thou hast come?' my old man asks Him, and answers the question for Him. 'No, Thou hast not; that Thou mayest not add to what has been said of old, and mayest not take from men the freedom which Thou didst exalt when Thou wast on earth. Whatsoever Thou revealest anew will encroach on men's freedom of faith; for it will be manifest as a miracle, and the freedom of their faith was dearer to Thee than anything in those days fifteen hundred years ago. Didst Thou not often say then, "I will make you free"?[4] But now Thou hast seen these "free" men,' the old man adds suddenly, with a pensive smile. 'Yes, we've paid dearly for it,' he goes on, looking sternly at Him, 'but at last we have completed that work in Thy name. For fifteen centuries we have been wrestling with Thy freedom, but now it is ended and over for good. Dost Thou not believe that it's over for good? Thou lookest meekly at me and deignest not even to be wroth with me. But let me tell Thee that now, today, people are more persuaded than ever that they have perfect freedom, yet they have brought their freedom to us and laid it humbly at our feet. But that has been our doing. Was this what Thou didst? Was this Thy freedom?'"

"I don't understand again," Alyosha broke in. "Is he ironical, is he laughing?"

"Not in the least! He claims it as a merit for himself and his Church that at last they have vanquished freedom and have done so to make men happy. 'For now' (he is speaking of the Inquisition, of course) 'for the first time it has become possible to think of the happiness of men. Man was made a rebel; and how can rebels be happy? Thou wast warned,' he says to Him. 'Thou hast had no lack of admonitions and warnings, but Thou didst not listen to those warnings; Thou didst reject the only way by which men might be made happy. But, fortunately, departing Thou didst hand on the work to us. Thou hast promised, Thou hast established by Thy word, Thou hast given to us the right to bind and to unbind,[5] and

---

4. "Ye shall know the truth, and the truth shall make you free," Jesus tells a group of listeners in John 8.32.
5. Jesus says to his disciples, "Whatsoever ye shall bind on earth shall be bound in heaven: and whatsoever ye shall loose on earth shall be loosed in heaven" (Matthew 18.18). See also Matthew 16.19 and John 20.23.

now, of course, Thou canst not think of taking it away. Why, then, hast Thou come to hinder us?'"

"And what's the meaning of 'no lack of admonitions and warnings'?" asked Alyosha.

"Why, that's the chief part of what the old man must say."

"'The wise and dread spirit, the spirit of self-destruction and nonexistence,' the old man goes on, 'the great spirit talked with Thee in the wilderness, and we are told in the books that he "tempted" Thee.[6] Is that so? And could anything truer be said than what he revealed to Thee in three questions and what Thou didst reject, and what in the books is called "the temptation"? And yet if there has ever been on earth a real thunderous miracle, it took place on that day, on the day of the three temptations. The statement of those three questions was itself the miracle. If it were possible to imagine simply for the sake of argument that those three questions of the dread spirit had perished utterly from the books, and that we had to restore them and to invent them anew, and to do so had gathered together all the wise men of the earth—rulers, chief priests, learned men, philosophers, poets—and had set them the task to invent three questions, such as would not only fit the occasion, but express in three words, three human phrases, the whole future history of the world and of humanity—dost Thou believe that all the wisdom of the earth united could have invented anything in depth and force equal to the three questions which were actually put to Thee then by the wise and mighty spirit in the wilderness? From those questions alone, from the miracle of their statement, we can see that we have here to do not with the fleeting human intelligence, but with the absolute and eternal. For in those three questions the whole subsequent history of mankind is, as it were, brought together into one whole, and foretold, and in them are united all the unsolved historical contradictions of human nature. At the time it could not be so clear, since the future was unknown; but now that fifteen hundred years have passed, we see that everything in those three questions was so justly grasped and foretold, and has been so truly fulfilled, that nothing can be added to them or taken from them.

"'Judge Thyself who was right—Thou or he who questioned Thee then? Remember the first question; its meaning, though not the exact words, was this: "Thou wouldst go into the world, and art going with empty hands, with some promise of freedom which men in their simplicity and their natural unruliness cannot even understand, which they fear and dread—for nothing has ever been more insupportable for a man and a human society than freedom. But seest Thou these stones in this parched and barren wilderness? Turn them into bread, and mankind will run after Thee like a flock, grateful and obedient, though forever trembling, lest Thou withdraw Thy hand and deny them Thy bread."[7] But Thou wouldst not deprive man of freedom and didst reject the offer, thinking, what is that freedom worth, if obedience is bought with bread? Thou didst reply that man lives not by bread alone. But dost Thou know that for the sake of that earthly bread the spirit of the earth will rise up against Thee and will

---

6. See note 5 on p. 62.
7. A reference to the first temptation of Christ, described in Matthew 4.3–4. Dostoevsky discussed the lure of turning stones into bread in an 1876 letter to a correspondent (see p. 655).

strive with Thee and overcome Thee, and all will follow him, crying, "Who can compare with this beast? He has given us fire from heaven!"[8] Dost Thou know that the ages will pass, and humanity will proclaim by the lips of their sages that there is no crime, and therefore no sin; there is only hunger?[9] "Feed men, and then ask of them virtue!" that's what they'll write on the banner, which they will raise against Thee, and with which they will destroy Thy temple. Where Thy temple stood will rise a new building; the terrible tower of Babel will be built again, and though, like the one of old, it will not be finished, yet Thou mightest have prevented that new tower and have cut short the sufferings of men for a thousand years; for they will come back to us after a thousand years of agony with their tower. They will seek us again, hidden underground in the catacombs, for we shall again be persecuted and tortured. They will find us and cry to us, "Feed us, for those who have promised us fire from heaven haven't given it!" And then we shall finish building their tower, for he finishes the building who feeds them. And we alone shall feed them in Thy name, declaring falsely that it is in Thy name. Oh, never, never can they feed themselves without us! No science will give them bread so long as they remain free. In the end they will lay their freedom at our feet, and say to us, "Make us your slaves, but feed us." They will understand themselves, at last, that freedom and bread enough for all are inconceivable together, for never, never will they be able to share between them! They will be convinced, too, that they can never be free, for they are weak, vicious, worthless and rebellious. Thou didst promise them the bread of Heaven, but, I repeat again, can it compare with earthly bread in the eyes of the weak, ever sinful and ignoble race of man? And if for the sake of the bread of Heaven thousands and tens of thousands shall follow Thee, what is to become of the millions and tens of thousands of millions of beings who will not have the strength to forego the earthly bread for the sake of the heavenly? Or dost Thou care only for the tens of thousands of the great and strong, while the millions, numerous as the sands of the sea,[1] who are weak but love Thee, must exist only for the sake of the great and strong? No, we care for the weak too. They are sinful and rebellious, but in the end they too will become obedient. They will marvel at us and look on us as gods, because we are ready to endure the freedom which they have found so dreadful and to rule over them—so awful it will seem to them to be free. But we shall tell them that we are Thy servants and rule them in Thy name. We shall deceive them again, for we will not let Thee come to us again. That deception will be our suffering, for we shall be forced to lie. This is the significance of the first question in the wilderness, and this is what Thou hast rejected for the sake of that freedom which Thou hast exalted above everything. Yet in this question lies hid the

---

8. Ivan again combines Christian and Greek mythological images. In the Book of Revelation John describes a vision of two beasts. People worshiped the first beast, saying "Who is like unto the beast?" (Revelation 13.4). "And I beheld another beast," John recounts, "And he doeth great wonders, so that he maketh fire come down from heaven on earth in the sight of men" (13.11, 13.13). The theme of bringing fire from heaven also derives from the myth of Prometheus.

9. The idea that crime and other forms of aberrant or antisocial behavior are directly and exclusively caused by environmental factors became a commonplace among the Russian intelligentsia in the 1860s.

1. The expression "numerous as the sands of the sea" is found several times in the Bible. See, for example, Revelation 20.8, in which John predicts that Satan will gather great forces, "the number of whom is as the sands of the sea."

great secret of this world. Choosing "bread," Thou wouldst have satisfied the universal and everlasting craving of humanity individually and together as one—to find someone to worship. So long as man remains free he strives for nothing so incessantly and so painfully as to find someone to worship. But man seeks to worship what is established beyond dispute, so that all men would agree at once to worship it. For these pitiful creations are concerned not only to find what one or the other can worship, but to find something that all would believe in and worship; what is essential is that all may be *together* in it. This craving for *community* of worship is the chief misery of every man individually and of all humanity from the beginning of time. For the sake of common worship they've slain each other with the sword. They have set up gods and challenged one another, "Put away your gods and come and worship ours, or we will kill you and your gods!" And so it will be to the end of the world, even when gods disappear from the earth; they will fall down before idols just the same. Thou didst know, Thou couldst not but have known, this fundamental secret of human nature, but Thou didst reject the one infallible banner which was offered Thee to make all men bow down to Thee alone—the banner of earthly bread; and Thou hast rejected it for the sake of freedom and the bread of Heaven. Behold what Thou didst further. And all again in the name of freedom! I tell Thee that man is tormented by no greater anxiety than to find someone quickly to whom he can hand over that gift of freedom with which this ill-fated being is born. But only one who can appease their conscience can take over their freedom. In bread there was offered Thee an invincible banner; give bread, and man will worship Thee, for nothing is more certain than bread. But if someone else gains possession of his conscience—oh! then he will cast away Thy bread and follow after him who has ensnared his conscience. In that Thou wast right. For the secret of man's being is not only to live but to have something to live for. Without a stable conception of the object of life, man would not consent to go on living, and would rather destroy himself than remain on earth, though he had bread in abundance. That is true. But what happened? Instead of taking men's freedom from them, Thou didst make it greater than ever! Didst Thou forget that man prefers peace, and even death, to freedom of choice in the knowledge of good and evil? Nothing is more seductive for man than his freedom of conscience, but nothing is a greater cause of suffering. And behold, instead of giving a firm foundation for setting the conscience of man at rest forever, Thou didst choose all that is exceptional, vague and enigmatic; Thou didst choose what was utterly beyond the strength of men, acting as though Thou didst not love them at all—Thou who didst come to give Thy life for them! Instead of taking possession of men's freedom, Thou didst increase it, and burdened the spiritual kingdom of mankind with its sufferings forever. Thou didst desire man's free love, that he should follow Thee freely, enticed and taken captive by Thee. In place of the rigid ancient law, man must hereafter with free heart decide for himself what is good and what is evil, having only Thy image before him as his guide.[2] But didst Thou not know he would at last reject even Thy image

2. The "rigid ancient law" refers to Judaism. From the Christian perspective, Judaism represents an older law or covenant, one surpassed by the covenant of Christ. The centrality of love in the Christian covenant is put forward in Romans 13.8–10, which concludes "love is the fulfilling of the law."

and Thy truth, if he is weighed down with the fearful burden of free choice? They will cry aloud at last that the truth is not in Thee, for they could not have been left in greater confusion and suffering than Thou hast caused, laying upon them so many cares and unanswerable problems. So that, in truth, Thou didst Thyself lay the foundation for the destruction of Thy kingdom, and no one is more to blame for it. Yet what was offered Thee? There are three powers, three powers alone, able to conquer and to hold captive forever the conscience of these impotent rebels for their happiness—those forces are miracle, mystery and authority. Thou hast rejected all three and hast set the example for doing so. When the wise and dread spirit set Thee on the pinnacle of the temple and said to Thee, "If Thou wouldst know whether Thou art the Son of God then cast Thyself down, for it is written: the angels shall hold him up lest he fall and bruise himself, and Thou shalt know then whether Thou art the Son of God and shalt prove then how great is Thy faith in Thy Father." But Thou didst refuse and wouldst not cast Thyself down.[3] Oh! of course, Thou didst proudly and well, like God; but the weak, rebellious race of men, are they gods? Oh, Thou didst know then that in taking one step, in making one movement to cast Thyself down, Thou wouldst be tempting God and have lost all Thy faith in Him, and wouldst have been dashed to pieces against that earth which Thou didst come to save. And the wise spirit that tempted Thee would have rejoiced. But I ask again, are there many like Thee? And couldst Thou believe for one moment that men, too, could face such a temptation? Is the nature of men such, that they can reject miracle, and at the great moments of their life, the moments of their deepest, most agonizing spiritual difficulties, cling only to the free verdict of the heart? Oh, Thou didst know that Thy deed would be recorded in books, would be handed down to remote times and the utmost ends of the earth, and Thou didst hope that man, following Thee, would cling to God and not ask for a miracle. But Thou didst not know that when man rejects miracle he rejects God too; for man seeks not so much God as the miraculous. And as man cannot bear to be without the miraculous, he will create new miracles of his own for himself, and will worship deeds of sorcery and witchcraft, though he might be a hundred times over a rebel, heretic and infidel. Thou didst not come down from the Cross when they shouted to Thee, mocking and reviling Thee, "Come down from the cross and we will believe that Thou art He."[4] Thou didst not come down, for again Thou wouldst not enslave man by a miracle, and didst crave faith given freely, not based on miracle. Thou didst crave for free love and not the base raptures of the slave before the might that has overawed him forever. But Thou didst think too highly of men therein, for they are slaves, of course, though rebellious by nature. Look round and judge; fifteen centuries have passed, look upon them. Whom hast Thou raised up to Thyself? I swear, man is weaker and baser by nature than Thou hast believed him! Can he, can he do what Thou didst? By showing him so much respect, Thou didst, as it were, cease to feel for him, for Thou didst ask far too much from him—thou who hast

---

3. A paraphrase of the second temptation of Christ, found in Matthew 4.5–7. Satan says to Jesus: "If thou be the Son of God, cast thyself down: for it is written, He shall give his angels charge concerning thee: and in their hands they shall bear thee up, lest at any time thou dash thy foot against a stone."
4. Paraphrase of Matthew 27.39–44.

loved him more than Thyself! Respecting him less, Thou wouldst have asked less of him. That would have been more like love, for his burden would have been lighter. He is weak and vile. What though he is every- where now rebelling against our power, and proud of his rebellion? It is the pride of a child and a schoolboy. They are little children rioting and barring out the teacher at school. But their childish delight will end; it will cost them dear. They will cast down temples and drench the earth with blood. But they will see at last, the foolish children, that, though they are rebels, they are impotent rebels, unable to keep up their own rebellion. Bathed in their foolish tears, they will recognize at last that He who created them rebels must have meant to mock at them. They will say this in despair, and their utterance will be a blasphemy which will make them more unhappy still, for man's nature cannot bear blasphemy, and in the end always avenges it on itself. And so unrest, confusion and unhappiness—that is the present lot of man after Thou didst bear so much for their freedom! Thy great prophet tells in vision and in image, that he saw all those who took part in the first resurrection and that there were of each tribe twelve thou- sand.[5] But if there were so many of them, they must have been not men but gods. They had borne Thy cross, they had endured scores of years in the barren, hungry wilderness, living upon locusts and roots[6]—and Thou may- est indeed point with pride at those children of freedom, of free love, of free and splendid sacrifice for Thy name. But remember that they were only some thousands, and gods at that; and what of the rest? And how are the other weak ones to blame, because they could not endure what the strong have endured? How is the weak soul to blame that it is unable to receive such terrible gifts? Canst Thou really have come only to the elect and for the elect? But if so, it is a mystery and we cannot understand it. And if it is a mystery, we too have a right to preach a mystery, and to teach them that it's not the free judgment of their hearts, not love that matters, but a mystery which they must follow blindly, even against their con- science. So we have done. We have corrected Thy work and have founded it upon *miracle, mystery,* and *authority.* And men rejoiced that they were again led like sheep, and that the terrible gift that had brought them such suffering, was, at last, lifted from their hearts. Were we right teaching them this? Speak! Did we not love mankind, so meekly acknowledging their feebleness, lovingly lightening their burden, and permitting their weak nature even sin with our sanction? Why hast Thou come now to hin- der us? And why dost Thou look silently and searchingly at me with Thy mild eyes? Be angry. I don't want Thy love, for I love Thee not. And what use is it for me to hide anything from Thee? Don't I know to Whom I am speaking? All that I can say is known to Thee already. I can see it in Thine eyes. And is it for me to conceal from Thee our mystery? Perhaps it is Thy will to hear it from my lips. Listen, then. We are not working with Thee, but with *him*—that is our mystery. It's long—eight centuries—since we have been on *his* side and not on Thine. Just eight centuries ago, we took from him what Thou didst reject with scorn, that last gift he offered Thee, showing Thee all the kingdoms of the earth.[7] We took from him Rome

---

5. See Revelation 7.2–9.
6. An allusion to Matthew 3.1–4.
7. A reference to the third and last temptation put forth by Satan to Jesus in the wilderness, the offer of political power.

and the sword of Caesar, and proclaimed ourselves sole rulers of the earth, though hitherto we have not been able to complete our work.[8] But whose fault is that? Oh, the work is only beginning, but it has begun. It has long to await completion and the earth has yet much to suffer, but we shall triumph and shall be Caesars, and then we shall plan the universal happiness of man. But Thou mightest have taken even then the sword of Caesar. Why didst Thou reject that last gift? Hadst Thou accepted that last counsel of the mighty spirit, Thou wouldst have accomplished all that man seeks on earth—that is, someone to worship, someone to keep his conscience, and some means of uniting all in one unanimous and harmonious anthill, for the craving for universal unity is the third and last anguish of men. Mankind as a whole has always strived to organize a universal state. There have been many great nations with great histories, but the more highly they were developed the more unhappy they were, for they felt more acutely than other people the craving for worldwide union. The great conquerors, Tamerlane[9] and Genghis Khan,[1] whirled like hurricanes over the face of the earth striving to subdue its people, and they too were but the unconscious expression of the same craving for universal unity. Hadst Thou taken the world and Caesar's purple, Thou wouldst have founded the universal state and have given universal peace. For who can rule men if not he who holds their conscience and their bread in his hands? We have taken the sword of Caesar, and in taking it, of course, have rejected Thee and followed *him*. Oh, ages are yet to come of the confusion of free thought, of their science and cannibalism. For having begun to build their tower of Babel without us, they will end, of course, with cannibalism. But then the beast will crawl to us and lick our feet and spatter them with tears of blood. And we shall sit upon the beast and raise the cup, and on it will be written, "Mystery."[2] But then, and only then, the reign of peace and happiness will come for men. Thou art proud of Thine elect, but Thou hast only the elect, while we give rest to all. And besides, how many of those elect, those mighty ones who could become elect, have grown weary waiting for Thee, and have transferred and will transfer the powers of their spirit and the warmth of their heart to the other camp, and end by raising their *free* banner against Thee. Thou didst Thyself lift up that banner. But with us all will be happy and will no more rebel nor destroy one another as under Thy freedom. Oh, we shall persuade them that they will only become free when they renounce their freedom to us and submit to us. And shall we be right or shall we be lying? They will be convinced that we are right, for they will remember the horrors of slavery

---

8. The temporal power of the Roman Catholic Popes can be traced back to 754, when Pepin the Short, King of the Franks, granted Ravenna to Pope Stephen III. Ivan's poem takes place eight centuries later, in the sixteenth century.
9. Born in present-day Uzbekistan, Tamerlane (1336–1405) conquered territory that extended from present-day southeastern Turkey to northwestern India. Millions of people were slaughtered in his campaigns.
1. Genghis Khan (c. 1162–1227) united nomadic central Asian tribes, then conquered vast territories stretching from the Caspian Sea to the Pacific. His descendents extended the Mongol Empire into Europe.
2. Ivan combines references to Biblical and secular sources: see Pushkin's poem "The Covetous Knight" and the beasts described in Revelation 13 and 17. Revelation 17 describes a vision of a corrupt woman, a "great whore," riding a beast. She holds "a golden cup in her hand full of abominations and filthiness of her fornication: And upon her forehead was a name written, MYSTERY, BABYLON THE GREAT, THE MOTHER OF HARLOTS AND ABOMINATIONS OF THE EARTH" (17.1, 4–5). When he says "we shall raise the cup," the Grand Inquisitor identifies himself— and by extension Roman Catholicism—with the woman riding the beast.

and confusion to which Thy freedom brought them. Freedom, free thought and science, will lead them into such straits and will bring them face to face with such marvels and insoluble mysteries, that some of them, the fierce and rebellious, will destroy themselves, others, rebellious but weak, will destroy one another, while the rest, weak and unhappy, will crawl fawning to our feet and whine to us: "Yes, you were right, you alone possess His mystery, and we come back to you, save us from ourselves!" Receiving bread from us, they will of course see clearly that we take the bread made by their hands from them, to give it to them, without any miracle. They will see that we do not change the stones to bread, but in truth they will be more thankful for taking it from our hands than for the bread itself! For they will remember only too well that in the old days, without our help, even the bread they made turned to stones in their hands, while since they have come back to us, the very stones have turned to bread in their hands. Too, too well they know the value of complete submission! And until men know that, they will be unhappy. Who is most to blame for their not knowing it, speak? Who scattered the flock and sent it astray on unknown paths? But the flock will come together again and will submit once more, and then it will be once for all. Then we shall give them the quiet humble happiness of weak beings such as they are by nature. Oh, we shall persuade them at last not to be proud, for Thou didst lift them up and thereby taught them to be proud. We shall show them that they are weak, that they are only pitiful children, but that childlike happiness is the sweetest of all. They will become timid and will look to us and huddle close to us in fear, as chicks to the hen. They will marvel at us and will be awestricken before us, and will be proud at our being so powerful and clever, that we have been able to subdue such a turbulent flock of thousands of millions. They will tremble impotently before our wrath, their minds will grow fearful, they will be quick to shed tears like women and children, but they will be just as ready at a sign from us to pass to laughter and rejoicing, to happy mirth and childish song. Yes, we shall set them to work, but in their leisure hours we shall make their life like a child's game, with children's songs and innocent dance. Oh, we shall allow them even sin, they are weak and helpless, and they will love us like children because we allow them to sin. We shall tell them that every sin will be redeemed, if it is done with our permission, that we allow them to sin because we love them, and the punishment for these sins we take upon ourselves. And we shall take it upon ourselves, and they will adore us as their saviors who have taken on themselves their sins before God. And they will have no secrets from us. We shall allow or forbid them to live with their wives and mistresses, to have or not to have children—according to whether they have been obedient or disobedient—and they will submit to us gladly and cheerfully. The most painful secrets of their conscience, all, all they will bring to us, and we shall have an answer for all. And they will be glad to believe our answer, for it will save them from the great anxiety and terrible agony they endure at present in making a free decision for themselves. And all will be happy, all the millions of beings except the hundred thousand who rule over them. For only we, we who guard the mystery, shall be unhappy. There will be thousands of millions of happy babes, and a hundred thousand sufferers who have taken upon themselves the curse of the knowledge of good and evil. Peacefully they will die, peacefully they will expire in Thy name, and beyond the grave they will find nothing but death. But we shall keep the secret, and for their happiness we shall entice them with the reward of heaven and eternity. Though if there were anything in the other world, it certainly would not be for such as they. It is prophesied that Thou wilt come again in victory, Thou wilt come with Thy chosen, the proud and strong, but we will say that they have only saved themselves, but we have saved all.[3] We are told that the harlot who sits upon the beast, and holds in her hands the *mystery*, shall be put to shame, that the weak will rise up again, and will rend her royal purple and will strip naked her 'loathsome' body.[4] But then I will stand up and point out to Thee the thousand millions of happy children who have known no sin. And we who have taken their sins upon us for their happiness will stand up before Thee and say: "Judge us if Thou canst and darest." Know that I fear Thee not. Know that I too have been in the wilderness, I too have lived on roots and locusts, I too prized the freedom with which Thou hast blessed men, and I too was striving to stand among Thy elect, among the strong and powerful, thirsting "to make up the number."[5] But I awakened and would not serve madness. I turned back and joined the ranks of those *who have corrected Thy work*. I left the proud and went back to the humble, for the happiness of the humble. What I say to Thee will come to pass, and our dominion will be built up. I repeat, tomorrow Thou shalt see that obedient flock who at a sign from me will hasten to heap up the hot cinders about the pile on which I shall burn Thee for coming to hinder us. For if anyone has ever deserved our fires, it is Thou. Tomorrow I shall burn Thee. *Dixi.*'"[6]

Ivan stopped. He was carried away as he talked and spoke with excitement; when he had finished, he suddenly smiled.

Alyosha had listened in silence; towards the end he was greatly moved and seemed several times on the point of interrupting, but restrained himself. Now his words came with a rush.

"But . . . that's absurd!" he cried, flushing. "Your poem is in praise of Jesus, not in blame of Him—as you meant it to be. And who will believe you about freedom? Is that the way to understand it? That's not the idea of it in the Orthodox Church . . . That's Rome, and not even the whole of Rome, it's false—those are the worst of the Catholics, the Inquisitors, the Jesuits! . . . And there could not be such a fantastic figure as your Inquisitor. What are these sins of mankind they take on themselves? Who are these keepers of the mystery who have taken some curse upon themselves for the happiness of mankind? When have they been seen? We know the Jesuits, they are spoken ill of, but surely they are not what you describe? They are not that at all, not at all. . . . They are simply the Romish army for the earthly sovereignty of the world in the future, with

---

3. According to Biblical passages describing the second coming of Christ, the elect shall be saved and the rest condemned. See Matthew 24.30–31 and Revelation 12.7–11, 17.14, and 19.19–21.
4. The book of Revelation describes the punishment awaiting the woman riding the beast, the "great whore" or city of Babylon. See Revelation 17.16, Revelation 18, and Revelation 19.1–3.
5. The Grand Inquisitor claims to have had an existence similar to that of John the Baptist, who lived in the wilderness and "did eat locusts and wild honey" (Mark 1.6). For John the Baptist's role as prophet and baptizer of Christ, see Matthew 3.1–15 and Mark 1.1–9. References to the elect can be found in Matthew 24.22, 24.24, and 24.31; Mark 13.20, 13.22, and 13.27. Several passages in the Book of Revelation specify the number of the elect as one hundred and forty-four thousand. See Revelation 14.1–4 and 7.4–8.
6. "I have spoken" (Latin).

the Pontiff of Rome for Emperor . . . that's their ideal, but there's no sort of mystery or lofty sorrow about it. . . . It's simple lust for power, for filthy earthly gain, for domination—something like a universal serfdom with them as masters—that's all they stand for. They don't even believe in God perhaps. Your suffering inquisitor is a mere fantasy . . ."

"Wait, wait," laughed Ivan, "how excited you are! A fantasy you say, let it be so! Of course it's a fantasy. But allow me to say: do you really think that the Roman Catholic movement of the last centuries is actually nothing but the lust for power, for filthy earthly gain? Is that Father Païssy's teaching?"

"No, no, on the contrary, Father Païssy did once say something even rather similar as you . . . but of course it's not the same, not a bit the same," Alyosha suddenly corrected himself.

"A precious bit of information, in spite of your 'not a bit the same.' I ask you why your Jesuits and Inquisitors have united simply for vile material gain? Why can there not be among them one martyr oppressed by great sorrow and loving humanity? You see, only suppose that there was one such man among all those who desire nothing but filthy material gain—if there's only one like my old inquisitor, who had himself eaten roots in the desert and made frenzied efforts to subdue his flesh to make himself free and perfect. But yet all his life he loved humanity, and suddenly his eyes were opened, and he saw that it is no great moral blessedness to attain perfection and freedom, if at the same time one gains the conviction that millions of God's beings have been created as a mockery, that they will never be capable of using their freedom, that these poor rebels can never turn into giants to complete the tower, that it was not for such geese that the great idealist dreamt his dream of harmony. Seeing all that he turned back and joined—the intelligent people. Surely that could have happened?"

"Joined whom, what intelligent people?" cried Alyosha, completely carried away. "They have no such great intelligence and no mysteries and secrets. . . . Perhaps nothing but Atheism, that's all their secret. Your inquisitor does not believe in God, that's his secret!"

"What if it is so! You finally guessed it. It's perfectly true that that's the whole secret, but isn't that suffering, at least for a man like that, who has wasted his whole life in the desert and yet could not shake off his incurable love of humanity? In his old age he reached the clear conviction that nothing but the advice of the great dread spirit could build up any tolerable sort of life for the feeble, unruly, 'incomplete, specimen beings created in jest.' And so, convinced of this, he sees that he must follow the counsel of the wise spirit, the dread spirit of death and destruction, and therefore accept lying and deception, and lead men consciously to death and destruction, and yet deceive them all the way so that they may not notice where they are being led, that the poor blind ones may at least on the way think themselves happy. And note, the deception is in the name of Him in Whose ideal the old man had so fervently believed all his life long. Is not that tragic? And if only one such stood at the head of the whole army 'filled with the lust for power only for the sake of filthy gain'—would not one such be enough to make a tragedy? More than that, one such standing at the head is enough to create the actual leading idea of the Roman Church with all its armies and Jesuits, its highest idea. I tell you frankly that I firmly believe that there has always been such a man among those who stood at the head of the movement. Who knows, there may have been some such even among the Roman popes. Who knows, perhaps the spirit of that accursed old man who loves mankind so obstinately in his own way, is to be found even now in a whole multitude of such old men, existing not by chance but by agreement, as a secret league formed long ago for the guarding of the mystery, to guard it from the weak and the unhappy, so as to make them happy. No doubt it is so, and so it must be indeed. I fancy that even among the Masons[7] there's something of the same mystery at the bottom, and that that's why the Catholics so detest the Masons as their rivals breaking up the unity of the idea, while it is so essential that there should be one flock and one shepherd. . . . But from the way I defend my idea I seem like an author who can't take your criticism. Enough of it."

"You are perhaps a Mason yourself!" broke suddenly from Alyosha. "You don't believe in God," he added, speaking this time very sorrowfully. Besides, it seemed to him that his brother was looking at him ironically. "How does your poem end?" he asked, suddenly looking down. "Or was it the end?"

"I meant to end it like this. When the Inquisitor ceased speaking he waited some time for his prisoner to answer him. His silence weighed down upon him. He saw that the prisoner had listened intently and quietly all the time, looking gently in his face and evidently not wishing to reply. The old man longed for Him to say something, however bitter and terrible. But He suddenly approached the old man in silence and softly kissed him on his bloodless aged lips. That was all his answer. The old man shuddered. His lips moved. He went to the door, opened it, and said to Him: 'Go, and come no more. . . . come not at all, never, never!' And he let Him out 'into the dark squares of the town.'[8] The prisoner went away."

"And the old man?"

"The kiss glows in his heart, but the old man adheres to his idea."

"And you with him, you too?" cried Alyosha, mournfully. Ivan laughed.

"Why, it's all nonsense, Alyosha, it's only a senseless poem of a senseless student, who could never write two lines of verse. Why do you take it so seriously? Surely you don't suppose I am going straight off to the Jesuits, to join the swarm of men who are correcting his work? Good Lord, it's no business of mine. I told you, all I want is to live on to thirty, and then—dash the cup to the ground!"

"But the little sticky leaves, and the precious tombs, and the blue sky, and the woman you love! How will you live, how will you love them?" Alyosha cried sorrowfully. "With such a hell in your heart and your head, how can you? No, that's just what you are going away for, to join them . . . if not, you will kill yourself, you can't endure it!"

"There is a strength to endure everything," Ivan said with a cold smile.

"What strength?"

7. Freemasonry is an international fraternal order, with rituals and symbols derived from medieval stonemason guilds. It lacks a fixed doctrine, but members typically strive for moral self-improvement and aspire to improve society; belief in a supreme being is a prerequisite for membership, which is exclusively male. The first Russian Masonic lodges appeared in the 1730s. Churches and governments were frequently hostile to Freemasonry as an international organization that eluded their control.

8. An inexact quotation from Pushkin's poem "Recollection" ("Vospominanie," 1828).

"The strength of the Karamazov—the strength of the Karamazov baseness."

"To sink into debauchery, to stifle your soul with corruption, yes?"

"Possibly even that . . . only perhaps till I am thirty I shall escape it, and then."

"How will you escape it? By what will you escape it? That's impossible with your ideas."

"In the Karamazov way, again."

"'Everything is permitted,' you mean?[9] Everything is permitted, is that it?"

Ivan scowled, and all at once turned strangely pale.

"Ah, you've caught up yesterday's phrase, which so offended Miüsov—and which brother Dmitri pounced upon so naïvely and paraphrased!" he smiled queerly. "Yes, if you like, 'everything is permitted' since the word has been said. I won't deny it. And Mitenka's version isn't bad."

Alyosha looked at him in silence.

"I thought, brother, that going away from here I have you at least," Ivan said suddenly, with unexpected feeling; "but now I see that there is no place for me even in your heart, my dear hermit. The formula, 'all is permitted,' I won't renounce—will you renounce me for that, yes?"

Alyosha got up, went to him and softly kissed him on the lips.

"That's plagiarism," cried Ivan, highly delighted. "You stole that from my poem. Thank you though. Get up, Alyosha, it's time we were going, both of us."

They went out, but stopped when they reached the entrance of the restaurant.

"Listen, Alyosha," Ivan began in a resolute voice, "if I am really able to care for the sticky little leaves I shall only love them, remembering you. It's enough for me that you are somewhere here, and I shan't lose my desire for life yet. Is that enough for you? Take it as a declaration of love if you like. And now you go to the right and I to the left.[1] And it's enough, do you hear, enough. I mean even if I don't go away tomorrow (I think I certainly shall go) and we meet again, don't say a word more on these subjects. I beg that particularly. And about brother Dmitri too, I ask you specially never speak to me again," he added, with sudden irritation; "it's all exhausted, it has all been said over and over again, hasn't it? And I'll make you one promise in return for it. When at thirty, I want to 'dash the cup to the ground,' wherever I may be I'll come to have one more talk with you, even though it were from America, you may be sure of that. I'll come on purpose. It will be very interesting to have a look at you, to see what you'll be by that time. It's rather a solemn promise, you see. And we really may be parting for seven years or ten. Come, go now to your *Pater Seraphicus*,[2] he is dying. If he dies without you, you will be angry with me for having kept you. Good-bye, kiss me once more; that's right, now go."

Ivan turned suddenly and went his way without looking back. It was just as brother Dmitri had left Alyosha the day before, though the parting had

---

9. See p. 65.
1. An allusion to Genesis 13.9. The left is traditionally associated with the devil.
2. "Angelic Father" (Latin). This term may be a reference to Goethe's *Faust*; it also refers to Saint Francis of Assisi (1181/82–1226), a patron saint of animals and founder of the Franciscan Order. Like Zosima, Francis was born into wealth and privilege but abandoned his inheritance for a life of poverty and preaching. For discussion of why Ivan refers to Zosima as Pater Seraphicus, see the complete version of Vetlovskaya, "Alyosha Karamazov."

been very different. This strange little observation flashed, like an arrow, through Alyosha's sad mind, sad and sorrowful at this moment. He waited a little, looking after his brother. For some reason he suddenly noticed that his brother Ivan swayed as he walked and that his right shoulder looked lower than his left. He had never noticed it before. But suddenly he turned too, and almost ran to the monastery. It was nearly dark, and he felt almost frightened; something new was growing up in him for which he could not account. The wind had risen again as on the previous evening, and the ancient pines murmured gloomily about him when he entered the hermitage woods. He almost ran. "*Pater Seraphicus*—he got that name from somewhere—where from?" Alyosha wondered. "Ivan, poor Ivan, and when shall I see you again? . . . Here is the hermitage. Yes, yes, that he is, Pater Seraphicus, he will save me—from him and forever!"

Several times afterwards in his life he wondered how he could on leaving Ivan so completely forget his brother Dmitri, though he had that morning, only a few hours before, so firmly resolved to find him and not to give up doing so, even if it meant he would be unable to return to the monastery that night.

Chapter VI

For a While a Very Obscure One

And Ivan Fyodorovich, on parting from Alyosha, went home to Fyodor Pavlovich's house. But, strange to say, he was suddenly overcome by unbearable depression, which, moreover, grew greater at every step he took towards the house. There was nothing strange in his being depressed; what was strange was that Ivan Fyodorovich could not have said what was the cause of it. He had often been depressed before, and there was nothing surprising at his feeling so at such a moment, when he had broken off with everything that had brought him here, and was preparing that day to make a new start and enter upon a new, unknown future. He would again be as solitary as ever, and though he had great hopes, and great—too great— expectations from life, he could not have given any definite account of his hopes, his expectations, or even his desires. Yet at that moment, though the apprehension of the new and unknown certainly found place in his heart, what was worrying him was something quite different. "Is it loathing for my father's house?" he wondered. "Quite likely; I am so sick of it; and though it's the last time I shall cross its hateful threshold, still I loathe it. . . . No, it's not that either. Is it the parting with Alyosha and the conversation I had with him? For so many years I've been silent with the whole world and not deigned to speak, and all of a sudden I reel off a rigmarole like that." It certainly might have been the youthful vexation of youthful inexperience and vanity, vexation at having failed to express himself, especially with such a being as Alyosha, on whom his heart had certainly been reckoning. No doubt that came in, that vexation, it must have done indeed; but yet that was not it, that was not it either. "I feel sick with depression and yet I can't tell what I want. Better not think, perhaps . . ."

Ivan Fyodorovich tried "not to think," but that, too, was no use. What made his depression so vexatious and irritating was that it had a kind of casual, external character—he felt that. Some person or thing seemed to be standing out somewhere, just as something will sometimes obtrude itself upon the eye, and though one may be so busy with work or conversation that for a long time one does not notice it, yet it irritates and almost torments one till at last one realizes, and removes the offending object, often quite a trifling and ridiculous one—some article left about in the wrong place, a handkerchief on the floor, a book not replaced on the shelf, and so on. At last, feeling very cross and ill-humored, Ivan Fyodorovich arrived home, and suddenly, about fifteen paces from the garden gate, he guessed what was fretting and worrying him.

On a bench in the gateway the lackey Smerdyakov was sitting, enjoying the coolness of the evening, and at the first glance at him Ivan Fyodorovich knew that the lackey Smerdyakov was on his mind, and that it was this man that his soul loathed. It all dawned upon him suddenly and became clear. Just before, when Alyosha had been telling him of his meeting with Smerdyakov, he had felt a sudden twinge of gloom and loathing, which had immediately stirred responsive anger in his heart. Afterwards, as he talked, Smerdyakov had been forgotten for the time; but still he had been in his mind, and as soon as Ivan Fyodorovich parted from Alyosha and was walking home, the forgotten sensation began to obtrude itself again. "Is it possible that a miserable scoundrel like that can worry me so much?" he wondered, with unbearable spite.

The thing was that Ivan Fyodorovich had indeed come of late to feel an intense dislike for the man, especially during the last few days. He had even begun to notice in himself a growing feeling that was almost of hatred for this being. Perhaps this process of hatred was accentuated by the fact that when Ivan Fyodorovich first came to the neighborhood he had felt quite differently. Then Ivan Fyodorovich had taken a kind of special interest in Smerdyakov, and had even found him suddenly very original. He had encouraged him to talk to him, although he had always wondered at a certain incoherence, or rather restlessness in his mind, and could not understand what it was that so continually and insistently worked upon the brain of "the contemplative." They discussed philosophical questions and even how there could have been light on the first day when the sun, moon, and stars were only created on the fourth day, and how that was to be understood. But Ivan Fyodorovich soon saw that, though the sun, moon, and stars might be an interesting subject, yet that it was quite secondary to Smerdyakov, and that he was looking for something altogether different. In one way and another, he began to betray a boundless vanity, and a wounded vanity, too, and that Ivan Fyodorovich disliked. It had first given rise to his aversion. Later on, there had been trouble in the house. Grushenka had come on the scene, and there had been the scandals with his brother Dmitri—they discussed that, too. But though Smerdyakov always talked of that with great excitement, it was impossible to discover what he desired to come of it. There was, in fact, something surprising in the illogicality and incoherence of some of his desires, accidentally betrayed and always vaguely expressed. Smerdyakov was always inquiring, putting certain indirect but obviously premeditated questions, but what his object was he did not explain, and usually at the most important moment he would break off and relapse into silence or pass to another subject. But what finally irritated Ivan Fyodorovich most and confirmed his dislike for him was the peculiar revolting familiarity which Smerdyakov began to show more and more markedly. Not that he forgot himself and was rude; on the contrary, he always spoke very respectfully, yet he had obviously begun to consider— goodness knows why!—that there was some sort of understanding between him and Ivan Fyodorovich. He always spoke in a tone that suggested that those two had some kind of compact, some secret between them, that had at some time been expressed on both sides, only known to them and beyond the comprehension of those mortals bustling around them. But for a long while Ivan Fyodorovich did not recognize the real cause of his growing dislike and he had only lately realized what was at the root of it. With a feeling of disgust and irritation he tried to pass in at the gate without speaking or looking at Smerdyakov. But Smerdyakov rose from the bench, and from that action alone, Ivan Fyodorovich knew instantly that he wanted particularly to talk to him. Ivan Fyodorovich looked at him and stopped, and the fact that he did stop, instead of passing by, as he meant to the minute before, drove him to fury. With anger and repulsion he looked at Smerdyakov's eunuch-like, sickly face, with the little curls combed forward on his forehead. His slightly squinting left eye winked and grinned as though to say, "Where are you going? You won't pass by; you see that we two intelligent people have something to say to each other." Ivan Fyodorovich shuddered: "Get away, you scoundrel, what have I to do with you, fool!" was on the tip of his tongue, but to his profound astonishment he heard himself say,

"Is my father still asleep, or has he woken up?" He asked the question softly and meekly, to his own surprise, and suddenly, again to his own surprise, sat down on the bench. For an instant he felt almost frightened; he remembered it afterwards. Smerdyakov stood facing him, his hands behind his back, looking at him with assurance and almost severity.

"His honor is still asleep," he articulated deliberately ("You were the first to speak, not I," he seemed to say). "I am surprised at you, sir," he added, after a pause, dropping his eyes affectedly, setting his right foot forward, and playing with the tip of his polished boot.

"Why are you surprised at me?" Ivan asked abruptly and sullenly, doing his utmost to restrain himself, and suddenly realizing, with disgust, that he felt intense curiosity and would not, on any account, have gone away without satisfying it.

"Why don't you go to Chermashnya, sir?" Smerdyakov suddenly raised his eyes and smiled familiarly. "Why I smile you must understand of yourself, if you are an intelligent man," his screwed-up left eye seemed to say.

"Why should I go to Chermashnya?" Ivan asked in surprise.

Smerdyakov was silent again.

"Fyodor Pavlovich himself has so begged you to, sir," he said at last, slowly and apparently attaching no significance to his answer. "I put you off with a secondary reason," he seemed to suggest, "simply to say something."

"What the devil, speak more clearly, what do you want?" Ivan Fyodorovich cried angrily at last, passing from meekness to violence.

Smerdyakov drew his right foot up to his left, pulled himself up, but still looked at him with the same serenity and the same little smile.

"Substantially nothing, sir—but just by way of conversation."

Another silence followed. They did not speak for nearly a minute. Ivan Fyodorovich knew that he ought to get up and show anger, and Smerdyakov stood before him and seemed to be waiting as though to see whether he would be angry or not. So at least it seemed to Ivan Fyodorovich. At last he moved to get up. Smerdyakov seemed to seize the moment.

"I'm in an awful position, Ivan Fyodorovich. I don't know how to help myself," he said resolutely and distinctly, and at his last word he sighed. Ivan Fyodorovich sat down again.

"They are both utterly crazy, sir, they are no better than little children, sir," Smerdyakov went on. "I am speaking of your parent and your brother Dmitri Fyodorovich. Here Fyodor Pavlovich will get up directly and begin worrying me every minute, 'Has she come? Why hasn't she come?' and so on up till midnight and even after midnight. And if Agrafena Alexandrovna doesn't come (for very likely she does not mean to come at all) then he will be at me again tomorrow morning, 'Why hasn't she come? When will she come?'—as though I were to blame for it. On the other side it's no better, sir. As soon as it gets dark, or even before, your brother will appear with his weapon in his hands: 'Look out, you rogue, you soup maker. If you miss her and don't let me know she's been—I'll kill you before anyone.' When the night's over, in the morning, he, too, like Fyodor Pavlovich, begins torturing me like a torturer. 'Why hasn't she come? Will she come soon?' And he, too, thinks me to blame because his lady hasn't come. And every day and every hour they get angrier and angrier, so that I sometimes think I shall kill myself in a fright, sir. I can't depend upon them, sir."

"And why have you meddled? Why did you begin to spy for Dmitri Fyodorovich?" said Ivan Fyodorovich irritably.

"How could I help meddling, sir? Though, indeed, I haven't meddled at all, if you want to know the truth of the matter. I kept quiet from the very beginning, not daring to answer; but he picked on me to be his servant Licharda.[4] He has had only one thing to say since: 'I'll kill you, you scoundrel, if you miss her.' I suppose for certain, sir, that I shall have a long fit tomorrow."

"What do you mean by 'a long fit'?"

"A long fit, lasting a long time, sir—several hours, or perhaps a day or two, sir. Once it went on for three days. I fell from the garret that time. The struggling ceased and then began again, and for three days I couldn't come back to my senses. Fyodor Pavlovich sent for Herzenstube, the doctor here, and he put ice on my head and tried another remedy, too. . . . I might have died, sir."

"But they say one can't tell with epilepsy when a fit is coming. What makes you say you will have one tomorrow?" Ivan Fyodorovich inquired, with a peculiar, irritable curiosity.

"That's just so. You can't tell beforehand, sir."

"Besides you fell from the garret then."

4. A character in the *Tale of Bova*, a chivalric romance derived from the thirteenth-century French story of *Beuve de Hantone* (*Bevis of Hampton* in English). This character is a servant implicated in the murder of his master. A version known as the *Tale of Bova Korolevich* was extremely popular in Russia. Here, Smerdyakov says that he plays the role of Licharda (Richard), the servant, to Dmitri.

"I climb up to the garret every day. I might fall from the garret again tomorrow. And, if not, I might fall down the cellar steps, sir. I have to go into the cellar every day, too, sir."

Ivan Fyodorovich took a long look at him.

"You are talking nonsense, I see, and I don't quite understand you," he said softly, but with a sort of menace. "Do you mean to pretend to be ill tomorrow for three days, eh?"

Smerdyakov, who was looking at the ground again, and playing with the toe of his right foot, set the foot down, moved the left one forward, and, grinning, articulated:

"Even if I were able to play such a trick, sir, that is, pretend to have a fit, sir—and it would not be difficult for a man accustomed to them—I would have a perfect right to use such a means to save my life from death, sir. For even if Agrafena Alexandrovna comes to see his father while I am ill, his honor can't blame a sick man for not telling him. He'd be ashamed to."

"What the devil!" Ivan Fyodorovich suddenly cried, his face twisting with anger, "Why are you always so afraid for your life? All my brother Dmitri's threats are only hasty words and mean nothing. He won't kill you; it's not you he'll kill!"

"He'd kill me first of all, sir, like a fly. But even more than that, I am afraid I shall be taken for an accomplice of his when he does something crazy to his father."

"Why should you be taken for an accomplice?"

"They'll think I am an accomplice, because I let him know the signals as a great secret, sir."

"What signals? Whom did you tell? Devil take you, speak more clearly."

"I'm bound to admit the fact," Smerdyakov drawled with pedantic composure, "that I have a secret with Fyodor Pavlovich in this business. As you know yourself (if only you do know it) he has for several days past locked himself in as soon as night or evening comes on. Of late you've been going upstairs to your room early every evening, and yesterday you did not come down at all, sir, and so perhaps you don't know how carefully he has begun to lock himself in at night, and even if Grigory Vasilyevich comes to the door he won't open to him till he hears his voice. But Grigory Vasilyevich does not come, because I wait upon him alone in his room now, sir. That's the arrangement he made himself ever since this to-do with Agrafena Alexandrovna began. But at night, by his orders, I go away to the lodge so that I don't get to sleep till midnight, but am on the watch, getting up and walking about the yard, waiting for Agrafena Alexandrovna to come. For the last few days he's been perfectly frantic expecting her. What he argues is, sir, she is afraid of him, Dmitri Fyodorovich (Mitka, as he calls him) 'and so,' says he, 'she'll come the back way, late at night, to me. You look out for her,' says he, 'till midnight and later; and if she does come, you run up and knock at my door or at the window from the garden. Knock at first twice, rather gently, like this, one, two, and then three times more quickly, tap-tap-tap, then,' says he, 'I shall understand at once that she has come, and will open the door to you quietly.' Another signal he gave me in case anything unexpected happens. At first, two quick knocks, one, two, and then, after an interval, another much louder. Then he will understand that something has happened suddenly and that I must see him, and he will open to me so that I can go and speak to him. That's all in case Agrafena Alexandrovna can't come herself, but sends a message. Besides, Dmitri Fyodorovich might come, too, so I must let him know he is near. His honor is awfully afraid of Dmitri Fyodorovich, so that even if Agrafena Alexandrovna had come and were locked in with him, and Dmitri Fyodorovich were to turn up anywhere near at the time, I should be bound to let him know at once, knocking three times. So that the first signal of five knocks means Agrafena Alexandrovna has come, while the second signal of three knocks means 'something important to tell you.' His honor has shown me them several times and explained them. And as in the whole universe no one knows of these signals but myself and his honor, sir, so he'd open the door without the slightest hesitation and without calling out (he is awfully afraid of calling out aloud). Well, those signals are known to Dmitri Fyodorovich too, now."

"How are they known? Did you tell him? How dared you tell him?"

"It was through fright I did it, sir. How could I dare to keep it back from him? Dmitri Fyodorovich kept persisting every day, 'You are deceiving me, you are hiding something from me! I'll break both your legs for you.' So I told him those secret signals that he might see my slavish devotion, and might be satisfied that I was not deceiving him, but was telling him all I could."

"If you think that he'll make use of those signals and try to get in, don't let him in."

"But if I should be laid up with a fit, sir, how could I prevent his coming in then, sir, even if I dared prevent him, knowing how desperate he is?"

"What the devil! How can you be so sure you are going to have a fit, devil take you? Are you laughing at me?"

"How could I dare laugh at you, and am I in a mood for laughing with this fear on me? I feel I am going to have a fit. I have a presentiment. Fright alone will bring it on."

"What the devil! If you are laid up, Grigory will be on the watch. Let Grigory know beforehand; he will be sure not to let him in."

"I would never dare to tell Grigory Vasilyevich about the signals without orders from my master. And as for Grigory Vasilyevich's hearing him and not admitting him, he has been ill ever since yesterday, and Martha Ignatyevna intends to give him medicine tomorrow. They've just arranged it. It's a very strange remedy of hers. Martha Ignatyevna knows of a preparation and always keeps it, sir. It's a strong thing made from some herb. She has the secret of it, sir, and she always gives it to Grigory Vasilyevich three times a year, sir, when his lumbago's so bad he is almost paralyzed by it. Then she takes a towel, wets it with the stuff, and rubs his whole back for half an hour till it's quite red and swollen, and what's left in the bottle she gives him to drink with a special prayer, sir; but not quite all, for on such occasions she leaves some for herself, and drinks it herself. And as they never take strong drink, sir, I assure you they both fall asleep at once and sleep sound a very long time. And when Grigory Vasilyevich wakes up he is perfectly well after it, but Martha Ignatyevna always has a headache from it, sir. So, if Martha Ignatyevna carries out her intention tomorrow, they won't hear anything and hinder Dmitri Fyodorovich. They'll be asleep, sir."

"What nonsense! And it all seems to happen at once, as though it were planned. You'll have a fit and they'll both be unconscious," cried Ivan

Fyodorovich. "But aren't you trying to arrange it so?" broke from him suddenly, and he frowned threateningly.

"How could I, sir? . . . And why should I, when it all depends on Dmitri Fyodorovich and his plans? . . . If he means to do anything, he'll do it; but if not, I won't be thrusting him upon his father."

"And why should he go to father, especially on the sly, if, as you say yourself, Agrafena Alexandrovna won't come at all?" Ivan Fyodorovich went on, turning white with anger. "You say that yourself, and all the while I've been here, I've felt sure it was all the old man's fancy, and the creature won't come to him. Why should Dmitri break in on him if she doesn't come? Speak! I want to know what you are thinking."

"You know yourself why he'll come, sir. What's the use of what I think? His honor will come simply because he is in a rage or suspicious on account of my illness perhaps, and he'll dash in, as he did yesterday through impatience to search the rooms, to see whether she hasn't escaped him on the sly. He is perfectly well aware, too, that Fyodor Pavlovich has a big envelope with three thousand rubles in it, tied up with ribbon and sealed with three seals. On it is written in his own hand, 'To my angel Grushenka, if she will come,' to which he added three days later, 'for my little chicken.' There's no knowing what that might do, sir."

"Nonsense!" shouted Ivan Fyodorovich, almost beside himself. "Dmitri won't come to steal money and kill my father to do it. He might have killed him yesterday on account of Grushenka, like the frantic, savage fool he is, but he won't steal."

"He is in very great need of money now—the greatest need, Ivan Fyodorovich. You don't know in what need he is," Smerdyakov explained, with perfect composure and remarkable distinctness. "He looks on that three thousand as his own, too. He said so to me himself. 'My father still owes me just three thousand,' he said. And besides that, consider, Ivan Fyodorovich, there is something else perfectly true, sir. It's as good as certain, so to say, that Agrafena Alexandrovna will force him, if only she cares to, to marry her—the master himself, I mean Fyodor Pavlovich, sir—if only she cares to, and of course she may care to. All I've said is that she won't come, but maybe she's looking for more than that, sir—I mean, to be mistress here. I know myself that Samsonov, her merchant, was laughing with her about it, telling her quite openly that it would not be at all a stupid thing to do. And she's got plenty of sense, sir. She wouldn't marry a beggar like Dmitri Fyodorovich. So, taking that into consideration, Ivan Fyodorovich, reflect that then neither Dmitri Fyodorovich nor yourself and your brother, Alexey Fyodorovich, would have anything after the master's death, not a ruble, for Agrafena Alexandrovna would marry him simply to get hold of the whole, all the money there is. But if your father were to die now, there'd be some forty thousand for sure, even for Dmitri Fyodorovich whom he hates so, for he's made no will. . . . Dmitri Fyodorovich knows all that very well."

A sort of shudder passed over Ivan Fyodorovich's face. He suddenly flushed.

"Then why on earth," he suddenly interrupted Smerdyakov, "do you advise me to go to Chermashnya? What did you mean by that? If I go away, you see what will happen here." Ivan Fyodorovich drew his breath with difficulty.

"Precisely so, sir," said Smerdyakov, softly and reasonably, watching Ivan Fyodorovich intently, however.

"What do you mean by 'precisely so'?" Ivan Fyodorovich questioned him, with a menacing light in his eyes, restraining himself with difficulty.

"I spoke because I felt sorry for you. If I were in your place I should simply throw it all up . . . rather than stay on in such a position, sir," answered Smerdyakov, with the most candid air looking at Ivan Fyodorovich's flashing eyes. They were both silent.

"You seem to be a perfect idiot, and what's more . . . an awful scoundrel, too!" Ivan Fyodorovich rose suddenly from the bench. He was about to pass straight through the gate, but he stopped short and turned to Smerdyakov. Something strange followed. Ivan Fyodorovich, in a sudden paroxysm, bit his lip, clenched his fists, and, in another minute, would have flung himself on Smerdyakov. The latter, anyway, noticed it at the same moment, started, and shrank back. But the moment passed without mischief to Smerdyakov, and Ivan Fyodorovich turned in silence, as it seemed in perplexity, to the gate.

"I am going away to Moscow tomorrow, if you care to know—early tomorrow morning. That's all!" he suddenly said angrily, loudly, and clearly, and wondered himself afterwards what need there was to say this then to Smerdyakov.

"That's the best thing you can do, sir," he responded, as though he had expected to hear it; "except that you can always be telegraphed for from Moscow, sir, if anything should happen here."

Ivan stopped again, and again turned quickly to Smerdyakov. But a change had passed over him, too. All his familiarity and carelessness had completely disappeared. His face expressed attention and expectation, intent but timid and cringing.

"Haven't you something more to say—something to add?" could be read in the intent gaze he fixed on Ivan Fyodorovich.

"And couldn't I be sent for from Chermashnya, too—in case anything happened?" Ivan Fyodorovich shouted suddenly, for some unknown reason raising his voice terribly.

"From Chermashnya, too . . . you could be sent for, sir," Smerdyakov muttered, almost in a whisper, looking disconcerted, but gazing intently into Ivan Fyodorovich's eyes.

"Only Moscow is further and Chermashnya is nearer. Is it to save my spending money on the fare, or to save my going so far out of my way, that you insist on Chermashnya?"

"Precisely so, sir . . ." muttered Smerdyakov, with a breaking voice. He looked at Ivan Fyodorovich with a revolting smile, and again made ready to draw back. But to his astonishment Ivan Fyodorovich suddenly broke into a laugh, and went through the gate still laughing. Anyone who had seen his face at that moment would have known that he was not laughing from lightness of heart, and he could not have explained himself what he was feeling at that instant. He moved and walked as though in a nervous frenzy.

Chapter VII

"It's Always Interesting Speaking
with an Intelligent Man"

And in the same nervous frenzy, too, he spoke. Meeting Fyodor Pavlovich in the drawing room as soon as he went in, he shouted to him, waving his hands, "I am going upstairs to my room, not in to you. Good-bye!" and passed by, trying not even to look at his father. Very possibly the old man was too hateful to him at that moment; but such an unceremonious display of hostility was a surprise even to Fyodor Pavlovich. And the old man evidently wanted to tell him something at once and had come to meet him in the drawing room on purpose. Receiving this amiable greeting, he stood still in silence and with an ironical air watched his son going upstairs, till he passed out of sight.

"What's the matter with him?" he promptly asked Smerdyakov, who had followed Ivan Fyodorovich.

"Angry about something, sir. Who can tell?" he muttered evasively.

"Ah, the devil! Let him be angry then! Bring in the samovar, and get along with you. Look sharp! No news?"

Then followed a series of questions such as Smerdyakov had just complained of to Ivan Fyodorovich, all relating to his expected visitor, and these questions we will omit. Half an hour later the house was locked, and the crazy old man was wandering alone through the rooms in excited expectation of hearing every minute the five knocks agreed upon, now and then peering out into the darkness, seeing nothing.

It was very late, but Ivan Fyodorovich was still awake and reflecting. He sat up late that night, till two o'clock. But we will not give an account of his thoughts, and this is not the place to look into that soul—its turn will come. And even if one tried, it would be very hard to give an account of them, for there were no thoughts in his brain, but something very vague, and, above all, intense excitement. He felt himself that he had lost his bearings. He was fretted, too, by all sorts of strange and almost surprising desires; for instance, after midnight he suddenly had an intense irresistible inclination to go down, open the door, go to the lodge and beat Smerdyakov. But if he had been asked why, he could not have given any exact reason, except perhaps that he loathed the lackey as one who had insulted him more gravely than anyone in the world. On the other hand, he was more than once that night overcome by a sort of inexplicable humiliating terror, which he felt positively paralyzed his physical powers. His head ached and he was giddy. A feeling of hatred was rankling in his heart, as though he meant to avenge himself on someone. He even hated Alyosha, recalling the conversation he had just had with him. At moments he hated himself intensely. Of Katerina Ivanovna he almost forgot to think, and wondered greatly at this afterwards, especially as he remembered perfectly that when he had protested so valiantly to Katerina Ivanovna that he would go away next day to Moscow, something had whispered in his heart, "That's nonsense, you are not going, and it won't be so easy to tear yourself away as you are boasting now." Remembering that night long afterwards, Ivan recalled with peculiar repulsion how he had suddenly got up from the sofa and stealthily, as though he were afraid of being watched, had opened the door, gone out on the staircase and listened to Fyodor Pavlovich stirring down below, had listened a long while—some five minutes—with a sort of strange curiosity, holding his breath while his heart throbbed. And why he had done all this, why he was listening, he could not have said. That "action" all his life afterwards he called "loathsome," and at the bottom of his heart, he thought of it as the basest action of his life. For Fyodor Pavlovich himself he did not even feel any hatred at that moment, but was simply intensely curious to know how he was walking down there below and what he must be doing now. He wondered and imagined how he must be peeping out of the dark windows and stopping in the middle of the room, listening, listening—for someone to knock. Ivan Fyodorovich went out onto the stairs twice to listen like this. About two o'clock when everything was quiet, and even Fyodor Pavlovich had gone to bed, Ivan Fyodorovich had got into bed, firmly resolved to fall asleep at once, as he felt fearfully exhausted. And he did fall asleep at once, and slept soundly without dreams, but waked early, at seven o'clock, when it was broad daylight. Opening his eyes, he was surprised to feel himself extraordinarily vigorous. He jumped up at once and dressed quickly; then dragged out his trunk and began packing immediately. His linen had come back from the laundress the previous morning. Ivan Fyodorovich positively smiled at the thought that everything was helping his sudden departure. And his departure certainly was sudden. Though Ivan Fyodorovich had said the day before (to Katerina Ivanovna, Alyosha, and Smerdyakov) that he was leaving next day, yet he remembered that he had no thought of departure when he went to bed, or, at least, had not dreamed that his first act in the morning would be to pack his trunk. At last his trunk and bag were ready. It was about nine o'clock when Martha Ignatyevna came in with her usual inquiry, "Where will your honor take your tea, in your own room or downstairs?" He looked almost cheerful, but there was about him, about his words and gestures, something hurried and scattered. Greeting his father affably, and even inquiring specially after his health, though he did not wait to hear his answer to the end, he announced that he was starting off in an hour to return to Moscow for good, and begged him to send for the horses. His father heard this announcement with no sign of surprise, and forgot in an unmannerly way to show regret at losing him. Instead of doing so, he flew into a great flutter at the recollection of some important business of his own.

"What a fellow you are! Not to tell me yesterday! Never mind; we'll manage it all the same. Do me a great service, my dear boy. Go to Chermashnya on the way. It's only to turn to the left from the station at Volovya, only another eight little miles and you come to Chermashnya."

"I'm sorry, I can't. It's fifty miles to the railway and the train starts for Moscow at seven o'clock tonight. I can only just catch it."

"You'll catch it tomorrow or the day after, but today turn off to Chermashnya. It won't put you out much to humor your father! If I hadn't had something to keep me here, I would have run over myself long ago, for I have some important and pressing business there. But here I . . . it's not the time for me to go now . . . you see, I have a woodlot there, in two sections, one in Begichev and one in Dyachkino, lying fallow. The Maslovs, an old merchant and his son, will give only eight thousand for the timber.

But last year I just missed a purchaser who would have given twelve, but he's not from around here, that's the trouble. There's no getting anyone around here to buy it. The Maslovs have it all their own way. One has to take what they'll give, because no one here dares bid against them. The priest at Ilyinskoe wrote to me last Thursday that a merchant called Gorstkin, a man I know, had turned up. What makes him valuable is that he is not from these parts, but from Pogryobov, so he is not afraid of the Maslovs. He says he will give me eleven thousand for the grove. Do you hear? But he'll only be here, the priest writes, for a week altogether, so you must go at once and make a bargain with him."

"Well, you write to the priest; he'll make the bargain."

"He can't do it. He has no eye for business. He is a perfect treasure, I'd give him twenty thousand to take care of it for me without a receipt; but he has no eye for business, he is a perfect child, a crow could deceive him. And yet he is a learned man, would you believe it? This Gorstkin looks like a peasant, he wears a blue caftan, but as for character, he's an out and out scoundrel. That's the common complaint. He is a liar, that's the trouble. Sometimes he tells such lies that you wonder why he is doing it. He told me the year before last that his wife was dead and that he had married another, and would you believe it, there was not a word of truth in it? His wife has never died at all, she is alive to this day and gives him a beating twice a week. So what you have to find out is whether he is lying or speaking the truth, when he says he wants to buy it and would give eleven thousand."

"I shall be no use in such a business. I have no eye either."

"Stay, wait a bit! You will be of use, for I will tell you the signs by which you can judge about Gorstkin. I've done business with him a long time. You see, you must watch his beard; he has a nasty, thin, red beard. If his beard shakes when he talks and he gets cross, it's all right, he is saying what he means, he wants to do business. But if he strokes his beard with his left hand and grins—he is trying to cheat you. Don't watch his eyes, you won't find out anything from his eyes, he is a deep one, a rogue—but watch his beard! I'll give you a note and you show it to him. He's called Gorstkin, though his real name is Lyagavy;[4] but don't call him so, he will be offended. If you come to an understanding with him, and see it's all right, write here at once. You need only write: 'He's not lying.' Stand out for eleven thousand; one thousand you can knock off, but not more. Just think! there's a difference between eight thousand and eleven thousand. It's as good as picking up three thousand; it's not so easy to find a purchaser, and I'm in desperate need of money. Only let me know it's serious, and I'll run over and fix it up. I'll snatch the time somehow. But what's the good of my galloping over, if it's all a notion of the priest's? Come, will you go?"

"Oh, I can't spare the time. You must excuse me."

"Come, you might oblige your father. I won't forget it. You've no heart, any of you—that's what it is! What's a day or two to you? Where are you going now—to Venice? Your Venice will keep another two days. I would have sent Alyoshka, but what use is Alyoshka in a thing like that? I send you just because you are an intelligent man. Do you suppose I don't see

4. The name *Gorstkin* may be derived from *gorst'* (handful); *lyagavy* means setter or spaniel.

that? You know nothing about timber, but you've got an eye. All that's needed is to see whether the man is in earnest. I tell you, watch his beard—if his beard shakes you know he is in earnest."

"You force me to go to that damned Chermashnya yourself, then?" cried Ivan Fyodorovich, with a malignant smile.

Fyodor Pavlovich did not catch, or would not catch, the malignancy, but he caught the smile.

"Then you'll go, you'll go? I'll scribble the note for you at once."

"I don't know whether I shall go. I don't know. I'll decide on the way."

"Nonsense! Decide at once. My dear fellow, decide! If you settle the matter, write me a line; give it to the priest and he'll send it on to me at once. And I won't delay you more than that. You can go to Venice. The priest will give you horses back to Volovya station . . ."

The old man was simply delighted. He wrote the note, and sent for the horses. A light lunch was brought in, with brandy. When Fyodor Pavlovich was pleased, he usually became expansive, but today he seemed to restrain himself. Of Dmitri Fyodorovich, for instance, he did not say a word. He was quite unmoved by the parting, and seemed, in fact, at a loss for something to say. Ivan Fyodorovich noticed this particularly. "He must be bored with me," he thought. Only when accompanying his son out on to the steps, the old man began to fuss about. He would have kissed him, but Ivan Fyodorovich made haste to hold out his hand, obviously avoiding the kiss. His father saw it at once, and instantly pulled himself up.

"Well, good luck to you, good luck to you!" he repeated from the steps. "You'll come again some time or other? Mind you do come. I shall always be glad to see you. Well, Christ be with you!"

Ivan Fyodorovich got into the carriage.

"Good-bye, Ivan! Don't be too hard on me!" the father called for the last time.

The whole household came out to take leave—Smerdyakov, Martha and Grigory. Ivan gave them ten rubles each. When he had seated himself in the carriage, Smerdyakov jumped up to arrange the rug.

"You see . . . I am going to Chermashnya," broke suddenly from Ivan Fyodorovich. Again, as the day before, the words seemed to drop of themselves, and he laughed, too, a peculiar, nervous laugh. He remembered it long after.

"It's a true saying then, that 'it's always interesting speaking with an intelligent man,'" answered Smerdyakov firmly, giving Ivan Fyodorovich a penetrating look.

The carriage rolled away. Nothing was clear in the traveler's soul, but he looked eagerly around him at the fields, at the hills, at the trees, at a flock of geese flying high overhead in the bright sky. And all of a sudden he felt very happy. He tried to talk to the driver, and he felt intensely interested in an answer the peasant made him; but a minute later he realized that he was not catching anything, and that he had not really even taken in the peasant's answer. He was silent, and it was pleasant even so. The air was fresh, pure and cool, the sky bright. The images of Alyosha and Katerina Ivanovna floated into his mind. But he softly smiled, blew softly on the friendly phantoms, and they flew away. "There's plenty of time for them," he thought. They reached the station quickly, changed horses, and galloped to Volovya. "Why is it interesting speaking with an intelligent man?

What did he mean by that?" The thought seemed suddenly to clutch at his breathing. "And why did I tell him I was going to Chermashnya?" They reached Volovya Station. Ivan Fyodorovich got out of the carriage, and the drivers stood round him bargaining over the journey of eight miles to Chermashnya. He told them to harness the horses. He went into the station house, looked round, glanced at the overseer's wife, and suddenly went back to the entrance.

"I won't go to Chermashnya. Am I too late to reach the railway by seven, brothers?"

"We shall just do it. Shall we get the carriage out?"

"At once. Will any one of you be going to the town tomorrow?"

"To be sure. Mitri here will."

"Can you do me a service, Mitri? Go to my father's, to Fyodor Pavlovich Karamazov, and tell him I haven't gone to Chermashnya. Can you?"

"Of course I can. I've known Fyodor Pavlovich a long time."

"And here's something for you, for I daresay he won't give you anything," said Ivan Fyodorovich, laughing gaily.

"You may depend on it he won't." Mitri laughed too. "Thank you, sir. I'll be sure to do it."

At seven o'clock Ivan Fyodorovich got into the train and set off for Moscow. "Away with the past. I've done with the old world forever, and may I have no news, no echo, from it. To a new life, new places, and no looking back!" But instead of delight his soul was filled with such gloom, and his heart ached with such anguish, as he had never known in his life before. He was thinking all the night. The train flew on, and only at daybreak, when he was approaching Moscow, he suddenly roused himself from his meditation.

"I am a scoundrel!" he whispered to himself.

Meanwhile Fyodor Pavlovich remained well satisfied at having seen his son off. For two hours afterwards he felt almost happy, and sat drinking brandy. But suddenly something happened which was very annoying and unpleasant for everyone in the house, and completely upset Fyodor Pavlovich's equanimity at once. Smerdyakov went to the cellar for something and fell down from the top of the steps. Fortunately, Martha Ignatyevna was in the yard and heard him in time. She did not see the fall, but heard his scream—the strange, peculiar scream, long familiar to her—the scream of the epileptic falling in a fit. They could not tell whether the fit had come on him at the moment he was descending the steps, so that he must have fallen unconscious, or whether it was the fall and the shock that had caused the fit in Smerdyakov, who was known to be liable to them. They found him at the bottom of the cellar steps, writhing in convulsions and foaming at the mouth. It was thought at first that he must have broken something—an arm or a leg—and hurt himself, but "God had preserved him," as Martha Ignatyevna expressed it—nothing of the kind had happened. But it was difficult to get him out of the cellar, into God's light. They asked the neighbors to help and managed it somehow. Fyodor Pavlovich himself was present at the whole ceremony. He helped, evidently alarmed and upset. The sick man did not regain consciousness; the convulsions ceased for a time, but then began again, and everyone concluded that the same thing would happen as had happened a year before, when he accidentally fell from the garret. They remembered that ice had been put on his head then. There was still ice in the cellar, and Martha Ignatyevna had some brought up. In the evening, Fyodor Pavlovich sent for Doctor Herzenstube, who arrived at once. He was an elderly and most estimable old man, and the most careful and conscientious doctor in the province. After careful examination, he concluded that the fit was a very violent one and might have serious consequences; that meanwhile he, Herzenstube, did not fully understand it, but that by tomorrow morning, if the present remedies were unavailing, he would venture to try something else. The invalid was taken to the lodge, to a room next to Grigory's and Martha Ignatyevna's. Then Fyodor Pavlovich had one misfortune after another to put up with that day. Martha Ignatyevna cooked the dinner, and the soup, compared with Smerdyakov's, was no "better than dishwater," and the fowl was so dried up that it was impossible even to chew it. To her master's bitter, though deserved, reproaches, Martha Ignatyevna replied that the fowl was a very old one to begin with, and that she had never been trained as a cook. In the evening there was another trouble in store for Fyodor Pavlovich; he was informed that Grigory, who had not been well for the last three days, was completely laid up by his lumbago. Fyodor Pavlovich finished his tea as early as possible and locked himself up alone in the house. He was in terrible excitement and suspense. That evening he reckoned on Grushenka's coming almost as a certainty. He had received from Smerdyakov that morning an assurance "that she had promised to come without fail." The incorrigible old man's heart throbbed with excitement; he paced up and down his empty rooms listening. He had to be on the alert. Dmitri Fyodorovich might be on the watch for her somewhere, and when she knocked on the window (Smerdyakov had informed him two days before that he had told her where and how to knock) the door must be opened at once. She must not be a second in the passage, for fear—which God forbid!—that she should be frightened and run away. Fyodor Pavlovich had much to think of, but never had his heart been steeped in such voluptuous hopes. This time he could say almost certainly that she would come!

Book Six

THE RUSSIAN MONK

Chapter I

Elder Zosima and His Visitors

When with an anxious and aching heart Alyosha went into his elder's cell, he stood still almost astonished: instead of a sick man at his last gasp, perhaps unconscious, as he had feared to find him, he saw him sitting up in his chair and, though weak and exhausted, his face was bright and cheerful, he was surrounded by visitors and engaged in a quiet and joyful conversation. But he had only got up from his bed a quarter of an hour before Alyosha's arrival; his visitors had gathered together in his cell earlier, waiting for him to wake, having received a most confident assurance from Father Païssy that "the teacher would get up, and as he had himself promised in the morning, converse once more with those dear to his heart." This promise and indeed every word of the dying elder's Father Païssy put implicit trust in. If he had seen him unconscious, if he had seen him breathe his last, and yet had his promise that he would rise up and say good-bye to him, he would not have believed perhaps even in death, but would still have expected the dead man to recover and fulfill his promise. In the morning as he lay down to sleep, Father Zosima had told him positively: "I shall not die without the delight of another conversation with you, beloved of my heart. I shall look once more on your dear faces and pour out my heart to you once again." The monks, who had gathered for this probably last conversation with Father Zosima, had all been his devoted friends for many years. There were four of them; Father Iosif and Father Païssy, Father Mikhail, the warden of the hermitage, a man not very old and far from being learned. He was of humble origin, of strong will and steadfast faith, of austere appearance, but of deep tenderness, though he obviously concealed it as though he were almost ashamed of it. The fourth, Father Anfim, was a very old and humble little monk of the poorest peasant class. He was almost illiterate, and very quiet, scarcely speaking to anyone. He was the humblest of the humble, and looked as though he had been frightened by something great and awful beyond the scope of his intelligence. Father Zosima had a great affection for this timorous man, and always treated him with marked respect, though perhaps there was no one he had known to whom he had said less, in spite of the fact that he had spent years wandering about holy Russia with him. That was very long ago, forty years before, when Father Zosima first began his life as a monk in a poor and little monastery at

Kostroma,[1] and when, shortly after, he had accompanied Father Anfim on his pilgrimage to collect alms for their poor monastery. The whole party were in the bedroom which, as we mentioned before, was very small, so that there was scarcely room for the four of them (in addition to Porfiry, the novice, who stood) to sit round Father Zosima on chairs brought from the sitting room. It was already beginning to get dark, the room was lighted up by the lamps and the candles before the icons. Seeing Alyosha standing embarrassed in the doorway, Father Zosima smiled at him joyfully and held out his hand.

"Welcome, my quiet one, welcome, my dear, here you are too. I knew you would come."

Alyosha went up to him, bowed down before him to the ground and wept. Something surged up from his heart, his soul was quivering, he wanted to sob.

"Come, don't weep over me yet," Father Zosima smiled, laying his right hand on his head. "You see I am sitting up talking; maybe I shall live another twenty years yet, as that dear good woman from Vishegorye, with her little Lizaveta in her arms, wished me yesterday. God bless the mother and the little girl Lizaveta," he crossed himself. "Porfiry, did you take her offering where I told you?"

He meant the sixty kopecks brought him the day before by the good-humored woman to be given "to someone poorer than me." Such offerings, always of money gained by personal toil, are made by way of penance voluntarily undertaken. The elder had sent Porfiry the evening before to a widow, whose house had been burned down lately, and who after the fire had gone with her children begging alms. Porfiry hastened "to reply that he had given the money, as he had been instructed, from an unknown benefactress."

"Get up, my dear boy," the elder went on to Alyosha. "Let me look at you. Have you been home and seen your brother?" It seemed strange to Alyosha that he asked so confidently and precisely, about one of his brothers only— but which one? Then perhaps he had sent him out both yesterday and today for the sake of that brother.

"I have seen one of my brothers," answered Alyosha.

"I mean the elder one, to whom I bowed down."

"I only saw him yesterday and could not find him today," said Alyosha.

"Make haste to find him, go again tomorrow and make haste, leave everything and make haste. Perhaps you may still have time to prevent something terrible. I bowed down yesterday to the great suffering in store for him."

He was suddenly silent and seemed to be pondering. The words were strange. Father Iosif, who had witnessed the scene yesterday, exchanged glances with Father Païssy. Alyosha could not resist asking:

"Father and teacher," he began with extreme emotion, "your words are too obscure. . . . What is this suffering in store for him?"

"Don't inquire. I seemed to see something terrible yesterday . . . as though his whole future were expressed in his eyes. A look came into his eyes . . . so that I was instantly horror-stricken at what that man is preparing for himself. Once or twice in my life I've seen such a look in a man's

1. A midsized city in north-central Russia.

face . . . reflecting as it were his future fate, and that fate, alas, came to pass. I sent you to him, Alexey, for I thought your brotherly face would help him. But everything and all our fates are from the Lord. 'Except a corn of wheat fall into the ground and die, it abideth alone; but if it die, it bringeth forth much fruit.' Remember that. You, Alexey, I've many times silently blessed for your face, know that," added the elder with a gentle smile. "This is what I think of you, you will go forth from these walls, but will live like a monk in the world. You will have many enemies, but even your foes will love you. Life will bring you many misfortunes, but you will find your happiness in them, and will bless life and will make others bless it—which is what matters most. Well, that is your character. Fathers and teachers," he addressed his friends with a tender smile, "I have never till today told even him why the face of this youth is so dear to me. Now I will tell you. His face has been as it were a remembrance and a prophecy for me. At the dawn of my life when I was a child I had an elder brother who died before my eyes at seventeen. And later on in the course of my life I gradually became convinced that that brother had been for a guidance and a sign from on high for me. For had he not come into my life, I should never perhaps, so I fancy at least, have become a monk and entered on this precious path. He appeared first to me in my childhood and here at the end of my pilgrimage, he seems to have come to me over again. It is marvelous, fathers and teachers, that Alexey, who has some, though not a great, resemblance in face, seems to me so like him spiritually, that many times I have taken him for that young man, my brother, mysteriously come back to me at the end of my pilgrimage, as a reminder and an inspiration. So that I positively wondered at so strange a dream in myself. Do you hear this, Porfiry?" he turned to the novice who waited on him. "Many times I've seen in your face as it were a look of mortification that I love Alexey more than you. Now you know why that was so, but I love you too, know that, and many times I grieved at your mortification. I should like to tell you, dear friends, of that youth, my brother, for there has been no presence in my life more precious, more significant and touching. My heart is full of tenderness, and I look at my whole life at this moment as though living through it again . . ."

Here I must observe that this last conversation of Father Zosima with the friends who visited him on the last day of his life had been partly preserved in writing. Alexey Fyodorovich Karamazov wrote it down from memory, some time after his elder's death. But whether this was only the conversation that took place then, or whether he added to it in his notes from previous conversations with his teacher as well, this I cannot determine; moreover Father Zosima's talk goes on without interruption in these notes, as though he told his life to his friends in the form of a story, although there is no doubt, according to later accounts, that it in fact went somewhat differently, for the conversation that evening was general, and though the guests did not interrupt their host much, they too talked, taking part in the conversation, and perhaps even spoke of themselves and recounted something, besides, there could not have been such continuity in this narrative, because the elder sometimes gasped for breath, lost his voice, and even lay down on his bed, though he didn't fall asleep, and his guests did not leave their places. Once or twice the conversation was interrupted by Father Païssy's reading the Gospel. It is worthy of note, too, that no one of them supposed that he would die that night, for on that evening of his life after his deep sleep in the day he seemed suddenly to have found new strength, which kept him up through this long conversation. It was like a last effort of love[2] which gave him incredible energy; only for a little time, however, for his life was cut short suddenly . . . But of that later. I will only add now that I have preferred to confine myself to the account given by Alexey Fyodorovich Karamazov, without going into the details of the conversation. It will be shorter and not so fatiguing, though of course, as I must repeat, Alyosha took a great deal from previous conversations and added them to it.

Chapter II

Notes of the Life in God[3] of the Deceased Hieromonk, the Elder Zosima, Taken from His Own Words by Alexey Fyodorovich Karamazov

Biographical Information

(a) FATHER ZOSIMA'S BROTHER

Beloved fathers and teachers, I was born in a distant province in the north, in the town of V——. My father was a nobleman by birth, but of no great distinction or position. He died when I was only two years old, and I don't remember him at all. He left my mother a small house built of wood, and some capital, not much, but sufficient to keep her and her children in comfort. There were two of us, my elder brother Markel and I, Zinovy. He was eight years older than I was, of hasty irritable temperament, but kindhearted and not sarcastic. He was remarkably silent, especially at home with me, his mother, and the servants. He did well at school, but did not get on with his schoolfellows, though he never quarreled, at least so my mother has told me. Six months before his death, when he was seventeen, he made friends with a political exile who had been banished from Moscow to our town for freethinking, and led a solitary existence there. He was a good scholar who had gained distinction in philosophy in the university. Something made him take a fancy to Markel, and he used to ask him to see him. The young man would spend whole evenings with him during that winter, till the exile was summoned to Petersburg to take up his post again at his own request, as he had powerful friends. It was the beginning of Lent, and Markel would not fast, he was rude and laughed at it. "That's all silly twaddle and there is no God," he said, horrifying my mother, the servants, and me too. For though I was only nine, I too was aghast at hearing such words. We had four servants, all serfs, bought in the name of a landowner who was a friend of ours. I remember my mother selling one of the

---

2. "Effort of love" translates *umilenie*, a rich term which conveys deep feeling, movement of heart and soul, and tenderness.
3. "Life" translates the Russian term *zhitie*, the formal hagiographical genre of the saint's life. For the significance of the *zhitie* in the depiction of Zosima, see Nathan Rosen, "Style and Structure in *The Brothers Karamazov*," p. 724.

four, the cook Afimya, who was lame and elderly, for sixty paper rubles, and hiring a free servant to take her place.[4] In the sixth week in Lent, my brother, who was never strong and had a tendency to consumption, was suddenly taken ill. He was tall but thin and delicate-looking, and of very pleasing countenance. I suppose he caught cold; anyway the doctor, who came, soon whispered to my mother that it was galloping consumption, that he would not live through the spring. My mother began weeping, and careful not to alarm my brother she entreated him to go to church, to confess and take the sacrament, as he was still able to move about. This made him angry, and he said something profane about the church. He grew thoughtful, however; he guessed at once that he was seriously ill, and that that was why his mother was begging him to confess and take the sacrament. He had been aware, indeed, for a long time past, that he was far from well, and had a year before coolly observed at dinner to our mother and me, "My life won't be long among you, I may not live another year," which seemed now like a prophecy. Three days passed and Holy Week had come. And on Tuesday morning my brother began going to church. "I am doing this simply for your sake, mother, to please and comfort you," he said. My mother wept with joy and grief, "his end must be near," she thought, "if there's such a change in him." But he was not able to go to church long, he took to his bed, so he had to confess and take the sacraments at home. It was a late Easter, and the days were bright, fine, and full of fragrance. I remember he used to cough all night and sleep badly, but in the morning he dressed and tried to sit up in an armchair. That's how I remember him sitting, quiet and gentle, smiling, his face bright and joyous, in spite of his illness. He completely changed spiritually—what a wonderful transformation had suddenly begun in him! The old nurse would come in and say, "Let me light the lamp before the icon, my dear." And formerly he would not have allowed it and would have even blown it out. "Light it, light it, dear, I was a wretch to have prevented your doing it. You are praying when you light the lamp, and I am praying when I rejoice seeing you. So we are praying to the same God." Those words seemed strange to us, and mother would go to her room and weep, but when she went in to him she wiped her eyes and looked cheerful. "Mother, don't weep, darling," he would say, "I've long to live yet, long to rejoice with you, and life is glad and joyful." "Ah, dear boy, how can you talk of joy when you lie feverish at night, coughing as though you would tear yourself to pieces." "Don't cry, mother," he would answer, "life is paradise, and we are all in paradise, but we won't see it, if we would, we should have heaven on earth the next day." Everyone wondered at his words, he spoke so strangely and decidedly; we were all touched and wept. Friends came to see us. "Dear ones," he would say to them, "what have I done that you should love me so, how can you love anyone like me, and how was it I did not know, I did not appreciate it before?" When the servants came in to him he would say continually, "Dear, kind people, why are you doing so much for me, do I deserve to be waited on? If it were God's will for me to live, I would wait on you, for all men should wait on one another." Mother shook her head as she listened. "My darling, it's your

---

4. Silver rubles were worth about twice as much as paper money in the first half of the nineteenth century. Prior to the emancipation, a free servant was an individual who was not owned by a master.

illness makes you talk like that." "Mother, my joy," he would say, "there must be servants and masters, but if so I will be the servant of my servants, the same as they are to me. And another thing, mother, every one of us has sinned against all men, and I more than any." Mother positively smiled at that, smiled through her tears. "Why, how could you have sinned against all men, more than all? Robbers and murderers have done that, but what sin have you committed yet, that you hold yourself more guilty than all?" "Mother, little heart of mine," he said (he had begun using such strange caressing words at that time), "little heart of mine, my joy, believe me, everyone is really responsible to all men for all men and for everything. I don't know how to explain it to you, but I feel it is so, painfully even. And how is it we went on then living, getting angry and not knowing?" So he would get up every day, more and more sweet and joyous and full of love. When the doctor, an old German called Eisenschmidt, came: "Well, doctor, have I another day in this world?" he would ask, joking. "You'll live many days yet," the doctor would answer, "and months and years too." "Months and years!" he would exclaim. "Why reckon the days? One day is enough for a man to know all happiness. My dear ones, why do we quarrel, try to outshine each other and keep grudges against each other? Let's go straight into the garden, walk and play there, love, appreciate, and kiss each other, and glorify life." "Your son cannot last long," the doctor told my mother, as she accompanied him to the door. "The disease is affecting his brain." The windows of his room looked out into the garden, and our garden was a shady one, with old trees in it which were coming into bud. The first birds of spring were flitting in the branches, chirruping and singing at the windows. And looking at them and admiring them, he began suddenly begging their forgiveness too, "Birds of heaven, happy birds, forgive me, for I have sinned against you too." None of us could understand that at the time, but he shed tears of joy. "Yes," he said, "there was such a glory of God all about me; birds, trees, meadows, sky, only I lived in shame and dishonored it all and did not notice the beauty and glory." "You take too many sins on yourself," mother used to say, weeping. "Mother, my joy, it's for joy, not for grief I am crying. Though I can't explain it to you, I like to humble myself before them, for I don't know how to love them enough. If I have sinned against everyone, yet all forgive me, too, and that's heaven. Am I not in heaven now?"

And there was a great deal more I don't remember. I remember I went once into his room when there was no one else there. It was a bright evening, the sun was setting, and a slanting ray lit up the whole room. He beckoned me, and I went up to him, he put his hands on my shoulders and looked into my face tenderly, lovingly; he said nothing for a minute, only looked at me like that: "Well," he said, "run and play now, live for me." I went out then and ran to play. And many times in my life afterwards I remembered with tears how he told me to live for him. There were many other marvelous and beautiful words of his, though we did not understand them at the time. He died the third week after Easter. He was fully conscious though he could not talk; up to his last hour he did not change. He looked happy, his eyes beamed and sought us, he smiled at us, beckoned us. There was a great deal of talk even in the town about his death. I was impressed by all this at the time, but not too much so, though I cried a great deal at his funeral. I was young then, a child, but a lasting impression, a hidden feeling of it all, remained in my heart, ready to rise up and respond when the time came. So indeed it happened.

(b)   OF THE HOLY SCRIPTURES IN THE LIFE OF FATHER ZOSIMA

I was left alone with my mother. Her friends began advising her to send me to Petersburg as other parents did. "You have only one son now," they said, "and have a fair income, and perhaps you will be depriving him of a brilliant career if you keep him here." They suggested I should be sent to Petersburg to the Cadet Corps, that I might afterwards enter the Imperial Guard.[5] My mother hesitated for a long time, it was awful to part with her only child, but she made up her mind to it at last, though not without many tears, believing she was acting for my happiness. She brought me to Petersburg and put me into the Cadet Corps, and I never saw her again; for she too died three years afterwards, and all those three years she grieved and trembled over us both. From the house of my childhood I have brought nothing but precious memories, for there are no memories more precious than those of early childhood in one's first home. And that is almost always so if there is any love and harmony in the family at all. Indeed, precious memories may remain even of a bad home, if only the heart knows how to find what is precious. With my memories of home I count, too, my memories of the Bible, which, child as I was, I was very eager to read at home. I had a book of Scripture history then with excellent pictures, called *A Hundred and Four Stories from the Old and New Testament,*[6] and I learned to read from it. I have it lying on my shelf now, I keep it as a precious relic of the past. But even before I learned to read, I remember first being moved to devotional feeling at eight years old. My mother took me alone to the house of the Lord, to mass (I don't remember where my brother was at the time) on the Monday before Easter. It was a clear day, and I remember today, as though I saw it now, how the incense rose from the censer and softly floated upwards and, overhead in the cupola, mingled in rising waves with the sunlight that streamed in at the narrow little window. I was stirred by the sight, and for the first time in my life I consciously received the seed of God's word in my heart. A youth came out into the middle of the church carrying a big book, so large that at the time it seemed to me he could barely even carry it. He laid it on the lectern, opened it, and began reading, and suddenly for the first time I understood something read in the church of God.[7] In the land of Uz, there lived a man, righteous and God-fearing, and he had great wealth, so many camels, so many sheep and asses, and his children feasted, and he loved them very much and prayed for them. "It may be that my sons have sinned in their feasting." Now the devil came before the Lord together with the sons of God, and said to the Lord that he had gone up and down the earth and under the earth. "And hast thou considered my servant Job?" God asked of him. And God boasted to the devil, pointing to his great and holy

5. The Cadet Corps trained boys aged ten to eighteen for careers as military officers. After completing coursework in subjects such as catechism, math, physics, drawing, marching, fencing, and dancing, graduates could enter military academies.
6. Zosima refers to a real book, the Russian translation of *Hundert und vier Heilige Geschichten aus dem Alten und Neuen Testament* (1714) by the Pietist theologian Johannes Hübner. Dostoevsky knew this book well as a child.
7. In the following passage, Zosima provides a highly idiosyncratic paraphrase of the Biblical Book of Job.

servant. And the devil laughed at God's words. "Give him over to me and Thou wilt see that Thy servant will murmur against Thee and curse Thy name." And God gave up the just man He loved so, to the devil. And the devil smote his children and his cattle and scattered his wealth, all of a sudden like a thunderbolt from heaven. And Job rent his mantle and fell down upon the ground and cried aloud, "Naked came I out of my mother's womb, and naked shall I return into the earth; the Lord gave and the Lord has taken away. Blessed be the name of the Lord forever and ever." Fathers and teachers, forgive my tears now, for all my childhood rises up again before me, and I breathe now as I breathed then, with the breast of a little child of eight, and I feel as I did then, awe and wonder and gladness. The camels at that time caught my imagination, and Satan, who talked like that with God, and God who gave His servant up to destruction, and His servant crying out: "Blessed be Thy name although Thou dost punish me," and then the soft and sweet singing in the church: "Let my prayer rise up before Thee," and again incense from the priest's censer and the kneeling and the prayer. Ever since then—only yesterday I took it up—I've never been able to read that sacred tale without tears. And how much that is great, mysterious and unfathomable there is in it! Afterwards I heard the words of mockery and blame, proud words, "How could God give up the most loved of His saints for the diversion of the devil, take from him his children, smite him with sore boils so that he cleansed the corruption from his sores with a potsherd—and for no object except to boast to the devil? 'See what My saint can suffer for My sake.'" But the greatness of it lies just in the fact that it is a mystery—that the passing earthly show and the eternal verity are brought together in it. In the face of the earthly truth, the eternal truth is accomplished. The Creator, just as on the first days of creation He ended each day with praise: "that is good that I have created," looks upon Job and again praises His creation. And Job praising the Lord, serves not only Him but all His creation for generations and generations, and forever and ever, since for that he was ordained. Good heavens, what a book it is, and what lessons there are in it! What a book the Bible is, what a miracle, what strength is given with it to man. It is like a mold cast of the world and man and human nature, everything is there, and a law for everything for all the ages. And what mysteries are solved and revealed; God raises Job again, gives him wealth again. Many years pass by, and he has other children and loves them. But how could he love those new ones when those first children are no more, when he has lost them? Remembering them, how could he be fully happy with those new ones, however dear the new ones might be? But he could, he could. It's the great mystery of human life that old grief passes gradually into quiet tender joy. The mild serenity of age takes the place of the riotous blood of youth. I bless the rising sun each day, and, as before, my heart sings to meet it, but now I love even more its setting, its long slanting rays and the soft tender gentle memories that come with them, the dear images from the whole of my long happy life—and over all the Divine Truth, softening, reconciling, forgiving! My life is ending, I know that well, but every day that is left me I feel how my earthly life is in touch with a new infinite, unknown, but approaching life, the nearness of which sets my soul quivering with rapture, my mind glowing and my heart weeping with joy. Friends and teachers, I have heard more than once, and of late one may hear it more often, that the priests, and above all the village priests, are complaining on all sides of their miserable income and their humiliating lot. They plainly state, even in print—I've read it myself—that they are unable to teach the Scriptures to the people because of the smallness of their means, and if Lutherans and heretics come and lead the flock astray, they let them lead them astray because they have so little to live upon. May the Lord increase the sustenance that is so precious to them, for their complaint is just, too. But of a truth I say, if anyone is to blame in the matter, half the fault is ours. For he may be short of time, he may say truly that he is overwhelmed all the while with work and services, but still it's not all the time, even he has an hour a week to remember God. And he does not work the whole year round. Let him gather round him once a week, some hour in the evening, if only the children at first—the fathers will hear of it and they too will begin to come. There's no need to build halls for this, let him take them into his own cottage. They won't spoil his cottage, they would only be there one hour. Let him open that book and begin reading it without grand words or superciliousness, without condescension to them, but gently and kindly, being glad that he is reading to them and that they are listening with attention, loving the words himself, only stopping from time to time to explain words that are not understood by the peasants. Don't be anxious, they will understand everything, the orthodox heart will understand all! Let him read them about Abraham and Sarah, about Isaac and Rebecca, of how Jacob went to Laban and wrestled with the Lord in his dream and said, "This place is dreadful"— and he will impress the devout mind of the peasant.[8] Let him read, especially to the children, how the brothers sold Joseph, the tender boy, the dreamer and prophet, into bondage, and told their father that a wild beast had devoured him, and showed him his blood-stained clothes.[9] Let him read them how the brothers afterwards journeyed into Egypt for corn, and Joseph, already a great ruler, unrecognized by them, tormented them, accused them, kept his brother Benjamin, and all through love: "I love you, and loving you I torment you." For he remembered all his life how they had sold him to the merchants in the burning desert by the well, and how, wringing his hands, he had wept and besought his brothers not to sell him as a slave in a strange land. And how, seeing them again after many years, he loved them beyond measure, but he harassed and tormented them in love. He left them at last not able to bear the suffering of his heart, flung himself on his bed and wept. Then, wiping his tears away he went out to them joyful and told them, "Brothers, I am your brother Joseph!" Let him read them further how happy old Jacob was on learning that his darling boy was still alive, and how he went to Egypt leaving his own country, and died in a foreign land, bequeathing his great prophecy that had lain mysteriously hidden in his meek and timid heart all his life, that from his offspring, from Judah, will come the great hope of the world, the Messiah and Savior. Fathers and teachers, forgive me and don't

8. The story of Abraham and Sarah is told throughout the book of Genesis, beginning with 11.29–31; for Isaac and Rebecca, see Genesis 24. The expression "How dreadful is this place!" occurs in Genesis 28.17. For Jacob wrestling with an angel, see Genesis 32.24–32.
9. The account of Joseph being sold by his brothers is found in Genesis 37; for Joseph being reunited with his brothers in Egypt, see Genesis 45; for Jacob's reunion with Joseph in Egypt, see Genesis 45.25–28; 46; for Jacob's blessing see Genesis 49:10.

be angry, that like a little child I've been babbling of what you know long ago, and can teach me a hundred times more skillfully. I only speak from rapture, and forgive my tears, for I love the Bible. Let him too weep, the priest of God, and be sure that the hearts of his listeners will throb in response. Only a little tiny seed is needed—drop it into the heart of the peasant and it won't die, it will live in his soul all his life, it will be hidden in the midst of his darkness, in the midst of the stench of his sin, like a bright spot, like a great reminder. And there's no need of much teaching or explanation, he will understand it all simply. Do you suppose that the peasants don't understand? Try reading them the touching story of the fair Esther and the haughty Vashti; or the miraculous story of Jonah in the whale.[1] Don't forget either the parables of Our Lord, choose especially from the Gospel of St. Luke (that is what I did) and then from the Acts of the Apostles the conversion of Saul[2] (that you mustn't leave out on any account), and from the *Lives of the Saints*, for instance, the life of Alexey, the man of God and, greatest of all, the happy martyr and the seer of God, Mary of Egypt[3]—and you will penetrate their hearts with these simple tales. Give one hour a week to it in spite of your poverty, only one little hour. And you will see for yourself that our people are benevolent and grateful, and will repay you a hundredfold. Mindful of the kindness of their priest and the moving words they have heard from him, they will of their own accord help him in his fields and in his house, and will treat him with more respect than before—so that it will even increase his worldly well-being too. The thing is so simple that sometimes one is even afraid to put it into words, for fear of being laughed at, and yet how true it is! One who does not believe in God will not believe in God's people. He who believes in God's people will see His Holiness too, even though he had not believed in it till then. Only the people and their future spiritual power will convert our atheists, who have torn themselves away from their native soil. And what is the word of Christ without an example? The people will perish without the word of God, for their soul thirsts for His word and every beautiful perception. In my youth, long ago, nearly forty years ago, I traveled all over Russia with Father Anfim, collecting funds for our monastery, and we stayed one night on the bank of a great navigable river with some fishermen. A good-looking peasant lad, about eighteen, joined us; he had to hurry back next morning to pull a merchant's barge along the bank. I noticed him looking straight before him with clear and tender eyes. It was a bright, warm, still, July night, a cool mist rose from the broad river, we could hear the splash of a fish, the birds were still, all was hushed and beautiful, everything praying to God. Only we two were not sleeping, the lad and I, and we talked of the beauty of this world of God's and of the great mystery of it. Every blade of grass, every insect, ant, and golden bee, all so amazingly know their path, though they have not intelligence, they bear witness to the mystery of God and con-

---

1. See the Biblical books of Esther and Jonah.
2. Saul (d. 64–65 C.E.) was a Jewish citizen of Rome, born in the city of Tarsus (located in present-day Turkey). He actively persecuted Christians until he experienced a vision, described in Acts 9.1–20, which inspired him to convert to Christianity and take the name Paul.
3. When she was twelve years old, Mary of Egypt (c. 344–421 C.E.) ran away to Alexandria, where she became notorious as a dissolute woman. She eventually converted to Christianity and spent the last forty-seven years of her life as an ascetic hermit in the desert. Saint Zosimas encountered her in the desert as a very old woman. She is the patron saint of penitent women.

tinually accomplish it themselves. I saw the dear lad's heart was moved. He told me that he loved the forest and the forest birds. He was a bird-catcher, knew the note of each of them, could call each bird. "I know nothing better than to be in the forest," said he, "though all things are good." "Truly," I answered him, "all things are good and wonderful, because all is truth. Look," said I, "at the horse, that great beast that is so near to man; or the lowly, pensive ox, which feeds him and works for him; look at their faces, what meekness, what devotion to man, who often beats them mercilessly. What gentleness, what confidence and what beauty in their faces! It's touching to know that there's no sin in them, for all, all except man, is sinless, and Christ has been with them before us." "Why," asked the boy, "is Christ with them too?" "It cannot but be so," said I, "since the Word is for all. All creation and all creatures, every leaf is striving to the Word, singing glory to God, weeping to Christ, unconsciously accomplishing this by the mystery of their sinless life. Yonder," said I, "in the forest wanders the dreadful bear, fierce and menacing, and yet innocent in it." And I told him how once a bear came to a great saint who had taken refuge in a tiny cell in the wood.[4] And the great saint pitied him, went up to him without fear and gave him a piece of bread. "Go along," said he, "Christ be with you," and the savage beast walked away meekly and obediently, doing no harm. And the lad was delighted that the bear had walked away without hurting the saint, and that Christ was with him too. "Ah," said he, "how good that is, how good and beautiful is all God's work!" He sat musing softly and sweetly. I saw he understood. And he slept beside me a light and sinless sleep. May God bless youth! And I prayed for him as I went to sleep. Lord, send peace and light to Thy people!

(c)   RECOLLECTIONS OF THE ADOLESCENCE AND YOUTH OF FATHER
ZOSIMA WHILE HE WAS STILL IN THE WORLD. THE DUEL

I spent a long time, almost eight years, in the military cadet school at Petersburg, and with my new education there, many of my childish impressions grew dimmer, though I forgot nothing. I picked up so many new habits and opinions that I was transformed into a cruel, absurd, almost savage being. A surface polish of courtesy and society manners I did acquire together with the French language. But we all, myself included, looked upon the soldiers in our service as cattle. I was perhaps worse than the rest in that respect, for I was so much more impressionable than my companions. By the time we left the school as officers, we were ready to shed our blood for the honor of the regiment, but no one of us had any knowledge of the real meaning of honor, and if anyone had known it, he would have been the first to ridicule it. Drunkenness, debauchery and devilry were what we almost prided ourselves on. I don't say that we were bad by nature, all these young men were good fellows, but they behaved badly, and I worst of all. What made it worse for me was that I had come into my own money, and so I flung myself into a life of pleasure, and plunged headlong into all the recklessness of youth. I was fond of reading, yet strange to say, the Bible was the one book I never opened at that time,

---

4. An episode from the *Life* of Saint Sergius of Radonezh (c. 1314–1392)

though I always carried it about with me, and I was never separated from it; in very truth I was keeping that book "for the day and the hour, for the month and the year,"[5] though I knew it not. After four years of this life, I chanced to be in the town of K—— where our regiment was stationed at the time. We found the people of the town hospitable, rich and fond of entertainments. I met with a cordial reception everywhere, as I was of a lively temperament and was known to be well off, which always goes a long way in the world. And then a circumstance happened which was the beginning of it all. I formed an attachment to a beautiful and intelligent young girl of noble and lofty character, the daughter of people much respected. They were well-to-do people of influence and position. They always gave me a cordial and friendly reception. I fancied that the young lady looked on me with favor and my heart was aflame at such an idea. Later on I saw and fully realized that I perhaps was not so passionately in love with her at all, but only recognised the elevation of her mind and character, which I could not indeed have helped doing. I was prevented, however, from making her an offer at the time by my selfishness, I was loath to part with the allurements of my free and licentious bachelor life in the heyday of my youth, and with my pockets full of money. I did drop some hint as to my feelings, however, though I put off taking any decisive step for a time. Then, all of a sudden, we were ordered off for two months to another district. On my return two months later, I found the young lady already married to a rich neighboring landowner, a very amiable man, still young though older than I was, connected with the best Petersburg society, which I was not, and of excellent education, which I also was not. I was so overwhelmed at this unexpected circumstance that my mind was positively clouded. And the main thing was that, as I learned then, the young landowner had been a long while betrothed to her, and I had indeed met him many times in her house, but blinded by my own merits I had noticed nothing. And this particularly mortified me; almost everybody had known all about it, while I knew nothing. I was filled with sudden irrepressible fury. With flushed face I began recalling how often I had been on the point of declaring my love to her, and as she had not attempted to stop me or to warn me, she must, I concluded, have been laughing at me all the time. Later on, of course, I reflected and remembered that she had been very far from laughing at me; on the contrary, she used to turn off any courting on my part with a jest and begin talking of other subjects; but at that moment I was incapable of reflecting and became inflamed with vengefulness. I am surprised to remember that my wrath and revengeful feelings were extremely oppressive and repugnant to my own nature, for being of an easy temper, I found it difficult to be angry with anyone for long, and so I had to work myself up artificially and became at last revolting and absurd. I waited for an opportunity and succeeded in insulting my "rival" in the presence of a large company. I insulted him on a perfectly extraneous pretext, jeering at his opinion upon an important event—it

---

5. Zosima borrows this phrase from the book of Revelation, where it is predicted that God will send death and destruction for many at the Second Coming. "I heard a voice from the four horns of the golden altar which is before God, Saying to the sixth angel which had the trumpet, Loose the four angels which are bound in the great river Euphrates. And the four angels were loosed, which were prepared for an hour, and a day, and a month, and a year, for to slay the third part of men" (9.13–15).

was in the year 1826[6]—and my jeer was, so people said, clever and effective. Then I forced him to ask for an explanation, and behaved so rudely that he accepted my challenge in spite of the vast inequality between us, as I was younger, a person of no consequence, and of inferior rank. I learned afterwards for a fact that it was from a jealous feeling on his side also that my challenge was accepted; he had been rather jealous of me on his wife's account before their marriage; he thought now that if he submitted to be insulted by me and refused to accept any challenge, and if she heard of it, she might begin to despise him and waver in her love for him. I soon found a second in a comrade, an ensign of our regiment. In those days though duels were severely punished, yet dueling was a kind of fashion among the officers—so strong and deeply rooted will a brutal prejudice sometimes be.

It was the end of June, and our meeting was to take place at seven o'clock the next day on the outskirts of the town—and then something happened that in very truth was the turning point of my life. In the evening, returning home in a savage and brutal humor, I flew into a rage with my orderly Afanasy, and gave him two blows in the face with all my might, so that it was covered with blood. He had not long been in my service and I had struck him before, but never with such ferocious cruelty. And, believe me, though it's forty years ago, I recall it now with shame and pain. I went to bed and slept for about three hours; when I woke up the day was breaking. I got up—I did not want to sleep any more—I went to the window—opened it, it looked out upon the garden; I saw the sun rising; it was warm and beautiful, the birds were singing. What's the meaning of it, I thought, I feel in my heart as it were something vile and shameful? Is it because I am going to shed blood? No, I thought, I feel it's not that. Can it be that I am afraid of death, afraid of being killed? No, that's not it, that's not it at all. . . . And suddenly I knew at once what it was; it was because I had beaten Afanasy the evening before! It all rose suddenly before my mind, it all was as it were repeated over again; he stood before me and I was beating him straight on the face and he was holding his arms stiffly down, his head erect, his eyes fixed upon me as though on parade. He staggered at each blow and did not even dare to raise his hands to protect himself. That is what a man has been brought to, and that was a man beating a fellow man! What a crime! It was as though a sharp needle had pierced me right through. I stood as if I were struck dumb, while the sun was shining, the leaves were rejoicing and sparkling and the birds were trilling the praise of God. . . . I hid my face in my hands, fell on my bed and broke into a storm of tears. And then I remembered my brother Markel and what he said on his deathbed to his servants: "My dear ones, why do you wait on me, why do you love me, am I worth your waiting on me?" Yes, am I worth it? flashed through my mind. After all what am I worth, that another man, like me, made in the likeness and image of God, should serve me? For the first time in my life this question forced itself upon me. He had said, "Mother, my little heart, in truth we are each responsible to all for all, it's only that men don't know this. If they knew it, the world would be a paradise at once." "God, can that too be false?" I thought as I wept. "In

6. Probably a reference to an unsuccessful revolt against Nicholas I (1796–1855, r. 1825–55) that took place in December 1825 and subsequently became known as the Decembrist uprising. Nicholas crushed the uprising; the rebels were executed, imprisoned, or exiled to Siberia.

truth, perhaps, I am more than all others responsible for all, a greater sinner than all men in the world." And all at once the whole truth in its full
light appeared to me: what was I going to do? I was going to kill a good,
intelligent, noble man, who had done me no wrong, and by depriving his
wife of happiness for the rest of her life, I should be torturing and killing
her too. I lay thus in my bed with my face in the pillow, heedless how the
time was passing. Suddenly my second, the ensign, came in with the pistols to fetch me. "Ah," said he, "it's a good thing you are up already, it's
time we were off, come along!" I did not know what to do and hurried to
and fro undecided; we went out to the carriage, however. "Wait here a
minute," I said to him. "I'll be back directly, I have forgotten my purse."
And I ran back alone, straight to Afanasy's little room. "Afanasy," I said, "I
gave you two blows on the face yesterday, forgive me," I said. He started as
though he were frightened, and looked at me; and I saw that it was not
enough, and on the spot, in my full officer's uniform, I dropped at his feet
and bowed my head to the ground. "Forgive me," I said. Then he was completely aghast. "Your honor . . . sir, what are you doing? Am I worth it?"
And he burst out crying as I had done before, hid his face in his hands,
turned to the window and shook all over with his sobs. I flew out to my
comrade and jumped into the carriage. "Ready," I cried. "Have you ever
seen a conqueror?" I asked him. "Here is one before you." I was in ecstasy,
laughing and talking all the way, I don't remember what about. He looked
at me. "Well, brother, you are a plucky fellow, you'll keep up the honor of
the uniform, I can see." So we reached the place and found them there,
awaiting us. We were placed twelve paces apart; he had the first shot. I
stood gaily, looking him full in the face; I did not twitch an eyelash, I
looked lovingly at him, for I knew what I would do. His shot just grazed my
cheek and ear. "Thank God," I cried, "no man has been killed," and I
seized my pistol, turned back and flung it far away into the wood. "That's
the place for you," I cried. I turned to my adversary. "Forgive me, young
fool that I am, sir," I said, "for my unprovoked insult to you and for forcing
you to fire at me. I am ten times worse than you and more, maybe. Tell
that to the person whom you hold dearest in the world." I had no sooner
said this than they all three shouted at me. "Upon my word," cried my
adversary, in great anger, "if you did not want to fight, why did not you let
me alone?" "Yesterday I was a fool, today I know better," I answered him
gaily. "As to yesterday, I believe you, but as for today, it is difficult to agree
with your opinion," said he. "Bravo," I cried, clapping my hands. "I agree
with you there too, I have deserved it!" "Will you shoot, sir, or not?" "No, I
won't," I said, "if you like, fire at me again, but it would be better for you
not to fire." The seconds, especially mine, were shouting too: "Can you
disgrace the regiment like this, facing your antagonist and begging his
forgiveness! If I'd only known this!" I stood facing them all, not laughing
now. "Gentlemen," I said, "is it really so surprising in these days to find a
man who can repent of his stupidity and publicly confess his wrongdoing?" "But not in a duel," cried my second again. "That's what's so surprising," I said. "For I ought to have owned my fault as soon as I got here,
before he had fired a shot, before leading him into a great and mortal sin;
but we have made our life so grotesque, that to act in that way would have
been almost impossible, for only after I have faced his shot at the distance
of twelve paces could my words have any significance for him, and if I had

spoken before, he would have said 'he is a coward, the sight of the pistols had frightened him, no use to listen to him.' Gentlemen," I cried suddenly, speaking straight from my heart, "look around you at the gifts of God, the clear sky, the pure air, the tender grass, the birds; nature is beautiful and sinless, and we, only we, are godless and foolish, and we don't understand that life is a paradise, for we have only to understand that and it will at once be fulfilled in all its beauty, we shall embrace each other and weep." I would have said more but I could not; my voice broke with the sweetness and youthful gladness of it, and there was such bliss in my heart as I had never known before in my life. "All this is rational and edifying," said my antagonist, "and in any case you are an original person." "You may laugh," I said to him, laughing too, "but afterwards you will approve of me." "Oh, I am ready to approve of you now," said he; "will you shake hands, for I believe you are genuinely sincere." "No," I said, "not now, later on when I have grown worthier and deserve your esteem, then shake hands and you will do well." We went home, my second upbraiding me all the way, while I kissed him. All my comrades heard of the affair at once and gathered together to pass judgment on me the same day. "He has disgraced the uniform," they said; "let him resign his commission." Some stood up for me: "He faced the shot," they said. "Yes, but he was afraid of his other shot and begged for forgiveness." "If he had been afraid of being shot, he would have shot his own pistol first before asking forgiveness, while he flung it loaded into the forest. No, there's something else in this, something original." I enjoyed listening and looking at them. "My dear friends and comrades," said I, "don't worry about my resigning my commission, for I have done so already. I have sent in my papers this morning and as soon as I get my discharge I shall go into a monastery—it's with that object I am leaving the regiment." When I had said this every one of them burst out laughing. "You should have told us of that first, that explains everything, we can't judge a monk." They laughed and could not stop themselves, and not scornfully, but kindly and merrily. They all felt friendly to me at once, even those who had been sternest in their censure, and all the following month, before my discharge came, they could not make enough of me. "Ah, you monk," they would say. And everyone said something kind to me, they began trying to dissuade me, even to pity me: "What are you doing to yourself?" "No," they would say, "he is a brave fellow, he faced fire and could have fired his own pistol too, but he had a dream the night before that he should become a monk, that's why he did it." It was the same thing with the society of the town. Till then I had been kindly received, but had not been the object of special attention, and now all came to know me at once and invited me; they laughed at me, but they loved me. I may mention that although everybody talked openly of our duel, the authorities took no notice of it, because my antagonist was a near relation of our general, and as there had been no bloodshed and no serious consequences, and as I resigned my commission, they turned it into a joke. And I began then to speak aloud and fearlessly, regardless of their laughter, for it was always kindly and not spiteful laughter. These conversations mostly took place in the evenings, in the company of ladies; women particularly liked listening to me then and they made the men listen. "But how can I possibly be responsible for all?" everyone would laugh in my face. "Can I, for instance, be responsible for you?" "You may well not know it," I would answer, "since the whole world has long been going on a different line, since we consider the veriest lies as truth and demand the same lies from others. Here I have for once in my life acted sincerely and, well, you all look upon me as a madman. Though you are friendly to me, yet, you see, you all laugh at me." "But how can we help being friendly to you?" said my hostess, laughing. The room was full of people. All of a sudden rose the young lady on whose account the duel had been fought and whom only lately I had intended to be my future wife. I had not noticed her coming into the room. She got up, came to me and held out her hand. "Let me tell you," she said, "that I am the first not to laugh at you, but on the contrary I thank you with tears and express my respect for you and for your action then." Her husband too came up and then they all approached me and almost kissed me. My heart was filled with joy, but my attention was especially caught by a middle-aged man who came up to me with the others. I knew him by name already, but had never made his acquaintance nor exchanged a word with him till that evening.

(d) THE MYSTERIOUS VISITOR

He had long been an official in the town; he was in a prominent position, respected by all, rich and had a reputation for benevolence. He subscribed considerable sums to the almshouse and the orphan asylum; he was very charitable, too, in secret, a fact which only became known after his death. He was a man of about fifty, almost stern in appearance and not much given to conversation. He had been married some ten years and his wife, who was still young, had borne him three children. Well, I was sitting alone in my room the following evening, when my door suddenly opened and this very gentleman walked in.

I must mention, by the way, that I was no longer living in my former quarters. As soon as I resigned my commission, I took rooms with an old lady, the widow of a government clerk. My landlady's servant waited upon me, for I had moved into her rooms simply because on my return from the duel I had sent Afanasy back to the regiment, as I felt ashamed to look him in the face after my last interview with him. So prone is the man of the world to be ashamed of any righteous action.

"I have," said my visitor, "with great interest listened to you speaking in different houses the last few days and I wanted at last to make your personal acquaintance, so as to talk to you more intimately. Can you, dear sir, grant me this great service?" "I can, with the greatest pleasure and I shall look upon it as an honor." I said this, though I felt almost dismayed, so greatly was I impressed from the first moment by the appearance of this man. For though other people had listened to me with interest and attention, no one had come to me before with such a serious, stern and concentrated expression. And now he had come to see me in my rooms. He sat down. "You are, I see, a man of great strength of character," he said; "as you have dared to serve the truth, even when by doing so you risked incurring the contempt of all." "Your praise is, perhaps, excessive," I replied. "No, it's not excessive," he answered; "believe me, such a course of action is far more difficult than you think. It is that which has impressed me, and it is only on that account that I have come to you," he continued. "Tell me, please, that is if you are not annoyed by my perhaps unseemly curiosity, what were your exact sensations, if you can recall them, at the moment when you made up your mind to ask forgiveness at the duel? Do not think my question frivolous; on the contrary, I have in asking the question a secret motive of my own, which I will perhaps explain to you later on, if it is God's will that we should become more intimately acquainted."

All the while he was speaking, I looked him straight in the face and I suddenly felt a complete trust in him and great curiosity on my side also, for I felt that there was some strange secret in his soul.

"You ask what were my exact sensations at the moment when I asked my opponent's forgiveness," I answered; "but I had better tell you from the beginning what I have not yet told anyone else." And I described all that had passed between Afanasy and me, and how I had bowed down to the ground at his feet. "From that you can see for yourself," I concluded, "that at the time of the duel it was easier for me, for I had made a beginning already at home, and when once I had started on the road, to go further along it was far from being difficult, but even became a source of joy and happiness."

I liked the way he looked at me as he listened. "All that," he said, "is exceedingly interesting. I will come to see you again and again." And from that time forth he came to see me nearly every evening. And we should have become greater friends, if only he had ever talked of himself. But about himself he scarcely ever said a word, yet continually asked me about myself. In spite of that I became very fond of him and spoke with perfect frankness to him about all my feelings; for, thought I, what need have I to know his secrets, since I can see without that that he is a good man. Moreover, though he is such a serious man and my senior, he comes to see a youngster like me and treats me as his equal. And I learned a great deal that was profitable from him, for he was a man of lofty mind. "That life is a paradise," he said to me suddenly, "that I have long been thinking about"; and all at once he added, "I think of nothing else indeed." He looked at me and smiled. "I am more convinced of it than you are, I will tell you later why." I listened to him and thought that he evidently wanted to tell me something. "Paradise" he went on, "lies hidden within all of us—here it lies hidden in me now, and if I will it, it will be revealed to me tomorrow and for all time." I looked at him; he was speaking with great emotion and gazing mysteriously at me, as if he were questioning me. "And that we are all responsible to all for all, apart from our own sins, you were quite right in thinking that, and it is wonderful how you could comprehend it in all its significance at once. And in very truth, so soon as men understand that, the Kingdom of Heaven will be for them not a dream, but a living reality." "And when," I cried out to him bitterly, "when will that come to pass? and will it ever come to pass? Is not it simply a dream of ours?" "What then, you don't believe it," he said. "You preach it and don't believe it yourself. Believe me, this dream, as you call it, will come to pass without doubt; it will come, but not now, for every process has its law. It's a spiritual, psychological process. To transform the world, to recreate it afresh, men must turn into another path psychologically. Until you have become really, in actual fact, a brother to everyone, brotherhood will not come to pass. No sort of scientific teaching, no kind of common interest, will ever teach men to share property and privileges with equal consideration for all.

Everyone will think his share too small and they will always envy, complain, and attack one another. You ask when it will come to pass; it will come to pass, but first we have to go through the period of *isolation*." "What do you mean by isolation?" I asked him. "Why, the isolation that prevails everywhere, above all in our age—it has not fully developed, it has not reached its limit yet. For everyone strives to keep his individuality as apart as possible, wishes to secure the greatest possible fullness of life for himself; but meantime all his efforts result not in attaining fullness of life but suicide, for instead of self-realization he ends by arriving at complete isolation. All mankind in our age have split up into units, they all keep apart, each in his own groove; each one holds aloof, hides himself and hides what he has, from the rest, and he ends by being repelled by others and repelling them. He heaps up riches by himself and thinks, 'how strong I am now and how secure,' and in his madness he does not understand that the more he heaps up, the more he sinks into self-destructive impotence. For he is accustomed to rely upon himself alone and to cut himself off from the whole; he has trained himself not to believe in the help of others, in men and in humanity, and only trembles for fear he should lose his money and the privileges that he has won for himself. Everywhere in these days men have, in their mockery, ceased to understand that the true security is to be found in social solidarity rather than in isolated individual effort. But this terrible individualism must inevitably have an end, and all will suddenly understand how unnaturally they are separated from one another. It will be the spirit of the time, and people will marvel that they have sat so long in darkness without seeing the light. And then the sign of the Son of Man will be seen in the heavens.[7] . . . But, until then, we must keep the banner flying. Sometimes even if he has to do it alone, and his conduct seems to be crazy, a man must set an example, and so draw men's souls out of their solitude, and spur them to some act of brotherly love even if he seems to be a holy fool, so that the great idea may not die . . ."

Our evenings, one after another, were spent in such stirring and fervent talk. I gave up society and visited my neighbors much less frequently. Besides, my vogue was somewhat over. I say this, not as blame, for they still loved me and treated me good-humoredly, but there's no denying that fashion is a great power in society. I began to regard my mysterious visitor with admiration, for besides enjoying his intelligence, I began to perceive that he was brooding over some plan in his heart, and was perhaps preparing himself for a great deed. Perhaps he liked my not showing curiosity about his secret, not seeking to discover it by direct question nor by insinuation. But I noticed at last that he seemed to show signs of wanting to tell me something. This had become quite evident, indeed, about a month after he first began to visit me. "Do you know," he said to me once, "that people are very inquisitive about us in the town and wonder why I come to see you so often. But let them wonder, for *soon all will be explained*." Sometimes an extraordinary agitation would come over him, and almost always on such occasions he would get up and go away. Sometimes he would fix a long piercing look upon me, and I thought "he will say something directly now." But he would suddenly begin talking of something

---

7. A reference to the second coming of Christ. See Matthew 24.30.

ordinary and familiar. He often complained of headache too. One day, quite unexpectedly indeed, after he had been talking with great fervor a long time, I saw him suddenly turn pale, and his face worked convulsively, while he stared persistently at me.

"What's the matter?" I said: "do you feel ill?"—he had just been complaining of headache.

"I . . . do you know . . . I murdered someone."

He said this and smiled with a face as white as chalk. "Why is it he is smiling?" The thought flashed through my mind before I realized anything else. I too turned pale.

"What are you saying?" I cried.

"You see," he said, with a pale smile, "how much it has cost me to say the first word. Now I have said it, I feel I've taken the first step and shall go on."

For a long while I could not believe him, and I did not believe him at that time, but only after he had been to see me three days running and told me all about it. I thought he was mad, but ended by being convinced, to my great grief and amazement. His crime was a great and terrible one. Fourteen years before, he had murdered the widow of a landowner, a wealthy and handsome young woman who had a house in our town. He fell passionately in love with her, declared his feeling and tried to persuade her to marry him. But she had already given her heart to another man, an officer of noble birth and high rank in the service, who was at that time away at the front,[8] though she was expecting him soon to return. She refused his offer and begged him not to come and see her. After he had ceased to visit her, he took advantage of his knowledge of the house to enter at night through the garden by the roof, at great risk of discovery. But as often happens, a crime committed with extraordinary audacity is more successful than others. Entering the garret through the skylight, he went down the ladder, knowing that the door at the bottom of it was sometimes, through the negligence of the servants, left unlocked. He hoped to find it so, and so it was. He made his way in the dark to her bedroom, where a light was burning. As though on purpose, both her maids had gone off to a birthday party in the same street, without asking leave. The other servants slept in the servants' quarters or in the kitchen on the ground floor. His passion flamed up at the sight of her asleep, and then vindictive, jealous anger took possession of his heart, and like a drunken man, beside himself, he thrust a knife into her heart, so that she did not even cry out. Then with devilish and criminal cunning he contrived that suspicion should fall on the servants. He was so base as to take her purse, to open her chest with keys from under her pillow, and to take some things from it, doing it all as it might have been done by an ignorant servant, leaving valuable papers and taking only money. He took some of the larger gold things, but left smaller articles that were ten times as valuable. He took with him, too, some things for himself as remembrances, but of that later. Having done this awful deed, he returned by the way he had come. Neither the next day, when the alarm was raised, nor at any time after in his life, did anyone dream of suspecting that he was the criminal! Indeed no one knew of his love for her, for he was always reserved and

---

8. Since the events described take place around 1812, this would refer to Napoléon's invasion of Russia.

silent and had no friend to whom he would have opened his heart. He was looked upon simply as an acquaintance, and not a very intimate one, of the murdered woman, as for the previous fortnight he had not even visited her. A serf of hers called Pyotr was at once suspected, and every circumstance confirmed the suspicion. The man knew—indeed his mistress did not conceal the fact—that having to send one of her serfs as a recruit she had decided to send him, as he had no relations and his conduct was unsatisfactory.[9] People had heard him angrily threatening to murder her when he was drunk in a tavern. Two days before her death, he had run away, staying no one knew where in the town. The day after the murder, he was found on the road leading out of the town, dead drunk, with a knife in his pocket and his right hand happened to be stained with blood. He declared that his nose had been bleeding, but no one believed him. The maids confessed that they had gone to a party and that the street door had been left open till they returned. And a number of similar details came to light, throwing suspicion on the innocent servant. They arrested him, and he was tried for the murder; but a week after the arrest, the prisoner fell sick of a fever and died unconscious in the hospital. There the matter ended, left to God's will, and the judges and the authorities and everyone in the town remained convinced that the crime had been committed by no one but the servant who had died in the hospital. And after that the punishment began.

My mysterious visitor, now my friend, told me that at first he was not in the least troubled by pangs of conscience. He was miserable a long time, but not for that reason; only from regret that he had killed the woman he loved, that she was no more, that in killing her he had killed his love, while the fire of passion was still in his veins. But of the innocent blood he had shed, of the murder of a fellow human being, he scarcely thought. The thought that his victim might have become the wife of another man was insupportable to him, and so, for a long time, he was convinced in his conscience that he could not have acted otherwise. At first he was troubled at the arrest of the servant, but his illness and death soon set his mind at rest, for the man's death was apparently (so he reflected at the time) not owing to his arrest or his fright, but a chill he had taken on the day he ran away, when he had lain all night dead drunk on the damp ground. The theft of the money and other things troubled him little, for he argued that the theft had not been committed for gain but to avert suspicion. The sum stolen was small, and he shortly afterwards subscribed the whole of it, and much more, towards the funds for maintaining an almshouse in the town. He did this on purpose to set his conscience at rest about the theft, and it's a remarkable fact that for a long time he really was at peace—he told me this himself. He entered then upon a career of great activity in the service, volunteered for a difficult and laborious duty, which occupied him two years, and being a man of strong will almost forgot the past. Whenever he recalled it, he tried not to think of it at all. He became active in philanthropy too, founded and helped to maintain many institutions in the town, did a good deal in the two capi-

---

9. Before the Emancipation, landowners acted as draft agents for the state. Responsible for providing the government with recruits from among their serfs, they often abused this role as a way to get rid of undesirables. Being drafted into the army was viewed as a terrible calamity by the recruit and his family.

tals, and in both Moscow and Petersburg was elected a member of philanthropic societies. At last, however, he began brooding over the past,
and the strain of it was too much for him. Then he was attracted by a fine
and intelligent girl and soon after married her, hoping that marriage
would dispel his lonely depression, and that by entering on a new life and
scrupulously doing his duty to his wife and children, he would escape
from old memories altogether. But the very opposite of what he expected
happened. He began, even in the first month of his marriage, to be continually fretted by the thought, "My wife loves me—but what if she
knew?" When she first told him that she would soon bear him a child,
he was troubled. "I am giving life, but I have taken life." Children came.
"How dare I love them, teach and educate them, how can I talk to them
of virtue? I have shed blood." They were splendid children, he longed to
caress them; "and I can't look at their innocent candid faces, I am unworthy." At last he began to be bitterly and ominously haunted by the blood
of his murdered victim, by the young life he had destroyed, by the blood
that cried out for vengeance. He had begun to have awful dreams. But,
being a man of fortitude, he bore his suffering a long time, thinking: "I
shall redeem everything by this secret agony." But that hope too, was vain;
the longer it went on, the more intense was his suffering. He was respected
in society for his active benevolence, though everyone was overawed by his
stern and gloomy character. But the more he was respected, the more
intolerable it was for him. He confessed to me that he had thoughts of
killing himself. But he began to be haunted by another idea—an idea
which he had at first regarded as impossible and unthinkable, though
at last it got such a hold on his heart that he could not shake it off. He
dreamed of rising up, going out and confessing in the face of all men that
he had committed murder. For three years this dream had pursued him,
haunting him in different forms. At last he believed with his whole heart
that if he confessed his crime, he would heal his soul and would be at
peace forever. But this belief filled his heart with terror, for how could he
carry it out? And then came what happened at my duel. "Looking at you,
I have made up my mind." I looked at him.

"Is it possible," I cried, clasping my hands, "that such a trivial incident
could give rise to such a resolution in you?"

"My resolution has been growing for the last three years," he answered,
"and your story only gave the last touch to it. Looking at you, I reproached
myself and envied you," he said this to me almost sullenly.

"But you won't be believed," I observed; "it's fourteen years ago."

"I have proofs, great proofs. I shall show them."

Then I cried and kissed him.

"Tell me one thing, one thing," he said (as though it all depended upon
me), "my wife, my children! My wife may die of grief, and though my children won't lose their rank and property, they'll be a convict's children and
forever! And what a memory, what a memory of me I shall leave in their
hearts!"

I said nothing.

"And to part from them, to leave them forever? It's forever, you know,
forever!"

I sat still and repeated a silent prayer. I got up at last, I felt afraid.

"Well?" He looked at me.

"Go!" said I, "proclaim it to the world. Everything passes, only the truth remains. Your children will understand, when they grow up, the nobility of your resolution."

He left me that time as though he had made up his mind. Yet for more than a fortnight afterwards, he came to me every evening, still preparing himself, still unable to bring himself to the point. He made my heart ache. One day he would come determined and say fervently:

"I know it will be heaven for me, heaven, the moment I confess. Fourteen years I've been in hell. I want to suffer. I will take my suffering and begin to live. You can pass through the world doing wrong, but there's no turning back. Now I dare not love my neighbor nor even my own children. Good God, my children will understand, perhaps, what my suffering has cost me and will not condemn me! God is not in strength but in truth."

"All will understand your great deed," I said to him, "if not at once, they will understand later; for you have served truth, the higher truth, not the earthly one."

And he would go away seeming comforted, but next day he would come again, bitter, pale, sarcastic.

"Every time I come to you, you look at me so inquisitively as though to say, 'He has still not proclaimed it!' Wait a bit, don't despise me too much. It's not such an easy thing to do, as you would think. Perhaps I shall not do it at all. You won't go and inform against me then, will you?"

And far from looking at him with indiscreet curiosity, I was afraid to look at him at all. I was quite ill from anxiety, and my soul was full of tears. I could not sleep at night.

"I have just come from my wife," he went on. "Do you understand what the word 'wife' means? When I went out, the children called to me, 'Good-bye, papa, hurry back to read *The Children's Magazine*[1] with us.' No, you don't understand that! No one is wise from another man's woe."

His eyes were glittering, his lips were twitching. Suddenly he struck the table with his fist so that everything on it danced—it was the first time he had done such a thing, he was such a mild man.

"But need I?" he exclaimed, "must I! No one has been condemned, no one has been sent to Siberia in my place, the man died of fever. And I've been punished by my sufferings for the blood I shed. And they won't believe me, they won't believe my proofs. Need I confess, need I? I am ready to go on suffering all my life for the blood I have shed, if only my wife and children may be spared. Will it be just to ruin them with me? Aren't we making a mistake? What is right in this case? And will people recognize it, will they appreciate it, will they respect it?"

"Good Lord!" I thought to myself, "he is thinking of other people's respect at such a moment!" And I felt so sorry for him then, that I believe I would have shared his fate if it could have comforted him. I saw he was beside himself. I was aghast, realizing with my heart as well as my mind what such a resolution meant.

"Decide my fate!" he exclaimed again.

---

1. Several journals with this title, consisting of reading material for children, were published in eighteenth- and nineteenth-century Russia.

"Go and proclaim," I whispered to him. My voice failed me, but I whispered it firmly. I took up the New Testament from the table, the Russian translation, and showed him the Gospel of St. John, chapter 12, verse 24:

"Verily, verily, I say unto you, except a corn of wheat fall into the ground and die, it abideth alone: but if it die, it bringeth forth much fruit." I had just been reading that verse when he came in.

He read it.

"That's true," he said, but he smiled bitterly. "It's terrible the things you find in those books," he said, after a pause. "It's easy enough to thrust them upon one. And who wrote them? Can they have been written by men?"

"The Holy Spirit wrote them," said I.

"It's easy for you to prate," he smiled again, this time almost with hatred. I took the book again, opened it in another place and showed him the Epistle to the Hebrews, chapter 10, verse 31. He read: "It is a fearful thing to fall into the hands of the living God."

He read it and simply flung down the book. He was even trembling all over.

"An awful text," he said. "There's no denying you've picked out fitting ones." He rose from the chair. "Well!" he said, "Good-bye, perhaps I won't come again . . . we shall meet in heaven. So I have been for fourteen years 'in the hands of the living God,' that's how one must think of those fourteen years. Tomorrow I will beseech those hands to let me go."

I wanted to take him in my arms and kiss him, but I did not dare—his face was contorted and somber. He went away. "Good God," I thought, "what has he gone to face!" I fell on my knees before the icon and wept for him before the Holy Mother of God, our swift defender and helper. I was half an hour praying in tears, and it was late, about midnight. Suddenly I saw the door open and he came in again. I was surprised.

"Where have you been?" I asked him.

"I think," he said, "I've forgotten something . . . my handkerchief, I think. . . . Well, even if I've not forgotten anything, let me stay a little."

He sat down. I stood over him. "You sit down, too," said he. I sat down. We sat still for two minutes; he looked intently at me and suddenly smiled—I remembered that—then he got up, embraced me warmly and kissed me.

"Remember," he said, "how I came to you a second time. Dost thou hear, remember it!"

For the first time he addressed me with the familiar pronoun. And he went out. "Tomorrow," I thought.

And so it was. I did not know that evening that the next day was his birthday. I had not been out for the last few days so I had no chance of hearing it from anyone. On that day he always had a great gathering, everyone in the town went to it. It was the same this time. After dinner he walked into the middle of the room, with a paper in his hand—a formal declaration to the chief of his department who was present. This declaration he read aloud to the whole assembly. It contained a full account of the crime, in every detail. "I cast myself out from men as a monster. God has visited me," he said in conclusion. "I want to suffer for my sin!" Then he brought out and laid on the table all the things he had been keeping for fourteen years, that he thought would prove his crime, the jewels belonging to the murdered woman which he had stolen to divert suspicion, a cross and a locket taken from her neck with a portrait of her betrothed in the locket, her notebook and two letters; one from her betrothed, telling her that he would soon be with her, and her unfinished answer left on the table to be sent off next day. He carried off these two letters—what for? Why had he kept them for fourteen years afterwards instead of destroying them as evidence against him? And this is what happened: everyone was amazed and horrified, everyone refused to believe it and thought that he was deranged, though all listened with intense curiosity. A few days later it was fully decided and agreed in every house that the unhappy man was mad. The legal authorities could not refuse to take the case up, but they too dropped it. Though the trinkets and letters made them ponder, they decided that even if they did turn out to be authentic, no charge could be based on those alone. Besides, she might have given him those things as a friend, or asked him to take care of them for her. I heard afterwards, however, that the genuineness of the things was proved by the friends and relations of the murdered woman, and that there was no doubt about them. Yet nothing was destined to come of it, after all. Five days later, all had heard that he was ill and that his life was in danger. The nature of his illness I can't explain, they said it was an affection of the heartbeat. But it became known that the doctors had been induced by his wife to investigate his mental condition also, and had come to the conclusion that it was a case of insanity. I betrayed nothing, though people ran to question me. But when I wanted to visit him, I was for a long while forbidden to do so, above all by his wife. "It's you who have caused his illness," she said to me; "he was always gloomy, but for the last year people noticed that he was peculiarly excited and did strange things, and now you have been the ruin of him. Your preaching has brought him to this; for the last month he was always with you." Indeed, not only his wife but the whole town was down on me and blamed me. "It's all your doing," they said. I was silent and indeed rejoiced at heart, for I saw plainly God's mercy to the man who had turned against himself and punished himself. I could not believe in his insanity. They let me see him at last, he insisted upon saying good-bye to me. I went in to him and saw at once that not only his days but his hours were numbered. He was weak, yellow, his hands trembled, he gasped for breath, but his face was full of tender and happy feeling.

"It is done!" he said. "I've long been yearning to see you, why didn't you come?"

I did not tell him that they would not let me see him.

"God has had pity on me and is calling me to Himself. I know I am dying, but I feel joy and peace for the first time after so many years. There was heaven in my heart from the moment I had done what I had to do. Now I dare to love my children and to kiss them. Neither my wife nor the judges, nor anyone has believed it. My children will never believe it either. I see in that God's mercy to them. I shall die, and my name will be without a stain for them. And now I feel God near, my heart rejoices as in Heaven. . . . I have done my duty."

He could not speak, he gasped for breath, he pressed my hand warmly, looking fervently at me. We did not talk for long, his wife kept peeping in at us. But he had time to whisper to me:

"Do you remember how I came back to you that second time, at midnight? I told you to remember it. You know what I came back for? I came to kill you!"

I started.

"I went out from you then into the darkness, I wandered about the streets, struggling with myself. And suddenly I hated you so that I could hardly bear it. Now, I thought, he is all that binds me, and he is my judge. I can't refuse to face my punishment tomorrow, for he knows all. It was not that I was afraid you would betray me (I never even thought of that) but I thought, 'How can I look him in the face if I don't proclaim my crime?' And if you had been at the other end of the earth, but alive, it would have been all the same, the thought was unendurable that you were alive knowing everything and condemning me. I hated you as though you were the cause, as though you were to blame for everything. I came back to you then, remembering that you had a dagger lying on your table. I sat down and asked you to sit down, and for a whole minute I pondered. If I had killed you, I should have been ruined by that murder even if I had not confessed the other. But I didn't think about that at all, and I didn't want to think of it at that moment. I only hated you and longed to revenge myself on you for everything. The Lord vanquished the devil in my heart. But let me tell you, you were never nearer death."

A week later he died. The whole town followed him to the grave. The chief priest made a speech full of feeling. All lamented the terrible illness that had cut short his days. But all the town was up in arms against me after the funeral, and people even refused to see me. Some, at first a few and afterwards more, began indeed to believe in the truth of his story, and they visited me and questioned me with great interest and eagerness, for man loves to see the downfall and disgrace of the righteous. But I held my tongue, and very shortly after, I left the town, and five months later by God's grace I entered upon the safe and blessed path, praising the unseen finger which had guided me so clearly to it. But every day, to this very day, I remember in my prayer to this day, the servant of God, Mikhail, who suffered so greatly.

Chapter III

From the Conversations and Exhortations of Elder Zosima

(e) SOMETHING ABOUT THE RUSSIAN MONK AND HIS POSSIBLE SIGNIFICANCE

Fathers and teachers, what is the monk? In the enlightened world the word is nowadays pronounced by some people with a jeer, and by others it is used as a term of abuse, and this contempt for the monk is growing. It is true, alas, it is true, that there are many sluggards, gluttons, profligates and insolent beggars among monks. Educated people point to these: "You are idlers, useless members of society, you live on the labor of others, you are shameless beggars." And yet how many meek and humble monks there are, yearning for solitude and fervent prayer in peace. These are less noticed, or passed over in silence. And how surprised men would be if I were to say that from these meek monks, who yearn for solitary prayer, the salvation of Russia will come perhaps once more. For they are in truth made ready in peace and quiet "for the day and the hour, the month and the year." Meanwhile, in their solitude, they keep the image of Christ fair and undefiled, in the purity of God's truth, from the times of the Fathers of old, the Apostles and the martyrs. And when the time comes they will show it to the tottering creeds of the world. That is a great thought. That star will rise out of the East.[2]

That is my view of the monk, and is it false? is it too proud? Look at the worldly and all who set themselves up above the people of God, has not God's image and His truth been distorted in them? They have science; but in science there is nothing but what is the object of sense. The spiritual world, the higher part of man's being is rejected altogether, dismissed with a sort of triumph, even with hatred. The world has proclaimed the reign of freedom, especially of late, but what do we see in this freedom of theirs? Nothing but slavery and self-destruction! For the world says: "You have desires and so satisfy them, for you have the same rights as the most rich and powerful. Don't be afraid of satisfying them and even multiplying your desires." That is the modern doctrine of the world. In that they see freedom. And what follows from this right of multiplication of desires? In the rich, *isolation* and spiritual suicide; in the poor, envy and murder; for they have been given rights, but have not been shown the means of satisfying their wants. They maintain that the world is getting more and more united, more and more bound together in brotherly community, as it overcomes distance and sets thoughts flying through the air. Alas, put no faith in such a bond of union. Interpreting freedom as the multiplication and rapid satisfaction of desires, men distort their own nature, for many senseless and foolish desires and habits and ridiculous fancies are fostered in them. They live only for mutual envy, for gluttony and ostentation. To have dinners, visits, carriages, rank and slaves to wait on one is looked upon as a necessity, for which life, honor and human feeling are sacrificed, and men even commit suicide if they are unable to satisfy it. We see the same thing among those who are not rich, while the poor drown their unsatisfied need and their envy in drunkenness. But soon they will drink blood instead of wine, they are being led on to it. I ask you is such a man free? I knew one 'champion of an idea' who told me himself that, when he was deprived of tobacco in prison, he was so wretched at the privation that he almost went and betrayed his 'idea' for the sake of getting tobacco again! And such a man says, "I am fighting for the cause of humanity." How can such a one fight, what is he fit for? He is capable perhaps of some action quickly over, but he cannot hold out long. And it's no wonder that instead of gaining freedom they have sunk into slavery, and instead of serving the cause of brotherly love and the union of humanity have fallen, on the contrary, into separation and isolation, as my mysterious visitor and teacher said to me in my youth. And therefore the idea of the service of humanity, of brotherly love and the solidarity of mankind, is more and more dying out in the world, and indeed this idea is sometimes treated with derision. For how can a man shake off his habits, what can become of him if he is in such bondage to the habit of satisfying the innumerable desires he has created for himself? He is isolated, and what concern has he with the rest of humanity? They have succeeded in

2. See Matthew 2.2.

accumulating a greater mass of objects, but the joy in the world has grown less.

The monastic way is very different. Obedience, fasting and prayer are laughed at, yet only through them lies the way to real, true freedom. I cut off my superfluous and unnecessary desires, I subdue my proud and wanton will and chastise it with obedience, and with God's help I attain freedom of spirit and with it spiritual joy. Who is more capable of conceiving a great idea and serving it—the rich man in his isolation or the man who has *freed himself* from the tyranny of material things and habits? The monk is reproached for his solitude, "You have secluded yourself within the walls of the monastery for your own salvation, and have forgotten the brotherly service of humanity!" But we shall see which will be most zealous in the cause of brotherly love. For it is not we, but they, who are in isolation, though they don't see that. Of old, leaders of the people came from among us, and why should they not again?[3] The same meek and humble ascetics will rise up and go out to work for the great cause. The salvation of Russia comes from the people. And the Russian monk has always been on the side of the people. We are isolated only if the people are isolated. The people believe as we do, and an unbelieving reformer will never do anything in Russia, even if he is sincere in heart and a genius. Remember that! The people will meet the atheist and overcome him, and Russia will be one and orthodox. Take care of the people and guard their hearts. Go on educating them quietly. That's your duty as monks, for this is a godbearing people.

(f) OF MASTERS AND SERVANTS, AND OF WHETHER IT IS
      POSSIBLE FOR THEM TO BE BROTHERS IN THE SPIRIT

Of course, I don't deny that there is sin in the peasants too. And the fire of corruption is spreading visibly, hourly, working from above downwards. The spirit of isolation is coming upon the people too. Kulaks and devourers of the commune are rising up.[4] Already the merchant grows more and more eager for rank, and strives to show himself cultured though he has not a trace of culture, and to this end meanly despises his old traditions, and is even ashamed of the faith of his fathers. He visits princes, though he is only a peasant corrupted. The peasants are rotting in drunkenness and cannot shake off the habit. And what cruelty to their wives, to their children even! All from drunkenness! I've seen in the factories children of ten, frail, rickety, bent and already depraved. The stuffy workshop, the din of machinery, work all day long, the vile language and the drink, the drink—is that what a little child's heart needs? He needs sunshine, childish play, good examples all about him, and at least a little love. There must be no more of this, monks, nor more torturing of children, rise up and preach that, make haste, make haste![5] But God will save Russia, for though the peasants are corrupted and cannot renounce their stinking sin, yet

3. Zosima probably refers to charismatic figures of the Russian Orthodox tradition such as St. Sergius and Tikhon of Zadonsk.
4. The word *kulak* ("fist") refers to a peasant who exploits other peasants. "Devourers of the commune" translates the Russian word *miroed*, which literally means "commune eater." Following the Emancipation, opportunities arose for some peasants to take advantage of others by lending money at high interest rates and buying up commune land.
5. Zosima's criticism of child labor may be an echo of Nekrasov's 1861 poem "Children Weeping."

they know that their stinking sin is cursed by God and that they do wrong in sinning. So that our people still believe in righteousness, have faith in God and weep tears of devotion. It is different with the upper classes. They, following science, want to base justice on reason alone, but not with Christ, as before, and they have already proclaimed that there is no crime, that there is no sin. And that's consistent, for if you have no God what is the meaning of crime? In Europe the people are already rising up against the rich with violence, and the leaders of the people are everywhere leading them to bloodshed, and teaching them that their wrath is righteous. But "their wrath is accursed, for it is cruel."[6] But God will save Russia as He has saved her many times. Salvation will come from the people, from their faith and their meekness. Fathers and teachers, watch over the people's faith and this will not be a dream. I've been struck all my life in our great people by their dignity, their true and seemly dignity. I've seen it myself, I can testify to it, I've seen it and marveled at it, I've seen it in spite of the degraded sins and poverty-stricken appearance of our peasantry. They are not servile, and even after two centuries of serfdom, they are free in manner and bearing, yet without insolence, and not revengeful and not envious. "You are rich and noble, you are clever and talented, well be so, God bless you. I respect you, but I know that I too am a man. By the very fact that I respect you without envy I prove my dignity as a man." In truth if they don't say this (for they don't know how to say this yet) that is how they *act*. I have seen it myself, I have known it myself, and, would you believe it, the poorer our Russian peasant is, the more noticeable is that serene goodness, for the rich among them are for the most part corrupted already, and much of that is due to our carelessness and indifference. But God will save His people, for Russia is great in her humility. I dream of seeing, and seem to see clearly already, our future. It will come to pass, that even the most corrupt of our rich will end by being ashamed of his riches before the poor, and the poor, seeing his humility, will understand and give way before him, will respond joyfully and kindly to his honorable shame. Believe me that it will end in that; things are moving to that. Equality is to be found only in the spiritual dignity of man, and that will only be understood among us. If we were brothers, there would be fraternity, but before that, they will never agree about the division of wealth. We preserve the image of Christ, and it will shine forth like a precious diamond to the whole world. So be it, so be it!

Fathers and teachers, a touching incident befell me once. In my wanderings I met in the town of K—— my old orderly, Afanasy. It was eight years since I had parted from him. He chanced to see me in the market-place, recognized me, ran up to me, and how delighted he was, he simply pounced on me: "Master dear, is it you? is it really you I see?" He took me home with him. He was no longer in the army, he was married and already had two little children. He and his wife earned their living hawking wares in the marketplace. His room was poor, but clean and joyful. He made me sit down, set the samovar,[7] sent for his wife, as though my appearance

---

6. In Genesis 49.1, Jacob commands his sons to gather around, "so that I may tell you that which shall befall you in the last days." Regarding his sons Simeon and Levi, he declares, "Cursed be their anger, for it was fierce; and their wrath, for it was cruel" (Genesis 49.7).

7. The samovar is a traditional Russian device for heating water for tea, consisting of a central metal urn with a vertical pipe filled with charcoal or other fuel and a spigot near the bottom.

were a festival for them. He brought me his children: "Bless them, father." "Is it for me to bless them? I am only a humble monk. I will pray for them. And for you, Afanasy Pavlovich, I have prayed every day since that day, for it all came from you," said I. And I explained that to him as well as I could. And what do you think? The man kept gazing at me and could not believe that I, his former master, an officer, was now before him in such a guise and position; it even made him shed tears. "Why are you weeping?" said I, "better rejoice over me, dear friend, whom I can never forget, for my path is a glad and joyful one." He did not say much, but kept sighing and shaking his head over me tenderly. "What has become of your fortune?" he asked. "I gave it to the monastery," I answered; "we live in common."

After tea I began saying good-bye, and suddenly he brought out half a ruble as an offering to the monastery, and another half-ruble I saw him thrusting hurriedly into my hand: "That's for you in your wanderings, it may be of use to you, father." I took his half-ruble, bowed to him and his wife, and went out rejoicing. And on my way I thought: "Here we are both now, he at home and I on the road, sighing and shaking our heads, no doubt, and yet smiling joyfully in the gladness of our hearts, remembering how God brought about our meeting." I have never seen him again since then. I had been his master and he my servant, but now when we exchanged a loving kiss with softened hearts, there was a great human bond between us. I have thought a great deal about that, and now what I think is this: is it so inconceivable that that grand and simple-hearted unity might in due time become universal among the Russian people? I believe that it will come to pass and that the time is at hand.

And of the servants I will add this, in old days when I was young I was often angry with servants; "the cook had served something too hot, the orderly had not brushed my clothes." But what taught me better then was a thought of my dear brother's, which I had heard from him in childhood: "Am I worth it, that another should serve me and be ordered about by me in his poverty and ignorance?" And I wondered at the time that such simple and self-evident ideas should be so slow to occur to our minds. It is impossible that there should be no servants in the world, but act so that your servant may be freer in spirit than if he were not a servant. And why cannot I be a servant to my servant and even let him see it, and that without any pride on my part or any mistrust on his? Why should not my servant be like my own kindred, so that I may take him into my family and rejoice in doing so? Even now this can be done, but it will lead to the grand unity of men in the future, when a man will not seek servants for himself, or desire to turn his fellow men into servants as he does now, but on the contrary, will long with his whole heart to be the servant of all, as the Gospel teaches.[8] And can it be a dream, that in the end man will find his joy only in deeds of enlightenment and mercy, and not in cruel pleasures as now, in gluttony, fornication, ostentation, boasting and envious rivalry of one with the other? I firmly believe that it is not and that the time is at

---

8. Reversal of roles—the great becoming the least, the master becoming the servant—is a theme encountered in the Gospels. In Matthew 23.11 Jesus declares to a crowd "he that is greatest among you shall be your servant;" In Mark 9.35 he tells his disciples "If any man desires to be first, the same shall be last of all, and servant of all." See also Mark 10.43. Dostoevsky discusses the relationship between master and servant in "Two Halves," *Diary*, August 1880, chapter 3, number 3.

hand. People laugh and ask: "When will that time come and does it look as if it is coming?" I believe that with Christ's help we shall accomplish this great thing. And how many ideas there have been on earth in the history of man which were unthinkable ten years before they appeared? Yet when their destined hour had come, they came forth and spread over the whole earth. So it will be with us, and our people will shine forth in the world, and all men will say: "The stone which the builders rejected has become the cornerstone of the building."[9] And we may ask the scornful themselves: if our hope is a dream, when will you build up your edifice and order things justly by your intellect alone, without Christ? If they declare that it is they who are advancing towards unity, only the most simple-hearted among them believe it, so that one may positively marvel at such simplicity. Of a truth, they have more fantastic dreams than we. They aim at justice, but, denying Christ, they will end by flooding the earth with blood, for blood cries out for blood, and he that taketh up the sword shall perish by the sword.[1] And if it were not for Christ's covenant, they would slaughter one another down to the last two men on earth. And those two last men would not be able to restrain each other in their pride, and the one would slay the other and then himself.[2] And that would come to pass, were it not for the promise of Christ that for the sake of the humble and meek the days shall be shortened.[3] While I was still wearing an officer's uniform after my duel, I talked about servants in general society, and I remember everyone was amazed at me: "What!" they asked, "are we to make our servants sit down on the sofa and offer them tea?" And I answered them: "Why not, sometimes at least." Everyone laughed. Their question was frivolous and my answer was not clear; but the thought in it was to some extent true.

(g)   OF PRAYER, OF LOVE, AND OF CONTACT WITH OTHER WORLDS

Young man, be not forgetful of prayer. Every time you pray, if your prayer is sincere, there will be new feeling and new meaning in it, which will give you fresh courage, and you will understand that prayer is education. Remember too, every day, and whenever you can, repeat to yourself, "Lord, have mercy on all who appear before Thee today." For every hour and every moment thousands of people leave life on this earth, and their souls appear before God. And how many of them depart in solitude, unknown, sad, dejected, that no one mourns for them or even knows whether they have lived or not. And behold, from the other end of the earth perhaps, your prayer for their rest will rise up to God though you knew them not

---

9. Zosima slightly changes the wording of Psalm 118.22: "The stone which the builders refused is become the head stone of the corner." See also Matthew 21.42.
1. When Jesus is placed under arrest, one of his companions draws a sword, eliciting the rebuke, "Put up again thy sword into his place: for all they that take the sword shall perish with the sword" (Matthew 26.52).
2. Zosima's description of the last men destroying each other may be indebted to George Gordon Byron's (1788–1824) poem "Darkness" (1816). Dostoevsky owned a volume of Lord Byron's poetry in Russian translation that contained this poem.
3. According to Jesus in the Gospels, God shortens the sufferings of the end of the world for the sake of the elect, but Zosima claims that it is for the sake of "the humble and meek." In response to his disciples' request that he describe how the world will end, Jesus says, "in those days shall be affliction, such as was not from the beginning of the creation . . . And except that the Lord had shortened those days, no flesh should be saved: but for the elect's sake, whom he hath chosen, he hath shortened the days" (Mark 13.19–20). See also Matthew 24.22.

nor they you. How touching it must be to a soul standing in dread before the Lord to feel at that instant that, for him too, there is one to pray, that there is a human being left on earth to love him too. And God will look on you both more graciously, for if you have had so much pity on him, how much more will He have pity Who is infinitely more loving and merciful than you. And He will forgive him for your sake.

Brothers, have no fear of men's sin, love a man even in his sin, for that is the semblance of divine love and is the highest love on earth. Love all God's creation, the whole and every grain of sand in it. Love every leaf, every ray of God's light. Love the animals, love the plants, love everything. If you love everything, you will perceive the divine mystery in things. Once you perceive it, you will begin to comprehend it better every day. And you will come at last to love the whole world with an all-embracing love. Love the animals: God has given them the rudiments of thought and joy untroubled. Do not trouble it, don't harass them, don't deprive them of their happiness, don't work against God's intent. Man, do not pride yourself on superiority to the animals; they are without sin, and you, with your greatness, defile the earth by your appearance on it, and leave the traces of your foulness after you— alas, it is true of almost every one of us! Love children especially, for they too are sinless like the angels; they live to soften and purify our hearts and as it were to guide us.[4] Woe to him who offends a child! Father Anfim taught me to love children. The kind, silent man used often on our wanderings to spend the pennies given us on sweets and cakes for the children. He could not pass by a child without emotion, that's the nature of the man.

At some thoughts one stands perplexed, especially at the sight of men's sin, and wonders whether one should use force or humble love. Always decide to use humble love. If you resolve on that once for all, you may subdue the whole world. Loving humility is marvelously strong, the strongest of all things and there is nothing else like it. Every day and every hour, every minute, walk round yourself and watch yourself, and see that your image is a seemly one. You pass by a little child, you pass by, spiteful, with ugly words, with wrathful heart; you may not have noticed the child, but he has seen you, and your image, unseemly and ignoble, may remain in his defenseless heart. You don't know it, but you may have sown an evil seed in him and it may grow, and all because you were not careful before the child, because you did not foster in yourself a careful, actively benevolent love. Brothers, love is a teacher; but one must know how to acquire it, for it is hard to acquire, it is dearly bought, it is won slowly by long labor. For we must love not only occasionally, for a moment, but forever. Everyone can love occasionally, even the wicked can. My brother asked the birds to forgive him; that sounds senseless, but it is right; for all is like an ocean, all is flowing and blending; a touch in one place sets up movement at the other end of the earth. It may be senseless to beg forgiveness of the birds, but birds would be happier at your side—a little happier, anyway—and children and all animals, if you yourself were nobler than you are now. It's all like an ocean, I tell you. Then you would pray to the

---

4. For Jesus' teachings regarding children, see Matthew 18.1–10 and Mark 10.13–15, where he instructs his disciples that children are first in the kingdom of heaven. Zosima's warning against harming a child is an echo of Matthew 18.6: "But whoso shall offend one of these little ones which believe in me, it were better for him that a millstone were hanged about his neck, and that he were drowned in the depth of the sea."

birds too, consumed by an all-embracing love, in a sort of transport, and pray that they too will forgive you your sin. Treasure this ecstasy, however senseless it may seem to men.

My friends, pray to God for gladness. Be glad as children, as the birds of heaven.[5] And let not the sin of men confound you in your doings. Fear not that it will wear away your work and hinder its being accomplished. Do not say, "Sin is mighty, wickedness is mighty, evil environment is mighty, and we are lonely and helpless, and evil environment is wearing us away and hindering our good work from being done." Fly from that dejection, children! There is only one means of salvation, then take yourself and make yourself responsible for all men's sins, that is the truth, you know, friends, for as soon as you sincerely make yourself responsible for everything and for all men, you will see at once that it is really so, and that you are to blame for everyone and for all things. But throwing your own indolence and impotence on others you will end by sharing the pride of Satan and murmuring against God. Of the pride of Satan what I think is this: it is hard for us on earth to comprehend it, and therefore it is so easy to fall into error and to share it, even imagining that we are doing something grand and fine. Indeed many of the strongest feelings and movements of our nature we cannot comprehend on earth. Let not that be a stumbling block, and think not that it may serve as a justification to you for anything. For the Eternal Judge asks of you what you can comprehend and not what you cannot. You will know that yourself hereafter, for you will behold all things truly then and will not dispute them. On earth, indeed, we are as it were astray, and if it were not for the precious image of Christ before us, we should be undone and altogether lost, as was the human race before the flood. Much on earth is hidden from us, but to make up for that we have been given a precious mystic sense of our living bond with the other world, with the higher heavenly world, and the roots of our thoughts and feelings are not here but in other worlds. That is why the philosophers say that we cannot apprehend the reality of things on earth. God took seeds from different worlds and sowed them on this earth, and His garden grew up and everything came up that could come up,[6] but what grows lives and is alive only through the feeling of its contact with other mysterious worlds. If that feeling grows weak or is destroyed in you, the heavenly growth will die away in you. Then you will be indifferent to life and even grow to hate it. That's what I think.

(h) CAN A MAN JUDGE HIS FELLOW CREATURES? OF FAITH TO THE END

Remember particularly that you cannot be a judge of anyone.[7] For no one can judge a criminal, until he recognizes that he is just such a criminal as

---

5. Zosima paraphrases and combines several Gospel passages that emphasize the necessity of innocence and utter dependence on God for salvation. In Luke 12.22–24, Jesus tells his disciples "Take no thought for your life, what ye shall eat; neither for the body, what ye shall put on. The life is more than meat, and the body is more than raiment. Consider the ravens: they neither sow nor reap . . . and God feedeth them: how much more are ye better than the fowls?" (see also Matthew 6.26). In Matthew 18.2–3, Jesus tells his disciples that they must become like children to enter the kingdom of heaven: "Verily I say unto you, Except ye be converted, and become as little children, ye shall not enter into the kingdom of heaven."
6. Seeds and sowing appear frequently in Gospel parables; see for example Matthew 13.3–8. Zosima also refers to Genesis 1.11–12.
7. The imperative to refrain from judgment runs throughout the Gospels, receiving its clearest expression in Matthew 7.1: "Judge not, that ye be not judged."

the man standing before him, and that he perhaps is more than all men to blame for that crime. When he understands that, he will be able to be a judge. Though that sounds absurd, it is true. If I had been righteous myself, perhaps there would have been no criminal standing before me. If you can take upon yourself the crime of the criminal your heart is judging, take it at once, suffer for him yourself, and let him go without reproach. And even if the law itself makes you his judge, act in the same spirit so far as possible, for he will go away and condemn himself more bitterly than you have done. If, after your kiss, he goes away untouched, mocking at you, do not let that be a stumbling block to you. It shows his time has not yet come, but it will come in due course. And if it come not, no matter; if not he, then another in his place will understand and suffer, and judge and condemn himself, and the truth will be fulfilled. Believe that, believe it without doubt; for in that lies all the hope and faith of the saints.

Work without ceasing. If you remember in the night as you go to sleep, "I have not done what I ought to have done," rise up at once and do it. If the people around you are spiteful and callous and will not hear you, fall down before them and beg their forgiveness; for in truth you are to blame for their not wanting to hear you. And if you cannot speak to them in their bitterness, serve them in silence and in humility, never losing hope. If all men abandon you and even drive you away by force, then when you are left alone fall on the earth and kiss it, water it with your tears and it will bring forth fruit even though no one has seen or heard you in your solitude. Believe to the end, even if all men went astray and you were left the only one faithful; bring your offering even then and praise God in your loneliness. And if two of you are gathered together—then there is a whole world, a world of living love. Embrace each other tenderly and praise God, for if only in you two His truth has been fulfilled.

If you sin yourself and grieve even unto death[8] for your sins or for your sudden sin, then rejoice for others, rejoice for the righteous man, rejoice that if you have sinned, he is righteous and has not sinned.

If the evildoing of men moves you to indignation and overwhelming distress, even to a desire for vengeance on the evildoers, shun above all things that feeling. Go at once and seek suffering for yourself, as though you were yourself guilty of that wrong. Accept that suffering and bear it and your heart will find comfort, and you will understand that you too are guilty, for you might have been a light to the evildoers, even as the one man sinless, and you were not a light to them. If you had been a light, you would have lightened the path for others too, and the evildoer might perhaps have been saved by your light from his sin. And even though your light was shining, yet you see men were not saved by it, hold firm and doubt not the power of the heavenly light.[9] Believe that if they were not saved, they will be saved hereafter. And if they are not saved hereafter, then their sons will be saved, for your light will not die even when you are dead. The righteous man departs, but his light remains. Men are always saved after the death of the deliverer. Men reject their prophets and slay them, but they love their martyrs and honor those whom they have slain.

8. An allusion to Christ's words to his disciples right before his arrest: "My soul is exceeding sorrowful, even unto death" (Matthew 26.38).
9. Zosima's words resonate with Biblical images of light, such as John 1.4–9.

You are working for the whole, you are acting for the future. Seek no reward, for great is your reward on this earth: the spiritual joy which is only vouchsafed to the righteous man. Fear not the great nor the mighty, but be wise and ever serene. Know measure, know the proper time, study that. When you are left alone, pray. Love to throw yourself on the earth and kiss it. Kiss the earth and love it with an unceasing, consuming love. Love all men, love everything. Seek that rapture and ecstasy. Water the earth with the tears of your joy and love those tears. Don't be ashamed of that ecstasy, prize it, for it is a gift of God and a great one; it is not given to many but only to the elect.

(i)   OF HELL AND HELLFIRE, A MYSTIC REFLECTION

Fathers and teachers, I ponder "What is hell?" I maintain that it is the suffering of no longer being able to love.[1] Once in infinite existence, immeasurable in time and space, a spiritual being was given on his coming to earth, the power of saying, "I am and I love." Once, only once, there was given him a moment of active *living* love and for that was earthly life given him, and with it times and seasons. And that happy being rejected the priceless gift, prized it and loved it not, scorned it and remained callous. Such a one, having left the earth, sees Abraham's bosom and talks with Abraham as we are told in the parable of the rich man and Lazarus,[2] and beholds heaven and can go up to the Lord. But that is just his torment, to rise up to the Lord without ever having loved, to be brought close to those who have loved when he has despised their love. For he sees clearly and says to himself, "Now I have understanding and though I now thirst to love, there will be nothing great, no sacrifice in my love, for my earthly life is over, and Abraham will not come even with a drop of living water[3] (that is the gift of earthly, active life) to cool the fiery thirst of spiritual love which burns in me now, though I despised it on earth; there is no more life for me and there will be no more time! Even though I would gladly give my life for others, it can never be, for that life is passed which can be sacrificed for love, and now there is a gulf fixed between that life and this existence."

They talk of hellfire in the material sense. I don't go into that mystery and I shun it. But I think if there were fire in material sense they would be glad of it, for, I imagine, that in material agony, their still greater spiritual agony would be forgotten for a moment. Moreover, that spiritual agony cannot be taken from them, for that suffering is not external but within them. And if it could be taken from them, I think they would be bitterer still in their unhappiness. For even if the righteous in Paradise forgave them, beholding their torments, and called them up to heaven in their infinite love, they would only multiply their torments, for they would arouse in them still more keenly a flaming thirst for responsive, active and grateful love which is now impossible. In the timidity of my heart I imagine, however, that the very recognition of this impossibility would serve at last to console them. For accepting the love of the righteous together with the

---

1. Zosima's reflections on hell as the inability to love appear to be influenced by the teachings of Isaac the Syrian. See p. 50.
2. The story of the rich man and Lazarus is told in Luke 16.19–31. See also p. 27.
3. Living water or the water of life is a key image and concept in the New Testament. See John 4.10.

impossibility of repaying it, by this submissiveness and the effect of this humility, they will attain at last, as it were, to a certain semblance of that active love which they scorned in life, to something like its outward expression. . . . I am sorry, friends and brothers, that I cannot express this clearly.

But woe to those who have slain themselves on earth, woe to the suicides! I believe that there can be none more miserable than they. They tell us that it is a sin to pray to God for them and outwardly the Church, as it were, renounces them, but in my secret heart I believe that we may pray even for them.[4] Love can never be an offense to Christ. For such as those I have prayed inwardly all my life, I confess it, fathers and teachers, and even now I pray for them every day.

Oh, there are some who remain proud and fierce even in hell, in spite of their certain knowledge and contemplation of the absolute truth; there are some fearful ones who have given themselves over to Satan and his proud spirit entirely. For such, hell is voluntary and ever consuming; they are tortured by their own choice. For they have cursed themselves, cursing God and life. They live upon their vindictive pride like a starving man in the desert sucking blood out of his own body.[5] But they are never satisfied, and they refuse forgiveness, they curse God Who calls them. They cannot behold the living God without hatred, and they cry out that the God of life should be annihilated, that God should destroy Himself and His own creation. And they will burn in the fire of their own wrath for ever and yearn for death and annihilation. But they will not attain to death. . . .

Here Alexey Fyodorovich Karamazov's manuscript ends. I repeat, it is incomplete and fragmentary. Biographical details, for instance, cover only Father Zosima's earliest youth. Of his teaching and opinions we find brought together sayings evidently uttered at different times and in response to various situations. His utterances during the last few hours have not been kept separate from the rest, but their general character can be gathered from what we have in Alexey Fyodorovich's manuscript.

The elder's death came in the end quite unexpectedly. For although those who were gathered about him that last evening realized that his death was approaching, yet it was difficult to imagine that it would come so suddenly. On the contrary, his friends, as I observed already, seeing him that night apparently so cheerful and talkative, were convinced that there was at least a temporary change for the better in his condition. Even five minutes before his death, they said afterwards wonderingly, it was impossible to foresee it. He seemed suddenly to feel an acute pain in his chest, he turned pale and pressed his hands to his heart. All rose from their seats and hastened to him. But though suffering, he still looked at them with a smile, sank slowly from his chair on his knees, then bowed his face to the earth, stretched out his arms and as though in joyful ecstasy,

---

4. The Russian Orthodox Church views suicide as the gravest of sins, because it is a rejection of God's gift of life: through the act of suicide, one renounces hope and cuts oneself off from God, making repentance and reconciliation impossible. The dead person may not have a Christian burial unless it is ruled that he or she was mentally impaired. Zosima flouts the Biblical injunction not to pray for those who commit "sin unto death," that is, a mortal sin such as suicide. See 1 John 5.16.
5. This image is probably borrowed from the writings of Isaac the Syrian.

praying and kissing the earth (as he taught), quietly and joyfully gave up
his soul to God.[6]

The news of his death spread at once through the hermitage and reached
the monastery. The nearest friends of the deceased and those whose duty
it was from their position began to lay out the corpse according to the
ancient ritual, and all the monks gathered together in the church. And
before dawn the news of the death reached the town. By the morning all
the town was talking of the event, and crowds were flocking from the town
to the monastery. But this subject will be treated in the next book; I will
only add here that before a day had passed something happened so unexpected, so strange, upsetting, and bewildering in its effect on the monks
and the townspeople, that after all these years, that day of general suspense is still vividly remembered in the town.

---

6. "Quietly and joyfully gave up his soul to God" is a common phrase in the hagiographical genre
of the saint's life. This is just one of many passages in Book Six in which Dostoevsky's novel is
permeated by the language of different genres.

Part Three

Book Seven

ALYOSHA

Chapter I

The Odor of Corruption[1]

The body of Father Zosima was prepared for burial according to the established ritual. As is well known, the bodies of dead monks and hermits are not washed. In the words of the Church Ritual: "If any one of the monks depart in the Lord, the monk designated (that is, whose office it is) shall wipe the body with warm water, making first the sign of the cross with a sponge on the forehead of the deceased, on the breast, on the hands and feet and on the knees, and that is enough." All this was done by Father Païssy, who then clothed the deceased in his monastic garb and wrapped him in his cloak, which was, according to custom, somewhat slit to allow of its being folded about him in the form of a cross. On his head he put a hood with an eight-cornered cross.[2] The hood was left open and the dead man's face was covered with black gauze. In his hand was put an icon of the Savior. Towards morning he was put in the coffin which had been made ready long before. It was decided to leave the coffin all day in the cell, in the larger room in which the elder used to receive his visitors and fellow monks. As the deceased was a hieromonk of the strictest rule, the Gospel, not the Psalter, had to be read over his body by hieromonks and hierodeacons. The reading was begun by Father Iosif immediately after the requiem service. Father Païssy desired later on to read the Gospel all day and night over his dead friend, but for the present he, as well as the Father Superintendent of the hermitage, was very busy and occupied, for something extraordinary, and unheard of, even "unseemly" excitement and impatient expectation began to be apparent in the monks, and the visitors from the monastery hostels, and the crowds of people flocking from the town. And as time went on, this grew more and more marked. Both the Superintendent and Father Païssy did their utmost to calm the general bustle and agitation. When it was fully daylight, some people began bringing their sick, in most cases children, with them from the town—as though they had been waiting expressly for this moment to do so, evidently persuaded that the dead elder's remains had a power of healing,[3] which would

---

1. The phrase "the odor of corruption" (*tletvornyi dukh*) occurs in Tyutchev's poem "I grob opushchen uzh v mogilu" (1836).
2. The Russian Orthodox cross differs from Western Christian representations, including two smaller crossbeams, raising the number of points from four to eight.
3. One of the most common motifs in the genre of the saint's life is the power of the holy man's relics to perform miracles, especially healing miracles.

be immediately made manifest in accordance with their faith. It was only then apparent how unquestionably everyone in our town had accepted Father Zosima during his lifetime as a great saint. And those who came were far from being all of the humbler classes. This intense expectation on the part of believers displayed with such haste, such openness, even with impatience and almost insistence, Father Païssy considered an evil temptation, and though he had long foreseen something of the sort, the actual manifestation of the feeling was beyond anything he had expected. When he came across any of the monks who displayed this excitement, Father Païssy began to reprove them. "Such immediate expectation of something extraordinary," he said, "shows a levity, possible to worldly people but unseemly in us." But little attention was paid him and Father Païssy noticed it uneasily. Yet he himself (if the whole truth must be told) secretly, at the bottom of his heart, cherished almost the same hopes and could not but be aware of it, though he was indignant at the too impatient expectation around him, and saw in it light-mindedness and vanity. Nevertheless, it was particularly unpleasant to him to meet certain persons, whose presence aroused in him great misgivings. In the crowd in the dead man's cell he noticed with inward aversion (for which he immediately reproached himself) the presence of Rakitin, for example, and of the monk from Obdorsk, who was still staying in the monastery. Of both of them Father Païssy felt for some reason suddenly suspicious—though, indeed, he might well have felt the same about others. The monk from Obdorsk was conspicuous as the most fussy in the excited crowd. He was to be seen everywhere; everywhere he asked questions, everywhere he listened, on all sides he whispered with a peculiar, mysterious air. His expression showed the greatest impatience and even a sort of irritation. As for Rakitin, he, as appeared later, had come so early to the hermitage at the special request of Madame Khokhlakova. As soon as that good-hearted but weak-minded woman, who could not herself have been admitted to the hermitage, woke and heard of the death of Father Zosima, she was overtaken with such intense curiosity that she promptly despatched Rakitin to the hermitage, to keep a careful lookout and report to her by letter every half hour or so *everything that takes place.* She regarded Rakitin as a most religious and devout young man. He was particularly clever in getting round people and assuming whatever part he thought most to their taste, if he detected the slightest advantage to himself from doing so. It was a bright, clear day and many of the visitors were thronging about the tombs, which were particularly numerous round the church and scattered here and there about the hermitage. As he walked round the hermitage, Father Païssy suddenly remembered Alyosha and that he had not seen him for some time, not since the night. And he had no sooner thought of him than he at once noticed him in the furthest corner of the hermitage garden, sitting on the tombstone of a monk who had been famous long ago for his saintliness. He sat with his back to the hermitage and his face to the wall, and seemed to be hiding behind the tombstone. Going up to him, Father Païssy saw that he was weeping quietly but bitterly, with his face hidden in his hands and that his whole frame was shaking with sobs. Father Païssy stood over him for a little.

"Enough, dear son, enough, dear," he pronounced with feeling at last. "Why do you weep? Rejoice and weep not. Don't you know that this is the greatest of *his* days? Think only where he is now, at this moment!"

Alyosha glanced at him, uncovering his face, which was swollen with crying like a child's, but turned away at once without uttering a word and hid his face in his hands again.

"Maybe it is well," said Father Païssy thoughtfully: "weep if you must, Christ has sent you those tears." "Your touching tears are but a relief to your spirit and will serve to gladden your dear heart," he added to himself, walking away from Alyosha, and thinking lovingly of him. He moved away quickly, however, for he felt that he too might weep looking at him. Meanwhile the time was passing; the monastery services and the requiems for the dead followed in their due course. Father Païssy again took Father Iosif's place by the coffin and began reading the Gospel. But before three o'clock in the afternoon that something took place to which I alluded at the end of the last book, something so unexpected by all of us and so contrary to the general hope, that, I repeat, this trivial incident has been minutely remembered to this day in our town and all the surrounding neighborhood. I may add here, for myself personally, that I feel it almost repulsive to recall that event which caused such frivolous agitation and was such a stumbling block to many, though in reality it was the most natural and trivial matter. I would, of course, have omitted all mention of it in my story, if it had not exerted a very strong influence on the heart and soul of the chief, *though future*, hero of my story, Alyosha, forming a crisis and turning point in his spiritual development, giving a shock to his intellect, which finally strengthened it for the rest of his life and gave it a definite aim.

And so, to return to our story. When before dawn they laid Father Zosima's body in the coffin and brought it into the front room, the question of opening the windows was raised among those who were around the coffin. But this suggestion made casually by someone was unanswered and almost unnoticed. Some of those present may perhaps have inwardly noticed it, only to reflect that the anticipation of decay and the odor of corruption from the body of such a saint was an actual absurdity, calling for compassion (if not a smile) for the lack of faith and the frivolity it implied. For they expected something quite different.[4] And, behold, soon after midday there were signs of something, at first only observed in silence by those who came in and out and were evidently each afraid to communicate the thought in his mind. But by three o'clock those signs had become so clear and unmistakable, that the news swiftly reached all the monks and visitors in the hermitage, promptly penetrated to the monastery, throwing all the monks into amazement, and finally, in the shortest possible time, spread to the town, exciting everyone in it, believers, and unbelievers alike. The unbelievers rejoiced, and as for the believers some of them rejoiced even more than the unbelievers, for "men love the downfall and disgrace of the righteous," as the deceased elder had said in one of his exhortations. The fact is that an odor of corruption began to come from the coffin, growing gradually more marked, and by three o'clock it was quite unmistakable. In all the past history of our monastery, no such scandal could be recalled, and in no other circumstances could such a scandal have been possible, as showed itself in unseemly disorder immediately after this discovery among the very monks themselves. Afterwards, even many years afterwards, some

---

4. The remains of holy men were believed to be incorruptible. The absence of signs of decomposition was interpreted as an indication of sainthood.

sensible monks were amazed and horrified, when they recalled that day, that the scandal could have reached such proportions. For in the past, monks of very holy life had died, God-fearing old men, whose saintliness was acknowledged by all, yet from their humble coffins, too, the odor of corruption had come, naturally, as from all dead bodies, but that had caused no scandal nor even the slightest excitement. Of course there had been, in former times, saints in the monastery whose memory was carefully preserved and whose relics, according to tradition, showed no signs of corruption. This fact was regarded by the monks as touching and mysterious, and the tradition of it was cherished as something blessed and miraculous, and as a promise, by God's grace, of still greater glory from their tombs in the future. One such, whose memory was particularly cherished, was an old monk, Job, who had died seventy years before at the age of a hundred and five. He had been a celebrated ascetic, rigid in fasting and silence, had died long ago, in the second decade of this century, and his tomb was pointed out to all visitors on their arrival with peculiar respect and mysterious hints of great hopes connected with it. (That was the very tomb on which Father Païssy had found Alyosha sitting in the morning.) Another memory cherished in the monastery was that of the famous Father Varsonofy, who had preceded Father Zosima in the eldership. He was revered during his lifetime as a crazy saint by all the pilgrims to the monastery. There was a tradition that both of these had laid in their coffins as though alive, that they had shown no signs of decomposition when they were buried and that there had been a holy light in their faces. And some people even insisted that a sweet fragrance came from their bodies. Yet, in spite of these edifying memories, it would be difficult to explain the frivolity, absurdity and malice that were manifested beside the coffin of Father Zosima. It is my private opinion that several different causes were simultaneously at work, one of which was the deeply rooted hostility to the institution of elders as a pernicious innovation, an antipathy hidden deep in the hearts of many of the monks. Even more powerful was jealousy of the dead man's saintliness, so firmly established during his lifetime that it was almost a forbidden thing to question it. For though the late elder had won over many hearts, more by love than by miracles, and had gathered round him a mass of loving adherents, nonetheless, in fact, rather the more on that account he had awakened jealousy and so had come to have bitter enemies, secret and open, not only in the monastery but in the world outside it. He did no one any harm, but "Why do they think him so saintly?" And that question alone gradually repeated gave rise at last to an intense, insatiable hatred of him. That I believe was why many people were extremely delighted at the smell of decomposition which came so quickly, for not a day had passed since his death. At the same time there were some among those who had been hitherto reverently devoted to the elder, who were almost mortified and personally affronted by this incident. This was how the thing happened.

As soon as signs of decomposition had begun to appear, the whole aspect of the monks betrayed their secret motives in entering the cell. They went in, stayed a little while and hastened out to confirm the news to the crowd of other monks waiting outside. Some of the latter shook their heads mournfully, but others did not even care to conceal the delight, which gleamed unmistakably in their malignant eyes. And now no one reproached them for it, no one raised his voice in protest, which was strange, for the majority of the monks had been devoted to the dead elder. But it seemed as though God had in this case let the minority get the upper hand for a time. Visitors from outside, particularly of the educated class, soon went into the cell, too, with the same spying intent. Of the peasantry few went into the cell, though there were crowds of them at the gates of the hermitage. After three o'clock the rush of worldly visitors was greatly increased and this was no doubt owing to the shocking news. People were attracted who would not otherwise have come on that day and had not intended to come, and among them were some personages of high standing. But external decorum was still preserved and Father Païssy, with a stern face, continued firmly and distinctly reading aloud the Gospel, apparently not noticing what was taking place around him, though he had, in fact, observed something unusual long before. But at last the murmurs, first subdued but gradually louder and more confident, reached even him. "It shows God's judgment is not as man's," Father Païssy heard suddenly. The first to give utterance to this sentiment was a layman, an elderly official from the town, known to be a man of great piety. But he only repeated aloud what the monks had long been whispering. They had long before formulated this damning conclusion, and the worst of it was that a sort of triumphant satisfaction at that conclusion became more and more apparent every moment. Soon they began to lay aside even external decorum and almost seemed to feel they had a sort of right to discard it. "And for what reason can *this* have happened," some of the monks said, at first with a show of regret; "he had a small frame and his flesh was dried up on his bones, what was there to decay?"

"It must be a sign from heaven," others hastened to add, and their opinion was adopted at once without protest. For it was pointed out, too, that if the odor had been natural, as in the case of every dead sinner, it would have been apparent later, after a lapse of at least twenty-four hours, but this hasty prematureness of corruption "was in excess of nature," and so the finger of God was evident. It was meant for a sign. This conclusion seemed irresistible. Gentle father hieromonk Iosif, the librarian, a great favorite of the dead man's, tried to reply to some of the evil speakers that "this is not held everywhere alike," and that the incorruptibility of the bodies of the just was not a dogma of the Orthodox Church, but only an opinion, and that even in the most Orthodox regions, at Athos for instance, they were not greatly confounded by the odor of corruption, and there the chief sign of the glorification of the saved was not bodily incorruptibility, but the color of the bones when the bodies have lain many years in the earth and have decayed in it. "And if the bones are yellow as wax, that is the great sign that the Lord has glorified the dead saint, if they are not yellow but black, it shows that God has not deemed him worthy of such glory—that is the belief in Athos, a great place, where the Orthodox doctrine has been preserved from of old, unbroken and in its greatest purity," said Father Iosif in conclusion. But the meek father's words had little effect and even provoked a mocking retort. "That's all pedantry and innovation, no use listening to it," the monks decided. "We stick to the old doctrine, there are all sorts of innovations nowadays, are we to follow them all?" added others. "We have had as many holy fathers as they had. There they are among the Turks, they have forgotten everything. Their doctrine has long been impure and they have no bells even," the most sneering added.[5] Father Iosif walked away grieving the more since he had put forward his own opinion with little confidence as though scarcely believing in it himself. He foresaw with distress that something very unseemly was beginning and that there were positive signs of disobedience. Little by little, all the sensible monks were reduced to silence like Father Iosif. And so it came to pass that all who loved the elder and had accepted with devout obedience the institution of the eldership were all at once terribly cast down and glanced timidly in one another's faces, when they met. Those who were hostile to the institution of elders, as a novelty, held up their heads proudly. "There was no odor of corruption from the late elder Varsonofy, but a sweet fragrance," they recalled malignantly. "But he gained that glory not because he was an elder, but because he was a holy man." And this was followed by a shower of criticism and even blame of Father Zosima. "His teaching was false; he taught that life is a great joy and not a vale of tears," said some of the more unreasonable. "He followed the fashionable belief, he did not recognize material fire in hell," others, still more unreasonable, added. "He was not strict in fasting, allowed himself sweet things, ate cherry jam with his tea, ladies used to send it to him. Is it for a monk of strict rule to drink tea?" could be heard among some of the envious. "He sat in pride," the most malignant declared vindictively; "he considered himself a saint and he took it as his due when people knelt before him." "He abused the sacrament of confession," the fiercest opponents of the institution of elders added in a malicious whisper. And among these were some of the oldest monks, strictest in their devotion, genuine ascetics, who had kept silent during the life of the deceased elder, but now suddenly unsealed their lips. And this was terrible, for their words had great influence on young monks who were not yet firm in their convictions. The monk from Obdorsk heard all this attentively, heaving deep sighs and nodding his head. "Yes, clearly Father Ferapont was right in his judgment yesterday," and at that moment Father Ferapont himself made his appearance, as though on purpose to increase the confusion.

I have mentioned already that he rarely left his wooden cell by the apiary. He was seldom even seen at church and they overlooked this neglect on the grounds of his holy foolishness, and did not keep him to the rules binding on all the rest. But if the whole truth is to be told, they hardly had a choice about it. For it would have been discreditable to insist on burdening with the common regulations so great an ascetic and hermit, who prayed day and night (he even dropped asleep on his knees). If they had insisted, the monks would have said "he is holier than all of us and he follows a rule harder than ours. And if he does not go to church, it's because he knows when he ought to; he has his own rule." It was to avoid the chance of these sinful murmurs Father Ferapont was left in peace. As everyone was aware, Father Ferapont particularly disliked Father Zosima. And now the news had reached him in his hut that "God's judgment is not the same as man's," and that something had happened which was "in excess of nature." It may well be supposed that among the first to run to him with the news was the guest from Obdorsk, who had visited him the

---

5. Mount Athos was ruled by the Ottoman Empire, or Turks, from the fall of Byzantium in 1453 until it was seized by Greece in 1912. The detail about the churches on Athos lacking bells is taken from Parfeny's *Pilgrimage*. See p. 30.

evening before and left his cell terror-stricken. I have mentioned above, that though Father Païssy, standing firm and immovable reading the Gospel over the coffin, could not hear nor see what was passing outside the cell, he gauged most of it correctly in his heart, for he knew the men surrounding him well. He was not shaken by it, but awaited what would come next without fear, watching with penetration and insight for the outcome of the general excitement. Suddenly an extraordinary uproar in the passage in open defiance of decorum burst on his ears. The door was flung open and Father Ferapont appeared in the doorway. Behind him there could be seen accompanying him a crowd of monks, together with many people from the town. They did not, however, enter the cell, but stood at the bottom of the steps, waiting to see what Father Ferapont would say or do. For they felt with a certain awe, in spite of their audacity, that he had not come for nothing. Standing in the doorway, Father Ferapont raised his arms, and under his right arm the keen inquisitive little eyes of the monk from Obdorsk peeped in. He alone, in his intense curiosity, could not resist running up the steps after Father Ferapont. The others, on the contrary, pressed further back in sudden alarm when the door was noisily flung open. Holding his hands aloft, Father Ferapont suddenly roared:

"Casting out I cast out!" and, turning in all directions, he began at once making the sign of the cross at each of the four walls and four corners of the cell in succession. All who accompanied Father Ferapont immediately understood his action. For they knew he always did this wherever he went, and that he would not sit down or say a word, till he had driven out the evil spirits.

"Satan, go hence! Satan, go hence!" he repeated at each sign of the cross. "Casting out I cast out," he roared again. He was wearing his coarse gown girt with a rope. His bare chest, covered with gray hair, could be seen under his hempen shirt. His feet were bare. As soon as he began waving his arms, the cruel irons he wore under his gown could be heard clanking. Father Païssy paused in his reading, stepped forward and stood before him waiting.

"What have you come for, worthy Father? Why do you offend against good order? Why do you disturb the peace of the flock?" he said at last, looking sternly at him.

"What have I come for? You ask why? What is your faith?" shouted Father Ferapont in his holy foolishness. "I've come here to drive out your visitors, the unclean devils. I've come to see how many have gathered here while I have been away. I want to sweep them out with a birch broom."

"You cast out the evil spirit, but perhaps you are serving him yourself," Father Païssy went on fearlessly. "And who can say of himself 'I am holy.' Can you, Father?"

"I am unclean, not holy. I would not sit in an armchair and would not have them bow down to me as an idol," thundered Father Ferapont. "Nowadays folks destroy the true faith. The dead man, your saint," he turned to the crowd, pointing with his finger to the coffin, "did not believe in devils. He gave purgatives to keep off the devils. And so they have become as common as spiders in the corners. And now he has begun to stink himself. In that we see a great sign from God."

This had indeed happened once during Father Zosima's lifetime. One of the monks was haunted in his dreams and, later on, in waking moments, by visions of evil spirits. When in the utmost terror he confided this to Father Zosima, the elder had advised continual prayer and rigid fasting. But when that was of no use, he advised him, while persisting in prayer and fasting, to take a special medicine. Many persons were shocked at the time and wagged their heads as they talked over it—and most of all Father Ferapont, to whom some of the censorious had hastened to report this "extraordinary" counsel on the part of the elder.

"Go away, Father!" said Father Païssy, in a commanding voice, "it's not for man to judge but for God. Perhaps we see here a 'sign' which neither you, nor I, nor any one of us is able to comprehend. Go, Father, and do not trouble the flock!" he repeated impressively.

"He did not keep the fasts according to the rule and therefore the sign has come. That is clear and it's a sin to hide it," the fanatic, carried away by a zeal that outstripped his reason, would not be quieted. "He was seduced by sweets, ladies brought them to him in their pockets, he sipped tea, he worshipped his belly, filling it with sweet things and his mind with haughty thought. . . . And for this he is put to shame. . . ."

"You speak lightly, Father!" Father Païssy too raised his voice. "I admire your fasting and severities, but you speak lightly like some frivolous youth, fickle and childish. Go away, Father, I command you!" Father Païssy thundered in conclusion.

"I will go," said Ferapont, seeming somewhat taken aback, but still as bitter. "You learned men! You are so clever you look down upon my nothingness. I came hither with little learning and here I have forgotten what I did know, God himself has preserved me in my weakness from your subtlety."

Father Païssy stood over him, waiting resolutely. Father Ferapont paused and, suddenly leaning his cheek on his hand despondently, pronounced in a singsong voice, looking at the coffin of the dead elder:

"Tomorrow they will sing over him 'Our Helper and Defender'—a splendid anthem—and over me when I die all they'll sing will be 'What earthly joy'—a little canticle,"[6] he added with tearful regret. "You are proud and puffed up, this is a vain place!" he shouted suddenly like a madman, and with a wave of his hand he turned quickly and quickly descended the steps. The crowd awaiting him below wavered; some followed him at once and some lingered, for the cell was still open, and Father Païssy, following Father Ferapont on to the steps, stood watching him. But the excited old fanatic was not completely silenced. Walking twenty steps away, he suddenly turned towards the setting sun, raised both his arms and, as though someone had cut him down, fell to the ground with a loud scream.

"My God has conquered! Christ has conquered with the setting sun!" he shouted frantically, stretching up his hands to the sun, and falling face downwards on the ground, he sobbed like a little child, shaken by his tears and spreading out his arms on the ground. Then all rushed up to him; there were exclamations and sympathetic sobs . . . a kind of frenzy seemed to take possession of them all.

---

6. When the body of a monk is carried out (from the cell to the church and then after the chanting from the church to the graveyard), the canticle "What earthly joy . . ." is sung. If the deceased was a hieromonk, the canon "Our Helper and Defender" is sung instead. [*Dostoevsky's note.*]

"This is the one who is a saint! This is the one who is a holy man!" some cried aloud, losing their fear. "This is he who should be an elder," others added malignantly.

"He wouldn't be an elder . . . he would refuse . . . he wouldn't serve a cursed innovation . . . he wouldn't imitate their foolery," other voices chimed in at once. And it is hard to say how far they might have gone, but at that moment the bell rang summoning them to service. All began crossing themselves at once. Father Ferapont, too, got up and crossing himself went back to his cell without looking round, still uttering exclamations which were utterly incoherent. A few followed him, but the greater number dispersed, hastening to service. Father Païssy let Father Iosif read in his place and went down. The frantic outcries of bigots could not shake him, but his heart was suddenly filled with melancholy for some special reason and he felt that. He stood still and suddenly wondered, "Why am I sad even to dejection?" and immediately grasped with surprise that his sudden sadness was due to a very small and special cause. In the crowd thronging at the entrance to the cell, he had noticed Alyosha and he remembered that he had felt at once a pang at heart on seeing him. "Can that boy mean so much to my heart now?" he asked himself, wondering. At that moment Alyosha passed him, hurrying away, but not in the direction of the church. Their eyes met. Alyosha quickly turned away his eyes and dropped them to the ground, and from the boy's look alone, Father Païssy guessed what a great change was taking place in him at that moment.

"Have you, too, fallen into temptation?" cried Father Païssy. "Can you be with those of little faith?" he added mournfully.

Alyosha stood still and gazed vaguely at Father Païssy, but quickly turned his eyes away again and again looked on the ground. He stood sideways and did not turn his face to Father Païssy, who watched his attentively.

"Where are you hastening? The bell calls to service," he asked again, but again Alyosha gave no answer.

"Are you leaving the hermitage? What, without asking leave, without asking a blessing?"

Alyosha suddenly gave a wry smile, cast a strange, very strange, look at the father to whom his former guide, the former sovereign of his heart and mind, his beloved elder, had confided him as he lay dying. And suddenly, still without speaking, waved his hand, as though not caring even to be respectful, and with rapid steps walked towards the gates away from the hermitage.

"You will come back again!" murmured Father Païssy, looking after him with sorrowful surprise.

Chapter II

A Critical Moment

Father Païssy, of course, was not wrong when he decided that his "dear boy" would come back again. Perhaps indeed, to some extent, he penetrated with insight into the true meaning of Alyosha's spiritual condition. Yet I must frankly admit that it would be very difficult for me to give a

clear account of that strange, vague moment in the life of the hero of my
tale whom I love so much and who was still so young. To Father Païssy's
sorrowful question, "Are you too with those of little faith?" I could of
course confidently answer for Alyosha no, he is not with those of little
faith. Quite the contrary. Indeed, all his trouble came from the fact that
he was of great faith. But still the trouble was there and was so agonizing
that even long afterwards Alyosha thought of that sorrowful day as one of
the bitterest and most fatal days of his life. If the question is asked: "Could
all his grief and disturbance have been only due to the fact that his elder's
body had shown signs of premature decomposition instead of at once performing miracles?" I must answer without beating about the bush, "Yes, it
certainly was." I would only beg the reader not to be in too great a hurry to
laugh at my young man's pure heart. I am far from intending to apologize
for him or to justify his innocent faith on the ground of his youth, or the
little progress he had made in his studies, or any such reason. I must
declare, on the contrary, that I have genuine respect for the qualities of
his heart. No doubt another youth, who received impressions cautiously,
whose love was lukewarm, and whose mind was too prudent for his age
(and therefore cheap), such a young man might, I admit, have avoided
what happened to my young man. But in some cases it is really more creditable to be carried away by an emotion, however unreasonable, which
springs from a great love, than to be unmoved. And this is even truer in
youth, for a young man who is always sensible is to be suspected and is of
little worth—that's my opinion! "But," reasonable people will exclaim perhaps, "every young man cannot believe in such a superstition and your
hero is no model for others." To this I reply again, yes! my young man had
faith, a faith holy and steadfast, but still I am not going to apologize for
him.

Don't you see: though I declared above, and perhaps too hastily, that I
would not explain, apologize for, or justify my hero, I see that some explanation is necessary for the understanding of the rest of my story. Let me
say then, it was not a question of miracles. There was no frivolous and
impatient expectation of miracles in his mind. And Alyosha needed no
miracles at the time, for the triumph of some preconceived idea—oh, no,
not at all—what he saw before all was one figure—the figure of his beloved
elder, the figure of that holy man whom he revered with such adoration.
The fact is that all the love that lay concealed in his pure young heart for
"everyone and everything" had, for the past year, been concentrated—
and perhaps wrongly so—primarily on one being, at least in the strongest
impulses of his heart, his beloved elder, now dead. It is true that being
had for so long been accepted by him as his ideal, that all his young
strength and energy could not but turn towards that ideal, even to the
forgetting at the moment "of everyone and everything." He remembered
afterwards how, on that terrible day, he had entirely forgotten his brother
Dmitri, about whom he had been so anxious and troubled the day before;
he had forgotten too to take the two hundred rubles to Ilyusha's father,
though he had so warmly intended to do so the preceding evening. But
again it was not miracles he needed but only "the higher justice" which
had been in his belief outraged by the blow that had so suddenly and cruelly wounded his heart. And what does it signify that this "justice" looked
for by Alyosha inevitably took the shape of miracles to be wrought imme-

diately by the ashes of his adored teacher? Why, everyone in the monastery cherished the same thought and the same hope, even those whose intellects Alyosha revered, Father Païssy himself, for instance. And so Alyosha, untroubled by doubts, clothed his dreams too in the same form as all the rest. And a whole year of life in the monastery had formed the habit of this expectation in his heart. But it was justice, justice, he thirsted for, not simply miracles. And now the man who should, he believed, have been exalted above everyone in the whole world, that man, instead of receiving the glory that was his due, was suddenly degraded and dishonored! What for? Who had judged him? Who could have decreed this? Those were the questions that wrung his inexperienced and virginal heart. He could not endure without mortification, without resentment even, that the holiest of holy men should have been exposed to the jeering and spiteful mockery of the frivolous crowd so inferior to him. Even had there been no miracles, had there been nothing marvelous to justify his hopes, why this indignity, why this humiliation, why this premature decay, "in excess of nature," as the spiteful monks said? Why this "sign from heaven," which they so triumphantly acclaimed in company with Father Ferapont, and why did they believe they had gained the right to acclaim it? Where is the finger of Providence? Why did Providence hide its face "at the most critical moment" (so Alyosha thought it), as though voluntarily submitting to the blind, dumb, pitiless laws of nature?

That was why Alyosha's heart was breaking, and, of course, as I have said already, the sting of it all was that the man he loved above everything on earth should be put to shame and humiliated! This murmuring may have been shallow and unreasonable in my hero, but I repeat again for the third time—and am prepared to admit that it, too, might be shallow—I am glad that my hero showed himself not too reasonable at that moment, for any man of sense will always come back to reason in time, but, if love does not gain the upper hand in a boy's heart at such an exceptional moment, when will it? I will not, however, omit to mention something strange, which came for a time to the surface of Alyosha's mind at this fatal and obscure moment. This new *something* was the harassing impression left by the conversation with his brother Ivan, which now persistently haunted Alyosha's mind. At this moment it haunted him. Oh, it was not that something of the fundamental, elemental, so to speak, faith of his soul had been shaken. He loved his God and believed in Him steadfastly, though he was suddenly murmuring against Him. Yet a vague but tormenting and evil impression left by his conversation with his brother Ivan the day before, suddenly revived again now in his soul and seemed forcing its way to the surface. It had begun to get dusk when Rakitin, crossing the pine copse from the hermitage to the monastery, suddenly noticed Alyosha, lying face downwards on the ground under a tree, not moving and apparently asleep. He went up and called him by his name.

"You here, Alexey? Can you have . . ." he began wondering but broke off. He had meant to say, "Can you have *come to this*?" Alyosha did not look at him, but from a slight movement Rakitin at once saw that he heard and understood him.

"What's the matter?" he went on; but the surprise in his face gradually passed into a smile that became more and more ironical.

"Listen, I've been looking for you for the last two hours. You suddenly disappeared. What are you about? What holy nonsense is this? You might just look at me . . ."

Alyosha raised his head, sat up and leaned his back against the tree. He was not crying, but there was a look of suffering and irritability in his face. He did not look at Rakitin, however, but looked away to one side of him.

"Do you know your face is quite changed? There's none of your famous mildness to be seen in it. Are you angry with someone? Have they been ill-treating you?"

"Let me alone," said Alyosha suddenly, with a weary gesture of his hand, still looking away from him.

"Oho! So that's how we are feeling! So you can shout at people like other mortals. That is a comedown from the angels. I say, Aloyshka, you have surprised me, do you hear? I mean it. It's long since I've been surprised at anything here. I always took you for an educated man . . ."

Alyosha at last looked at him, but vaguely, as though scarcely understanding what he said.

"Can you really be so upset simply because your old man has begun to stink? You don't mean to say you seriously believed that he was going to start pulling off miracles?" exclaimed Rakitin, genuinely surprised again.

"I believe, I believe, I want to believe, and I will believe, what more do you want?" cried Alyosha irritably.

"Nothing at all, my boy. What the devil, why no schoolboy of thirteen believes in that now. But still . . . ah, the devil. So now you are in a temper with your God, you are rebelling against Him; He didn't promote him. He hasn't bestowed the order of merit! Eh, what a bunch!"

Alyosha gazed a long while with his eyes half closed at Rakitin, and there was a sudden gleam in his eyes . . . but not of anger with Rakitin.

"I am not rebelling against my God; I simply 'don't accept His world.'" Alyosha suddenly smiled a forced smile.

"How do you mean, you don't accept the world?" Rakitin thought a moment over his answer. "What idiocy is this?"

Alyosha did not answer.

"Come, enough nonsense, now to business. Have you had anything to eat today?"

"I don't remember . . . I think I have."

"You ought to have something, to judge by your face. It makes one sorry to look at you. You didn't sleep all night either, I hear, you had a meeting in there. And then all this fuss and bother afterwards. Most likely you've had nothing to eat but a mouthful of holy bread. I've got some sausage in my pocket; I've brought it from the town in case of need, only you won't eat sausage. . . ."

"Give me some."

"Well! You really are going all out! Why, it's a regular mutiny, with barricades! Well, my boy, we must make the most of it. Come to my place . . . I wouldn't mind a drop of vodka myself, I am tired to death. Vodka is going too far for you, I suppose . . . or would you like some?"

"Give me some vodka too."

"Well, now! You surprise me, brother!" Rakitin looked at him in amazement. "Well, one way or another, vodka or sausage, this is a jolly fine chance and mustn't be missed. Come along."

Alyosha got up in silence and followed Rakitin.

"If your brother Vanechka could see this—wouldn't he be surprised! By the way, your brother Ivan Fyodorovich set off to Moscow this morning, did you know?"

"Yes," answered Alyosha listlessly, and suddenly the image of his brother Dmitri rose before his mind. But only for a minute, and though it reminded him of something that must not be put off for a moment, some duty, some terrible obligation, even that reminder made no impression on him, did not reach his heart and instantly faded out of his mind and was forgotten. But, a long while afterwards, Alyosha remembered this.

"Your brother Vanechka once declared that I was a 'liberal nonentity without any talent.' Once you, too, could not resist letting me know I was 'dishonorable.' Well! I would like to see what your talents and sense of honor will do for you now." This phrase Rakitin finished to himself in a whisper. "Ha, listen!" he said aloud, "let's go by the path beyond the monastery straight to the town. Hmm! I ought to go to Madame Khokhlakova's by the way. Just think, I've written to tell her everything that happened, and would you believe it, she answered me instantly in pencil (the lady has a passion for writing notes) that she would never have expected 'such conduct from a man of such a reverend character as Father Zosima.' That was her very word: 'conduct.' She is angry too. Eh, you are a bunch! Wait!" he cried suddenly again. He suddenly stopped and taking Alyosha by the shoulder made him stop too.

"Do you know, Alyoshka," he peeped inquisitively in his eyes, absorbed in a sudden new thought which had dawned on him, and though he was laughing outwardly he was evidently afraid to utter that new idea aloud, so difficult he still found it to believe in the strange and unexpected mood in which he now saw Alyosha. "Alyoshka, do you know where we had better go?" he brought out at last timidly, and insinuatingly.

"I don't care . . . where you like."

"Let's go to Grushenka, eh? Will you come?" pronounced Rakitin at last, trembling with timid suspense.

"Let's go to Grushenka," Alyosha answered calmly, at once, and this prompt and calm agreement was such a surprise to Rakitin that he almost started back.

"Well! Really!" he cried in amazement, but seizing Alyosha firmly by the arm he led him along the path still dreading that he would change his mind. They walked along in silence, Rakitin was positively afraid to talk.

"And how glad she will be, how delighted," he muttered, but lapsed into silence again. And indeed it was not to please Grushenka he was taking Alyosha to see her. He was a practical person and never undertook anything without a prospect of gain for himself. His object in this case was twofold, first a revengeful desire to see "the downfall of the righteous," and Alyosha's fall "from the saints to the sinners," over which he was already gloating in his imagination, and in the second place he had in view a certain material gain for himself, of which more will be said later.

"So the moment has come," he thought to himself with spiteful glee, "and we shall catch it on the fly, for it's just what we want."

Chapter III

An Onion

Grushenka lived in the busiest part of town, near the cathedral square, in a small wooden lodge in the courtyard belonging to the house of the widow Morozova. The house was a large stone building of two stories, old and very ugly. The widow led a secluded life with her two nieces, who were also elderly spinsters. She had no need to let her lodge, but everyone knew that she had taken in Grushenka as a lodger, four years before, solely to please her kinsman, the merchant Samsonov, who was known to be the girl's protector. It was said that the jealous old man's object in placing his "favorite" with the widow Morozova was that the old woman should keep a sharp eye on her new lodger's conduct. But this sharp eye soon proved to be unnecessary, and in the end the widow Morozova seldom met Grushenka and did not worry her by looking after her in any way. It is true that four years had passed since the old man had brought the slim, delicate, shy, timid, dreamy, and sad girl of eighteen from the chief town of the province, and much had happened since then. Little was known of the girl's history in the town and that little was vague. Nothing more had been learned during the last four years, even after many persons had become interested in the "extraordinary beauty" into whom Agrafena Alexandrovna had meanwhile developed. There were rumors that she had been betrayed by someone at seventeen, some sort of officer, and immediately afterwards abandoned by him. The officer had gone away and afterwards married, while Grushenka had been left in poverty and disgrace. It was said, however, that though Grushenka had been raised from destitution by the old man, Samsonov, she came of a respectable family belonging to the clerical class, that she was the daughter of some deacon or something of the sort.[7] And now after four years the sensitive, injured and pathetic little orphan had become a plump, rosy beauty of the Russian type, a woman of bold and determined character, proud and insolent. She had a good head for business, was acquisitive, saving and careful, and by fair means or foul had succeeded, it was said, in amassing a little fortune. There was only one point on which all were agreed. Grushenka was not easily to be approached and except her aged protector there had not been one man who could boast of her favors during those four years. It was a positive fact, for there had been a good many, especially during the last two years, who had attempted to obtain those favors. But all their efforts had been in vain and some of these suitors had been forced to beat an undignified and even comic retreat, owing to the firm and ironical resistance they met from the strong-willed young person. It was known too that the young person had, especially of late, been given to what is called "gesheft,"[8] and that she had shown marked abilities in that direction, so that many people began to call her a real Yid. It was not that she lent money on interest, but it was known, for instance, that she had for

---

7. Grushenka's social status is thus similar to that of Sofya Ivanovna, Fyodor Pavlovich's second wife. Rakitin was ashamed of his association with the clerical class, but in Grushenka's case, belonging to this class elevates her above the status of harlot which many in town ascribe to her.
8. "Gesheft" is Yiddish for "business" (from the German word *Geschäft*); it is used here to signify unscrupulous moneymaking.

some time past, in partnership with Fyodor Pavlovich Karamazov, actually invested in the purchase of bad debts for a trifle, a tenth of their nominal value, and afterwards had made out of them ten times their value. The ailing old widower Samsonov, a man of large fortune, was stingy and merciless. He tyrannized over his grown-up sons, but, for the last year during which he had lost the use of his swollen legs, he had fallen greatly under the influence of his protégée, whom he had at first kept strictly and in humble surroundings "on Lenten fare" as the wits said at the time. But Grushenka had succeeded in emancipating herself, while she established in him a boundless belief in her fidelity. The old man, now long since dead, had had a large business in his day and was also a noteworthy character, miserly and hard as flint. Though Grushenka's hold upon him was so strong that he could not live without her (it had been so especially for the last two years), he did not settle any considerable fortune on her and would not have been moved to do so, if she had threatened to leave him. But he had presented her with a small sum, and even that was a surprise to everyone when it became known. "You are a wench with brains," he said to her, when he gave her eight thousand rubles, "and you must look after yourself, but let me tell you that except your yearly allowance as before, you'll get nothing more from me to the day of my death, and I'll leave you nothing in my will either." And he kept his word; he died and left everything to his sons, whom, with their wives and children, he had treated all his life as servants. Grushenka was not even mentioned in his will. All this became known afterwards. He helped Grushenka with his advice to increase her capital and put business in her way. When Fyodor Pavlovich, who first came into contact with Grushenka over a piece of speculation, ended to his own surprise by falling madly in love with her, old Samsonov, gravely ill as he was, was immensely amused. It is remarkable that throughout their whole acquaintance Grushenka was absolutely and spontaneously open with the old man, and he seems to have been the only person in the world with whom she was so. Of late, when Dmitri Fyodorovich too had come on the scene with his love, the old man stopped laughing. On the contrary, he once gave Grushenka a stern and earnest piece of advice. "If you have to choose between the two, father or son, you'd better choose the old man, if only you make sure the old scoundrel will marry you and settle some fortune on you beforehand. But don't keep on with the captain, you'll get no good out of that." These were the very words of the old voluptuary, who felt already that his death was not far off and who actually died five months later. I will note, too, in passing, that although many in our town knew of the grotesque and monstrous rivalry of the Karamazovs, father and son, the object of which was Grushenka, scarcely anyone understood what really underlay her attitude to both of them. Even Grushenka's two servants (after the catastrophe of which we will speak later) testified in court that she received Dmitri Fyodorovich simply from fear because "he threatened to murder her." These servants were an old cook, ailing and almost deaf, who came from Grushenka's old home, and her granddaughter, a smart young girl of twenty, who performed the duties of a maid. Grushenka lived very economically and her surroundings were anything but luxurious. Her lodge consisted of three rooms furnished with old mahogany furniture in the fashion of the 1820s, belonging to her landlady.

It was quite dark when Rakitin and Alyosha entered her rooms, yet they were not lighted up. Grushenka was lying down in her drawing room on the big, hard, clumsy sofa, with a mahogany back. The sofa was covered with shabby and ragged leather. Under her head she had two white down pillows taken from her bed. She was lying stretched out motionless on her back with her hands behind her head. She was dressed as though expecting someone, in a black silk dress, with a dainty lace fichu on her head, which was very becoming. Over her shoulders was thrown a lace shawl pinned with a massive gold brooch. She certainly was expecting someone. She lay as though impatient and weary, her face rather pale and her lips and eyes hot, restlessly tapping the arm of the sofa with the tip of her right foot. The appearance of Rakitin and Alyosha caused a slight excitement. From the hall they could hear Grushenka leap up from the sofa and cry out in a frightened voice, "Who's there?" But the maid met the visitors and at once called back to her mistress.

"It's not him, ma'am, it's nothing, only other visitors."

"What can be the matter?" muttered Rakitin leading Alyosha into the drawing room. Grushenka was standing by the sofa as though still alarmed. A thick coil of her dark brown hair escaped from its lace covering and fell on her right shoulder, but she did not notice it and did not put it back till she had gazed at her visitors and recognized them.

"Ah, it's you, Rakitka? You quite frightened me. Whom have you brought? Who is this with you? Good heavens, you have brought him!" she exclaimed, recognizing Alyosha.

"Do send for candles!" said Rakitin, with the free-and-easy air of a most intimate friend, who is privileged to give orders in the house.

"Candles . . . of course, candles . . . Fenya, fetch him a candle . . . Well, you have chosen a moment to bring him!" she exclaimed again, nodding towards Alyosha, and turning to the mirror she began quickly fastening up her hair with both hands. She seemed displeased.

"Haven't I managed to please you?" asked Rakitin, instantly almost offended.

"You frightened me, Rakitka, that's what it is." Grushenka turned with a smile to Alyosha. "Don't be afraid of me, my dear Alyosha, you can't think how glad I am to see you, my unexpected visitor. But you frightened me, Rakitka, I thought it was Mitya breaking in. You see, I deceived him just now, I made him promise to believe me and I told him a lie. I told him that I was going to spend the evening with my old man, Kuzma Kuzmich, and should be there till late counting up his money. I always spend one whole evening a week with him making up his accounts. We lock ourselves in and he counts on the reckoning beads while I sit and put things down in the book. I am the only person he trusts. Mitya believes that I am there, but I came back and have been sitting locked in here, expecting some news. How was it Fenya let you in? Fenya, Fenya, run out to the gate, open it and look about whether the captain is to be seen! Perhaps he is hiding and spying, I am dreadfully frightened."

"There's no one there, Agrafena Alexandrovna, I've just looked out, I keep running to peep through the crack, I am in fear and trembling myself."

"Are the shutters fastened, Fenya? And we must draw the curtains— that's better!" She drew the heavy curtains herself. "He'd rush in at once

if he saw a light. I am afraid of your brother Mitya today, Alyosha."
Grushenka spoke loudly and, though she was alarmed, she seemed almost
in some sort of frenzy.

"Why are you so afraid of Mitenka today?" inquired Rakitin. "I would
have thought you were not timid with him, you'd twist him round your
little finger."

"I tell you, I am expecting news, priceless news, so I don't want Mitenka
at all. And he didn't believe, I feel he didn't, that I would stay at Kuzma
Kuzmich's. He must be in his ambush now, behind Fyodor Pavlovich's,
in the garden, watching for me. And if he's there, he won't come here,
so much the better! But I really have been to Kuzma Kuzmich's, Mitya
escorted me there. I told him I should stay there till midnight, and I asked
him to be sure to come at midnight to fetch me home. He went away and
I sat ten minutes with Kuzma Kuzmich and came back here again. Ugh, I
was afraid, I ran for fear of meeting him."

"And why are you so dressed up? What a curious cap you've got on!"

"How curious you are yourself, Rakitin! I tell you, I am expecting a
message. If the message comes, I shall fly, I shall gallop away and you will
see no more of me. That's why I am dressed up, so as to be ready."

"And where are you flying to?"

"If you know too much, you'll get old too soon."

"Upon my word! You are highly delighted . . . I've never seen you like
this before. You are dressed up as if you were going to a ball." Rakitin
looked her up and down.

"Much you know about balls."

"And do you know much about them?"

"I have seen a ball. The year before last, Kuzma Kuzmich's son was
married and I looked on from the gallery. Do you suppose I want to be
talking to you, Rakitka, while a prince like this is standing here.[9] Such a
visitor! Alyosha, my dear boy, I gaze at you and can't believe my eyes.
Good heavens, can you have come here to see me! To tell you the truth I
never had a thought of seeing you and I didn't think that you would ever
come and see me. Though this is not the moment now, I am awfully glad
to see you. Sit down on the sofa, here, that's right, my bright young moon.
I really can't take it in even now. . . . Eh, Rakitka, if only you had brought
him yesterday or the day before! But I am glad as it is! Perhaps it's better
he has come now, at such a moment, and not the day before yesterday."

She gaily sat down beside Alyosha on the sofa, looking at him with positive delight. And she really was glad, she was not lying when she said so.
Her eyes glowed, her lips laughed, but it was a good-natured merry laugh.
Alyosha had not expected to see such a kind expression on her face. . . .
He had hardly met her till the day before, he had formed an alarming idea
of her, and had been horribly struck the day before by the spiteful and
treacherous trick she had played on Katerina Ivanovna. He was greatly
surprised to find her now altogether different from what he had expected.
And, crushed as he was by his own sorrow, his eyes involuntarily rested on
her with attention. Her whole manner seemed changed for the better
since yesterday, there was scarcely any trace of that mawkish sweetness in

---

9. Many of Grushenka's expressions in this scene are drawn from Russian folklore. Saint Alexey
is referred to as a prince in Russian folk legends.

her speech, of those soft and mannered movements. Everything was simple, simple-hearted, her gestures were rapid, direct, confiding, but she was greatly excited.

"Dear me, how everything comes together today," she chattered on again. "And why I am so glad to see you, Alyosha, I couldn't say myself! If you ask me, I couldn't tell you."

"Come, don't you know why you're glad?" said Rakitin, grinning. "You always used to pester me to bring him, you'd some object, I suppose."

"I had a different object once, but now that's over, this is not the moment. I want you to have something nice, that's what! I am so good-natured now. You sit down, too, Rakitka, why are you standing? You've sat down already? There's no fear of Rakitushka's forgetting to look after himself. Look, Alyosha, he's sitting there opposite us, so offended that I didn't ask him to sit down before you. Ugh, Rakitka is such a one to take offense!" laughed Grushenka. "Don't be angry, Rakitka, I'm kind today. Why are you so depressed, Alyoshechka, are you afraid of me?" she peeped into his eyes with merry mockery.

"He's sad. The promotion has not been given," boomed Rakitin.

"What promotion?"

"His elder stinks."

"What do you mean, 'stinks'? You are talking some nonsense, you want to say something nasty. Be quiet, stupid! Let me sit on your knee, Alyosha, like this." She suddenly skipped forward and jumped, laughing, on his knee, like a nestling kitten, with her right arm about his neck. "I'll cheer you up, my pious boy. Yes, really, will you let me sit on your knee, you won't be angry? If you tell me, I'll get off."

Alyosha did not speak. He sat afraid to move, he heard her words, "If you tell me, I'll get off," but he did not answer, he seemed numb. But there was nothing in his heart such as Rakitin, for instance, watching him malignantly from his corner, might have expected or fancied. The great grief in his heart swallowed up every sensation that might have been aroused, and, if only he could have thought clearly at that moment, he would have realised that he had now the strongest armor to protect him from every lust and temptation. Yet in spite of the vague irresponsiveness of his spiritual condition and the sorrow that overwhelmed him, he could not help wondering at a new and strange sensation in his heart. This woman, this "dreadful" woman, had no terror for him now, none of that terror that had stirred in his soul at any passing thought of woman, if such thoughts occurred to him at all. On the contrary, this woman, dreaded above all women, sitting now on his knee, holding him in her arms, aroused in him now a quite different, unexpected, peculiar feeling, a feeling of the intensest and purest interest without a trace of fear, of his former terror. That was what instinctively surprised him.

"You've talked nonsense enough," cried Rakitin, "you'd much better give us some champagne. You owe it me, you know you do!"

"Yes, I really do. Do you know, Alyosha, I promised him champagne on the top of everything, if he'd bring you? I'll have some too! Fenya, Fenya, bring us the bottle Mitya left! Look sharp! Though I am so stingy, I'll stand a bottle, not for you, Rakitka, you're a toadstool, but he is a prince! And though my heart is full of something very different, so be it, I'll drink with you. I long for some dissipation."

"But what is the matter with you? And what is this message may I ask, or is it a secret?" Rakitin put in inquisitively, doing his best to pretend not to notice the snubs that were being continually aimed at him.

"Ech, it's not a secret, and you know it, too," Grushenka said, in a voice suddenly anxious, turning her head towards Rakitin, and drawing a little away from Alyosha, though she still sat on his knee with her arm round his neck. "My officer is coming, Rakitin, my officer is coming."

"I heard he was coming, but is he so near?"

"He is at Mokroe now, he'll send a messenger from there, so he wrote, I got a letter from him today. I am expecting the messenger every minute."

"You don't say so! Why at Mokroe?"

"That's a long story, I've told you enough."

"That Mitenka will really be up to something now—you bet! Does he know or doesn't he?"

"He know! Of course he doesn't. If he knew, there would be murder. But I am not afraid of that now, I am not afraid of his knife. Be quiet, Rakitka, don't remind me of Dmitri Fyodorovich, he has bruised my heart. And I don't want to think of that at this moment. I can think of Alyoshechka here, I can look at Alyoshechka . . . smile at me dear, cheer up, smile at my foolishness, at my pleasure. . . . Ah, he's smiling, he's smiling! How kindly he looks at me! And you know, Alyosha, I've been thinking all this time you were angry with me, because of the day before yesterday, because of that young lady. I was a cur, that's what. . . . But it's a good thing it happened so. It was a horrid thing, but a good thing too." Grushenka smiled dreamily and a little cruel line showed in her smile. "Mitya told me that she screamed out that I 'ought to be flogged.' I did insult her dreadfully. She sent for me, she wanted to make a conquest of me, to win me over with her chocolate. . . . No, it's a good thing it did end like that." She smiled again. "But I am still afraid of your being angry."

"Yes, that's really true," Rakitin put in suddenly with genuine surprise. "Alyosha, she is really afraid of a chicken like you."

"He is a chicken to you, Rakitka, that's what . . . because you've no conscience, that's what! You see, I love him with all my soul, that's what! Alyosha, do you believe I love you with all my soul?"

"Ah, you shameless woman! She is making you a declaration, Alexey!"

"Well, what of it, I love him!"

"And what about your officer? And the priceless message from Mokroe?"

"That is quite different."

"That's a woman's way of looking at it!"

"Don't you make me angry, Rakitka." Grushenka caught him up hotly. "This is quite different. I love Alyosha in a different way. It's true, Alyosha, I had sly designs on you before, for I am horrid, violent, but at other times I've looked upon you, Alyosha, as my conscience. I've kept thinking 'how anyone like that must despise a nasty thing like me.' I thought that the day before yesterday, as I ran home from the young lady's. I have thought of you a long time in that way, Alyosha, and Mitya knows, I've talked to him about it. Mitya understands. Would you believe it, I sometimes look at you and feel ashamed, utterly ashamed of myself. . . . And how, and since when, I began to think about you like that, I can't say, I don't remember . . ."

Fenya came in and put a tray with an uncorked bottle and three glasses of champagne on the table.

"Here's the champagne!" cried Rakitin. "You're excited, Agrafena Alexandrovna, and not yourself. When you've had a glass of champagne, you'll be ready to dance. Eh, they can't even do that properly," he added, looking at the bottle. "The old woman's poured it out in the kitchen and the bottle's been brought in warm and without a cork. Well, let me have some, anyway."

He went up to the table, took a glass, emptied it at one gulp and poured himself out another.

"One doesn't often stumble upon champagne," he said, licking his lips. "Now, Alyosha, take a glass, show what you can do! What shall we drink to? The gates of paradise? Take a glass, Grushka, you drink to the gates of paradise, too."

"What gates of paradise?"

She took a glass, Alyosha took his, tasted it and put it back.

"No, I'd better not," he smiled gently.

"And you bragged!" cried Rakitin.

"Well, if so, I won't either," chimed in Grushenka, "I really don't want any. You can drink the whole bottle alone, Rakitka. If Alyosha has some, I will."

"What touching sentimentality!" said Rakitin tauntingly, "and she's sitting on his knee, too! He's got something to grieve over, but what's the matter with you? He is rebelling against his God and ready to eat sausage . . ."

"How so?"

"His elder died today, Father Zosima, the saint."

"So Father Zosima is dead," cried Grushenka. "Good God, I did not know!" She crossed herself devoutly. "Goodness, what have I been doing, sitting on his knee like this at such a moment!" She started up as though in dismay, instantly slipped off his knee and sat down on the sofa. Alyosha fixed a long wondering look upon her and a light seemed to dawn in his face.

"Rakitin," he said suddenly, in a firm and loud voice; "don't taunt me with having rebelled against God. I don't want to feel angry with you, so you must be kinder, too. I've lost a treasure such as you have never had, and you cannot judge me now. You had much better look at her—do you see how she has pity on me? I came here to find a wicked soul—I felt drawn to evil because I was base and evil myself, and I've found a true sister, I have found a treasure—a loving heart. She had pity on me just now. . . . Agrafena Alexandrovna, I am speaking of you. You've raised my soul from the depths."

Alyosha's lips were quivering and he caught his breath.

"She has saved you, it seems," laughed Rakitin spitefully. "And she meant to get you in her clutches, do you realize that?"

"Wait, Rakitka." Grushenka jumped up. "Hush, both of you. Now I'll tell you all about it. Hush, Alyosha, your words make me ashamed, for I am bad and not good—that's what I am. And you hush, Rakitka, because you are telling lies. I had the low idea of trying to get him in my clutches, but now you are lying, now it's all different. And don't let me hear anything more from you, Rakitka." All this Grushenka said with extreme emotion.

"They are both crazy," said Rakitin, looking at them with amazement. "I feel as though I were in a madhouse. They're both getting so feeble they'll begin crying in a minute."

"I shall begin to cry, I shall," repeated Grushenka. "He called me his sister and I shall never forget that. Only let me tell you, Rakitka, though I am bad, I did give away an onion."

"An onion? Oh, the devil, you really are crazy."

Rakitin wondered at their exaltation. He was aggrieved and annoyed, though he might have reflected that for each of them everything that could shake their souls had just come together in a way that does not happen often in life. But though Rakitin was very sensitive about everything that concerned himself, he was very obtuse as regards the feelings and sensations of others—partly from his youth and inexperience, partly from his intense egoism.

"You see, Alyoshechka," Grushenka turned to him with a nervous laugh. "I was boasting when I told Rakitin I had given away an onion, but it's not to boast I tell you about it. It's only a story, but it's a nice story.[1] I used to hear it when I was a child from Matryona, my cook, who is still with me. It's like this. Once upon a time there was a woman and a very wicked woman she was. And she died and did not leave a single good deed behind. The devils caught her and plunged her into the lake of fire. So her guardian angel stood and wondered what good deed of hers he could remember to tell to God; 'she once pulled up an onion in her garden,' said he, 'and gave it to a beggar woman.' And God answered: 'You take that onion then, hold it out to her in the lake, and let her take hold and be pulled out. And if you can pull her out of the lake, let her come to Paradise, but if the onion breaks, then the woman must stay where she is.' The angel ran to the woman and held out the onion to her; 'Come,' said he, 'catch hold and I'll pull you out.' And he began cautiously pulling her out. He had just pulled her right out, when the other sinners in the lake, seeing she was being drawn out, began catching hold of her so as to be pulled out with her. But she was a very wicked woman and she began kicking them. 'I'm to be pulled out, not you. It's my onion, not yours.' As soon as she said that, the onion broke. And the woman fell into the lake and she is burning there to this day. So the angel wept and went away. So that's the story, Alyosha; I know it, by heart, for I am that wicked woman myself. I boasted to Rakitka that I had given away an onion, but to you I'll say: 'I've done nothing but give away *one* onion all my life, that's the only good deed I've done.' So don't praise me, Alyosha, don't think me good, I am bad, I'm a wicked woman and you make me ashamed if you praise me. Eh, I must confess everything. Listen, Alyosha. I was so anxious to get hold of you that I promised Rakitin twenty-five rubles if he would bring you to me. Stop, Rakitin, wait!" She went with rapid steps to the table, opened a drawer, pulled out a purse and took from it a twenty-five ruble bill.

"What nonsense! What nonsense!" cried Rakitin, disconcerted.

"Take it. Rakitka, I owe it you, there's no fear of your refusing it, you asked for it yourself." And she threw the bill to him.

---

1. In a letter to his editor Lyubimov written in September 1879, Dostoevsky explains that he heard the story of the onion from a peasant woman. He believed that it was being printed for the first time, but a similar version had appeared in a collection of Russian folk tales published in 1859.

"As if I'd refuse it," boomed Rakitin, obviously abashed, but carrying off his confusion with a swagger. "That will come in very handy; fools are made for an intelligent man's profit."

"And now hold your tongue, Rakitka, what I am going to say now is not for your ears. Sit down in that corner and keep quiet. You don't like us, so hold your tongue."

"What should I like you for?" Rakitin snarled, not concealing his ill-humor. He put the twenty-five ruble bill in his pocket and he felt ashamed at Alyosha's seeing it. He had reckoned on receiving his payment later, without Alyosha's knowing of it, and now, feeling ashamed, he lost his temper. Till that moment he had thought it discreet not to contradict Grushenka too flatly in spite of her snubbing, since he had something to get out of her. But now he, too, was angry:

"One loves people for some reason, but what have either of you done for me?"

"You should love people without a reason, as Alyosha does."

"How does he love you? How has he shown it, that you make such a fuss about it?"

Grushenka was standing in the middle of the room; she spoke with heat and there were hysterical notes in her voice.

"Hush, Rakitka, you know nothing about us! And don't dare to speak to me like that again. How dare you be so familiar? Sit in that corner and be quiet, as though you were my lackey! And now, Alyosha, I'll tell you the whole truth, that you may see what a creature I am! I am not talking to Rakitka, but to you. I wanted to ruin you, Alyosha, that's the holy truth; I quite meant to. I wanted to so much, that I bribed Rakitka to bring you. And why did I want to do such a thing? You knew nothing about it, Alyosha, you turned away from me, if you passed me, you dropped your eyes. And I've looked at you a hundred times before today, I began asking everyone about you. Your face haunted my heart. 'He despises me,' I thought, 'he won't even look at me.' And I felt it so much at last that I wondered at myself for being so frightened of a boy. I'll get him in my clutches and laugh at him. I was full of spite and anger. Would you believe it, nobody here dares talk or think of coming to Agrafena Alexandrovna with any evil purpose. Old Kuzma is the only man I have anything to do with here, I was bound and sold to him, Satan brought us together, but there has been no one else. But looking at you, I thought, I'll get him in my clutches and laugh at him. You see what a spiteful cur I am, and you called me your sister! And now that man who wronged me has come; I sit here waiting for a message from him. And do you know what that man has been to me? Five years ago, when Kuzma brought me here, I used to shut myself up, that no one might have sight or sound of me. I was a silly slip of a girl; I used to sit here sobbing, I used to lie awake all night, thinking: 'Where is he now, the man who wronged me? He is laughing at me with another woman, most likely. If only I could see him, if I could meet him again, I'd pay him back, I'd pay him back!' At night I used to lie sobbing into my pillow in the dark, and I used to brood over it, I used to tear my heart on purpose and gloat over my anger. 'I'll pay him back, I'll pay him back!' That's what I used to cry out in the dark. And when I suddenly thought that I could really do nothing to him, and that he was laughing at me then, or perhaps had utterly forgotten me, I would fling myself on the floor, melt into helpless tears, and lie there shaking till dawn. In the morning I would get up more spiteful than a dog, ready to tear the whole world to pieces. And then what do you think? I began saving money, I became hard-hearted, grew stout—grew wiser, would you say? No, no one in the whole world sees it, no one knows it, but when the night darkness comes on, I sometimes lie as I did five years ago, when I was a silly girl, clenching my teeth and crying all night, thinking: 'I'll pay him back, I'll pay him back!' Do you hear? Well then, now you understand me. A month ago a letter came to me—he was coming, he was a widower, he wanted to see me. It took my breath away, then I suddenly thought: 'If he comes and whistles to call me, I shall creep back to him like a little beaten dog.' I couldn't believe myself. Am I so abject? Shall I run to him or not? And I've been in such a rage with myself all this month that I am worse than I was five years ago. Do you see now, Alyosha, how violent, vindictive I am? I have shown you the whole truth! I played with Mitya to keep me from running to that other. Hush, Rakitka, it's not for you to judge me, I am not speaking to you. Before you came in, I was lying here waiting, brooding, deciding my whole future life, and you can never know what was in my heart. Yes, Alyosha, tell your young lady not to be angry with me for what happened the day before yesterday. . . . Nobody in the whole world knows what I am going through now, and no one ever can know. . . . For perhaps I shall take a knife with me today. I can't make up my mind . . ."

And at this "tragic" phrase Grushenka suddenly broke down, hid her face in her hands, flung herself on the sofa pillows, and sobbed like a little child. Alyosha got up and went to Rakitin.

"Misha," he said, "don't be angry. She wounded you, but don't be angry. You heard what she said just now? You mustn't ask too much of a human soul, one must be merciful . . ."

Alyosha said this at the instinctive prompting of his heart. He felt obliged to speak and he turned to Rakitin. If Rakitin had not been there, he would have spoken to the air. But Rakitin looked at him ironically and Alyosha stopped short.

"You were so primed up with your elder's teaching last night that now you have to let it off on me, Alyoshechka, little man of God!" said Rakitin, with a smile of hatred.

"Don't laugh, Rakitin, don't smile, don't talk of the dead—he was better than anyone in the world!" cried Alyosha, with tears in his voice. "I didn't speak to you as a judge but as the lowest of the judged. What am I beside her? I came here seeking my ruin, and said to myself, 'What does it matter?' in my cowardliness, but she after five years in torment, as soon as anyone says a word from the heart to her—it makes her forget everything, forgive everything, in her tears! The man who has wronged her has come back, he sends for her and she forgives him everything, and hastens joyfully to meet him and she won't take a knife with her. She won't! No, I am not like that. I don't know whether you are, Misha, but I am not like that. It's a lesson to me . . . She is more loving than we. . . . Have you heard her speak before of what she has just told us? No, you haven't; if you had, you'd have understood her long ago . . . and the person insulted the day before yesterday must forgive her, too! She will, when she knows . . . and she shall know. . . . This soul is not yet at peace with itself, one must be tender with it . . . there may be a treasure in that soul . . ."

Alyosha stopped, because he was out of breath. In spite of his ill-humor, Rakitin looked at him with astonishment. He had never expected such a tirade from the gentle Alyosha.

"She's found someone to plead her cause! Why, are you in love with her? Agrafena Alexandrovna, our monk's really in love with you, you've made a conquest!" he cried, with a coarse laugh.

Grushenka lifted her head from the pillow and looked at Alyosha with a tender smile shining on her face, which seemed somehow puffed up from her recent tears.

"Let him alone, Alyosha, my cherub, you see what he is, he is not a person for you to speak to. Mikhail Ospovich," she turned to Rakitin, "I meant to beg your pardon for being rude to you, but now I don't want to. Alyosha, come to me, sit down here." She beckoned to him with a happy smile. "That's right, sit here. Tell me," she took him by the hand and looked into his face, smiling, "tell me, do I love that man or not? the man who wronged me, do I love him or not? Before you came, I lay here in the dark, asking my heart whether I loved him. Decide for me, Alyosha, the time has come, it shall be as you say. Am I to forgive him or not?"

"But you have forgiven him already," said Alyosha, smiling.

"Yes, I really have forgiven him," Grushenka murmured thoughtfully. "What a base heart! To my base heart!" She snatched up a glass from the table, emptied it at a gulp, lifted it in the air and flung it on the floor. The glass broke with a crash. A little cruel line came into her smile.

"Perhaps I haven't forgiven him, though," she said, with a sort of menace in her voice, and she dropped her eyes to the ground as though she were talking to herself. "Perhaps my heart is only getting ready to forgive, I shall struggle with my heart. You see, Alyosha, I've grown to love my tears in these five years. . . . Perhaps I only love my resentment, not him . . ."

"Well, I wouldn't care to be in his shoes," hissed Rakitin.

"Well, you won't be, Rakitka, you'll never be in his shoes. You will shine my shoes, Rakitka, that's the place you are fit for. You'll never get a woman like me . . . and he won't either, perhaps . . ."

"Won't he? Then why are you dressed up like that?" said Rakitin, with a venomous sneer.

"Don't taunt me with dressing up, Rakitka, you don't know all that is in my heart! If I choose to tear off my finery, I'll tear it off at once, this minute," she cried in a resonant voice. "You don't know what that finery is for, Rakitka! Perhaps I shall see him and say: 'Have you ever seen me look like this before?' He left me a thin, consumptive crybaby of seventeen. I'll sit by him, fascinate him and work him up. 'Do you see what I am like now?' I'll say to him; 'well, and that's enough for you, my dear sir, there's many a slip twixt the cup and the lip!' That may be what the finery is for, Rakitka." Grushenka finished with a malicious laugh. "I'm violent and resentful, Alyosha, I'll tear off my finery, I'll destroy my beauty, I'll scorch my face, slash it with a knife, and turn beggar.[2] If I choose, I won't go anywhere now to see anyone. If I choose, I'll send Kuzma back all he has ever given me, tomorrow, and all his money and I'll go out slaving as

___

2. The acts of violence Grushenka threatens to commit against herself are stock elements recounted in the lives of saints who began as sinners.

a charwoman for the rest of my life. You think I wouldn't do it, Rakitka, that I would not dare to do it? I would, I would, I could do it directly, only don't exasperate me . . . and I'll send him about his business. I'll snap my fingers in his face, he shall never see me again!"

She uttered the last words in an hysterical scream, but broke down again, hid her face in her hands, buried it in the pillow and shook with sobs. Rakitin got up.

"It's time we were off," he said "it's late, we shall be shut out of the monastery."

Grushenka leapt up from her place.

"Surely you don't want to go, Alyosha!" she cried, in mournful surprise. "What are you doing to me? You've stirred up my feeling, tormented me, and now you'll leave me to face this night alone!"

"He can hardly spend the night with you! Though if he wants to, let him! I'll go alone," Rakitin scoffed jeeringly.

"Hush, evil tongue!" Grushenka cried angrily at him; "you never said such words to me as he has come to say."

"What has he said to you so special?" asked Rakitin irritably.

"I can't say, I don't know. I don't know what he said to me, it went straight to my heart; he has wrung my heart. . . . He is the first, the only one who has pitied me, that's what it is. Why did you not come before, you cherub?" She fell on her knees before him as though in a sudden frenzy. "I've been waiting all my life for someone like you, I knew that someone like you would come and forgive me. I believed that nasty as I am, someone would really love me, not only with a shameful love!"

"What have I done to you?" answered Alyosha bending over her with a tender smile, and gently taking her by the hands; "I only gave you an onion, nothing but a tiny little onion, that's all, that's all!"

He started to cry himself as he said it. At that moment there was a sudden noise in the passage, someone came into the hall. Grushenka jumped up seeming greatly alarmed. Fenya ran noisily into the room, crying out:

"Mistress, mistress darling, a messenger has galloped up," she cried, breathless and joyful. "A carriage from Mokroe for you, Timothy the driver, with a troika,[3] they are just putting in fresh horses. . . . A letter, here's the letter, mistress."

A letter was in her hand and she waved it in the air all the while she talked. Grushenka snatched the letter from her and carried it to the candle. It was only a note, a few lines. She read it in one instant.

"He has sent for me," she cried, her face white and distorted, with a wan smile; "he whistles! Crawl back, little dog!"

But only for one instant she stood as though hesitating; suddenly the blood rushed to her head and sent a glow to her cheeks.

"I will go," she cried; "five years of my life! Good-bye! Good-bye, Alyosha, my fate is sealed. Go, go, leave me all of you, don't let me see you again! Grushenka is flying to a new life. . . . Don't you remember evil against me either, Rakitka. I may be going to my death! Ugh! I feel as though I were drunk!"

---

3. A Russian sled or carriage with two wheels, called a troika because it is always pulled by three horses.

She suddenly left them and ran into her bedroom.

"Well, she has no thoughts for us now!" grumbled Rakitin. "Let's go, or we may hear that feminine shriek again. I am sick of all these tears and cries."

Alyosha mechanically let himself be led out. In the yard stood a covered cart. Horses were being taken out of the shafts, men were running to and fro with a lantern. Three fresh horses were being led in at the open gate. But when Alyosha and Rakitin reached the bottom of the steps, Grushenka's bedroom window was suddenly opened and she called in a ringing voice after Alyosha:

"Alyoshechka, give my greetings to your brother Mitenka and tell him not to remember evil against me, though I have brought him misery. And tell him too in my words: 'Grushenka has fallen to a scoundrel, and not to you, noble heart.' And add, too, that Grushenka loved him only one hour, only one short hour she loved him—so let him remember that hour all his life—say, 'Grushenka tells you to!'"

She ended in a voice full of sobs. The window was shut with a slam.

"Hmm, hmm!" growled Rakitin, laughing, "she ruins your brother Mitya and then tells him to remember it all his life! What ferocity!"

Alyosha made no reply, he seemed not to have heard. He walked fast beside Rakitin as though in a terrible hurry. He was lost in thought and moved mechanically. Rakitin felt a sudden twinge as though he had been touched on an open wound. He had expected something quite different by bringing Grushenka and Alyosha together. Something very different from what he had hoped for had happened.

"He is a Pole, that officer of hers," he began again, restraining himself; "and indeed he is not an officer at all now. He served in the customs in Siberia, somewhere on the Chinese frontier, some puny little beggar of a Pole, I expect. Lost his job, they say. He's heard now that Grushenka's saved a little money, so he's turned up again—that's the explanation of the mystery."

Again Alyosha seemed not to hear. Rakitin could not control himself.

"Well, so you've saved the sinner?" he laughed spitefully. "Have you turned the Magdalene onto the true path? Driven out the seven devils, eh?[4] So you see the miracles you were looking out for just now have come to pass!"

"Stop, Rakitin," Alyosha answered, with an aching heart.

"So you despise me now for those twenty-five rubles? I've sold my friend, you think. But you are not Christ, you know, and I am not Judas."

"Oh, Rakitin, I assure you I'd forgotten about it," cried Alyosha, "you remind me of it yourself . . ."

But this was the last straw for Rakitin.

"Devil take you all and each of you!" he yelled suddenly, "why the devil did I have anything to do with you? I don't want to know you from this time forward. Go alone, there's your road!"

---

4. Rakitin refers to the Gospel story of Mary Magdalene, who rejected a life of sin and became one of the most devoted followers of Christ. According to the Gospels, he performed an exorcism on her, expelling the "seven devils," and she was the first person to see him after his resurrection. See Mark 16.9 and Luke 8.1–2.

And he turned abruptly into another street, leaving Alyosha alone in the dark. Alyosha came out of the town and walked across the fields to the monastery.

Chapter IV
Cana of Galilee

It was very late, by monastery rules, when Alyosha returned to the hermitage; the doorkeeper let him in by a special entrance. It had struck nine o'clock—the hour of rest and repose after a day of such agitation for all. Alyosha timidly opened the door and went into the elder's cell where his coffin was now standing. There was no one in the cell but Father Païssy, reading the Gospel in solitude over the coffin, and the young novice Porfiry, who, exhausted by the previous night's conversation and the disturbing incidents of the day, was sleeping the deep sound sleep of youth on the floor of the other room. Though Father Païssy heard Alyosha come in, he did not even look in his direction. Alyosha turned to the right from the door to the corner, fell on his knees and began to pray.

His soul was overflowing but with mingled feelings; no single sensation stood out distinctly, on the contrary, one drove out another in a slow, continual rotation. But there was a sweetness in his heart and, strange to say, Alyosha was not surprised at it. Again he saw that coffin before him, the hidden dead figure so precious to him, but the weeping and poignant grief of the morning was no longer aching in his soul. As soon as he came in, he fell down before the coffin as before a holy shrine, but joy, joy was glowing in his mind and in his heart. The one window of the cell was open, the air was fresh and cool. "So the odor must have become stronger, if they opened the window," thought Alyosha. But even this thought of the odor of corruption, which had seemed to him so awful and humiliating a few hours before, no longer made him feel miserable or indignant. He began quietly praying, but he soon felt that he was praying almost mechanically. Fragments of thought floated through his soul, flashed like stars and went out again at once, to be succeeded by others. But yet there was reigning in his soul a sense of the wholeness of things—something steadfast and comforting—and he was aware of it himself. Sometimes he began praying ardently, he longed to pour out his thankfulness and love. . . . But when he had begun to pray, he passed suddenly to something else, and sank into thought, forgetting both the prayer and what had interrupted it. He began listening to what Father Païssy was reading, but worn out with exhaustion he gradually began to doze.

"*And the third day there was a marriage in Cana of Galilee,*" read Father Païssy.[5] "*And the mother of Jesus was there; And both Jesus was called, and his disciples, to the marriage.*"

"Marriage? What's that. . . . A marriage!" floated whirling through Alyosha's mind. "There is happiness for her, too. . . . She has gone to the feast. . . . No, she has not taken the knife. . . . That was only a "tragic"

---

5. According to John 2.1–11, Jesus performed his first miracle in the town of Cana in Galilee at a wedding feast, where he turned water into wine.

phrase. . . . Well . . . tragic phrases should be forgiven, they must be.
Tragic phrases comfort the heart. . . . Without them, sorrow would be too
heavy for men to bear. Rakitin has gone off to the back alley. As long as
Rakitin broods over his wrongs, he will always go off to the back alley. . . .
But the high road. . . . The road is wide and straight and bright as crystal,
and the sun is at the end of it. . . . Ah! . . . What's being read?" . . .

*"And when they wanted wine, the mother of Jesus saith unto him; 'They
have no wine'"* . . . Alyosha heard.

"Ah, yes, I was missing that, and I didn't want to miss it, I love that passage; it's Cana of Galilee, the first miracle. . . . Ah, that miracle! Ah, that
sweet miracle! It was not men's grief, but their joy Christ visited, He
worked His first miracle to help men's joy . . . 'He who loves men loves
their joy, too.' . . . *He* was always repeating that, it was one of his leading
ideas. . . . 'There's no living without joy,' Mitya says. . . . Yes, Mitya. . . .
'Everything that is true and beautiful is always full of forgiveness,' he
used to say that, too" . . .

*"Jesus saith unto her, Woman, what has it to do with thee or me? Mine
hour is not yet come. His mother saith unto the servants: Whatsoever he
saith unto you, do it."*

"Do it. . . . Joy, the joy of some poor, very poor, people. . . . Of course
they were poor, since they hadn't wine enough even at a wedding. . . .
The historians write that, in those days, the people living about the Lake
of Gennesaret[6] were the poorest that can possibly be imagined . . . and
another great heart of that other great being, His Mother, knew that He
had come not only to make His great terrible sacrifice. She knew that His
heart was open even to the simple, artless merrymaking of some obscure
and unlearned beings, who had warmly bidden Him to their poor wedding. 'Mine hour is not yet come,' He said, with a soft smile (He must
have smiled gently to her). And indeed was it to make wine abundant at
poor weddings He had come down to earth? And yet He went and did as
she asked Him. . . . Ah, he is reading again."

*"Jesus saith unto them, Fill the waterpots with water. And they filled them
up to the brim.*

*"And he saith unto them. Draw out now and bear unto the governor of
the feast. And they bare it.*

*"When the ruler of the feast had tasted the water that was made wine,
and knew not whence it was; [but the servants which drew the water knew]
the governor of the feast called the bridegroom.*

*"And saith unto him: Every man at the beginning doth set forth good
wine; and when men have well drunk, that which is worse; but thou hast
kept the good wine until now."*

"But what's this, what's this? Why is the room growing wider? . . . Ah,
yes . . . It's the marriage, the wedding . . . yes, of course. Here are the
guests, here are the young couple sitting, and the merry crowd and . . .
Where is the wise governor of the feast? But who is this? Who? Again the
walls are receding. . . . Who is getting up there from the great table?
What! . . . He here, too? But he's in the coffin . . . but he's here, too. He
has stood up, he sees me, he is coming here. . . . God!" . . .

---

6. Also known as the Sea of Galilee, the Lake of Gennesaret is mentioned several times in the
   Bible; see for example Luke 5.1.

Yes, he came up to him, to him, he, the little, thin old man, with tiny wrinkles on his face, joyful and laughing softly. There was no coffin now, and he was in the same dress as he had worn yesterday sitting with them, when the visitors had gathered about him. His face was uncovered, his eyes were shining. How was this then, he, too, had been called to the feast. He, too, at the marriage of Cana in Galilee. . . .

"Yes, my dear, I am called, too, called and bidden," he heard a soft voice saying over him. "Why have you hidden yourself here, out of sight? You come and join us too."

It was his voice, the voice of Father Zosima. And it must be he, since he called him! The elder raised Alyosha by the hand and he rose from his knees.

"We are rejoicing," the little, thin old man went on. "We are drinking the new wine, the wine of new, great gladness; do you see how many guests? Here are the bride and bridegroom, here is the wise governor of the feast, he is tasting the new wine. Why do you wonder at me? I gave an onion to a beggar, so I, too, am here. And many here have given only an onion each—only one little onion. . . . What are all our deeds? And you, my gentle one, you, my kind boy, you too have known how to give a famished woman an onion today. Begin your work, dear one, begin it, gentle one . . . Do you see our Sun, do you see Him?"

"I am afraid . . . I dare not look," whispered Alyosha.

"Do not fear Him. He is terrible in His greatness, awful in His sublimity, but infinitely merciful. He has made Himself like unto us from love and rejoices with us, He is changing the water into wine that the gladness of the guests may not be cut short. He is expecting new guests, He is calling new ones unceasingly forever and ever. . . . There they are bringing new wine. Do you see they are bringing the vessels . . ."

Something glowed in Alyosha's heart, something filled it till it ached, tears of rapture rose from his soul. . . . He stretched out his hands, uttered a cry and woke up.

Again the coffin, the open window, and the soft, solemn, distinct reading of the Gospel. But Alyosha did not listen to the reading. It was strange, he had fallen asleep on his knees, but now he was on his feet, and suddenly, as though thrown forward, with three firm rapid steps he went right up to the coffin. His shoulder brushed against Father Païssy without his noticing it. Father Païssy raised his eyes for an instant from his book, but looked away again at once, seeing that something strange was happening to the youth. Alyosha gazed for half a minute at the coffin, at the covered, motionless dead man that lay in the coffin, with the icon on his breast and the peaked hood with the octangular cross, on his head. He had only just been hearing his voice, and that voice was still ringing in his ears. He was listening, still expecting other words, but suddenly he turned sharply and went out of the cell.

He did not stop on the steps either, but went quickly down; his soul, overflowing with rapture, yearned for freedom, space, openness. The vault of heaven, full of soft, shining stars, stretched vast and fathomless above him. The Milky Way ran in two pale streams from the zenith to the horizon. The fresh, motionless, still night enfolded the earth. The white towers and golden domes of the cathedral gleamed out against the sapphire sky. The gorgeous autumn flowers, in the beds round the house, were slumbering till morning. The silence of earth seemed to melt into the silence of the heavens. The mystery of earth was one with the mystery of the stars. . . . Alyosha stood, gazed, and suddenly threw himself down on the earth.

He did not know why he embraced it. He could not have told why he longed so irresistibly to kiss it, to kiss it all. But he kissed it weeping, sobbing and watering it with his tears, and rapturously vowed to love it, to love it forever and ever. "Water the earth with the tears of your joy and love those tears," echoed in his soul. What was he weeping over? Oh! in his rapture he was weeping even over those stars, which were shining to him from the abyss of space, and "he was not ashamed of that ecstasy." There seemed to be threads from all those innumerable worlds of God, linking his soul to them, and it was trembling all over "in contact with other worlds." He longed to forgive everyone and for everything, and to beg forgiveness. Oh, not for himself, but for all men, for all and for everything. "And others are praying for me too," echoed again in his soul. But with every instant he felt clearly and, as it were, tangibly, that something firm and unshakable as that vault of heaven had entered into his soul. It was as though some idea had seized the sovereignty of his mind—and it was for all his life and forever and ever. He had fallen on the earth a weak youth, but he rose up a resolute champion, and he knew and felt it suddenly at the very moment of his ecstasy. And never, never, all his life long, could Alyosha forget that minute. "Someone visited my soul in that hour," he used to say afterwards, with implicit faith in his words.

Within three days he left the monastery in accordance with the words of his elder, who had bidden him to "sojourn in the world."

Book Eight

MITYA

Chapter I

Kuzma Samsonov

But Dmitri Fyodorovich, to whom Grushenka, flying away to a new life, had left her last greetings, "ordering" him to remember the hour of her love forever, knew nothing of what had happened to her, and was at that moment in a condition of feverish agitation and activity. For the last two days he had been in such an inconceivable state of mind that he might easily have fallen ill with brain fever, as he said himself afterwards. Alyosha had not been able to find him the morning before, and brother Ivan had not succeeded in meeting him at the tavern on the same day. The people at his lodgings, by his orders, concealed his movements. He had spent those two days literally rushing in all directions, "struggling with his destiny and trying to save himself," as he expressed it himself afterwards, and for some hours he even made a dash out of the town on urgent business, terrible as it was to him to lose sight of Grushenka for a moment. All this was explained afterwards in detail, and confirmed by documentary evidence; but for the present we will only note the most essential incidents of those two terrible days immediately preceding the awful catastrophe that broke so suddenly upon him.

Though Grushenka had, it is true, loved him for one little hour, genuinely and sincerely, yet she tortured him sometimes, cruelly and mercilessly. The worst of it was that he could never tell what she meant to do. To prevail upon her by force or kindness was also impossible: she would yield to nothing. She would only have become angry and turned away from him altogether, he knew that well already. He suspected, quite correctly, that she, too, was passing through an inward struggle, and was in a state of extraordinary indecision, that she was making up her mind to something, and unable to determine upon it. And so, not without good reason, he divined, with a sinking heart, that at moments she must simply hate him and his passion. And so, perhaps, it was, but what was distressing Grushenka he did not understand. For him the whole tormenting question lay between him and Fyodor Pavlovich.

Here, we must note, by the way, one certain fact: he was firmly persuaded that Fyodor Pavlovich would offer, or perhaps had offered, Grushenka lawful wedlock, and did not for a moment believe that the old voluptuary hoped to gain his object for three thousand rubles. Mitya had reached this conclusion from his knowledge of Grushenka and her character. That was

313

how it was that he could believe at times that all Grushenka's uneasiness rose from not knowing which of them to choose, which was more to her advantage. Strange to say, during those days it never occurred to him to think of the approaching return of the "officer," that is, of the man who had been such a fatal influence in Grushenka's life, and whose arrival she was expecting with such emotion and dread. It is true that of late Grushenka had been very silent about it. Yet he was perfectly aware of a letter she had received a month ago from her seducer, and had heard of it from her own lips. He partly knew, too, what the letter contained. In a moment of spite Grushenka had shown him that letter, but to her astonishment he attached hardly any consequence to it. It would be hard to say why this was. Perhaps, weighed down by all the hideous horror of his struggle with his own father for this woman, he was incapable of imagining any danger more terrible, at any rate for the time. He simply did not believe in a suitor who suddenly turned up again after five years' disappearance, still less in his speedy arrival. Moreover, in the "officer's" first letter which had been shown to Mitenka, the possibility of his new rival's visit was very vaguely suggested. The letter was very indefinite, high-flown, and full of sentimentality. It must be noted that Grushenka had concealed from him the last lines of the letter, in which his return was alluded to more definitely. He had, besides, noticed at that moment, he remembered afterwards, a certain involuntary proud contempt for this missive from Siberia[1] on Grushenka's face. Grushenka told him nothing of what had passed later between her and this rival; so that by degrees he had completely forgotten the officer's existence. He felt that whatever might come later, whatever turn things might take, his final conflict with Fyodor Pavlovich was close upon him, and must be decided before anything else. With a sinking heart he was expecting every moment Grushenka's decision, always believing that it would come suddenly, on the impulse of the moment. All of a sudden she would say to him: "Take me, I'm yours forever," and it would all be over. He would seize her and bear her away at once to the ends of the earth. Oh, then he would bear her away at once, as far, far away as possible; to the furthest end of Russia, if not of the earth, then he would marry her, and settle down with her *incognito*, so that no one would know anything about them, there, here, or anywhere. Then, oh, then, a new life would begin at once! Of this different, reformed and "virtuous" life ("it must, it must be virtuous") he dreamed feverishly at every moment. He thirsted for that resurrection and renewal. The filthy morass, in which he had sunk of his own free will, was too revolting to him, and, like very many men in such cases, he put faith above all in change of place. If only it were not for these people, if only it were not for these circumstances, if only he could fly away from this accursed place—he would be altogether regenerated, would enter on a new path. That was what he believed in, and for what he was yearning.

But all this could only be on condition of the first, the *happy* solution of the question. There was another possibility, a different and awful ending. Suddenly she might say to him; "Go away. I have just come to terms

---

1. A complex, parodying allusion to Pushkin's famous missive to Decembrist rebels exiled to Siberia (see also p. 257), "In the depths of Siberian Mines" ("Vo glubine sibirskikh rud," 1827). The effect is to mock the Poles.

with Fyodor Pavlovich. I am going to marry him and don't want you"—
and then . . . but then. . . . But Mitya did not know what would happen
then. Up to the last hour he didn't know. That must be said to his credit.
He had no definite intentions, had planned no crime. He was simply
watching and spying in agony, while he prepared himself for the first,
happy solution of his destiny. He drove away any other idea, in fact. But
for that ending a quite different anxiety arose, a new, incidental, but yet
fatal and insoluble difficulty presented itself.

If she were to say to him: "I'm yours; take me away," how could he take
her away? Where had he the means, the money to do it? It was just at this
time that all sources of revenue from Fyodor Pavlovich, doles which had
gone on without interruption for so many years, ceased. Grushenka had
money, of course, but with regard to this Mitya suddenly evinced extraordinary pride; he wanted to carry her away and begin the new life with her
himself, at his own expense, not at hers. He could not conceive of taking
her money, and the very idea caused him a pang of intense repulsion. I
won't enlarge on this fact or analyze it here, but confine myself to remarking that this was his attitude at the moment. All this may have arisen
indirectly and unconsciously from the secret stings of his conscience for
the money of Katerina Ivanovna that he had thievishly appropriated. "I've
been a scoundrel to one of them, and I shall be a scoundrel again to the
other directly," with his feeling then, as he explained after: "and when
Grushenka knows, she won't care for such a scoundrel." Where then was
he to get the means, where was he to get the fateful money? Without it,
all would be lost and nothing could be done, "and only because I hadn't
the money. Oh, the shame of it!"

To anticipate things: he did, perhaps, know where to get the money,
knew, perhaps, where it lay at that moment. I will say no more of this here,
as it will all become clear later. But his chief trouble, I must explain however obscurely, lay in the fact that to have the sum he knew of, to *have the
right* to take it, he must first restore Katerina Ivanovna's three thousand—
if not, "I'm a pocket thief, I'm a scoundrel, and I don't want to begin a new
life as a scoundrel," Mitya decided. And so he made up his mind to move
heaven and earth to return Katerina Ivanovna that three thousand, and
that *first of all*. The final stage of this decision, so to say, had been reached
only during the last hours, that is, after his last interview with Alyosha,
two days before, on the highway, on the evening when Grushenka had
insulted Katerina Ivanovna, and Mitya, after hearing Alyosha's account of
it, had admitted that he was a scoundrel, and told him to tell Katerina
Ivanovna so, "if it could be any comfort to her." After parting from his
brother on that night, he had felt in his frenzy that it would be better "to
murder and rob someone than fail to pay my debt to Katya. I'd rather
everyone thought me a robber and a murderer, I'd rather go to Siberia
than that Katya should have the right to say that I deceived her and stole
her money, and used her money to run away with Grushenka and begin a
virtuous new life! That I can't do!" So Mitya decided, grinding his teeth,
and he might well fancy at times that his brain would give way. But meanwhile he went on struggling. . . .

Strange to say, though one would have supposed there was nothing left
for him but despair—for what chance had he, with nothing in the world,
to raise such a sum?—yet to the very end he persisted in hoping that he

would get that three thousand, that the money would somehow come to him, of itself, as though it might drop from heaven. That is just how it is with people who, like Dmitri Fyodorovich, have never had anything to do with money, except to squander what had come to them by inheritance without any effort of their own, and have no notion how money is obtained. A whirl of the most fantastic notions took possession of his brain immediately after he had parted with Alyosha two days before, and threw his thoughts into a tangle of confusion. This is how it was he first hit upon a perfectly wild enterprise. And perhaps to men of that kind in such circumstances the most impossible, fantastic schemes occur first, and seem most practical. He suddenly determined to go to Samsonov, the merchant who was Grushenka's protector, and to propose a "scheme" to him, and by means of it to obtain from him at once the whole of the sum required. Of the commercial value of his scheme he had no doubt, not the slightest, and was only uncertain how Samsonov would look upon his scheme, supposing he were to consider it from any but the commercial point of view. Though Mitya knew the merchant by sight, he was not acquainted with him and had never spoken a word to him. But for some unknown reason he had long entertained the conviction that the old reprobate, who was lying at death's door, would perhaps not at all object now to Grushenka's securing a respectable position, and marrying a man "to be depended upon." And he believed not only that he would not object, but that this was what he desired, and, if opportunity arose, that he would be ready to help. From some rumor, or perhaps from some stray words of Grushenka's, he had gathered further that the old man would perhaps prefer him to Fyodor Pavlovich for Grushenka. Possibly many of the readers of my novel will feel that in reckoning on such assistance, and being ready to take his bride, so to speak, from the hands of her protector, Dmitri Fyodorovich showed great coarseness and want of delicacy. I will only observe that Mitya looked upon Grushenka's past as something completely passed. He looked on that past with infinite compassion and resolved with all the fervor of his passion that when once Grushenka told him she loved him and would marry him, it would mean the beginning of a new Grushenka and a new Dmitri Fyodorovich, free from every vice, and containing only virtue. They would forgive one another and would begin their lives afresh. As for Kuzma Samsonov, Dmitri looked upon him as a man who had exercised a fateful influence in that remote past of Grushenka's, though she had never loved him, and who was now himself "a thing of the past," completely done with, and, so to speak, nonexistent. Besides, Mitya hardly looked upon him as a man at all, for it was known to everyone in the town that he was only a shattered wreck, whose relations with Grushenka had changed their character and were now simply paternal, so to speak, and that this had been so for a long time. In any case there was much simplicity on Mitya's part in all this, for, in spite of all his vices, he was a very simple-hearted man. It was an instance of this simplicity that Mitya was seriously persuaded that, being on the eve of his departure for the next world, old Kuzma must sincerely repent of his past relations with Grushenka, and that she had no more devoted friend and protector in the world than this, now harmless, old man.

After his conversation with Alyosha, at the crossroads, he hardly slept all night, and, at ten o'clock next morning, he was at the house of Samsonov and telling the servant to announce him. It was a very large and gloomy old house, of two stories with a lodge and wings. In the lower story lived Samsonov's two married sons with their families, his old sister, and his unmarried daughter. In the lodge lived two of his clerks, one of whom also had a large family. Both the lodge and the lower story were over-crowded, but the old man kept the upper floor to himself, and would not even let the daughter live there with him, though she waited upon him, and in spite of her asthma was obliged at certain fixed hours, and at any time he might call her, to run upstairs to him from below. This upper floor contained a number of large rooms kept purely for show, furnished in the old-fashioned merchant style, with long, monotonous rows of clumsy mahogany chairs along the walls, with glass chandeliers under shades, and gloomy mirrors on the walls. All these rooms were entirely empty and unused, for the old man kept to one room, a small, remote bedroom, where he was waited upon by an old servant with a kerchief on her head,[2] and by a lad, who used to sit on the locker in the passage. Owing to his swollen legs, the old man could hardly walk at all, and was only rarely lifted from his leather armchair, when the old woman supporting him led up and down the room once or twice. He was morose and taciturn even with this old woman. When he was informed of the arrival of the "captain," he at once refused to see him. But Mitya persisted and sent his name up again. Samsonov questioned the lad minutely: What he looked like? Whether he was drunk? Was he going to make a row? The answer he received was that he was sober, but wouldn't go away. The old man again refused to see him. Then Mitya, who had foreseen this, and purposely brought pencil and paper with him, wrote clearly on the piece of paper the words: "On most important business closely concerning Agrafena Alexandrovna," and sent it up to the old man. After thinking a little Samsonov told the lad to take the visitor to the drawing room, and sent the old woman downstairs with a summons to his younger son to come upstairs to him at once. The younger son, a man over six foot and of exceptional physical strength, who was closely shaven and dressed in the German style, though his father still wore a caftan and a beard, came at once without a comment.[3] All the family trembled before the father. The old man had sent for this giant, not because he was afraid of the "captain" (he was by no means of a timorous temper), but in order to have a witness in case of an emergency. Supported by his son and the servant lad, he swept at last into the drawing room. It may be assumed that he felt considerable curiosity. The drawing room in which Mitya was awaiting him was a vast, dreary room that laid a weight of depression on the heart. It had a double row of windows, a gallery, mar-bled walls, and three immense chandeliers with glass lusters covered with shades. Mitya was sitting on a little chair at the entrance, awaiting his fate with nervous impatience. When the old man appeared at the opposite

---

2. This detail indicates that the household remains traditional instead of following contemporary Western fashions.

3. The deeply conservative Russian merchant class had traditionally distinguished itself from the rest of the population through distinctive habits of dress and grooming. Men typically allowed their beards to grow long and wore caftans, or long coats, over loose shirts and trousers. By the 1860s, however, some younger merchants preferred to adopt a Europeanized appearance. Samsonov's son signals his generational difference from his father by shaving his beard and wearing Western clothes, but he appears to obey his father in essentials—perhaps Dos-toevsky's commentary on the shallowness of such differences in style.

door, seventy feet away, Mitya jumped up at once, and with his long, military stride walked to meet him. Mitya was well dressed, in a frock coat, buttoned up, with a round hat and black gloves in his hands, just as he had been three days before at the elder's, at the family meeting with his father and brothers. The old man waited for him, standing dignified and unbending, and Mitya felt at once that he had looked him through and through as he advanced. Mitya was greatly impressed, too, with Samsonov's immensely swollen face. His lower lip, which had always been thick, hung down now, looking like a bun. He bowed to his guest in dignified silence, motioned him to an armchair by the sofa, and leaning on his son's arm he began lowering himself on to the sofa facing Mitya, groaning painfully, so that Mitya, seeing his painful exertions, immediately felt remorseful and sensitively conscious of his insignificance in the presence of the dignified person he had ventured to disturb.

"What is it you want of me, sir?" said the old man, deliberately, distinctly, severely, but courteously, when he was at last seated.

Mitya started, leaped up, but sat down again. Then he began at once speaking with loud, nervous haste, gesticulating, and in a positive frenzy. He was unmistakably a man driven into a corner, on the brink of ruin, catching at the last straw, ready to sink if he failed. Old Samsonov probably grasped all this in an instant, though his face remained cold and immovable as a statue's.

"Most honored sir, Kuzma Kuzmich, you have no doubt heard, more than once, of my disputes with my father, Fyodor Pavlovich Karamazov, who robbed me of my inheritance from my mother . . . seeing the whole town is gossiping about it . . . for here everyone's gossiping of what they shouldn't . . . and besides, it might have reached you through Grushenka . . . I beg your pardon, through Agrafena Alexandrovna . . . Agrafena Alexandrovna, the lady for whom I have the highest respect and esteem . . ." So Mitya began, and broke down at the first sentence. We will not reproduce his speech word for word, but will only summarize the gist of it. Three months ago, he said, he had of express intention (Mitya purposely used these words instead of "intentionally") consulted a lawyer in the chief town of the province, "a distinguished lawyer, Kuzma Kuzmich, Pavel Pavlovich Korneplodov. You have perhaps heard of him? A man of vast intellect, the mind of a statesman . . . he knows you, too . . . spoke of you in the highest terms . . ." Mitya broke down again. But these breaks did not deter him. He leaped instantly over the gaps, and struggled on and on. This Korneplodov, after questioning him minutely, and inspecting the documents he was able to bring (Mitya alluded somewhat vaguely to these documents, and slurred over the subject with special haste), reported that they certainly might take proceedings concerning the village of Chermashnya, which ought, he said, to have come to him, Mitya, from his mother, and so stun the old villain, his father . . . "because every door was not closed and justice might still find a loophole." In fact, he might reckon on an additional sum of six or even seven thousand rubles from Fyodor Pavlovich, as Chermashnya was worth, at least, twenty-five thousand, he might say twenty-eight thousand, in fact, "thirty, thirty, Kuzma Kuzmich, and, would you believe it, I didn't get seventeen from that heartless man!" So he, Mitya, had thrown the business up, for the time, knowing nothing about the law, but on coming here was struck dumb by a cross claim made upon him (here Mitya went adrift again, and again took a flying leap forward), "so will not you, excellent and honored Kuzma Kuzmich, be willing to take up all my claims against that unnatural monster, and pay me a sum of only three thousand? . . . You see, you cannot, in any case, lose over it. On my honor, my honor, I swear that. Quite the contrary, you may make six or seven thousand instead of three" . . . Above all, he wanted this concluded "that very day." "I'll do the business with you at a notary's, or whatever it is . . . in fact, I'm ready to do anything. . . . I'll hand over all the deeds . . . whatever you want, sign anything . . . and we could draw up the agreement at once . . . and if it were possible, if it were only possible, that very morning. . . . You could pay me that three thousand, for there isn't a capitalist in this town to compare with you, and so would save me from . . . would save me, in fact . . . for a good, I might say an honorable, action. . . . For I cherish the most honorable feelings for a certain person, whom you know well, and care for as a father. I would not have come, indeed, if it had not been as a father. And, indeed, three men are banging their heads together, for it's fate—that's a fearful thing, Kuzma Kuzmich! Realism, Kuzma Kuzmich, realism! Realism, Kuzma Kuzmich, realism! And as you've dropped out long ago, only two heads are left. I'm expressing it awkwardly, perhaps, but I'm not a literary man. That is, one of the heads is mine, and the other—that monster's. So you must choose. It's either I or the monster. It all lies in your hands—the fate of three lives, and the happiness of two. . . . Excuse me, I'm making a mess of it, but you understand . . . I see from your venerable eyes that you understand . . . and if you don't understand, I'm done for . . . so you see!"

Mitya broke off his absurd speech with that "so you see!" and jumping up from his seat, awaited the answer to his stupid proposal. At the last phrase he had suddenly and hopelessly realized that it had fallen flat, above all, that he had been talking utter nonsense. "How strange it is! On the way here it seemed all right, and now it's nothing but nonsense." The idea suddenly dawned on his despairing mind. All the while he had been talking, the old man sat motionless, watching him with an icy expression in his eyes. After keeping him for a moment in suspense, Kuzma Kuzmich pronounced at last, in the most decisive and chilling tone:

"Excuse me, we don't undertake such business."

Mitya suddenly felt his legs growing weak under him.

"What am I to do now, Kuzma Kuzmich?" he muttered, with a pale smile. "I'm done for now, don't you think?"

"Excuse me, sir . . ."

Mitya remained standing, staring motionless. He suddenly noticed a movement in the old man's face. He started.

"You see, sir, business of that sort's not in our line," said the old man slowly. "There's the court, and the lawyers—it's a perfect misery. But if you like, there is a man here you might apply to."

"My God, who is it! You resurrect me, Kuzma Kuzmich," Mitya suddenly stammered.

"He doesn't live here, and he's not here just now. He is a peasant, he does business in timber. His name is Lyagavy. He's been haggling with Fyodor Pavlovich for the last year, over your woodlot at Chermashnya. They can't agree on the price, maybe you've heard? Now he's come back again and is staying with the priest at Ilyinskoe, about eight miles from

the Volovya station. He wrote to me, too, about the business of the woodlot asking my advice. Fyodor Pavlovich means to go and see him, himself.
So if you were to be before Fyodor Pavlovich and to make Lyagavy the
offer you've made me, he might possibly . . ."

"A brilliant idea!" Mitya interrupted ecstatically. "He's the very man, it
would just suit him. He's haggling with him for it, being asked too much,
and here he would have all the documents entitling him to the property
itself. Ha-ha-ha!"

And Mitya suddenly went off into his short, wooden laugh, startling
Samsonov.

"How can I thank you, Kuzma Kuzmich?" cried Mitya effusively.

"Don't mention it," said Samsonov, inclining his head.

"But you don't know, you've saved me. Oh, it was a true presentiment
brought me to you. . . . so now to this priest!"

"No need of thanks, sir."

"I'll make haste and fly there. I'm afraid I've overtaxed your strength.
I shall never forget it. It's a Russian says that, Kuzma Kuzmich, a
R-r-russian!"

"To be sure!"

Mitya seized his hand to press it, but there was a malignant gleam in
the old man's eye. Mitya drew back his hand, but at once blamed himself
for his mistrustfulness. "It's because he's tired," he thought.

"For her sake! For her sake, Kuzma Kuzmich! You understand that it's
for her," he roared, his voice ringing through the room. He bowed, turned
sharply round, and with the same long stride walked to the door without
looking back. He was trembling with delight.

"Everything was on the verge of ruin and my guardian angel saved me,"
was the thought in his mind. And if such a businessman as Samsonov
(a most worthy old man, and what dignity!) had suggested this course,
then . . . then success was assured. He would fly off immediately. "I will
be back before night, I shall be back at night and the thing is done. Could
the old man have been laughing at me?" exclaimed Mitya, as he strode
towards his lodging. He could, of course, imagine nothing, but that the
advice was practical "from such a businessman" with an understanding
of the business, with an understanding of this Lyagavy (curious surname!).
Or—the old man was laughing at him. Alas! the second alternative was
the correct one. Long afterwards, when the catastrophe had happened,
old Samsonov himself confessed, laughing, that he had made a fool of the
"captain." He was a cold, spiteful and sarcastic man, liable to violent
antipathies. Whether it was the "captain's" excited face, or the foolish
conviction of the "rake and spendthrift," that he, Samsonov, could be
taken in by such a cock-and-bull story as his scheme, or jealousy over
Grushenka, in whose name this "scapegrace" had rushed in on him with
such a tale to get money—which worked on the old man I can't tell. But,
at the instant when Mitya stood before him, feeling his legs grow weak
under him, and frantically exclaiming that he was ruined, at that moment
the old man looked at him with intense spite, and resolved to make a
laughingstock of him. When Mitya had gone, Kuzma Kuzmich, white
with rage, turned to his son and bade him see to it that that beggar never
be seen again, and never admitted even into the yard, or else he'd . . .

Gifts

Annie - book, gtip, GF bracelet

Monica - bag? GF bracelet

Lindsay - poster? GF bracelet

Katie - GF bracelet.

He did not utter his threat. But even his son, who often saw him enraged, trembled with fear. For a whole hour afterwards, the old man was shaking with anger, and by evening he was worse, and sent for the doctor.

Chapter II

Lyagavy

So he must drive at full speed, and he did not have the money for horses, he had forty kopecks, and that was all, all that was left after so many years of prosperity! But he had at home an old silver watch which had long ceased to go. He snatched it up and carried it to a Jewish watchmaker who had a shop in the marketplace. The Jew gave him six rubles for it. "And I didn't expect even this much!" cried Mitya, ecstatically. (He was still in a state of ecstasy.) He seized his six rubles and ran home. At home he borrowed three rubles from the people of the house, who loved him so much that they were pleased to give it him, though it was all they had. Mitya in his excitement told them on the spot that his fate would be decided that day, and he described, in desperate haste, the whole "scheme" he had put before Samsonov, the latter's decision, his own hopes for the future, and so on. These people had been told many of their lodger's secrets before, and so looked upon him as a gentleman who was not at all proud, and almost one of *themselves*. Having thus collected nine rubles Mitya sent for posting horses to take him to the Volovya station. This was how the fact came to be remembered and established that "at midday, on the day before the event, Mitya didn't have a kopeck, and that he had sold his watch to get money and had borrowed three rubles from his landlords, all in the presence of witnesses."

I note this fact; later on it will be apparent why I do so.

Though he was radiant with the joyful anticipation that he would at last solve "all his difficulties," yet, as he drew near Volovya station, he trembled at the thought of what Grushenka might be doing in his absence. What if she made up her mind today to go to Fyodor Pavlovich? This was why he had gone off without telling her and why he left orders with his landlady not to let out where he had gone, if anyone came to inquire for him. "I must, I must get back tonight," he repeated, as he was jolted along in the cart, "and I daresay I shall have to bring this Lyagavy back here . . . to draw up the deed." So mused Mitya, with a throbbing heart, but alas! his dreams were not fated to be carried out.

To begin with, he was late, taking a short cut from Volovya station which turned out to be twelve miles instead of eight. Secondly, he did not find the priest at home at Ilyinskoe; he had gone off to a neighboring village. While Mitya, setting off there with the same exhausted horses, was looking for him, it was almost dark.

The priest, a shy and amiable looking little man, informed him at once that, though Lyagavy had been staying with him at first, he was now at Sukhoy Possyolok, that he was staying the night in the forester's cottage, as he was buying timber there too. At Mitya's urgent request that he would take him to Lyagavy at once, and by so doing "save him, so to speak," the priest agreed, after some demur, to conduct him to Sukhoy Possyolok; his curiosity was obviously aroused. But, unluckily, he advised their going on foot, as it would not be "much over" a half mile or so. Mitya, of course, agreed, and marched off with his yard-long strides, so that the poor priest almost ran after him. He was a very cautious man, though not old. Mitya at once began talking to him, too, of his plans, nervously and excitedly asking advice in regard to Lyagavy, and talking all the way. He turned off Mitya's questions with: "I don't know. Ah, I can't say. How can I tell?" and so on. When Mitya began to speak of his quarrel with his father over his inheritance, the priest was positively alarmed, as he was in some way dependent on Fyodor Pavlovich. He inquired, however, with surprise, why he called the peasant trader Gorstkin, Lyagavy, and obligingly explained to Mitya that, though the man's name really was Lyagavy, he was never called so, as he would be grievously offended at the name, and that he must be sure to call him Gorstkin, "or you'll do nothing with him; he won't even listen to you," said the priest in conclusion.

Mitya was somewhat surprised for a moment, and explained that that was what Samsonov had called him. On hearing this fact, the priest dropped the subject, though he would have done well to put into words his doubt whether, if Samsonov had sent him to that peasant, calling him Lyagavy, there was not something wrong about it, and he was exposing him to ridicule. But Mitya had no time to pause "over such trifles." He hurried, striding along, and only when he reached Sukhoy Possyolok he realized that they had come not a half mile, nor one and one-half, but at least two. This annoyed him, but he controlled himself.

They went into the hut. The forester, the priest's friend, lived in one half of the hut, and Gorstkin was lodging in the other, the better room the other side of the passage. They went into that room and lighted a tallow candle. The hut was extremely overheated. On the pine table there was a samovar that had gone out, a tray with cups, an empty rum bottle, a bottle of vodka partly full, and some half-eaten crusts of wheat bread. The visitor himself lay stretched at full length on the bench, with his coat crushed up under his head for a pillow, snoring heavily. Mitya stood in perplexity.

"Of course I must wake him. My business is too important. I've come in such haste. I'm in a hurry to get back today," he said in great agitation. But the priest and the forester stood in silence, not giving their opinion. Mitya went up and began trying to wake him himself; he tried vigorously, but the sleeper did not wake. "He's drunk," Mitya decided. "Good Lord! What am I to do? What am I to do?" And, terribly impatient, he began pulling him by the arms, by the legs, shaking his head, lifting him up and making him sit on the bench. Yet, after prolonged exertions, he could only succeed in getting the drunken man to utter absurd grunts, and violent but inarticulate oaths.

"No, you'd better wait a little," the priest pronounced at last, "for he's obviously not in a fit state."

"He's been drinking the whole day," the forester chimed in.

"Good heavens!" cried Mitya. "If only you knew how important it is to me and how desperate I am!"

"No, you'd better wait till morning," the priest repeated.

"Till morning? Mercy! that's impossible!"

And in his despair he was on the point of attacking the sleeping man again, but stopped short at once, realizing the uselessness of his efforts. The priest said nothing, the sleepy forester looked gloomy.

"What terrible tragedies realism contrives for people," said Mitya, in complete despair. The perspiration was streaming down his face. The priest seized the moment to put before him, very reasonably, that even if he succeeded in wakening the man, he would still be drunk and incapable of conversation. "And your business is important," he said, "so you'd certainly better put it off till morning." With a gesture of despair Mitya agreed.

"Father, I will stay here with a light, and seize the favorable moment. As soon as he wakes I'll begin. I'll pay you for the light," he said to the forester, "for the night's lodging, too; you'll remember Dmitri Karamazov. Only, Father, I don't know what we're to do with you. Where will you sleep?"

"No, I'm going home. I'll take his horse and get home," he said, indicating the forester. "And now I'll say good-bye. I wish you all success."

So it was settled. The priest rode off on the forester's horse, delighted to escape, though he shook his head uneasily, wondering whether he ought not next day to inform his benefactor Fyodor Pavlovich of this curious incident, "or he may in an unlucky hour hear of it, be angry, and withdraw his favor." The forester, scratching himself, went back to his room without a word, and Mitya sat on the bench to "catch the favorable moment," as he expressed it. Profound dejection clung about his soul like a heavy mist. A profound, intense dejection! He sat thinking, but could reach no conclusion. The candle burned dimly, a cricket chirped; it became insufferably close in the overheated room. He suddenly pictured the garden, the path behind the garden, the door of his father's house mysteriously opening and Grushenka running in. He leaped up from the bench.

"It's a tragedy!" he said, grinding his teeth. Mechanically he went up to the sleeping man and looked in his face. He was a lean, middle-aged peasant, with a very long face, dark blond curls, and a long, thin, reddish beard, wearing a blue cotton shirt and a black waistcoat, from the pocket of which peeped the chain of a silver watch. Mitya looked at his face with intense hatred, and for some unknown reason his curly hair particularly irritated him. What was insufferably humiliating was, that, after leaving things of such importance and making such sacrifices, he, Mitya, utterly worn out, should with business of such urgency be standing over this dolt on whom his whole fate depended, while he snored as though there were nothing the matter, as though he'd dropped from another planet. "Oh, the irony of fate!" cried Mitya, and, quite losing his head, he fell again to rousing the tipsy peasant. He roused him with a sort of ferocity, pulled him, pushed him, even beat him; but after five minutes of vain exertions, he returned to his bench in helpless despair, and sat down.

"Stupid! Stupid!" cried Mitya. "And how dishonorable it all is!" something made him add. His head began to ache horribly. "Should he give it up and go away altogether?" he wondered. "No, wait till tomorrow now. I'll stay on purpose. What else did I come for? Besides, I've no means of going. How am I to get away from here now? Oh, the idiocy of it!"

But his head ached more and more. He sat without moving, and unconsciously dozed off and fell asleep as he sat. He seemed to have slept two hours or more. He was awakened by his head aching so unbearably that he could have screamed. There was a hammering in his temples, and the top of his head ached. It was a long time before he could wake up fully and understand what had happened to him.

At last he realized that the room was full of charcoal fumes from the stove, and that he might die of suffocation. And the drunken peasant still lay snoring. The candle guttered and was about to go out. Mitya cried out, and ran staggering across the passage into the forester's room. The forester woke up at once, but hearing that the other room was full of fumes, to Mitya's surprise and annoyance, accepted the fact with strange unconcern, though he did go to see to it.

"But he's dead, he's dead! and . . . what am I to do then?" cried Mitya frantically.

They threw open the doors, opened a window and the chimney. Mitya brought a pail of water from the passage. First he wet his own head, then, finding a rag of some sort, dipped it into the water, and put it on Lyagavy's head. The forester still treated the matter contemptuously, and when he opened the window said grumpily: "It'll be all right, now." He went back to sleep, leaving Mitya a lighted lantern. Mitya fussed about the drunken peasant for half an hour, wetting his head, and gravely resolved not to sleep all night. But he was so worn out that when he sat down for a moment to take a breath, he closed his eyes, unconsciously stretched himself full length on the bench and slept like the dead.

It was dreadfully late when he awoke. It was somewhere about nine o'clock. The sun was shining brightly in the two little windows of the hut. The curly-headed peasant was sitting on the bench and had his coat on. He had another samovar and another bottle in front of him. Yesterday's bottle had already been finished, and the new one was more than half empty. Mitya jumped up and saw at once that the cursed peasant was drunk again, hopelessly and incurably. He stared at him for a moment with wide-open eyes. The peasant was silently and slyly watching him, with insulting composure, and even a sort of contemptuous condescension, so Mitya fancied. He rushed up to him.

"Excuse me, you see. . . . I . . . you've most likely heard from the forester here in the hut. I'm Lieutenant Dmitri Karamazov, the son of the old Karamazov whose woodlot you are buying."

"That's a lie!" said the peasant, calmly and confidently.

"A lie? You know Fyodor Pavlovich?"

"I don't know any of your Fyodor Pavloviches," said the peasant, speaking thickly.

"You're bargaining with him for the lot, for the lot. Do wake up, and collect yourself. Father Pavel of Ilyinskoe brought me here. You wrote to Samsonov, and he has sent me to you," Mitya gasped breathlessly.

"You're l-lying!" Lyagavy blurted out again. Mitya's legs went cold.

"For mercy's sake! It isn't a joke! You're tipsy, perhaps. Yet you can speak and understand . . . or else . . . I understand nothing!"

"You're a painter!"

"For mercy's sake! I'm Karamazov, Dmitri Karamazov. I have an offer to make you, an advantageous offer . . . very advantageous offer, concerning the woodlot!"

The peasant stroked his beard importantly.

"No, you've contracted for the job and turned out a scamp. You're a scoundrel!"

"I assure you you're mistaken," cried Mitya, wringing his hands in despair. The peasant still stroked his beard, and suddenly screwed up his eyes cunningly.

"No, you show me this: you tell me the law that allows roguery. D'you hear? You're a scoundrel! Do you understand that?"

Mitya stepped back gloomily, and suddenly "something seemed to hit him on the head," as he said afterwards. In an instant a light seemed to dawn in his mind, "a light was kindled and I grasped it all." He stood, stupefied, wondering how he, after all a man of intelligence, could have yielded to such folly, have been led into such an adventure, and have kept it up for almost twenty-four hours, fussing round this Lyagavy, wetting his head. "Why, the man's drunk, dead drunk, and he'll go on drinking now for a week; what's the use of waiting here? And what if Samsonov sent me here on purpose? What if she? . . . Oh, God, what have I done?"

The peasant sat watching him and grinning. Another time Mitya might have killed the fool in a fury, but now he felt as weak as a child. He went quietly to the bench, took up his overcoat, put it on without a word, and went out of the hut. He did not find the forester in the next room; there was no one there. He took fifty kopecks in small change out of his pocket and put them on the table for his night's lodging, the candle, and the trouble he had given. Coming out of the hut he saw nothing but forest all round. He walked haphazardly, not knowing which way to turn out of the hut, to the right or to the left. Hurrying there the evening before with the priest, he had not noticed the road. He had no revengeful feeling for anybody, even for Samsonov, in his heart. He strode along a narrow forest path, dazed, lost, with his "lost idea," without heeding where he was going. A child could have knocked him down, so weak was he in body and soul. He got out of the forest somehow, however, and a vista of fields, bare after the harvest, stretched as far as the eye could see. "What despair! What death all round!" he repeated striding on and on.

He was saved by meeting an old merchant who was being driven across country in a hired carriage. When he overtook him, Mitya asked the way, and it turned out that the old merchant, too, was going to Volovya. After some discussion they took Mitya along with them. Three hours later they arrived. At Volovya, Mitya at once ordered posting horses to drive to the town, and suddenly realized that he was appallingly hungry. While the horses were being harnessed, an omelette was prepared for him. He ate it all in an instant, ate a huge hunk of bread, ate a sausage, and swallowed three glasses of vodka. After eating, his spirits and his heart grew lighter. He flew towards the town, urged on the driver, and suddenly made a new and "unalterable" plan to procure that "accursed money" before evening. "And to think, only to think that a man's life should be ruined for the sake of that paltry three thousand!" he cried, contemptuously. "I'll settle it today." And if it had not been for the thought of Grushenka and of what might have happened to her, which never left him, he would perhaps have become quite cheerful again. . . . But the thought of her was stabbing him to the heart every moment, like a sharp knife. At last they arrived, and Mitya at once ran to Grushenka.

Chapter III

Gold Mines

This was the visit of Mitya of which Grushenka had spoken to Rakitin with such horror. She was just then expecting the "message," and was much relieved that Mitya had not been to see her that day or the day before. She hoped that "please God he won't come till I'm gone away," and he suddenly burst in on her. The rest we know already. To get him off her hands she suggested at once that he should walk with her to Samsonov's, where she said she absolutely must go "to settle his accounts," and when Mitya accompanied her at once, she said good-bye to him at the gate, making him promise to come at twelve o'clock to take her home again. Mitya, too, was delighted at this arrangement. If she was sitting at Samsonov's she could not be going to Fyodor Pavlovich's, "if only she's not lying," he added at once. But he thought she was not lying from what he saw. He was that sort of jealous man who, in the absence of the beloved woman, at once invents all sorts of awful fancies of what may be happening to her, and how she may be "betraying" him, but, when shaken, heartbroken, convinced of her faithlessness, he runs back to her; at the first glance at her face, her gay, laughing, affectionate face, he revives at once, lays aside all suspicion and with joyful shame abuses himself for his jealousy. After leaving Grushenka at the gate he rushed home. Oh, he had so much still to do that day! But a load had been lifted from his heart, anyway. "Now I must only make haste and find out from Smerdyakov whether anything happened there last night, whether, by any chance, she went to Fyodor Pavlovich; ugh!" floated through his mind. Before he had time to reach his lodging, jealousy had surged up again in his restless heart.

Jealousy! "Othello was not jealous, he was trustful," observed Pushkin.[4] And that remark alone is enough to show the deep insight of our great poet. Othello's soul was shattered and his whole outlook clouded simply because *his ideal was destroyed.* But Othello did not begin hiding, spying, peeping. He was trustful. On the contrary, he had to be led on, pushed on, excited with great difficulty before he could entertain the idea of deceit. The truly jealous man is not like that. It is impossible to picture to oneself the shame and moral degradation to which the jealous man can descend without a qualm of conscience. And yet it's not as though the jealous were all vulgar and base souls. On the contrary, a man of lofty feelings, whose love is pure and full of self-sacrifice, may yet hide under tables, bribe the vilest people, and be familiar with the lowest ignominy of spying and eavesdropping. Othello was incapable of reconciling himself to faithlessness—not incapable of forgiving it, but of reconciling himself to it—though his soul was as innocent and free from malice as a babe's. It is not so with the really jealous man. It is hard to imagine what a jealous man can reconcile himself to and overlook, and what he can forgive! The jealous are the readiest of all to forgive, and all women know it. The jealous man can forgive extraordinarily quickly (though, of course, after a violent scene), and he is able to forgive infidelity almost conclusively proved, the very

4. This remark is found in Pushkin's "Table-talk" from the 1830s.

kisses and embraces he has seen, if only he can somehow be convinced that it has all been "for the last time," and that his rival will vanish from that day forward, will depart to the ends of the earth, or that he himself will carry her away somewhere, where that dreaded rival will not get near her. Of course the reconciliation is only for an hour. For, even if the rival did disappear next day, he would invent another one and would be jealous of him. And one might wonder what there was in a love that had to be so watched over, what a love could be worth that needed such strenuous guarding. But that the jealous will never understand. And yet among them are men of noble hearts. It is remarkable, too, that those very men of noble hearts, standing hidden in some cupboard, listening and spying, never feel the stings of conscience at that moment, anyway, though they understand clearly enough with their "noble hearts" the shameful depths to which they have voluntarily sunk. At the sight of Grushenka, Mitya's jealousy vanished, and for an instant he became trustful and generous, and positively despised himself for his evil feelings. But that only proved that, in his love for that woman, there was an element of something far higher than he himself imagined, that it was not only a sensual passion, not only the "curve of her body," of which he had talked to Alyosha. But, as soon as Grushenka had gone, Mitya began to suspect her of all the low cunning of faithlessness, and he felt no sting of conscience at it.

And so jealousy surged up in him again. He had, in any case, to make haste. The first thing to be done was to get hold of at least a small, temporary loan of money. The nine rubles had almost all gone on his expedition. And, as we all know, one can't take a step without money. But he had thought over in the cart where he could get a loan. He had a brace of fine dueling pistols in a case, which he had not pawned till then because he prized them above all his possessions. In the Metropolis tavern he had some time ago made acquaintance with a young official and had learned that this very opulent bachelor was passionately fond of weapons. He used to buy pistols, revolvers, daggers, hang them on his wall and show them to acquaintances. He prided himself on them, and was quite a specialist on the mechanism of revolvers, how to load them, how to shoot them, and so on. Mitya, without stopping to think, went straight to him, and offered to pawn his pistols to him for ten rubles. The official, delighted, began trying to persuade him to sell them outright. But Mitya would not consent, so the young man gave him ten rubles, protesting that nothing would induce him to take interest. They parted friends. Mitya was in haste; he rushed towards Fyodor Pavlovich's by the back way, to his gazebo, to get hold of Smerdyakov as soon as possible. In this way the fact was established that three or four hours before a certain event, of which I shall speak later on, Mitya had not a farthing, and pawned for ten rubles a possession he valued, though, three hours later, he was in possession of thousands. . . . But I am anticipating.

From Marya Kondratyevna (the woman living near Fyodor Pavlovich's) he learned the very disturbing fact of Smerdyakov's illness. He heard the story of his fall in the cellar, his fit, the doctor's visit, Fyodor Pavlovich's anxiety; he heard with interest, too, that his brother Ivan Fyodorovich had set off that morning for Moscow. "Then he must have driven through Volovya before me," thought Dmitri Fyodorovich but he was terribly distressed about Smerdyakov. "What will happen now? Who'll keep watch for me? Who'll bring me word?" he thought. He began greedily questioning the women whether they had seen anything the evening before. They quite understood what he was trying to find out, and completely reassured him. No one had been there. Ivan Fyodorovich had been there through the night; "everything had been in perfect order." Mitya grew thoughtful. He would certainly have to keep watch today, but where? Here or at Samsonov's gate? He decided that he must be on the lookout both here and there, and meanwhile . . . meanwhile . . . The difficulty was that he had to carry out the new plan that he had made on the journey back. He was sure of its success, but he must not delay acting upon it. Mitya resolved to sacrifice an hour to it: "in an hour I shall know everything, I shall settle everything, and then, then, first of all to Samsonov's. I'll inquire whether Grushenka's there and instantly be back here again, stay till eleven, and then to Samsonov's again to bring her home." This is what he decided.

He flew home, washed, combed his hair, brushed his clothes, dressed, and went to Madame Khokhlakova's. Alas! he had built his hopes on her. He had resolved to borrow three thousand from that lady. And what was more, he felt suddenly convinced that she would not refuse to lend it to him. It may be wondered why, if he felt so certain, he had not gone to her at first, one of his own sort, so to speak, instead of to Samsonov, a man he did not know, who was not of his own class, and to whom he hardly knew how to speak. But the fact was that he had never known Madame Khokhlakova well, and had seen nothing of her for the last month, and that he knew she could not endure him. She had detested him from the first because he was engaged to Katerina Ivanovna, while she had, for some reason, suddenly conceived the desire that Katerina Ivanovna should throw him over, and marry the "charming, chivalrously educated Ivan Fyodorovich, who had such excellent manners." Mitya's manners she detested. Mitya positively laughed at her, and had once said about her that she was just as lively and at her ease as she was uncultivated. But that morning in the cart a brilliant idea had struck him: "If she is so anxious I should not marry Katerina Ivanovna"—and he knew she was positively hysterical upon the subject—"why should she refuse me now that three thousand, just to enable me to leave Katya and get away from her forever? These spoiled fine ladies, if they set their hearts on anything will spare no expense to satisfy their caprice. Besides, she's so rich," Mitya argued.

As for his "plan" it was just the same as before; it consisted of the offer of his rights to Chermashnya—but not with a commercial object, as it had been with Samsonov, not trying to lure the lady with the possibility of making a profit of six or seven thousand—but simply as a noble security for the debt. As he worked out this new idea, Mitya was enchanted with it, but so it always was with him in all his undertakings, in all his sudden decisions. He gave himself up to every new idea with passionate enthusiasm. Yet, when he mounted the steps of Madame Khokhlakova's house he felt a shiver of fear run down his spine. At that moment he saw fully, as a mathematical certainty, that this was his last hope, that if this broke down, nothing else was left him in the world but to "rob and murder someone for the three thousand." It was half past seven when he rang at the bell.

At first fortune seemed to smile upon him. As soon as he was announced he was received with extraordinary rapidity. "As though she were waiting for me," thought Mitya, and as soon as he had been led to the drawing room, the lady of the house herself ran in, and declared at once that she was expecting him.

"I was expecting you! I was expecting you! Though I'd no reason to suppose you would come to see me, as you will admit yourself. Yet, I did expect you. You may marvel at my instinct, Dmitri Fyodorovich, but I was convinced all the morning that you would come."

"That is certainly wonderful, Madame," observed Mitya, sitting down limply, "but I have come to you on a matter of great importance. . . . On a matter of supreme importance for me that is, Madame . . . for me alone . . . and I hasten . . ."

"I know you've come on most important business, Dmitri Fyodorovich; it's not a case of presentiment, no reactionary harking back to the miraculous (have you heard about Father Zosima?). This is a case of mathematics: you couldn't help coming, after all that has passed with Katerina Ivanovna; you couldn't, you couldn't, that's a mathematical certainty."

"The realism of actual life, Madame, that's what it is. But allow me to explain . . ."

"Realism indeed, Dmitri Fyodorovich. I'm all for realism now. I've seen too much of miracles. You've heard that Father Zosima is dead?"

"No, Madame, it's the first time I've heard of it." Mitya was a little surprised. The image of Alyosha rose to his mind.

"Last night, and only imagine . . ."

"Madame," interrupted Mitya, "I can imagine nothing except that I'm in a desperate position, and that if you don't help me, everything will fall through, and I will fall first of all. Excuse me, for the triviality of the expression, but I'm in a fever . . ."

"I know, I know that you're in a fever. You could hardly fail to be, and whatever you may say to me, I know beforehand. I have long been thinking over your destiny, Dmitri Fyodorovich, I am watching over it and studying it. . . . Oh, believe me, I'm an experienced doctor of the soul, Dmitri Fyodorovich."

"Madame, if you are an experienced doctor, I'm certainly an experienced patient," said Mitya, with an effort to be polite, "and I feel that if you are watching over my destiny in this way, you will come to my help in my ruin, and so allow me, at least to explain to you the plan with which I have ventured to come to you . . . and what I am hoping of you. . . . I have come, Madame . . ."

"Don't explain it. It's of secondary importance. But as for help, you're not the first I have helped, Dmitri Fyodorovich. You have most likely heard of my cousin, Madame Belmesova. Her husband was ruined, 'had come to grief,' as you characteristically express it, Dmitri Fyodorovich. I recommended him to take to horse breeding, and now he's doing well. Have you any idea of horse breeding, Dmitri Fyodorovich?"

"Not the faintest, Madame; ah, Madame, not the faintest!" cried Mitya, in nervous impatience, positively starting from his seat. "I simply implore you, Madame, to listen to me. Only give me two minutes of free speech that I may just explain to you everything, the whole plan with which I have come. Besides I am short of time. I'm in a fearful hurry," Mitya cried hysterically, feeling that she was just going to begin talking again, and hoping to cut her short. "I have come in despair . . . in the last gasp of despair, to beg you to lend me the sum of three thousand, a loan, but on safe, most safe security, madame, with the most trustworthy guarantees! Only let me explain . . ."

"You must tell me all that afterwards, afterwards!" Madame Khokhlakova with a gesture demanded silence in her turn, "and whatever you may tell me, I know it all beforehand; I've told you so already. You ask for a certain sum, for three thousand, but I can give you more, immeasurably more, I will save you, Dmitri Fyodorovich, but you must listen to me."

Mitya started from his seat again.

"Madame, will you really be so good!" he cried, with a strong feeling. "Good God, you've saved me! You have saved a man from a violent death, from a bullet. . . . My eternal gratitude . . ."

"I will give you more, infinitely more than three thousand!" cried Madame Khokhlakova, looking with a radiant smile at Mitya's ecstasy.

"Infinitely? But I don't need so much. I only need that fatal three thousand, and on my part I can give security for that sum with infinite gratitude, and I propose a plan which . . ."

"Enough, Dmitri Fyodorovich, it's said and done." Madame Khokhlakova cut him short, with the modest triumph of beneficence. "I have promised to save you, and I will save you. I will save you as I did Belmesov. What do you think of gold mines, Dmitri Fyodorovich?"

"Of the gold mines, Madame? I have never thought anything about them."

"But I have thought of them for you. Thought of them over and over again. I have been watching you for the last month. I've watched you a hundred times as you've walked past, saying to myself: that's a man of energy who ought to go to the gold mines. I've studied your gait and come to the conclusion: that's a man who would find mines."

"From my gait, Madame?" said Mitya, smiling.

"Yes, from your gait. You surely don't deny that character can be told from the gait, Dmitri Fyodorovich? Science supports the idea. I'm all for science and realism now. After all this business with Father Zosima, which has so upset me, from this very day I'm a realist and I want to devote myself to practical usefulness. I'm cured. 'Enough!' as Turgenev says."[5]

"But, Madame, the three thousand you so generously promised to lend me . . ."

"It is yours, Dmitri Fyodorovich," Madame Khokhlakova cut in at once. "The money is as good as in your pocket, not three thousand, but three million, Dmitri Fyodorovich, in less than no time. I'll make you a present of the idea: you shall find gold mines, make millions, return and become a man of action, and wake us up and lead us to better things. Are we to leave it all to the Yids? You will found institutions and enterprises of all sorts. You will help the poor, and they will bless you. This is the age of railways, Dmitri Fyodorovich. You'll become famous and indispensable to the Department of Finance, which is so badly off at present. The depreciation of the ruble[6] keeps me awake at night, Dmitri Fyodorovich; people don't know that side of me . . ."

---

5. Turgenev published a farewell to literature, "Enough. Fragment from the Notes of a Dead Artist" in 1864, but continued writing until his death in 1883. Dostoevsky had subjected Turgenev to critical sarcasm before, most notably in the character of the novelist Karmazinov in *Demons* (1872).
6. The paper ruble was not fully backed by precious metal holdings, and its depreciation was a frequent topic in the press in the 1860s and '70s.

"Madame, Madame!" Dmitrí Fyodorovich interrupted with an uneasy presentiment. "I shall indeed, perhaps, follow your advice, your wise advice, Madame. . . . I shall perhaps set off . . . to the gold mines. . . . I'll come and see you again about it . . . many times, indeed . . . but now, that three thousand you so generously . . . oh, that would set me free, and if you could today . . . you see, I haven't a minute, a minute to lose today . . ."

"Enough, Dmitri Fyodorovich, enough!" Madame Khokhlakova interrupted emphatically. "The question is, will you go to the gold mines or not; have you quite made up your mind? Answer mathematically."

"I will go, Madame, afterwards. . . . I'll go wherever you like . . . but now . . ."

"Wait!" cried Madame Khokhlakova. And jumping up and running to a handsome bureau with numerous little drawers, she began pulling out one drawer after another, looking for something with desperate haste.

"The three thousand," thought Mitya, his heart almost stopping, "and at once . . . without any papers or formalities . . . that's doing things in gentlemanly style! She's a splendid woman, if only she didn't talk so much!"

"Here!" cried Madame Khokhlakova, running back joyfully to Mitya, "here is what I was looking for!"

It was a tiny silver icon on a cord, such as is sometimes worn next to the skin with a cross.

"This is from Kiev, Dmitri Fyodorovich," she went on reverently, "from the relics of the holy martyr, Barbara.[7] Let me put it on your neck myself, and with it dedicate you to a new life, to a new career."

And she actually put the cord round his neck, and began arranging it. In extreme embarrassment, Mitya bent down and helped her, and at last he got it under his necktie and collar through his shirt to his chest.

"Now you can set off," Madame Khokhlakova pronounced, sitting down solemnly in her place again.

"Madame, I am so touched. I don't know how to thank you, indeed . . . for such kindness, but . . . if only you knew how precious time is to me. . . . That sum of money, for which I shall be indebted to your generosity. . . . Oh, Madame, since you are so kind, so touchingly generous to me" (Mitya exclaimed impulsively) "then let me reveal to you . . . though, of course, you've known it a long time . . . that I love somebody here. . . . I have been false to Katya . . . Katerina Ivanovna I should say. . . . Oh, I've behaved inhumanly, dishonorably to her, but I fell in love here with another woman . . . a woman whom you, Madame, perhaps, despise, for you know everything already, but whom I cannot leave on any account, and therefore that three thousand now . . ."

"Leave everything, Dmitri Fyodorovich," Madame Khokhlakova interrupted in the most decisive tone. "Leave everything, especially women. Mines are your goal, and there's no place for women there. Afterwards, when you come back rich and famous, you will find the girl of your heart in the highest society. That will be a modern girl, a girl of education and

---

7. Relics believed to be those of Saint Barbara (third or fourth century C.E.) were brought from Constantinople to Kiev in the twelfth century. Kiev, the current capital of Ukraine and a center of early eastern Slavic civilization, has long been a center of Eastern Orthodox faith.

advanced ideas. By that time the dawning woman question will have gained ground, and the new woman will have appeared."[8]

"Madame, that's not the point, not at all. . . ." Mitya clasped his hands in entreaty.

"Yes, it is, Dmitri Fyodorovich, just what you need; the very thing you're yearning for, though you don't realize it yourself. I am not at all opposed to the present woman movement, Dmitri Fyodorovich. The development of woman, and even the political emancipation of woman in the near future— that's my ideal. I've a daughter myself, Dmitri Fyodorovich, people don't know that side of me. I wrote a letter to the author, Shchedrin, on that subject. That author has taught me so much, so much about the vocation of woman. So last year I sent him an anonymous letter of two lines: 'I kiss and embrace you, my author, for the modern woman. Persevere.' And I signed myself, 'a Mother.' I thought of signing myself 'a contemporary Mother,' and hesitated, but I stuck to the simple 'Mother'; there's more moral beauty in that, Dmitri Fyodorovich. And the word 'contemporary' might have reminded him of *The Contemporary*—a painful recollection owing to the censorship. . . .[9] Good Heavens, what is the matter!"

"Madame!" cried Mitya, jumping up at last, clasping his hands before her in helpless entreaty. "You will make me weep if you delay what you have so generously . . ."

"Oh, do weep, Dmitri Fyodorovich, do weep! That's a noble feeling . . . such a path lies open before you! Tears will ease your heart, and later on you will return rejoicing. You will hasten to me from Siberia on purpose to share your joy with me . . ."

"But allow me, too!" Mitya cried suddenly. "For the last time I entreat you, tell me, can I have the sum you promised me today, if not, when may I come for it?"

"What sum, Dmitri Fyodorovich?"

"The three thousand you promised me . . . that you so generously . . ."

"Three thousand? Rubles? Oh, no, I haven't got three thousand," Madame Khokhlakova announced with serene amazement. Mitya was stupefied.

"Why, you said just now . . . you said . . . you said it was as good as in my hands . . ."

"Oh, no, you misunderstood me, Dmitri Fyodorovich. In that case you misunderstood me. I was talking of the gold mines. It's true I promised you more, infinitely more than three thousand, I remember it all now, but I was referring to the mines."

"But the money? The three thousand?" Dmitri Fyodorovich exclaimed, stupidly.

"Oh, if you meant money, I haven't any. I haven't a penny, Dmitri Fyodorovich. I'm quarreling with my steward about it, and I've just borrowed five hundred rubles from Miüsov, myself. No, no, I don't have any money. And, do you know, Dmitri Fyodorovich, if I had, I wouldn't give it to you. In the first place I never lend money. Lending money means losing friends. And I wouldn't give it to you particularly. I wouldn't give it to you,

8. Women's changing status in Russian society was a hotly debated topic in the 1860s and '70s.
9. Saltykov-Shchedrin published the revolutionary democratic journal *The Contemporary* until it was closed by the government censors in 1866. Later he edited *Notes of the Fatherland*, where he published a "Letter to Khokhlakova" in reply to Dostoevsky.

because I like you and want to save you, for all you need is the gold mines, the gold mines, the gold mines!"

"Oh, go to the devil!" Mitya suddenly let out a roar, and with all his might brought his fist down on the table.

"Aie! Aie!" cried Madame Khokhlakova in fright, and she flew to the other end of the drawing room.

Mitya spat on the floor, and strode rapidly out of the room, out of the house, into the street, into the darkness! He walked like one possessed, and beating himself on the breast, on the spot where he had struck himself two days previously, before Alyosha, the last time he saw him in the dark, on the road. What those blows upon his breast signified, *on that spot*, and what he meant by it—that was, for the time, a secret which was known to no one in the world, and had not been told even to Alyosha. But that secret meant for him more than disgrace; it meant ruin, suicide. So he had determined, if he did not get hold of the three thousand that would pay his debt to Katerina Ivanovna, and so remove from his breast, from *that spot on his breast*, the shame he carried upon it, that weighed on his conscience. All this will be fully explained to the reader later on, but now that his last hope had vanished, this man, so strong physically, burst out crying like a little child a few steps from the Khokhlakovs' house. He walked on, and not knowing what he was doing, wiped away his tears with his fist. In this way he reached the square, and suddenly became aware that he had stumbled against something. He heard a piercing wail from an old woman whom he had almost knocked down.

"Good Lord, you've nearly killed me! Why don't you look where you're going, rascal?"

"Why, it's you!" cried Mitya, recognizing the old woman in the dark. It was the old servant who waited on Samsonov, whom Mitya had particularly noticed the day before.

"And who are you, my good sir?" said the old woman in quite a different voice. "I don't know you in the dark."

"You live at Kuzma Kuzmich's. You're the servant there?"

"Just so, sir, I was only running out to Prokhorich's . . . But I don't know you now."

"Tell me, my good woman, is Agrafena Alexandrovna there now?" said Mitya, beside himself with suspense. "I saw her to the house some time ago."

"She has been there, sir. She stayed a little while, and went off again."

"What? Went away?" cried Mitya. "When did she go?"

"Why, as soon as she came. She only stayed a minute. She only told Kuzma Kuzmich a tale that made him laugh, and then she ran away."

"You're lying, damn you!" roared Mitya.

"Aie! Aie!" shrieked the old woman, but Mitya had vanished.

He ran with all his might to the house where Grushenka lived. At the moment he reached it, Grushenka was on her way to Mokroe. It was not more than a quarter of an hour after her departure. Fenya was sitting with her grandmother, the old cook, Matryona, in the kitchen when "the captain" ran in. Fenya uttered a piercing shriek on seeing him.

"You scream?" roared Mitya, "where is she?" But without giving the terror-stricken Fenya time to utter a word, he suddenly fell all of a heap at her feet.

"Fenya, for Christ's sake, tell me, where is she?"

"I don't know. Dmitri Fyodorovich, my dear, I don't know. You may kill me but I can't tell you." Fenya swore and protested. "You went out with her yourself not long ago . . ."

"She came back!"

"Indeed she didn't. By God I swear she didn't come back."

"You're lying!" shouted Mitya. "From your terror I know where she is."

He rushed away. Fenya in her fright was glad she had got off so easily. But she knew very well that it was only that he was in such haste, or she might not have fared so well. But as he ran, he surprised both Fenya and old Matryona by an unexpected action. On the table stood a brass mortar, with a pestle in it, a small brass pestle, not much more than six inches long. Mitya already had opened the door with one hand when, with the other, he snatched up the pestle, and thrust it in his side pocket and was off.

"Oh Lord! He's going to murder someone!" cried Fenya, flinging up her hands.

Chapter IV

In the Dark

Where was he running? Obviously, "where could she be except at Fyodor Pavlovich's? She must have run straight to him from Samsonov's, that was clear now. The whole intrigue, the whole deceit was evident." . . . It all rushed whirling through his mind. He did not run to Marya Kondra-tyevna's. "There was no need to go there . . . not the slightest need . . . he must raise no alarm . . . they would run and tell directly. . . . Marya Kon-dratyevna was clearly in the plot, Smerdyakov too, he too, all had been bought over!" He formed another plan of action: he ran a long way round Fyodor Pavlovich's house, crossing the lane, running down Dmitrovsky Street, then over the little bridge, and so came straight to the deserted alley at the back, which was empty and uninhabited, with, on one side the hurdle fence of a neighbor's kitchen garden, on the other, the strong high fence that ran all round Fyodor Pavlovich's garden. Here he chose a spot, apparently the very place, where, according to the tradition, he knew Stinking Lizaveta had once climbed over it: "If she could climb over it," the thought, God knows why, occurred to him, "surely I can." He did in fact jump up, and instantly contrived to catch hold of the top of the fence. Then he vigorously pulled himself up and sat astride on it. Close by, in the garden, stood the bathhouse, but from the fence he could see the lighted window of the house too. "Yes, the old man's bedroom is lit up. She's there!" and he leaped from the fence into the garden. Though he knew Grigory was ill and very likely Smerdyakov, too, and that there was no one to hear him, he instinctively hid himself, stood still, and began to listen. But there was dead silence on all sides and, as though by design, complete stillness, not the slightest breath of wind.

"And nought but the whispering silence,"[1] the line for some reason rose to his mind. "If only no one heard me jump over the fence! It seems

---

1. An inexact rendering of Book II, lines 415–19 from Pushkin's mock epic poem *Ruslan and Lyud-mila* (1820): "[She] does not sleep, redoubles attention, / Motionless looks into the darkness . . . / All is obscure, deathly silence! / [She] only hears the heart's throbbing . . . / And thinks . . . the silence whispers."

no one did." After standing still for a minute, he walked softly over the grass in the garden, avoiding the trees and shrubs. He walked slowly, creeping stealthily at every step, listening to his own footsteps. It took him five minutes to reach the lighted window. He remembered that just under the window there were several thick and high bushes of elder and white hazel. The door from the house into the garden, on the left-hand side, was shut; he had carefully looked purposely to see, in passing. At last he reached the bushes and hid behind them. He held his breath. "I must wait now," he thought, "to reassure them, in case they heard my footsteps and are listening. . . . If only I don't cough or sneeze."

He waited two minutes. His heart was beating violently, and, at moments, he could scarcely breathe. "No, this throbbing at my heart won't stop," he thought. "I can't wait any longer." He was standing behind a bush in the shadow. The light of the window fell on the front part of the bush. "How red the white hazel berries are!"[2] he murmured, not knowing why. Softly and noiselessly, step by step, he approached the window, and raised himself on tiptoe. All Fyodor Pavlovich's bedroom lay open before him. It was not a large room, and was divided in two parts by a red screen, "Chinese," as Fyodor Pavlovich used to call it. The word "Chinese" flashed into Mitya's mind, "and behind the screen, is Grushenka," thought Mitya. He began watching Fyodor Pavlovich, who was wearing his new striped-silk dressing gown, which Mitya had never seen, and a silk cord with tassels round the waist. A clean, dandified shirt of fine linen with gold studs peeped out under the collar of the dressing gown. On his head Fyodor Pavlovich had the same red bandage which Alyosha had seen. "He's all dressed up," thought Mitya. His father was standing near the window, apparently lost in thought. Suddenly he jerked up his head, listened a moment, and, hearing nothing, went up to the table, poured out half a glass of brandy from a decanter, and drank it off. Then he uttered a deep sigh, again stood still a moment, walked distractedly up to the mirror on the wall, with his right hand raised the red bandage on his forehead a little, and began examining his bruises and scars, which had not yet disappeared. "He's alone," thought Mitya, "in all probability he's alone." Fyodor Pavlovich moved away from the mirror, turned suddenly to the window and looked out. Mitya instantly slipped away into the shadow.

"She may be there behind the screen. Perhaps she's asleep by now," he thought, with a pang at his heart. Fyodor Pavlovich moved away from the window. "He's looking for her out of the window, so she's not there. Why should he stare out into the dark? He's wild with impatience." . . . Mitya slipped back at once, and fell to gazing in at the window again. The old man was sitting down at the table, apparently dejected. At last he put his elbow on the table, and laid his right cheek against his hand. Mitya watched him eagerly.

"He's alone, he's alone!" he repeated again. "If she were here, his face would be different." Strange to say, a queer, irrational vexation rose up in his heart that she was not here. "It's not that she's not here," he explained to himself, immediately, "but that I can't tell for certain whether she is or not." Mitya remembered afterwards that his mind was, at that moment, exceptionally clear, that he took in everything to the slightest detail, and missed no point. But a feeling of misery, the misery of uncertainty and

2. These lines have not been identified.

indecision was growing in his heart with every instant. "Is she here or not?" The angry doubt filled his heart, and suddenly, making up his mind, he put out his hand and softly knocked on the window frame. He knocked the signal the old man had agreed upon with Smerdyakov, twice slowly and then three times more quickly, tap-tap-tap, the signal that meant "Grushenka is here!" The old man started, jerked up his head, and, jumping up quickly, ran to the window. Mitya slipped away into the shadow. Fyodor Pavlovich opened the window and thrust his whole head out.

"Grushenka, is it you? Is it you?" he said, in a sort of trembling half-whisper. "Where are you, my little angel, where are you?" He was fearfully agitated and breathless.

"He's alone," Mitya decided.

"Where are you?" cried the old man again; and he thrust his head out further, thrust it out to the shoulders, gazing in all directions, right and left. "Come here, I've a little present for you. Come, I'll show you . . ."

"He means the three thousand," thought Mitya.

"But where are you? Are you at the door? I'll open it at once."

And the old man almost climbed out of the window, peering out to the right, where there was a door into the garden, trying to see into the darkness. In another second he would certainly have run out to open the door without waiting for Grushenka's answer. Mitya looked at him from the side without stirring. The old man's profile that he loathed so, his pendant Adam's apple, his hooked nose, his lips that smiled in sweet expectation, were all brightly lit up by the slanting lamplight falling on the left from the room. A horrible fury of hatred suddenly surged up in Mitya's heart, "There he was, his rival, the man who had tormented him, had ruined his life!" It was a rush of that sudden, furious, revengeful anger of which he had spoken, as though foreseeing it, to Alyosha, four days ago in the gazebo, in answer to Alyosha's question, "How can you say you'll kill our father?"

"I don't know, I don't know," he had said then. "Perhaps I shall not kill him, perhaps I shall. I'm afraid he'll suddenly be so loathsome to me *at that moment, with that face of his*. I hate his Adam's apple, his nose, his eyes, his shameless grin. I feel a personal repulsion. That's what I'm afraid of, that's what may be too much for me . . ."

This personal repulsion was growing unendurable. Mitya was beside himself. He suddenly pulled the brass pestle out of his pocket . . .

"God was watching over me then," Mitya himself said afterwards. At that very moment Grigory woke up on his bed of sickness. Earlier in the evening he had undergone the treatment which Smerdyakov had described to Ivan Fyodorovich. He had rubbed himself all over with vodka mixed with a secret very strong decoction, had drunk what was left of the mixture while his wife repeated a "certain prayer" over him, after which he had gone to bed. Martha Ignatyevna had tasted the stuff, too, and, being unused to strong drink, slept like the dead beside her husband. But Grigory woke up in the night, quite suddenly, and, after a moment's reflection, though he immediately felt a sharp pain in his back, he sat up in bed. Then he deliberated again, got up and dressed hurriedly. Perhaps his conscience was uneasy at the thought of sleeping while the house was unguarded "in such perilous times." Smerdyakov, exhausted by his fit, lay motionless in the next room. Martha Ignatyevna did not stir. "The stuff's been too much for the woman," Grigory thought, glancing at her, and groaning, he went out on the steps. No doubt he only intended to look out from the steps, for he was hardly able to walk, the pain in his back and his right leg was intolerable. But he suddenly remembered that he had not locked the little gate into the garden that evening. He was the most punctual and precise of men, a man who adhered to an unchangeable routine, and habits that lasted for years. Limping and writhing with pain he went down the steps and towards the garden. Yes, the gate stood wide open. Mechanically he stepped into the garden. Perhaps he fancied something, perhaps caught some sound, and, glancing to the left he saw his master's window open. No one was looking out of it then. "What's it open for? It's not summer now," thought Grigory, and suddenly, at that very instant he caught a glimpse of something extraordinary before him in the garden. Forty paces in front of him a man seemed to be running in the dark, a sort of shadow was moving very fast. "Good Lord!" cried Grigory beside himself, and forgetting the pain in his back, he hurried to intercept the running figure. He took a short cut, evidently he knew the garden better; the flying figure went towards the bathhouse, ran behind it and rushed to the garden fence. Grigory followed, not losing sight of him, and ran, forgetting everything. He reached the fence at the very moment the man was climbing over it. Grigory cried out, beside himself, pounced on him, and clutched his leg in his two hands.

Yes, his foreboding had not deceived him; he recognized him, it was he, the "monster-parricide"!

"Parricide!" the old man shouted so that the whole neighborhod could hear, but he had not time to shout more, he fell at once, as though struck by lightning. Mitya jumped back into the garden and bent over the fallen man. In Mitya's hands was the brass pestle, and he flung it mechanically in the grass. The pestle fell two paces from Grigory, not in the grass but on the path, in a most conspicuous place. For some seconds he examined the prostrate figure before him. The old man's head was covered with blood. Mitya put out his hand and began feeling it. He remembered afterwards clearly, that he had been awfully anxious "to make sure" whether he had broken the old man's skull, or simply "stunned" him with the pestle. But the blood was flowing horribly; and in a moment Mitya's fingers were drenched with the hot stream. He remembered taking out of his pocket the clean white handkerchief with which he had provided himself for his visit to Madame Khokhlakova, and putting it to the old man's head, senselessly trying to wipe the blood from his face and temples. But the handkerchief was instantly soaked with blood. "Good heavens! what am I doing it for?" thought Mitya, suddenly pulling himself together. "If I have broken his skull, how can I find out now? And what difference does it make now?" he added, hopelessly. "If I've killed him, I've killed him . . . you've come to grief, old man, so there you must lie!" he said aloud. And suddenly, turning to the fence, he vaulted over it into the lane and fell to running—the handkerchief soaked with blood he held, crushed up, in his right fist, and, as he ran, he thrust it into the back pocket of his coat. He ran headlong, and the few passersby who met him in the dark, in the streets, remembered afterwards that they had met a man running frenziedly that night. He flew back again to the widow

Morozova's house. Immediately after he had left it, that evening, Fenya
had rushed to the chief porter, Nazar Ivanovich, and begged him, for
Christ's sake, "not to let the captain in again today or tomorrow." Nazar
Ivanovich promised, but went upstairs to his mistress who had suddenly
sent for him, and meeting his nephew, a boy of twenty, who had recently
come from the country, on the way up told him to take his place, but forgot to mention "the captain." Mitya, running up to the gate, knocked.
The lad instantly recognized him, for Mitya had more than once tipped
him. Opening the gate at once, he let him in, and hastened to inform him
with a good-humored smile that "Agrafena Alexandrovna is not at home
now, you know."

"Where is she then, Prokhor?" asked Mitya, stopping short.

"She set off this evening, some two hours ago, with Timothy, to
Mokroe."

"What for?" cried Mitya.

"That I can't say. To see some officer. Someone invited her and horses
were sent to fetch her."

Mitya left him, and ran like a madman to Fenya.

Chapter V

A Sudden Decision

She was sitting in the kitchen with her grandmother; they were both
just going to bed. Relying on Nazar Ivanovich, they had not locked themselves in. Mitya ran in, pounced on Fenya and seized her firmly by the
throat.

"Speak at once! Where is she? With whom is she now, at Mokroe?" he
roared furiously.

Both the women squealed.

"Aie! I'll tell you. Aie, Dmitri Fyodorovich, darling, I'll tell you everything directly, I won't hide anything," gabbled Fenya, frightened to death;
"she's gone to Mokroe, to her officer."

"What officer?" roared Mitya.

"To her officer, the same one she used to know, the one who threw her
over five years ago," cackled Fenya, as fast as she could speak.

Mitya withdrew the hands with which he was squeezing her throat. He
stood facing her, pale as death, unable to utter a word, but his eyes
showed that he realized it all, all, from the first word, and guessed the
whole position. Poor Fenya was not in a condition at that moment to
observe whether he understood or not. She remained sitting on the trunk
as she had been when he ran into the room, trembling all over, holding
her hands out before her as though trying to defend herself. She seemed
to have grown rigid in that position. Her wide-open, scared eyes were
fixed immovably upon him. And to make matters worse, both his hands
were smeared with blood. On the way, as he ran, he must have touched
his forehead with them, wiping off the perspiration, so that on his forehead and his right cheek were bloodstained patches. Fenya was on the
verge of hysterics. The old cook had jumped up and was staring at him
like a madwoman, almost unconscious with terror.

Mitya stood for a moment, then mechanically sank on to a chair next to Fenya. He sat, not reflecting but, as it were, terror-stricken, benumbed. Yet everything was clear as day: that officer, he knew about him, he knew everything perfectly, he had known it from Grushenka herself, had known that a letter had come from him a month before. So that for a month, for a whole month this had been going on in secret from him, till the very arrival of this new man, and he had never thought of him! But how could he, how could he not have thought of him? Why was it he had forgotten this officer, like that, forgotten him as soon as he heard of him? That was the question that faced him like some monstrous thing. And he looked at this monstrous thing with horror, growing cold with horror.

But suddenly, as gently and mildly as a gentle and affectionate child, he began speaking to Fenya as though he had utterly forgotten how he had scared and hurt her just now. He fell to questioning Fenya with an extreme preciseness, astonishing in his position, and though the girl looked wildly at his bloodstained hands, she, too, with wonderful readiness and rapidity, answered every question as though eager to put the whole truth and nothing but the truth before him. Little by little, even with a sort of enjoyment, she began explaining every detail, not wanting to torment him, but, as it were, eager to be of the utmost service to him. She described the whole of that day, in great detail, the visit of Rakitin and Alyosha, how she, Fenya, had stood on the watch, how the mistress had set off, and how she had called out of the window to Alyosha to give him, Mitya, her greetings, and to tell him "to remember forever how she had loved him for an hour." Hearing of the message, Mitya suddenly smiled, and there was a flush of color on his pale cheeks. At the same moment Fenya said to him, not a bit afraid now to be inquisitive:

"Look at your hands, Dmitri Fyodorovich. They're all over blood!"

"Yes," answered Mitya mechanically. He looked carelessly at his hands and at once forgot them and Fenya's question. He sank into silence again. Twenty minutes had passed since he had run in. His first horror was over, but evidently some new fixed determination had taken possession of him. He suddenly stood up, smiling dreamily.

"What has happened to you, sir?" said Fenya, pointing to his hands again. She spoke compassionately, as though she felt very near to him now in his grief. Mitya looked at his hands again.

"That's blood, Fenya," he said, looking at her with a strange expression. "That's human blood, and, my God! why was it shed? But . . . Fenya . . . there's a fence here" (he looked at her as though setting her a riddle) "a high fence, and terrible to look at. But, at dawn tomorrow, 'when the sun flies high,' Mitya will leap over that fence. . . . You don't understand what fence, Fenya, and never mind. . . . You'll hear tomorrow and understand . . . and now, good-bye. I won't stand in her way. I'll step aside, I know how to step aside. Live, my joy. . . . You loved me for an hour, remember Mitenka Karamazov so forever. . . . She always used to call me Mitenka, do you remember?"

And with those words he went suddenly out of the kitchen. Fenya was almost more frightened at this sudden departure than she had been when he ran in and attacked her.

Just ten minutes later Dmitri Fyodorovich went in to Pyotr Ilyich Perkhotin, the young official with whom he had pawned his pistols. It was by now half past eight, and Pyotr Ilyich had finished his evening tea, and had just put his coat on again to go to the Metropolis to play billiards. Mitya caught him coming out. Seeing him with his face all smeared with blood, the young man uttered a cry of surprise.

"Good Lord! What's the matter with you?"

"I've come for my pistols," said Mitya quickly, "and brought you the money. And thanks very much. I'm in a hurry, Pyotr Ilyich, please make haste."

Pyotr Ilyich grew more and more surprised; he suddenly caught sight of a bundle of bills in Mitya's hand, and what was more, he had walked in holding the bills as no one walks in and no one carries money: he had them in his right hand, and held them outstretched as if to show them. Perkhotin's servant boy, who met Mitya in the passage, said afterwards that he walked into the passage in the same way, with the money outstretched in his hand, so he must have been carrying them like that even in the street. They were all rainbow-colored hundred-ruble bills, and the fingers holding them were covered with blood. When Pyotr Ilyich was questioned later on as to the sum of money, he said that it was difficult to judge at a glance, but that it might have been two thousand, or perhaps three, but it was a big, "fat" bundle. "Dmitri Fyodorovich," so he testified afterwards, "seemed unlike himself, too; not drunk, but, as it were, exalted, lost to everything, but at the same time, as it were, absorbed, as though pondering and searching for something and unable to come to a decision. He was in great haste, answered abruptly and very strangely, and at moments seemed not at all dejected but quite cheerful."

"But what *is* the matter with you? What's wrong?" cried Pyotr Ilyich, looking wildly at his guest. "How is it that you're all covered with blood? Have you had a fall? Look at yourself!"

He took him by the elbow and led him to the glass.

Seeing his bloodstained face, Mitya started and scowled wrathfully.

"Eh, the devil! That's the last straw," he muttered angrily, hurriedly changing the bills from his right hand to the left, and impulsively jerked the handkerchief out of his pocket. But the handkerchief turned out to be soaked with blood, too (it was the handkerchief he had used to wipe Grigory's face). There was scarcely a white spot on it, and it had not merely begun to dry, but had stiffened into a crumpled ball and could not be pulled apart. Mitya threw it angrily on the floor.

"Oh, the devil!" he said. "Don't you have a rag of some sort . . . to wipe my face?"

"So you're only stained, not wounded? You'd better wash," said Pyotr Ilyich. "Here's a washstand. I'll pour you out some water."

"A washstand? That's all right . . . but where am I to put this?" With the strangest perplexity he indicated his bundle of hundred-ruble bills, looking inquiringly at Pyotr Ilyich as though it were for him to decide what he, Mitya, was to do with his own money.

"In your pocket, or on the table here. They won't be lost."

"In my pocket? Yes, in my pocket. All right. . . . But I say, that's all nonsense," he cried, as though suddenly coming out of his absorption. "Look here, let's first settle that business of the pistols. Give them back to me. Here's your money . . . because I am in great need of them . . . and I haven't a minute, a minute to spare."

And taking the topmost bill from the bundle he held it out to Pyotr Ilyich.

"But I don't have enough change. Don't you have anything smaller?"

"No," said Mitya, looking again at the bundle, and as though not trusting his own words he turned over two or three of the topmost ones. "No, they're all alike," he added, and again he looked inquiringly at Pyotr Ilyich.

"How have you grown so rich?" the latter asked. "Wait, I'll send my boy to Plotnikov's, they close late—to see if they won't change it. Here, Misha!" he called into the passage.

"To Plotnikov's shop—splendid!" cried Mitya, as though struck by an idea. "Misha," he turned to the boy as he came in, "look here, run to Plotnikov's and tell them that Dmitri Fyodorovich sends his greetings, and will be there directly. . . . But listen, listen, tell them to have champagne, three cases ready before I come, and packed as it was to take to Mokroe. I took four cases with me then," he added (suddenly addressing Pyotr Ilyich); "they know all about it, don't you trouble, Misha," he turned again to the boy. "Stay, listen; tell them to put in cheese, Strasbourg pâté, smoked fish, ham, caviar, and everything, everything they've got, up to a hundred rubles, or a hundred and twenty as before. . . . But wait: don't let them forget dessert, sweets, pears, watermelons, two or three or four—no, one melon's enough, and chocolate, candy, toffee, fondants; in fact, everything I took to Mokroe before, three hundred rubles' worth with the champagne . . . let it be just the same again. And remember, Misha, if you are called Misha. . . . His name is Misha, isn't it?" He turned to Pyotr Ilyich again.

"Wait a minute," Pyotr Ilyich intervened, listening and watching him uneasily, "you'd better go yourself and tell them. He'll muddle it."

"He will, I see he will! Eh, Misha! Why, I was going to kiss you for the commission. . . . If you don't make a mistake, there's ten rubles for you, run along, make haste. . . . Champagne's the chief thing, let them bring up champagne. And brandy, too, and red and white wine, and all I had then. . . . They know what I had then."

"But listen!" Pyotr Ilyich interrupted with some impatience. "I say, let him simply run and change the money and tell them not to close, and you go and tell them. . . . Give him your bill. Be off, Misha! Put your best leg forward!" Pyotr Ilyich seemed to hurry Misha off on purpose, because the boy remained standing with his mouth and eyes wide open, apparently understanding little of Mitya's orders, gazing up with amazement and terror at his bloodstained face and the trembling bloodstained fingers that held the bills.

"Well, now come and wash," said Pyotr Ilyich, sternly. "Put the money on the table or else in your pocket. . . . That's right, come along. But take off your coat."

And beginning to help him off his coat, he cried out again:

"Look, your coat's covered with blood, too!"

"That . . . it's not the coat. It's only a little here on the sleeve. . . . And that's only here where the handkerchief lay. It must have soaked through. I must have sat on the handkerchief at Fenya's, and the blood's come through," Mitya explained at once with astounding ingenuousness. Pyotr Ilyich listened, frowning.

"Well, you must have been up to something; you must have been fighting with someone," he muttered.

They began to wash. Pyotr Ilyich held the jug and poured out the water. Mitya, in desperate haste, scarcely soaped his hands (they were trembling, and Pyotr Ilyich remembered it afterwards). But the young official insisted on his soaping them thoroughly and rubbing them more. He seemed to exercise more and more sway over Mitya, as time went on. It may be noted in passing that he was a young man of sturdy character.

"Look, you haven't got your nails clean. Now rub your face; here, on your temples, by your ear. . . . Will you go in that shirt? Where are you going? Look, all the cuff of your right sleeve is covered with blood."

"Yes, it's all bloody," observed Mitya, looking at the cuff of his shirt.

"Then change your shirt."

"I don't have time. You see I'll . . ." Mitya went on with the same confiding ingenuousness, drying his face and hands on the towel, and putting on his coat. "I'll turn it up at the wrist. It won't be seen under the coat. . . . You see!"

"Tell me now, what game have you been up to? Have you been fighting with someone? In the tavern again, as before? Have you been beating that captain again?" Pyotr Ilyich asked him reproachfully. "Whom have you been beating now . . . or killing, perhaps?"

"Nonsense!" said Mitya.

"Why 'nonsense'?"

"Don't worry," said Mitya, and he suddenly laughed. "I smashed an old woman in the marketplace just now."

"Smashed? An old woman?"

"An old man!" cried Mitya, looking Pyotr Ilyich straight in the face, laughing, and shouting at him as though he were deaf.

"Devil take it! An old woman, an old man . . . Did you kill someone?"

"We made up. Had a fight—then made up. In a place I know of. We parted friends. A fool. . . . He's forgiven me. . . . He's sure to have forgiven me by now . . . if he had got up, he wouldn't have forgiven me"— Mitya suddenly winked—"only, devil take him, you know, I say, Pyotr Ilyich, devil take him! Don't worry about him! I don't want to just now!" Mitya snapped out, resolutely.

"Whatever do you want to go picking quarrels with everyone for? . . . Just as you did with that captain over some trifles. . . . You've been fighting and now you're rushing off on the spree—that's just like you! Three cases of champagne—what do you want all that for?"

"Bravo! Now give me the pistols. Upon my honor I don't have time now. I should like to have a chat with you, my dear boy, but I don't have time. And there's no need, it's too late for talking. Where's my money? Where have I put it?" he cried, thrusting his hands into his pockets.

"You put it on the table . . . yourself. . . . Here it is. Had you forgotten? Money's like trash or water to you, it seems. Here are your pistols. It's an odd thing, at six o'clock you pledged them for ten rubles, and now you've got thousands. Two or three I should say."

"Three, you bet," laughed Mitya, stuffing the notes into the side pocket of his trousers.

"You'll lose it like that. Have you found a gold mine?"

"The mines? The gold mines?" Mitya shouted at the top of his voice and went off in a roar of laughter. "Would you like to go to the mines,

Perkhotin? There's a lady here who'll stump up three thousand for you, if only you'll go. She did it for me, she's so awfully fond of gold mines. Do you know Madame Khokhlakova?"

"I don't know her, but I've heard of her and seen her. Did she really give you three thousand? Did she really?" said Pyotr Ilyich, eyeing him dubiously.

"As soon as the sun flies high tomorrow, as soon as Phoebus, ever young, flies upwards, praising and glorifying God,[3] you go to her, this Madame Khokhlakova, and ask her whether she did stump up that three thousand or not. Try and find out."

"I don't know on what terms you are . . . since you say it so positively, I suppose she did give it to you. You've got the money in your paw, but instead of going to Siberia you're spending it all. . . . Where are you really off to now, eh?"

"To Mokroe."

"To Mokroe? But it's night!"

"Once the lad had all, now the lad has nought,"[4] cried Mitya suddenly.

"How 'nought'? You say that with all those thousands!"

"I'm not talking about thousands. Damn thousands! I'm talking of the female character.

> Fickle is the heart of woman
> Treacherous and full of vice;[5]

I agree with Ulysses. That's what he says."

"I don't understand you!"

"Am I drunk?"

"Not drunk, but worse."

"I'm drunk in spirit, Pyotr Ilyich, drunk in spirit! But that's enough!"

"What are you doing, loading the pistol?"

"I'm loading the pistol."

Unfastening the pistol case, Mitya actually opened the powder horn, and carefully sprinkled and rammed in the charge. Then he took the bullet and before inserting it, held it in two fingers in front of the candle.

"Why are you looking at the bullet?" asked Pyotr Ilyich, watching him with uneasy curiosity.

"Oh, a fancy. Why, if you meant to put that bullet in your brain, would you look at it or not?"

"Why look at it?"

"It's going into my brain, so it's interesting to look and see what it's like. But that's foolishness, a moment's foolishness. Now that's done," he added, putting in the bullet and driving it home with the ramrod. "Pyotr Ilyich, my dear fellow, that's nonsense, all nonsense, and if only you knew what nonsense! Give me a little piece of paper now."

---

3. Dmitri combines classical Greek mythology with Biblical texts. Phoebus is one of the names of Apollo, the Greek god of the sun; "praising and glorifying God" alludes to several passages in the Bible, such as Psalm 66.2, Luke 2.20, and Acts 3.8.
4. Dmitri quotes a Russian folk ballad.
5. These verses are spoken by Ulysses in Tyutchev's 1851 poem "The Wake" ("Pominki"). Tyutchev's poem is an adaptation of Schiller's "Victory Celebration" ("Das Siegesfest," 1803). Ulysses is the Latin name for Odysseus, whose attempt to return home to his wife and son after the Trojan War is recounted in Homer's epic *The Odyssey* (c. 700 B.C.E.).

"Here's some paper."

"No, a clean new piece, writing paper. That's right."

And taking a pen from the table, Mitya rapidly wrote two lines, folded the paper in four, and thrust it in his waistcoat pocket. He put the pistols in the case, locked it up, and kept it in his hand. Then he looked at Pyotr Ilyich with a slow, thoughtful smile.

"Now, let's go," he said.

"Where are we going? No, wait a minute. . . . Are you thinking of putting that bullet in your brain, perhaps?" Pyotr Ilyich asked uneasily.

"I was fooling about the bullet! I want to live. I love life! You may be sure of that. I love golden-haired Phoebus and his warm light. . . . Dear Pyotr Ilyich, do you know how to step aside?"

"What do you mean by 'stepping aside'?"

"Making way. Making way for a dear being, and for one I hate. And to let the one I hate become dear—that's what making way means! And to say to them: God bless you, go your way, pass on, while I . . ."

"While you?"

"That's enough, let's go."

"Upon my word. I'll tell someone to prevent your going there," said Pyotr Ilyich, looking at him. "What are you going to Mokroe for, now?"

"There's a woman there, a woman, that's enough for you, Pyotr Ilych, enough!"

"Listen, though you're such a savage I've always liked you. . . . I feel anxious."

"Thanks, old fellow. I'm a savage you say. Savages, savages! That's what I am always saying. Savages! Why, here's Misha! I was forgetting him."

Misha ran in, post haste, with a handful of bills in change, and reported that everyone was in a bustle at the Plotnikovs'; "They're carrying down the bottles, and the fish, and the tea; it will all be ready directly." Mitya seized ten rubles and handed it to Pyotr Ilyich, then tossed another ten-ruble note to Misha.

"Don't dare to do such a thing!" cried Pyotr Ilyich. "I won't have it in my house, it's a bad, demoralizing habit. Put your money away. Here, put it here, why waste it? It would come in handy tomorrow, and I daresay you'll be coming to me to borrow ten rubles again. Why do you keep putting the bills in your side pocket? Ah, you'll lose them!"

"I say, my dear fellow, let's go to Mokroe together."

"What should I go for?"

"I say, let's open a bottle at once, and drink to life! I want to drink, and especially to drink with you. I've never drunk with you, have I?"

"Very well, we can go to the Metropolis. I was just going there."

"I haven't time for that. Let's drink at the Plotnikovs', in the back room. Shall I ask you a riddle?"

"Ask away."

Mitya took the piece of paper out of his waistcoat pocket, unfolded it and showed it. In a large, distinct hand was written:

"I punish myself for my whole life, my whole life I punish!"

"I certainly will speak to someone. I'll go at once," said Pyotr Ilyich, after reading the paper.

"You won't have time, dear boy, come and have a drink. March!"

Plotnikov's shop was at the corner of the street next door but one to Pyotr Ilyich's. It was the largest grocery shop in our town, and by no means a bad one, belonging to some rich merchants. They kept everything that could be got in a Petersburg shop, grocery of all sorts, wines "bottled by the brothers Eliseyev," fruits, cigars, tea, coffee, sugar, and so on. There were three shop assistants and two errand boys always employed. Though our part of the country had grown poorer, the landowners had gone away, and trade had got worse, yet the grocery stores flourished as before, every year with increasing prosperity; there were plenty of purchasers for their goods. They were awaiting Mitya with impatience in the shop. They had vivid recollections of how he had bought, three or four weeks ago, wine and goods of all sorts to the value of several hundred rubles, paid for in cash (they would never have let him have anything on credit, of course). They remembered that then, as now, he had had a bundle of hundred-ruble bills in his hand, and had scattered them at random, without bargaining, without reflecting, or caring to reflect what use so much wine and provisions would be to him. The story was told all over the town that driving off then with Grushenka to Mokroe he had "spent three thousand in one night and the following day, and had come back from the spree without a penny, cleaned out." He had picked up a whole troop of gypsies (encamped in our neighborhood at the time), who for two days got money without stint out of him while he was drunk, and drank expensive wine without stint. People used to tell, laughing at Mitya, how he had given champagne to grimy-handed peasants, and feasted the village women and girls on sweets and Strasbourg pâté. Though to laugh at Mitya to his face was rather a risky proceeding, there was much laughter behind his back, especially in the tavern, at his own ingenuous public avowal that all he had got out of Grushenka by this "escapade" was "permission to kiss her foot, and that was the utmost she had allowed him."

By the time Mitya and Pyotr Ilyich reached the shop, they found a troika[6] with three horses harnessed abreast with bells, and with Andrey, the driver, ready waiting for Mitya at the entrance. In the shop they had almost entirely finished packing one box of provisions, and were only waiting for Mitya's arrival to nail it down and put it in the cart. Pyotr Ilyich was astounded.

"Where did this troika come from in such a hurry?" he asked Mitya.

"I met Andrey as I ran to you, and told him to drive straight here to the shop. There's no time to lose. Last time I drove with Timothy, but Timothy now has gone on before me with a certain enchantress. Shall we be very late, Andrey?"

"They'll only get there an hour at most before us, not even that maybe. I got Timothy ready to start. I know how he'll go. Their pace won't be ours, Dmitri Fyodorovich. How could it be? They won't get there an hour earlier!" Andrey, a lanky, red-haired driver, a lad wearing a full-skirted coat, and with a caftan on his arm, replied warmly.

"Fifty rubles for vodka if we're only an hour behind them."

"I'll guarantee the time, Dmitri Fyodorovich. Ech, they won't be half an hour before us, let alone an hour."

6. See note 3 on p. 307.

Though Mitya bustled about seeing after things, he gave his orders strangely, as it were disconnectedly, and inconsecutively. He began a sentence and forgot the end of it. Pyotr Ilyich found himself obliged to come to the rescue.

"Four hundred rubles' worth, not less than four hundred rubles' worth, just as it was then," commanded Mitya. "Four cases of champagne, not a bottle less."

"What do you want with so much? What's it for? Wait!" cried Pyotr Ilyich. "What's this box? What's in it? Surely there isn't four hundred rubles' worth here?"

The officious shopmen began explaining with oily politeness that the first box contained only half a case of champagne, and only "the most indispensable articles" such as appetizers, sweets, toffee, and so on. But the main part of the "comestibles" ordered would be packed and sent off, as on the previous occasion, in a special cart, also with three horses, traveling at full speed, so that it would arrive "not more than an hour later than Dmitri Fyodorovich himself."

"Not more than an hour! Not more than an hour! And put in more toffee and fondants. The girls there are so fond of it," Mitya insisted hotly.

"The fondants are all right. But what do you want with four cases of champagne? One would be enough," said Pyotr Ilyich, almost angry. He began bargaining, asking for a bill of the goods, and refused to be satisfied. But he succeeded only in saving a hundred rubles. In the end it was agreed that only three hundred rubles' worth should be sent.

"Well, you may go to the devil!" said Pyotr Ilyich, as though suddenly thinking differently of it. "What's it to do with me? Throw away your money, since it's cost you nothing!"

"This way, my accountant, this way, don't be angry." Mitya drew him into a room at the back of the shop. "They'll give us a bottle here directly. We'll taste it. Ech, Pyotr Ilyich, come along with me, for you're a nice fellow, the sort I like."

Mitya sat down on a wicker chair, before a little table, covered with a filthy dinner napkin. Pyotr Ilyich sat down opposite, and the champagne soon appeared, and oysters were suggested to the gentlemen. "First class oysters, the last lot in."

"To the devil with the oysters. I don't eat them. And we don't need anything," snapped Pyotr Ilyich, almost angrily.

"There's no time for oysters," said Mitya. "And I'm not hungry. Do you know, friend," he said suddenly, with feeling, "I have never liked all this disorder."

"Who does like it? Three cases of champagne for peasants, upon my word, that's enough to make anyone angry!"

"That's not what I mean. I'm talking of a higher order. There's no order in me, no higher order. But . . . that's all over. There's no need to grieve about it. It's too late, damn it! My whole life has been disorder, and one must set it in order. Is that a pun, eh?"

"You're raving, not making puns!"

"Glory be to God in Heaven,
Glory be to God in me . . .

That verse came from my heart once, it's not a verse, but a tear. . . . I wrote it myself . . . not while I was pulling the captain's beard, though . . ."

"Why do you bring him in all of a sudden?"

"Why do I bring him in? Foolery! All things come to an end; all things are made equal. That's the long and short of it."

"You know, I keep thinking of your pistols."

"That's all foolery, too! Drink, and don't be fanciful. I love life. I've loved life too much, shamefully much. Enough! Let's drink to life, dear boy, I propose the toast. Why am I pleased with myself? I'm a scoundrel, but I'm satisfied with myself. And yet I'm tortured by the thought that I'm a scoundrel, but satisfied with myself. I bless creation. I'm ready to bless God and His creation directly, but . . . I must kill one noxious insect for fear it should crawl and spoil life for others. . . . Let us drink to life, dear brother. What can be more precious than life? Nothing, nothing! To life, and to one queen of queens."

"Let's drink to life and to your queen, too, if you like."

They drank a glass each. Although Mitya was excited and expansive, yet he was melancholy, too. It was as though some heavy, overwhelming anxiety were weighing upon him.

"Misha . . . here's your Misha come! Misha, come here, my boy, drink this glass to Phoebus, the golden-haired, of tomorrow morn . . ."

"What are you giving it to him for?" cried Pyotr Ilyich, irritably.

"Yes, yes, yes, let me! I want to!"

"E—ech!"

Misha emptied the glass, bowed, and ran out.

"He'll remember it afterwards," Mitya remarked. "Woman, I love woman! What is woman? The queen of creation! I am sad, I am sad, Pyotr Ilyich. Do you remember Hamlet? 'I am so sad, so sad, Horatio . . . Oh, poor Yorick!'[7] Perhaps that's me, Yorick? Yes, I'm Yorick now, and a skull afterwards."

Pyotr Ilyich listened in silence. Mitya, too, was silent for awhile.

"What dog's that you've got here?" he asked the shopman, casually, noticing a pretty little lapdog with dark eyes, sitting in the corner.

"It belongs to Barbara Alexyeevna, the mistress," answered the clerk. "She brought it and forgot it here. It must be taken back to her."

"I saw one like it . . . in the regiment . . ." murmured Mitya dreamily, "only that one had its hind leg broken. . . . By the way, Pyotr Ilyich, I wanted to ask you: have you ever stolen anything in your life?"

"What a question!"

"Oh, I didn't mean anything. From somebody's pocket, you know. I don't mean government money, everyone steals that, and no doubt you do, too . . ."

"You go to the devil."

"I'm talking of other people's money. Stealing straight out of a pocket? Out of a purse, eh?"

"I stole twenty kopecks from my mother when I was nine years old. I took it off the table on the sly, and held it tight in my hand."

"Well, and what happened?"

---

7. Dmitri paraphrases Shakespeare's *Hamlet* V.1.

"Oh, nothing. I kept it three days, then I felt ashamed, confessed and gave it back."

"And what then?"

"Naturally I was whipped. But why do you ask? Have you stolen something?"

"I have," said Mitya, winking slyly.

"What have you stolen?" inquired Pyotr Ilyich curiously.

"I stole twenty kopecks from my mother when I was nine years old, and gave it back three days later." After he said this, Mitya suddenly got up.

"Dmitri Fyodorovich, won't you come now?" called Andrey from the door of the shop.

"Are you ready? We'll come!" Mitya started. "One last tale and . . . [8] Andrey, a glass of vodka as we leave. Give him some brandy as well! That box" (the one with the pistols) "put under my seat. Good-bye, Pyotr Ilyich, think kindly of me."

"But you're coming back tomorrow?"

"Of course."

"Will you settle the little bill now?" cried the clerk, springing forward.

"Oh yes, the bill. Of course."

He pulled the bundle of bills out of his pocket again, picked out three hundred rubles, threw them on the counter, and ran hurriedly out of the shop. Everyone followed him out, bowing and wishing him good luck. Andrey, clearing his throat from the brandy he had just swallowed, jumped up on the box. But Mitya was only just taking his seat when suddenly, to his surprise, he saw Fenya before him. She ran up panting, clasped her hands before him with a cry, and plumped down at his feet.

"Dmitri Fyodorovich, dear good Dmitri Fyodorovich, don't harm my mistress! And it was I who told you all about it! . . . And don't murder him, he's the former one, hers! He'll marry Agrafena Alexandrovna now. That's why he's come back from Siberia. Dmitri Fyodorovich, dear, don't take another's life!"

"Tut—tut—tut! That's it, is it? So you're off there to make trouble!" muttered Pyotr Ilyich. "Now, it's all clear, as clear as daylight. Dmitri Fyodorovich, give me your pistols at once if you mean to behave like a man," he shouted aloud to Mitya. "Do you hear, Dmitri?"

"The pistols? Wait a bit, brother, I'll throw them into the pool on the road," answered Mitya. "Fenya, get up, don't kneel to me. Mitya won't hurt anyone, the silly fool won't hurt anyone again. But I say, Fenya," he shouted, after having taken his seat. "I hurt you just now, so forgive me and have pity on me, forgive a scoundrel. . . . But it doesn't matter if you don't. It's all the same now. Now then, Andrey, look alive, fly along full speed!"

Andrey whipped up the horses, and the bells began ringing.

"Good-bye, Pyotr Ilyich! My last tear is for you! . . ."

"He's not drunk, but he keeps babbling like a lunatic," Pyotr Ilyich thought as he watched him go. He had half a mind to stay and see the cart packed with the remaining wines and provisions, knowing that they would deceive and defraud Mitya. But, suddenly feeling vexed with

---

8. These words are spoken by the monk Pimen, a character in Pushkin's drama *Boris Godunov* (1825).

himself, he turned away with a curse and went to the tavern to play billiards.

"He's a fool, though he's a good fellow," he muttered as he went. "I've heard of that officer, Grushenka's former flame. Well, if he has turned up. . . . Ech, those pistols! What the devil, I'm not his nurse, am I? Let them do what they like! Besides, it'll all come to nothing. They're loud-mouths, that's all. They'll drink and fight, fight and make friends again. Are those really men who mean business? What does he mean by 'I'm stepping aside, I'm punishing myself'? It'll come to nothing! He's shouted such phrases a thousand times, drunk, in the taverns. But now he's not drunk. 'Drunk in spirit'—they're fond of fine phrases, the scoundrels. Am I his nurse? He must have been fighting, his whole mug was bloody. With whom? I shall find out at the Metropolis. And his handkerchief was soaked in blood. . . . Fooh, the devil, it's still lying on my floor. . . . curse it!"

He reached the tavern in the foulest of humors and at once made up a game. The game cheered him. He played a second game, and suddenly began telling one of his partners that Dmitri Karamazov had cash again, something like three thousand rubles, and had gone to Mokroe again to spend it with Grushenka. . . . This news aroused almost unexpected curiosity in his listeners. They all began to speak about it, not laughing, but somehow with a strange gravity. They even stopped playing.

"Three thousand? But where can he have got three thousand?"

Questions were asked. The story of Madame Khokhlakova's present was received with skepticism.

"Hasn't he robbed the old man, that's the question?"

"Three thousand! There's something odd about it."

"He boasted aloud that he would kill his father; we all heard him, here. And it was three thousand he talked about . . ."

Pyotr Ilyich listened. All at once he became short and dry in his answers. He said not a word about the blood on Mitya's face and hands, though he had meant to speak of it at first.

They began a third game, and by degrees the talk about Mitya died away. But by the end of the third game, Pyotr Ilyich felt no more desire for billiards; he laid down the cue, and without having supper as he had intended, he walked out of the tavern. When he reached the marketplace he stood still in perplexity, wondering at himself. He suddenly realized that what he wanted was to go to Fyodor Pavlovich's and find out if anything had happened there. "On account of some stupid nonsense—as it's sure to turn out—am I going to wake up the household and make a scandal? Fooh, the devil, am I their nurse or what?"

In a foul humor he went straight home, and suddenly remembered Fenya. "Eh, the devil, I ought to have questioned her just now," he thought with vexation, "I should have heard everything." And the desire to speak to her, and so find out, became so pressing and importunate that when he was halfway home he turned abruptly and went towards the house where Grushenka lodged. Going up to the gate he knocked. The sound of the knock in the silence of the night sobered him and made him feel annoyed. And no one answered him; everyone in the house was asleep. "And I shall be making a fuss!" he thought, with a feeling of positive discomfort. But instead of going away altogether, he fell to knocking again with all his might, filling the street with clamor.

"Not coming? Well, I will wake them up, I will!" he muttered at each knock, fuming at himself, but at the same time he redoubled his knocks on the gate.

Chapter VI

"I Am Coming, Too!"

But Dmitri Fyodorovich was speeding along the road. It was a little more than twelve miles to Mokroe, but Andrey's three horses galloped at such a pace that the distance might be covered in an hour and a quarter. It was as though the swift motion suddenly revived Mitya. The air was fresh and cool, there were big stars shining in the sky. It was the very night, and perhaps the very hour, in which Alyosha fell on the earth, and "rapturously swore to love it forever and ever." But all was confusion, confusion, in Mitya's soul, and although many things were goading his heart, at that moment his whole being was yearning for her, his queen, to whom he was flying to look on her for the last time. One thing I can say for certain; his heart did not waver for one instant. I shall perhaps not be believed when I say that this jealous lover felt not the slightest jealousy of this new man, new rival, this officer, who seemed to have sprung out of the earth. If any other had appeared on the scene, he would have been jealous at once, and would perhaps have stained his terrible hands with blood again. But as he flew through the night, he felt no envy, no hostility even, for the man who had been her first lover. . . . It is true he had not yet seen him. "Here there was no room for dispute; it was her right and his; this was her first love which, after five years, she had not forgotten; so she had loved him only for those five years, and I, how do I come in? What right have I? Step aside, Mitya, and make way! What am I now? Now everything is over apart from the officer—even if he had not appeared, everything would be over . . ."

These words would roughly have expressed his feelings, if he had been capable of reasoning. But he could not reason at that moment. His present resolution had arisen without reasoning. At Fenya's first words, it had sprung from feeling, and been adopted in a flash, with all its consequences. And yet, in spite of his resolution, there was confusion in his soul, an agonizing confusion: his resolution did not give him peace. There was so much behind that tortured him. And it seemed strange to him, at moments, to think that he had written his own sentence of death with pen and paper: "I punish myself," and the paper was lying there in his pocket, ready; the pistol was loaded; he had already resolved how, next morning, he would meet the first warm ray of "golden-haired Phoebus." And yet he could not be rid of the past, of all that he had left behind and that tortured him. He felt that miserably, and the thought of it sank into his heart with despair. There was one moment when he felt an impulse to stop Andrey, to jump out of the cart, to pull out his loaded pistol, and to make an end of everything without waiting for the dawn. But that moment flew by like a spark. The troika flew on, "devouring space," and as he drew near his goal, again the thought of her, of her alone, took more and more complete possession of his soul, chasing away the fearful specters that had been haunting it. Oh, how he longed to look upon her, if only for a moment, if only from a distance! "She's now with *him*," he thought, "now I shall see what she looks like with him, her first love, and that's all I want." Never had this woman, who was such a fateful influence in his life, aroused such love in his breast, such new and unknown feeling, surprising even to himself, a feeling tender to devoutness, to self-effacement before her! "I will efface myself!" he said, in a rush of almost hysterical ecstasy.

They had been galloping nearly an hour. Mitya was silent, and though Andrey was, as a rule, a talkative peasant, he did not utter a word, either. He seemed afraid to talk, he only whipped up smartly his three lean, but mettlesome, bay horses. Suddenly Mitya cried out in horrible anxiety:

"Andrey! What if they're asleep?"

This thought fell upon him like a blow. It had not occurred to him before.

"It may well be that they're gone to bed, by now, Dmitri Fyodorovich."

Mitya frowned as though in pain. Yes, indeed . . . he was rushing there . . . with such feelings . . . while they were asleep . . . she was asleep, perhaps, there too. . . . And angry feeling surged up in his heart.

"Drive on, Andrey! Whip them up! Look alive!" he cried, beside himself.

"But maybe they're not in bed!" Andrey reconsidered after a pause. "Timothy said there were a lot of them there . . ."

"At the station?"

"Not at the posting station, but at Plastunov's, at the inn, where they let out horses, too,"

"I know. So you say there are a lot of them? How's that? Who are they?" cried Mitya, greatly dismayed at this unexpected news.

"Well, Timothy was saying they're all gentlefolk. Two from our town— who they are I can't say—and there are two others, strangers, maybe more besides. I didn't ask particularly. They've set to playing cards, so Timothy said."

"Cards?"

"So, maybe they're not in bed if they're at cards. It's most likely not more than eleven."

"Quicker, Andrey! Quicker!" Mitya cried again, nervously.

"May I ask you something, sir?" said Andrey, after a pause. "Only I'm afraid of angering you, sir."

"What is it?"

"Why, Fedos'ia Markovna threw herself at your feet just now, and begged you not to harm her mistress, and someone else, too . . . so you see, sir . . . It's I am taking you there . . . forgive me, sir, it's my conscience . . . maybe it's stupid of me to speak of it . . ."

Mitya suddenly seized him by the shoulders from behind.

"Are you a driver? A driver?" he asked frantically.

"Yes, sir . . ."

"Then you know that one has to make way. What would you say to a driver who wouldn't make way for anyone, but would just drive on and crush people? No, a driver mustn't run over people. One can't run over a man. One can't spoil people's lives. And if you have spoiled a life—punish yourself. . . . If you've spoiled a life, if only you've ruined any one's life— punish yourself and go away."

These phrases burst from Mitya almost hysterically. Though Andrey was surprised at him, he kept up the conversation.

"That's right, Dmitri Fyodorovich, you're quite right, one mustn't crush or torment a man, or any kind of creature, for every creature is created by God. Take a horse, for instance, for some folks, even among us drivers, drive anyhow. Nothing will restrain them, they just force it along."

"To hell?" Mitya suddenly interrupted, and went off into his abrupt, short laugh. "Andrey, simple soul," he seized him firmly by the shoulders again, "tell me, will Dmitri Fyodorovich Karamazov go to hell, or not, what do you think?"

"I don't know, dear man, it depends on you, for you are . . . you see, sir, when the Son of God was nailed on the Cross and died, He went straight down to hell from the Cross, and set free all sinners that were tormented. And hell groaned, because it thought that it would get no more sinners. And then God said to hell: 'Don't groan, hell, for you shall have all the mighty of the earth, the rulers, the chief judges, and the rich men, and shall be filled up as you have been in all the ages till I come again.' Those were His very words . . ."[9]

"A peasant legend, splendid! Capital! Whip up the left, Andrey!"

"So you see, sir, who it is hell's for," said Andrey, whipping up the left horse, "but you're like a little child . . . that's how we look on you . . . and though you're hasty-tempered, sir, yet God will forgive you for your kind heart."

"And you, do you forgive me, Andrey?"

"What should I forgive you for, sir? You've never done me any harm."

"No, for everyone, for everyone, you here alone, on the road, will you forgive me for everyone? Speak, simple peasant heart!"

"Oh, sir! I feel afraid of driving you, your talk is so strange."

But Mitya did not hear. He was frantically praying and muttering to himself.

"Lord, receive me, with all my lawlessness, and do not condemn me. Let me pass by Thy judgment . . . do not condemn me, for I have condemned myself, do not condemn me, for I love Thee, O Lord. I am a wretch, but I love Thee. If Thou sendest me to hell, I shall love Thee there, and from there I shall cry out that I love Thee forever and ever. . . . But let me love to the end. . . . Here and now for just five hours . . . till the first ardent ray of Thy day . . . for I love the queen of my soul . . . I love her and I cannot help loving her. Thou seest my whole heart. . . . I shall gallop up, I shall fall before her and say, 'You are right to pass on and leave me. Farewell and forget your victim . . . never fret yourself about me!'"

"Mokroe!" cried Andrey, pointing ahead with his whip.

Through the pale darkness of the night loomed a solid black mass of buildings, flung down, as it were, on the vast plain. The village of Mokroe numbered two thousand inhabitants, but at that hour all were asleep, and only here and there a few lights still twinkled.

"Drive on, Andrey, I am coming!" Mitya exclaimed, feverishly.

---

9. Such stories about Christ's descent into hell, based on apocryphal sources, circulated widely in Russia.

"They're not asleep," said Andrey again, pointing with his whip to the Plastunovs' inn, which was at the entrance to the village. The six windows, looking on the street, were all brightly lit up.

"They're not asleep," Mitya repeated, joyously. "Quicker, Andrey! Gallop! Drive up with a dash! Set the bells ringing! Let all know that I have come. I'm coming! I'm coming, too!" Mitya kept exclaiming frenziedly.

Andrey lashed his exhausted team into a gallop, drove with a dash and pulled up his steaming, panting horses at the high flight of steps. Mitya jumped out of the cart just as the innkeeper, on his way to bed, peered out from the steps curious to see who had arrived.

"Trifon Borisich, is that you?"

The innkeeper bent down, looked intently, ran down the steps, and rushed up to the guest with obsequious delight.

"Dmitri Fyodorovich, your honor! Do I see you again?"

Trifon Borisich was a thickset, healthy peasant, of middle height, with a rather fat face. His expression was severe and uncompromising, especially with the peasants of Mokroe, but he had the power of assuming the most obsequious countenance, when he had an inkling that it was in his interest. He dressed in Russian style, with a shirt buttoning down on one side, and a full-skirted coat. He had saved a good sum of money, but was forever dreaming of improving his position. More than half the peasants were in his clutches, everyone in the neighborhood was in debt to him. From the neighboring landowners he bought and rented lands which were worked by the peasants, in payment of debts which they could never shake off. He was a widower, with four grown-up daughters. One of them was already a widow and lived in the inn with her two children, his grandchildren, and worked for him like a charwoman. Another of his daughters was married to a petty official and in one of the rooms of the inn, on the wall could be seen among the family photographs a miniature photograph of this official in uniform and official epaulettes. The two younger daughters used to wear fashionable blue or green dresses, fitting tight at the back, and with trains a yard long, on Church holidays or when they went to pay visits. But next morning they would get up at dawn, as usual, sweep out the rooms with a birch broom, empty the slops, and clean up after lodgers. In spite of the thousands of rubles he had saved, Trifon Borisich was very fond of emptying the pockets of a drunken guest, and, remembering that not a month ago he had, in twenty-four hours, made two if not three hundred rubles out of Dmitri, when he had come on his escapade with Grushenka, he met him now with an eager welcome, scenting his prey the moment Mitya drove up to the steps.

"Dmitri Fyodorovich, dear sir, we see you once more!"

"Wait, Trifon Borisich," began Mitya, "first and foremost, where is she?"

"Agrafena Alexandrovna?" The innkeeper understood at once, looking sharply into Mitya's face. "She's here, too . . ."

"With whom? With whom?"

"Some strangers. One is an official gentleman, a Pole, to judge from his speech. He sent the horses for her from here; and there's another with him, a friend of his, or a fellow traveler, there's no telling. He's dressed like a civilian."

"Well, are they feasting? Have they money?"

"Poor sort of a feast! Nothing to boast of, Dmitri Fyodorovich."

"Nothing to boast of? And who are the others?"

"They're two gentlemen from the town. . . . They've come back from Cherny, and are putting up here. One's quite a young gentleman, a relative of Mr. Miüsov, he must be, but I've forgotten his name . . . and I expect you know the other, too, the landowner Maximov. He's been on a pilgrimage, so he says, to the monastery in the town. He's traveling with this young relation of Mr. Miüsov."

"Is that all?"

"Yes."

"Wait, listen, Trifon Borisich. Tell me the chief thing: What of her? How is she?"

"Oh, she's only just come. She's sitting with them."

"Is she cheerful? Is she laughing?"

"No. I think she's not laughing much. She's sitting quite bored. She's combing the young gentleman's hair."

"The Pole—the officer?"

"He's not young, and he's not an officer, either. Not him, sir. It's the young gentleman that's Mr. Miüsov's relation . . . I've forgotten his name."

"Kalganov?"

"That's it, Kalganov!"

"All right. I'll see for myself. Are they playing cards?"

"They have been playing, but they've stopped. They've been drinking tea, the official gentleman asked for liqueurs."

"Wait, Trifon Borisich, wait, my good soul, I'll see for myself. Now answer one more question: are the gypsies here?"

"There's no sign of gypsies at all now, Dmitri Fyodorovich, the authorities have driven them away, but there are Yids around, they play the hammered dulcimer and fiddle in Rozhdestvenskaya,[1] so one could send for them now. They'd come."

"Send for them. Certainly send for them!" cried Mitya. "And you can get the girls together as you did then. Marya especially, Stepanida, too, and Arina. Two hundred rubles for a chorus!"

"Oh, for a sum like that I can get all the village together, though by now they're asleep. Are the peasants here worth such kindness, Dmitri Fyodorovich, or the girls either? To spend a sum like that on such coarseness and rudeness! What's the good of giving a peasant a cigar to smoke, the stinking ruffian! And the girls are all lousy. Besides, I'll get my daughters up for nothing, let alone a sum like that. They've only just gone to bed, I'll give them a kick and set them singing for you. You gave the peasants champagne to drink the other time, e-ech!"

For all his pretended compassion for Mitya, Trifon Borisich had hidden half a case of champagne on the last occasion, and had picked up a hundred-ruble bill under the table, and squeezed it in his fist. And so it remained in his fist.

"Trifon Borisich, I sent more than one thousand flying last time I was here. Do you remember?"

"You did send it flying. I may well remember. You must have left three thousand behind you."

"Well, I've come to do the same again, do you see?"

---

1. *Rozhdestvenskaya* means "nativity." Russian villages often bore the name of their church.

And he pulled out his roll of bills, and held them up before the inn-keeper's nose.

"Now, listen and remember. In an hour's time the wine will arrive, appetizers, pies, and sweets—bring them all up at once. That box Andrey has is to be brought up at once, too. Open it, and serve champagne immediately. And the girls, we must have the girls, Marya especially."

He turned to the cart and pulled out the box of pistols.

"Here, Andrey, let's settle. Here's fifteen rubles for the drive, and fifty for vodka . . . for your readiness, for your love. . . . Remember the gentleman Karamazov!"

"I'm afraid, your honor," faltered Andrey. "Give me five rubles extra, but more I won't take. Trifon Borisich, bear witness. Forgive my foolish words . . ."

"What are you afraid of?" asked Mitya, scanning him. "Well, go to the devil, if that's it!" he cried, flinging him five rubles. "Now, Trifon Borisich, take me up quietly and let me first get a look at them, so that they don't see me. Where are they? In the blue room?"

Trifon Borisich looked apprehensively at Mitya, but at once obediently did his bidding. Leading him into the hall, he went himself into the first large room, adjoining that in which the visitors were sitting, and took the light away. Then he stealthily led Mitya in, and put him in a corner in the dark, whence he could freely watch the company without being seen. But Mitya did not look long, and, indeed, he could not see them, he saw her, his heart throbbed violently, and all was dark before his eyes. She was sitting sideways to the table in a low chair, and beside her, on the sofa, was the pretty youth, Kalganov. She was holding his hand and seemed to be laughing, while he, seeming vexed and not looking at her, was saying something in a loud voice to Maximov, who sat on the other side of the table, facing Grushenka. Maximov was laughing violently at something. On the sofa sat *he*, and on a chair by the sofa there was another stranger. The one on the sofa was lolling backwards, smoking a pipe, and Mitya had an impression of a stoutish broad-faced short little man, who was apparently angry about something. His friend, the other stranger, struck Mitya as extraordinarily tall, but he could make out nothing more. He caught his breath. He could not bear it for a minute, he put the pistol case on a chest, and with a throbbing heart he walked, growing numb and faint of heart, straight into the blue room to face the company.

"Aie!" shrieked Grushenka, the first to notice him.

Chapter VII

The Former and Indisputable One

With his long, rapid strides, Mitya walked straight up to the table.

"Gentlemen," he said in a loud voice, almost shouting, yet stammering at every word, "I . . . I'm all right! Don't be afraid!" he exclaimed, "I'm all right, all right," he turned suddenly to Grushenka, who had shrunk back in her chair towards Kalganov, and clasped his hand tightly. "I . . . I'm coming, too. I'm here till morning. Gentlemen, may a passing traveler . . .

stay with you till morning? Only till morning, for the last time, in this same room?"

So he finished, turning to the fat little man, with the pipe, sitting on the sofa. The latter removed his pipe from his lips with dignity and observed severely:

"*Panie*,[2] we're here in private. There are other rooms."

"Why, it's you, Dmitri Fyodorovich! What do you mean?" answered Kalganov suddenly. "Sit down with us. How are you?"

"Delighted to see you, dear . . . and precious fellow, I always thought a lot of you." Mitya responded, joyfully and eagerly, at once holding out his hand across the table.

"Aie! How tight you squeeze! You've quite broken my fingers," laughed Kalganov.

"He always squeezes like that, always," Grushenka put in gaily, with a timid smile, seeming suddenly convinced from Mitya's face that he was not going to make a scene. She was watching him with intense curiosity and still some uneasiness. She was struck by something about him, and indeed the last thing she expected of him was that he would come in and speak like this at such a moment.

"Good evening," the landowner Maximov ventured mawkishly, on the left. Mitya rushed up to him, too.

"Good evening. You're here too! How glad I am to find you here, too! Gentlemen, gentlemen, I . . ." (He addressed the *pan* with the pipe again, evidently taking him for the most important person present.) "I flew here. . . . I wanted to spend my last day, my last hour in this room, in this very room . . . where I, too, adored . . . my queen. . . . Forgive me, *panie*," he cried wildly, "I flew here and vowed. . . . Oh, don't be afraid, it's my last night! Let's drink to our good understanding. They'll bring the wine at once. . . . I brought this with me." (For some reason he suddenly pulled out his bundle of bills.) "Allow me, *panie*! I want to have music, singing, a revel, as we had before. But the worm, the unnecessary worm, will crawl away, and there'll be no more of him. I will commemorate my day of joy on my last night."

He was almost choking. There was so much, so much he wanted to say, but strange exclamations were all that came from his lips. The *pan* gazed fixedly at him, at the bundle of bills in his hand; looked at Grushenka, and was in evident perplexity.

"If my suverin lady is permitting . . ." he began.

"What does 'suverin' mean? 'Sovereign,' I suppose?" interrupted Grushenka. "I can't help laughing at you, the way you talk. Sit down, Mitya, what are you talking about? Don't frighten us, please. You won't frighten us, will you? If you won't, I am glad to see you . . ."

"Me, me frighten you?" cried Mitya, flinging up his hands. "Oh, pass me by, go your way, I won't hinder you!" And suddenly he surprised them all, and no doubt himself as well, by flinging himself on a chair, and bursting into tears, turning his head away to the opposite wall, while his arms clasped the back of the chair tight, as though embracing it.

2. Throughout this chapter, the two Polish characters interlace their speech with Polish words and Russian words that have been Polonized or are pronounced with Polish accents, an effect impossible to convey in translation. *Pan* means "sir" or "gentleman"; *pani* is analogous to "Miss" or "Mrs."; *panie* is the form of direct address for a gentleman, and *panovie* for "gentlemen."

"Come, come, what a fellow you are!" cried Grushenka reproachfully. "That's just how he comes to see me—he begins talking, and I can't make out what he means. He cried like that once before, and now he's crying again! It's shameful! Why are you crying? *As though you had anything to cry for!*" she added enigmatically, emphasizing each word with some irritability.

". . . I'm not crying. . . . Well, good evening!" he instantly turned round in his chair, and suddenly laughed, not his abrupt, wooden laugh but a long, quivering, inaudible nervous laugh.

"Well, there you are again. . . . Come, cheer up, cheer up." Grushenka said to him persuasively. "I'm very glad you've come, very glad, Mitya, do you hear, I'm very glad! I want him to stay here with us," she said peremptorily, addressing the whole company, though her words were obviously meant for the man sitting on the sofa. "I wish it, I wish it! And if he goes away I shall go, too!" she added with flashing eyes.

"What my queen commands is law!" pronounced the Pole, gallantly kissing Grushenka's hand. "I beg you, *panie*, to join our company," he added politely, addressing Mitya.

Mitya was jumping up with the obvious intention of delivering another tirade, but the words did not come.

"Let's drink, *panie*," he blurted out instead of making a speech. Everyone laughed.

"Good heavens! I thought he was going to begin again!" Grushenka exclaimed nervously. "Do you hear, Mitya," she went on insistently, "don't prance about, but it's nice you've brought the champagne. I want some myself, and I can't bear liqueurs. And best of all, you've come yourself. We were fearfully dull here. . . . You've come for a spree again, I suppose? But put your money in your pocket. Where did you get such a lot?"

Mitya had been, all this time, holding in his hand the crumpled bundle of bills on which the eyes of all, especially of the *pan*s, were fixed. He thrust them hurriedly and embarrassedly into his pocket. He flushed. At that moment the innkeeper brought in an uncorked bottle of champagne, and glasses on a tray. Mitya snatched up the bottle, but he was so bewildered that he did not know what to do with it. Kalganov took it from him and poured out the champagne.

"Another! Another bottle!" Mitya cried to the innkeeper, and, forgetting to clink glasses with the *pan* whom he had so solemnly invited to drink to their good understanding, he drank off his glass without waiting for anyone else. His whole countenance suddenly changed. The solemn and tragic expression with which he had entered vanished completely, and a look of something childlike came into his face. He seemed to have become suddenly gentle and subdued. He looked shyly and happily at everyone, with a continual nervous little laugh, and the blissful expression of a little dog who has done wrong, been petted, and let in again. He seemed to have forgotten everything, and was looking round at everyone with a childlike smile of delight. He looked at Grushenka, laughing, continually, and bringing his chair close up to her. By degrees he had gained some idea of the two *pan*s, though he had formed no definite conception of them yet. The *pan* on the sofa struck him by his dignified demeanor and his Polish accent; and, above all, by his pipe. "Well, what of it? It's a good thing he's smoking a pipe," he reflected. The *pan*'s puffy, middle-aged face, with its tiny nose and very thin, pointed, dyed and impudent looking mustache, had not so far roused the faintest doubts in Mitya. He was not even particularly struck by the *pan*'s absurd wig made in Siberia, with lovelocks foolishly combed forward over the temples. "I suppose it's all right since he wears a wig," he went on, musing blissfully. The other, younger *pan*, who was staring insolently and defiantly at the company and listening to the conversation with silent contempt, still only impressed Mitya by his great height, which was terribly disproportionate to that of the *pan* on the sofa. "If he stood up he'd be six foot three." The thought flitted through Mitya's mind. It occurred to him, too, that this *pan* must be the friend of the other, as it were, a "bodyguard," and no doubt the big *pan* was at the disposal of the little *pan* with the pipe. But this all seemed to Mitya perfectly right and not to be questioned. In his mood of doglike submissiveness all feeling of rivalry had died away. Grushenka's mood and the enigmatic tone of some of her words he completely failed to grasp. All he understood, with thrilling heart, was that she was kind to him, that she had forgiven him, and made him sit by her. He was beside himself with delight, watching her sip her glass of champagne. The silence of the company seemed somehow to strike him, however, and he looked round at everyone with expectant eyes. "Why are we sitting here though, gentlemen? Why don't you begin doing something?" his smiling eyes seemed to ask.

"He keeps lying, and we were all laughing," Kalganov began suddenly, as though divining his thoughts and pointing to Maximov.

Mitya immediately stared at Kalganov and then at Maximov.

"He's lying?" he laughed his short, wooden laugh, seemingly suddenly delighted at something—"ha, ha!"

"Yes. Would you believe it, he will have it that all our cavalry officers in the twenties married Polish women. That's awful rot, isn't it?"

"Polish women?" repeated Mitya, perfectly ecstatic.

Kalganov was well aware of Mitya's attitude to Grushenka, and he guessed about the *pan*, too, but that did not much interest him, perhaps did not even interest him at all; what he was interested in was Maximov. He had come here with Maximov by chance, and he met the *pan*s here at the inn for the first time in his life. Grushenka he knew before, and had once been with someone to see her; but she had not taken to him. But here she looked at him very affectionately: before Mitya's arrival, she had been making much of him, but he seemed somehow to be unmoved by it. He was a young man, not over twenty, dressed like a dandy, with a very charming fair-skinned face, and splendid thick, fair hair. From his fair face looked out beautiful pale blue eyes, with an intelligent and sometimes even deep expression, beyond his age indeed, although the young man sometimes looked and talked quite like a child, and was not at all ashamed of it, even when he was aware of it himself. As a rule he was very odd, even capricious, though always friendly. Sometimes there was something fixed and obstinate in his expression. He would look at you and listen, seeming all the while to be persistently dreaming over something else. Often he was listless and lazy, at other times he would grow excited, sometimes, apparently, over the most trivial matters.

"Only imagine, I've been taking him about with me for the last four days," he went on, indolently drawling his words, quite naturally though, without the slightest affectation. "Ever since your brother, do you remember, shoved him off the carriage and sent him flying. That made me take an interest in him at the time, and I took him into the country, but he keeps talking such rot I'm ashamed to be with him. I'm taking him back."

"The *pan* has never seen a Polish *pani*, and says what is impossible," the *pan* with the pipe observed to Maximov.

The *pan* with the pipe spoke Russian fairly well, much better, anyway, than he pretended. If he used Russian words, he always distorted them into a Polish form.

"But I was married to a Polish *pani* myself," tittered Maximov in reply.

"But did you serve in the cavalry? You were talking about the cavalry. Were you a cavalry officer?" put in Kalganov at once.

"Was he a cavalry officer indeed? Ha, ha!" cried Mitya, listening eagerly, and turning his inquiring eyes to each as he spoke, as though there were no knowing what he might hear from each.

"No, no, sir, you see, sir," Maximov turned to him. "What I mean is that those pretty Polish ladies, sir . . . when they danced the mazurka with our Uhlans[3] . . . when one of them dances a mazurka with a Uhlan she immediately jumps on his knee like a kitten, sir . . . a little white one . . . and the pan-father and pan-mother look on and allow it. . . . They allow it . . . and next day the Uhlan comes and offers her his hand. . . . That's how it is, sir . . . offers her his hand, he-he!" Maximov ended, tittering.

"The *pan* is a *lajdak*!"[4] The tall *pan* on the chair growled suddenly and crossed one leg over the other. Mitya's eye was caught by his huge greased boot, with its thick, dirty sole. The dress of both the *pans* looked rather greasy.

"Well, now it's *lajdak*! What's he scolding about?" said Grushenka, suddenly vexed.

"*Pani* Agrippina, what the *pan* saw in Poland were servant girls, and not ladies of good birth," the *pan* with the pipe observed to Grushenka.

"You can bet on that," the tall *pan* snapped contemptuously.

"What next! Let him talk! People talk, why hinder them? It makes it cheerful," Grushenka said crossly.

"I'm not hindering them, *pani*," said the *pan* in the wig significantly, with a long look at Grushenka, and relapsing into dignified silence he sucked his pipe again.

"No, no, the *pan* spoke the truth," Kalganov got excited again, as though it were a question of vast import. "He's never been in Poland, so how can he talk about it? I suppose you weren't married in Poland, were you?"

"No, sir, in the province of Smolensk, sir. Only, a Uhlan had brought her to Russia before that, my future wife, that is, sir, with her pan-mamma and her *tante*,[5] and another female relation with a grown-up son. He brought her straight from Poland and . . . gave her up to me. He was a lieutenant in our regiment, a very nice young man. At first he meant to marry her himself. But he didn't marry her, because she turned out to be lame."

"So you married a lame woman?" cried Kalganov.

---

3. Originally a Polish folk dance, the mazurka was popular among the European upper classes as a ballroom dance throughout the eighteenth and nineteenth centuries. Uhlans were members of cavalry units in the Russian army.
4. Scoundrel (Polish).
5. Aunt (French and German).

"Yes, sir. They both deceived me a little bit at the time, and concealed it. I thought she was hopping; she kept hopping . . . I thought it was her high spirits."

"So pleased she was going to marry you!" yelled Kalganov, in a ringing, childish voice.

"Yes, sir, so pleased. But it turned out to be quite a different cause. Afterwards, when we were married, after the wedding, that very evening, she confessed, and very touchingly asked forgiveness. 'I once jumped over a puddle,' she said, 'in the years of my youth, and injured my little foot, he-he!'"

Kalganov went off into the most childish laughter, almost falling on the sofa. Grushenka, too, laughed. Mitya was at the pinnacle of happiness.

"Do you know, that's the truth, he's not lying now," exclaimed Kalganov, turning to Mitya; "and do you know, he's been married twice; it's his first wife he's talking about. But his second wife, do you know, ran away, and is alive now."

"Is it possible?" said Mitya, turning quickly to Maximov with an expression of the utmost astonishment.

"Yes, sir. She did run away, sir. I've had that unpleasant experience," Maximov modestly assented, "with a monsieur, sir. And what was worse, she'd had all my little property transferred to her beforehand. 'You're an educated man,' she said to me. 'You can always make your living.' She settled my business with that. A venerable bishop once said to me: 'One of your wives was lame, but the other was too lightfooted,' he-he!"

"Listen, listen!" cried Kalganov, bubbling over, "if he's telling lies—and he often is—he's only doing it to amuse us all. There's no harm in that, is there? You know, I sometimes like him. He's awfully low, but it's natural to him, eh? Don't you think so? Some people are low for some reason, to get some profit, but he's simply so, from nature. Imagine, he claims (he was arguing about it all the way yesterday) that Gogol wrote *Dead Souls*[6] about him. Do you remember, there's a landowner called Maximov in it, whom Nozdryov thrashed. He was charged, do you remember, 'for inflicting bodily injury with rods on the landowner Maximov in a drunken condition.' Would you believe it, he claims that he was that Maximov and that it was he who got thrashed! Now can it be so? Chichikov made his journey, at the very latest, at the beginning of the twenties, so that the dates don't fit. He couldn't have been thrashed then, he couldn't, could he?"

It was difficult to imagine what Kalganov was excited about, but his excitement was genuine. Mitya followed his lead without protest.

"Well, but if they did thrash him!" he cried, laughing.

"It's not that they thrashed me exactly, sir, but just so . . ." Maximov suddenly put in.

"What do you mean 'just so'? Either they thrashed you or they didn't."

"*Ktura godzina, panie?*" (What time is it?) the *pan* with the pipe asked the tall *pan* on the chair, with a bored expression. The other shrugged his shoulders in reply. Neither of them had a watch.

---

6. Gogol's novel *Dead Souls* (1842) is recognized as a comic masterpiece. The scene in question occurs in chapter IV.

"Why not talk? Let other people talk. Must other people not talk because you're bored?" Grushenka flew at him with evident intention of finding fault. Something seemed to flash upon Mitya's mind for the first time. This time the *pan* answered with unmistakable irritability.

"*Pani*, I didn't oppose it. I didn't say anything."

"All right then. Come, tell us your story," Grushenka cried to Maximov. "Why are you all silent?"

"There's nothing to tell, it's all so foolish, ma'am," answered Maximov at once, with evident satisfaction, mincing a little. "Besides, all that's by way of allegory in Gogol, for he's made all the names have a meaning. Nozdryov was really called Nosov, and Kuvshinikov had quite a different name, he was called Shkvornev. Fenardi really was called Fenardi,[7] only he wasn't an Italian but a Russian, Petrov, gentlemen, and Mam'selle Fenardi was a pretty girl with her pretty little legs in tights, and she had a little short skirt with spangles, gentlemen, and she kept turning round and round, only not for four hours but for four minutes only, gentlemen, and she bewitched everyone . . ."

"But what were you beaten for, why were you beaten?" cried Kalganov.

"For Piron!"[8] answered Maximov.

"What Piron?" cried Mitya.

"The famous French writer, Piron. We were all drinking then, a big party of us, in a tavern at that very fair. They'd invited me, and first of all I began quoting epigrams. 'Is that you, Boileau? What a funny get-up!'[9] and Boileau answers that he's going to a masquerade, that is to the baths, he-he! And they took it to themselves, so I made haste to repeat another, very sarcastic, well known to all educated people:

> Yes, Sappho and Phaon are we!
> But one grief is weighing on me.
> You don't know your way to the sea![1]

They were still more offended and began abusing me in the most unseemly way for it. And as luck would have it, to set things right, I began telling a very cultivated anecdote about Piron, how he was not accepted into the French Academy, and to revenge himself wrote his own epitaph:

> *Ci-gît Piron qui ne fut rien*
> *Pas même académicien.*[2]

They seized me and thrashed me."

"But what for? What for?"

---

7. Kuvshinikov, Nozdryov, and Maximov are characters in *Dead Souls*. Fenardi, a famous magician of the 1820s, is also mentioned in Gogol's novel.
8. See p. 121.
9. From the 1814 poem "Epigram na perevod poemy 'L'art poetique'" ("Epigram to the translation of *L'art poétique*") by the fabulist Ivan Krylov (1769–1844). Nicolas Boileau-Despréaux (1636–1711), French poet and critic, author of *L'art Poetique* (*The Art of Poetry*, 1674).
1. Taken from Konstantin Batyushkov's (1787–1855) satirical poem about a woman poet, "Madrigal novoi Saphe" ("Madrigal to the New Sappho," 1809). Sappho: Greek lyric poet (c. 630–570 B.C.E.). In Greek mythology, Phaon was a boatman who worked in the island of Lesbos, the home of Sappho. According to legend, Sappho fell in love with him.
2. "Here lies Piron, who was nothing / Not even a member of the Academy" (French). The French Academy refused to elect Piron a member. These lines are quoted by Nikolay Karamzin (1766–1826) in his *Letters of a Russian Traveler* (1797, 1801). Karamzin, a prolific writer, journal editor, and historian, was one of Dostoevsky's favorite authors.

"For my education. People can thrash a man for anything," Maximov concluded, briefly and sententiously.

"Eh, that's enough! That's all stupid, I don't want to listen. I thought it would be amusing," Grushenka cut them short, suddenly. Mitya started, and at once stopped laughing. The tall *pan* rose upon his feet and, with the haughty air of a man bored and out of his element, began pacing from corner to corner of the room, his hands behind his back.

"Ah, he can't sit still," said Grushenka, looking at him contemptuously. Mitya began to feel anxious. He noticed besides that the *pan* on the sofa was looking at him with an irritable expression.

"*Pan!*" cried Mitya, "let's drink, *panie!* And the other *pan*, too! Let us drink, *panovie!*" In a flash he had pulled three glasses towards him, and filled them with champagne. "To Poland, *panovie*, I drink to your Poland, to the Polish land!" cried Mitya.

"*Bardzo mi to milo, panie, wypijem*" (I shall be delighted, *panie*, let's drink), said the *pan* on the sofa, with dignity and affable condescension, and he took his glass.

"And the other *pan*, what's his name? Drink, most illustrious, take your glass!" Mitya urged.

"*Pan* Vrublevsky," put in the *pan* on the sofa.

Pan Vrublevsky came up to the table, swaying as he walked.

"To Poland, *panovie!*" cried Mitya, raising his glass. "Hurrah!"

All three drank. Mitya seized the bottle and again poured out three glasses.

"Now to Russia, *panovie*, and let us be brothers!"

"Pour out some for us," said Grushenka; "I'll drink to Russia, too!"

"So will I," said Kalganov.

"And I would, too . . . to Russia, the old grandmother!"[3] tittered Maximov.

"All! All!" cried Mitya. "Landlord, some more bottles!"

The other three bottles Mitya had brought with him were put on the table. Mitya filled the glasses.

"To Russia! Hurrah!" he shouted again. All drank the toast except the *pan*s, and Grushenka tossed off her whole glass at once. The *pan*s did not touch theirs.

"How's this, *panovie?*" cried Mitya, "won't you drink it?"

Pan Vrublevsky took the glass, raised it, and said with a resonant voice: "To Russia as she was before 1772."[4]

"Come, that's better!" cried the other *pan* in Polish, and they both emptied their glasses at once.

"You're fools, you *panovie*," broke suddenly from Mitya.

"*Panie!*" shouted both the *pan*s menacingly, setting on Mitya like a couple of cocks. *Pan* Vrublevsky was specially furious.

"Can one help loving one's own country?" he shouted in Polish.

"Be silent! Don't quarrel! I won't have any quarreling!" cried Grushenka imperiously, and she stamped her foot on the floor. Her face glowed,

---

3. An allusion to the final line of the novel *The Precipice* (1869) by Ivan Goncharov (1812–1891), which refers to Russia as a grandmother.
4. A reference to the first partition of Poland, when Prussia, Austria, and Russia divided Poland among themselves. Poland lost almost one third of its territory in the partition.

her eyes were shining. The effects of the glass she had just drunk were apparent. Mitya was terribly alarmed.

"*Panovie*, forgive me! It was my fault, I'm sorry. Vrublevsky, *pan* Vrublevsky, I'm sorry."

"Hold your tongue, you, anyway! Sit down, you stupid!" Grushenka scolded with angry annoyance.

Everyone sat down, all were silent, looking at one another.

"Gentlemen, I was the cause of it all," Mitya began again, unable to make anything of Grushenka's words. "Come, why are we sitting here? What shall we do . . . to amuse ourselves again?"

"Ach, it's certainly anything but amusing!" Kalganov mumbled lazily.

"Let's play faro again, sir, as we did just now," Maximov tittered suddenly.

"Faro? Splendid!" cried Mitya. "If only the *panovie* . . .

"It's lite,[5] *panovie*," the *pan* on the sofa responded, as it were unwillingly.

"That's true," assented *Pan* Vrublevsky.

"Lite? What do you mean by 'lite'?" asked Grushenka.

"Late, *pani*, late, 'a late hour,' I mean," the *pan* on the sofa explained.

"It's always late with them. They can never do anything!" Grushenka almost shrieked in her anger. "They're dull themselves, so they want others to be dull. Before you came, Mitya, they were just as silent and kept turning up their noses at me."

"My goddess!" cried the *pan* on the sofa in Polish, "I see you're not well-disposed to me, that's why I'm gloomy. I'm ready, *panie*," added he, addressing Mitya.

"Begin, *panie*," Mitya assented, pulling his money out of his pocket, and laying two hundred-ruble bills on the table. "I want to lose a lot to you. Take your cards. Make the bank."

"We'll get cards from the landlord, *panie*," said the little *pan*, gravely and emphatically.

"That's much the best way," chimed in *Pan* Vrublevsky in Polish.

"From the landlord? Very good, I understand, let's get them from him, that's clever of you, *panovie*. Cards!" Mitya shouted to the landlord.

The landlord brought in a new, unopened pack, and informed Mitya that the girls were getting ready, and that the Yids with the hammered dulcimer would also most likely be here soon; but the troika with the provisions had not yet arrived. Mitya jumped up from the table and ran into the next room to give orders, but only three girls had arrived, and Marya was not there yet. And he did not know himself what orders to give and why he had run out. He only told them to take out of the box the presents for the girls, the sweets, the toffee and the fondants. "And vodka for Andrey, vodka for Andrey!" he cried in haste. "I was rude to Andrey!" Suddenly Maximov, who had followed him out, touched him on the shoulder.

"Give me five rubles," he whispered to Mitya. "I'll stake something at faro, too, he-he!"

"Capital! Splendid! Take ten, here!"

Again he took all the bills out of his pocket and picked out one for ten rubles. "And if you lose that, come again, come again."

5. An attempt to convey Polish pronunciation, as is the use of "plices" for "places," below.

"Very good, sir," Maximov whispered joyfully, and he ran back again. Mitya too, returned, apologizing for having kept them waiting. The *pans* had already sat down, and opened the pack. They looked much more amiable, almost cordial. The *pan* on the sofa had lit another pipe and was preparing to deal. He wore an air of solemnity.

"To your plices, *panovie!*" cried *Pan* Vrublevsky.

"No, I'm not going to play any more," observed Kalganov, "I've lost fifty rubles to them just now."

"The *pan* had no luck, perhaps the *pan* will be lucky this time," the *pan* on the sofa observed in his direction.

"How much in the bank? To cover?" asked Mitya.

"That depends, *panie*, maybe a hundred, maybe two hundred, as much as you will stake."

"A million!" laughed Mitya.

"The *Pan* Captain has heard of *Pan* Podvysotsky, perhaps?"[6]

"What Podvysotsky?"

"In Warsaw there was a bank and anyone comes and stakes against it. Podvysotsky comes, sees a thousand gold pieces, stakes against the bank. The banker says, '*Panie* Podvysotsky, are you laying down the gold, or must we trust to your honor?' 'To my honor, *panie*,' says Podvysotsky. 'So much the better.' The banker deals. Podvysotsky wins. 'Take it, *panie*,' says the banker, and pulling out the drawer he gives him a million. 'Take it, *panie*, this is your gain.' There was a million in the bank. 'I didn't know that,' says Podvysotsky, '*Panie* Podvysotsky,' said the banker, 'you pledged your honor and we pledged ours.' Podvysotsky took the million."

"That's not true," said Kalganov.

"*Panie* Kalganov, in gentlemanly society one doesn't say such things."

"As if a Polish gambler would give away a million!" cried Mitya, but checked himself at once. "Forgive me, *panie*, it's my fault again, he would, he would give away a million, for honor, for Polish honor. You see how I talk Polish, ha-ha! Here, I stake ten rubles, on the jack."

"And I put a ruble on the queen, the queen of hearts, the pretty little *panienochka*,[7] he-he!" laughed Maximov, pulling out his queen, and, as though trying to conceal it from everyone, he moved right up and crossed himself hurriedly under the table. Mitya won. The ruble won, too.

"Press it!" cried Mitya.

"I'll bet another ruble, a single stake," Maximov muttered gleefully, hugely delighted at having won a ruble.

"Lost!" shouted Mitya. "Double on the seven!"

The seven too lost.

"Stop," Kalganov said suddenly.

"Double, double," Mitya doubled his stakes, and each time he doubled the stake, the card he doubled lost. The ruble stakes kept winning.

"Double!" shouted Mitya, furiously.

"You've lost two hundred, *panie*. Will you take another hundred?" the *pan* on the sofa inquired.

---

6. In a letter to his editor Lyubimov from November 16, 1879, Dostoevsky claims to have heard the following anecdote from several Poles.
7. Polish *panienka* (miss), with a Russian diminutive suffix.

"What? Lost two hundred already? Then another two hundred! All doubles!"

And pulling his money out of his pocket, Mitya was about to fling two hundred rubles on the queen, when Kalganov suddenly covered it with his hand.

"That's enough!" he shouted in his ringing voice.

"What's the matter?" Mitya stared at him.

"That's enough! I don't want you to play any more. Don't!"

"Why?"

"Because I don't. Just spit and come away. That's why. I won't let you go on playing."

Mitya gazed at him in astonishment.

"Give it up, Mitya. He may be right. You've lost a lot as it is," said Grushenka, with a strange note in her voice. Both *pans* suddenly rose from their seats with a deeply offended air.

"Are you joking, *panie*?" said the short *pan*, looking severely at Kalganov.

"How dare you!" *Pan* Vrublevsky, too, growled at Kalganov.

"Don't dare to shout like that," cried Grushenka. "Ah, you turkey cocks!"

Mitya looked at each of them in turn. But something in Grushenka's face suddenly struck him, and at the same instant something new flashed into his mind—a strange new thought!

"*Pani* Agrippina," the little *pan* was beginning, crimson with anger, when Mitya suddenly went up to him and slapped him on the shoulder.

"Most illustrious one, two words with you."

"What do you want?"

"In the next room, I've two words to say to you, something pleasant, very pleasant. You'll be glad to hear it."

The little *pan* was taken aback and looked apprehensively at Mitya. He agreed at once, however, on condition that *Pan* Vrublevsky went with them.

"The bodyguard? Let him come, and I want him, too. I must have him!" cried Mitya. "March, *panovie*!"

"Where are you going?" asked Grushenka, anxiously.

"We'll be back in one moment," answered Mitya.

There was a sort of boldness, a sudden confidence shining in his eyes. His face had looked very different when he entered the room an hour before. He led the *pans* not into the large room where the chorus of girls was assembling and the table was being set, but into the bedroom on the right, where the trunks and packages were kept, and there were two large beds, with pyramids of cotton pillows on each. There was a lighted candle on a small wooden table in the corner. The *pan* and Mitya sat down to this table, facing each other, while the huge Vrublevsky stood beside them, his hands behind his back. The *pans* looked severe but were evidently inquisitive.

"What can I do for you, *panie*?" lisped the little *pan*.

"Well, look here, *panie*, I won't keep you long. There's money for you," he pulled out his bills. "Would you like three thousand? Take it and go your way."

The *pan* gazed, open-eyed at Mitya, with a searching look.

"*Trzy* thousand, *panie*?" He exchanged glances with Vrublevsky.

"*Trzy, panovie, trzy!* Listen, *panie*, I see you're a sensible man. Take three thousand and go to the devil, and Vrublevsky with you—d'you hear? But, at once, this very minute, and forever. You understand that, *panie*, forever. Here's the door, you go out of it. What have you got there, an overcoat, a fur coat? I'll bring it out to you. They'll get the horses out directly, and then—good-bye, *panie!*"

Mitya awaited an answer with assurance. He had no doubts. An expression of extraordinary resolution passed over the *pan's* face.

"And the money, *panie?*"

"The money, *panie?* Five hundred rubles I'll give you this moment for the journey, and as a first installment, and twenty-five hundred tomorrow, in the town—I swear on my honor, I'll get it, I'll get it at any cost!" cried Mitya.

The Poles exchanged glances again. The short *pan's* face looked more forbidding.

"Seven hundred, seven hundred, not five hundred, at once, this minute, cash down!" Mitya added, feeling something wrong. "What's the matter, *panie?* Don't you trust me? I can't give you the whole three thousand right away. If I give it to you now, you may come back to her tomorrow. . . . Besides, I haven't got the three thousand with me. I've got it at home in town," faltered Mitya, his spirit sinking at every word he uttered. "Upon my word, the money's there, hidden."

In an instant an extraordinary sense of personal dignity showed itself in the little *pan's* face.

"What next?" he asked ironically. "For shame!" and he spat on the floor. *Pan* Vrublevsky spat too.

"You do that, *panie*," said Mitya, recognizing with despair that all was over, "because you hope to make more out of Grushenka? You're a couple of capons, that's what you are!"

"This is a mortal insult!" The little *pan* turned as red as a crab, and he went out of the room, briskly, as though unwilling to hear another word. Vrublevsky swung out after him, and Mitya followed, confused and crestfallen. He was afraid of Grushenka, afraid that the *pan* would at once raise an outcry. And so indeed he did. The *pan* walked into the room and threw himself in a theatrical attitude before Grushenka.

"*Pani* Agrippina, I have received a mortal insult!" he exclaimed in Polish. But Grushenka suddenly lost all patience, as though they had wounded her in the tenderest spot.

"Speak Russian! Speak Russian!" she cried, "not another word of Polish! You used to talk Russian. You can't have forgotten it in five years." She flushed with anger.

"*Pani* Agrippina . . ."

"My name's Agrafena, Grushenka, speak Russian or I won't listen!" The *pan* gasped with offended dignity, and quickly and pompously delivered himself in broken Russian:

"*Pani* Agrafena, I came here to forget the past and forgive it, to forget all that has happened till today . . ."

"Forgive? Come here to forgive me?" Grushenka cut him short, jumping up from her seat.

"Just so, *pani*, I'm not pusillanimous, I'm magnanimous. But I was astounded when I saw your lovers. *Pan* Mitya offered me three thousand, in the other room, to depart. I spat in the *pan's* face."

"What? He offered you money for me?" cried Grushenka, hysterically. "Is it true, Mitya? How dare you? Am I for sale?"

"*Panie, panie!*" yelled Mitya, "she's pure and shining, and I have never been her lover! That's a lie . . ."

"How dare you defend me to him?" shrieked Grushenka. "It wasn't virtue kept me pure, and it wasn't that I was afraid of Kuzma, but that I might hold up my head when I met him, and tell him he's a scoundrel. And did he actually refuse the money?"

"He was taking it, taking it!" cried Mitya; "only he wanted to get the whole three thousand at once, and I could only give him seven hundred right away."

"I see: he heard I had money, and came here to marry me!"

"*Pani* Agrippina!" cried the little *pan*. "I'm—a knight, I'm—a nobleman, and not a *lajdak*. I came here to make you my wife and I find you a different woman, perverse and shameless."

"Oh, go back where you came from! I'll tell them to turn you out and you'll be turned out," cried Grushenka, furious. "I've been a fool, a fool, to have been miserable these five years! And it wasn't for his sake, it was my spite made me miserable. And this isn't he at all! Was he like this? It might be his father! Where did you get your wig from? He was a falcon, but this is a gander.[8] He used to laugh and sing to me. . . . And I've been crying for five years, damned fool that I am, base, shameless fool!"

She sank back in her low chair and hid her face in her hands. At that instant the chorus of Mokroe girls began singing in the room on the left—a rollicking dance song.

"This is Sodom!" *Pan* Vrublevsky roared suddenly. "Landlord, send the shameless hussies away!"

The landlord, who had been for some time past inquisitively peeping in at the door, hearing shouts and guessing that his guests were quarreling, at once entered the room.

"What are you shouting for? D'you want to split your throat?" he said, addressing Vrublevsky, with surprising rudeness.

"Swine!" bellowed *Pan* Vrublevsky.

"Swine? And what sort of cards were you playing with just now? I gave you a pack and you hid it. You played with marked cards! I could send you to Siberia for playing with false cards, d'you know that, for it's just the same as counterfeit bills . . ." And going up to the sofa he thrust his fingers between the sofa back and the cushion, and pulled out an unopened pack of cards.

"Here's my pack unopened!" He held it up and showed it to all in the room. "From where I stood I saw him slip my pack away, and put his in place of it—you're a cheat and not a gentleman!"

"And I twice saw the *pan* change a card!" cried Kalganov.

"How shameful! How shameful!" exclaimed Grushenka, clasping her hands, and blushing for genuine shame. "Good Lord, he's come to that!"

"I thought so, too!" said Mitya. But before he had uttered the words, *Pan* Vrublevsky, with an embarrassed and infuriated face, shook his fist at Grushenka, shouting:

"You low harlot!"

8. Common images from Russian folk songs.

Mitya flew at him at once, clutched him in both hands, lifted him in the air, and in one instant had carried him into the room on the right, from which they had just come.

"I've laid him on the floor, there!" he announced, returning at once, gasping with excitement. "He's struggling, the scoundrel! But he won't come back, no fear of that! . . ." He closed one half of the folding doors, and holding the other ajar called out to the little Pole:

"Most illustrious excellence, will you be pleased to retire as well?"

"My dear Dmitri Fyodorovich," said Trifon Borisich, "make them give you back the money you lost. It's as good as stolen from you."

"I don't want my fifty rubles back," Kalganov declared suddenly.

"I don't want my two hundred, either," cried Mitya, "I wouldn't take it for anything! Let him keep it as a consolation."

"Bravo, Mitya! Well done, Mitya!" cried Grushenka, and there was a terribly malicious note in her exclamation. The little *pan*, crimson with fury, but still mindful of his dignity, was making for the door, but he stopped short and said suddenly, addressing Grushenka in Polish:

"*Pani*, if you want to come with me, come. If not, good-bye."

And swelling with indignation and importance he went to the door. This was a man of character: he had so good an opinion of himself that after all that had passed, he still expected that the *pani* would follow him. Mitya slammed the door after him.

"Lock it," said Kalganov. But the key clicked on the other side, they had locked it from within.

"Bravo!" exclaimed Grushenka maliciously and mercilessly. "Bravo! Serves them right!"

Chapter VIII

Delirium

What followed was almost an orgy, a feast to which all were welcome. Grushenka was the first to call for wine. "I want to drink. I want to be quite drunk, as we were before. Do you remember, Mitya, do you remember how we made friends here last time!" Mitya himself was almost delirious, feeling that "his happiness" was at hand. But Grushenka was continually sending him away from her: "Go and enjoy yourself. Tell them to dance, to make merry, 'let the stove and cottage dance';[9] as we had it last time," she kept exclaiming. She was tremendously excited. And Mitya hastened to obey her. The chorus were in the next room. The room in which they had been sitting till that moment was too small, and was divided in two by cotton curtains, behind which was a huge bed with a puffy feather mattress and a pyramid of cotton pillows. In all four rooms for visitors there were beds. Grushenka settled herself just at the door. Mitya set an easy chair for her. She had sat in the same place to watch the dancing and singing "the time before," when they had their spree there. All the girls who had come had been there then; the Yids with fiddles and zithers had come, too, and at last the long-expected cart had arrived with the wines and provisions.

9. A phrase from a popular Russian folk song.

Mitya bustled about. All sorts of people began coming into the room to look on, peasants and their women, who had been roused from sleep and attracted by the hopes of another marvelous entertainment such as they had enjoyed a month before. Mitya remembered their faces, greeting and embracing everyone he knew. He uncorked bottles and poured out wine for everyone who presented himself. Only the girls were very eager for the champagne. The men preferred rum, brandy, and, above all, hot punch. Mitya had chocolate made for all the girls, and ordered that three samovars should be kept going all night to provide tea and punch for everyone to help himself. In short, there began something disorderly and absurd, but Mitya was in his natural element, and the more absurd it became, the more his spirits rose. If the peasants had asked him for money at that moment, he would have pulled out his bills and given them away right and left. This was probably why the landlord, Trifon Borisich, kept hovering about Mitya to protect him. He seemed to have given up all idea of going to bed that night, though he drank little, only one glass of punch, and kept a sharp lookout on Mitya's interests in his own way. He intervened in the nick of time, civilly and obsequiously persuading Mitya not to give away "cigars and Rhine wine," and, above all, money to the peasants as he had done before. He was very indignant, too, at the peasant girls drinking liqueurs, and eating sweets. "They're a lousy lot, Dmitri Fyodorovich," he said. "I'd give them a kick with my knee, every one of them, and order them to consider it an honor—that's all they're worth!" Mitya remembered Andrey again, and ordered punch to be sent out to him. "I was rude to him just now," he repeated with a sinking, softened voice. Kalganov did not want to drink, and at first did not care for the girls' singing; but after he had drunk a couple of glasses of champagne he became extraordinarily lively, strolling about the room, laughing and praising the music and the songs, admiring everyone and everything. Maximov, blissfully drunk, never left his side. Grushenka, too, was beginning to get drunk. Pointing to Kalganov, she said to Mitya: "What a dear, charming boy he is!" And Mitya, delighted, ran to kiss Kalganov and Maximov. Oh, great were his hopes! She had said nothing yet, and seemed, indeed, purposely to refrain from speaking. But she looked at him from time to time with caressing and ardent eyes. At last she suddenly gripped his hand and drew him vigorously to her. She was sitting at the moment in the low chair by the door.

"How was it you came just now, eh? How you walked in! . . . I was so frightened. So you wanted to give me up to him, did you? Did you really want to?"

"I didn't want to spoil your happiness!" Mitya faltered blissfully. But she did not need his answer.

"Well, go and enjoy yourself . . ." she sent him away once more. "Don't cry, I'll call you back again."

He ran off, and she listened to the singing and looked at the dancing, though her eyes followed him wherever he went. But in another quarter of an hour she called him once more and again he ran back to her.

"Come, sit beside me, tell me, how did you hear about me, and my coming here yesterday? From whom did you first hear it?"

And Mitya began telling her all about it, disconnectedly, incoherently, feverishly. He spoke strangely, often frowning, and stopping abruptly.

"What are you frowning at?" she asked.

"Nothing. . . . I left a man ill there. I'd give ten years of my life for him to get well, to know he was all right!"

"Well, never mind him, if he's ill. So you meant to shoot yourself tomorrow! What a silly boy! What for? I like such reckless fellows as you," she lisped, her speech beginning to get thick. "So you would go any length for me, eh? Did you really mean to shoot yourself tomorrow, you stupid? No, wait a little. Tomorrow I may have something to say to you. . . . I won't say it today, but tomorrow. You'd like it to be today? No, I don't want to today. Well, go along now, go and amuse yourself."

Once, however, she called him, as it were, puzzled and uneasy.

"Why are you sad? I see you're sad. . . . Yes, I see it," she added, looking intently into his eyes. "Though you keep kissing the peasants and shouting, I see something. No, be merry. I'm merry; you be merry, too. . . . I love somebody here. Guess who it is. Ah, look, my boy has fallen asleep, poor dear, he's had too much."

She meant Kalganov. He was, in fact, drunk, and had dropped asleep for a moment, sitting on the sofa. But he was not merely drowsy from drink; he felt suddenly dejected, or, as he said, "bored." He was intensely depressed by the girls' songs, which, as the drinking went on, gradually became coarse and more reckless. And the dances were as bad. Two girls dressed up as bears, and a lively girl, called Stepanida, with a stick in her hand, acted the part of keeper, and began to "show them." "Look alive, Marya, or you'll get the stick!" The bears rolled on the ground at last in the most unseemly fashion, amid roars of laughter from the closely packed crowd of men and women. "Well, let them! Let them!" said Grushenka sententiously, with a blissful expression on her face. "When they do get a day to enjoy themselves, why shouldn't people be happy?" But Kalganov looked as though he had been besmirched with dirt. "It's swinish, all this populism," he murmured, moving away; "it's their spring revels when it's light all night in summer."[1] He particularly disliked one "new" song to a jaunty dance tune. It described how a gentleman came and tried his luck with the girls, to see whether they would love him:[2]

> The master came to try the girls:
> Would they love him, would they not?

But the girls could not love the master:

> He would beat me cruelly
> And such love won't do for me.

Then a gypsy comes along and he, too, tries:

> The gypsy came to try the girls:
> Would they love him, would they not?

But they couldn't love the gypsy either:

> He would be a thief, I fear,
> And would cause me many a tear.

1. Pre-Christian summer solstice celebrations persisted (and persist) in many parts of Europe.
2. In his November 16, 1879, letter to Lyubimov, Dostoevsky writes that he took this song "from nature" ("s natury"), and claims that it is "definitely an image of the newest peasant creation." The song was available in a volume of Russian folk songs published in Moscow in 1870.

And many more men come to try their luck, among them a soldier:

> The soldier came to try the girls:
> Would they love him, would they not?

But the soldier is rejected with contempt:

> The soldier he would strap his pack
> And after him I . . .

here followed an indecent line, sung with absolute frankness and causing a sensation in the audience. The song ends with a merchant:

> The merchant came to try the girls:
> Would they love him, would they not?

And it appears that he wins their love because:

> The merchant will make gold for me
> And his queen I will gladly be.

Kalganov was positively indignant:

"That's just a song of yesterday," he said aloud. "Who writes such things for them? They might just as well have had a railway man or a Yid come to try his luck with the girls; they'd have won out over all." And, almost as though it were a personal affront, he declared, on the spot, that he was bored, sat down on the sofa and immediately fell asleep. His pretty little face looked rather pale, as it fell back on the sofa cushion.

"Look how pretty he is," said Grushenka, taking Mitya up to him. "I was combing his hair just now; his hair's like flax, and so thick . . ."

And, bending over him tenderly, she kissed his forehead. Kalganov instantly opened his eyes, looked at her, stood up, and with the most anxious air inquired where Maximov was.

"So that's who it is you want." Grushenka laughed. "Stay with me a minute. Mitya, run and find his Maximov."

Maximov, it appeared, could not tear himself away from the girls, only running away from time to time to pour himself out a glass of liqueur. He had drunk two cups of chocolate. His face was red, and his nose was crimson; his eyes were moist, and mawkishly sweet. He ran up and announced that he was going to dance the sabotière.[3]

"They taught me all those well-bred, aristocratic dances when I was little . . ."

"Go, go with him, Mitya, and I'll watch from here how he dances," said Grushenka.

"No, no, I'm coming to look on, too," exclaimed Kalganov, brushing aside in the most naïve way Grushenka's offer to sit with him. They all went to look on. Maximov danced his dance. But it roused no great admiration in anyone but Mitya. It consisted of nothing but skipping and hopping, kicking up the feet, and at every skip Maximov slapped the upturned sole of his foot. Kalganov did not like it at all, but Mitya kissed the dancer.

"Thanks. You're tired perhaps? What are you looking for here? Would you like some sweets? A cigar, perhaps?"

---

3. The sabotière was a folk dance, not an aristocratic dance. *Sabot* means wooden shoe or clog in French.

"A cigarette, sir."

"Don't you want a drink?"

"I'll just have a liqueur, sir . . . Have you any chocolates?"

"Yes, there's a heap of them on the table there. Choose one, my dear soul!"

"I like one with vanilla, sir . . . for old people. He-he!"

"No, brother, we've none of that special sort."

"I say," the old man bent down to whisper in Mitya's ear. "That girl there, little Marya, he-he! How would it be if you were to help me make friends with her?"

"So that's what you're after! No, brother, that won't do!"

"I'd do no harm to anyone," Maximov muttered disconsolately.

"Oh, all right, all right. They only come here to dance and sing, you know, brother. But damn it all, wait a bit! . . . Eat and drink and be merry, meanwhile. Don't you want money?"

"Later on perhaps," smiled Maximov.

"All right, all right . . ."

Mitya's head was burning. He went outside to the wooden balcony which ran round the whole building on the inner side, overlooking the courtyard. The fresh air revived him. He stood alone in the dark, in a corner, and suddenly clutched his head in both hands. His scattered thoughts came together; his sensations blended into a whole and threw a sudden light into his mind. A fearful and terrible light! "If I'm to shoot myself, why not now?" passed through his mind. "Why not go for the pistols, bring them here, and here, in this dark, dirty corner, make an end?" Almost a minute he stood, undecided. A few hours earlier, when he had been dashing here, he was pursued by disgrace, by the theft he had committed, and that blood, that blood! . . . But yet it was easier for him then. Then everything was over: he had lost her, given her up. She was gone for him— oh, then his death sentence had been easier for him; at least it had seemed necessary, inevitable, for what had he to stay on earth for? But now? Was it the same as then? Now one phantom, one terror at least was at an end: that first, rightful lover, that fateful figure had vanished, leaving no trace. The terrible phantom had suddenly turned into something so small, so comic; it had been carried into the bedroom and locked in. It would never return. She was ashamed, and from her eyes he could see now whom she loved. Now he had everything to make life happy . . . but he could not go on living, he could not; oh, damnation! "Oh, God! restore to life the man I knocked down at the fence! Let this fearful cup pass from me![4] Lord, thou hast wrought miracles for such sinners as me! But what, what if the old man's alive? Oh, then the shame of the other disgrace I would wipe away. I would restore the stolen money. I'd give it back; I'd get it somehow. . . . No trace of that shame will remain except in my heart forever! But no, no; oh, impossible cowardly dreams! Oh, damnation!"

Yet it was as if a ray of some kind of bright hope shone to him in the darkness. He jumped up and ran back to the room—to her, to her, his queen forever! Was not one hour, one moment of her love worth all the rest of life, even in the agonies of disgrace? This wild question clutched at

---

4. Dmitri's words echo those spoken by Christ on the eve of his crucifixion. See Matthew 26.39, Mark 14.36, and Luke 22.42.

his heart. "To her, to her alone, to see her, to hear her, to think of nothing, to forget everything, if only for that night, for an hour, for a moment!" Just as he turned from the balcony into the passage, he came upon the landlord, Trifon Borisich. He thought he looked gloomy and worried, and fancied he had come to find him.

"What is it, Trifon Borisich? are you looking for me?"

"No, sir." The landlord seemed disconcerted. "Why should I be looking for you? Where have you been?"

"Why do you look so glum? You're not angry, are you? Wait a bit, you shall soon get to bed. . . . What's the time?"

"It'll be three o'clock. Past three, it must be."

"We'll stop soon. We'll stop."

"Don't mention it; it doesn't matter. Keep it up as long as you like . . ."

"What's the matter with him?" Mitya wondered for an instant, and he ran back to the room where the girls were dancing. But she was not there. She was not in the blue room either; there was no one but Kalganov asleep on the sofa. Mitya peeped behind the curtain—she was there. She was sitting in the corner, on a trunk. Bent forward, with her head and arms on the bed close by, she was crying bitterly, doing her utmost to stifle her sobs that she might not be heard. Seeing Mitya, she beckoned him to her, and when he ran to her, she grasped his hand tightly.

"Mitya, Mitya, I loved him, you know," she began in a whisper. "How I have loved him these five years, all that time! Did I love him or only my own spite? No, him, him! It's a lie that it was my spite I loved and not him. Mitya, I was only seventeen then; he was so kind to me, so merry; he used to sing to me. . . . Or so it seemed to a silly girl like me. . . . And now, O Lord, it's not the same man. Even his face is not the same; he's different altogether. I wouldn't have recognized him. I drove here with Timothy, and all the way I was thinking how would I meet him, what would I say to him, how would we look at one another. My soul was faint, and all of a sudden it was just as though he had emptied a pail of dirty water over me. He talked to me like a schoolmaster, all so grave and learned; he met me so solemnly that I was struck dumb. I couldn't get a word in. At first I thought he was ashamed to talk before his great big Pole. I sat staring at him and wondering why I couldn't say a word to him now. It must have been his wife that ruined him; you know he threw me up to get married. She must have changed him like that. Mitya, how shameful it is! Oh, Mitya, I'm ashamed, I'm ashamed for all my life. Curse it, curse it, curse those five years!" And again she burst into tears, but clung tight to Mitya's hand and did not let it go.

"Mitya, darling, stay, don't go away. I want to say one word to you," she whispered, and suddenly raised her face to him. "Listen, tell me who it is I love? I love one man here. Who is that man? That's what you must tell me." A smile lighted up her face that was swollen with weeping, and her eyes shone in the half darkness. "A falcon flew in, and my heart sank. 'Fool! that's the man you love!' That was what my heart whispered to me at once. You came in and all grew bright. What's he afraid of? I wondered. For you were frightened; you couldn't speak. It's not them he's afraid of— could you be frightened of any one? It's me he's afraid of, I thought, only me. So Fenya told you, you little stupid, how I called to Alyosha out of the window that I'd loved Mitenka for one hour, and that I was going now to love . . . another. Mitya, Mitya, how could I be such a fool as to think I could love anyone after you? Do you forgive me, Mitya? Do you forgive me or not? Do you love me? Do you love me?"

She jumped up and held him with both hands on his shoulders. Mitya, dumb with rapture, gazed into her eyes, at her face, at her smile, and suddenly clasped her tightly in his arms and kissed her passionately.

"You will forgive me for having tormented you? It was through spite I tormented you all. It was for spite I drove the old man out of his mind. . . . Do you remember how you drank at my house one day and broke the wine glass? I remembered that and I broke a glass today and drank 'to my vile heart.' Mitya, my falcon, why don't you kiss me? He kissed me once, and now he draws back and looks and listens. Why listen to me? Kiss me, kiss me hard, that's right. If you love, well then love! I'll be your slave now, your slave for the rest of my life. It's sweet to be a slave. Kiss me! Beat me, ill-treat me, do what you will with me. . . . Oh, how I deserve to be tormented. Stop, wait, afterwards, I won't have that . . ." she suddenly thrust him away. "Go along, Mitya, I'll come and have some wine, I want to be drunk, I'm going to get drunk and dance; I must, I must!"

She tore herself away from him and disappeared behind the curtain. Mitya followed like a drunken man. "Yes, come what may—whatever may happen now, for one minute I'd give the whole world," he thought. Grushenka did, in fact, toss off a whole glass of champagne at one gulp, and suddenly became very tipsy. She sat down in the same chair as before, with a blissful smile on her face. Her cheeks were glowing, her lips were burning, her flashing eyes were moist; there was passionate appeal in her eyes. Even Kalganov felt a stir at the heart and went up to her.

"Did you feel how I kissed you when you were asleep just now?" she said thickly. "I'm drunk now, that's what it is. . . . And aren't you drunk? And why isn't Mitya drinking? Why don't you drink, Mitya? I'm drunk, and you don't drink . . ."

"I am drunk! I'm drunk as it is . . . drunk with you . . . and now I'll be drunk with wine, too."

He drank off another glass, and—he thought it strange himself—that glass made him completely drunk. He was suddenly drunk, although till that moment he had been quite sober, he remembered that. From that moment everything whirled about him, as though he were delirious. He walked, laughed, talked to everybody, without knowing what he was doing. Only one persistent burning sensation made itself felt continually, "like a red-hot coal in his heart,"[5] he said afterwards. He went up to her, sat beside her, gazed at her, listened to her. . . . She became very talkative, kept calling everyone to her, and beckoned to different girls out of the chorus. When the girl came up, she either kissed her, or made the sign of the cross over her. In another minute she might have cried. She was greatly amused by the "little old man," as she called Maximov. He ran up every minute to kiss her hands, "each little finger," and finally he danced another dance to an old song, which he sang himself. He danced with special vigor to the refrain:

---

5. A paraphrase from one of Dostoevsky's favorite poems, Pushkin's "Prophet" (1826). Dostoevsky's reading of the poem at an October 19, 1880, charity event caused a sensation.

> The little pig says—oink, oink, oink,
> The little calf says—moo, moo, moo,
> The little duck says—quack, quack, quack,
> The little goose says—ga, ga, ga.
> The hen goes strutting through the halls,
> Troo-roo-roo-roo-roo, she'll say,
> Troo-roo-roo-roo-roo, she'll say![6]

"Give him something, Mitya," said Grushenka. "Give him a present, he's poor, you know. Ah, the poor, the insulted. . . . Do you know, Mitya, I shall go into a nunnery. No, I really shall one day. Alyosha said something to me today that I shall remember all my life. . . . Yes. . . . But today let us dance. Tomorrow to the nunnery, but today we'll dance. I want to play today, good people, and what of it? God will forgive us. If I were God, I'd forgive everyone: 'My dear sinners, from this day forth I forgive you.' I'm going to beg forgiveness: 'Forgive me, good people, a silly wench.' I'm a beast, that's what I am. But I want to pray. I gave a little onion. Wicked as I've been, I want to pray. Mitya, let them dance, don't stop them. Everyone in the world is good. Everyone—even the worst of them. The world's a nice place. Though we're bad the world's all right. We're good and bad, good and bad. . . . Come, tell me, I've something to ask you; come here everyone, and I'll ask you: Why am I so good? You know I am good. I'm very good. . . . Come, why am I so good?" So Grushenka babbled on, getting more and more drunk. At last she announced that she was going to dance, too. She got up from her chair, staggering. "Mitya, don't give me any more wine—if I ask you, don't give it to me. Wine doesn't give peace. Everything's going round, the stove, and everything. I want to dance. Let everyone see how I dance . . . let them see how beautifully I dance . . ."

She really meant it. She pulled a white cambric handkerchief out of her pocket, and took it by one corner in her right hand, to wave it in the dance. Mitya ran to and fro, the girls were quiet, and got ready to break into a dancing song at the first signal. Maximov, hearing that Grushenka wanted to dance, squealed with delight, and ran skipping about in front of her, humming:

> With legs so slim and sides so trim
> And its little tail curled tight.[7]

But Grushenka waved her handkerchief at him and drove him away.

"Shh! Mitya, why don't they come? Let everyone come . . . to look on. Call them in, too, that were locked in. . . . Why did you lock them in? Tell them I'm going to dance. Let them look on, too . . ."

Mitya walked with a drunken swagger to the locked door, and began knocking to the Poles with his fist.

"Hi, you . . . Podvysotskys! Come, she's going to dance. She calls you."

"*Lajdak!*" one of the Poles shouted in reply.

"You're a *lajdak* yourself! You're a petty Polish scoundrel, that's what you are."

---

6. Similar verses can be found in Russian folk songs.
7. Similar verses are found in a popular folk song included in a collection of Russian riddles published in Saint Petersburg in 1876.

"Stop laughing at Poland," said Kalganov sententiously. He too was drunk.

"Be quiet, boy! If I call him a scoundrel, it doesn't mean that I called all Poland so. One *lajdak* doesn't make a Poland. Be quiet, my pretty boy, have a candy."

"Ach, what fellows! As though they were not men. Why won't they make friends?" said Grushenka, and went forward to dance. The chorus broke into "Ah, my hall, my hall!"[8] Grushenka flung back her head, half opened her lips, smiled, waved her handkerchief, and suddenly, with a violent lurch, stood still in the middle of the room, looking bewildered.

"I'm weak . . ." she said in an exhausted voice. "Forgive me. . . . I'm weak, I can't . . . I'm sorry."

She bowed to the chorus, and then began bowing in all directions.

"I'm sorry. . . . Forgive me . . ."

"The lady's been drinking. The pretty lady has been drinking," voices were heard saying.

"The lady's drunk too much," Maximov explained to the girls, giggling.

"Mitya, lead me away . . . take me," said Grushenka helplessly. Mitya pounced on her, snatched her up in his arms, and carried the precious burden through the curtains. "Well, now I'll leave," thought Kalganov, and walking out of the blue room, he closed the two halves of the door after him. But the orgy in the larger room went on and grew louder and louder. Mitya laid Grushenka on the bed and kissed her on the lips.

"Don't touch me . . ." she faltered, in an imploring voice. "Don't touch me, till I'm yours. . . . I've told you I'm yours, but don't touch me . . . spare me. . . . With them here, with them close, you mustn't. He's here. It's nasty here . . ."

"I'll obey you! I won't think of it . . . I worship you!" muttered Mitya. "Yes, it's nasty here, it's abominable." And still holding her in his arms, he sank on his knees by the bedside.

"I know, though you're a brute, you're generous," Grushenka articulated with difficulty. "It must be honorable . . . it shall be honorable for the future . . . and let us be honest, let us be good, not brutes, but good . . . take me away, take me far away, do you hear? I don't want it to be here, but far, far away . . ."

"Oh, yes, yes, it must be!" said Mitya, pressing her in his arms. "I'll take you and we'll fly away. . . . Oh, I'd give my whole life for one year only to know about that blood!"

"What blood?" asked Grushenka, bewildered.

"Nothing," muttered Mitya, through his teeth. "Grusha, you wanted to be honest, but I'm a thief. But I've stolen money from Katka. . . . Disgrace, a disgrace!"

"From Katka, from that young lady? No, you didn't steal it. Give it back to her, take it from me. . . . Why make a fuss? Now everything of mine is yours. What does money matter? We shall waste it anyway. . . . Folks like us are bound to waste money. But we'd better go and work the earth. I want to dig the earth with my own hands. We must work, do you hear? Alyosha said so. I won't be your mistress, I'll be faithful to you, I'll be your slave, I'll work for you. We'll go to the young lady and bow down to her

8. A popular dance song.

together, so that she may forgive us, and then we'll go away. And if she won't forgive us, we'll go anyway. Take her her money and love me. . . . Don't love her. . . . Don't love her any more. If you love her, I shall strangle her. . . . I'll put out both her eyes with a needle . . ."

"I love you. I love only you. I'll love you in Siberia . . ."

"Why Siberia? Never mind, Siberia if you like. I don't care . . . we'll work . . . there's snow in Siberia. . . . I love driving in the snow . . . and must have bells. . . . Do you hear, there's a bell ringing? Where is that bell ringing? There are people coming. . . . Now it's stopped."

She closed her eyes, exhausted, and suddenly fell asleep for an instant. There had certainly been the sound of a bell in the distance, but the ringing had ceased. Mitya let his head sink on her breast. He did not notice that the bell had ceased ringing, nor did he notice that the songs had ceased, and that instead of singing and drunken clamor there was deathly silence in the house. Grushenka opened her eyes.

"What's the matter? Was I asleep? Yes . . . a bell . . . I've been asleep and dreamed I was driving over the snow with bells, and I dozed. I was with someone I loved, with you. And far, far away. I was holding you and kissing you, nestling close to you. I was cold, and the snow glistened. . . . You know how the snow glistens at night when the moon shines. It was as though I was not on earth. I woke up, and my dear one is close to me. How sweet that is . . ."

"Close to you," murmured Mitya, kissing her dress, her bosom, her hands. And suddenly he had a strange fancy: it seemed to him that she was looking straight before her, not at him, not into his face, but over his head, with an intent, almost uncanny fixity. An expression of wonder, almost of alarm, came suddenly into her face.

"Mitya, who is that looking at us?" she whispered suddenly. Mitya turned, and saw that someone had, in fact, parted the curtains and seemed to be watching them. And not one person alone, it seemed. He jumped up and walked quickly to the intruder.

"Here, come to us, come here," said a voice, speaking not loudly, but firmly and peremptorily.

Mitya passed to the other side of the curtain and stood stock still. The room was filled with people, but not those who had been there before. An instantaneous shiver ran down his back, and he shuddered. He recognized all those people instantly. That tall, stout old man in the overcoat and forage cap with a cockade—was the police captain, Mikhail Makarovich. And that "consumptive-looking" trim dandy, "who always has such polished boots"—that was the deputy prosecutor. "He has a chronometer worth four hundred rubles; he showed it to me." And that small young man in spectacles. . . . Mitya forgot his surname though he knew him, had seen him: he was the "district attorney" from the "Jurisprudence," who had only lately come to the town. And this man—the inspector of police, Mavriky Mavrikyevich, a man he knew well. And those fellows with the badges, why are they here? And those other two. . . . peasants. . . . And there at the door Kalganov with Trifon Borisich. . . .

"Gentlemen! What's this for, gentlemen?" began Mitya, but suddenly, as though beside himself, not knowing what he was doing, he cried aloud, at the top of his voice:

"I un—der—stand!"

The young man in spectacles moved forward suddenly, and stepping up to Mitya, began with dignity, though hurriedly:

"We have to make . . . in brief, I beg you to come this way, this way to the sofa. . . . It is absolutely imperative that you should give an explanation."

"The old man!" cried Mitya frantically. "The old man and his blood! . . . I understand."

And he sank, almost fell, on a chair close by, as though he had been mown down by a scythe.

"You understand? He understands it! Monster and parricide! Your father's blood cries out against you!" the old captain of police roared suddenly, stepping up to Mitya. He was beside himself, crimson in the face and quivering all over.

"This is impossible!" cried the small young man. "Mikhail Makarovich, Mikhail Makarovich, this won't do! . . . I beg you'll allow me to speak. I should never have expected such behavior from you . . ."

"This is delirium, gentlemen, raving delirium," cried the captain of police; "look at him: drunk, at this time of night, in the company of a disreputable wench, with the blood of his father on his hands. . . . It's delirium! delirium!"

"I beg you most earnestly, dear Mikhail Makarovich, to restrain your feelings," the prosecutor said in a rapid whisper to the old police captain, "or I shall be forced to resort to . . ."

But the little attorney did not allow him to finish. He turned to Mitya, and delivered himself in a loud, firm, dignified voice:

"Ex-Lieutenant Karamazov, it is my duty to inform you that you are charged with the murder of your father, Fyodor Pavlovich Karamazov, perpetrated this night . . ."

He said something more, and the prosecutor, too, put in something, but though Mitya heard them he did not understand them. He stared at them all with wild eyes.

Book Nine

THE PRELIMINARY INVESTIGATION

Chapter I

The Beginning of the Official Perkhotin's Career

Pyotr Ilyich Perkhotin, whom we left knocking as loud as he could at the strong locked gates of the widow Morozova's house, ended, of course, by making himself heard. Fenya, who had been so frightened two hours ago, and who still from agitation and "thinking" could not make up her mind to go to bed, was frightened once again almost to the point of hysterics by the furious knocking at the gate. Though she had herself seen him drive away, she fancied that it must be Dmitri Fyodorovich knocking again, no one else could knock so "savagely." She ran to the house porter, who had already woken up and gone out to the gate, and began imploring him not to open it. But having questioned Pyotr Ilyich, and learned that he wanted to see Fenya on very "important business," the man made up his mind at last to let him in. Pyotr Ilyich was admitted into Fenya's kitchen but the girl begged him to allow the house porter to be present, "because of her misgivings." He began questioning her and at once learned the most vital fact, that is, that when Dmitri Fyodorovich had run out to look for Grushenka, he had snatched up a pestle from the mortar, and that when he returned, the pestle was not with him and his hands were smeared with blood. "And the blood was simply dripping, dripping from him, dripping!" Fenya kept exclaiming. This horrible detail was simply the product of her disordered imagination. But although not "dripping," Pyotr Ilyich had himself seen those hands stained with blood, and had helped to wash them. Moreover, the question he had to decide was not how soon the blood had dried, but where Dmitri Fyodorovich had run with the pestle, or rather, whether it really was to Fyodor Pavlovich's, and what might be concluded from that. Pyotr Ilyich persisted in returning to this point, and though he found out nothing conclusive, yet he carried away a conviction that Dmitri Fyodorovich could have gone nowhere but to his father's house, and that therefore *something* must have happened there. "And when he came back," Fenya added with excitement, "I told him the whole story, and then I began asking him, 'Why have you got blood on your hands, Dmitri Fyodorovich?' and he answered that that was human blood, and that he had just killed someone. He confessed it all to me, and suddenly ran off like a madman. I sat down and began thinking, where's he run off to now like a madman? He'll go to Mokroe, I thought, and kill my mistress there. I ran out to beg him not to kill her. I was running to his lodgings, but I looked at Plotnikov's shop, and saw him just setting off, and there was no blood on his hands then." (Fenya had noticed this and remembered it.) Fenya's old grandmother confirmed her evidence as far as she was capable. After asking some further questions, Pyotr Ilyich left the house, even more upset and uneasy than he had been when he entered it.

The most direct and the easiest thing for him to do would have been to go straight to Fyodor Pavlovich's, to find out whether anything had happened there, and if so, what; and only to go to the police captain, as Pyotr Ilyich firmly intended doing, when he had satisfied himself of the fact. But the night was dark, Fyodor Pavlovich's gates were strong, and he would have to knock again. His acquaintance with Fyodor Pavlovich was of the slightest, and what if, after he had been knocking, they opened to him, and nothing had happened, and Fyodor Pavlovich in his jeering way would go telling the story all over the town, how a stranger, called Perkhotin, had broken in upon him at midnight to ask if anyone had killed him. It would make a scandal. And scandal was what Pyotr Ilyich dreaded more than anything in the world. Yet the feeling that possessed him was so strong, that though he stamped his foot angrily and swore at himself, he set off again, not to Fyodor Pavlovich's but to Madame Khokhlakova's. He decided that if she denied having just given Dmitri Fyodorovich three thousand rubles, he would go straight to the police captain, but if she admitted having given him the money, he would go home and let the matter rest till next morning. It is, of course, perfectly evident that there was even more likelihood of causing scandal by going at eleven o'clock at night to a fashionable lady, a complete stranger, and perhaps rousing her from her bed to ask her an amazing question, than by going to Fyodor Pavlovich. But that is just how it is, sometimes, especially in cases like the present one, with the decisions of the most precise and phlegmatic people. Pyotr Ilyich was by no means phlegmatic at that moment. He remembered all his life how a haunting uneasiness gradually gained possession of him, growing more and more painful and driving him on, against his will. Yet he kept cursing himself, of course, all the way for going to this lady, but "I will get to the bottom of it, I will!" he repeated for the tenth time, grinding his teeth, and he carried out his intention. It was exactly eleven o'clock when he entered Madame Khokhlakova's house. He was admitted into the yard pretty quickly, but, in response to his inquiry whether the lady was still up, the porter could give no answer, except that she was usually in bed by that time. "Ask at the top of the stairs. If the lady wants to receive you, she'll receive you. If she won't, she won't." Pyotr Ilyich went up, but did not find things so easy here. The lackey was unwilling to take in his name, but finally called a maid. Pyotr Ilyich politely but insistently begged her to inform her lady that an official, living in the town, called Perkhotin, had called on particular business, and that, if it were not of the greatest importance, he would not have ventured to come. "Tell her in those words, in those words exactly," he asked the girl. She went away. He remained waiting in the entry. Madame Khokhlakova herself was already in her bedroom, though not yet asleep. She had felt upset ever since Mitya's visit, and had a presentiment that she would not get through the night without the migraine headache which always, with her, followed such excitement. She was surprised on hearing the announcement from the maid. She irritably declined to see him, however, though the unexpected visit at such an hour, of an "official living in the town," who was a total stranger, roused her feminine curiosity intensely. But this time Pyotr Ilyich was as obstinate as a mule. He begged the maid most earnestly to take another message "in these very words": "That he had come on business of the greatest importance, and that Madame Khokhlakova might have cause to regret it later, if she refused to see him now." "I plunged headlong," he described it afterwards. The maid, gazing at him in amazement, went to take his message again. Madame Khokhlakova was impressed. She thought a little, asked what he looked like, and learned that he was "very well dressed, young and so polite." We may note, parenthetically, that Pyotr Ilyich was a rather good-looking young man, and well aware of the fact. Madame Khokhlakova made up her mind to see him. She was in her dressing-gown and slippers, but she flung a black shawl over her shoulders. "The official" was asked to walk into the drawing room, the very room in which Mitya had been received shortly before. The lady came to meet her visitor, with a sternly inquiring countenance, and, without asking him to sit down, began at once with the question: "What do you want?"

"I have ventured to disturb you, Madame, on a matter concerning our common acquaintance, Dmitri Fyodorovich Karamazov," Perkhotin began. But he had hardly uttered the name, when the lady's face showed signs of acute irritation. She almost shrieked, and interrupted him in a fury:

"How much longer am I to be tormented by that awful man?" she cried hysterically. "How dare you, sir, how could you venture to disturb a lady who is a stranger to you, in her own house at such an hour! . . . And to force yourself upon her to talk of a man who came here, to this very drawing room, only three hours ago, to murder me, and went stamping out of the room, as no one would go out of a decent house. Let me tell you, sir, that I shall lodge a complaint against you, that I will not let it pass. Kindly leave me at once . . . I am a mother. . . . I . . . I . . ."

"Murder! then he tried to murder you, too?"

"Why, has he killed somebody else?" Madame Khokhlakova asked impulsively.

"If you would kindly listen, Madame, for half a moment, I'll explain it all in a couple of words," answered Perkhotin, firmly. "At five o'clock this afternoon Dmitri Fyodorovich borrowed ten rubles from me, and I know for a fact he had no money. Yet at nine o'clock, he came to see me with a bundle of hundred-ruble bills in his hand, about two or three thousand rubles. His hands and face were all covered with blood, and he looked like a madman. When I asked him where he had got so much money, he answered that he had just received it from you, that you had given him a sum of three thousand to go to the gold mines . . ."

Madame Khokhlakova's face suddenly assumed an expression of intense and painful excitement.

"Good God! He must have killed his old father!" she cried, clasping her hands. "I never gave him any money, never! Oh, run, run! . . . Don't say another word! Save the old man . . . run to his father . . . run!"

"Excuse me, Madame, then you did not give him money? You remember for a fact that you did not give him any money?"

"No, I didn't, I didn't! I refused to give it to him, for he could not appreciate it. He ran out in a fury, stamping. He rushed at me, but I slipped away . . . And let me tell you, as I wish to hide nothing from you now, that he even spat at me, can you imagine? But why are we standing? Ah, sit down. . . . Excuse me, I . . . or better run, run, you must run and save the poor old man from an awful death!"

"But if he has killed him already?"

"Ah, good heavens, yes! Then what are we to do now? What do you think we must do now?"

Meantime she had made Pyotr Ilyich sit down and sat down herself, facing him. Briefly, but fairly clearly, Pyotr Ilyich told her the history of the affair, that part of it at least which he had himself witnessed. He described, too, his visit to Fenya, and told her about the pestle. All these details produced an overwhelming effect on the distracted lady, who kept uttering shrieks, and covering her face with her hands. . . .

"Would you believe it, I foresaw all this! I have that special faculty, whatever I imagine comes to pass. And how often, how often, I've looked at that awful man and always thought, that man will end by murdering me. And now it's happened . . . that is, if he hasn't murdered me, but only his own father, it's only because the finger of God preserved me, and what's more, he was ashamed to murder me because, on this very place, I put the holy icon from the relics of the holy martyr, Saint Barbara, on his neck. . . . And to think how near I was to death at that minute, I went close up to him and he stretched out his neck to me! . . . Do you know, Pyotr Ilyich (I think you said your name was Pyotr Ilyich), I don't believe in miracles, but that icon and this unmistakable miracle with me now—that shakes me, and I'm ready to believe in anything you like. Have you heard about Father Zosima? . . . But I don't know what I'm saying . . . and imagine, with the icon on his neck he spat at me. . . . He only spat, it's true, he didn't murder me and . . . he dashed away! But what shall we do, what must we do now? What do you think?"

Pyotr Ilyich got up, and announced that he was going straight to the police captain, to tell him all about it, and leave him to do what he thought fit.

"Oh, he's an excellent man, excellent! Mikhail Makarovich, I know him. Of course, he's the person to go to. How practical you are, Pyotr Ilyich! How well you've thought of everything! I should never have thought of it in your place!"

"Especially as I know the police captain very well, too," observed Pyotr Ilyich, who still continued to stand, and was obviously anxious to escape as quickly as possible from the impulsive lady, who would not let him say good-bye and go away.

"And be sure, be sure," she prattled on, "to come back and tell me what you see there, and what you find out . . . what comes to light . . . how they'll try him . . . and what he's condemned to . . . Tell me, we have no capital punishment, have we? But be sure to come, even if it's at three o'clock at night, at four, at half past four. . . . Tell them to wake me, to wake me, to shake me, if I don't get up. . . . But, good heavens, I shan't sleep! But wait, hadn't I better come with you?"

"No—no, madame. But if you would write three lines with your own hand, stating that you did not give Dmitri Fyodorovich money, it might, perhaps, be of use . . . in case it's needed . . ."

"To be sure!" Madame Khokhlakova skipped, delighted, to her bureau. "And you know I'm simply struck, amazed at your resourcefulness, your good sense in such affairs. Are you in government here? I'm delighted to think that you're in the service here!"

And still speaking, she scribbled on half a sheet of notepaper the following lines in a large hand:

"I've never in my life lent to that unhappy man, Dmitri Fyodorovich Karamazov (for, in spite of all, he is unhappy) three thousand rubles today. I've never given him money, never! That I swear by all that's holy in our world!"

"K. KHOKHLAKOVA."

"Here's the note!" she turned quickly to Pyotr Ilyich. "Go, save him. It's a noble deed on your part!"

And she made the sign of the cross three times over him. She ran out to accompany him to the passage.

"How grateful I am to you! You can't think how grateful I am to you for having come to me, first. How is it I haven't met you before? I shall feel flattered at seeing you at my house in the future. How delightful it is that you are in government service here! . . . Such precision! Such practical ability! . . . They must appreciate you, they must understand you. If there's anything I can do, believe me . . . oh, I love young people! I'm in love with young people! The younger generation are the one prop of our suffering Russia. Her one hope. . . . Oh, go, go!" . . .

But Pyotr Ilyich had already run away or she would not have let him go so soon. Yet Madame Khokhlakova had made a rather agreeable impression on him, which had somewhat softened his anxiety at being drawn into such an unpleasant affair. Tastes differ, as we all know. "She's by no means so elderly," he thought, feeling pleased, "on the contrary I should have taken her for her daughter."

As for Madame Khokhlakova, she was simply enchanted by the young man. "Such sense! such exactness! in so young a man! in our day! and all that with such manners and appearance! People say the young people of today are no good for anything, but here's an example!" etc., etc. So she simply forgot this "dreadful affair," and it was only as she was getting into bed, that, suddenly recalling "how near death she had been," she exclaimed: "Ah, it is awful, awful!" But she fell at once into a sound, sweet sleep. I would not, however, have dwelt on such trivial and irrelevant details, if this eccentric meeting of the young official with the by no means elderly widow, had not subsequently turned out to be the foundation of the whole career of that practical and precise young man. His story is remembered to this day with amazement in our town, and I shall perhaps have something to say about it, when I have finished my long history of the Karamazov brothers.

Chapter II

The Alarm

Our police captain, Mikhail Makarovich Makarov, a retired lieutenant colonel, redesignated a state councilor,[1] was a widower and an excellent man. He had only come to us three years previously, but had won general esteem, chiefly because he "knew how to keep society together." He was never without visitors, and could not have got along without them. Someone or other was always dining with him; without a couple of guests, or even just one, he would not sit down to table. He gave regular dinners, too, on all sorts of occasions, sometimes most surprising ones. Though the fare was not elegant, it was abundant. The fish pies were excellent, and the wine made up in quantity for what it lacked in quality. The first room his guests entered was a well-appointed billiard room, with pictures of English racehorses, in black frames on the walls, an essential decoration, as we all know, for a bachelor's billiard room. There was card-playing every evening at his house, if only at one table. But at frequent intervals, all the society of our town, with the mammas and young ladies, assembled at his house to dance. Though Mikhail Makarovich was a widower, he did not live alone. His widowed daughter lived with him, with her two unmarried daughters, grown-up girls, who had finished their education. They were of pleasant appearance and lively character, and though everyone knew they would have no dowry, they attracted all the young men of fashion to their grandfather's house. Mikhail Makarovich was by no means very efficient in his work, though he performed his duties no worse than many others. To speak plainly, he was a man of rather narrow education. His understanding of the limits of his administrative power could not always be relied upon. It was not so much that he failed to grasp certain reforms enacted during the present reign, as that he made conspicuous blunders in his interpretation of them. This was not from any special lack of intelligence, but from carelessness, for he was always in too great a hurry to go into the subject. "I have the heart of a soldier rather than of a civilian," he used to say of himself. He had not even formed a definite idea of the fundamental principles of the reforms connected with the emancipation of the serfs, and only picked it up, so to speak, from year to year, involuntarily increasing his knowledge by practice. And yet he was himself a landowner. Pyotr Ilyich knew for certain that he would meet some of Mikhail Makarovich's visitors there that evening, but he didn't know which. As it happened, at that moment the prosecutor, and Varvinsky, our district doctor, a young man, who had only just come to us from Petersburg after taking a brilliant degree at the Academy of Medicine,[2] were playing whist at the police captain's. Ippolit Kirillovich, the prosecutor (he was really the deputy prosecutor, but we always called him the prosecutor), was rather a peculiar man, of about thirty-five, inclined to be con-

---

1. Lieutenant colonel (*podpolkovnik*) was the seventh rank in the military Table of Ranks; court councilor occupied the fifth rung in the civil Table.
2. Founded in 1758 as the medical faculty of Moscow University, the Academy of Medicine was the highest medical institution in Russia. In the 1850s and '60s, the public began to associate the Academy with freethinking and atheism.

sumptive, and married to a fat and childless woman. He was vain and irritable, though he had a good intellect, and even a kind heart. It seemed that all that was wrong with him was that he had a better opinion of himself than his ability warranted. And that made him seem constantly uneasy. He had, moreover, certain higher, even artistic, leanings, towards psychology, for instance, a special study of the human heart, a special gift of cognition regarding the criminal and his crime. He cherished a grievance on this ground, considering that he had been passed over in the service, and being firmly persuaded that in higher spheres he had not been properly appreciated, and had enemies. In gloomy moments he even threatened to give up his post, and practice as a lawyer in criminal cases. The unexpected Karamazov case agitated him profoundly: "It was a case that might well be talked about all over Russia." But I am anticipating.

Nikolay Parfenovich Nelyudov, the young district attorney, who had come from Petersburg only two months before, was sitting in the next room with the young ladies. People talked about it afterwards and wondered that all the gentlemen should, as though intentionally, on the evening of "the crime" have been gathered together at the house of the executive authority. Yet it was perfectly simple and happened quite naturally. Ippolit Kirillovich's wife had had toothache for the last two days, and he was obliged to go out to escape from her groans. The doctor, from the very nature of his being, could not spend an evening except at cards. Nikolay Parfenovich Nelyudov had been intending for the last three days to drop in that evening at Mikhail Makarovich's, so to speak casually, so as slyly to startle the elder granddaughter, Olga Mikhailovna, by showing that he knew her secret, that he knew it was her birthday, and that she was trying to conceal it on purpose, so as not to be obliged to give a dance. He anticipated a great deal of merriment, many playful jests about her age, and her being afraid to reveal it, about his knowing her secret and telling everybody, and so on. The charming young man was a great adept at such teasing; the ladies had christened him "the naughty man," and he seemed to be delighted at the name. He was extremely well bred, however, of good family, education and feelings, and, though leading a life of pleasure, his sallies were always innocent and in good taste. He was short and weak and delicate looking. On his white, slender, little fingers he always wore a number of big, glittering rings. When he was engaged in his official duties, he always became extraordinarily grave, as though realizing his position and the sanctity of the obligations laid upon him. He had a special gift for mystifying murderers and other criminals of the peasant class during interrogation, and if he did not win their respect, he certainly succeeded in arousing their wonder.

Pyotr Ilyich was simply dumbfounded when he went into the police captain's. He saw instantly that everyone knew. They had positively thrown down their cards, all were standing up and talking. Even Nikolay Parfenovich had left the young ladies and ran in, looking urgent and ready for action. Pyotr Ilyich was met with the astounding news that old Fyodor Pavlovich really and in fact had been murdered that evening in his own house, murdered and robbed. The news had only just reached them in the following manner.

Martha Ignatyevna, the wife of old Grigory, who had been knocked senseless near the fence, was sleeping soundly in her bed and might well have slept till morning after the draught she had taken. But, all of a sudden she woke up, no doubt roused by a fearful epileptic scream from Smerdyakov, who was lying in the next room unconscious. That scream always preceded his fits, and always terrified and upset Martha Ignatyevna. She could never get accustomed to it. She jumped up and ran half-awake to Smerdyakov's room. But it was dark there, and she could only hear the invalid beginning to gasp and struggle. Then Martha Ignatyevna herself screamed out and was going to call her husband, but suddenly realized that when she had got up, he was not beside her in bed. She ran back to the bedstead and began groping with her hands, but the bed was really empty. Then he must have gone out—where? She ran to the steps and timidly called him. She got no answer, of course, but she caught the sound of groans far away in the garden in the stillness of the night. She listened. The groans were repeated, and it was evident they came from the garden. "Good Lord! Just as it was with Lizaveta Smerdyashchaya!" she thought distractedly. She went timidly down the steps and saw that the gate into the garden was open. "He must be out there, poor dear," she thought. She went up to the gate and all at once she distinctly heard Grigory calling her by name, "Martha! Martha!" in a weak, moaning, dreadful voice. "Lord, preserve us from harm!" Martha Ignatyevna murmured, and ran towards the voice, and that was how she found Grigory. However, she found him not by the fence where he had been knocked down, but about twenty paces off. It appeared later that he had crawled away on coming to himself, and probably had been a long time getting so far, losing consciousness several times. She noticed at once that he was covered with blood, and screamed at the top of her voice. Grigory was muttering incoherently: "He has murdered . . . his father murdered. . . . Why scream, silly . . . run . . . fetch someone . . ."

But Martha continued screaming, and seeing that her master's window was open and that there was a candle alight in the window, she ran there and began calling Fyodor Pavlovich. But peeping in at the window, she saw a fearful sight. Her master was lying on his back, motionless, on the floor. His light-colored dressing gown and white shirt were soaked with blood. The candle on the table brightly lighted up the blood and the motionless dead face of Fyodor Pavlovich. Terror-stricken, Martha rushed away from the window, ran out of the garden, drew the bolt of the big gate, and ran headlong by the back way to the neighbor, Marya Kondratyevna. Both mother and daughter were asleep, but they woke up at Martha's desperate and persistent screaming and knocking at the shutter. Martha, shrieking and screaming incoherently, managed to tell them the main fact, and to beg for assistance. It happened that Thomas had come back from his wanderings and was staying the night with them. They got him up immediately and all three ran to the scene of the crime. On the way, Marya Kondratyevna remembered that at about eight o'clock she heard a dreadful scream from their garden, and this was no doubt Grigory's scream, "Parricide!" uttered when he caught hold of Mitya's leg. "Some one person screamed out and then was silent," Marya Kondratyevna explained as she ran. Running to the place where Grigory lay, the two women with the help of Thomas carried him to the lodge. They lighted a candle and saw that Smerdyakov was no better, that he was writhing in convulsions, his eyes fixed in a squint, and that foam was flowing from his lips. They moistened Grigory's forehead with water mixed with vinegar, and the water revived him at once. He asked immediately: "Is the master murdered?" Then Thomas and both the women ran to the house and saw this time that not only the window, but also the door into the garden was wide open, though Fyodor Pavlovich had for the last week locked himself in every night and did not allow even Grigory to come in on any pretext. Seeing that door open, they were afraid to go in to Fyodor Pavlovich "for fear anything should happen afterwards." And when they returned to Grigory, the old man told them to go straight to the police captain. Marya Kondratyevna ran there and gave the alarm to the whole party at the police captain's. She arrived only five minutes before Pyotr Ilyich, so that his story came, not as his own surmise and theory, but as the direct confirmation, by a witness, of the theory held by all, as to the identity of the criminal (a theory he had in the bottom of his heart refused to believe till that moment).

It was resolved to act with energy. The deputy police inspector of the town was commissioned to take four witnesses, to enter Fyodor Pavlovich's house and there to open an inquiry on the spot, according to the regular forms, which I will not go into here. The district doctor, a zealous man, new to his work, almost insisted on accompanying the police captain, the prosecutor, and the district attorney. I will note briefly that Fyodor Pavlovich was found to be quite dead, with his skull battered in. But with what? Most likely with the same weapon with which Grigory had been attacked later. And immediately that weapon was found, Grigory, to whom all possible medical assistance was at once given, described in a weak and breaking voice how he had been knocked down. They began looking with a lantern by the fence and found the brass pestle dropped in a most conspicuous place on the garden path. There were no signs of disturbance in the room where Fyodor Pavlovich was lying. But by the bed, behind the screen, they picked up from the floor a big and thick envelope with the inscription: "A present of three thousand rubles for my angel Grushenka, if she is willing to come." And below had been added by Fyodor Pavlovich, "For my little chicken." There were three seals of red sealing wax on the envelope, but it had been torn open and was empty; the money had been removed. They found also on the floor a piece of narrow pink ribbon, with which the envelope had been tied up. One piece of Pyotr Ilyich's evidence made a great impression on the prosecutor and the district attorney, namely, his idea that Dmitri Fyodorovich would shoot himself before daybreak, that he had resolved to do so, had spoken of it to Pyotr Ilyich, had taken the pistols, loaded them before him, written a letter, put it in his pocket, etc. When Pyotr Ilyich, though still unwilling to believe in it, threatened to tell someone so as to prevent the suicide, Mitya had answered grinning: "You'll be too late." So they must make haste to Mokroe to find the criminal, before he really did shoot himself. "That's clear, that's clear!" repeated the prosecutor in great excitement. "That's just the way with mad fellows like that: 'I shall kill myself tomorrow, so I'll make merry till I die!'"

The story of how he had bought the wine and provisions excited the prosecutor more than ever. "Do you remember the fellow that murdered a merchant called Olsufyev, gentlemen? He stole fifteen hundred, went at once to have his hair curled, and then, without even hiding the money, carrying it almost in his hand in the same way, he went off to the girls."[3] All were delayed, however, by the inquiry, the search, and the formalities, etc., in the house of Fyodor Pavlovich. It all took time and so, two hours before starting, they sent on ahead to Mokroe the officer of the rural police, Mavriky Mavrikyevich Shmertsov,[4] who had arrived in the town the morning before to get his pay. He was instructed to avoid raising the alarm when he reached Mokroe, but to keep constant watch over the "criminal" till the arrival of the proper authorities, also to procure witnesses for the arrest, policemen and so on. Mavriky Mavrikyevich did as he was told, preserving his incognito, and giving no one but his old acquaintance, Trifon Borisovich, the slightest hint of his secret business. He had spoken to him just before Mitya met the landlord in the balcony, looking for him in the dark, and noticed at once a change in Trifon Borisovich's face and voice. So neither Mitya nor anyone else knew that he was being watched. The box with the pistols had been carried off by Trifon Borisovich and put in a suitable place. Not until after four o'clock, almost at sunrise, did all the officials, the police captain, the prosecutor, the district attorney, drive up in two carriages, each drawn by three horses. The doctor remained at Fyodor Pavlovich's to perform a postmortem next day on the body. But he was particularly interested in the condition of the servant, Smerdyakov. "Such violent and protracted epileptic fits, recurring continually for two days, are rarely to be met with, and are of interest to science," he declared enthusiastically to his companions, and, as they left, they laughingly congratulated him on his find. The prosecutor and the district attorney distinctly remembered the doctor's saying that Smerdyakov could not outlive the night.

After these long, but, I think, necessary explanations, we will return to that moment of our tale at which we broke off.

Chapter III

The Soul's Journey through Torments. The First Torment.[5]

And so Mitya sat looking wildly at the people round him, not understanding what was said to him. Suddenly he got up, flung up his hands and shouted aloud:

"I'm not guilty! I'm not guilty of that blood! I'm not guilty of my father's blood. . . . I meant to kill him. But I'm not guilty. Not I."

But he had hardly said this, before Grushenka rushed from behind the curtain and flung herself at the police captain's feet.

"It was my fault, accursed I am! Mine! My wickedness!" she cried, in a heart-rending voice, bathed in tears, stretching out her clasped hands

---

3. Ippolit Kirillovich refers to the case of one Zaitsev, an eighteen-year-old who robbed and killed a merchant in November 1878 to steal from his store. The case was reported in the January 1879 issue of the journal *The Voice*.
4. This name may be based on the German word *Schmerz* (pain).
5. According to the teachings of some Church fathers, after death the soul must pass through a period of torments before reaching its final destination. In Russian Orthodox belief, the soul may be intercepted by evil spirits who subject it to various trials on its way toward heaven.

towards them. "He did it through me. I tortured him and drove him to it. I tortured that poor old man that's dead, too, in my wickedness, and brought him to this! It's my fault, mine first, mine most, my fault!"

"Yes, it's your fault! You're the chief criminal! You fury! You harlot! You're the most to blame!" shouted the police captain, threatening her with his hand. But he was quickly and resolutely suppressed. The prosecutor positively seized hold of him.

"This is absolutely irregular, Mikhail Makarovich!" he cried. "You are positively hindering the inquiry. . . . You're ruining the case . . ." he almost gasped.

"Follow the regular course! Follow the regular course!" cried Nikolay Parfenovich, fearfully excited too, "otherwise it's absolutely impossible! . . ."

"Judge us together!" Grushenka cried frantically, still kneeling. "Punish us together. I will go with him now, if it's to death!"

"Grusha, my life, my blood, my holy one!" Mitya fell on his knees beside her and held her tight in his arms. "Don't believe her," he cried, "she's not guilty of anything, of any blood, of anything!"

He remembered afterwards that he was forcibly dragged away from her by several men, and that she was led out, and that when he recovered himself he was sitting at the table. Beside him and behind him stood the men with badges. Facing him on the other side of the table sat Nikolay Parfenovich, the district attorney. He kept persuading him to drink a little water out of a glass that stood on the table. "That will refresh you, that will calm you. Be calm, don't be frightened," he added, extremely politely. Mitya (he remembered it afterwards) became suddenly intensely interested in his big rings, one with an amethyst, and another with a transparent bright yellow stone, of great brilliance. And long afterwards he remembered with wonder how those rings had riveted his attention through all those terrible hours of interrogation, so that he was utterly unable to tear himself away from them and dismiss them, as things that had nothing to do with his position. On Mitya's left side, in the place where Maximov had been sitting at the beginning of the evening, the prosecutor was now seated and on Mitya's right hand, where Grushenka had been, was a rosy-cheeked young man in a sort of shabby hunting jacket, with ink and paper before him. This was the secretary of the district attorney, who had brought him with him. The police captain was now standing by the window at the other end of the room, beside Kalganov, who was sitting there.

"Drink some water," said the district attorney softly, for the tenth time.

"I have drunk it, gentlemen, I have . . . but . . . come, gentlemen, crush me, punish me, decide my fate!" cried Mitya, staring with terribly fixed wide-open eyes at the district attorney.

"So you positively declare that you are not guilty of the death of your father, Fyodor Pavlovich?" asked the district attorney, softly but insistently.

"Not guilty. I am guilty of other blood, of the blood of another old man, but not of my father's. And I weep for it! I killed, I killed the old man and knocked him down. . . . But it's hard to have to answer for that blood with other blood, with terrible blood of which I am not guilty. . . . It's a terrible accusation, gentlemen, a knockout blow. But who has killed my father, who has killed him? Who can have killed him if I didn't? It's marvelous, extraordinary, impossible."

"Yes, who can have killed him?" the district attorney was beginning, but Ippolit Kirillovich, the assistant prosecutor, but for the sake of brevity we will call him the prosecutor, glancing at him, addressed Mitya.

"You need not worry yourself about the old servant, Grigory Vasilyevich. He is alive, he has recovered, and in spite of the terrible blows inflicted, according to his own and your evidence, by you, there seems no doubt that he will live, so the doctor says, at least."

"Alive? He's alive?" Mitya suddenly shouted, flinging up his hands. His whole face beamed. "Lord, I thank Thee for the miracle Thou hast wrought for me, a sinner and evildoer. That's an answer to my prayer. I've been praying all night." And he crossed himself three times. He was almost breathless.

"So from this Grigory we have received such important evidence concerning you, that . . ." the prosecutor would have continued, but Mitya suddenly jumped up from his chair.

"One minute, gentlemen, for God's sake, one minute; I will run to her—"

"Excuse me, at this moment it's quite impossible," Nikolay Parfenovich almost shrieked. He, too, leaped to his feet. Mitya was seized by the men with the badges, but he sat down on his own accord. . . .

"Gentlemen, what a pity! I wanted to see her for one minute only; I wanted to tell her that it has been washed away, it has gone, that blood that was weighing on my heart all night, and that I am not a murderer now! Gentlemen, she is my betrothed!" he said ecstatically and reverently, looking round at them all. "Oh, thank you, gentlemen! Oh, in one minute you have given me new life, resurrected me! . . . That old man used to carry me in his arms, gentlemen. He used to wash me in the tub when I was a baby three years old, abandoned by everyone, he was my own father!"

"And so you . . ." the district attorney began.

"Allow me, gentlemen, allow me one minute more," interposed Mitya, putting his elbows on the table and covering his face with his hands. "Let me have a moment to think, let me breathe, gentlemen. All this is horribly upsetting, horribly. A man is not a drum, gentlemen!"

"Drink a little more water," murmured Nikolay Parfenovich. Mitya took his hands from his face and laughed. His eyes were confident. He seemed completely transformed in a moment. His whole tone was changed; he was once more the equal of these men, with all of whom he was acquainted, as though they had all met the day before, when nothing had happened, at some social gathering. We may note in passing that, on his first arrival, Mitya had been made very welcome at the police captain's, but later, during the last month especially, Mitya had hardly called at all, and when the police captain met him, in the street, for instance, Mitya noticed that he frowned and only bowed out of politeness. His acquaintance with the prosecutor was less intimate, though he sometimes paid his wife, a nervous and fanciful lady, polite visits, without quite knowing why, and she always received him graciously and had, for some reason, taken an interest in him up to the last. He had not had time to get to know the district attorney, though he had met him and talked to him twice, each time about the fair sex.

"You're a most skillful investigator, I see, Nikolay Parfenovich," cried Mitya, laughing gaily, "but I can help you now. Oh, gentlemen, I am resurrected, and don't be offended at my addressing you so simply and directly. I'm rather drunk, too, I'll tell you that frankly. I believe I've had the honor . . . the honor and pleasure of meeting you, Nikolay Parfenovich, at my kinsman Miüsov's. Gentlemen, gentlemen, I don't pretend to be on equal terms with you. I understand, of course, in what character I am sitting before you. Oh, of course, there's a horrible suspicion . . . hanging over me . . . if Grigory has given evidence. . . . A horrible suspicion! It's awful, awful, I understand that! But to business, gentlemen, I am ready, and we will make an end of it in one moment; for, listen, listen, gentlemen! Since I know I'm innocent, we can put an end to it in a minute. Can't we? Can't we?"

Mitya spoke much and quickly, nervously and effusively, as though he positively took his listeners to be his best friends.

"So, for the present, we will write that you absolutely deny the charge brought against you," said Nikolay Parfenovich, impressively, and bending down to the secretary he dictated to him in an undertone what to write.

"Write it down? You want to write that down? Well, write it; I consent, I give my full consent, gentlemen, only . . . do you see. . . . Stay, stay, write this. Of disorderly conduct I am guilty, of violence on a poor old man I am guilty. And there is something else at the bottom of my heart, of which I am guilty, too—but that you need not write down" (he turned suddenly to the secretary) "that's my personal life, gentlemen, that doesn't concern you, the bottom of my heart, that's to say. . . . But of the murder of my old father I'm not guilty. That's a wild idea. It's quite a wild idea! . . . I will prove you that and you'll be convinced directly. . . . You will laugh, gentlemen. You'll laugh yourself at your suspicion! . . ."

"Be calm, Dmitri Fyodorovich," said the district attorney, evidently trying to allay Mitya's excitement by his own composure. "Before we go on with our inquiry, I should like, if you will consent to answer, to hear you confirm the statement that you disliked your father, Fyodor Pavlovich, that you were involved in continual disputes with him. Here at least, a quarter of an hour ago, you exclaimed that you wanted to kill him: 'I didn't kill him,' you said, 'but I wanted to kill him'?"

"Did I exclaim that? Ach, that may be so, gentlemen! Yes, unhappily, I did want to kill him . . . many times I wanted to . . . unhappily, unhappily!"

"You wanted to. Would you consent to explain what motives precisely led you to such a sentiment of hatred for your parent?"

"What is there to explain, gentlemen!" Mitya shrugged his shoulders sullenly, looking down. "I have never concealed my feelings. All the town knows about it—everyone knows in the tavern. Only lately I declared them in Father Zosima's cell. . . . And the very same day, in the evening I beat my father. I nearly killed him, and I swore I'd come again and kill him, before witnesses. . . . Oh, a thousand witnesses! I've been shouting it aloud for the last month, anyone can tell you that! . . . The fact stares you in the face, it speaks for itself, it cries aloud, but, feelings, gentlemen, feelings are another matter. You see, gentlemen" (Mitya frowned), "it seems to me that about feelings you've no right to question me. I know that you are bound by your office, I quite understand that, but that's my affair, my private, intimate affair, yet . . . since I haven't concealed my feelings in the past . . . in the tavern, for instance, I've talked to everyone, so . . . so I won't make a secret of it now. You see, I understand, gentlemen, that there are terrible facts against me in this business. I told everyone that I'd kill him, and now, all of a sudden, he's been killed. So it must have been me! Ha, ha! I can make allowances for you, gentlemen, I can quite make allowances. I'm shocked to the epidermis myself, for who can have murdered him, if not I? That's what it comes to, isn't it? If not I, who can it be, who? Gentlemen, I want to know, I insist on knowing!" he exclaimed suddenly. "Where was he murdered? How was he murdered? How, and with what? Tell me," he asked quickly, looking at the two lawyers.

"We found him in his study, lying on his back on the floor, with his head battered in," said the prosecutor.

"That's horrible!" Mitya shuddered and, putting his elbows on the table, hid his face in his right hand.

"We will continue," interposed Nikolay Parfenovich. "So what was it that impelled you to this sentiment of hatred? You have asserted in public, I believe, that it was based upon jealousy?"

"Well, yes, jealousy. And not only jealousy."

"Disputes about money?"

"Yes, about money, too."

"There was a dispute about three thousand rubles, I think, which you claimed as part of your inheritance?"

"Three thousand! More, more," cried Mitya hotly; "more than six thousand, more than ten, perhaps. I told everyone so, shouted it at them. But I made up my mind to let it go at three thousand. I was desperately in need of that three thousand . . . so the bundle of bills for three thousand that I knew he kept under his pillow, ready for Grushenka, I considered as simply stolen from me. Yes, gentlemen, I looked upon it as mine, as my own property . . ."

The prosecutor looked significantly at the district attorney, and had time to wink at him on the sly.

"We will return to that subject later," said the district attorney promptly. "You will allow us to note that point and write it down; that you looked upon that money as your own property?"

"Write it down, by all means. I know that's another fact that tells against me, but I'm not afraid of facts and I tell them against myself. Do you hear? Do you know, gentlemen, you take me for a different sort of man from what I am," he added, suddenly, gloomy and dejected. "You have to deal with a man of honor, a man of the highest honor; above all—don't lose sight of it—a man who's done a lot of nasty things, but has always been, and still is, honorable at bottom, in his inner being. I don't know how to express it. That's just what's made me wretched all my life, that I yearned to be honorable, that I was, so to speak, a martyr to a sense of honor, seeking for it with a lantern, with the lantern of Diogenes[6] and yet, all my life I've been doing filthy things like all of us, gentlemen . . . that is like me alone. That was a mistake, like me alone, me alone! . . . Gentlemen, my head aches . . ."

---

6. Diogenes of Sinope (c. 412–323 B.C.E.), Greek philosopher. According to legend, he once walked through the streets of Athens carrying a lantern in broad daylight to illustrate the difficulty of finding an honest man.

His brows contracted with pain. "You see, gentlemen, I couldn't bear the look of him, there was something in him ignoble, impudent, trampling on everything sacred, something sneering and irreverent, loathsome, loathsome. But now that he's dead, I feel differently."

"How do you mean?"

"I don't feel differently, but I wish I hadn't hated him so."

"You feel penitent?"

"No, not penitent, don't write that. I'm not much good myself, I'm not very beautiful, so I had no right to consider him repulsive. That's what I mean! Write that down, if you like."

Saying this Mitya became very mournful. He had grown more and more gloomy as the inquiry continued. At that moment another unexpected scene followed. Though Grushenka had been removed, she had not been taken far away, only into the room next to the blue room, in which the examination was proceeding. It was a little room with one window, just beyond the large room in which they had danced and feasted so lavishly. She was sitting there with no one by her but Maximov, who was terribly depressed, terribly scared, and clung to her side, as though for security. At their door stood one of the peasants with a badge on his breast. Grushenka was crying, and suddenly her grief was too much for her, she jumped up, flung up her arms, and with a loud wail, "oh, sorrow, my sorrow," rushed out of the room to him, to her Mitya, and so unexpectedly that they had not time to stop her. Mitya, hearing her cry, trembled, jumped up, and with a yell rushed impetuously to meet her, not knowing what he was doing. But they were not allowed to come together, though they saw one another. He was seized by the arms. He struggled, and tried to tear himself away. It took three or four men to hold him. She was seized too, and he saw her stretching out her arms to him, crying aloud as they carried her away. When the scene was over, he came to himself again, sitting in the same place as before, opposite the district attorney, and crying out to them:

"What do you want with her? Why do you torment her? She's done nothing, nothing! . . ."

The attorneys tried to soothe him. About ten minutes passed like this. At last Mikhail Makarovich, who had been absent, came hurriedly into the room, and said in a loud and excited voice to the prosecutor:

"She's been removed, she's downstairs. Will you allow me to say one word to this unhappy man, gentlemen? In your presence, gentlemen, in your presence."

"By all means, Mikhail Makarovich," answered the district attorney. "In the present case we have nothing against it."

"Listen, Dmitri Fyodorovich, my dear fellow," began the police captain, and there was a look of warm, almost fatherly, feeling for the luckless prisoner on his excited face, "I took your Agrafena Alexandrovna downstairs myself, and confided her to the care of the landlord's daughters, and that old fellow Maximov is with her all the time. And I soothed her, do you hear? I soothed and calmed her. I impressed on her that you have to clear yourself, so she mustn't hinder you, must not depress you, or you may lose your head and say the wrong thing in your evidence. In fact, I talked to her and she understood. She's a sensible girl, my boy, a good-hearted girl, she would have kissed my old hands, begging help for you. She sent me herself, to tell you not to worry about her. And I must go, my dear fellow, I must go and tell her that you are calm and comforted about her. And so you must be calm, do you understand? I was unfair to her; she is a Christian soul, gentlemen, yes, I tell you, she's a gentle soul, and not to blame for anything. So what am I to tell her, Dmitri Fyodorovich, will you sit quiet or not?"

The good-natured police captain said a great deal that was irregular, but Grushenka's grief, human grief, touched his good-natured heart, and tears stood in his eyes. Mitya jumped up and rushed towards him.

"Forgive me, gentlemen, oh, allow me, allow me!" he cried. "You've the heart of an angel, an angel, Mikhail Makarovich, I thank you for her. I will, I will be calm, cheerful, in fact. Tell her, in the infinite kindness of your heart, that I am cheerful, quite cheerful, that I shall be laughing in a minute, knowing that she has a guardian angel like you. I shall be finished with all this directly, and as soon as I'm free, I'll be with her, she'll see, let her wait. Gentlemen," he said, turning to the two attorneys, "now I'll open my whole soul to you; I'll pour out everything. We'll finish this off directly, finish it off gaily. We shall laugh at it in the end, won't we? But, gentlemen, that woman is the queen of my heart. Oh, let me tell you that. That one thing I'll tell you now. . . . I see I'm with honorable men. She is my light, she is my holy one, and if only you knew! Did you hear her cry, 'I'll go to death with you'? And what have I, a penniless beggar, done for her? Why such love for me? How can a clumsy, ugly brute like me, with my ugly face, deserve such love, that she is ready to go to exile with me? And how she fell down at your feet for my sake, just now? . . . and yet she's proud and has done nothing! How can I help adoring her, how can I help crying out and rushing to her as I did just now? Gentlemen, forgive me! But now, now I am comforted!"

And he sank back in his chair and covering his face with his hands, burst into tears. But they were happy tears. He recovered himself instantly. The old police captain seemed much pleased, and the jurists also. They felt that the examination was passing into a new phase. When the police captain went out, Mitya was positively gay.

"Now, gentlemen, I am at your disposal, entirely at your disposal. And . . . if it were not for all these trivial details, we should understand one another in a minute. I'm at those details again. I'm at your disposal, gentlemen, but I declare that we must have mutual confidence, you in me and I in you, or there'll be no end to it. I speak in your interests. To business, gentlemen, to business, and don't rummage in my soul; don't tease me with trifles, but only ask me about facts and what matters, and I will satisfy you at once. And devil take the details!"

So spoke Mitya. The interrogation began again.

Chapter IV

The Second Torment

"You don't know how you encourage us, Dmitri Fyodorovich, by your readiness to answer," said Nikolay Parfenovich, with an animated air, and obvious satisfaction beaming in his very prominent, short-sighted, light gray eyes, from which he had removed his spectacles a moment before. "And you have made a very just remark about the mutual confidence, without which it is sometimes positively impossible to get on in cases of such importance, if the suspected party really hopes and desires to defend himself and is in a position to do so. We, on our side, will do everything in our power, and you can see for yourself how we are conducting the case. You approve, Ippolit Kirillovich?" He turned to the prosecutor.

"Oh, undoubtedly," replied the prosecutor. His tone was somewhat cold, compared with Nikolay Parfenovich's impulsiveness.

I will note once for all: Nikolay Parfenovich, who had but lately arrived among us, had from the first felt marked respect for Ippolit Kirillovich, our prosecutor, and had become almost his bosom friend. He was almost the only person who put implicit faith in Ippolit Kirillovich's extraordinary talents as a psychologist and orator and in the justice of his grievance. He had heard of him in Petersburg. On the other hand, young Nikolay Parfenovich was the only person in the whole world whom our "unappreciated" prosecutor genuinely liked. On their way to Mokroe they had time to come to an understanding about the present case. And now as they sat at the table, the sharp-witted junior caught and interpreted every indication on his senior colleague's face, every glance, or wink, or half a word.

"Gentlemen, only let me tell my own story and don't interrupt me with trivial questions and I'll tell you everything in a moment," said Mitya excitedly.

"Excellent! Thank you. But before we proceed to listen to your communication, will you allow me to inquire as to another little fact of great interest to us. I mean the ten rubles you borrowed yesterday at about five o'clock on the security of your pistols, from your friend, Pyotr Ilyich Perkhotin."

"I pledged them, gentlemen. I pledged them for ten rubles. What more? That's all about it. As soon as I got back to town I pledged them."

"You got back to town? Then had you been out of town?"

"Yes, I went on a journey of twenty-five miles into the country. Didn't you know?"

The prosecutor and Nikolay Parfenovich exchanged glances.

"Well, how would it be if you began your story with a systematic description of all you did yesterday, from the morning onwards? Allow us, for instance, to inquire why you were absent from the town, and just when you left and when you came back—all those facts."

"You should have asked me like that from the beginning," cried Mitya, laughing aloud, "and if you like, we won't begin from yesterday, but from the morning of the day before; then you'll understand how, why, and where I went. I went the day before yesterday, gentlemen, to a merchant of the town, called Samsonov, to borrow three thousand rubles from him on safe security. It was a pressing matter, gentlemen, it was a sudden necessity."

"Allow me to interrupt you," the prosecutor put in politely. "Why were you in such pressing need for just that sum, three thousand?"

"Oh, gentlemen, you needn't go into details, how, when and why, and why just so much money, and not so much, and all that rigmarole. Why, it'll run to three volumes, and then you'll want an epilogue!"

Mitya said all this with the good-natured but impatient familiarity of
a man who is anxious to tell the whole truth and is full of the best
intentions.

"Gentlemen!" he corrected himself hurriedly—"don't be vexed with me
for my restiveness, I beg you again. Believe me once more, I feel the
greatest respect for you and understand the true position of affairs. Don't
think I'm drunk. I'm quite sober now. And, besides, being drunk would be
no hindrance. With me it's you know, like the saying:

> 'When he is sober, he is a fool;
> When he is drunk, he is wise man.'

Ha, ha! But I see, gentlemen, it's not the proper thing to make jokes to
you, till we've had our explanation, I mean. And I've my own dignity to
keep up, too. I quite understand the difference for the moment. I am,
after all, in the position of a criminal, and so, far from being on equal
terms with you. And it's your business to watch me. I can't expect you to
pat me on the head for what I did to Grigory, for one can't break old men's
heads with impunity. I suppose you'll put me away for him for six months,
or a year perhaps, in a house of correction. I don't know what the punishment is—but it will be without loss of the rights of my rank, without loss
of my rank, Mr. Prosecutor, won't it? So you see, gentlemen, I understand
the distinction between us. . . . But you must see that you could puzzle
God Himself with such questions. 'How did you step? Where did you
step? When did you step? And on what did you step?' I shall get mixed up,
if you go on like this, and you will put it all down against me. And what
will that lead to? To nothing! And even if it's nonsense I'm talking now,
let me finish, and you, gentlemen, being men of honor and refinement, will
forgive me! I'll finish by asking you, gentlemen, to drop that regulation
method of questioning. I mean, beginning from some miserable trifle,
how I got up, what I had for breakfast, how I spat, and where I spat, and so
distracting the attention of the criminal, suddenly stun him with an overwhelming question, 'Whom did you murder? Whom did you rob?' Ha, ha!
That's your regulation method, that's where all your cunning comes in. You
can put peasants off their guard like that, but not me. I know the tricks.
I've been in the service, too. Ha, ha, ha! You're not angry, gentlemen? You
forgive my impertinence?" he cried, looking at them with a good nature
that was almost surprising. "It's only Mitka Karamazov, you know, so you
can overlook it. It would be inexcusable in a sensible man; but you can forgive it in Mitka. Ha, ha!"

Nikolay Parfenovich listened, and laughed, too. Though the prosecutor
did not laugh, he kept his eyes fixed keenly on Mitya, as though anxious
not to miss the least little word, the least movement, the least twitch of
the least feature on his face.

"That's how we have treated you from the beginning," said Nikolay
Parfenovich, still laughing. "We haven't tried to put you out by asking how
you got up in the morning and what you had for breakfast. We began,
indeed, with questions of the greatest importance."

"I understand. I saw it and appreciated it, and I appreciate still more
your present kindness to me, an unprecedented kindness, worthy of your
noble hearts. We three here are gentlemen, and let everything be on the
footing of mutual confidence between educated, well-bred people, who

have the common bond of noble birth and honor. In any case, allow me to look upon you as my best friends at this moment of my life, at this moment when my honor is assailed. That's no offense to you, gentlemen, is it?"

"On the contrary. You've expressed all that so well, Dmitri Fyodorovich," Nikolay Parfenovich answered with dignified approbation.

"And enough of those trivial questions, gentlemen, all those tricky questions!" cried Mitya enthusiastically. "Or there's simply no knowing where we shall get to! Is there?"

"I will follow your sensible advice entirely," the prosecutor interposed, addressing Mitya. "But I don't withdraw my question, however. It is now vitally important for us to know exactly why you needed that sum, I mean precisely three thousand."

"Why I needed it? . . . Oh, for one thing and another. . . . Well, it was to pay a debt."

"A debt to whom?"

"That I absolutely refuse to answer, gentlemen. Not because I couldn't, or because I wouldn't dare, or because it would be damaging, for it's all a paltry matter and absolutely trifling, but—I won't, because it's a matter of principle; that's my private life, and I won't allow any intrusion into my private life. That's my principle. Your question has no bearing on the case, and whatever has nothing to do with the case is my private affair. I wanted to pay a debt. I wanted to pay a debt of honor, but to whom I won't say."

"Allow me to make a note of that," said the prosecutor.

"By all means. Write down that I won't say, that I won't. Write that I would think it dishonorable to say. Ech! you can write it; you've nothing else to do with your time."

"Allow me to caution you, sir, and to remind you once more, if you are unaware of it," the prosecutor began, with a peculiar and stern impressiveness, "that you have a perfect right not to answer the questions put to you now, and we on our side, have no right to extort an answer from you, if you decline to give it for one reason or another. That is entirely a matter for your personal decision. But it is our duty, on the other hand, in such cases as the present, to explain and set before you the degree of injury you will be doing yourself by refusing to give this or that piece of evidence. After which I will beg you to continue."

"Gentlemen, I'm not angry . . . I . . ." Mitya muttered in a rather disconcerted tone. "Well, gentlemen, you see, that Samsonov to whom I went then . . ."

Of course, we will not reproduce his account of what is known to the reader already. Mitya was impatiently anxious not to omit the slightest detail. At the same time he was in a hurry to get it over. But as he gave his evidence it was written down, and therefore they continually had to stop him. Dmitri Fyodorovich disliked this, but submitted; got angry, though still good-humoredly. He did, it is true, exclaim, from time to time, "Gentlemen, that's enough to drive an angel out of patience!" Or, "Gentlemen, it's no good your irritating me." But even though he exclaimed he still preserved for a time his genially expansive mood. So he told them how Samsonov had made a fool of him two days before. (He had completely realized by now that he had been fooled.) The sale of his watch for six rubles to obtain money for the journey was something new to the attorneys. They were at once greatly interested, and even, to Mitya's intense indignation, thought it necessary to write the fact down as a secondary confirmation of the circumstance that he had hardly a cent in his pocket at the time. Little by little Mitya began to grow gloomy. Then, after describing his journey to see Lyagavy, the night spent in the stifling hut, and so on, he came to his return to the town. Here he began, without being particularly urged, to give a minute account of the agonies of jealousy he endured on Grushenka's account. He was heard with silent attention. They inquired particularly into the circumstance of his having an observation post in Marya Kondratyevna's house at the back of Fyodor Pavlovich's garden to keep watch on Grushenka, and of Smerdyakov's bringing him information. They laid particular stress on this, and noted it down. Of his jealousy he spoke warmly and at length, and though inwardly ashamed at exposing his most intimate feelings, so to speak, to "public ignominy," he evidently overcame his shame in order to tell the truth. The frigid severity with which the district attorney, and still more the prosecutor, stared intently at him as he told his story, disconcerted him at last considerably. "That boy, Nikolay Parfenovich, to whom I was talking nonsense about women only a few days ago, and that sickly prosecutor are not worth my telling this to," he reflected mournfully. "It's ignominious. 'Be patient, humble, hold thy peace.'"[7] He wound up his reflections with that line. But he pulled himself together to go on again. When he came to telling of his visit to Madame Khokhlakova, he even regained his spirits and even wished to tell a little anecdote of that lady which had nothing to do with the case. But the district attorney stopped him, and politely suggested that he should pass on to "more essential matters." At last, when he described his despair and told them how, when he left Madame Khokhlakova's, he thought that he'd "get three thousand if he had to murder someone to do it," they stopped him again and noted down that he had "meant to murder someone." Mitya let them write it without protest. At last he reached the point in his story when he suddenly learned that Grushenka had deceived him and had returned from Samsonov's as soon as he left her there, though she had said that she would stay there till midnight. "If I didn't kill Fenya then, gentlemen, it was only because I hadn't time," broke from him suddenly at that point in his story. That, too, was carefully written down. Mitya waited gloomily, and was beginning to tell how he ran into his father's garden when the district attorney suddenly stopped him, and opening the big portfolio that lay on the sofa beside him he brought out the brass pestle.

"Do you recognise this object?" he asked, showing it to Mitya.

"Oh, yes," he smiled gloomily. "Of course I recognize it. Let me have a look at it. . . . Devil take it, never mind!"

"You have forgotten to mention it," observed the district attorney.

"Ah, the devil! I wouldn't have concealed it from you. Do you suppose I could have managed without it? It simply escaped my memory."

"Be so good as to tell us precisely how you came to arm yourself with it."

"Certainly I will be so good, gentlemen."

---

7. An inexact quotation from the poem "Silentium" ("Silence," 1833) by Tyutchev, quoted further on p. 400.

And Mitya described how he took the pestle and ran.

"But what object had you in view in arming yourself with such a weapon?"

"What object? No object. I just picked it up and ran off."

"What for, if you had no object?"

Mitya was seething with vexation. He looked intently at "the boy" and smiled gloomily and malignantly. He was feeling more and more ashamed at having told "such people" the story of his jealousy so sincerely and with such effusion.

"To hell with the pestle!" broke from him suddenly.

"But still . . ."

"Oh, to keep off dogs. . . . Oh, because it was dark. . . . In case anything turned up."

"But have you ever on previous occasions taken a weapon with you when you went out, since you're so afraid of the dark?"

"Ugh! damn it all, gentlemen! There's positively no talking to you!" cried Mitya, exasperated beyond endurance, and turning to the secretary, crimson with anger, he said quickly, with a note of fury in his voice:

"Write down at once . . . at once . . . 'that I snatched up the pestle to go and kill my father . . . Fyodor Pavlovich . . . by hitting him on the head with it!' Well, now are you satisfied, gentlemen? Are your minds relieved?" he said, glaring defiantly at the attorneys.

"We quite understand that you made that statement just now through exasperation with us and the questions we put to you, which you consider trivial, though they are, in fact, essential," the prosecutor remarked drily in reply.

"Well, upon my word, gentlemen! Yes, I took the pestle. . . . What does one pick things up for at such moments? I don't know what for. I snatched it up and ran—that's all. It's shameful, gentlemen, *passons*,[8] or I declare I won't tell you any more."

He sat with his elbows on the table and his head in his hand. He sat sideways to them and gazed at the wall, struggling against a bad feeling. He had, in fact, an awful inclination to get up and declare that he wouldn't say another word, "not if you hang me for it."

"You see, gentlemen," he said at last, with difficulty controlling himself, "you see. I listen to you and am haunted by a dream. . . . It's a dream I have sometimes, you know. . . . I often dream it—it's always the same . . . that someone is hunting me, someone I'm awfully afraid of . . . that he's hunting me in the dark, in the night . . . tracking me, and I hide somewhere from him, behind a door or cupboard, hide in a degrading way, and the worst of it is, he always knows where I am, but he pretends not to know where I am on purpose, to prolong my agony, to enjoy my terror. . . . That's just what you're doing now. It's just like that!"

"Is that the sort of thing you dream about?" inquired the prosecutor.

"Yes, it is. Don't you want to write it down?" said Mitya, with a distorted smile.

"No; no need to write it down. But still you do have curious dreams."

"It's not a question of dreams now, gentlemen—this is realism, this is real life! I'm a wolf and you're the hunters. Well, hunt him down!"

8. "Enough of that" (French).

"You are wrong to make such comparisons . . ." began Nikolay Parfenovich, with extraordinary softness.

"No, I'm not wrong, not at all!" Mitya flared up again, though his outburst of wrath had obviously relieved his heart. He grew more good-humored at every word. "You may not trust a criminal or a man on trial tortured by your questions, but an honorable man, the honorable impulses of the heart (I say that boldly!)—no! That you must believe you have no right indeed . . . but—

> Be patient, humble, hold thy peace.
> Be silent, heart,

Well, shall I go on?" he broke off gloomily.

"If you'll be so kind," answered Nikolay Parfenovich.

Chapter V

The Third Torment

Though Mitya spoke sullenly, it was evident that he was trying more than ever not to forget or miss a single detail of his story. He told them how he had leaped over the fence into his father's garden; how he had gone up to the window; told them all that had passed under the window. Clearly, precisely, distinctly, he described the feelings that troubled him during those moments in the garden when he longed so terribly to know whether Grushenka was with his father or not. But, strange to say, both attorneys listened now with a sort of awful reserve, looked coldly at him, asked few questions. Mitya could gather nothing from their faces. "They're angry and offended," he thought. "Well, to hell with them!" When he described how he made up his mind at last to give the "signal" to his father that Grushenka had come, so that he would open the window, the lawyers paid no attention to the word "signal," as though they entirely failed to grasp the meaning of the word in this connection: so much so, that Mitya noticed it. Coming at last to the moment when, seeing his father peering out of the window, his hatred flared up and he pulled the pestle out of his pocket, he suddenly, as though of design, stopped short. He sat gazing at the wall and was aware that their eyes were fixed upon him.

"Well?" said the district attorney. "You pulled out the weapon and . . . and what happened then?"

"Then? Why, then I murdered him . . . hit him on the head and cracked his skull. . . . I suppose that's your story. That's it!" His eyes suddenly flashed. All his smothered wrath suddenly flamed up with extraordinary violence in his soul.

"Our story?" repeated Nikolay Parfenovich. "Well—and yours?"

Mitya dropped his eyes and was silent a long time.

"My story, gentlemen? Well, it was like this," he began softly. "Whether it was someone's tears, or my mother prayed to God, or a good angel kissed me at that instant, I don't know. But the devil was conquered. I rushed from the window and ran to the fence. My father was alarmed and, for the first time, he saw me then, cried out, and sprang back from the window. I remember that very well. I ran across the garden to the fence . . . and there Grigory caught me, when I was sitting on the fence."

At that point he raised his eyes at last and looked at his listeners. They seemed to be staring at him with perfectly unruffled attention. A sort of paroxysm of indignation seized on Mitya's soul.

"Why, you're laughing at me at this moment, gentlemen!" he broke off suddenly.

"What makes you think that?" observed Nikolay Parfenovich.

"You don't believe one word—that's what! I understand, of course, that I have come to the vital point. The old man's lying there now with his skull broken, while I—after dramatically describing how I wanted to kill him, and how I snatched up the pestle—I suddenly ran away from the window. A poem! In verse! As though one could believe a fellow on his word. Ha, ha! You are scoffers, gentlemen!"

And he swung his whole body round on his chair so that the chair creaked.

"And did you notice," asked the prosecutor suddenly, as though not observing Mitya's excitement, "did you notice when you ran away from the window, whether the door into the garden was open?"

"No, it was not open."

"It was not?"

"It was shut. And who could open it? Bah! the door. Wait a bit!" he seemed suddenly to bethink himself, and almost with a start:

"Why, did you find the door open?"

"Yes, it was open."

"Why, who could have opened it if you did not open it yourselves?" cried Mitya, greatly astonished.

"The door stood open, and your father's murderer undoubtedly went in at that door, and, having accomplished the crime, went out again by the same door," the prosecutor pronounced deliberately, as though chiseling out each word separately. "That is perfectly clear. The murder was committed in the room and *not through the window*; that is absolutely certain from the examination that has been made, from the position of the body, and everything. There can be no doubt of that circumstance."

Mitya was absolutely dumbfounded.

"But that's utterly impossible!" he cried, completely at a loss. "I . . . I didn't go in. . . . I tell you positively, definitely, the door was shut the whole time I was in the garden, and when I ran out of the garden. I only stood at the window and saw him through the window. That's all, that's all. . . . I remember to the last minute. And if I didn't remember, it would be just the same. I know it, for no one knew the *signals* except Smerdyakov, and me, and the dead man. And he wouldn't have opened the door to anyone in the world without the signals."

"Signals? What signals?" asked the prosecutor, with greedy, almost hysterical, curiosity. He instantly lost all trace of his reserve and dignity. He asked the question with a sort of cringing timidity. He scented an important fact of which he had known nothing, and was already filled with dread that Mitya might be unwilling to disclose it.

"So you didn't know!" Mitya winked at him with a malicious and mocking smile. "What if I won't tell you? From whom could you find out? No one knew about the signals except my father, Smerdyakov, and me: that was all. Heaven knew, too, but it won't tell you. But it's an interesting fact. There's no knowing what you might build on it. Ha, ha! Take comfort, gentlemen, I'll reveal it. You've some foolish idea in your hearts. You don't know the man you have to deal with! You have to do with a prisoner who gives evidence against himself, to his own damage! Yes, for I'm a knight of honor and you—are not."

The prosecutor swallowed this without a murmur. He was trembling with impatience to hear the new fact. Minutely and exactly Mitya told them everything about the signals invented by Fyodor Pavlovich for Smerdyakov. He told them exactly what every tap on the window meant, tapped the signals on the table, and when Nikolay Parfenovich said that he supposed he, Mitya, had tapped the signal "Grushenka has come," when he tapped to his father, he answered precisely that he had tapped that signal, that "Grushenka had come."

"So now you can build up your tower," Mitya broke off, and again turned away from them contemptuously.

"So no one knew of the signals but your late parent, you, and the servant Smerdyakov? And no one else?" Nikolay Parfenovich inquired once more.

"Yes. The servant Smerdyakov, and heaven. Write down about heaven. That may be of use. Besides, you will need God yourselves."

And they had already, of course, begun writing it down. But while they wrote, the prosecutor said suddenly, as though hitting on a new idea:

"But if Smerdyakov also knew of these signals and you absolutely deny all responsibility for the death of your father, was it not he, perhaps, who knocked the signal agreed upon, induced your father to open to him, and then . . . committed the crime?"

Mitya turned upon him a look of profound irony and intense hatred. His silent stare lasted so long that it made the prosecutor blink.

"You've caught the fox again," commented Mitya at last; "you've got the rascal by the tail. Ha, ha! I see right through you, Mr. Prosecutor. You thought, of course, that I should jump at that, catch at your prompting, and shout with all my might, 'Aie, it's Smerdyakov; he's the murderer.' Admit that's what you thought. Admit it, and I'll go on."

But the prosecutor did not admit it. He held his tongue and waited.

"You're mistaken. I'm not going to shout 'it's Smerdyakov,'" said Mitya.

"And you don't even suspect him?"

"Why, do you suspect him?"

"He is suspected, too."

Mitya fixed his eyes on the floor.

"Joking apart," he brought out gloomily. "Listen. From the very beginning, almost from the moment when I ran out to you from behind the curtain, I've had the thought of Smerdyakov in my mind. I've been sitting here, shouting that I'm innocent and thinking all the time 'Smerdyakov!' I can't get Smerdyakov out of my head. In fact, I, too, thought of Smerdyakov just now; but only for a second. Almost at once I thought, 'No, it's not Smerdyakov.' It's not his doing, gentlemen."

"In that case is there anybody else you suspect?" Nikolay Parfenovich inquired cautiously.

"I don't know anyone it could be, whether it's the hand of Heaven or of Satan, but . . . not Smerdyakov," Mitya jerked out with decision.

"But what makes you affirm so confidently and emphatically that it's not he?"

"From my conviction—my impression. Because Smerdyakov is a man of the most abject character and a coward. He's not a coward, he's the epitome of all the cowardice in the world walking on two legs. He was born of a chicken. When he talked to me, he was always trembling for fear I would kill him, though I never raised my hand against him. He fell at my feet and blubbered; he has kissed these very boots, literally, beseeching me 'not to frighten him.' Do you hear? 'Not to frighten him.' What a thing to say! Why, I offered him money. He's a puling chicken—sickly, epileptic, weak-minded—a child of eight could thrash him. He has no character worth talking about. It's not Smerdyakov, gentlemen. He doesn't care for money; he wouldn't take my presents. Besides, what motive had he for murdering the old man? Why, he may be his son, you know—his natural son. Do you know that?"

"We have heard that legend. But you are your father's son, too, you know; yet you yourself told everyone you meant to murder him."

"That's a thrust! And a nasty, mean one, too! I'm not afraid! Oh, gentlemen, isn't it too base of you to say that to my face? It's base, because I told you that myself. I not only wanted to murder him, but I might have done it. And, what's more, I went out of my way to tell you of my own accord that I nearly murdered him. But, you see, I didn't murder him, you see, my guardian angel saved me—that's what you have not taken into account. And that's why it's so base of you, so base! For I didn't kill him, I didn't kill him, I didn't kill him! Do you hear, I did not kill him."

He was almost choking. He had not been so moved before during the whole interrogation.

"And what has he told you, gentlemen—Smerdyakov, I mean?" he added suddenly, after a pause. "May I ask that question?"

"You may ask any question," the prosecutor replied with frigid severity, "any question relating to the facts of the case, and we are, I repeat, bound to answer every inquiry you make. We found the servant Smerdyakov, concerning whom you inquire, lying unconscious in his bed, in an epileptic fit of extreme severity, that had recurred, possibly, ten times. The doctor who was with us told us, after seeing him, that he may possibly not outlive the night."

"Well, if that's so, the devil must have killed my father," broke suddenly from Mitya, as though until that moment he had been asking himself: "Was it Smerdyakov or not?"

"We will come back to this later," Nikolay Parfenovich decided. "Now, wouldn't you like to continue your statement?"

Mitya asked for a rest. His request was courteously granted. After resting, he went on with his story. But he was evidently depressed. He was exhausted, mortified and morally shaken. To make things worse the prosecutor exasperated him, as though intentionally, by vexatious interruptions about "trifling points." Scarcely had Mitya described how, sitting on the wall, he had struck Grigory on the head with the pestle, while the old man had hold of his left leg, and how he had then jumped down to look at him, when the prosecutor stopped him to ask him to describe exactly how he was sitting on the wall. Mitya was surprised.

"Oh, I was sitting like this, astride, one leg on one side of the wall and one on the other."

"And the pestle?"

"The pestle was in my hand."

"Not in your pocket? Do you remember that precisely? Was it a violent blow you gave him?"

"It must have been a violent one. But why do you ask?"

"Would you mind sitting on the chair just as you sat on the wall then and showing us just how you moved your arm, and in what direction?"

"You're making fun of me, aren't you?" asked Mitya, looking haughtily at his interrogator; but the latter did not flinch. Mitya turned abruptly, sat astride on his chair, and swung his arm.

"This was how I struck him? That's how I killed him! What more do you want?"

"Thank you. May I trouble you now to explain why you jumped down, with what object, and what you had in view?"

"Oh, hang it! . . . I jumped down to look at the man I'd hurt . . . I don't know what for!"

"Though you were so excited and were running away?"

"Yes, though I was excited and running away."

"You wanted to help him?"

"Help! . . . Yes, perhaps I did want to help him. . . . I don't remember."

"You don't remember? Then you didn't quite know what you were doing?"

"Not at all. I remember everything—every detail. I jumped down to look at him, and wiped his face with my handkerchief."

"We have seen your handkerchief. Did you hope to restore him to consciousness?"

"I don't know whether I hoped it. I simply wanted to make sure whether he was alive or not."

"Ah! You wanted to be sure? Well, what then?"

"I'm not a doctor. I couldn't decide. I ran away thinking I'd killed him. And now he's recovered."

"Excellent," commented the prosecutor. "Thank you. That's all I wanted. Kindly proceed."

Alas! it never entered Mitya's head to tell them, though he remembered it, that he had jumped back from pity, and standing over the prostrate figure had even uttered some words of regret: "You've come to grief, old man—there's no help for it. Well, there you must lie." The prosecutor could only draw one conclusion: that the man had jumped back "at such a moment and in such excitement" simply with the object of ascertaining whether the *only* witness of his crime were dead; that he must therefore have been a man of great strength, coolness, decision and foresight even at such a moment," . . . and so on. The prosecutor was satisfied: "I've provoked the nervous fellow by 'trifles' and he has said more than he meant to."

With painful effort Mitya went on. But this time he was pulled up immediately by Nikolay Parfenovich.

"How were you able to run to the servant, Fedos'ia Markovna, with your hands so covered with blood, and, as it appears, your face too?"

"Why, I didn't notice the blood at all at the time," answered Mitya.

"That's quite likely. It does happen sometimes." The prosecutor exchanged glances with Nikolay Parfenovich.

"I simply didn't notice. You're quite right there, prosecutor," Mitya assented suddenly. Next came the account of Mitya's sudden determination to "step aside" and "make way for their happiness." But he could not make up his mind to open his heart to them as before, and tell them about "the queen of his soul." He disliked speaking of her before these chilly persons "who were fastening on him like bugs." And so in response to their reiterated questions he answered briefly and abruptly:

"Well, I made up my mind to kill myself. What had I left to live for? That question stared me in the face. Her first rightful lover had come back, the man who wronged her but who'd hurried back to offer his love, after five years and atone for the wrong with marriage. . . . So I knew it was all over for me. . . . And behind me disgrace, and that blood— Grigory's. . . . What had I to live for? So I went to redeem the pistols I had pledged, to load them and put a bullet in my brain tomorrow."

"And a grand feast the night before?"

"Yes, a grand feast the night before. "Eh, the devil, gentlemen, hurry up and finish it. I meant to shoot myself not far from here, beyond the village, and I'd planned to do it at five o'clock in the morning. And I had a note in my pocket already. I wrote it at Perkhotin's when I loaded my pistols. Here's the letter. Read it! It's not for you I tell it," he added contemptuously. He took it from his waistcoat pocket and flung it on the table. The attorneys read it with curiosity, and, as is usual, added it to the papers connected with the case.

"And you didn't even think of washing your hands at Perkhotin's? You were not afraid then of arousing suspicion?"

"What suspicion? Suspicion or not, I should have galloped here just the same, and shot myself at five o'clock, and you wouldn't have been in time to do anything. If it hadn't been for what's happened to my father, you would have known nothing about it, and wouldn't have come here. Oh, it's the devil's doing. It was the devil murdered father, it was through the devil that you found it out so soon. How did you manage to get here so quick? It's marvelous, a dream!"

"Mr. Perkhotin informed us that when you came to him, you held in your hands . . . your blood-stained hands . . . your money . . . a lot of money . . . a bundle of hundred-ruble bills, and that his servant boy saw it too."

"That's true, gentlemen. I remember it was so."

"Now, there's one little point presents itself. Can you inform us," Nikolay Parfenovich began, with extreme gentleness, "where did you get so much money all of a sudden, when it appears from the facts, from the reckoning of time, that you had not been home?"

The prosecutor's brows contracted at the question being asked so plainly, but he did not interrupt Nikolay Parfenovich.

"No, I didn't go home," answered Mitya, apparently perfectly composed, but looking at the floor.

"Allow me then to repeat my question," Nikolay Parfenovich went on as though creeping up to the subject. "Where were you able to procure such a sum all at once, when, by your own confession, at five o'clock the same day you . . ."

"I was in want of ten rubles and pledged my pistols with Perkhotin, and then went to Madame Khokhlakova to borrow three thousand which she wouldn't give me, and so on, and all the rest of it," Mitya interrupted sharply. "Yes, gentlemen, I was in want of it, and suddenly thousands turned up, eh? Do you know, gentlemen, you're both afraid now 'what if he won't tell us where he got it?' That's just how it is. I'm not going to tell you, gentlemen. You've guessed right. You'll never know," said Mitya, chipping out each word with extraordinary determination. The attorneys were silent for a moment.

"You must understand, Mr. Karamazov, that it is of vital importance for us to know," said Nikolay Parfenovioh, softly and suavely.

"I understand; but still I won't tell you."

The prosecutor, too, intervened, and again reminded him that the prisoner was at liberty to refuse to answer questions, if he thought it to his interest, and so on. But in view of the damage he might do himself by his silence, especially in a question of such importance as . . .

"And so on, gentlemen, and so on. Enough! I've heard that rigmarole before," Mitya interrupted again. "I can see for myself how important it is, and that this is the vital point, and still I won't say."

"What is it to us? It's not our business, but yours. You are doing yourself harm," observed Nikolay Parfenovich nervously.

"You see, gentlemen, joking apart"—Mitya lifted his eyes and looked firmly at them both—"I had an inkling from the first that we should come to loggerheads at this point. But at first when I began to give my evidence, it was all still far away and misty; it was all floating, and I was so simple that I began with the supposition of 'mutual confidence existing between us.' Now I can see for myself that such confidence is out of the question, for in my case we were bound to come to this cursed fence. And now we've come to it! It's impossible and there's an end of it! But I don't blame you. You can't believe it all simply on my word. I understand that, of course."

He relapsed into gloomy silence.

"Couldn't you, without abandoning your resolution to be silent about the chief point, could you not, at the same time, give us some slight hint as to the nature of the motives which are strong enough to induce you to refuse to answer, at a point so full of danger to you?"

Mitya smiled mournfully, almost dreamily.

"I'm much more good-natured than you think, gentlemen. I'll tell you the reason why and give you that hint, though you don't deserve it. I won't speak of that, gentlemen, because it would be a stain on my honor. The answer to the question where I got the money would expose me to far greater disgrace than the murder and robbing of my father, if I had murdered and robbed him. That's why I can't tell you. I can't for fear of disgrace. What, gentlemen, are you going to write that down?"

"Yes, we'll write it down," lisped Nikolay Parfenovich.

"You ought not to write that down about 'disgrace.' I only told you that in the goodness of my heart. I needn't have told you. I made you a present of it, so to speak, and you pounce upon it at once. Oh, well, write—write what you like," he concluded, with scornful disgust. "I'm not afraid of you and I can still hold up my head before you."

"And can't you tell us the nature of that disgrace?" Nikolay Parfenovich hazarded.

The prosecutor frowned darkly.

"No, no, *c'est fini*,[9] don't trouble yourself. It's not worthwhile soiling one's hands. I have soiled myself enough through you as it is. You're not worth it—no one is . . . Enough, gentlemen. I'm not going on."

This was said too peremptorily. Nikolay Parfenovich did not insist further, but from Ippolit Kirillovich's eyes he saw that he had not given up hope.

"Can you not, at least, tell us what sum you had in your hands when you went into Mr. Perkhotin's—how many rubles exactly?"

"I can't tell you that."

"You spoke to Mr. Perkhotin, I believe, of having received three thousand from Madame Khokhlakova."

"Perhaps I did. Enough, gentlemen. I won't say how much I had."

"Will you be so good then as to tell us how you came here and what you have done since you arrived?"

"Oh! you might ask the people here about that. But I'll tell you if you like."

He proceeded to do so, but we won't repeat his story. He told it drily and curtly. Of the raptures of his love he said nothing, but told them that he abandoned his determination to shoot himself, owing to "new factors in the case." He told the story without going into motives or details. And this time the attorneys did not trouble him much. It was obvious that there was no essential point of interest to them here.

"We shall verify all that. We will come back to it during the examination of the witnesses, which will, of course, take place in your presence," said Nikolay Parfenovich in conclusion. "And now allow me to request you to lay on the table everything in your possession, especially all the money you still have with you."

"My money, gentlemen? Certainly. I understand that that is necessary. I'm surprised, indeed, that you haven't inquired about it before. It's true I couldn't get away anywhere. I'm sitting here where I can be seen. But here's my money—count it—take it. That's all, I think."

He turned it all out of his pockets; even the small change—two pieces of twenty kopecks—he pulled out of his waistcoat pocket. They counted the money, which amounted to eight hundred and thirty-six rubles, and forty kopecks.

"And is that all?" asked the district attorney.

"Yes."

"You stated just now in your evidence that you spent three hundred rubles at Plotnikov's. You gave Perkhotin ten, your driver twenty, here you lost two hundred, then . . ."

Nikolay Parfenovich reckoned it all up. Mitya helped him readily. They recollected every penny and included it in the reckoning. Nikolay Parfenovich hurriedly added up the total.

"With this eight hundred you must have had about fifteen hundred at first?"

"I suppose so," snapped Mitya.

"How is it they all assert there was much more?"

"Let them assert it."

9. "That's all" (French).

"But you asserted it yourself."

"Yes, I did, too."

"We will compare all this with the evidence of other persons not yet examined. Don't be anxious about your money. It will be properly taken care of and be at your disposal at the conclusion of . . . what is beginning . . . if it appears, or, so to speak, is proved that you have undisputed right to it. Well, and now . . ."

Nikolay Parfenovich suddenly got up, and informed Mitya firmly that it was his duty and obligation to conduct a minute and thorough search "of your clothes and everything else . . ."

"By all means, gentlemen. I'll turn out all my pockets, if you like."

And he did, in fact, begin turning out his pockets.

"It will be necessary to take off your clothes, too."

"What! Undress! Ugh! Damn it. Won't you search me as I am? Can't you?"

"It's utterly impossible, Dmitri Fyodorovich. You must take off your clothes."

"As you like," Mitya submitted gloomily; "only, please, not here, but behind the curtains. Who will search them?"

"Behind the curtains, of course."

Nikolay Parfenovich bent his head in assent. His small face wore an expression of peculiar solemnity.

Chapter VI

The Prosecutor Catches Mitya

Something utterly unexpected and amazing to Mitya followed. He could never, even a minute before, have conceived that anyone could behave like that to him, Mitya Karamazov! What was worst of all, there was something humiliating in it, and on their side something "supercilious and scornful." It was nothing to take off his coat, but he was asked to undress further, or rather not asked but "commanded," he quite understood that. From pride and contempt he submitted without a word. Several peasants accompanied the attorneys and remained on the same side of the curtain. "To be ready if force is required," thought Mitya, "and perhaps for some other reason, too."

"Well, must I take off my shirt, too?" he asked sharply, but Nikolay Parfenovich did not answer. He was busily engaged with the prosecutor in examining the coat, the trousers, the waistcoat and the cap; and it was evident that they were both much interested in the scrutiny. "They make no bones about it," flashed through Mitya's mind, "they don't keep up the most elementary politeness."

"I ask you for the second time—need I take off my shirt or not?" he said, still more sharply and irritably.

"Don't trouble yourself. We will tell you what to do," Nikolay Parfenovich said, and his voice was positively peremptory, or so it seemed to Mitya.

Meantime a consultation was going on in undertones between the attorneys. There turned out to be on the coat, especially on the left side at the back, huge patches of blood, dry, hardened, and still stiff. There were bloodstains on the trousers, too. Nikolay Parfenovich, moreover, in the presence of the peasant witnesses, passed his fingers along the collar, the cuffs, and all the seams of the coat and trousers, obviously looking for something—money, of course. He didn't even hide from Mitya his suspicion that he was capable of sewing money up in his clothes. "He treats me not as an officer but as a thief," Mitya muttered to himself. They communicated their ideas to one another with amazing frankness. The secretary, for instance, who was also behind the curtain, fussing about and listening, called Nikolay Parfenovich's attention to the cap, which they were also fingering. "You remember Gridyenko, the clerk," observed the secretary. "Last summer he received the wages of the whole office, and pretended to have lost the money when he was drunk. And where was it found? Why, in just such pipings in his cap. The hundred-ruble bills were screwed up in little rolls and sewed in the piping." Both attorneys remembered Gridyenko's case perfectly well, and so laid aside Mitya's cap, and decided that all his clothes must be more thoroughly examined later.

"Excuse me," cried Nikolay Parfenovich, suddenly, noticing that the right cuff of Mitya's shirt was turned in, and covered with blood, "excuse me, what's that, blood?"

"Yes," Mitya jerked out.

"That is, what blood . . . and why is the cuff turned in?"

Mitya told him how he had got the sleeve stained with blood looking after Grigory, and had turned it inside when he was washing his hands at Perkhotin's.

"You must take off your shirt, too. That's very important as material evidence."

Mitya flushed red and flew into a rage.

"What, am I to stay naked?" he shouted.

"Don't disturb yourself. We will arrange something. And meanwhile take off your socks."

"You're not joking? Is that really necessary?" Mitya's eyes flashed.

"We are in no mood for joking," countered Nikolay Parfenovich sternly.

"Well, if I must . . ." muttered Mitya, and sitting down on the bed, he took off his socks. He felt unbearably awkward. All were clothed, while he was naked, and strange to say, when he was undressed he felt somehow guilty in their presence, and was almost ready to believe himself that he was inferior to them, and that now they had a perfect right to despise him. "When all are undressed, one is somehow not ashamed, but when one's the only one undressed and everybody is looking, it's degrading," he kept repeating to himself, again and again. "It's like a dream, I've sometimes dreamed of being in such degrading positions." It was a misery to him to take off his socks. They were very dirty, and so were his underclothes, and now everyone could see it. And what was worse, he disliked his feet. All his life he had thought both his big toes hideous. He particularly loathed the coarse, flat, crooked nail on the right one, and now they would all see it. Feeling intolerably ashamed made him, at once and intentionally, coarser. He pulled off his shirt, himself.

"Would you like to look anywhere else if you're not ashamed to?"

"No, there's no need to, at present."

"Well, am I to stay naked like this?" he added savagely.

"Yes, that can't be helped for the time . . . Kindly sit down here for a while. You can wrap yourself in a quilt from the bed, and I . . . I'll see to all this."

All the things were shown to the witnesses. The report of the search was drawn up, and at last Nikolay Parfenovich went out, and the clothes were carried out after him. Ippolit Kirillovich went out, too. Mitya was left alone with the peasants, who stood in silence, never taking their eyes off him. Mitya wrapped himself up in the quilt. He felt cold. His bare feet stuck out, and he couldn't pull the quilt over so as to cover them. Nikolay Parfenovich seemed to be gone a long time, "an insufferable time." "He thinks of me as a puppy," thought Mitya, gnashing his teeth. "That rotten prosecutor has gone, too, contemptuous no doubt, it disgusts him to see me naked!" Mitya imagined, however, that his clothes would be examined and returned to him. But what was his indignation when Nikolay Parfenovich came back with quite different clothes, brought in behind him by a peasant.

"Here are clothes for you," he observed airily, seeming well satisfied with the success of his mission. "Mr. Kalganov has kindly provided these for this unusual emergency, as well as a clean shirt. Luckily he had them all in his trunk. You can keep your own socks and underclothes."

Mitya flew into a passion.

"I won't have other people's clothes!" he shouted menacingly, "give me my own!"

"It's impossible!"

"Give me my own. Devil take Kalganov and his clothes, too!"

It was a long time before they could persuade him. But they succeeded somehow in quieting him down. They impressed upon him that, his clothes being stained with blood, must be "included with the other material evidence," and that they "had not even the right to let him have them now . . . taking into consideration the possible outcome of the case." Mitya at last understood this. He subsided into gloomy silence and hurriedly dressed himself. He merely observed, as he put them on, that the clothes were much better than his old ones, and that he disliked "gaining by the change." It was, besides, "ridiculously narrow. Am I to be dressed up like a fool . . . for your amusement!"

They urged upon him again that he was exaggerating, that Kalganov was only a little taller, so that only the trousers might be a little too long. But the coat turned out to be really tight in the shoulders.

"Devil take it! I can hardly button it," Mitya grumbled. "Be so good as to tell Mr. Kalganov from me that I didn't ask for his clothes, and it's not my doing that they've dressed me up like a clown."

"He quite understands that, and is sorry . . . I mean, not sorry to lend you his clothes, but sorry about all this business," mumbled Nikolay Parfenovich.

"Confound his sorrow! Well, where now, or am I to go on sitting here?"

He was asked to go back to the "other room." Mitya went in, scowling with anger, and trying to avoid looking at any one. Dressed in another man's clothes he felt himself disgraced, even in the eyes of the peasants, and of Trifon Borisovich, whose face appeared, for some reason, in the doorway, and vanished immediately. "He's come to look at me dressed up like a mummer," thought Mitya. He sat down on the same chair as before. He had an absurd nightmarish feeling, as though he were out of his mind.

"Well, what now? Are you going to flog me? That's all that's left for you," he said, clenching his teeth and addressing the prosecutor. He would not turn to Nikolay Parfenovich, as though he disdained to speak to him. "He looked too closely at my socks, and turned them inside out on purpose to show everyone how dirty my underclothes were—the scoundrel!"

"Well, now we must proceed to the examination of witnesses," observed Nikolay Parfenovich, as though in reply to Mitya's question.

"Yes," said the prosecutor thoughtfully, as though reflecting on something.

"We've done what we could in your interest, Dmitri Fyodorovich," Nikolay Parfenovich went on, "but having received from you such an uncompromising refusal to explain to us the source from which you obtained the money found upon you, we are, at the present moment . . ."

"What is the stone in your ring?" Mitya interrupted suddenly, as though awakening from a reverie. He pointed to one of the three large rings adorning Nikolay Parfenovich's right hand.

"Ring?" repeated Nikolay Parfenovich with surprise.

"Yes, that one . . . on your middle finger, with the little veins in it, what stone is that?" Mitya persisted, like a peevish child.

"That's a smoky topaz," said Nikolay Parfenovich, smiling. "Would you like to look at it? I'll take it off . . ."

"No, don't take it off!" cried Mitya furiously, suddenly waking up, and angry with himself. "Don't take it off . . . there's no need. . . . The devil. . . . Gentlemen, you've sullied my heart! Can you suppose that I would conceal it from you, if I really had killed my father, that I would shuffle, lie, and hide myself? No, that's not like Dmitri Karamazov, that he couldn't do, and if I were guilty, I swear I wouldn't have waited for your coming, or for the sunrise as I meant at first, but would have destroyed myself before this, without waiting for the dawn! I know that about myself now. I couldn't have learned so much in twenty years as I've found out in this accursed night! . . . And would I have been like this on this night, and at this moment, sitting with you, could I have talked like this, could I have moved like this, could I have looked at you and at the world like this, if I had really been the murderer of my father, when the very thought of having accidentally killed Grigory gave me no peace all night—not from fear—oh, not simply from fear of your punishment! The disgrace of it! And you expect me to be open with such scoffers as you, who see nothing and believe in nothing, blind moles and scoffers, and to tell you another nasty thing I've done, another disgrace, even if that would save me from your accusation! No, better Siberia! The man who opened the door to my father and went in at that door, he killed him, he robbed him. Who was he—I'm racking my brains and can't think who. But I can tell you it was not Dmitri Karamazov, and that's all I can tell you, and that's enough, enough, leave me alone. . . . Exile me, punish me, but don't bother me any more. I'll say no more. Call your witnesses!"

Mitya uttered his sudden monologue as though he were determined to be absolutely silent for the future. The prosecutor watched him the whole time and only when he had ceased speaking, observed, as though it were the most ordinary thing, with the most frigid and composed air:

"Oh, about the open door of which you spoke just now, we may as well inform you, by the way, now, of a very interesting piece of evidence of the greatest importance both to you and to us, that has been given us by Grigory, the old man you wounded. On his recovery, he clearly and emphatically stated, in reply to our questions, that when, on coming out to the steps, and hearing a noise in the garden, he made up his mind to go into it through the little gate which stood open, before he noticed you running, as you have told us already, in the dark from the open window where you saw your father, he, Grigory, glanced to the left, and, while noticing the open window, observed at the same time, much nearer to him, the door, standing wide open—that door which you have stated to have been shut the whole time you were in the garden. I will not conceal from you that Grigory himself confidently affirms and bears witness that you must have run from that door, though, of course, he did not see you do so with his own eyes, since he only noticed you first some distance away in the garden, running towards the fence."

Mitya had leapt up from his chair half way through this speech.

"Nonsense!" he yelled, in a sudden frenzy, "it's a bare-faced lie. He couldn't have seen the door open because it was shut. He's lying!"

"I consider it my duty to repeat that he is firm in his statement. He does not waver. He adheres to it. We've cross-examined him several times."

"Precisely. I have cross-examined him several times," Nikolay Parfenovich confirmed warmly.

"It's false, false! It's either an attempt to slander me, or the hallucination of a madman," Mitya still shouted. "He's simply raving, from loss of blood, from the wound. He must have fancied it when he came to. . . . He's raving."

"Yes, but he noticed the open door, not when he came to after his injuries, but before that, as soon as he went into the garden from the lodge."

"But it's false, it's false! It can't be so! He's slandering me from spite. . . . He couldn't have seen it . . . I didn't come from the door," gasped Mitya.

The prosecutor turned to Nikolay Parfenovich and said to him impressively:

"Confront him with it."

"Do you recognize this object?"

Nikolay Parfenovich laid upon the table a large and thick official envelope, on which three seals still remained intact. The envelope was empty, and slit open at one end. Mitya stared at it with open eyes.

"It . . . it must be that envelope of my father's, the envelope that contained the three thousand rubles . . . and if there's inscribed on it, allow me, 'For my little chicken' . . . yes—three thousand!" he shouted, "do you see, three thousand, do you see?"

"Of course, we see. But we didn't find the money in it. It was empty, and lying on the floor by the bed, behind the screen."

For some seconds Mitya stood as though thunderstruck.

"Gentlemen, it's Smerdyakov!" he shouted suddenly, at the top of his voice. "It's he who's murdered him! He's robbed him! No one else knew where the old man hid the envelope. It's Smerdyakov, that's clear, now!"

"But you, too, knew of the envelope and that it was under the pillow."

"I never knew it. I've never seen it. This is the first time I've looked at it. I've only heard of it from Smerdyakov. . . . He was the only one who knew where the old man kept it hidden, I didn't know . . ." Mitya was completely breathless.

"But you told us yourself that the envelope was under your deceased father's pillow. You especially stated that it was under the pillow, so you must have known it."

"We've got it written down," confirmed Nikolay Parfenovich.

"Nonsense! It's absurd! I'd no idea it was under the pillow. And perhaps it wasn't under the pillow at all. . . . It was just a chance guess that it was under the pillow. What does Smerdyakov say? Have you asked him where it was? What does Smerdyakov say? that's the chief point. . . . And I went out of my way to tell lies against myself. . . . I told you without thinking that it was under the pillow, and now you . . . Oh, you know how one says the wrong thing, without meaning it. No one knew but Smerdyakov, only Smerdyakov, and no one else. . . . He didn't even tell me where it was! But it's his doing, his doing; there's no doubt about it, he murdered him, that's as clear as daylight now," Mitya exclaimed more and more frantically, repeating himself incoherently, and growing more and more exasperated and excited. "You must understand that, and arrest him at once. . . . He must have killed him while I was running away and while Grigory was unconscious, that's clear now. . . . He gave the signal and father opened to him . . . for no one but he knew the signal, and without the signal father would never have opened the door. . . ."

"But you're again forgetting the circumstance," the prosecutor observed, still speaking with the same restraint, though with a note of triumph, "that there was no need to give the signal if the door already stood open when you were there, while you were in the garden . . ."

"The door, the door," muttered Mitya, and he stared speechless at the prosecutor. He sank back helpless in his chair. All were silent.

"Yes, the door! . . . It's a phantom! God is against me!" he exclaimed, staring before him in complete stupefaction.

"Come, you see," the prosecutor went on with dignity, "and you can judge for yourself, Dmitri Fyodorovich. On the one hand we have the evidence of the open door from which you ran out, a fact which overwhelms you and us. On the other side your incomprehensible, persistent, and, so to speak, obdurate silence with regard to the source from which you obtained the money which was so suddenly seen in your hands, when only three hours earlier, on your own testimony, you pledged your pistols for the sake of ten rubles! In view of all these facts, judge for yourself. What are we to believe, and what can we depend upon? And don't accuse us of being 'frigid, cynical, scoffing people,' who are incapable of believing in the generous impulses of your heart. . . . Try to enter into our position . . ."

Mitya was indescribably agitated. He turned pale.

"Very well!" he exclaimed suddenly, "I will tell you my secret. I'll tell you where I got the money! . . . I'll reveal my shame, that I may not have to blame myself or you hereafter."

"And believe me, Dmitri Fyodorovich," put in Nikolay Parfenovich, in a little voice of almost pathetic delight, "that every sincere and complete confession on your part at this moment may, later on, have an immense influence in your favor, and may, indeed, moreover . . ."

But the prosecutor gave him a slight shove under the table, and he checked himself in time. Mitya, it is true, had not heard him.

Chapter VII

Mitya's Great Secret. Received with Hisses

"Gentlemen," he began, still in the same agitation, "I want to make a full confession: that money was *my own*."

The attorneys' faces even lengthened. That was not at all what they expected.

"How do you mean?" faltered Nikolay Parfenovich, "when at five o'clock on the same day, by your own admission . . ."

"To the devil with five o'clock on the same day and my own admission. That's nothing to do with it now! That money was my own, my own, that is, stolen by me . . . not mine, I mean, but stolen by me, and it was fifteen hundred rubles, and I had it on me all the time, all the time . . ."

"But where did you get it?"

"I took it off my neck, gentlemen, off this very neck . . . it was here, round my neck, sewn up in a rag, and I'd had it round my neck a long time, it's a month since I put it round my neck . . . to my shame and disgrace!"

"And from whom did you . . . appropriate it?"

"You mean, 'steal it'? Speak out plainly now. Yes, I consider that I practically stole it, but, if you prefer, I 'appropriated it.' I consider I stole it. And last night I stole it finally."

"Last night? But you said that it's a month since you . . . obtained it? . . ."

"Yes. But not from my father. Not from my father, don't be uneasy. I didn't steal it from my father, but from her. Let me tell you without interrupting. It's hard to do, you know. You see, a month ago, I was sent for by Katerina Ivanovna Verkhovtseva, formerly my betrothed. Do you know her?"

"Yes, of course."

"I know you know her. She's a noble soul, noblest of the noble. But she has hated me ever so long, oh, ever so long . . . and hated me with good reason, good reason!"

"Katerina Ivanovna!" Nikolay Parfenovich exclaimed with amazement. The prosecutor, too, stared.

"Oh, don't take her name in vain! I'm a scoundrel to bring her into it. Yes, I've seen that she hated me . . . a long while. . . . From the very first, even that evening at my lodging . . . but enough, enough. You're unworthy even to know of that. No need of that at all. . . . I need only tell you that she sent for me a month ago, gave me three thousand rubles to send to her sister and another relation in Moscow (as though she couldn't have sent it off herself!), and I . . . it was just at that fatal moment in my life when I . . . Well, in fact, when I'd just come to love another, *her*, she's sitting down below now, Grushenka. I carried her off here to Mokroe then, and wasted here in two days half that damned three thousand, but the other half I kept on me. Well, I've kept that other half, that fifteen hundred like a locket round my neck, but yesterday I undid it, and spent it. What's left of it, eight hundred rubles, is in your hands now, Nikolay Parfenovich. That's what's left from the fifteen hundred I had yesterday."

"Excuse me. How's that? Why, when you were here a month ago you spent three thousand, not fifteen hundred, everybody knows that."

"Who knows it? Who counted the money? Did I let anyone count it?"

"Why, you told everyone yourself that you'd spent exactly three thousand."

"It's true, I did. I told the whole town so, and the whole town said so. And here, at Mokroe, too, everyone reckoned it was three thousand. Yet I didn't spend three thousand, but fifteen hundred. And the other fifteen hundred I sewed into a little bag. That's how it was, gentlemen. That's where I got that money yesterday . . ."

"This is almost miraculous," murmured Nikolay Parfenovich.

"Allow me to inquire," observed the prosecutor at last, "have you informed anyone whatever of this circumstance before, I mean that you had fifteen hundred left about you a month ago?"

"I told no one."

"That's strange. Do you mean absolutely no one?"

"Absolutely no one. No one and nobody."

"What was your reason for this reticence? What was your motive for making such a secret of it? To be more precise: You have told us at last your secret, in your words, so 'disgraceful,' though in reality—that is, of course, comparatively speaking—this action, that is, the appropriation of three thousand rubles belonging to someone else, and, of course, only for a time is, in my view at least, only an act of the greatest reck- lessness and not so disgraceful, when one takes into consideration your character. , , , Even admitting that it was an action in the highest degree discreditable, still, discreditable is not 'disgraceful.' . . . Many people have already guessed, during this last month, about the three thousand of Miss Verkhovtseva's that you have spent, and I had heard the legend myself, apart from your confession. . . . Mikhail Makarov- ich, for instance, had heard it, too, so that indeed, it was scarcely a legend, but the gossip of the whole town. There are indications, too, if I am not mistaken, that you confessed this yourself to someone, I mean that the money was from Miss Verkhovtseva and so, it's extremely sur- prising to me that hitherto, that is, up to the present moment, you have made such an extraordinary secret of the fifteen hundred you say you put by, apparently connecting a feeling of positive horror with that secret. . . . It's not easy to believe that it could cost you such distress to confess such a secret. . . . You cried out, just now, that Siberia would be better than confessing it . . ."

The prosecutor ceased speaking. He was provoked. He did not conceal his vexation, which was almost spite, and poured out everything that had accumulated, not even caring about the beauty of his style, that is, dis- connectedly and even almost incoherently.

"It's not the fifteen hundred that's the disgrace, but that I put it apart from the rest of the three thousand," said Mitya firmly.

"Why," smiled the prosecutor irritably. "What is there disgraceful, to your thinking, in your having set aside half of the three thousand you had discreditably, if you prefer, 'disgracefully,' appropriated? Your taking the three thousand is more important than what you did with it. And by the way, why did you do that—why did you set apart that half, for what pur- pose, for what object did you do it? Can you explain that to us?"

"Oh, gentlemen, the purpose is the whole point!" cried Mitya. "I put it aside because I was vile, that is, because I was calculating, and to be calculating in such a case is vile . . . and that vileness has been going on a whole month."

"It's incomprehensible."

"I wonder at you. But I'll make it clearer. Perhaps it really is incomprehensible. You see, attend to what I say. I appropriate three thousand entrusted to my honor, I spent it on a spree, say I spend it all, and next morning I go to her and say, 'Katya, I've done wrong, I've squandered your three thousand,' well, is that right? No, it's not right—it's dishonest and cowardly, I'm a beast, with no more self-control than a beast, that's so, isn't it? But still I'm not a thief? Not a downright thief, you'll admit! I squandered it, but I didn't steal it. Now a second, rather more favorable alternative: follow me carefully, or I may get confused again—my head's going round—and so for the second alternative: I spend here only fifteen hundred out of the three thousand, that is, only half. Next day I go and take that half to her: 'Katya, take this fifteen hundred from me, I'm a low beast, and an untrustworthy scoundrel, for I've wasted half the money, and I shall waste this, too, so keep me from temptation!' Well, what of that alternative? I would be a beast and a scoundrel, and whatever you like; but not a thief, not altogether a thief, or I would not have brought back what was left, but have kept that, too. She would see at once that since I brought back half, I would pay back what I'd spent, that I would never give up trying to, that I would work to get it and pay it back. So in that case I would be a scoundrel, but not a thief, you may say what you like, not a thief!"

"I admit that there is a certain distinction," said the prosecutor, with a cold smile. "But it's strange that you see such a vital difference."

"Yes, I see a vital difference! Every man may be a scoundrel, and perhaps every man is a scoundrel, but not everyone can be a thief, it takes an arch-scoundrel to be that. Oh, of course, I don't know how to make these fine distinctions . . . but a thief is lower than a scoundrel, that's my conviction. Listen, I carry the money about me a whole month, I may make up my mind to give it back tomorrow, and I'm a scoundrel no longer, but I cannot make up my mind, you see, though I make up my mind every day, and every day spur myself on to do it, and yet for a whole month I can't bring myself to it, you see. Is that right to your thinking, is that right?"

"Certainly, that's not right, that I can quite understand, and that I don't dispute," answered the prosecutor with reserve. "And let us give up all discussions of these subtleties and distinctions, and, if you will be so kind, get back to the point. And the point is, that you have still not told us, although we've asked you, why, in the first place, you halved the money, squandering one half and hiding the other? For what purpose exactly did you hide it, what did you mean to do with that fifteen hundred? I insist upon that question, Dmitri Fyodorovich."

"Yes, of course!" cried Mitya, striking himself on the forehead; "forgive me, I'm troubling you, and am not explaining the chief point, or you'd understand in a minute, for it's just the motive of it that's the disgrace! You see, it was all to do with the old man, my dead father. He was always pestering Agrafena Alexandrovna, and I was jealous; I thought then that she was hesitating between me and him. So I kept thinking every day, suppose she were to make up her mind all of a sudden, suppose she were to stop tormenting me, and were suddenly to say to me, 'I love you, not him; take me to the other end of the world.' And I'd only forty kopecks; how could I take her away, what could I do? Why, I'd be lost. You see, I didn't know her then, I didn't understand her, I thought she wanted money, and that she wouldn't forgive my poverty. And so I fiendishly counted out the half of that three thousand, sewed it up, calculating on it, sewed it up before I was drunk, and after I had sewn it up, I went off to get drunk on the rest. Yes, that was base. Do you understand now?"

Both attorneys laughed aloud.

"I would have called it sensible and moral on your part not to have squandered it all," chuckled Nikolay Parfenovich, "for after all what does it amount to?"

"Why, that I stole it, that's what it amounts to! Oh, God, you horrify me by not understanding! Every day that I had that fifteen hundred sewn up round my neck, every day and every hour I said to myself, 'You're a thief! you're a thief!' Yes, that's why I've been so savage all this month, that's why I fought in the tavern, that's why I attacked my father, it was because I felt I was a thief. I couldn't make up my mind, I didn't dare even to tell Alyosha, my brother, about that fifteen hundred: I felt I was such a scoundrel and such a pickpocket. But, do you know, while I carried it I said to myself at the same time every hour: 'No, Dmitri Fyodorovich, you may yet not be a thief.' Why? Because I might go next day and pay back that fifteen hundred to Katya. And only yesterday I made up my mind to tear my amulet off my neck, on my way from Fenya's to Perkhotin. I hadn't been able till that moment to bring myself to it. And it was only when I tore it off that I became a definitive and unquestionable thief, a thief and a dishonest man for the rest of my life. Why? Because, with that I destroyed, too, my dream of going to Katya and saying, 'I'm a scoundrel, but not a thief!' Do you understand now? Do you understand?"

"What was it made you decide to do it yesterday?" Nikolay Parfenovich interrupted.

"Why? It's absurd to ask. Because I had condemned myself to die at five o'clock this morning, here, at dawn. I thought it made no difference whether I died a thief or a man of honor. But I see it's not so, it turns out that it does make a difference. Believe me, gentlemen, what has tortured me most during this night has not been the thought that I'd killed the old servant, and that I was in danger of Siberia just when my love was being rewarded, and Heaven was open to me again. Oh, that did torture me, but not in the same way; not so much as the damned consciousness that I had torn that damned money off my breast at last and spent it, and had become a downright thief! Oh, gentlemen, I tell you again, with a bleeding heart, I have learned a great deal this night. I have learned that it's not only impossible to live a scoundrel, but impossible to die a scoundrel. . . . No, gentlemen, one must die honest . . ."

Mitya was pale. His face had a haggard and exhausted look, in spite of his being intensely excited.

"I am beginning to understand you, Dmitri Fyodorovich," the prosecutor said slowly, in a soft and almost compassionate tone. "But all this, if you'll excuse my saying so, is a matter of nerves, in my opinion . . . your overwrought nerves, that's what it is. And why, for instance, should you not have saved yourself such misery for almost a month, by going and returning that fifteen hundred to the lady who had entrusted it to you? And why could you not have explained things to her, and in view of your position, which you describe as being so awful, why could you not have had recourse to the plan which would so naturally have occurred to one's mind, that is, after honorably confessing your errors to her, why could you not have asked her to lend you the sum needed for your expenses, which, with her generous heart, she would certainly not have refused you in your distress, especially if it had been with some guarantee, or even on the security you offered to the merchant Samsonov, and to Madame Khokhlakova. I suppose you still regard that security as of value?"

Mitya suddenly crimsoned.

"Surely you don't think me such an out and out scoundrel as that? You can't be speaking in earnest?" he said, with indignation, looking the prosecutor straight in the face, and seeming unable to believe his ears.

"I assure you I'm in earnest. . . . Why do you imagine I'm not serious?" It was the prosecutor's turn to be surprised.

"Oh, how base that would have been! Gentlemen, do you know, you are torturing me! Let me tell you everything, so be it. I'll confess all my infernal wickedness, but to put you to shame, and you'll be surprised yourself at the depths of ignominy to which a medley of human passions can sink. You must know that I already had that plan myself, that plan you spoke of, just now, prosecutor! Yes, gentlemen, I, too, have had that thought in my mind all this current month, so that I was on the point of deciding to go to Katya—I was base enough for that. But to go to her, to tell her of my treachery, and for that very treachery, to carry it out, for the expenses of that treachery, to beg for money from her, Katya (to beg, do you hear, to beg), and to go straight from her to run away with the other, the rival, who hated and insulted her—to think of it! You must be mad, prosecutor!"

"Mad I am not, but I did speak in haste, without thinking . . . of that feminine jealousy . . . if there could be jealousy in this case, as you assert . . . yes, perhaps there is something of the kind," said the prosecutor, smiling.

"But that would have been so infamous!" Mitya brought his fist down on the table fiercely. "That would have raised such a stench! Yes, do you know that she might have given me that money, yes, and she would have given it too; she'd have given it to satisfy her vengeance, to show her contempt for me, for hers is an infernal nature, too, and she's a woman of great wrath. I'd have taken the money, too, oh, I would have taken it; I would have taken it, and then, for the rest of my life . . . oh, God! Forgive me, gentlemen, I'm making such an outcry because I've had that thought in my mind so much lately, only the day before yesterday, that night when I was having all that bother with Lyagavy, and afterwards yesterday, all day yesterday, I remember, till that happened . . ."

"Till what happened?" put in Nikolay Parfenovich inquisitively, but Mitya did not hear it.

"I have made you an awful confession," Mitya said gloomily in conclusion. "You must appreciate it, and what's more, you must respect it, for if not, if that leaves your souls untouched, then you've simply no respect for me, gentlemen, I tell you that, and I shall die of shame at having confessed it to men like you! Oh, I shall shoot myself! Yes, I see, I see already that you don't believe me. What, you want to write that down, too?" he cried in dismay.

"Yes, what you said just now," said Nikolay Parfenovich, looking at him in surprise, "that is, that up to the last hour you were still contemplating going to Miss Verkhovtseva to beg that sum from her. . . . I assure you, that's a very important piece of evidence for us, Dmitri Fyodorovich, I mean for the whole case . . . and particularly for you, particularly important for you."

"Have mercy, gentlemen!" Mitya flung up his hands, "Don't write that, anyway; have some shame. Here I've torn my heart asunder before you, and you seize the opportunity and are rummaging in the wounds of both halves. . . . Oh, my God!"

In despair he hid his face in his hands.

"Don't worry yourself so, Dmitri Fyodorovich," observed the prosecutor, "everything that is written down will be read over to you afterwards, and what you don't agree to we'll alter as you like. But now I'll ask you one little question for the third time. Has no one, absolutely no one, heard from you of that money you sewed up? That, I must tell you, is almost impossible to believe."

"No one, no one, I told you so before, or you've not understood anything! Let me alone!"

"Very well, this matter is bound to be explained, and there's plenty of time for it, but meantime, consider; we have perhaps a dozen witnesses that you yourself spread it abroad, and even shouted almost everywhere about the three thousand you'd spent here; three thousand, not fifteen hundred. And now, too, when you got hold of the money you had yesterday, you gave many people to understand that you had brought three thousand with you."

"You've got not dozens, but hundreds of witnesses, two hundred witnesses, two hundred have heard it, thousands have heard it!" cried Mitya.

"Well, you see, all bear witness to it. And the word *all* means something."

"It means nothing. I talked rot, and everyone began repeating it."

"But what need have you to 'talk rot,' as you call it?"

"The devil knows. From bravado perhaps . . . at having wasted so much money. . . . To try and forget that money I had sewn up, perhaps . . . yes, that was why . . . damn it . . . how often will you ask me that question? Well, I told a fib, and that was the end of it, once I'd said it, I didn't care to correct it. What does a man tell lies for sometimes?"

"That's very difficult to decide, Dmitri Fyodorovich, what makes a man tell lies," observed the prosecutor impressively. "Tell me, though, was that 'amulet,' as you call it, on your neck, a big thing?"

"No, not big."

"How big, for instance?"

"If you fold a hundred-ruble bill in half, that would be the size."

"You'd better show us the remains of it. You must have them somewhere."

"Eh, the devil . . . what nonsense . . . I don't know where they are."

"But excuse me: where and when did you take it off your neck? According to your own evidence you didn't go home."

"When I was going from Fenya's to Perkhotin's, on the way I tore it off my neck and took out the money."

"In the dark?"

"What should I want a light for? I did it with my fingers in one minute."

"Without scissors, in the street?"

"In the marketplace I think it was. Why scissors? It was an old rag. It was torn in a minute."

"Where did you put it afterwards?"

"I dropped it there."

"Where was it, exactly?"

"In the marketplace, in the marketplace! The devil knows whereabouts. What do you want to know for?"

"That's extremely important, Dmitri Fyodorovich. It would be material evidence in your favor. How is it you don't understand that? Who helped you to sew it up a month ago?"

"No one helped me. I did it myself."

"Can you sew?"

"A soldier has to know how to sew. No knowledge was needed to do that."

"Where did you get the material, that is, the rag in which you sewed the money?"

"Are you laughing at me?"

"Not at all. And we are in no mood for laughing, Dmitri Fyodorovich."

"I don't know where I got the rag from—somewhere, I suppose."

"I would have thought you couldn't have forgotten it?"

"Upon my word, I don't remember. I might have torn a bit off my linen."

"That's very interesting. We might find in your lodgings tomorrow the shirt or whatever it is from which you tore the rag. What sort of rag was it, cloth or linen?"

"Goodness only knows what it was. Wait a bit. . . . I believe I didn't tear it off anything. It was a bit of calico. . . . I believe I sewed it up in a cap of my landlady's."

"In your landlady's cap?"

"Yes. I took it from her."

"How did you get it?"

"You see, I remember once taking a cap for a rag, perhaps to wipe my pen on. I took it without asking, because it was a worthless rag. I tore it up, and I took the notes and sewed them up in it. I believe it was in that very rag I sewed it. An old piece of calico, washed a thousand times."

"And you remember that for certain now?"

"I don't know whether for certain. I think it was in the cap. But, hang it, what does it matter?"

"In that case your landlady will remember that the thing was lost?"

"No, she won't, she didn't miss it. It was an old rag, I tell you, an old rag not worth a cent."

"And where did you get the needle and thread?"

"I'll stop now. I won't say any more. Enough of it!" said Mitya, losing his temper at last.

"It's strange that you should have so completely forgotten where you threw the 'amulet' in the marketplace."

"Give orders for the marketplace to be swept tomorrow, and perhaps you'll find it," said Mitya sneering. "Enough, gentlemen, enough!" he decided, in an exhausted voice. "I see you don't believe me! Not for a moment! It's my fault, not yours. I ought not to have been so ready. Why, why did I degrade myself by confessing my secret to you? It's a joke to you. I see that from your eyes. You led me on to it, prosecutor! Sing a hymn of triumph if you can. . . . Curse you, you torturers!"

He bent his head, and hid his face in his hands. The attorneys were silent. A minute later he raised his head and looked at them almost vacantly. His face now expressed complete, hopeless, despair, and he sat mute and passive as though hardly conscious of what was happening. In the meantime they had to finish what they were doing. They had to begin examining the witnesses immediately. It was by now eight o'clock in the morning. The lights had been extinguished long ago. Mikhail Makarovich and Kalganov, who had been continually in and out of the room all the while the interrogation had been going on, had now both gone out again. The attorneys, too, looked very tired. It was a wretched morning, the whole sky was overcast, and the rain streamed down in buckets. Mitya gazed blankly out of the window.

"May I look out of the window?" he asked Nikolay Parfenovich, suddenly.

"Oh, as much as you like," the latter replied.

Mitya got up and went to the window. The rain lashed against the little greenish panes of the window. He could see the muddy road just below the window, and further away, in the rainy mist, a row of poor, black, dismal huts, looking even blacker and poorer in the rain. Mitya thought of "Phoebus the golden-haired," and how he had meant to shoot himself at his first ray. "Perhaps it would be even better on a morning like this," he thought with a smile, and suddenly, flinging his hand downwards, he turned to his "torturers."

"Gentlemen," he cried, "I see that I am lost! But she? Tell me about her, I beseech you. Surely she need not be ruined with me? She's innocent, you know, she was out of her mind when she cried last night 'it's all my fault!' She's done nothing, nothing! I've been grieving over her all night as I sat with you. . . . Can't you, won't you tell me what you are going to do with her now?"

"You can set your mind quite at rest on that score, Dmitri Fyodorovich," the prosecutor answered at once, with evident alacrity. "We have, so far, no grounds for interfering with the lady in whom you are so interested. I trust that it may be the same in the later development of the case. . . . On the contrary, we'll do everything that lies in our power in that matter. Set your mind completely at rest."

"Gentlemen, I thank you. I knew that you were honest, straightforward people in spite of everything. You've taken a load off my heart. . . . Well, what are we to do now? I'm ready."

"Well, we ought to make haste. We must pass to examining the witnesses without delay. That must be done in your presence and therefore . . ."

"Shouldn't we have some tea first?" interposed Nikolay Parfenovich, "I think we've deserved it!"

They decided that if tea were ready downstairs (Mikhail Makarovich had, no doubt gone down to get some) they would have a glass and then "go on and on," putting off their proper breakfast until a more favorable opportunity. Tea really was ready below, and was soon brought up. Mitya at first refused the glass that Nikolay Parfenovich politely offered him, but afterwards he asked for it himself and drank it greedily. He looked surprisingly exhausted. It might have been supposed from his herculean strength that one night of carousing, even accompanied by the most violent emotions, could have had little effect on him. But he felt that he could hardly hold his head up, and from time to time all the objects about him seemed heaving and dancing before his eyes. "A little more and I shall begin raving," he said to himself.

Chapter VIII

The Evidence of the Witnesses. The Babe

The examination of the witnesses began. But we will not continue our story in such detail as before. And so we will omit how Nikolay Parfenovich impressed on every witness called that he must give his evidence in accordance with truth and conscience, and that he would afterwards have to repeat his evidence on oath, how every witness was called upon to sign the protocol of his evidence, and so on. We will only note that the point principally insisted upon in the examination was the question of the three thousand rubles, that is, was the sum spent here, at Mokroe, by Dmitri Fyodorovich on the first occasion, a month before, three thousand or fifteen hundred? And again had he spent three thousand or fifteen hundred yesterday? Alas, all the evidence given by everyone turned out to be against Mitya. There was not one in his favor, and some witnesses introduced new, almost crushing facts, in contradiction of Mitya's story. The first witness examined was Trifon Borisich. He was not in the least abashed as he stood before the attorneys. He had, on the contrary, an air of stern and severe indignation with the accused, which gave him an appearance of truthfulness and personal dignity. He spoke little, and with reserve, waited to be questioned, answered precisely and deliberately. Firmly and unhesitatingly he bore witness that the sum spent a month before could not have been less than three thousand, that all the peasants about here would testify that they had heard the sum of three thousand mentioned by Mitri Fyodorich himself. "What a lot of money he flung away on the gypsy girls alone. He wasted a thousand, I daresay, on them alone."

"I don't believe I gave them five hundred," was Mitya's gloomy comment on this. "It's a pity I didn't count the money at the time, but I was drunk . . ."

Mitya was sitting sideways with his back to the curtains. He listened gloomily, with a melancholy and exhausted air, as though he would say: "Oh, say what you like. It makes no difference now."

"More than a thousand went on them, Mitri Fyodorovich," retorted Trifon Borisovich firmly. "You flung it about at random and they picked it up. They were a rascally, thievish lot, horse stealers, they've been driven away from here, or maybe they'd bear witness themselves how much they got from you. I saw the sum in your hands, myself—count it I didn't, you didn't let me, that's true enough—but by the look of it I would say it was far more than fifteen hundred . . . fifteen hundred, indeed! We've seen money too. We can judge amounts . . ."

As for the sum spent yesterday he asserted that Dmitri Fyodorovich had told him, as soon as he arrived, that he had brought three thousand with him.

"Come now, is that so, Trifon Borisich?" replied Mitya. "Surely I didn't declare so positively that I'd brought three thousand?"

"You did say so, Mitri Fyodorovich. You said it before Andrey. Andrey himself is still here. Send for him. And in the hall, when you were treating the chorus, you shouted straight out that you would leave your sixth thousand here—that is with what you spent before, we must understand. Stepan and Semyon heard it, and Pyotr Fomich Kalganov, too, was standing beside you at the time. Maybe he'd remember it . . ."

The evidence as to the sixth thousand made an extraordinary impression on the two examiners. They were delighted with this new mode of reckoning, three and three made six, three thousand then and three now made six, that was clear.

They questioned all the peasants suggested by Trifon Borisovich, Stepan and Semyon, the driver Andrey, and Kalganov. The peasants and the driver hesitatingly confirmed Trifon Borisich's evidence. They noted down, with particular care, Andrey's account of the conversation he had had with Mitya on the road: "'Where,' says he, 'am I, Dmitri Fyodorovich, going, to Heaven or to Hell, and shall I be forgiven in the next world or not?'" The "psychologist" Ippolit Kirillovich heard this with a subtle smile, and ended by recommending that these remarks as to where Dmitri Fyodorovich would go should be "included in the case."

Kalganov, when called, came in reluctantly, frowning and ill-humored, and he spoke to the attorneys as though he had never met them before in his life, though they were acquaintances whom he had been meeting every day for a long time past. He began by saying that "he knew nothing about it and didn't want to." But it appeared that he had heard of the sixth thousand, and he admitted that he had been standing close by at the moment. As far as he could see he "didn't know" how much money Mitya had in his hands. He affirmed that the Poles had cheated at cards. In reply to reiterated questions he stated that, after the Poles had been turned out, Mitya's position with Agrafena Alexandrovna had certainly improved, and that she had said that she loved him. He spoke of Agrafena Alexandrovna with reserve and respect, as though she had been a lady of the best society, and did not once allow himself to call her Grushenka. In spite of the young man's obvious repugnance at giving evidence, Ippolit Kirillovich examined him at great length, and only from him learned all the details of what made up Mitya's "romance," so to speak, on that night. Mitya did not once stop Kalganov. At last they let the young man go, and he left the room with unconcealed indignation.

The Poles, too, were examined. Though they had gone to bed in their room, they had not slept all night, and on the arrival of the police officers they hastily dressed and got ready, realizing that they would certainly be sent for. They gave their evidence with dignity, though not without some fear. The little *pan* turned out to be a retired official of the twelfth class,[1]

_____
1. In other words, close to the bottom of the Table of Ranks.

who had served in Siberia as a veterinary surgeon. His name was Mussy-alovich. *Pan* Vrublevsky turned out to be an uncertified dentist. Although Nikolay Parfenovich asked him questions on entering the room they both addressed their answers to Mikhail Makarovich, who was standing on one side, taking him in their ignorance for the most important person and in command, and addressed him at every word as "*Panie* Colonel." Only after several reproofs from Mikhail Makarovich himself, they grasped that they had to address their answers only to Nikolay Parfenovich. It turned out that they could speak Russian quite correctly except for their accent in some words. Of his relations with Grushenka, past and present, *Pan* Mussyalovich spoke proudly and warmly, so that Mitya was roused at once and declared that he would not allow the "scoundrel" to speak like that in his presence! *Pan* Mussyalovich at once called attention to the word "scoundrel," and begged that it should be put down in the deposition. Mitya fumed with rage.

"He's a scoundrel! A scoundrel! You can put that down. And put down, too, that, in spite of the deposition I still declare that he's a scoundrel!" he cried.

Though Nikolay Parfenovich did insert this in the deposition, he showed the most praiseworthy tact and management. After sternly repri-manding Mitya, he cut short all further inquiry into the romantic aspect of the case, and hastened to pass to what was essential. One piece of evi-dence given by the *pans* roused special interest in the attorneys: that was how, in that very room, Mitya had tried to buy off *Pan* Mussyalovich, and had offered him three thousand rubles to resign his claims, seven hun-dred rubles down, and the remaining twenty-three hundred "to be paid next day in the town." He had sworn at the time that he had not the whole sum with him at Mokroe, but that his money was in the town. Mitya observed hotly that he had not said that he would be sure to pay him the remainder next day in the town. But *Pan* Vrublevsky confirmed the state-ment, and Mitya, after thinking for a moment admitted, frowning, that it must have been as the *pans* stated, that he had been excited at the time, and might indeed have said so. The prosecutor positively pounced on this piece of evidence. It seemed to establish for the prosecution (and they did, in fact, base this deduction on it) that half, or a part of, the three thousand that had come into Mitya's hands might really have been left somewhere hidden in the town, or even, perhaps, somewhere here, in Mokroe. This would explain the circumstance, so ticklish for the prosecution, that only eight hundred rubles were to be found in Mitya's hands. This circumstance had been the one piece of evidence which, insignificant as it was, had hitherto told, to some extent, in Mitya's favor. Now this one piece of evi-dence in his favor had broken down. In answer to the prosecutor's inquiry, where he would have got the remaining twenty-three hundred rubles, since he himself had denied having more than fifteen hundred, Mitya confidently replied that he had meant to offer the "little Pole," not money, but a formal deed of conveyance of his rights to the village of Chermash-nya, those rights which he had already offered to Samsonov and Madame Khokhlakova. The prosecutor positively smiled at the "innocence of this subterfuge."

"And you imagine he would have accepted such a deed as a substitute for twenty-three hundred rubles in cash?"

"He certainly would have accepted it," Mitya snapped heatedly. "Why, look here, he might have grabbed not two thousand, but four or six, for it. He would have put little lawyers, Polacks and little Yids, onto the job, and might have got, not three thousand, but the whole property out of the old man."

The evidence of *Pan* Mussyalovich was, of course, entered into the deposition in the fullest detail. Then they let the *pans* go. The incident of the cheating at cards was hardly touched upon. Nikolay Parfenovich was too well pleased with them, as it was, and did not want to worry them with trifles, moreover, it was nothing but a foolish, drunken quarrel over cards. There had been drinking and disorder enough, that night. . . . So the two hundred rubles remained in the pockets of the *pans*.

Then the little old man Maximov was summoned. He came in timidly, approached with little steps, looking very disheveled and depressed. He had, all this time, taken refuge below with Grushenka, sitting dumbly beside her, and "now and then he'd begin blubbering over her and wiping his eyes with a blue check handkerchief," as Mikhail Makarovich described afterwards. So that she, herself, began trying to pacify and comfort him. The old man at once confessed that he had done wrong, that he had borrowed "ten rubles in my poverty, sir," from Dmitri Fyodorovich, and that he was ready to pay it back. To Nikolay Parfenovich's direct question, had he noticed how much money Dmitri Fyodorovich held in his hand, as he must have been able to see the sum better than anyone when he took the note from him, Maximov, in the most positive manner, declared that there was twenty thousand.

"Have you ever seen so much as twenty thousand before, then?" inquired Nikolay Parfenovich, with a smile.

"To be sure I have, sir, not twenty, but seven, when my wife mortgaged my little property. She'd only let me look at it from a distance, boasting of it to me. It was a very thick bundle, all rainbow-colored bills. And Dmitri Fyodorovich's were all rainbow-colored . . ."

He was not kept long. At last it was Grushenka's turn. Nikolay Parfenovich was obviously apprehensive of the effect her appearance might have on Dmitri Fyodorovich, and he muttered a few words of admonition to him, but Mitya bowed his head in silence, giving him to understand "that he would not make a scene." Mikhail Makarovich, himself, led Grushenka in. She entered with a stern and gloomy face, that looked almost composed, and sat down quietly on the chair offered her by Nikolay Parfenovich. She was very pale, she seemed to be cold, and wrapped herself closely in her magnificent black shawl. She was suffering from a slight feverish chill—the first symptom of the long illness which followed that night. Her grave air, her direct earnest look and quiet manner made a very favorable impression on everyone. Nikolay Parfenovich was even a little bit "fascinated." He admitted himself, when talking about it afterwards, that only then had he seen "how handsome the woman was," for, though he had seen her several times before, he had always looked upon her as something of a "provincial hetaera."[2] "She has the manners of the best society," he said enthusiastically, gossiping about her in a circle of

---

2. In ancient Greece a hetaera was an unmarried, educated woman who led a free lifestyle; the word came to indicate a woman of loose behavior.

ladies. But this was received with positive indignation by the ladies, who immediately called him a "naughty man," to his great satisfaction. As she entered the room, Grushenka only glanced for an instant at Mitya, who looked at her uneasily. But her face reassured him at once. After the first inevitable inquiries and warnings, Nikolay Parfenovich asked her, hesitating a little, but preserving the most courteous manner, on what terms she was with the retired lieutenant, Dmitri Fyodorovich Karamazov. To this Grushenka firmly and quietly replied:

"He was an acquaintance. He came to see me as an acquaintance during the past month."

To further inquisitive questions she answered plainly and with complete frankness, that, though "at times" she had thought him attractive, she had not loved him, but had enticed him as well as "the little old man" "in my vile spite," that she had seen that Mitya was very jealous of Fyodor Pavlovich and everyone else; but that had only amused her. She had never meant to go to Fyodor Pavlovich, she had simply been laughing at him. "I had no thoughts for either of them all this last month, I was expecting another man who had wronged me. But I think," she said in conclusion, "that there's no need for you to inquire about that, nor for me to answer you, for that's my own business."

Nikolay Parfenovich immediately acted upon this hint. He again dismissed the "romantic" aspect of the case and passed to the serious one, that is, to the question of most importance, concerning the three thousand rubles. Grushenka confirmed the statement that three thousand rubles had certainly been spent on the first carousal at Mokroe, and, though she had not counted the money herself, she had heard that it was three thousand from Dmitri Fyodorovich's own lips.

"Did he tell you that alone, or before someone else, or did you only hear him speak of it to others in your presence?" the prosecutor inquired immediately.

To which Grushenka replied that she had heard him say so before other people, and had heard him say so when they were alone.

"Did he say it to you alone once, or several times?" inquired the prosecutor, and learned that he had told Grushenka so several times.

Ippolit Kirillovich was very well satisfied with this piece of evidence. Further examination elicited that Grushenka knew, too, where that money had come from, and that "Dmitri Fyodorovich had got it from Katerina Ivanovna."

"And did you never, once, hear that the money spent a month ago was not three thousand, but less, and that Dmitri Fyodorovich had saved half that sum for his own use?"

"No, I never heard that," answered Grushenka.

It was explained further that Mitya had, on the contrary, often told her during that month that he didn't have a kopeck. "He was always expecting to get some from his father," said Grushenka in conclusion.

"Did he never say before you . . . casually, or in a moment of irritation," Nikolay Parfenovich put in suddenly, "that he intended to make an attempt on his father's life?"

"Ach, he did say so," sighed Grushenka.

"Once or several times?"

"He mentioned it several times, always in anger."

"And did you believe he would do it?"

"No, I never believed it," she answered firmly. "I had faith in his noble heart."

"Gentlemen, allow me," cried Mitya suddenly, "allow me to say one word to Agrafena Alexandrovna, in your presence."

"You can speak," Nikolay Parfenovich assented.

"Agrafena Alexandrovna!" Mitya got up from his chair, "have faith in God and in me: I am not guilty of my father's murder!"

Having uttered these words Mitya sat down again on his chair. Grushenka stood up and crossed herself devoutly before the icon.

"Thanks be to Thee, O Lord," she said, in a voice thrilled with emotion, and still standing, she turned to Nikolay Parfenovich and added: "As he has spoken now, believe it! I know him. He'll say anything as a joke or from obstinacy, but he'll never deceive you against his conscience. He's telling the whole truth, you may believe it."

"Thanks, Agrafena Alexandrovna, you've given me fresh courage," Mitya responded in a quivering voice.

As to the money spent the previous day, she declared that she did not know what sum it was, but had heard him tell several people that he had three thousand with him. And to the question where he got the money, she said that he had told her that he had "stolen" it from Katerina Ivanovna, and that she had replied to that that he hadn't stolen it, and that he must pay the money back next day. On the prosecutor's asking her emphatically whether the money he said he had stolen from Katerina Ivanovna was what he had spent yesterday, or what he had squandered there a month ago, she declared that he meant the money spent a month ago, and that that was how she understood him.

Grushenka was at last released, and Nikolay Parfenovich informed her impulsively that she might at once return to the town and that if he could be of any assistance to her, with horses for example, or if she would care for an escort he . . . would be . . .

"I thank you sincerely," said Grushenka, bowing to him, "I'm going with this little old man, the landowner, I am driving him back to town with me, and meanwhile, if you'll allow me, I'll wait below to hear what you decide about Dmitri Fyodorovich."

She went out. Mitya was calm, and even looked more cheerful, but only for a moment. He felt more and more oppressed by a strange physical weakness. His eyes were closing with fatigue. The examination of the witness was, at last, over. They proceeded to a final revision of the deposition. Mitya got up, moved from his chair to the corner by the curtain, lay down on a large chest covered with a rug, and instantly fell asleep.

He had a strange dream, utterly out of keeping with the place and the time. He was driving somewhere in the steppes, where he had been stationed long ago, and a peasant was driving him in a cart with a pair of horses, through snow and sleet. He was cold, it was early in November, and the snow was falling in big wet flakes, melting as soon as it touched the earth. And the peasant drove him smartly, snapping his whip, he had a fair, long beard. He was not an old man, somewhere about fifty, and he had on a gray peasant's smock. And there, not far off was a village, he could see the very black huts, and half the huts were burned down, there were only the charred beams sticking up. And as they drove in, there were peasant women drawn up along the road, a lot of women, a whole row, all thin and wan, with their faces a sort of brownish color, especially one at the edge, a tall, bony woman, who looked forty, but might have been only twenty, with a long thin face. And in her arms was a little baby crying. And her breasts must have been so dried up that there was not a drop of milk in them. And the child cried and cried, and held out its little bare arms, with its little fists blue from cold.

"Why are they crying? Why are they crying?" Mitya asked, as they dashed briskly by.

"It's the babe," answered the driver, "the babe weeping."[3]

And Mitya was struck by his saying, in his peasant way, "the babe," and he liked the peasant's calling it a "babe." There seemed more pity in it. "But why is it weeping?" Mitya persisted stupidly, "why are its little arms bare? Why don't they wrap it up?"

"The babe's cold, its little clothes are frozen and don't warm it."

"But why is it? Why?" stupid Mitya still persisted.

"Why, they're poor people, burned out. They've no bread. They're begging because they've been burned out."

"No, no," Mitya, as it were, still did not understand. "Tell me: why it is those poor mothers stand there, why are people poor, why is the babe poor, why is the steppe barren, why don't they hug each other and kiss, why don't they sing songs of joy, why are they so dark from black misery, why don't they feed the babe?"

And he felt that, though his questions were unreasonable and senseless, yet he wanted to ask just that, and he had to ask it just in that way. And he felt also that a passion of pity, such as he had never known before, was rising in his heart, and he wanted to cry, that he wanted to do something for them all, so that the babe should weep no more, so that the dark-faced, dried-up mother should not weep, that no one should shed tears again from that moment, and he wanted to do it at once, at once, regardless of all obstacles, with all the Karamazov recklessness.

"And I'm coming with you. I won't leave you now for the rest of my life, I'm coming with you," he heard close beside him Grushenka's tender voice, full of emotion. And his whole heart glowed, and he struggled forward towards the light, and he longed to live, to live, to go on and on, towards the new, beckoning light, and to hasten, hasten, now, at once!

"What! Where?" he exclaimed opening his eyes, and sitting up on the chest, as though he had revived from a swoon, smiling brightly. Nikolay Parfenovich was standing over him, suggesting that he should hear the deposition read aloud and sign it. Mitya guessed that he had been asleep an hour or more, but he did not hear Nikolay Parfenovich. He was suddenly struck by the fact that there was a pillow under his head, which hadn't been there when he had leaned back, exhausted, on the chest.

"Who put that pillow under my head? Who was so kind?" he cried, with a sort of ecstatic, grateful feeling, and tears in his voice, as though some great kindness had been shown him. He never found out who this kind man was, perhaps one of the peasant witnesses, or Nikolay Parfenovich's little secretary, had compassionately thought to put a pillow under his

---

3. The theme of the babe weeping is taken from Nekrasov, "Children Weeping" (see also note 3 on p. 94).

head, but his whole soul was quivering with tears. He went to the table
and said that he would sign whatever they liked.

"I've had a good dream, gentlemen," he said somehow strangely, with a
sort of new face, as if lit up with joy.

Chapter IX

They Carry Mitya Away

When the deposition had been signed, Nikolay Parfenovich turned solemnly to the prisoner and read him the indictment, setting forth, that in
such a year, on such a day, in such a place, the district attorney of such-
and-such a district court, having examined so-and-so (to wit, Mitya)
accused of this and of that (all the charges were carefully written out) and
having considered that the accused, not pleading guilty to the charges
made against him, had brought forward nothing in his defense, while the
witnesses, so-and-so, and so-and-so, and the circumstances such-and-such
testify against him, acting in accordance with such-and-such articles of
the Statutes, and so on, has ruled, that, in order to preclude such-and-such
(Mitya) from all means of evading pursuit and judgment he be detained in
such-and-such a prison, which he hereby notifies to the accused and communicates a copy of this same indictment to the deputy prosecutor, and so
on, and so on. In brief, Mitya was informed that he was, from that moment,
a prisoner, and that he would be driven at once to town, and there shut up
in a very unpleasant place. Mitya listened attentively, and only shrugged
his shoulders.

"Well, gentlemen, I don't blame you. I'm ready. . . . I understand that
there's nothing else for you to do."

Nikolay Parfenovich informed him gently that he would be escorted at
once by the rural police officer, Mavriky Mavrikyevich, who happened to
be on the spot. . . .

"Wait," Mitya interrupted, suddenly, and impelled by uncontrollable
feeling he pronounced, addressing all in the room: "Gentlemen, we're all
cruel, we're all monsters, we all make men weep, and mothers, and babes
at the breast, but of all, let it be settled here, now, of all I am the lowest
viper! I've sworn to amend every day of my life, beating my breast, and
every day I've done the same filthy things. I understand now that such
men as I need a blow, a blow of destiny to catch them as with a noose,
and bind them by a force from without. Never, never should I have risen
of myself! But the thunderbolt has fallen.[4] I accept the torment of accusation, and my public shame, I want to suffer and by suffering I shall be
purified. Perhaps I shall be purified, gentlemen, what? But listen, for the
last time, I am not guilty of my father's blood. I accept my punishment,
not because I killed him, but because I meant to kill him, and perhaps I
really might have killed him. Still I mean to fight it out with you, I warn
you of that. I'll fight it out with you to the end, and then God will decide.

---

4. Dmitri quotes a Russian proverb: "The peasant won't cross himself until the thunder claps"
(*Poka grom ne grianet, muzhik ne perekrestitsia*). Dostoevsky cites this proverb in his November
16 letter to Lyubimov, where he describes Dmitri's character.

Good-bye, gentlemen, don't be vexed with me for having shouted at you during the examination. Oh, I was still such a fool then. . . . In another minute I shall be a prisoner, but now, for the last time, as a free man, Dmitri Karamazov offers you his hand. Saying good-bye to you, I say it to all men."

His voice quivered and he stretched out his hand, but Nikolay Parfenovich, who happened to stand nearest to him, with a sudden, almost nervous movement, hid his hands behind his back. Mitya instantly noticed this, and started. He let his outstretched hand fall at once.

"The preliminary inquiry is not yet over," Nikolay Parfenovich faltered, somewhat embarrassed. "We will continue it in town, and I, for my part, of course, am ready to wish you all success . . . in your defense. . . . As a matter of fact, Dmitri Fyodorovich, I've always been disposed to regard you as, so to speak, more unfortunate than guilty. All of us here, if I may make bold to speak for all, we are all ready to recognize that you are, at bottom, a young man of honor, but, alas, one who has been carried away by certain passions to a somewhat excessive degree . . ."

Nikolay Parfenovich's little figure was positively majestic by the time he had finished speaking. It struck Mitya that in another minute this "boy" would take his arm, lead him to another corner, and renew their conversation about "girls." But many quite irrelevant and inappropriate thoughts sometimes occur even to a prisoner when he is being led out to execution.[5]

"Gentlemen, you are good, you are humane, may I see *her* to say 'good-bye' for the last time?" asked Mitya.

"Certainly, but considering . . . in fact, now it's impossible except in the presence of . . ."

"Be present, if you like!"

Grushenka was brought in, but the farewell was brief, and of few words, and did not at all satisfy Nikolay Parfenovich. Grushenka made a deep bow to Mitya.

"I have told you I am yours, and I will be yours. I will follow you forever, wherever they may send you. Farewell; you are guiltless, though you've been your own undoing."

Her lips quivered, tears flowed from her eyes.

"Forgive me, Grusha, for my love, for ruining you, too, with my love."

Mitya would have said something more, but he broke off and went out. He was at once surrounded by men who kept a constant watch on him. At the bottom of the steps to which he had driven up with such a dash the day before with Andrey's three horses, two carts stood in readiness. Mavriky Mavrikyevich, a sturdy, thickset man with a wrinkled face, was annoyed about something, some sudden irregularity. He was shouting angrily. He asked Mitya to get into the cart with somewhat excessive surliness. "When I stood him drinks in the tavern, the man had quite a different face,"

---

5. Dostoevsky frequently inserts elements from his own well-known biography into his novels. He was sentenced to death for his participation in the Petrashevsky Circle, a group of intellectuals who met to discuss topics such as Utopian Socialism in the 1840s. Dostoevsky stood before the firing squad on December 22, 1849; at the last minute, Nicholas I commuted the sentence to hard labor. The idea that a condemned man being led to execution may be subject to irrelevant thoughts is also put forth by the character Prince Myshkin in Dostoevsky's novel *The Idiot*.

thought Mitya, as he got in. At the gates there was a crowd of people, peasants, women and drivers. Trifon Borisovich came down the steps too. All stared at Mitya.

"Forgive me at parting, good people!" Mitya shouted suddenly from the cart.

"Forgive us too!" he heard two or three voices.

"Good-bye to you, too, Trifon Borisich!"

But Trifon Borisich did not even turn round. He was, perhaps, too busy. He, too, was shouting and fussing about something. It appeared that everything was not yet ready in the second cart, in which two constables were to accompany Mavriky Mavrikyevich. The peasant who had been ordered to drive the second cart was pulling on his coat, stoutly maintaining that it was not his turn to go, but Akim's. But Akim was not to be seen. They ran to look for him. The peasant persisted and asked them to wait.

"You see what our peasants are, Mavriky Mavrikyevich. They have no shame!" exclaimed Trifon Borisich. "Akim gave you twenty-five kopecks the day before yesterday. You've drunk it all and now you cry out. I'm simply surprised at your good nature, with our low peasants, Mavriky Mavrikyevich, that's all I can say."

"But what do we want a second cart for?" Mitya put in. "Let's start with the one, Mavriky Mavrikyevich. I won't be unruly, I won't run away from you, old fellow. What do we want an escort for?"

"I'll trouble you, sir, to learn how to speak to me if you've never been taught. I'm not 'old fellow' to you, and you can keep your advice for another time!" Mavriky Mavrikyevich snapped out savagely, as though glad to vent his wrath.

Mitya was reduced to silence. He flushed all over. A moment later he felt suddenly very cold. The rain had ceased, but the dull sky was still overcast with clouds, and a keen wind was blowing straight in his face. "I've caught a cold," thought Mitya, twitching his shoulders.

At last Mavriky Mavrikyevich, too, got into the cart, sat down heavily, and, as though without noticing it, squeezed Mitya into the corner. It is true that he was out of humor and greatly disliked the task that had been laid upon him.

"Good-bye, Trifon Borisich!" Mitya shouted again, and felt himself, that he had not called out this time from good nature, but involuntarily, from resentment.

But Trifon Borisich stood proudly, with both hands behind his back, and staring straight at Mitya with a stern and angry face, he made no reply.

"Good-bye, Dmitri Fyodorovich, good-bye!" he heard all at once the voice of Kalganov, who had suddenly darted out. Running up to the cart he held out his hand to Mitya. He had no cap on. Mitya had time to seize and press his hand.

"Good-bye, dear fellow! I won't forget your generosity," he cried warmly. But the cart moved and their hands parted. The bell began ringing—they carried Mitya away.

Kalganov ran back, sat down in a corner, bent his head, hid his face in his hands, and burst out crying. For a long while he sat like that, crying as though he were a little boy instead of a young man of twenty. Oh, he believed almost without doubt in Mitya's guilt! "What are these people, what kind of people can there be after this!" he exclaimed incoherently, in bitter despondency, almost despair. At that moment he did not even want to live in the world. "Is it worth it? Is it worth it?" exclaimed the youth in his grief.

Part Four

Book Ten

BOYS

Chapter I

Kolya Krasotkin

The beginning of November. We had eleven degrees of frost, without snow, but a little dry snow had fallen on the frozen ground during the night, and a "dry and sharp" wind[1] was lifting and blowing it along the dreary streets of our town, especially about the marketplace. It was a dull morning, but the snow had ceased. Not far from the marketplace, close to Plotnikov's shop, there stood a small house, very clean both inside and out. It belonged to Mrs. Krasotkina, the widow of a former provincial secretary,[2] who had died long ago, almost fourteen years ago. His widow, a lively still attractive little lady of thirty,[3] was living in her neat little house on her "private means." She lived in respectable seclusion; she was of a soft but fairly cheerful disposition. She was about eighteen at the time of her husband's death; she had been married only a year and had just borne him a son. From the day of his death she had devoted herself heart and soul to the bringing up of her precious treasure, her boy Kolya. Though she had loved him passionately those fourteen years, he had caused her far more suffering than happiness. She trembled and fainted with terror almost every day, afraid he would fall ill, would catch cold, do something naughty, climb on a chair and fall off it, and so on and so on. When Kolya began going to school, the mother devoted herself to studying all the sciences with him so as to help him, and go through his lessons with him. She hastened to make the acquaintance of the teachers and their wives, even made up to Kolya's schoolfellows, and fawned upon them in the hope of thus saving Kolya from being teased, laughed at, or beaten by them. She went so far that the boys actually began to mock at him on her account, and taunt him with being a "mamma's boy." But the boy could hold his own. He was a resolute boy, "tremendously strong," as was rumored in his class, and which soon proved to be the fact; he was agile, strong-willed, and of an audacious and enterprising temper. He was good at lessons, and there was a rumor in the school that he could beat the teacher, Dardanelov, at arithmetic and universal history. Though he looked down upon everyone,

---

1. The phrase "dry and sharp" wind is a quotation from Nekrasov's 1846 poem "Before the Rain" (*Pered dozhdem*).
2. A provincial secretary occupied the twelfth grade in the Table of Ranks.
3. Dostoevsky originally planned to make Kolya twelve years old; when he adjusted this character's age upward, he forgot to change the mother's age accordingly. See Dostoevsky's letter to Lyubimov April 13, 1880.

he was a good comrade and not supercilious. He accepted his schoolfellows' respect as his due, but was friendly with them. Above all, he knew where to draw the line. He could restrain himself on occasion, and in his relations with the teachers he never overstepped that last mystic limit beyond which a prank became disorder, rebellion, and lawlessness. But he was very, very fond of mischief on every possible occasion as much so as the smallest boy in school, and not so much for the sake of mischief as for creating a sensation, inventing something, doing something effective, flashy, and conspicuous. Above all, he was extremely vain. He knew how to place even his mother in a submissive relationship to him, he was almost despotic in his control of her. She submitted to him, oh, she had submitted to him long ago. The one thought unendurable to her was that her boy "doesn't love her enough." She was always fancying Kolya was "unfeeling" to her, and at times, dissolving into hysterical tears, she used to reproach him with his coldness. The boy disliked this, and the more demonstrations of feeling were demanded of him the more he seemed intentionally to avoid them. Yet it was not intentional on his part but instinctive—it was his character. His mother was mistaken; he was very fond of her. He only disliked "sheepish sentimentality," as he expressed it in his schoolboy language. There was a bookcase in the house containing a few books that had been his father's. Kolya was fond of reading, and had read several of them by himself. His mother did not mind that and only wondered sometimes at seeing the boy staying for hours by the bookcase poring over a book instead of going to play. And in that way Kolya read some things unsuitable for his age. Though the boy, as a rule, knew where to draw the line in his mischief, he had of late begun to play pranks that caused his mother serious alarm. It is true there was nothing immoral in what he did, but a wild mad recklessness. It happened that July, during the summer holidays, that the mother and son went to another district, forty-five miles away, to spend a week with a distant relation, whose husband was an official at the railway station (the very station, the nearest one to our town, from which a month later Ivan Fyodorovich Karamazov set off for Moscow). There Kolya began by carefully investigating every detail connected with the railway, knowing that he could impress his schoolfellows when he got home with his newly acquired knowledge. But there happened to be some other boys in the place with whom he soon made friends. Some of them lived at the station,[4] others in the neighborhood; there were six or seven of them, all between twelve and fifteen, and two of them came from our town. The boys played together, and on the fourth or fifth day of Kolya's stay at the station, a mad bet was made by the foolish boys. Kolya, who was almost the youngest of the party and rather looked down upon by the others in consequence, was moved by vanity or by reckless bravado to bet them two rubles that he would lie down between the rails at night when the eleven o'clock train was due, and would lie there without moving while the train rolled over him at full speed. It is true they made a preliminary study, from which it appeared that it was possible to lie so flat between the rails that the train could pass over without touching, but to lie there was no joke! Kolya maintained stoutly that

---

4. Children living at the station might be children of railroad employees, or of innkeepers and shopkeepers who worked there.

he would. At first they laughed at him, called him a little liar, a braggart, but that only egged him on. What piqued him most was that these boys of fifteen turned up their noses at him too superciliously, and were at first disposed to treat him as "a small boy," not fit to associate with them, and that was an unendurable insult. And so it was resolved to go in the evening, half a mile from the station, so that the train might have time to get up full speed after leaving the station. The boys assembled. It was a pitch dark night without a moon. At the time fixed, Kolya lay down between the rails. The five others who had taken the bet waited among the bushes below the embankment, their hearts beating with suspense, which was followed by alarm and remorse. At last they heard in the distance the rumble of the train leaving the station. Two red lights gleamed out of the darkness; the monster roared as it approached.

"Run, run away from the rails," the boys cried to Kolya from the bushes, breathless with terror. But it was too late: the train darted up and flew past. The boys rushed to Kolya. He lay without moving. They began pulling at him, lifting him up. He suddenly got up from the roadbed and walked away without a word. Then he explained that he had lain there as though he were insensible to frighten them, but the fact was that he really had lost consciousness, as he confessed long after to his mother. In this way his reputation as "a desperate character" was established forever. He returned home to the station as white as a sheet. Next day he had a slight attack of nervous fever, but he was in high spirits and well pleased with himself. The incident did not become known at once, but when they came back to the town it penetrated to the school and even reached the ears of the masters. But then Kolya's mother hastened to entreat the masters on her boy's behalf, and in the end Dardanelov, a respected and influential teacher, exerted himself in his favor, and the affair was ignored. Dardanelov was a bachelor, not yet an old man, who had been passionately in love with Mrs. Krasotkina for many years past, and had once already, about a year previously, ventured, trembling with fear and the delicacy of his sentiments, to offer her most respectfully his hand in marriage. But she refused him resolutely, feeling that to accept him would be an act of treachery to her son, though Dardanelov had, to judge from certain mysterious symptoms, reason for believing that he was not an object of aversion to the charming but too chaste and tenderhearted widow. Kolya's mad prank seemed to have broken the ice, and Dardanelov was rewarded for his intercession by a suggestion of hope. The suggestion, it is true, was a faint one, but then Dardanelov was such a paragon of purity and delicacy that it was enough for the time being to make him perfectly happy. He was fond of the boy, though he would have felt it beneath him to try and win him over, and was severe and strict with him in class. Kolya, too, kept him at a respectful distance. He learned his lessons perfectly; he was second in his class, was reserved with Dardanelov, and the whole class firmly believed that Kolya was so good at universal history that he could "beat" even Dardanelov. Kolya did indeed ask him the question, "Who founded Troy?" to which Dardanelov had made a very vague reply, referring to the movements and migrations of races, to the remoteness of the period, to the mythical legends. But the question, "Who had founded Troy?" that is, what individuals, he could not answer, and even for some reason regarded the question as idle and frivolous. But the boys remained convinced that Dardanelov did not know who founded Troy. Kolya had read of the founders of Troy in Smaragdov, whose history was among the books in his father's bookcase. In the end all the boys became interested in the question, who it was that had founded Troy, but Krasotkin would not tell his secret, and his reputation for knowledge remained unshaken.

After the incident on the railway a certain change came over Kolya's attitude to his mother. When Anna Fyodorovna (the widow Krasotkina) heard of her son's exploit, she almost went out of her mind with horror. She had such terrible attacks of hysterics, lasting with intervals for several days, that Kolya, seriously alarmed at last, promised on his honor that such pranks should never be repeated. He swore on his knees before the holy icon, and swore by the memory of his father, at Mrs. Krasotkina's instance, and the "manly" Kolya burst into tears like a boy of six, from "feelings." And all that day the mother and son were constantly rushing into each other's arms sobbing. Next day Kolya woke up as "unfeeling" as before, but he had become more silent, more modest, sterner, and more thoughtful. Six weeks later, it is true, he got into another scrape, which even brought his name to the ears of our justice of the peace, but it was a scrape of quite another kind, amusing, foolish, and he did not, as it turned out, take the leading part in it, but was only implicated in it. But of this later. His mother still fretted and trembled, but the more uneasy she became, the greater were the hopes of Dardanelov. It must be noted that Kolya understood and divined what was in Dardanelov's heart and, of course, despised him profoundly for his "feelings"; he had in the past been so tactless as to show this contempt before his mother, hinting vaguely that he knew what Dardanelov was after. But from the time of the railway incident his behavior in this respect also was changed; he did not allow himself the remotest allusion to the subject and began to speak more respectfully of Dardanelov before his mother, which the sensitive woman at once appreciated with boundless gratitude. But at the slightest mention of Dardanelov by a visitor in Kolya's presence, she would flush as pink as a rose from shame. At such moments Kolya would either stare out of the window scowling, or would investigate the state of his boots, or would shout angrily for "Perezvon,"[5] the big, shaggy, mangy dog, which he had picked up a month before, brought home, and kept for some reason secretly indoors, not showing him to any of his schoolfellows. He bullied him frightfully, teaching him all sorts of tricks, so that the poor dog howled for him whenever he was absent at school, and when he came in, whined with delight, rushed about as if he were crazy, begged, lay down on the ground pretending to be dead, and so on; in fact, showed all the tricks he had taught him, not at the word of command, but simply from the zeal of his excited and grateful heart.

I have forgotten, by the way, to mention that Kolya Krasotkin was the boy stabbed in the thigh with a penknife by the boy already known to the reader as the son of Captain Snegiryov. Ilyusha had been defending his father when the schoolboys jeered at him, shouting the nickname of "wisp of tow."

---

5. The term *perezvon* refers to chime- or bell-ringing for Orthodox services.

Chapter II

Children

And so on that frosty, snowy, and windy morning in November, the boy Kolya Krasotkin was sitting at home. It was Sunday and there was no school. It had just struck eleven, and he particularly wanted to go out "on very urgent business," but he was left alone in charge of the house, for it so happened that all its elder inmates were absent owing to a sudden and singular event. Mrs. Krasotkina had let two little rooms, separated from the rest of the house by a passage, to a doctor's wife with her two small children. This lady was the same age as Anna Fyodorovna, and a great friend of hers. Her husband, the doctor, had left a year before, going first to Orenburg and then to Tashkent[6] and for the last six months she had not heard a word from him. Had it not been for her friendship with Mrs. Krasotkina, which was some consolation to the forsaken lady, she would certainly have completely dissolved away in tears. And now, to add to her misfortunes, Katerina, her only servant, was suddenly moved the evening before to announce, to her mistress's amazement, that she proposed to bring a child into the world before morning. It seemed almost miraculous to everyone that no one had noticed the probability of it before. The astounded doctor's wife decided to move Katerina while there was still time to an establishment in the town kept by a midwife for such emergencies. As she set great store by her servant, she promptly carried out this plan and remained there looking after her. By the morning all Mrs. Krasotkina's friendly sympathy and energy were called upon to render assistance and appeal to someone for help in the case. So both the ladies were absent from home, the Krasotkins' servant, Agatha, had gone out to the market, and Kolya was thus left for a time to protect and look after the "kids," that is, the son and daughter of the doctor's wife, who were left alone. Kolya was not afraid of taking care of the house, besides he had Perezvon, who had been told to lie down without moving, under the bench in the hall. Every time Kolya, walking to and fro through the rooms, came into the hall, the dog shook his head and gave two loud and insinuating taps on the floor with his tail, but alas! the whistle did not sound to release him. Kolya looked sternly at the luckless dog, who relapsed again into obedient rigidity. The one thing that troubled Kolya was "the kids." He looked, of course, with the utmost scorn on Katerina's unexpected adventure, but he was very fond of the bereaved "kiddies," and had already taken them a picture book. Nastya, the elder, a girl of eight, could read, and Kostya, the boy, aged seven, was very fond of being read to by her. Krasotkin could, of course, have provided more diverting entertainment for them. He could have made them stand side by side and played soldiers with them, or send them hiding all over the house. He had done so more than once before and was not above doing it, so much so that a report once spread at school that Krasotkin played horses with the little lodgers

---

6. Orenburg is a city southeast of Moscow on the Ural river, near present-day Kazakhstan. Tashkent, now the capital of Uzbekistan, was militarily annexed to the Russian Empire in 1865 and became the capital of Russian Turkistan.

at home, prancing with his head on one side like a trace horse. But Krasotkin haughtily parried this thrust, pointing out that to play horses with boys of one's own age, boys of thirteen, would certainly be disgraceful "these days," but, that he did it for the sake of "the kids" because he liked them, and no one had a right to call him to account for his feelings. The two "kids" adored him. But on this occasion he was in no mood for games. He had very important business of his own before him, something almost mysterious. Meanwhile time was passing and Agatha, with whom he could have left the children, would not come back from market. He had several times already crossed the hall, opened the door of the lodgers' room and looked anxiously at the kids who were sitting over the book, as he had bidden them. Every time he opened the door they grinned at him, hoping he would come in and would do something delightful and amusing. But Kolya was preoccupied and did not go in. At last it struck eleven and he made up his mind, once for all, that if that "damned" Agatha did not come back within ten minutes he would go out without waiting for her, making the "kids" promise, of course, to be brave when he was away, not to be naughty, not to cry from fright. With this idea he put on his padded winter overcoat with its catskin fur collar, slung his satchel round his shoulder, and, regardless of his mother's constantly reiterated entreaties that he always put on galoshes in such cold weather, he looked at them contemptuously as he crossed the hall and went out with only his boots on. Perezvon, seeing him in his outdoor clothes, began tapping vigorously on the floor with his tail, nervously. Twitching all over, he even uttered a plaintive whine. But Kolya, seeing his dog's passionate excitement, decided that it was a breach of discipline, kept him for another minute under the bench, and only when he had opened the door into the hall did he whistle for him. The dog leaped up like a mad creature and rushed bounding before him rapturously. Kolya opened the door to peep at the "kids." They were both sitting as before at the table, not reading but warmly disputing about something. The children often argued together about various exciting problems of life, and Nastya, being the elder, always got the best of it. If Kostya did not agree with her, he almost always appealed to Kolya Krasotkin, and his verdict was regarded as infallible by both of them. This time the kids' discussion rather interested Krasotkin, and he stood still in the hall to listen. The children saw he was listening and that made them dispute with even greater energy.

"I shall never, never believe," Nastya prattled, "that the old women find babies among the cabbages in the kitchen garden. It's winter now and there are no cabbages, and so the old woman couldn't have taken Katerina a daughter."

"Whew!" Kolya whistled to himself.

"Or perhaps they do bring babies from somewhere, but only to those who are married."

Kostya stared at Nastya and listened, pondering profoundly.

"Nastya, how silly you are," he said at last, firmly and calmly. "How can Katerina have a baby when she isn't married?"

Nastya was exasperated.

"You know nothing about it," she snapped irritably. "Perhaps she has a husband, only he is in prison, so now she's got a baby."

"But is her husband in prison?" the matter-of-fact Kostya inquired gravely.

"Or, I tell you what," Nastya interrupted impulsively, completely rejecting and forgetting her first hypothesis. "She has no husband, you are right there, but she wants to be married, and so she's been thinking of getting married, and thinking and thinking of it till now she's got it, that is, not a husband but a baby."

"Well, perhaps so," Kostya agreed, entirely vanquished. "But you didn't say so before. So how could I tell?"

"Come, kiddies," said Kolya, stepping into the room. "You're terrible people, I see."

"And Perezvon with you!" grinned Kostya, and began snapping his fingers and calling Perezvon.

"I am in a difficulty, kids," Krasotkin began solemnly, "and you must help me. Agatha must have broken her leg, since she has not turned up till now, that's certain. I must go out. Will you let me go?"

The children looked anxiously at one another. Their smiling faces showed signs of uneasiness, but they did not yet fully grasp what was expected of them.

"You won't be naughty while I am gone? You won't climb on the cupboard and break your legs? You won't be frightened alone and cry?"

A look of profound despondency came into the children's faces.

"And I could show you something as a reward, a little copper cannon which can be fired with real gunpowder."

The children's faces instantly brightened. "Show us the cannon," said Kostya, beaming all over.

Krasotkin put his hand in his satchel, and pulling out a little bronze cannon stood it on the table.

"Ah, you are bound to ask that! Look, it's on wheels." He rolled the toy along on the table. "And it can be fired off, too. It can be loaded with shot and fired off."

"And could it kill anyone?"

"It can kill anyone; you've only got to aim at anybody," and Krasotkin explained where the powder had to be put, where the shot should be rolled in, showed a tiny hole like a touch hole, and told them that it recoiled when it was fired. The children listened with intense interest. What particularly struck their imagination was that the cannon recoiled.

"And have you got any powder?" Nastya inquired.

"Yes."

"Show us the powder, too," she drawled with a smile of entreaty.

Krasotkin dived again into his satchel and pulled out a small flask containing a little real gunpowder. He had some shot, too, in a folded piece of paper. He even uncorked the flask and shook a little powder into the palm of his hand.

"One has to be careful there's no fire about, or it would blow up and kill us all,' Krasotkin warned them sensationally.

The children gazed at the powder with an awestricken alarm that only intensified their enjoyment. But Kostya liked the shot better.

"And does the shot burn?" he inquired.

"No, it doesn't."

"Give me a little shot," he asked in an imploring voice.

"I'll give you a little shot; here, take it, but don't show it to your mother till I come back, or she'll be sure to think it's gunpowder, and will die of fright and give you a thrashing."

"Mother never does whip us," Nastya observed at once.

"I know, I only said it for the beauty of style. And don't you ever deceive your mother except just this once, until I come back. And so, kiddies, can I go out? You won't be frightened and cry when I'm gone?"

"We sha-all cry," drawled Kostya, on the verge of tears already.

"We shall cry, we shall be sure to cry," Nastya chimed in with timid haste.

"Oh, children, children, how fraught with peril are your years![7] There's no help for it, chickens, I shall have to stay with you I don't know how long. And time is passing, time is passing, oogh!"

"Tell Perezvon to pretend to be dead!" Kostya begged.

"There's no help for it, we must have recourse to Perezvon. *Ici,*[8] Perezvon." And Kolya began giving orders to the dog, who performed all his tricks. He was a rough-haired dog, of medium size, with a coat of a sort of lilac gray color. He was blind in his right eye, and his left ear was torn. He whined and jumped, stood and walked on his hind legs, lay on his back with his paws in the air, rigid as though he were dead. While this last performance was going on, the door was opened and Agatha, Mrs. Krasotkina's servant, a stout woman of forty, marked with smallpox, appeared in the doorway. She had come back from market and had a bag full of provisions in her hand. Holding up the bag of provisions in her left hand she stood still to watch the dog. Though Kolya had been so anxious for her return, he did not cut short the performance, and after keeping Perezvon dead for the appropriate time, at last he whistled to him. The dog jumped up and began bounding about in his joy at having done his duty.

"Only think, a dog!" Agatha observed sententiously.

"Why are you late, female?" asked Krasotkin sternly.

"Female, indeed! Go on with you, you brat."

"Brat?"

"Yes, a brat. What is it to you if I'm late; if I'm late, you may be sure I have good reason," muttered Agatha, busying herself about the stove, without a trace of anger or displeasure in her voice. She seemed quite pleased, in fact, to enjoy a skirmish with her merry young master.

"Listen, you frivolous old woman," Krasotkin began, getting up from the sofa, "can you swear by all you hold sacred in the world and something else besides, that you will watch vigilantly over the kids in my absence? I am going out."

"And what am I going to swear for?" laughed Agatha. "I shall look after them without that."

"No, you must swear on your eternal salvation. Else I won't go."

"Well, don't then. What does it matter to me? It's cold out; stay at home."

"Kids," Kolya turned to the children, "this woman will stay with you till I come back or till your mother comes, for she ought to have been back

7. The opening words of a fable by Ivan Dmitryev (1760–1837), "The Rooster, the Cat, and the Little Mouse" (1802).
8. "Here" (French).

long ago. She will give you some lunch, too. You'll give them something, Agatha, won't you?"

"That I can do."

"Good-bye, chickens, I go with my heart at rest. And you, granny," he added gravely, in an undertone, as he passed Agatha, "I hope you'll spare their tender years and not tell them any of your old woman's nonsense about Katerina. *Ici,* Perezvon!"

"Get along with you!" retorted Agatha, really angry this time. "Ridiculous boy! You want a whipping for saying such things, that's what you want!"

Chapter III
The Schoolboy

But Kolya did not hear her. At last he could go out. As he went out at the gate he looked round him, shrugged up his shoulders, and saying "It is freezing," went straight along the street and turned off to the right towards the marketplace. When he reached the last house but one before the marketplace he stopped at the gate, pulled a whistle out of his pocket, and whistled with all his might as though giving a signal. He did not have to wait more than a minute before a rosy-cheeked boy of about eleven, wearing a warm, neat, and even stylish coat, darted out to meet him. This was Smurov, a boy in the preparatory class (two classes below Kolya Krasotkin), son of a well-to-do official. Apparently he was forbidden by his parents to associate with Krasotkin, who was well known to be a desperately naughty boy, so Smurov was obviously slipping out on the sly. He was—if the reader has not forgotten—one of the group of boys who two months before had thrown stones at Ilyusha. He was the one who told Alyosha Karamazov about Ilyusha.

"I've been waiting for you for the last hour, Krasotkin," said Smurov stolidly, and the boys strode towards the marketplace.

"I am late," answered Krasotkin, "I was detained by circumstances. You won't be thrashed for coming with me?"

"Well, really! I'm never thrashed! And you've got Perezvon with you?"

"Yes."

"You're taking him, too?"

"Yes."

"Ah! if it were only Zhuchka!"

"That's impossible. Zhuchka doesn't exist. Zhuchka is lost in the mists of obscurity."

"Ah! couldn't we do this?" Smurov suddenly stood still. "You see Ilyusha says that Zhuchka was a shaggy, grayish, smoky-looking dog like Perezvon. Couldn't you tell him this is Zhuchka, and he might believe you?"

"Boy, shun a lie, that's one thing; even with a good object—that's another. Above all, I hope you've not told them anything about my coming."

"Heaven forbid! I know what I am about. But you won't comfort him with Perezvon," said Smurov, with a sigh. "You know his father, the captain, 'the wisp of tow,' told us that he was going to bring him a real mastiff pup, with a black nose, today. He thinks that would comfort Ilyusha; but I doubt it."

"And how is Ilyusha?"

"Ah, he is bad, very bad! I believe he has consumption: he is quite conscious, but his breathing! His breathing's gone wrong. The other day he asked to have his boots on to be led round the room. He tried to walk, but he couldn't stand. 'Ah, I told you before, father,' he said, 'that those boots were no good. I could never walk properly in them.' He fancied it was his boots that made him stagger, but it was simply weakness, really. He won't live another week. Herzenstube is looking after him. Now they are rich again—they've got heaps of money."

"They are rogues."

"Who are rogues?"

"Doctors and the whole crew of quacks collectively, and also, of course, individually. I reject medicine. It's a useless institution. I mean to go into all that. But what's that sentimentality you've got up there? The whole class seems to be there every day?"

"Not the whole class: it's only about ten of us who go to see him every day. There's nothing in that."

"What I don't understand in all this is the part that Alexey Karamazov is taking in it. His brother's going to be tried tomorrow or next day for such a crime, and yet he has so much time to spend on sentimentality with boys."

"There's no sentimentality about it. You are going yourself now to make it up with Ilyusha."

"Make it up with him? What an absurd expression! But I allow no one to analyze my actions."

"And how pleased Ilyusha will be to see you! He has no idea that you are coming. Why was it, why was it you wouldn't come all this time?" Smurov cried with sudden warmth.

"My dear boy, that's my business, not yours. I am going on my own because I choose to, but you've all been hauled there by Alexey Karamazov—there's a difference, you know. And how do you know? I may not be going to make it up at all. It's a stupid expression."

"It's not Karamazov at all; it's not his doing. Our fellows began going there of themselves. Of course, they went with Karamazov at first. And there's been nothing of that sort—no silliness. First one went, and then another. His father was awfully pleased to see us. You know he will simply go out of his mind if Ilyusha dies. He sees that Ilyusha's dying. And he seems so glad we've made it up with Ilyusha. Ilyusha asked after you, that was all. He just asks and says no more. His father will go out of his mind or hang himself. He behaved like a madman before. You know he is a very decent man. We made a mistake then. It's all the fault of that parricide who beat him then."

"Karamazov's a riddle to me all the same. I might have made his acquaintance long ago, but I like to be aloof in some cases. Besides, I have a theory about him which I must work out and verify."

Kolya subsided into dignified silence. Smurov, too, was silent. Smurov, of course, worshipped Krasotkin and never dreamed of putting himself on a level with him. Now he was tremendously interested at Kolya's saying that he was "going of himself" to see Ilyusha. He felt that there must be some mystery in Kolya's suddenly taking it into his head to go to see him that day. They crossed the marketplace, in which at that hour were many loaded wagons from the country and a great number of live fowls. The market women were selling rolls, cottons and thread, etc., in their booths. These Sunday markets were naïvely called "fairs" in the town, and there were many such fairs during the year. Perezvon ran about in the wildest spirits, sniffing about first on one side, then the other. When he met other dogs they zealously smelled each other over according to the rules of canine etiquette.

"I like to watch such realism, Smurov," said Kolya suddenly. "Have you noticed how dogs sniff at one another when they meet? It seems to be a law of their nature."

"Yes; it's a funny habit."

"No, it's not funny; you are wrong there. There's nothing funny in nature, however funny it may seem to man with his prejudices. If dogs could reason and criticize us they'd be sure to find just as much that would be funny to them, if not far more, in the social relations of men, their masters—far more, indeed. I repeat that, because I am convinced that there is far more foolishness among us. That's Rakitin's idea—a remarkable idea. I am a Socialist, Smurov."

"And what is a Socialist?" asked Smurov.

"That's when all are equal and all have property in common, there are no marriages, and everyone has any religion and laws he likes best,[9] and all the rest of it. You are not old enough to understand yet. It's cold, though."

"Yes, eight above. Father looked at the thermometer just now."

"Have you noticed, Smurov, that in the middle of winter we don't feel so cold even when it's zero as we do now, in the beginning of winter, when there is a sudden cold wave, eight above, especially when there is not much snow. It's because people are not used to it. Everything is habit with men, everything even in their social and political relations. Habit is the great motive power. What a funny-looking peasant!"

Kolya pointed to a tall peasant, with a good-natured countenance, in a long sheepskin coat, who was standing by his wagon, clapping together his hands, in their shapeless leather gloves, to warm them. His long fair beard was all white with frost.

"That peasant's beard's frozen," Kolya cried in a loud provocative voice as he passed him.

"Lots of people's beards are frozen," the peasant replied, calmly and sententiously.

"Don't provoke him," observed Smurov.

"It's all right; he won't be cross; he's a nice fellow. Good-bye, Matvey."

"Good-bye."

"Is your name Matvey?"

"Yes. Didn't you know?"

"No, I didn't. It was a guess."

"You don't say so! You are a schoolboy, I suppose?"

"Yes."

9. This may be a parodying allusion to a story cycle by Saltykov-Shchedrin, "Whatever Each Likes Best: Stories, Scenes, Reflections and Aphorisms" (*Kak komu ugodno. Rasskazi, stseny, razmyshleniia i aforizmy*), published in *The Contemporary* in 1863.

"You get whipped, I expect?"

"Nothing to speak of—sometimes."

"Does it hurt?"

"Well, yes, it does."

"Ech, what a life!" The peasant heaved a sigh from the bottom of his heart.

"Good-bye, Matvey."

"Good-bye. You are a nice lad, that you are."

The boys went on.

"That was a nice peasant," Kolya observed to Smurov. "I like talking to the peasants, and am always glad to do them justice."

"Why did you tell a lie, pretending we are thrashed?" asked Smurov.

"I had to say that to please him."

"How do you mean?"

"You know, Smurov, I don't like being asked the same thing twice. I like people to understand at the first word. Some things can't be explained. According to a peasant's notions, schoolboys are whipped, and must be whipped. What would a schoolboy be, if he were not whipped? And if I were to tell him we are not, he'd be disappointed. But you don't understand that. One has to know how to talk to the peasants."

"Only don't tease them, please, or you'll get into another scrape as you did about that goose."

"So you're afraid?"

"Don't laugh, Kolya. Of course, I'm afraid. My father would be awfully cross. I am strictly forbidden to go out with you."

"Don't be uneasy, nothing will happen this time. Hullo, Natasha!" he shouted to a market woman in one of the booths.

"Call me Natasha! What next! My name is Marya," the middle-aged market woman shouted at him.

"I am so glad it's Marya. Good-bye!"

"Ah, you young rascal! A brat like you to carry on so!"

"I'm in a hurry. I can't stay now. You shall tell me next Sunday." Kolya waved his hand at her, as though she had attacked him and not he her.

"I've nothing to tell you next Sunday. You set upon me, you impudent thing. I didn't say anything," bawled Marya. "You want a whipping, that's what you want, you saucy jackanapes!"

There was a roar of laughter among the other market women round her. Suddenly a man in a violent rage darted out from the arcade of shops close by. He was a young man, not a native of the town, with dark, curly hair and a long, pale face, marked with smallpox. He wore a long blue coat and a peaked cap, and looked like a merchant's clerk. He was in a state of stupid excitement and brandished his fist at Kolya.

"I know you," he cried angrily, "I know you!"

Kolya stared at him. He could not recall when he could have had a row with the man. But he had been in so many rows on the street that he could hardly remember them all.

"Do you?" he asked sarcastically.

"I know you! I know you!" the man repeated idiotically.

"So much the better for you. Well, it's time I was going. Good-bye!"

"You are at your saucy pranks again?" cried the man. "You are at your saucy pranks again? I know, you are at it again!"

"It's not your business, brother, if I am at my saucy pranks again," said Kolya, standing still and scanning him.

"Not my business?"

"No; it's not your business."

"Whose then? Whose then? Whose then?"

"It's Trifon Nikitich's business now, not yours."

"What Trifon Nikitich?" asked the youth, staring with loutish amazement at Kolya, but still angry as ever.

"Have you been to the Church of the Ascension?" he suddenly asked him, with stern emphasis.

"What Church of Ascension? What for? No, I haven't," said the young man, somewhat taken aback.

"Do you know Sabaneyev?" Kolya went on even more emphatically and even more severely.

"What Sabaneyev? No, I don't know him."

"Well, then you can go to the devil," said Kolya, cutting short the conversation, and turning sharply to the right he strode quickly on his way as though he disdained further conversation with a dolt who did not even know Sabaneyev.

"Stop, hey! What Sabaneyev?" the young man recovered from his momentary stupefaction and was as excited as before. "What did he say?" He turned to the market women with a silly stare.

The women laughed.

"You can never tell what he's after," said one of them.

"What Sabaneyev is it he's talking about?" the young man repeated, still furious and brandishing his right arm.

"It must be a Sabeneyev who worked for the Kuzmichovs, that's who it must be," one of the women suggested.

The young man stared at her wildly.

"For the Kuzmichovs?" repeated another woman. "But his name wasn't Trifon. His name's Kuzma, not Trifon; but the boy said Trifon Nikitich, so it can't be the same."

"His name is not Trifon and not Sabaneyev, it's Chizhov," put in suddenly a third woman, who had hitherto been silent, listening gravely. "Alexey Ivanich is his name. Chizhov, Alexey Ivanich."

"Not a doubt about it, it's Chizhov," a fourth woman emphatically confirmed the statement.

The bewildered youth gazed from one to another.

"But what did he ask for, what did he ask for, good people?" he cried almost in desperation. "'Do you know Sabaneyev?' says he. And who the devil's to know who is Sabaneyev?"

"You're a senseless fellow. I tell you it's not Sabaneyev, but Chizhov, Alexey Ivanich Chizhov, that's who it is!" one of the women shouted at him impressively.

"What Chizhov? Who is he? Tell me, if you know."

"That tall, sniveling fellow who used to sit in the market in the summer."

"And what's your Chizhov to do with me, good people, eh?"

"How can I tell what he's to do with you?" put in another. "You ought to know yourself what you want with him, if you make such a clamor about him. He spoke to you, he did not speak to us, you stupid. Don't you really know him?"

"Know whom?"

"Chizhov."

"The devil take Chizhov and you with him. I'll give him a hiding, that I will. He was laughing at me!"

"Will give Chizhov a hiding! More likely he will give you one. You are a fool, that's what you are!"

"Not Chizhov, not Chizhov, you spiteful, mischievous woman. I'll give the boy a hiding. Catch him, catch him, he was laughing at me!"

The women guffawed. But Kolya was by now a long long way off, marching along with a triumphant air. Smurov walked beside him, looking round at the shouting group far behind. He, too, was in high spirits, though he was still afraid of getting into some scrape in Kolya's company.

"What Sabaneyev did you mean?" he asked Kolya, foreseeing what his answer would be.

"How do I know? Now there'll be a hubbub among them all day. I like to stir up fools in every class of society. There's another blockhead, that peasant there. You know, they say 'there's no one stupider than a stupid Frenchman,' but a stupid Russian shows it in his face just as much. Can't you see it all over his face that he is a fool, that peasant, eh?"

"Let him alone, Kolya. Let's go on."

"Nothing could stop me, now I am once off. Hey, good morning, peasant!"

A sturdy-looking peasant, with a round, simple face, and grizzled beard, who was walking by, raised his head and looked at the boy. He seemed not quite sober.

"Good morning, if you are not laughing at me," he said deliberately in reply.

"And if I am?" laughed Kolya.

"Well, a joke's a joke. Laugh away. I don't mind. There's no harm in a joke."

"I beg your pardon, brother, it was a joke."

"Well, God forgive you!"

"Do you forgive me, too?"

"I quite forgive you. Go along."

"I say, you seem a clever peasant."

"Cleverer than you," the peasant answered unexpectedly with the same gravity.

"I doubt it," said Kolya, somewhat taken aback.

"It's true though."

"Perhaps it is."

"It is, brother."

"Good-bye, peasant!"

"Good-bye!"

"There are all sorts of peasants," Kolya observed to Smurov, after a brief silence. "How could I tell I had hit on a clever one? I am always ready to recognize intelligence in the peasantry."

In the distance the cathedral clock struck half past eleven. The boys made haste and they walked as far as Captain Snegiryov's lodging, a considerable distance, quickly and almost in silence. Twenty paces from the house Kolya stopped and told Smurov to go on ahead and ask Karamazov to come out to him.

"One must sniff round a bit first," he observed to Smurov.

"Why ask him to come out?" Smurov protested. "You go in; they will be awfully glad to see you. What's the sense of getting acquainted in the frost out here?"

"I know why I want to see him out here in the frost," Kolya cut him short in the despotic tone he was fond of adopting with "small boys," and Smurov ran to do his bidding.

Chapter IV

Zhuchka

Kolya leaned against the fence with an air of dignity, waiting for Alyosha to appear. Yes, he had long wanted to meet him. He had heard a great deal about him from the boys, but hitherto he had always maintained an appearance of disdainful indifference when he was mentioned, and he had even "criticized" what he heard about Alyosha. But secretly he had a great longing to make his acquaintance; there was something sympathetic and attractive in all he was told about Alyosha. So the present moment was important: to begin with, he had to show himself at his best, to show his independence. "Or, he'll think of me as thirteen and take me for a boy, like the rest of them. And what are these boys to him? I shall ask him when I get to know him. It's a pity I am so short, though. Tuzikov is younger than I am, yet he is half a head taller. But I have an intelligent face. I am not good-looking. I know I'm hideous, but I have an intelligent face. I mustn't talk too freely; if I fall into his arms all at once, he may think . . . Tfoo! how horrible if he should think . . . !"

Such were the thoughts that excited Kolya while he was doing his utmost to assume the most independent air. What distressed him most was his being so short; he did not mind so much his "hideous" face, as being so short. On the wall in a corner at home he had the year before made a pencil mark to show his height, and every two months since, he anxiously measured himself against it to see how much he had gained. But, alas! he grew very slowly, and this sometimes reduced him almost to despair. His face was in reality by no means "hideous"; on the contrary, it was rather attractive, with a fair, pale skin, freckled. His small, lively gray eyes had a fearless look, and often glowed with feeling. He had rather high cheekbones; small, very red, but not very thick, lips; his nose was small and unmistakably turned up. "I've a regular pug nose, a regular pug nose," Kolya used to mutter to himself when he looked in the mirror, and he always left it with indignation. "But perhaps I haven't got an intelligent face?" he sometimes thought, doubtful even of that. But it must not be supposed that his mind was preoccupied with his face and his height. On the contrary, however bitter the moments before the mirror were to him, he quickly forgot them, and forgot them for a long time, "abandoning himself entirely to ideas and to real life," as he formulated his activities to himself.

Alyosha came out quickly and hastened up to Kolya. Before he reached him, Kolya could see that his face was somehow quite joyful. "Can he be so glad to see me?" Kolya wondered, feeling pleased. We may note here, in passing, that Alyosha's appearance had undergone a complete change

since we saw him last. He had abandoned his cassock and was now wearing a well-cut coat and a soft, round hat, and his hair had been cropped
short. All this was very becoming to him, and he looked quite handsome.
His charming face always had a good-humored expression; but there was
a gentleness and serenity in his good humor. To Kolya's surprise, Alyosha
came out to him just as he was, without an overcoat. He had evidently
come in haste. He held out his hand to Kolya at once.

"Here you are at last! How anxious we've been to see you!"

"There were reasons which you shall know directly. Anyway, I am glad
to make your acquaintance. I've long been hoping for an opportunity, and
have heard a great deal about you," Kolya muttered, a little breathless.

"We should have met anyway. I've heard a great deal about you, too;
but you've been a long time coming here."

"Tell me, how are things going?"

"Ilyusha is very ill. He is certainly dying."

"How awful! You must admit that medicine is a fraud, Karamazov," cried
Kolya warmly.

"Ilyusha has mentioned you often, very often, even in his sleep, in
delirium, you know. One can see that you used to be very, very dear to
him . . . before the incident . . . with the knife. . . . Then there's another
reason. . . . Tell me, is that your dog?"

"Yes, Perezvon."

"Not Zhuchka?" Alyosha looked at Kolya with eyes full of pity. "Is she
lost forever?"

"I know you would all like it to be Zhuchka. I've heard all about it."
Kolya smiled mysteriously. "Listen, Karamazov, I'll tell you all about it.
That's what I came for; that's what I asked you to come out here for, to
explain the whole episode to you before we go in," he began with animation. "You see, Karamazov, Ilyusha came into the preparatory class last
spring. Well, you know what our preparatory class is—a lot of small boys.
They began teasing Ilyusha at once. I am two classes higher up, and, of
course, I only look on at them from a distance. I saw the boy was weak and
small, but he wouldn't give in to them; he fought with them. I saw he was
proud, and his eyes were full of fire. I like children like that. And they
teased him all the more. The worst of it was he was horribly dressed at the
time, his breeches were too small for him, and there were holes in his
boots. They teased him about it; they jeered at him. That I can't stand. I
stood up for him at once, and gave it to them hot. I beat them, but they
adore me, do you know, Karamazov?" Kolya boasted impulsively; "but I am
always fond of children. I've two chickens on my hands at home now—
that's what detained me today. So they stopped beating Ilyusha and I took
him under my protection. I saw the boy was proud. I tell you that, the boy
was proud; but in the end he became slavishly devoted to me: he did my
slightest bidding, obeyed me as though I were God, tried to copy me. In
the intervals between the classes he used to run to me at once, and I'd go
about with him. On Sundays, too. They always laugh when an older boy
makes friends with a younger one like that; but that's a prejudice. If it's my
fancy, that's enough. I am teaching him, developing him. Why shouldn't I
develop him if I like him? Here you, Karamazov, have taken up with all
these nestlings. I see you want to influence the younger generation—to
develop them, to be of use to them, and I assure you this trait in your

character, which I knew by hearsay, attracted me more than anything. Let us get to the point, though. I noticed that there was a sort of softness and sentimentality coming over the boy, and you know I have a positive hatred of this sheepish sentimentality, and I have had it since birth. There were contradictions in him, too: he was proud, but he was slavishly devoted to me, and yet all at once his eyes would flash and he'd refuse to agree with me; he'd argue, fly into a rage. I used sometimes to propound certain ideas; I could see that it was not so much that he disagreed with the ideas, but that he was simply rebelling against me, because I was cool in responding to his endearments. And so, in order to train him properly, the tenderer he was, the colder I became. I did it on purpose: that was my idea. My object was to form his character, to lick him into shape, to make a man of him . . . and besides . . . no doubt, you understand me at a word. Suddenly I noticed for three days in succession he was downcast and dejected, not because of my coldness, but for something else, something more important. I wondered what the tragedy was. I have pumped him and found out that he had somehow got to know Smerdyakov, who was lackey to your late father—it was before his death, of course—and he taught the little fool a silly trick—that is, a brutal, nasty trick. He told him to take a piece of bread, to stick a pin in it, and throw it to one of those hungry dogs who snap up anything without biting it, and then to watch and see what would happen. So they prepared a piece of bread like that and threw it to Zhuchka, that shaggy dog there's been such a fuss about. The people of the house it belonged to never fed it at all, though it barked all day. (Do you like that stupid barking, Karamazov? I can't stand it.) So it rushed at the bread, swallowed it, and began to squeal; it turned round and round and ran away, squealing as it ran out of sight. That was Ilyusha's own account of it. He confessed it to me, and cried bitterly. He hugged me, shaking all over. He kept on repeating 'He ran away squealing': the sight of that haunted him. He was tormented by remorse, I could see that. I took it seriously. I determined to give him a lesson for other things as well. So I must confess I wasn't quite straightforward, and pretended to be more indignant perhaps than I was. 'You've done a nasty thing,' I said, 'you are a scoundrel. I won't tell anyone, of course, but I shall have nothing more to do with you for awhile. I'll think it over and let you know through Smurov' (that's the boy who's just come with me; he's always ready to do anything for me) 'whether I will have anything to do with you in the future or whether I give you up for good as a scoundrel.' He was tremendously upset. I must confess I felt I'd gone too far as I spoke, but there was no help for it. I did what I thought best at the time. A day or two after, I sent Smurov to tell him that I would not speak to him again. That's what we call it when two schoolfellows refuse to have anything more to do with one another. Secretly I only meant to give him the silent treatment for a few days and then, if I saw signs of repentance, to hold out my hand to him again. That was my intention. But what do you think happened? He heard Smurov's message, his eyes suddenly flashed. "'Tell Krasotkin from me,' he cried, 'that I will throw bread with pins to all the dogs—all—all of them!' 'So he's got a little free spirit, we must smoke it out of him.' And I began to treat him with contempt; whenever I met him I turned away or smiled sarcastically. And just then that affair with his father happened. You remember the 'wisp of tow'? You must realize that he was fearfully worked up by what had happened already. The boys, seeing I'd given him up, set on him and taunted him, shouting, 'Wisp of tow, wisp of tow!' And he had soon regular skirmishes with them, which I am very sorry for. They seem to have given him one very bad beating. One day he flew at them all as they were coming out of school. I stood a few yards off, looking on. And, I swear, I don't remember that I laughed; it was quite the other way, I felt awfully sorry for him, in another minute I would have run up to take his part. But he suddenly met my eyes. I don't know what he imagined; but he pulled out a penknife, rushed at me, and struck at my thigh, here in my right leg. I didn't move. I don't mind confessing I am plucky sometimes, Karamazov. I simply looked at him contemptuously, as though to say, 'this is how you repay all my kindness! Do it again, if you like, I'm at your service.' But he didn't stab me again; he broke down, he was frightened at what he had done, he threw away the knife, burst out crying, and ran away. I did not snitch on him, of course, and I made them all keep quiet, so it wouldn't come to the ears of the masters. I didn't even tell my mother till it had healed up. And the wound was a mere scratch. And then I heard that the same day he'd been throwing stones and had bitten your finger—but you understand now what a state he was in! Well, it can't be helped: it was stupid of me not to come and forgive him—that is, to make it up with him—when he was taken ill. I am sorry for it now. But I had a special reason. So now I've told you all about it . . . but I'm afraid it was stupid of me."

"Oh, what a pity," exclaimed Alyosha, with feeling, "that I didn't know before what terms you were on with him, or I'd have come to you long ago to beg you to go to him with me. Would you believe it, when he was feverish he talked about you in delirium. I didn't know how much you were to him! And you've really not succeeded in finding that dog? His father and the boys have been hunting all over the town for it. Would you believe it, since he's been ill, I've three times heard him repeat with tears, 'It's because I killed Zhuchka, papa, that I am ill now. God is punishing me for it.' He can't get that idea out of his head. And if the dog were found and proved to be alive, then, perhaps, he might even be resurrected by joy. We have all rested our hopes on you."

"Tell me, what made you hope that I would be the one to find him?" Kolya asked, with great curiosity. "Why did you reckon on me rather than anyone else?"

"There was a report that you were looking for the dog, and that you would bring it when you'd found it. Smurov said something of the sort. We've all been trying to persuade Ilyusha that the dog is alive, that it's been seen. The boys brought him a live hare: he just looked at it, with a faint smile, and asked them to set it free in the fields. And so we did. His father has just this moment come back, bringing him a mastiff pup, hoping to comfort him with that; but I think it only makes it worse."

"Tell me, Karamazov, what sort of man is the father? I know him, but what do you make of him—a mountebank, a buffoon?"

"Oh, no; there are people of deep feeling who have been somehow crushed. Buffoonery in them is a form of resentful irony against those to whom they daren't speak the truth, from having been for years humiliated and intimidated by them. Believe me, Krasotkin, that sort of buffoonery is sometimes tragic in the extreme. His whole life now is centered on Ilyusha, and if Ilyusha dies, he will either go mad with grief, or kill himself. I feel almost certain of that when I look at him now."

"I understand you, Karamazov. I see you understand human nature," Kolya added, with feeling.

"And as soon as I saw you with a dog, I thought it was Zhuchka you were bringing."

"Wait a bit, Karamazov, perhaps we shall find it yet; but this is Perezvon. I'll let him go in now and perhaps it will amuse Ilyusha more than the mastiff pup. Wait a bit, Karamazov, you will know something in a minute. But, I say, I am keeping you here!" Kolya cried suddenly. "You have no overcoat on in this bitter cold. You see what an egoist I am. Oh, we are all egoists, Karamazov!"[1]

"Don't trouble; it is cold, but I don't often catch cold. Let us go in though, and, by the way, what is your name? I know you are called Kolya, but what else?"

"Nikolay—Nikolay Ivanovich Krasotkin, or, as they say in official documents 'Krasotkin son.'" Kolya laughed for some reason, but added suddenly. "Of course I hate my name Nikolay."

"Why so?"

"It's so trivial, so ordinary."

"You are thirteen?" asked Alyosha.

"No, fourteen—that is, I shall be fourteen very soon, in a couple of weeks. I'll confess one weakness of mine, Karamazov, just to you, since it's our first meeting, so that you may understand my character at once. I hate being asked my age, more than that . . . and in fact . . . there's a libelous story going around about me, that last week I played robbers with the preparatory boys. It's a fact that I did play with them, but it's a perfect libel to say I did it for my own amusement. I have reasons for believing that you've heard the story; but I wasn't playing for my own amusement, it was for the sake of the children, because they couldn't think of anything to do by themselves. But they've always got some silly tale. This is an awful town for gossip, I can tell you."

"But what if you had been playing for your own amusement, what's the harm?"

"Come, I say, for my own amusement! You don't play horsey, do you?"

"But you must look at it like this," said Alyosha, smiling. "Grown-up people go to the theater and there the adventures of all sorts of heroes are represented—sometimes there are robbers and battles, too—and isn't that just the same thing, in a different form, of course? And young people's games of soldiers or robbers in their playtime are also art in its first stage. You know, they spring from the growing artistic instincts of the young. And sometimes these games are much better than performances in the theater, the only difference is that people go there to look at actors, while in these games the young people are the actors themselves. But that's only natural."

"You think so? Is that your conviction?" Kolya looked at him intently. "Oh, you know, that's rather an interesting view. When I go home, I'll

---

1. The theory of rational egoism, developed by Chernyshevsky in his novel *What Is to be Done?*, posits that each individual inexorably pursues his self-interest. The theory was popular with the revolutionary-democratic youth and was one of Dostoevsky's favorite objects of satire.

think it over. I'll admit I thought I might learn something from you. I've come to learn of you, Karamazov," Kolya concluded, in a voice full of spontaneous feeling.

"And I of you," said Alyosha, smiling and pressing his hand.

Kolya was much pleased with Alyosha. What struck him most was that he treated him exactly like an equal and that he talked to him just as if he were "quite grown up."

"I'll show you a trick now, Karamazov, it's a theatrical performance, too," he said, laughing nervously. "That's why I've come."

"Let us go first to the people of the house, on the left. All the boys leave their coats in there, because the room is small and hot."

"Oh, I'm only coming in for a minute. I'll keep on my overcoat. Perezvon will stay here in the passage and be dead. *Ici*, Perezvon, lie down and be dead! You see how he's dead. I'll go in first and explore, then I'll whistle to him when I think fit, and you'll see, he'll dash in like mad. Only Smurov must not forget to open the door at the moment. I'll arrange it all and you'll see a trick . . ."

Chapter V

At Ilyusha's Bedside

The room inhabited by the family of the retired captain Snegiryov is already familiar to us. It was close and crowded at that moment with a number of visitors. Several boys were sitting with Ilyusha and, though all of them like Smurov were prepared to deny that it was Alyosha who had brought them and reconciled them with Ilyusha, it was really the fact. All the art he had used had been to take them, one by one, to Ilyusha, without "sheepish sentimentality," appearing to do so casually and without design. It was a great consolation to Ilyusha in his suffering. He was greatly touched by seeing the almost tender affection and sympathy shown him by these boys, who had been his enemies. Krasotkin was the only one missing and his absence was a heavy load on Ilyusha's heart. Perhaps the bitterest of all his bitter memories was his stabbing Krasotkin, who had been his one friend and protector. Clever little Smurov, who was the first to make up with Ilyusha, thought it was so. But when Smurov hinted to Krasotkin that Alyosha wanted to come and see him about something, the latter cut him short, bidding Smurov tell "Karamazov" at once that he knew best what to do, that he wanted no one's advice, and that, if he went to see Ilyusha, he would choose his own time, for he had "his own reasons." That was two weeks before this Sunday. That was why Alyosha had not been to see him, as he had meant to. But though he waited, he sent Smurov to him twice again. Both times Krasotkin met him with a curt, impatient refusal, sending Alyosha a message not to bother him any more, that if he came himself, he, Krasotkin, would not go to Ilyusha at all. Up to the very last day, Smurov did not know that Kolya meant to go to Ilyusha that morning, and only the evening before, as he parted from Smurov, Kolya abruptly told him to wait at home for him next morning, for he would go with him to the Snegiryovs', but warned him on no account to say he was coming, as he wanted to drop in casually. Smurov obeyed.

Smurov's fancy that Kolya would bring back the lost dog was based on the words Kolya had dropped that "they must be asses not to find the dog, if it were alive." When Smurov, waiting for an opportunity, timidly hinted at his guess about the dog, Krasotkin flew into a violent rage. "I'm not such an ass as to go hunting about the town for other people's dogs when I've got my own Perezvon! And how can you imagine a dog could be alive after swallowing a pin? Sheepish sentimentality, that's what it is!"

For the last two weeks Ilyusha had not left his little bed under the icons in the corner. He had not been to school since the day he met Alyosha and bit his finger. He was taken ill the same day, though for a month afterwards he was sometimes able to get up and walk about the room and hall. But lately he had become so weak that he could not move without help from his father. His father was terribly concerned about him. He even gave up drinking and was almost crazy with terror that his boy would die. And often, especially after leading him round the room on his arm and putting him back to bed, he would run to a dark corner in the hall and, leaning his head against the wall, he would break into paroxysms of violent weeping, stifling his sobs that they might not be heard by Ilyushechka.

Returning to the room, he would usually begin doing something to amuse and comfort his precious boy, he would tell him stories, funny anecdotes, or would mimic comic people he had happened to meet, even imitate the howls and cries of animals. But Ilyusha could not bear to see his father fooling and playing the buffoon. Though the boy tried not to show how he disliked it, he saw with an aching heart that his father was an object of contempt, and he was continually haunted by the memory of the "wisp of tow" and that "terrible day." Nina, Ilyusha's gentle, crippled sister, did not like her father's buffoonery either (Barbara Nikolaevna had been gone for some time past to Petersburg to study at the University). But the half-imbecile mother was greatly diverted and laughed heartily when her husband began capering about or performing something. It was the only way she could be amused; all the rest of the time she grumbled and complained that now everyone had forgotten her, that no one treated her with respect, that she was slighted, and so on. But during the last few days she had completely changed. She began looking constantly at Ilyusha's bed in the corner and seemed lost in thought. She was more silent, quieter, and, if she cried, she cried quietly so as not to be heard. The captain noticed the change in her with mournful perplexity. She did not like the boys' visits at first, but later on their merry shouts and stories began to divert her, and at last she liked them so much that, if the boys had given up coming, she would have felt dreary without them. When the children told some story or played a game, she laughed and clapped her hands. She called some of them to her and kissed them. She was particularly fond of Smurov. As for the captain, the presence in his room of the children, who came to cheer up Ilyusha, filled his heart from the first with ecstatic joy. He even hoped that Ilyusha would now get over his depression, and that that would hasten his recovery. In spite of his alarm about Ilyusha, he had not, till lately, felt one minute's doubt that his boy would suddenly recover. He met his little visitors with homage, waited upon them hand and foot, he was ready to be their horse and even began letting them ride on his back, but Ilyusha did not like the game and it was given up. He began buying little things for them, gingerbread and nuts, gave them tea and cut them sandwiches. It must be noted that all this time he had plenty of money. He had taken the two hundred rubles from Katerina Ivanovna just as Alyosha had predicted he would. And afterwards Katerina Ivanovna, learning more about their circumstances and Ilyusha's illness, visited them herself, made the acquaintance of the family and succeeded in fascinating the half-imbecile mother. Since then she had been lavish in helping them, and the captain, terror-stricken at the thought that his boy might be dying, forgot his pride and humbly accepted her assistance. All this time Doctor Herzenstube, who was called in by Katerina Ivanovna, came punctually every other day, but little was gained by his visits and he dosed the invalid mercilessly. But on that Sunday morning a new doctor was expected, who had come from Moscow, where he had a great reputation. Katerina Ivanovna had sent for him from Moscow at great expense, not expressly for Ilyusha, but for another object of which more will be said in its place hereafter. But, as he had come, she had asked him to see Ilyusha as well, and the captain had been told to expect him. He hadn't the slightest idea that Kolya Krasotkin was coming, though he had long wished for a visit from the boy for whom Ilyusha was fretting. At the moment when Krasotkin opened the door and came into the room, the captain and all the boys were round Ilyusha's bed, looking at a tiny mastiff pup, which had only been born the day before, though the captain had spoken for it a week ago to comfort and amuse Ilyushechka, who was still fretting over the lost and probably dead Zhuchka. Ilyusha, who had heard three days before that he was to be presented with a puppy, not an ordinary puppy, but a pedigreed mastiff (a very important point, of course), tried from delicacy of feeling to pretend that he was pleased. But his father and the boys could not help seeing that the puppy only served to recall to his little heart the thought of the unhappy dog he had tormented. The puppy lay beside him feebly moving and he, smiling sadly, stroked it with his thin, pale, wasted hand. Clearly he liked the puppy, but . . . it wasn't Zhuchka; if he could have had Zhuchka and the puppy, too, then he would have been completely happy.

"Krasotkin!" cried one of the boys suddenly. He was the first to see him come in. Krasotkin's entrance made a general sensation; the boys moved away and stood on each side of the bed, so that he could get a full view of Ilyushechka. The captain ran eagerly to meet Kolya.

"Please come in . . . you are welcome!" he said hurriedly. "Ilyusha, Mr. Krasotkin has come to see you!"

But Krasotkin, shaking hands with him hurriedly, instantly showed his full knowledge of the manners of good society. He turned first to the captain's wife sitting in her armchair, who was very ill-humored at the moment, and was grumbling that the boys stood between her and Ilyusha's bed and did not let her see the new puppy. With the greatest courtesy he made her a bow, clicked his heels, and then turning to Nina, he made her, as the only other lady present, a similar bow. This polite behavior made an extremely favorable impression on the sick lady.

"There, you can see at once he is a young man that has been well brought up," she commented aloud, throwing up her hands; "but as for our other visitors they come in one on the top of another."

"How do you mean, mamma, one on the top of another, how is that?" muttered the captain affectionately, though a little anxious on her account.

"That's how they ride in. They get on each other's shoulders in the hall and prance in like that on a respectable family. Strange sort of visitors!"

"But who's come in like that, mamma?"

"Why, that boy came in riding on that one's back and this one on that one's."

Kolya was already by Ilyusha's bedside. The sick boy turned visibly paler. He raised himself in the bed and looked intently at Kolya. Kolya had not seen his little friend for two months, and he was overwhelmed at the sight of him. He had never imagined that he would see such a wasted, yellow face, such enormous, feverishly glowing eyes and such thin little hands. He saw, with grieved surprise, Ilyusha's rapid, hard breathing and dry lips. He stepped close to him, held out his hand, and almost overwhelmed, he said:

"Well, old man . . . how are you?" But his voice failed him, he couldn't achieve an appearance of ease; his face suddenly twitched and the corners of his mouth quivered. Ilyusha smiled a pitiful little smile, still unable to utter a word. Something moved Kolya to raise his hand and pass it over Ilyusha's hair.

"Never mind!" he murmured softly to him to cheer him up, or perhaps not knowing why he said it. For a minute they were silent again.

"What's this you've got, a new puppy?" Kolya said suddenly, in a most callous voice.

"Ye-es," answered Ilyusha in a long whisper, gasping for breath.

"A black nose, that means he'll be fierce, a good house dog," Kolya observed gravely and stolidly, as if the only thing he cared about was the puppy and its black nose. But in reality he still had to do his utmost to control his feelings not to burst out crying like "a child," and do what he would he could not control it. "When it grows up, you'll have to keep it on the chain, I'm sure."

"He'll be a huge dog!" cried one of the boys.

"Of course he will," "a mastiff," "large," "like this," "as big as a calf," shouted several voices.

"As big as a calf, as a real calf," chimed in the captain. "I got one like that on purpose, one of the fiercest breed, and his parents are huge and very fierce, they stand as high as this from the floor. . . . Sit down here, on Ilyusha's bed, or here on the bench. You are welcome, we've been hoping to see you a long time . . . You were so kind as to come with Alexey Fyodorovich?"

Krasotkin sat on the edge of the bed, at Ilyusha's feet. Though he had perhaps prepared a free-and-easy opening for the conversation on his way, now he completely lost the thread of it.

"No . . . I came with Perezvon. I've got a dog now, called Perezvon. A Slavonic name. He's out there . . . if I whistle, he'll run in. I've brought a dog too," he said, addressing Ilyusha all at once. "Do you remember Zhuchka, old man?" he suddenly fired the question at him.

Ilyushechka's little face quivered. He looked with an agonized expression at Kolya. Alyosha, standing at the door, frowned and signed to Kolya not to speak of Zhuchka, but he did not or would not notice.

"Where . . . is Zhuchka?" Ilyusha asked in a broken voice.

"Oh, well, my boy, your Zhuchka's lost and done for!"

Ilyusha did not speak, but he fixed an intent gaze once more on Kolya. Alyosha, catching Kolya's eye, signed to him vigorously again, but he turned away his eyes pretending not to have noticed.

"It must have run away and died somewhere. It must have died after an appetizer like that," Kolya pronounced pitilessly, though he seemed a little breathless. "But I've got a dog, Perezvon . . . A Slavonic name. . . . I've brought him to show you."

"I don't want him!" said Ilyusha suddenly.

"No, no, you really must see him . . . it will amuse you. I brought him on purpose. . . . He's the same sort of shaggy dog. . . . You allow me to call in my dog, Madame?" he suddenly addressed Mrs. Snegiryova, with inexplicable excitement in his manner.

"I don't want him, I don't want him!" cried Ilyusha, with a mournful laceration in his voice. There was a reproachful light in his eyes.

"Perhaps, sir," the captain started up from the chest by the wall on which he had just sat down, "you'd better, sir . . . another time," he muttered, but Kolya could not be restrained. He hurriedly shouted to Smurov, "Open the door," and as soon as it was open, he blew his whistle. Perezvon dashed headlong into the room.

"Jump, Perezvon, beg! Beg!" shouted Kolya, jumping up, and the dog stood erect on his hind legs by Ilyusha's bedside. What followed was a surprise to everyone: Ilyusha started, lurched violently forward, bent over Perezvon and gazed at him, faint with suspense.

"It's . . . Zhuchka!" he cried suddenly, in a voice breaking with joy and suffering.

"And who did you think it was?" Krasotkin shouted with all his might, in a ringing, happy voice, and bending down he seized the dog and lifted him up to Ilyusha.

"Look, old man, you see, blind in one eye and the left ear is torn, just the marks you described to me. It was by that I found him. I found him right then, quickly. He did not belong to anyone!" he explained, turning quickly to the captain, to his wife, to Alyosha and then again to Ilyusha. "He used to live in the Fedotovs' backyard. Though he made his home there, they did not feed him. He was a stray dog that had run away from the village . . . I found him. . . . You see, old man, he couldn't have swallowed what you gave him. If he had, he must have died, he must have! So he must have spat it out, since he is alive. You did not see him do it. But the pin pricked his tongue, that is why he squealed. He ran away squealing and you thought he'd swallowed it. He might well squeal, because the skin of dogs' mouths is so tender . . . tenderer than in men, much tenderer!" Kolya cried impetuously, his face glowing and radiant with delight.

Ilyusha could not speak. White as a sheet, he gazed open-mouthed at Kolya, with his great eyes almost popping out of his head. And if Krasotkin, who had no suspicion of it, had known what a disastrous and fatal effect such a moment might have on the sick child's health, nothing would have induced him to play such a trick on him. But Alyosha was perhaps the only person in the room who realized it. As for the captain he behaved like a small child.

"Zhuchka! It's Zhuchka!" he cried in a blissful voice. "Ilyusha, this is Zhuchka, your Zhuchka! Mamma, this is Zhuchka!" He was almost weeping.

"And I never guessed!" cried Smurov regretfully. "Bravo, Krasotkin, I said he'd find the dog and here he's found him."

"Here he's found him!" another boy repeated gleefully.

"Krasotkin's great!" cried a third voice.

"He's great, he's great!" cried the other boys, and they began clapping.

"Wait, wait," Krasotkin did his utmost to shout above them all. "I'll tell you how it happened, that's the whole point. I found him, I took him home and hid him at once. I kept him locked up at home and did not show him to anyone till today. Only Smurov had known for the last two weeks, but I assured him this dog was called Perezvon and he did not guess. And meanwhile I taught the dog all sorts of tricks. You should only see all the things he can do! I trained him so as to bring you a well-trained dog, in good condition, old man, so as to be able to say to you, 'See, old man, what a fine dog your Zhuchka is now!' Do you have a bit of meat, he'll show you a trick that will break you up laughing. A piece of meat, haven't you got any?"

The captain ran across the hall to the landlady, where their cooking was done. Not to lose precious time, Kolya, in desperate haste, shouted to Perezvon "dead!" And the dog immediately turned round and lay on his back with its four paws in the air. The boys laughed, Ilyusha looked on with the same suffering smile, but the person most delighted with the dog's performance was "mamenka." She laughed at the dog and began snapping her fingers and calling it, "Perezvon, Perezvon!"

"Nothing will make him get up, nothing!" Kolya cried triumphantly, proud of his success. "He won't move for all the shouting in the world, but if I call to him, he'll jump up in a minute. *Ici*, Perezvon!"

The dog leaped up and bounded about, whining with delight. The captain ran back with a piece of cooked beef.

"Is it hot?" Kolya inquired hurriedly, with a businesslike air, taking the meat. "Dogs don't like hot things. No, it's all right. Look, everybody, look, Ilyushechka, look, old man; why aren't you looking? He does not look at him, now I've brought him."

The new trick consisted in making the dog stand motionless with his nose out and putting a tempting morsel of meat just on his nose. The luckless dog had to stand without moving, with the meat on his nose, as long as his master chose to keep him, without a movement, perhaps for half an hour. But he kept Perezvon only for a brief moment.

"Paid for!" cried Kolya, and the meat passed in a flash from the dog's nose to his mouth. The audience, of course, expressed enthusiasm and surprise.

"Can you really have put off coming all this time simply to train the dog?" exclaimed Alyosha, with an involuntary note of reproach in his voice.

"Simply for that!" answered Kolya, with perfect simplicity. "I wanted to show him in all his glory."

"Perezvon! Perezvon," called Ilyusha suddenly, snapping his thin fingers and beckoning to the dog.

"What is it? Let him jump up on the bed! *Ici*, Perezvon!" Kolya slapped the bed and Perezvon darted up to Ilyusha. The boy threw both arms round his head and Perezvon instantly licked his cheek. Ilyusha crept close to him, stretched himself out in bed and hid his face in the dog's shaggy coat.

"Dear, dear!" kept exclaiming the captain. Kolya sat down again on the edge of the bed.

"Ilyusha, I can show you another trick. I've brought you a little cannon. You remember, I told you about it before and you said how much you'd like to see it. Well, here, I've brought it to you."

And Kolya hurriedly pulled out of his satchel the little bronze cannon. He hurried, because he was happy himself. Another time he would have waited till the sensation made by Perezvon had passed off, now he hurried on regardless of all consideration. "You are all happy now," he felt, "so here's something to make you happier!" He was perfectly enchanted himself.

"I've been coveting this thing for a long while; it's for you, old man, it's for you. It belonged to Morozov, it was no use to him, he had it from his brother. I swopped a book from father's bookcase for it, *A Kinsman of Mahomet or Salutary Folly*,[2] a scandalous book published in Moscow a hundred years ago, before they had any censorship. And Morozov has a taste for such things. He was grateful to me, too . . ."

Kolya held the cannon in his hand so that all could see and admire it. Ilyusha raised himself, and, with his right arm still round the dog, he gazed enchanted at the toy. The sensation was even greater, when Kolya announced that he had gunpowder too, and that it could be fired off at once "if it won't alarm the ladies." "Mamenka" immediately asked to look at the toy closer and her request was granted. She was much pleased with the little bronze cannon on wheels and began rolling it to and fro on her lap. She readily gave permission for the cannon to be fired, without any idea of what she had been asked. Kolya showed the powder and the shot. The captain, as a military man, undertook to load it, putting in a minute quantity of powder. He asked that the shot might be put off till another time. The cannon was put on the floor, aiming towards an empty part of the room, three grains of powder were thrust into the touch hole and a match was put to it. A magnificent explosion followed. Mamenka was startled, but at once laughed with delight. The boys gazed in speechless triumph. But the captain, looking at Ilyusha, was more enchanted than any of them. Kolya picked up the cannon and immediately presented it to Ilyusha, together with the powder and the shot.

"I got it for you, for you! I've been keeping it for you a long time," he repeated once more in his delight.

"Oh, give it to me! No, give me the cannon!" Mamenka began begging like a little child. Her face showed a piteous fear that she would not get it. Kolya was disconcerted. The captain fidgeted uneasily.

"Mamochka, mamochka," he ran to her, "the cannon's yours, of course, but let Ilyusha have it, because it's a present to him, but it's just as good as yours. Ilyusha will always let you play with it, it shall belong to both of you, both of you."

"No, I don't want it to belong to both of us, I want it to be mine altogether, not Ilyusha's," persisted mamma, on the point of tears.

"Take it, mamma, here, keep it!" Ilyusha cried. "Krasotkin, may I give it to my mamma?" he turned to Krasotkin with an imploring face, as though he were afraid he might be offended at his giving his present to someone else.

---

2. A first-person account of a Frenchman's amorous adventures in Constantinople, translated from French and published in Moscow in 1785.

"Of course, you may," Krasotkin assented heartily, and, taking the cannon from Ilyusha, he handed it himself to mamenka with a polite bow. She was so touched that she cried.

"Ilyushechka, darling, he's the one who loves his mamochka!" she said tenderly, and at once began wheeling the cannon to and fro on her lap again.

"Mamenka, let me kiss your hand." The captain darted up to her at once and did so.

"And I never saw such a charming fellow as this nice boy," said the grateful lady, pointing to Krasotkin.

"And I'll bring you as much powder as you like, Ilyusha. We make the powder ourselves now. Borovikov found out how it's made—twenty-four parts of saltpeter, ten of sulphur and six of birchwood charcoal. It's all pounded together, mixed into a paste with water and rubbed through a sieve—that's how it's done."

"Smurov told me about your powder, only father says it's not real gunpowder," responded Ilyusha.

"Not real?" Kolya flushed. "It burns. I don't know, of course."

"No, sir, I didn't mean that," put in the captain with a guilty face. "I only said that real powder is not made like that, but that's nothing, it can be made that way, too."

"I don't know, you know best. We lighted some in a pomatum jar, it burned splendidly, it all burned away leaving only a tiny ash. But that was only the paste, and if you rub it through . . . but of course you know best, I don't know. . . . And Bulkin's father thrashed him on account of our powder, did you hear?" he turned to Ilyusha.

"Yes," answered Ilyusha. He listened to Kolya with immense interest and enjoyment.

"We had prepared a whole bottle of it and he used to keep it under his bed. His father saw it. He said it might explode, and thrashed him on the spot. He was going to make a complaint against me to the masters. He is not allowed to go about with me now, no one is allowed to go about with me now. Smurov is not allowed to either, I've got a bad name with everyone. They say I'm a 'desperate character,'" Kolya smiled scornfully. "It all began from what happened on the railway."

"Ah, we've heard of that exploit of yours, too," cried the captain. "How could you lie still on the line? It is possible you weren't the least afraid, lying there under the train? Weren't you frightened?"

The captain was abject in his flattery of Kolya.

"N-not particularly," answered Kolya carelessly. "What's blasted my reputation more than anything here was that cursed goose," he said, turning again to Ilyusha. But though he assumed an unconcerned air as he talked, he still could not control himself and was continually missing the note he tried to keep up.

"Ah! I heard about the goose!" Ilyusha laughed, beaming all over. "They told me, but I didn't understand. Did they really take you to the court?"

"The most stupid, trivial affair, they made a mountain out of a molehill as they always do," Kolya began carelessly. "I was walking through the marketplace here one day, just when they'd driven in the geese. I stopped and looked at them. All at once a fellow, who is an errand boy at Plotnikov's now, looked at me and said, 'What are you looking at the geese for?' I looked at him, he was a stupid, round-mugged fellow of twenty. I am always on the side of the people, you know. I like talking to the peasants. . . . We've fallen behind the people—that's an axiom.[3] I believe you are laughing, Karamazov?"

"No, heaven forbid, I am listening," said Alyosha with a most good-natured air, and the sensitive Kolya was immediately reassured.

"My theory, Karamazov, is clear and simple," he hurried on again, looking pleased. "I believe in the people and am always glad to give them their due, but I am not for spoiling them, that is a *sine qua non*[4] . . . But I was telling you about the goose. So I turned to the fool and answered, 'I am wondering what the goose thinks about.' He looked at me quite stupidly, 'And what does the goose think about?' he asked. 'Do you see that cart full of oats?' I said. 'The oats are dropping out of the sack, and the goose has put its neck right under the wheel to gobble them up—do you see?' 'I see that quite well,' he said. 'Well,' said I, 'if that cart were to move on a little, would it break the goose's neck or not?' 'It'd be sure to break it,' and he grinned all over his face, highly delighted. 'Come on then,' said I, 'let's try.' 'Let's,' he said. And it did not take us long to arrange: he stood at the bridle without being noticed, and I stood on one side to direct the goose. And the owner wasn't looking, he was talking to someone, so I had nothing to do, the goose thrust its head in after the oats of itself, under the cart, just under the wheel. I winked at the lad, he tugged at the bridle, and crack! The goose's neck was broken in half. And, as luck would have it, all the peasants saw us at that moment and they kicked up a shindy at once. 'You did that on purpose!' 'No, not on purpose.' 'Yes, you did, on purpose!' Well, they shouted, 'Take him to the justice of the peace!' They took me, too. 'You were there, too,' they said, 'you helped, you're known all over the market!' And, for some reason, I really am known all over the market," Kolya added conceitedly. "We all went off to the justice's, they brought the goose, too. The fellow was crying in a great funk, simply blubbering like a woman. And the farmer kept shouting that you could kill any number of geese like that. Well, of course, there were witnesses. The justice of the peace settled it in a minute, that the farmer was to be paid a ruble for the goose, and the fellow to have the goose. And he was warned not to play such pranks again. And the fellow kept blubbering like a woman, 'It wasn't me,' he said, 'it was he who egged me on,' and he pointed to me. I answered with the utmost composure that I hadn't egged him on, that I simply stated the general proposition, had spoken hypothetically. The justice of the peace smiled and was vexed with himself at once for having smiled. 'I'll complain to your masters about you, so that in the future you won't waste your time on such general propositions, instead of sitting at your books and learning your lessons.' He didn't complain to the masters, that was a joke, but the matter was noised abroad and came to the ears of the masters. Their ears are long, you know! The classical master, Kolbasnikov, was particularly shocked about it, but Dardanelov got me off again. But Kolbasnikov is savage with everyone now like a green ass. Did you know, Ilyusha, he is just married, got a dowry of a thousand

3. Professions of faith in the common people were platitudes of the Russian oppositional press of the 1860s and 70s.
4. An essential or indispensable element or condition (Latin).

rubles, and his bride's a regular fright of the first rank and the last degree. The third class fellows wrote an epigram on it.

> Astounding news has reached the class,
> Kolbasnikov has been an ass.

And so on, awfully funny, I'll bring it to you later on. I say nothing against Dardanelov, he is a learned man, there's no doubt about it. I respect men like that and it's not because he stood up for me."

"But you took him down a peg about the founders of Troy!" Smurov put in suddenly, unmistakably proud of Krasotkin at such a moment. He was particularly pleased with the story of the goose.

"Did you really take him down a peg?" the captain inquired, in a flattering way. "On the question of who founded Troy, sir? We heard of it, Ilyusha told me about it at the time."

"He knows everything, papa, he knows more than any of us!" put in Ilyushechka; "he only pretends to be like that, but really he is top in every subject . . ."

Ilyusha looked at Kolya with infinite happiness.

"Oh, that's all nonsense about Troy, a trivial matter. I consider this an unimportant question," said Kolya with haughty humility. He had by now completely recovered his dignity, though he was still a little uneasy. He felt that he was greatly excited and that he had talked about the goose, for instance, with too little reserve, while Alyosha had looked serious and had not said a word all the time. And the vain boy began by degrees to have a rankling fear that Alyosha was silent because he despised him, and thought he was showing off before him. If he dared to think anything like that Kolya would . . .

"I regard the question as quite a trivial one," he rapped out again, proudly.

"And I know who founded Troy," a boy, who had not spoken before, said suddenly, to the surprise of everyone. He was silent and seemed to be shy. He was a pretty boy of about eleven, called Kartashov. He was sitting near the door. Kolya looked at him with dignified amazement. The fact was that the identity of the founders of Troy had become a secret for the whole school, a secret which could only be discovered by reading Smaragdov, and no one had Smaragdov but Kolya. One day when Kolya's back was turned, Kartashov hastily opened Smaragdov, which lay among Kolya's books, and immediately lighted on the passage relating to the foundation of Troy. This was a good while ago, but he felt uneasy and could not bring himself to announce publicly that he, too, knew who had founded Troy, afraid of what might happen and of Krasotkin's somehow putting him to shame over it. But now he couldn't resist saying it. For weeks he had been longing to.

"Well, who did found it?" asked Kolya, turning to him with haughty superciliousness. He saw from his face that he really did know and at once made up his mind how to take it. There was, so to speak, a discordant note in the general harmony.

"Troy was founded by Teucer, Dardanus, Ilius and Tros," the boy rapped out at once, and in the same instant he blushed, blushed so, that it was painful to look at him. But the boys stared at him, stared at him for a whole minute, and then all the staring eyes turned at once and were fastened upon Kolya, who was still scanning the audacious boy with disdainful composure.

"In what sense did they found it?" he deigned to comment at last. "And what is meant by founding a city or a state? What did they do—did they go and each lay a brick, do you suppose?"

There was laughter. The offending boy turned from pink to crimson. He was silent and on the point of tears. Kolya held him so for a minute.

"Before you talk of a historical event like the foundation of a nationality, you must first understand what you mean by it," he admonished him in stern incisive tones. "But I attach no consequence to these old wives' tales and I don't think much of universal history in general," he added carelessly, addressing the company generally.

"Universal history, sir?" the captain inquired, looking almost scared.

"Yes, universal history! It's the study of the successive follies of mankind and nothing more.[5] The only subjects I respect are mathematics and natural science," said Kolya.[6] He was showing off and he stole a glance at Alyosha; his was the only opinion he was afraid of there. But Alyosha was still silent and still serious as before. If Alyosha had said a word it would have stopped him, but Alyosha was silent and "it might be the silence of contempt" and that finally irritated Kolya.

"The classical languages, too . . . they are simply madness, nothing more. You seem to disagree with me again, Karamazov?"

"I don't agree," said Alyosha, with a faint smile.

"The study of the classics, if you ask my opinion, is simply a police measure, that's the only reason why it has been introduced into our schools."[7] By degrees Kolya began to get breathless again. "Latin and Greek were introduced because they are a bore and because they stupefy the intellect. It was dull before, so what could they do to make things duller? It was senseless enough before, so what could they do to make it more senseless? So they thought of Greek and Latin. That's my entire opinion of them, I hope I shall never change it," Kolya finished abruptly. His cheeks were flushed.

"That's true," assented Smurov suddenly, in a ringing tone of conviction. He had listened attentively.

"And yet he is first in Latin himself," cried one of the group of boys suddenly.

"Yes, papa, he says that and yet he is first in Latin," echoed Ilyusha.

"What of it?" Kolya thought fit to defend himself, though the praise was very sweet to him. "I plug away at Latin, because I have to, because I

---

5. "History is the study of the successive follies of mankind and nothing more" is from Voltaire's "Essay on the Manners and Spirit of Nations" (1756).
6. Segments of Russian society that considered themselves progressive were typically critical of traditional humanistic education, and advocated study of the natural sciences instead. See for example the writings of Dmitri Pisarev (1840–1868), a leader of the revolutionary democratic movement. Dostoevsky firmly believed in the value of humanistic learning. In his 1872–75 notebooks, he writes that Peter the Great's emphasis on technical education resulted in an "unusual narrowing and paucity of thought," whereas the high respect accorded to the humanities in the Renaissance was accompanied by "great technological discoveries (printing press, gunpowder) . . . and a broadening of human thought (the discovery of America, the Reformation, discoveries in astronomy and so on)" [15:582].
7. The study of classical languages in Russian secondary schools was in fact promoted as an antidote to freethinking by Count Dmitri Andreevich Tolstoy (1823–1889), a reactionary Minister of Popular Enlightenment. The relative merit of scientific and practical education as opposed to the study of the humanities was hotly debated in the Russian press of the 1860s–70s.

promised my mother to pass my examination, and I think that whatever you do, it's worth doing it well. But in my soul I have a profound contempt for the classics and all that vileness. . . . You don't agree, Karamazov?"

"Why 'vileness'?" Alyosha smiled again.

"Well, all the classical authors have been translated into all languages, so it was not for the sake of studying the classics they introduced Latin, but solely as a police measure, to stupefy the intelligence. So what can one call it but vileness?"

"Why, who taught you all this?" cried Alyosha, surprised at last.

"In the first place I am capable of thinking for myself without being taught. Besides, what I said just now about the classics being translated our teacher Kolbasnikov has said to the whole of the third class."

"The doctor has come!" cried Nina, who had been silent till then.

A carriage belonging to Madame Khokhlakova drove up to the gate. The captain, who had been expecting the doctor all the morning, rushed headlong out to meet him. Mamenka pulled herself together and assumed a dignified air. Alyosha went up to Ilyusha and began setting his pillows straight. Ninochka, from her invalid chair, anxiously watched him putting the bed tidy. The boys hurriedly took leave. Some of them promised to come again in the evening. Kolya called Perezvon and the dog jumped off the bed.

"I won't go away, I won't go away," Kolya said hastily to Ilyusha. "I'll wait in the passage and come back when the doctor's gone, I'll come back with Perezvon."

But by now the doctor had entered, an important-looking person with long, dark whiskers and a shiny, shaven chin, wearing a bearskin coat. As he crossed the threshold he stopped, taken aback; he probably fancied he had come to the wrong place. "How is this? Where am I?" he muttered, not removing his coat nor his peaked sealskin cap. The crowd, the poverty of the room, the washing hanging on a line in the corner, puzzled him. The captain, bent double, was bowing low before him.

"It's here, sir, here, sir," he muttered cringingly; "it's here, you've come right, sir, you were coming to us . . ."

"Sne-gi-ryov?" the doctor said loudly and pompously. "Mr. Snegiryov— is that you?"

"That's me, sir!"

"Ah!"

The doctor looked round the room with a squeamish air once more and threw off his coat, displaying to all eyes the grand decoration of his neck. The captain caught the fur coat in the air, and the doctor took off his cap.

"Where is the patient?" he asked emphatically.

Chapter VI

Precocity

"What do you think the doctor will say to him?" Kolya asked quickly. "What a repulsive mug, though, hasn't he? I can't stand medicine!"

"Ilyusha will die. I think that's certain," answered Alyosha mournfully.

"They are frauds! Medicine's a fraud! I am glad to have made your acquaintance, though, Karamazov. I wanted to know you for a long time. I am only sorry we meet in such sad circumstances."

Kolya had a great inclination to say something even warmer and more demonstrative, but he felt ill at ease. Alyosha noticed this, smiled, and pressed his hand.

"I've long learned to respect you as a rare person," Kolya muttered again, faltering and uncertain. "I have heard you are a mystic and have been in the monastery. I know you are a mystic but . . . that hasn't put me off. Contact with real life will cure you.[8] . . . It's always so with characters like yours."

"What do you mean by mystic? Cure me of what?" Alyosha was rather astonished.

"Oh, God, and all the rest of it."

"What, don't you believe in God?"

"Oh, I've nothing against God. Of course, God is only a hypothesis, but . . . I admit that He is needed . . . for the order of the universe and all that . . . and that if there were no God He would have to be invented,"[9] added Kolya, beginning to blush. He suddenly fancied that Alyosha might think he was trying to show off his knowledge and to prove that he was "grown up." "I haven't the slightest desire to show off my knowledge to him," Kolya thought indignantly. And all of a sudden he felt horribly annoyed.

"Frankly, I can't stand all these discussions," he said with a final air. "It's possible for one who doesn't believe in God to love mankind, don't you think so?[1] Didn't Voltaire not believe in God and love mankind?" ("I am at it again," he thought to himself.)

"Voltaire believed in God, though not very much, I think, and I don't think he loved mankind very much either," said Alyosha quietly, gently, and quite naturally, as though he were talking to someone of his own age, or even older. Kolya was particularly struck by Alyosha's apparent diffidence about his opinion of Voltaire. He seemed to be leaving the question for him, little Kolya, to settle.

"Have you read Voltaire?" Alyosha finished.

"No, not to say read. . . . But I've read *Candide*[2] in the Russian translation . . . in an absurd, grotesque, old translation . . . (At it again! again!)"

"And did you understand it?"

"Oh, yes, everything. . . . That is . . . Why do you suppose I shouldn't understand it? There's a lot of nastiness in it, of course. . . . Of course I can understand that it's a philosophical novel and written to advocate an idea. . . ." Kolya was getting muddled by now. "I am a Socialist, Karam-

---

8. Kolya's mumbling about mysticism and real life may be a parody of passages from Belinsky's infamous "Letter to N. V. Gogol" (1847). Dostoevsky knew this text well; he had read it aloud before members of the Petrashevsky Circle, a fact the government used against him at his trial in 1849.

9. See p. 27.

1. Kolya again paraphrases a passage from Belinsky's "Letter to Gogol," in which Belinsky maintains that Voltaire was a better Christian than any priest or Church figure because he fought fanaticism.

2. *Candide, or Optimism* (1759), a philosophical novel by Voltaire. Dostoevsky was polemically engaged with the ideas of this novel throughout his life. On December 24, 1877, he composed a list of projects he hoped to complete; among them was the ambition to write a "Russian Candide." (15:409).

azov, I am an incurable Socialist,"[3] he announced suddenly, apropos of nothing.

"A Socialist?" smiled Alyosha. "But when have you had time to become one? Why, I thought you are only thirteen?"

Kolya winced.

"In the first place I am not thirteen, but fourteen, fourteen in two weeks," he flushed angrily, "and in the second place I am at a complete loss to understand what my age has to do with it. The question is what are my convictions, not what is my age, isn't it?"[4]

"When you are older, you'll understand for yourself the influence of age on convictions. I fancied, too, that you were not expressing your own ideas," Alyosha answered serenely and modestly, but Kolya interrupted him hotly:

"Come, you want obedience and mysticism. You must admit that the Christian religion, for instance, has only been of use to the rich and the powerful to keep the lower classes in slavery, that's so, isn't it?"[5]

"Ah, I know where you read that, and I am sure someone told you so!" cried Alyosha.

"I say, what makes you think I read it? And certainly no one told me so. I can think for myself. . . . I am not opposed to Christ, if you like. He was a most humane person, and if He were alive today, He would be found in the ranks of the revolutionists, and would perhaps play a conspicuous part. . . . There's no doubt about that."[6]

"Oh, where, where did you get that from? What fool have you made friends with?" exclaimed Alyosha.

"Come, the truth will out! It has so chanced that I have often talked to Mr. Rakitin, of course, but . . . old Belinsky said that, too, so they say."

"Belinsky? I don't remember. He hasn't written that anywhere."

"If he didn't write it, they say he said it. I heard that from a . . . but never mind."

"And have you read Belinsky?"

"Well, no . . . I haven't read all of him, but . . . I read the passage about Tatyana, why she didn't go off with Onegin."[7]

"Didn't go off with Onegin? Surely, you don't . . . understand that already?"

"Why, you seem to take me for the child Smurov," said Kolya, with a grin of irritation. "But please don't suppose I am such a revolutionist. I

---

3. The phrase "I am an incurable socialist" may be a reference to Alexander Herzen's "Letter to Alexander I," published in the journal *Polar Star* in 1855.

4. A similar passage occurs in the 1860 story "A Little Demon" (*Besynok*) by Vsevolod Krestovsky (1840–1895), published in the journal *The Torch* (*Svetoch*) in 1861 and dedicated to Dostoevsky. Krestovsky's story focuses on the complex psychology of an adolescent girl. Dostoevsky and Krestovsky became acquainted in 1859, and Krestovsky's works were published in *Time* and *Epoch*. Krestovsky's story furnished the title for Book 11, Chapter III of *The Brothers Karamazov*.

5. Kolya again paraphrases passages from Belinsky's "Letter to Gogol," in which Belinsky writes that the Russian Orthodox Church was always "a support of the knout and sycophant of despotism."

6. Kolya once again paraphrases Belinsky's "Letter to Gogol," in which Belinsky writes of Christ: "He was the first to proclaim to people the teaching of freedom, equality, and brotherhood." Dostoevsky himself, in the chapter "Old People" in his 1873 *Diary of a Writer*, had reported hearing Belinsky say this.

7. Tatyana, who had been in love with Onegin as a young girl but was rebuffed by him, was later married off to an older man. When Onegin reappears in her life and declares his love for her, she refuses him on the grounds that she has been given to another. Both Belinsky and Dostoevsky published analyses of *Eugene Onegin*; Belinsky was highly critical of Tatiana's loyalty to her husband, whereas Dostoevsky praised it. See also p. 140.

often disagree with Mr. Rakitin. Though I mention Tatyana, I am not at all for the emancipation of women. I acknowledge that women are subservient creatures and must obey. *Les femmes tricottent,*[8] as Napoleon said." Kolya, for some reason, smiled. "And on that question at least I am quite of one mind with that pseudo-great man. I think, too, that to leave one's own country and fly to America is base, worse than base—silly. Why go to America when one may be of great service to humanity here?[9] Now especially. There's a perfect mass of fruitful activity open to us. That's what I answered."

"What do you mean? Answered whom? Has someone suggested your going to America already?"

"I must confess, they've been at me to go, but I declined. That's between ourselves, of course, Karamazov; do you hear, not a word to anyone. I say this only to you. I am not at all anxious to fall into the clutches of the secret police and take lessons at the Chain bridge,

> Long will you remember
> The house at the chain bridge.[1]

Do you remember? It's splendid. Why are you laughing? You don't suppose I am fibbing, do you?" ("What if he should find out that I have only that one number of *The Bell*[2] in father's bookcase, and haven't read any more of it?" Kolya thought with a shudder.)

"Oh, no, I am not laughing and don't suppose for a moment that you are lying. No, indeed, I can't suppose so, for all this alas! is perfectly true. But tell me, have you read Pushkin, *Onegin,* for instance? . . . You spoke just now of Tatyana."

"No, I haven't read it yet, but I want to read it. I have no prejudices, Karamazov; I want to hear both sides. What makes you ask?"

"Oh, nothing."

"Tell me, Karamazov, have you an awful contempt for me?" Kolya rapped out suddenly and drew himself up before Alyosha, as though he were on parade. "Be so kind as to tell me, without beating about the bush."

"I have a contempt for you?" Alyosha looked at him wondering. "What for? I am only sad that a charming nature such as yours should be perverted by all this crude nonsense before you have begun life."

"Don't be anxious about my nature," Kolya interrupted, not without complacency. "But it's true that I am stupidly sensitive, crudely sensitive. You smiled just now, and I fancied you seemed to . . ."

"Oh, my smile meant something quite different. I'll tell you why I smiled. Not long ago I read the criticism made by a German who had lived in Russia, on our students and youth of today. 'Show a Russian schoolboy,'

---

8. "Women knit" (French).
9. Life in America and the possibility of emigration were topics frequently addressed in the Russian press of the 1860s and 70s. Kolya's reference to America would remind readers of episodes in Chernyshevsky's novel *What Is to be Done?* describing the emigration of one of the main characters.
1. The headquarters of the Tsarist secret police were located near the Chain Bridge in Saint Petersburg. "Secret police" is a translation of *tret'ego otdeleniia,* or "third department" of the Imperial Chancellery, founded by Nicholas I in 1826. Kolya recites part of an anti-government satire by Dmitri Minaev (1835–1889) on a venture in workers' education, located near the secret police headquarters and the Chain Bridge.
2. A Russian-language newspaper published in London by Herzen and his friend and collaborator Nikolay Ogarev (1813–1877) from 1857–67. *The Bell* was illegal in Russia but widely read there in smuggled copies.

he writes, 'a map of the stars, which he knows nothing about, and he will give you back the map next day with corrections on it.' No knowledge and unbounded conceit—that's what the German meant to say about the Russian schoolboy."

"Yes, that's perfectly right," Kolya laughed suddenly, "truthissimo! exactly so! Bravo the German. But the Kraut did not see the good side, what do you think? Conceit may be, that comes from youth, that will be corrected if need be, but, on the other hand, there is an independent spirit almost from childhood, boldness of thought and conviction, and not the spirit of these sausage makers, groveling before authority. . . . But the German was right all the same. Bravo the German! But Germans ought to be strangled all the same. Though they are so good at sciences and learning they ought to be strangled."

"Strangled, what for?" smiled Alyosha.

"Well, perhaps I am talking nonsense, I agree. I am awfully childish sometimes, and when I am pleased about anything I can't restrain myself and am ready to talk any nonsense. But, I say, we are chattering away here about nothing, and that doctor has been a long time in there. But perhaps he's examining the "mamasha" and that poor crippled Ninochka. I like that Ninochka, you know. She whispered to me suddenly as I was coming away, 'Why didn't you come before?' And in such a voice, so reproachfully! I think she is awfully nice and pathetic."

"Yes, yes! Well, you'll be coming often, you will see what she is like. It would do you a great deal of good to know people like that, to learn to value a great deal which you will find out from knowing these people," Alyosha observed warmly. "That would have more effect on you than anything."

"Oh, how I regret and blame myself for not having come sooner!" Kolya exclaimed, with bitter feeling.

"Yes, it's a great pity. You saw for yourself how delighted the poor child was to see you. And how he fretted for you to come!"

"Don't tell me! You make it worse! But it serves me right. What kept me from coming was my conceit, my egoistic vanity, and the beastly willfulness, which I never can get rid of, though I've been struggling with it all my life. I see that now. I am a scoundrel in lots of ways, Karamazov!"

"No, you have a charming nature, though it's been distorted, and I quite understand why you have had such an influence on this noble, morbidly sensitive boy," Alyosha answered warmly.

"And you say that to me!" cried Kolya; "and would you believe it, I thought—I've thought several times since I've been here—that you despised me! If only you knew how I prize your opinion!"

"But are you really so sensitive? At your age! Would you believe it, just now, when you were telling your story, I thought, as I watched you, that you must be very sensitive!"

"You thought so? What an eye you've got, I say! I bet that was when I was talking about the goose. That was just when I fancied you had a great contempt for me for being in such a hurry to show off, and for a moment I quite hated you for it, and began talking like a fool. Then I fancied—just now, here—when I said that if there were no God He would have to be invented, that I was in too great a hurry to display my knowledge, especially as I got that phrase out of a book. But I swear I wasn't showing off out of vanity, though I really don't know why, out of joy, yes, I believe it was from joy . . . though it's perfectly disgraceful for anyone to be gushing with joy, I know that. But I am convinced now that you don't despise me; it was all my imagination. Oh, Karamazov, I am profoundly unhappy. I sometimes fancy all sorts of things, that everyone is laughing at me, the whole world, and then I feel ready to overturn the whole order of things."

"And you torment everyone about you," smiled Alyosha.

"Yes, I torment everyone about me, especially my mother. Karamazov, tell me, am I very ridiculous now?"

"Don't think about that, don't think of it at all!" cried Alyosha. "And what does ridiculous mean? Isn't everyone constantly being or seeming ridiculous? Besides, nearly all clever people now are fearfully afraid of being ridiculous, and that makes them unhappy. All I am surprised at is that you should be feeling that so early, though I've observed it for some time past, and not only in you. Nowadays the very children have begun to suffer from it. It's almost a sort of insanity. The devil has taken the form of that vanity and entered into the whole generation; it's simply the devil," added Alyosha, without a trace of the smile that Kolya, staring at him, expected to see. "You are like everyone else," said Alyosha, in conclusion, "that is, like very many others. Only you must not be like everybody else, that's all."

"Even if everyone is like that?"

"Yes, even if everyone is like that. You be the only one not like it. You really are not like everyone else, here you are not ashamed to confess to something bad and even ridiculous. And who will admit so much in these days? No one. And people have even ceased to feel the impulse to self-criticism. Don't be like everyone else, even if you were the only one who is not like everyone else."

"Splendid! I was not mistaken in you. You know how to console one. Oh, how I have longed to know you, Karamazov. I've long been eager for this meeting. Can you really have thought about me, too? You said just now that you thought of me, too?"

"Yes, I'd heard of you and had thought of you, too . . . and if it's partly vanity that makes you ask, it doesn't matter."

"Do you know, Karamazov, our talk has been like a declaration of love," said Kolya, in a bashful and melting voice. "That's not ridiculous, is it?"

"Not at all ridiculous, and if it were ridiculous, it wouldn't matter, because it's been a good thing." Alyosha smiled brightly.

"But do you know, Karamazov, you must admit that you are a little ashamed yourself, now. . . . I see it by your eyes." Kolya smiled with a sort of sly happiness.

"Why ashamed?"

"Well, why are you blushing?"

"It was you made me blush," laughed Alyosha, and he really did blush. "Oh, well, I am a little ashamed, goodness knows why, I don't know . . ." he muttered almost embarrassed.

"Oh, how I love you and admire you at this moment just because you are rather ashamed! Because you are just like me," cried Kolya, in positive ecstasy. His cheeks glowed, his eyes beamed.

"You know, Kolya, you will be very unhappy in your life," something made Alyosha say suddenly.

"I know, I know. How you know it all beforehand!" Kolya agreed at once.

"But you will bless life on the whole, all the same."

"Just so, hurrah! You are a prophet. Oh, we shall get on together, Karamazov! Do you know, what delights me most, is that you treat me quite like an equal. But we are not equals, no, we are not, you are better! But we shall get on. Do you know, all this last month I've been saying to myself, 'either we shall be friends at once, forever, or we shall part enemies to the grave!'"

"And saying that, of course, you loved me," Alyosha laughed gaily.

"I did. I loved you awfully. I've been loving and dreaming of you. And how do you know it all beforehand? Ah, here's the doctor. Goodness! What will he tell us? Look at his face!"

Chapter VII

Ilyusha

The doctor came out of the room again, muffled in his fur coat and with his cap on his head. His face looked almost angry and disgusted, as though he were afraid of getting dirty. He cast a cursory glance round the hall, looking sternly at Alyosha and Kolya as he did so. Alyosha waved from the door to the coachman, and the carriage that had brought the doctor drove up. The captain darted out after the doctor, and, bowing, almost cringing, stopped him to get the final opinion. The poor fellow looked utterly crushed; there was a scared look in his eyes.

"Your Excellency, your Excellency . . . is it possible?" he began, but could not go on and clasped his hands in despair. Yet he still gazed imploringly at the doctor, as though a word from him might still change the poor boy's fate.

"I can't help it, I am not God!" the doctor answered offhand, though with the customary impressiveness.

"Doctor . . . your Excellency . . . and will it be soon, soon?"

"You must be prepared for anything," said the doctor incisively, emphasizing each syllable, and dropping his eyes he was about to step out to the coach.

"Your Excellency, for Christ's sake," the terror-stricken captain stopped him again. "Your Excellency! but can nothing, absolutely nothing save him now?"

"It's not in my hands now," said the doctor impatiently, "but hmm. . . ." he stopped suddenly. "If you could, for instance . . . send . . . your patient . . . at once, without delay" (the words "at once, without delay," the doctor uttered with an almost wrathful sternness that made the captain start) "to Sy-ra-cuse, the change to the new be-ne-ficial climatic conditions might possibly effect . . ."

"To Syracuse!" cried the captain, unable to grasp what was said.

"Syracuse is in Sicily," Kolya jerked out suddenly in explanation. The doctor looked at him.

"Sicily! your Excellency," faltered the captain, "but you've seen"—he spread out his hands, indicating his surroundings—"mamenka and my family?"

"N-no, Sicily is not the place for the family, the family should go to the Caucasus in the early spring . . . your daughter must go to the Caucasus, and your wife . . . after a course of the waters in the Caucasus for her rheumatism . . . must be sent straight to Paris to the psy-chi-a-trist Lepelletier;[3] I could give you a note to him, and then . . . there might be a change . . ."

"Doctor, doctor! But you see!" The captain flung wide his hands again despairingly, indicating the bare wooden walls of the hall.

"Well, that's not my business," smiled the doctor. "I have only told you the answer of me-di-cal sci-ence to your question as to possible treatment. As for the rest, to my regret . . ."

"Don't be afraid, apothecary, my dog won't bite you," Kolya rapped out loudly, noticing the doctor's rather uneasy glance at Perezvon, who was standing in the doorway. There was a wrathful note in Kolya's voice. He used the word apothecary instead of doctor *on purpose*, and, as he explained afterwards, "I used it to insult him."

"What's that?" The doctor flung up his head, staring with surprise at Kolya. "Who's this?" he addressed Alyosha, as though asking him to explain.

"It's Perezvon's master, apothecary, don't worry about me," Kolya said incisively again.

"Perezvon," repeated the doctor, perplexed.

"He hears the bell, but where it is he cannot tell. Good-bye, apothecary, we shall meet in Syracuse."

"Who's this? Who's this?" The doctor flew into a terrible rage.

"He is a schoolboy, doctor, he is a mischievous boy; take no notice of him," said Alyosha, frowning and speaking quickly. "Kolya, hold your tongue!" he cried to Krasotkin. "Take no notice of him, doctor," he repeated, rather impatiently.

"He needs a thrashing, a good thrashing!" The doctor stamped in a perfect fury.

"And you know, apothecary, my Perezvon might bite!" said Kolya, turning pale, with quivering voice and flashing eyes. "*Ici*, Perezvon!"

"Kolya, if you say another word, I'll have nothing more to do with you," Alyosha cried peremptorily.

"Apothecary, there is only one man in the world who can command Nikolay Krasotkin—this is the man" (Kolya pointed to Alyosha). "I obey him, good-bye!"

He stepped forward, opened the door, and quickly went into the inner room. Perezvon flew after him. The doctor stood still for five seconds in amazement, looking at Alyosha; then, with a curse, he went out quickly to the carriage, repeating aloud, "This is . . . this is . . . I don't know what it is!" The captain darted forward to help him into the carriage. Alyosha followed Kolya into the room. He was already by Ilyusha's bedside. The sick boy was holding his hand and calling for his father. A minute later the captain, too, came back.

"Papa, papa, come . . . we . . ." Ilyusha faltered in violent excitement, but apparently unable to go on, he flung his wasted arms round papa and Kolya, uniting them in one embrace, and hugging them as tightly as he could. The captain suddenly began to shake with dumb sobs, and Kolya's lips and chin twitched.

---

3. Almire René Jacques Lepelletier (1790–1880), well-known Parisian physiologist, regarded especially for his studies on physiology and philosophy.

"Papa, papa! How sorry I am for you, papa!" Ilyusha moaned bitterly.

"Ilyushechka . . . darling . . . the doctor said . . . you would be all right . . . we shall be happy . . . the doctor . . ." the captain began.

"Ah, papa! I know what the new doctor said to you about me. . . . I saw!" cried Ilyusha, and again he hugged them both with all his strength, hiding his face on papa's shoulder.

"Papa don't cry, and when I die get a good boy, another one . . . choose one of them all, a good one, call him Ilyusha and love him instead of me . . ."

"Hush, old man, you'll get well," Krasotkin cried suddenly, in a voice that sounded angry.

"But don't ever forget me, papa," Ilyusha went on, "come to my grave . . . and papa, bury me by our big stone, where we used to go for our walk, and come to me there with Krasotkin in the evening . . . and Perezvon . . . I shall expect you. . . . Papa, papa!"

His voice broke. They were all three silent, still embracing. Ninochka was crying, quietly in her chair, and at last seeing them all crying, mamma, too, burst into tears.

"Ilyushechka, Ilyushechka!" she exclaimed.

Krasotkin suddenly released himself from Ilyusha's embrace.

"Good-bye, old man, mother expects me back to dinner," he said quickly. "What a pity I did not tell her! She will be dreadfully anxious. . . . But after dinner I'll come back to you for the whole day, for the whole evening, and I'll tell you all sorts of things, all sorts of things. And I'll bring Perezvon, but now I will take him with me, because he will begin to howl when I am away and bother you. Good-bye!"

And he ran out into the hall. He didn't want to cry, but in the hall he burst into tears. Alyosha found him crying.

"Kolya, you must be sure to keep your word and come, or he will be terribly disappointed," Alyosha said emphatically.

"I will! Oh, how I curse myself for not having come before," muttered Kolya, crying, and no longer ashamed of it. At that moment the captain flew out of the room, and at once closed the door behind him. His face looked frenzied, his lips were trembling. He stood before the two lads and flung up his arms.

"I don't want a good boy! I don't want another boy!" he muttered in a wild whisper, clenching his teeth. "If I forget thee, Jerusalem, may my tongue . . ."[4]

He broke off with a sob and sank on his knees before the wooden bench. Pressing his fists against his head, he began sobbing with absurd whimpering cries, doing his utmost that his cries should not be heard in the room. Kolya ran out into the street.

"Good-bye, Karamazov. Will you come yourself?" he cried sharply and angrily to Alyosha.

"I will certainly come in the evening."

"What was that he said about Jerusalem? . . . What did he mean by that?"

---

4. Captain Snegiryov quotes Psalm 137.5–6: "If I forget thee, O Jerusalem, let my right hand forget her cunning. If I do not remember thee, let my tongue cleave to the roof of my mouth; if I prefer not Jerusalem above my chief joy."

"It's from the Bible. 'If I forget thee, Jerusalem,' that is, if I forget all that is most precious to me, if I let anything take its place, then may . . ."

"I understand, that's enough! Be sure you come! *Ici*, Perezvon!" he cried with positive ferocity to the dog, and with rapid strides he went home.

Book Eleven

BROTHER IVAN FYODOROVICH

Chapter I

At Grushenka's

Alyosha went towards the cathedral square to the widow Morozova's house to see Grushenka, who had sent Fenya to him early in the morning with an urgent message begging him to come. Questioning Fenya, Alyosha learned that her mistress had been particularly distressed since the previous day. During the two months that had passed since Mitya's arrest, Alyosha had called frequently at the widow Morozova's house, both from his own inclination and to take messages for Mitya. Three days after Mitya's arrest, Grushenka was taken very ill and was ill for nearly five weeks. For one whole week she was unconscious. She was very much changed—thinner and a little sallow, though she had for the past two weeks been well enough to go out. But to Alyosha her face was even more attractive than before, and he liked to meet her eyes when he went in to see her. A look of firmness and intelligent purpose had developed in her face. There were signs of spiritual transformation in her, and a steadfast, fine and humble determination that nothing could shake could be discerned in her. There was a small vertical line between her brows which gave her charming face a look of concentrated thought, almost austere at the first glance. There was scarcely a trace of her former frivolity. It seemed strange to Alyosha, too, that in spite of the calamity that had overtaken the poor girl, betrothed to a man who had been arrested for a terrible crime, almost at the instant of their betrothal, in spite of her illness and the almost inevitable sentence hanging over Mitya, Grushenka had yet not lost her youthful cheerfulness. There was a soft light in the once proud eyes, though . . . though, at times, they gleamed with the old vindictive fire when she was visited by one disturbing thought stronger than ever in her heart. The object of that uneasiness was the same as ever—Katerina Ivanovna, of whom Grushenka had even raved when she lay in delirium. Alyosha knew that she was fearfully jealous of her. Yet Katerina Ivanovna had not once visited Mitya in his prison, though she might have done it whenever she liked. All this created a difficult problem for Alyosha, for he was the only person to whom Grushenka opened her heart and from whom she was continually asking advice. Sometimes he was incapable of telling her anything.

Full of anxiety he entered her lodging. She was at home. She had returned from seeing Mitya half an hour before, and from the rapid movement with which she leaped up from her chair to meet him he saw that she had been expecting him with great impatience. A pack of cards dealt for a game of "fools" lay on the table. A bed had been made up on the leather sofa on the other side and Maximov lay, half-reclining, on it. He wore a dressing gown and a cotton nightcap, and was evidently ill and weak, though he was smiling blissfully. When the homeless little old man returned with Grushenka from Mokroe two months before, he had simply stayed on and was still staying with her. He arrived with her in rain and sleet, sat down on the sofa, drenched and scared, and gazed mutely at her with a timid, appealing smile. Grushenka, who was in terrible grief and in the first stage of fever, almost forgot his existence in all she had to do the first half hour after her arrival. Suddenly she chanced to look at him intently: he laughed a pitiful, helpless little laugh. She called Fenya and told her to give him something to eat. All that day he sat in the same place, almost without stirring. When it got dark and the shutters were closed, Fenya asked her mistress,

"Is the gentleman going to stay the night, mistress?"

"Yes; make him a bed on the sofa," answered Grushenka.

Questioning him more in detail, Grushenka learned from him that he had literally nowhere to go, and that "Mr. Kalganov, my benefactor, told me straight that he wouldn't receive me again and gave me five rubles." "Well, God bless you, you'd better stay then," Grushenka decided in her grief, smiling compassionately at him. Her smile wrung the old man's heart and his lips twitched with grateful tears. And so the wandering sponger had stayed with her ever since. He did not leave the house even when she was ill. Fenya and her grandmother, the cook, did not turn him out, but went on serving him meals and making up his bed on the sofa. Grushenka had grown used to him, and coming back from seeing Mitya (whom she had begun to visit in prison before she was really well) she would sit down and begin talking to "Maximushka" about trifling matters, to keep her from thinking of her sorrow. The old man turned out to be a good storyteller on occasions, so that at last he became necessary to her. Grushenka saw scarcely anyone else beside Alyosha, who did not come every day and never stayed long. Her old merchant lay seriously ill at this time, "at his last gasp" as they said in the town, and he did, in fact, die a week after Mitya's trial. Three weeks before his death, feeling the end approaching, he made his sons, their wives and children, come upstairs to him at last and bade them not leave him again. From that moment he gave strict orders to his servants not to admit Grushenka and to tell her if she came, "The master wishes you long life and happiness and tells you to forget him." But Grushenka sent almost every day to inquire after him.

"You've come at last!" she cried, flinging down the cards and joyfully greeting Alyosha, "and Maximushka's been scaring me that perhaps you wouldn't come. Ah, how I need you! Sit down to the table. What will you have—coffee?"

"Yes, please," said Alyosha, sitting down at the table. "I am very hungry."

"That's right. Fenya, Fenya, coffee," cried Grushenka. "It's been made a long time ready for you. And bring some little pies, and mind they are hot. Do you know, we've had a storm over those pies today. I took them to the prison for him, and would you believe it, he threw them back to me: he would not eat them. He flung one of them on the floor and stamped on it. So I said to him: 'I will leave them with the warder; if you don't eat them before evening, it will be because your venomous spite is enough for you!' With that I went away. We quarreled again, would you believe it? Whenever I go we quarrel."

Grushenka said all this in one breath in her agitation. Maximov, feeling nervous, at once smiled and looked on the floor.

"What did you quarrel about this time?" asked Alyosha.

"I didn't expect it in the least. Only fancy, he is jealous of the Pole. 'Why are you keeping him?' he said. 'So you've begun keeping him.' He is jealous, jealous of me all the time, jealous eating and sleeping! He even took it into his head to be jealous of Kuzma last week."

"But he knew about the Pole before?"

"Yes, but there it is. He has known about him from the very beginning, but today he suddenly got up and began to curse him. I am ashamed to repeat what he said. The fool! Rakitka went in as I came out. Perhaps Rakitka is egging him on. What do you think?" she added carelessly.

"He loves you, that's what it is; he loves you so much. And now he is particularly worried."

"I should think he might be, with the trial tomorrow. And I went to him to say something about tomorrow, for I dread to think what's going to happen then. You say that he is worried, but how worried I am! And he talks about the Pole! What a fool! He is not jealous of Maximushka yet, anyway."

"My wife was dreadfully jealous over me, too, ma'am" Maximov put in his little word.

"Jealous of you?" Grushenka laughed in spite of herself. "Of whom could she have been jealous?"

"Of the servant girls."

"Hold your tongue, Maximushka, I am in no laughing mood now, I feel angry. Don't ogle the pies. I won't give you any; they are not good for you, and I won't give you any vodka either. I have to look after him, too, just as though I kept an almshouse," she laughed.

"I don't deserve your kindness, ma'am. I am worthless," said Maximov, with tears in his voice. "You would do better spend your kindness on people of more use than me."

"Ech, everyone is of use, Maximushka, and how can we tell who's of most use. If only that Pole didn't exist, Alyosha. He's taken it into his head to fall ill, too, today. I've been to see him also. And I shall send him some pies, too, on purpose. I hadn't sent him any, but Mitya accused me of it, so now I shall send some! Ah, here's Fenya with a letter! Yes, it's from the Poles—begging again!"

Pan Mussyalovich had indeed sent an extremely long and characteristically eloquent letter in which he begged her to lend him three rubles. In the letter was enclosed a receipt for the sum, with a promise to repay it within three months, signed by *Pan* Vrublevsky as well. Grushenka had received many such letters, accompanied by such receipts, from her former lover during the two weeks of her convalescence. But she knew that the two *pans* had been to ask after her health during her illness. The first letter Grushenka got from them was a long one, written on large notepaper and with a big family crest on the seal. It was so obscure and rhetorical that Grushenka put it down before she had read half, unable to make head or tail of it. She could not attend to letters then. The first letter was followed next day by another in which *Pan* Mussyalovich begged her for a loan of two thousand rubles for a very short period. Grushenka left that letter, too, unanswered. A whole series of letters had followed—one every day—all as pompous and rhetorical, but the loan asked for, gradually diminishing, dropped to a hundred rubles, then to twenty-five, to ten, and finally Grushenka received a letter in which both the *pans* begged her for only one ruble and included a receipt signed by both. Then Grushenka suddenly felt sorry for them, and at dusk she went round herself to their lodgings. She found the two Poles in great poverty, almost destitution, without food or fuel, without cigarettes, in debt to their landlady. The two hundred rubles they had carried off from Mitya at Mokroe had soon disappeared. But Grushenka was surprised at their meeting her with arrogant dignity and self-assertion, with the greatest punctilio and pompous speeches. Grushenka simply laughed, and gave her former admirer ten rubles. Then, laughing, she told Mitya of it and he was not in the least jealous. But ever since, the *pans* had attached themselves to Grushenka and bombarded her daily with requests for money and she had always sent them small sums. And now that day Mitya had suddenly taken it into his head to be fearfully jealous.

"Like a fool, I went round to him just for a minute, on the way to see Mitya, for he is ill, too, my former *pan*," Grushenka began again with nervous haste. "I was laughing, telling Mitya about it. 'Imagine,' I said, 'my *pan* had the happy thought to sing his old songs to me on the guitar. He thought I would be touched and marry him!' Mitya leaped up swearing. . . . So, there, I'll send the pies to the *pans*! Fenya, is it that little girl they've sent? Here, give her three rubles and wrap up a dozen pies, and tell her to take them. And you, Alyosha, be sure to tell Mitya that I did send them the pies."

"I wouldn't tell him for anything," said Alyosha, smiling.

"Ech! You think he is unhappy about it. Why, he's jealous on purpose. He doesn't care," said Grushenka bitterly.

"On purpose?" asked Alyosha.

"I tell you you are silly, Alyosha, that's what. You know nothing about it, with all your intelligence, that's what. I am not offended that he is jealous of a girl like me. I would be offended if he were not jealous. I am like that. I am not offended at jealousy. I have a fierce heart, too. I can be jealous myself. Only what offends me is that he doesn't love me at all. I tell you he is jealous now on *purpose*. Am I blind? Don't I see? He began talking to me just now of that woman, Katka, saying she was this and that, how she had ordered a doctor from Moscow for him, to try and save him; how she had ordered the best counsel, the most learned one, too. So he loves her, if he'll praise her to my face, more shame to him! He's treated me badly himself, so he attacked me, to make out I am in fault first and to throw it all on me. 'You were with your Pole before me, so I can't be blamed for Katka,' that's what it amounts to. He wants to throw the whole blame on me. He attacked me on purpose, on purpose, I tell you, but I'll . . ."

Grushenka could not finish saying what she would do. She hid her eyes in her handkerchief and sobbed violently.

"He doesn't love Katerina Ivanovna," said Alyosha firmly.

"Well, whether he loves her or not, I'll soon find out for myself," said Grushenka, with a menacing note in her voice, taking the handkerchief from her eyes. Her face was distorted. Alyosha saw sorrowfully that from being mild and serene, it had become sullen and spiteful.

"Enough of this foolishness," she said suddenly; "it's not for that I sent for you. Alyosha, darling, tomorrow—what will happen tomorrow? That's what worries me! And it's only me it worries! I look at everyone and no one is thinking of it. No one cares about it. Are you thinking about it even? Tomorrow he'll be tried, you know. Tell me, how will he be tried? You know it's the lackey, the lackey that killed him! Good heavens! Can they condemn him in place of the lackey and will no one stand up for him? They haven't troubled the lackey at all, have they?"

"He's been severely cross-examined," observed Alyosha thoughtfully; "but everyone came to the conclusion it was not he. Now he is lying very ill. He has been ill ever since that attack. Really ill," added Alyosha.

"Oh, dear! couldn't you go to that counsel yourself and tell him the whole thing by yourself? He's been brought from Petersburg for three thousand rubles, they say."

"We gave these three thousand together—brother Ivan, Katerina Ivanovna and I—but she paid two thousand for the doctor from Moscow herself. The counsel Fetyukovich[1] would have charged more, but the case has become known all over Russia; it's talked of in all the papers and journals. Fetyukovich agreed to come more for the glory of the thing, because the case has become so notorious. I saw him yesterday."

"Well? Did you talk to him?" Grushenka put in eagerly.

"He listened and said nothing. He told me that he had already formed his opinion. But he promised to give my words consideration."

"Consideration! Ah, they are swindlers! They'll ruin him. And why did she send for the doctor?"

"As an expert. They want to prove that Mitya's mad and committed the murder when he didn't know what he was doing." Alyosha smiled gently, "but Mitya won't agree to that."

"Yes; but that would be the truth if he had killed him!" cried Grushenka. "He was mad then, perfectly mad, and that was my fault, wretch that I am! But, of course, he didn't do it, he didn't do it! And they are all against him, the whole town. Even Fenya's evidence went to prove he had done it. And the people at the shop, and that official, and at the tavern, too, before, people had heard him say so! They are all, all against him, all crying out against him."

"Yes, there's a fearful accumulation of evidence," Alyosha observed grimly.

"And Grigory—Grigory Vasilyevich—sticks to his story that the door was open, persists that he saw it—there's no shaking him. I went and talked to him myself. He's rude about it, too."

"Yes, that's perhaps the strongest evidence against him," said Alyosha.

---

1. The character Fetyukovich was partly inspired by famous lawyers of Dostoevsky's day: Vladimir Spasovich (1829–1906), a professor of law at the University of Saint Petersburg and defense attorney in the Kroneberg child abuse case (see p. 649), and P. A. Alexandrov (1836–1893), the defense lawyer for Vera Zasulich in 1878. Zasulich (1849–1919), a student radical, attempted to assassinate a Russian general in 1877. See also note 1, p. 553.

"And as for Mitya's being mad, he certainly seems like it now," Grushenka began with a peculiarly anxious and mysterious air. "Do you know, Alyosha, I've been wanting to talk to you about it for a long time. I go to him every day and simply wonder at him. Tell me, now, what do you suppose he's always talking about? He talks and talks and I can make nothing of it. I fancied he was talking of something intellectual that I couldn't understand in my foolishness. Only he suddenly began talking to me about a 'babe'—that is, about some child. 'Why is the babe poor?' he said. 'It's for that babe I am going to Siberia now. I am not a murderer, but I must go to Siberia!' What that meant, what babe, I couldn't tell for the life of me. Only I cried when he said it, because he said it so nicely. He cried himself, and I cried, too. He suddenly kissed me and made the sign of the cross over me. What did it mean, Alyosha, tell me? What is this 'babe'?"

"It must be Rakitin, who's been going to see him lately," smiled Alyosha, "though . . . that's not Rakitin's doing. I didn't see Mitya yesterday. I'll see him today."

"No, it's not Rakitka; it's his brother Ivan Fyodorovich upsetting him. It's his going to see him, that's what it is," Grushenka began, and suddenly broke off. Alyosha gazed at her in amazement.

"Ivan's going? Has he been to see him? Mitya told me himself that Ivan hasn't been once."

"There . . . there! What a girl I am! Blurting things out!" exclaimed Grushenka, confused and suddenly blushing. "Wait, Alyosha, hush! Since I've said so much I'll tell the whole truth—he's been to see him twice, the first time directly he arrived. He rushed here from Moscow at once, of course, before I was taken ill; and the second time was a week ago. He told Mitya not to tell you about it, under any circumstances; and not to tell anyone, in fact. He came secretly."

Alyosha sat plunged in thought, considering something. The news evidently impressed him.

"Brother Ivan doesn't talk to me of Mitya's case," he said slowly. "He's said very little to me these last two months. And whenever I go to see him, he seems vexed at my coming, so I haven't been to see him for the last three weeks. Hm! . . . if he was there a week ago . . . there certainly has been a change in Mitya this week."

"There has been a change," Grushenka assented quickly. "They have a secret, they have a secret! Mitya told me himself there was a secret, and such a secret that Mitya can't rest. Before then, he was cheerful—and, indeed, he is cheerful now—but when he shakes his head like that, you know, and strides about the room and keeps pulling at the hair on his right temple with his right hand, I know there is something on his mind worrying him. . . . I know! He was cheerful before, though, indeed, he is cheerful today."

"But you said he was worried."

"Yes, he is worried and yet cheerful. He keeps on being irritable for a minute and then cheerful and then irritable again. And you know, Alyosha, I constantly wonder at him—with this awful thing hanging over him, he sometimes laughs at such trifles as though he were a baby himself."

"And did he really tell you not to tell me about Ivan? Did he say 'don't tell him'?"

"Yes, he told me 'don't tell him.' It's you that Mitya's most afraid of. Because it's a secret: he said himself it was a secret. Alyosha, darling, go to him and find out what their secret is and come and tell me," Grushenka besought him with sudden eagerness. "Set my mind at rest that I may know the worst that's in store for poor me. That's why I sent for you."

"You think it's something to do with you? If it were, he wouldn't have told you there was a secret."

"I don't know. Perhaps he wants to tell me, but doesn't dare to. He warns me. There is a secret, he tells me, but he won't tell me what it is."

"What do you think yourself?"

"What do I think? It's the end for me, that's what I think. They all three have been plotting my end, for Katka's in it. It's all Katka, it all comes from her. She is this and that means that I am not. He tells me that beforehand—warns me. He is planning to throw me over, that's the whole secret. They've planned it together, the three of them—Mitya, Katka, and Ivan Fyodorovich. Alyosha, I've been wanting to ask you a long time. A week ago he suddenly told me that Ivan was in love with Katka, because he often goes to see her. Did he tell me the truth or not? Tell me, on your conscience, tell me the worst."

"I won't tell you a lie. Ivan is not in love with Katerina Ivanovna, I think."

"Oh, that's what I thought! He is lying to me, shameless deceiver, that's what it is! And he was jealous of me just now, so as to put the blame on me afterwards. He is stupid, he can't disguise what he is doing; he is so open, you know. . . . But I'll give it to him, I'll give it to him! 'You believe I did it,' he said. He said that to me, to me. He reproached me with that! God forgive him! You wait, I'll make it hot for Katka at the trial! I'll just say a word then . . . I'll tell everything then!"

And again she cried bitterly.

"This I can tell you for certain, Grushenka," Alyosha said, getting up. "First, that he loves you, loves you more than anyone in the world, and you only, believe me. I know. I do know. The second thing is that I don't want to worm his secret out of him, but if he'll tell me of his own will today, I will tell him straight out that I have promised to tell you. Then I'll come to you today and tell you. Only . . . it seems to me . . . Katerina Ivanovna has nothing to do with it, and that the secret is about something else. That's certain. It isn't likely it's about Katerina Ivanovna, it seems to me. Good-bye for now."

Alyosha shook hands with her. Grushenka was still crying. He saw that she put little faith in his consolation, but she was better for having had her sorrow out, for having spoken of it. He was sorry to leave her in such a state of mind, but he was in haste. He had a great many things to do still.

Chapter II

An Ailing Little Foot

The first of these things was at the house of Madame Khokhlakova, and he hurried there to get it over as quickly as possible and not to be too late for Mitya. Madame Khokhlakova had been slightly ailing for the last three weeks: her foot had for some reason swollen up, and though she was not in bed, she lay all day half-reclining on the couch in her boudoir, in a fascinating but decorous *déshabillé*.[2] Alyosha had once noted with innocent amusement that, in spite of her illness, Madame Khokhlakova had begun to be rather dressy—caps, bows, little jackets, had made their appearance, and he had an inkling of the reason, though he dismissed such ideas from his mind as frivolous. During the last two months the young official, Perkhotin, had become a regular visitor at the house. Alyosha had not called for four days and he was in haste to go straight to Liza, as it was with her he had to speak, for Liza had sent a maid to him the previous day, specially asking him to come to her "about something very important," a request which, for certain reasons, had interest for Alyosha. But while the maid went to take his name in to Liza, Madame Khokhlakova heard of his arrival from someone, and immediately sent to beg him to come to her "just one minute." Alyosha reflected that it was better to accede to the mamasha's request, or else she would be sending down to Liza's room every minute that he was there. Madame Khokhlakova was lying on a couch. She was particularly smartly dressed and was evidently in a state of extreme nervous excitement. She greeted Alyosha with cries of rapture.

"It's ages, ages, perfect ages since I've seen you! It's a whole week—only think of it! Ah, but you were here only four days ago, on Wednesday. You have come to see Lise. I'm sure you meant to slip into her room on tiptoe, without my hearing you. My dear, dear Alexey Fyodorovich, if you only knew how worried I am about her! But of that later, though that's the most important thing, of that later. Dear Alexey Fyodorovich, I trust you implicitly with my Liza. Since the death of Father Zosima—God rest his soul!" (She crossed herself) "—I look upon you as a monk, though you look charming in your new suit. Where did you find such a tailor in these parts? No, no, that's not the chief thing—of that later. Forgive me for sometimes calling you Alyosha; an old woman like me may take liberties," she smiled coquettishly; "but that will do later, too. The important thing is that I shouldn't forget what is important. Please remind me of it yourself. As soon as my tongue runs away with me, you just say 'the important thing?' Ach! how do I know now what is of most importance? Ever since Lise took back her promise—her childish promise, Alexey Fyodorovich— to marry you, you've realized, of course, that it was only the playful childish fantasy of a sick little girl who had been so long confined to her chair— thank God, she can walk now! . . . that new doctor Katya sent for from Moscow for your unhappy brother, who will tomorrow . . . But why speak of tomorrow? I am ready to die at the very thought of tomorrow. Ready to die of curiosity. . . . In short, that doctor was with us yesterday and saw Lise. . . . I paid him fifty rubles for the visit. But that's not the point, that's not the point again. You see, I'm mixing everything up. I am in such a hurry. Why am I in a hurry? I don't understand. It's awful how I seem growing unable to understand anything. Everything seems mixed up in a sort of tangle. I am afraid you are so bored you will jump up and run away, and that will be all I shall see of you. Goodness! Why are we sitting here and no coffee? Yulia, Glafira, coffee!"

---

2. A state of semi-undress or inappropriate dress. Although it is daytime and she is receiving visitors, Madame Khokhlakova wears a fancy nightgown.

Alyosha hastened to thank her, and announced that he had just had coffee.

"Where?"

"At Agrafena Alexandrovna's."

"At . . . at that woman's? Ah, it's she who has brought ruin on everyone. I know nothing about it though. They say she has become a saint, though it's rather late in the day. She had better have done it before. What use is it now? Hush, hush, Alexey Fyodorovich, for I have so much to say to you that I am afraid I shall tell you nothing. This awful trial . . . I shall certainly go, I am making arrangements. I shall be carried there in my chair; besides I can sit up. I shall have servants with me. And, you know, I am a witness. How shall I speak, how shall I speak? I don't know what I shall say. One has to take an oath, doesn't one?"

"Yes; but I don't think you will be able to go."

"I can sit up. Ah, you put me out; ah! this trial, this savage act, and then they are all going to Siberia, some are getting married, and all this so quickly, so quickly, everything's changing, and at last—nothing. All grow old and have death to look forward to. Well, so be it! I am weary. This Katya, *cette charmante personne*,[3] has disappointed all my hopes. Now she is going to follow one of your brothers to Siberia, and your other brother is going to follow her, and will live in the nearest town, and they will all torment one another. It drives me out of my mind. Worst of all—the publicity. The story has been told a million times over in all the papers in Moscow and Petersburg. Ah! yes, would you believe it, there's a paragraph that I was a 'dear friend' of your brother's—I don't want to repeat the horrid word. Just imagine, just imagine!"

"Impossible! Where was the paragraph? What did it say?"

"I'll show you right now. I got the paper and read it yesterday. Here, in the Petersburg paper *Gossip*.[4] The paper began coming out this year. I am awfully fond of gossip, and I subscribed to it, and now—this is what gossip comes to! to my own misfortune. Here it is, here, this passage. Read it."

And she handed Alyosha a sheet of newspaper which had been under her pillow.

It was not exactly that she was upset, she seemed overwhelmed, and perhaps everything really was mixed up in a lump in her head. The paragraph was very typical, and must have been a great shock to her, but, fortunately perhaps, she was unable to keep her mind fixed on any one subject at that moment, and so might race off in a minute to something else and quite forget the newspaper.

Alyosha was well aware that the story of the terrible case had spread all over Russia. And, good heavens! what wild reports and despatches about his brother, about all the Karamazovs, and even about himself he had read in the course of those two months. One paper had even stated that he had gone into a monastery and become a monk, in horror at his brother's crime. Another contradicted this, and stated that he and his elder, Father Zosima, had broken into the monastery chest and "made tracks from the monastery." The present paragraph in the paper *Gossip* was under the

3. "That charming person" (French).
4. Possibly an allusion to the journal *Rumors* (*Molva*), published in Saint Petersburg 1879–81 and at times critical of Dostoevsky's views.

heading, "The Karamazov Case at Skotoprigonevsk."[5] (That, alas! was the name of our little town. I had hitherto kept it concealed.) It was brief, and Madame Khokhlakova was not directly mentioned in it. No names appeared, in fact. It was merely stated that the criminal, whose approaching trial was making such a sensation—retired army captain, an idle swaggerer, and reactionary bully—was continually involved in amorous intrigues, and particularly popular with certain ladies "who were pining in solitude." One such lady, a pining widow, who tried to seem young though she had a grown-up daughter, was so fascinated by him that only two hours before the crime she offered him three thousand rubles, on condition that he would elope with her to the gold mines. But the criminal, counting on escaping punishment, had preferred to murder his father to get the three thousand, rather than go off to Siberia with the middle-aged charms of his pining lady. This playful paragraph finished, of course, with an outburst of generous indignation at the wickedness of parricide and at the lately abolished institution of serfdom. Reading it with curiosity, Alyosha folded up the paper and handed it back to Madame Khokhlakova.[6]

"Well, that must be me," she hurried on again. "Of course I am meant. Scarcely more than an hour before, I suggested gold mines to him, and here they talk of 'middle-aged charms' as though that were my motive! He writes that out of spite. God Almighty forgive him for the middle-aged charms, as I forgive him! You know it's . . . do you know who it is? It's your friend Rakitin."

"Perhaps," said Alyosha, "though I've heard nothing about it."

"It's he, it's he! No 'perhaps' about it. You know I turned him out of the house. . . . You know all that story, don't you?"

"I know that you asked him not to visit you in the future, but why it was, I haven't heard . . . from you, at least."

"Ah, then you've heard it from him! He abuses me, I suppose, abuses me dreadfully?"

"Yes, he does; but then he abuses everyone. But why you've given him up I haven't heard from him either. I meet him very seldom now, indeed. We are not friends."

"Well, then, I'll tell you all about it. There's no help for it, I repent, for there is one point in which I was perhaps to blame. Only a little, little point, so little that perhaps it doesn't count. You see, my dear boy"— Madame Khokhlakova suddenly looked arch and a charming, though enigmatic, smile played about her lips—"you see, I suspect . . . You must forgive me, Alyosha. I am like a mother to you. . . . No, no; quite the contrary. I speak to you now, as though you were my father—mother's quite out of place. Well, it's as though I were confessing to Father Zosima, that's just it. I called you a monk just now. Well, that poor young man, your friend, Rakitin (Mercy on us! I can't be angry with him. I feel cross, but not very), that frivolous young man, would you believe it, seems to have taken it into his head to fall in love with me. I only noticed it later. At first—a month ago—he only began to come more often to see me, almost every day; though, of course, we were acquainted before. I knew nothing

---

5. Based on the word *skotoprigonka*, Russian for stockyard or cattle yard.
6. Rakitin's article is a parody of a certain type of exposé journalism common in the liberal and radical Russian press of the 1860s–70s.

about it . . . and suddenly it dawned upon me, and I began to notice things with surprise. You know, two months ago, that modest, charming, excellent young man, Pyotr Ilyich Perkhotin, who's in the service here, began to be a regular visitor at the house. You met him here ever so many times yourself. And he is an excellent, earnest young man, isn't he? He comes once every three days, not every day (though I should be glad to see him every day), and always so well dressed. Altogether, I love young people, Alyosha, talented, modest, like you, and he has almost the mind of a statesman, he talks so charmingly, and I shall certainly, certainly try and get a promotion for him. He is a future diplomat. On that awful day he almost saved me from death by coming in the night. And your friend Rakitin comes in such boots, and always stretches them out on the carpet. . . . In short, he began hinting at his feelings, in fact, and one day, as he was going, he squeezed my hand terribly hard. My foot began to swell right after he pressed my hand like that. He had met Pyotr Ilyich here before, and would you believe it, he was constantly gibing at him, gibing at him, growling at him, for some reason. I simply looked at the way they went on together and laughed inwardly. So suddenly I was sitting here alone—no, I was laid up then, well, suddenly I was lying here alone and Rakitin comes in, and imagine, brought me some verses of his own composition—a short poem, on my bad foot: that is, he described my foot in a poem. Wait a minute—how did it go?

A captivating little foot
Started suddenly to ail,[7]

it began somehow like that. I can never remember poetry. I've got it here. I'll show it to you later. But it's a charming thing—charming; and, you know, it's not only about the foot; it had a good moral, too, a charming idea, only I've forgotten it; in fact, it was just the thing for an album. So, of course, I thanked him, and he was evidently flattered. I'd hardly had time to thank him when in comes Pyotr Ilyich, and Mikhail Ivanovich suddenly looked as black as night. I could see that Pyotr Ilyich was in the way, for Mikhail Ivanovich certainly wanted to say something after giving me the verses. I had a presentiment of it; but Pyotr Ilyich came in. I showed Pyotr Ilyich the verses and didn't say who was the author. But I am convinced, I am convinced, that he guessed, though he won't admit it to this day, and declares he had no idea. But he says that on purpose. Pyotr Ilyich began to laugh at once, and fell to criticizing it. 'Wretched doggerel,' he said they were, 'some seminarian must have written them,' and with such vehemence, such vehemence! Then, instead of laughing, your friend flew into a rage. 'Good gracious!' I thought, 'they'll fly at each other.' 'It was I who wrote them,' said he. 'I wrote them as a joke,' he said, 'for I think it degrading to write verses. . . . But they are good poetry. They want to put a monument to your Pushkin for writing about women's feet,[8] while I wrote with a

---

7. These verses of Rakitin's, and those on p. 498, are a parody of a parody of Pushkin written by Minaev. The effect is to mock the contempt for Pushkin expressed by Minaev, an "exposé poet" (*oblichitel'ny poet*) of questionable talent. Russian radicals of the 1860s generally expressed contempt for Pushkin and the high culture he had come to represent.
8. Plans for a monument to Pushkin had begun in the early 1860s and gained momentum in the mid-1870s; the monument was finally unveiled in June 1880, and Dostoevsky played a prominent role in the ceremonies. The speech he delivered at the event created a sensation, and was published in the August 1880 issue of the *Diary of a Writer*.

moral purpose, and you,' said he, 'are an advocate of serfdom. You have no humane ideas,' said he. 'You have no modern, enlightened feelings, you are uninfluenced by progress, you are a mere official,' he said, 'and you take bribes.' Then I began screaming and imploring them. And, you know, Pyotr Ilyich is anything but a coward. He at once took up the most gentlemanly tone, looked at him sarcastically, listened, and apologized. 'I'd no idea,' said he. 'I shouldn't have said it, if I had known. I should have praised it. Poets are all so irritable,' he said. In short, he laughed at him under the cover of the most gentlemanly tone. He himself explained to me afterwards that it was all sarcastic. I thought he was in earnest. Only as I lay there, just as before you now, I thought, 'would it, or would it not, be the proper thing for me to turn Mikhail Ivanovich out for shouting so rudely at a visitor in my house?' And, would you believe it, I lay here, shut my eyes, and wondered, would it be the proper thing or not. I kept worrying and worrying, and my heart began to beat, and I couldn't make up my mind whether to make an outcry or not. One voice seemed to be telling me, 'speak,' and the other 'no, don't speak.' And no sooner had the second voice said that than I cried out, and fainted. Of course, there was a fuss. I got up suddenly and said to Mikhail Ivanovich, 'It's painful for me to say it, but I don't wish to see you in my house again.' So I turned him out. Ah! Alexey Fyodorovich, I know myself I did wrong. I was putting it on. I wasn't angry with him at all really; but I suddenly fancied—that was what did it—that it would be such a fine scene. . . . And yet, believe me, it was quite natural, for I really shed tears and cried for several days afterwards, and then suddenly, one afternoon, I forgot all about it. So it's two weeks since he's been here, and I kept wondering whether he would come again. I wondered even yesterday, then suddenly last night came this *Gossip*. I read it and gasped. Who could have written it? He must have written it. He went home, sat down, wrote it on the spot, sent it, and they put it in. It was two weeks ago, you see. But, Alyosha, it's awful how I keep talking and don't say what I want to say. Ah! the words come of themselves!"

"It's very important for me to be in time to see my brother today," Alyosha faltered.

"To be sure, to be sure! You bring it all back to me. Listen, what is an aberration?"

"What aberration?" asked Alyosha, wondering.

"In the legal sense. An aberration in which everything is pardonable. Whatever you do, you will be acquitted at once."[9]

"What do you mean?"

"I'll tell you. This Katya . . . Ah! she is a charming, charming being, only I never can make out who it is she is in love with. She was with me some time ago and I couldn't get anything out of her. Especially as she won't talk to me except on the surface now. In short, she is always talking about my health and nothing else, and she takes up such a tone with me, too. I simply said to myself, 'Well, so be it. I don't care' . . . Oh, yes. I was talking of aberration: this doctor has come. You know a doctor has come? Of course you know it—the one who discovers madmen. You wrote for

9. Dostoevsky was extremely critical of what he perceived to be the routine abuse of the insanity defense in the newly reformed Russian legal system of the 1860s and 70s, and wrote frequently about this topic in his *Diary of a Writer*.

him. No, it wasn't you, but Katya. It's all Katya! Well, you see, a man may be sitting perfectly sane and suddenly have an aberration. He may be conscious and know what he is doing and yet be in a state of aberration. And there's no doubt that Dmitri Fyodorovich was suffering from aberration. They found out about aberration as soon as the law courts were reformed. It's all the good effect of the reformed law courts. The doctor has been here and questioned me about that evening, about the gold mines. 'How did he seem then?' he asked me. He must have been in a state of aberration. He came in shouting, 'Money, money, three thousand! Give me three thousand!' and then went away and immediately did the murder. 'I don't want to murder him,' he said, and he suddenly went and murdered him. That's why they'll acquit him, because he struggled against it and yet he murdered him."

"But he didn't murder him," Alyosha interrupted rather sharply. He felt more and more sick with anxiety and impatience.

"Yes, I know it was that old man Grigory murdered him."

"Grigory?" cried Alyosha.

"Yes, yes; it was Grigory. He lay as Dmitri Fyodorovich struck him down, and then got up, saw the door open, went in and killed Fyodor Pavlovich."

"But why, why?"

"Suffering from aberration. When he recovered from the blow Dmitri Fyodorovich gave him on the head, he was suffering from aberration: he went and committed the murder. As for his saying he didn't, he very likely doesn't remember. Only, you know, it'll be better, ever so much better, if Dmitri Fyodorovich murdered him. And that's how it must have been, though I say it was Grigory. It certainly was Dmitri Fyodorovich, and that's better, ever so much better! Oh! not better that a son should have killed his father, I don't defend that. Children ought to honor their parents, and yet it would be better if it were he, as you'd have nothing to cry over then, for he did it when he was unconscious or rather when he was conscious, but did not know what he was doing. Let them acquit him— that's so humane, and would show what a blessing reformed law courts are. I knew nothing about it, but they say they have been so a long time. And when I heard it yesterday, I was so struck by it that I wanted to send for you at once. And if he is acquitted, make him come straight from the law courts to dinner with me, and I'll have a party of friends, and we'll drink to the reformed law courts. I don't believe he'd be dangerous; besides, I'll invite a great many friends, so that he could always be led out if he did anything. And then he might be made a justice of the peace or something in another town, for those who have been in trouble themselves make the best judges. And, besides, who isn't suffering from aberration, nowadays?—you, I, all of us are in a state of aberration, and there are ever so many examples of it: a man sits singing a song, suddenly something annoys him, he takes a pistol and shoots the first person he comes across, and no one blames him for it. I read that lately, and all the doctors confirm it. The doctors are always confirming; they confirm anything. Why, my Lise is in a state of aberration. She made me cry again yesterday, and the day before, too, and today I suddenly realized that it's all due to aberration. Oh, Lise grieves me so! I believe she's quite mad. Why did she send for you? Did she send for you or did you come of your own accord?"

"Yes, she sent for me, and I am just going to see her." Alyosha got up resolutely.

"Oh, my dear, dear Alexey Fyodorovich, perhaps that's what's most important," Madame Khokhlakova cried, suddenly bursting into tears. "God knows I trust Lise to you with all my heart, and it's no matter her sending for you on the sly, without telling her mother. But forgive me, I can't trust my daughter so easily to your brother Ivan Fyodorovich, though I still consider him the most chivalrous young man. But only fancy, he's been to see Lise and I knew nothing about it!"

"How? What? When?" Alyosha was exceedingly surprised. He had not sat down again and listened standing.

"I will tell you, that's perhaps why I asked you to come, for I don't know now why I did ask you to come. Well, Ivan Fyodorovich has only been to see me twice, since he came back from Moscow. First time he came as a friend to call on me, and the second time, more recently, Katya was here and he came because he heard she was here. I didn't, of course, expect him to come often, knowing what a lot he has to do as it is, *vous comprenez, cette affaire et la mort terrible de votre papa.*[1] But I suddenly heard he'd been here again, not to see me but to see Lise. That's six days ago now. He came, stayed five minutes, and went away. And I didn't hear of it till three days afterwards from Glafira, so it was a great shock to me. I sent for Lise right away. She laughed. 'He thought you were asleep,' she said, 'and came in to me to ask after your health.' Of course, that's how it happened. But Lise, Lise, mercy on us, how she distresses me! Would you believe it, one night, four days ago, just after you saw her last time, and had gone away, she suddenly had a fit, screaming, shrieking, hysterics! Why is it I never have hysterics? Then, next day another fit and the same thing on the third, and yesterday too, and then yesterday that aberration. She suddenly screamed out, 'I hate Ivan Fyodorovich. I insist on your never letting him come to the house again.' I was struck dumb at these amazing words, and answered, 'On what grounds could I refuse to see such an excellent young man, a young man of such learning too, and so unfortunate,' for all this business is a misfortune, isn't it? She suddenly burst out laughing at my words, and so rudely, you know. Well, I was pleased, I thought I had amused her and the fits would pass off, especially as I wanted to refuse to see Ivan Fyodorovich anyway on account of his strange visits without my knowledge, and meant to ask him for an explanation. But early this morning Liza awoke and flew into a rage with Yulia and, would you believe it, slapped her in the face. That's monstrous, I am always polite to my servants. And an hour later she was hugging Yulia's feet and kissing them. She sent a message to me, that she wasn't coming to see me at all, and would never come and see me again, and when I dragged myself down to her, she rushed to kiss me, crying, and as she kissed me, she pushed me out of the room without saying a word, so I couldn't find out what was the matter. Now, dear Alexey Fyodorovich, I rest all my hopes on you, and, of course, my whole life is in your hands. I simply beg you to go to Lise and find out everything from her, as you alone can, and come back and tell me—me, her mother, for you understand it will be the death of me, simply the death of me, if this goes on, or else I shall run away. I can stand no more. I have patience; but I may

---

1. "You understand, this business and the terrible death of your father" (French).

lose patience, and then . . . then something awful will happen. Ah, dear me! At last, Pyotr Ilyich!" cried Madame Khokhlakova, beaming all over as she saw Perkhotin enter the room. "You are late, you are late! Well, sit down, speak, put us out of suspense. What does the counsel say? Where are you off to, Alexey Fyodorovich?"

"To Lise."

"Oh, yes. You won't forget, you won't forget what I asked you? It's a question of life and death!"

"Of course, I won't forget, if I can . . . but I am so late," muttered Alyosha, beating a hasty retreat.

"No, be sure, be sure to come in; don't say 'if you can.' I shall die if you don't," Madame Khokhlakova called after him, but Alyosha had already left the room.

Chapter III

A Little Demon

Going in to Liza, he found her half reclining in the invalid chair, in which she had been wheeled when she was unable to walk. She did not move to meet him, but her sharp keen eyes were simply riveted on his face. There was a feverish look in her eyes, her face was pale and yellow. Alyosha was amazed at the change that had taken place in her in three days. She was positively thinner. She did not hold out her hand to him. He touched the thin, long fingers which lay motionless on her dress, then he sat down facing her, without a word.

"I know you are in a hurry to get to the prison," Liza said curtly, "and mamma's kept you there for hours, she's just been telling you about me and Yulia."

"How do you know?" asked Alyosha.

"I've been listening. Why do you stare at me? I want to listen and I do listen, there's no harm in that. I don't apologize."

"You are upset about something?"

"On the contrary, I am very happy. I've only just been reflecting for the thirtieth time what a good thing it is I refused you and shall not be your wife. You are not fit to be a husband. If I were to marry you and give you a note to take to the man I loved after you, you'd take it and be sure to give it to him and bring an answer back, too. If you were forty, you would still go on carrying my love letters for me."

She suddenly laughed.

"There is something spiteful and yet open-hearted about you," Alyosha smiled to her.

"The open-heartedness consists in my not being ashamed of myself with you. What's more, I don't want to feel ashamed with you, just with you. Alyosha, why is it I don't respect you? I am very fond of you, but I don't respect you. If I respected you, I wouldn't talk to you without shame, would I?"

"No."

"But do you believe that I am not ashamed with you?"

"No, I don't believe it."

Liza laughed nervously again; she spoke rapidly.

"I sent your brother, Dmitri Fyodorovich, some candy in prison. Alyosha, you know, you are quite handsome! I shall love you awfully for having so quickly allowed me not to love you."

"Why did you send for me today, Lise?"

"I wanted to tell you of a longing I have. I should like someone to torture me, marry me and then torture me, deceive me and go away. I don't want to be happy."

"You are in love with disorder?"

"Yes, I want disorder. I keep wanting to set fire to the house. I keep imagining how I'll creep up and set fire to the house on the sly, it must be on the sly. They'll try to put it out, but it'll go on burning. And I shall know and say nothing. Ah, what silliness! And how bored I am!"

She waved her hand with a look of repulsion.

"It's your luxurious life," said Alyosha, softly.

"Is it better then to be poor?"

"Yes, it is better."

"That's what your late monk taught you. That's not true. Let me be rich and all the rest poor, I'll eat candy and drink cream and not give any to anyone else. Ach, don't speak, don't say anything," she waved her hand at him, though Alyosha had not opened his mouth. "You've told me all that before, I know it all by heart. It bores me. If I am ever poor, I shall murder somebody, and even if I am rich, I may murder someone, perhaps— why do nothing! But do you know, I should like to reap, cut the rye?[2] I'll marry you, and you shall become a peasant, a real peasant; we'll keep a colt, shall we? Do you know Kalganov?"

"Yes."

"He is always wandering about, dreaming. He says, why live in real life, it's better to dream. One can dream the most delightful things, but real life is a bore. But he'll be married soon for all that, he's declared his love to me already. Can you spin tops?"

"Yes."

"Well, he's just like a top: he wants to be wound up and set spinning and then to be lashed, lashed, lashed with a whip. If I marry him, I'll keep him spinning all his life. You are not ashamed to be with me?"

"No."

"You are awfully cross, because I don't talk about holy things. I don't want to be holy. What will they do to me in the next world for the greatest sin?[3] You must know all about that."

"God will censure you." Alyosha was watching her steadily.

"That's just what I should like. I would go up and they would censure me and I would burst out laughing in their faces. I would dreadfully like to set fire to the house, Alyosha, to our house; you still don't believe me?"

"Why? There are children of twelve who have a longing to set fire to something and they do set things on fire too. It's a sort of disease."

"That's not true, that's not true, there may be children, but that's not what I mean."

---

2. Extremely difficult agricultural work.
3. According to Christian doctrine, the greatest sin is blasphemy against the Holy Spirit; see Matthew 12.31–32.

"You take evil for good; it's a passing crisis, it's the result of your illness, perhaps."

"You do despise me though! It's simply that I don't want to do good, I want to do evil, and it has nothing to do with illness."

"Why do evil?"

"So that everything might be destroyed. Ah, how good it would be if everything were destroyed! You know, Alyosha, I sometimes think of doing a fearful lot of harm and everything bad, and I would do it for a long while on the sly and suddenly everyone would find it out. Everyone would stand round and point their fingers at me and I would look at them all. That would be awfully pleasant. Why would it be so pleasant, Alyosha?"

"I don't know. It's a craving to destroy something good or, as you say, to set fire to something. It happens sometimes."

"I not only say it, I shall do it."

"I believe you."

"Ah, how I love you for saying you believe me. And you are not lying one little bit. But perhaps you think that I am saying all this on purpose to annoy you?"

"No, I don't think that . . . though perhaps there is a little desire to do that in it, too."

"There is a little. I never can tell lies to you," she declared, with a strange fire in her eyes.

What struck Alyosha above everything was her earnestness. There was not a trace of humor or jesting in her face now, though, in the old days, fun and gaiety never deserted her even at her most "earnest" moments.

"There are moments when people love crime," said Alyosha thoughtfully.

"Yes, yes! You have expressed my thought, they love crime, everyone loves crime, they love it always, not at some 'moments.' You know, it's as though people have made an agreement to lie about it and have lied about it ever since. They all declare that they hate evil, but secretly they all love it."

"And are you still reading nasty books?"

"Yes, I am. Mamma reads them and hides them under her pillow and I steal them."

"Aren't you ashamed to destroy yourself?"

"I want to destroy myself. There's a boy here, who lay down between the railway lines when the train was passing. Lucky fellow! Listen, your brother is being tried now for murdering his father and everyone loves his having killed his father."

"Loves his having killed his father?"

"Yes, loves it, everyone loves it! Everybody says it's so awful, but secretly they simply love it. I for one love it."

"There is some truth in what you say about everyone," said Alyosha softly.

"Oh, what ideas you have!" Liza shrieked in delight. "And you a monk, too! You wouldn't believe how I respect you, Alyosha, for never telling lies. Oh, I must tell you a funny dream of mine. I sometimes dream of devils. It's night, I am in my room with a candle and suddenly there are devils all over the place, in all the corners, under the table, and they open the doors, there's a crowd of them behind the doors and they want to come and seize me. And they are just coming, just seizing me. But I suddenly cross myself and they all draw back, though they don't go away altogether, they stand at the doors and in the corners, waiting. And suddenly I have a frightful longing to revile God aloud, and so I begin, and then they come crowding back to me, delighted, and seize me again and I cross myself again and they all draw back. It's awful fun, it takes one's breath away."

"I've had the same dream, too," said Alyosha suddenly.

"Really?" cried Liza, surprised. "Listen, Alyosha, don't laugh, that's awfully important. Could two different people have the same dream?"

"It seems they can."

"Alyosha, I tell you, it's awfully important," Liza went on, with really excessive amazement. "It's not the dream that's important, but your having the same dream as me. You never lie to me, don't lie now: is it true? You are not laughing?"

"It's true."

Liza seemed extraordinarily impressed and for half a minute she was silent.

"Aloysha, come and see me, come and see me more often," she said suddenly, in a supplicating voice.

"I'll always come to see you, all my life," answered Alyosha firmly.

"You are the only person I can talk to, you know," Liza began again. "I talk to no one but myself and you. Only you in the whole world. And to you more readily than to myself. And I am not a bit ashamed with you, not a bit. Alyosha, why am I not ashamed with you, not a bit? Alyosha, is it true that at Easter the Yids steal children and kill them?"[4]

"I don't know."

"I have a book here in which I read about the trial of a Yid, who took a child of four years old and cut off the fingers from both hands, and then crucified him on the wall, hammered nails into him and crucified him, and afterwards, when he was tried, he said that the child died soon, within four hours. That was 'soon'! He said the child moaned, kept on moaning and he stood admiring it. That is good!"

"Good?"

"Good. I sometimes imagine that it was I who crucified him. He would hang there moaning and I would sit opposite him eating pineapple compote. I am awfully fond of pineapple compote. Do you like it?"

Alyosha looked at her in silence. Her pale, sallow face was suddenly contorted, her eyes burned.

"You know, when I read about that Yid I shook with sobs all night. I kept imagining how the little child cried and moaned (little boys of four understand, you know) and all the while the thought of pineapple compote haunted me. In the morning I wrote a letter to a certain person, begging him *particularly* to come and see me. He came and I suddenly told him all

4. Russian has one word, *paskha*, that means both Passover and Easter. Liza refers to "blood libel," the myth that Jews kidnap and ritually murder Christian children at Passover. Reports of such murders and accounts of the trials of Jews accused of blood libel occasionally circulated in the press. In March 1879, a case of alleged ritual murder was tried in the Georgian city of Kutaisi. The defendants, young Jewish men accused of abducting and murdering a young girl, were acquitted. Responding to their acquittal, Dostoevsky wrote, "How disgusting that the Kutaisi Yids were acquitted. They were undoubtedly guilty" (March 28, 1879, letter to O. A. Novikova [30.1:59]). For analysis of Dostoevsky's relationship to the blood libel myth, see Maxim D. Shrayer, "The Jewish Question in *The Brothers Karamazov*," in *A New Word on* The Brothers Karamazov, ed. Robert Louis Jackson (Evanston: Northwestern UP, 2004).

about the child and the pineapple compote. *All* about it, *all*, and said that
'it was good.' He laughed and said it really was good. Then he got up and
went away. He was only here five minutes. Did he despise me? Did he
despise me? Tell me, tell me, Alyosha, did he despise me or not?" She sat up
on the couch, with flashing eyes.

"Tell me," Alyosha asked anxiously, "did you send for that person?"

"Yes, I did."

"Did you send him a letter?"

"Yes."

"Simply to ask about that, about that child?"

"No, not about that at all. But when he came, I asked him about that at
once. He answered, laughed, got up and went away."

"That person behaved honorably," Alyosha murmured.

"And did he despise me? Did he laugh at me?"

"No, for perhaps he believes in the pineapple compote himself. He is
very ill now, too, Lise."

"Yes, he does believe in it," said Liza, with flashing eyes.

"He doesn't despise anyone," Alyosha went on. "Only he does not
believe anyone. If he doesn't believe in people, of course, he does despise
them."

"Then he despises me, me?"

"You, too."

"That's good." Liza seemed to grind her teeth. "When he went out
laughing, I felt that it was good to be despised. The child with fingers cut
off is good and to be despised is good . . ."

And she laughed at Alyosha's face, a feverish malicious laugh.

"Do you know, Alyosha, do you know, I would like . . . Alyosha save
me!" she suddenly jumped from the couch, rushed to him and seized him
with both hands. "Save me!" she almost groaned. "Is there anyone in the
world I could tell what I've told you! I've told you the truth, the truth. I
shall kill myself, because I loathe everything! I don't want to live, because
I loathe everything! I loathe everything, everything. Alyosha, why don't
you love me in the least?" she finished in a frenzy.

"But I do love you!" answered Alyosha warmly.

"And will you weep over me, will you?"

"Yes."

"Not because I won't be your wife, but simply weep for me?"

"Yes."

"Thank you! It's only your tears I want. Everyone else may punish me
and trample me under foot, everyone, everyone, not excepting *anyone*.
For I don't love anyone. Do you hear, not anyone! On the contrary, I hate
everybody! Go, Alyosha, it's time you went to your brother," she tore herself away from him suddenly.

"How can I leave you like this?" said Alyosha, almost in alarm.

"Go to your brother, the prison will be shut, go, here's your hat. Give
my love to Mitya, go, go!"

And she almost forcibly pushed Alyosha out of the door. He looked at
her with pained surprise, when he was suddenly aware of a letter in his
right hand, a tiny letter folded up tight and sealed. He glanced at it and
instantly read the address "to Ivan Fyodorovich Karamazov." He looked
quickly at Liza. Her face had become almost menacing.

"Give it to him, you must give it to him!" she ordered him, frenzied and trembling. "Today, at once, or I'll poison myself! That's why I sent for you." And she slammed the door quickly. The bolt clicked. Alyosha put the note in his pocket and went straight downstairs, without going back to Madame Khokhlakova, forgetting her, in fact. As soon as Alyosha had gone, Liza unbolted the door, opened it a little, put her finger in the crack and slammed the door with all her might, pinching her finger. Ten seconds afterwards, releasing her finger, she walked softly, slowly to her chair, sat up straight in it and looked intently at her blackened finger and at the blood that oozed from under the nail. Her lips were quivering and she kept whispering rapidly to herself:

"I am a wretch, wretch, wretch, wretch!"

Chapter IV

A Hymn and a Secret

It was quite late (and how long is a November day?) when Alyosha rang at the prison gate. It was beginning to get dusk. But Alyosha knew that he would be admitted without difficulty. Things were managed in our little town, as everywhere else. At first, of course, on the conclusion of the preliminary inquiry, relations and a few other persons could only obtain interviews with Mitya by going through certain inevitable formalities. But later, though the formalities were not relaxed, exceptions were made for at least some of Mitya's visitors. So much so, that sometimes the interviews with the prisoner in the room set aside for the purpose were practically private. These exceptions, however, were few in number: only Grushenka, Alyosha and Rakitin were treated like this. But the captain of the police, Mikhail Makarovich, was very favorably disposed to Grushenka. His abuse of her at Mokroe weighed on the old man's conscience, and when he learned the whole story, he completely changed his view of her. And, strange to say, though he was firmly persuaded of his guilt, yet after Mitya was once in prison, the old man came to take a more and more lenient view of him. "He was a man of good heart, perhaps," he thought, "who, like a Swede, had come to grief from drinking and dissipation."[5] His first horror had been succeeded by pity. As for Alyosha, the police captain was very fond of him and had known him for a long time. Rakitin, who had of late taken to coming very often to see the prisoner, was one of the most intimate acquaintances of the "police captain's young ladies," as he called them, and was always hanging about their house. He gave lessons in the house of the prison superintendent, too, who, though scrupulous in the performance of his duties, was a kind-hearted old man. Alyosha, again, had an intimate acquaintance of long standing with the superintendent, who was fond of talking to him, generally on "sacred subjects." He respected Ivan Fyodoro-

---

5. The Russian original is *"propal, kak shved pod Poltavoi"* ("he fell like a Swede at Poltava"), a common saying. Mikhail Makarovich expresses a view of Swedes that was common in Russia at the time. Following an era of protracted military conflict, which ended when Peter the Great defeated Sweden at the battle of Poltava in 1720, the Russian state employed Swedes in efforts to Westernize the country. Russians typically perceived Swedes as either drunken and debauched or cold, efficient workers.

vich, and stood in awe of his opinion, though he was a great philosopher himself: "self-taught," of course. But Alyosha had an irresistible attraction for him. During the last year the old man had taken to studying the Apocryphal Gospels,[6] and constantly talked over his impressions with his young friend. He used to come and see him in the monastery and discussed it for hours together with him and with the monks. So even if Alyosha were late at the prison, he had only to go to the superintendent and everything was made easy. Besides, everyone in the prison, down to the humblest warder, had grown used to Alyosha. The sentry, of course, did not trouble him so long as the authorities were satisfied.

When Mitya was summoned from his cell, he always went downstairs, to the place set aside for interviews. As Alyosha entered the room he came upon Rakitin, who was just taking leave of Mitya. They were both talking loudly. Mitya was laughing heartily as he saw him out, while Rakitin seemed grumbling. Rakitin did not like meeting Alyosha, especially of late. He scarcely spoke to him, and bowed to him stiffly. Seeing Alyosha enter now, he frowned and looked away, as though he was entirely absorbed in buttoning his big, warm, fur-trimmed overcoat. Then he began looking at once for his umbrella.

"I must mind not to forget my belongings," he muttered, simply to say something.

"Mind you don't forget other people's belongings," said Mitya, as a joke, and laughed at once at his own wit. Rakitin fired up instantly.

"You'd better give that advice to your own family, who've always been a slave-driving lot, and not to Rakitin," he cried, suddenly trembling with anger.

"What's the matter? I was joking!" cried Mitya. "Foo, the devil! They are all like that," he turned to Alyosha, nodding towards Rakitin's hurriedly retreating figure. "He was sitting here, laughing and cheerful, and all at once he boils up like that. He didn't even nod to you. Have you broken with him completely? Why are you so late? I've not been simply waiting, but thirsting for you the whole morning. But never mind. We'll make up for it now."

"Why does he come here so often? Surely you are not such great friends?" asked Alyosha. He, too, nodded at the door through which Rakitin had disappeared.

"Great friends with Rakitin? No, not as much as that. Is it likely—a pig like that? He considers I am . . . a scoundrel. They can't understand a joke either, that's the worst of such people. They never understand a joke, and their souls are dry, dry and flat; they remind me of prison walls when I was first brought here. But he is an intelligent fellow, very intelligent. Well, Alexey, it's all over with me now."

He sat down on the bench and made Alyosha sit down beside him.

"Yes, the trial's tomorrow. Do you really have no hope, brother?" Alyosha said, with an apprehensive feeling.

"What are you talking about?" said Mitya, looking at him rather uncertainly. "Oh, you mean the trial! Damn it all! Till now we've been talking of things that don't matter, about this trial, but I haven't said a word to you about the chief thing. Yes, the trial is tomorrow; but it wasn't the trial

6. Gospels not recognized by an official church as sacred text.

I meant, when I said it was all over with me. Why do you look at me so critically?"

"What do you mean, Mitya?"

"Ideas, ideas, that's all! Ethics! What is ethics?"

"Ethics?" asked Alyosha, wondering.

"Yes; is it a science?"

"Yes, there is such a science . . . but . . . I confess I can't explain to you what sort of science it is."

"Rakitin knows. Rakitin knows a lot, devil take him! He's not going to be a monk. He means to go to Petersburg. There he'll go in for criticism of an elevating tendency. Who knows, he may be of use and make his own career, too. Ough! they are first-rate, these people, at making a career! Devil take ethics! I am done for, Alexey, I am, you man of God! I love you more than anyone. It rends my heart to yearn to look at you, that's what. Who was Karl Bernard?"

"Karl Bernard?" Alyosha was surprised again.

"No, not Karl. Wait, I made a mistake. Claude Bernard.[7] What is that? Chemistry or what?"

"He must be a scientist," answered Alyosha; "but I must say I can't tell you much about him, either. I've heard of him as a scientist, but what sort I don't know."

"Well, devil take him, then! I don't know either," swore Mitya. "A scoundrel of some sort, most likely. They are all scoundrels. And Rakitin will make his way. Rakitin will get on anywhere; he is another Bernard. Ugh, these Bernards! They are all over the place."

"But what is the matter?" Alyosha asked insistently.

"He wants to write an article about me, about my case, and so begin his literary career. That's what he comes for; he said so himself. He wants to prove some theory. He wants to say that 'he couldn't help murdering his father, he was corrupted by his environment,' and so on. He explained it all to me. He is going to put in a tinge of Socialism, he says. But there, devil take him, he can put in a tinge, if he likes, I don't care. He can't bear brother Ivan, he hates him. He's not fond of you, either. But I don't turn him out, for he is an intelligent fellow. Awfully conceited though. I said to him just now, 'The Karamazovs are not blackguards, but philosophers; for all true Russians are philosophers, and though you've studied, you are not a philosopher—you are a low fellow.' He laughed, so maliciously. And I said to him, '*de ideabus non est disputandum.*'[8] Isn't that rather good? At least I've become a classicist, you see!" Mitya laughed suddenly.

"Why is it all over with you? You said so just now," Alyosha interposed.

"Why is it all over with me? Hmm . . . The fact of it is . . . if you take it as a whole, I am sorry to lose God—that's why it is."

"What do you mean by 'sorry to lose God'?"

"Imagine: inside, in the nerves, in the head—that is, these nerves are there in the brain . . . (devil take them!) there are sort of little tails, the

7. French scientist, physiologist, and pathologist (1813–1878), proponent of the experimental method. His writings and ideas were well-known in Russia, and a Russian translation of his *An Introduction to the Study of Experimental Medicine* (1865) was published by Dostoevsky's friend and collaborator Nikolay Strakhov (1828–1896) in 1866.
8. Mitya parodies the well-known Latin aphorism "*de gustibus non est disputandum*" (there is no arguing about tastes).

little tails of those nerves, and as soon as they begin quivering . . . that is, you see, I look at something with my eyes and then they begin quivering, those little tails . . . and when they quiver, then an image appears . . . it doesn't appear at once, but an instant, a second, passes . . . and then something like a moment appears; that is, not a moment—devil take the moment—but an image; that is, an object, or an action, devil take it—that's why I see and then think, because of those tails, not at all because I've got a soul, and that I am some sort of image and likeness. All that is nonsense. Mikhail explained it all to me yesterday, brother, and it simply bowled me over. It's magnificent, Alyosha, this science! A new man's arising—that I understand. . . . And yet I am sorry to lose God!"

"Well, that's a good thing, anyway," said Alyosha.

"That I am sorry to lose God! It's chemistry, brother, chemistry! There's no help for it, your reverence, you must make way for chemistry. And Rakitin does dislike God. Ough! doesn't he dislike Him! That's the sore point with all of them. But they conceal it. They tell lies. They pretend. 'Will you preach this in your reviews?' I asked him. 'Oh, well, if I did it openly, they won't let it through,' he said. He laughed. 'But what will become of men then?' I asked him, 'without God and immortal life? All things are permitted then, they can do what they like?' 'Didn't you know?' he said laughing, 'an intelligent man can do what he likes,' he said. 'An intelligent man knows his way about, but you've put your foot in it, committing a murder, and now you are rotting in prison.' He says that to my face! A regular pig! I used to kick such people out, but now I listen to them. He talked a lot of sense, too. Writes well. He began reading me an article last week. I copied out three lines of it. Wait a minute. Here it is."

Mitya hurriedly pulled out a piece of paper from his pocket and read:

"'In order to determine this question, it is above all essential to put one's personality in contradiction to one's reality.' Do you understand that?"

"No, I don't," said Alyosha. He looked at Mitya and listened to him with curiosity.

"I don't understand either. It's dark and obscure, but clever. 'Everyone writes like that now,' he says, 'it's the effect of their environment.' They are afraid of the environment. He writes poetry, too, the scoundrel. He's written in honor of Madame Khokhlakova's foot. Ha, ha, ha!"

"I've heard about it," said Alyosha.

"Have you? And have you heard the poem?"

"No."

"I've got it. Here it is. I'll read it to you. You don't know—I haven't told you—there's quite a story about it. He's a rascal! Three weeks ago he began to tease me. 'You've got yourself into a mess, like a fool, for the sake of three thousand, but I'm going to collar a hundred and fifty thousand. I am going to marry a widow and buy a house in Petersburg.' And he told me he was courting Madame Khokhlakova. She hadn't much brains in her youth, and now at forty she has lost what she had. 'But she's awfully sentimental,' he says; 'that's how I shall get hold of her. When I marry her, I shall take her to Petersburg and there I shall start a newspaper.' And his mouth was simply watering in a nasty, sensual way, the beast, watering not for Khokhlakova, but for the hundred and fifty thousand. And he made me believe it. He came to see me every day. 'She is coming round,' he declared. He was beaming with delight. And then, all of a sudden, he was turned out of the house. Perkhotin's carrying everything before him, bravo! I could kiss the foolish woman for turning him out of the house. And he had written this doggerel. 'It's the first time I've soiled my hands with writing poetry,' he said.[9] 'It's to win her heart, so it's in a good cause. When I get hold of the foolish woman's fortune, I can be of great social utility.' They have this social justification for every nasty thing they do! 'Anyway it's better than your Pushkin's poetry,' he said, 'for I've managed to advocate civic sorrow even in that.' I understand what he means about Pushkin, I quite see that, if he really was a man of talent and only wrote about women's feet. But wasn't Rakitin stuck up about his doggerel! The vanity of these fellows! 'On the convalescence of the swollen foot of the object of my affections'—he thought of that for a title. He's a nimble fellow!

> A captivating little foot,
> Though swollen and red and tender!
> The doctors come and plasters put,
> But still they cannot mend her.
>
> Yet, 'tis not for her foot I dread—
> A theme for Pushkin's muse more fit—
> It's not her foot, it is her head:
> I tremble for her loss of wit!
>
> For as her foot swells, strange to say,
> Her intellect is on the wane—
> Oh, for some remedy I pray
> That may restore both foot and brain![1]

He is a pig, a regular pig, but it turned out playfully for the scoundrel! And he really has put in a progressive idea. And wasn't he angry when she kicked him out! He was gnashing his teeth!"

"He's taken his revenge already," said Alyosha. "He's written a paragraph about Madame Khokhlakova."

And Alyosha told him briefly about the paragraph in *Gossip*.

"That's his doing, that's his doing!" Mitya assented frowning. "That's him! These paragraphs . . . I know . . . the insulting things that have been written about Grushka, for instance. . . . And about Katya, too. . . . Hmm!"

He walked across the room with a harassed air.

"Brother, I cannot stay long," Alyosha said, after a pause. "Tomorrow will be a great and awful day for you, the judgment of God will be accomplished . . . I am amazed at you, you walk about here, talking of I don't know what . . ."

"No, don't be amazed at me," Mitya broke in warmly. "Am I to talk of that stinking dog? Of the murderer? We've talked enough of him. I don't

---

9. Rakitin expresses the contempt for poetry, and art in general, that was common to those who advocated "utilitarian" aesthetics, the view that art is justified only when it serves social goals. Dostoevsky was deeply opposed to such a view of art and argued against it in the essay "Mr. ——bov and the Question of Art," published in *Time* in 1861.

1. Rakitin's poem is another parody of a Minaev parody of Pushkin, this time of Pushkin's poem "City of Luxury, City of Poverty" (1828).

want to say more of the stinking son of Stinking Lizaveta![2] God will kill him, you will see, hush!"

He went up to Alyosha excitedly and kissed him. His eyes glowed.

"Rakitin wouldn't understand it," he began in a sort of exaltation; "but you, you'll understand it all. That's why I was thirsting for you. You see, there's so much I've been wanting to tell you for ever so long, here, within these peeling walls, but I haven't said a word about what matters most; the moment never seems to have come. Now I can wait no longer. I must pour out my heart to you. Brother, these last two months I've found in myself a new man. A new man has risen up in me. He was hidden in me, but would never have come to the surface, if it hadn't been for this blow from heaven. I am afraid! And what do I care if I spend twenty years in the mines, breaking out ore with a hammer? I am not a bit afraid of that—it's something else I am afraid of now: that that new man may leave me. Even there, in the mines, underground, I may find a human heart in another convict and murderer by my side, and I may make friends with him, for even there one may live and love and suffer. One may resurrect and revive a frozen heart in that convict, one may wait upon him for years, and at last bring up from the dark depths a lofty soul, a feeling, suffering creature; one may bring forth an angel, resurrect a hero! There are so many of them, hundreds of them, and we are all responsible for them. Why was it I dreamed of that 'babe' at such a moment? 'Why is the babe so poor?' That was a sign to me at that moment. It's for the babe I'm going. Because we are all responsible for all. For all the 'babes,' for there are big children as well as little children. All are 'babes.' I go for all, because someone must go for all. I didn't kill father, but I've got to go. I accept it. It's all come to me here, here, within these peeling walls. There are numbers of them there, hundreds of them underground, with hammers in their hands. Oh, yes, we shall be in chains and there will be no freedom, but then, in our great sorrow, we shall rise again to joy, without which man cannot live nor God exist, for God gives joy: it's His privilege—a grand one. Ah, man should be dissolved in prayer! What would I be underground there without God? Rakitin lies! If they drive God from the earth, we shall shelter Him underground. One cannot exist in prison without God; it's even more impossible than out of prison. And then we men underground will sing from the bowels of the earth a tragic hymn to God, with Whom is joy. Hail to God and His joy! I love Him!"

Mitya was almost gasping for breath as he uttered his wild speech. He turned pale, his lips quivered, and tears rolled down his cheeks.

"Yes, life is full, there is life even underground," he began again. "You wouldn't believe, Alexey, how I want to live now, what a thirst for existence and consciousness has sprung up in me within these peeling walls. Rakitin doesn't understand that; all he cares about is building a house and letting flats. But I've been longing for you. And what is suffering? I am not afraid of it, even if it were beyond reckoning. I am not afraid of it now. I was afraid of it before. Do you know, perhaps I won't answer at the trial at all. . . . And I seem to have such strength in me now, that I think I could stand anything, any suffering, only to be able to say and to repeat

2. Dmitri's words may echo a popular folk legend based on the Gospel story of the rich and poor Lazarus, published in Saint Petersburg in 1860.

to myself every moment, 'I exist.' In thousands of agonies—I exist. I'm tormented on the rack—but I exist! Though I sit alone on a post—I exist! I see the sun, and if I don't see the sun, I know it's there. And there's a whole life in that, in knowing that the sun is there. Alyosha, my cherub, all these philosophies are the death of me, devil take them! Brother Ivan . . ."

"What of brother Ivan?" interrupted Alyosha, but Mitya did not hear.

"You see, I never had any of these doubts before, but it was all hidden away in me. It was perhaps just because ideas I did not understand were surging up in me, that I used to drink and fight and rage. It was to stifle them in myself, to still them, to smother them. Brother Ivan is not Rakitin, there is an idea in him. Brother Ivan is a sphinx and is silent; he is always silent. It's God that torments me. That's the only thing that torments me. What if He doesn't exist? What if Rakitin's right—that it's an idea made up by men? Then, if He doesn't exist, man is the chief of the earth, of the universe. Magnificent! Only how is he going to be good without God? That's the question. I always come back to that. For whom is man going to love then? To whom will he be thankful? To whom will he sing the hymn? Rakitin laughs. Rakitin says that one can love humanity without God. Well, only a sniveling idiot can maintain that. I can't understand it. Life's easy for Rakitin. 'You'd better think about the extension of civic rights, or even of keeping down the price of meat. You will show your love for humanity more simply and directly by that, than by philosophy.' I answered him, 'Well, but you, without a God, are more likely to raise the price of meat, if it suits you, and make a ruble on every kopeck.' He lost his temper. But after all, what is goodness? Answer me that, Alexey. Virtue is one thing with me and another with a Chinese, so it's a relative thing. Or isn't it? Is it not relative? A treacherous question! You won't laugh if I tell you it's kept me awake two nights. I only wonder now how people can live and think nothing about it. Vanity! Ivan has no God. He has an idea. It's beyond me. But he is silent. I believe he is a freemason. I asked him, but he is silent. I wanted to drink from the springs of his soul—he was silent. But once he did drop a word."

"What did he say?" Alyosha took it up quickly.

"I said to him, 'Then everything is permitted, if it is so?' He frowned. 'Fyodor Pavlovich, our papenka,' he said, 'was a little pig, but his ideas were right enough.' That was what he dropped. That was all he said. That was going one better than Rakitin."

"Yes," Alyosha assented bitterly. "When was he with you?"

"Of that later, now I must speak of something else. I have said nothing about Ivan to you before. I put it off to the last. When my business here is over and the verdict has been given, then I'll tell you something. I'll tell you everything. We have something tremendous on hand. . . . And you will be my judge in it. But don't begin about that now; be silent. You talk of tomorrow, of the trial; but, would you believe it, I know nothing about it."

"Have you talked to the counsel?"

"What's the use of the counsel? I told him all about it. He's a soft, city-bred rogue—a Bernard! But he doesn't believe me—not a bit of it. Only imagine, he believes I did it. I see it. 'In that case,' I asked him, 'why have you come to defend me?' Hang them all! They've got a doctor down, too, want to prove I'm mad. I won't have that! Katerina Ivanovna wants to do her 'duty' to the end, whatever the strain!" Mitya smiled bitterly. "The cat! A fierce heart! She knows that I said of her at Mokroe that she was a woman of 'great wrath.' They repeated it. Yes, the facts against me have grown numerous as the sands of the sea. Grigory sticks to his point. Grigory's honest, but a fool. Many people are honest because they are fools: that's Rakitin's idea. Grigory's my enemy. And there are some people who are better as foes than friends. I mean Katerina Ivanovna. I am afraid, oh, I am afraid she will tell how she bowed to the ground after that forty-five hundred. She'll pay it back to the uttermost farthing.[3] I don't want her sacrifice; they'll put me to shame at the trial. I wonder how I can stand it. Go to her, Alyosha, ask her not to speak of that in the court, can't you? But damn it all, it doesn't matter! I shall get through somehow. I don't pity her. It's her own doing. She deserves what she gets. I shall have my own story to tell, Alexey." He smiled bitterly again. "Only . . . only Grusha, Grusha! Good Lord! Why should she have such suffering to bear?" he exclaimed suddenly, with tears. "Grusha's killing me; the thought of her's killing me, killing me. She was with me just now . . ."

"She told me she was very much grieved by you today."

"I know. Devil take me for my character! It was jealousy. I was sorry, I kissed her as she was going. I didn't ask her forgiveness."

"Why didn't you?" exclaimed Alyosha.

Suddenly Mitya laughed almost mirthfully.

"God preserve you, my dear boy, from ever asking forgiveness for a fault from a woman you love. From one you love especially, however greatly you may have been in fault. For a woman—devil only knows what to make of a woman: I know something about them, anyway. But try acknowledging you are in fault to a woman, say, 'I am sorry, forgive me,' and a shower of reproaches will follow! Nothing will make her forgive you simply and directly, she'll humble you to the dust, bring forward things that have never happened, recall everything, forget nothing, add something of her own, and only then forgive you. And even the best, the best of them do it. She'll scrape up all the scrapings and load them on your head. They are ready to flay you alive, I tell you, every one of them, all these angels without whom we cannot live! I tell you plainly and openly, dear boy, every decent man ought to be under some woman's thumb. That's my conviction—not conviction, but feeling. A man ought to be magnanimous, and it's no disgrace to a man! No disgrace to a hero, not even a Caesar! But don't ever beg her pardon all the-same for anything. Remember that rule given you by your brother Mitya, who's come to ruin through women. No, I'd better make it up to Grusha somehow, without begging pardon. I worship her, Alexey, worship her. Only she doesn't see it. No, she still thinks I don't love her enough. And she tortures me, tortures me with her love. The past was nothing! In the past it was only those infernal curves of hers that tortured me, but now I've taken all her soul into my soul and through her I've become a man myself. Will they marry us? If they don't, I shall die of jealousy. I imagine something every day. . . . What did she say to you about me?"

Alyosha repeated all Grushenka had said to him that day. Mitya listened, made him repeat things, and seemed pleased.

---

3. Dmitri uses language from the Sermon on the Mount; see Matthew 5.23–26.

"Then she is not angry at my being jealous?" he exclaimed. "That's a woman for you! 'I've a fierce heart myself!' Ah, I love such fierce hearts, though I can't bear anyone's being jealous of me. I can't endure it. We shall fight. But I shall love her, I shall love her infinitely. Will they marry us? Do they let convicts marry? That's the question. And without her I can't exist . . ."

Mitya walked frowning across the room. It was almost dark. He suddenly seemed terribly worried.

"So there's a secret, she says, a secret? We have got up a plot against her, and 'Katka' is mixed up in it, she thinks. No, my good Grushenka, that's not it. You are very wide of the mark, in your foolish feminine way. Alyosha, darling, well, here goes! I'll tell you our secret!"

He looked round, went close up quickly to Alyosha, who was standing before him, and whispered to him with an air of mystery, though in reality no one could hear them: the old warder was dozing in the corner, and not a word could reach the ears of the soldiers on guard.

"I will tell you all our secret!" Mitya whispered hurriedly. "I meant to tell you later, for how could I decide on anything without you? You are everything to me. Though I say that Ivan is superior to us, you are my cherub. It's your decision that will decide it. Perhaps it's you that is superior and not Ivan. You see, it's a question of conscience, question of the higher conscience—the secret is so important that I can't settle it myself, and I've put it off till I could speak to you. But anyway it's too early to decide now, for we must wait for the verdict. As soon as the verdict is given, you shall decide my fate. Don't decide it now. I'll tell you now. You listen, but don't decide. Stand and keep quiet. I won't tell you everything. I'll only tell you the idea, without details, and you keep quiet. Not a question, not a movement. You agree? But, goodness, what shall I do with your eyes? I'm afraid your eyes will tell me your decision, even if you don't speak. Oo! I'm afraid! Alyosha, listen! Brother Ivan suggests my *escaping*. I won't tell you the details: it's all been thought out: it can all be arranged. Hush, don't decide, I aim to go to America with Grusha. You know I can't live without Grusha! What if they won't let her follow me to Siberia? Do they let convicts get married? Brother Ivan thinks not. And without Grusha what would I do there underground with a hammer? I would only smash my skull with the hammer! But on the other hand, my conscience? I would have run away from suffering. A sign has come, I reject the sign. I have a way of purification and I turn my back on it. Ivan says that in America, 'with good inclinations' I can be of more use than underground. But what becomes of our hymn from underground? What's America? America is vanity again! And there's a lot of swindling in America, too, I expect. I would have run away from crucifixion! I tell you, you know, Alexey, because you are the only person who can understand this. There's no one else. It's folly, madness to others, all I've told you of the hymn. They'll say I'm out of my mind or a fool. I am not out of my mind and I am not a fool. Ivan understands about the hymn, too. He understands, only he doesn't answer—he is silent. He doesn't believe in the hymn. Don't speak, don't speak. I see how you look! You have already decided. Don't decide, spare me! I can't live without Grusha. Wait till after the trial!"

Mitya ended beside himself. He held Alyosha with both hands on his shoulders, and his yearning, feverish eyes were fixed on his brother's.

"They don't let convicts marry, do they?" he repeated for the third time in a supplicating voice.

Alyosha listened with extreme surprise and was deeply moved.

"Tell me one thing," he said, "is Ivan very keen on it, and whose idea was it?"

"His, his, and he insists! He didn't come to see me at first, then he suddenly came a week ago and he began about it right away. He insists terribly. He doesn't ask me, but orders me. He doesn't doubt of my obeying him, though I showed him all my heart as I have to you, and told him about the hymn, too. He told me he'd arrange it; he's found out about everything. But of that later. He wants it to the point of hysterics. It's all a matter of money: there'll be ten thousand for the escape and twenty thousand for America. And he says we can arrange a magnificent escape for ten thousand."

"And he told you on no account to tell me?" Alyosha asked again.

"To tell no one, and especially not you; on no account to tell you. He is afraid, no doubt, that you'll stand before me as my conscience. Don't tell him I told you. Don't tell him, for anything."

"You are right," Alyosha pronounced; "it's impossible to decide anything before the trial is over. After the trial you'll decide by yourself. Then you'll find that new man in yourself and he will decide."

"A new man, or a Bernard who'll decide à la Bernard, for I believe I'm a contemptible Bernard myself," said Mitya, with a bitter grin.

"But, brother, have you no hope then of being acquitted?"

Mitya shrugged his shoulders convulsively and shook his head.

"Alyosha, darling, it's time you were going," he said, with a sudden haste. "There's the superintendent shouting in the yard. He'll be here directly. We are late; it's irregular. Embrace me quickly. Kiss me! Sign me with the cross, darling, for the cross I have to bear tomorrow."

They embraced and kissed.

"Ivan," said Mitya suddenly, "suggests my escaping; but, of course, he believes I did it."

A mournful smile came on to his lips.

"Have you asked him whether he believes it?" asked Alyosha.

"No, I haven't. I wanted to, but I couldn't. I didn't have the courage. But I saw it from his eyes. Well, good-bye!"

Once more they kissed hurriedly, and Alyosha was just going out, when Mitya suddenly called him back.

"Stand facing me! That's right!" And again he seized Alyosha, putting both hands on his shoulders. His face became suddenly quite pale, so that it was dreadfully apparent, even through the gathering darkness. His lips twitched, his eyes fastened upon Alyosha.

"Alyosha, tell me the whole truth, as you would before God. Do you believe I did it? Do you, do you in yourself, believe it? The whole truth, don't lie!" he cried desperately.

Everything seemed to heave in front of Alyosha, and he felt something like a stab at his heart.

"Hush! What do you mean?" he faltered helplessly.

"The whole truth, the whole, don't lie!" repeated Mitya.

"I've never for one instant believed that you were the murderer!" broke in a shaking voice from Alyosha's breast, and he raised his right hand in

the air, as though calling God to witness his words. Mitya's whole face
was lit up with bliss.

"Thank you!" he articulated slowly, as though letting a sigh escape him
after fainting. "Now you have given me new life. Would you believe it, till
this moment I've been afraid to ask you, you, even you. Well, go! You've
given me strength for tomorrow. God bless you! Well, go along! Love
Ivan!" was Mitya's last word.

Alyosha went out in tears. Such distrustfulness in Mitya, such lack of
confidence even to him, to Alyosha—all this suddenly opened before Alyosha an unsuspected depth of hopeless grief and despair in the soul of his
unhappy brother. Intense, infinite compassion overwhelmed him instantly.
There was a poignant ache in his torn heart. "Love Ivan"—he suddenly
recalled Mitya's words. And he was going to Ivan. He badly wanted to see
Ivan all day. He was as much worried about Ivan as about Mitya, and more
than ever now.

Chapter V

Not You, Not You!

On the way to Ivan he had to pass the house where Katerina Ivanovna was
living. There was light in the windows. He suddenly stopped and resolved
to go in. He had not seen Katerina Ivanovna for more than a week. But
now it struck him that Ivan might be with her, especially on the eve of the
terrible day. Ringing, and mounting the staircase, which was dimly lighted
by a Chinese lantern, he saw a man coming down, and as they met, he
recognized him as his brother. So he was just coming from Katerina
Ivanovna.

"Ah, it's only you," said Ivan Fyodorovich drily. "Well, good-bye! You
are going to her?"

"Yes."

"I don't advise you to; she's 'upset' and you'll upset her more."

A door was instantly flung open above, and a voice cried suddenly:

"No, no! Alexey Fyodorovich, have you come from him?"

"Yes, I have been with him."

"Has he sent me any message? Come up, Alyosha, and you, Ivan Fyodorovich, you must come back, you must. Do you hear?"

There was such a peremptory note in Katya's voice that Ivan Fyodorovich, after a moment's hesitation, made up his mind to go back with
Alyosha.

"She was eavesdropping," he murmured angrily to himself, but Alyosha
heard it.

"Excuse my keeping my overcoat on," said Ivan Fyodorovich, going into
the drawing room. "I won't sit down. I won't stay more than a minute."

"Sit down, Alexey Fyodorovich," said Katerina Ivanovna, though she
remained standing. She had changed very little during this time, but there
was an ominous gleam in her dark eyes. Alyosha remembered afterwards
that she had struck him as particularly good-looking at that moment.

"What did he ask you to tell me?"

"Only one thing," said Alyosha, looking her straight in the face, "that you would spare yourself and say nothing at the trial of what" (he was a little confused) ". . . passed between you . . . at the time of your first acquaintance . . . in that town."

"Ah! that I bowed down to the ground for that money!" She broke in with a bitter laugh. "Why, is he afraid for me or for himself? He asks me to spare—whom? Him or myself? Tell me, Alexey Fyodorovich!"

Alyosha watched her intently, trying to understand her.

"Both yourself and him," he answered softly.

"I am glad to hear it," she snapped out maliciously, and she suddenly blushed. "You don't know me yet, Alexey Fyodorovich," she said menacingly. "And I don't know myself yet. Perhaps you'll want to trample me under foot after my examination tomorrow."

"You will give your evidence honorably," said Alyosha; "that's all that's wanted."

"Women are often dishonorable," she snarled. "Only an hour ago I was thinking I felt afraid to touch that monster . . . as though he were a viper . . . but no, he is still a human being to me! But did he kill? Was it he who killed?" she cried, all of a sudden, hysterically, turning quickly to Ivan Fyodorovich. Alyosha saw at once that she had asked Ivan Fyodorovich that question before, perhaps only a moment before he came in, and not for the first time, but for the hundredth, and that they had ended by quarreling.

"I've been to see Smerdyakov. . . . It was you, you who persuaded me that he murdered his father. It's only you I believed!" she continued, still addressing Ivan Fyodorovich. He gave her a sort of strained smile. Alyosha started at her tone. He had not suspected such familiar intimacy between them.

"Well, that's enough, anyway," Ivan cut short the conversation. "I am going. I'll come tomorrow." And turning at once, he walked out of the room and went straight downstairs. With an imperious gesture, Katerina Ivanovna suddenly seized Alyosha by both hands.

"Follow him! Overtake him! Don't leave him alone for a minute!" she said, in a hurried whisper. "He's mad! Don't you know that he's mad? He is in a fever, nervous fever. The doctor told me so. Go, run after him. . . ."

Alyosha jumped up and ran after Ivan Fyodorovich, who was not fifty paces ahead of him.

"What do you want?" He turned quickly on Alyosha, seeing that he was running after him. "She told you to catch up to me, because I'm mad. I know it all by heart," he added irritably.

"She is mistaken, of course; but she is right, that you are ill," said Alyosha. "I was looking at your face just now. You look very ill, Ivan."

Ivan walked on without stopping. Alyosha followed him.

"And do you know, Alexey Fyodorovich, how people do go out of their mind?" Ivan asked in a voice suddenly quiet, without a trace of irritation, with a note of the simplest curiosity.

"No, I don't. I suppose there are all kinds of insanity."

"And can one observe that one's going mad oneself?"

"I imagine one can't see oneself clearly in such circumstances," Alyosha answered with surprise. Ivan paused for half a minute.

"If you want to talk to me, please change the subject," he said suddenly.

"Oh, while I think of it, I have a letter for you," said Alyosha timidly, and he took Liza's note from his pocket and held it out to Ivan. They were just under a lamp post. Ivan recognized the handwriting at once.

"Ah, from that little demon!" he laughed maliciously, and, without opening the envelope, he tore it into bits and threw it in the air. The bits were scattered by the wind.

"She's not sixteen yet, I believe, and already offering herself," he said contemptuously, striding along the street again.

"How do you mean, offering herself?" exclaimed Alyosha.

"As wanton women offer themselves, to be sure."

"How can you, Ivan, how can you?" Alyosha cried warmly in a grieved voice. "She is a child; you are insulting a child! She is ill; she is very ill, too. She is on the verge of insanity, too, perhaps . . . I had to give you her letter . . . I had hoped to hear something from you . . . that would save her."

"You'll hear nothing from me. If she is a child I am not her nurse. Be quiet, Alexey. Don't go on about her. I am not even thinking about it."

They were silent again for a moment.

"She will be praying all night now to the Mother of God to show her how to act tomorrow at the trial," he suddenly spoke sharply and spitefully again.

"You . . . you mean Katerina Ivanovna?"

"Yes. Whether she's to save Mitenka or ruin him. She'll pray for light from above. She can't make up her mind for herself, you see. She has not had time to decide yet. She takes me for her nurse, too. She wants me to sing lullabys to her."

"Katerina Ivanovna loves you, brother," said Alyosha sadly.

"Perhaps; but I am not very keen on her."

"She is suffering. Why do you . . . sometimes say things to her that give her hope?" Alyosha went on, with timid reproach. "I know that you've given her hope. Forgive me for speaking to you like this," he added.

"I can't behave to her as I ought—break off altogether and tell her so straight out," said Ivan, irritably. "I must wait till sentence is passed on the murderer. If I break off with her now, she will avenge herself on me by ruining that scoundrel tomorrow at the trial, for she hates him and knows she hates him. It's all a lie—lie upon lie! As long as I don't break off with her, she goes on hoping, and she won't ruin that monster, knowing how I want to get him out of trouble. If only that damned verdict would come!"

The words "murderer" and "monster" echoed painfully in Alyosha's heart.

"But how can she ruin Mitya?" he asked, pondering on Ivan's words. "What evidence can she give that would ruin Mitya?"

"You don't know that yet. She's got a document in her hands, in Mitenka's own writing, that proves mathematically that he did murder Fyodor Pavlovich."

"That's impossible!" cried Alyosha.

"Why is it impossible? I've read it myself."

"There can't be such a document!" Alyosha repeated warmly. "There can't be, because he's not the murderer. It's not he who murdered father, not he!"

Ivan Fyodorovich suddenly stopped.

"Who is the murderer then, according to you?" he asked, with apparent coldness, and a certain haughty note even sounded in the tone of his question.[4]

"You know who," Alyosha pronounced in a low penetrating voice.

"Who? You mean the myth about that crazy idiot, the epileptic, Smerdyakov?"

Alyosha suddenly felt himself trembling all over.

"You know who," broke helplessly from him. He could scarcely breathe.

"Who? Who?" Ivan cried almost fiercely. All his restraint suddenly vanished.

"I only know one thing," Alyosha went on, still almost in a whisper, "*it was not you* who killed father."

"Not you! What do you mean by 'not you'?" Ivan was thunderstruck.

"It was not you who killed father, not you!" Alyosha repeated firmly.

The silence lasted for half a minute.

"I know I didn't. Are you raving?" said Ivan, with a pale, distorted smile. His eyes were riveted on Alyosha. They were standing again under a lamp post.

"No, Ivan. You've told yourself several times that you are the murderer."

"When did I say so? I was in Moscow. . . . When have I said so?" Ivan faltered helplessly.

"You've said so to yourself many times, when you've been alone during these two dreadful months," Alyosha went on softly and distinctly as before. Yet he was speaking now, as it were, not of himself, not of his own will, but obeying some irresistible command. "You have accused yourself and have confessed to yourself that you are the murderer and no one else. But you didn't murder, you are mistaken: you are not the murderer. Do you hear? It was not you! God has sent me to tell you so."

They were both silent. The silence lasted a whole long minute. They were both standing still, gazing into each other's eyes. They were both pale. Suddenly Ivan began trembling all over, and clutched Alyosha's shoulder.

"You've been in my room!" he whispered hoarsely. "You've been there at night, when he came. . . . Confess . . . have you seen him, have you seen him?"

"Whom do you mean—Mitya?" Alyosha asked, bewildered.

"Not him, devil take the monster!" Ivan shouted, in a frenzy. "Do you know that he visits me? How did you find out? Speak!"

"Who is *he*? I don't know whom you are talking about," Alyosha faltered, beginning to be alarmed.

"Yes, you do know . . . or how could you . . . ? It's impossible that you don't know."

Suddenly he seemed to check himself. He stood still and seemed to reflect. A strange grin contorted his lips.

"Brother," Alyosha began again, in a shaking voice, "I have said this to you, because you'll believe my word, I know that. I tell you for your whole life: it was *not you*! You hear, for your whole life. God has put it into my

---

4. Ivan suddenly switches from the intimate to the formal second person address, from *ty* to *vy*.

heart to say this to you, even though it may make you hate me from this hour."

But by now Ivan Fyodorovich had apparently regained his self-control.

"Alexey Fyodorovich," he said, with a cold smile, "I can't endure prophets and epileptics—messengers from God especially—and you know that only too well. I break off all relations with you from this moment and probably forever. I beg you to leave me at this crossing. It's the way to your lodgings, too. You'd better be particularly careful not to come to me today! Do you hear?"

He turned and walked on with a firm step, not looking back.

"Brother," Alyosha called after him, "if anything happens to you today, turn to me before anyone!"

But Ivan made no reply. Alyosha stood under the lamp post at the crossing, till Ivan had vanished into the darkness. Then he turned and walked slowly homewards. Both Alyosha and Ivan were living in lodgings; neither of them was willing to live in Fyodor Pavlovich's empty house. Alyosha had a furnished room in the house of some tradesmen. Ivan lived some distance from him. He had taken a roomy and fairly comfortable lodge attached to a fine house that belonged to a well-to-do lady, the widow of an official. But his only attendant was a deaf and rheumatic old crone who went to bed at six o'clock every evening and got up at six in the morning. Ivan Fyodorovich had become remarkably indifferent to his comforts of late, and very fond of being alone. He did everything for himself in the one room he lived in, and rarely entered any of the other rooms in his abode. He reached the gate of the house and had his hand on the bell, when he suddenly stopped. He felt that he was still trembling all over with anger. Suddenly he let go of the bell, turned back with a curse, and walked with rapid steps in the opposite direction. He walked a mile and a half to a tiny, slanting, wooden house, almost a hut, where Marya Kondratyevna, the neighbor who used to come to Fyodor Pavlovich's kitchen for soup and to whom Smerdyakov had once sung his songs and played on the guitar, was now lodging. She had sold their little house, and was now living here with her mother in what was practically a hut. Smerdyakov, who was ill—almost dying—had been with them ever since Fyodor Pavlovich's death. It was to him Ivan Fyodorovich was going now, drawn by a sudden and irresistible prompting.

Chapter VI

The First Meeting with Smerdyakov

This was the third time that Ivan had been to see Smerdyakov since his return from Moscow. The first time he had seen him and talked to him after the catastrophe was on the first day of his arrival, then he had visited him once more, two weeks later. But his visits had ended with that second one, so that it was now over a month since he had seen him. And he had scarcely heard anything of him. Ivan Fyodorovich had only returned five days after his father's death, so that he was not present at the funeral, which took place the day before he came back. The cause of his delay was that Alyosha, not knowing his Moscow address, had to apply to Katerina Ivanovna to telegraph to him, and she, not knowing his address either, telegraphed to her sister and aunt, reckoning on Ivan Fyodorovich's going to see them as soon as he arrived in Moscow. But he did not go to them till four days after his arrival. When he got the telegram, he at once, of course, came flying back to us. The first to meet him was Alyosha, and Ivan was greatly surprised to find that in opposition to the general opinion of the town, he refused to entertain a suspicion against Mitya, and spoke openly of Smerdyakov as the murderer. Later on, after seeing the police captain and the prosecutor, and hearing the details of the charge and the arrest, he was still more surprised at Alyosha, and ascribed his opinion only to his exaggerated brotherly feeling and sympathy with Mitya, of whom Alyosha, as Ivan knew, was very fond. By the way, let us say a word or two of Ivan's feeling towards his brother Dmitri Fyodorovich. He positively disliked him, at most, felt sometimes a compassion for him, and even that was mixed with great contempt, almost repugnance. Mitya's whole personality, even his appearance, was extremely unattractive to him. Ivan looked with indignation on Katerina Ivanovna's love for his brother. Yet he went to see Mitya on the first day of his arrival, and that interview, far from shaking Ivan's belief in his guilt, positively strengthened it. He found his brother agitated, nervously excited. Mitya had been talkative, but very absent-minded and incoherent. He used violent language, accused Smerdyakov, and was fearfully muddled. He talked principally about the three thousand rubles, which he said had been "stolen" from him by his father. "The money was mine, it was my money," Mitya kept repeating. "Even if I had stolen it, I would have had the right." He hardly contested the evidence against him, and if he tried to turn a fact to his advantage, it was in an absurd and incoherent way. He hardly seemed to wish to defend himself to Ivan or anyone else. Quite the contrary, he was angry and proudly scornful of the charges against him; he was continually firing up and abusing every one. He only laughed contemptuously at Grigory's evidence about the open door, and declared that it was "the devil that opened it." But he could not bring forward any coherent explanation of the fact. He even succeeded in insulting Ivan Fyodorovich during their first interview, telling him sharply that it was not for people who declared that "everything was permitted," to suspect and question him. Altogether he was anything but friendly with Ivan Fyodorovich on that occasion. Immediately after that interview with Mitya, Ivan Fyodorovich went for the first time to see Smerdyakov.

In the railway train, flying back from Moscow, he kept thinking of Smerdyakov and of his last conversation with him on the evening before he went away. Many things seemed to him puzzling and suspicious. But when he gave his evidence to the district attorney Ivan Fyodorovich said nothing, for the time, of that conversation. He put that off till he had seen Smerdyakov, who was at that time in the hospital. Doctor Herzenstube and Varvinsky, the doctor he met in the hospital, confidently asserted in reply to Ivan Fyodorovich's persistent questions, that Smerdyakov's epileptic attack was unmistakably genuine, and were even surprised at his question: "Could he have been shamming on the day of the catastrophe?" They gave him to understand that the attack was an exceptional one, the fits persisting and recurring several times, so that the patient's life was positively in danger, and it was only now, after they had applied remedies, that they could assert with confidence that the patient would survive. "Though it might well be," added Doctor Herzenstube, "that his reason would be impaired for a considerable period, if not permanently." On Ivan Fyodorovich's asking impatiently whether that meant that he was now mad, they told him that this was not yet the case, in the full sense of the word, but that certain abnormalities were perceptible. Ivan Fyodorovich decided to find out for himself what those abnormalities were. At the hospital he was at once allowed to see the patient. Smerdyakov was lying on a bunk in a separate ward. There was one other bunk in the room, and in it lay a tradesman of the town, swollen with dropsy,[5] who was obviously almost dying; he could be no hindrance to their conversation. Smerdyakov grinned uncertainly on seeing Ivan Fyodorovich, and for the first instant seemed nervous. So at least Ivan Fyodorovich fancied. But that was only momentary. For the rest of the time he was struck, on the contrary, by Smerdyakov's composure. From the first glance Ivan Fyodorovich had no doubt that he was very ill. He was very weak; he spoke slowly, seeming to move his tongue with difficulty; he was much thinner and sallower. Throughout the interview, which lasted twenty minutes, he kept complaining of headache and of pain in all his limbs. His thin eunuch-like face seemed to have become so tiny; his hair was ruffled, and in place of the crest of curls in front stood up a thin tuft of hair. But in the left eye, which was screwed up and seemed to be insinuating something, Smerdyakov showed himself unchanged. "It's always interesting speaking with an intelligent man." Ivan was reminded of that at once. He sat down on the stool at his feet. Smerdyakov, with painful effort, shifted his position in bed, but he was not the first to speak. He remained dumb, and did not even look much interested.

"Can you talk to me?" asked Ivan Fyodorovich. "I won't tire you much."

"Certainly I can," mumbled Smerdyakov, in a faint voice.

"Has your honor been back long?" he added patronizingly, as though encouraging a nervous visitor.

"I only arrived today. . . . To see the mess you are in here."

Smerdyakov sighed.

"Why do you sigh, you knew of it all along?" Ivan Fyodorovich blurted out.

Smerdyakov was stolidly silent for a while.

"How could I help knowing, sir? It was clear beforehand. But how could I tell it would turn out like that?"

"What would turn out? Don't prevaricate! You've foretold you'd have a fit; on the way down to the cellar, you know. You mentioned the very spot."

"Have you said so at the examination yet?" Smerdyakov queried with composure.

Ivan Fyodorovich felt suddenly angry.

"No. I haven't yet, but I certainly shall. You must explain a great deal to me, my man, and let me tell you, I am not going to let you play with me!"

5. A condition known as edema today, the accumulation of excess lymph fluid causing swelling, occurring most frequently in the feet and ankles.

"Why should I play with you, sir, when I put my whole trust in you, as in God Almighty?" said Smerdyakov, with the same composure, only for a moment closing his eyes.

"In the first place," began Ivan Fyodorovich, "I know that epileptic fits can't be foretold beforehand. I've inquired; don't try and take me in. You can't foretell the day and the hour. How was it you told me the day and the hour beforehand, and about the cellar, too? How could you tell that you would fall down the cellar stairs in a fit, if you didn't sham a fit on purpose?"

"I had to go to the cellar anyway, sir, several times a day, indeed," Smerdyakov drawled deliberately. "I fell from the garret just in the same way a year ago, sir. It's quite true you can't foretell the day and hour of a fit beforehand, but you can always have a presentiment of it."

"But you did foretell the day and the hour!"

"In regard to my epilepsy, your honor, you had much better inquire of the doctors here, sir. You can ask them whether it was a real fit or a sham; it's no use my saying any more about it."

"And the cellar? How could you know beforehand of the cellar?"

"You don't seem able to get over that cellar! As I was going down to the cellar, I was in terrible dread and doubt. What frightened me most was losing you and being left without defense in all the world. So I went down into the cellar thinking, 'Here it'll come on directly, it'll strike me down directly, shall I fall?' And it was through this fear, sir, that I suddenly felt the spasm that always comes . . . and so I went flying. All that and all my previous conversation with you at the gate the evening before, when I told you how frightened I was and spoke of the cellar, sir. I told all that to Doctor Herzenstube and Nikolay Parfenovich, the district attorney, and it's all been written down in the deposition. And the doctor here, Mr. Varvinsky, maintained to all of them that it was just the thought of it brought it on, the apprehension that I might fall. It was just then that the fit seized me. And so they've written it down, that it's just how it must have happened, simply from fear, sir."

As he finished, Smerdyakov drew a deep breath, as though exhausted.

"Then you have said all that in your evidence?" said Ivan Fyodorovich, somewhat taken aback. He had meant to frighten him with the threat of repeating their conversation, and it appeared that Smerdyakov had already reported it all himself.

"What have I to be afraid of? Let them write down the whole truth," Smerdyakov pronounced firmly.

"And have you told them every word of our conversation at the gate?"

"No, not every word, that is, sir."

"And did you tell them that you can sham fits, as you boasted then?"

"No, I didn't tell them that either, sir."

"Tell me now, why did you send me then to Chermashnya?"

"I was afraid you'd go away to Moscow, Chermashnya is nearer, anyway, sir."

"You are lying, you suggested my going away yourself; you told me to get out of the way of misfortune."

"That was simply out of affection and my sincere devotion to you, foreseeing trouble in the house, to spare you. Only I wanted to spare myself even more, sir. That's why I told you to get out of misfortune's way, that you might understand that there would be trouble in the house, and would remain at home to protect your father."

"You might have said it more directly, you fool!" Ivan Fyodorovich suddenly fired up.

"How could I have said it more directly then, sir? It was simply my fear that made me speak, and you might have been angry, too. I might well have been apprehensive that Dmitri Fyodorovich would make a scene and carry away that money, for he considered it as good as his own, but who could tell that it would end in a murder like this? I thought that he would only carry off the three thousand that lay under the master's mattress, sir, in the envelope, sir, and you see, he's murdered him. How could you guess it either, your honor?"

"But if you say yourself that it couldn't be guessed, how could I have guessed and stayed at home? Why are you confusing things?" said Ivan Fyodorovich pondering.

"You might have guessed from my sending you to Chermashnya and not to Moscow."

"How could I guess it from that?"

Smerdyakov seemed much exhausted, and again he was silent for a minute.

"You might have guessed, sir, from the fact of my asking you not to go to Moscow, but to Chermashnya, sir, that I wanted to have you nearer, for Moscow's a long way off, and Dmitri Fyodorovich, knowing you are not far off, would not be so bold. And if anything had happened, you might have come to protect me, too, for I warned you of Grigory Vasilyevich's illness, and that I was afraid of having a fit. And when I explained those knocks to you, by means of which one could go in to the deceased, and that Dmitri Fyodorovich knew them all through me, I thought that you would guess yourself that he would be sure to do something, and so wouldn't go to Chermashnya even, but would stay."

"He talks very coherently," thought Ivan Fyodorovich, "though he does mumble; what's the derangement of his faculties that Herzenstube talked of?"

"You are being cunning with me, devil take you!" he exclaimed, getting angry.

"But I thought at the time that you guessed it completely," Smerdyakov parried with the simplest air.

"If I'd guessed it, I would have stayed," cried Ivan Fyodorovich, flaring up again.

"Why, sir, I thought that it was because you guessed it that you went away in such a hurry, only to get out of misfortune, sir, only to run away and save yourself in your fright."

"You think that everyone is as great a coward as yourself?"

"Forgive me, sir, I thought you were like me."

"Of course, I ought to have guessed," Ivan said in agitation, "and I did guess there was some vileness brewing on your part . . . only you are lying, you are lying again," he cried, suddenly recollecting. "Do you remember how you went up to the carriage and said to me, 'It's always interesting speaking with an intelligent man'? So you were glad I went away, since you praised me?"

Smerdyakov sighed again and again. A trace of color came into his face.

"If I was pleased," he articulated rather breathlessly, "it was simply because you agreed not to go to Moscow, but to Chermashnya. For it was nearer, anyway. Only when I said these words to you, it was not by way of praise, but of reproach. You didn't understand it."

"What reproach?"

"Why, that foreseeing such a calamity you deserted your own father, and would not protect us, for I might have been arrested at any time for stealing that three thousand, sir."

"Devil take you!" Ivan swore again. "Wait, did you tell the prosecutor and the district attorney about those knocks?"

"I told them everything just as it was, sir."

Ivan Fyodorovich was again inwardly amazed.

"If I thought of anything then," he began again, "it was solely of some vileness on your part. Dmitri might kill him, but that he would steal—I did not believe that then. . . . But I was prepared for any vileness from you. You told me yourself you could sham a fit. What did you say that for?"

"It was just through my simplicity, and I never have shammed a fit on purpose in my life. And I only said so then to boast to you. It was just foolishness. I liked you so much then, and was open-hearted with you."

"My brother directly accuses you of the murder and theft."

"What else is left for him to do?" said Smerdyakov, with a bitter grin. "And who will believe him with all the proofs against him? Grigory Vasilyevich saw the door open, sir. What can he say after that? But never mind him! He is trembling to save himself."

He slowly ceased speaking, and suddenly, as though on reflection, added:

"And look here again, sir. He wants to throw it on me and make out that it is the work of my hands—I've heard that already, sir. But as to my being clever at shamming a fit: would I have told you beforehand that I could sham one, if I really had had such a design against your father? If I had been planning such a murder could I have been such a fool as to give such evidence against myself beforehand? And to his own son, too! Upon my word, sir! Is that likely? As if that could be, such a thing has never happened. No one hears this talk of ours now, except Providence itself, sir, and if you were to tell about it to the prosecutor and Nikolay Parfenovich you might defend me completely by doing so, for who would be likely to be such a criminal, if he is openhearted beforehand? Anyone can see that."

"Well," and Ivan Fyodorovich got up to cut short the conversation, struck by Smerdyakov's last argument. "I don't suspect you at all, and I think it's absurd indeed to suspect you. On the contrary, I am grateful to you for setting my mind at rest. Now I am going, but I'll come again. Meanwhile, good-bye. Get well. Is there anything you want?"

"I am very thankful for everything, sir. Martha Ignatyevna does not forget me, and provides me anything I want, according to her kindness. Good people visit me every day."

"Good-bye. But I won't say anything of your being able to sham a fit, and I don't advise you to, either," something made Ivan say suddenly.

"I quite understand, sir. And if you don't speak of that, I shall say nothing of that conversation of ours at the gate."

Then it happened that Ivan Fyodorovich went out, and only when he had gone a dozen steps along the corridor, he suddenly felt that there was an insulting significance in Smerdyakov's last words. He was almost on the point of turning back, but it was only a passing impulse, and muttering, "nonsense!" he went out of the hospital. His chief feeling was one of relief at the fact that it was not Smerdyakov, but Mitya, who had committed the murder, though he might have been expected to feel the opposite. He did not want to analyze the reason for this feeling, and even felt a positive repugnance at prying into his sensations. He felt as though he wanted to make haste to forget something. In the following days he became totally convinced of Mitya's guilt, as he got to know all the weight of evidence against him. There was the evidence of people of no importance, Fenya and her mother, for instance, but the effect of it was almost overpowering. As for Perkhotin, the people at the tavern, and at Plotnikov's shop, as well as the witnesses at Mokroe, their evidence seemed conclusive. It was the details that were so damning. The secret of the "knocks" impressed the prosecutor and the district attorney almost as much as Grigory's evidence as to the open door. Grigory's wife, Martha, in answer to Ivan Fyodorovich's questions, declared that Smerdyakov had been lying all night the other side of the partition wall. "He was not three paces from our bed," and that although she was a sound sleeper she waked several times and heard him moaning. "He was moaning the whole time, moaning continually." Talking to Herzenstube, and giving it as his opinion that Smerdyakov was not mad at all but only rather weak, he only evoked from the old man a subtle smile. "Do you know how he spends his time now?" he asked, "learning lists of French words by heart. He has an exercise book under his pillow with the French words written out in Russian letters for him by someone, he, he, he!" Ivan Fyodorovich ended by dismissing all doubts. He could not think of his brother Dmitri without repulsion. Only one thing was strange, however. Alyosha persisted that Dmitri was not the murderer, and that "in all probability" Smerdyakov was. Ivan always felt that Alyosha's opinion meant a great deal to him, and so he was astonished at it now. Another thing that was strange was that Alyosha did not make any attempt to talk about Mitya with Ivan, that he never began on the subject and only answered his questions. This, too, struck Ivan Fyodorovich particularly. But he was very much preoccupied at that time with something quite apart from that. On his return from Moscow, he abandoned himself hopelessly to his mad and consuming passion for Katerina Ivanovna. This is not the time to begin to speak of this new passion of Ivan Fyodorovich's which left its mark on all the rest of his life: this would furnish the subject for another tale, for another novel, which I may perhaps never write. But I cannot omit to mention here that when Ivan Fyodorovich on leaving Katerina Ivanovna with Alyosha, as I've related already, told him, "I am not keen on her," it was an absolute lie: he loved her madly, though at times he hated her so that he might have murdered her. Many causes helped to bring about this feeling. Shattered by what had happened with Mitya, she rushed on Ivan Fyodorovich's return to meet him as her one salvation. She was hurt, insulted and humiliated in her feelings. And here the man had come back to her, who had loved her so ardently before (oh, she knew that very well), and whose heart and intellect she considered so superior to her own. But the sternly virtuous girl did not abandon herself altogether to the man she loved, in spite of the Karamazov recklessness of his passions and the great fascination he had for her. She was continually tormented at the same time by remorse for having betrayed Mitya, and in moments of discord and violent anger (and they were numerous) she told Ivan so plainly. This was what he had called to Alyosha "lies upon lies." There was, of course, much that was false in it, and that angered Ivan Fyodorovich more than anything. . . . But of all this later. He did, in fact, for a time almost forget Smerdyakov's existence, and yet, two weeks after his first visit to him, he began to be haunted by the same strange thoughts as before. It's enough to say that he was continually asking himself why it was that on that last night in Fyodor Pavlovich's house he had crept out on to the stairs like a thief and listened to hear what his father was doing below. Why had he recalled that afterwards with repulsion; why, next morning, had he been suddenly so depressed on the journey; why, as he reached Moscow, had he said to himself "I am a scoundrel"? And now he almost thought that these tormenting thoughts would make him even forget Katerina Ivanovna, so completely did they take possession of him again! It was just after thinking this, that he met Alyosha in the street. He stopped him at once, and put a question to him:

"Do you remember when Dmitri burst in after dinner and beat father, and afterwards I told you in the yard that I reserved 'the right to desire' . . . tell me, did you think then that I desired father's death or not?"

"I did think so," answered Alyosha, softly.

"It was so, too; it was not a matter of guessing. But didn't you think then that what I wished was just that 'one viper should devour another'; that is, just that Dmitri should kill father, and as soon as possible . . . and that I myself was even prepared to help to bring that about?"

Alyosha turned rather pale, and looked silently into his brother's eyes.

"Speak!" cried Ivan, "I want above everything to know what you thought then. I want the truth, the truth!" He drew a deep breath, looking angrily at Alyosha before his answer came.

"Forgive me, I did think that, too, at the time," whispered Alyosha, and he did not add a single "mitigating circumstance."

"Thanks," snapped Ivan, and, leaving Alyosha, he went quickly on his way. From that time Alyosha noticed that Ivan began obviously to avoid him and seemed to have taken a dislike to him, so much so that Alyosha gave up going to see him. Immediately after that meeting with him, Ivan Fyodorovich had not gone home, but went straight to Smerdyakov again.

Chapter VII

The Second Visit to Smerdyakov

By that time Smerdyakov had been discharged from the hospital. Ivan Fyodorovich knew his new lodging, the dilapidated little wooden house, divided in two by a hall on one side of which lived Marya Kondratyevna and her mother, and on the other, Smerdyakov. No one knew on what terms he lived with them, whether as a friend or as a lodger. It was supposed afterwards that he had come to stay with them as Marya Kondratyevna's betrothed, and was living there for a time without paying for board or lodging. Both mother and daughter had the greatest respect for him and looked upon him as greatly superior to themselves. Ivan Fyodorovich knocked, and, on the door being opened, went into the hall. By Marya

Kondratyevna's directions he went straight to the better room on the left, occupied by Smerdyakov. There was a tiled stove in the room and it was extremely hot. The walls were covered with blue wallpaper, which was a good deal torn, however, and in the cracks under it cockroaches swarmed in amazing numbers, so that there was a continual rustling from them. The furniture was very scanty: two benches against each wall and two chairs by the table. The table of plain wood was covered with a cloth with pink patterns on it. There was a pot of geraniums on each of the two little windows. In the corner there was a case of icons. On the table stood a little copper samovar with many dents in it, and a tray with two cups. But Smerdyakov had finished tea and the samovar was out. He was sitting at the table on a bench. He was looking at an exercise book and slowly writing with a pen. There was a bottle of ink by him and a flat iron candlestick, but with a stearine candle. Ivan Fyodorovich saw at once from Smerdyakov's face that he had completely recovered from his illness. His face was fresher, fuller, his hair stood up jauntily in front and was plastered down at the sides. He was sitting in a motley, padded dressing gown, rather dirty and frayed, however. He had spectacles on his nose, which Ivan Fyodorovich had never seen him wearing before. This trifling circumstance suddenly redoubled Ivan Fyodorovich's anger: "A creature like that and wearing spectacles!" Smerdyakov slowly raised his head and looked intently at his visitor through his spectacles; then he slowly took them off and rose from the bench, but by no means respectfully, almost lazily, doing the least possible required by common civility. All this struck Ivan instantly, he took it all in and noted it at once—most of all the look in Smerdyakov's eyes, positively malicious, churlish and haughty. "What do you want to intrude for?" it seemed to say; "we settled everything then, why have you come again?" Ivan could scarcely control himself.

"It's hot here," he said, still standing, and unbuttoned his overcoat.

"Take off your coat, sir," Smerdyakov conceded.

Ivan took off his coat and threw it on a bench. With trembling hands, he took a chair, moved it quickly to the table and sat down. Smerdyakov managed to sit down on his bench before him.

"To begin with, are we alone?" Ivan Fyodorovich asked sternly and impulsively. "Can they overhear us in there?"

"No one can hear anything. You've seen for yourself, sir, there's a hall."

"Listen, my good fellow, what was that you babbled, as I was leaving the hospital, that if I said nothing about your faculty of shamming fits, you wouldn't tell the district attorney all our conversation at the gate. What do you mean by *all*? What could you mean by it? Were you threatening me? Have I entered into some sort of compact with you? Do you suppose I am afraid of you?"

Ivan Fyodorovich said this in a perfect fury, giving him to understand with obvious intention that he scorned any subterfuge or indirectness and meant to show his cards. Smerdyakov's eyes gleamed resentfully, his left eye winked and he at once gave his answer, with his habitual composure and deliberation: "You want to have everything above board, very well, you shall have it," he seemed to say.

"This is what I meant then, and this is why I said that, that you, knowing beforehand of this murder of your own parent, left him to his fate, and that people mightn't after that conclude any evil about your feelings and perhaps of something else, too—that's what I promised not to tell the authorities."

Though Smerdyakov spoke without haste and obviously was controlling himself, yet there was something in his voice, determined and emphatic, resentful and insolently defiant. He stared impudently at Ivan Fyodorovich, who for a moment seemed to see spots before his eyes.

"How? What? Are you out of your mind?"

"I'm perfectly in possession of all my faculties, sir."

"Do you suppose I *knew* of the murder?" Ivan Fyodorovich cried at last, and he brought his fist violently down on the table. "What do you mean by 'something else, too'? Speak, scoundrel!"

Smerdyakov was silent and still scanned Ivan Fyodorovich with the same insolent stare.

"Speak, you stinking rogue, what is that 'something else, too'?"

"The 'something else' I meant was that you probably too were very desirous of your parent's death."

Ivan Fyodorovich jumped up and struck him with all his might on the shoulder, so that he fell back against the wall. In an instant his face was bathed in tears. Saying, "It's a shame, your honor, to strike a sick man," he covered his eyes with a very dirty and used blue checked handkerchief and sank into quiet weeping. A minute passed.

"That's enough! Stop," Ivan Fyodorovich said peremptorily, sitting down again. "Don't make me lose all patience."

Smerdyakov took the rag from his eyes. Every line of his puckered face reflected the insult he had just received.

"So you thought then, you scoundrel, that together with Dmitri I meant to kill my father?"

"I didn't know what thoughts were in your mind then, sir," said Smerdyakov resentfully; "and so I stopped you then at the gate to sound you out on that very point, sir."

"To sound what, what?"

"Why, that very circumstance, whether you wanted your father to be murdered or not?"

What infuriated Ivan Fyodorovich more than anything was the aggressive, insolent tone to which Smerdyakov persistently adhered.

"It was you who murdered him!" he cried suddenly.

Smerdyakov smiled contemptuously.

"You know of yourself, for a fact, that it wasn't I who murdered him. And I should have thought that there was no need to speak of it again to an intelligent man."

"But why, why had you such a suspicion about me at the time?"

"As you know already, it was simply from fear, sir. For I was in such a position, shaking with fear, that I suspected everyone. I resolved to sound you out, too, for I thought if you wanted the same as your brother, then the business was as good as settled and I would be crushed like a fly, too."

"Look here, you didn't say that two weeks ago."

"I meant the same when I talked to you in the hospital, only I thought you'd understand without wasting words, and that being such an intelligent man you wouldn't care to talk of it openly."

"What next! Come answer, answer, I insist: what was it . . . what could I have done to put such a degrading suspicion into your base soul?"

"As for the murder, you couldn't have done that, sir, and didn't want to, but as for wanting someone else to do it, that was just what you did want."

"And how coolly, how coolly he speaks! But why should I have wanted it, what grounds had I for wanting it?"

"What grounds had you? What about the inheritance, sir?" said Smerdyakov sarcastically, and as it were vindictively. "Why, after your parent's death there was at least forty thousand to come to each of you, and very likely more, but if Fyodor Pavlovich got married then to that lady, Agrafena Alexandrovna, she would have had all his capital made over to her directly after the wedding, for she's plenty of sense, sir, so that your parent would not have left you two rubles between the three of you. And were they far from a wedding, either? Not a hairsbreadth: that lady had only to lift her little finger and he would have run after her to church, with his tongue out."

Ivan Fyodorovich restrained himself with painful effort.

"Very good," he commented at last, "you see, I haven't jumped up, I haven't knocked you down, I haven't killed you. Speak on. So, according to you, I had fixed on brother Dmitri to do it, I was reckoning on him?"

"How could you help reckoning on him, sir? If he killed him, then he would lose all the rights of a nobleman, his rank and property, and would go off to exile, sir, so his share of the inheritance would come to you and your brother Alexey Fyodorovich, in equal parts, so you'd each have not forty, but sixty thousand each. There's not a doubt you did reckon on Dmitri Fyodorovich."

"What I put up with from you! Listen, villain, if I had reckoned on anyone then, it would have been on you, not on Dmitri, and I swear I did expect some vileness from you . . . at the time . . . I remember my impression!"

"I thought, too, for a minute, at the time, that you were reckoning on me as well," said Smerdyakov, with a sarcastic grin. "So that it was just by that more than anything you showed me what was in your mind. For if you had a foreboding about me and yet went away, you as good as said to me, 'You can murder my parent, I won't hinder you!'"

"You scoundrel! So that's how you understood it!"

"It was all that going to Chermashnya. Why! You were meaning to go to Moscow and refused all your father's entreaties to go to Chermashnya— and simply at a foolish word from me you consented at once! What reason had you to consent to Chermashnya, sir? Since you went to Chermashnya with no reason, simply at my word, it shows that you must have expected something from me."

"No, I swear I didn't!" shouted Ivan, grinding his teeth.

"You didn't, sir? Then you ought, as your father's son, to have had me taken to jail and thrashed at once for my words then . . . or at least, to have given me a punch in the face on the spot, but you were not a bit angry, if you please, and at once in a friendly way acted on my foolish word and went away, sir, which was utterly absurd, for you ought to have stayed to save your parent's life. How could I help drawing my conclusions?"

Ivan sat scowling, both his fists convulsively pressed on his knees.

"Yes, I am sorry I didn't punch you in the face," he said with a bitter smile. "I couldn't have taken you to jail just then. Who would have believed me and what charge could I bring against you? But the punch in the face . . . oh, I'm sorry I didn't think of it. Though blows are forbidden, I should have pounded your ugly face to a jelly."

Smerdyakov looked at him almost with relish.

"In the ordinary occasions of life," he said in the same complacent and sententious tone in which he had taunted Grigory and argued with him about religion at Fyodor Pavlovich's table, "in the ordinary occasions of life, blows on the face are forbidden nowadays by law and people have given them up, but in exceptional occasions of life people still fly to blows, not only among us but all over the world, be it even the total Republic of France, just as in the time of Adam and Eve, sir, and they will never stop, but you, even in an exceptional case, did not dare, sir."

"What are you learning French words for?" Ivan nodded towards the exercise book lying on the table.

"Why shouldn't I learn them so as to improve my education, supposing that I may myself chance to go some day to those happy parts of Europe."

"Listen, monster," Ivan's eyes flashed and he trembled all over. "I am not afraid of your accusations, you can say what you like about me, and if I don't beat you to death, it's simply because I suspect you of that crime and I'll drag you to justice. I'll unmask you."

"To my thinking, you'd better keep quiet, sir, for what can you accuse me of, considering my absolute innocence; and who would believe you? Only if you begin, I shall tell everything, too, for I must defend myself."

"Do you think I am afraid of you now?"

"If the court doesn't believe all I've said to you just now, sir, the public will, and you will be ashamed."

"That's as much as to say 'It's always interesting speaking with an intelligent man,' eh?" snarled Ivan.

"You hit the mark, indeed. And you will be intelligent, sir."

Ivan Fyodorovich got up, shaking all over with indignation, put on his coat, and without replying further to Smerdyakov, without even looking at him, walked quickly out of the cottage. The cool evening air refreshed him. There was a bright moon in the sky. A nightmare of ideas and sensations filled his soul. "Shall I go at once and give information against Smerdyakov? But what information can I give? He is not guilty, anyway. On the contrary, he'll accuse me. And in fact why did I set off for Chermashnya then? What for? What for?" Ivan asked himself. "Yes, of course, I was expecting something and he is right . . ." And he remembered for the hundredth time how, on that last night in his father's house, he had listened on the stairs. But he remembered it now with such anguish that he stood still on the spot as though he had been stabbed. "Yes, I expected it then, that's true! I wanted the murder, I did want the murder! Did I want the murder? Did I want it? I must kill Smerdyakov! If I don't dare kill Smerdyakov now, life is not worth living!" Ivan Fyodorovich did not go home, but went straight to Katerina Ivanovna and alarmed her by his appearance. He was like a madman. He repeated all his conversation with Smerdyakov, every syllable of it. He couldn't be calmed, however much she tried to soothe him: he kept walking about the room, speaking strangely, disconnectedly. At last he sat down, put his elbows on the table, leaned his head on his hands and pronounced this strange sentence:

"If it's not Dmitri, but Smerdyakov who's the murderer, I share his guilt, for I put him up to it. Whether I did, I don't know yet. But if he is the murderer, and not Dmitri, then, of course, I am the murderer, too."

When Katerina Ivanovna heard that, she got up from her seat without a word, went to her writing table, opened a box standing on it, took out a sheet of paper and laid it before Ivan. This was the document of which Ivan Fyodorovich spoke to Alyosha later on as a "mathematical proof" that brother Dmitri had killed his father. This was the letter written by Mitya to Katerina Ivanovna when he was drunk, on the very evening he met Alyosha at the crossroads on the way to the monastery, after the scene at Katerina Ivanovna's, when Grushenka had insulted her. Then, parting from Alyosha, Mitya had rushed to Grushenka. I don't know whether he saw her, but in the evening he was at the Metropolis, where he got thoroughly drunk. Then he asked for pen and paper and wrote a document of weighty consequence to himself. It was a wordy, disconnected, frantic letter, a "drunken" letter in fact. It was like the talk of a drunken man, who, on his return home, begins with extraordinary heat telling his wife or one of his household how he has just been insulted, what a scoundrel had just insulted him, what a fine fellow he is on the other hand, and how he will make that scoundrel pay; and all that at great length, with great excitement and incoherence, with drunken tears and blows on the table. The letter was written on a dirty piece of ordinary paper of the cheapest kind. It had been provided by the tavern and there were figures scrawled on the back of it. There was evidently not space enough for his drunken verbosity and Mitya not only filled the margins but had written the last line right across the rest. The letter ran as follows:

Fatal Katya!
  Tomorrow I will get the money and repay your three thousand and farewell, woman of great wrath, but farewell too my love! Let us make an end! Tomorrow I shall try and get it from everyone, and if I can't borrow it, I give you my word of honor I shall go to my father and break his skull and take the money from under the pillow, if only Ivan has gone. If I had to go to Siberia for it, I'll give you back your three thousand. And farewell. I bow down to the ground before you, for I've been a scoundrel to you. Forgive me! No, better not forgive me, you'll be happier and so shall I! Better Siberia than your love, for I love another woman and you got to know her too well today, so how can you forgive? I will murder the man who's robbed me! I'll leave you all and go to the East so as to see no one again. Not *her* either, for you are not my only tormentress, she is too. Farewell!
  P.S.—I write my curse, but I adore you! I hear it in my heart. One string is left, and it vibrates. Better tear my heart in two! I shall kill myself, but first of all that cur. I shall tear three thousand from him and fling it to you. Though I've been a scoundrel to you, I am not a thief! You can expect three thousand. The cur keeps it under his mattress, in pink ribbon. I am not a thief, but I'll murder my thief. Katya, don't look disdainful. Dmitri is not a thief, but a murderer! He has murdered his father and ruined himself to hold his ground, rather than endure your pride. And he doesn't love you.

P.P.S.—I kiss your feet, farewell!

P.P.P.S.—Katya, pray to God that someone'll give me the money. Then I shall not be steeped in gore, and if no one does—I shall! Kill me!

> Your slave and enemy,
> D. KARAMAZOV.

When Ivan read this "document," he was convinced. So then it was his brother, not Smerdyakov. And if not Smerdyakov, then not he, Ivan. This letter at once assumed in his eyes the aspect of a mathematical proof. There could be no longer the slightest doubt of Mitya's guilt. The suspicion never occurred to Ivan, by the way, that Mitya might have committed the murder in conjunction with Smerdyakov, and indeed it did not fit in with the facts. Ivan was completely reassured. The next morning he only thought of Smerdyakov and his gibes with contempt. A few days later he positively wondered how he could have been so horribly distressed at his suspicions. He resolved to dismiss him with contempt and forget him. So passed a month. He made no further inquiry about Smerdyakov, but twice he happened to hear that he was very ill and out of his mind. "He'll end in madness," the young doctor, Varvinsky, observed about him and Ivan remembered this.

During the last week of that month Ivan himself began to feel very ill. He went to consult the Moscow doctor who had been sent for by Katerina Ivanovna just before the trial. And just at that time his relations with Katerina Ivanovna became acutely strained. They were like two enemies in love with one another. Katerina Ivanovna's "returns" to Mitya, that is, her brief but violent revulsions of feeling in his favor, drove Ivan to perfect frenzy. Strange to say, until that last scene described above, when Alyosha came from Mitya to Katerina Ivanovna, Ivan had never once, during that month, heard her express a doubt of Mitya's guilt, in spite of those "returns" that were so hateful to him. It is remarkable, too, that while he felt that he hated Mitya more and more every day, he realized that it was not on account of Katya's "returns" that he hated him, but just *because he was the murderer of his father!* He was conscious of this and fully recognized it to himself. Nevertheless, he went to see Mitya ten days before the trial and proposed to him a plan of escape—a plan he had obviously thought over a long time. He was partly impelled to do this by a sore place still left in his heart from a phrase of Smerdyakov, that it was to his, Ivan's, advantage that his brother should be convicted, as that would increase his inheritance and Alyosha's from forty to sixty thousand rubles. He determined to sacrifice thirty thousand on arranging Mitya's escape. On his return from seeing him, he was very mournful and dispirited, he suddenly began to feel that he was anxious for Mitya's escape, not only to heal that sore place by sacrificing thirty thousand, but for another reason. "Is it because I am as much a murderer at heart?" he asked himself. Something very deep down seemed burning and rankling in his soul. His pride above all suffered cruelly all that month. But of that later. . . .

When, after his conversation with Alyosha, Ivan Fyodorovich suddenly decided with his hand on the bell of his lodging to go to Smerdyakov, he obeyed a sudden and peculiar impulse of indignation. He suddenly remembered how Katerina Ivanovna had only just cried out to him in

Alyosha's presence: "It was you, you, persuaded me of his" (that is, Mitya's) "guilt!" Ivan was thunderstruck when he recalled it. He had never once tried to persuade her that Mitya was the murderer, on the contrary, he had suspected himself in her presence, that time when he came back from Smerdyakov. It was *she*, she, who had produced that "document" and proved his brother's guilt. And now she suddenly exclaimed: "I've been at Smerdyakov's myself!" When had she been there? Ivan had known nothing of it. So she was not at all so sure of Mitya's guilt! And what could Smerdyakov have told her? What, what, had he said to her? His heart burned with violent anger. He could not understand how he could, half an hour before, have let those words pass and not have cried out at the moment. He let go of the bell and rushed off to Smerdyakov. "Perhaps I shall kill him this time," he thought on the way.

Chapter VIII

The Third and Last Meeting with Smerdyakov

When he was halfway there, the keen dry wind that had been blowing early that morning rose again, and a fine, thick, dry snow began falling heavily. It did not lie on the ground, but was whirled about by the wind and soon there was a regular snowstorm. There were scarcely any lamp posts in the part of the town where Smerdyakov lived. Ivan strode alone in the darkness, unconscious of the storm, instinctively picking out his way. His head ached and there was a painful throbbing in his temples. He felt that his hands were twitching convulsively. Not far from Marya Kondratyevna's little house, Ivan Fyodorovich suddenly came upon a solitary drunken little peasant. He was wearing a coarse and patched coat, and was walking in zigzags, grumbling and swearing to himself. Then suddenly he would begin singing in a husky drunken voice:

> Ach, Vanka's gone to Petersburg,
> I won't wait till he comes back.

But he broke off every time at the second line and began swearing again; then he would begin the same song again. Ivan felt an intense hatred for him before he had thought about him at all. Suddenly he realized his presence and felt an irresistible impulse to knock him down. At that moment they met, and the peasant with a violent lurch fell full tilt against Ivan, who pushed him back furiously. The peasant went flying backwards and fell like a log on the frozen ground. He uttered one plaintive "O-oh!" and then was silent. Ivan stepped up to him. He was lying on his back, without movement or consciousness. "He will freeze," thought Ivan, and he went on his way to Smerdyakov's.

In the hall, Marya Kondratyevna, who ran out to open the door with a candle in her hand, whispered that Pavel Fyodorovich (that is, Smerdyakov) was very ill; "it's not that he's laid up, sir, but he seems not himself, and he even told us to take the tea away; he wouldn't have any."

"Why, is he making a row?" asked Ivan coarsely.

"Oh, dear, no, quite the contrary, sir, he's very quiet. Only please don't talk to him too long," Marya Kondratyevna begged him.

Ivan Fyodorovich opened the door and stepped into the room.

It was overheated as before, but there were changes in the room. One of the benches at the side had been removed, and in its place had been put a large old mahogany leather sofa, on which a bed had been made up, with fairly clean white pillows. Smerdyakov was sitting on the sofa, wearing the same dressing gown. The table had been brought out in front of the sofa, so that there was hardly room to move. On the table lay a thick book with a yellow cover, but Smerdyakov was not reading it. He seemed to be sitting doing nothing. He met Ivan with a slow silent gaze, and was apparently not at all surprised at his coming. There was a great change in his face; he was much thinner and sallower. His eyes were sunken and there were dark circles under them.

"Why, you really are ill?" Ivan Fyodorovich stopped short. "I won't keep you long, I won't even take off my coat. Where can one sit down?"

He went to the other end of the table, moved up a chair and sat down on it.

"Why do you look at me without speaking? I've only come with one question, and I swear I won't go without an answer. Has the young lady, Katerina Ivanovna, been with you?"

Smerdyakov still remained silent, looking quietly at Ivan as before. Suddenly, he waved his hand and turned his face away.

"What's the matter with you?" cried Ivan.

"Nothing."

"What do you mean by 'nothing'?"

"Yes, she has. It's no matter to you. Let me alone."

"No, I won't let you alone. Tell me, when was she here?"

"Why, I'd quite forgotten about her," said Smerdyakov, with a scornful smile, and turning his face to Ivan again, he stared at him with a look of frenzied hatred, the same look that he had fixed on him at their last interview, a month before.

"You seem very ill yourself, your face is sunken; you don't look like yourself," he said to Ivan.

"Never mind my health, tell me what I ask you."

"But why are your eyes so jaundiced? The whites are quite yellow. Are you so troubled?"

He smiled contemptuously and suddenly laughed outright.

"Listen, I've told you I won't go away without an answer!" Ivan cried, intensely irritated.

"Why do you keep pestering me? Why do you torment me?" said Smerdyakov, with a look of suffering.

"Oh, the devil! I have nothing to do with you. Just answer my question and I'll go away."

"I have no answer to give you," said Smerdyakov, looking down again.

"You may be sure I'll make you answer!"

"Why are you so uneasy?" Smerdyakov stared at him, not simply with contempt, but almost with a revulsion. "Is this because the trial begins tomorrow? Nothing will happen to you, can't you believe that at last? Go home, go to bed and sleep in peace, don't be afraid of anything."

"I don't understand you. . . . What have I to be afraid of tomorrow?" Ivan articulated in astonishment, and suddenly a chill breath of fear did in fact pass over his soul. Smerdyakov measured him with his eyes.

"You don't understand?" he drawled reproachfully. "It's a strange thing an intelligent man should care to play such a farce!"

Ivan looked at him speechless. The startling, incredibly supercilious tone of this man who had once been his lackey was extraordinary in itself. He had not taken such a tone even at their last interview.

"I tell you, you've nothing to be afraid of. I won't say anything about you, there's no proof against you. I say, how your hands are trembling. Why are your fingers moving like that? Go home, *you* did not murder him."

Ivan started. He remembered Alyosha.

"I know it was not I," he faltered.

"Do you?" Smerdyakov caught him up again.

Ivan jumped up and seized him by the shoulder.

"Tell me everything, you viper! Tell me everything!"

Smerdyakov was not in the least scared. He only riveted his eyes on Ivan with insane hatred.

"Well, it was you who murdered him, if that's it," he whispered furiously.

Ivan sank back on his chair, as though pondering something. He laughed malignantly.

"You mean my going away. What you talked about last time?"

"You stood before me last time and understood it all, and you understand it now."

"All I understand is that you are mad."

"Aren't you tired of it? Here we are face to face; what's the use of going on keeping up a farce to each other? Are you still trying to throw it all on me, to my face? *You* murdered him; you are the real murderer, I was only your instrument, your faithful servant Licharda,[6] and it was following your words I did it."

"*Did* it? Why, did you murder him?" Ivan turned cold.

Something seemed to give way in his brain, and he shuddered all over with a cold shiver. Then Smerdyakov himself looked at him wonderingly; probably the genuineness of Ivan's horror struck him.

"You don't mean to say you really did not know?" he faltered mistrustfully, looking with a forced smile into his eyes. Ivan still gazed at him, and seemed unable to speak.

> Ach, Vanka's gone to Petersburg,
> I won't wait till he comes back,

suddenly echoed in his head.

"Do you know, I am afraid that you are a dream, a phantom sitting before me," he muttered.

"There's no phantom here, but only us two and one other. No doubt he is here, that third, between us."

"Who is he? Who is here? What third person?" Ivan Fyodorovich cried in alarm, looking about him, his eyes hastily searching in every corner.

"That third is God Himself, sir, Providence, sir. He is the third beside us now. Only don't look for him, you won't find him."

"It's a lie that you killed him!" Ivan shouted madly. "You are mad, or teasing me again!"

6. See p. 233.

Smerdyakov, as before, watched him curiously, with no sign of fear. He could still scarcely get over his incredulity; he still fancied that Ivan "knew everything" and was trying to "throw it all on him to his face."

"Wait a minute, sir," he said at last in a weak voice, and suddenly bringing up his left leg from under the table, he began turning up his trouser leg. He was wearing long white stockings and slippers. Slowly he took off his garter and fumbled to the bottom of his stocking. Ivan gazed at him, and suddenly shuddered in a paroxysm of terror.

"Madman!" he cried, and rapidly jumping up, he drew back, so that he knocked his back against the wall and stood up against it, stiff and straight. He looked with insane terror at Smerdyakov, who, entirely unaffected by his terror, continued fumbling in his stocking, as though he were making an effort to get hold of something with his fingers and pull it out. At last he got hold of it and began pulling it out, Ivan Fyodorovich saw that it was a piece of paper, or perhaps a roll of papers. Smerdyakov pulled it out and laid it on the table.

"Here," he said quietly.

"What is it?" responded Ivan, trembling.

"Kindly look at it, sir," Smerdyakov answered, still in the same low tone.

Ivan stepped up to the table, took up the roll of paper and began unfolding it, but suddenly he drew back his fingers, as though from contact with some loathsome, terrible viper.

"Your hands keep twitching, sir," observed Smerdyakov, and he deliberately unfolded the bundle himself. Under the wrapper were three packets of hundred-ruble bills.

"They are all here, sir, all the three thousand rubles; you need not count them. Take them," Smerdyakov suggested to Ivan, nodding at the notes. Ivan sank back in his chair. He was as white as a handkerchief.

"You frightened me . . . with your stocking," he said, with a strange grin.

"Can you really, can you really not have known till now?" Smerdyakov asked once more.

"No, I did not know. I kept thinking of Dmitri. Brother, brother! Ach!" He suddenly clutched his head in both hands. "Listen. Did you kill him alone? With my brother's help or without my brother?"

"It was only with you, with your help, sir, I killed him, and Dmitri Fyodorovich is quite innocent."

"All right, all right. Talk about me later. Why do I keep on trembling? I can't speak properly."

"You were bold enough then, sir. You said 'everything was permitted,' and how frightened you are now," Smerdyakov muttered in surprise. "Won't you have some lemonade? I'll ask for some at once. It's very refreshing, sir. Only I must hide this first."

And again he motioned at the bills. He was just going to get up and call at the door to Marya Kondratyevna to make some lemonade and bring it them, but, looking for something to cover up the notes that she might not see them, he first took out his handkerchief, and as it turned out again to be very dirty and used, took up the big yellow book that Ivan had noticed at first lying on the table, and put it over the money. The book was *The Sayings of the Holy Father Isaac the Syrian.*[7] Ivan read it mechanically.

7. See p. 50.

"I won't have any lemonade," he said. "Talk of me later. Sit down and tell me how you did it. Tell me all about it."

"You'd better take off your greatcoat, sir, or you'll be too hot."

Ivan Fyodorovich, as though he'd only just thought of it, flung off his overcoat, and, without getting up from his chair, threw it on the bench.

"Speak, please, speak."

He seemed calmer. He waited, feeling sure that Smerdyakov would tell him *all* about it.

"How it was done?" sighed Smerdyakov. "It was done in a most natural way, following your very words, sir."

"Of my words later," Ivan broke in again, apparently with complete self-possession, firmly uttering his words, and not shouting as before. "Only tell me in detail how you did it. Everything, as it happened. Don't forget anything. The details, above everything, the details, I beg you."

"You'd gone away, then I fell into the cellar, sir."

"In a fit or in a sham one?"

"A sham one, naturally, sir. I shammed it all. I went quietly down the steps to the very bottom and lay down quietly, sir, and as I lay down I gave a scream, and thrashed about, till they carried me out."

"Wait! And were you shamming all along, afterwards, and in the hospital?"

"No, not at all, sir. Next day, in the morning, before they took me to the hospital, I had a real attack and a more violent one than I've had for years. For two days I was totally unconscious."

"All right, all right. Go on."

"They laid me on the bed. I knew I'd be on the other side of the partition, for whenever I was ill, Martha Ignatyevna used to put me there, near them. She's always been very kind to me from my birth up, sir. At night I moaned, but quietly, sir. I kept expecting Dmitri Fyodorovich to come."

"Expecting him? To come to you?"

"Not to me. I expected him to come into the house, for I'd no doubt that he'd come that night, for being without me and getting no news, he'd be sure to come and climb over the fence, as he used to, and do something."

"And if he hadn't come?"

"Then nothing would have happened, sir. I would never have brought myself to it without him."

"All right, all right . . . speak more intelligibly, don't hurry; above all, don't leave anything out!"

"I expected him to kill Fyodor Pavlovich, sir. I thought that was certain, for I had prepared him for it . . . during the last few days. . . . He knew about the knocks, that was the chief thing. With his suspiciousness and the fury which had been growing in him all those days, he was bound to get into the house by means of those taps. That was inevitable, so I was expecting him, sir."

"Wait," Ivan interrupted, "if he had killed him, he would have taken the money and carried it away; you must have considered that. What would you have got by it afterwards? I don't see."

"But he would never have found the money, sir. That was only what I told him, that the money was under the mattress. But that wasn't true. It had been lying in a box. And afterwards I suggested to Fyodor Pavlovich, as I was the only person he trusted, to hide the envelope with the money in the corner behind the icons, for no one would have guessed that place, especially if they came in a hurry. So that's where the envelope lay, in the corner behind the icons. It would have been absurd to keep it under the mattress; the box, anyway, could be locked. But all believe it was under the mattress. A stupid thing to believe, sir. So if Dmitri Fyodorovich had committed the murder, finding nothing, he would either have run away in a hurry, afraid of every sound, as always happens with murderers, or he would have been arrested, sir. So I could always have clambered up to the icons and have taken away the money next morning or even that night, and it would have all been put down to Dmitri Fyodorovich. I could reckon upon that."

"But what if he did not kill him, but only knocked him down?"

"If he did not kill him, of course, I would not have ventured to take the money, and nothing would have happened. But I calculated that he would beat him senseless, and I would have time to take it then, and then I'd make out to Fyodor Pavlovich that it was no one but Dmitri Fyodorovich who had taken the money after beating him."

"Wait . . . I am getting mixed up. Then it was Dmitri after all who killed him, you only took the money?"

"No, he didn't kill him. Well, I might as well have told you now that he was the murderer. . . . But I don't want to lie to you now, because . . . because if you really haven't understood till now, as I see for myself, and are not pretending, so as to throw your guilt on me to my very face, you are still responsible for it all, since you knew of the murder, sir, and charged me to do it, sir, and went away knowing all about it. And so I want to prove to your face this evening that you are the only real murderer in the whole affair, sir, and I am not the real murderer, though I did kill him. You are the rightful murderer."

"Why, why, am I the murderer? Oh, God!" Ivan cried, unable to restrain himself at last, and forgetting that he had put off discussing himself till the end of the conversation. "You still mean Chermashnya? Wait, tell me, why did you want my consent, if you really took Chermashnya for consent? How will you explain that now?"

"Assured of your consent, I would have known that you wouldn't make an outcry over those three thousand being lost, even if I'd been suspected, instead of Dmitri Fyodorovich, or as his accomplice; on the contrary, you would have protected me from others. . . . And when you got your inheritance you would have rewarded me when you were able, all the rest of your life. For you'd have received your inheritance through me, sir, seeing that if he had married Agrafena Alexandrovna, you wouldn't have had a cent."

"Ah! Then you intended to torment me all my life afterwards," snarled Ivan. "And what if I hadn't gone away then, but had informed against you?"

"What could you have informed? That I persuaded you to go to Chermashnya? That's all nonsense, sir. Besides, after our conversation you would either have gone away or have stayed. If you had stayed, nothing would have happened. I would have known that you didn't want it done, and would have attempted nothing. Since you went away, it meant you assured me that you wouldn't dare to inform against me at the trial, and that you'd overlook my having the three thousand. And, indeed, you couldn't have prosecuted me afterwards, because then I would have told it all in the court; that is, not that I had stolen the money or killed him—I would not have said that—but that you'd put me up to the theft and the murder, though I didn't consent to it. That's why I needed your consent, so that you couldn't have cornered me afterwards, sir, for what proof could you have had? I could always have cornered you, revealing your eagerness for your father's death, and I tell you the public would have believed it all, and you would have been ashamed for the rest of your life."

"Was I so eager then, was I?" Ivan snarled again.

"To be sure you were, and by your consent you silently sanctioned my doing it." Smerdyakov looked resolutely at Ivan. He was very weak and spoke slowly and wearily, but some hidden inner force urged him on. He evidently had some design. Ivan felt that.

"Go on," he said. "Tell me what happened that night."

"What more is there to tell, sir! I lay there and I thought I heard the master shout. And before that Grigory Vasilyevich had suddenly got up and came out, and he suddenly gave a scream, and then all was silence and darkness. I lay there waiting, my heart beating; I couldn't bear it. I got up at last, sir, went out. I saw the window open on the left into the garden, and I stepped to the left to listen whether he was sitting there alive, and I heard the master moving about, sighing, so I knew he was alive, sir. Ech! I thought. I went to the window and shouted to the master, 'It's I.' And he shouted to me, 'He's been here, he's been here; he's run away.' He meant Dmitri Fyodorovich had been there. 'He's killed Grigory!' 'Where?' I whispered. 'There, in the corner,' he pointed. He was whispering, too. 'Wait a bit,' I said. I went to the corner of the garden to look, and there I came upon Grigory Vasilyevich lying by the wall, covered with blood, senseless. So it's true that Dmitri Fyodorovich has been here, was the thought that came into my head, and I determined on the spot to make an end of it, as Grigory Vasilyevich, even if he were alive, would see nothing of it, as he lay there senseless. The only risk was that Martha Ignatyevna might wake up. I felt that at the moment, but the longing to get it done came over me, till I could scarcely breathe. I went back to the window to the master and said, 'She's here, she's come; Agrafena Alexandrovna has come, wants to be let in.' And he started like a baby. 'Where is she?' he fairly gasped, but couldn't believe it. 'She's standing there,' said I, 'open.' He looked out of the window at me, half believing and half distrustful, but afraid to open. 'Why he is afraid of me now,' I thought. And it was funny. I thought of knocking on the window frame those taps we'd agreed upon as a signal that Grushenka had come, in his presence, before his eyes. He didn't seem to believe my words, but as soon as he heard the taps, he ran at once to open the door. He opened it. I would have gone in, but he stood in the way to prevent me passing. 'Where is she? Where is she?' He looked at me, all of a tremble. Well, thought I, if he's so frightened of me as all that, that's bad! And my legs went weak with fright that he wouldn't let me in or would call out, or Martha Ignatyevna would run up, or something else might happen. I don't remember now, but I must have stood pale, facing him. I whispered to him, 'Why, she's there, there, under the big window, how is it you don't see her?' I said. 'Bring her then, bring her.' 'She's afraid,' said I, 'she was frightened at the noise, she's hidden in the bushes; go and call to her yourself from the study.' He ran to the window, put the candle in the window. 'Grushenka,' he cried, 'Grushenka, are you here?' Though he cried that, he didn't want to lean out of the window, he didn't want to move away from me, for he was panic-stricken; he was so frightened he didn't dare to turn his back on me, 'Why, here she is,' said I. I went up to the window and leaned right out of it. 'Here she is, she's in the bush, laughing at you, don't you see her?' He suddenly believed it; he was all of a shake—he was awfully crazy about her—and he leaned right out of the window. I snatched up that iron paperweight from his table; do you remember, weighing about three pounds. I swung it and hit him on the top of the skull with the corner of it. He didn't even cry out. He only sank down suddenly, and I hit him again and a third time. And the third time I knew I'd broken his skull. He suddenly rolled on his back, face upwards, covered with blood. I looked round. There was no blood on me, not a spot. I wiped the paperweight, put it back, went up to the icons, took the money out of the envelope, and flung the envelope on the floor and the pink ribbon beside it. I went out into the garden all of a tremble, straight to the apple tree with a hollow in it—you know that hollow. I'd marked it long before and put a rag and a piece of paper ready in it. I wrapped all the notes in the rag and stuffed it deep down in the hole. And there it stayed for over two weeks. I took it out later, when I came out of the hospital. I went back to my bed, lay down and thought, 'If Grigory Vasilyevich has been killed outright, it may be a bad job for me, but if he is not killed and recovers, it will be first rate, for then he'll bear witness that Dmitri Fyodorovich had been here, and so he must have killed him and taken the money.' Then I began groaning with suspense and impatience, so as to wake Martha Ignatyevna as soon as possible. At last she got up, and she rushed to me, but when she saw Grigory Vasilyevich was not there, she ran out, and I heard her scream in the garden. And that set it all going and set my mind at rest."

The narrator stopped. Ivan had listened all the time in dead silence without stirring or taking his eyes off him. As he told his story Smerdyakov glanced at him from time to time, but for the most part kept his eyes averted. When he had finished he was evidently agitated and was breathing hard. Perspiration stood out on his face. But it was impossible to tell whether it was remorse he was feeling, or what.

"Wait," cried Ivan, pondering. "What about the door? If he only opened the door to you, how could Grigory have seen it open before? For Grigory saw it before you went."

It was remarkable that Ivan spoke quite amicably, in a different tone, not angry as before, so if anyone had opened the door at that moment and peeped in at them, he would certainly have concluded that they were talking peaceably about some ordinary, though interesting, subject.

"As for that door and Grigory Vasilyevich's having seen it open, that's only his fancy," said Smerdyakov, with a wry smile. "He is not a man, I assure you, but an obstinate mule. He didn't see it, but fancied he had seen it, and there's no shaking him. It's just our luck he took that notion into his head, for they can't fail to convict Dmitri Fyodorovich after that."

"Listen . . ." said Ivan Fyodorovich, beginning to seem bewildered again and making an effort to grasp something. "Listen. There are a lot of questions I want to ask you, but I forget them . . . I keep forgetting and getting mixed up. Yes! Tell me this at least, why did you open the envelope and leave it there on the floor? Why didn't you simply carry off the envelope? . . . While you were telling me, I thought you spoke about it as though it were the right thing to do . . . but why, I can't understand . . ."

"I did that for a good reason, sir. For if a man had known all about it, as I did for instance, if he'd seen that money before, and perhaps had put them in that envelope himself, and had seen the envelope sealed up and addressed, with his own eyes, if such a man had done the murder, what would have made him tear open the envelope afterwards, especially in such desperate haste, since he'd know for certain the money must be in the envelope? No, if the robber had been someone like me, he'd simply have put the envelope straight in his pocket and got away with it as fast as he could, sir. But it'd be quite different with Dmitri Fyodorovich. He only knew about the envelope by hearsay; he had never seen it, and if he'd found it, for instance, under the mattress, he'd have torn it open as quickly as possible to make sure the money was in it. And he'd have thrown the envelope down, without having time to think that it would be evidence against him. Because he was not an habitual thief, sir, and had never directly stolen anything before, for he is a gentleman born, sir, and if he did bring himself to steal, it would not be regular stealing, but simply taking what was his own, for he'd told the whole town he meant to before, and had even bragged aloud before everyone that he'd go and take his property from Fyodor Pavlovich. I didn't say that openly to the prosecutor when I was being examined, but quite the contrary, I brought him to it by a hint, as though I didn't see it myself, and as though he'd thought of it himself and I hadn't prompted him; so that Mr. Prosecutor's mouth positively watered at my suggestion, sir."

"But can you possibly have thought of all that on the spot?" cried Ivan Fyodorovich, overcome with astonishment. He looked at Smerdyakov again with alarm.

"Mercy on us! Could anyone think of it all in such a desperate hurry? It was all thought out beforehand."

"Well . . . well, it was the devil who helped you!" Ivan Fyodorovich cried again. "No, you are not a fool, you are far more intelligent than I thought . . ."

He got up, obviously intending to walk across the room. He was in terrible distress. But as the table blocked his way, and there was hardly room to pass between the table and the wall, he only turned round where he stood and sat down again. Perhaps the impossibility of moving irritated him, as he suddenly cried out almost as furiously as before.

"Listen, you miserable, contemptible man! Don't you understand that if I haven't killed you, it's simply because I am keeping you to answer tomorrow at the trial. God sees," Ivan raised his hand, "perhaps I, too, was guilty; perhaps I really had a secret desire for my father's . . . death, but I swear I was not as guilty as you think, and perhaps I didn't urge you on at all. No, no, I didn't urge you on! But no matter, I will give evidence against myself tomorrow, at the trial. I'm determined to! I shall tell everything, everything. But we'll make our appearance together. And whatever you may say against me at the trial, whatever evidence you give, I'll face it, I am not afraid of you. I'll confirm it all myself! But you must confess, too! You must, you must, we'll go together. That's how it shall be!"

Ivan said this solemnly and resolutely, and from his flashing eyes alone it could be seen that it would be so.

"You are ill, sir, I see, you are quite ill, sir. Your eyes are yellow," Smerdyakov commented, without the least irony, with apparent sympathy in fact.

"We'll go together," Ivan repeated. "And if you won't go, no matter, I'll go alone."

Smerdyakov paused as though pondering.

"There'll be nothing of the sort, sir, and you won't go, sir," he concluded at last positively.

"You don't understand me," Ivan exclaimed reproachfully.

"You'll be too much ashamed, sir, if you confess it all. And, what's more, it will be no use at all, for I shall say straight out that I never said anything of the sort to you, and that you are either ill (and it looks like it, too), or that you're so sorry for your brother that you are sacrificing yourself to save him and have invented it all against me, because your whole life you've thought no more of me than if I'd been a fly, and not a man. And who will believe you, and what single proof have you got?"

"Listen, you showed me that money just now to convince me."

Smerdyakov lifted the book off the bills and laid it on one side.

"Take the money away with you," Smerdyakov sighed.

"Of course I shall take it. But why do you give it to me, if you committed the murder for the sake of it?" Ivan looked at him with great surprise.

"I don't want it, sir," Smerdyakov articulated in a shaking voice, with a gesture of refusal. "I did have an idea of beginning a new life with that money in Moscow or, better still, abroad. I did dream of it, chiefly because 'all things are permitted.' That was quite right what you taught me, for you talked a lot to me about that. For if there's no everlasting God, there's no such thing as virtue, and there's no need of it. You were right there. So that's how I looked at it."

"Did you come to that by yourself?" asked Ivan, with a wry smile.

"With your guidance, sir."

"And now, I suppose, you believe in God, since you are giving back the money?"

"No, sir, I don't believe," whispered Smerdyakov.

"Then why are you giving it back?"

"Stop . . . that's enough!" Smerdyakov waved his hand again. "You used to say yourself that everything was permitted, so now why are you so upset, too? You even want to go and give evidence against yourself. . . . Only there'll be nothing of the sort! You won't go to give evidence," Smerdyakov decided with conviction.

"You'll see," said Ivan.

"It isn't possible. You are very intelligent, sir. You are fond of money, I know that, sir. You like to be respected, too, for you're very proud; you are far too fond of female charms, too, and you care most of all about living in undisturbed comfort, without having to bow to anyone—that's what you care most about. You won't want to spoil your life forever by taking such a disgrace on yourself. You are like Fyodor Pavlovich, sir, you are more like him sir, more like him than any of his children; you've the same soul as he had."

"You are not stupid," said Ivan, seeming struck. The blood rushed to his face. "I used to think you were stupid. You are serious now!" he observed, looking suddenly at Smerdyakov with a different expression.

"It was your pride made you think I was stupid. Take the money."

Ivan took the three rolls of bills and put them in his pocket without wrapping them in anything.

"I shall show them at the court tomorrow," he said.

"Nobody will believe you, as you've plenty of money of your own now; you may simply have taken it out of your cashbox and brought it to the court."

Ivan rose from his seat.

"I repeat," he said, "the only reason I haven't killed you is that I need you for tomorrow, remember that, don't forget it!"

"Well, kill me. Kill me now, sir," Smerdyakov said, all at once looking strangely at Ivan. "You won't dare do that even!" he added, with a bitter smile. "You won't dare to do anything, you, sir, who used to be so bold!"

"Till tomorrow," cried Ivan, and moved to go out.

"Wait a moment. . . . Show them to me again."

Ivan took out the bills and showed them to him. Smerdyakov looked at them for ten seconds.

"Well, you can go," he said, with a wave of his hand. "Ivan Fyodorovich!" he called after him again.

"What do you want?" Ivan turned without stopping.

"Good-bye, sir!"

"Till tomorrow!" Ivan cried again, and he walked out of the cottage.

The snowstorm was still raging. He walked the first few steps boldly, but suddenly began staggering. "It's something physical," he thought with a grin. Something like joy was springing up in his heart. He was conscious of unbounded resolution; he would make an end of the wavering that had so tortured him of late. His mind was made up, "and now it will not be changed," he thought with relief. At that moment he stumbled against something and almost fell down; stopping short, he made out at his feet the peasant he had knocked down, still lying senseless and motionless. The snow had almost covered his face. Ivan suddenly seized him and lifted him in his arms. Seeing a light in the little house to the right he went up, knocked at the shutters, and asked the man to whom the house belonged to help him carry the peasant to the police station, promising him three rubles. The man got ready and came out. I won't describe in detail how Ivan Fyodorovich succeeded in his object, bringing the peasant to the police station and arranging for a doctor to see him at once, providing with a liberal hand for the expenses. I will only say that this business took a whole hour, but Ivan Fyodorovich was well content with it. His mind wandered and worked incessantly. "If I had not taken my decision so firmly for tomorrow," he reflected with satisfaction, "I would not have stayed a whole hour to look after the peasant, but would have passed by, without caring about his being frozen. I am quite capable of watching myself, by the way," he thought at the same instant, with still greater satisfaction, "although they have decided that I am going out of my mind!" Just as he reached his own house he stopped short, asking himself suddenly whether he hadn't better go at once now to the prosecutor and tell him everything. He decided the question by turning back to the house. "Everything together tomorrow!" he whispered to himself, and, strange to say, almost all his gladness and self-satisfaction passed in one instant. As he entered his own room he felt something like a touch of ice on his heart, like a recollection or, more exactly, a reminder, of something agonizing and revolting that was in that room now, at that moment, and had been there before. He sank wearily on his sofa. The old woman brought him a samovar; he made tea, but did not touch it. He dismissed the woman for the night. He sat on the sofa and felt giddy. He felt that he was ill and helpless. He was beginning to drop asleep, but got up uneasily and walked across the room to shake off his drowsiness. At moments he fancied he was delirious, but it was not illness that he thought of most. Sitting down again, he began looking round, as though searching for something. This happened several times. At last his eyes were fastened intently on one point. Ivan smiled, but an angry flush suffused his face. He sat a long time in his place, his head propped on both arms, though he looked sideways at the same point, at the sofa that stood against the opposite wall. There was evidently something, some object, that irritated him there, worried him and tormented him.

Chapter IX

The Devil. Ivan Fyodorovich's Nightmare

I am not a doctor, but yet I feel that the moment has come when I must inevitably give the reader some account of the nature of Ivan Fyodorovich's illness. Anticipating events I can say at least one thing: he was at that moment on the very eve of an attack of brain fever. Though his health had long been affected, it had offered a stubborn resistance to the fever which in the end gained complete mastery over it. Though I know nothing of medicine, I venture to hazard the suggestion that he really had perhaps, by a terrible effort of will, succeeded in delaying the attack for a time, hoping, of course, to check it completely. He knew that he was unwell, but he loathed the thought of being ill at that fatal time, at the approaching crisis in his life, when he needed to have all his wits about him, to say what he had to say boldly and resolutely and "to justify himself to himself." He had, however, consulted the new doctor, who had been brought from Moscow by a fantastic notion of Katerina Ivanovna's to which I have referred already. After listening to him and examining him the doctor came to the conclusion that he was actually suffering from some disorder of the brain, and was not at all surprised by an admission which Ivan had reluctantly made him. "Hallucinations are quite likely in your condition," the doctor opined, "though it would be better to verify them . . . you must take steps at once, without a moment's delay, or things will go badly with you." But Ivan Fyodorovich did not follow this judicious advice and did not take to his bed to be nursed. "I am walking about, so I am strong enough, if I drop, it'll be different then, anyone may nurse me who likes," he decided, dismissing the subject. And so he was sitting almost conscious himself of his delirium and, as I have said already, looking persistently at some object on the sofa against the opposite wall. Someone appeared to be sitting there, though goodness knows how he had come in, for he had not been in the room when Ivan Fyodorovich came into it, on his return from Smerdyakov. This was a person or, more accurately speaking, a Russian gentleman of a particular kind, no longer young, *qui frisait la cinquantaine*,[8] as the French say, with rather long, still thick, dark hair, slightly streaked with gray, and a small pointed beard. He was wearing a brownish reefer jacket, rather shabby, evidently made by a good tailor though, and of a fashion at least three years old, that had been discarded by smart and well-to-do people for the last two years. His linen and his long scarflike necktie were all such as are worn by people who aim at being stylish, but on closer inspection his linen was not too clean and his wide scarf was very threadbare. The visitor's checked trousers were of excellent cut, but were too light in color and too tight for the present fashion. His soft fluffy white hat was out of keeping with the season. In brief there was every appearance of gentility on straitened means. It looked as though the gentleman belonged to that class of idle landowners who used to flourish in the times of serfdom. He had unmistakably been, at some time, in good and fashionable society, had once had good connections, had possibly preserved them indeed, but, after a gay youth, becoming gradually impoverished on the abolition of serfdom, he had sunk into the position of a toady, a sponger of the best class, wandering from one good old friend to another and received by them for his companionable and accommodating disposition and as being, after all, a gentleman who could be asked to sit down with anyone, though, of course, not in a place of honor. Such gentlemen of accommodating temper and dependent position, who can tell a story, take a hand at cards, and who have a distinct aversion for any duties that may be forced upon them, are usually solitary creatures, either bachelors or widowers. Sometimes they have children, but if so, the children are always brought up at a distance, at some aunt's, to whom these gentlemen never allude in good society, seeming ashamed of the relationship. They gradually lose sight of their children altogether, though at intervals they receive a birthday or Christmas letter from them and sometimes even answer it. The countenance of the unexpected visitor was not so much good-natured as accommodating and ready to assume any amiable expression as occasion might arise. He had no watch, but he had a tortoise shell lorgnette on a black ribbon. On the middle finger of his right hand was a massive gold ring with a cheap opal stone in it. Ivan Fyodorovich was angrily silent and would not begin the conversation. The visitor waited and sat exactly like a poor relation who had come down from his room to keep his host company at tea, and was discreetly silent, seeing that his host was frowning and preoccupied. But he was ready for any affable conversation as soon as his host should begin it. All at once his face expressed a sudden solicitude.

"I say," he began to Ivan Fyodorovich, "excuse me, I only mention it to remind you. You went to Smerdyakov's to find out about Katerina Ivanovna, but you came away without finding out anything about her, you probably forgot . . ."

"Ah, yes," suddenly broke from Ivan and his face grew gloomy with uneasiness. "Yes, I'd forgotten . . . but it doesn't matter now, never mind,

8. "Who was approaching fifty" (French). In the original, the devil is referred to as a *dzhentl'men*, which conveys a sense of irony.

till tomorrow," he muttered to himself, "and you," he added, addressing his visitor irritably, "I would have remembered that myself in a minute, for that was just what was tormenting me! Why do you interfere, as if I would believe that you prompted me, and that I didn't remember it on my own?"

"Don't believe it then," said the gentleman, smiling amicably, "what's the good of believing against your will? Besides, proofs are no help to believing, especially material proofs. Thomas believed, not because he saw Christ risen, but because he wanted to believe, before he saw. Look at the spiritualists, for instance.[9] . . . I am very fond of them . . . imagine, they think that they serve the cause of religion, because the devils show them their horns from the other world. That, they say, is a material proof, so to speak, of the existence of another world. The other world and material proofs, what next! And if you come to that, does proving there's a devil prove that there's a God? I want to join an idealist society, I'll lead the opposition in it, I'll say I am a realist, but not a materialist, he-he!"

"Listen." Ivan Fyodorovich suddenly got up from the table. "I seem to be delirious . . . I am delirious, in fact, talk any nonsense you like, I don't care! You won't drive me to fury, as you did last time. But I feel somehow ashamed . . . I want to walk about the room . . . I sometimes don't see you and don't even hear your voice as I did last time, but I always guess what you are prating, for it's I, *I myself speaking, not you.* Only I don't know whether I was dreaming last time or whether I really saw you. I'll wet a towel and put it on my head and perhaps you'll vanish into air."

Ivan Fyodorovich went into the corner, took a towel, and did as he said, and with a wet towel on his head began walking up and down the room.

"I am so glad you treat me so familiarly," the visitor began.

"Fool," laughed Ivan, "do you suppose I should stand on ceremony with you? I am in good spirits now, though I have a pain in my forehead . . . and in the top of my head . . . only please don't talk philosophy, as you did last time. If you can't take yourself off, talk of something amusing. Talk gossip, you are a sponger, you ought to talk gossip. What a nightmare to have! But I am not afraid of you. I'll get the better of you. I won't be taken to a madhouse!"

"*C'est charmant,*[1] sponger. Yes, I am in my natural shape. For what am I on earth but a sponger? By the way, I listen to you and am rather surprised to find you are actually beginning to take me for something real, not simply your fancy, as you persisted in declaring last time . . ."

"Never for one minute have I taken you for reality," Ivan cried with a sort of fury. "You are a lie, you are my illness, you are a phantom. It's only that I don't know how to destroy you and I see I must suffer for a time. You are my hallucination. You are the incarnation of myself, but only of one side of me . . . of my thoughts and feelings, but only the nastiest and stupidest of them. From that point of view you might be of interest to me, if only I had time to waste on you . . ."

"Excuse me, excuse me, I'll catch you. When you flew out at Alyosha under the lamp post this evening and shouted to him. 'You learned it

9. Spiritualism enjoyed a vogue in Russia in the 1870s. Dostoevsky was very interested in the psychological sources of belief in spiritualism; he attended a séance in 1876 and wrote about spiritualism's appeal in his *Diary of a Writer.* See for example January 1876, chapter 3, number 2, "Spiritualism. Something about Devils."
1. "That's delightful" (French).

from *him*! How do you know that *he* visits me?' You were thinking of me then. So for one brief moment you did believe that I really exist," the gentleman laughed blandly.

"Yes, that was a moment of weakness . . . but I couldn't believe in you. I don't know whether I was asleep or awake last time. Perhaps I was only dreaming then and didn't see you really at all . . ."

"And why were you so surly with Alyosha just now? He is a dear; I've treated him badly over Father Zosima."

"Don't talk of Alyosha! How dare you, you lackey!" Ivan laughed again.

"You scold me, but you laugh—that's a good sign. But you are ever so much more polite than you were last time and I know why: that great resolution of yours . . ."

"Don't speak of my resolution," cried Ivan, savagely.

"I understand, I understand, *c'est noble, c'est charmant*, you are going to defend your brother and to sacrifice yourself . . . *C'est chevaleresque.*"[2]

"Hold your tongue, I'll kick you!"

"I won't be altogether sorry, for then my object will be attained. If you kick me, you must believe in my reality, for people don't kick ghosts. Joking apart, it doesn't matter to me, scold if you like, though it's better to be a trifle more polite even to me. 'Fool, lackey!' My, what words!"

"Scolding you, I scold myself," Ivan laughed again, "You are myself, myself, only with a different mug. You just say what I am thinking . . . and are incapable of saying anything new!"

"If I am like you in my way of thinking, it's all to my credit," the gentleman declared, with delicacy and dignity.

"You choose out only my worst thoughts, and what's more, the stupid ones. You are stupid and vulgar. You are awfully stupid. No, I can't put up with you! What am I to do, what am I to do!" Ivan said through his clenched teeth.

"My dear friend, above all things I want to behave like a gentleman and to be recognized as such," the visitor began in an attack of some sort of deprecating and simple-hearted pride, typical of a sponger. "I am poor, but . . . I won't say very honest, but . . . it's an axiom generally accepted in society that I am a fallen angel. I certainly can't conceive how I can ever have been an angel. If I ever was, it must have been so long ago that there's no harm in forgetting it. Now I only prize the reputation of being a gentlemanly person and live as I can, trying to make myself agreeable. I love men genuinely, oh! I've been greatly calumniated! Here when I stay with you from time to time, my life gains a kind of reality and that's what I like most of all. You see, like you, I suffer from the fantastic and so I love the realism of earth. Here, with you, everything is circumscribed, here all is formulated and geometrical, while we have nothing but indeterminate equations! I wander about here dreaming. I like dreaming. Besides, on earth I become superstitious. Please don't laugh, that's just what I like, to become superstitious. I adopt all your habits here: I've grown fond of going to the public baths, would you believe it? and I go and steam myself with merchants and priests. What I dream of is becoming incarnate once for all and irrevocably in the form of some merchant's wife weighing two hundred fifty pounds, and of believing all she believes.

2. "That's noble, that's delightful," "that's chivalrous" (French).

My ideal is to go to church and offer a candle in simple-hearted faith, upon my word it is. Then there would be an end to my sufferings. I like being doctored too; in the spring there was an outbreak of smallpox and I went and got vaccinated in a foundling hospital—if only you knew how I enjoyed myself that day. I subscribed ten rubles to the cause of the Slavs![3] . . . But you are not listening. Do you know, you are not at all well this evening? I know you went yesterday to that doctor . . . well, what about your health? What did the doctor say?"

"Fool!" Ivan snapped out.

"But you are clever, anyway. You are scolding again? I didn't ask out of sympathy. You needn't answer. Now rheumatism has come in again . . ."

"Fool!" repeated Ivan.

"You keep saying the same thing; but I had such an attack of rheumatism last year that I remember it to this day."

"The devil have rheumatism!"

"Why not, if I sometimes put on fleshly form? I put on fleshly form and I take the consequences. Satan *sum et nihil humanum a me alienum puto.*"[4]

"What, what? Satan *sum et nihil humanum* . . . that's not bad for the devil!"

"I am glad I've pleased you at last."

"But you didn't get that from me," Ivan stopped suddenly, seeming struck. "That never entered my head, that's strange."

"*C'est du nouveau, n'est-ce pas?*[5] This time I'll act honestly and explain it to you. Listen, in dreams and especially in nightmares, from indigestion or anything, a man sometimes sees such artistic visions, such complex and real actuality, such events, even a whole world of events, woven into such a plot, with such unexpected details from the most exalted matters to the last button on a cuff, as I swear Leo Tolstoy could not create.[6] Yet such dreams are sometimes seen not by writers, but by the most ordinary people, officials, journalists, priests. . . . The subject is a complete enigma. A statesman confessed to me, indeed, that all his best ideas came to him when he was asleep. Well, that's how it is now, though I am your hallucination, yet just as in a nightmare, I say original things which had not entered your head before. So I don't repeat your ideas, yet I am only your nightmare, nothing more."

"You are lying. Your aim is to convince me you exist apart and are not my nightmare, and now you are asserting you are a dream."

"My dear fellow, I've adopted a special method today, I'll explain it to you afterwards. Wait, where did I break off? Oh, yes! I caught cold then, only not here but yonder."

"Where is yonder? Tell me, will you be here long? Can't you go away?" Ivan exclaimed almost in despair. He ceased walking to and fro, sat down on the sofa, leaned his elbows on the table again and held his head tight

---

3. See note 6, p. 206.
4. "I am the devil, and nothing human is foreign to me" (Latin). Ivan's devil parodies a well-known saying by the Roman philosopher Terence (c. 185–159 B.C.E.): "*homo sum, humani nihil a me alienum puto*" ("I am a man, and nothing human is alien to me").
5. "That's something new, isn't it?" (French).
6. Leo Tolstoy (1828–1910), author of the novels *War and Peace* (1865–69) and *Anna Karenina* (1873–77) as well as short stories, essays, and plays. Dostoevsky viewed the literary accomplishments of his great contemporary with deep ambivalence as well as respect, and objected vigorously to the pacifism and negative view of Russia's participation in the Balkan War set forth in *Anna Karenina*.

in both hands. He pulled the wet towel off and flung it away in vexation. It was evidently of no use.

"Your nerves are out of order," observed the gentleman, with a carelessly easy, though perfectly polite, air. "You are angry with me even for being able to catch cold, though it happened in a most natural way. I was hurrying then to a diplomatic soirée at the house of a lady of high rank in Petersburg, who was aiming at influence in the Ministry. Well, an evening suit, white tie, gloves, though I was God knows where and had to fly through space to reach your earth. . . . Of course, it took only an instant, but you know a ray of light from the sun takes fully eight minutes, and fancy in an evening suit and open waistcoat. Spirits don't freeze, but when one's in fleshy form, well . . . in brief, I didn't think, and set off, and you know in those ethereal spaces, in the water that is above the firmament,[7] there's such a frost . . . that is, what frost, at least one can't call it frost, you can imagine, 150 degrees below zero! You know the game the village girls play—they invite the unwary to lick an ax at thirty degrees below zero, the tongue instantly freezes to it and the dupe tears the skin off, so the tongue bleeds. But that's only in 30 degrees, in 150 degrees I imagine it would be enough to put your finger on the ax and it would be the end of it . . . if only there could be an ax there."

"And can there be an ax there?" Ivan Fyodorovich interrupted, carelessly and disdainfully. He was exerting himself to the utmost not to believe in the delusion and not to sink into complete insanity.

"An ax?" the guest interrupted in surprise.

"Yes, what would become of an ax there?" Ivan Fyodorovich cried suddenly, with a sort of savage and insistent obstinacy.

"What would become of an ax in space? *Quelle idée!*[8] If it were to fall to any distance, it would begin, I think, flying round the earth without knowing why, like a satellite. The astronomers would calculate the rising and the setting of the ax, *Gatzuk*[9] would put it in his calendar, that's all."

"You are stupid, awfully stupid," said Ivan peevishly. "Fib more intelligently or I won't listen. You want to get the better of me by realism, to convince me that you exist, but I don't want to believe you exist! I won't believe it!"

"But I am not lying, it's all the truth; the truth is unhappily hardly ever witty. I see you persist in expecting something great of me, and perhaps something beautiful.[1] That's a great pity, for I only give what I can . . ."

"Don't talk philosophy, you ass!"

"Philosophy, indeed, when all my right side is numb and I am moaning and groaning. I've tried all the medical faculty: they can diagnose beautifully, they have the whole of your disease at their fingertips, but they've no idea how to cure you. There was an enthusiastic little student here, 'You may die,' said he, 'but you'll know perfectly what disease you are dying of!' And then what a way they have of sending people to specialists. 'We only diagnose,' they say, 'but go to such-and-such a specialist, he'll cure you.' The old doctor who used to cure all sorts of disease has com-

---

7. The waters above the firmament appear in Genesis 1.7–8.
8. "What an idea!" (French).
9. An almanac published in Moscow in the 1870s and 80s by A. A. Gattsuk (1832–1891).
1. References to the great or lofty and beautiful (*velikoe i prekrasnoe*) in Dostoevsky are usually allusions to Schiller.

pletely disappeared, I assure you, now there are only specialists and they all advertise in the newspapers. If anything is wrong with your nose, they send you to Paris: there, they say, is a European specialist who cures noses. If you go to Paris, he'll look at your nose; I can only cure your right nostril, he'll tell you, for I don't cure the left nostril, that's not my specialty, but go to Vienna, there there's a specialist who will cure your left nostril.[2] What are you to do? I fell back on popular remedies, a German doctor advised me to rub myself with honey and salt in the bathhouse. Solely to get an extra bath I went, smeared myself all over and it did me no good at all. In despair I wrote to Count Mattei in Milan.[3] He sent me a book and some drops, bless him, and, only fancy, Hoff's malt extract cured me! I bought it by accident, drank a bottle and a half of it, and I was ready to dance, it took it away completely. I made up my mind to write to the papers to thank him, I was prompted by a feeling of gratitude, and only fancy, it led to no end of bother: not a single paper would take my letter. 'It would be very reactionary,' they said, 'no one will believe it. *Le diable n'existe point.*[4] You'd better remain anonymous,' they advised me. What use is a letter of thanks if it's anonymous? I laughed with the men at the newspaper office. 'It's reactionary to believe in God in our days,' I said, 'but I am the devil, so I may be believed in.' 'We quite understand that,' they said. 'Who doesn't believe in the devil? Yet it won't do, it might injure our reputation. As a joke, if you like.' But I thought as a joke it wouldn't be very witty. So it wasn't printed. And do you know, I have felt sore about it to this day. My best feelings, gratitude, for instance, are literally denied me simply from my social position."

"Philosophical reflections again?" Ivan snarled malignantly.

"God preserve me from it, but one can't help complaining sometimes. I am a slandered man. You upbraid me every moment with being stupid. One can see you are young. My dear fellow, intelligence isn't the only thing! I have naturally a kind and merry heart. 'I also write vaudevilles of all sorts.'[5] You seem to take me for Khlestakov grown old, but my fate is a far more serious one. Before time was, by some decree which I could never make out, I was predestined 'to deny' and yet I am genuinely good-hearted and not at all inclined to negation.[6] 'No, you must go and deny, without denial there's no criticism and what would a journal be without a column of criticism?' Without criticism it would be nothing but one 'hosannah.' But nothing but hosannah is not enough for life, the hosannah must be tried in the crucible of doubt and so on, in the same style. But I don't meddle in that, I didn't create it, I am not answerable for it. Well, they've chosen their scapegoat, they've made me write the column of criticism and so life was made possible. We understand that comedy; I, for instance, simply and directly demand that I be annihilated. No, live, I

---

2. This passage disparaging specialists may have been inspired by Voltaire's philosophical story *Zadig, or, the Book of Fate: An Eastern Tale* (1747), about a doctor who says he can cure only right eyes.
3. Count Mattei (1809–1896) was a famous nineteenth-century Italian medical specialist, highly esteemed by upper-class Europeans.
4. "The devil doesn't exist at all" (French).
5. This line is spoken by the character Khlestakov in Gogol's comedy *The Inspector General* (1836). Through a series of misunderstandings, Khlestakov deceives an entire provincial town into thinking he is an inspector general, a much higher rank than he actually possesses.
6. An allusion to Mephistopheles, who says "I am the spirit who always denies" in Goethe's *Faust* (I.1338).

am told, for there'd be nothing without you. If everything in the universe were sensible, nothing would happen. There would be no events without you, and there must be events. So against the grain I serve to produce events and do what's irrational because I am commanded to. For all their indisputable intelligence, men take this farce as something serious, and that is their tragedy. They suffer, of course . . . but then they live, they live a real life, not a fantastic one, for suffering is life. Without suffering what would be the pleasure of it? It would be transformed into an endless church service; it would be holy, but tedious. But what about me? I suffer, but still, I don't live. I am x in an indeterminate equation. I am a sort of phantom in life who has lost all ends and beginnings,[7] and who has even forgotten his own name. You are laughing—no, you are not laughing, you are angry again. You are forever angry, all you care about is intelligence, but I repeat again that I would give away all this super-stellar life, all the ranks and honors, simply to be transformed into the soul of a merchant's wife weighing two hundred fifty pounds and set candles at God's shrine."

"Then even you don't believe in God?" said Ivan, with a smile of hatred.

"What can I say—that is, if you are in earnest . . ."

"Is there a God or not?" Ivan cried with the same savage intensity.

"Ah, then you are in earnest! My dear fellow, upon my word I don't know. There! I've said it now!"

"You don't know, but you see God? No, you are not someone apart, you are *myself*, you are *I* and nothing more! You are rubbish, you are my fancy!"

"Well, if you like, I have the same philosophy as you, that would be true. *Je pense, donc je suis*,[8] I know that for a fact, all the rest, all these worlds, God and even Satan—all that is not proved, to my mind. Does all that exist of itself, or is it only an emanation of myself, a logical development of my ego which alone has existed forever:[9] but I make haste to stop, for it seems you are about to jump up and start fighting."

"You'd better tell me some anecdote!" said Ivan miserably.

"There is an anecdote precisely on our subject, or rather a legend, not an anecdote. You reproach me with unbelief, you see, you say, yet you don't believe. But, my dear fellow, I am not the only one like that. We are all in a muddle over there now and all through your science. Once there used to be atoms, five senses, four elements, and then everything hung together somehow. There were atoms in the ancient world even, but since we've learned that you've discovered the chemical molecule and protoplasm and the devil knows what, we had to tuck in our tails. There's a regular muddle, and, above all, superstition, scandal; there's as much scandal among us as among you, you know; a little more in fact, and denunciations, indeed, for we have a certain department where particular 'information' is received.[1] Well, this wild legend belongs to our middle ages—not yours, but ours—and no one believes it even among us, except the old ladies of two hundred fifty pounds, not your old ladies I mean, but ours. We have everything you have, I am revealing one of our secrets out

---

7. *Ends and Beginnings* is the title of an 1862–63 collection of essays by Herzen.
8. "I think, therefore I am" (French), the famous words of the French mathematician, scientist, and philosopher René Descartes (1596–1650) in his book *Discourse on the Method* (1637).
9. The devil's speculations on the reality of phenomena external to the ego are indebted to the subjective idealism of the philosopher Johann Gottlieb Fichte (1762–1814).
1. See note 1, p. 468.

of friendship for you; though it's forbidden. This legend is about Paradise. There was, they say, here on earth a thinker and philosopher. 'He rejected everything, laws, conscience, faith,'[2] and, above all, the future life. He died; he expected to go straight to darkness and death and he found a future life before him. He was astounded and indignant. 'This contradicts my principles!' he said. And he was punished for that . . . that is, you must excuse me, I am just repeating what I heard myself, it's only a legend . . . he was sentenced to walk a quadrillion kilometers in the dark (we've adopted the metric system, you know) and when he has finished that quadrillion, the gates of heaven would be opened to him and he'll be forgiven . . ."

"And what tortures have you in the other world besides the quadrillion kilometers?" asked Ivan, with a strange eagerness.

"What tortures? Ah, don't ask. In old days we had all sorts, but now they have taken chiefly to moral punishments—'the stings of conscience' and all that nonsense. We got that, too, from you, from the 'mellowing of your manners.'[3] And who's the better for it? Only those who have got no conscience, for how can they be tortured by conscience when they have none? But decent people who have conscience and a sense of honor suffer for it. Reforms, when the ground has not been prepared for them, especially if they are institutions copied from abroad, do nothing but mischief! The ancient fire was better. Well, this man, who was condemned to the quadrillion kilometers, stood still, looked round and lay down across the road. 'I won't go, I refuse on principle!' Take the soul of an enlightened Russian atheist and mix it with the soul of the prophet Jonah,[4] who sulked for three days and nights in the belly of the whale, and you get the character of that thinker who lay across the road."

"What did he lie on there?"

"Well, I suppose there was something to lie on. You are not laughing?"

"Bravo!" cried Ivan, still with the same strange eagerness. Now he was listening with an unexpected curiosity. "Well, is he lying there now?"

"That's the point, that he isn't. He lay there almost a thousand years and then he got up and went on."

"What an ass!" cried Ivan, laughing nervously and still seeming to be pondering something intently. "Does it make any difference whether he lies there forever or walks the quadrillion kilometers? It would take a billion years to walk it?"

"Much more than that, I haven't got a pencil and paper or I could work it out. But he got there long ago and that's where the story begins."

"What, he got there? But how did he get the billion years to do it?"

"Why, you keep thinking of our present earth! But our present earth may have been repeated a billion times. Why, it's become extinct, been frozen; cracked, broken to bits, disintegrated into its elements, again 'the water above the firmament,' then again a comet, again a sun, again from the sun it becomes earth—and the same sequence may have been repeated

2. A reference to Griboedov's Woe from Wit, IV. iv.
3. An allusion to eighteenth-century debates, most notably between Voltaire and Rousseau, on whether morals improve or decline with the progress of civilization; it may also be a polemical stab at Saltykov-Shchedrin's Unfinished Conversations (1875).
4. According to the Bible, God commanded Jonah to go to Nineveh, but he disobeyed and took a boat to another country. God sent a fearful storm and Jonah told the sailors to throw him overboard to calm the waves; they did so, and he spent three days in the belly of a whale. See Jonah 1.1–17.

endlessly and exactly the same to every detail, most unseemly and insufferably tedious . . ."

"Well, well, what happened when he arrived?"

"Why, the moment the gates of Paradise were open and he walked in,
before he had been there two seconds, by the clock, (though to my thinking his watch must have long dissolved into its elements on the way), he
cried out that those two seconds were worth walking not a quadrillion
kilometers but a quadrillion of quadrillions, raised to the quadrillionth
power! In fact, he sang 'hosannah' and overdid it so, that some persons
there of lofty ideas wouldn't shake hands with him at first—he'd become
too rapidly reactionary, they said. The Russian temperament. I repeat, it's
a legend. I give it for what it's worth. So that's the sort of ideas we have on
such subjects even now."

"I've caught you!" Ivan cried, with an almost childish delight, as though
he had succeeded in remembering something at last. "That anecdote
about the quadrillion years, I made up myself! I was seventeen then, I was
in high school. I made up that anecdote and told it to a schoolfellow called
Korovkin, it was at Moscow. . . . The anecdote is so characteristic that I
couldn't have taken it from anywhere. I thought I'd forgotten it . . . but
I've unconsciously recalled it—I recalled it myself—it was not you telling
it! Thousands of things are unconsciously remembered like that even
when people are being taken to be executed[5] . . . it's come back to me in a
dream. You are that dream! You are a dream and do not exist!"

"From the vehemence with which you deny my existence," laughed the
gentleman, "I am convinced that you believe in me."

"Not in the slightest! I haven't a hundredth part of a grain of faith in
you!"

"But you have the thousandth of a grain. Homeopathic doses perhaps
are the strongest. Confess that you have faith even to the ten-thousandth
of a grain."

"Not for one minute," cried Ivan furiously. "But I should like to believe
in you," he added strangely.

"Aha! There's an admission! But I am good-natured. I'll come to your
assistance again. Listen, it was I who caught you, not you me. I told you
your anecdote you'd forgotten, on purpose, so as to destroy your faith in
me completely."

"You are lying. The object of your visit is to convince me of your
existence!"

"Just so. But hesitation, suspense, conflict between belief and disbelief—
is sometimes such torture to a conscientious man, such as you are, that
it's better to hang oneself at once. Knowing that you are inclined to
believe in me, I administered some disbelief by telling you that anecdote.
I lead you to belief and disbelief by turns, and I have my motive in it. It's
the new method, sir. As soon as you disbelieve in me completely, you'll
begin assuring me to my face that I am not a dream but a reality. I know
you. Then I shall have attained my object, which is an honorable one. I
shall sow in you only a tiny grain of faith and it will grow into an oak
tree—and such an oak tree that, sitting on it, you will long to enter the

---

5. This idea about the experience of a condemned criminal is also set forth by Prince Myshkin in
   The Idiot.

ranks of 'the hermit monks and chaste women,'[6] for that is what you are secretly longing for. You'll dine on locusts, you'll wander into the wilderness to save your soul!"

"Then it's for the salvation of my soul you are working, is it, you scoundrel?"

"One must do a good deed sometimes. How ill-humored you are!"

"Buffoon! did you ever tempt those holy men who ate locusts and prayed seventeen years in the wilderness till they were overgrown with moss?"

"My dear fellow, I've done nothing else. One forgets the whole world and all the worlds, and sticks to one such saint, because he is a very precious diamond. One such soul, you know, is sometimes worth a whole constellation. We have our arithmetic, you know. The conquest is precious! And some of them, on my word, are not inferior to you in culture, though you won't believe it. They can contemplate such depths of belief and disbelief at the same moment that sometimes it really seems that they are within a hairsbreadth of being 'turned upside down,' as the actor Gorbunov says."[7]

"Well, did you fail, did you get your nose pulled?"

"My friend," observed the visitor sententiously, "it's better to get off with your nose pulled than without a nose at all, as an afflicted marquis observed not long ago (he must have been treated by a specialist) in confession to his spiritual father—a Jesuit. I was present, it was simply charming. 'Give me back my nose!' he said, and he beat his breast. 'My son,' said the priest evasively, 'all things are accomplished in accordance with the inscrutable decrees of Providence, and what seems a misfortune sometimes leads to extraordinary, though unapparent, benefits. If stern destiny has deprived you of your nose, it's to your advantage that no one can ever pull you by your nose. 'Holy father, that's no comfort,' cried the despairing marquis. 'I'd be delighted to have my nose pulled every day of my life, if it were only in its proper place.' 'My son,' sighs the priest, 'you can't expect every blessing at once. This is murmuring against Providence, who even in this has not forgotten you, for if you repine as you repined just now, declaring you'd be glad to have your nose pulled for the rest of your life, your desire has already been fulfilled indirectly, for when you lost your nose, you were led by the nose.'"[8]

"Foo, how stupid!" cried Ivan.

"My dear friend, I only wanted to amuse you. But I swear that's the genuine Jesuit casuistry and I swear that it all happened word for word as I've told you. It happened lately and gave me a great deal of trouble. The unhappy young man shot himself that very night when he got home. I was by his side till the very last moment. Those Jesuit confessionals are really my most delightful diversion at melancholy moments. Here's another incident that happened only the other day. A little blonde Norman

---

6. A reference to a poem by Pushkin, "Desert Fathers and Chaste Women" (*Ottsy pustynniki i zheny neporochny*, 1836), which was itself inspired by a prayer of Ephrem the Syrian, a fourth-century theologian and hymnist.

7. The actor Ivan Gorbunov (1831–1895) performed in the Little Theater and the Alexandrinsky Theater of Saint Petersburg; he was also well-known as a theater historian, author, and folk storyteller. Dostoevsky was personally acquainted with him.

8. The loss of the nose is a common symptom of second-stage syphilis. This play on words derives from an 1821 epigram by Pushkin; such jokes and puns were dated by Dostoevsky's time.

girl of twenty—a buxom, unsophisticated beauty that would make your mouth water—comes to an old priest. She bends down and whispers her sin into the grating. 'Why, my daughter, have you fallen again already?' cries the priest. 'O Sancta Maria, what do I hear! Not the same man this time, how long will this go on? Aren't you ashamed!' 'Ah, mon père,' answers the sinner with tears of penitence, 'ça lui fait tant de plaisir, et à moi si peu de peine!'[9] Just imagine, such an answer! I drew back. It was the cry of nature, better than innocence itself, if you like. I absolved her sin on the spot and was turning to go, but I was forced to turn back. I heard the priest at the grating making an appointment with her for the evening—though he was an old man hard as flint, he fell in an instant! It was nature, the truth of nature asserted its rights! What, you are turning up your nose again? Angry again? I don't know how to please you . . ."

"Leave me alone, you are beating on my brain like a haunting nightmare," Ivan moaned miserably, helpless before his apparition. "I am bored with you, agonizingly and insufferably. I would give anything to be able to shake you off!"

"I repeat, moderate your expectations, don't demand of me 'everything great and beautiful'[1] and you'll see how well we shall get on," said the gentleman impressively. "You are really angry with me for not having appeared to you in a red glow, 'with thunder and lightning,' with scorched wings,[2] but have shown myself in such a modest form. You are wounded, in the first place, in your aesthetic feelings, and, secondly, in your pride. How could such a vulgar devil visit such a great man as you! Yes, there is that romantic strain in you, that was so derided even by Belinsky.[3] I can't help it, young man, as I got ready to come to you I did think as a joke of appearing in the figure of a retired general who had served in the Caucasus, with a star of the Lion and the Sun on my coat.[4] But I was positively afraid of doing it, for you'd have thrashed me for daring to pin the Lion and the Sun on my coat, instead of, at least, the Polar Star or Sirius.[5] And you keep on saying I am stupid, but, mercy on us! I make no claim to be equal to you in intelligence. Mephistopheles declared to Faust that he desired evil, but did only good.[6] Well, he can say what he likes, it's quite the opposite with me. I am perhaps the one man in all of nature who loves the truth and genuinely desires good. I was there when the Word, Who died on the cross, rose up into Heaven bearing on His bosom the soul of

9. "Ah father, it gives him so much pleasure and me so little trouble!" (French). Based on an anonymous epigram about a French actress, Jeanne-Catherine Gaussin (1711–1767). The episode described here between a priest and a young woman is similar to an episode in Évariste de Parny's (1753–1814) mock epic War of the Gods (1799).
1. See note 1, p. 538.
2. The phrase "with thunder and lightning" may quote an apocryphal text. The image of "scorched wings" evokes a passage from Lermontov's verse epic The Demon (1842).
3. Belinsky was extremely critical of Romanticism, and publicly rejected Dostoevsky's novella The Double (1846) as insufficiently realistic.
4. "Retired General" translates otstavnoi deistvitel'nyi statskii sovetnik, the fourth rank in the civil Table of Ranks. The star of the Lion and the Sun is a medal of that chivalric order, an honor bestowed by the Persian court to foreign dignitaries who distinguished themselves in service to Persia and occasionally awarded to Russian bureaucrats serving in the Caucasus.
5. The Polar Star is the medallion of the Order of the Polar Star, established by Frederick I of Sweden in 1748. The devil is making a play on words, for Polar Star was the literary almanac of the Decembrists (published 1823–25); it was also the title of a literary and sociopolitical collection published by Herzen and Ogarev. The devil implies that Ivan expects him to hold revolutionary views.
6. Mephistopheles speaks these words in Goethe's Faust I.1336.

the penitent thief.[7] I heard the joyful shrieks of the cherubim singing and screaming hosannah and the thunderous howl of the seraphim[8] which shook heaven and all creation, and I swear to you by all that's sacred, I longed to join the choir and shout hosannah with them all. The word had almost escaped me, had almost broken from my lips . . . you know how susceptible and aesthetically impressionable I am. But common sense—oh, a most unhappy trait in my character—kept me in due bounds and I let the moment pass! For what would have happened, I reflected, what would have happened after my hosannah? Everything on earth would have been extinguished at once and no events could have occurred. And so, solely from a sense of duty and my social position, I was forced to suppress the good moment and to stick to my nasty task. Somebody takes all the credit of what's good for himself, and nothing but nastiness is left for me. But I don't envy the honor of a life of idle imposture, I am not ambitious. Why am I, of all beings in the world, doomed to be cursed by all decent people and even to be kicked, for if I put on mortal form I am bound to take such consequences sometimes? I know, of course, there's a secret in it, but they won't tell me the secret for anything, for then perhaps, seeing the meaning of it, I might bawl hosannah, and the indispensable minus would disappear at once, and good sense would reign supreme throughout the whole world. And that, of course, would mean the end of everything, even of magazines and newspapers, for who would subscribe to them? I know that at the end of all things I shall be reconciled. I, too, shall walk my quadrillion and learn the secret. But till that happens I am sulking and fulfill my destiny though it's against the grain—that is, to ruin thousands for the sake of saving one. How many souls have had to be ruined and how many honorable reputations destroyed for the sake of that one righteous man, Job, over whom they made such a fool of me in old days. Yes, till the secret is revealed, there are two sorts of truth for me—one, their truth, yonder, which I know nothing about so far and the other my own. And there's no knowing which will turn out the better. . . . Are you asleep?"

"I might well be," Ivan groaned angrily. "All my stupid ideas—outgrown, thrashed out long ago, and flung aside like a dead carcass—you present to me as something new!"

"There's no pleasing you! And I thought I would fascinate you by my literary style. That hosannah in the skies really wasn't bad, was it? And then that ironical tone à la Heine, eh?"

"No, I was never such a lackey! How then could my soul beget a lackey like you?"

"My dear fellow, I know a most charming and attractive young Russian gentleman, a young thinker and a great lover of literature and art, the author of a promising poem entitled 'The Grand Inquisitor.' I was only thinking of him!"

"I forbid you to speak of 'The Grand Inquisitor,'" cried Ivan, crimson with shame.

7. The Word is Christ, who according to Luke 23.43, was crucified along with two thieves, and promised one of them that he would be with Christ in paradise.
8. Cherubim and seraphim are angels that occupy the highest rungs in the heavenly hierarchy. Seraphim are characterized by flames, cherubim by wisdom and knowledge. For the descriptions of Christ's death on the cross on which this passage relies, see Matthew 27, Luke 23, and Mark 15.

"And the 'Geological Cataclysm.' Do you remember? That was a poem, now!"

"Hold your tongue, or I'll kill you!"

"You'll kill me? No, excuse me, I will speak. I came to treat myself to that pleasure. Oh, I love the dreams of my ardent young friends, quivering with eagerness for life! 'There are new men,' you decided last spring, when you were meaning to come here, 'they propose to destroy everything and begin with cannibalism. Stupid fellows, they didn't ask my advice! I maintain that nothing need be destroyed, that we only need to destroy the idea of God in man, that's how we have to set to work. It's that, that we must begin with. Oh, blind race of men who have no understanding! As soon as men have all of them denied God—and I believe that period, analogous with geological periods, will come to pass—the old conception of the universe will fall of itself without cannibalism and what's more the old morality, and then everything will begin anew. Men will unite to take from life all it can give, but only for joy and happiness in the present world. Man will be lifted up with a spirit of divine Titanic pride and the man-god will appear. From hour to hour extending his conquest of nature infinitely by his will and his science, man will feel such lofty joy from hour to hour in doing it that it will make up for all his old dreams of the joys of heaven. Everyone will know that he is mortal and will accept death proudly and serenely like a God. His pride will teach him that it's useless for him to repine at life's being a moment, and he will love his brother without need of reward. Love will be sufficient only for a moment of life, but the very consciousness of its momentariness will intensify its fire, which now is dissipated in dreams of eternal love beyond the grave' . . . and so on and so on in the same style. Charming!"

Ivan sat with his eyes on the floor, and his hands pressed to his ears, but he began trembling all over. The voice continued.

"The question now is, my young thinker reflected, is it possible that such a period will ever come? If it does, everything is determined and humanity is settled forever. But as, owing to man's inveterate stupidity, this cannot come about for at least a thousand years, everyone who recognizes the truth even now may legitimately order his life as he pleases, on the new principles. In that sense, 'all things are permitted' for him. What's more, even if this period never comes to pass, since there is no God and no immortality anyway, the new man may well become the man-god, even if he is the only one in the whole world, and promoted to his new position, he may lightheartedly overstep all the barriers of the old morality of the old slave-man, if necessary. There is no law for God. Where God stands, the place is holy. Where I stand will be at once the foremost place . . . 'all things are permitted' and that's the end of it! That's all very charming; but if you want to swindle why do you want a moral sanction for doing it? But that's our modern Russian all over. He can't bring himself to swindle without a moral sanction. He is so in love with truth . . ."

The visitor talked, obviously carried away by his own eloquence, speaking louder and louder and looking ironically at his host. But he did not succeed in finishing; Ivan suddenly snatched a glass from the table and flung it at the orator.

"*Ah, mais c'est bête enfin,*"[9] cried the latter, jumping up from the sofa and shaking the drops of tea off himself. "He remembers Luther's inkstand![1] He takes me for a dream and throws glasses at a dream! It's like a woman! I suspected you were only pretending to stop up your ears."

A loud, persistent knocking was suddenly heard at the window. Ivan Fyodorovich jumped up from the sofa.

"Do you hear? You'd better open," cried the visitor; "it's your brother Alyosha with the most interesting and surprising news, I'll be bound!"

"Be silent, deceiver, I knew it was Alyosha, I felt he was coming, and of course he has not come for nothing; of course he brings 'news,'" Ivan exclaimed frantically.

"Open, open to him. There's a snowstorm and he is your brother. *Monsieur sait-il le temps qu'il fait? C'est à pas mettre un chien dehors.*"[2]

The knocking continued. Ivan wanted to rush to the window, but something seemed to fetter his arms and legs. He strained every effort to break his chains, but in vain. The knocking at the window grew louder and louder. At last the chains were broken and Ivan Fyodorovich leapt up from the sofa. He looked round him wildly. Both candles had almost burned out, the glass he had just thrown at his visitor stood before him on the table, and there was no one on the sofa opposite. The knocking on the window frame went on persistently, but it was by no means so loud as it had seemed in his dream, on the contrary, it was quite subdued.

"It was not a dream! No, I swear it was not a dream, it all happened just now!" cried Ivan Fyodorovich. He rushed to the window and opened the movable pane.

"Alyosha, I told you not to come," he cried fiercely to his brother. "In two words, what do you want? In two words, do you hear?"

"An hour ago Smerdyakov hanged himself," Alyosha answered from the yard.

"Come round to the steps, I'll open at once," said Ivan, going to open the door to Alyosha.

Chapter X

"It Was He Who Said That!"

Alyosha, coming in, told Ivan that a little over an hour ago Marya Kondratyevna had run to his rooms and informed him Smerdyakov had taken his own life. "I went in to clear away the samovar and he was hanging on a nail in the wall." On Alyosha's inquiring whether she had informed the police, she answered that she had told no one, "but I flew straight to you, I've run all the way." She seemed perfectly crazy, Alyosha reported, and was shaking like a leaf. When Alyosha ran with her to the cottage, he found Smerdyakov still hanging. On the table lay a note: "I destroy my

---

9. "Oh, but that's stupid, after all" (French).
1. Martin Luther (1483–1546), leader of the Protestant Reformation, reported frequent visions of the devil, in whose existence he firmly believed. In one well-known instance, Luther became enraged at the devil's taunts and hurled an inkstand at him.
2. "Does the gentleman know what the weather is like? You wouldn't put a dog out in it" (French).

life of my own will and desire, not to blame anyone." Alyosha left the note on the table and went straight to the police captain and told him all about it. "And from him I've come straight to you," said Alyosha, in conclusion, looking intently into Ivan's face. He had not taken his eyes off him while he told his story, as though struck by something in his expression.

"Brother," he cried suddenly, "you must be terribly ill. You look and don't seem to understand what I tell you."

"It's a good thing you came," said Ivan, as though brooding, and not hearing Alyosha's exclamation. "I knew he had hanged himself."

"From whom?"

"I don't know. But I knew. Did I know? Yes, he told me. He told me so just now."

Ivan stood in the middle of the room, and still spoke in the same brooding tone, looking at the ground.

"Who is *he*?" asked Alyosha, involuntarily looking round.

"He's slipped away."

Ivan raised his head and smiled softly.

"He was afraid of you, of a dove like you. You are a 'pure cherub.'[3] Dmitri calls you a cherub. Cherub! . . . the thunderous howl of the seraphim. What are seraphim? Perhaps a whole constellation. But perhaps that constellation is only a chemical molecule. There's a constellation of the Lion and the Sun. Don't you know it?"

"Brother, sit down," said Alyosha in alarm. "For goodness' sake, sit down on the sofa! You are delirious; put your head on the pillow, that's right. Would you like a wet towel on your head? Perhaps it will do you good."

"Give me the towel: it's here on the chair. I just threw it down there."

"It's not here. Don't worry yourself. I know where it is—here," said Alyosha, finding a clean towel folded up and unused, by Ivan's dressing table in the other corner of the room. Ivan looked strangely at the towel: recollection seemed to come back to him for an instant.

"Wait"—he got up from the sofa—"an hour ago I took that new towel from there and wetted it. I wrapped it round my head and threw it down here . . . How is it it's dry? There was no other."

"You put that towel on your head?" asked Alyosha.

"Yes, and walked up and down the room an hour ago . . . Why have the candles burned down so? What's the time?"

"Nearly twelve."

"No, no, no!" Ivan cried suddenly. "It was not a dream. He was here; he was sitting here, on that sofa. When you knocked at the window, I threw a glass at him . . . this one. Wait a minute. I was asleep last time, but this dream was not a dream. It has happened before. I have dreams now, Alyosha . . . yet they are not dreams, but reality. I walk about, talk and see . . . though I am asleep. But he was sitting here, on that sofa there. . . . He is frightfully stupid, Alyosha, frightfully stupid." Ivan laughed suddenly and began pacing about the room.

"Who is stupid? Of whom are you talking, brother?" Alyosha asked anxiously again.

---

3. In Christian symbolism, the dove indicates the presence of the Holy Spirit, before whom unclean spirits must give way. The phrase "pure cherub" may be a quotation from Lermontov's *Demon* and the Russian translation of Schiller's ode "To Joy," quoted earlier by Dmitri.

"The devil! He's taken to visiting me. He's been here twice, almost three times. He taunted me with being angry at his being a simple devil and not Satan, with scorched wings, in thunder and lightning. But he is not Satan: that's a lie. He is an impostor. He is simply a devil—a paltry, trivial devil. He goes to the baths. If you undressed him, you'd be sure to find he had a tail, long and smooth like a Great Dane's, a yard long, dun color.[4] . . . Alyosha, you are cold. You've been in the snow. Would you like some tea? What? Is it cold? Shall I tell her to bring some? *C'est à ne pas mettre un chien dehors . . .*"

Alyosha ran to the washing stand, wetted the towel, persuaded Ivan to sit down again, and put the wet towel round his head. He sat down beside him.

"What were you telling me earlier about Liza?" Ivan began again. (He was becoming very talkative.) "I like Liza. I said something nasty about her. It was a lie. I like her . . . I am afraid for Katya tomorrow. I am more afraid of her than of anything. On account of the future. She will cast me off tomorrow and trample me under foot. She thinks that I am ruining Mitya from jealousy on her account! Yes, she thinks that! But it's not so. Tomorrow the cross, but not the gallows. No, I won't hang myself. Do you know, I can never commit suicide, Alyosha. Is it because I am base? I am not a coward. Is it from love of life? How did I know that Smerdyakov had hanged himself? Yes, it was *he* told me so."

"And you are quite convinced that there has been someone here?" asked Alyosha.

"Yes, on that sofa in the corner. You would have driven him away. You did drive him away: he disappeared when you arrived. I love your face, Alyosha. Did you know that I loved your face? And *he* is myself, Alyosha. All that's base in me, all that's mean and contemptible. Yes, I am a romantic. He guessed it . . . though it's a libel. He is frightfully stupid; but it's to his advantage. He has cunning, animal cunning—he knew how to infuriate me. He kept taunting me with believing in him, and that was how he made me listen to him. He fooled me like a boy. He told me a great deal that was true about myself, though. I would never have owned it to myself. Do you know, Alyosha," Ivan added in an intensely earnest and confidential tone. "I should be awfully glad to think that it was *he* and not I."

"He has worn you out," said Alyosha, looking compassionately at his brother.

"He's been teasing me! And you know he does it so cleverly, so cleverly. 'Conscience! What is conscience? I make it up for myself. Why am I tormented by it? From habit. From the universal habit of mankind for seven thousand years. So let us give it up, and we shall be gods.' It was he who said that, it was he who said that!"

"And not you, not you?" Alyosha could not help shouting, looking frankly at his brother. "Never mind him, anyway; have done with him and forget him. And let him take with him all that you curse now, and never come back!"

"Yes, but he is spiteful. He laughed at me. He was impudent, Alyosha," Ivan said, with a shudder of offense. "But he was unfair to me, unfair to me about lots of things. He told lies about me to my face. 'Oh, you are

---

4. According to folk belief, the devil can assume any form, and frequently appears as a cat or dog.

going to perform an act of heroic virtue: to confess you murdered your father, that the lackey murdered him at your instigation.'"

"Brother," Alyosha interposed, "restrain yourself. It was not you who murdered him. It's not true!"

"That's what he says, he, and he knows it. 'You are going to perform an act of heroic virtue, and you don't believe in virtue; that's what tortures you and makes you angry, that's why you are so vindictive.' He said that to me about me and he knows what he says."

"It's you who say that, not he," exclaimed Alyosha mournfully, "and you say it because you are ill and delirious, tormenting yourself."

"No, he knows what he says. 'You are going out of pride,' he says. 'You'll stand up and say it was I who killed him, and why do you writhe with horror? You are lying! I despise your opinion, I despise your horror!' He said that about me. 'And do you know you are longing for their praise—"he is a criminal, a murderer, but what a generous soul; he wanted to save his brother and he confessed."' That's a lie, Alyosha!" Ivan cried suddenly, with flashing eyes. "I don't want the low rabble to praise me, I swear I don't! That's a lie! That's why I threw the glass at him and it broke against his ugly face."

"Brother, calm yourself, stop!" Alyosha entreated him.

"Yes, he knows how to torment one. He's cruel," Ivan went on, unheeding. "I had an inkling from the first what he came for. 'Granting that you go through pride, still you had a hope that Smerdyakov might be convicted and sent to Siberia, and Mitya would be acquitted, while you would only be punished with *moral* condemnation' ('Do you hear?' he laughed then)— 'and some people will praise you. But now Smerdyakov's dead, he has hanged himself, and who'll believe you alone? But yet you are going, you are going, you'll go all the same, you've decided to go. What are you going for now?' That's awful, Alyosha. I can't endure such questions. Who dare ask me such questions?"

"Brother," interposed Alyosha. His heart sank with terror, but he still seemed to hope to bring Ivan to reason, "how could he have told you of Smerdyakov's death before I came, when no one knew of it and there was no time for anyone to know of it?"

"He told me," said Ivan firmly, refusing to admit a doubt. "It was all he did talk about, if you come to that. 'And it would be all right if you believed in virtue,' he said. 'No matter if they disbelieve you, you are going for the sake of principle. But you are a little pig like Fyodor Pavlovich and what do you want with virtue? Why do you want to go meddling if your sacrifice is of no use to anyone? Because you don't know yourself why you go! Oh, you'd give a great deal to know yourself why you go! And can you have made up your mind? You've not made up your mind. You'll sit all night deliberating whether to go or not. But you will go; you know you'll go. You know that whichever way you decide, the decision does not depend on you. You'll go because you won't dare not to go. Why won't you dare? You must guess that for yourself. That's a riddle for you!' He got up and went away. You came and he went. He called me a coward, Alyosha! *Le mot de l'énigme*[5] is that I am a coward. 'It is not for such eagles to soar above the earth.' It was he who added that—he! And Smerdyakov said the same. He

---

5. "The answer to the riddle" (French).

must be killed! Katya despises me, I've seen that for a month past, even Liza will begin to despise me! 'You are going in order to be praised.' That's a brutal lie! And you despise me too, Alyosha. Now I am going to hate you again! And I hate the monster, too! I hate the monster! I don't want to save the monster. Let him rot in Siberia! He's begun singing a hymn! Oh, tomorrow I'll go, stand before them, and spit in their faces!"

He jumped up in a frenzy, flung off the towel, and fell to pacing up and down the room again. Alyosha recalled what he had just said. "I seem to be sleeping awake. . . . I walk, I speak, I see, but I am asleep." It seemed to be just like that now. Alyosha did not leave him. The thought passed through his mind to run for a doctor, but he was afraid to leave his brother alone: there was no one to whom he could leave him. By degrees Ivan lost consciousness completely at last. He still went on talking, talking incessantly, but quite incoherently, and even articulated his words with difficulty. Suddenly he staggered violently; but Alyosha was in time to support him. Ivan let him lead him to his bed. Alyosha undressed him somehow and put him to bed. He sat watching over him for another two hours. The sick man slept soundly, without stirring, breathing softly and evenly. Alyosha took a pillow and lay down on the sofa, without undressing.

As he fell asleep he prayed for Mitya and Ivan. He began to understand Ivan's illness. "The anguish of a proud determination. A deep conscience!" God, in Whom he disbelieved, and His truth were gaining mastery over his heart, which still refused to submit. "Yes," the thought floated through Alyosha's head as it lay on the pillow, "yes, since Smerdyakov is dead, no one will believe Ivan's evidence; but he will go and give it." Alyosha smiled softly. "God will conquer!" he thought. "Either he will rise up in the light of truth, or . . . he'll perish in hate, revenging on himself and on everyone his having served the cause he does not believe in," Alyosha added bitterly, and again he prayed for Ivan.

Book Twelve

A JUDICIAL ERROR

Chapter I

The Fatal Day

At ten o'clock in the morning of the day following the events I have described, the trial of Dmitri Karamazov began in our district court.[1]

I hasten to emphasize the fact that I am far from esteeming myself capable of reporting all that took place at the trial in full detail, or even in the actual order of events. I imagine that to mention everything and to explain it properly would fill a volume, even a very large one. And so I trust I may not be reproached for confining myself to what struck me personally, and what I especially remembered. I may have selected as of most interest what was of secondary importance, and may have omitted the most prominent and essential details. But I see I shall do better not to apologize. I will do my best and the reader will see for himself that I have done all I can.

And, to begin with, before entering the court, I will mention what surprised me most on that day. Indeed, as it appeared later, everyone was surprised at it, too. We all knew that the affair had aroused great interest, that everyone was burning with impatience for the trial to begin, that it had been a subject of talk, conjecture, exclamation and surmise for the last two months in local society. Everyone knew, too, that the case had become known throughout Russia, but yet we had not imagined that it had aroused such burning, such intense, interest in everyone, not only among ourselves, but all over Russia. This became evident at the trial this day. Visitors had arrived not only from the chief town of our province, but from several other Russian towns, as well as from Moscow and Petersburg. Among them were lawyers, ladies, and even several distinguished personages. Every ticket of admission had been snatched up. A special place behind the table at which the three judges sat was set apart for the most distinguished and important of the men visitors; a row of armchairs had been placed there—something exceptional, which had never been allowed before. A large proportion—not less than half of the public—were ladies, local and visiting. There was such a large number of lawyers from all parts that they did not know where to seat them, for every ticket had long since been eagerly sought, begged for, and distributed. I saw at the

1. The description of Dmitri's trial was partly inspired by the March 1878 trial of Vera Zasulich, a young radical who was tried for shooting and wounding General Trepov, Chief of Police in Saint Petersburg. Dostoevsky attended the trial as a member of the press. See also note 1, p. 479.

end of the room, behind the platform, a special partition hurriedly put up, behind which all these lawyers were admitted, and they thought themselves lucky to have standing room there, for all chairs had been removed for the sake of space, and the crowd behind the partition stood throughout the case closely packed, shoulder to shoulder. Some of the ladies, especially those who came from a distance, made their appearance in the gallery very smartly dressed, but the majority of the ladies were oblivious even of dress. Their faces betrayed hysterical, greedy, almost morbid, curiosity. A peculiar fact—established afterwards by many observations—was that almost all the ladies, or, at least the vast majority of them, were on Mitya's side and in favor of his being acquitted. This was perhaps chiefly owing to his reputation as a conqueror of female hearts. It was known that two women rivals were to appear in the case. One of them—Katerina Ivanovna—was an object of general interest. All sorts of extraordinary tales were told about her, amazing anecdotes of her passion for Mitya, in spite of his crime. Her pride and "aristocratic connections" were particularly insisted upon (she had called upon scarcely anyone in the town). People said she intended to petition the Government for leave to accompany the criminal to Siberia and to be married to him somewhere in the mines. The appearance of Grushenka in court was awaited with no less impatience, as Katerina Ivanovna's rival. The public was looking forward with anxious curiosity to the meeting of the two rivals—the proud aristocratic girl and "the hetaera."[2] But Grushenka was a more familiar figure to the ladies of the district than Katerina Ivanovna. They had already seen "the woman who had ruined Fyodor Pavlovich and his unhappy son," and all, almost without exception, wondered how father and son could be so in love with "such a very common, ordinary Russian woman, who was not even pretty." In brief, there was a great deal of talk. I know for a fact that there were several serious family quarrels on Mitya's account in our town. Many ladies quarreled violently with their husbands over differences of opinion about the dreadful case, and it was only natural that the husbands of these ladies, far from being favorably disposed to the prisoner, should enter the court bitterly prejudiced against him. In fact, one may say pretty certainly that the masculine, as distinguished from the feminine part of the audience were biased against the prisoner. There were numbers of severe, frowning, even vindictive, faces, and they were in the majority. Mitya, indeed, had managed to offend many people during his stay in the town. Some of the visitors were, of course, in excellent spirits and quite unconcerned as to the fate of Mitya personally. But all were interested in the trial, and the majority of the men were certainly hoping for the punishment of the criminal, except perhaps the lawyers, who were more interested in the legal than in the moral aspect of the case. Everybody was excited at the presence of the celebrated lawyer, Fetyukovich. His talent was well known, and this was not the first time he had defended notorious criminal cases in the provinces. And if he defended them, such cases became celebrated and long remembered all over Russia. There were stories, too, about our prosecutor and about the President of the Court. It was said that Ippolit Kirillovich was in a tremor at meeting Fetyukovich, and that they had been enemies from the beginning of their careers in

2. See note 2, p. 425.

Petersburg, that though our sensitive prosecutor, who always considered that he had been aggrieved by someone in Petersburg because his talents had not been properly appreciated, had been resurrected in spirit over the Karamazov case, and was even dreaming of resurrecting his flagging fortunes by means of it; Fetyukovich, they said, was his one anxiety. But these rumors were not quite just. Our prosecutor was not one of those men who lose heart in the face of danger. On the contrary, his self-confidence increased with the increase of danger. It must be noted that our prosecutor was in general too hasty and morbidly impressionable. He would put his whole soul into some case and work at it as though his whole fate and his whole fortune depended on its result. This was the subject of some ridicule in the legal profession, for just by this characteristic our prosecutor had gained a wider notoriety than could have been expected from his modest position. People laughed particularly at his passion for psychology. In my opinion, they were wrong, and our prosecutor was, I believe, a man and a character of greater depths than was generally supposed. But with his delicate health he had failed to make his mark at the outset of his career and had never made up for it later.

As for the President of our Court, I can only say that he was a humane and cultured man, who had a practical knowledge of his work and progressive views. He was rather ambitious, but did not concern himself greatly about his future career. The great aim of his life was to be a man of advanced ideas. He was, too, a man of connections and property. He felt, as we learned afterwards, rather strongly about the Karamazov case, but from a social, not from a personal standpoint. He was interested in it as a social phenomenon, in its classification and its character as a product of our social conditions, as typical of the national character, and so on, and so on. His attitude to the personal aspect of the case, to its tragic significance and the persons involved in it, including the prisoner, was rather indifferent and abstract, as was perhaps fitting, indeed.

The court was packed and overflowing long before the judges made their appearance. Our court is the best hall in the town—spacious, lofty, and good for sound. On the right of the judges, who were on a raised platform, a table and two rows of chairs had been put ready for the jury. On the left was the place for the prisoner and the counsel for the defense. In the middle of the court, near the judges, was a table with the "material proofs." On it lay Fyodor Pavlovich's white silk dressing gown, stained with blood; the fatal brass pestle with which the supposed murder had been committed; Mitya's shirt, with a bloodstained sleeve; his coat, stained with blood in patches behind the pocket in which he had put his hand-kerchief; the handkerchief itself, stiff with blood and by now quite yellow; the pistol loaded by Mitya at Perkhotin's with a view to suicide, and taken from him on the sly at Mokroe by Trifon Borisovich; the envelope in which the three thousand rubles had been put ready for Grushenka, the narrow pink ribbon with which it had been tied, and many other articles I don't remember. In the body of the hall, at some distance, came the seats for the public. But in front of the balustrade a few chairs had been placed for witnesses who remained in the court after giving their evidence. At ten o'clock the three judges arrived—the President, one honorary justice of the peace, and one other. The prosecutor, of course, entered immediately after. The President was a short, stout, thick-set man of fifty, with a dyspeptic complexion, dark hair turning gray and cut short, and a red ribbon, of what Order I don't remember. The prosecutor struck me and the others, too, as looking particularly pale, almost green. His face seemed to have grown suddenly thinner, perhaps in a single night, for I had seen him looking as usual only two days before. The President began by asking the court whether all the jury were present. But I see I can't go on like this, partly because some things I did not hear, others I did not notice, and others I have forgotten, but most of all because, as I have said before, I have literally no time or space to mention everything that was said and done. I only know that neither side, that is, neither the prosecution nor the defense objected to very many of the jurymen. I remember the composition of the jury—four were petty officials of the town, two were merchants, and six peasants and artisans of the town. I remember, long before the trial, questions were continually asked with some surprise, especially by ladies, "Can such a delicate, complex and psychological case be submitted for decision to petty officials and even peasants?" And "What can an official, still more a peasant, understand in such an affair?" All the four officials in the jury were, in fact, men of no consequence and of low rank. Except one who was rather younger, they were gray-headed men, little known in society, who had vegetated on a pitiful salary, and who probably had elderly, unpresentable wives and crowds of children, perhaps even without shoes and stockings. At most, they spent their leisure over cards and, of course, had never read a single book. The two merchants looked respectable, but were strangely silent and stolid. One of them was close-shaven, and was dressed in German style; the other had a small, gray beard, and wore a red ribbon with some sort of a medal upon it around his neck. There is no need to speak of the artisans and the peasants. The artisans of Skotoprigonevsk are almost peasants, and even work on the land. Two of them also wore German dress, and perhaps for that reason, were dirtier and more uninviting looking than the others. So that one might well wonder, as I did as soon as I had looked at them, "what men like that could possibly make of such a case?" Yet their faces made a strangely imposing, almost menacing, impression; they were stern and frowning.

At last the President opened the case of the murder of the retired titular councilor, Fyodor Pavlovich Karamazov.[2] I don't quite remember how he described him. The bailiff was told to bring in the prisoner, and Mitya made his appearance. There was a hush through the court. One could have heard a fly. I don't know how it was with others, but Mitya made a most unfavorable impression on me. He looked terribly dandyish in a brand-new frock coat. I heard afterwards that he had ordered it in Moscow expressly for the occasion from his own tailor, who had his measurements. He wore immaculate black kid gloves and exquisite linen. He walked in with his yard-long strides, looking stiffly straight in front of him, and sat down in his place with a most unperturbed air. At the same moment the counsel for defense, the celebrated Fetyukovich, entered, and a sort of subdued hum passed through the court. He was a tall, spare man, with long thin legs, with extremely long, thin, pale fingers, clean-shaven face, straight brushed, rather short hair, and thin lips that were at times

---

2. Fyodor Pavlovich held the ninth grade in the Table of Ranks.

curved into something between a sneer and a smile. He looked about forty. His face would have been pleasant, if it had not been for his eyes, which, in themselves small and inexpressive, were set remarkably close together, with only the thin, long nose as a dividing line between them. In fact, there was something strikingly birdlike about his face. He was in evening dress and white tie.[3] I remember the President's first questions to Mitya, about his name, his calling, and so on. Mitya answered sharply, and his voice was so unexpectedly loud that it made the President start and look at the prisoner with surprise. Then followed a list of persons who were to take part in the proceedings—that is, of the witnesses and experts. It was a long list. Four of the witnesses were not present—Miüsov, who had given evidence at the preliminary inquiry, but was now in Paris; Madame Khokhlakova and Maximov, who were absent through illness; and Smerdyakov, through his sudden death, of which an official statement from the police was presented. The news of Smerdyakov's death produced a sudden stir and whisper in the court. Many of the audience, of course, had not heard of the sudden suicide. What struck people most was Mitya's sudden outburst. As soon as the statement of Smerdyakov's death was made, he suddenly cried out aloud from his place:

"He was a dog and died like a dog!"

I remember how his counsel rushed to him, and how the President addressed him, threatening to take stern measures, if such outbursts were repeated. Mitya nodded and in a subdued voice repeated several times abruptly to his counsel, with no show of regret:

"I won't again, I won't. It escaped me. I won't do it again."

And, of course, this brief episode did him no good with the jury or the public. His character was displayed, and it spoke for itself. It was under the influence of this incident that the indictment was read.

It was rather short, but circumstantial. It only stated the chief reason why he had been arrested, why he must be tried, and so on. Yet it made a great impression on me. The clerk read it loudly and distinctly. The whole tragedy was suddenly unfolded before us, concentrated, in bold relief, in a fatal and pitiless light. I remember how immediately after it had been read, the President asked Mitya in a loud impressive voice:

"Defendant, how do you plead?"

Mitya suddenly rose from his seat.

"I plead guilty to drunkenness and dissipation," he exclaimed, again in a startling, almost frenzied, voice, "to idleness and debauchery. I meant to become an honest man for good, just at the moment when I was struck down by fate. But I am not guilty of the death of that old man, my enemy and my father. No, no, I am not guilty of robbing him! I could not be. Dmitri Karamazov is a scoundrel, but not a thief."

He sat down again, visibly trembling all over. The President again briefly but impressively admonished him to answer only what was asked, and not to go off into irrelevant and frenzied exclamations. Then he ordered the case to proceed. All the witnesses were led up to take the oath. Then I saw them all together. The brothers of the prisoner were, however, allowed to give evidence without taking the oath. After an exhortation from the priest and the President, the witnesses were led away and were made to sit

3. Appropriate attire for a trial at the time.

as far as possible apart from one another. Then they began calling them up one by one.

Chapter II

Dangerous Witnesses

I do not know whether the witnesses for the defense and for the prosecution were separated into groups by the President, and whether it was arranged to call them in a certain order. But no doubt it was so. I only know that the witnesses for the prosecution were called first. I repeat, I don't intend to describe all the questions step by step. Besides, my account would be to some extent superfluous, because in the speeches for the prosecution and for the defense the whole course of the evidence was brought together and set in a strong and significant light, and I took down parts of those two remarkable speeches in full, and will quote them in due course, together with one extraordinary and quite unexpected episode, which occurred before the final speeches, and undoubtedly influenced the sinister and fatal outcome of the trial. I will only observe that from the first moments of this "trial" one peculiar characteristic of the case was conspicuous and observed by all, that is, the overwhelming strength of the prosecution as compared with the arguments the defense had to rely upon. Everyone realized it from the first moment that the facts began to group themselves round a single point, and the whole horrible and bloody crime was gradually revealed. Everyone, perhaps, felt from the first that the case was beyond dispute, that there was no doubt about it, that there could be really no discussion, and that the defense was only a matter of form, and that the criminal was guilty, obviously and conclusively guilty. I imagine that even the ladies, who were so impatiently longing for the acquittal of the fascinating defendant, were at the same time, without exception, convinced of his guilt. What's more, I believe they would have been mortified if his guilt had not been so firmly established, as that would have lessened the effect of the closing scene of the criminal's acquittal. That he would be acquitted all the ladies, strange to say, were firmly persuaded up to the very last moment. "He is guilty, but he will be acquitted, from motives of humanity, in accordance with the new ideas, the new sentiments that had come into fashion," and so on, and so on. And that was why they had crowded into the court so impatiently. The men were more interested in the contest between the prosecutor and the famous Fetyukovich. All were wondering and asking themselves what could even a talent like Fetyukovich's make of such a desperate case; and so they followed his achievements, step by step, with concentrated attention. But Fetyukovich remained an enigma to all up to the very end, up to his speech. Persons of experience suspected that he had some design, that he was working towards some object, but it was almost impossible to guess what it was. His confidence and self-reliance were unmistakable, however. Every one noticed with pleasure, moreover, that he, after so short a stay, not more than three days, perhaps, among us, had so wonderfully succeeded in mastering the case and "had studied it to a turn." People described with relish, afterwards, how cleverly he had "taken down" all the witnesses for the prosecution, and as far as possible perplexed them and, what's more, had aspersed their reputation and so depreciated the value of their evidence. But it was supposed that he did this rather by way of sport, so to speak, for professional glory, to show nothing had been omitted of the accepted trial methods, for all were convinced that he could do no real good by such disparagement of the witnesses, and probably was more aware of this than anyone, having some idea of his own in the background, some concealed weapon of defense, which he would suddenly reveal when the time came. But meanwhile, conscious of his strength, he seemed to be diverting himself. So, for instance, when Grigory, Fyodor Pavlovich's old servant, who had given the most damning piece of evidence "about the open door into the garden," was examined, the counsel for the defense positively fastened upon him when his turn came to question him. It must be noted that Grigory entered the hall with a composed and almost stately air, not the least disconcerted by the majesty of the court or the vast audience listening to him. He gave evidence with as much confidence as though he had been talking with his Martha, only perhaps more respectfully. It was impossible to make him contradict himself. The prosecutor questioned him first in detail about the family life of the Karamazovs. The family picture stood out in lurid colors. It was plain to ear and eye that the witness was guileless and impartial. In spite of his profound reverence for the memory of his deceased master, he yet bore witness that he had been unjust to Mitya and "hadn't brought up his children as he should. He'd have been devoured by lice when he was little, if it hadn't been for me," he added, describing Mitya's early childhood. "It wasn't fair either of the father to wrong his son over his mother's property, which was by right his." In reply to the prosecutor's question what grounds he had for asserting that Fyodor Pavlovich had wronged his son in their money relations, Grigory, to the surprise of everyone, had no proof at all to bring forward, but he still persisted that the arrangement with the son was "unfair," and that he ought "to have paid him several thousand rubles more." I must note, by the way, that the prosecutor asked this question whether Fyodor Pavlovich had really kept back part of Mitya's inheritance with marked persistence of all the witnesses who could be asked it, not excepting Alyosha and Ivan, but he obtained no exact information from anyone; all alleged that it was so, but were unable to bring forward any distinct proof. Grigory's description of the scene at the dinner table, when Dmitri had burst in and beaten his father, threatening to come back to kill him, made a sinister impression on the court, especially as the old servant's composure in telling it, his parsimony of words and peculiar phraseology were as effective as eloquence. He observed that he was not angry with Mitya for having knocked him down and struck him on the face; he had forgiven him long ago, he said. Of the deceased Smerdyakov he observed, crossing himself, that he was a lad of ability, but stupid and afflicted, and, worse still, an atheist, and that it was Fyodor Pavlovich and his elder son[4] who had taught him atheism. But he defended Smerdyakov's honesty almost with warmth, and related how Smerdyakov had once found the master's money in the yard, and, instead of concealing it, had taken it to his master, who had rewarded him with a "gold piece" for it, and trusted

4. Grigory erroneously refers to Ivan as the elder son.

him implicitly from that time forward. He maintained obstinately that the door into the garden had been open. But he was asked so many questions that I can't recall them all. At last the counsel for the defense began to cross-examine him, and the first question he asked was about the envelope in which Fyodor Pavlovich was supposed to have put three thousand rubles for "a certain person." "Have you ever seen it, you, who were for so many years in close attendance on your master?" Grigory answered that he had not seen it and had never heard of the money from anyone "till everybody was talking about it." This question about the envelope Fetyukovich put to everyone who could conceivably have known of it, as persistently as the prosecutor asked his question about Dmitri's inheritance, and got the same answer from all, that no one had seen the envelope, though many had heard of it. From the beginning everyone noticed Fetyukovich's persistence on this subject.

"Now, with your permission I'll ask you a question," Fetyukovich said, suddenly and unexpectedly. "Of what was that balsam, or, rather, decoction, made, which, as we learn from the preliminary inquiry, you used on that evening to rub your lumbago, in the hope of curing it?"

Grigory looked blankly at the questioner, and after a brief silence muttered "there was saffron in it."

"Nothing but saffron? Don't you remember any other ingredient?"

"There was milfoil in it, too."

"And pepper perhaps?" Fetyukovich queried.

"Yes, there was pepper, too."

"Et cetera. And all dissolved in vodka?"

"In pure alcohol."

There was a faint sound of laughter in the court.

"Well, well, in pure alcohol, even. After rubbing your back, I believe, you drank what was left in the bottle with a certain pious prayer, known only to your wife?"

"I did."

"Did you drink much? Roughly speaking, a wine glass or two?"

"It might have been a tumblerful."

"A tumblerful, even. Perhaps a tumbler and a half?"

Grigory did not answer. He seemed to see what was meant.

"A glass and a half of neat alcohol—is not at all bad, don't you think? You might see 'the gates of heaven open,'[5] not only the door into the garden?"

Grigory remained silent. There was another laugh in the court. The President made a movement.

"Do you know for a fact," Fetyukovich persisted, "whether you were awake or not when you saw the open door?"

"I was on my legs."

"That's not a proof that you were awake." (There was again laughter in the court.) "Could you have answered at that moment, if anyone had asked you a question—for instance, what year it is?"

"I don't know."

"And what year is it, Anno Domini, do you know?"

Grigory stood with a perplexed face, looking straight at his tormentor. Strange to say, it appeared he really did not know what year it was.

---

5. An inexact quotation from Revelation 4.1.

"But perhaps you can tell how many fingers you have on your hands?"

"I am a servant," Grigory said suddenly, in a loud and distinct voice. "If my betters think fit to make game of me, it is my duty to suffer it."

Fetyukovich was a little taken aback, and the President intervened, reminding him that he must ask more relevant questions. Fetyukovich bowed with dignity and said that he had no more questions to ask of the witness. The public and the jury, of course, were left with a grain of doubt in their minds as to the evidence of a man who might, while undergoing a certain cure, have seen "the gates of heaven," and who did not even know what year he was living in. But before Grigory left the box another episode occurred. The President, turning to the prisoner, asked him whether he had any comment to make on the evidence of the last witness.

"Except about the door, all he has said is true," cried Mitya, in a loud voice. "For combing the lice off me, I thank him; for forgiving my blows, I thank him. The old man has been honest all his life and as faithful to my father as seven hundred poodles."

"Prisoner, be careful in your language," the President admonished him.

"I am not a poodle," Grigory muttered.

"All right, it's I who am a poodle myself," cried Mitya. "If it's an insult, I take it to myself and I beg his pardon. I was a beast and cruel to him. I was cruel to Aesop, too."

"What Aesop?" the President asked sternly again.

"Oh, Pierrot . . . my father, Fyodor Pavlovich."

The President again and again warned Mitya impressively and very sternly to be more careful in his language.

"You are injuring yourself in the opinion of your judges."

The counsel for the defense was equally clever in dealing with the evidence of Rakitin. I may remark that Rakitin was one of the leading witnesses and one to whom the prosecutor attached great significance. It appeared that he knew everything; his knowledge was amazing, he had been everywhere, seen everything, talked to everybody, knew every detail of the biography of Fyodor Pavlovich and all the Karamazovs. Of the envelope, it is true, he had only heard from Mitya himself. But he described minutely Mitya's exploits in the Metropolis, all his compromising doings and sayings, and told the story of Captain Snegiryov's "wisp of tow." But even Rakitin could say nothing positive about Mitya's inheritance, and confined himself to contemptuous generalities. "Who could tell which of them was to blame, and who was in debt to the other, with their crazy Karamazov way of muddling things so that no one could make head or tail of it?" He attributed the tragic crime to the habits that had become ingrained by ages of serfdom and the distressed condition of Russia, due to the lack of appropriate institutions. He was, in fact, allowed some latitude of speech. This was the first occasion on which Rakitin showed what he could do, and he attracted notice. The prosecutor knew that the witness was preparing a magazine article on the case, and afterwards in his speech, as we shall see later, quoted some ideas from the article, showing that he had seen it already. The picture drawn by the witness was a gloomy and sinister one, and greatly strengthened the case for the prosecution. Altogether, Rakitin's discourse fascinated the public by its independence and the extraordinary nobility of his ideas. There were even two or three outbreaks of applause when he spoke of serfdom and the distressed condition of Russia. But Rakitin, in his youthful ardor, made a slight blunder, of which the counsel for the defense at once adroitly took advantage. Answering certain questions about Grushenka, and carried away by the loftiness of his own sentiments and his success, of which he was, of course, conscious, he went so far as to speak somewhat contemptuously of Agrafena Alexandrovna as "the kept mistress of Samsonov." He would have given a good deal to take back his words afterwards, for Fetyukovich tripped him up on it at once. And it was all because Rakitin had not reckoned on the lawyer having been able to become so intimately acquainted with every detail in so short a time.

"Allow me to ask," began the counsel for the defense, with the most affable and even respectful smile, "you are, of course, the same Mr. Rakitin whose pamphlet, *The Life of the Deceased Elder, Father Zosima*, published by the diocesan authorities, full of profound and religious reflections and preceded by an excellent and devout dedication to the Bishop, I have just read with such pleasure?"[6]

"I did not write it for publication . . . it was published afterwards," muttered Rakitin, for some reason fearfully disconcerted and almost ashamed.

"Oh, that's excellent! A thinker like you can, and indeed ought to, take the widest view of every social question. Your most instructive pamphlet has been widely circulated through the patronage of the Bishop, and has been of appreciable service. . . . But this is the chief thing I would like to learn from you. You stated just now that you were very intimately acquainted with Miss Svetlova." (It must be noted that Grushenka's surname was "Svetlova." I heard it for the first time that day, during the case.)

"I cannot answer for all my acquaintances. . . . I am a young man . . . and who can answer for everyone he meets?" cried Rakitin, flushing all over.

"I understand, I quite understand!" cried Fetyukovich, as though he, too, were embarrassed and in haste to excuse himself. "You, like any other, might well be interested in an acquaintance with a young and beautiful woman who would readily entertain the flower of local youth, but . . . I only wanted to know . . . it has come to my knowledge that Miss Svetlova was particularly anxious a couple of months ago to make the acquaintance of the younger Karamazov, Alexey Fyodorovich, and promised you twenty-five rubles, if you would bring him to her in his monastic dress. And that actually took place on the evening of the day on which the terrible crime, which is the subject of the present trial, was committed. You brought Alexey Karamazov to Miss Svetlova, and did you receive the twenty-five rubles from Miss Svetlova as a reward, that's what I wanted to hear from you?"

"It was a joke. . . . I don't see of what interest that can be to you. . . . I took it for a joke . . . meaning to give it back later . . ."

"Then you did take . . . But you have not given it back yet . . . or have you?"

6. This episode in Rakitin's life is drawn from the biography of Grigory Eliseev (see p. 76). A former seminarian and professor of church history, Eliseev rejected religion in favor of left-wing political activism, ultimately becoming a leading contributor to *The Contemporary*. In his early years, however, he wrote books sympathetic to the Orthodox Church, a fact later used by the right-wing press to discredit him with his associates on the radical left.

"That's of no consequence," muttered Rakitin, "I refuse to answer such questions. . . . Of course I shall give it back."

The President intervened, but Fetyukovich declared he had finished questioning Mr. Rakitin. Mr. Rakitin left the witness stand with something of a stain upon his character. The effect left by the lofty idealism of his speech was somewhat marred, and Fetyukovich's expression, as he watched him walk away, seemed to suggest to the public that "this is a specimen of the lofty-minded persons who accuse him." I remember that this incident, too, did not pass off without an outbreak from Mitya. Enraged by the tone in which Rakitin had referred to Grushenka, he suddenly shouted "Bernard!" When, after Rakitin's cross-examination, the President asked the prisoner if he had anything to say, Mitya cried loudly:

"Since I've been arrested, he has borrowed money from me! He is a contemptible Bernard and opportunist, and he doesn't believe in God; he took the Bishop in!"

Mitya, of course, was pulled up again for the intemperance of his language, but Rakitin was done for. Captain Snegiryov's evidence was a failure, too, but from quite a different reason. He appeared in ragged and dirty clothes, muddy boots, and in spite of the vigilance and preliminary "expertise" of the police officers, he suddenly turned out to be hopelessly drunk. On being asked about Mitya's attack upon him, he refused to answer.

"God bless him. Ilyushechka told me not to. God will repay me yonder."

"Who told you not to tell? Of whom are you talking?"

"Ilyushechka, my little son. 'Papochka, papochka, how he insulted you!' He said that at the stone. Now he is dying . . ."

The captain suddenly began sobbing, and plumped down on his knees before the President. He was hurriedly led away amidst the laughter of the public. The effect prepared by the prosecutor did not come off at all.

Fetyukovich went on making the most of every opportunity, and amazed people more and more by his minute knowledge of the case. Thus, for example, Trifon Borisovich made a great impression, of course, very prejudicial to Mitya. He calculated almost on his fingers that on his first visit to Mokroe, Mitya must have spent three thousand rubles, "or very little less. Just think what he squandered on those gypsy girls alone! And as for our lousy peasants, it wasn't a case of flinging half a ruble in the street, he made them presents of twenty-five rubles each, at least, he didn't give them less. And what a lot of money was simply stolen from him! And if anyone did steal, he did not leave a receipt. How could one catch the thief when he was flinging his money away all the time? Our peasants are robbers, you know; they have no care for their souls. And the way he went on with the girls, our village girls! They're completely set up since then, I tell you, they used to be poor." He recalled, in fact, every item of expense and added it all up. So the theory that only fifteen hundred had been spent and the rest had been put aside in a little bag seemed inconceivable. "I saw three thousand as clear as a penny in his hands, I saw it with my own eyes; I should think I ought to know how to reckon money," cried Trifon Borisovich, doing his best to satisfy the "authorities." When Fetyukovich had to cross-examine him, he scarcely tried to refute his evidence, but began asking him about an incident at the first carousal at Mokroe, a month before the arrest, when Timothy and another peasant called Akim had

picked up on the floor in the passage a hundred rubles dropped by Mitya
when he was drunk, and had given them to Trifon Borisovich, and received
a ruble each from him for doing so. "Well," asked the lawyer, "did you give
that hundred rubles back to Mr. Karamazov?" Trifon Borisovich shuffled in
vain. . . . He was obliged, after the peasants had been examined, to admit
the finding of the hundred rubles, only adding that he had religiously
returned it all to Dmitri Fyodorovich "in perfect honesty, and it's only
because his honor was totally drunk, sir, at the time, he wouldn't remember it." But, as he had denied the incident of the hundred rubles till the
peasants had been called to prove it, his evidence as to returning the
money to Mitya, was naturally regarded with great suspicion. So one of
the most dangerous witnesses brought forward by the prosecution was
again discredited. The same thing happened with the Poles. They took up
an attitude of pride and independence; they vociferated loudly that they
had both been in the service of the Crown, and that "*Pan* Mitya" had
offered them three thousand "to buy their honor," and that they had seen
a large sum of money in his hands. *Pan* Mussyalovich introduced a terrible number of Polish words into his sentences, and seeing that this only
increased his consequence in the eyes of the President and the prosecutor,
grew more and more pompous, and ended by speaking in Polish altogether. But Fetyukovich caught them, too, in his snares: Trifon Borisovich,
recalled, was forced, in spite of his evasion, to admit that *Pan* Vrublevsky
had substituted another pack of cards for the one he had provided, and
that *Pan* Mussyalovich had cheated during the game. Kalganov confirmed
this, and both *pans* left the witness stand with damaged reputations, even
amidst laughter from the public. Then exactly the same thing happened
with almost all the most dangerous witnesses. Fetyukovich succeeded in
casting a slur on all of them, and dismissing them with a certain derision.
The lawyers and experts were lost in admiration, and were only at a loss to
understand what good purpose could be served by it, for all, I repeat, felt
that the case for the prosecution could not be refuted, but was growing
more and more tragically overwhelming. But from the confidence of the
"great magician" they saw that he was serene, and they waited, feeling that
"such a man" had not come from Petersburg for nothing, and that he was
not a man to return unsuccessful.

Chapter III

Medical Expertise and a Pound of Nuts

The evidence of the medical experts, too, was of little use to the accused.
And it appeared later that Fetyukovich had not reckoned much upon it.
The medical line of defense had only been taken up through the insistence of Katerina Ivanovna, who had sent for a celebrated doctor from
Moscow on purpose. The case for the defense could, of course, lose nothing by it and might, with luck, gain something from it. There was, however,
an element of comedy about it, through the difference of opinion of the
doctors. The medical experts were the famous doctor from Moscow, our
doctor, Herzenstube, and the young doctor, Varvinsky. The two latter
appeared also as witnesses for the prosecution. The first to be called in

the capacity of expert was Doctor Herzenstube. He was a gray and bald-ing old man of seventy, of middle height and sturdy build. He was much esteemed and respected by everyone in the town. He was a conscien-tious doctor and an excellent and pious man, a Herrnhuter or Moravian brother,[7] I am not quite sure which. He had been living amongst us for many years and behaved with wonderful dignity. He was a kind-hearted and humane man. He treated the sick poor and peasants for nothing, visited them in their slums and huts, and left money for medicine, but he was as obstinate as a mule. If once he had taken an idea into his head, there was no shaking it. Almost everyone in the town was aware, by the way, that the famous doctor had, within the first two or three days of his presence among us, uttered some extremely offensive allusions to Doctor Herzenstube's qualifications. Though the Moscow doctor asked twenty-five rubles for a visit, several people in the town were glad to take advan-tage of his arrival, and rushed to consult him regardless of expense. All these had, of course, been previously patients of Doctor Herzenstube, and the celebrated doctor had criticized his treatment with extreme harsh-ness. Finally, he had asked the patients as soon as he saw them, "Well, who has been cramming you with nostrums? Herzenstube? Ha, ha!" Doc-tor Herzenstube, of course, heard all this, and now all the three doctors made their appearance, one after another, to be examined. Doctor Her-zenstube roundly declared that the abnormality of the defendant's mental faculties was self-evident. Then giving his ground for this opinion, which I omit here, he added that the abnormality was not only evident in many of the defendant's actions in the past, but was apparent even now at this very moment. When he was asked to explain how it was apparent now at this moment, the old doctor, with simple-hearted directness, pointed out that the defendant on entering the court had "an extraordinary air, remark-able in the circumstances"; that he had "marched in like a soldier, looking straight before him, though it would have been more natural for him to look to the left where, among the public, the ladies were sitting, seeing that he was a great admirer of the fair sex and must be thinking much of what the ladies are saying of him now," the old man concluded in his peculiar language. I must add that he spoke Russian readily, but every phrase was formed in German style, which did not, however, trouble him, for it had always been a weakness of his to believe that he spoke Russian perfectly, better indeed than Russians. And he was very fond of using Russian proverbs, always declaring that the Russian proverbs were the best and most expressive sayings in the whole world. I may remark, too, that in conversation through absentmindedness he often forgot the most ordinary words, which sometimes went out of his head, though he knew them perfectly. The same thing happened, though, when he spoke Ger-man, and at such times he always waved his hand before his face as though trying to catch the lost word, and no one could induce him to go on speaking till he had found the missing word. His remark that the pris-oner ought to have looked at the ladies on entering roused a whisper of amusement in the audience. All our ladies were very fond of our old

7. Herrnhuterism was a Protestant religious movement that began in the eighteenth century in Herrnhut, Saxony, eventually spreading to Russia as well. Emphasizing the need for prayer, continual spiritual introspection, and moral education, Herrnhuterism derived from the teachings of the Moravian Brotherhood, a movement founded in Bohemia in 1457.

doctor; they knew, too, that having been all his life a bachelor and a religious man of exemplary conduct, he looked upon women as lofty and ideal beings. And so his unexpected observation struck everyone as very strange.

The Moscow doctor, being questioned in his turn, definitely and emphatically repeated that he considered the defendant's mental condition abnormal in "the highest degree." He talked at length and with erudition of "aberration" and "mania," and argued that, from all the facts collected, the defendant had undoubtedly been in a condition of aberration for several days before his arrest, and, if the crime had been committed by him, it must, even if he were conscious of it, have been almost involuntary, as he had not the power to control the morbid impulse that possessed him. But apart from temporary aberration, the doctor diagnosed mania, which promised, in his words, to lead to complete insanity in the future. (It must be noted that I report this in my own words; the doctor made use of very learned and professional language.) "All his actions are in contravention of common sense and logic," he continued. "Not to refer to what I have not seen, that is, the crime itself and the whole catastrophe, the day before yesterday, while he was talking to me, he had an unaccountably fixed look in his eye. He laughed unexpectedly when there was nothing to laugh at. He showed continual and inexplicable irritability, using strange words, 'Bernard!' 'Ethics!' and others equally inappropriate." But the doctor detected mania, above all, in the fact that the prisoner could not even speak of the three thousand rubles, of which he considered himself to have been cheated, without extraordinary irritation, though he could speak comparatively lightly of other misfortunes and grievances. According to all accounts, he had even in the past, whenever the subject of the three thousand rubles was touched on, flown into a perfect frenzy, and yet he was reported to be a disinterested and not grasping man. "As to the opinion of my learned colleague," the Moscow doctor added ironically in conclusion, "that the defendant would, on entering the court, have naturally looked at the ladies and not straight before him, I will only say that, apart from the playfulness of this theory, it is radically unsound. For though I fully agree that the defendant, on entering the court where his fate will be decided, would not naturally look straight before him in that fixed way, and that that may really be a sign of his abnormal mental condition, at the same time I maintain that he would naturally not look to the left at the ladies, but, on the contrary, to the right to find his defense counsel, on whose help all his hopes rest and on whose defense all his future depends." The doctor expressed his opinion positively and emphatically. But the unexpected pronouncement of Doctor Varvinsky gave the last touch of comedy to the difference of opinion between the experts. In his opinion the defendant was now, and had been all along, in a perfectly normal condition, and, although he certainly must have been in a nervous and exceedingly excited state before his arrest, this might have been due to several perfectly obvious causes, jealousy, anger, continual drunkenness, and so on. But this nervous condition would not involve the mental "aberration" of which mention had just been made. As to the question whether the defendant should have looked to the left or to the right on entering the court, "in his modest opinion," the defendant would naturally look straight before him on entering the court, as he had in fact done, since that was where the judges, on whom his fate depended, were sitting. So that it was just by looking straight before him that he showed his perfectly normal state of mind at the present. The young doctor concluded his "modest" testimony with some heat.

"Bravo, apothecary!" cried Mitya, from his seat, "just so!"

Mitya, of course, was checked, but the young doctor's opinion had a decisive influence on the judges and on the public, and, as appeared afterwards, everyone agreed with him. But Doctor Herzenstube, when called as a witness, was quite unexpectedly of use to Mitya. As an old resident in the town who had known the Karamazov family for years, he furnished some facts of great value for the prosecution, and suddenly, as though recalling something, he added:

"But the poor young man might have had a very different life, for he had a good heart both in childhood and after childhood, that I know. But the Russian proverb says, 'If a man has one head, it's good, but if another intelligent man comes to visit him, it would be better still, for then there will be two heads and not only one.'"

"One head is good, but two are better," the prosecutor put in impatiently. He knew the old man's habit of talking slowly and deliberately, regardless of the impression he was making and of the delay he was causing, and highly prizing his flat, Kraut-ish, and always gleefully complacent German wit. The old man was fond of making jokes.

"Oh, yes, that's what I say," he went on stubbornly. "A single head is good, but two are much better, but he did not meet another head with wits, and his own wits went. Where did they go? I've forgotten the word." He went on, passing his hand before his eyes, "Oh, yes, *spazieren.*"

"For a walk?"

"Oh, yes, for a walk, that's what I say. Well, his wits went for a walk and fell in such a deep hole that he lost himself. And yet he was a grateful and sensitive boy. Oh, I remember him very well, a little chap so high, left neglected by his father in the backyard, when he ran about without boots on his feet, and his little breeches hanging by one button."

A note of feeling and tenderness suddenly came into the honest old man's voice. Fetyukovich positively started, as though scenting something and caught at it instantly.

"Oh, yes, I was a young man then. . . . I was . . . well, I was forty-five then, and had only just come here. And I was so sorry for the boy then; I asked myself why shouldn't I buy him a pound of . . . a pound of what? I've forgotten what it's called. A pound of what children are very fond of, what is it, what is it?" The doctor began waving his hands again. "It grows on a tree and is gathered and given to everyone . . ."

"Apples?"

"Oh, no, no. You have a dozen of apples, not a pound. . . . No, there are a lot of them, and all little. You put them in the mouth and crack."

"Nuts?"

"Quite so, nuts, that's what I say," the doctor repeated in the calmest way as though he had been at no loss for a word. "And I bought him one pound of nuts, for no one had ever bought the boy a pound of nuts before. And I lifted my finger and said to him, 'Boy, *Gott der Vater.*' He laughed and said, '*Gott der Vater.*' . . . '*Gott der Sohn.*' He laughed again and lisped '*Gott der Sohn.*' '*Gott der heilige Geist.*'[8] Then he laughed again and said as best he could: '*Gott der heilige Geist.*' I went away, and two days after I happened to be passing, and he shouted to me on his own, 'Uncle, *Gott der Vater, Gott der Sohn,*' and he had only forgotten '*Gott der heilige Geist.*' But I reminded him of it and I felt very sorry for him again. But he was taken away, and I did not see him again. Twenty-three years passed. I am sitting one morning in my study, a white-haired old man, when there walks into the room a blooming young man, whom I would never have recognized, but he held up his finger and said, laughing, '*Gott der Vater, Gott der Sohn, und Gott der heilige Geist.* I have just arrived and have come to thank you for that pound of nuts, for no one else ever bought me a pound of nuts; you are the only one that ever did.' And then I remembered my happy youth and the poor child in the yard, without boots on his feet, and my heart was touched and I said, 'You are a grateful young man, for you have remembered all your life the pound of nuts I bought you in your childhood.' And I embraced him and blessed him. And I shed tears. He laughed, but he shed tears, too . . . for the Russian often laughs when he ought to be weeping. But he did weep; I saw it. And now, alas! . . ."

"And I am weeping now, German, I am weeping now, too, you saintly man," Mitya cried suddenly from his place.

In any case the anecdote made a certain favorable impression on the public. But the chief sensation in Mitya's favor was created by the evidence of Katerina Ivanovna, which I will describe directly. Indeed, when the witnesses *à décharge,*[9] that is, called by the defense, began giving evidence, fortune seemed all at once markedly more favorable to Mitya, and what was particularly striking, this was a surprise even to the counsel for the defense. But before Katerina Ivanovna was called, Alyosha was examined, and he recalled a fact which seemed to furnish positive evidence against one important point made by the prosecution.

Chapter IV

Fortune Smiles on Mitya

It came quite as a surprise even to Alyosha himself. He was not required to take the oath, and I remember that both sides addressed him very gently and sympathetically. It was evident that his good reputation had preceded him. Alyosha gave his evidence modestly and with restraint, but his warm sympathy for his unhappy brother was unmistakable. In answer to one question, he sketched his brother's character as that of a man, violent-tempered perhaps and carried away by his passions, but at the same time honorable, proud and generous, capable of self-sacrifice, if necessary. He admitted, however, that, through his passion for Grushenka and his rivalry with his father, his brother had been of late in an intolerable position. But he repelled with indignation the suggestion that his brother

---

8. "God the Father, God the Son, God the Holy Spirit" (German).
9. A juridical term, literally "to lighten (the charge)" (French), referring to a witness called by the defense.

might have committed a murder for the sake of gain, though he recognized that the three thousand rubles had become almost an obsession with Mitya; that he looked upon them as part of the inheritance he had been cheated of by his father, and that, indifferent as he was to money as a rule, he could not even speak of that three thousand without rage and fury. As for the rivalry of the two "persons," as the prosecutor expressed it—that is, of Grushenka and Katya—he answered evasively and was even unwilling to answer one or two questions altogether.

"Did your brother tell you, anyway, that he intended to kill your father?" asked the prosecutor. "You can refuse to answer if you think necessary," he added.

"He did not tell me so directly," answered Alyosha.

"How so? Did he indirectly?"

"He spoke to me once of his hatred for our father and his fear that at an extreme moment . . . at a moment of disgust he might perhaps murder him."

"And you believed him?"

"I am afraid to say that I did. But I never doubted that some higher feeling would always save him at the fatal moment, as it has indeed saved him, for it was *not he* who killed my father," Alyosha said firmly, in a loud voice that was heard throughout the court. The prosecutor started like a warhorse at the sound of a trumpet.

"Let me assure you that I fully believe in the complete sincerity of your conviction and do not explain it by or identify it with your affection for your unhappy brother. Your peculiar view of the whole tragic episode is known to us already from the preliminary investigation. I won't attempt to conceal from you that it is highly individual and contradicts all the other evidence collected by the prosecution. And so I think it essential to press you to tell me what facts have led you to this conviction of your brother's innocence and of the guilt of another person against whom you gave evidence at the preliminary inquiry?"

"I only answered the questions asked me at the preliminary inquiry," replied Alyosha, slowly and calmly. "I made no accusation against Smerdyakov on my own account."

"Yet you gave evidence against him?"

"I was led to do so by my brother Dmitri's words. I was told what took place at his arrest and how he had pointed to Smerdyakov before I was examined. I believe absolutely that my brother is innocent, and if he didn't commit the murder, then . . ."

"Then Smerdyakov? Why Smerdyakov? And why are you so completely persuaded of your brother's innocence?"

"I cannot help believing my brother. I know he wouldn't lie to me. I saw from his face he wasn't lying."

"Only from his face? Is that all the proof you have?"

"I have no other proof."

"And of Smerdyakov's guilt have you no proof whatever but your brother's word and the expression of his face?"

"No, I have no other proof."

The prosecutor dropped the examination at this point. The impression left by Alyosha's evidence on the public was most disappointing. There had been talk about Smerdyakov before the trial; someone had heard something, someone had pointed out something else, it was said that Alyosha had gathered together some extraordinary proofs of his brother's innocence and Smerdyakov's guilt, and after all there was nothing, no evidence except certain moral convictions so natural in a brother.

But Fetyukovich began his cross-examination. On his asking Alyosha when it was that the prisoner had told him of his hatred for his father and that he might kill him, and whether he had heard it, for instance, at their last meeting before the catastrophe, Alyosha started as he answered, as though only just recollecting and understanding something.

"I remember one circumstance now which I'd quite forgotten myself. It wasn't clear to me at the time, but now . . ."

And, obviously only now for the first time struck by an idea, he recounted eagerly how, at his last interview with Mitya that evening under the tree, on the road to the monastery, Mitya had struck himself on the breast, "the upper part of the breast," and had repeated several times that he had a means of regaining his honor, that that means was here, here on his breast. "I thought, when he struck himself on the breast, he meant that it was in his heart," Alyosha continued, "that he might find in his heart strength to save himself from some awful disgrace which was awaiting him and which he did not dare confess even to me. I must confess I did think at the time that he was speaking of our father, and that the disgrace he was shuddering at was the thought of going to our father and doing some violence to him. Yet it was just then that he pointed to something on his breast, so that I remember the idea struck me at the time that the heart is not on that part of the breast, but below, and that he struck himself much too high, just below the neck, and kept pointing to that place. My idea seemed stupid to me at the time, but he was perhaps pointing then to that little bag in which he had fifteen hundred rubles!"

"Just so," Mitya suddenly cried from his place. "That's right, Alyosha, I was striking it with my fist!"

Fetyukovich flew to him in haste entreating him to keep quiet, and at the same instant pounced on Alyosha. Alyosha, carried away himself by his recollection, warmly expressed his theory that this disgrace was probably just that fifteen hundred rubles on him, which he might have returned to Katerina Ivanovna as half of what he owed her, but which he had yet determined not to repay her and to use for another purpose—namely, to enable him to elope with Grushenka, if she consented.

"It is so, it must be so," exclaimed Alyosha, in sudden excitement. "My brother cried several times that half of the disgrace, half of it (he said *half* several times) he could free himself from at once, but that he was so unhappy in his weakness of will that he wouldn't do it . . . that he knew beforehand he was incapable of doing it!"

"And you clearly, confidently remember that he struck himself just on this part of the breast?" Fetyukovich asked eagerly.

"Clearly and confidently, for I thought at the time, 'Why does he strike himself up there when the heart is lower down,' and the thought seemed stupid to me at the time . . . I remember its seeming stupid . . . it flashed through my mind. That's what brought it back to me just now. How could I have forgotten it till now! It was that little bag he meant when he said he had the means but wouldn't give back that fifteen hundred. And when he was arrested at Mokroe he cried out—I know, I was told it—that he considered it the most disgraceful act of his life that when he had the means of repaying Katerina Ivanovna half (half, note!) what he owed her, he yet could not bring himself to repay the money and preferred to remain a thief in her eyes rather than part with it. And what torture, what torture that debt has been to him!" Alyosha exclaimed in conclusion.

The prosecutor, of course, intervened. He asked Alyosha to describe once more how it had all happened, and several times insisted on the question, had the prisoner seemed to point to anything. Perhaps he had simply struck himself with his fist on the breast?

"But it was not with his fist," cried Alyosha; "he pointed with his fingers and pointed here, very high up. . . . How could I have so completely forgotten it till this moment!"

The President asked Mitya what he had to say to the last witness's evidence. Mitya confirmed it, saying that he had been pointing to the fifteen hundred rubles which were on his breast, just below the neck, and that that was, of course, the disgrace, "A disgrace I cannot deny, the most shameful act of my whole life," shouted Mitya. "I might have repaid it and didn't repay it. I preferred to remain a thief in her eyes rather than give it back. And the most shameful part of it was that I knew beforehand I wouldn't give it back! You are right, Alyosha! Thanks, Alyosha!"

So Alyosha's cross-examination ended. What was important and striking about it was that one fact at least had been found, and even though this were only one tiny bit of evidence, a mere hint at evidence, it did go some little way towards proving that the amulet had existed and had contained fifteen hundred rubles and that the prisoner had not been lying at the preliminary inquiry when he alleged at Mokroe that those fifteen hundred rubles were "his own." Alyosha was glad. With a flushed face he moved away to the seat assigned to him. He kept repeating to himself: "How was it I forgot! How could I have forgotten it! And what made it come back to me now?"

Katerina Ivanovna was called to the witness stand. As she entered something extraordinary happened in the court. The ladies clutched their lorgnettes and opera glasses. There was a stir among the men: some stood up to get a better view. Everybody alleged afterwards that Mitya had turned "white as a sheet" on her entrance. All in black, she advanced modestly, almost timidly. It was impossible to tell from her face that she was agitated; but there was a resolute gleam in her dark and gloomy eyes. I may remark that many people mentioned that she was extremely good-looking at that moment. She spoke softly but clearly, so that she was heard all over the court. She expressed herself with composure, or at least tried to appear composed. The President began his examination discreetly and very respectfully, as though afraid to touch on "certain chords," and showing consideration for her great unhappiness. But in answer to one of the first questions Katerina Ivanovna replied firmly that she had been formerly betrothed to the defendant "until he left me of his own accord . . ." she added quietly. When they asked her about the three thousand she had entrusted to Mitya to post to her relations, she said firmly, "I didn't give him the money simply to send it off. I felt at the time that he was in great need of money. . . . I gave him the three thousand on the understanding that he would post it within the month if he cared to. There was no need for him to worry himself about that debt afterwards."

I will not repeat all the questions asked her and all her answers in detail. I will only give the substance of her evidence.

"I was firmly convinced that he would send off that sum as soon as he got money from his father," she went on. "I have never doubted his disinterestedness and his honesty . . . his scrupulous honesty . . . in money matters. He felt quite certain that he would receive the money from his father, and spoke to me several times about it. I knew he had a feud with his father and have always believed that he had been unfairly treated by his father. I don't remember any threat by him against his father. He certainly said nothing, made no such threat before me. If he had come to me at that time, I should have at once relieved his anxiety about those unlucky three thousand rubles, but he had given up coming to see me . . . and I myself was put in such a position . . . that I could not invite him. . . . And I had no right, indeed, to be exacting as to that money," she added suddenly, and there was a ring of resolution in her voice. "I was once indebted to him for assistance in money for more than three thousand, and I took it, although I could not at that time foresee that I would ever be in a position to repay my debt."

There was a note of defiance in her voice. It was then Fetyukovich began his cross-examination.

"Did that take place not here, but at the beginning of your acquaintance?" Fetyukovich suggested cautiously, feeling his way, instantly scenting something favorable. I must mention in parenthesis that, though Fetyukovich had been brought from Petersburg partly at the instance of Katerina Ivanovna herself, he knew nothing about the episode of the five thousand rubles given her by Mitya, and of her "bowing to the ground to him." She concealed this from him and said nothing about it! And that was strange. It may be pretty certainly assumed that she herself did not know till the very last minute whether she would speak of that episode in the court, and waited for the inspiration of the moment.

No, I can never forget those moments! She began telling her story. She told *everything*, the whole episode that Mitya had told Alyosha, and her "bowing to the ground," and her reason. She told about her father and her going to Mitya, and did not in one word, in a single hint, suggest that Mitya had himself, through her sister, proposed they should "send him Katerina Ivanovna" to fetch the money. She generously concealed that and was not ashamed to make it appear as though she had of her own impulse run to the young officer, relying on something . . . to beg him for the money. It was something tremendous! I turned cold and trembled as I listened. The hall was hushed, trying to catch each word. It was something unexampled. Even from such a self-willed and contemptuously proud girl as she was, such an extremely frank avowal, such sacrifice, such self-immolation, seemed incredible. And for what, for whom? To save the man who had deceived and insulted her and to help, in however small a degree, in saving him, by creating a strong impression in his favor. And, indeed, the figure of the young officer who, with a respectful bow to the innocent girl, handed her his last five thousand rubles—all he had in the world— was thrown into a very sympathetic and attractive light, but . . . I had a painful misgiving at heart! I felt that calumny might come of it later (and it did, in fact, it did). It was repeated all over the town afterwards with spiteful laughter that the story was perhaps not quite complete—that is, in the statement that the officer had let the young lady depart "with nothing but a respectful bow." It was hinted that something was here omitted. "And even if nothing had been omitted, if this were the whole story," the most highly respected of our ladies maintained, "even then it's very doubtful whether it was creditable for a young girl to behave in that way, even for the sake of saving her father." And can Katerina Ivanovna, with her intelligence, her morbid sensitiveness, have failed to understand that people would talk like that? She must have understood it, yet she made up her mind to tell everything. Of course, all these nasty little suspicions as to the truth of her story only arose afterwards and at the first moment all were deeply impressed by it. As for the judges and the lawyers, they listened in reverent, almost shamefaced silence to Katerina Ivanovna. The prosecutor did not venture upon even one question on the subject. Fetyukovich made a low bow to her. Oh, he was almost triumphant! Much ground had been gained. For a man to give his last five thousand on a generous impulse and then for the same man to murder his father at night for the sake of robbing him of three thousand—the idea seemed too incongruous. Fetyukovich felt that now the charge of robbery, at least, was as good as disproved. "The case" was thrown into quite a different light. There was a wave of sympathy for Mitya. As for him . . . I was told that once or twice, while Katerina Ivanovna was giving her evidence, he started to jump up from his seat, sank back again, and hid his face in his hands. But when she had finished, he suddenly cried in a sobbing voice, stretching his hands out to her:

"Katya, why have you ruined me?"

And his sobs were audible all over the court. But he instantly restrained himself, and cried again:

"Now I am condemned!"

Then he sat rigid in his place, with his teeth clenched and his arms across his chest. Katerina Ivanovna remained in the court and sat down in her place. She was pale and sat with her eyes cast down. Those who were sitting near her declared that for a long time she shivered all over as though in a fever. Grushenka was called.

I am approaching the sudden catastrophe which was perhaps the final cause of Mitya's ruin. For I am convinced, so is everyone—all the lawyers said the same afterwards—that if the episode had not occurred, the prisoner would at least have been recommended to mercy. But of that later. A few words first about Grushenka.

She, too, was dressed entirely in black, with her magnificent black shawl on her shoulders. She walked to the witness stand with her smooth, noiseless tread, with the slightly swaying gait common in women of full figure. She looked steadily at the President, turning her eyes neither to the right nor to the left. To my thinking she was very good-looking at that moment, and not at all pale, as the ladies alleged afterwards. They declared, too, that she had a concentrated and spiteful expression. I believe that she was simply irritated and painfully conscious of the contemptuous and inquisitive eyes of our scandal-loving public. She was proud and could not stand contempt. She was one of those people who flare up, angry and eager to retaliate, at the mere suggestion of contempt. There was an element of timidity, too, of course, and inward shame at her own timidity, so it was not strange that her tone kept changing. At one moment it was angry, contemptuous and rough, and at another there was a sincere note of self-condemnation. Sometimes she spoke as though she were taking a desperate plunge; as though she felt, "I don't care what happens. I'll say it. . . ." Of her acquaintance with Fyodor Pavlovich, she remarked curtly, "That's all nonsense, and was it my fault that he would pester me?" But a minute later she added, "It was all my fault. I was laughing at them both—at the old man and at him, too—and I brought both of them to this. It was all on account of me it happened." Samsonov's name came up somehow. "That's nobody's business," she snapped at once, with a sort of insolent defiance. "He was my benefactor; he took me when I hadn't a shoe to my foot, when my family had turned me out." The President reminded her, though very politely, that she must answer the questions directly, without going off into irrelevant details. Grushenka crimsoned and her eyes flashed.

The envelope with the bills in it she had not seen, but had only heard from "that wicked wretch" that Fyodor Pavlovich had an envelope with bills for three thousand in it. "But that was all foolishness. I was only laughing. I wouldn't have gone to him for anything."

"To whom are you referring as 'that wicked wretch'?" inquired the prosecutor.

"The lackey, Smerdyakov, who murdered his master and hanged himself last night."

She was, of course, at once asked what ground she had for such a definite accusation; but it appeared that she, too, had no grounds for it.

"Dmitri Fyodorovich told me so himself; you can believe him. The woman who came between us has ruined him; she is the cause of it all, let me tell you." Grushenka added. She seemed to be quivering with hatred, and there was a vindictive note in her voice.

She was again asked to whom she was referring.

"The young lady, Katerina Ivanovna there. She sent for me, offered me chocolate, tried to fascinate me. There's not much true shame about her, I can tell you that . . ."

At this point the President checked her sternly, begging her to moderate her language. But the jealous woman's heart was burning in her, and she did not care what she did.

"During the arrest at Mokroe," the prosecutor asked, recollecting, "everyone saw and heard you run out of the next room and cry out: 'It's all my fault. We'll go to Siberia together!' So you already believed him to have murdered his father?"

"I don't remember what I felt at the time," answered Grushenka. "Everyone was crying out that he had killed his father, and I felt that it was my fault, that it was on my account he had murdered him. But when he said he wasn't guilty, I believed him at once, and I believe him now and always shall believe him. He is not the man to tell a lie."

Fetyukovich began his cross-examination. I remember that among other things he asked about Rakitin and the twenty-five rubles "you paid him for bringing Alexey Fyodorovich Karamazov to see you."

"There was nothing strange about his taking the money," sneered Grushenka, with angry contempt. "He was always coming to me for money: he used to get thirty rubles a month at least out of me, chiefly for luxuries: he had enough to keep him without my help."

"What led you to be so liberal to Mr. Rakitin?" Fetyukovich asked, in spite of an uneasy movement on the part of the President.

"Why, he is my cousin. His mother was my mother's sister. But he's always begged me not to tell anyone here of it, he is so dreadfully ashamed of me."

This new fact was a complete surprise to everyone; no one in the town nor in the monastery, not even Mitya, knew of it. I was told that Rakitin turned purple with shame where he sat. Grushenka had somehow heard before she came into the court that he had given evidence against Mitya, and so she was angry. The whole effect on the public, of Rakitin's speech, of his noble sentiments, of his attacks upon serfdom and the political disorder of Russia, was this time cancelled and destroyed. Fetyukovich was satisfied: it was another godsend. Grushenka's cross-examination did not last long and, of course, there could be nothing particularly new in her evidence. She left a very disagreeable impression on the public; hundreds of contemptuous eyes were fixed upon her, as she finished giving her evidence and sat down again in the court, at a good distance from Katerina Ivanovna. Mitya was silent throughout her evidence. He sat as though turned to stone, with his eyes fixed on the ground.

Ivan Fyodorovich was called to give evidence.

Chapter V

A Sudden Catastrophe

I may note that he had been called before Alyosha. But the usher of the court announced to the President that, owing to an attack of illness or some sort of fit, the witness could not appear at the moment, but was ready to give his evidence as soon as he recovered. But no one seemed to have heard it and it only came out later. His entrance was for the first moment almost unnoticed. The principal witnesses, especially the two rival ladies, had already been questioned. Curiosity was satisfied for the time; the public was feeling almost fatigued. Several more witnesses were still to be heard, who probably had little information to give after all that had been given. Time was passing. Ivan Fyodorovich walked up with extraordinary slowness, looking at no one, and with his head bowed, as though plunged in gloomy thought. He was irreproachably dressed, but his face made a painful impression, on me at least: there was an earthy look in it, a look like a dying man's. His eyes were lusterless; he raised them and looked slowly round the court. Alyosha jumped up from his seat and moaned "Ah!" I remember that, but it was hardly noticed.

The President began by informing him that he was a witness not on oath, that he might answer or refuse to answer, but that, of course, he must bear witness according to his conscience, and so on and so on. Ivan Fyodorovich listened and looked at him blankly, but his face gradually relaxed into a smile, and as soon as the President, looking at him in astonishment, finished, he laughed outright.

"Well, and what else?" he asked in a loud voice.

There was a hush in the court; there was a feeling of something strange. The President showed signs of uneasiness.

"You . . . are perhaps still unwell?" he began, looking everywhere for the bailiff.

"Don't trouble yourself, your excellency, I am well enough and can tell you something interesting," Ivan Fyodorovich answered with sudden calmness and respectfulness.

"You have some special communication to make?" the President went on, still mistrustfully.

Ivan Fyodorovich looked down, waited a few seconds and, raising his head, answered, almost stammering:

"No . . . I haven't. I have nothing particular."

They began asking him questions. He answered, as it were reluctantly, with extreme brevity, with a sort of disgust which grew more and more marked, though he answered rationally. To many questions he answered that he did not know. He knew nothing of his father's money relations with Dmitri Fyodorovich. "I wasn't interested in the subject," he added. Threats to murder his father he had heard from the defendant. Of the money in the envelope he had heard from Smerdyakov.

"The same thing over and over again," he interrupted suddenly, with a look of weariness. "I have nothing particular to tell the court."

"I see you are unwell and understand your feelings," the President began.

He turned to the prosecutor and the counsel for the defense to invite them to examine the witness, if necessary, when Ivan Fyodorovich suddenly asked in an exhausted voice:

"Let me go, your excellency, I feel very ill."

And with these words, without waiting for permission, he turned to walk out of the court. But after taking four steps he stood still, as though he had reached a decision, smiled slowly, and went back.

"I am like the peasant girl, your excellency . . . you know. How does it go? 'I'll stand up if I like, and I won't if I don't.'[1] They were trying to put on her sarafan[2] to take her to church to be married, and she said, 'I'll stand up if I like, and I won't if I don't.' . . . It's in some book about our folklore."

"What do you mean by that?" the President asked severely.

"Why, this," Ivan Fyodorovich suddenly pulled out a roll of bills. "Here's the money . . . the bills that lay in that envelope" (he nodded towards the table on which lay the material evidence) "for the sake of which father was murdered. Where shall I put them? Mr. Bailiff, take them."

The bailiff took the whole roll and handed it to the President.

"How could this money have come into your possession if it is the same money?" the President asked wonderingly.

"I got them from Smerdyakov, from the murderer, yesterday. . . . I was with him just before he hanged himself. It was he, not my brother, who killed our father. He murdered him and I incited him to do it . . . Who doesn't desire his father's death?"

"Are you in your right mind?" broke involuntarily from the President.

"I should think I am in my right mind . . . in the same nasty mind as you . . . and as all these . . . ugly faces." He turned suddenly to the audience. "My father has been murdered and they pretend they are horrified,"

---

1. Many Russian wedding songs contain such themes and phrases, through which the bride declares her independence. A song with similar phrases had been published in a collection of Russian songs in Saint Petersburg in 1839.
2. A long dress worn by Russian peasant women.

he snarled, with furious contempt. "They keep up the sham with one another. Liars! They all desire the death of their fathers. One viper devours another. . . . If there hadn't been a parricide, they'd have been angry and gone home ill-humored. It's a spectacle they want! 'Bread and Circuses.'[3] Though I am one to talk! Have you any water? Give me a drink for Christ's sake!" He suddenly clutched his head.

The bailiff at once approached him. Alyosha jumped up and cried, "He is ill. Don't believe him: he has brain fever." Katerina Ivanovna rose impulsively from her seat and, rigid with horror, gazed at Ivan Fyodorovich. Mitya stood up and greedily looked at his brother and listened to him with a wild, twisted smile.

"Don't disturb yourselves. I am not mad, I am only a murderer," Ivan began again. "You can't expect eloquence from a murderer," he added suddenly for some reason and laughed twistedly.

The prosecutor bent over to the President in obvious dismay. The two other judges communicated in agitated whispers. Fetyukovich pricked up his ears as he listened: the hall was hushed in expectation. The President seemed suddenly to recollect himself.

"Witness, your words are incomprehensible and impossible here. Calm yourself, if you can, and tell your story . . . if you really have something to tell. How can you confirm your statement . . . if indeed you are not delirious?"

"That's just it. I have no proof. That cur Smerdyakov won't send you proofs from the other world . . . in an envelope. You think of nothing but envelopes—one is enough. I have no witnesses . . . except one, perhaps," he smiled thoughtfully.

"Who is your witness?"

"He has a tail, your excellency, and that would be irregular! *Le diable n' existe point!*[4] Don't pay attention: he is a paltry, pitiful devil," he added suddenly. He ceased laughing and spoke as it were, confidentially. "He is here somewhere, no doubt—under that table with the material evidence on it, perhaps. Where should he sit if not there? You see, listen to me. I told him I don't want to keep quiet, and he talked about the geological cataclysm . . . idiocy! Come, release the monster . . . he's been singing a hymn. That's because his heart is light! It's like a drunken man in the street bawling how 'Vanka went to Petersburg,' and I would give a quadrillion quadrillions for two seconds of joy. You don't know me! Oh, how stupid all this business is! Come, take me instead of him! I didn't come for nothing. . . . Why, why is everything so stupid? . . ."

And he began slowly, and as it were reflectively, looking round him again. But the court was all excitement by now. Alyosha rushed towards him, but the bailiff had already siezed Ivan Fyodorovich by the arm.

"What are you doing?" he cried, staring into the man's face, and suddenly seizing him by the shoulders, he flung him violently to the floor. But the police were on the spot and he was seized. He screamed furiously. And

---

3. The Caesars provided bread and circuses (*panem et circenses*) to the people of Imperial Rome to keep them content. The juxtaposition of bread and water here is significant, signaling the distinction between materialism (bread) and the "living water" of Christian faith; see, for example, John 4.10.
4. "The devil doesn't exist at all!" (French).

all the time he was being removed, he yelled and screamed something incoherent.

The whole court was thrown into confusion. I don't remember everything as it happened, I was excited myself and could not follow. I only know that afterwards, when everything was quiet again and everyone understood what had happened, the bailiff came in for a reprimand, though he very reasonably explained that the witness had been quite well, that the doctor had seen him an hour ago, when he had a slight attack of giddiness, but that, until he had come into the court, he had talked quite consecutively, so that nothing could have been foreseen—that he had, in fact, insisted on giving evidence. But before everyone had completely regained their composure and recovered from this scene, it was followed by another. Katerina Ivanovna had an attack of hysterics. She sobbed, shrieking loudly, but refused to leave the court, struggled, and besought them not to remove her. Suddenly she cried to the President:

"There is more evidence I must give at once . . . at once! Here is a document, a letter . . . take it, read it quickly, quickly! It's a letter from that monster . . . that man there, there!" she pointed to Mitya. "It was he who killed his father, you will see that directly. He wrote to me how he would kill his father! But the other one is ill, he is ill, he is delirious! I have seen that he is delirious for three days!" She kept crying out, beside herself.

The bailiff took the document she held out to the President, and she, dropping into her chair, hiding her face in her hands, began convulsively and noiselessly sobbing, shaking all over, and stifling every sound for fear she should be ejected from the court. The document she had handed up was that letter Mitya had written at the Metropolis tavern, which Ivan Fyodorovich had spoken of as a "mathematical proof." Alas! its mathematical conclusiveness was recognized, and had it not been for that letter, Mitya might have escaped his doom or, at least, that doom would have been less terrible. It was, I repeat, difficult to notice every detail. What followed is still confused in my mind. The President must, I suppose, have at once passed on the document to the judges, the jury, and the lawyers on both sides. I only remember how they began examining the witness. On being gently asked by the President whether she had recovered sufficiently, Katerina Ivanovna exclaimed impetuously:

"I am ready, I am ready! I am quite equal to answering you," she added, evidently still afraid that she would somehow be prevented from giving evidence. She was asked to explain in detail what this letter was and under what circumstances she received it.

"I received it the day before the crime was committed, but he wrote it the day before that, at the tavern—that is, two days before he committed the crime. Look, it is written on some sort of bill!" she shouted breathlessly. "He hated me at the time, because he had behaved contemptibly and was running after that creature . . . and because he owed me that three thousand. . . . Oh! he was humiliated by that three thousand on account of his own baseness! This is how it happened about that three thousand. I beg you, I beseech you, to hear me. Three weeks before he murdered his father, he came to me one morning. I knew he was in need of money, and what he wanted it for. Yes, yes—to win that creature and carry her off. I knew then that he had been false to me and meant to abandon me, and it was I, I, who gave him that money, who offered it to him on the pretext of his sending it to my sister in Moscow. And as I gave it to him, I looked him in the face and said that he could send it when he liked, 'in a month's time would do.' How, how could he have failed to understand that I was practically telling him to his face, 'You want money to be false to me with your creature, so here's the money for you. I give it to you myself. Take it, if you have so little honor as to take it!' I wanted to prove what he was, and what happened? He took it, he took it, and squandered it with that creature in one night. . . . But he knew, he knew that I knew all about it. I assure you he understood, too, that I gave him that money to test him, to see whether he was so lost to all sense of honor as to take it from me. I looked into his eyes and he looked into mine, and he understood it all and he took it—he carried off my money!"

"That's true, Katya," Mitya roared suddenly, "I looked into your eyes and I knew that you were dishonoring me, and yet I took your money. Despise me as a scoundrel, despise me, all of you! I've deserved it!"

"Defendant," cried the President, "another word and I will order you to be removed."

"That money was a torment to him," Katya went on with impulsive haste. "He wanted to repay it to me. He wanted to, that's true; but he needed money for that creature, too. So he murdered his father, but he didn't repay me, and went off with her to that village where he was arrested. There, again, he squandered the money he had stolen after the murder of his father. And a day before the murder he wrote me this letter. He was drunk when he wrote it. I saw it at once, at the time. He wrote it from spite, and feeling certain, positively certain, that I would never show it to anyone, even if he did kill him, or else he wouldn't have written it. For he knew I wouldn't want to revenge myself and ruin him! But read it, read it attentively—more attentively, please—and you will see that he had described it all in his letter, all beforehand, how he would kill his father and where his money was kept. Look, please, don't overlook that, there's one phrase there, 'I shall kill him as soon as Ivan has gone away.' So he thought it all out beforehand how he would kill him," Katerina Ivanovna pointed out to the court with venomous and malignant triumph. Oh! it was clear she had studied every line of that letter and detected every meaning underlining it. "If he hadn't been drunk, he wouldn't have written to me; but, look, everything is written there beforehand, just as he committed the murder after. The whole scenario!" she exclaimed frantically.

She was reckless now of all consequences to herself, though, no doubt, she had foreseen them even a month ago, for even then, perhaps, shaking with anger, she had pondered whether to show it at the trial or not. Now she had taken the fatal plunge. I remember that the letter was read aloud by the clerk, right afterwards, I believe. It made an overwhelming impression. They asked Mitya whether he admitted having written the letter.

"It's mine, mine!" cried Mitya. "I wouldn't have written it, if I hadn't been drunk! . . . We've hated each other for many things, Katya, but I swear, I swear I loved you even while I hated you, and you didn't love me!"

He sank back on his seat, wringing his hands in despair. The prosecutor and counsel for the defense began cross-examining her, chiefly to ascertain what had induced her to conceal such a document and to give her evidence in quite a different tone and spirit just before.

"Yes, yes. I was telling lies just now, I was lying against my honor and my conscience, but I wanted to save him, for he has hated and despised me so!" Katya shouted like a madwoman. "Oh, he has despised me horribly, he has always despised me, and do you know, he has despised me from the very moment that I bowed down to him for that money. I saw that. . . . I felt it at once at the time, but for a long time I wouldn't believe it. How often I have read it in his eyes 'you came of your own will, though.' Oh, he didn't understand, he had no idea why I ran to him, he can suspect nothing but baseness, he judged me by himself, he thought everyone was like himself!" Katya hissed furiously, in a perfect frenzy. "And he only wanted to marry me because I'd inherited a fortune, because of that, because of that! I always suspected it was because of that! Oh, he is a brute! He was always convinced that I would be trembling with shame all my life before him, because I went to him then, and that he had a right to despise me forever for it, and so to be superior to me—that's why he wanted to marry me! That's so, that's all so! I tried to conquer him by my love—a love that knew no bounds. I even tried to forgive his faithlessness; but he understood nothing, nothing! How could he understand indeed? He is a monster! I only received that letter the next evening: it was brought me from the tavern—and only that morning, only that morning I wanted to forgive him everything, everything—even his treachery!"

The President and the prosecutor, of course, tried to calm her. I can't help thinking that they felt ashamed of taking advantage of her hysteria and of listening to such avowals. I remember hearing them say to her, "We understand how hard it is for you; be sure we are able to feel for you," and so on, and so on. And yet they dragged the evidence out of the raving, hysterical woman. She described at last with extraordinary clearness, which is so often seen, though only for a moment, in such overwrought states, how Ivan Fyodorovich had been nearly driven out of his mind during the last two months trying to save "the monster and murderer," his brother.

"He tortured himself," she exclaimed, "he was always trying to minimize his brother's guilt and confessing to me that he, too, had never loved his father, and perhaps desired his death himself. Oh, he has a deep, deep conscience! He tormented himself with his conscience! He told me everything, everything! He came every day and talked to me as his only friend. I have the honor to be his only friend!" she cried suddenly with a sort of defiance, and her eyes flashed. "He had been twice to see Smerdyakov. One day he came to me and said, 'If it was not my brother, but Smerdyakov committed the murder' (for the legend was circulating everywhere that Smerdyakov had done it) 'perhaps I too am guilty, for Smerdyakov knew I didn't like my father and perhaps believed that I desired my father's death.' Then I brought out that letter and showed it him. He was entirely convinced that his brother had done it, and he was overwhelmed by it. He couldn't endure the thought that his own brother was a parricide! Only a week ago I saw that it was making him ill. During the last few days he has talked incoherently in my presence. I saw his mind was giving way. He walked about, raving; he was seen muttering in the streets. The doctor from Moscow, at my request, examined him the day before yesterday and told me that he was on the eve of brain fever—and all on his account, on account of this monster! And last night he learned that Smerdyakov was dead! It was such a shock that it drove him out of his mind . . . and all through this monster, all for the sake of saving the monster!"

Oh, of course, such an outpouring, such an avowal is only possible once in a lifetime—at the hour of death, for instance, on the way to the scaffold. But it was in Katya's character, and it was such a moment in her life. It was the same impetuous Katya who had thrown herself on the mercy of a young profligate to save her father; the same Katya who had just before, in her pride and chastity, sacrificed herself and her maidenly modesty before all these people, telling of Mitya's generous conduct, in the hope of softening his fate a little. And now, again, she sacrificed herself but this time it was for another, and perhaps only now—perhaps only at this moment—she felt and knew how dear that other was to her! She had sacrificed herself in terror for him, conceiving all of a sudden that he had ruined himself by his confession that it was he who had committed the murder, not his brother, she had sacrificed herself to save him, to save his good name, his reputation! And yet one terrible doubt occurred to one— was she lying in her description of her former relations with Mitya?—that was the question. No, she had not intentionally slandered him when she cried that Mitya despised her for her bowing down to him! She believed it herself. She had been firmly convinced, perhaps ever since that bow, that the simple-hearted Mitya, who even then adored her, was laughing at her and despising her. She had loved him with an hysterical, lacerated love only from pride, from wounded pride, and that love was not like love, but more like revenge. Oh! perhaps that lacerated love would have grown into real love, perhaps Katya longed for nothing more than that, but Mitya's faithlessness had wounded her to the bottom of her heart, and her heart could not forgive him. The moment of revenge had come upon her suddenly, and all that had been accumulating so long and so painfully in the offended woman's breast burst out all at once and unexpectedly. She betrayed Mitya, but she betrayed herself, too. And no sooner had she given full expression to her feelings than the tension of course was over and she was overwhelmed with shame. Hysterics began again: she fell on the floor, sobbing and screaming. She was carried out. At that moment Grushenka, with a wail, rushed towards Mitya before they had time to prevent her.

"Mitya," she wailed, "your serpent has destroyed you! There, she has shown you what she is!" she shouted to the judges, shaking with anger. At a signal from the President they seized her and tried to remove her from the court. She wouldn't allow it. She fought and struggled to get back to Mitya. Mitya uttered a cry and struggled to get to her. He was overpowered.

Yes, I think the ladies who came to see the spectacle must have been satisfied—the spectacle had been a rich one. Then I remember the Moscow doctor appeared on the scene. I believe the President had previously sent the bailiff to arrange for medical aid for Ivan Fyodorovich. The doctor announced to the court that the sick man was suffering from a dangerous attack of brain fever and that he must be at once removed. In answer to questions from the prosecutor and the counsel for the defense he said that the patient had come to him of his own accord the day before yesterday and that he had warned him that he had such an attack coming on, but he had not consented to be looked after. "He was certainly not in a normal state of mind: he told me himself that he saw visions when he was awake, that he met several persons in the street, who were dead, and that Satan visited him every evening," said the doctor, in conclusion. Having given his evidence, the celebrated doctor withdrew. The letter produced by Katerina Ivanovna was added to the material proofs. After some deliberation, the judges decided to proceed with the trial and to enter both the unexpected pieces of evidence (given by Ivan Fyodorovich and Katerina Ivanovna) in the deposition.

But I will not detail the evidence of the other witnesses, who only repeated and confirmed what had been said before, though all with their characteristic peculiarities. I repeat, all was brought together in the prosecutor's speech, which I shall quote immediately. Everyone was excited, everyone was electrified by the late catastrophe, and all were awaiting the speeches for the prosecution and the defense with intense impatience. Fetyukovich was obviously shaken by Katerina Ivanovna's evidence. But the prosecutor was triumphant. When all the evidence had been taken, the court was adjourned for almost an hour. I believe it was just eight o'clock when the President returned to his seat and our prosecutor, Ippolit Kirillovich, began his speech.

Chapter VI

The Prosecutor's Speech. Sketches of Character

Ippolit Kirillovich began his speech, trembling with nervousness, with cold sweat on his forehead, feeling hot and cold all over by turns. He described this himself afterwards. He regarded this speech as his *chef d'œuvre*,[5] the *chef d'œuvre* of his whole life, as his swan song. He died, it is true, nine months later of rapid consumption, so that he had the right, as it turned out, to compare himself to a swan singing his last song if he had a premonition of his death. He had put his whole heart and all the brain he had into that speech. And poor Ippolit Kirillovich unexpectedly revealed that at least some feeling for the public welfare and "the eternal question" lay concealed in him. Where his speech really excelled was in its sincerity. He genuinely believed in the defendant's guilt; he was accusing him not as an official duty only, and in calling for vengeance he quivered with a genuine passion "for the security of society." Even the ladies in the audience, though they remained hostile to Ippolit Kirillovich, admitted that he made an extraordinary impression on them. He began in a shaky, breaking voice, but it soon gained strength and filled the court to the end of his speech. But as soon as he had finished, he almost fainted.

"Gentlemen of the jury," began the prosecutor, "this case has made a stir throughout Russia. But what is there to wonder at, what is there so peculiarly horrifying in it for us? Particularly for us? We are so accustomed to such crimes! That's what's so horrible, that such dark deeds have ceased to horrify us. What ought to horrify us is that we are so accustomed to it, and not this or that isolated crime. What are the causes of our indifference, our lukewarm attitude to such deeds, to such signs of the

---

5. "Masterpiece" (French).

times, ominous of an unenviable future? Is it our cynicism, is it the premature exhaustion of intellect and imagination in a society that is sinking
into decay, in spite of its youth? Is it that our moral principles are shattered to their foundations, or is it, perhaps, a complete lack of such principles among us? I cannot answer such questions; nevertheless they are
disturbing, and every citizen not only should, but must, suffer through
them. Our newborn and still timid press has done good service to the public already, for without it we would never have heard in some detail, at
least, of the horrors of unbridled violence and moral degradation which
are continually made known by the press, not merely to those who attend
the new jury courts established in the present reign,[6] but to everyone. And
what do we read almost daily? Of things beside which the present case
grows pale, and seems almost commonplace. But what is most important
is that the majority of our national crimes of violence bear witness to some
general, some widespread evil, now so general among us that it is difficult
to contend against it. One day we see a brilliant young officer of high
society, at the very outset of his life and career, in a cowardly underhand
way, without a pang of conscience, murdering an official who had once
been his benefactor, and the servant girl, to steal his own IOU and what
ready money he could find on him; 'it will come in handy for my pleasures
in the fashionable world and for my career in the future.'[7] After murdering
them, he puts pillows under the head of each of his victims; he goes away.
Next, a young hero decorated for bravery kills the mother of his chief and
benefactor, on the highway, like a robber, and to urge his companions
to join him he asserts that 'she loves him like a son, and so will follow all
his directions and take no precautions.' Granted that he is a monster, yet
I dare not say in these days that he is a unique monster. Another man will
not commit the murder, but will feel and think just like him, and is just as
dishonorable as he in soul. In silence, alone with his conscience, he asks
himself perhaps: 'What is honor, and isn't the condemnation of bloodshed
a prejudice?' Perhaps people will cry out against me that I am morbid,
hysterical, that it is a monstrous slander, that I am exaggerating, that I am
delirious. Let them say so—and heavens! I would be the first to rejoice if
it were so! Oh, don't believe me, think of me as morbid, but remember my
words; if only a tenth, if only a twentieth part of what I say is true—even
so it's awful! Look, gentlemen, look how our young people commit suicide,
without asking themselves Hamlet's question what there is beyond, without a sign of such a question, as though all that relates to the soul and to
what awaits us beyond the grave had long been erased in their minds and
buried under the sands.[8] Look, finally, at our vice, at our sensualists.
Fyodor Pavlovich, the luckless victim in the present case, was almost an
innocent babe compared with many of them. And yet we all knew him, 'he
lived among us!'[9] . . . Yes, one day perhaps the leading intellects of Russia
and of Europe will study the psychology of Russian crime, for the subject

---

6. The Judicial Reforms of 1864 implemented public trial by jury in Russia. See also p. 20.
7. Ippolit Kirillovich refers to the case of one Karl von Landsberg, who borrowed a great deal of
   money and then killed his creditor when he was unable to repay the loan. His trial took place
   in July 1879, and the case was extensively reported in *The Voice*.
8. See Hamlet's monologue in III.1. Dostoevsky refers to Hamlet's contemplation of immortality
   in the January 1876 *Diary*, chapter 1, number 1, "In Place of a Foreword."
9. The first line of Pushkin's untitled 1834 poem dedicated to the Polish Romantic poet Adam
   Mickiewicz (1798–1855).

is worth it. But this study will come later, at leisure, when all the tragic topsyturvydom of today is further behind us, so that it's possible to examine it with more insight and more impartiality than people like myself, for example, can do. Now we are either horrified or pretend to be horrified, though we really gloat over the spectacle, and love strong and eccentric sensations which tickle our cynical, pampered idleness. Or, finally, like little children, we brush the dreadful ghosts away and hide our heads in the pillow so as to forget them in our sports and merriment. But yet we must one day begin life in sober earnest, we, too, must look at ourselves as a society; it's time we too tried to grasp at least something of our social position, or at least to make a beginning in that direction. A great writer of the last epoch, at the end of his greatest work, personifying Russia in a swift troika galloping to an unknown goal, exclaims, 'Oh, troika, birdlike troika, who invented thee!'[1] and adds, in proud ecstasy, that all the peoples of the world stand aside respectfully to make way for the recklessly galloping troika to pass. That may be, gentlemen, they may stand aside, respectfully or not, but in my poor opinion the great writer ended his book in this way either in a fit of childish and naïve optimism, or simply in fear of the censorship of the day. For if the troika were drawn by his heroes, Sobakevich, Nozdryov, Chichikov, it could reach no rational goal with such horses, no matter who might be driving it. And those were the horses of an older generation, ours are worse specimens still . . ."

At this point Ippolit Kirillovich's speech was interrupted by applause. The liberal significance of this simile was appreciated. The applause was, it's true, of brief duration, so that the President did not think it necessary to caution the public, and only looked severely in the direction of the offenders. But Ippolit Kirillovich was encouraged; he had never been applauded before! He had been all his life unable to get a hearing, and now he suddenly had an opportunity of securing the ear of all Russia.

"What after all, is this Karamazov family, which has suddenly gained such an unenviable notoriety throughout Russia?" he continued. "Perhaps I am exaggerating too much, but it seems to me that certain fundamental features of our educated class of today are reflected in this family picture—oh, not all the elements, and only, of course, in miniature, 'like the sun in a drop of water,'[2] but something is reflected nevertheless, something is expressed nevertheless. Think of that unhappy, depraved, unbridled old man, who has met with such a melancholy end, the 'father of a family.' Beginning life of noble birth, but as a poor little sponger, through an unexpected marriage he came into a small fortune. A petty knave, a toady and buffoon, a fairly good, though undeveloped, intelligence, he was, above all, a moneylender, who grew bolder with growing prosperity. His abject and servile characteristics disappeared, his malicious and sarcastic cynicism was all that remained, and his sensuality. On the spiritual side he was undeveloped, while his thirst for life was extraordinary. He saw nothing in life but sensual pleasure, and he brought his children up to be the same. He had no feelings for his duties as a father. He ridiculed those duties. He left his little children to the servants, and was glad to be

---

1. Ippolit Kirillovich refers to Gogol and his novel *Dead Souls*. A troika appears at the conclusion of *Dead Souls* as a metaphor for Russia.
2. A quotation from the poem "God" (1784) by the Russian poet Gavrila Derzhavin (1743–1816).

rid of them, forgot about them completely. The old man's maxim was *après moi le déluge*.[3] He was an example of everything that is opposed to civic duty, of the most complete and malignant individualism. 'The world may burn for all I care, so long as I am all right,' and he was all right; he was content, he was eager to go on living in the same way for another twenty or thirty years. He swindled his own son and spent his money, his maternal inheritance, on trying to get his own son's mistress from him. No, I don't intend to leave the defendant's defense altogether to my talented colleague from Petersburg. I will speak the truth myself, I can well understand what resentment he had heaped up in his son's heart against him. But enough, enough of that unhappy old man; he has had his reward.[4] Let us remember, however, that he was a father, and one of the typical fathers of today. Do I insult society in saying that he is typical of many modern fathers? Alas! many modern fathers only differ in not openly professing such cynicism as his, for they are better educated, more cultured, but their philosophy is essentially the same as his.[5] Perhaps I am a pessimist, but you have agreed to forgive me. Let us agree beforehand, you need not believe me, do not believe me but let me speak and do not believe me. Let me say what I have to say, however, and remember something of my words. But now for the children of this father, this head of a family. One of them is the defendant before us, all the rest of my speech will deal with him. Of the other two I will speak only cursorily. Of the other two, the elder is one of those modern young men of brilliant education and vigorous intellect, who has, however, lost all faith in everything. He has denied and already rejected much, too much in life, exactly like his father. We have all heard him, he was a welcome guest in local society. He never concealed his opinions, quite the contrary in fact, which justifies me in speaking rather openly of him now, of course, not as an individual, but as a member of the Karamazov family. Another personage closely connected with the case died here by his own hand last night at the edge of the town. I mean an afflicted idiot, formerly the servant, and possibly the illegitimate son of Fyodor Pavlovich, Smerdyakov. At the preliminary inquiry, he told me with hysterical tears how that young Karamazov, Ivan Fyodorovich, had horrified him by his spiritual audacity. 'Everything in the world is permitted according to him, and nothing must be forbidden in the future—that is what he always taught me.' I believe that idiot was driven out of his mind by this theory, though, of course, the epileptic attacks from which he suffered, and this terrible catastrophe that struck their house, have helped to unhinge his faculties. But that idiot dropped one very interesting observation, which would have done credit to a more intelligent observer, and that is, indeed, why I've mentioned it, 'If there is one of the sons that is like Fyodor Pavlovich in character, it is Ivan Fyodorovich.' With that remark I conclude my sketch of his character, feeling it indelicate to continue further. Oh, I don't want to draw any further conclusions and croak like a raven over the young man's future. We've seen today in this court that the direct force of truth lives in his young heart, that family feeling

---

3. "After me, the flood" (French), a saying attributed to Louis XIV of France.
4. An echo of Matthew 6.5, where Jesus speaks about "hypocrites": "Verily I say unto you, They have their reward."
5. Dostoevsky discusses modern Russian fathers extensively in his *Diary*; see for example the July/August 1877 issue.

has not been destroyed in him by lack of faith and cynicism, which has come to him rather by inheritance than by the exercise of independent thought. Then the third son. Oh, he is still a youth, devout and modest, in contradistinction to his elder brother's gloomy and destructive theory of life, seeking to cling, so to speak, to the 'ideas of the people,' or to what goes by that clever name in some theoretical circles of our thinking intellectual classes. He clung to the monastery, you see, and was within an ace of becoming a monk. He seems to me to have betrayed unconsciously, and so early, that timid despair which leads so many in our unhappy society, who dread cynicism and its corrupting influences, and mistakenly attribute all the mischief to European enlightenment, to return to their 'native soil,'[6] as they say, to the bosom, so to speak, of their mother earth, like frightened children, yearning to fall asleep on the withered bosom of their decrepit mother, and to sleep there forever, only to escape the horrors that terrify them. For my part I wish the excellent and gifted young man every success; I trust that his youthful idealism and impulse towards the ideas of the people may never degenerate, as often happens, on the moral side into gloomy mysticism, and on the political into blind chauvinism—two elements which are even a greater menace to Russia than the premature decay, due to misunderstanding and gratuitous adoption of European enlightenment, from which his elder brother is suffering."

Two or three people started to clap at the mention of chauvinism and mysticism. Ippolit Kirillovich had been, indeed, carried away by his own eloquence. All this had little to do with the case in hand, to say nothing of the fact of its being somewhat vague, but the indignant and consumptive man was overcome by the desire to express himself once in his life. People said afterwards that he was actuated by unworthy motives in his criticism of Ivan Fyodorovich, because the latter had on one or two occasions got the better of him in argument, and Ippolit Kirillovich, remembering it, tried now to take his revenge. But I don't know whether it was true. All this was only introductory, however, and the speech passed to more direct consideration of the case.

"But to come to the eldest son of the father of a contemporary family," Ippolit Kirillovich went on. "He is the defendant before us. We have his life and his deeds and his actions, too, before us; the fatal day has come and all has been brought to the surface, all has been disclosed. In contradistinction to his brothers' 'Europeanism' and 'the principles of the people,' he seems to represent Russia directly—oh, not all Russia, not all! God preserve us, if it were! Yes, here she is, our mother Russia, the very scent and smell of her. Oh, we are spontaneous, we are a marvelous mingling of good and evil, we are lovers of enlightenment and Schiller, yet we brawl in taverns and pluck out the beards of our boon companions. Oh, we, too, can be good and noble, but only when all goes well with us. What is more, we can be carried off our feet, positively carried off our feet by noble ideals, but only if they come of themselves, if they fall from heaven for us, if they need not be paid for. We dislike paying for anything, but we are very fond of receiving, and that's so with us in everything. Oh, give us

6. The term "native soil" refers to a movement initiated to some degree by Dostoevsky. In the early 1860s Dostoevsky, together with his brother Mikhail and collaborators at their journals *Time* and *Epoch*, articulated a vision of Russian culture which extolled the value of native institutions and the wisdom of the non-Westernized peasantry.

every possible good in life (we couldn't be content with less), and in particular put no obstacle in our way, and we will show that we, too, can be good and noble. We are not greedy, no, but we must have money, a great deal of money, and you will see how generously, with what scorn of filthy lucre, we will fling it all away in the reckless dissipation of one night. But if we do not get it, we will show what we are ready to do to get it when we are in great need of it. But all this later, let us take events in their chronological order. First, there is before us a poor abandoned child, running about the backyard 'without boots on his feet,' as our worthy and esteemed fellow citizen, of foreign origin, alas! expressed it just now. I repeat it again, I yield to no one the defense of the accused. I am here to prosecute him, but to defend him also. Yes, I, too, am human; I, too, can weigh the influence of home and childhood on the character. But the boy grows up, he becomes a youth, a young man, and becomes an officer; for a duel and other reckless conduct he is exiled to one of the remote frontier towns of our blessed Russia. There he led a wild life as an officer. And, of course, a big ship needs broad waters, he needs money, money before all things, and so after prolonged disputes he comes to a settlement with his father, and the last six thousand are sent to him. A letter is in existence in which he practically gives up his claim to the rest and settles his conflict with his father over the inheritance upon the payment of this six thousand. Then came his meeting with a young girl of lofty character and brilliant education. Oh, I do not venture to repeat the details; you have only just heard them. Honor, self-sacrifice were shown there, and I will be silent. The figure of the young officer, frivolous and profligate, doing homage to true nobility and to lofty ideal, was shown in a very sympathetic light before us. But the other side of the coin was unexpectedly turned to us immediately after in this very court. Again I will not venture to conjecture why it happened so, and will refrain from analysis, but there were causes. The same person, bathed in tears of long-concealed indignation, alleged that he, he of all men, had despised her for her action, which, though incautious, reckless perhaps, was still dictated by lofty and generous motives. He, he, the girl's betrothed, looked at her with that smile of mockery, which was more insufferable from him than from anyone. And knowing that he had already deceived her (he had deceived her, believing that she was bound to endure everything from him, even treachery), she intentionally offered him three thousand rubles, and clearly, too clearly, let him understand that she was offering him money to deceive her. 'Well, will you take it or not, are you so lost to shame?' was the dumb question in her scrutinizing eyes. He looked at her, saw clearly what was in her mind (he's admitted here before you that he understood it all), appropriated that three thousand unconditionally, and squandered it in two days with the new object of his affections. What are we to believe then? The first legend of the young officer sacrificing his last cent in a noble impulse of generosity and doing reverence to virtue, or the other side of the coin, which is so revolting? As a rule, between two extremes one has to find the mean, but in the present case this is not true. The probability is that in the first case he was genuinely noble, and in the second as genuinely base. And why? Because he was of the broad Karamazov character—that's just what I am leading up to—capable of combining the most incongruous contradictions, and simultaneously contemplating both abysses, the abyss above us, the abyss of the highest ideals, and the abyss below us, the abyss of the lowest and foulest degradation. Remember the brilliant remark made by a young observer who has observed the Karamazov family at close quarters, and profoundly—Mr. Rakitin: 'The sense of their own degradation is as essential to these reckless, unbridled natures as the sense of their lofty generosity.' And that's true, they continually and unceasingly need this unnatural mixture. Two extremes, two extremes, gentlemen, at the same moment, or they are miserable and dissatisfied and their existence is incomplete. They are wide, wide as mother Russia; they include everything and put up with everything. By the way, gentlemen of the jury, we've just touched upon that three thousand rubles, and I will venture to anticipate things a little. Can you conceive that a man like that, on receiving that sum and in such a way, at the price of such shame, such disgrace, such utter degradation, could have been capable that very day of setting apart half that sum, that very day, and sewing it up in a little bag, and would have had the firmness of character to carry it about with him for a whole month afterwards, in spite of every temptation and his extreme need of it! Neither in drunken debauchery in taverns, nor when he was flying into the country, trying to get from God knows whom, the money so essential to him to remove the object of his affections from being tempted by his rival, his father, did he bring himself to touch that little bag. Why, if only to avoid abandoning his mistress to the temptations of the rival of whom he was so jealous, he would have been certain to have opened that bag and to have stayed at home to keep constant watch over his beloved, and to await the moment when she would say to him at last 'I am yours,' and to fly with her far from their fatal present surroundings. But no, he did not touch his talisman, and what is the reason he gives for it? The chief reason, as I have just said, was that when she would say 'I am yours, take me where you will,' he might have the wherewithal to take her. But that first reason, in the defendant's own words, was of little weight beside the second. While I have that money on me, he said, I am a scoundrel, not a thief, for I can always go to my insulted betrothed, and, laying down half the sum I have fraudulently appropriated, I can always say to her, 'You see I've squandered half your money, and shown I am a weak and immoral man, and, if you like, a scoundrel' (I use the defendant's own expressions), 'but though I am a scoundrel, I am not a thief, for if I had been a thief, I wouldn't have brought you back this half of the money, but would have taken it as I did the other half!' A marvelous explanation of the fact! This frantic, but weak man, who could not resist the temptation of accepting the three thousand rubles at the price of such disgrace, this very man suddenly develops the most stoical firmness, and carries about thousands of rubles without daring to touch them. Does that fit in at all with the character we have analyzed? No, and I venture to tell you how the real Dmitri Karamazov would have behaved in such circumstances, if he really had brought himself to put away the money. At the first temptation—for instance, to entertain the woman with whom he had already squandered half the money—he would have unpicked his little bag and have taken out, let us say, first, one hundred rubles, for why should he have taken back precisely half the money, that is, fifteen hundred rubles; why not fourteen hundred? He could just as well have said then that he was a scoundrel and not a thief, because he brought back fourteen hundred rubles. Then another time he would have unpicked it again and taken out another hundred, and then a third, and then a fourth, and before the end of the month he would have taken the last bill but one, feeling that if he took back only a hundred it would answer the purpose, he would be a scoundrel but not a thief. I've spent twenty-nine hundred but at least I've brought one back, and a thief would have stolen it all. And finally, when he would spend the next to last bill, then he would have looked at this last bill, and have said to himself, 'It's really not worthwhile to give back one hundred; let's spend that, too!' That's how the real Dmitri Karamazov, as we know him, would have behaved. One cannot imagine anything more incongruous with the actual fact than this legend of the little bag. Nothing could be more inconceivable. But we shall return to that later."

After touching upon what had come out in the proceedings concerning the financial relations of father and son, and arguing again and again that it was utterly impossible, from the facts known, to determine who was in the wrong, Ippolit Kirillovich passed to the evidence of the medical experts in reference to Mitya's fixed idea about the three thousand owing him.

Chapter VII

A Historical Survey

"The medical experts have strived to convince us that the defendant is out of his mind and a maniac. I maintain that he is in his right mind, but that that is even worse, and that if he had not been, he might have behaved more intelligently. As for his being a maniac, that I would agree with, but only in one point, that very point the medical experts indicated, that is, his fixed idea about the three thousand rubles supposedly owed him by his father. Yet I think one might find a much simpler cause than his tendency to insanity. For my part I agree thoroughly with the young doctor who maintained that the defendant's mental faculties have always been and are normal, and that he has only been irritable and exasperated. That is just the point. The object of the defendant's continual and violent anger was not the sum itself; there was a special motive at the bottom of it. That motive is jealousy!" Here Ippolit Kirillovich described at length the defendant's fatal passion for Grushenka. He began from the moment when the defendant went to the "young person's" lodgings "to beat her"—"I use his own expression," the prosecutor explained—"but instead of beating her, he remained there, at her feet. That was the beginning of the passion. At the same time the defendant's father, too, was captivated by the same young person—an amazing and fatal coincidence, for they both lost their hearts to her simultaneously, though both had known and met her before. And she inspired in both of them the most violent, characteristically Karamazov passion. We have her own confession: 'I was laughing at both of them.' Yes, the sudden desire to make a jest of both of them came over her, formerly she didn't want to, but now the notion suddenly came to her mind, and she conquered both of them at once. The old man, who worshipped money, at once set aside three thousand rubles as a reward for one visit from her, but soon after that he was led to such a state that he would have been happy to lay his property and his name at her feet, if only she would become his lawful wife. We have good evidence of this. As for the defendant, the tragedy of his fate is evident; it is before us. But such was the young person's 'game.' The enchantress even gave the unhappy young man no hope, for hope, true hope, was withheld until the last moment, when he knelt before her, stretching out hands that were already stained with the blood of his father and rival. It was in that position that he was arrested. 'Send me to Siberia with him, I have brought him to this, I am most to blame,' the woman herself cried, in genuine remorse at the moment of his arrest. The talented young man, to whom I have referred already, Mr. Rakitin, who has undertaken to describe this trial, characterized this heroine in brief and impressive terms: 'She was disillusioned early in life, deceived and ruined by a betrothed, who seduced and abandoned her. She was left in poverty, cursed by her respectable family, and taken under the protection of a wealthy old man, whom she still, however, considers as her benefactor. There was perhaps much that was good in her young heart, but it was embittered too early. She grew calculating and heaped up money. She grew sarcastic and resentful against society.' After this sketch of her character it may well be understood that she might laugh at both of them simply from mischief, from malice. After a month of hopeless love and moral degradation, during which he betrayed his betrothed and appropriated money entrusted to his honor, the defendant was driven almost to frenzy, almost to madness by continual jealousy—and of whom? His father! And the worst of it was that the crazy old man was alluring and enticing the object of his affection by means of that very three thousand rubles, which the son looked upon as his own property, part of his inheritance from his mother, of which his father was cheating him. Yes, I admit it was hard to bear! It might well drive a man to madness. It was not the money, but the fact that this money was used with such revolting cynicism to ruin his happiness!"

Then the prosecutor went on to describe how the idea of murdering his father had entered the defendant's head, and illustrated his theory with facts.

"At first we only talked about it in taverns—we were talking about it all that month. Ah, we like being always surrounded with company, and we like to tell our companions everything, even our most diabolical and dangerous ideas; we like to share every thought with others at once, and expect, for some reason, that those we confide in will meet us with perfect sympathy, enter into all our troubles and anxieties, take our part and not oppose us in anything. If not, we fly into a rage and smash up everything in the tavern." (Then followed the anecdote about Captain Snegiryov.) "Those who saw and heard the defendant began to think at last that he might mean more than shouts and threats to his father, and that such a frenzy might turn threats into actions." (Here the prosecutor described the meeting of the family at the monastery, the conversations with Alyosha, and the horrible scene of violence when the defendant had rushed into his father's house just after dinner.)

"I cannot positively assert," the prosecutor continued, "that the defendant fully premeditated and intended to murder his father, before that incident. Yet the idea had several times presented itself to him, and he had deliberated on it—for that we have facts, witnesses, and his own words. I confess, gentlemen of the jury," he added, "that till today I have been uncertain whether to attribute to the defendant conscious premeditation of the crime that occurred to him. I was firmly convinced that he had frequently pictured the fatal moment beforehand, but had only pictured it, contemplating it as a possibility. He had not definitely considered when and how he might commit the crime. But I was only uncertain till today, till that fatal document was presented to the court just now by Miss Verkhovtseva. You yourselves heard that young lady's exclamation, 'it is the plan, the scenario of the murder!' That is how she defined that miserable, drunken letter of the unhappy defendant. And, in fact, from that letter we see that the whole fact of the murder was premeditated. It was written two days before, and so we know now for a fact that, forty-eight hours before the perpetration of his terrible design, the defendant swore that, if he could not get money next day, he would murder his father in order to take the envelope with the money from under his pillow, 'from the envelope with the pink ribbon, as soon as Ivan had left.' 'As soon as Ivan had gone away'—you hear that; so he had thought everything out, weighing every circumstance, and he carried it all out just as he had written it. The proof of premeditation is conclusive; the crime must have been committed for the sake of the money, that is stated clearly, that is written and signed. The defendant does not deny his signature. I shall be told he was drunk when he wrote it. But that does not diminish the value of the letter, quite the contrary; he wrote when drunk what he had planned when sober. Had he not planned it when sober, he would not have written it when drunk. I shall be asked: Then why did he talk about it in taverns? A man who *premeditates* such a crime is silent and keeps it to himself. Yes, but he talked about it before he had formed a plan and premeditated it, when he had only the desire, only the impulse to it was ripening. Afterwards he talked less about it. On the evening he wrote that letter at the Metropolis tavern, contrary to his custom he was silent, though he had been drinking. He did not play billiards, he sat in a corner, talked to no one. He did indeed turn a local shopman out of his seat, but that was done almost unconsciously, out of habit, because he could never enter a tavern without making a disturbance. It is true that after he had made the final decision, he must have felt apprehensive that he had talked too much about his design beforehand, and that this might lead to his arrest and prosecution afterwards, when he had accomplished his design. But there was nothing for it; he could not take his words back, but his luck had served him before, it would serve him again. We believed in our lucky star, you know! I must confess, too, that he did a great deal to avoid the fatal catastrophe. 'Tomorrow I shall try and borrow the money from everyone,' as he writes in his peculiar language, 'and if they won't give it to me, there will be bloodshed.' Again written while drunk and again carried out while sober, just as it was set down."

Here Ippolit Kirillovich passed to a detailed description of all Mitya's efforts to borrow the money in order to avoid the crime. He described his visit to Samsonov, his journey to Lyagavy, all of which were attested to. "Harassed, jeered at, hungry, after selling his watch to pay for the journey (though he tells us he had fifteen hundred rubles on him—a likely story), tortured by jealousy at having left the object of his affections in the town, suspecting that she would go to Fyodor Pavlovich in his absence, he returned at last to the town, to find, to his joy, that she had not been near his father. He accompanied her himself to her protector. (Strange to say, he doesn't seem to have been jealous of Samsonov, which is psychologically interesting.) Then he hastens back to his ambush in the back gardens, and there learns that Smerdyakov is in a fit, that the other servant is ill—the coast is clear and he knows the 'signals'—what a temptation! Still he resists it; he goes off to a lady who has for some time been residing in the town, and who is highly esteemed among us, Madame Khokhlakova. That lady, who had long watched his career with compassion, gave him the most judicious advice, to give up his dissipated life, his unseemly love affair, the waste of his youth and vigor in taverns and debauchery, and to set off to Siberia to the gold mines: 'that would be an outlet for your turbulent energies, your romantic character, your thirst for adventure.'" After describing the result of this conversation and the moment when the defendant learnt that Grushenka had not remained at Samsonov's, the sudden frenzy of the luckless man, worn out with jealousy and nervous exhaustion, at the thought that she had deceived him and was now with his father, Ippolit Kirillovich concluded by dwelling upon the fatal influence of chance. "Had the maid told him that her mistress was at Mokroe with her former lover, nothing would have happened. But she lost her head, she could only swear and protest her ignorance, and if the defendant did not kill her on the spot, it was only because he flew in pursuit of his false mistress. But note, frantic as he was, he took with him a brass pestle. Why that? Why not some other weapon? But since he had been contemplating his plan and preparing himself for it for a whole month, he would snatch up anything like a weapon that caught his eye. He had realized for a month past that any object of the kind would serve as a weapon, so he instantly, without hesitation, recognized that it would serve his purpose. So it was by no means unconsciously, by no means involuntarily, that he snatched up that fatal pestle. And then we find him in his father's garden—the coast is clear, there are not witnesses, darkness and jealousy. The suspicion that she was there, with him, with his rival, in his arms, and perhaps laughing at him at that moment—took his breath away. And it was not mere suspicion, why talk of suspicion—the deception was open, obvious. She must be there, in that lighted room, she must be behind the screen; and the unhappy man would have us believe that he stole up to the window, peeped respectfully in, and discreetly withdrew, for fear something terrible and immoral should happen. And he tries to persuade us of that, us, who understand his character, who know his state of mind at the moment, and that he knew the signals by which he could at once enter the house." At this point Ippolit Kirillovich temporarily interrupted his argument and found it necessary to expatiate on Smerdyakov, in order to demolish completely the suspected connection of Smerdyakov with the murder, and have done with that idea once and for all. He did this very circumstantially, and everyone realized that, although he professed to despise that suspicion, he thought the subject of great importance.

Chapter VIII

A Treatise on Smerdyakov

"To begin with, what was the source of this suspicion?" Ippolit Kirillovich began with this question. The first person who cried out that Smerdyakov had committed the murder was the defendant himself at the moment of his arrest, yet from that time to this he had not brought forward a single fact to confirm the charge, not only a single fact, but even anything that might be considered by human thought to be the faintest suggestion of a fact. The charge is confirmed by three persons only—the two brothers of the defendant and Miss Svetlova. The elder of these brothers expressed his suspicions only today, when he was undoubtedly suffering from brain fever. But we know that for the last two months he has completely shared our conviction of his brother's guilt and did not attempt to combat that idea. But of that later. The younger brother has admitted that he has not the slightest fact to support his notion of Smerdyakov's guilt, and has only been led to that conclusion from the defendant's own words and "the expression of his face." Yes, that astounding piece of evidence has been brought forward twice today by him. Miss Svetlova was even more astounding. 'What the defendant tells you, you must believe; he is not a man to tell a lie.' That is all the evidence against Smerdyakov produced by these three persons, who are all deeply concerned in the defendant's fate. And yet the theory of Smerdyakov's guilt has been noised about, has been and is still maintained. Can you believe it, can you imagine it?"

Here Ippolit Kirillovich thought it necessary to describe briefly the personality of the late Smerdyakov, "who had cut short his life in a fit of insanity." He depicted him as a man of weak intellect, with a smattering of education, who had been thrown off his balance by philosophical ideas above his level and certain modern theories of duty and obligation which he learned in practice from the reckless life of his master, who was also perhaps his father—Fyodor Pavlovich; and, theoretically, from various strange philosophical conversations with his master's elder son, Ivan Fyodorovich, who readily indulged in this diversion, probably feeling dull or wishing to amuse himself, and finding no better target. "He spoke to me himself of his spiritual condition during the last few days at his father's house," Ippolit Kirillovich explained; "but others too have borne witness to it—the defendant himself, his brother, and the servant Grigory—that is, all who knew him well. Moreover, Smerdyakov, whose health was shaken by his attacks of epilepsy, was 'cowardly as a chicken.' 'He fell at my feet and kissed them,' the defendant himself has told us, before he realized how damaging such a statement was to himself. 'He is an epileptic chicken,' he declared about him in his characteristic language. And the defendant chose him for his confidant (we have his own word for it) and he frightened him into consenting at last to act as a spy and informant for him. In that capacity of domestic spy he deceived his master, revealing to the defendant the existence of the envelope with the bills in it and the signals by means of which he could get into the house. How could he help telling him, indeed? 'He would have killed me, I could see that he would have killed me,' he said at the inquiry, trembling and shaking even before us, though his tormentor was by that time arrested and could do him no harm. 'He suspected me at every instant. In fear and trembling I hastened to tell him every secret to pacify him, that he might see that I had not deceived him and let me off alive.' Those are his own words. I wrote them down and I remember them. 'When he began shouting at me, I would fall on my knees.' He was naturally very honest and enjoyed the complete confidence of his master, ever since he had restored him some money he had lost. So it may be supposed that the poor fellow suffered pangs of remorse at having deceived his master, whom he loved as his benefactor. Persons severely afflicted with epilepsy are, so the most skillful psychiatrists tell us, always prone to continual and morbid self-reproach. They worry over their 'guilt' about something and toward someone, they are tormented by pangs of conscience, often entirely without cause; they exaggerate and often invent all sorts of faults and crimes. And here we have a man of that type who had really been driven to wrongdoing by terror and intimidation. He had, besides, a strong presentiment that something bad would be the outcome of the situation that was developing before his eyes. When Fyodor Pavlovich's eldest son, Ivan Fyodorovich, was leaving for Moscow, just before the catastrophe, Smerdyakov begged him to remain, though he was too timid to tell him plainly and obviously what he feared. He confined himself to hints, but his hints were not understood. It must be observed that he looked on Ivan Fyodorovich as a protector, whose presence in the house was a guarantee that no harm would come to pass. Remember the phrase in Dmitri Karamazov's 'drunken' letter, 'I shall kill the old man, if only Ivan goes away.' So Ivan Fyodorovich's presence seemed to everyone a guarantee of peace and order in the house. But he went away, and within an hour of his young master's departure Smerdyakov was taken with an epileptic fit. But that's perfectly intelligible. Here I must mention that Smerdyakov, oppressed by terror and despair of a sort, had felt during those last few days that one of the fits from which he had suffered before at moments of strain might be coming upon him again. The day and hour of such an attack cannot, of course, be foreseen, but every epileptic can feel beforehand that he is likely to have one. So the doctors tell us. And so, as soon as Ivan Fyodorovich had driven out of the yard, Smerdyakov, depressed by his lonely, so to speak, and unprotected position, went to the cellar. He went down the stairs wondering if he would have a fit or not, and what if it were to come upon him at once. And that very apprehension, that very wonder, brought on the spasm in his throat that always precedes such attacks, and he fell headlong unconscious into the cellar. And in this perfectly natural occurrence people over-shrewdly try to detect a suspicion, a hint that he was shamming an attack *on purpose*. But, if it were on purpose, the question arises at once, what was his motive? What was he reckoning on? What was he aiming at? I say nothing about medicine: science, I am told, may lie, may make mistakes: the doctors were not able to discriminate between the counterfeit and the real. That may be so, that may be so, but answer me one question: what motive had he for such a counterfeit? Could he, had he been plotting the murder, have desired to attract the attention of the household by having a fit just before? You see, gentlemen of the jury, on the night of the murder, there were five persons in Fyodor Pavlovich's—Fyodor Pavlovich himself (but he did not kill himself, that's evident); then his servant, Grigory, but he was almost killed himself; the third person was Grigory's wife, Martha Ignatyevna, but it would be simply shameful to imagine her murdering her master. Two persons are left—the defendant and Smerdyakov. But, if we are to believe the defendant's statement that he is not the murderer, then Smerdyakov must have been, for there is no other alternative, no one else can be found. That, that is what accounts for the 'artful,' astounding accusation against the unhappy idiot who committed suicide yesterday. Precisely because, and for the sole reason that, there was no one else. Had a shadow of suspicion rested on anyone else, had there been any sixth person, I am persuaded that even the defendant would have been ashamed to accuse Smerdyakov, and would have accused that sixth person, for to charge Smerdyakov with that murder is perfectly absurd.

"Gentlemen, let us lay aside psychology, let us lay aside medicine, let us even lay aside logic, let us turn only to the facts and see what the facts tell us. If Smerdyakov killed him, how did he do it? Alone or with the assistance of the prisoner? Let us consider the first alternative—that he did it alone. If he had killed him it must have been with some object, for some advantage to himself. But not having a shadow of the motive that the defendant had for the murder—hatred, jealousy, and so on— Smerdyakov could only have murdered him for the sake of gain, in order to appropriate the three thousand rubles he had seen his master put in the envelope. And yet he tells another person—and a person most closely interested, that is, the defendant—everything about the money and the signals, where the envelope lay, what was written on it, what it was tied up with, and, above all, told him of those signals by which he could enter the house. Did he do this simply to betray himself, or to invite a rival to the same enterprise, one who would be anxious to get that envelope for himself? 'Yes,' I shall be told, 'but he betrayed it from fear.' But how do you explain this? A man who could conceive such an audacious, savage act, and carry it out, tells facts which are known to no one else in the world, and which, if he held his tongue, no one would ever have guessed! No, however cowardly he might be, if he had plotted such a crime, nothing would have induced him to tell anyone about the envelope and the signals, for that was as good as betraying himself beforehand. He would have invented something, he would have told some lie if he had been forced to give information, but he would have been silent about that. For, I repeat, on the other hand, if he had said nothing about the money but had committed the murder and stolen the money, no one in the world could have charged him with murder for the sake of robbery, since no one but he had seen the money, no one but he knew of its existence in the house. Even if he had been accused of the murder, it could only have been thought that he had committed it from some other motive. But since no one had observed any such motive in him beforehand, and everyone saw, on the contrary, that his master was fond of him and honored him with his confidence, he would, of course, have been the last to be suspected. People would have suspected first the man who had a motive, a man who had himself declared he had such motives, who had made no secret of it; they would, in fact, have suspected the son of the murdered man, Dmitri Fyodorovich. Had Smerdyakov killed and robbed him, and the son been accused of it, that would, of course, have suited Smerdyakov. Yet are we to believe that, though plotting the murder, he told that son, Dmitri, about the money, the envelope, and the signals? Is that logical? Is that clear?

"When the day of the murder planned by Smerdyakov came, we have him falling downstairs in a *feigned* fit—with what object? In the first place that Grigory, who had been intending to take his medicine, might put it off and remain on guard, seeing there was no one to look after the house, and, in the second place, I suppose, that his master seeing that there was no one to guard him, and in terror of a visit from his son, might redouble his vigilance and precaution. And, most of all, I suppose that he, Smerdyakov, disabled by the fit, might be carried from the kitchen, where he always slept, apart from all the rest, and where he could go in and out as he liked, to Grigory's room at the other end of the lodge, where he was always put, shut off by a screen three paces from their own bed. This was the immemorial custom established by his master and the kind-hearted Martha Ignatyevna, whenever he had a fit. There, lying behind the screen, he would most likely, to keep up the sham, have begun groaning, and so keeping them awake all night (as Grigory and his wife testified). And all this, we are to believe, that he might more conveniently get up and murder his master!

"But I shall be told that he shammed illness on purpose that he might not be suspected and that he told the defendant of the money and the signals to tempt him to commit the murder, and when he had murdered him and had gone away with the money making a noise, most likely, and waking people, Smerdyakov got up, am I to believe, and went in—what for? To murder his master a second time and carry off the money that had already been stolen? Gentlemen, are you laughing? I am ashamed to put forward such suggestions, but, incredible as it seems, that's just what the defendant alleges. When he had left the house, had knocked Grigory down and raised an alarm, he tells us Smerdyakov got up, went in and murdered his master and stole the money! I won't press the point that Smerdyakov could hardly have reckoned on this beforehand, and have foreseen that the furious and exasperated son would simply come to peep in respectfully, though he knew the signals, and beat a retreat, leaving Smerdyakov his booty. Gentlemen of the jury, I put this question to you in earnest; when was the moment when Smerdyakov could have committed his crime? Name that moment, or you can't accuse him.

"But, perhaps, the fit was a real one, the sick man suddenly recovered, heard a shout, and went out. Well—what then? He looked about him and said, 'Why not go and kill the master?' And how did he know what had happened, since he had been lying unconscious till that moment? But there's a limit to these flights of fancy.

"'Quite so,' some astute people will tell me, 'but what if they were in agreement? What if they murdered him together and shared the money— what then?'

"A weighty suspicion, truly! And the facts to confirm it are astounding: one commits the murder and takes all the trouble while his accomplice lies on one side shamming a fit, apparently to arouse suspicion in everyone, alarm in his master and alarm in Grigory. It would be interesting to know what motives could have induced the two accomplices to form such an insane plan. But perhaps it was not a case of active complicity, on Smerdyakov's part, but so to speak only of passive acquiescence; perhaps

Smerdyakov was intimidated and agreed not to prevent the murder, and foreseeing that he would be blamed for letting his master be murdered, without screaming for help or resisting, he may have obtained permission from Dmitri Karamazov to get out of the way by shamming a fit—'you may murder him as you like; it's nothing to me.' But even if it were so, since in any case this attack of Smerdyakov's was bound to throw the household into confusion, Dmitri Karamazov could never have agreed to such a plan. I will waive that point however. Supposing that he did agree, it would still follow that Dmitri Karamazov is the murderer, the direct murderer and the instigator, and Smerdyakov is only a passive accomplice, and not even an accomplice, but merely acquiesced against his will through terror, but the court would certainly be able to distinguish that, but what do we see? As soon as he is arrested the prisoner instantly throws all the blame on Smerdyakov, and accuses him *alone*, not accusing him of being his accomplice, but of being himself the murderer. 'He did it alone,' he says. 'He murdered and robbed him. It was the work of his hands.' Strange sort of accomplices who begin to accuse one another at once! It simply can't be! And think of the risk for Karamazov. After committing the murder, and he is the main murderer and the other is not the main one, while his accomplice lay in bed, he throws the blame on the invalid. But that one, the one who lay in bed, might well have resented it and in self-preservation might well have confessed the truth. 'We both participated, but I didn't murder, I only agreed and allowed it out of fear.' For he, Smerdyakov, might well have seen that the court would at once judge how far he was responsible, and so he might well have reckoned that if he were punished, it would be far less severely than the real murderer. But in that case he would have been certain to make a confession, yet he has not done so. Smerdyakov never hinted at their complicity, though the actual murderer persisted in accusing him and declaring that he had committed the crime alone. What's more, Smerdyakov at the inquiry volunteered the statement that it was *he* who had told the prisoner of the envelope of money and of the signals, and that, but for him, he would have known nothing about them. If he had really been a guilty accomplice, would he so readily have made this statement at the inquiry, that is, that he himself told the accused? On the contrary, he would have tried to conceal it, to distort the facts or minimize them. But he was far from distorting or minimizing them. No one but an innocent man, who had no fear of being charged with complicity, could have acted as he did. And in a fit of melancholy arising from his disease and this catastrophe he hanged himself yesterday. He left a note written in his peculiar language, 'I destroy myself of my own will and inclination, not to blame anyone.' What would it have cost him to add: 'I am the murderer, not Karamazov'? But he did not add that: did he have enough conscience for one thing, but not the other?

"And what followed? Notes for three thousand rubles were brought into the court just now, and we are glad that they were the same that lay in the envelope now on the table before us, and that the witness had received them from Smerdyakov the day before. But I need not recall the painful scene, though I will make one or two comments, selecting such trivial ones as might not be obvious at first sight to everyone, and so may be overlooked. In the first place, Smerdyakov must have given back the money and hanged himself yesterday from remorse. (Since he would only have hanged himself from remorse.) And he confessed his guilt to Ivan Karamazov only yesterday, as the latter informs us. If it were not so, indeed, why should Ivan Fyodorovich have kept silence till now? And so, if he has confessed, then why, I ask again, did he not avow the whole truth in the last letter he left behind, knowing that the innocent defendant had to face this terrible trial the next day? The money alone is no proof. A week ago, quite by chance, the fact came to the knowledge of myself and two other persons in this court that Ivan Fyodorovich had sent two five-percent coupons of five thousand each—that is, ten thousand in all—to the chief town of the province to be changed. I only mention this to point out that anyone may have money, at a particular time, and if he brings in three thousand rubles it can't be proved that these bills are the same, that is, precisely those that were in Fyodor Pavlovich's envelope. Finally, Ivan Karamazov, after receiving yesterday a communication of such importance from the real murderer, did not stir. Why didn't he report it at once? Why did he put it all off till morning? I think I have a right to conjecture why. His health had been giving way for a week past: he had admitted to a doctor and to his most intimate friends that he was suffering from hallucinations and seeing phantoms of the dead: he was on the eve of the attack of brain fever by which he has been stricken down today. In this condition he suddenly heard of Smerdyakov's death, and at once reflected, 'The man is dead, I can throw the blame on him and save my brother. I have money. I will take a roll of bills and say that Smerdyakov gave them to me before his death.' You will say that was dishonorable: it's dishonorable to slander even the dead, and even to save a brother. True, but what if he slandered him unconsciously? What if, finally unhinged by the sudden news of the lackey's death, he imagined it really was so? You saw the recent scene: you have seen the witness's condition. He was standing up and was speaking, but where was his mind? The fever-stricken man's testimony was followed by the document, the defendant's letter written two days before the crime to Miss Verkhovtseva, and containing a complete scenario of the murder. Why, then, are we looking for any other scenario and those who constructed them? The crime was committed precisely according to this scenario, and by none other than the writer of it. Yes, gentlemen of the jury, it went off without a hitch! We did not run respectfully and timidly away from our father's window, though we were firmly convinced that the object of our affections was with him. No, that is absurd and unlikely! He went in and murdered him. Most likely he killed him in anger, burning with resentment, as soon as he looked on his hated rival. But having killed him, probably with one blow of the brass pestle, and having convinced himself, after careful search, that she was not there, he did not, however, forget to put his hand under the pillow and take out the envelope with the money, the torn cover of which lies now on the table before us. I mention this fact that you may note one, to my thinking, very characteristic circumstance. Had he been an experienced murderer and had he committed the murder for the sake of gain only, well, would he have left the torn envelope on the floor as it was found, beside the corpse? Well, had it been Smerdyakov, for instance, murdering his master to rob him, he would have simply carried away the envelope with him, without troubling himself to open it over his victim's corpse, for he would have known for certain that the money was in the envelope—it had been put in and sealed up in his presence—

and had he taken the envelope with him, no one would ever have known of the robbery. I ask you, gentlemen of the jury, would Smerdyakov have behaved in that way? Would he have left the envelope on the floor? No, this was the action of a frantic murderer, a murderer who was not a thief and had never stolen before that day, who snatched the money from under the pillow, not like a thief stealing them, but as though seizing his own property from the thief who had stolen it. For that was the idea which had become almost an insane obsession in Dmitri Karamazov in regard to that money. And pouncing upon the envelope, which he had never seen before, he tore it open to make sure whether the money was in it, and ran away with the money in his pocket, even forgetting to consider that he had left an astounding piece of evidence against himself in that torn envelope on the floor. All because it was Karamazov, not Smerdyakov, he didn't think, he didn't reflect, and how could he? He ran away; he heard behind him the servant cry out; the old man caught him, stopped him and was felled to the ground by the brass pestle. The defendant, moved by pity, leaped down to look at him. Would you believe it, he tells us that he leaped down out of pity, out of compassion, to see whether he could do anything for him. Was that a moment to show compassion? No; he jumped down simply to make certain whether the only witness of his crime were dead or alive. Any other feeling, any other motive would be unnatural. Note that he took trouble over Grigory, wiped his head with his handkerchief and, convincing himself he was dead, he ran to the house of his mistress, dazed and covered with blood. How was it he never thought that he was covered with blood and would be at once detected? But the defendant himself assures us that he did not even notice that he was covered with blood. That may be believed, that is very possible, that always happens at such moments with criminals. On one point they will show diabolical cunning, while another will escape them altogether. But he was thinking at that moment of one thing only—where was *she*? He wanted to find out at once where she was, so he ran to her lodging and learned an unexpected and astounding piece of news—she had gone off to Mokroe with her 'former' one, the 'rightful' one!"

Chapter IX

Psychology at Full Steam. The Galloping Troika. The Finale of the Prosecutor's Speech

Ippolit Kirillovich had chosen the historical method of exposition, beloved by all nervous orators, who find in its limitations a check on their own eager rhetoric. At this moment in his speech he went off into a dissertation on Grushenka's "first and rightful lover," and brought forward several interesting thoughts on this theme. "Karamazov, who had been frantically jealous of everyone, collapsed, so to speak, and effaced himself at once before this first lover. What makes it all the more strange is that he seems to have hardly thought of this new danger to himself, looming in the person of this unexpected rival. But he had looked upon him as a remote danger, and Karamazov always lives only in the present. Possibly he regarded him

as a fiction. But his wounded heart grasped instantly that the woman had
been concealing this new rival and deceiving him, because he was anything but a fiction to her, because he was the one hope of her life. Grasping this instantly, he resigned himself. Gentlemen of the jury, I cannot
help dwelling on this unexpected trait in the character of the defendant,
who, it would seem, would be totally incapable of manifesting it. He suddenly evinces an irresistible desire for justice, a respect for woman and
recognition of her right to love. And all this at the very moment when he
had stained his hands with his father's blood for her sake! It is also true
that the blood he had shed was already crying out for vengeance, for, after
having ruined his soul and his life in this world, he was forced to ask himself at that same instant what he was and what he could be *now* to her, to
that being, dearer to him than his own soul, in comparison with that 'former' and 'rightful' lover who had returned penitent, with new love, to the
woman he had once betrayed, with honorable offers, with the promise of
a reformed and happy life. And he, luckless man, what could he give her
now, what could he offer her? Karamazov understood all this, understood
that all ways were barred to him by his crime and that he was a criminal
under sentence, and not a man with life before him! This thought crushed
and destroyed him. And so he instantly flew to one frantic plan, which, to
a man of Karamazov's character, must have appeared the one inevitable
way out of his terrible position. That way out was suicide. He ran for the
pistols he had left in pledge with his friend Perkhotin and on the way, as
he ran, he pulled out of his pocket the money for the sake of which he had
stained his hands with his father's blood. Oh, now he needed money more
than ever. Karamazov would die, Karamazov would shoot himself and it
would be remembered! To be sure, we are poets, to be sure, we have
burned the candle at both ends all our life. 'To her, to her! and there, oh,
there I will give a feast to the whole world, such as never was before, that
will be remembered and talked of long after! In the midst of shouts of wild
merriment, reckless gypsy songs and dances we shall raise the glass and
drink to the woman we adore and her new-found happiness! And then, on
the spot, at her feet, we shall dash out our brains before her and punish
ourselves! She will remember Mitya Karamazov sometimes, she will see
how Mitya loved her, she will feel for Mitya!' Here we see in excess a love
of effect, a romantic despair and sentimentality, and the wild recklessness
of the Karamazovs. Yes, but there is something else, gentlemen of the jury,
something that cries out in the soul, throbs incessantly in the mind, and
poisons his heart unto death—that *something* is conscience, gentlemen of
the jury, its judgment, its terrible torments! The pistol will settle everything, the pistol is the only way out! But *beyond*—I don't know whether
Karamazov wondered at that moment 'What lies beyond,' and whether a
Karamazov could, like Hamlet, wonder 'What lies beyond.' No, gentlemen
of the jury, they have their Hamlets, but we, so far, have only our Karamazovs!" Here Ippolit Kirillovich drew a minute picture of Mitya's preparations, the scene at Perkhotin's, at the shop, with the drivers. He quoted
numerous words and actions, confirmed by witnesses, and the picture
made a terrible impression on the audience. The guilt of this harassed and
desperate man stood out clear and convincing, when the facts were brought
together. "What need had he of precaution? Two or three times he almost
confessed, hinted at it, all but spoke out." (Then followed the evidence

given by witnesses.) "He even cried out to the peasant who drove him, 'Do you know, you are driving a murderer!' But it was impossible for him to speak out, he had to get to Mokroe and there to finish his romance. But what was awaiting the luckless man? Almost from the first minute at Mokroe he saw and finally understood completely that his invincible rival was perhaps by no means so invincible, that the toast to their new-found happiness was not desired and would not be acceptable. But you know the facts, gentlemen of the jury, from the preliminary inquiry. Karamazov's triumph over his rival was complete and here—oh, here his soul passed into quite a new phase, perhaps the most terrible phase through which his soul has passed or will pass. One may say with certainty, gentlemen of the jury," the prosecutor exclaimed, "that outraged nature and the criminal heart bring their own vengeance more completely than any earthly justice. What's more, justice and punishment on earth positively alleviate the punishment of nature and are, indeed, essential to the soul of the criminal at such moments, as its salvation from despair. For I cannot imagine the horror and moral suffering of Karamazov when he learned that she loved him, that for his sake she had rejected her 'first' and 'rightful' lover, that she was summoning him, Mitya, to a new life, that she was promising him happiness—and when? When everything was over for him and nothing was possible!

"By the way, I will note in parenthesis a point of importance for the light it throws on the defendant's position at the moment. This woman, this love of his, had been till the last moment, till the very instant of his arrest, a being unattainable, passionately desired by him but unattainable. Yet why did he not shoot himself then, why did he relinquish his design and even forget where his pistol was? It was just that passionate desire for love and the hope of satisfying it that restrained him. Throughout the heat of their revels he kept close to his adored mistress, who was reveling with him and was more charming and seductive to him than ever—he did not leave her side, abasing himself in his homage before her. His passion might well, for a moment, stifle not only the fear of arrest, but even the torments of conscience. For a moment, oh, only for a moment. I can picture the state of mind of the criminal hopelessly enslaved by three influences— first, the influence of drink, of noise and excitement, of the thud of the dance and the scream of the song, and of her, flushed with wine, singing and dancing and laughing to him! Secondly, the hope in the background that the fatal end might still be far off, that not till next morning, at least, would they come and take him. So he had a few hours and that's much, very much! In a few hours one can think of many things. I imagine that he felt something like what criminals feel when they are being taken to the scaffold.[7] They have another long, long street to pass down and at a walking pace, past thousands of people. Then there will be a turning into another street and only at the end of that street the dread place of execution! It seems to me that at the beginning of the journey the condemned man, sitting on his shameful cart, must feel that he has infinite life still before him. The houses recede, the cart moves on—oh, that's nothing, it's still far to the turning into the second street and he still looks boldly to right and to left at those thousands of callously curious people with their

---

7. Prince Myshkin describes a condemned man's experience in these terms in *The Idiot*.

eyes fixed on him, and he still fancies that he is just such a man as they. But now the turning comes to the next street. Oh, that's nothing, nothing, there's still a whole street before him. And however many houses have been passed, he will still think: 'There are still a lot of houses left.' And so to the very end, to the very scaffold. This, I imagine, is how it was with Karamazov then. 'They've not had time yet,' he must have thought, 'I may still find some way out, oh, there's still time to make some plan of defense, and now, now—she is so fascinating!'

"His soul was full of confusion and dread, but he managed, however, to put aside half his money and hide it somewhere—I cannot otherwise explain the disappearance of quite half of the three thousand he had just taken from his father's pillow. He had been in Mokroe more than once before, he had caroused there for two days together already, he knew the old big house with all its passages and outbuildings. I imagine that part of the money was hidden in that house, not long before the arrest, in some crevice, under some floor, in some corner, under the roof. With what object? I shall be asked. Why, the catastrophe may take place at once, of course; he hadn't yet considered how to meet it, he hadn't the time, his head was throbbing and his heart was with *her*, but money—money was indispensable in any case! With money a man is always a man. Perhaps such foresight at such a moment may strike you as unnatural? But he assures us himself that a month before, at another critical and exciting moment, he had halved his money and sewn it up in a little bag. And though that was not true, as we shall prove directly, it shows the idea was a familiar one to Karamazov, he had contemplated it. What's more, when he declared at the inquiry that he had put fifteen hundred rubles in a bag (which never existed) he may have invented that little bag on the inspiration of the moment, because he had two hours before divided his money and hidden half of it at Mokroe till morning, in case of emergency, simply not to have it on himself. Two extremes, gentlemen of the jury, remember that Karamazov can contemplate two extremes and both at once. We have looked in the house, but we haven't found the money. It may still be there or it may have disappeared the next day and be in the prisoner's hands now. In any case he was at her side, on his knees before her, she was lying on the bed, he had his hands stretched out to her and he had so entirely forgotten everything that he did not even hear the men coming to arrest him. He hadn't time to prepare any line of defense in his mind. He and his mind were caught unawares."

"And there he is before his judges, before the arbiters of his destiny. Gentlemen of the jury, there are moments in the execution of our duties when it is terrible for us to face a man, terrible on his account, too! The moments of contemplating that animal fear, when the criminal sees that all is lost, but still struggles, still means to struggle, the moments when every instinct of self-preservation rises up in him at once and he looks at you with a piercing glance, with questioning and suffering eyes, studies you, your face, your thoughts, uncertain on which side you will strike, and his distracted mind frames thousands of plans in an instant, but he is still afraid to speak, afraid of giving himself away! This torment of the soul, this animal thirst for self-preservation, these humiliating moments of the human spirit, are awful, and sometimes arouse horror and compassion for the criminal even in the lawyer. And this was what we all witnessed then. At first he was thunderstruck and in his terror dropped some very compromising phrases. 'Blood! I've deserved it!' But he quickly restrained himself. He had not prepared what he was to say, what answer he was to make, he had nothing but a bare denial ready. 'I am not guilty of my father's death.' That was our fence for the moment and behind it we hoped to throw up a barricade of some sort. His first compromising exclamations he hastened to explain by declaring that he was responsible for the death of the servant Grigory only. 'Of that bloodshed I am guilty, but who has killed my father, gentlemen, who has killed him? Who can have killed him, *if not I?*' Do you hear, he asked us that, us, who had come to ask him that question! Do you hear that phrase uttered with such premature haste—'if not I'—the animal cunning, the naïveté, the Karamazov impatience of it? 'I didn't kill him and you mustn't think I did! I wanted to kill him, gentlemen, I wanted to kill him,' he hastens to admit (he was in a hurry, in a terrible hurry), 'but still I am not guilty, it is not I who murdered him.' He concedes to us that he wanted to murder him, as though to say, you can see for yourselves how truthful I am, so you'll believe all the sooner that I didn't murder him. Oh, in such cases the criminal is often amazingly shallow and credulous. At that point one of the lawyers asked him, as it were incidentally, the most simple question, 'Wasn't it Smerdyakov who killed him?' Then, as we expected, he was horribly angry at our having anticipated him and caught him unawares, before he had time to pave the way to choose and snatch the moment when it would be most natural to bring in Smerdyakov's name. He rushed at once to the other extreme, as he always does, and began to assure us that Smerdyakov could not have killed him, was not capable of it. But don't believe him, that was only his cunning; he didn't really give up the idea of Smerdyakov; on the contrary, he meant to bring him forward again; for, indeed, he had no one else to bring forward, but he would do that later, because for the moment that line was spoiled for him. He would bring him forward perhaps next day, or even a few days later, choosing an opportunity to cry out to us, 'You know I was more skeptical about Smerdyakov than you, you remember that yourselves, but now I am convinced. He killed him, he must have done it!' And for the present he falls back upon a gloomy and irritable denial. Impatience and anger prompted him, however, to the most inept and incredible explanation of how he looked into his father's window and how he respectfully withdrew. The worst of it was that he was unaware of the position of affairs, of the evidence given by Grigory. We proceeded to search him. The search angered, but encouraged him, the whole three thousand had not been found on him, only half of it. And no doubt only at that moment of angry silence and denial does the idea of the little bag jump into his head for the first time in his life. No doubt he was conscious himself of the improbability of the story and strove painfully to make it sound more likely, to weave it into a romance that would sound plausible. In such cases the first duty, the chief task of the investigating attorneys, is to prevent the criminal being prepared, to pounce upon him unexpectedly so that he may blurt out his cherished ideas in all their simplicity, improbability and inconsistency. The criminal can only be made to speak by the sudden and apparently incidental communication of some new fact, of some circumstance of great importance in the case, of which he had no previous idea and could not have foreseen. We had such a fact in readiness, oh, it was long ready—that was Grigory's evidence about the open door through which the defendant had run out. He had completely forgotten about that door and had not even suspected that Grigory could have seen it. The effect of it was amazing. He leapt up and shouted to us, 'Then Smerdyakov murdered him, it was Smerdyakov!' and so betrayed the basis of the defense he was keeping back, and betrayed it in its most improbable shape, for Smerdyakov could only have committed the murder after he had knocked Grigory down and run away. When we told him that Grigory saw the door was open before he fell down, and had heard Smerdyakov behind the screen as he came out of his bedroom—Karamazov was positively crushed. My esteemed and witty colleague, Nikolay Parfenovich, told me afterwards that he was almost moved to tears at the sight of him. And to improve matters, the prisoner hastened to tell us about the much-talked-of little bag—so be it, you shall hear this romance! Gentlemen of the jury, I have told you already why I consider this romance not only an absurdity, but the most improbable invention that could have been brought forward in the circumstances. If one tried on a bet to invent the most unlikely story, one could hardly find anything more incredible. The worst of such stories is that the triumphant romancers can always be put to confusion and crushed by the very details in which real life is so rich and which these unhappy and involuntary storytellers neglect as insignificant trifles. Oh, they have no thought to spare for such details, their minds are concentrated on their grand invention as a whole and someone dares to suggest such a trifle to them! But that's how they are caught. The prisoner was asked the question, 'Where did you get the stuff for your little bag and who made it for you?' 'I made it myself.' 'And where did you get the linen?' The prisoner was positively offended, he thought it almost insulting to ask him such a trivial question, and would you believe it, his resentment was genuine, genuine! But they are all like that. 'I tore it off my shirt.' 'Then we shall find that shirt among your linen tomorrow, with a piece torn off.' And only fancy, gentlemen of the jury, if we really had found that torn shirt (and how could we have failed to find it in his chest of drawers or trunk?) that would have been a fact, a material fact in support of his statement! But he was incapable of that reflection. 'I don't remember, it may not have been off my shirt, I sewed it up in one of my landlady's caps.' 'What sort of a cap?' 'It was an old cotton rag of hers lying about.' 'And do you remember that clearly?' 'No, I don't.' And he was angry, very angry, and yet imagine not remembering it! At the most terrible moments of man's life, for instance when he is being led to execution, he remembers just such trifles. He will forget anything but some green roof that has flashed past him on the road, or a jackdaw on a cross—that he will remember. He concealed the making of that little bag from his household, he must have remembered his humiliating fear that someone might come in and find him needle in hand, how at the slightest sound he slipped behind the screen (there is a screen in his lodgings). But, gentlemen of the jury, why do I tell you all this, all these details, trifles?" cried Ippolit Kirillovich suddenly. "Just because the defendant still persists in these absurdities to this moment. He has not explained anything since that fatal night two months ago, he has not added one actual illuminating fact to his former fantastic statements; all those are trivialities. 'You must believe it on my honor.' Oh, we are glad to believe it, we are eager to believe it, even if only on his word of honor! Are we jackals thirsting for human blood? Show us a single fact in the defendant's favor and we shall rejoice; but let it be a substantial, real fact, and not a conclusion drawn from the defendant's expression by his own brother, or that when he beat himself on the breast he must have meant to point to the little bag, in the darkness, too. We shall rejoice at the new fact, we shall be the first to repudiate our charge, we shall hasten to repudiate it. But now justice cries out and we persist, we cannot repudiate anything." Here Ippolit Kirillovich passed to his finale. He looked as though he was in a fever, he spoke of the blood that cried for vengeance, the blood of the father murdered by his son, with the base motive of robbery! He pointed to the tragic and glaring consistency of the facts. "And whatever you may hear from the talented and celebrated counsel for the defense," Ippolit Kirillovich could not resist adding, "whatever eloquent and touching appeals may be made to your sensibilities, remember that at this moment you are in a temple of justice. Remember that you are the champions of our justice, the champions of our holy Russia, of her principles, her family, everything that she holds sacred! Yes, you represent Russia here at this moment, and your verdict will be heard not in this hall only but will re-echo throughout the whole of Russia, and all Russia will hear you, as her champions and her judges, and she will be encouraged or disheartened by your verdict. Do not disappoint Russia and her expectations. Our fatal troika dashes on in her headlong flight perhaps to destruction and in all Russia for long past men have stretched out imploring hands and called a halt to its furious reckless course. And if other nations stand aside from that troika that may be, not from respect, as the poet would fain believe, but simply from horror, note that. From horror, perhaps from disgust. And well it is that they stand aside, but maybe they will cease one day to do so and will form a firm wall confronting the hurrying apparition and will check the frenzied rush of our recklessness, for the sake of their own safety, enlightenment and civilization. Already we have heard voices of alarm from Europe, they already begin to sound. Do not tempt them! Do not heap up their growing hatred by a sentence justifying the murder of a father by his son!"

In short, though Ippolit Kirillovich was genuinely moved, he wound up his speech with this rhetorical appeal—and the effect produced by him was extraordinary. When he had finished his speech, he went out hurriedly and, as I have mentioned before, almost fainted in the adjoining room. There was no applause in the court, but serious persons were pleased. The ladies were not so well satisfied, though even they were pleased with his eloquence, especially as they had no apprehensions as to the upshot of the trial and had full trust in Fetyukovich. "He will speak at last and of course carry all before him." Everyone looked at Mitya; he sat silent through the whole of the prosecutor's speech, clenching his teeth, with his hands clasped, and his head bowed. Only from time to time he raised his head and listened, especially when Grushenka was spoken of. When the prosecutor mentioned Rakitin's opinion of her, a smile of contempt and anger passed over his face and he murmured rather audibly "the Bernards!" When Ippolit Kirillovich described how he had questioned and tortured him at Mokroe, Mitya raised his head and listened with intense curiosity. At one point he seemed about to jump up and cry out, but controlled himself and only shrugged his shoulders disdainfully. People talked afterwards of the end of the speech, of the prosecutor's feat in examining the prisoner at Mokroe and jeered at Ippolit Kirillovich. "The man could not resist boasting of his abilities," they said.

The court was adjourned, but only for a short interval, a quarter of an hour or twenty minutes at most. There was a hum of conversation and exclamations in the audience. I remember some of them.

"A solid speech," a gentleman in one group observed gravely.

"He brought in too much psychology," said another voice.

"But it was all true, the absolute truth!"

"Yes, he is first rate at it."

"He summed it all up."

"Yes, he summed us up, too," chimed in another voice. "Do you remember, at the beginning of his speech, making out we were all like Fyodor Pavlovich?"

"And at the end, too. But that was all rot."

"And obscure too."

"He was a little too much carried away."

"It's unjust, it's unjust, sir."

"No, it was smartly done, anyway. He's had long to wait, but he'd had his say, he-he!"

"What will the counsel for the defense say?"

In another group I heard:

"He had no business to make a thrust at the Petersburg man like that; 'appealing to your sensibilities'—do you remember?"

"Yes, that was awkward of him."

"He was in too great a hurry."

"He is a nervous man."

"We laugh, but what must the defendant be feeling?"

"Yes, what must it be for Mitenka?"

In a third group:

"What lady is that, the fat one, with the lorgnette, sitting at the end?"

"She is a general's wife, divorced, I know her."

"That's the one, with the lorgnette."

"She is not good for much."

"Oh, no, she is a piquant little woman."

"Two places beyond her there is a little fair woman, she is prettier."

"They caught him smartly at Mokroe, didn't they, eh?"

"Oh, it was smart enough. We've heard it before, how often he has told the story at people's houses!"

"And he couldn't resist doing it now. That's vanity."

"He is a man with a grievance, he-he!"

"Yes, and quick to take offense. And there was too much rhetoric, such long sentences."

"Yes, he tries to alarm us, he kept trying to alarm us. Do you remember about the troika? Something about 'They have Hamlets, but we have, so far, only Karamazovs!' That was cleverly said!"

"That was to propitiate the liberals. He is afraid of them."

"Yes, and he is afraid of the jurist, too."

"Yes, what will Mr. Fetyukovich say?"

"Whatever he says, he won't get round our peasants."

"Do you think so?"

A fourth group:

Martin's bookmarks are a bit excessive...

"What he said about the troika was good, that piece about the other nations."

"And that was true what he said about other nations not standing it."

"What do you mean?"

"Why, in the English Parliament a Member got up last week and speaking about the Nihilists asked the Ministry whether it was not high time to intervene, to educate this barbarous people.[8] Ippolit was thinking of him, I know he was. He was talking about that last week."

"Not an easy job."

"Not an easy job? Why not?"

"Why, we'd shut up Kronstadt[9] and not let them have any wheat. Where would they get it?"

"In America. They get it from America now."

"Nonsense!"

But the bell rang, all rushed to their places. Fetyukovich mounted the tribune.

Chapter X

The Defense Attorney's Speech.
An Argument That Cuts Both Ways

All was hushed as the first words of the famous orator rang out. The eyes of the audience were fastened upon him. He began very simply and directly, with an air of conviction, but not the slightest trace of conceit. He made no attempt at eloquence, at pathos, or emotional phrases. He was like a man speaking in a circle of intimate and sympathetic friends. His voice was a fine one, sonorous and attractive, and there was something genuine and simple in the very sound of it. But everyone realized at once that the speaker might suddenly rise to genuine pathos and "pierce the heart with untold power."[1] His language was perhaps more irregular than Ippolit Kirillovich's, but he spoke without long phrases, and indeed, with more precision. One thing did not please the ladies: he kept bending forward, especially at the beginning of his speech, not exactly bowing, but as though he were about to dart at his listeners, bending his long back in half, as though there were a spring in the middle of that long and narrow back that enabled him to bend at right angles. At the beginning of his speech he spoke rather disconnectedly, without system, one may say, dealing with facts separately, though, at the end, these facts formed a whole. His speech might be divided into two parts, the first consisting of criticism in refutation of the charge, sometimes malicious and sarcastic.

---

8. The term "nihilist" first entered popular usage in Russia through Turgenev's novel *Fathers and Children* (see also p. 54). One character in that novel defines a nihilist as someone "who approaches everything from a critical point of view." When used by an upper-class member of Russian society, as it appears to be here, "nihilist" was a term of opprobrium. To such people, nihilists represented radical young people opposed to all the existing institutions of Russian life. See Ivan Turgenev, *Fathers and Children*, ed. Michael R. Katz (New York: W. W. Norton, 2009), p. 18.

English preoccupation with Russian nihilists was a feature of the late 1870s, so this reference is an anachronism.

9. An island naval base in the Gulf of Finland, about 18 miles west of Saint Petersburg.

1. From Pushkin's 1830 poem, "Answer to an Anonymous Correspondent."

But in the second half he suddenly changed his tone, and even his manner, and at once rose to pathos. The audience seemed on the lookout for it, and quivered with enthusiasm. He went straight to the point, and began by saying that although he practiced in Petersburg, he had more than once visited provincial towns as attorney for the defense, when he was convinced they were innocent or at least felt it beforehand. "That is what has happened to me in the present case," he explained. "From the very first accounts in the newspapers I was struck by something which strongly prepossessed me in the defendant's favor. Briefly, what interested me most was a fact which often occurs in legal practice, but rarely, I think, in such an extreme and peculiar form as in the present case. I ought to formulate that peculiarity only at the end of my speech, but I will do so at the very beginning, for it is my weakness to go to work directly, not keeping my effects in reserve and economizing my material. That may be imprudent on my part, but at least it's sincere. What I have in my mind is this: there is an overwhelming chain of evidence against the defendant, and at the same time not one fact that will stand criticism, if it is examined separately. As I followed the case more closely in the papers and reports my idea was more and more confirmed, and I suddenly received from the defendant's relatives a request to undertake his defense. I at once hurried here, and here I became completely convinced. It was to break down this terrible chain of facts, and to show that each piece of evidence taken separately was unproved and fantastic, that I undertook the case."

So began counsel for the defense and then suddenly exclaimed:

"Gentlemen of the jury, I am new to this district. I have no preconceived ideas. The defendant, a man of turbulent and unbridled temper, has not insulted me. But he has insulted perhaps hundreds of persons in this town, and so prejudiced many people against him beforehand. Of course I recognize that the moral sentiment of local society is justly excited against him. The defendant is of turbulent and violent temper. Yet he was received in society here; he was even welcome in the family of my highly talented friend, the prosecutor." *Nota bene*. At these words there were two or three laughs in the audience, quickly suppressed, but noticed by all. All of us knew that the prosecutor received Mitya against his will, solely because he had somehow interested his wife—a lady of the highest virtue and moral worth, but fanciful, capricious, and fond of opposing her husband, especially in trifles. Mitya's visits, however, had not been frequent. "Nevertheless I venture to suggest," the defense attorney continued, "that in spite of his independent mind and just character, my opponent may have formed a mistaken prejudice against my unfortunate client. Oh, that is so natural; the unfortunate man has only too well deserved such prejudice. Outraged morality, and still more outraged aesthetic feeling, is often relentless. We have all heard in the highly talented prosecutor's speech a stern analysis of the defendant's character and conduct, and his severe critical attitude to the case was evident. And, what's more, he went into psychological subtleties in order to explain the essence of the matter to us, into which he could not have entered, if he had the least conscious and malicious prejudice against the defendant. But there are things which are even worse, even more fatal in such cases, than the most malicious and consciously unfair attitude. It is worse if we are carried away by a certain artistic instinct, so to speak, by the desire for artistic creation, so to speak, the composition of a novel, especially if God has endowed us with psychological insight. Before I started on my way here, I was warned in Petersburg, and was myself aware, that I should find a talented opponent whose psychological insight and subtlety had gained him peculiar renown in legal circles of recent years. But profound as psychology is, it's a knife that cuts both ways." (Laughter among the public.) "You will, of course, forgive me my comparison; I can't boast of eloquence. But I will take as an example any point in the prosecutor's speech. The defendant, running away in the garden in the dark, climbed over the fence, was seized by the servant, and knocked him down with a brass pestle. Then he jumped back into the garden and spent five minutes over the man, trying to discover whether he had killed him or not. And the prosecutor refuses to believe the defendant's statement that he ran to old Grigory out of pity. 'No,' he says, 'such sensibility is impossible at such a moment, that's unnatural; he ran to find out whether the only witness of his crime was dead or alive, and so showed that he had committed the murder, since he would not have run back for any other reason.' Here you have psychology; but let us take the same psychology and apply it to the case the other way round, and our result will be no less probable. The murderer, we are told, leaped down to find out, as a precaution, whether the witness was alive or not, yet he had left in his murdered father's study, as the prosecutor himself argues, an amazing piece of evidence in the shape of a torn envelope, with an inscription that there had been three thousand rubles in it. 'If he had carried that envelope away with him, no one in the world would have known of that envelope and of the money in it, and that the money had been stolen by the prisoner.' Those are the prosecutor's own words. So on one side you see a complete absence of precaution, a man who has lost his head and run away in a fright, leaving that clue on the floor, and two minutes later, when he has killed another man, we are entitled to assume the most heartless and calculating foresight in him. But even admitting this was so, it is psychological subtlety, I suppose, that discerns that under certain circumstances I become as bloodthirsty and keensighted as a Caucasian eagle,[2] while at the next I am as timid and blind as a mole. But if I am so bloodthirsty and cruelly calculating that when I kill a man I only run back to find out whether he is alive to witness against me, why should I spend five minutes looking after my victim at the risk of encountering other witnesses? Why soak my handkerchief, wiping the blood off his head so that it may be evidence against me later? If he were so cold-hearted and calculating, why not hit the servant on the head again and again with the same pestle so as to kill him outright and relieve himself of all anxiety about the witness? Again, though he ran to see whether the witness was alive, he left another witness on the path, that brass pestle which he had taken from the two women, and which they could always recognize afterwards as theirs, and testify that he had taken it from them. And it is not as though he had forgotten it on the path, dropped it through carelessness or haste, no, we had flung away our weapon, for it was found fifteen paces from where Grigory lay. Why did we do so? Just because we were grieved at

2. In Greek myth, the Caucasian eagle was the child of Typhon, a giant winged monster with a hundred heads, and Echidna, a half-woman, half-snake. The eagle was sent by Zeus to eat Prometheus's liver each day, after the liver had regenerated itself at night; it was eventually killed by Heracles.

having killed a man, an old servant; and we flung away the pestle in vexation, with a curse, as a murderous weapon. That's how it must have been, what other reason could we have had for throwing it so far? And if he was capable of feeling grief and pity at having killed a man, it shows that he was innocent of his father's murder. Had he murdered him, he would never have run to another victim out of pity; then he would have felt differently; his thoughts would have been centered on self-preservation. He would have had none to spare for pity, that is beyond doubt. On the contrary, I repeat, he would have broken his skull instead of spending five minutes looking after him. There was room for pity and good feeling just because his conscience had been clear till then. Here we have a different psychology. I have purposely resorted to this method, gentlemen of the jury, to show that you can prove anything by it. It all depends on who makes use of it. Psychology lures even most serious people into romancing, and quite unconsciously. I am speaking of excessive psychology, of the abuse of psychology, gentlemen."

Sounds of approval and laughter, at the expense of the prosecutor, were again audible in the court. I will not repeat the speech for the defense in detail; I will only quote some passages from it, some leading points.

Chapter XI

There Was No Money. There Was No Robbery

There was one point that struck everyone in the defense attorney's speech. He flatly denied the existence of the fatal three thousand rubles, and consequently the possibility of their having been stolen.

"Gentlemen of the jury," he began. "Every new and unprejudiced observer must be struck by a characteristic peculiarity in the present case, namely, the charge of robbery, and the complete impossibility of proving that there was anything to be stolen. We are told that money was stolen—three thousand rubles—but whether those rubles ever existed, nobody knows. Consider, how have we heard of that sum, and who has seen it? The only person who saw it and stated that it had been put in the envelope, was the servant, Smerdyakov. He had spoken of it to the defendant and his brother, Ivan Fyodorovich, before the catastrophe. Miss Svetlova, too, had been told of it. But not one of these three persons had actually seen the money, no one but Smerdyakov had seen it. Here the question arises, if it's true that it did exist, and that Smerdyakov had seen it, when did he see it for the last time? What if his master had taken it from under his bed and put it back in his cash box without telling him? Note, that according to Smerdyakov's story the money was kept under the mattress; the defendant must have pulled it out, and yet the bed was absolutely unrumpled; that is carefully recorded in the deposition. How could the prisoner have found the money without disturbing the bed? How could he have helped soiling with his bloodstained hands the fine and spotless linen with which the bed had been purposely made? But I shall be asked; what about the envelope on the floor? Yes, it's worth saying a word or two about that envelope. I was somewhat surprised just now to hear the highly talented prosecutor declare of his own will—of his own will, observe—when he tried to show the absurdity of considering Smerdyakov the murderer, that but for that envelope, but for its being left on the floor, no one in the world would have known of the existence of that envelope and the money in it, and therefore of the defendant's having stolen it. And so that torn scrap of paper with its inscription is, by the prosecutor's own admission, the sole proof on which the charge of robbery rests, 'otherwise no one would have known of the robbery, nor perhaps even of the money.' But is the mere fact that that scrap of paper was lying on the floor a proof that there was money in it, and that that money had been stolen? Yet, it will be objected, Smerdyakov had seen the money in the envelope. But when, when had he seen it for the last time, I ask you that? I talked to Smerdyakov, and he told me that he had seen the money two days before the catastrophe. Then why not imagine that old Fyodor Pavlovich, locked up alone in impatient and hysterical expectation of the object of his adoration, may have whiled away the time by breaking open the envelope and taking out the money. 'What's the use of the envelope,' he may have asked himself, 'she won't believe the notes are there, but when I show her the thirty rainbow-colored bills in one roll, it will make more impression, you may be sure, it will make her mouth water.' And so he tears open the envelope, takes out the money, and flings the envelope on the floor, conscious of being the owner and untroubled by any fears of leaving evidence. Listen, gentlemen, could anything be more likely than this theory and such an action? Why is it out of the question? But if anything of the sort could have taken place, the charge of robbery falls to the ground; if there was no money, there was no robbery. If the envelope on the floor may be taken as evidence that there had been money in it, why may I not maintain the opposite, that the envelope was on the floor precisely because the money had been taken from it by its owner? But I shall be asked what became of the money if Fyodor Pavlovich took it out of the envelope since it was not found when the police searched the house? In the first place, part of the money was found in the cash box, and secondly, he might have taken it out that morning or the evening before to make some other use of it, to give or send it away; he may have changed his idea, his plan of action completely, without thinking it necessary to announce the fact to Smerdyakov beforehand. And if there is the barest possibility of such an explanation, how can the defendant be so positively accused of having committed murder for the sake of robbery, and of having actually carried out that robbery? This is encroaching on the domain of romance. If it is maintained that something has been stolen, the thing must be produced, or at least its existence must be proved beyond doubt. Yet no one had ever seen the money. Not long ago in Petersburg a young man of eighteen, hardly more than a boy, who had a small stand in the market, went in broad daylight into a moneychanger's shop with an ax, and with extraordinary, typical audacity killed the master of the shop and carried off fifteen hundred rubles.[3] Five hours later he was arrested, and, except fifteen rubles he had already managed to spend, the whole sum was found on him. Moreover, the shopman, on his return to the shop after the murder, informed the police not only of the exact sum stolen, but even of the bills and gold coins of which that sum was made up, and those very bills and coins were found on the criminal. This was followed by a full and genuine confession on the part of the murderer that he had killed the man and had taken these very bills. That's what I call evidence, gentlemen of the jury! In that case I know, I see, I touch the money, and cannot deny its existence. Is it the same in the present case? And yet it is a question of life and death, of a man's fate. Yes, I shall be told, but he was carousing that night, squandering money; he was shown to have had fifteen hundred rubles—where did he get the money? But the very fact that only fifteen hundred could be found, and the other half of the sum could nowhere be discovered, shows that that money was not the same, and had never been in any envelope. By strict calculation of time it was proved at the preliminary inquiry that the prisoner ran straight from those women servants to Perkhotin's without going home, and that he had been nowhere. So he had been all the time in company and therefore could not have divided the three thousand in half and hidden half in the town. It's just this consideration that has led the prosecutor to assume that the money is hidden in some crevice at Mokroe. Why not in the dungeons of the castle of Udolpho,[4] gentlemen? Isn't this supposition really too fantastic and too much of a romance? And observe, if that supposition breaks down, the whole charge of robbery is scattered to the winds, for in that case what could have become of the other fifteen hundred rubles? By what miracle could they have disappeared, since it's proved that the prisoner went nowhere else? And we are ready to ruin a man's life with such romances! I shall be told that he could not explain where he got the fifteen hundred that he had, and everyone knew that he was without money before that night. Who knew it, pray? The defendant has made a clear and unflinching statement of the source of that money, and if you will have it so, gentlemen of the jury, nothing can be more probable than that statement, and more consistent with the temper and spirit of the defendant. The prosecutor is charmed with his own romance. A man of weak will, who had brought himself to take the three thousand so insultingly offered by his betrothed, could not, we are told, have set aside half and sewn it up, but would, even if he had done so, have unpicked it every two days and taken out a hundred, and so would have spent it all in a month. All this, you will remember, was put forward in a tone that brooked no contradiction. But what if the thing happened quite differently? What if you've been weaving a romance, and about quite a different kind of man? That's just it, you have invented quite a different man! I shall be told, perhaps, there are witnesses that he spent on one day all that three thousand given him by Miss Verkhovtseva a month before the catastrophe, so he could not have divided the sum in half. But who are these witnesses? The value of their evidence has been shown in court already. Besides, in another man's hand a crust always seems larger, and not one of these witnesses counted that money; they all judged simply at sight. And the witness Maximov has testified that the defendant had twenty thousand in his hand. You see, gentlemen of the jury, psychology is a two-edged weapon. Let me turn the other edge now and see what comes of it. A month before the catastrophe the prisoner was entrusted by Miss Verkhovtseva with three thousand

---

4. From Ann Radcliffe's (1764–1823) Gothic novel, *The Mysteries of Udolpho* (1794). Dostoevsky read Radcliffe's novels with enthusiasm as a child.

rubles to send off by mail. But the question is: is it true that they were entrusted to him in such an insulting and degrading way as was proclaimed just now? The first statement made by Miss Verkhovtseva on the subject was different, completely different. In the second statement we heard only cries of resentment and revenge, cries of long-concealed hatred. And the very fact that the witness gave her first evidence incorrectly, gives us a right to conclude that her second piece of evidence may have been incorrect also. The prosecutor will not, dare not (his own words) touch on that story. So be it. I will not touch on it either, but will only venture to observe that if a lofty and high-principled person, such as that highly respected Miss Verkhovtseva unquestionably is, if such a person, I say, allows herself suddenly in court to contradict her first statement, with the obvious motive of ruining the defendant, it is clear that this evidence has been given not impartially, not coolly. Have not we the right to assume that a revengeful woman might have exaggerated much? Yes, she may well have exaggerated, in particular, the insult and humiliation of her offering him the money. No, it was offered in such a way that it was possible to take it, especially for a man so easygoing as the defendant. Above all, he expected to receive shortly from his father the three thousand rubles that he reckoned was owing to him. It was unreflecting of him, but it was just his irresponsible want of reflection that made him so confident that his father would give him the money, that he would get it, and so could always despatch the money entrusted to him by Miss Verkhovtseva and repay the debt. But the prosecutor refuses to allow that he could the same day have set aside half the money and sewn it up in a little bag: 'That's not his character,' he tells us, 'he couldn't have had such feelings.' But you yourself were shouting that Karamazov is broad, you yourself shouted about the two extreme abysses which a Karamazov can contemplate at once. Karamazov is just such a two-sided nature, fluctuating between two abysses, that even when moved by the most violent craving for riotous gaiety, he can control himself, if something strikes him on the other side. And on the other side is love—that new love which had flamed up in his heart, and for that love he needed money; oh, far more than for carousing with his mistress. If she were to say to him, 'I am yours, I won't have Fyodor Pavlovich,' then he must have money to take her away. That was more important than carousing. Could a Karamazov fail to understand it? That anxiety was just what he was suffering from—what is there improbable in his laying aside that money and concealing it in case of emergency? But time passed, and Fyodor Pavlovich did not give the defendant the expected three thousand; on the contrary, the latter heard that he meant to use this sum to seduce the woman he, the defendant, loved. 'If Fyodor Pavlovich doesn't give the money,' he thought, 'I shall be put in the position of a thief before Katerina Ivanovna.' And then the idea presented itself to him that he would go to Miss Verkhovtseva, lay before her the fifteen hundred rubles he still carried round his neck, and say, 'I am a scoundrel, but not a thief.' So here we have already a twofold reason why he should guard that sum of money as the apple of his eye, why he shouldn't unpick the little bag, and spend it a hundred at a time. Why should you deny the defendant a sense of honor? Yes, he has a sense of honor, granted that it's misplaced, granted it's often mistaken, yet it exists and amounts to a passion, and he has proved that. But now the affair becomes even more complex; his jealous torments reach a climax, and those same two questions torture his fevered brain more and more: 'If I repay Katerina Ivanovna, where can I find the means to go off with Grushenka?' If he behaved wildly, drank, and made disturbances in the taverns in the course of that month, it was perhaps because he was wretched and strained beyond his powers of endurance. These two questions became so acute that they drove him at last to despair. He sent his younger brother to beg for the last time for the three thousand rubles, but without waiting for a reply, burst in himself and ended by beating the old man in the presence of witnesses. After that he had no prospect of getting it from anyone; his father would not give it to him after that beating. The same evening he struck himself on the breast, just on the upper part of the breast where the little bag was, and swore to his brother that he had the means of not being a scoundrel, but that still he would remain a scoundrel, for he foresaw that he would not use that means, that he wouldn't have the character, that he wouldn't have the willpower to do it. Why, why does the prosecutor refuse to believe the evidence of Alexey Karamazov, given so genuinely and sincerely, so spontaneously and convincingly? And why, on the contrary, does he force me to believe in money hidden in a crevice, in the dungeons of the castle of Udolpho? The same evening, after his talk with his brother, the defendant wrote that fatal letter, and that letter is the chief, the most stupendous proof of the defendant's having committed robbery! 'I shall beg from everyone, and if I don't get it I shall murder my father and shall take the envelope with the pink ribbon on it from under his mattress as soon as Ivan has gone.' A full scenario of the murder, we are told, so it must have been he. 'It has all been done as he wrote,' cries the prosecutor. But in the first place, it's the letter of a drunken man and written in great irritation; secondly, he writes of the envelope what he has heard from Smerdyakov again, for he has not seen the envelope himself; and thirdly, he wrote it indeed, but how can you prove that he did it? Did the prisoner take the envelope from under the pillow, did he find the money, did that money exist indeed? And was it to get money that the prisoner ran off, if you remember? He ran off posthaste not to steal, but to find out where she was, the woman who had crushed him. He was not running to carry out a scenario, to carry out what he had written, that is, not for an act of premeditated robbery, but he ran suddenly, spontaneously, in a jealous fury. Yes! I shall be told, but when he got there and murdered him he seized the money, too. But did he murder him after all? The charge of robbery I repudiate with indignation. A man cannot be accused of robbery, if it's impossible to state accurately what he has stolen; that's an axiom. But did he murder him without robbery, did he murder him at all? Is that proved? Isn't that, too, a romance?"

Chapter XII

And There Was No Murder Either

"Allow me, gentlemen of the jury, to remind you that a man's life is at stake and that you must be very careful. We have heard the prosecutor himself admit that until today he hesitated to accuse the defendant of a full and conscious premeditation of the crime; he hesitated till he saw that fatal drunken letter which was produced in court today. 'All was done as written.' But, I repeat again, he was running to her, to seek her, solely to find out where she was. That's a fact that can't be disputed. Had she been at home, he would not have run away, but would have remained at her side, and so would not have done what he promised in the letter. He ran unexpectedly and accidentally, and by that time very likely he did not even remember his 'drunken' letter. 'He snatched up the pestle,' they say, and you will remember how a whole edifice of psychology was built on that pestle—why he was bound to look at that pestle as a weapon, to snatch it up, and so on, and so on. A very commonplace idea occurs to me at this point: What if that pestle had not been in sight, had not been lying on the shelf from which it was snatched by the defendant, but had been put away in a cupboard? It would not have caught the defendant's eye, and he would have run away without a weapon, with empty hands, and then he would certainly not have killed anyone. How then can I look upon the pestle as a proof of his arming himself and of premeditation? Yes, but he talked in the taverns of murdering his father, and two days before, on the evening when he wrote his drunken letter, he was quiet and only quarreled with a shopman in the tavern, because a 'Karamazov could not help quarreling'! But my answer to that is, that, if he was planning such a murder in accordance with his letter, he certainly would not have quarreled even with a shopman, and probably would not have gone into the tavern at all, because a person plotting such a crime seeks quiet and retirement, because to efface himself, to avoid being seen and heard, that he might be forgotten about, and that not from calculation, but from instinct. Gentlemen of the jury, the psychological method is a two-edged weapon, and we, too, can use it. As for all this shouting in taverns throughout the month, don't we often hear children, or drunkards coming out of taverns shout, 'I'll kill you'? but they don't murder anyone. And that fatal letter—isn't that simply drunken irritability, too? Isn't that simply the shout of the brawler outside the tavern, 'I'll kill you! I'll kill the lot of you!' Why not, why could it not be that? What reason have we to call that letter 'fatal' rather than absurd? Because his father has been found murdered, because a witness saw the defendant running out of the garden with a weapon in his hand, and was knocked down by him: therefore, we are told, everything was done as he had planned in writing, and the letter was not 'absurd,' but 'fatal.' Now, thank God! we've come to the real point: 'since he was in the garden, he must have murdered him.' In those few words: 'since he *was*, then he *must*' lies the whole case for the prosecution. He was there, so he must have. And what if there is no *must* about it, even if he was there? Oh, I admit that the chain of evidence—the coincidences—are really suggestive. But examine all these facts separately, regardless of their connection. Why, for instance, does the prosecution refuse to admit the truth of the defendant's statement that he ran away from his father's window? Remember the sarcasm in which the prosecution indulged at the expense of the respectful and 'pious' sentiments which suddenly came over the murderer. But what if there were something of the sort, a piety of feeling, if not respectfulness of feeling? 'My mother must have been praying for me at that moment,' were the defendant's words at the preliminary inquiry, and so he ran away as soon as he convinced himself that Miss Svetlova was not in his father's house. 'But he could not convince himself by looking through the window,' the prosecution objects. But why couldn't he? Why? The window opened at the signals given by the defendant. Some word might have been uttered by Fyodor Pavlovich, some exclamation which showed the defendant that she was not there. Why should we assume everything as we imagine it, as we make up our minds to imagine it? A thousand things may happen in reality which elude the subtlest novelist. 'Yes, but Grigory saw the door open and so the defendant certainly was in the house, therefore he killed him.' Now about that door, gentlemen of the jury. . . . Observe that we have only the statement of one witness as to that door, and he was at the time in such a condition, that . . . But supposing the door was open; supposing the defendant has lied in denying it, from an instinct of self-defense, natural in his position; supposing he did go into the house—well, what then? How does it follow that because he was there he committed the murder? He might have dashed in, run through the rooms; might have pushed his father away; might have struck him; but as soon as he had made sure Miss Svetlova was not there, he may have run away rejoicing that she was not there and that he had not killed his father. And it was perhaps just because he had escaped from the temptation to kill his father, because he had a clear conscience and was rejoicing at not having killed him, that he was capable of a pure feeling, the feeling of pity and compassion, and leaped off the fence a minute later to the assistance of Grigory after he had, in his excitement, knocked him down. With terrible eloquence the prosecutor has described to us the dreadful state of the defendant's mind at Mokroe when love again appeared before him calling him to new life, while love was impossible for him because he had his father's bloodstained corpse behind him and beyond that corpse—retribution. And yet the prosecutor allowed him love, which he explained, according to his method, talking about his drunken condition, about a criminal being taken to execution, about it being still far off, and so on and so on. But again I ask, Mr. Prosecutor, have you not invented a new personality? Is the defendant so coarse and heartless as to be able to think at that moment of love and of dodges to escape punishment, if his hands were really stained with his father's blood? No, no, no! As soon as it was made plain to him that she loved him and called him to her side, promising him new happiness, oh! then, I protest, he must have felt the impulse to suicide doubled, trebled, and must have killed himself, if he had his father's murder on his conscience. Oh, no! he would not have forgotten where his pistols lay! I know the defendant: the savage, stony heartlessness ascribed to him by the prosecution is inconsistent with his character. He would have killed himself, that's certain. He did not kill himself just because 'his mother's prayers had saved him,' and he was innocent of his father's blood. He was troubled, he was grieving that night at Mokroe only about old Grigory and praying to God that the old man would recover, that his blow had not been fatal, and that he would not have to suffer for it. Why not accept such an interpretation of the facts? What trustworthy proof have we that the defendant is lying? But we shall be told at once again, 'There is his father's corpse! If he ran away without murdering him, who did murder him?'

"Here, I repeat, you have the whole logic of the prosecution. Who murdered him, if not he? There's no one to put in his place. Gentlemen of the jury, is that really so? Is it positively, actually true that there is no one else at all? We've heard the prosecution count on its fingers all the persons who were in that house that night. They were five in number; three of them, I agree, could not have been responsible—the murdered man himself, old Grigory, and his wife. There are left then the defendant and Smerdyakov, and the prosecutor dramatically exclaims that the defendant pointed to Smerdyakov because he had no one else to fix on, that had there been a sixth person, even a phantom of a sixth person, he would have abandoned the charge against Smerdyakov at once in shame and have accused the other. But, gentlemen of the jury, why may I not draw the very opposite conclusion? There are two persons—the defendant and Smerdyakov. Why can I not say that you accuse my client, simply because you have no one else to accuse? And you have no one else only because you have determined to exclude Smerdyakov from all suspicion. It's true, indeed, Smerdyakov is accused only by the prisoner, his two brothers, and Miss Svetlova. But there are others who accuse him: there are vague rumors of a question, of a suspicion, an obscure report, a feeling of expectation. Finally, we have the evidence of a combination of facts very suggestive, though, I admit, inconclusive. In the first place we have precisely on the day of the catastrophe that fit, for the genuineness of which the prosecutor, for some reason, has felt obliged to make a careful defense. Then Smerdyakov's sudden suicide on the eve of the trial. Then the equally startling evidence given in court today by the elder of the defendant's brothers, who had believed in his guilt, but has today produced a bundle of bills and proclaimed Smerdyakov as the murderer. Oh, I fully share the court's and the prosecution's conviction that Ivan Karamazov is suffering from brain fever, that his statement may really be a desperate effort, planned in delirium, to save his brother by throwing the guilt on the dead man. But again Smerdyakov's name is pronounced, again there is a suggestion of mystery. There is something unexplained, incomplete. And perhaps it may one day be explained. But we won't go into that now. Of that later. The court has resolved to go on with the trial, but, meantime, I might make a few remarks about the character sketch of Smerdyakov drawn with subtlety and talent by the prosecutor. But while I admire his talent I cannot agree with him. I have visited Smerdyakov. I have seen him and talked to him, and he made a very different impression on me. He was weak in health, it is true; but in character, in spirit, he was by no means the weak man the prosecution has made him out to be. I found in him no trace of the timidity on which the prosecutor so insisted. There was no simplicity about him at all. I found in him, on the contrary, an extreme mistrustfulness concealed under a mask of naïveté, and an intelligence of considerable range. The prosecution was too simple in taking him for weak-minded. He made a very definite impression on me: I left him with the conviction that he was a distinctly spiteful being, excessively ambitious, vindictive, and intensely envious. I made some inquiries: he resented his parentage, was ashamed of it, and would clench his teeth when he remembered that he was the son of 'stinking Lizaveta.' He was disrespectful to the servant Grigory and his wife, who had cared for him in his childhood. He cursed and jeered at Russia. He dreamed of going to France and becoming a Frenchman. He often used to say that he hadn't the means to do so. I fancy he loved no one but himself and had a strangely high opinion of himself. His conception of culture was limited to good clothes, clean shirt fronts and polished boots. Believing himself to be the illegitimate son of Fyodor Pavlovich (there is evidence of this) he might well have resented his position, compared with that of his master's legitimate sons. They had everything, he nothing. They had all the rights, they had the inheritance, while he was only the cook. He told me himself that he had helped Fyodor Pavlovich to put the notes in the envelope. The destination of that sum—a sum which would have made his career—must have been hateful to him. Moreover, he saw three thousand rubles in new rainbow-colored bills. (I asked him about that on purpose.) Oh, beware of showing an ambitious and envious man a large sum of money at once! And it was the first time he had seen so much money in the hands of one man. The sight of the rainbow-colored bundle may have made a morbid impression on his imagination, but with no immediate results. The highly talented prosecutor, with extraordinary subtlety, sketched for us all the arguments for and against the hypothesis of Smerdyakov's guilt, and asked us in particular what motive he had in feigning a fit. But he may not have been feigning at all, the fit may have happened quite naturally, but it may have passed off quite naturally, and the sick man may have recovered, not completely perhaps, but still regaining consciousness, as happens with epileptics. The prosecution asks at what moment could Smerdyakov have committed the murder. But it is very easy to point out that moment. He might have woken up from deep sleep (for he was only asleep—an epileptic fit is always followed by a deep sleep) at that moment when old Grigory shouted at the top of his voice 'Parricide!' That extraordinary shout in the dark and stillness may have woken Smerdyakov, whose sleep may have been less sound at the moment: he might naturally have woken up an hour before. Getting out of bed, he goes almost unconsciously and with no definite motive towards the sound to see what's the matter. His head is still clouded with his attack, his faculties are half asleep; but, once in the garden, he walks to the lighted windows and he hears terrible news from his master, who would be, of course, glad to see him. His mind sets to work at once. He hears all the details from his frightened master, and gradually in his disordered brain there shapes itself an idea—terrible, but seductive and irresistibly logical. To kill the old man, take the three thousand, and throw all the blame on to his young master. Who would be accused if not the young master, how could it not be he, he was there, there is all the evidence. A terrible lust for money, for booty, might seize upon him as he realized his security from detection. Oh! these sudden and irresistible impulses come so often when there is a favorable opportunity, and especially with murderers who have had no idea of committing a murder beforehand. And Smerdyakov may have gone in and carried out his plan. With what weapon? Why, with any stone picked up in the garden. But what for, with what object? Why, the three thousand which means a career for him. Oh, I am not contradicting myself—the money may have existed. And perhaps Smerdyakov alone knew where to find it, where his master kept it. And the covering of the money—the torn envelope on the floor? Just now, when the prosecutor was explaining his extremely subtle theory that only an inexperienced thief like Karamazov would have left the envelope on the floor, and not one like Smerdyakov, who would never have left a piece of evidence like that against himself, I thought as I listened that I was hearing something very familiar, and, would you believe it, I have heard that very argument, that very conjecture, of how Karamazov would have behaved, precisely two days before, from Smerdyakov himself. What's more, it struck me at the time. I fancied that there was an artificial simplicity about him; that he was in a hurry to suggest this idea to me that I might fancy it was my own. He insinuated it, as it were. Did he not insinuate the same idea to the prosecution? Did he not also suggest it to the highly talented prosecutor? I shall be asked, 'What about the old woman, Grigory's wife? She heard the sick man moaning close by, all night.' Yes, she heard it, but that evidence is extremely unreliable. I knew a lady who complained bitterly that she had been kept awake all night by a dog in the yard. Yet the poor beast, it appeared, had only yelped two or three times in the night. And that's natural. If anyone is asleep and hears a groan he wakes up, annoyed at being waked, but instantly falls asleep again. Two hours later, again a groan, he wakes up and falls asleep again; and the same thing again two hours later—three times altogether in the night. Next morning the sleeper wakes up and complains that someone has been groaning all night and keeping him awake. And it is bound to seem so to him: the intervals of two hours of sleep he does not remember, he only remembers the moments of waking, so he feels he has been woken up all night. But why, why, asks the prosecution, did not Smerdyakov confess in his last letter? 'Why did his conscience prompt him to one step and not to both?' But, excuse me, conscience implies penitence, and the suicide may not have felt penitence, but only despair. Despair and penitence are two very different things. Despair may be vindictive and irreconcilable, and the suicide, laying his hands on himself, may well have felt redoubled hatred for those whom he had envied all his life. Gentlemen of the jury, beware of a judicial error! What is there unlikely in all I have put before you just now? Find the error in my reasoning; find the impossibility, the absurdity. And if there is but a shade of possibility, but a shade of probability in my propositions, do not condemn him. And is there only a shade? I swear by all that is sacred, I fully believe in the explanation of the murder I have just put forward. What troubles me and makes me indignant is that of all the mass of facts heaped up by the prosecution against the defendant, there is not a single one certain and irrefutable. And yet the unhappy man is to be ruined by the accumulation of these facts. Yes, the accumulated effort is awful: the blood, the blood dripping from his fingers, the blood-stained shirt, the dark night resounding with the shout 'Parricide!' and the old man falling with a broken head. And then the mass of phrases, statements, gestures, shouts! Oh! this has so much influence, it can so bias the mind; but, gentlemen of the jury, can it bias your minds? Remember, you have been given absolute power, the power to bind and to loose, but the greater the power, the more terrible its responsibility. I do not draw back one iota from what I have said just now, but suppose for one moment I agreed with the prosecution that my luckless client had stained his hands with his father's blood. This is only an hypothesis, I repeat; I never for one instant doubt his innocence. But, so be it, I assume that my client is guilty of parricide. Even so, hear what I have to say. I have it in my heart to say something more to you, for I feel that there must be a great conflict in your hearts and minds. . . . Forgive my referring to your hearts and minds, gentlemen of the jury, but I want to be truthful and sincere to the end. Let us all be sincere!"

At this point the speech was interrupted by rather loud applause. The last words, indeed, were pronounced with a note of such sincerity that everyone felt that he really might have something to say, and that what he was about to say would be of the greatest consequence. But the President, hearing the applause, in a loud voice threatened to clear the court if such an incident were repeated. Every sound was hushed and Fetyukovich began in a new voice full of feeling quite unlike the tone he had used hitherto.

Chapter XIII

An Adulterer of Thought

"It's not only the accumulation of facts that threatens my client with ruin, gentlemen of the jury," he began sonorously, "no, what is really threatening my client with ruin is one fact—the dead body of his father! Had it been an ordinary case of murder you would have rejected the charge in view of the triviality, the incompleteness, and the fantastic character of the evidence, if you examine each part of it separately; or, at least, you would have hesitated to ruin a man's life simply from the prejudice against him which he has, alas! only too well deserved. But it's not an ordinary case of murder, it's a case of parricide. That impresses men's minds, and to such a degree that the very triviality and incompleteness of the evidence becomes less trivial and less incomplete even to an unprejudiced mind. How can such a defendant be acquitted? What if he committed the murder and gets off unpunished? That is what everyone, almost involuntarily, instinctively, feels at heart. Yes, it's a fearful thing to shed a father's blood—the father who has begotten me, loved me, not spared his life for me, grieved over my illnesses from childhood up, troubled all his life for my happiness, and has lived in my joys, in my successes. To murder such a father—that's inconceivable. Gentlemen of the jury, what is a father—a real father? What is the meaning of that great word? What is the great idea in that name? We have just indicated in part what a true father is and what he ought to be. In the case in which we are now so deeply occupied and over which our hearts are aching—in the present case, the father, Fyodor Pavlovich Karamazov, in no way corresponds to that conception of a father to which we have just referred. That's the misfortune. And indeed some fathers are like a misfortune. Let us examine this misfortune rather more closely: we must shrink from nothing, gentlemen of the jury, considering the importance of the decision you have to make. It's our particular duty not to shrink from any idea, like children or frightened women, as the highly talented prosecutor happily expresses it. But in the course of his heated speech my esteemed opponent (and he was my opponent before I opened my lips) exclaimed several times, 'Oh, I will not yield the defense of the defendant to the advocate who has come down from Petersburg. I am the prosecution, but I am also the counsel for the defense!' He exclaimed that several times, but forgot to mention that if this terrible defendant was for twenty-three years so grateful for a mere pound of nuts given him by the only man who had been kind to him, as a child in his father's house, might not such a man well

have remembered for twenty-three years how he ran in his father's backyard, 'without boots on his feet and with his little trousers hanging by one
button'—to use the expression of the humane doctor, Herzenstube? Oh,
gentlemen of the jury, why need we look more closely at this 'misfortune,'
why repeat what we all know already? What did my client meet with when
he arrived here, at his father's house, and why depict my client as a heartless egoist and monster? He is uncontrolled, he is wild and unruly—we
are trying him now for that—but who is responsible for his life? Who is
responsible for his having received such an unseemly bringing up, in spite
of his excellent disposition and his grateful and sensitive heart? Did anyone train him to be reasonable? Was he enlightened by study? Did anyone
love him ever so little in his childhood? My client was left to the care of
Providence like a beast of the field. He thirsted, perhaps, to see his father
after long years of separation. A thousand times he may, perhaps, recalling
his childhood, have driven away the loathsome phantoms that haunted his
childish dreams and with all his heart he may have longed to embrace and
to forgive his father! And what awaited him? He was met by cynical taunts,
suspicions and wrangling about money. He heard nothing but revolting
talk and vicious precepts uttered daily 'over the brandy,' and at last he saw
his father enticing his mistress from him with his own money, the son's
own money! Oh, gentlemen of the jury, that was cruel and revolting! And
that old man was always complaining of the disrespect and cruelty of his
son. He slandered him in society, injured him, calumniated him, bought
up his unpaid debts to get him thrown into prison. Gentlemen of the jury,
people like my client, who are fierce, unruly, and uncontrolled on the surface, are sometimes, most frequently indeed, exceedingly tender-hearted,
only they don't express it. Don't laugh, don't laugh at my idea! The talented
prosecutor laughed mercilessly just now at my client's loving Schiller—
loving the 'sublime and beautiful!' I would not have laughed at that in
his place, in the prosecutor's place. Yes, such natures—oh, let me speak in
defense of such natures, so often and so cruelly misunderstood—these
natures often thirst for tenderness, goodness, and justice, as it were, in
contrast to themselves, their unruliness, their ferocity—they thirst for it
unconsciously, but they do thirst for it. Passionate and fierce on the surface, they are painfully capable of loving woman, for instance, and with a
spiritual and elevated love. Again do not laugh at me, this is very often the
case in such natures. But they cannot hide their passions—sometimes very
coarse—and that is conspicuous and is noticed, but the inner man is
unseen. Their passions are quickly exhausted; but, by the side of a noble
and lofty creature that seemingly coarse and rough man seeks a new life,
seeks to correct himself, to be better, to become noble and honorable, 'sublime and beautiful,' however much the expression has been ridiculed. I said
just now that I would not venture to touch upon my client's engagement to
Miss Verkhovtseva. But I may say half a word. What we heard just now was
not evidence, but only the scream of a frenzied and revengeful woman, and
it was not for her—oh, not for her!—to reproach him with treachery, for
she has betrayed him! If she had had but a little time for reflection she
would not have given such evidence. Oh, do not believe her! No, my client is not a 'monster,' as she called him! The crucified Lover of Mankind
on the eve of His Crucifixion said: 'I am the Good Shepherd. The good

shepherd giveth his life for his sheep, so that none of them might be lost.'[5] Let not a man's soul be lost through us! I asked just now what does 'father' mean, and exclaimed that it was a great word, a precious name. But one must use words honestly, gentlemen of the jury, and I venture to call things by their right names, by their proper designation: such a father as the murdered old Karamazov cannot be called a father and does not deserve to be. Filial love for an unworthy father is an absurdity, an impossibility. Love cannot be created from nothing: only God can create something from nothing. 'Fathers, provoke not your children to wrath,' the apostle writes, from a heart glowing with love.[6] It's not for the sake of my client that I quote these sacred words, I mention them for all fathers. Who has authorized me to preach to fathers? No one. But as a man and a citizen I make my appeal—*vivos voco*![7] We are not long on earth, we do many evil deeds and say many evil words. So let us all catch a favorable moment when we are all together to say a good word to each other. That's what I am doing: while I am in this place I take advantage of my opportunity. Not for nothing is this tribune given to us by the highest authority—all Russia hears us! I am not speaking only for the fathers here present, I cry aloud to all fathers: 'Fathers, provoke not your children to wrath.' Yes, let us first fulfill Christ's injunction ourselves and only then venture to expect it of our children. Otherwise we are not fathers, but enemies of our children, and they are not our children, but our enemies, and we have made them our enemies ourselves. 'What measure ye mete it shall be measured unto you again'— it's not I who say that, it's the Gospel precept, measure to others according as they measure to you. How can we blame children if they measure us according to our measure? Not long ago a servant girl in Finland was suspected of having secretly given birth to a child. She was watched, and a box of which no one knew anything was found in the corner of the loft, behind some bricks. It was opened and inside was found the body of a newborn child which she had killed. In the same box were found the skeletons of two other babies which, according to her own confession, she had killed at the moment of their birth. Gentlemen of the jury, was she a mother to her children? She gave birth to them, indeed; but was she a mother to them? Would anyone venture to give her the sacred name of mother? Let us be bold, gentlemen of the jury, let us be audacious even; it's our duty to be so at this moment and not to be afraid of certain words and ideas like Moscow merchants' wives who are afraid of 'metal' and 'brimstone.'[8] No, let us prove that the progress of the last few years has touched even us, and let us say plainly, the father is not merely he who begets the child, but he who begets it and does his duty by it. Oh, of course, there is the other meaning, there is the other interpretation of the word 'father,' which insists

5. By referring to Jesus as "the crucified Lover of Mankind," Fetyukovich implies that Jesus was merely mortal, in contradiction to the Christian belief that Jesus was divine as well as human. In John 10.11, Jesus says, "I am the good shepherd: the good shepherd giveth his life for the sheep."
6. In Colossians 3.21, the apostle Paul commands, "Fathers, provoke not your children to anger, lest they be discouraged." Fetyukovich omits to mention the passage that immediately precedes this, in which Paul exhorts children to obey their parents: "Children, obey your parents in all things: for this is well pleasing unto the Lord." See also Ephesians 6.1–4.
7. "I call upon the living" (Latin), part of the epigraph to Schiller's poem "The Song of the Bell" (Das Lied von der Glocke, 1798). This was also the slogan of *The Bell* (see p. 468).
8. In the play *Hard Days* (*Tiazhelye dni*, 1863) by Alexander Ostrovsky (1823–1886); the words *metal* and *brimstone* elicit ignorant and superstitious reactions from the characters (act II, scene 2). These words are associated with Biblical passages such as Luke 17.29: "But the same day that Lot went out of Sodom it rained fire and brimstone from heaven, and destroyed them all."

that any father, even though he be a monster, even though he be the enemy of his children, still remains my father simply because he begot me. But this is, so to speak, the mystical meaning which I cannot comprehend with my intellect, but can only accept by faith, or, better to say, *on faith*, like many other things which I do not understand, but which religion bids me believe. But in that case let it be kept outside the sphere of actual life. In the sphere of actual life, which has, indeed, its own rights, but also lays upon us great duties and obligations, in that sphere, if we want to be humane—Christian, in fact—we must, and ought to, act only upon convictions justified by reason and experience, which have been passed through the crucible of analysis; in a word, we must act rationally, not insanely, and not as though in dream and delirium, that we may not do harm, that we may not ill-treat and ruin a man. Then it will be real Christian work, not only mystic, but rational and philanthropic. . . ."

There was violent applause at this passage from many parts of the court, but Fetyukovich waved his hands as though imploring them to let him finish without interruption. The court relapsed into silence at once. The orator went on.

"Do you suppose, gentlemen of the jury, that our children as they grow up and begin to reason can avoid such questions? No, they cannot, and we will not impose on them an impossible restriction. The sight of an unworthy father involuntarily suggests tormenting questions to a youth, especially when he compares him with the excellent fathers of his companions. The conventional answer to this question is: 'He begot you, and you are his flesh and blood, and therefore you are bound to love him.' The youth involuntarily reflects: 'But did he love me when he begot me?' he asks, wondering more and more.[9] 'Was it for my sake he begot me? He did not know me, not even my sex, at that moment, at the moment of passion, inflamed by wine, perhaps, and he has only transmitted to me a propensity to drunkenness—that's all he's done for me. . . . Why am I bound to love him, simply for begetting me when he has cared nothing for me all my life after?' Oh, perhaps those questions strike you as coarse and cruel, but do not expect an impossible restraint from a young mind. 'Drive nature out of the door and it will fly in at the window,'[1] and, above all, let us not be afraid of 'metal' and 'brimstone,' but decide the question according to the dictates of reason and humanity and not of mystic ideas. How shall it be decided? Why, like this. Let the son stand before his father and ask him, 'Father, tell me, why must I love you? Father, show me that I must love you,' and if that father is able to answer him and show him good reason, we have a real, normal, parental relation, not resting on mystical prejudice, but on a rational, responsible and strictly humanitarian basis. But if he does not, there's an end to the family tie. He is not a father to him, and the son has a right to look upon him as a stranger, and even an enemy. Our tribune, gentlemen of the jury, ought to be a school of true and sound ideas!"

Here the orator was interrupted by irrepressible and almost frantic applause. Of course, it was not the whole audience, but a good half of it applauded. The fathers and mothers present applauded. Shrieks and

---

9. Fetyukovich loosely paraphrases lines spoken by Franz Moor in Schiller's *The Robbers*, act I, scene I and act IV, scene 2.
1. This line appears in Karamzin's 1803 free translation of "A Cat Turned into a Woman," by the French fabulist Jean de La Fontaine (1621–1695).

exclamations were heard from the gallery, where the ladies were sitting. Handkerchiefs were waved. The President began ringing his bell with all his might. He was obviously irritated by the behavior of the audience, but did not venture to clear the court as he had threatened. Even persons of high position, old men with stars on their breasts, sitting on specially reserved seats behind the judges, applauded the orator and waved their handkerchiefs. So that when the noise died down, the President confined himself to repeating his stern threat to clear the court, and Fetyukovich, excited and triumphant, continued his speech.

"Gentlemen of the jury, you remember that awful night of which so much has been said today, when the son got over the fence into his father's house and stood face to face with the enemy and persecutor who had begotten him. I insist most emphatically it was not for money he ran to his father's house: the charge of robbery is an absurdity, as I proved before. And it was not to murder him he broke into the house, oh, no! If he had had that design he would, at least, have taken the precaution of arming himself beforehand. The brass pestle he caught up instinctively without knowing why he did it. Granted that he deceived his father by tapping at the window, granted that he made his way in—I've said already that I do not for a moment believe that legend, but let it be so, let us suppose it for a moment. Gentlemen, I swear to you by all that's holy, if it had not been his father, but an ordinary enemy, he would, after running through the rooms and satisfying himself that the woman was not there, have made off, posthaste, without doing any harm to his rival. He would have struck him, pushed him away perhaps, nothing more, for he had no thought and no time to spare for that. What he wanted to know was where she was. But his father, his father! The mere sight of the father who had hated him from his childhood, had been his enemy, his persecutor, and now his unnatural rival, was enough! A feeling of hatred came over him involuntarily, irresistibly, clouding his reason. It all surged up in one moment! It was an impulse of madness and insanity, but also an impulse of nature, irresistibly and unconsciously (like everything in nature) avenging the violation of its eternal laws. But even then he did not murder him—I maintain that, I cry that aloud!—no, he only brandished the pestle in a burst of indignant disgust, not meaning to kill him, not knowing that he would kill him. Had he not had this fatal pestle in his hand, he would have only knocked his father down perhaps, but would not have killed him. As he ran away, he did not know whether he had killed the old man he had knocked down. Such a murder is not a murder. Such a murder is not a parricide. No, the murder of such a father cannot be called parricide. Such a murder can only be reckoned parricide by prejudice. But I appeal to you again and again from the depths of my soul; did this murder actually take place? Gentlemen of the jury, if we convict and punish him, he will say to himself: 'These people have done nothing for my bringing up, for my education, nothing to improve my lot, nothing to make me better, nothing to make me a man. These people have not given me to eat and to drink, have not visited me in prison and nakedness,[2] and here they have

---

2. Fetyukovich loosely paraphrases Jesus' words to his disciples regarding the end of the world, when the elect will inherit the earth: "For I was an hungred, and ye gave me meat: I was thirsty, and ye gave me drink: I was a stranger, and ye took me in: Naked, and ye clothed me: I was sick, and ye visited me: I was in prison, and ye came unto me" (Matthew 25.35–36).

sent me to penal servitude. I am even, I owe them nothing now, and owe no one anything forever and ever. They are wicked and I will be wicked. They are cruel and I will be cruel!' That is what he will say, gentlemen of the jury. And I swear, by finding him guilty you will only make it easier for him: you will ease his conscience, he will curse the blood he has shed and will not regret it. At the same time you will destroy in him the possibility of becoming a new man, for he will remain in his wickedness and blindness all his life. But do you want to punish him fearfully, terribly, with the most awful punishment that could be imagined, and at the same time to save him and regenerate his soul? If so, overwhelm him with your mercy! You will see, you will hear how he will tremble and be horror-struck. 'How can I endure this mercy? How can I endure so much love? Am I worthy of it?' That's what he will exclaim. Oh, I know, I know that heart, that wild but grateful heart, gentlemen of the jury! It will bow before your mercy; it thirsts for a great and loving action, it will flame up and be resurrected forever. There are souls which, in their limitation, blame the whole world. But subdue such a soul with mercy, show it love, and it will curse its past, for there are many good impulses in it. Such a heart will expand and see that God is merciful and that men are good and just. He will be horror-stricken; he will be crushed by remorse and the vast obligation laid upon him henceforth. And he will not say then, 'I am even,' but will say, 'I am guilty in the sight of all men and am more unworthy than all.' With tears of penitence and poignant, tender anguish, he will exclaim: 'Others are better than I, they wanted to save me, not to ruin me!' Oh, this act of mercy is so easy for you, for in the absence of anything like real evidence it will be too awful for you to pronounce: 'Yes, he is guilty.' Better acquit ten guilty men than punish one innocent man![3] Do you hear, do you hear that majestic voice from the past century of our glorious history? It is not for an insignificant person like me to remind you that the Russian court does not exist for the punishment only, but also for the salvation of the fallen man! Let other nations think of retribution and the letter of the law, we will cling to the spirit and the meaning—the salvation and the reformation of the lost. If this is true, if Russia and her justice are such, she may go forward with good cheer! Do not try to scare us with your frenzied troikas from which all the nations stand aside in disgust. Not a runaway troika, but the stately chariot of Russia will move calmly and majestically to its goal. In your hands is the fate of my client, in your hands is the fate of Russian justice. You will defend it, you will save it, you will prove that there are men to watch over it, that it is in good hands!"

Chapter XIV

The Peasants Stand Up for Themselves

That was how Fetyukovich concluded, and the enthusiasm of the audience burst like an irresistible storm. It was out of the question to stop it: the women wept, many of the men wept too, even two important personages

---

3. A loose rendition of lines from Peter the Great's Code of Martial Law (1716), repeated in *The Complete Code of Laws of the Russian Empire*, published in Saint Petersburg in 1876.

shed tears. The President submitted, and even postponed ringing his bell: "the suppression of such an enthusiasm would be the suppression of something sacred," as the ladies cried afterwards. The orator himself was genuinely touched. And it was at this moment that Ippolit Kirillovich got up to make certain objections. People looked at him with hatred. "What? What's the meaning of it? He positively dares to make objections," the ladies babbled. But if the whole world of ladies, including his wife, had protested he could not have been stopped at that moment. He was pale, he was shaking with emotion, his first words, his first phrases were even unintelligible, he gasped for breath, could hardly speak clearly, lost the thread. But he soon recovered himself. Of this closing argument of his I will quote only a few sentences.

". . . . I am reproached with having woven a romance. But what is this defense if not one romance on the top of another? All that was lacking was poetry. Fyodor Pavlovich, while waiting for his mistress, tears open the envelope and throws it on the floor. We are even told what he said while engaged in this amazing act. Is not this a flight of fancy? And what proof have we that he had taken out the money? Who heard what he said? The weak-minded idiot, Smerdyakov, transformed into a Byronic hero, avenging society for his illegitimate birth—isn't this a romance in the Byronic style?[4] And the son who breaks into his father's house and murders him without murdering him is not even a romance—this is a sphinx setting us a riddle which he cannot solve himself. If he murdered him, he murdered him, and what's the meaning of his murdering him without having murdered him—who can make head or tail of this? Then we are admonished that our tribune is a tribune of true and sound ideas and from this tribune of 'sound ideas' is heard a solemn declaration that to call the murder of a father 'parricide' is nothing but a prejudice! But if parricide is a prejudice, and if every child is to ask his father why he is to love him, what will become of us? What will become of the foundations of society? What will become of the family? Parricide, it appears, is only a bogey of Moscow merchants' wives. The most precious, the most sacred guarantees for the destiny and future of Russian justice are presented to us in a perverted and frivolous form, simply to attain an object—to obtain the justification of something which cannot be justified. 'Oh, crush him by mercy,' cries the counsel for the defense; but that's all the criminal wants, and tomorrow it will be seen how much he is crushed. And is not the counsel for the defense too modest in asking only for the acquittal of the defendant? Why not found a charity in the honor of the parricide to commemorate his exploit among future generations? Religion and the Gospel are corrected— that's all mysticism, we are told, and ours is the only true Christianity which has been subjected to the analysis of reason and common sense. And so they set up before us a false semblance of Christ! '*What measure ye mete so it shall be meted unto you again*,' cries the counsel for the defense, and instantly deduces that Christ teaches us to measure as it is measured to us—and this from the tribune of truth and sound sense! We peep into

---

4. Byron's poetry was associated with a specific type of hero: talented, passionate, and rebellious; characterized by a lack of respect for social institutions, rank, and propriety; arrogant and ultimately self-destructive. Ippolit Kirillovich may also refer specifically to Byron's poem "Parisina" (1816), in which an illegitimate son is condemned to death for having an affair with his father's wife.

the Gospel only on the eve of making speeches, in order to dazzle the audience by our acquaintance with what is, anyway, a rather original composition, which may be of use to produce a certain effect—all to serve the purpose! But what Christ commands us is something very different: He bids us beware of doing this, because the wicked world does this, but we ought to forgive and to turn the other cheek, and not to measure to our persecutors as they measure to us. This is what our God has taught us and not that to forbid children to murder their fathers is a prejudice. And we will not from the tribune of truth and good sense correct the Gospel of our Lord, Whom the counsel for the defense deigns to call only 'the crucified lover of humanity,' in opposition to all orthodox Russia, which calls to Him, 'For Thou art our God!'"[5]

At this the President intervened and checked the over zealous speaker, begging him not to exaggerate, not to overstep the bounds, and so on, as presidents always do in such cases. The audience, too, was uneasy. The public was restless: there were even exclamations of indignation. Fetyukovich did not so much as reply; he only mounted the tribune to lay his hand on his heart and, with an offended voice, utter a few words full of dignity. He only touched again, lightly and ironically, on "romancing" and "psychology," and in an appropriate place quoted, "Jupiter, you are angry, therefore you are wrong," which provoked a burst of approving laughter in the audience, for Ippolit Kirillovich was by no means like Jupiter.[6] Then, of the accusation that he was teaching the young generation to murder their fathers, Fetyukovich observed, with great dignity, that he would not even answer. As for the prosecutor's charge of uttering unorthodox opinions, and calling Christ merely 'the crucified lover of humanity' rather than 'God,' and that could not be expressed from this 'tribune of truth and good sense,' Fetyukovich noted that it was a personal "insinuation" and that he had expected in this court to be secure from accusations "damaging to my reputation as a citizen and a loyal subject." But at these words the President pulled him up, too, and Fetyukovich concluded his rejoinder with a bow, amid a hum of approbation in the court. And Ippolit Kirillovich was, in the opinion of our ladies, "crushed for good."

Then the defendant was allowed to speak. Mitya stood up, but said very little. He was fearfully exhausted, physically and mentally. The look of strength and independence with which he had entered in the morning had almost disappeared. He seemed as though he had passed through an experience that day, which had taught him for the rest of his life something very important he had not understood till then. His voice was weak, he did not shout as before. In his words there was a new note of humility, defeat and submission.

"What am I to say, gentlemen of the jury? The hour of judgment has come for me, I feel the hand of God upon me! The end has come to an erring man! But, before God, I repeat to you, I am innocent of my father's blood! For the last time I repeat, it wasn't I who killed him! I erred, but I loved what is good. Every instant I strove to reform, but I lived like a wild beast. I thank the prosecutor, he told me many things about myself that I

---

5. Ippolit Kirillovich accuses Fetyukovich of denying the divinity of Christ, in sharp defiance of Orthodox doctrine; "for Thou art our God" is a common phrase in Orthodox prayers.
6. Jupiter was the supreme deity in Roman mythology, the patron deity of the Roman state.

did not know; but it's not true that I killed my father, the prosecutor is mistaken. I thank my counsel, too. I cried listening to him; but it's not true that I killed my father, and he needn't have supposed it. And don't believe the doctors. I am perfectly sane, only my heart is heavy. If you spare me, if you let me go, I will pray for you. I will be a better man. I give you my word before God I will! And if you will condemn me, I'll break my sword over my head myself and kiss the pieces.[7] But spare me, do not rob me of my God! I know myself, I shall rebel! My heart is heavy, gentlemen . . . spare me!"

He almost fell back in his place: his voice broke: he could hardly articulate the last phrase. Then the judges proceeded to put the questions and began to ask both sides to formulate their conclusions. But I will not describe the details. At last the jury rose to retire for consultation. The President was very tired, and so his last charge to the jury was rather feeble. "Be impartial, don't be influenced by the eloquence of the defense, but yet weigh the arguments. Remember that there is a great responsibility laid upon you," and so on and so on. The jury withdrew and the court adjourned. People could get up, move about, exchange their accumulated impressions, refresh themselves at the buffet. It was very late, almost one o'clock at night, but nobody went away. The strain was so great that no one could think of repose. All waited with sinking hearts, although, however, not everyone's heart was sinking. The ladies were simply in a state of hysterical impatience, but their hearts were untroubled: "Acquittal is inevitable." They all prepared themselves for a dramatic moment of general enthusiasm. I must admit there were many among the men, too, who were convinced that an acquittal was inevitable. Some were pleased, others frowned, while some were simply dejected: they did not want an acquittal! Fetyukovich himself was confident of his success. He was surrounded by people congratulating him and fawning upon him.

"There are," he said to one group, as I was told afterwards, "there are invisible threads that bind the counsel for the defense with the jury. One feels during one's speech if they are being formed. I was aware of them. They exist. Our cause is won. Set your mind at rest."

"What will our peasants say now?" said one stout, cross-looking, pock-marked gentleman, a landowner of the neighborhood, approaching a group of gentlemen engaged in conversation.

"But they are not all peasants. There are four government clerks among them."

"Yes, there are clerks," said a member of the district council, joining the group.

"And do you know that Nazaryov, the merchant with the medal, a juryman?"

"What of him?"

"He is a man with brains."

"But he never speaks."

"He is no great talker, but so much the better. There's no need for the Petersburg man to teach him: he could teach all Petersburg himself. He's the father of twelve children. Think of that!"

---

7. As part of the ritual of being drummed out of the army, a sword would be broken over the condemned soldier.

"But really, do you suppose they won't acquit him?" one of our young officials exclaimed in another group.

"They'll acquit him for certain," said a resolute voice.

"It would be shameful, disgraceful, not to acquit him!" cried the official. "Suppose he did murder him—there are fathers and fathers! And, besides, he was in such a frenzy. . . . He really may have done nothing but swing the pestle in the air, and so knocked the old man down. But it was a pity they dragged the lackey in. That was simply an absurd theory! If I'd been in Fetyukovich's place, I would simply have said straight out: 'He murdered him; but he is not guilty, and you can go to the devil!'"

"That's what he did, only without saying, 'Go to the devil!'"

"No, Mikhail Semyonich, he almost said that, too," put in a third voice.

"Why, gentlemen, in Lent an actress was acquitted in our town who had cut the throat of her lover's lawful wife."[8]

"Oh, but she did not finish cutting it."

"That makes no difference. She began cutting it."

"What did you think of what he said about children? Splendid, wasn't it?"

"Splendid!"

"And about mysticism, too!"

"Oh, drop mysticism, do!" cried someone else; "think of Ippolit and his fate from this day forth. His wife will scratch his eyes out tomorrow for Mitenka's sake."

"Is she here?"

"What an idea! If she'd been here she'd have scratched them out in court. She is at home with toothache. He, he, he!"

"He, he, he!"

In a third group:

"I daresay they will acquit Mitenka, after all."

"I wouldn't be surprised if he turns the Metropolis upside down tomorrow. He will be drinking for ten days!"

"Oh, the devil!"

"The devil's bound to have a hand in it, where should he be if not here?"

"Well, gentlemen, I admit it was eloquent. But still it's not the thing to break your father's head with a pestle! Or what are we coming to?"

"The chariot! Do you remember the chariot?"

"Yes; he turned a cart into a chariot!"

"And tomorrow he will turn a chariot into a cart, just to suit his purpose."

"What clever people there are nowadays. Is there any justice to be had in Russia?"

But the bell rang. The jury deliberated for exactly an hour, neither more nor less. A profound silence reigned in the court as soon as the public had taken their seats. I remember how the jurymen walked into the court. At last! I won't repeat the questions in order, and, indeed, I have forgotten them. I remember only the answer to the President's first and chief question: "Did the accused commit the murder for the sake of robbery and with premeditation?" (I don't remember the exact words.) There was a complete

8. A reference to the case of Anastasya Kairova, who was acquitted of attempted murder. Dostoevsky discussed the Kairova case extensively in the May 1876 issue of his *Diary*.

hush. The foreman of the jury, the youngest of the clerks, pronounced, in a clear, loud voice, amidst the deathlike stillness of the court:

"Yes, guilty!"

And the same answer was repeated to every question: "Yes, guilty!" and without the slightest extenuating comment. This no one had expected; almost everyone had reckoned upon a recommendation for mercy, at least. The deathlike silence in the court was not broken—all seemed petrified: those who desired his conviction as well as those who had been eager for his acquittal. But that was only for the first instant, and it was followed by a fearful hubbub. Many of the men in the audience were pleased. Some were rubbing their hands with no attempt to conceal their joy. Those who disagreed with the verdict seemed crushed, shrugged their shoulders, whispered, but still seemed unable to realize this. But how shall I describe the state the ladies were in? I thought they would create a riot. At first they could scarcely believe their ears. Then suddenly the whole court rang with exclamations: "What's the meaning of it? What next?" They leaped up from their places. They seemed to fancy that it might be at once reconsidered and reversed. At that instant Mitya suddenly stood up and cried in a heartrending voice, stretching his hands out before him:

"I swear by God and His dreadful Day of Judgment, I am not guilty of my father's blood! Katya, I forgive you! Brothers, friends, have pity on the other woman!"

He could not go on, and broke into a terrible sobbing wail that was heard all over the court in a voice not his own, in a new, surprising voice that suddenly emerged from God knows where. From the furthest corner at the back of the gallery came a piercing shriek—it was Grushenka. She had succeeded in begging admittance to the court again before the beginning of the attorneys' speeches. Mitya was taken away. The passing of the sentence was deferred till next day. The whole court was in a hubbub but I did not wait to hear. I only remember a few exclamations I heard on the steps as I went out.

"He'll have a twenty years' trip to the mines!"[9]

"Not less."

"Well, our peasants have stood up for themselves."

"And have done in our Mitenka!"

End of the fourth and last part.

9. According to Russian law of the time, Dmitri would have received life in prison for the premeditated murder of his father. Dostoevsky may have assigned him to twenty years in prison because this was the sentence received by Ilynsky, one of the prototypes for Dmitri. Ilynsky, one of Dostoevsky's fellow prisoners in Siberian labor camp, was serving twenty years for the murder of his father; he was later acquitted.

EPILOGUE

Chapter I

Plans to Save Mitya

Five days after the trial, very early in the morning, before nine o'clock, Alyosha went to Katerina Ivanovna's to make final arrangements on a matter of great importance to both of them and to give her a message. She sat and talked to him in the very room in which she had once received Grushenka. In the next room Ivan Fyodorovich lay unconscious in a high fever. Katerina Ivanovna had immediately after the scene at the trial ordered the sick and unconscious man to be carried to her house, disregarding the inevitable gossip and general disapproval of the public. One of the two relations who lived with her had departed to Moscow immediately after the scene at the court, the other remained. But even if both had gone away, Katerina Ivanovna would have adhered to her resolution, and would have gone on nursing the sick man and sitting by him day and night. Varvinsky and Herzenstube attended him. The famous doctor had gone back to Moscow, refusing to give an opinion as to the probable outcome of the illness. Though the doctors encouraged Katerina Ivanovna and Alyosha, it was evident that they could not yet give them positive hopes of recovery. Alyosha came to see his sick brother twice a day. But this time he had specially urgent business, and he foresaw how difficult it would be to approach the subject, yet he was in great haste: he had another engagement that could not be put off for that same morning, and he had to hurry. They had been talking for a quarter of an hour. Katerina Ivanovna was pale and very fatigued, yet at the same time in a state of terrible, sickly excitement: she had a presentiment of the reason why Alyosha had come to her.

"Don't worry about his decision," she said, with confident emphasis to Alyosha. "One way or another he is bound to come to it: he must escape! That unhappy man, that hero of honor and conscience—not he, not Dmitri Fyodorovich, but the man lying on the other side of that door, who has sacrificed himself for his brother," Katya added, with flashing eyes, "told me the whole plan of escape long ago. You know he has already entered into negotiations. . . . I've told you something already. . . . You see, it will probably come off at the third stopping place from here, when the party of prisoners is taken to Siberia. Oh, it's a long way off yet. Ivan Fyodorovich has already visited the superintendent of the third stop. But we don't know yet who will be in charge of the party, and it's impossible to find that out so long beforehand. Tomorrow perhaps I will show you in detail the whole plan which Ivan Fyodorovich left me on the eve of the trial in case of need. . . . That was when—do you remember?—you found us quarreling. He had just gone downstairs, but seeing you I made him come back; do you remember? Do you know what we were quarreling about then?"

"No, I don't," said Alyosha.

"Of course he did not tell you: it was about that plan of escape. He had told me the main idea three days before, and we began quarreling about it at once and quarreled for three days. We quarreled because when he told me that, if Dmitri Fyodorovich were convicted he would escape abroad with that creature, I suddenly felt furious—I can't tell you why, I don't know myself why . . . Oh, of course, I was furious then about that creature, that creature, and that she, too, should go abroad with Dmitri!" Katerina Ivanovna exclaimed suddenly, her lips quivering with anger. "As soon as Ivan Fyodorovich saw that I was furious about that creature, he instantly imagined I was jealous of her and that I therefore still loved Dmitri. That is how our first quarrel began. I would not give an explanation, I could not ask forgiveness; I could not bear to think that such a man could suspect me of still loving that . . . and when I myself had told him long before that I did not love Dmitri, that I loved no one but him! It was only anger against that creature that made me angry with him. Three days later, on the evening you came, he brought me a sealed envelope, which I was to open at once, if anything happened to him. Oh, he foresaw his illness! He told me that the envelope contained the details of the escape, and that if he died or was taken dangerously ill, I was to save Mitya alone. Then he left me money, nearly ten thousand—the very same to which the prosecutor referred in his speech, having learned from someone that he had sent them to be changed. I was suddenly tremendously impressed to find that Ivan Fyodorovich had not given up his idea of saving his brother, and was confiding this plan of escape to me, though he was still jealous of me and still convinced that I loved Mitya. Oh, that was a sacrifice! No, you cannot fully understand the greatness of such self-sacrifice, Alexey Fyodorovich. I wanted to fall at his feet in reverence, but I thought at once that he would take it only for my joy at the thought of Mitya's being saved (and he certainly would have imagined that!), and I was so exasperated at the mere possibility of such an unjust thought on his part that I lost my temper again, and instead of kissing his feet, flew into a fury again! Oh, I am unhappy! It's my character, my awful, unhappy character! Oh, you will see, I shall end by driving him, too, to abandon me for another with whom he can get on better, like Dmitri. But . . . no, I could not bear it, I would kill myself. And when you came in then, and when I called to you and told him to come back, I was so enraged by the look of contempt and hatred he turned on me that—do you remember?—I cried out to you that it was *he, he alone* who had persuaded me that his brother Dmitri was murderer! I said that malicious thing on purpose to wound him again, he had never, never persuaded me that his brother was a murderer, on the contrary, it was I, I who persuaded him! Oh, my temper was the cause of everything! I paved the way to that hideous scene at the trial. He wanted to show me that he was an honorable man, and that, even if I loved his brother, he would not ruin him for revenge or jealousy. So he came to the court . . . I am the cause of it all, I alone am to blame!"

Katya never had made such confessions to Alyosha before, and he felt that she was now at that stage of unbearable suffering when even the proudest heart painfully crushes its pride and falls vanquished by grief. Oh, Alyosha knew another terrible reason of her present misery, though she had carefully concealed it from him during those days since the trial; it would have been for some reason too painful to him if she had been brought so low as to speak to him now about that. She was suffering for her "treachery" at the trial, and Alyosha felt that her conscience was impelling her to confess it to him, to him, Alyosha, with tears and cries and hysterical writhings on the floor. But he dreaded that moment and longed to spare her. It made the commission on which he had come even more difficult. He spoke of Mitya again.

"It's all right, it's all right, don't be anxious about him!" she began again, sharply and stubbornly. "All that is only momentary, I know him, I know his heart only too well. You may be sure he will consent to escape. It's not as though it would be immediately; he will have time to make up his mind to it. Ivan Fyodorovich will be well by that time and will manage it all himself, so that I shall have nothing to do with it. Don't be anxious; he will consent to run away. He has agreed already: do you suppose he would give up his creature? And they won't let her go to him in prison, so he is bound to escape. It's you he's most afraid of, he is afraid you won't approve of his escape on moral grounds. But you must generously *allow* it, if your sanction is so necessary," Katya added with venom. She paused and smiled.

"He talks about some hymn," she went on again, "some cross he has to bear, some duty; I remember Ivan Fyodorovich told me a great deal about it, and if you knew how he talked!" Katya cried suddenly, with feeling she could not repress, "if you knew how he loved that wretched man at the moment he told me, and how he hated him, perhaps, at the same moment! And I heard his story and his tears with sneering disdain. Oh, creature! It is I who am the creature, me! It is I who am responsible for his fever. But that man in prison is he ready for suffering?" Katya concluded irritably. "And can such a man suffer? Men like him never suffer!"

There was a note of hatred and contemptuous repulsion in her words. And yet it was she who had betrayed him. "Perhaps because she feels how she's guilty towards him she hates him at moments," Alyosha thought to himself. He hoped that it was only "at moments." In Katya's last words he detected a challenging note, but he did not take it up.

"I sent for you this morning especially to make you promise to persuade him yourself. Or do you, too, consider that to escape would be dishonorable, unvalorous, or how would . . . unchristian, perhaps?" Katya added, even more defiantly.

"Oh, no. I'll tell him everything," muttered Alyosha. "He asks you to come and see him today," he blurted out suddenly, looking her steadily in the face. She started, and drew back a little from him on the sofa.

"Me? Can that be?" she faltered, turning pale.

"It can and ought to be!" Alyosha began emphatically, growing more animated. "He needs you particularly just now. I would not have opened the subject and worried you beforehand, if it were not necessary. He is ill, he is beside himself, he keeps asking for you. It is not to be reconciled with you that he wants you, but only that you would go and show yourself at his door. So much has happened to him since that day. He realizes how guilty beyond all reckoning he is towards you. He does not ask your forgiveness; 'it's impossible to forgive me,' he says himself, but only that you would show yourself in his doorway."

"You're suddenly . . ." faltered Katya. "I had a presentiment all these days that you would come with that message. I knew he would ask me to come. It's impossible!"

"Let it be impossible, but do it. Only think, he realizes for the first time how he has offended you, the first time in his life; he had never grasped it before so fully. He said, 'If she refuses to come I shall be unhappy all my life.' Do you hear? though he is condemned to penal servitude for twenty years, he is still planning to be happy—is not that piteous? Think—you must visit him; though he is ruined, he is innocent," broke like a challenge from Alyosha. "His hands are clean, there is no blood on them! For the sake of his infinite sufferings in the future visit him now. Go, lead him on his way into the darkness—stand at his door, that is all. . . . You must do it, you *must!*" Alyosha concluded, laying immense stress on the word "must."

"I must . . . but I cannot . . ." Katya moaned. "He will look at me. . . . I can't."

"Your eyes ought to meet. How will you live all your life, if you don't make up your mind to do it now?"

"Better suffer all my life."

"You must go, you *must* go," Alyosha again emphasized implacably.

"But why today, why at once? . . . I can't leave the patient . . ."

"You can for a moment. It will only be a moment. If you don't come, he will be in delirium by tonight. I would not tell you a lie; have pity on him!"

"Have pity on *me!*" Katya said, with bitter reproach, and she burst into tears.

"Then you will come," said Alyosha firmly, seeing her tears. "I'll go and tell him you will come at once."

"No, don't tell him so on any account," cried Katya in alarm. "I will come, but don't tell him beforehand, for perhaps I may go, but not go in . . . I don't know yet . . ."

Her voice failed her. She gasped for breath. Alyosha got up to go.

"And what if I meet anyone?" she said suddenly, in a low voice, turning white again.

"That's just why you must go now, to avoid meeting anyone. There will be no one there, I can tell you that for certain. We will expect you," he concluded emphatically, and went out of the room.

Chapter II

For a Moment the Lie Becomes Truth

He hurried to the hospital where Mitya was lying now. The day after his fate was determined, Mitya had fallen ill with nervous fever, and was sent to the prison division of the town hospital. But at the request of several persons (Alyosha, Madame Khokhlakova, Liza, etc.), Doctor Varvinsky had put Mitya not with other prisoners, but in a separate little room, the one where Smerdyakov had been. It is true that there was a sentinel at the other end of the corridor, and there was a grating over the window, so that Varvinsky could be at ease about the indulgence he had shown, which was not quite legal; but he was a kindhearted and compassionate young man. He knew how hard it would be for a man like Mitya to pass at once so suddenly into the society of robbers and murderers, and that he must get used to it by degrees. The visits of relations and friends were informally sanctioned by the doctor and superintendant, and even by the police captain. But only Alyosha and Grushenka had visited Mitya. Rakitin had tried to force his way in twice, but Mitya emphatically asked Varvinsky not to admit him.

Alyosha found him sitting on his bunk in a hospital dressing gown, rather feverish, with a towel, soaked in vinegar and water, on his head. He looked at Alyosha as he came in with an indefinite expression, but there was a shade of something like dread discernible in it.

He had become terribly preoccupied since the trial; sometimes he would be silent for half an hour together, and seemed to be pondering something heavily and painfully, oblivious of everything about him. If he roused himself from his brooding and began to talk, he always spoke with a kind of abruptness and never of what he really wanted to say. He looked sometimes with a face of suffering at his brother. He seemed to be more at ease with Grushenka than with Alyosha. It is true, he scarcely spoke to her at all, but as soon as she came in, his whole face lit up with joy.

Alyosha sat down beside him on the bunk in silence. This time Mitya was waiting for Alyosha in suspense, but he did not dare ask him the question. He felt it almost unthinkable that Katya would consent to come, and at the same time he felt that if she did not come, something inconceivable would happen. Alyosha understood his feelings.

"Trifon Borisich," Mitya began nervously, "has pulled his whole inn to pieces, I am told. He's taken up the flooring, pulled apart the planks, split up all the gallery, I am told. He is seeking treasure all the time—the fifteen hundred rubles which the prosecutor said I'd hidden there. He began playing these tricks, they say, as soon as he got home. Serve him right, the swindler! The guard here told me yesterday; he comes from there."

"Listen," began Alyosha. "She will come, but I don't know when. Perhaps today, perhaps in a few days, that I can't tell. But she will come, she will, that's certain."

Mitya started, would have said something, but was silent. The news had a tremendous effect on him. It was evident that he would have liked terribly to know what had been said, but he was afraid to ask. Something cruel and contemptuous from Katya would have cut him like a knife at that moment.

"This was what she said among other things; that I must be sure to set your conscience at rest about escaping. If Ivan is not well by then she will see to it all herself."

"You've spoken of that already," Mitya observed musingly.

"And you have repeated it to Grusha," observed Alyosha.

"Yes," Mitya admitted. "She won't come this morning." He looked timidly at his brother. "She won't come till the evening. While I told her yesterday that Katya was taking measures, she was silent, but she set her mouth. She only whispered, 'Let her!' She understood that it was important. I did not dare to try her further. She understands now, I think, that Katya no longer cares for me, but loves Ivan."

"Does she?" broke from Alyosha.

"Perhaps she does not. Only she is not coming this morning," Mitya hastened to explain again; "I asked her to do something for me. You know, brother Ivan is superior to all of us. He ought to live, not us. He will recover."

"Would you believe it, though Katya is alarmed about him, she scarcely doubts that he will," said Alyosha.

"That means that she is convinced he will die. It's because she is frightened she's so sure he will get well."

"Ivan has a strong constitution, and I, too, believe there's every hope that he will get well," Alyosha observed anxiously.

"Yes, he will get well. But she is convinced that he will die. She has a great deal of sorrow to bear . . ."

A silence followed. Something very important was tormenting Mitya.

"Alyosha, I love Grusha terribly," he said suddenly in a shaking voice, full of tears.

"They won't let her go out *there* to you," Alyosha put in at once.

"And there is something else I wanted to tell you," Mitya went on, with a sudden ring in his voice. "If they beat me on the way or *there*, I won't submit to it. I will kill someone, and will be shot for it. And this will be going on for twenty years! They speak to me rudely as it is. The sentinel speaks to me without ceremony. I've been lying here all night, passing judgment on myself. I am not ready! I am not able to resign myself. I wanted to sing a 'hymn'; but if a guard speaks rudely to me, I have not the strength to bear it. For Grusha I would bear anything . . . anything except blows, that is. . . . But she won't be allowed to come *there*."

Alyosha smiled gently.

"Listen, brother, once for all," he said. "This is what I think about it. And you know that I would not tell you a lie. Listen: you are not ready, and such a cross is not for you. What's more, you don't need such a great martyr's cross when you are not ready for it. If you had murdered our father, it would grieve me that you should reject your cross. But you are innocent, and such a cross is too much for you. You wanted to regenerate another man in yourself by suffering. I say, only remember that other man always, all your life and wherever you escape to; and that will be enough for you. Your refusal of that great cross will only serve to make you feel all your life an even greater duty, and that constant feeling will do more for your regeneration, perhaps, than if you went *there*. For there you would not endure it and would begin to grumble, and perhaps at last would say: 'I am even.' The advocate was right about that. Such heavy burdens are not for all men.[1] For some they are impossible. These are my thoughts about it, if you need them. If other men would have to answer for your escape, officers or soldiers, then I would not have 'allowed' you," smiled Alyosha. "But they declare—the superintendent of that stop told Ivan himself—that if it's well managed there will be no great inquiry, and that they can get off easily. Of course, bribing is dishonest even in such a case, but I can't undertake to judge about it, because if Ivan and Katya commissioned me to act for you, I know I would go and give bribes. I must tell you the truth. And so I can't judge your own action. But let me assure you that I shall never condemn you. And it would be a strange thing if I could judge you in this. Now I think I've gone into everything."

"But I do condemn myself!" cried Mitya. "I shall escape, that was settled apart from you; could Mitka Karamazov do anything but run away?

---

1. In Matthew 23.4, Jesus reproaches those who would impose heavy burdens on others: "For they bind heavy burdens and grievous to be borne, and lay them on men's shoulders; but they themselves will not move them with one of their fingers." See also Luke 11.46.

But I shall condemn myself, and I will pray for my sin forever. That's how the Jesuits talk, isn't it? Just as we are doing?"

"Yes," Alyosha smiled gently.

"I love you for always telling the whole truth and never hiding anything," cried Mitya, with a joyful laugh. "So I've caught my Alyosha being jesuitical. I must kiss you for that. Now listen to the rest; I'll open the other side of my heart to you. This is what I planned and decided. If I run away, even with money and a passport, and even to America, I would be cheered up by the thought that I am not running away for pleasure, not for happiness, but to another exile as bad, perhaps, as Siberia. It is as bad, Alyosha, it is! I hate that America, damn it, already. Even though Grusha will be with me. Just look at her; is she an American? She is Russian, Russian to the marrow of her bones; she will be homesick for the motherland, and I shall see every hour that she is suffering for my sake, that she has taken up that cross for me. And what harm has she done? And how shall I, too, put up with the rabble out there, though they may be better than I, every one of them. I hate that America already! And though they may be wonderful at machinery, every one of them, damn them, they are not my people, they are not of my soul. I love Russia, Alyosha, I love the Russian God, though I am a scoundrel myself. I'll croak there!" he exclaimed, his eyes suddenly flashing. His voice was trembling with tears.

"So this is what I've decided, Alyosha, listen!" he began again, mastering his emotion. "As soon as I arrive there with Grusha, we will set to work at once on the land, in solitude, somewhere very remote, with wild bears. There must be some remote parts even there. I am told there are still Redskins there, somewhere, on the edge of the horizon. So to the country of the *Last of the Mohicans*,[2] and there we'll tackle the grammar at once, Grusha and I. Work and grammar—that's how we'll spend three years. And by that time we shall speak English like any Englishman. And as soon as we've learned it—good-bye to America! We'll run here to Russia as American citizens. Don't be uneasy—we would not come to this little town. We'd hide somewhere, a long way off, in the north or in the south. I will be changed by that time, and she will, too, in America. The doctors shall make me some sort of wart on my face—what's the use of their being so mechanical!—or else I'll put out one eye, let my beard grow a yard, and I will turn gray, fretting for Russia. I daresay they won't recognize us. And if they do, let them send us to Siberia—I don't care. It will show it's our fate. We'll work on the land here, too, somewhere in the wilds, and I'll make up as an American all my life. But we shall die on our own soil. That's my plan, and it won't be altered. Do you approve?"

"I approve," said Alyosha, not wanting to contradict him. Mitya paused for a minute and said suddenly:

"And how they worked it up at the trial! Didn't they work it up!"

"Even if they hadn't, you would have been convicted just the same," said Alyosha, with a sigh.

"Yes, people are sick of me here! God bless them, but it's hard," Mitya moaned miserably.

---

2. Historical novel (1826) by James Fenimore Cooper (1789–1851) which influenced the image of America in Russia. Dostoevsky owned a copy of Cooper's complete works in French translation.

Again there was silence for a minute.

"Alyosha, put me out of my misery at once!" he exclaimed suddenly. "Tell me, is she coming now, or not? Tell me? What did she say? How did she say it?"

"She said she would come, but I don't know whether she will come today. It's hard for her, you know!" Alyosha looked timidly at his brother.

"I should think it is hard for her! Alyosha, it will drive me out of my mind. Grusha keeps looking at me. She understands. My God, calm my heart: what is it I want? I want Katya! Do I understand what I want? It's the impious Karamazov abandon! No, I am not fit for suffering. I am a scoundrel, that's all one can say!"

"Here she is!" cried Alyosha.

At that instant Katya appeared in the doorway. For a moment she stood still, gazing at Mitya with a dazed expression. He leaped impulsively to his feet, and a scared look came into his face. He turned pale, but a timid, pleading smile appeared on his lips at once, and with an irresistible impulse he held out both hands to Katya. Seeing it, she flew impetuously to him. She seized him by the hands, and almost by force made him sit down on the bed. She sat down beside him, and still keeping his hands pressed them violently, convulsively. Several times they both strove to speak, but stopped short and again gazed speechless with a strange smile, their eyes fastened on one another. So passed two minutes.

"Have you forgiven me or not?" Mitya faltered at last, and at the same moment turning to Alyosha, his face distorted with joy, he shouted to him, "Do you hear what I am asking, do you hear?"

"That's what I loved you for, that you are generous at heart!" broke suddenly from Katya. "My forgiveness is no good to you, nor yours to me; whether you forgive me or not, you will always be a sore place in my soul, and I in yours—so it must be . . ." She stopped to take breath.

"What have I come for?" she began again with nervous haste: "to embrace your feet, to press your hands like this, till it hurts—you remember how in Moscow I used to squeeze them—to tell you again that you are my god, my joy, to tell you that I love you madly," she nearly moaned in anguish, and suddenly pressed his hand greedily to her lips. Tears streamed from her eyes.

Alyosha stood speechless and confounded; he had never expected what he was seeing.

"Love is over, Mitya!" Katya began again, "but the past is painfully dear to me. Know that forever. But now let what might have been come true for one minute," she faltered, with a drawn smile, looking into his face joyfully again. "You love another woman, and I love another man, and yet I shall love you eternally, and you will love me; do you know that? Do you hear? Love me, love me all your life!" she cried, with a quiver almost of menace, in her voice.

"I shall love you, and . . . do you know, Katya," Mitya began, drawing a deep breath at each word, "do you know, five days ago, that same evening, I loved you. . . . When you fell down and were carried out . . . All my life! So it will be, so it will be eternally . . ."

So they murmured to one another frantic words, almost meaningless, perhaps not even true, but at that moment it was all true, and they both believed what they said implicitly.

"Katya," cried Mitya suddenly, "do you believe I murdered him? I know you don't believe it now, but then . . . when you gave evidence. . . . Surely, surely, you did not believe it!"

"I did not believe it even then! I've never believed it. I hated you, and for a moment I persuaded myself. While I was giving evidence I persuaded myself and believed it, but when I'd finished speaking I stopped believing it at once. Don't doubt that! I have forgotten that I came here to punish myself," she said, with a new expression in her voice, quite unlike the loving tones of a moment before.

"Woman, yours is a heavy burden," broke, as it were, involuntarily from Mitya.

"Let me go," she whispered. "I'll come again. It's more than I can bear now."

She was getting up from her place, but suddenly uttered a loud scream and staggered back. Grushenka walked suddenly and noiselessly into the room. No one had expected her. Katya moved swiftly to the door, but when she reached Grushenka, she stopped suddenly, turned as white as chalk and moaned softly, almost in a whisper:

"Forgive me!"

Grushenka stared at her and, pausing for an instant, in a vindictive, venomous voice, answered:

"We are wicked, my girl, you and I! We are both wicked! As though we could forgive one another! Save him, and I'll worship you all my life."

"You won't forgive her!" cried Mitya, with frantic reproach.

"Don't be anxious, I'll save him for you!" Katya whispered rapidly, and she ran out of the room.

"And you could refuse to forgive her when she begged your forgiveness herself?" Mitya exclaimed bitterly again.

"Mitya, don't dare to blame her; you have no right to!" Alyosha cried hotly.

"Her proud lips spoke, not her heart," Grushenka brought out in a tone of disgust. "If she saves you I'll forgive her everything . . ."

She stopped speaking, as though suppressing something. She could not yet recover herself. She had come in, as appeared afterwards, accidentally, with no suspicion of what she would meet.

"Alyosha, run after her!" Mitya cried to his brother; "tell her . . . I don't know . . . don't let her go away like this!"

"I'll come to you again at nightfall," said Alyosha, and he ran after Katya. He overtook her outside the hospital grounds. She was walking fast, but as soon as Alyosha caught her up she said quickly:

"No, before that woman I can't punish myself! I asked her forgiveness because I wanted to punish myself to the bitter end. She would not forgive me. . . . I like her for that!" she added, in an unnatural voice, and her eyes flashed with fierce anger.

"My brother did not expect this in the least," muttered Alyosha. "He was sure she would not come . . ."

"No doubt. Let us leave that," she snapped. "Listen: I can't go with you to the funeral now. I've sent them flowers for the little coffin. I think they still have money. If necessary, tell them I'll never abandon them. . . . Now leave me, leave me, please. You are late as it is—the bells are ringing for late mass. . . . Leave me, please!"

Chapter III

Ilyushechka's Funeral. The Speech at the Stone

He really was late. They had waited for him and had already decided to bear the pretty flower-decked little coffin to the church without him. It was the coffin of poor little Ilyushechka. He had died two days after Mitya was sentenced. At the gate of the house Alyosha was met by the shouts of the boys, Ilyusha's schoolfellows. They had all been impatiently expecting him and were glad that he had come at last. There were about twelve of them, they all had their schoolbags or satchels on their shoulders. "Papa will cry, be with papa," Ilyusha had told them as he lay dying, and the boys remembered it. Kolya Krasotkin was the foremost of them.

"How glad I am you've come, Karamazov!" he cried, holding out his hand to Alyosha. "It's awful here. It's really horrible to see it. Snegiryov is not drunk, we know for a fact he's had nothing to drink today, but he seems as if he were drunk . . . I am always manly, but this is awful. Karamazov, if I am not keeping you, one question before you go in?"

"What is it, Kolya?" said Alyosha, stopping.

"Is your brother innocent or guilty? Was it he who killed your father or was it the lackey? As you say, so it will be. I haven't slept for the last four nights for thinking of it."

"The lackey killed him, my brother is innocent," answered Alyosha.

"That's what I said," the boy Smurov cried suddenly.

"So he will perish an innocent victim for truth!" exclaimed Kolya; "though he is ruined he is happy! I could envy him!'

"What do you mean? How can you? Why?" cried Alyosha surprised.

"Oh, if I, too, could sacrifice myself some day for truth!" said Kolya with enthusiasm.

"But not in such a cause, not with such disgrace and such horror!" said Alyosha.

"Of course . . . I would like to die for all humanity, and as for disgrace, I don't care about that—our names may perish.[3] I respect your brother!"

"And so do I!" the boy who had once declared that he knew who had founded Troy cried suddenly and unexpectedly out of the crowd, and he blushed up to his ears like a peony as he had done on that occasion.

Alyosha went into the room. Ilyusha lay with his hands folded and his eyes closed in a blue coffin with a white frill round it. His thin face was hardly changed at all, and strange to say there was practically no smell from the corpse. The expression of his face was serious and, as it were, thoughtful. His hands, crossed over his breast, looked particularly beautiful, as though chiseled in marble. There were flowers in his hands and the coffin, inside and out, was decked with flowers, which had been sent early in the morning by Liza Khokhlakova. But there were flowers too from Katerina Ivanovna, and when Alyosha opened the door, the captain had a bunch in his trembling hands and was strewing them again over his dear

---

3. Kolya quotes the revolutionary French politician and orator Pierre Victurnien Vergniaud (1753–1793), who declared: "Perissent nos noms, pourvu que la chose publique soit sauvée!" (Let our names perish, as long as the public good is saved!)

boy. He scarcely glanced at Alyosha when he came in, and he would not
look at any one, even at his crazy weeping wife, "mamochka," who kept trying to stand on her crippled legs to get a closer look at her dead boy.
Ninochka had been pushed in her chair by the boys close up to the coffin.
She sat with her head pressed to it and she too was no doubt quietly weeping. Snegiryov's face looked eager, yet bewildered and exasperated. There
was something crazy about his gestures and the words that broke from him.
"Old man, dear old man!" he exclaimed every minute, gazing at Ilyusha. It
was his habit to call Ilyusha "old man," as a term of affection when he was
alive.

"Papa, give me a flower, too; take that white one out of his hand and
give it to me," the crazy "mamochka" begged, whimpering. Either because
the little white rose in Ilyusha's hand had caught her fancy or because
she wanted one from his hand to keep in memory of him, she moved restlessly, stretching out her hands for the flower.

"I won't give it to anyone, I won't give you anything," Snegiryov cried callously. "They are his flowers, not yours! Everything is his, nothing is yours!"

"Papa, give mamma a flower!" said Ninochka, suddenly lifting her face
wet with tears.

"I won't give away anything, and to her less than anyone! She didn't
love him. She took away his little cannon and he gave it to her," the captain broke into loud sobs at the thought of how Ilyusha had given up his
cannon to his mother. The poor, crazy woman was bathed in noiseless
tears, hiding her face in her hands. The boys, seeing that the father would
not leave the coffin and that it was time to carry it out, stood around it in
a close circle and began to lift it up.

"I don't want him to be buried in the churchyard," Snegiryov wailed
suddenly; "I'll bury him by the stone, by our stone! Ilyusha told me to. I
won't let him be carried out!"

He had been saying for the last three days that he would bury him by the
stone, but Alyosha, Krasotkin, the landlady, her sister and all the boys
interfered.

"What an idea, bury him by a heathen stone, as though he had hanged
himself," the old landlady said sternly. "There in the churchyard the
ground has been crossed. He'll be prayed for there. One can hear the
singing in church and the deacon reads so plainly and verbally that it will
reach him every time just as though it were read over his grave."

At last the captain made a gesture of despair as though to say, "Take
him where you will." The boys raised the coffin, but as they passed the
mother, they stopped for a moment and lowered it that she might say
good-bye to Ilyusha. But on seeing that precious little face, which for the
last three days she had only looked at from a distance, she trembled all
over and her gray head began twitching spasmodically over the coffin.

"Mamma, make the sign of the cross over him, give him your blessing,
kiss him," Ninochka cried to her. But her head still twitched like an
automaton and with a face contorted with burning grief she began, without a word, beating her breast with her fist. They carried the coffin past
her. Ninochka pressed her lips to her brother's for the last time as they
bore the coffin by her. As Alyosha went out of the house he begged the
landlady to look after those who were left behind, but she interrupted
him before he had finished.

"To be sure, I'll stay with them, we are Christians, too." The old woman wept as she said it.

They had not far to carry the coffin to the church, not more than three hundred paces. The day was still, clear; it was frosty, but just slightly. The church bells were still ringing. Snegiryov ran fussing and distracted after the coffin, in his old, short, almost summer little coat, with his head bare and his soft, old, wide-brimmed hat in his hand. He seemed in a state of bewildered anxiety, at one minute stretching out his hand to support the head of the coffin and only hindering the bearers, then running alongside and trying to find a place for himself there. A flower fell on the snow and he rushed to pick it up, as though God only knew what depended on the loss of that flower.

"And the crust of bread, we've forgotten the crust!" he cried suddenly in terrible fright. But the boys reminded him at once that he had taken the crust of bread already and that it was in his pocket. He instantly pulled it out and was reassured.

"Ilyushecka told me to, Ilyushecka," he explained at once to Alyosha. "He was lying there one night, and I was sitting by him, and he suddenly told me: Papochka, when my grave is filled up crumble a piece of bread on it so that the sparrows may fly down, I'll hear them and it will cheer me up not to be lying alone."

"That's a good thing," said Alyosha, "we must often take some."

"Every day, every day!" said the captain quickly, seeming cheered at the thought.

They reached the church at last and set the coffin in the middle of it. The boys surrounded it and remained reverently standing so, all through the service. It was an old and rather poor church, many of the icons were without settings, but such churches are the best for praying in. During the mass Snegiryov became somewhat calmer, though at times he had outbursts of the same unconscious and, as it were, incoherent anxiety. At one moment he went up to the coffin to set straight the cover or the wreath, then, when a candle fell out of the candlestick, he rushed to replace it and spent a terribly long time fumbling over it. Then he subsided and stood quietly by the coffin with a look of blank uneasiness and perplexity. After the Epistle[4] he suddenly whispered to Alyosha, who was standing beside him, that the Epistle had not been read *properly* but did not explain what he meant. During the prayer, "Like the Cherubim," he joined in the singing but did not go on to the end, and, falling on his knees, he pressed his forehead to the stone floor and lay so for a long while. At last came the funeral service and candles were distributed. The distracted father began fussing about again, but the touching and impressive funeral prayers moved and roused his soul. He seemed suddenly to shrink together and broke into rapid, short sobs, which he tried at first to smother, but at last he sobbed aloud. When they began taking leave of the dead and closing the coffin, he flung his arms about, as though he would not allow them to cover Ilyushechka, and began greedily and persistently kissing his dead boy on the lips. At last they succeeded in persuading him to come away from the step, but suddenly he impulsively stretched out his hand and snatched a few flowers from the coffin. He looked at them and some new

4. A reading from the Bible.

idea seemed to dawn upon him, so that he apparently forgot about the main thing for a minute. Gradually he seemed to sink into brooding and did not resist when the coffin was lifted up and carried to the grave. It was an expensive one in the churchyard close to the church; Katerina Ivanovna had paid for it. After the customary rites the gravediggers lowered the coffin. Snegiryov with his flowers in his hands bent down so low over the open grave that the boys caught hold of his coat in alarm and pulled him back. But he did not seem to understand fully what was happening. When they began filling up the grave, he suddenly pointed anxiously at the falling earth and began trying to say something, but no one could make out what he meant, and he stopped suddenly. Then he was reminded that he must crumble the bread and he was awfully excited, snatched up the bread and began pulling it to pieces and flinging the morsels on the grave. "Come, fly down birds, fly down, little sparrows!" he muttered anxiously. One of the boys observed that it was awkward for him to crumble the bread with the flowers in his hands and suggested he should give them to someone to hold for a time. But he would not do this and even seemed suddenly alarmed for his flowers, as though they wanted to take them from him altogether, and after looking at the grave and, as it were, satisfying himself that everything had been done and the bread had been crumbled, he suddenly, to the surprise of everyone, turned, quite composedly even, and made his way homewards. But his steps became more and more hurried, he almost ran. The boys and Alyosha kept up with him.

"The flowers are for mamochka, the flowers are for mamochka! I was unkind to mamochka," he began exclaiming suddenly. Someone called to him to put on his hat as it was cold. But he flung the hat in the snow as though he were angry and kept repeating, "I don't want the hat, I don't want the hat!" Smurov picked it up and carried it after him. All the boys were crying, and Kolya and the boy who discovered Troy most of all, and though Smurov, with the captain's hat in his hand, was crying bitterly too, he managed, as he ran, to snatch up a piece of red brick that lay on the snow of the path, to fling it at the flock of sparrows that was flying by. He missed them, of course, and went on crying as he ran. Halfway, Snegiryov suddenly stopped, stood still for half a minute, as though struck by something, and suddenly turning back to the church, ran towards the deserted grave. But the boys instantly overtook him and caught hold of him on all sides. Then he fell helpless on the snow as though he had been knocked down, and struggling, sobbing, and wailing, he began crying out, "Ilyushechka, old man, dear old man!" Alyosha and Kolya tried to make him get up, soothing and persuading him.

"Captain, stop, a brave man must endure," muttered Kolya.

"You'll spoil the flowers," said Alyosha, "and 'mamochka' is expecting them, she is sitting crying because you would not give her any from Ilyushechka before. Ilyusha's little bed is still there . . ."

"Yes, yes, mamochka!" Snegiryov suddenly recollected again, "they'll take away the bed, they'll take it away," he added as though alarmed that they really would. He jumped up and ran homewards again. But it was not far off and they all came running together. Snegiryov opened the door hurriedly and called to his wife with whom he had so cruelly quarreled just before:

"Mamochka, dear, Ilyushecka has sent you these flowers, your poor little crippled feet!" he cried, holding out to her a little bunch of flowers that had been frozen and broken while he was struggling in the snow. But at that instant he saw in the corner, by the little bed, Ilyusha's little boots, which the landlady had put tidily side by side. Seeing the old, patched, rusty-looking, stiff boots he flung up his hands and rushed to them, fell on his knees, snatched up one boot and, pressing his lips to it, began kissing it greedily, crying, "Ilyushecka, old man, dear old man, where are your little feet?"

"Where have you taken him away? Where have you taken him?" the lunatic screamed in a heartrending voice. Nina, too, broke into sobs. Kolya ran out of the room, the boys followed him. At last Alyosha too went out. "Let them weep," he said to Kolya, "it's no use trying to comfort them just now. Let us wait a minute and then go back."

"No, it's no use, it's awful," Kolya assented. "Do you know, Karamazov," he suddenly dropped his voice so that no one could hear them, "I feel dreadfully sad, and if it were only possible to resurrect him, I'd give anything in the world to do it."

"Ah, so would I," said Alyosha.

"What do you think, Karamazov, had we better come back here tonight? He'll be drunk, you know."

"Perhaps he will. Let us come together, just the two of us, that will be enough, to spend an hour with them, with the mother and Nina. If we all come together we shall remind them of everything again," Alyosha advised.

"The landlady is laying the table for them now—there'll be a funeral dinner or something, the priest is coming; shall we go back to it, Karamazov?"

"Of course," said Alyosha.

"It's all so strange, Karamazov, such grief and then suddenly pancakes—it all seems so unnatural in our religion."

"They are going to have salmon too," the boy who had discovered Troy suddenly observed in a loud voice.

"I beg you most earnestly, Kartashov, not to interrupt again with your stupidities, especially when no one is talking to you and no one cares to know whether you exist or not," Kolya snapped out irritably. The boy flushed crimson but did not dare to reply. Meantime they were strolling slowly along the path and suddenly Smurov exclaimed:

"There's Ilyusha's stone, under which they wanted to bury him!"

They all stopped silently by the big stone. Alyosha looked and the whole picture of what Snegiryov had described to him that day, how Ilyushechka, weeping and hugging his father, had cried, "Papochka, papochka, how he insulted you," rose at once before his imagination. Something seemed to shake in his soul. With a serious and earnest expression he looked from one to another of the bright, pleasant faces of Ilyusha's schoolfellows, and suddenly said to them:

"I should like to say one word to you, here at this place."

The boys stood round him and at once bent attentive and expectant eyes upon him.

"Gentlemen, we shall soon part. I shall be for some time with my two brothers, of whom one is going to Siberia and the other is lying at death's door. But soon I shall leave this town, perhaps for a long time. So we shall part, gentlemen. Let us make a compact, here, at Ilyusha's stone, that we will never forget first, Ilyushecka, and second, one another. And whatever happens to us later in life, if we don't meet for twenty years afterwards, let us always remember how we buried the poor little boy at whom we once threw stones, do you remember, by the bridge? and afterwards we all grew so fond of him. He was a fine boy, a kindhearted, brave boy, he felt for his father's honor and stood up for his father when he was insulted. And so in the first place, we will remember him, boys, all our lives. And even if we are occupied with most important things, if we attain to honor or fall into some great misfortune—still let us never forget how good it was once here, when we were all together, united by a good and kind feeling which made us, for the time we were loving that poor boy, better perhaps than we are. My little doves[5]—let me call you so, for you are very like them, those pretty little blue-gray birds, at this minute as I look at your good dear faces. My dear little children, perhaps you won't understand what I am saying to you, because I often speak very unintelligibly, but you'll remember it all the same and will agree with my words someday. You must know that there is nothing higher and stronger and more wholesome and useful for life in the future than some good memory, especially a memory of childhood, from the parental home. People talk to you a great deal about your education, but some beautiful, sacred memory, preserved from childhood, is perhaps the best education. If a man carries many such memories with him into life, then he is saved for his whole life. And if we have only one good memory left in our heart, even that may serve someday as our salvation. Perhaps we may even grow wicked later on, we may even be unable to refrain from a bad action, may laugh at people's tears and at those people who say as Kolya did just now, 'I want to suffer for all men,' and may even jeer spitefully at such people. But however bad we may become—which God forbid—yet, when we recall how we buried Ilyusha, how we loved him in his last days, and how we have been talking like friends all together, at this stone, the cruelest and most mocking of us—if we do become so—will not dare to laugh inwardly at having been kind and good at this moment! What's more, perhaps, that one memory may keep him from great evil, and he will reflect and say, 'Yes, I was good and brave and honest then.' Let him laugh to himself, that's no matter, a man often laughs at what's good and kind; that's only from thoughtlessness; but I assure you, gentlemen, that as he laughs he will say at once in his heart, 'No, I do wrong to laugh, for that's not a thing to laugh at!'"

"That will certainly be so, I understand you, Karamazov!" cried Kolya, with flashing eyes. The boys were moved and they, too, wanted to say something, but they restrained themselves, looking attentively and tenderly at the speaker.

"I say this in case we become bad," Alyosha went on, "but there's no reason why we should become bad, is there, gentlemen? Let us be, first and above all, kind, then honest, and then let us never forget each other. I say that again. I give you my word, gentlemen, that for my part I'll never forget one of you; every face looking at me now I shall remember even for thirty years. Just now Kolya said to Kartashov that we did not care to know 'whether he exists or not.' But I cannot forget that Kartashov exists and that he is not blushing now as he did when he discovered Troy, but is looking at me with his nice, kind, happy little eyes. Gentlemen, my dear

5. See p. 150.

gentlemen, let us all be generous and brave like Ilyushechka, intelligent, brave, and generous like Kolya (though he will be ever so much more intelligent when he is grown up), and let us all be as bashful but also as smart and sweet as Kartashov. But why am I talking about those two! You are all dear to me, gentlemen, from this day forth, I have a place in my heart for you all, and I beg you to keep a place in your hearts for me! Well, and who has united us in this kind, good feeling which we shall remember and intend to remember all our lives, who, if not Ilyushechka, the good boy, the dear boy, the boy precious to us now and unto ages of ages! Let us never forget him, and may his memory be eternal and good in our hearts now and unto ages of ages!"[6]

"Yes, yes, eternal, eternal," the boys cried in their ringing voices, with faces rendered soft with emotion.

"Let us remember his face, and his clothes, and his poor little boots, his coffin and his unhappy, sinful father, and how boldly he stood up for him alone against the whole school."

"We will, we will remember!" cried the boys. "He was brave, he was good!"

"Ah, how I loved him!" exclaimed Kolya.

"Ah, little children, ah, dear friends, don't be afraid of life! How good life is when one does something good and just!"

"Yes, yes," the boys repeated ecstatically.

"Karamazov, we love you!" a voice, probably Kartashov's, cried impulsively.

"We love you, we love you!" they all caught it up. There were little tears in the eyes of many of them.

"Hurrah for Karamazov!" Kolya shouted ecstatically.

"And may the dead boy's memory live eternally!" Alyosha added again with feeling.

"Eternal memory!" the boys chimed in again.

"Karamazov!" cried Kolya, "can it really be true what religion says, that we shall all rise from the dead, and shall live, and see each other again, everyone, and Ilyushechka?"

"Certainly we shall all rise again, certainly we shall see each other and gladly, joyfully will tell each other all that has happened," Alyosha answered, half laughing, half ecstatic.

"Ah, how good it will be!" broke from Kolya.

"Well, now we will finish talking and go to his funeral dinner. Don't be put out at our eating pancakes—it's something ancient, eternal, and there's something good in that," laughed Alyosha. "Well, let us go! And now we go hand in hand."

"And eternally so, all our lives hand in hand! Hurrah for Karamazov!" Kolya cried once more ecstatically and once more all the boys joined in his exclamation.

THE END

---

6. These final passages evoke the liturgical language of the Orthodox funeral service, in which the prayer "Eternal Memory" is sung.

CONTEXTS

VISSARION BELINSKY

Vissarion Grigoryevich Belinsky (1811–1848), a leading literary and social critic, played an extremely important role in Dostoevsky's life: he was the first to acclaim Dostoevsky's literary talent in the 1840s, and was according to Dostoevsky's own account a great influence on him as a young man. Initially a champion of Hegel's philosophy of history, Belinsky eventually expressed outrage over aspects of his secular theodicy. Extensive excerpts of Belinsky's impassioned letters were published in the 1870s. His views were well known among Russian intellectuals and were probably one source of inspiration for Ivan Karamazov's rebellion.

Letter to V. P. Botkin[†]

The fate of the subject, the individual, the personality is more important than the fate of the entire world . . . No thank you, Yegor Fedorych [Hegel], with all due respect for your philosophical cap; let me inform you, with all respect for your philosophical philistinism, that if I did succeed in reaching the top of the evolution ladder, I would demand even there an account from you of all the victims of the conditions of life and history, of all the victims of accident, superstition, the Inquisition, Phillip II, etc., etc.; otherwise I will throw myself headlong from the top rung. I will not have happiness if you give it to me gratis unless I feel assured about every one of my blood brothers, the bone of my bone and the flesh of my flesh. Disharmony is said to be a condition of harmony: that may be very profitable and pleasant for megalomaniacs, but certainly not for those whose fates are destined to express the idea of disharmony . . . What does it matter to me that I am convinced that reason will triumph, that things will improve in the future, if fate has ordained me to be a witness to the triumph of chance, unreason, and brute force?

F. M. DOSTOEVSKY

Excerpt from Dostoevsky's *Diary of a Writer*: The Kroneberg Case[‡]

I think everyone has heard of the Kroneberg case that was tried in the circuit court in Petersburg last month, and that everyone has read the newspaper reports and commentaries. It was an extremely interesting case, and the newspaper accounts were remarkably heated.* * *

I will recapitulate the facts: according to the indictment, a father flogged a child, his seven-year-old daughter, too cruelly, and he had treated her cruelly before. A stranger, a woman from the lower classes, could not

---

† Letter to V. P. Botkin, March 1841, in Kenneth Lantz, *The Dostoevsky Encyclopedia* (Westport, CT and London: Greenwood Press, 2004), 33.

‡ From *The Writer's Diary* (*Dnevnik pisatelya*; Paris: YMCA Press, 1951), II: 66–101, trans. Ralph Matlaw.

stand the cries of the tortured girl who (according to the indictment) had cried "daddy! daddy!" for a quarter of an hour while she was being flogged. The flogging, according to the testimony of one expert, turned out to be with "Spitzruten" (rods) rather than switches, that is, something completely unsuitable for a seven-year-old. They lay in court among the material exhibits and could be seen by everyone, even by Mr. Spasovich[1] himself. Incidentally, the indictment mentioned that when the father was asked to remove at least a certain twig before the flogging he replied, "No, that will add vigor to it." It is also known that after the punishment the father almost fainted himself.* * *

The counsel for the defense was Mr. Spasovich. He is a man of talent. Whenever anyone speaks of him, they universally say "That is a man of talent." I am very glad of that. I will note that Mr. Spasovich was appointed by the court to conduct the defense, and therefore he conducted the defense under some coercion, so to speak . . .

* * *

It is well known that Mr. Spasovich is also a remarkably gifted lawyer. His speech in this case is, in my estimation, the height of art; nevertheless, it left an almost disgusting impression on me. You see, I begin with complete sincerity. But the problem lay in that falseness of all the circumstances of the case that grouped themselves around Mr. Spasovich, and from which he could in no way extricate himself by the very force of things; that is my view, and therefore everything that was strained and tormenting in his position as defense counsel necessarily was also reflected in his speech. The case was so set up that a verdict of guilty would have exposed his client to a heavy, incommensurate penalty. And a misfortune would have occurred: a family destroyed, everyone left unprotected, and everyone unhappy. His client was charged with "torture," and that was the charge that was dreadful. Mr. Spasovich started right off by rejecting any notion of torture. "There was no torture, there was no harm whatsoever done to the child!" He denied everything: the rods, the bruises, the blows, the blood, the integrity of the witnesses for the prosecution, everything, everything, a very bold stratagem, an onslaught, so to speak, on the jurors' conscience, but Mr. Spasovich knows his strength. He even rejected the child, its infancy, he even destroyed and tore up by its roots the pity for it in the hearts of his auditors. The cries that continued for a quarter of an hour during the flogging "daddy! daddy!" (even if it had been five minutes)— everything disappeared, and in its place appeared a "mischievous little girl, with a rosy face, smiling, cunning, spoiled, and with secret vices." Listeners practically forgot that she was seven years old; Mr. Spasovich artfully confiscated her age as the single thing most dangerous to him. When he had destroyed all that, he naturally obtained a verdict of acquittal, but what could he do, "what if the jury had found his client guilty"? So that of course he could not worry about the means or use genteel methods. "A lofty end justifies any means." But let us examine that remarkable speech in detail, you will see that it is well worth it. * * *

From the first words you feel that you are in contact with an extraordinary talent, with a force. Mr. Spasovich reveals himself from the begin-

1. See p. 479 [Editor's note].

ning, is the first to point out to the jury the weakness of the defense he has undertaken, reveals its weakest part, that which he fears most of all. * * *

"Gentlemen of the jury," Mr. Spasovich began, "I do not fear the decision of the tribunal or the prosecutor's charges. I fear an abstract idea, a phantom, I fear that the crime, as it has been called, has as its object a weak defenseless creature. The very words 'torturing a child' arouse, in the first place, a feeling of great compassion for the child, and in the second, just as great a feeling of indignation against him who tortured it."

Very clever. Extraordinary sincerity. The auditor, who is bristling, prepared beforehand to hear something that inevitably would be very tricky, devious, deceptive, who had just said to himself, "Well, friend, let's see how you're going to deceive me," is suddenly struck by the man's practically being totally defenseless. The supposed trickster needs defense himself and, moreover, from you, from those he was prepared to deceive! Thus Mr. Spasovich immediately breaks the ice of mistrust and percolates into your heart, even though it may be just a single drop. True, he spoke about a *phantom*, said that he was only afraid of a "phantom," that is to say, practically a prejudice; you haven't heard anything else, but already you are ashamed that you may be thought to be a man with prejudices. Isn't that right? Very clever.

"Gentlemen of the jury," Mr. Spasovich continued, "I am not a partisan of flogging. I can quite understand that *a system of education may be introduced* (don't worry, these are all new expressions and are taken verbatim from various pedagogical papers), from which flogging will be barred. Nevertheless, I have as little expectation of the complete and unconditional eradication of physical punishment as I have of the expectation that you will have no further function in trials because there will be a cessation of punishable crimes and the destruction of that law which must exist in the family as in the state."

Thus the whole trial seems to concern only a flogging, not a bundle of switches, not rods. You look carefully, you listen—no, the man is speaking seriously, he is not joking. In other words, this whole Sodom has been raised about the question whether a little twig should or should not be used at a certain age. Is it worthwhile to have been convened for that? True, he is not a partisan of flogging; he proclaims it himself, but yet—

"In the normal course of things normal methods are used. In the present case, abnormal means were unquestionably used. But if you look into the circumstances that brought about those means, if you take into account the nature of the child, the temperament of the father, the goal that guided him during the punishment, you will understand a great deal in this case, and once you have understood, you will exonerate him, because a *profound* understanding of the case inevitably leads to much being explained and seeming natural, not requiring criminal prosecution. That is my task: to explain the incident."

That is, don't you see, "punishment," not "torture," he himself says that a father is being tried only because he whipped his child too painfully. Oh, what a state of things we've come to! But if you look more deeply . . . That's just it, neither the tribunal nor the prosecutor was able to look deeper. But as soon as we, the jury, look into it, we will acquit him, because he himself says "a profound understanding will lead to acquittal," and that *profound understanding* of course exists only among us on the jury bench. * * * In short, "flatter, flatter," an old, commonplace trick, but then the most dependable one.

After that, Mr. Spasovich turned directly to the presentation of the history of the case and began *ab ovo*.[2] Of course, we will not repeat it word for word. * * *

* * *

But the pillars, the real Pillars of Hercules, begin where Mr. Spasovich reaches the "father's righteous anger."

"When this nasty habit had been discovered in the girl," Mr. Spasovich said (that is, the habit of lying), "in addition to all her other faults, when the father found out that she *stole*, he really became very angry. I believe that *each one of you would become just as angry*, and I think that to prosecute a father because he punished his child painfully *but for good reason*— is to render a disservice to the family, is to render a disservice to the state, for the state can only be solid when it is supported by the solidity of the family. If the father became indignant, he was completely within his rights.

* * *

In conclusion Mr. Spasovich said something very shrewd: "In conclusion, I take the liberty of stating that in my opinion the whole charge against Kroneberg is framed entirely incorrectly, that is to say in such a way, that the questions that will be put to you cannot be answered at all."

That is really clever; that is the essence of the case and from it stems all its falseness. But Mr. Spasovich adds even a few more quite solemn words on the subject: "I take it that all of you will admit that the family exists, that parental authority exists."

On that point I will take the liberty of introducing one very small point, and that only in passing.

We Russians are a young nation. We are only beginning to live, though we have already lived a thousand years, but a large ship needs broad horizons. We are a fresh nation and we have no sacred things *quand-même*.[3] We love our sacred things but only because they are really holy. We do not merely insist on them in order to defend *l'Ordre*.[4] Our sacred things remain so by our faith, not by their utility. We would not even defend such sacred things if we stopped having faith in them, like the ancient priests who, at the end of paganism, defended their idols, whom they had long since stopped considering gods. Not a single one of our sacred things needs fear free investigation, precisely because it is solid in reality. We love the sanctity of the family when it is really sacred, and not because the solidity of the state is founded on it. * * * But there must be measure and limits in everything, and we are ready to understand that. I am not a jurist, but I cannot fail to note a profound falseness in the Kroneberg case. Something was wrong here, something must have been different, regardless of who was actually guilty. Mr. Spasovich is profoundly correct

2. "From the egg," i.e., from the very beginning (Latin) [*Editor's note*].
3. "Notwithstanding" (French) [*Editor's note*].
4. "The system" (French) [*Editor's note*].

when he spoke of the framing of the question. However, that solves nothing. Perhaps we need a profound and *independent* review of our laws on that point, in order to fill gaps and to fit the character of our society.

F. M. DOSTOEVSKY

Selections from Dostoevsky's Letters[†]

No. 357. To A. N. Maykov.[1] *Florence, December 11, 1868*[2]

* * * Now I have in mind a huge novel entitled *Atheism* (for God's sake, that's strictly between us), but before I can start on it I have to read practically a whole library of atheists, Catholics, and Orthodox. Even with complete freedom for work it would take at least two years. I have a [central] character: a Russian, one of our society, *getting on in years*, not very educated but also not uneducated, with a certain distinction in rank,— *suddenly*, in his later years, loses faith in God. All his life he had devoted himself to work completely, never went astray, and to the age of forty-five didn't distinguish himself in any way. (A psychological riddle: deep feelings, a man, and a Russian man.) Loss of faith in God has a colossal effect on him. (The action of the novel, the background, is very extensive.) He scuttles among the younger generation, the atheists, the Slavophiles and Westerners, among Russian fanatics and hermits, among the clergy; he happens to fall into the clutches of a Jesuit, a propagator of the faith, a Pole, moves on from him into the depths of the flagellant sectants—and toward the end discovers Christ and the Russian earth, the Russian Christ and the Russian God. For God's sake, don't tell anyone; but as far as I'm concerned, I'd die happy if I could finish this final novel, for I would have expressed myself completely. Ah, my friend! I have a completely different notion of actuality and realism than our realists and critics. My idealism is more real than theirs. God! If one were to relate meaningfully what we Russians have gone through in the last ten years of our spiritual development, wouldn't the realists exclaim that it was a fantasy! But that is the fundamental, basic realism! That's just what realism is, only deeper, while theirs merely skims the surface. Isn't Lyubim Tortsov[3] really insignificant— and that's the only ideal thing that their realism has allowed them. Realism is a profound thing—no question about it! You won't explain a hundredth part of real, actual facts through their realism. While we, with our idealism, have even predicted facts. It has happened.

---

† All letters are taken from the *Polnoe sobranie sochinenii*. All dates are Old Style (Julian Calendar). Footnotes are by the editor.
1. See p. 96. Dostoevsky corresponded frequently with Maykov while living abroad, 1867–71; these letters contain valuable information about the evolution of his ideas and literary projects.
2. Trans. Ralph E. Matlaw.
3. A character in Ostrovsky's play *Poverty Is No Crime* (1854). The poet and literary critic Apollon Grigoryev (1822–1864), Dostoevsky's friend and collaborator at *Time* and *Epoch*, had praised this character as a representative of humility.

No. 387. To A. N. Maykov. Dresden, March 25, 1870[4]

* * * I promised *The Dawn* something good and I want to do it well.[5] That piece for *The Dawn* has matured in my mind for two years. It is the same idea I have already written to you about. It will be my last novel, about the size of *War and Peace*, and with an idea you would approve, at least judging by our previous conversations. That novel will consist of five large parts (each about 250 pages—the plan has matured in my mind for two years). The stories are completely separate from each other, so they might even be sold separately. The first novel I have earmarked for Kashpirev:[6] its action takes place in the 1840's. The general title for the novel is *The Life of a Great Sinner*, but each novel will have a separate title. The main question, which will run through all the parts—is the very one I have struggled with consciously and unconsciously all my life—the existence of God. Through the course of his life my hero is at times an atheist, then a believer, then a fanatic and a sectant, then again an atheist. The second part will take place entirely in a monastery. I have put all my hopes in this second tale. Perhaps it will finally be said that I have not merely written trifles. (I confess it to you alone, Apollon Nikolaevich—I want to make the main figure of the second tale Tikhon Zadonsky,[7] under a different name, of course, but yet the bishop will live peacefully in the monastery. A thirteen-year-old boy, who participated in a criminal act, mature and corrupted—don't worry—I know the type—(of our educated circle), the future hero of the whole novel is placed in the monastery for instruction. The little wolf and child-nihilist meets Tikhon * * *

(I am an expert in that field and I know the Russian monastery since childhood). But Tikhon and the child are the main thing. For God's sake don't tell anyone the contents of that second volume. (I never tell anyone my plans in advance, I'm somehow ashamed. But I confess myself to you.) Let others consider it worthless, but for me it is a treasure. Do not tell anyone about Tikhon. I wrote Strakhov[8] about the monastery, but didn't mention Tikhon. Perhaps I will create a grandiose, *positive*, holy figure. That's no longer a Konstanzhoglo or the German (I forget his name) in *Oblomov*.[9] How do we know, perhaps it is precisely Tikhon who is our *positive* Russian type our literature is seeking and not Lavretsky, not Chichikov, not Rakhmetov and the others, and not the Lopukhovs, not the Rakhmetovs.[1] Actually I won't create anything, I will merely present the real Tikhon, whom I long ago took into my heart with rapture. But I consider even that an important achievement if I am successful. Don't tell anyone. But I have to be in Russia for the second novel, for the monas-

4. Trans. Ralph Matlaw.
5. *The Dawn* (*Zarya*) was a conservative journal published in Saint Petersburg, 1869–71. Dostoevsky sympathized with the journal's ideology and contributed the novella *The Eternal Husband* to its pages in 1870.
6. Publisher of *The Dawn*.
7. See p. 31.
8. Strakhov collaborated with Dostoevsky at *Time* and was a proponent of the native soil movement (see p. 586).
9. Kostanzhoglo is a positive but flat character in Gogol's *Dead Souls*; "the German" is Stolz, a half-Russian, half-German character in Goncharov's 1861 novel *Oblomov*.
1. Characters in, respectively, Turgenev's *A Nest of Gentry* (1859), Gogol's *Dead Souls*, and Chernyshevsky's *What Is to Be Done?*

tery. Oh, if it were to turn out successfully! The first novel is the hero's childhood. Of course it isn't about children; there is a romance.* * *

No. 619. To V. A. Alekseev.[2] Petersburg, June 7, 1876[3]

You raise a shrewd question, particularly as it must be answered at length. In itself the matter is clear. The devil's temptation contains three colossal, eternal questions, and after eighteen centuries there are no more difficult, that is, shrewd, ideas than these, and they still cannot be resolved.

"Stones and bread" signify the contemporary social question, *environment*. It isn't prophecy, it has always existed. "How should one approach the ruined poor, who out of hunger and oppression resemble beasts rather than humans—go to them and preach to the starving the avoidance of sin, humility, chastity—would it not be better to *feed* them first? It would be more humane. They come to preach to you too, but then you are the Son of God, the whole world awaited you eagerly; then act as the foremost in mind and fairness, give all of them food, give them *security*, give them a social structure that will guarantee them bread and order forever, and only then ask them not to sin. If they then sin they would be ungrateful, whereas now they sin out of hunger. It is sinful even to ask them to refrain.

You are the Son of God, consequently you can do anything. Here are stones, look, how many. All You need do is command, and the stones will be turned to bread.

Command also that the earth will bear without labor, teach people a science or teach them a procedure that will secure their lives henceforth. Do you really not believe that man's greatest vices and misfortunes arose from hunger, cold, poverty, and the impossible struggle for survival?"

That is the first idea the evil spirit proposed to Christ. Admit that it is difficult to deal with it. Contemporary *socialism* in Europe, and here, constantly dismisses Christ, and concerns itself first of all with *bread*, calls upon science and maintains that the only reasons for all man's miseries are *poverty*, the struggle for survival, "the environment ruined him."

To that Christ replied, "Man does not live by bread alone," that is, he stated as well the axiom of man's spiritual origin. The devil's idea could only apply to the beast in man, while Christ knew that by bread alone you cannot animate man. If there were no spiritual life, no ideal of Beauty, man would pine away, die, go mad, kill himself or give himself to pagan fantasies. And as Christ, the ideal of Beauty in Himself and his Word, he decided it was better to implant the ideal of Beauty in the soul. If it exists in the soul, each would be the brother of everyone else and then, of course, working for each other, all would also be rich. Whereas if you gave them bread, they might become enemies to each other out of boredom.

But suppose you gave them Beauty and Bread at the same time? Then you would deprive man of *work, individuality, self-sacrifice and the sacrifice*

2. V. A. Alekseev, a singer at the Mariinsky Opera, had asked Dostoevsky what he meant by calling the concern of Pisareva, a recent suicide, with the small amount of money she left "the final expression of the greatest prejudice of contemporary youth, who value material means above everything, dream of stones turned into bread." Alekseev points out that in the *Gospels* the stones were not turned to bread. Dostoevsky discusses Pisareva in the May 1876 issue of his *Diary of a Writer*. See chapter 2, number 2, "One Inappropriate Thought."
3. Trans. Ralph Matlaw.

of one's goods for one's neighbor, in short, all life, the ideal of life would be taken away. And therefore it is better to proclaim only the spiritual ideal.

The proof that this brief excerpt from the New Testament concerns precisely this idea and not merely Christ's being hungry and the devil's advising him to take *stone* and command it to become bread, the proof lies precisely in that Christ answered by disclosing the secret of man's nature "Man does not live by bread alone" (that is, like the animals).

If the matter merely concerned assuaging Christ's hunger, why speak of the spiritual nature of man in general? And for that matter, had He wished, He could have obtained bread earlier, without the devil's counsel. Incidentally, consider current ideas by Darwin and others on man's descent from the monkey. Without going into any theories Christ proclaimed outright that there is a spiritual realm in man apart from the animal. So what does it matter—let man descend from wherever you like (the Bible doesn't explain how God fashioned man from clay or made him from stone) but on the contrary that God *breathed into his nostrils the breath of life* (but badly, that man might turn into a beast again through his sins).

Your obedient servant, F. Dostoevsky.

P.S. Pisareva studied with, and frequented, contemporary youth, where there is no question of religion, but where they dream of socialism, that is, of a structure of the world where there will first of all be bread and bread will be divided equally and there will be no property. According to my observations these socialists, while waiting for the future structure of society without individual responsibility, are in the meantime terribly fond of money and even value it immoderately, but precisely for the significance they attach to it.

No. 731. To N. L. Ozmidov. Petersburg, February 1878[4]

Now imagine that there is no God or immortality of the soul (immortality of the soul and God—it is all one, one and the same idea). Tell me, then why I should live well, do good, if I die completely on earth? Without immortality the whole matter is simply to reach my term.* * * And if that's so, then why should I (if I rely on my cunning and intelligence, in order to not get caught) not knife others, not plunder, not rob, or, if not knife others, why shouldn't I just live at the expense of others, solely for my own belly? After all I will die, and everything will die, there won't be anything! In this way it turns out that the human organism alone does not fall under the general axiom and lives exclusively *in order to destroy itself*, and not for its preservation and feeding. For what kind of society is it, if all its members are enemies to each other? A terrible nonsense ensues. Add to that, on top of all this, *my I*, which understands everything. If it understands all this, that is, the whole earth and its axiom, then, of course, this *my I* is higher than all this, at the very least is not contained by this alone, but goes as it were to the side, above all this, judges and cognizes it. But in that case this *I* not only is not subject to the earthly axiom, the

---

4. Ozmidov wrote Dostoevsky in January 1878 to express his regret at the cessation of the *Diary*. He was especially disappointed that the discussion of immortality begun in the December 1876 issue, where Dostoevsky wrote about the "necessity and inevitability of belief in immortality," would not be continued.

earthly law, but comes out of them, has a law above them. Where is this law? Not on earth, where everything is finished and everything dies without a trace and without resurrection. Isn't there a hint about the immortality of the soul? If it did not exist, then would you yourself, Nikolay Lukich, worry about it, write letters, seek it? This means that you cannot handle your own *I*: it does not fit into the earthly order of things, but is always seeking something else that it belongs to, outside of this world.

No. 737. To an anonymous correspondent. Petersburg, March 27, 1878

From your letter I conclude that you are a good mother and are much concerned about your growing child. But why you need solutions to the questions you send me—I can't understand. You set yourself too much and worry painfully. The matter can be handled much more simply. * * * Be good, and let your child understand that you are good (himself, without hints), and let him remember that you were good; then, believe me, you will fulfill your obligation to him for his whole life, because directly through your goodness he will learn what good is. And for this he will remember your image with great respect his whole life, and, perhaps, with tenderness too. And even if you do much that is bad, that is at the very least frivolous, painful, and even ridiculous, then he *without doubt* will forgive you for your badness, sooner or later, in his memory of you, for the sake of the good which he will remember. Know also, that you cannot do more for him. Indeed this is more than enough. The memory of the *good* in his parents, that is of their goodness, truth, honesty, compassion, the absence of false shame and if possible the absence of lies—all this will make a different person out of him sooner or later, believe it.

* * *

Imagine that your child, grown to fifteen or sixteen years, comes to you (from bad companions at school, for example) and asks you or his father such a question: "Why should I love you and why should this be my duty?" Believe me, no knowledge or questions will help you then, and you won't have any answer for him at all. And therefore it will be necessary to act so that *he never comes to you* with such a question. But this will be possible only if he really loves you, spontaneously (*neposredstvenno*), so that the question will not even occur to him.

* * *

No. 732. To V. V. Mikhailov.[5] Petersburg, March 16, 1878[6]

* * * You indicated in your last letter that you would have no objection to writing me again. I value that highly, and *I count on you*. What interests me particularly in your letter is that you love children, have lived among children a great deal, and do so even now. Here, then, is my request, dear Vladimir Vasilyevich: I have conceived and will soon start writing a large novel where, among other things, children, particularly youngsters aged

5. Trans. Ralph Matlaw.
6. Mikhailov was a well-known teacher and pedagogue who in the 1860s had published articles about child-rearing.

approximately seven to fifteen, will play a great role. Many children will be introduced. I am studying them and have studied them all my life, and love them dearly, and have children myself. But the observations of a man like yourself would be very valuable to me (I understand that). So write me *about children*—everything you know. Both about Petersburg children who call you "uncle" and Elizavetgrad children, and *about whatever you know*. (Incidents, habits, answers, sayings and puns, traits, relation to the family, misdeeds and innocence; their nature and the teacher, Latin, etc., etc.,—in short what you know.) You will help me greatly, I shall be very grateful and will await your correspondence eagerly. * * *

No. 749. To N. M. Dostoevsky. Petersburg, Tuesday, May 16, 1878[7]

My very dear brother Nikolay Mikhailovich, today our Alyosha died from a sudden attack of epilepsy, which he had never had before. Yesterday he was still merry, sang, ran around, and today he is laid out for burial. The attack started at 9:30 in the morning, and at 2:30 Lyoshechka died. He will be buried Thursday the 18th in the Great Okhtensky Cemetery. Good-bye, Kolya, pity Lyosha, you petted him frequently (remember how he imitated a drunk, "Vanka the foo'"?). I have never felt so sad. We all grieve.

Your brother, F. Dostoevsky

No. 782. To N. A. Lyubimov. Staraya Russa,[8] May 10, 1879[9]

Today I sent off to you at the *Russian Messenger* forty pages (minimum) of the text of *The Brothers Karamazov* for the forthcoming May issue of the *Russian Messenger*.[1]

That is the fifth book, entitled *Pro and Contra*, but not all of it, only half. The second half of that fifth book will be sent (in time) for the June issue, and will consist of fifty pages. I had to divide this fifth book of my novel into two issues of the *Russian Messenger* because in the first place, even if I put all my efforts into it I would hardly be able to finish it before the end of May (it took too long to get everything together and to move to Staraya Russa)—and therefore I would not have time to see the proofs, which is the most important thing of all for me, and in the second place, this fifth book is in my view the culminating point of the novel and must be finished with particular care. Its meaning, as you will see from the text I sent, is the depiction of extreme blasphemy and the kernel of the idea of destruction of our time, in Russia, among our youth who have broken away from reality, and together with the blasphemy and anarchy, their refutation in the last words of the Elder Zosima, a character in the novel, which I am preparing at the moment. Since the difficulty of the task I have undertaken is obvious, you will of course understand, esteemed Nikolay Alexeevich, and will forgive my preferring to stretch it over two issues rather than to spoil the culminating chapter by my rushing it. The whole chapter will be

---

7. Trans. Ralph Matlaw.
8. A small town 150 miles from Saint Petersburg, Staraya Russa was a model for Skotoprigonevsk. Dostoevsky and his family spent summers there in the 1870s.
9. Trans. Ralph Matlaw.
1. Dostoevsky uses the term "sheets" (signatures), the unit used for serial rights. A "printed sheet" consisted of sixteen pages, more specifically, 40,000 typographical characters. The figures have been rounded off to end in 5 or 0. Dostoevsky received 300 rubles a sheet for his last novel.

full of movement. In the text I sent you I merely depict the character of one of the leading figures in the novel who expresses his fundamental convictions. These convictions are precisely that which I recognize as the synthesis of contemporary Russian anarchism. The refutation not of God, but of the meaning of His creation. All socialism comes from and began with the refutation of the meaning of historical reality and arrived at a program of destruction and anarchism. The original anarchists were, in many instances, people of sincere convictions. My hero chooses a theme I consider irrefutable: the senselessness of children's suffering, and develops from it the absurdity of all historical reality. I don't know whether I executed it well but I know that the figure of my hero is a real one to the utmost degree. (I was reproached for many figures in *Demons* as being fantastic but later, would you believe it, they were justified by reality, so they must have been apprehended correctly. K. P. Pobedonostsev,[1] for example, told me of two or three incidents about imprisoned anarchists which strikingly resembled what I depicted in *Demons*.) Everything my hero says in the text I sent you is based on reality. All the anecdotes about children took place, existed, were published in the press, and I can cite the places, I invented nothing. The general who ran down the child with his hunting dogs and that whole incident is a real fact and was published last year, I think in the *Archive*, and was reprinted in many newspapers. My hero's blasphemy will be triumphantly refuted in the next (June) issue, on which I am now working with fear, trembling, and veneration, since I consider my task (the destruction of anarchism) a civic deed. Wish me success, esteemed Nikolay Alexeevich.

I await the proofs with great impatience. Address: F. M. Dostoevsky, Staraya Russa.

In the text I sent there does not seem to be a single *indecent* word. There is only the bit about the tormentors who were raising a five-year-old child and smeared *it with its feces* because she didn't ask to be taken up during the night. But I ask you, I beg you not to strike that. It comes from a current criminal trial. The word "feces" was retained in all the newspapers (only two months ago in the *Voice*). It can't be toned down, Nikolay Alexeevich, that would be too, too sad! After all, we're not writing for ten-year-old children. But I am sure you would have stuck to my text even without my request.

* * *

No. 784. To Konstantin Pobedonostsev. Staraya Russa, May 1879

The thing is that this book is the culminating one in my novel, it's called *Pro and Contra*, and the point of the book is blasphemy and the refutation of blasphemy. The blasphemy is finished and sent off, but I'll send the refutation for the June book. I took the blasphemy as I myself have felt it and understood it, in its strongest form, that is, just as it occurs with us now in our Russia with the *entire* (almost) upper class, and primarily among the youth, that is, the scientific and philosophical refutation of the existence of God is already cast aside, today's *practical socialists* don't

---

1. Konstantin Pobedonostsev (1827–1907), Procurator of the Holy Synod. Dostoevsky corresponded with him during composition of *The Brothers Karamazov*.

engage in this at all (as people did for the whole last century and in the first half of the present one). On the other hand God's creation, God's world and *the meaning of it* are *rejected* at full force. * * * I flatter myself with the hope that even in this abstract theme I have not betrayed realism. The refutation of this (not direct, that is, not face to face) appears in the last words of the dying elder. Many critics have accused me of not taking the right themes in my novels, not realistic enough ones, etc. I, on the other hand, don't know of anything more realistic than precisely such themes . . .

* * *

No. 785. To N. A. *Lyubimov. Staraya Russa, June 11, 1879*[2]

Two days ago I sent to the office of the *Russian Messenger* the continuation of the *Karamazovs* for the June issue (the ending of the fifth book, *Pro and Contra*). In it is concluded what is said by "a mouth speaking great things and blasphemies."[3] A contemporary *nay-sayer*, one of the most vehement, openly declares himself in favor of the devil's counsel and maintains that it insures mankind's happiness more than Christ. It is an *omen*, and a striking one for Russian, stupid socialism (but terrible, because our youth is in it): bread, the tower of Babel (that is, the future reign of socialism) and the total enslavement of the freedom of conscience—that is what the desperate nay-sayer and atheist comes to. The difference lies in that our socialists (and you know very well that it is not merely the underground nihilists) are conscious Jesuits and liars who do not admit that their ideal is the ideal of coercing human consciousness and reducing humanity to a herd of cattle, while my socialist (Ivan Karamazov) is a sincere man, who admits openly that he agrees with the "Grand Inquisitor's" view of humanity and that Christ's faith (seemingly) raised man much higher than he in fact is. The question is brought to a head: "Do you despise humanity or respect it, you, its future saviors?"

And they give the impression of doing all this in the name of love for humanity. "Christ's law is difficult and abstract, unbearable for weak men," and in place of the law of Freedom and Enlightenment, they bring them the law of chains and enslavement by bread.

The next book will cover the Elder Zosima's death and his conversations with friends before he dies. It is not a sermon but rather a story, the tale of his own life. If it succeeds I'll accomplish something good: I'll force them to realize that a pure, ideal Christian is not something abstract, but graphically real, possible, standing before our eyes, and that Christianity is the only refuge from all its ills for the Russian land. I pray God it may succeed, it will be a moving thing, if I only have enough inspiration. And the main theme is one that could not even occur to any of today's writers and poets, therefore something completely *original*. The whole novel is written for its sake, if it will only come off, that's what worries me now! I will unfailingly send it for the *July* issue, and also no later than July tenth. I'll try my very best. * * *

2. Trans. Ralph Matlaw.
3. Revelation 13.5.

No. 807. To N. A. Lyubimov. Ems, Germany, August 7, 1879[4]

I rush to enclose *the sixth book of the Karamazovs, all of it,* for publication in the eighth (August) issue of the *Russian Messenger.* I have entitled this sixth book *"The Russian Monk"*—a daring and challenging title, since all our hostile critics will cry out: "Is this what the Russian monk is like, how dare he to place him on such a pedestal?" But it's all the better if they cry out, isn't it? (And I'm sure they won't refrain.) But I reckon that I did not transgress against reality: it is true not only as an ideal but also as the reality.

Only I don't know whether I succeeded. I reckon myself that I wasn't able to express one tenth of what I wanted. Nevertheless, I look upon this *sixth* book as the culminating point of the novel. Of course, many of Elder Zosima's exhortations (or one might better say the manner of their expression) belong to him, that is, to the way he is depicted artistically. Though I completely share the thoughts he expresses, if I had expressed them as coming *from me* personally, I would have expressed them in a different form and in different style. But he *could not* express himself either in a different style *or in a different spirit* than that which I gave him. Otherwise there would have been no artistic character. Such, for example, are the Elder's reflections on *The Russian Monk, Of Masters and Servants, Can a Man Judge His Fellow Creatures,* and so on. I took a character and a figure out of ancient Russian monks and saints: for all their profound humility, they have infinite, naïve hopes for the future of Russia, for its moral and even political predestination. Didn't Saint Sergius, the Metropolitans Peter and Alexey[5] always have Russia in mind in that sense?

I ask you in particular (*I beg you*), esteemed Nikolay Alexeevich, to give the proofs to a dependable proofreader, as I will not be able to correct them in my absence. I especially ask you to pay close attention to the proofs for pages ten to seventeen inclusive (the chapter entitled *Of the Holy Scriptures in the Life of Father Zosima*). It is an enraptured and poetic chapter, the prototype is taken from several exhortations of Tikhon Zadonsky, while the naïveté of the exposition is taken from the *Pilgrimages* of the monk Parfeny. Correct them yourself, esteemed Nikolay Alexeevich, do me that great favor—When the proof is done for the whole book, show it to M. N. Katkov.[6] I would like him to read it and give me his opinion, for I value his opinion highly.

I trust you will find nothing, as editor, to delete or correct in this book, not the slightest word, I guarantee it.

I also ask you particularly to keep all the divisions into chapters and *subchapters* as I have them. At this point there is introduced into the novel what is someone else's manuscript (The Notes of Alexey Karamazov) and of course Alexey Karamazov divides his manuscript according to his own notions. Here I add a *nota bene* of complaint: in the June issue, in the chapter "The Grand Inquisitor," all my rubrics were omitted, and even more, the whole thing was published without a break, ten pages in a row, without even *paragraph indentations.* That distressed me greatly, and I make this bitter complaint to you.

---

4. Trans. Ralph Matlaw.
5. Fourteenth-century ecclesiastics.
6. Mikhail Katkov (1818–1887), editor of the *Russian Messenger.*

I will infallibly send the following, seventh book, entitled "Grushenka," with which the second part of the Karamazovs will end this year, from Staraya Russa around the tenth of September. I plan this book for two issues of the *Russian Messenger*, September and October. There will only be 65 pages altogether in the seventh book, so that for September there will be only 32 pages, not more, but nothing can be done: there are two separate episodes in this seventh book, two separate stories, as it were. However, with the completion of the second part the *spirit and idea* of the novel will be completely *filled out*. If it doesn't come off, it will be my fault as an artist. I will postpone the third part of the novel (no larger than the first) until next year, as I already wrote you. My health interfered, my health! So the second part somehow comes out disproportionately long. But nothing could be done, that's how it turned out.

No. 817. To Konstantin Pobedonostsev. Ems, August 24, 1879[7]

* * * Your opinion of what you have read in the Karamazovs (so far as the force and vividness of the published material is concerned) gratified me greatly. But at the same time you raise the *most crucial* question: my reply to all these atheistic propositions has not yet appeared, and it must be made. That's precisely it and my worry now and all my disquiet lies in that. For I proposed to make the sixth book, *The Russian Monk*, which will appear August 31, the answer to that whole *negative side*. And for that reason I tremble for it in this sense: will it be answer *enough?* The more so as it is not a direct point for point answer to the propositions previously expressed (in the Grand Inquisitor and earlier) but an oblique one. Something completely opposite to the world view expressed earlier appears in this part, but again it appears not point by point but so to speak in artistic form. And that is what worries me, that is, will I be understood and will I achieve anything of my aim? In addition there were the demands of art: it was necessary to present a modest and majestic figure, but life is full of the comic and is only majestic in its external sense, so that I was necessarily forced, for artistic reasons, to touch also on the most banal aspects of the monk's biography, in order to maintain artistic realism. Then there are several exhortations of the monk that will be thought absurd because they are too exalted. Of course they are absurd in the ordinary sense, but in another, inner sense they are just. In any case, I am very uneasy and would greatly appreciate your opinion, for I value your opinion highly. I wrote it with a great deal of love. * * *

No. 820. To N. A. Lyubimov. Staraya Russa, September 16, 1879[8]

With this I am sending to the *Russian Messenger* the *seventh book* of the Karamazovs for the September issue, forty-one pages.

* * *

I beg you, Nikolay Alexeevich, not to delete anything in this Book. And there is no reason to: *everything is in order*. There is only one little word (about the dead body): *he stank*. But it is said by Father Ferapont, and he

7. Trans. Ralph Matlaw.
8. Trans. Ralph Matlaw.

can't speak differently, and even if he could say *smelled* he would not, but would say *stank*. Leave it, *for God's sake*. There is nothing else. Except perhaps about the purgative. But that is well written and moreover it is significant as an important accusation. The last chapter (which I'll send later), *Cana of Galilee*, is the most significant in the whole book, perhaps even in the whole novel. With this posting I am finished with the monastery. There will be nothing more about the monastery. The following Book (for October) will end that Part, and then there will be a break, as I have already informed you.

* * * One small *nota bene* in any case: for heaven's sake don't imagine that I could permit myself, in my work, even the slightest doubt in the miraculous efficacy of reliques. The matter concerns only the reliques of the defunct monk Zosima, but that is something completely different. A commotion similar to the one I described once occurred on Mt. Athos and is briefly related with touching naïveté in the "Pilgrimages" of Monk Parfeny.

P.S. Esteemed Nikolay Alexeevich, I particularly beg you to proofread the legend of *the little onion* carefully. That is a gem, taken down by me from a peasant woman, and of course published *for the first time*. At least I have never heard it until now.

No. 824. To E. N. Lebedeva.[9] Petersburg, November 8, 1879[1]

Dear Madame:

The servant Smerdyakov killed old Karamazov. All the details will become clear as the novel progresses. Ivan Fyodorovich participated in the murder only obliquely and remotely, only by failing (intentionally) to inform Smerdyakov during their conversation before his departure for Moscow and clearly and categorically expressing his repugnance for the crime Smerdyakov conceived (which Ivan Fyodorovich clearly saw and had a presentiment of) and thus *seemed to permit* Smerdyakov to commit that crime. Smerdyakov had to have that *permission*, the reason for which will again become clear in the rest of the novel. Dmitri Fyodorovich is completely innocent of his father's murder.

When Dmitri Karamazov jumped down from the fence and started to wipe the blood from the head of the old servant he had wounded, by that very act and his words: "You've come to grief old man," etc., he already seems to indicate to the reader that he is *not* the parricide. Had he killed the father and then ten minutes later Grigory, he wouldn't have jumped off the fence to go to the servant he had knocked down, except possibly to convince himself that a vital witness of his crime had been destroyed. But besides that, he seems to feel compassion for him, says: "You've come to grief, old man," etc. Had he killed the father, he would not have stood over the servant's body with words of pity. The plot is not the only important thing for the reader, but also some knowledge of the human soul (psychology), which every author is entitled to expect from the reader.

In any case, I am flattered by your interest in my work.

9. Trans. Ralph Matlaw.
1. This reader was apparently puzzled by the segment of the novel published in the October issue of the *Russian Messenger*. The installment ends in the middle of the chapter "In the Dark," with the line "He suddenly pulled the brass pestle out of his pocket . . ." (p. 336). She wrote Dostoevsky asking for clarification about the murder, and received this reply.

No. 825. To N. A. Lyubimov. Petersburg, November 16, 1879[2]

Yesterday I sent off the end of the eighth book of the *Karamazovs*, and you have probably already received it at the office. Once again I apologize profusely for the delay. Suddenly many completely new characters appeared in that eighth book, though fleetingly, but each had to be sketched as fully as possible, and therefore the book turned out longer than I had originally anticipated and also took longer, so that this time my delay came as a surprise even to me. I particularly ask you to look at the proofreading, esteemed Nikolay Alexeevich, so that it may be done just as splendidly as it has been up to now.

I wrote you that I would finish in November and stop until next year, but meantime circumstances have changed since *I will send yet a new ninth book for the December issue* and therewith conclude that Part. The fact is that I originally wanted to limit myself to a *judicial inquiry*, at the trial. But discussing the matter with a certain prosecutor (who has wide experience), I suddenly noticed that a whole part of our criminal trials, an extremely curious and extremely hobbling part (a sore spot of our criminal trials) would thereby disappear completely, without a trace, from the novel. That part of the trial is called a *Preliminary Investigation*, with its old-fashioned routine and new abstraction in the figures of our young advocates, district attorneys, etc. And therefore, in order to complete the Part, I am writing a different ninth book, entitled "A *Preliminary Investigation*," which I will get to you in December, as early as possible. Moreover, I will mark Mitya Karamazov's character even more strongly: he purifies his heart and conscience under the threat of misfortune and false accusation. He accepts punishment in his heart not for what he has done, but for being so dissipated that he could have, and wanted to commit the crime for which he will be falsely found guilty by a judicial error. A thoroughly Russian character: unless there's thunder, the peasant won't cross himself. His spiritual purification begins during the several hours of the preliminary investigation, to which this ninth book is devoted. It is very important to me as the author. There is one inconvenience: the whole book will probably occupy only 25 pages. But it will turn out whole and well finished.

And so I will present that ninth book in December, and at the same time an apology[3] to the periodical (for publication), about carrying over the completion of the novel to next year, about which (letter) I already wrote you last summer. I definitely want to publish that letter, it weighs on my conscience.

*   *   *

No. 827. To N. A. Lyubimov. Petersburg, December 8, 1879[4]

Again I am terribly at fault toward you and the *Russian Messenger*: the ninth Book of the *Karamazovs* that I so positively promised for Decem-

---

2. Trans. Ralph Matlaw.
3. Since the novel had been promised for 1879, Dostoevsky felt he had placed the periodical in an uncomfortable position, for readers would have to subscribe for another year if they wanted the balance of the novel.
4. Trans. Ralph Matlaw.

ber—I cannot send in December. The reason is—I have worked so hard I have become ill, that the theme of the book (A Preliminary Investigation) has stretched out and become more complex, and mainly, mainly—that this book has turned out for me to be one of the most important in the novel and demands (I can see it) such careful polishing that if I shortened it or messed it up I would harm myself as a writer now and forever. And even the idea of my novel would suffer, and it is dear to me. Everyone is reading my novel, I receive letters about it, the young are reading it, high society reads it, critics praise or abuse it, and I have never had such a success, to judge by the effect it has made. That is why I want to finish it well.

And therefore, please forgive me, if you can. I will send this ninth book to you for the January issue. * * *

No. 887. To N. A. Lyubimov. Staraya Russa, August 10, 1880[5]

* * * I consider the 6th, 7th, and 8th chapters of Book 11 successful. But I don't know how you will regard the 9th chapter, esteemed Nikolay Alexeevich. Perhaps you'll call it too characteristic! But I really did not want to be eccentric. I am duty bound to tell you that I have gotten opinions from doctors (more than one) long ago. They confirm that not only similar nightmares but even hallucinations are possible before "brain fever." My hero, of course, also sees hallucinations, but he confuses them with his nightmares. This is not only a physical (diseased) trait, when a man begins at times to stop differentiating between reality and the imagined (which has happened to everyone at least once a lifetime), but it is also a spiritual trait, corresponding to the hero's character: denying the reality of the phantom, he insists on its reality when the phantom disappears. *Tormented by disbelief, he (unconsciously) at the same time wishes that the phantom were something real and not a fantasy.*

Though why do I bother to explain? You will see everything for yourself when you read it, highly esteemed Nikolay Alexeevich. But forgive my *Devil*: it's only a devil, a petty devil, and not Satan with "fallen wings." I don't think the chapter will be too boring, though it is longish. I also don't think the censor could object to anything, except perhaps two tiny words: "the cherubim's *hysterical shrieks*." I beg you to leave it that way. After all, it's the *devil* who says it, and he can't speak otherwise. If it can't be done, substitute *joyful shouts* for *hysterical shrieks*. But is *shrieks* impossible? Otherwise it would be very prosaic and out of character.

I don't think anything else my devil prattles would raise objections from the censor. Though the two stories about the *confessionals* are indiscreet, they don't seem at all obscene. Doesn't Mephistopheles babble the same sort of thing in both parts of *Faust*?

I think Ivan's spiritual state is adequately explained in the tenth and last chapter, and therefore the nightmare in the ninth is, too. I again repeat that I checked the medical condition with doctors.

Brain fever strikes my hero with a virulent attack precisely at the moment he gives his testimony in court (that will be in the following, twelfth, book). * * *

---

5. Trans. Ralph Matlaw.

No. 896. To N. A. Lyubimov. Staraya Russa, September 8, 1880[6]

No matter how I tried to finish and send you all of the *twelfth* and last book of the Karamazovs so that it might be printed at one time, I finally saw that I couldn't do it. I broke it off at a place where the narrative could present something complete (though perhaps not as effective), and the action breaks off for a while anyway. That is "The Trial." I don't think I made any *technical* mistakes in the story. I consulted two prosecutors before hand. I stopped the story at the recess before the "Closing Arguments." There remain the speeches of the prosecutor and the counsel for the defense—and these must be done as well as possible, the more so as both the lawyer and prosecutor are presented by me in part as types of our contemporary court (though not based on anyone specifically), with their morality, liberalism, and view of their task. I am occupied with those two speeches now, and they, together with the "Verdict," will conclude the twelfth and *last* part of the novel. There remains an Epilogue of 25 pages. But I have the firm intention and desire to publish the end of Part Four *together with the Epilogue.*

No. 907. To N. A. Lyubimov. Petersburg, November 8, 1880[7]

I am sending off to the *Russian Messenger* the concluding *Epilogue* of the Karamazovs, which ends the novel. Altogether 31 sheets and probably not more than 28 pages of the journal. * * *

Well, and now the novel is finished! I worked on it for three years, published it for two—a great moment for me. Toward Christmas I want to issue a separate edition. It is in great demand, both here and by other book dealers in Russia. They've even sent money.

You will permit me not to bid you farewell. After all, I intend to live and write for another 20 years. Think kindly of me. * * *

F. M. DOSTOEVSKY

From Dostoevsky's *Notebooks*†

KATERINA IVANOVNA. SELF-INVENTION. A person fails to live throughout his life but invents himself.

KARAMAZOVS. Those villains have mocked me for an *uneducated* and retrograde faith in God. Those blockheads have never even conceived so powerful a rejection of God as exists in the Inquisitor and the preceding chapter, to which *the whole book* will serve as answer. After all, I do not believe in God like a fool (a fanatic). And they wanted to teach me, and mocked my backwardness! Their stupid sort never even conceived a rejection as powerful as the one I overcame. And they are going to teach me!

THE DEVIL. (A psychological and *detailed* critical explanation of Ivan Fyodorovich and the devil's appearing.) Ivan Fyodorovich is profound, he

6. Trans. Ralph Matlaw.
7. Trans. Ralph Matlaw.
† From F. M. Dostoevsky, *Biografiya, pis'ma, i zametki iz zapisnoy knizhki* (Petersburg, 1883), pp. 359, 368–75, and *Literaturnoe nasledstvo*, 83 (Moscow, 1971), p. 671. Trans. Ralph E. Matlaw.

isn't one of the contemporary atheists who merely show the narrowness of their world-view and the dullness of their dull little capacities in their disbelief.

ALL ARE NIHILISTS. Nihilism has appeared among us because we *are all nihilists*. Only the new, original form of its appearance has scared us. (We are all, to the last man, Fyodor Pavloviches.)

TO KAVELIN.[1] * * * I cannot consider someone who burns heretics a moral man, for I do not admit your thesis that morality means accord with one's inner convictions. My moral image and ideal is Christ. I ask you—did he burn heretics? No. Therefore burning heretics is an immoral action.

The Inquisitor is immoral by the very fact that the idea of burning heretics could dwell in his heart, in his conscience. * * *

* * * the tenacious and constant belief of mankind in *contact with other worlds* is also highly significant. It cannot be dismissed by a stroke of the pen, by the same means you used to dismiss the question of Russia. * * *

The Inquisitor and the chapter on children. In view of these chapters you might still have treated me in a scholarly fashion, but not with such condescension so far as philosophy is concerned, though philosophy is not my specialty. And throughout Europe there *has not been* and does not exist so powerful an *expression* [of these ideas] from the atheistic point of view as mine. It is clear that I do not believe in Christ and preach Him like a child, but my *hosannah* has passed through a great *furnace of doubt*, as my devil says in the same book. But perhaps you didn't read *The Karamazovs*—that's something else, and then I beg your pardon.

---

1. A projected reply to the historian and jurist Konstantin Kavelin (1818–1885), who had attacked Dostoevsky's view in an "Open Letter" in the *Russian Messenger*, November, 1880. [*Editor's note.*]

CRITICISM

RALPH E. MATLAW

On Translating *The Brothers Karamazov*

There is no more exasperating, nor perhaps rewarding, way of confronting a text than to attempt a translation: exasperating, because one immediately becomes aware of the impossibility of the task; rewarding, because one discovers, given a worthy text, the immense verbal artistry that one confronts, of levels of meaning and implication that sometimes emerge only in the laborious process of re-expression in a recalcitrant idiom that perforce distorts the original. I had thought of translating the novel. A brief attempt showed me the folly of that undertaking. Fortunately, the standard translation into English, made by Mrs. Garnett[1] more than sixty years ago, is excellent. It is, for a variety of reasons I will detail, deficient in certain respects (here remedied), and has frequently been slighted both by those who read Russian and note certain lapses, sometimes trivial, sometimes quite crucial, and by those who do not read Russian but who clearly feel that something has been distorted by Mrs. Garnett or, if not distorted, presented in a way that lets one glimpse the discrepancy between her literary talents and those of the authors she has translated, Pushkin, Gogol, Turgenev, Dostoevsky, Tolstoy, Chekhov, and others. However, no single person has rendered greater service to Russian literature than Mrs. Garnett so far as the English reader is concerned and, indeed, she thereby becomes a major figure in literary history.

* * *

The religious essence and overtones of the book create innumerable difficulties for the translator. We no longer have the Bible at our fingertips and find it much more difficult to achieve—and to catch—the Biblical and theological echoes that reverberate in the original, not merely in recognizing texts or references (for in his *Notebooks* and in the novel itself Dostoevsky indicates that people do not know the Gospels and even those in the monastery make mistakes), but in conveying the verbal peculiarities that constant exposure to the Bible and the speech of clerics involves. Mrs. Garnett, closer to that tradition, has been most successful precisely in conveying the religious "aura" of the book.

Even here, however, a number of comments are necessary. A Russian word may convey several meanings, only one of which is available in a single English word. The chapter title "The Breath of Corruption" points toward a less physical concept than does mine, "The Odor of Corruption." Dostoevsky was concerned with the physical as well as the spiritual, but insisted on the former in his concern that the censor pass the word "stink." There is even a kind of bonus in my version, since it may faintly suggest to some readers the "odor of sanctity" which is one of the problems the chapter examines.

The most difficult words to render consistently are those that appear in both the religious and legal aspects of the book and determine key

---

1. A prolific translator of Dostoevsky, Tolstoy, Chekhov, and other Russian writers, the Englishwoman Constance Garnett (1861–1946) was instrumental in making the Russian classics available to readers in Britain and the United States. [*Editor's note.*]

themes: guilt, judgment, confession. They are perhaps seen quintessen-
tially when Mitya faces, and one of the lawyers refers to, his "terrible
trial." The ecclesiastic meaning of the same two words is "the Last Judgment," and every Russian reader would be aware of it. But it can only be
rendered in its secular sense. "Confession" is a sacrament but also a legal
concept and, in addition, an ordinary locution. In Russian the meanings
are distinct, in English identical. Where the meaning is clearly one or the
other, there is no problem. But when Mitya makes his "Confession of an
Ardent Heart" (and it must be "ardent" rather than "passionate" to maintain Dostoevsky's imagery of fire and light) the ecclesiastic word is used,
while a secular term, even a colloquial term (rendered in this case as
"admission") is used by Ivan. Similarly, there are "miracles," "mysteries,"
and "secrets," which Dostoevsky distinguishes, but a Russian "mystery"
may also be a "sacrament," and it may be a mystery in a detective sense as
well as a religious one. Here, as elsewhere, Dostoevsky is always consistent in his usage, but the translator cannot be. Moreover, when a word is
particularly important, Dostoevsky will repeat it several times and call
attention to it to insure the reader's paying heed.

The crucial cluster is the word "guilt" along with its derivatives and
attendant ideas. In the legal sense, guilt and sentencing or judgment are
clear, at least linguistically. But ethically and morally their implication
differs. Since the leading idea of the novel is that "we are all responsible for
everyone and everything," it would not have done to translate the word
"responsible" as "guilty," for that would both limit the meaning and introduce an unwarranted legal note, perhaps also a more specifically psychi-
atric connotation than Dostoevsky may have intended. Indeed, the same
word "guilty" (*vinovat*) colloquially and most frequently means "excuse me"
in Russian or, to get a closer shade of meaning, "pardon me." Dostoevsky
studiously avoids this usage throughout the novel. Similarly, "to judge, condemn, blame" may be the same word in Russian but must be distinguished
in English according to context, so that again certain overtones disappear.
Only slightly less troublesome is the fervor, gentility, kindness, the melting of the heart in the Russian "*umilenie*," a word with strong religious
overtones but also used descriptively. Vladimir Nabokov has suggested—
incorrectly—that it is the French "*attendrissement*," but that is only a
partial meaning and we have no equivalent for the French word either.

There are at least two words connected with the religious vocabulary
that require some explanation. The first is "*klikushka*," the "possessed,"
"screaming"[2] woman whose disease is explained in "Peasant Women Who
Have Faith," a term used disparagingly by Karamazov for his second wife.
It does not sound nearly so aberrant in Russian. Incidentally, the problem
is not unique to Russia, nor does it necessarily require a laying on of
hands by a cleric. It is worth noting in these days of equal rights that the
"*couvade*" existed, and exists, among certain French peasants (and in other
nationalities), wherein the woman went back to the fields after giving birth
while the husband took to his bed for a week. Another accepted institution in Russia was that of the "*yurodivy*," the "fool in Christ," the religious
madman exemplified in Father Ferapont. The term is also used with various secular shades of contempt and disparagement, as madman, fool,

2. Translated as "shriekers" in this edition. [*Editor's note.*]

hysterical, weak-minded, exultation (applied to Alyosha, and to his mother), with never quite the same implication in English, for the notion itself is foreign.

In other areas, too, the English sometimes overstates Dostoevsky's point. Smerdyakov is a lackey. With two exceptions he is always so designated, rather than as a servant or a footman, while Grigory never is. The word was less contemptuous in Dostoevsky's time than it is now, and could be used simply to designate a particular kind of servant, which Smerdyakov, as cook, is not. But it also contained the pejorative sense that has in effect now become the primary meaning in both languages, and by his consistency Dostoevsky emphasizes what is later called Smerdyakov's "lackey soul." The stench of his soul is implicit each time his name is given in Russian, for his name, is derived from "stink," and its physical counterpart may be felt in the pomades and lotions and dandyish dress he affects to disguise his exterior, which at the end yield to his filthy dressing-gown and snot-fouled handkerchief. The contempt for his lackey's soul may also be glimpsed in the contemptuous designation of a serf or slave in the nineteenth century as "*smerd*." Altogether it is a name with considerable implication. It may be indicated in French by mere transliteration but requires explanation in English.

Smerdyakov's peculiar abjectness, the fawning, mincing, unctuous speech, his false humility, we may sometimes get in English, as in Dickens's Uriah Heep, but hardly with the range possible in Russian. One of the obvious devices is the use of "sir" or "ma'am," done in Russian by the addition of the letter "s" to almost any word—"*nyet-s*" and "*da-s*," both monosyllables, mean "no, sir (or ma'am)" and "yes, sir (or ma'am)." It may be done for emphasis once or twice by anyone in normal discourse but becomes the mark of a special servility when overused, and it becomes particularly annoying in Smerdyakov in conjunction with the rest of his affected speech. The effect is quite different in Captain Snegiryov, who coins a name for himself I have given as "Yessirov" ("Sigma-userov" is more exact but requires footnoting), who consciously uses it as a means of self-abasement and self-humiliation. It is used by the pretentious Marya Kondratevna (what a marvelous touch that Smerdyakov has a female admirer!), and in the pitiful Maximov, living on others' charity and speaking as a dependent is expected to. I have introduced what may strike some readers as too many "sir's" but I have by no means put in each "s" of the Russian. Again Dostoevsky is artistically consistent. In certain vital speeches both Smerdyakov and Snegiryov fail to use "sir," and that very absence alerts the reader to something important.

Maximov's speech is typical, at least in literature, of the poor relations, hangers-on, dependents that are known in Russian as "*prizhival'shchiki*," those hangers-on who lived at the expense, and the whim, of others. When they were buffoons like Maximov or Fyodor Karamazov in his youth, assuring their keep by demeaning themselves, they may well be called "toadies,"[3] though that word probably no longer conveys a sense of an accepted institution, as Roman "parasites"—hangers-on—also were. The exemplar of a more modest form of the toady, who characterizes himself as a "*prizhival'shchik*," is one of Dostoevsky's most stupendous creations,

---

3. Translated as "spongers" in this edition. [*Editor's note.*]

Ivan's devil. (Incidentally, since the father was of the same ilk of parasites, it is surprising that no one has analyzed in detail what this may mean, either for an understanding of Ivan or for the novel as a whole.) The term "toady," however, could hardly be applied in English, as it is in Russian, to Karamazov's second wife, who, before leaving her dependent's position by marrying Karamazov, had attempted to leave it by committing suicide. It was clearly a difficult and humiliating way of existing, with little comfort in the larger view expressed by a well-meaning character in Chekhov, "We are all God's *prizhival'shchiki*."

Among the varieties of speech and styles in the novel, each suited to the character, one of the most difficult to convey is that of the Prosecuting Attorney. Mrs. Garnett had eliminated so many of his repetitions, his elliptical sentence structure, his inability to state a point logically and succinctly, that he emerged a much better lawyer and thinker than Dostoevsky ever meant him to be. I have reinstated all the passages and have tried to follow Dostoevsky exactly, not an easy task, because if the attorney gets tangled up in his own rhetoric, the translator may overstate the attorney's deficiencies in another direction. Suffice it to say that Dostoevsky expended great effort and ingenuity in showing the muddled thought and obtuse psychologizing of the prosecutor in the fabric of his speech, and some of this at least is now conveyed in English. Dostoevsky himself comments in the novel on the attorney's style, modestly calling attention through the narrator to its shortcomings, as he does on that of the defense attorney's. Much as Dostoevsky despised Fetyukovich's prototype[4] (whom he denied using as a model), he not only manages to capture the essentials of his style but perhaps makes it even more effective.

We come next to problems of diminutives, common ways of conveying affection, politeness, good humor, or deference in Russian, which may, however, also have a pejorative cast. It is quite natural to refer to "birdies" and "little this" or "little that" in Russian, but it sounds somewhat childish or silly, if not downright idiotic, in English, and I have made no attempt to indicate each time a diminutive was used. Excessive use creates a cloying sentimentality even in Russian, and totters on the annoying in the Snegiryov sections and in some of Elder Zosima's homilies. The saccharine quality may be used with deliberate effect, as Dostoevsky demonstrates in the first meeting between Grushenka and Katerina Ivanovna. * * *

Russians use a variety of diminutives in names, particularly children's names. In general, the longer the diminutive form, the greater the affection shown. Thus Ilyusha Snegiryov has a further degree of diminutive—Ilyushechka—when his father shows even greater attachment. His legal name, Il'ya, is not used at all. Alyosha in some emotive exchanges with his father and with Grushenka becomes Alyoshechka but is never quite transformed into the babyish forms Dostoevsky uses in reporting the death of his own son. Dmitri, usually Mitya, can become Mitka or Mitenka, each time with a slightly different shade of meaning, connected with his age, character, and particular circumstance. In brief, by the use of such diminutives Dostoevsky can convey both the attitude of the speaker and a particular quality of the character: his youth, something childish, something endearing, something not quite formal, or merely a degree of friend-

4. See p. 479. [*Editor's note.*]

ship or respect. One tends to think of Alyosha rather than of Alexey or Alexey Fyodorovich, of Grushenka (Mitya's "Grusha" betokens an even closer feeling) rather than Agrafena Alexandrovna, of Dmitri in some of his doings as Mitya, in others as Dmitri, in still others as Dmitri Karamazov, with still another level available in Russian and discussed shortly. But Ivan is only Ivan or Ivan Fyodorovich and I have had to reintroduce the two or three times he is called Vanya or Vanka by his father for an important reason: when on his way to Smerdyakov Ivan hears the peasant singing "Vanka's gone to Petersburg" the Russian reader would automatically recognize that Vanka is a diminutive of Ivan and might thus be led to consider another implication of the passage.

Diminutives are only one peculiarity of Russian names. In addition to the given name, everyone has a patronymic ("son of," "daughter of"). This permits at least one further level of formality. In the late nineteenth century the family name was rarely used in social discourse and even in certain forms of address and reference, for the name and patronymic approximate our "Mr." or "Mrs." That prefix is rare, for people would be addressed by their military or civil rank or a designation of their social status as a member of the nobility, middle class, and so on. The use of the family name alone is perfectly acceptable, for example among schoolmates, comrades, and the like, but it can convey a lesser sense of derogation than in English: when Fetyukovich refers to Grushenka at the trial he merely gives her family name. It sounds cruder in English than in Russian; the French can convey a slightly different insinuation by "la Svetlova." Russian has a form of address (*gospozha*) that designates an adult female, whether single or married, for which there is unfortunately no longer a word in English (formerly "mistress" was an exact equivalent). It is used by Fetyukovich for Katerina Ivanovna, and by the prosecuting attorney for Grushenka. To maintain this hierarchy I have used "Miss" for the two rivals, have retained the original translator's "Madame" Khokhlakova, and left "Mrs." for the few instances when wives of commoners are mentioned. The family name alone for peripheral characters like Rakitin, Maximov, and Perkhotin is not merely one of convenience but also of a certain distance in attitude.

Patronymics and names in general should present problems in translation, and certain shades of attitude, for example in the difference between Trifon Borisovich and Trifon Borisich—since the "ov" is usually not pronounced anyway—cannot be conveyed in English. So, too, Barbara Nikolaevna Snegiryova occasionally is "Nikolavna." Here they are vital: It is possible to refer to a single hero as Raskolnikov, but if one were to write "Karamazov" a further distinction is necessary as four characters share the name. The patronymic offers a solution that may seem unduly cumbersome in English, where Ivan is clearly Ivan, Dmitri is Dmitri, and so on. But in Russian, certainly in the narrative portions, and frequently in direct address, they cannot be mentioned without their patronymics, and I have reintroduced them into Mrs. Garnett's translation. The reason is that Dostoevsky himself hammers away at their brotherhood and their connection with their father Fyodor, who on at least one vital occasion forgets who is a half-brother and who a full, and hints at a different alignment. Each time the two elder brothers' names appear in the narrative, and frequently in conversation, almost invariably for Ivan, Ivan is Ivan

Fyodorovich and Dmitri is Dmitri Fyodorovich. Occasionally, Dostoevsky omits the patronymic. Sometimes it may be accidental, sometimes—as in Ivan's conversation with the devil—by design. I have always followed his usage, without concern for inconsistency or worries about his intentions.

When any of the brothers refer to another by his first name (not by a diminutive), without the patronymic, he frequently finds it necessary to add "brother," or perhaps to substitute it for the patronymic. I have turned it at the beginning of the novel into "my brother Ivan (Dmitri)" because in today's quaint idiom the lack of possessive pronoun may convey a different meaning. The patronymic may become annoying in English but it is necessary. The reader can gauge the effect for himself. Ivan is always Ivan Fyodorovich, but Dmitri is Mitya as well as Dmitri Fyodorovich. When Alyosha is called Alexey Fyodorovich there is a slight shock not because of the formality, but because it reminds one of the family connection. It is even more striking when Kolya and the schoolboys call him "Karamazov," which he unquestionably is.

The Karamazov brothers, however, are four. We read that old Karamazov was amused that townspeople added the patronymic Fyodorovich to Smerdyakov's Christian name, but tolerated it even though he denied paternity. The lackey is always called by the family name Fyodor devised, Smerdyakov, and it must really come as a shocking reminder that he too is a member of the family when Marya Kondratevna—the only one in the book—addresses him as "Pavel Fyodorovich." The patronymic emphasizes brotherhood, and in more than merely the legal sense. Onomastics (the study of the forms of proper names) are crucial. The family name, the given names, the names of other characters always point to something significant. Dostoevsky distributed his spiritual and intellectual strivings and shortcomings, his physical drives and his disease among the four brothers. He endowed his favorite character with the name of his recently deceased young boy, Alexey; to Dmitri he gave his sensuality, to Ivan his dialectical and rational skills, to Smerdyakov his epilepsy; and to old Karamazov, the source from which the novel turbulently flows, the father of us all, the creator of the novel assigned his own name, Fyodor—Theodore, "the gift of God"! Indeed!

* * *

I will add a personal prejudice. *The Brothers Karamazov* hinges on the killing of a father, on patricide. For some inexplicable reason, "parricide" has taken its place in the original translation and become hallowed by the translation of Freud's article as "Dostoevsky and Parricide." I have let it stand because I have always been amused by the notion of Grigory's shouting "Parricide" at the fleeing figure who turns out to be Mitya. It is certainly Dostoevsky's intent that all should think Mitya culpable, and he emphasizes it in the shout. My amusement stems from the Russian "*ottseubiytsa*," which is perfectly colloquial but sounds like an exclamation that might more naturally issue from a Samurai or a Kamikaze pilot than from a Russian servant in the provinces. "Parricide" is bad enough, "patricide" even worse. The Germans are luckier: instead of the learned word, Grigory can rattle out the machine-gun burst: "*Vatertöter*"!

I have deleted one line of Mrs. Garnett's translation, the very last of the novel, "Hurrah for Karamazov!", an addition of her own. Dostoevsky was not modest about the book. When the prosecutor makes the invidious comparison "They have their Hamlets but we only have our Karamazovs," the reader may italicize the names, make them titles, and consider their preeminence in their respective literatures and in world literature. But the affirmative shout that ends the novel, "Hurrah for Karamazov" is only an acoustic effect, to be imagined by the reader, not a real line. The book is replete with such effects, the most notable being the silence just before the murder, which prompts Mitya to think of a verse "and only the silence whispers." Dostoevsky's conclusion is an audible chorus ("they all chimed in"), not a repetition of the shout itself. And it is clearly a more apt conclusion than a cheer for a Karamazov. The ending emphasizes unity and brotherhood, not the individual that has brought it about, not the family whose deeds have set it in motion, not the author who takes a final bow.

VALENTINA A. VETLOVSKAYA

Alyosha Karamazov and the Hagiographic Hero[†]

"The main narrative is the second," explains the narrator of *The Brothers Karamazov* in his introductory remarks, "—it is the action of my hero in our day, at the very present time. The first novel takes place thirteen years ago, and it is hardly even a novel, but only a period in my hero's early youth. I cannot do without this first novel, because much in the second would be unintelligible without it."[1]

Clearly Dostoevsky conceived of his work in the form of two novels, of which the second (not known to us) is the main one. It follows that without this second novel much in the first cannot be entirely comprehensible. It is essential, therefore, that we seek out and consider elements which might provide some clue to the overall structure of the two novels. In this way the balance of parts in our presentation will not be upset, and we shall avoid making secondary things primary and primary ones secondary.

We may note at the outset that Dostoevsky wrote his introductory remarks in 1878, that is, when beginning his work on *The Brothers Karamazov*. The idea of a continuation of the novel, then, was not an afterthought, the result of work already accomplished; rather, it preceded the writing of the part of the work we know. The elements of the work's overall structure, then, its foundation, must certainly be in place in the work as we know it—indeed, they must even be partially visible. Otherwise the reader would not have been informed in the introduction that the two novels have the "essential unity of the whole"; in fact, there would be no question at all of any essential unity.

The introductory remarks provide some indication of the sense of the whole. The opening phrase of the introduction speaks of a biography: "In beginning the biography of my hero, Aleksey Fyodorovich Karamazov," etc. The narrator continues: "I have two novels and only one biography." What is important here, first, is that the narrator-author conceives of the

† From *Dostoevsky: New Perspectives*, ed. Robert Louis Jackson, pp. 206–226. Trans. by Pollack and Fusso Reprinted by permission of the Russian Authors' Society.
1. *The Brothers Karamazov*, trans. by Constance Garnett, Modern Library, 1950, xviii. All subsequent references are to this edition. (Translator's note.)

whole as a biography, and, second, that Aleksey Fyodorovich Karamazov is the center of this biography. The preeminence of precisely this hero is emphasized throughout the entire story, in spite of the fact that the first novel is called *The Brothers Karamazov*.

The first line of the novel, closely related to the introduction, reads as follows: "Aleksey Fyodorovich Karamazov was the third son of . . . a land-owner . . . in our district." The main hero is singled out. Further, the introductory story of Alyosha appears in a special chapter entitled, "The Third Son, Alyosha." By contrast, the more laconic and dry accounts of Dmitry and Ivan appear in chapters that seem to diminish rather than accentuate the importance of these heroes: "He Gets Rid of his Eldest Son," "The Second Marriage and the Second Family" (here Fyodor Pavlovich is in the foreground).

We may recall at this point that the word used for "biography," *zhizneopisanie*, signifies "*vita*." The narrator of *The Brothers Karamazov* emerges—not obtrusively, but clearly enough—as the narrator of a *vita*, with his "main" hero, Alyosha, as hero-saint.[2] The point deserves special emphasis. In this connection I. P. Eryomin has written about the life of Theodosius of Pechersk:

> From his first appearance in Nestor's Chronicle, Theodosius of Pechersk is presented to the reader in the "seraphic" image of the ideally positive Christian hero-saint. And he continues in the same basic image through the entire *vita*, accompanied by prayerfully reverential epithets. . . . Even in early youth, he is "one of God's elect," an "earthly angel" and a "heavenly human being." "Drawn to God's love," even in childhood he reveals virtues not usually possessed by an ordinary person in such a totality; he performs acts that go beyond all norms of everyday human conduct: these acts—his spiritual exploits—evoke pious consternation in some people, in others, "unreasoning ones," reproaches and even derision.[3]

The basic motifs and, in part, the tone of the preliminary characterization of Alyosha remind the reader of the typical hagiographical tale. Thus, Alyosha has been living in the monastery "for the past year, . . . and seemed willing to be cloistered there for the rest of his life." "He was . . . an early lover of humanity," the narrator further explains, "and that he adopted the monastic life was simply because at that time it struck him, so to say, as the ideal escape for his soul, struggling from the darkness of worldly wickedness to the light of love." The narrator will return to this motif again.

The opposition of the "darkness of earthly malice" and the "light of love," and of (earthly) darkness and (heavenly) light in general, is a metaphor common to the *vita* narrative, and one that goes back to the evangelists' texts. (This opposition is consistently pursued up to the end of the novel.)

2. A. L. Volynsky, in connection with the portrait characterization of Alyosha in the novel, noted the latter circumstance: "His [Alyosha's—V. V.] quiet gaze, the longish . . . oval of his face, the animation of expression—all this merges into the sort of icon-like image found in old tsarist documents—an image in which there is nothing provocative, nothing sharply individual." A. L. Volynskii, *Tsarstvo Karamazovykh* (St. Petersburg, 1901), 148–49.
3. Eryomin, I. P., "K kharakteristike Nestora kak pisatelia," in his *Literatura drevnei Rusi* (Moscow–Leningrad, 1966), 30.

Like the typical hero of a hagiographic narrative, even in early youth Alyosha feels the urge to depart from the vain world, because earthly passions are alien to him.

The complex relations between the ideal hero of the *vita* and the surrounding world make this hero strange to ordinary people and ordinary perception. This is the way Alyosha is presented to the reader. The narrator speaks right away of a strangeness, a certain eccentricity in him, but at the same time explains that these qualities do not, nevertheless, signify isolation: ". . . on the contrary, it happens sometimes that such a person [the eccentric—V. V.], I dare say, carries within himself the very heart of the universal, and the rest of the men of his epoch have for some reason been temporarily torn from it. . . ." As a result Alyosha is both set off against other people (this is typical for the hero of a *vita*), and closely linked to them, because it is impossible to go far from the "heart," impossible to entirely break off from it. Such a twist is unusual for a *vita*.

The desire for seclusion, the unchildlike pensiveness and concentration of the young Alyosha, his alienation from the playfulness and joyfulness typical of children, pointed out by the narrator, develop the same idea of the hero's "strangeness" and "eccentricity." Such a development is also typical of the *vita* narrative.[4] But the "gift for arousing a special love for oneself," confirmed many times subsequently, is a sign of that side of Alyosha's character that, despite any strangeness (or, perhaps, because of that strangeness), makes him dear to all people.

"He never tried to show off among his schoolfellows" is the slightly altered expression of the motif of humility, the absence of pride typical of the hero of the *vita*. This motif is reiterated in the report that Alyosha "never resented an insult. It would happen that an hour after the offence he would address the offender or answer some question with as trustful and candid an expression as though nothing had happened between them" (I, 1, iv).

The absence of pride, along with the complete indifference to worldly goods (money, for example, both his own and that of others) is emphasized by the words: "Another feature characteristic of him—and very much so—was that he never worried about whose means he was living on. In this respect he was the complete opposite of his older brother Ivan Fyodorovich. . . ." With regard to this lack of the vain and sensitive pride with which his older brother is endowed, the narrator considers it necessary to note again the strangeness, the "apparent" holy-foolery of his "main" and "beloved" hero. (It is important that this holy-foolery comes not from indifference or incivility in relation to others but, on the contrary, from an extreme and perhaps naïve trustfulness and sympathy toward people.)

Alyosha's "wild fanatical modesty and chastity" also belongs to the obligatory attributes of the hero of the *vita*—another feature that makes him strange from an ordinary point of view and that, for example, makes "all his schoolfellows from the bottom class to the top want to mock at him" and to look upon him "with compassion" (I, 1, iv).

---

4. See, for example, Nestor's account of the childhood of Theodosius: "Neither did he draw near to playing children, as is the habit of young people, but lo he abhorred their games." *Kievo-Pecherskii paterik*, introduction and notes by Prof. Dm. Abramovich (Kiev, 1931), 23.

In general, the motifs that are enumerated here exhaust the preliminary characterization of Alyosha. They are all marked and coordinated with the usual representation of the hero of the *vita*, who, even in childhood, exhibits the uncommon characteristics of the future great ascetic and saint.

Other motifs, too, are heard, in a very muffled form, but nevertheless from the beginning—motifs that contrast with those just introduced and that are apparently intended to point not just to the future great ascetic, but also to the future (perhaps also great) sinner.[5] Rather than analyzing them, however, let us merely say that the motives that compel Alyosha to elect the monastery as the lot most congenial to him also make this choice rather flimsy. The hero aspires to "truth" and to "great deeds" and wants to achieve these things as hastily as possible but, starting from this same aspiration, others go the opposite road. Alyosha "was convinced of the existence of God and immortality" (I, 1, v), but after some time he could be "convinced" by something else (after all, he is only beginning to live). Alyosha encounters an extraordinary elder in the monastery and falls in love with him (I, 1, iv, v), but this encounter is fortuitous. Moreover, too strong a feeling of love for the elder alone is not such an unconditionally good thing as it might at first appear. These and similar considerations all arise in the reader's mind not at once, but only later, when the motifs of Alyosha's preliminary characterization begin to recur. Acquiring additional hints and associations, they take on an ambiguous character, leading the reader to contemplate the idea of turns for the worse in the fate of the main hero.

For example, the teachings of the elder make it clear that belief in God, which inspires the young hero, acquires the force of conviction only when it is the result of "the experience of active love" (I, 2, iv). This "active" love is "a harsh and dreadful thing," it is "labor and fortitude, and thus for some people, perhaps, a whole science." Such a love the elder contrasts with "contemplative" love, which "is greedy for immediate action, rapidly performed and in the sight of all" (I, 2, iv).

With the exception of the moment of self-admiration (which is in no way connected with Alyosha), everything in the characterization of "contemplative" love corresponds to the feeling with which Alyosha enters on the "monastic road." The hero is not yet ready for an "active" love, for the "harsh and dreadful," for "labor and fortitude." Therefore his choice, despite the fact that it is natural for this essentially saintly hero, has as yet the most hasty and preliminary character. It perhaps serves as a premonitory allusion to the future, but it is not very important in the present, for the hero begins directly from that with which he should have ended.

As a result the image of the main hero of the "biography" is presented as mobile, capable of further change, and lacking that schematic straightforwardness and fixity of form which burdens the typical hero of a *vita*. Let us stress that this changeability and mobility is indicated not so much in spite of the hagiographic canon, as within its boundaries, thanks to the ambiguity, created by the narration, of certain motifs originating in that canon.

It is precisely because Alyosha is not yet ready to serve God and the "truth," as he then imagined it, that the elder sends his "quiet boy" out of

---

5. During the last period of his life, as is well known, Dostoevsky was extremely interested in the idea of writing a *Life of a Great Sinner*.

the monastery: "This is not your place for the time. I bless you for great service in the world. Yours will be a long pilgrimage . . . You will have to bear *all* before you come back. There will be much to do. But I don't doubt you, and so I send you forth . . . Work, work unceasingly . . ." (I, 2, vii). The fact that Alyosha is really still too young, unstable, and unconfirmed in his (still naïve) beliefs, is corroborated yet again by his reaction to the elder's words. "Alyosha started, when the elder said, '. . . leave the monastery. Go away for good.'" The hero is perplexed, confused, frightened. "But how could he be left without him [the elder—V. V.]? How could he live without seeing and hearing him? Where should he go? He had told him not to weep, and to leave the monastery. Good God! It was long since Alyosha had known such anguish" (I, 2, vii).

The above-cited motifs (on the one hand, the hero's uncommonness even in early youth, his decision to go into a monastery; on the other, his lack of inner preparation for this exploit, his dispatch into the world for such preparation) signify that in this case we are dealing with the organic combination in one character of the two usual types of hagiographic hero. The first type is the hero who senses, almost from infancy, his lofty calling, and subsequently follows it without swerving (like Theodosius of Pechersk or Sergius of Radonezh). The second type is the hero who turns to God and gives himself up to the same asceticism after many trials, mistakes and errors (Ephraim Sirin). Alyosha's dispatch from the monastery does confront him with this set of trials, for in relation to the hero of the *vita*, the world can only appear in its tempting aspect.

After the presentation of the main hero, a motif arises that links his name with that of Aleksey the Man of God. This motif is at first heard obliquely. The hero of the *vita*, widely known in its time, is only recalled to the reader's mind. The occasion for this reminder is the elder's conversation with one of the devout women, who is wasting away with grief over her dead boy. To the elder's question as to what her son was called, the mother answers:

"Aleksey, Father."
"A sweet name. After Aleksey, the Man of God?"
"Of God, Father, of God, Aleksey the Man of God!"
"What a saint he was! I will remember him, mother . . ." (I, 2, iii)

Since the name of the main hero has already been mentioned and he himself has been presented to the reader in a hagiographic halo, the reminder of Aleksey the Man of God brings to mind certain details of the "biography" that support the idea of Alyosha's closeness to the hagiographic hero mentioned here.

Aleksey the Man of God was born in Rome; his parents were rich and distinguished Romans: "Under the emperors Arcadius and Honorius, at the end of the fourth century, there lived in Rome a distinguished man by the name of Euphimian, and his wife Aglaida. . . .'[6] In the version of the

6. *Izbrannye zhitiia sviatykh, kratko izlozhennye po rukovodstvu Chetikh Minei*, 2nd ed., revised and supplemented, (Moscow, 1860), March 17. This edition was in Dostoevsky's library. See L. Grossman, *Biblioteka Dostoevskogo* (Odessa, 1919), 154. Especially interested in the *vita* of Aleksey the Man of God, Dostoevsky undoubtedly did not limit himself to the short exposition of it in this edition. The *Lives of the Saints* by Dimitrius of Rostov and the *Prologue*, quite authoritative and accessible in their time, were well known to him.

life found in the *Lives of the Saints* by Dimitrius of Rostov, we read: "There was in ancient Rome a pious man by the name of Euphimian, at the time of the pious emperors Arcadius and Honorius, great among the nobles and exceedingly wealthy. . . ." In the *Prologue* version of the life of Aleksey the Man of God we read: "He was from ancient Rome, the son of Euphimian the patrician, his mother was Aglaida. . . ."[7]

Clearly it is not by chance that it is precisely in the chapter, "The Third Son, Alyosha," that the portrait of Fyodor Pavlovich is given, which ends with the words: "He was fond indeed of making fun of his own face, though, I believe, he was well satisfied with it. He used particularly to point to his nose, which was not very large, but very delicate and conspicuously aquiline. 'A regular Roman nose,' he used to say, 'with my goitre I've quite the countenance of an ancient Roman patrician of the decadent period'" (I, 1, iv). To be sure, the evident resemblance between Fyodor Pavlovich and the father of the ancient hero of the *vita*, who was by habit quite pious, is confined to this casual remark.

Of course, this remark is important in general as well: it likens the present to the past, gives the "particular" a broad significance, because the "confusion," decay, and "fall" of present-day Russian life is related here to the "fall" of ancient Rome. If the analogy is continued, however, then a rebirth out of this "fall," like the rebirth of ancient (pagan) Rome, must appear on the paths of Christianity. Moreover, because Rome was unable to deal with this problem in its own time, since, as Ivan explains, "Rome . . . retained too much of pagan civilization and culture" (I, 2, v), then clearly the problem stands now before the "fallen" and also decaying Russia. All this is in accordance with Slavophile ideas and the Slavophile conception of the history of the West and Russia, with which Dostoevsky sympathized. If one believes the testimony of Vladimir Solovyov, these themes should have been strongly heard in the second novel.[8] In the first novel they are only hinted at, and they are not the themes that are important for us now. We are interested in Alyosha and his connections with the hero of the ancient *vita*. It is likely that Fyodor Pavlovich's claim to resemblance to the ancient Roman is, in this respect, a significant detail.

* * *

Dostoevsky, though not overly concerned with formal matters (the precise reproduction of the sequence of hagiographical motifs and their literal transmission), nonetheless has adhered to the hagiographic outline in the most important points of Alyosha's story. The elder, for example, sends Alyosha back not only to his father and brothers (Alyosha himself recalls his deceased mother and upon arrival seeks out her grave), but also to his (here, it is true, future) bride.

The complexity of Alyosha's relations with Liza Khokhlakova is noted from the very beginning: Alyosha's attachment to Liza countervails his lofty goals.

---

7. Both the *vita* in the edition of Dimitrius of Rostov and the *Prologue* redaction are cited according to the texts included by V. P. Adrianova-Perets in the appendix to her *Zhitie Alekseia cheloveka bozhiia v drevnei russkoi literature i narodnoi slovesnosti* (Petrograd, 1917), 501, 512.
8. VI. Solov'ev, *Tri rechi v pamiati Dostoevskogo (1881–1883 gg.)* (Moscow, 1884), 20–21.

"Why do you make fun of him [Alyosha—V. V.] like that, naughty girl?" the elder says to her. Liza suddenly and quite unexpectedly blushed. Her eyes flashed and her face became quite serious. She began speaking quickly and nervously in a warm and resentful voice: "Why has he forgotten everything, then? . . . No, now he's saving his soul! Why have you put that long gown on him? If he runs he'll fall."

And suddenly she hid her face in her hands and went off into terrible, uncontrollable . . . laughter. The elder listened to her with a smile, and blessed her tenderly. . . .

"I will certainly send him," the elder decided (I, 2, iv).

Let us note that it is hardly by chance that Alyosha's future bride and spouse is called Liza. In the Russian versions of the life of Aleksey the Man of God, the name of the bride and spouse of the saint is not mentioned, but several variants of the sacred poem speak either of Katerina or of Lizaveta:

> The father permitted him to wed
> A princess renowned and promised to him,
> Lizaveta by name.[9]

In the elder's conversation with the devout women, where the name of Aleksey the Man of God is heard for the first time, the name of Lizaveta is heard as well:

"Is that your little girl?"
"My little girl, Father, Lizaveta."
"May the Lord bless you both, you and your babe Lizaveta . . ."
He blessed them all and bowed low to them (I, 2, iii).

The chapter "A Lady of Little Faith" (following "Devout Peasant Women") involves four characters: elders (Alyosha's spiritual father, Father Zosima; Liza's mother, Mme Khokhlakova) and minors (Alyosha, Liza). In view of the consistency of motifs, Alyosha's link with Aleksey the Man of God and Liza's with Lizaveta, the bride and spouse of the saint in the Russian sacred poem, can be assumed, while the elder's firm intention to send Alyosha to Liza after her mother's words and her own takes on the character of a betrothal. Subsequently this betrothal is confirmed. Alyosha says to Liza: "I shall be leaving the monastery altogether in a few days. If I go into the world, I must marry. I know that. *He* [the elder, Dostoevsky's emphasis— V. V.] told me to marry, too. Whom could I marry better than you—and who would have me except you? I have been thinking it over" (II, 5, i).

* * *

In accordance with the spirit and meaning of the *vita* and the poem about Saint Aleksey, Alyosha Karamazov's rapprochement with the world

9. *Kaliki perekhozhie. Sbornik stikhov i issledovanie P. Bessonova* (Moscow, 1861), var. No. 28 (hereinafter the variants of the sacred poem about Aleksey the Man of God from the collections of Kireevsky, Bessonov and Varentsov are indicated in the text of the book). We basically rely on the texts of Bessonov, because Dostoevsky could not have missed them: the collection was widely known. Dostoevsky was apparently also familiar with the editions of P. Kireevsky (*Russkie narodnye pesni sobrannye Petrom Kireevskim*), Part 1 (Moscow, 1848) and V. Varentsov (*Sbornik russkikh dukhovnykh stikhov, sostavlennyi V. Varentsovym* (St. Petersburg, 1860), in each of which there is also a variant of the poem that interests us. . . .

VALENTINA A. VETLOVSKAYA

and his relations at first turns out to be a trial for him. The narrative is constructed so that after the scene in the monastery, which serves as the starting point of the action, Alyosha is sent on errands by first one, then another character; he listens to others' stories, usually filled with perturbation and grief, that cast doubt on the affirmation of God's endless love, charity, and beneficence. The tempting character of these encounters, commissions, and confessions is conveyed through various motifs.

Among these motifs, the indication of Alyosha's suffering (in contrast to his joyful sojourn in the monastery and his communion with the elder) is one of the most constant and important ones. "This request [of Katerina Ivanovna—V. V.] and the necessity of going had at once aroused an uneasy feeling in his heart, and this feeling had grown more and more painful all the morning . . ." (I, 3, iii). So begins Alyosha's ascetic life in the world and his "ordeals." On the way to Katerina Ivanovna, Alyosha's brother Mitya stops him:

> "I might have sent anyone, but I wanted to send an angel. . . ."
> "Did you really mean to send me?" cried Alyosha with a distressed expression (I, 3, iii).

Alyosha's suffering, which reveals the gravity of others' appeals and commissions for this "quiet boy," is contrasted with the joy of those who, voluntarily or not, tempt Alyosha: "'Oh, gods,' exclaims, again, Mitya, 'I thank you for sending him to me by the back way, and he came to me like the golden fish to the silly old fishermen in the fable!'" (I, 3, iii). "'Here he is! Here he is!' yelled Fyodor Pavlovich, highly delighted at seeing Alyosha. 'Join us. Sit down. Coffee is a lenten dish, but it's hot and good. I don't offer you brandy, you're keeping the fast. But would you like some? No; I'd better give you some of our famous liqueur. . . . Now we've a treat for you, in your own line, too. It'll make you laugh. Balaam's ass has begun talking to us here . . .'" (I, 3, vi). "Alyosha left his father's house," the narrator further recounts, "feeling even more exhausted and dejected in spirit than when he had entered it. . . . He felt something bordering upon despair, which he had never known till then" (I, 3, x).

The world into which Alyosha is sent by the elder disturbs and torments the young hero.

> Why, why, had he gone forth? Why had he sent him "into the world"? thinks Alyosha, returning to the monastery the very first day of his "travels." Here was peace. Here was holiness. But there was confusion, there was darkness in which one lost one's way and went astray at once . . . (I, 3, xi).

The day after this sorrowful return Father Paisy, again seeing Alyosha off "into the world," pronounces unexpected parting words: "Remember, young man, unceasingly . . . that worldly science, which has become a great power, has . . . analyzed everything divine handed down to us in the holy books. After this cruel analysis the learned of this world have nothing left of all that was sacred of old" (II, 4, i). Hastening to "protect the young soul entrusted to him," Father Paisy speaks words that are of the utmost importance for an understanding of subsequent events: ". . . you are young," he addresses Alyosha, "and the temptations of the world are great and beyond your strength to endure" (II, 4, i).

Alyosha's meeting with his father, then with the schoolchildren, then the "lacerations," of which the gravest is the last (the confession of Captain Snegiryov, in which the theme of the innocently suffering child is heard), continues the grave series of "temptations" of Alyosha. The gloomy impressions from his first days of acquaintance with the world, even before the conversation with his brother Ivan, behind whom stands "worldly science," make Alyosha let slip a phrase expressing something that was "already undoubtedly tormenting him": "And perhaps I don't even believe in God" (II, 5, i).

Alyosha's sudden confession, on the one hand, and Father Paisy's warning, on the other, uttered on the same day as the brothers' meeting in the tavern, both have a very direct relation to that meeting. Ivan's tempting speech, which comes along with the other temptations but is stronger than they are, is addressed to the hero, who is already disturbed by the world's "darkness." Here the suffering child, familiar to the reader and to Alyosha through the captain's confession, arises once more on the lips of the "learned" Ivan, now as a kind of "emblem" and basic argument of "worldly science," which has left "nothing . . . of all that was sacred of old." Having told Alyosha about the general and the persecuted child Ivan asks:

> "Well—what did he deserve? To be shot? To be shot for the satisfaction of our moral feelings? Speak, Alyosha!"
> "To be shot," murmured Alyosha, lifting his eyes to Ivan with a pale, twisted smile.
> "Bravo!" cried Ivan, delighted. "If even you say so . . ." (II, 5, 4).

The delight of the atheist Ivan, in accordance with the author's conception, must not only indicate temptation, as did earlier the delight of Mitya or Fyodor Pavlovich, but also compromise Alyosha's words in the eyes of the reader: this delight signifies that here Alyosha proves to be too close to his older brother. Ivan continues thus: "You're a pretty monk! So there is a little devil sitting in your heart, Alyosha Karamazov!" In the author's opinion, the reader must guess that if even the atheist Ivan perceives no sanctity in Alyosha's reaction ("Shoot him!"), and begins to speak of a "devil," then it must be that there is no such sanctity.

Fulfilling others' requests, listening to others (above all his brother Ivan), Alyosha gives way to temptation. The "darkness" of the world does not remain alien to this hero's heart, and not only because he is too young, but also because Alyosha, as he himself explains more than once, is a Karamazov. Notwithstanding his strangeness, Alyosha is the same sort of man as everyone else (in contrast to the *vita* and the poem, in the novel this motif is carried out quite definitely). The very deep affinity of the "angel" Alyosha for the other "sinners" presumes, for the young and inexperienced hero, the possibility of committing the same errors as the others. "Yes, yes, it is he, it is Pater Seraphicus, he will save me—from him and forever!" (II, 5, v)—races helplessly through Alyosha's mind when he hurries to the monastery after the conversation with Ivan.

The death of Father Zosima and everything that follows it is a trial that makes Alyosha's heart overflow with suffering, and provokes his reproaches and indignation. Speaking of these events, the narrator distinguishes two circumstances that "exerted a very strong influence on the heart and soul of the main . . . hero of the story" (III, 7, i). The first is Ivan's pernicious influence on Alyosha. "Oh, it was not that something of the fundamental, elemental, so to speak, faith of his soul had been shaken. . . . Yet a vague but tormenting and evil impression left by his conversation with Ivan the day before, suddenly revived again now in his soul and seemed forcing its way to the surface of his consciousness" (III, 7, ii). Outraged by the injustice of Heaven in relation to the deceased elder, Alyosha repeats Ivan's words: "I am not rebelling against my God; I simply 'don't accept His world.'" The blasphemy of these words on the lips of the young ascetic is obvious. ". . . This is a jolly fine chance and mustn't be missed . . ." Rakitin immediately decides (III, 7, ii). The second circumstance that the narrator emphasizes (both justifying and condemning Alyosha) is that Alyosha loved his spiritual father, Father Zosima, too much: "The fact is that all the love that lay concealed in his pure young heart for everyone and everything had, for the past year, been concentrated—and perhaps wrongly so—on one being, now deceased. It is true that that being had for so long been accepted by him as his ideal, that all his young strength and energy could not but turn towards that ideal, even to the forgetting at the moment of everyone and everything" (III, 7, ii). These explanations by the narrator are extremely important.

Growing indignant and grumbling, Alyosha, like Ivan, demands "supreme justice," which, in the young hero's opinion, has been "violated." Instead of the glory and triumph of the deceased righteous man, whom he loved with an exceptional love, Alyosha sees this righteous man "degraded and dishonored" (III, 7, 2). The narrator insistently strives to show that Alyosha's error (his grumbling and indignation) is rooted in the exceptional nature of his love, which—in its own way, of course, but essentially the same as with Ivan—destroys the living connection between things. Alyosha involuntarily forgets that his elder belongs entirely to the world, "sinful" and "stinking" in its sins, and thus bears the guilt for its ugliness along with everyone else. According to the logic of the narration it emerges that the elder bears this guilt to an even greater degree than do others: remitting others' sins, he takes them upon his own soul and, consequently, answers for them, for it is clearly only under such a condition that he has the right to forgive others.[1] The idea of the connection between each person and everyone else, and the responsibility of each for everyone, repeated many times by the elder himself during his life, underlies the artistic narrative here as well. But it is precisely this idea that Alyosha has forgotten in his grief.

---

1. N. Kostomarov retells a legend, communicated to him by F. I. Buslaev and known here and in the West in many variants, about a sinner who killed his father and seduced his mother. He seeks a priest who could remit his sin: "The sinner went to several priests to beg forgiveness, but *since not one could bring himself to forgive him and take responsibility for such a sin, he killed them. . . .*" (N. Kostomarov, "Iz mogil'nykh predanii. Legenda o krovosmesitele," *Sovremennik*, 1860, Vol. LXXX, Section I, 223). In the apocryphal "Voprosy Ioanna Bogoslova Avraamu na Eleonskoi gore," to the question whether the priest takes the sins of the confessor upon himself, the following answer is given: "If a son steals with his father, do they not bind him together with his father, and lead them both to trial, and don't they both pay for that theft? Child, *those also, the sin of the confessor and the priest, the sin is common to both, doing that he answers for him and takes his sins upon himself.*" N. S. Tikhonravov, *Pamiatniki starinnoi russkoi literatury, izdavaemye grafom Gr. Kushelevym-Bezborodko*, 210; cf. "Voprosy sv. Ioanna Bogoslova o zhivykh i mertvykh . . . ," in *Pamiatniki starinnoj russkoi literatury, izdavaemye grafom Gr. Kushelevym-Bezborodko*, Issue 3 (St. Petersburg, 1862), 116. In the light of these parallels, the "breath of corruption" revealed after Zosima's death signifies that the "stink of sins," his own and others', no longer burden the elder. The italics in the quotations are mine.

If Alyosha had loved the elder more "correctly," that is, not with an exceptional love but in the same way that he loved others, he would not have found grounds in the righteous man's "shame" for the condemnation of "God's world." Everything in this world is connected. And just as there are none who are completely righteous, so there are none who are completely sinful. For this reason the scene of Alyosha and Grushenka, coming after the scene of the young hero's bitter suffering, harmoniously complements the story about the righteous man's "shame." Here the sinful woman unexpectedly reveals a degree of love, reverence for sanctity, and compassion for her dispirited brother that, considering her "incorrect" view of things, would not be supposed of her. Thanks to this, Grushenka is able to encourage Alyosha: the loftiness of her soul, made manifest "at that moment," is the essential link in the chain of phenomena that, according to the author's conception, makes their entire relationship not frightfully incongruous but comforting and harmonious.

Alyosha's dream ("Cana of Galilee") naturally concludes these scenes. The boundlessness of God's love for all people and the joy of those who are united by this love are manifested here to the young ascetic as if before his very eyes. The link of everyone with each other, salutary and joyful when God is among people (a circumstance which must be construed in a broad sense), staggers Alyosha's soul with ecstasy. The idea of the primordial beauty and purity of "God's world," and of the responsibility of all people for the fact that they make this beautiful world vicious, is what the author tries to emphasize in "Cana of Galilee." It is just this idea that Alyosha suddenly grasps, "for the rest of his life and forever and ever": "What was he weeping over? Oh! in his rapture he was weeping even over those stars, which were shining to him from the abyss of space . . . He longed to forgive everyone and for everything, and to beg forgiveness. Oh, not for himself, but for all men, for all and for everything. 'And others are praying for me too,' echoed again in his soul. . . . He had fallen on the earth a weak boy, but he rose up a resolute champion, and he knew and felt it suddenly at the very moment of his ecstasy" (III, 7, iv).

Thus the young ascetic's passionate and exceptional love for his spiritual father yields, at this important moment, to a just as passionate love for the world and for all people without exception. "He who loves everyone alike in compassion and indifferently," reasons Isaak Sirin, mentioned and quoted in *The Brothers Karamazov*, "has achieved perfection."[2] Alyosha (not intellectually, but emotionally) finds a way out of suffering in the joyful acceptance of "God's world," and in union with everything and everyone. This loving union with people, the intimate inclusion of them all (including the most sinful) in his soul eliminates the contradiction between love of God and love of people—the basic contradiction overcome by the hero of the ancient *vita*, Aleksey the Man of God. For such an unqualified love, the possibility of which is indicated by the moment of Alyosha's ecstasy, is itself, in the author's conception, divine love.

2. Isaak Sirin [Isaac the Syrian], *Slova podvizhnicheskie* (Moscow, 1858), 60. This idea is repeated: "When [a man—V. V.] sees all people . . . as good, and no one seems to him impure or defiled, then he is truly pure in heart" (*ibid.*, p. 141). Among the surviving notes for the novel we read: "Elder: The main thing is not to lie. Not to store up possessions, to love (Damaskin, Sirin).'" F. M. Dostoevsky, *Polnoe sobranie sochinenii v tridtsati tomakh*, vol. XV (Leningrad, 1976), 320. He probably had in mind the discussions of genuine love by Ioann Damaskin and Isaak Sirin.

"'Someone visited my soul in that hour,' Alyosha would say afterwards, with firm faith in his words" (III, 7, iv). "'Brothers,' the elder used to teach, 'have no fear of men's sin. Love a man even in his sin, for that is the semblance of Divine Love and is the highest love on earth. Love all God's creation, the whole and every grain of sand in it. . . . Love the animals, love the plants, love everything. If you love everything, you will perceive the divine mystery in things. Once you perceive it, you will begin to comprehend it better every day. And you will come at last to love the whole world with an all-embracing love'" (II, 6, iii).[3]

If the moment of Alyosha's ecstasy is prolonged (as the words of the elder prophesy) or if this moment really acquires the greatest significance in the hero's life (as the narrator foretells), the world will cease to play its tempting role for the young ascetic. When this world is revealed to the hero in the beauty and harmony of all its relations, and not in an ugly conglomeration of absurdities, when it evokes an ecstatic rapture, then there is no place for the condemnation of its creator. Dostoevsky clearly tries to carry out this idea.

True, it is possible that the moment of Alyosha's ecstasy before "God's world" is only an anticipation. It is possible that subsequently Alyosha will turn from the "correct road" once more. All this is possible. But if Alyosha does turn from this road, then it would certainly be in order for him to enter onto it later, once and for all. It is precisely this outcome that the logic of the artistic narrative demands.

A person who joyfully takes into his soul the entire world ("both the whole, and every grain of sand") without exception, accepting all people in spite of their "stinking sin," loving it all with an equally deep love, in other words, a person who comprehends the beauty and blessing of God's creation and along with it the beauty and blessing of the creator, is, of course, a "man of God." The world and God are harmoniously reconciled in the soul of this hero.

So Alyosha emerges (or must emerge) from the grave trial to which the "divine" elder sends him. And thus Dostoevsky interprets the central figure and the central confrontation of the *vita* of Aleksey the Man of God against a new background. In the continuation of the novel about Alyosha this interpretation would, it is likely, appear more clearly, but even now it is sufficiently obvious.

---

3. Zosima's words, like the concluding scene of "Cana of Galilee," particularly rely on Isaak Sirin's discussion of higher perfection, included in the "passion of a man's heart for all creation, for men, for birds, for animals, for demons and all creatures" (Isaak Sirin, *Slova podvizhnicheskie*, 299).

WILLIAM MILLS TODD III

The Brothers Karamazov and the Poetics of Serial Publication[†]

* * *

In this paper, which will be programmatic and somewhat hortatory, I would like to address certain issues involved in the publication and reception of *The Brothers Karamazov*, which appeared in sixteen installments in *The Russian Herald* over a period of almost two years, January 1879 to November 1880. This makes *The Brothers Karamazov* Dostoevsky's longest serialized novel (and thus his most demanding for his readers). Since, as he admitted, it was also the novel that he had least drafted as he began serialization, it was in many ways the most demanding for him, and his need for ongoing research into such topics as the investigative process as well as his personal problems forced him no less than eleven times to miss the month's installment of a "book" (*kniga*) and several times to change his plans for the novel as it unfolded.[1]

Many fine studies of the novel have already examined its beginnings in Dostoevsky's plans from the late 1860's, in Dostoevsky's creative interaction with works (such as Schiller's) which he had read and reread since childhood, or in Dostoevsky's life history. Other important studies, for the most part more recent ones, have read the novel as an integral text, an artistic whole comprised of various structures. The questions of part and whole, text and context, which these two types of research have raised make it all the more interesting to return to a consideration of the novel's serial publication, in connection with which these questions arose. Compelling invitations to such a study may be found in Dostoevsky's "tactical" correspondence with his editor (the word *taktika* is Dostoevsky's),[2] in the reactions of his contemporaries to the parts as they appeared, and in the opening lines of the novel, which thematize the relationship of individual elements (such as Alesha) to the whole and which promise the reader that the project underway is itself only part of a larger one.[3]

Even scholars who devote their energies to intrinsic analyses of the separate, one-volume edition of the text might find reason to examine the serial publication of *The Brothers Karamazov*. First, the separate edition, which appeared immediately after the serialization was completed and which serves as the basis for modern editions, preserves many aspects of the novel's serial form: titles, subtitles, segmentation, and format, even

† From *Dostoevsky Studies: Journal of the International Dostoevsky Society*, Vol. 7 (1986), 87–93. Reprinted by permission of the author.

1. For a description of his plan for serialization see F. M. Dostoevskii, *Pis'ma IV. 1878–1881*, ed. A. S. Dolinin (Moscow: GIKhL, 1959): 31. Letter of 11 July 1878 to S. A. Iur'ev.

2. Dostoevskii, *Pis'ma IV*, 61. Letter to V. F. Putsykovich of 11 June 1879. Dostoevsky's letters to his editor, N. A. Liubimov, which appear in this volume, are invaluable for an understanding of the novel's serialization.

3. For a contemporary reader's reaction to the problems of whole and part posed by serial publication, see K. P. Pobedonostsev's letter of 16 August 1879 to Dostoevsky, in Leonid Grossman, "Dostoevskii i pravitel' stvennye krugi 1870-kh godov," *Literaturnoe nasledstvo*, 15 (1934): 139.

   Exceptions to the neglect of serial publication appear in the excellent commentaries to *The Brothers Karamazov* in F. M. Dostoevskii, *Polnoe sobranie sochinenii v tridtsati tomakh* (Leningrad: Nauka, 1972–), 2: 411–47. Subsequent references to this addition will appear in parentheses in the text.

when the format was a typesetter's mistake, as was the case with the single uninterrupted paragraph of "The Grand Inquisitor."[4] In preserving his serial form, Dostoevsky differed from such Western writers as Dickens, Thackeray, or Trollope, who would dissolve and regroup the parts of their serials into new wholes as they prepared separate editions.[5] Second, the separate edition of *The Brothers Karamazov* preserves the mnemonic strategies (summaries, repeated phrases, recurring imagery) which Dostoevsky used to enable his initial readers to bridge the gaps between installments.[6] The devices which made it possible for readers to control nearly two years of reading prove not unhelpful for readers encountering the 700-page assembled text. Third, the initial critical response to the novel, which has set important issues for modern scholarship, frequently addressed the uncompleted novel.[7] Dostoevsky himself, who had only written several books of the novel when he began serialization, could react to this criticism as he continued to write and, in fact, entertained the possibility of responding to his critics in a letter to the editor of *The Russian Herald* which appeared at the end of the first year of serialization.[8] Finally, the demands of serial publication increased the myriad tensions that were involved in nineteenth-century fiction-writing, tensions between the parties in the literary process (such as writers and editors and censors), between the novel's status as both a material object and an intellectual-artistic phenomenon, between the economic needs and interests of writers and publishers and their ideological concerns, between the need to seize the public's attention and to create art of the highest level, between ongoing engagement with the issues of the day and attempts to realize artistic insights of enduring value, between the integrity of the novel's parts and their place in the larger whole, or, to put it somewhat differently, between the part's place in an issue of a periodical and its place in the novel. * * *

A large issue in the poetics of serialization is the generic one, for while novels and periodicals had intertwined as publishing enterprises in Western Europe since at least the early eighteenth century, many different forms of serialization had evolved, each placing different special demands upon writers, readers, and publishers.[9] The crudest of these distinctions in serialized form involved the length of the part, and these ranged from the several-hundred-page parts of the "triple-decker" novels that were the staple of the English lending libraries between the 1830's and 1880's, to the 32-page monthly parts popularized by Dickens, to the 5-page installment in such weekly magazines as *All the Year Round*, to the quarter-page feuilletons which graced the so-called *rez-de-chaussée* of the French daily newspapers or the *podval* of the Russian ones. In mid-century Russia, the favored form had become the monthly installment in the "thick journal,"

4. Dostoevskii, *Pis'ma IV*, 92. Letter to N. A. Liubimov of 7 August 1879.
5. J. A. Sutherland, *Victorian Novelists and Publishers* (Chicago: U of Chicago P, 1976): 204.
6. See, in this regard, the analysis of the novel's "inherent relationships" and "narrative structure" in Robert L. Belknap, *The Structure of* The Brothers Karamazov (The Hague: Mouton, 1967), Ch. 2 and 4.
7. For a survey of some of the more than thirty reviews the novel received as it was being serialized, see the commentaries to the novel in Dostoevskii, *Polnoe sobranie sochinenii*, 16: 487–501.
8. Dostoevskii, *Pis'ma IV*, 122. Letter to N. A. Liubimov of 8 December 1879.
9. *Robinson Crusoe*, for example, appeared as 78 installments in a pirated edition in *The Original London Post, or Heathcot's Intelligence*, 7 October 1719 to 30 March 1720.
   On the rise of seriality and related problems, see Lennard J. Davis, *Factual Fictions: The Origins of the English Novel* (New York: Columbia UP, 1983), Ch. 4–5.

such as *The Russian Herald*, an installment ranging in length from thirty to a hundred or so pages, permitting the novel to be serialized during the course of a subscription year.

As could well be imagined, these differing lengths proved compatible in varying degrees with the talents of individual writers. A master of surprise or suspense, such as Dickens or Wilkie Collins, could work very well within the limits of a five-page installment. A more discursive writer—a George Eliot—could find such shorter boundaries impossibly constricting and a threat to artistic dignity.[1] It was significant for the development of Russian fiction that the predominant mode of serialization between the 1840's and 1880's, the monthly "thick journals" allowed their novelists considerably more latitude—in length of the part, in frequency of their appearance, and in duration of the novel. Even here, however, there were norms, and Dostoevsky could boast with near accuracy that he had, up until *The Brothers Karamazov*, completed his novels during one subscription year.[2] When *The Brothers Karamazov* and *Anna Karenina* spilled over into two and three subscription years, the publisher of *The Russian Herald*, not beloved by the Russian intelligentsia in the best of times, was accused of defrauding his subscribers, and Dostoevsky felt obliged to print a letter of apology in the December 1879 issue.[3] Yet two contemporary novels appeared at a much more dilatory pace: Mel'nikov's anthropological novel *In the Hills* was supported by *The Russian Herald* during seven years (1875–1881) and Saltykov-Shchedrin's loosely constructed *Golovlevs* continued for six years (1876–1881) in *The National Annals* (*Otochestvennye zapiski*).

Differences of length and frequency of installments as well as differences between the types of periodical or part publication in which the nineteenth-century novels appeared called for different types of plotting. Because some of the most striking serials of the century were those, such as the *romans-feuilletons*, which featured swift action, sensational criminality, and intricate intrigue, scholarly attention has been drawn to the impact of this form of writing upon the novels of such writers as Dostoevsky, who worked in longer and more flexible serial forms, and in forms in which the problem of selling the individual parts or renewing subscriptions quarterly did not play a role, as it did with French and Russian daily newspapers or with the part publications of such English novelists as Dickens and Thackeray.[4]

1. For information on these modes of serialization in Western Europe, see Sutherland, *Victorian Novelists and Publishers*; Kathleen Tillotson, *Novels of the Eighteen-Forties* (Oxford 1954): 21–47; and Peter Brooks, *Reading for the Plot: Design and Intention in Narrative* (New York: Vintage Books, 1984), Ch. 6.
2. Dostoevskii, *Pis'ma IV*, 30–31. Letter of 11 July 1878 to S. A. Iur'ev.
3. Dostoevskii, *Pis'ma IV*, 122. Letter to N. A. Liubimov of 8 December 1879.
   For a reader's complaint about Katkov's practices, see the letter of F. M. Tolstoi to O. F. Miller of 17 July 1879, in L. R. Lanskoi, "Pis'ma o Dostoevskom," *Literaturnoe nasledstvo*, 86 (1973): 488.
4. On Dostoevsky and the *romans-feuilletons*, see L. P. Grossman, "Kompozitsiia v romane Dostoevskogo," *Vestnik Evropy* 2 (1916): 121–56; and Donald Fanger, *Dostoevsky and Romantic Realism: A Study of Dostoevsky in Relation to Balzac, Dickens, and Gogol* (Cambridge, Mass.: Harvard UP, 1965).
   On fluctuating subscriptions to part publications, see Tillotson, *Novels of the Eighteen-Forties*, 34–35. On the quarterly subscriptions to the French dailies see Brooks, *Reading for the Plot*, 147.
   On the Russian dailies and the fiction they published, see Jeffrey Brooks, *When Russia Learned to Read: Literacy and Popular Literature, 1861–1917* (Princeton: Princeton UP, 1985), Ch. 4.

* * * The Dostoevskian installment was, he intended, a "book," although four books (V, VIII, XI, XII) were, with the author's permission, divided into two installments. Each installment, he promised Liubimov, his long-suffering editor, would have "a finished character. That is, no matter how large or small the fragment, it would include something whole and finished."[5] This phrase "whole and finished" echoes throughout Dostoevsky's correspondence, as does the phrase "I write in books."[6] And while one may see such insistence on artistic integrity as a tactical gambit for preventing Liubimov from making the kind of editorial decisions that had disfigured *Crime and Punishment, The Possessed,* and the works of other writers, it does point toward a principle of organization that can be discovered in the parts, namely the attempt to give a thematic or conceptual unity to each installment.[7] One can see this striving for unity in the rigor with which the individual books realize the thematics of their titles, which in all but three cases suggest not concrete individuals, but categories of public event ("a judicial error"), of character ("the sensualists"), or of psychology ("lacerations"). Dostoevsky positively revelled in the finished quality of Book X ("Boys"): "I am very satisfied that the book . . . is so separate and episodic: the reader will not have such pretentions (to criticism?) as if in the most unfinished place one had suddenly broken off and placed the words 'to be continued.'"[8] Recent scholarship has shown how, in fact, a variety of structural principles (repeated images and situations, parallels in characterization, and fragments of quotations) tie Book X to the rest of the novel.[9] My point here is that Dostoevsky's strategies of serialization impelled the reader to perform this integration at the level of thematic inference and not at the level of story or "who done it." The reactions of his readers that have been collected in volume 86 of *Literaturnoe nasledstvo* show his success in provoking such thematic interpretation of the individual parts and of the novel as an unfolding whole.

Dostoevsky's reluctance to employ the serial writer's tricks is particularly evident in the conclusions to his installments, where, relatively speaking, he avoids the heavy-handed building of suspense that figured so prominently in the shorter serial forms. There are, to be sure, exceptions to this. Book VI ("The Russian Monk") does end with the narrator's attempts to arouse suspense by forewarning the reader about the "something unexpected, strange, alarming, and contradictory" which would soon occur (14: 294), but this is so trite by comparison with the general solemnity of Book VI that it as much calls attention to the gossipy, misguided townsfolk (including here the narrator) as it produces serious suspense. It is, in any case, more restrained than the typical installment ending of Dostoevsky's contemporaries, of which a convenient example may be provided by another fiction serialized in *The Russian Herald,* K. Orlovsky's novella *Redemption (Iskuplenie):* "'Poor Girl!' thought Vologdin, 'She pit-

5. Dostoevskii, *Pis'ma IV,* 50. Letter to N. A. Liubimov of 30 April 1879.
6. *Cf.* Dostoevsky's letters of 7 August 1879, 8 September 1879, 16 September 1879, 17 November 1879, and 29 April 1880. "I write in books"—letters of 16 November 1879 and 2 December 1879.
7. Note Dostoevsky's use of the following terms: "theme" *(tema,* letters of 19 May 1879, 11 June 1879, and 8 December 1879), "thought" *(mysl',* letter of 10 May 1879), "sense" *(smysl,* letters of 19 May 1879 and 29 April 1880), and "culminating point" *(kul'minatsionnaia tochka,* letters of 30 April 1879, 10 May 1879, 19 May 1879, 8 July 1879, 7 August 1879, and 9 August 1879).
8. Letter to N. A. Liubimov of 29 April 1880.
9. Robert Belknap, "The Rhetoric of an Ideological Novel," in William Mills Todd III, ed., *Literature and Society in Imperial Russia: 1800–1914* (Stanford: Stanford UP, 1978): 172–201.

ies me, but if she only knew to whom she has given her first love, and how dearly I would give to deliver her from what awaits her!'"[1]

Likewise, Dostoevsky avoids the serial writer's surprise endings. The only exception comes at the end of Book VIII ("Mitia"), but here the sudden arrest of Dmitri provides a thematically appropriate ending for a book which has been shaped by extravagant plans, depths of despair, murder, assault, drunkenness, and Dmitri's mad chase after a parodistic resurrection (14: 336). It could be argued, since these decisions are a matter of interpretation, that Book IV ends with a surprise, namely Captain Snegyrev rejecting Alesha's offer of money (14: 193). To be surprised by this conclusion, however, would be to have missed the psychological patterns which had been so rigorously developed during this book, entitled "Lacerations." And Dostoevsky, as we see from a testy letter to a reader who failed to understand such patterns, insisted that his readers master his psychology: "Not only the plot of a novel is important for a reader, but also a certain knowledge of the human soul (psychology), which each author has a right to expect from the reader."[2]

More typical of Dostoevsky's methods of concluding an installment, be it a book or part of a book, are endings on moments of relaxation or endings which return to a theme of the book. Several parts end on moments of joy or reconciliation for Alesha (III, VII, X, Epilogue). Book XI ("Brother Ivan Fedorovich") ends on an uncertain note, Alesha's recognition that Ivan could follow two paths—live in reconciliation or perish in hatred—but this uncertainty concludes a book devoted to Ivan's alternating rejection of and turning toward a number of characters, and it, therefore, rounds off Book IX thematically.[3]

So far I have been discussing the installments as parts of the novel *The Brothers Karamazov*. But one of the "defamiliarizing" benefits of studying the serialization of the novel would be the opportunity that it affords to see the novel as contemporaries saw it during its first two years in the public sphere, as a contribution to a "thick journal," *The Russian Herald*.[4] The editors of the journal made sure that the novel would be framed by never placing Dostoevsky's installment at either the front or the back, but always toward the middle of the monthly issue, thereby forcing readers to at least notice the other contributions as they made their way to the novel.

For modern readers, whose sense of the differences between imaginative literature and journalism may be strong and whose only encounter with novels has been through the medium of the book, the reading of a serialized novel within its environment can be a powerful experience of heteroglossia. Beside the installments of *The Brothers Karamazov*, for example, appeared essays on biological science, ecology, technology, pedagogy, jurisprudence, prison organization, politics, philosophy, history, literature, and music. Memoirs, especially ones concerning Russia's wars in the Balkans and in the Caucasus, played a prominent part, as one would

1. K. Orlovskii, "Iskuplenie," *Russkii vestnik* 150 (November 1880): 336.
2. Letter to E. N. Lebedeva of 8 November 1879.
3. In a personal communication G. F. Fridlender has called my attention to the importance of Dostoevsky's monthly issues of *The Diary of a Writer* as a laboratory for developing different techniques of closure and suspense besides those offered by the *roman-feuilleton*.
4. On the "thick journals" (*tolstye zhurnaly*), a term used by Belinsky as early as 1840, see Robert A. Maguire, *Red Virgin Soil: Soviet Literature in the 1920s* (Princeton: Princeton UP, 1968), Ch. 2.

expect from the political orientation of the journal's editors. How, and, indeed, whether, these essays and the chapters of the novel came into contact for Dostoevsky, his editors, and his readers, remains a critical problem, and one which I can only touch upon briefly here.

The range of possibilities for such contact between fiction and essay or memoir is very great, and it would by no means necessarily have been uniform for all of the participants in the literary process. Assuming that the journal was publishing a novel of great appeal, as was the case with *The Brothers Karamazov*, one could imagine a situation of minimal contact, or virtual disjuncture, in which the editors would take the fiction for its public appeal, the author would accept their offer for the honorarium involved, and the readers would turn directly to the serialized novel, ignoring the journal's other pieces. The other extreme, one of maximal contact, or coincidence, might involve the editors publishing an ideologically acceptable text for an author who would share that ideology, following the journal's other pieces and referring to them in a variety of ways and taking part in the journal's polemics with other journals for readers who would be interested in all of the journal's pieces and in its struggles with competing periodicals and ideologies.

Predictably enough, a hundred years of Dostoevsky scholarship and further research have demonstrated, not without controversy, that the case with *The Russian Herald*, *The Brothers Karamazov*, and its many readers rests somewhere between the extremes of disjuncture and coincidence. Although Dostoevsky's attitude toward Katkov and *The Russian Herald* was not uniformly positive during the years in which the novel was written and published and although there would have been purely financial reasons for giving *The Russian Herald* his new novel, he also wrote of his relations to the journal in terms of values, describing himself as a contributor (*sotrudnik*) to the journal, praising some of Liubimov's political contributions to it, and yet mentioning that his own views did not totally coincide with Katkov's. Beyond this, Leonid Grossman has shown that the novel incorporated many of the themes, characters, and incidents that characterized works by other members of Katkov's stable.[5] Other studies have shown how Dostoevsky waged polemical warfare with the chief ideological rival of *The Russian Herald*, *The National Annals*, and with its editor, Saltykov-Shchedrin.[6]

For the purposes of a poetics of journal serialization, one would have to move beyond these valuable influence or author studies, however, to study the interplay between the installments of *The Brothers Karamazov* and other contributions to *The Russian Herald* not as isolated elements in a thematic repertoire, but as statements belonging to institutionalized discourses. In this way one would study not only the relationship of particular parts of the lawyers' speeches to particular courtroom speeches that Dostoevsky had covered as a reporter, not only the relationship of particular parts of Zosima's life (Book VI) to particular moments in the lives of other elders that Dostoevsky had studied. Nor could one be satisfied with indicating the mere presence of parallels between sections of the novel

5. Grossman, "Dostoevskii i pravitel'stvennye krugi 1870-kh godov."
6. S. S. Borshchevskii, *Shchedrin i Dostoevskii: istoriia ikh ideinoi bor'by* (Moscow: GIKhL, 1956), Ch. X.

and other types of contribution to the thick journal. One would also want to show how *The Brothers Karamazov* had articulated (often parodistically), approached, and otherwise played with the strategies of judicial, hagiographical, theological, medical, psychological, or sociological discourse, discourses which were embodied in the other contributions to the journal. The lawyers' speeches, the doctors' analyses, the narrator's characterological generalizations, Ivan's article and "poem," the courtroom testimony and articles of Rakitin, and the biographies by Alesha and Rakitin are but several of the places where the novel makes contact with other types of writing in the journal. The provisional thematic closure of Dostoevsky's installments—provisional because later installments can reopen the topics—allows the novel to approach these other discourses and to risk absorption into them, yet (ultimately) to separate itself from them, because, among other reasons, the novelistic representations inevitably present human life as "open" or "unfinished" in contradistinction to the institutionalized discourses which present it as closed and determinate. In this investigation of the interplay between novel and journal, Ivan and Rakitin serve as important figures of border-transgression because of the articles within the novel within the journal that they write.

A second aspect of this interplay of discourses would involve the extent to which other contributions to *The Russian Herald* themselves reacted to aspects of the novel. This is too large a topic to be more than adumbrated here, but a representative place for the investigation to touch upon would concern the presentation of other monks in *The Russian Herald*, of which two followed Dostoevsky's treatment of Zosima in Book VI (August 1879): Konstantin Leont'ev's biography of Father Kliment (November and December 1879), whose asceticism and stern rejection of comfort stand in opposition to Zosima's all-embracing love, and "D.B.'s" biography of Archimandrite Pimen' (December 1880), a rather dry account of a monk who strived for erudition and who fulfilled administrative roles in the monastery, unlike, again, Zosima. Such examples of implicit dialogue within the journal would make it possible to present the novel's position as one of neither ideological coincidence nor disjuncture with its medium, but rather of dynamic interaction.

*   *   *

Serialization of The Brothers Karamazov

January 1879	"From the Author," Books I, II
February 1879	Book III
March 1879	
April 1879	Book IV
May 1879	Book V, 1–4
June 1879	Book V, 5–7
July 1879	
August 1879	Book VI
September 1879	Book VII
October 1879	Book VIII, 1–4
November 1879	Book VIII, 5–8
December 1879	(apology for delay)

January 1880	Book IX
February 1880	
March 1880	
April 1880	Book X
May 1880	
June 1880	
July 1880	Book XI, 1–5
August 1880	Book XI, 6–10
September 1880	Book XII, 1–5
October 1880	Book XII, 6–14
November 1880	Epilogue

VLADIMIR KANTOR

Pavel Smerdyakov and Ivan Karamazov: The Problem of Temptation[†]

* * *

The opinion that Pavel Smerdyakov is nothing other than an obedient tool in the hands of Ivan Karamazov, no more than the executor of his evil will, was already voiced in the nineteenth century by Orest Miller: 'Unfortunate Smerdyakov, having blindly subordinated himself to Ivan's ideal . . . committed the crime.'[1] Since then, with various degrees of complexity and evidence but most often simply in passing (for this is, after all, a secondary question; what interests us in the novel is the conflict between Good and Evil, the Grand Inquisitor, etc.), it is affirmed that 'Smerdyakov is only the practical agent of criminality. Behind him in Dostoevsky's novel the figure of Ivan Karamazov rises up, whose ideas and concepts, the author assures us, prompted Smerdyakov to the crime, and justified and even elevated the murderer in his own eyes.'[2] In this way, laying the entire responsibility on one character, we utterly free up the other from any responsibility at all. When we do this, the direct unambiguous murderer turns out to be Ivan; pursuing the logic of this thought, Ivan becomes the 'carrier of evil' in the poetic world of the novel. In V. E. Vetlovskaya's profound and authoritative study, this position is summed up in the following words: 'Thus Alyosha (and the reader), in listening to Ivan, hear the devil himself.'[3] But if this is the case, then Ivan's nature appears completely monosemantic—and all his torments, self-accusations, the ambivalence and multiple meanings of his words and actions must be considered insubstantial and unessential; the structure of his image is thereby simplified, as is the understanding of guilt and responsibility upon which Dostoevsky insisted: The entire figurative structure of the novel is very noticeably disrupted. The genetic link between Smerdyakov

---

[†] From *Dostoevsky and the Christian Tradition*, pp. 189–220, ed. George Pattison and Diane Oenning Thompson. Copyright © 2001 Cambridge University Press. Reprinted with the permission of Cambridge University Press.
1. O. Miller, *Russkie pisateli posle Gogolia*, vol. 1 (St Petersburg, 1900), 264.
2. Ya. S. Belinkis, *F. M. Dostoevskii* (Leningrad, 1960), 51. I deliberately cite a popular brochure to indicate the widespread prevalence of this point of view.
3. V. E. Vetlovskaya, *Poetika romana 'Brat'ia Karamazovy'* (Leningrad, 1977), 100.

and the devil ('lackeydom') and the manifest repetitiousness of the images that connect them are revealed as accidental and artistically non-obligatory; the conversations between Ivan and Smerdyakov, and later between Ivan and the devil who is tempting him, become meaningless nonsense if the hero himself is an unconditional force for evil ('the devil').

* * *

If we endorse the point of view on Smerdyakov that he is a passive murderer, a blind tool in someone else's hand, a person merely carrying out Ivan's plan, then we will enter naturally into a contradiction with the poetic and worldview-shaping concepts that govern Dostoevsky's cosmos, a cosmos resting on the fact that each person bears full responsibility for his or her own acts, regardless of the social level from which he comes and no matter how undeveloped he may be. Speaking of the peasant who drove his wife to suicide, Dostoevsky proclaims:

> 'Lack of development, dullness of mind—have pity, it's the environment!'—this is what the peasant's lawyer has insisted. But millions of peasants live like that and not all of them hang their wives by the feet! One must, all the same, draw a line < . . . > Then on the other hand, here's an educated man, and suddenly he hangs his wife up. No, you've prevaricated enough, gentlemen lawyers, with your 'environment'! (21, 23)[4]

It is possible to forgive a person a great deal (Mitya). To forgive is possible, but one cannot remove responsibility from him, and not only for an act but also for an intention (Ivan). According to Dostoevsky, the 'environment', the external circumstances of a human being, do not define and do not justify. Yet here we end up with Smerdyakov having been forced into committing the murder by extraneous circumstances (for another person's will is an external cause), and he himself is not guilty.

It is also worth remembering that we have here a novel about the *brothers* Karamazov, where each possesses his own life motif and ideational motif, and that this novel is not about three brothers but four—since Smerdyakov, as we are given to believe at several points in the novel, is the illegitimate son of Fyodor Pavlovich and thus the half-brother of the central heroes. What is more, if Ivan and Mitya reveal themselves to be vacillating, inconstant natures, seeking good and truth but committing misdemeanours and crimes along the way, then Alyosha, from one side, and Smerdyakov, from the other, function like firm orientation points of good and evil. Immediately after Mitya's 'Confession of an Ardent Heart' (Book 3, 3–5) and long before Ivan expounds to Alyosha his understanding of how the world is made ('Pro and Contra'), Smerdyakov, in the chapter 'Disputation' (*Contraverza*) (that is, argument, conflict; it is characteristic that the Latin titles emphasise the closeness of the problems posed by the legitimate and the illegitimate brother, Ivan and Pavel) also sets forth his credo in a 'quarrel'. However, unlike Ivan, who tries to weigh and evaluate in his heart the pro as well as the contra, Smerdyakov is monosemantic

---

4. Notes in the text are to the *Polnoe sobranie sochinenii*. English translation of this passage can be found in Lantz, 145 [*Editor's note*].

and pronounces an apologia to perfidy, his own sort of 'justification of evil'.[5] It is not by chance (as I try to show below) that Ivan *swings* between Alyosha and Smerdyakov.

Smerdyakov is not a madman, not crazy; even less is he a 'weak-minded idiot', as he is called by the residents of the town—although he does have the falling sickness, he is an epileptic. It was he who thought out and subtly executed not only the plan with the envelope, which he ripped open and threw out just as someone would have done who didn't know whether there was money in it—thus strengthening suspicions against Mitya; he also successfully played through the performance of his epileptic fit. In endowing Smerdyakov with epilepsy, just as he did his favourite hero Prince Myshkin, Dostoevsky emphasises precisely his isolation and separateness from the sphere of the 'healthy' Rakitins (Rakitin, incidentally, with his mediocrity and his strong worldly mind, recalls Ganya Ivolgin),[6] and takes him 'out of the ranks' of ordinary everyday persons. But Smerdyakov is the opposite of Myshkin. In Dostoevsky's view, epilepsy develops in a person, in certain instances, a heightened keenness of mind and penetration, which can then be used for either good or evil deeds. Everything depends wholly on the person's moral foundation.[7]

* * *

The strength of Dostoevsky, that which permitted him to divine the collisions of the future, lay in his moral maximalism, the fact that he imposed on a person—especially as regards questions of life and death—the entire fullness of moral responsibility, allowing no transfer of it to another's shoulders. If we remember that Smerdyakov is intimately tied to the major problem of the novel, patricide, it becomes clear that one can call him a secondary character only with difficulty: he must be scrutinised more intently, in keeping with the writer's own scale of values.

But at the same time he cannot be scrutinised separately, for he is Ivan's double and thus becomes comprehensible only alongside him. A 'double', however, is in no sense a 'hero of the second order'. A double is of course more one-dimensional, more monosemantic, but this does not at all mean he is subordinated to the hero; on the contrary, as a rule it is the other way around. Recall Robert Louis Stevenson's *Strange Case of Dr Jekyll and Mr Hyde*, in which Mr Hyde, created out of all the evil sides of the doctor's soul, gradually gained the upper hand. Recall also that in Dostoevsky's own Petersburg poem, *The Double*, Golyadkin Junior turns out to be more decisive, more resourceful, more base, and in the end rubs out Golyadkin Senior, who still preserved some elements of decency, which in fact proved an obstacle to his 'success.' But in that short novel, the double is a double in the full sense of the word, duplicating not only the outer image but even the name and patronymic of the hero. In *The Brothers Karamazov* the issue is more complicated. But there too the double is vitally linked with the hero, with several of his desires that are unacknowledged even by the hero himself, yet he is linked not linearly, not

5. T. S. Karlova, *Dostoevskii i russkii sud* (Kazan, 1975), 159.
6. A minor character in Dostoevsky's *The Idiot*.
7. Thomas Mann noted this double nature of illness in connection with his discussions of Dostoevsky. See T. Mann, *Sobranie sochinenii v 10–ti tt*, vol. 9 (Moscow, 1960), 509–11.

in a 'frontal' way, and this creates difficulties in making sense out of their interrelations. Smerdyakov, Mikhail Bakhtin notes, 'gradually gains control over Ivan's voice, which the latter is concealing from himself. Smerdyakov is able to govern this voice precisely because Ivan's consciousness *does not look in that direction and does not want to look there*' [my emphasis, V. K.].[8] In any event and no matter what, the double is never identified with the author's lyrical hero (that is, with a hero whose task it is to resolve metaphysical problems of personality). If we declare Smerdyakov to be a simple executor of other people's ideas, then the entire complicated dialectic of the hero's interrelations falls away, the reason for Ivan's torments becomes incoherent or banal, and the conflict between two wills struggling over him disappears (the 'It's not you!' spoken by Alyosha and the 'But you are the main murderer!' spoken by Smerdyakov)— that is, what falls away is the internal tension that Mitya speaks of when he says: When 'the devil is struggling with God', then 'the field of battle is the hearts of men' (14, 100).

'Ivan is a riddle', says Alyosha (14, 209). It is impossible not to agree with him, because, beginning with his 'fateful arrival' in the town—'which served as starting-point for so many consequences', as the narrator puts it—right up to his final 'fatal' deposition in court, the other characters and even more the readers try to figure Ivan out and get to the bottom of him (14, 12). Ivan, it seems, feels more keenly than the others a hatred of 'Karamazovism', whose embodiment, for him, is his father and his brother Mitya: 'One reptile will devour another, and good riddance to them both!' (14, 129). But is that the solution Dostoevsky himself accepts? And can we be sure that Ivan's desire to rid himself of the pollution of 'Karamazovism' by his father's death is his own actual final position?

The fact is that Ivan is a riddle not only for others but also for himself. He cannot define himself in any way, and this is the cause of his constant vacillation, inner turmoil, the absence in him of any precise position on life that so confused Smerdyakov. In the elder Zosima's cell (a visit that Ivan had insisted upon, during which he conversed with the elder 'in a modest and restrained manner, with visible courtesy'), Ivan first sets forth for the reader, although still in compressed form, his own credo, as if awaiting the elder's advice and evaluation both of his idea and of himself. At this point the elder suddenly says to Ivan, apropos of his idea that if God and immortality do not exist then all is permitted, that Ivan has thought up this idea 'from desperation':

> —This question is not yet resolved for you, and in this lies your great grief, for it insistently demands resolution . . .
> —And can it be resolved in myself? Resolved in a positive direction?—Ivan Fyodorovich continued to ask, somewhat strangely, looking at the elder with an inexplicable smile.
> —If it cannot be resolved in a positive direction, then it will never be resolved negatively either—for you yourself know this quality of your heart; therein lies the whole of its torment. (14, 65)

---

8. M. M. Bakhtin, *Problemy poetiki Dostoevskogo* (Moscow, 1963), 427.

Apparently the elder's point of view coincided with Ivan's point of view on himself, because after these words he 'suddenly rose from his chair, went up to him, received his blessing, and, having kissed his hand, returned silently to his place. His expression was firm and serious' (14, 65).

What sort of inner struggle is tormenting Ivan? In the chapters 'The Brothers Get Acquainted', 'Rebellion' and 'The Grand Inquisitor', Dostoevsky presents Ivan with the opportunity to develop his understanding of God, the world, society, his own self, and possible routes for restructuring the world.

Ivan begins his confession with the admission that at the basis of his being lies an elemental, unreasoning 'Karamazovian' thirst for life, which transcends all human derangements and disillusionments, even despair, even the feeling that the whole world is a 'disordered, accursed, perhaps even demonic chaos' (14, 209). This feature, as Ivan himself says, is 'in part Karamazovian', and in this thirst he resembles his father. However, in Ivan the thirst for life emerges as a consciously articulated force—and we begin to understand that this 'Karamazovian' elemental quality contains a life-creating potency of incredible energy, but one not bounded by forms and not oriented in a positive direction.

> —I'm terribly glad that you want to live so much,—Alyosha exclaimed. 'I think that everyone should love life before all else in the world.'
> —Love life more than the meaning of it?
> —Absolutely, love it before logic, as you say, it must absolutely be before logic, because only then will I grasp its meaning. I've long imagined this is how it is. Half the deed is done, Ivan, and already acquired: you love to live. Now you need only try at the second half, and you are saved. (14, 210)

In contrast to old Fyodor Pavlovich, Ivan seeks this meaning, for he cannot reconcile himself with the world's disharmony: 'I want to see with my own eyes how the doe lies down with the lion and how the murdered man will rise up and embrace his murderer' (14, 222). But the world is so cruel, and human sufferings so innumerable, tormenting, and without exit (especially the unjust and heartrending sufferings of children), that Dostoevsky's hero demands vengeance and retribution. And this vengeance he refuses to cede to God, to the God who says: 'Vengeance is mine, and mine the retribution' (Deut. 32:35). Ivan paraphrases the utterance, turning it back on himself: 'I need retribution, otherwise I will put an end to myself. Retribution not in the infinite wherever and whenever, but here and now, on earth, so that I can see it myself' (14, 222). According to Ivan, God cannot find—and does not have the right to find—a justification for human sufferings. This whole complex of ideas is formulated by Ivan in the aphorism with which he opened his conversation with Alyosha: 'It's not that I do not accept God, understand that, it is the world created by Him, it is God's world that I do not accept and will not agree to accept' (14, 214). Since God was not able to establish the world on humane principles, Ivan takes upon himself full responsibility for this world. But can a person—alone—take upon himself such a responsibility? Does not such despotic individualism in fact signify a rejection of real—that is, human-scale—responsibility for one's own actions? This is one of the most important questions posed in the novel.

Ivan's theomachist[9] zeal produced a very strong impression on Dostoevsky's contemporaries, even on those who did not accept the novel as a whole. Ivan Karamazov was entered into the ranks of such images of world literature as Job, Lucifer, Byron's Cain and Manfred, Lermontov's Demon.[1] Of all these parallels, perhaps the one that deserves the most attention is that between Ivan Karamazov and the Biblical theomach Job. In his novels Dostoevsky often provides distinctive hints to guide us towards those works of world literature meant to serve as commentary, as a tuning-fork to the events and heroes that he represents. For example, in *The Idiot*, Pushkin's verse about the 'Poor Knight' that Aglaya recites functions in this way, permitting the author to highlight the knightly, Don-Quixotic service of Prince Myshkin to his ideal. In *The Brothers Karamazov*, immediately after Ivan's confession to Alyosha (the chapters 'Rebellion' and 'The Grand Inquisitor') and his conversation with Smerdyakov ('It is always interesting to have a talk with a clever man') there follows the book 'A Russian Monk', where the elder Zosima names as the most important spiritual impact on his life the legend of Job, the righteous man 'who had cried out to God' after his countless sufferings but who in the end was forgiven by God. The elder not only recalls the legend but retells it, in his own interpretation, omitting, as if deliberately, the hero's theomachic speeches, which constitute three-quarters of the Book of Job. And most likely this is no accident, inasmuch as the utterances of Ivan Karamazov and those of the Biblical hero coincide to a striking extent. Just like Ivan, tempted by his own misfortunes and by the misfortunes of the world, so does Job accuse God:

> He destroyeth the sinless and the guilty. If He suddenly strikes with the scourge, he will laugh at the torments of the innocent. The earth is given into the hand of the wicked; he covereth the faces of the judges thereof. If not He, then who? (Job 9: 22–24)

He does not reject God, but enters into argument with him: 'Surely I would speak to the Almighty, and I desire to contend with God' (Job 13:3). The nineteenth-century reader (whom Dostoevsky addressed), who knew the Bible if only through the catechism in the secondary school curriculum, would inevitably have detected not only the omissions in the elder's version of the story but also, having recalled the words of Job—tempted, with God's permission, by Satan—he would correlate them with Ivan's words and understand that in this instance Ivan is not the tempter, but the tempted. The theme of Job, it should be noted, was of constant interest to Dostoevsky. As early as 1875, in a letter to his wife, he wrote: 'I'm

---

9. Theomachy usually refers to battles among gods, such as are described in the Homeric epics. It also means opposition to God or the divine will, or the desire to destroy belief in God [*Editor's note*].

1. One of the prerevolutionary critics wrote: 'The grandiose figure of Ivan, who, like Job, declares: "O, if only man could enter into competition with God, as a human son with his nearest of kin", eclipses the naive Alyosha and the seductively sweet teachings of the elder Zosima' (D. V. Filosofov, *Staroe i novoe* [Moscow, 1912], 182). Unfortunately, this similarity is only named and hinted at, not disclosed and explicated. Victor Shklovsky made reference to the link between Job and this novel in an equally transitory way; he writes only that Job 'rebelled against the structure of the world: this rebellion also helped the late Dostoevsky of *The Brothers Karamazov*' (V. Shklovskii, *Tetiva. O neskhodstve skhodnogo* [Moscow, 1970], 232).

reading the Book of Job, and it casts me into feverish ecstasy; I throw down my work, I pace my room for hours on end, almost weeping . . . this book, Anya, it's strange, this book was one of the first to make a deep impression in my life, when I was still a little child!' (29, i, 43). The motif of Job is also heard in *The Adolescent*, in the teachings of Makar Dolgoruky (13, 330). Doubtless too, while pondering 'The Life of a Great Sinner' (which in a way is a threshold for *The Brothers Karamazov*), Dostoevsky could not refrain from turning to what is almost the sole Biblical image of a theomachic righteous man. This parallel, in any case, demonstrates one of the reasons for the author's respectfully serious attitude towards his hero-rebel. Dostoevsky is writing his own variant of a man tormented by the Divine structure of the world, and that man's path to self-knowledge and to knowledge of the meaning of the world. A path that is far from easy.

* * *

In his early novel *The Double*, Dostoevsky attempted to depict for the first time a situation where certain, albeit the very worst, wishes and feelings of the hero could appear to him as living an entirely autonomous and independent life. Dostoevsky himself considered the phenomenon of the double one of his most important artistic ideas—but one that he could not come to terms with in his youth. In particular it was difficult to resolve whether all these nasty feelings picked up by the double actually belonged to the personality-core of the hero, or whether they were somehow borrowed, alien, external. This problem received its ultimate sociophilosophical and artistic resolution in the writer's last novel.

I begin, therefore, with the double.

The first mention of Smerdyakov is made by Mitya, who because of him arrives late at the family gathering in the elder's cell: 'The servant Smerdyakov, who was sent by my father, to my persistent question about the time, answered me twice in the most decisive tone that the meeting had been set for one o'clock' (14, 63). Thus, even before his first appearance in the pages of the novel, Smerdyakov is connected in the reader's mind with some sort of confusion, with the substitution of something false for what is real—and although it is still not clear whether this confusion is deliberate or accidental, in any event it has led to a certain tension. But for the nonce this is all only in passing. Then the author remarks about the birth of Smerdyakov in the second chapter of the third book ('Stinking Lizaveta'), albeit only in connection with the filthiest act of Fyodor Pavlovich. About Smerdyakov himself the narrator so far communicates no details at all, putting his trust in the fact that 'something about him will somehow come off by itself in the further course of the narrative' (14, 93). Only in the sixth chapter of this same book does the narrator finally tell us about Smerdyakov. A secondary figure, clearly. Yet all the same, at a certain moment all our attention is focused on him. During his conversations with Ivan . . . But by that point Smerdyakov himself is already winning for himself a secondary role. He declares to Ivan: 'I was only your stooge, your faithful servant Licharda, I committed the deed according to your word' (15, 59). With such persistence does he refuse for himself a primary role, which would carry with it responsibility, that—if only out of a feeling of contradiction—it is worth analysing this situation further.

Destructive and centrifugal forces exist in the common people. Dostoevsky knew this and did not conceal it. Recall the scene at 'Mokroe', recall Fedka the Convict from *Demons*, the sort of bandit on whom the Bakuninites[2] placed their hopes, or the convicts from the *Notes from the House of the Dead*. There was yet another characteristically national type, in Dostoevsky's opinion, and that was the 'contemplator':

> suddenly, having piled up impressions for many years, he would cast off everything and set out for Jerusalem, to wander and save himself; or perhaps he would suddenly burn down his native village, or perhaps both the one and the other would happen together. There are a good number of 'contemplators' among the people. One such contemplator was probably Smerdyakov. (14, 117)

By his psychological makeup, then, Smerdyakov resembles similar types coming from the people. But Smerdyakov is not a moujik, not a peasant, he is a lackey. 'Lackeydom', in Dostoevsky's view, is spiritual spinelessness, a lack of autonomy accompanied by the remarkable ability to look after one's own material interests. Genetically, the lackey in Russia is a product of the serf-owning era: a person severed from the people, living in the noble's house but not on an equal footing with the nobleman, that is, a person occupying an ill-defined and degraded position, neither one thing nor the other. In the post-Reform period, so Dostoevsky believed, this phenomenon became widespread. Inadequate education and its utilitarian bent gave rise to a mass of so-called 'half-educated people', torn from popular culture, from 'folk truth' ('Can a Russian peasant have a feeling against an educated person? Because of his lack of education, he cannot have any feeling at all' Smerdyakov mutters), but who at the same time were not elevated to higher spiritual questions (thus this same Smerdyakov reproaches Gogol: 'It's all about lies, what's written there') (14, 205, 116). A line can be drawn through the novel connecting a whole series of characters most unpleasant to the author, and all of them falling under the rubric of 'lackey'—beginning with Fyodor Pavlovich and ending with the devil. For Dostoevsky, the lackey is the embodiment of Russia's evil. It is characteristic that Smerdyakov, the illegitimate son of Fyodor Pavlovich, resembles him more closely than do the other children. Old Karamazov relies on him, does not acknowledge his paternity, but nevertheless, suspicious and not overfond of his two older legitimate children, 'somehow even loved him, although the young man looked at him just as askance as the others did, and was silent all the time' (14, 116). And it is precisely Smerdyakov who bears the full patrilinear name (compare Fyodor Pavlovich and Pavel Fyodorovich), continuing the family tradition of lackeydom. After all, Fyodor Pavlovich in his youth was a hanger-on, that is, a lackey of the same sort. And Smerdyakov also dreams of amassing his own little capital, just like his father.

There is, however, an essential difference. If, for Fyodor Pavlovich, lackeydom is one of the facets of his external profile, then for Smerdyakov this concept emerges as a qualitative, pivotal characteristic of his personality. 'He is a lackey and a boor', Ivan lets drop about Smerdyakov, and the

---

2. Fedka the convict is a minor character in *Demons* (1872). Followers of Mikhail Bakunin were known as Bakuninites. See p. 14 [*Editor's note*].

latter sensed that 'lackey' was not only the name of his position and duties but also that the word described him himself, his personality: 'And they refer to me as a stinking lackey' (14, 122). Smerdyakov harbours a feeling of his own chosenness and superiority over the rest of the world: 'He was extremely unsociable and silent. Not because he was uncivilised or in any sense shy, no, on the contrary he was an arrogant character who seemed to despise everyone' (14, 114). But a sense of having been thwarted in his rights draws a sharp boundary between him and the others: 'I could have done still otherwise, ma'am, I could have known still otherwise, ma'am, if it weren't for my fate since childhood' (14, 204). For all his 'solitude', old Karamazov sometimes experienced the need for a 'trustworthy person'. Smerdyakov, however, experienced no need for any contact with another at all; he was 'unsociable', the narrator tells us, 'and felt not the slightest need for any society' (14, 15–16). Here the boundary is drawn most sharply of all. For Dostoevsky takes Smerdyakov's aloneness, his isolation from the world, to the point of grotesque, raising it to a symbol. After Smerdyakov returned from studying in Moscow it was noticed that he 'had suddenly somehow aged extraordinarily, his face had wrinkled most inappropriately for his age, he had grown yellow and had begun to resemble a eunuch . . . He despised the female sex, . . . and held himself aloof from them, almost inapproachable' (14, 115). In vain did Fyodor Pavlovich ask him: ' "Do you want me to find you a wife?" . . . But Smerdyakov only paled from vexation at such words and did not answer' (14, 116). If 'Karamazovism', and especially old Karamazov himself, is an embodiment (for all the cruelty and spiritual emptiness of sensuousness) of the spontaneous and elemental, in its own way a natural life-creating principle which perhaps, in time, could be reined in morally, then against the backdrop of Karamazovian sensuousness, Smerdyakov appears symbolically sterile.

But Dostoevsky insists that 'Smerdyakovism' is a product of 'Karamazovism', its new stage; that death-bearing Smerdyakov is the result of elemental Karamazovian animal energies. Out of an elemental thirst for life which cared not one whit about another human being there is born, in the natural order of things, a merciless and calculating murderer. Smerdyakov is inseparably linked with the Karamazovs, and a sufficiently candid— symbolically candid—hint to that effect is provided by Rakitin. Speaking of the elder Zosima's bow to Mitya, Rakitin notes: 'In my opinion, the old man really is farseeing: he's sniffed a crime. Something stinks in your family' (14, 73). The surname (Smerdyakov) signifying a bad smell, Ivan's words about a 'stinking lackey', and the emphasis given to Smerdyakov's own fastidious concern for his toilette (as if trying to cease being a 'stinking' lackey, 'Smerdyakov spent almost all his salary on clothes, pomade, perfumes and other such things')—all this involuntarily suggests associations with the odour of decay (the elder had 'sniffed it out') emanating from the 'nice little family' of Karamazovs (14, 116). We add that, according to Dal',[3] a *smerd* is a 'person from the mob, lowborn, a moujik, a special category or class of slaves, of unfree servants; later a serf'. The evaluative nuance of the word from which Dostoevsky produced the name Smerdya-

---

3. The lexicographer Vladimir Dal' (1801–1872) traveled extensively throughout Russia, collecting and publishing folk sayings and fairy tales. His *Tolkovyi slovar' zhivago velikorusskogo iazyka* (*Explanatory Dictionary of the Live Great Russian Language*, 1863–66) remains a preeminent resource for the linguistic study of nineteenth-century Russia [*Editor's note*].

kov is easy enough to understand, and is linked with Russia's primary evil as most Russian writers saw it: the slavery of serfdom. Smerdyakov is a former slave who wants to straighten himself out. And as Konstantin Aksakov had warned, 'a slave in revolt is more dangerous than a wild beast, he exchanges his fetters for a knife . . .'

If the Karamazovs are constantly on view, then Smerdyakov is constantly in the shadows. A slave hides out before his time, before his rebellion begins; alien to him are the free word and the open act. Old Karamazov 'acts monstrously', Mitya boozes it up and creates scandal after scandal in the taverns, Ivan shocks society with his theories and Alyosha astonishes everyone by becoming a novice in the monastery, but through all this Smerdyakov is not noted for any reprehensible behaviour at all—on the contrary, all his negative qualities, which are well known in town, serve him as a justification and even work to his benefit. The reader, for example, firmly knows that Smerdyakov is a coward, an atheist, always ready to betray anyone out of fear for his own skin. But what is remarkable is that Smerdyakov doesn't hide this; quite the opposite, he tells it to everyone, even to the public prosecutor. Thus, during the trial the prosecutor, as if taking it for granted, says of him: 'In the capacity of domestic spy he betrayed his master, communicated to the accused both the existence of the packet with the money and the signs which were to be used to gain access to the master' (15, 136). And all of that, they say, was done out of fear of Mityenka, who threatened to kill him. All this is taken to be the truth. But at the same time the reader knows that Smerdyakov tells the truth with the purpose of hiding it. Everyone sees his authentic face, which is the face of a coward and a scoundrel, and this turns out to be the most reliable guarantee that he will remain above suspicion. Which is to say, the face simultaneously turns out to be, as it were, a mask.

Smerdyakov usually speaks what he wants to say, sometimes in hints, sometimes straight out, at times even in such a way that one can understand and grasp his meaning fully. But one only has to seize him by the arm; he won't hide anything, he'll admit that he indeed did speak this or that, but then it will become clear that his truth was at the same time a mask, albeit a compulsory mask, which evil circumstances had forced him to put on. And he bears no responsibility for it.

It is no accident that when at last he lays all his cards on the table before Ivan ('The third and final meeting with Smerdyakov'), it is clear that he has communicated nothing new about himself to the reader at all. Moreover, not only has he communicated nothing to the reader but also nothing to the local society as well, even though it would have been shocked by this information had it been made public; they knew about all this unconsciously anyway. The defence attorney, who had gathered together all the town gossip and rumours, speaks thus in court about Smerdyakov:

> Definitely an embittered being, exaggeratedly ambitious, vengeful and burning with envy. I collected some information: he hated his origins, was ashamed of his birth and gnashed his teeth whenever he remembered that he 'descended from Stinking Lizaveta'. He was disrespectful toward the servant Grigory and his wife, who had been his benefactors during his childhood. He cursed Russia and ridiculed her. He dreamed of emigrating to France in order to remake himself into a Frenchman. He spoke much and often about that earlier, saying

that he lacked the means for doing so. It seems to me that he loved no one except himself, and that he held himself in strangely high regard. He saw enlightenment in good clothes, in clean shirt-fronts and in polished boots. Considering himself (and there are facts to support this) the illegitimate son of Fyodor Pavlovich, he might well have despised his position vis-à-vis the legitimate children of his master; everything goes to them, you see, and to him nothing, they had all the rights, they had the inheritance, while he was only a cook. (15, 164–65)

The defence attorney even puts forth the hypothesis that Smerdyakov did the killing. But it remains a hypothesis, he does not insist on it, although he does exclaim: 'Is there anything untrue or unlikely in all that I have just now presented and described to you?' (15, 166). But immediately afterwards, he all the same presumes that the murder was committed by Mitya.

The excessive hypothetical quality in this supposition that Smerdyakov was the murderer even spreads to an analysis of his face. His face again seems to be a mask, not his true face. Thus does the prosecutor object to the defence attorney in his final statement, and with full justification: 'The feebleminded idiot Smerdyakov, transformed into some sort of Byronic hero, avenging himself on society for his illegitimacy—isn't this really only a poem in the Byronic fashion?' (15, 174).

Relevant here are humorous scenes like this: at carnival time, two masks meet; the people beneath the masks start a conversation and then, having decided to introduce themselves and get acquainted, they remove their masks. Under his stupid or terrifying mask one of them has a normal face; the other has the same mask. The mask was a *mould* of the face.

As V. E. Vetlovskaya has aptly observed, in his ideas Smerdyakov is very close to the Grand Inquisitor: 'The Grand Inquisitor says essentially the same thing as Smerdyakov. He also justifies his personal baseness and treachery before God, and does so on the same foundations, that is, resorting to conclusions about universal human weakness, insignificance, and people's ineradicable sinfulness.'[4] But this observation speaks not only to the lackey-like essence of the Grand Inquisitor and to a certain part of Ivan's soul (for the Grand Inquisitor is his creation); it also speaks to the fact that in Ivan's soul there is a mundane corroboration and intensifying in evil's direction, evil not as his product but as his double, it is independent of him although he feels its closeness to him, he feels their mutual attraction.

Smerdyakov sets out his credo (in the chapter 'Disputation') especially for Ivan's benefit, giving him, as it were, the first hints of its existence and potentials ('Ivan!' Fyodor Pavlovich suddenly shouted. 'Bend your ear down now. All this was concocted for you' [14, 118]. The independence and, in its own way, originality of Smerdyakov's judgments on the legitimacy and legal inviolability of treason is emphasised both by the narrator, when speaking of the 'contemplators', and by Fyodor Pavlovich, who comments on Smerdyakov's original way of thinking with some surprise: 'Here Balaam's ass thinks, thinks, and the devil knows what he'll think himself up to!' (14, 122). Thus does he sum up the utterances of his illegitimate

4. Vetlovskaya, *Poetika romana 'Brat'ia Karamazovy'*, 90.

son. Listening in to these words one must not forget that the devil is one of the characters of the novel. Perhaps the power of evil does indeed know about the lackey's evil intentions ('the devil knows . . . what he'll think himself up to'), but so far Ivan Karamazov has not guessed him out.

All the same, what is it that attracts this 'Jesuit'—this vain, embittered, secretive, pettily envious and vengeful person—to Ivan, who despises him? Smerdyakov is introduced into the action as it were in passing, during dinner. Fyodor Pavlovich, Alyosha and Ivan are at table. The narrator notes that for some time Smerdyakov had very rarely been present at dinner, but 'from the time of Ivan Fyodorovich's arrival in town he began to be present at dinner almost every day' (14, 117). Fyodor Pavlovich, a malicious person and a sensualist but who, during apertures in his sensuality, could be a very observant man, hit upon the true definition of Smerdyakov's partiality for Ivan: 'Smerdyakov now slips in every day around dinnertime, you are so *interesting* to him [my emphasis, V. K.], what have you done to endear yourself to him?—Fyodor Pavlovich added.' Ivan wants to give it another word: 'He's taken it into his head to respect me' (14, 122). But Fyodor Pavlovich, who has studied Smerdyakov, does not agree: 'You see, I know that he cannot endure me, as he cannot anyone, and just as he cannot endure you, although it seems to you that he's "taken it into his head to respect you". Alyoshka all the more, Alyoshka he despises' (14, 122). This motif of the presumed respect that Smerdyakov bears toward Ivan stretches throughout the entire novel. The usual representation of the situation is that Smerdyakov began to respect Ivan and fell under his spiritual influence. Smerdyakov himself speaks of this, so that the prosecutor, quoting his words (and we already know that Smerdyakov was able to wind the prosecutor around his finger, for example, concerning the empty packet that was thrown on the floor, and most importantly concerning the murder itself), declares:

> He [Smerdyakov], with hysterical tears, told me at the preliminary investigation how this young Karamazov, Ivan Fyodorovich, horrified him with his spiritual impudence. 'Everything, he says, in his view, is permitted, everything in the world, and nothing should be forbidden in advance—that's what he was teaching me.' It seems that he's become an idiot because of this thesis, which he was *taught*, and finally he went out of his mind (15, 126–27) [my emphasis, V. K].

As we noted earlier, this same idea is often encountered in the scholarship on Dostoevsky.[5] But is it in fact correct?

'They spoke about philosophical questions and even about why the earth was illuminated on the first day if the sun, moon, and stars were created only on the fourth day, and how one should understand that properly; but Ivan Fyodorovich was soon convinced that the sun, moon and stars, although these were interesting topics, were for Smerdyakov absolutely tertiary, and that he needed something absolutely other' (14, 243). So, Smerdyakov is not interested in pure theory. What does interest him, then? 'Smerdyakov all the time inquired, asked indirect and apparently premeditated questions, but for what purpose he didn't explain, and

---

5. See, for example, in N. Chirkov: 'The entire irresistible fatal nature of the relations between Ivan and Smerdyakov comes down to the fact that the latter is a spiritual product of Ivan' (N. M. Chirkov, *O stile Dostoevskogo* [Moscow, 1967], 273).

during the most fervent moment of his questioning he would often either fall silent or suddenly pass over to something else altogether' (14, 243). This does not suggest overall that Smerdyakov had studied any special topic—more likely he had not studied—but it does suggest that he *was studying* Ivan himself. And for his part he reacted very ironically to Ivan's ideas. 'They were of the opinion that I would rebel; they were mistaken, sir. If there had been such a sum in my pocket, I would have long ago been gone'—so Smerdyakov confesses frankly to the maid (14, 205).

There is no way that Ivan could have failed to guess this. After all, Ivan knew about even these words of Smerdyakov, which Alyosha had accidentally overheard. (The chapter 'The Brothers Get Acquainted' follows the chapter 'Smerdyakov with a Guitar'.)

> Alyosha told his brother quickly and *in detail* about his meeting with Smerdyakov. Ivan suddenly began to listen with a very concerned air, *even requestioning* him on some points [emphasis mine, V. K.]. < . . . > Ivan frowned and fell into thought.
> –Did you frown because of Smerdyakov?—asked Alyosha.
> –Yes, because of him. The devil take him. (14,211)

Something, apparently, has begun to trouble Ivan in his relations with Smerdyakov. He rejects him as evil ('the devil take him'). But he does not succeed in thinking his troubled state of mind through to the end. It is as if the lackey has cast a spell on him. After his conversation with Alyosha in the tavern, Ivan runs into Smerdyakov and wants to walk past him:

> –'Out of my sight, you scoundrel, what sort of company am I for you, you fool!'—was about to fly off his tongue, but *to his great surprise* what came off his tongue was something quite different:
> –What's with father, is he sleeping or has he woken up?—he spoke quietly and with *unexpected* composure, *and suddenly, also wholly unexpectedly,* he sat down on the bench. For a moment he became almost terrified, he remembered it later. [my emphasis, V. K.] (14, 244)

What's happening here? It is as if some irrational forces have entered into the action, and Ivan is not in a condition to resist them. Smerdyakov almost forces Ivan to give him a sanction for the murder.

In a letter about the unfinished novel to one of his female correspondents, Dostoevsky explained the relationship between Smerdyakov and Ivan *as regards* the murder in the following way:

> The servant Smerdyakov murdered old Karamazov. All the details will be explained in the further course of the novel. Ivan Fyodorovich participated in the murder *only indirectly* and *at a distance*, solely by the fact that he refrained (intentionally) from bringing Smerdyakov to reason during a conversation with him before departing for Moscow, he refrained from expressing to him clearly and categorically *his disgust at the evil deed being planned by him* (which Ivan Fyodorovich saw and clearly had premonitions of) and thus, *as it were, permitted* Smerdyakov to commit the crime. *Such permission* was indispensible for Smerdyakov, and again, it will subsequently be explained why. (30, i, 129)[6]

6. The letter to E. N. Lebedeva is dated 8 November 1879.

Let us assume that Smerdyakov heard Ivan's inner voice, a voice hidden from others and from his own self as well; let us assume that he guessed Ivan's desire for the death of his father, which reflected his theory that 'all was permitted'. But let us then consider carefully to what extent this theory corresponded, in Dostoevsky's artistic plan, to the core of that hero's personality, and whether or not the theory was adequate to his unselfish and passionate desire for world harmony.

Strictly speaking, the thesis 'all is permitted' reflects the essence of the behaviour of Fyodor Pavlovich Karamazov in the world, a man able to descend 'to the ultimate limit of any nastiness', fearing only 'those pranks which the court might punish' (14, 80). But theory, of course, is more logically consistent.

It is probably no accident that, scattered throughout the novel, there are lines of dialogue emphasising the similarity between Ivan and Fyodor Pavlovich. Pointing to Ivan, old Karamazov himself, for example, exclaims: 'This is my son, flesh of my flesh, of my most beloved flesh' (14, 66). But for precisely that reason does he fear Ivan more than he does Mitya ('I'm afraid of Ivan; I'm afraid of Ivan more than I am of the other one') (14, 130). 'You, sir, of all the children most resemble Fyodor Pavlovich, your soul is the same as his, sir'—so Smerdyakov assures Ivan in their final conversation, and Ivan, struck by this, answers: 'You're not stupid' (15, 68). Smerdyakov is both right and not right; he again, as it were, moves himself off into the shadows. But we can say that if Smerdyakov continued Fyodor Pavlovich's *practical* line, then Ivan gave sense to that practice *theoretically*. We recall that in his 'serious' questioning of God's world, Fyodor Pavlovich orients towards Ivan's position.

Ivan hopes, apparently, that the destructive force of the thesis 'all is permitted' will in the final analysis destroy 'Karamazovism' as well. But the coincidence of his theory with his father's practice is significant. In his notebooks for 1880–81, Dostoevsky wrote that 'the entire novel serves' as an answer to the torments of Ivan's idea (27, 48). This aim is served by an explanation of the genesis of the idea 'all is permitted', the fact that it belongs 'to this world.'

But does Ivan himself endorse this idea to the end? There are good reasons to doubt that he does. All of Ivan's words, especially in his confession to Alyosha, are constructed in a tensely interrogative form, with maximal sharpness, as if the answer were intended to convince *him* of something and not only Alyosha; he himself is still in the process of deciding. What is more, one could say that the entire novel is structured as a struggle between Ivan and the evil that is tempting him. It is characteristic that the concluding idea of his theomachic torment—of which Dostoevsky wrote, not without pride: 'Even in Europe there is not and *has not been* such power of atheistic *expressions*' (27, 86)—he accomplishes not in the indicative mood (that is, once having firmly decided), but in the subjunctive: 'There is no virtue *if* there is no immortality' [my emphasis, V. K.]. Recall the words of the elder Zosima, with which Ivan agreed: 'This idea is not yet resolved in your heart and is tormenting it' (14, 65). 'In him there is a great and unresolved thought', Alyosha says of Ivan (14, 76). And even Ivan himself emphasises the indeterminacy, the unfinalisability of his purely theoretical ideas, not realised in practice: 'The mind prevaricates and hides. The mind is a scoundrel' (14, 215). However, this 'subjunctiveness' of the conclusion uttered by him is not noticed by other people. Others take his words as an affirmative, even as an imperative, utterance: ' "You were bold back then, you kept saying back then that 'everything is permitted', sir; and now you're so frightened!" Smerdyakov murmured, marveling' (15, 61). It is this absence of self-definition in Ivan that leads to the tragedy.

'Ivan Fyodorovich is deep', the writer noted about his hero (27, 48). And the whole horror of Ivan's struggle with God, his rebellion, a horror acknowledged by him himself ('One cannot live by rebellion, and I want to live'), is that he has nothing upon which he can innerly rely for support (14, 223). Facing him is emptiness. Thus the desire to hang on 'until thirty' and then 'fling the goblet to the floor' (14, 209, 239). No matter how much one reads into Ivan's words, and no matter how much one tries to read out of them, what is it, really, that he wishes to present to society in the sense of a higher truth? It's not revolution, of course, with its concrete social tasks for the reconstruction of the world. Dostoevsky found the exact word, *bunt*, rebellion, to which Pushkin in his time attached the epithets 'senseless and merciless'. And in reality, rebellion, vengeance, a denial of everything whatsoever without clear cognisance of the end result of one's actions, will take on a senseless and merciless character, 'creating anarchy in the realm of morality' (Karl Marx and Friedrich Engels), no matter how excellent and fine the feelings emanating from the rebel (*buntovshchik*). Precisely the absence in Ivan of a positive, life-structuring principle permits others not to notice the depth of his ethical questioning. For that reason, what for Ivan himself is a problem becomes for Smerdyakov an axiom—for the absence of theoretical clarity greatly facilitates the selfish utilisation of the idea Ivan utters. 'A slave in a rebellion is more dangerous than wild beasts . . .'

Ivan himself does not believe overall in the possibility of a practical realisation of the idea that 'all is permitted', which is linked, in his opinion, to 'anthropophagy', to the full-scale denial of the world. And when he informs Smerdyakov that he is going to Chermashnya, it is as if he is continuing (for himself) his own strange theoretical game, as if he is posing to himself the same question all the time: but is this possible in reality? It is Smerdyakov who provokes him to a seriousness that Ivan did not want to notice, but which in a strange way hypnotises him:

> When he had already taken a seat in the carriage, Smerdyakov ran up to straighten the rug.
> —You see, I'm going to Chermashnya,—*somehow suddenly burst* from Ivan Fyodorovich, and *just as on the day before*, it flew out by itself, accompanied by a sort of nervous chuckle. He kept remembering it for a long time afterwards.
> —So it's true what people say, that it's always interesting to have a talk with an intelligent man,—Smerdyakov replied *firmly*, giving Ivan Fyodorovich a *penetrating* look [my emphasis, V. K.]. (14, 254)

As soon as he had driven out of the courtyard and put some distance between himself and Smerdyakov, his internal battle begins with the 'lackey', the 'slave', the *smerd*, as if some charm had fallen off him. But it is a strange struggle . . . Proud and inflexible Ivan would like to prove to himself his independence from the lackey . . . But here, like a schoolboy before his teacher, what happens is precisely the opposite of what is promised.

> –And why did I announce to him that I was going to Chermashnya?—They pulled up to Volovya station, Ivan Fyodorovich got out of the carriage, the coachmen clustered around him. They haggled over the price to Chermashnya, twenty versts on a country road, in a hired carriage. Ivan gave orders to harness up. He entered the station, looked around, glanced at the stationmaster's wife and then suddenly walked back out on the porch.
> –I don't need to go to Chermashnya. Brothers, can I make it to the train station by seven o'clock? (14, 255)

In place of a real act or confrontation, which would turn into a crime, he is simply running from Smerdyakov and his deeds, away, to Moscow, in order to cleanse himself more quickly. This is almost a physical need, for there is this feeling of moral filth; he has forgotten about his father. At first he doesn't even think that his words, his conclusions have now taken on the indisputability of a mathematical formula: Smerdyakov is no theoretician. And it seems to Ivan that everything that had happened was a nightmare, a dream, that he was theorising as before, that he had only to get away and to get a grip on himself, and then he would figure it all out at his leisure. 'At seven o'clock in the evening Ivan Fyodorovich boarded the train and flew toward Moscow. 'Away with all the past, the old world is done with forever, and may I *never hear another word or echo* from it!' [Smerdyakov had hinted to him 'that from Moscow, sir, you can be bothered by telegraph from here, in any event, sir'] 'To a new world, to new places, without looking back!' [my emphasis, V. K.] (14, 255).

But Ivan is already visited by the premonition that it will not be so easy to disentangle oneself from Smerdyakov and his deeds. And:

> instead of delight there descended on his soul such terrible darkness, and such grief gnawed at his heart, such as he had never experienced in his entire life. He sat thinking the entire night; the train car sped on, and only at daybreak, already entering Moscow, did he suddenly come to.
> —I am a scoundrel!—he whispered to himself. (14, 255)

In these words we hear an acknowledgment that by his flight Ivan did not rid himself of Smerdyakov, did not save himself from the lackey who was pursuing him. On the contrary, having shamefully refused to be where his presence was required, he betrayed himself to another's will and, like a 'scoundrel', having avoided the responsibility of making a decision, escaped from the 'field of battle', from the field where a battle was being waged between good and evil. In these words Ivan's hidden conscience resounds, the voice of his personality-core that has not yet been eroded by evil; the lackey, the slave cannot conquer the hero and ideologist completely, the norms of morality do not permit the hero to accept as obligatory the conclusions of his theory 'all is permitted'.

* * * But here is a curious thing: that not for a single moment do we cease believing in Ivan, in the possibility of his overcoming the pollution which has surrounded him (if not now, then at some point in the future), and this despite the fact that it is precisely to him that the devil appears and it is he who succumbs to the temptation of Smerdyakov. It would seem that Ivan should call forth the narrator's most active dislike, but Ivan's thirst for world harmony is so sincere and all-encompassing that neither the narrator nor the elder Zosima, the author's ideal hero, can refuse sympathy to this atheist. 'A deep conscience' is what Alyosha says about him at the end of the novel (15, 89). Quite possibly these words of Zosima refer directly to Ivan: 'Do not hate atheists, false preachers, materialists, even the malicious ones and not only the good ones, for there are many good ones even there, particularly in our times' (14, 149). In this we hear above all Dostoevsky's own faith in the all-conquering force of good, especially in the young people 'of the most recent time', who for the official literature and state press were simply a swarm of 'godless atheists'. Dostoevsky himself saw the primary evil in the mass of 'semi-educated' people who had appeared in the post-reform transitional era, a sort of moral lumpenproletariat that was tempting Russia. It is no accident that as soon as Smerdyakov departs from the pages of the novel, the devil appears—who, as it were, plays the double to the 'lackey' who has committed suicide. It is this evil, which had led him astray in a maze as a wood sprite in the fairy tale leads travellers astray on the road, that Ivan must overcome. But how? Can he do it? To do this he must first solve the riddle of his own self.

The obstacle to this self-unriddling is Ivan's pride. Taking on himself responsibility for the entire cosmos, entering into a debate with God over the management of the universe, Ivan does not assume responsibility for the small, weak people nearby: 'So am I my brother Dmitry's keeper?' he remarks, in Cain-like hatred and indifference to his brother (14, 211). 'If she's a child, then I'm not her nurse', is how he steps indifferently over the spiritual sufferings of Lise (15, 38). And how much that symbolic scene is worth, where he flings away from him the drunken peasant who has turned up under his feet, so that the latter falls on the 'frozen ground'. Ivan passes by indifferently, although he knows that the little peasant will 'freeze'! In the same category one might locate his desire for the death of his father. It seems to him simpler to clear away 'Karamazovism' from the path than to spend the effort trying to awaken the human being in his father, as Alyosha tries to do, who urges his father to find a good principle in himself and who believes that an awakening is possible ('You're not a malicious person, but a corrupted one', he tells his father [14, 158]. But for this, constant daily effort is necessary—and not only effort, but also an acknowledgment of the fact that he is the same as other people, weak and sinful, and not the proud lawgiver of the universe; for this it is necessary to love one's neighbour, the concrete living human being, and not all humanity as a whole. And such responsibility is heavier and more serious.

After the murder had been committed, Ivan says to Smerdyakov that he came 'to disentangle the mess you have made here', in this way placing himself outside the events that have occurred. It is as if he senses that if he turns out to be implicated, then he will have to admit that he is the same as the others, and perhaps even worse. 'If it wasn't Dmitry who killed, but Smerdyakov < . . . > then, of course, I am also a murderer' (15, 54). But only by passing through this realisation, Dostoevsky suggests, can he overcome evil and break through to his own self, to what is best in him, to that genuine responsibility for one's neighbours that every person must bear. And only then will Ivan understand *who* the real murderer is, and his passionate dreams for world happiness will acquire a real-life ground, for they will be united with everyday life expressed in a constant pattern of behaviour.

It is apparently no accident that the unearthly, rather abstract and overly eloquent dream of Ivan's about universal happiness is perceived by Smerdyakov as a hidden desire of personal gain. To Ivan's question, why he (Ivan) wished the death of his father, Smerdyakov 'venomously and even vindictively' answered: 'And the inheritance, sir? . . . After all, then, after your parent, there would be coming to each of the three brothers maybe forty thousand or a little more' (15, 52). Smerdyakov (like Rakitin, who also suspects Ivan of material greed) is one dimensional. He judges Ivan by his own measurement. As we have already noted, his face and his mask absolutely coincide, therefore he does not even suspect the multiple meanings possible for human personality and is capable of seeing in another person only the 'external crust', the socially conditioned features. Smerdyakov cannot hear Ivan's inner voice. And it is no accident that to no one but Alyosha did Ivan speak about his thirst for world harmony, whereas he frequently expressed aloud, and even 'on one local, largely female, social occasion', the idea that 'if God didn't exist, then all is permitted.' Thus Smerdyakov is repeating not some secret, hidden voice of Ivan's but that which had been turned outwards, to the surface. One might sooner say that Ivan expresses the hidden voice of post-reform Russian society, where families were disintegrating, where trade in human honour and dignity was continuing and even intensifying, where, just as before, everything was held in the servile fetters of a still-viable serfdom and high society and where, in essence, everything was permitted to the strong of this world, where in the hearts and minds the idea of 'arbitrary will' reigned supreme.

In other words: Smerdyakov repeats that which does not belong to the personality-core of Ivan, he repeats only those fixed ideas conditioned by society which the hero, as it were, has accumulated and releases to the surface. This is the meaning of 'doubleness' in the novel. The theory 'all is permitted' is like a chemically cleansed 'Karamazovism' that has received its theoretical expression, to the extent that 'Karamazovism' is the quintessence of the societal disintegration then underway. But Smerdyakov tries to persuade Ivan that he exists wholly and essentially in this theory, that he and Ivan are one—and Ivan, horrified at this circumstance, asks the lackey: 'What sort of alliance do you think I entered into with you, what is this, do you think I'm afraid of you?' (15, 51). Smerdyakov is convinced that Ivan did enter in to such an alliance, for 'it is always interesting to have a talk with an intelligent man.' Thus Ivan faces a double task: to understand that his idea is itself lackey-like, secondary, non-autonomous, to see his fault in the fact that he shared this idea, spoke it out, and thereby took on his share of responsibility for murder; but, at the same time, he must understand that his potential is not exhausted by this idea.

At this point in the struggle for Ivan, two forces collide: from one side, Alyosha; from the other, Smerdyakov and then the devil. Alyosha is described in the novel as the antithesis of Ivan (Christ appears to him, the devil to Ivan), but it is precisely he who attempts to help Ivan cleanse himself from those foreign ideas which to Ivan have seemed like his own. If these words really express the essence of Ivan, then he is the real murderer of his father; if they do not, then somewhere there exists the real murderer. Alyosha confirms that the murderer is Smerdyakov—not Mitya and not Ivan. And what is most important, he tries to convince Ivan of this, in order, so to speak, to dis-identify him from Smerdyakov, from his double. As Bakhtin justly notes, 'Alyosha foresees that Ivan is by himself a 'deep conscience', that sooner or later he will give himself the categorical answer, 'I did the killing'. And according to Dostoevsky's creative plan, he could not give himself any other answer. And that is why Alyosha's word proves so useful, precisely as the word of the *other*'.[7] Alyosha's words, addressed to Ivan, are full of such force and energy that they constitute perhaps the most passionate utterance of Alyosha's in the novel.

> Ivan Fyodorovich suddenly stopped.
> —Then who is the murderer, in your opinion?—he asked for some reason with obvious coldness, and a certain arrogant note sounded in the very tone of the question.
> —You yourself know who,—Alyosha said softly and with conviction.
> —Who? You mean that fable about the crazy idiot epileptic? About Smerdyakov?—
> Alyosha suddenly felt how he was trembling all over.
> —You yourself know who,—escaped him helplessly. He was breathless. (15, 39)

And Ivan, mentioning Smerdyakov (let's even assume he was the murderer) as no more than a worthless plaything of his own will and passion, awaits the blow from his brother. He knows full well that Alyosha does not believe in Mitya's guilt. Which means only one person remains: he himself, Ivan.

> —So who? Who?—Ivan cried out, almost fiercely. All his reserve suddenly vanished.
> —I know only one thing,—Alyosha said, still in the same almost whisper. —It was *not you* who killed father.
> —'Not you'! What do you mean by 'not you?'—Ivan was dumbfounded.
> —It was not you who killed father, not you,—Alyosha repeated firmly. The silence lasted for half a minute.
> —But I know very well it was not me—are you raving?—Ivan muttered with a pale and crooked grin. He fastened his eyes on Alyosha. Both were standing under a streetlamp.
> —No, Ivan, you've told yourself several times that you are the murderer.
> —When did I say that? When I was in Moscow . . . When did I say that?—Ivan stammered, quite at a loss.
> —You've said it to yourself many times while you were alone during these past terrible two months,—Alyosha continued, as softly and as distinctly as before. But he was now speaking not, as it were, out of himself, not of his own will, but obeying some sort of irresistible command.—You accused yourself and confessed to yourself that the murderer is none other than you. *But it was not you who killed him, you are mistaken, the murderer is not you, do you hear me, not you! God has sent me to tell you that*— [my emphasis, V. K.] (15, 40)

---

7. Bakhtin, *Problemy poetiki Dostoevskogo*, 441.

These words sound almost like an incantation intended to liberate and cleanse Ivan's soul from despair. Recall that he has been in despair from the very beginning of the novel. This had already been noticed by the elder. Alyosha appears at the optimally necessary moment for him, when not only Ivan but the reader too is definitively confused by all that has happened. And he speaks this not only to Ivan, but also to the reader and to all future criticism.

It is apparently again no accident that structurally in the novel, immediately after this discussion with Alyosha, there follows the three conversations with Smerdyakov, who, on the contrary, attempts to persuade Ivan that they, the two of them, are identical, and that Ivan is the real and only murderer:

> —We're sitting here just the two of us, so what's the use of putting on an act, playing a comedy? Or do you still want to shift it all on to me alone, right to my face? *You killed him, you are the chief killer, and I was just your stooge, your faithful servant Licharda, and I committed the deed according to your word* [my emphasis, V. K.]. (15, 59)

After almost every word of this retelling of the murder, Smerdyakov inserts, in diverse variations, the phrase: 'It was all done in the most natural manner, sir, from your very words.' And he carries out his story entirely from that point of view: 'I want to prove it to your face this very night *that in all this the chief murderer is you alone, sir, and I'm not the real chief one, although I did do the killing. But it's you who are the most lawful murderer!* [my emphasis, V. K.] (15, 63).

But after Alyosha's words, part of Dostoevsky's intention is that it must at last become clear to the reader that Ivan is a spiritual cover-up for Smerdyakov, just as Mitya turned out to be a juridical cover-up. The lackey does not wish to bear any sort of responsibility. That is why he needed Ivan's *permission*, about which Dostoevsky had written. He had himself declared that nothing would have happened if Mitya hadn't come. But Ivan too entered into his plan. This plan had been too fastidiously, too autonomously worked out. When he told Ivan his actions and the counter-measures he had taken against possible suspicions towards his person, Ivan asked in horror:

> —But is it really possible that you could have thought of all that right there on the spot?—Ivan exclaimed, beside himself with astonishment. Again he looked fearfully at Smerdyakov.
> —Have pity on me, sir, how could I have thought all of that up, when everything was in such a flurry? *It was all thought out beforehand,*— Smerdyakov blurted out [my emphasis, V. K.] (15, 66)

Smerdyakov is not only not a passive executor of Ivan's idea; he is also not an agitated, divided nature tormented by the evil surrounding him (as is Ivan). Smerdyakov is an active carrier of evil, which has drawn into the elemental forces of criminality not only Ivan. Remember how the young boy Ilyusha suffers because he thinks he has killed the dog Zhuchka. 'That's why I'm ill, papa, because I killed Zhuchka back then, for that God has punished me', he says over and over again to his father (14, 482). There are many guilty parties in the illness and death of Ilyushechka, but only one who tried to destroy the pure soul of the boy by drawing him into a wicked deed—and that was Smerdyakov. 'He had somehow managed to make friends with the lackey of your late father, with Smerdyakov', Kolya Krasotkin explains the story to Alyosha (14, 480). 'He taught the little fool a stupid trick, that is, a mean trick, a vile trick, how to take a piece of bread, the soft part, shove a pin into it, and then toss it to some mongrel, the kind of dog who's so hungry he'd swallow anything without chewing it, and then watch what happens. So they fixed up such a little piece and threw it to that same shaggy Zhuchka' (14, 480). Ilyushechka suffers from that beastly act, but Smerdyakov, who in childhood had liked to hang cats in secret, doesn't even recall the episode. And for us, this temptation by Smerdyakov of a child (Ilyushechka) is in its essentials an enlightening parallel to the temptation of an adult (Ivan). The real criminal is Smerdyakov, but the entire weight of moral blame and responsibility falls on his accomplices. In this way they are linked by evil, and a great deal of spiritual strength is necessary to separate out oneself and one's participation in this evil act (the crime).

Smerdyakov, and then the devil (his new hypostasis) manage to convince Ivan that he is the authentic murderer of his father. Ivan communicates to Alyosha the devil's words:

> —Oh, you are going to perform a virtuous deed, you will announce that you killed your father, that the lackey killed your father at your instruction.'
> —Brother,—Alyosha interrupted.—Stop. It wasn't you who killed him. That's not true!
> —He says it, and he knows it,—Ivan repeated, as if mechanically. (15, 87)

Ivan's soul is divided, and the devil, personifying the dark side of this soul, tries to persuade it that it too does not believe in good. 'You are going to perform a virtuous deed, but you don't even believe in virtue—that's what infuriates you and torments you; that's why you're so vindictive' (15, 87). This is not quite true, but it is important to the devil to strengthen Ivan in evil, because Ivan's very approach to testify in court is already almost senseless, since Smerdyakov has hanged himself. Alyosha, who does not believe that Ivan is the murderer, nevertheless does not try to hinder Ivan from going to court and repenting, because to remain where he is means not only to hide from responsibility but also to be identified definitively with Smerdyakov. That's what Smerdyakov wanted from Ivan, and that's what the devil, speaking of the senselessness of any appearance at court, wants as well: 'Here Smerdyakov has died, hanged himself, so who is going to believe you in court on your own?' the devil remarks ironically, making fun of him because he cannot become a real murderer, that is, indifferently survive another's death ('it's not for such eagles to soar above the earth!') (15, 88).

Ivan struggles with the devil with all his strength, but the deed of evil has gone so far he is no longer able to disentangle himself from his clutches. And although Ivan goes to repent, in order to master the devil, their struggle, one might say, finishes with a certain advantage accruing to the dark principle. The strength of autonomous will, of all-destroying arbitrary wilfulness, turns out to be helpless in a conflict with evil. Ivan mastered his pride by going to court, but by degrading his pride—as is often the case with Dostoevsky's heroes—he rages all the more angrily against the entire world and slandered himself more than was true or just, identifying himself with Smerdyakov, all exactly as Alyosha had feared. Having announced that Smerdyakov and not Mitya was the murderer, Ivan clarifies: 'He killed, and I instructed him to kill' (15, 116). Ivan identifies himself with Smerdyakov and the truth of repentance becomes a demonic farce, definitively confirming Mitya in the murder. Because after Ivan's speech incriminating himself, Katerina Ivanovna, frightened for her beloved (Ivan), destroys Mitya with her own evidence. It is no accident that Ivan names as his single witness the *devil*.

> –Who is your witness?
> –He has a tail, your honour, you wouldn't allow him in! < . . . >
> Pay no attention to him, he's a wretched, petty devil,—he added, as it were confidentially.—He's probably here somewhere, under that table there, with the material evidence, where else would he be sitting if not there? (15, 117)

Mastering his pride, Ivan declares that his idea is a vile, lackey-like one and as such belongs not to him but to all of vile society. This step was necessary. But Ivan is not yet strong enough to take one more step and to repudiate the idea. The effort to master his pride cost him his reason.

> –Who doesn't wish the death of his father?
> –Are you in your right mind?—inadvertently escaped from the judge.
> –That's just it, I am in my right mind < . . . > and in a vile mind, the same sort of mind that you all have < . , , > you vile mugs!—He turned suddenly to the public.—A father's been murdered, and they pretend to be frightened,—he growled with savage contempt.—They'll make all sorts of faces at each other. Liars! Everyone wants his father dead! (15, 117)

At the end of his speech he shouts out with the 'ferocious howl' of one possessed (as V. E. Vetlovskaya has observed). Here it is perhaps worth making one closing observation.

Ivan arrives at an idea that is very precious to Dostoevsky: that everyone is guilty for everything; but he arrives at it somehow strangely, as it were, from the other end. For him this is the possibility to lighten, or perhaps to remove altogether, his *personal* guilt and responsibility—because, by accusing himself, he can in no way *understand* his guilt. He refused to acknowledge spiritual 'Karamazovism' as a product of his own self, and consequently as part of his own essence, but to sever himself from it and to disidentify himself from Smerdyakov was something he could not manage to do. Thus Ivan's guilt in a certain sense turns out to be deeper and more difficult than if he had simply taught Smerdyakov his ideas; his proud mind, conditioned, in Dostoevsky's view, to despise people, did not give him the chance to look intently at those surrounding him, to understand them.

> –You're not stupid,—Ivan muttered, as if struck by something; his blood rose to his face.—Earlier I thought you were stupid. But you're serious now!—he remarked, suddenly looking at Smerdyakov in a new way.
> –It was from pride that you thought I was stupid. (15, 68)

Such is the ending of the 'third, and final, meeting with Smerdyakov', and revelation came too late. That which is absolutely clear to Alyosha and on which he insists ('The lackey killed, but my brother is innocent') from the very beginning of this tragic murder is not at all clear to Ivan (15, 189). The absence in his spiritual make-up of authentic inner freedom hinders him from breaking through to Alyosha's simplicity and clarity. Ivan's guilt and disaster is that in trying to find the path to an overcoming of the world's evil, he turns to the destructive elemental force of his thesis 'all is permitted', not realising that at the basis of this thesis lies a well-hidden *greed*. It is not accidental that the organiser of the destructive act is the greedy lackey Smerdyakov. Ivan falls from the frying pan into the fire, from 'Karamazovism' to 'Smerdyakovism'.

In his battle with repellent 'Karamazovism', Ivan does not expect that the external world contains anything capable of helping him: 'the people's truth'. Truth and goodness, according to Dostoevsky, are categories that function outside the bounds of the greed of the world. And the 'people's truth', contained in the image and idea of Christ, is not able to suppress the truth of personality, Dostoevsky believed; it can only come to its aid. The torments of a lonely mind lead the hero to madness. But in these torments there is a radiant force. They indicate to the reader Ivan's moral purity, which he cannot see in himself. Tyutchev (cited by Ivan in his tale of the Grand Inquisitor) wrote:

> It is not given to us to predict,
> How our word will resound,
> And we are given compassion
> As we are given grace.[8]

Ivan Karamazov's problem is the problem of a person's responsibility for a word uttered by him, a problem that has resounded tragically in the fate of Russia in the twentieth century. Ivan was not able to predict how his word would echo or resound. But the hero's spiritual torments give him the right, at least, to the reader's compassion and, perhaps, to the involuntary sympathy of the author. The realist Dostoevsky, whose 'hosannah' passed 'through a great crucible of doubts', decided all the same to sympathise secretly with his hero-theomach (27, 86). Not by accident does Mitya say in the epilogue, 'Listen, brother Ivan will surpass all of us . . . He'll get well' (15, 184). Alyosha is more cautious, but hope has not abandoned him either: 'And I too very much hope that he will get well' (15, 185). And we must assume that in Dostoevsky, this means more than physical health. According to Dostoevsky, Christianity is the path to freedom. The Revolutionary-nihilists subordinate themselves to collective and party commands, for they are afraid of freedom and therefore they cannot take the path of Christ. Ivan, like Job, has a chance of reconciliation with God since he is free. Evidently, through the 'crucible of doubts' he too will arrive at his 'Hosanna'. Once he has renounced his egoism, he has only to look after others and pray for them. And then what is written in the Bible will take place: 'After Job had prayed for his friends, the Lord made him prosperous again and gave him twice as much as he had before' (Job 42:10). Only in this way can Ivan recover his spiritual health.

---

8. These lines are from Tyutchev's lyric, 'It is not given to us to predict', dated 27 February 1869. F. I. Tyutchev, *Stikhotvoreniia: Pis'ma: Vospominaniia sovremennikov* (Moscow, 1988), 132.

EDWARD WASIOLEK

Dmitry and Katerina[†]

In the confession of an ardent heart, Dmitry tells Alyosha—he is our ears—what Katya means to him. But he tells only what he knows, and she means more to him than he knows. The relations between them bristle with paradoxes. A high-minded, well-educated, rich girl insists on an engagement with an impoverished, dissolute army officer. When Dmitry basely repays her generosity by stealing her money and spending it on a wild orgy with another girl, Katerina rises nobly to forgiveness. Throughout the novel she stands ready to bear everything for his sake: vice, theft, unfaithfulness, insult, and even marriage to Grushenka. Despite all this, Dmitry not only is incorrigibly ungrateful but unaccountably sees her love and sacrifice as oppressive burdens. Katerina's "goodness" drives him to murder. The incriminating letter he writes Katya threatening his father's life makes this clear. In that letter he states that only by paying her back the money he had stolen from her could he preserve his honor, and if he could not get the money any other way, he would kill his father to get it. If the Elder's bow stays Dmitry's hand against his father, Katya's had originally moved it and continues to move it throughout the novel. The first meeting with Katerina begins with a bow, as low and as long as the Elder's bow of expiation. It is characteristic of Dostoevsky that he uses the same gesture for opposite meanings, as if to emphasize that the act remains without significance until we ourselves choose the significance.

On the simplest level it would appear that Katerina is sacrificing herself out of gratitude for Dmitry's noble gesture in saving her father and sparing her. This is the way that Alyosha understands her motives and her relations with Dmitry. As he goes to see Katya at her request early in the novel, he tells himself: "The girl's aims were of the noblest, he knew that. She was trying to save his brother Dmitry simply through generosity (*velikodushie*), though he had already behaved badly to her." And this is the way he understands it in his conversation with Dmitry, when his brother tells him about his first meeting with Katya: he assures Dmitry that Katerina loves him, and not Ivan. When Dmitry tells him about the 3,000 rubles that he had stolen from Katerina, Alyosha says:

> "Katerina Ivanovna will understand it all," Alyosha said solemnly. "She'll understand how great this trouble is and will forgive. She has a lofty mind, and no one could be more unhappy than you. She'll see that for herself."

Yet even while Alyosha is convinced that Katerina's motives are lofty, pure, and sincere, he has moments of uneasiness. From the very beginning, something about her troubles him. On his way to his first meeting with her, even while paying justice to her fine qualities, "a shiver began to run down his back as soon as he drew near her house." When he sees her, he sees pride, self-confidence, and strong will in her face. Her black burning eyes are set beautifully in a thin, pale, almost yellow face, and he sees

† From *Dostoevsky: The Major Fiction*, pp. 151–60. © 1964 Massachusetts Institute of Technology. Published by the MIT Press.

why Dmitry could easily fall in love with her. But he also sees unclearly
something that makes it unlikely for Dmitry to love her for a long time.
He tells his brother: "Perhaps you will always love her, but perhaps you
will not always be happy with her." But he no sooner says this than he
feels ashamed of himself. Later, when he goes to her with Dmitry's farewell message, he feels that his first impression must have been wrong. As
she comes out to meet him, he sees in her face only simplicity, goodness,
and sincerity.

Again and again Alyosha tries to take her as she sees herself, but each
time he is stopped by a feeling he cannot understand. He swings from
facing up to his doubt about Katerina's motives to feeling ashamed of
having that doubt. Alyosha is our ears and our eyes, and the difficulty he
has in understanding Katerina is our difficulty. And the difficulty is great.
Engaged to Dmitry, Katerina regards him as a repugnant monster; determined to save him, she plots his ruin; frantic to keep him faithful, she
provokes his betrayal of her. It is she who almost saves him at the trial,
and it is she who most irrevocably ruins him legally by the letter she produces in which he had uttered threats against his father's life. Throughout
her relations with Dmitry, her fitful character sweeps her from love to
hate, generosity to spite, arrogance to submissiveness. She is all contradiction, flailing each action with its opposite. There is something in her relations with Dmitry that she cannot forgive, something that drives her to
pursue him with an unrelenting, self-punishing love. She herself best
expresses it in Mrs. Khokhlokov's drawing room before Ivan and Alyosha,
when after a night of shame and rage at Grushenka's insult, she triumphantly announces that she will bear that too out of love for Dmitry:

> "I've already decided, even if he marries that—creature" (she began
> solemnly), "whom I never, never can forgive, *even then I will not aban-
> don him.* Henceforward I will never, never abandon him!" she cried,
> breaking into a sort of pale, hysterical ecstasy. "Not that I would run
> after him continually, get in his way and worry him. Oh, no! I will go
> away to another town—where you like—but I will watch over him
> all my life—I will watch over him all my life unceasingly. When he
> becomes unhappy with that woman, and that is bound to happen
> quite soon, let him come to me and he will find a friend, a sister. . . .
> Only a sister, of course, and so forever; but he will learn at least that
> that sister is really his sister, who loves him and has sacrificed all
> her life to him. I will gain my point. I will insist on his knowing me
> and confiding entirely in me, without reserve," she cried, in a sort of
> frenzy. "I will be a god to whom he can pray—and that, at least, he
> owes me for his treachery and for what I suffered yesterday through
> him. And let him see that all my life I will be true to him and the
> promise I gave him, in spite of his being untrue and betraying me."

It is this something that Alyosha finally understands as he listens to
Katerina's final decision, even though he had been firmly convinced up
to the previous night that she loved Dmitry: "Alyosha had till the evening
before implicitly believed that Katerina Ivanovna had a steadfast and
passionate love for Dmitry; but he had only believed it till the evening
before." When he had awakened that morning—after dreaming of Grushenka all night—the word *nadryv* is on his lips. It is this word that startles

him when it is used by Mrs. Khokhlokov about Katerina's love for Dmitry, and which—while listening to Katerina—sparks his illumination. For as he excitedly expresses it to the startled Katerina, her love for Dmitry is a love from *nadryv*, that is, a self-punishing love, delighting in its self-hurt, needing the hurt, and only masquerading as love. Ivan provides a further illumination: "Believe me, Katerina Ivanovna, you love only him. And the more he insults you, the more you love him—that's your 'laceration.' You love him just as he is; you love him for insulting you. If he reformed, you'd give him up at once and cease to love him. But you need him so as to contemplate continually your heroic fidelity and to reproach him for infidelity. And it all comes from your pride."

Alyosha and Ivan tell us what Katerina's love is, but they do not tell us why it is so. We can begin to understand why by going back—as indeed Katerina and Dmitry keep going back—to that first fateful meeting. The scene had ended with Dmitry's heroic and successful struggle to overcome the noxious Karamazov insect of passion within him. The tragic relations between them have their seeds in that success, or rather in the gesture that accompanies the "triumph" of Dmitry: Dmitry's long bow of respect, and Katerina's low bow of respectful gratitude. They know it, and the fateful bow is insisted upon by both of them in their conversations.

Katerina Ivanovna is convinced that Dmitry hates her, and he hates her because he had compelled her to bow to him. She explains the reason for "his hatred" for her in this way:

> Oh, he has despised me horribly, he has always despised me, and do you know, he has despised me from the very moment that I bowed down to him for that money. I saw that. I felt it at once at the time, but for a long time I wouldn't believe it. How often have I read in his eyes. "You came of yourself, though."

Forgetting that it was she, not Dmitry, who had insisted on marriage, Katerina adds: "He was always convinced that I should be trembling with shame all my life before him, because I went to him then, and that he had a right to despise me forever for it, and so to be superior to me—that's why he wanted to marry me." Despite his contempt and monstrous ingratitude, "I tried to conquer him by my love, a love that knew no bounds. I even tried to forgive his faithlessness; but he understood nothing, nothing! How could he understand indeed? He is a monster!"

But the truth is that the hate and contempt that she ascribes to Dmitry is the hate and contempt she herself feels for him. This is, I think, clear to the reader who can pierce the rather transparent attempt to hide her own hate by giving the hate and all base qualities to Dmitry and all noble qualities to herself. In the notebooks to *The Brothers Karamazov* Dostoevsky makes the hatred she feels explicit. He writes of her in the first sketch of the scene: "Oh, he laughed at me because of that long, low bow. I hated him." It is his bow, out of respect to her, that hurts. For with the bow Dmitry changes from one who abases and humiliates to one who respects and forgives. And she hates the long low bow she must return, for it acknowledges his triumph over her.

We can now understand Katerina's paradoxical and contradictory motives, for once we perceive the subtle deceptions she has drawn over her feelings, perhaps without knowing it, we can see that her motives and actions have followed consistently from what the bowing scene meant to her. Katerina wishes only to hurt because her meeting with Dmitry is compounded of nothing but hurt. She is humiliated in having to appeal for help to the repugnant sensualist, and she is humiliated in having to receive the respectful bow from him. The heroic sacrifice of Dmitry in overcoming the noxious Karamazov insect within him by his deep bow of respect is not an act of sacrifice executed in selflessness and taken in gratitude, but an act of sacrifice given and taken as a subtle and exquisite insult. It is sacrifice used as insult; and ravishment, by comparison, would have been kind. After Dmitry's respectful bow, Katerina carries away in her heart the intolerable burden of an act of sacrifice and the desire to repay it with an equally intolerable act of sacrifice. Is it any wonder, then, that she is obsessed, from this point on, with only one idea: to save Dmitry, to sacrifice herself wholly and fully, to repay the burning insult of sacrifice with the burning insult of sacrifice. The oscillations between arrogance and submissiveness, love and hate, and unselfishness and spitefulness are not the struggle of a proud nature between its good intentions and, as has been usually suggested, the selfish impulses of its spirit. The love no less than the hate, and the submissiveness no less than the arrogance, are needed to bring to her feet a Dmitry ruined and shamed before all, but contrite and nobly forgiven by her. As a consequence, she courts his betrayal, provokes his humiliations of her, works for his shame, and plots her own injury. The more sunken Dmitry is, the stronger her spirit is in lifting him; the deeper the injury to herself, the more lofty her forgiveness; and the more lofty her forgiveness, the sweeter her repayment of the insult of Dmitry's respectful bow.

Dmitry understands this. He understands why she gives him the 3,000 rubles when she knows that he will use it to carry Grushenka away. He knows that she gives him the money to destroy his honor and to provoke his humiliations of her. And he understands that she wants to be dishonored, so that her forgiveness will be all the nobler. How else is one to explain his agonized cry, "Katya, why have you destroyed me!" when at the trial he hears with dismay her generous account of their first meeting. As Katerina tells Alyosha, she is ready to bear all for his sake. Referring to the 3,000 rubles Dmitry had "stolen" from her, Katerina says: "Let him be ashamed of himself, let him be ashamed of other people's knowing, but not of my knowing. He can tell God everything without shame. Why is it he still does not understand how much I am ready to bear for his sake? . . . I want to save him forever."

What Katerina cannot bear is the possibility of a Dmitry who does not want to be forgiven. This is why, for instance, she becomes hysterical when Alyosha, after a meeting with Dmitry in the garden adjoining the Karamazov house, comes to convey to her Dmitry's "good-bye." Katerina is startled by the word "good-bye" and insists that Alyosha must have made a mistake in giving her the message. In the face of Alyosha's assurances that there has been no mistake, since Dmitry has asked him three times not to forget it, Katerina flushes and insists that Dmitry must not have said it deliberately but in a moment of reckless indecision. "He's merely in despair, and I can still save him," she infers exultantly.

It is at this point in the narration that translations blur this intention to trace back the drama of insult and repayment to Dmitry's respectful bow. The word "good-bye" (Magarshack has "good-bye" and Garnett "give his compliments") is in Russian the verb *klanyat'sya*, that is, "good-bye" by bowing. The Russian word expresses at once the sense of parting and recalls to Katerina the insulting respectful bow of the first meeting, when the same verb was used in a different aspect. The blurring in translation of Dostoevsky's intention is unfortunate since a phrase like "to bow out" would have caught, as does the Russian, both the sense of parting and a reminder of the fateful bow. Is it any wonder, then, that Katerina clings almost hysterically to the possibility of some mistake in Alyosha's message, which doubles the intolerable insult by recalling the first sacrifice and severing the possibility of repayment.

Dmitry, as the dissolute officer who struggled against the Karamazov sensuality within him, seemed unconscious of the enormity of the insult he had offered the proud girl, although in the ecstasy of self-satisfaction after she leaves, when he almost stabs himself with his sword, Dostoevsky hints that Dmitry has shared in the intention to insult. The Dmitry who reminds Katerina that she is rich and he but a poor rake, when she writes her letter of declaration of love for him, is also conscious of Katerina's motives. At times his awareness comes out sharply, though involuntarily, as when he retorts to Alyosha's assurance that Katerina loves him, and not Ivan: "She loves her virtue, and not me." He is always sorry for statements of this kind, ashamed of his base nature that erupts in criticism of Katerina, when morally he considers himself infinitely below her. Yet, despite his conscious intentions, he insists again and again in reminding her of the bow. In his last incriminating letter to her, he returns once again to the bow: "Farewell, I bow down to the ground [*Klanyayus' do zemli*] before you, for I've been a scoundrel to you. Forgive me! No, better not forgive me, you'll be happier, and so shall I! Better Siberia than your love." Better murder and prison than such love! Such love and sacrifice, and the bow that symbolizes them, are not purifying and uplifting but abasing and persecuting. They are not Zossima's love, nor is Katerina's bow Zossima's bow. Zossima's bow stays the hand of the murderer; Katerina's raises it. What is wrong with such a love?

Katerina loves Dmitry from *nadryv*, and in this word Dostoevsky catches the vortex of her emotions and motives; with this word he points to one of his most penetrating insights into human motives. Dostoevsky devotes all of Book Four of Part Two to examples of *nadryv*, pointing to something that Ferapont, Captain Snegirev, Katerina, and little Ilyusha have in common. Magarshack has ineptly translated the word as "heartache," Garnett less ineptly as "laceration." It is impossible to think of a translation more misleading than Magarshack's. It is romantic and trivial in connotation, and wholly inappropriate to what sears Katerina's breast. Garnett's translation is not much more helpful, but it is not the positive hindrance Magarshack's translation is.

The word comes from the verb *nadryvat'*, which means—apart from its literal meaning of tearing things apart, like paper—"to strain or hurt oneself by lifting something beyond one's strength." To this must be added Dostoevsky's special use of the word to mean a *purposeful* hurting of oneself, and to this, an explanation of the purpose. *Nadryv* is for Dostoevsky a purposeful and pleasurable self-hurt. Father Ferapont's ascetic deprivations are a self-denial from *nadryv*. He "hurts" himself, so that he can hurt the other monks; he needs the "indulgent" monks (which his exercises in asceticism create) as much as Katerina needs a fallen Dmitry. Father Ferapont's ascetic deprivations are weapons of humiliation of others and exaltation of self. Captain Snegirev's *nadryv* is more pathetic and less violent than Father Ferapont's, but it shares some of the same quality. He deliberately hurts himself—when he stamps on the money Alyosha offers him and which he needs so desperately—because of the beautiful and noble image he has of himself at that moment.

Nadryv is for Dostoevsky a primal psychological fact. It is the impulse in the hearts of men that separates one man from another, the impulse we all have to make the world over into the image of our wills. Katerina *loves* from *nadryv*; Father Ferapont *fasts* from *nadryv*; Captain Snegirev *loves* *honor* from *nadryv*. Dostoevsky shows this basic psychological characteristic working to corrupt what seem to be good motives. From the Underground Man on, one of the premises of Dostoevsky's mature dialectic has been that the Will will subvert the best and highest motives to its own purposes. *Nadryv* is Dostoevsky's mature pointing to the psychological impulse that works to corrupt everything to its own purposes.

Ivan has his *nadryv* also, for his hurt is his bruised sense of justice. He raises *nadryv* to a level of universal revolt against God.

NATHAN ROSEN

Style and Structure in *The Brothers Karamazov*: The Grand Inquisitor and the Russian Monk†

The two crucial sections of *The Brothers Karamazov*, according to Dostoevsky, are Books V and VI, centering on the Grand Inquisitor and the Russian monk respectively. Both these sections, which Dostoevsky characterized in his letters as "culminating points," occur one-third of the way through the novel, so they do not culminate in anything except the main action of the novel. They are "culminating points" only as the *pro* and *contra* of an ideological debate, crystallizing the main issues in the novel. Such ideological debates can also be found at the beginning of the Book of Job and Goethe's *Faust*, works specifically mentioned in *The Brothers Karamazov*. Dostoevsky's ideological debate differs sharply in certain respects.

First, the debate takes place on earth, and God and Satan are replaced by mortals; we are in the modern world in which heaven and hell are within us. Second, the two protagonists do not confront each other but appear in successive books; they do not really "talk" to one another. (Alyosha Karamazov is the more or less passive listener in each case.) Third, the debate is, according to all critics, one-sided, with the victory clearly won by the Grand Inquisitor. And finally, critical attention has been concentrated almost entirely on the Grand Inquisitor; "The Russian Monk" section has been ignored except by the theologically minded. This is all the more remarkable and unjust since Dostoevsky declares that *both* are "cul-

† From *Russian Literature Triquarterly*, Vol. 1, No. 1 (1971), 352–63. Reprinted by permission of Ardis Publishers.

minating points" in the novel. His statement should be respected and given the attention it deserves. How strange that Dostoevsky should compose a debate in which Satan wins so obviously! Why include the debate at all? When critics like Rozanov,[1] Camus, D. H. Lawrence, and Rahv ignore this question, they not only misunderstand the Grand Inquisitor and the Russian Monk, but the whole novel as well.

The misinterpretation began with Rozanov's celebrated (and overrated) book, *The Legend of the Grand Inquisitor*, first published in 1894, with a third edition in 1906. Rozanov explained that although "The Grand Inquisitor" is "only an episode . . . its connection with the plot of this novel is so weak that one can study it as a separate work." To make up for this structural weakness in the novel, however, "there is an inner connection: The Legend constitutes the essence of the whole work, which is merely grouped around it like variations on its theme." Philip Rahv, writing sixty years later, does not even trouble to mention the novel: "The Legend," he says, "lends itself to analysis, quite apart from its local narrative setting, as a unique essay in the philosophy of history." It is therefore not surprising to find "The Grand Inquisitor" published separately as a modern "relevant" classic whose life and meaning are independent of the novel. For such readers "The Grand Inquisitor" becomes identical with *The Brothers Karamazov*, the very essence of it—precisely what Rozanov maintains. And the very opposite of what Dostoevsky sought to achieve in writing the novel: a defense of Christianity as the only true way of life in our time.

Let us examine two implications in Rozanov's argument. If, as he says, "The Legend" is the essence of the whole novel, one must conclude that it could have been inserted anywhere in the novel without suffering any important change in meaning. As a matter of fact, Rozanov fails to notice just where "The Legend" is placed. It occurs immediately after Ivan Karamazov shows his strength of will by breaking off with Katerina Ivanovna, who wishes to be his "grand inquisitor"; and he is about to order champagne "to celebrate my first hour of freedom." He is therefore one of the elect, capable of free choice, and unlike the submissive majority. Nor does Rozanov note what follows "The Legend": the meeting with Smerdyakov in which Ivan tacitly authorizes the murder of the father. After Ivan's noble obsession with the suffering of mankind it is surprising that he should add to that suffering by killing his father. This becomes a damaging commentary on the meaning of "The Grand Inquisitor." And Ivan's personal vindictiveness about his father is doubled or reinforced by Smerdyakov's. Thus the context of "The Grand Inquisitor"—what precedes and what follows it—adds to its meaning.

A second implication of Rozanov's argument: if "The Legend" is the essence of the novel, then the author of "The Legend"—Ivan Karamazov—must be the central character in the novel. Rozanov says this without any qualification. Yet the novel is entitled *The Brothers Karamazov*; Zosima bows before Mitya, not Ivan; and indeed Mitya is the major figure in the action of the novel. Ivan is only one element. To concentrate upon him means to disregard the major part of the novel.

---

1. Vasily Rozanov (1856–1919), Russian writer and philosopher.

Rozanov and other critics could have regained their perspective if they had reminded themselves that the novel has *two* culminating "points" and one of them is "The Russian Monk." But they have unanimously chosen to disregard this section, dismissing it as mawkish and unctuous, a sentimental lyrical effusion, pallid, abstract, lacking in drama. The most charitable evaluation was made by E. H. Carr: "Ivan's denunciation of God remains more powerful and cogent than the defence which is put into the mouths of Zosima and Alyosha." Other critics, like Mochulsky and Wasiolek, silently pass over the artistic weaknesses of "The Russian Monk" but draw upon it as a reservoir of Dostoevsky's favorite ideas on religion. Religious commentators have, of course, worked thoroughly over this section, treating its ideas with veneration but ignoring its relation to the novel.

Could Dostoevsky have known so much less than his critics? Could he have supposed that "The Russian Monk" was an adequate, i.e., artistically persuasive refutation of the views of the Grand Inquisitor? And if it was not an adequate refutation, why did he retain it? These questions can best be answered by examining "The Russian Monk" and "The Grand Inquisitor" from an artistic standpoint rather than as intellectual debating propositions.

Ivan's arraignment of God is found in the three chapters "The Brothers Make Friends," "Rebellion," and "The Grand Inquisitor." These chapters are overwhelming in their intellectual and artistic power, and Dostoevsky was justly proud of what he had achieved. "My hero," he remarked, "takes a theme which *in my opinion* [Dostoevsky's emphasis] is irrefutable: the senselessness of the suffering of children, and draws from it the absurdity of the whole of historical actuality." Ivan's indictment is therefore irrefutable as an intellectual position. As to the artistic merit of these chapters Dostoevsky was also proud: "In all Europe," he exulted, "there have been no expressions of atheism, past or present, as powerful as mine."

Not only is the intellectual argument irrefutable, but it is vividly dramatized with the aid of actual newspaper reports on Turkish atrocities and horror stories of every kind. When a Russian general orders a serf boy to be torn to pieces by hunting dogs while the boy's mother is forced to watch, Alyosha has a traumatic experience; the meek apostle of Zosima cries out that the general should be shot! The journalistic reports are followed by a vivid and startling drama: the confrontation between Christ and the Grand Inquisitor in the dungeons of the Inquisition. The confrontation reaches a climax when Christ silently kisses the Inquisitor and departs; Christ's mission on earth—to correct the work of the Grand Inquisitor—is left unfinished, and the Inquisitor is free to carry on his diabolic work of stamping out freedom in the world. What could be more crushing to Father Zosima's (and Dostoevsky's) philosophy? Pobedonostsev, the head of the Russian church, was so disturbed by the power of the Grand Inquisitor's arguments that he anxiously wrote Dostoevsky to find out what refutation was possible. (*The Brothers Karamazov* was being published serially in a conservative magazine.) Dostoevsky replied that the refutation would appear that very month (August, 1879) under the title "The Russian Monk."

Although Dostoevsky had worked longer on this section than any other (more than three months) he was worried about its success. "Will it be adequate as a refutation?" he wrote Pobedonostsev. "Especially as the answer is not direct, not a point-by-point refutation of what had been said previously in 'The Grand Inquisitor' and before, but only indirectly . . . so to say, in an artistic picture." There was also the problem of the "absurdity" of Zosima's views for the modern reader. And there were "artistic obligations: I had to present a modest and august figure, whereas life is full of the comic and is only august when looked at from within, so that willy-nilly, due to the demands of art, I had to deal in the biography of my monk with the most vulgar and commonplace aspects so as not to weaken artistic realism."

Nevertheless there is little that is realistic in "The Russian Monk." On the level of intellectual argument there is, as Dostoevsky admitted, no attempt at a refutation since no intellectual refutation was possible. The refutation is indirect, "an artistic picture." It consisted originally of a series of three narratives entitled "From the Life (*Zhitie*) of the Deceased Monk and Priest, the Elder Zosima." Dostoevsky later added a second part, "Conversations and Teachings of the Elder Zosima."

"The Russian Monk" is indeed a saint's life (*zhitie*), that is, it is not a reliable factual biography, but a sort of dramatized sermon, the most popular genre in old Russian literature. The *zhitie* depicted the life and teachings of a holy person, usually idealized, with standardized and selected details to make the moral lesson as striking as possible. Events in the holy person's life that diverged from the didactic goal were omitted. If necessary elements in his life were lacking, they would be added. Legends and miracles were associated with the saint, testifying to his spiritual power. The life was usually written by disciples of the saint. When Zosima's biography, set down by his disciple Alyosha, is described as a *zhitie*, we must be prepared (as Alyosha himself was) for the introduction of the miraculous.

The second half of "The Russian Monk," a sermon, was also in keeping with the *zhitie* since it presented the *teachings* of the saint.

Let us examine the three narratives related by Zosima about his life before his conversion.

The first story is about Markel, Zosima's elder brother, an atheist who underwent a death-bed conversion at Easter. Nothing is said about his character or his past that could supply the basis for the sudden conversion. It remains a mystery.

The second story has to do with a duel contrived by Zosima before his conversion. He wishes to revenge himself on an innocent young man. The night before the duel Zosima savagely beats up his own orderly. On the morning of the duel he recalls the beating with shame, recalls Markel's conversion, and refuses to duel. There is no explanation of the change in his behavior between night and morning. It remains a mystery.

The last story is a confession made to Zosima by a mysterious stranger. Rebuffed by a girl he loved, the stranger had killed the girl and had managed to plant incriminating evidence on a servant who died soon after. The murderer then married, had children, and lived an irreproachable life as father, husband, and citizen. "And after that the punishment began." He began to suffer an intolerable isolation, walled off even from members of his family. This isolation reminds the reader of Raskolnikov after the murder of the pawnbroker, but there is an important difference.

Raskolnikov's reaction can be understood from the strength of his religious background, his close ties with his mother and sister, his obsession with the suffering of the poor. But nothing of this sort—nothing about the past or nature of the mysterious stranger—is introduced to make plausible his growing isolation. It remains a mystery.

In all three stories what could have made the conversions persuasive—psychological motivation—is missing. We are given not so much an artistic picture as a frame without a picture. And it is equally clear that this omission was deliberate. It is as if Dostoevsky wished to emphasize mystery as a dimension of human experience, even if this had to be done at the expense of the "artistic realism" which had so preoccupied him in his letter to Pobedonostsev. Yet, given the genre of the *zhitie*, the lack of realism could be expected.

Between the first and second of these stories is a short essay entitled "Of the Holy Scriptures in the Life of Father Zosima." This essay deals principally with the influence on the young Zosima of the Old Testament stories, especially the Book of Job. Two things are noteworthy in his account of the Book of Job: he retells the story in great detail, and he leaves much out. What is left out is revealing: Job's vehement insistence on his own innocence, his demand for a personal encounter with God to plead his innocence, and God's reply as the Voice in the Whirlwind. That is to say, Job's integrity and independence, his intellectual and spiritual energy—which in the end win God's favor—these are left out. Zosima's own emphasis is quite different, and rather surprising. He discusses Job's children, whom Satan destroyed as part of the testing of Job, and then the new children that Job received at the end:

> What mysteries are solved and revealed; God raises Job again, gives him wealth again. Many years pass by, and he has other children and loves them. But how could he love those new ones when those first children are no more, when he has lost them. Remembering them, how could he be fully happy with those new ones, however dear the new ones might be? But he could, he could. It's the great mystery of human life that old grief passes gradually into quiet tender joy.

The emphasis throughout is on children, perhaps as an indirect answer to Ivan's obsession with the suffering of children, but note how Zosima has shifted the emphasis: from the theological question of why Job must suffer and why must his children die (to vindicate God before Satan), Zosima shifts to a psychological question: how can Job recover from the loss of his first children and love the new children which God has provided for him? It turns out that this too is a mystery, the mystery of the healing power of time upon sorrow, but this mystery is at any rate psychologically valid, attested to by experience.

Thus Zosima offers as a sacred remembrance from his childhood a version of the Book of Job carefully pruned of Job's defiance and intellectual challenge of God, and also of God's reaction to this challenge, which involves the power of coercion. There is also the mystery of human nature whereby Job manages to forget his first children and love the new children. This essay easily blends into the three stories that emphasize the mystery of conversion, the enigma of human nature.

The second half of "The Russian Monk" consists of the teachings of Zosima: a long abstract series of exhortations, a rapturous, poetic, and at times sentimental sermon. Since it is abstract, it has even less artistic effect than the three stories related by Zosima. By adding this sermon, did Dostoevsky intend to strengthen the refutation he had made in the three stories?

At first glance the answer would seem to be no. I have mentioned, however, that Dostoevsky worked longer on "The Russian Monk" than on any other section of the novel. In exasperation he wrote his wife: "For a long time this Elder has been sitting on my neck, from the very beginning of the summer he has tormented me." The difficulty does not seem to be in theme or construction but in style. In creating Zosima's life and teachings Dostoevsky labored to reproduce the style of the *zhitie*. "This chapter is rapturous and poetical," wrote Dostoevsky to his editor. "The prototype [for Zosima] was in some teachings of Tikhon Zadonsky, and the naivete of the exposition was taken from the book on the wanderings of Father Parfeny." Dostoevsky's concern with style is also clear in another part of his letter:

> Even though I am in full agreement with the ideas that he [Zosima] expresses, if I had to express them personally *with my own voice*, I would have done so in a different form and in different words. He *couldn't* have used other words or spoken in a *different spirit* than what I have given him. Otherwise he would not have been an artistically created person. . . . I have taken this person and figure from old Russian monks and saints: in deep humility he holds limitless, naive hopes for the future of Russia.

We are indebted to two scholars, Pletnev and Komarovich, for intensive studies of Dostoevsky's sources for the style of "The Russian Monk." In addition to Zadonsky and Parfeny, Dostoevsky made use of Biblical texts, recollections of his visit to the saintly elder Amvrosy at the Optina Pustin monastery, various lives of the saints, etc. In short, a mosaic of old Russian literary style. Even Parfeny's memoirs, although written in the nineteenth century, follow the traditions of old Russian literature. Yet the question must be raised: if Dostoevsky wishes to refute the views of the Grand Inquisitor, and indirectly by an artistic picture, why choose a consciously archaic style which would seem to set the refutation even more distantly into the past?

This question can be resolved by examining the style. The prose is rhythmic, sounds and words are repeated, especially *umilenie* (tender emotion) as noun, verb, adjective, and adverb. *Umilenie*: the cult of tears and of the heart, which is so characteristic of Zosima. The effect of *umilenie*, according to Pletnev, "is to melt sin away and in the joyous tears of the repentant sinner arises the new man." The sinner's tears are joyous because he knows he is being forgiven. Much of this came from Parfeny's book, but the studied repetition of tears, heart, tender emotion in "The Russian Monk" seems to me to have a special function. The reader is being acted on to open his heart as well. There are other stylistic examples that produce the same effect. Zosima often uses caressing diminutives, which are not characteristic of old Russian literature but do reinforce the impression of a warm-hearted open person who lives by his heart. Sentences often begin with verbs followed by noun-subjects, building up parallel structures as, for example, in Zosima's account of how he later met his orderly Afanasy or Zosima's version of the Book of Job:

> *Byla u menia togda kniga, sviashchennaia istoriia . . .*
> *Posetilo menia nekotoroe proniknovenie dukhovnoe . . .*
> *Povela matushka menia odnogo . . . vo khram Gospoden' . . .*
> *Smotrel ia umilenno . . .*
> *Vyshel na sredinu khrama otrok s bol'shoiu knigoi . . .*
> *Byl muzh v zemle Un . . .*

Such parallel verb-subject structures recall the word order in lives of saints or Russian folklore. Also common is the practice of beginning each sentence with "and"—reminiscent of the Bible. Modern Russian and Church Slavic unobtrusively blend as in: *"Na vsiak den' i chas, na vsiakuiu minutu . . ."* ["Every day and hour every minute . . ."]. *Vsiak den'* is Church Slavic, *vsiakuiu minutu* is Russian. The Russian reader may vaguely recall that the phrase *navsiak den'* parallels the structure of *"Izhe na vsiakoe vremia i na vsiakii chas . . ."* ["Who at any time and at any hour . . ."], and is part of an important daily prayer, the Great Doxology (*Velikoe Slavoslovie*). The whole chapter consists of such deft reminders. And associated with these recollected words and sounds is an esthetic picture. Zosima remembers that as an eight-year-old boy he heard the story of Job read in church for the first time, while "the incense rose from the censer and softly floated upwards and, overhead in the cupola, mingled in rising waves with the sunlight that streamed in the little window."

The function of Zosima's style is not only to assure its "realism"—a style that authenticates his profession—but by verbal legerdemain it works on the Russian reader's *unconscious*, making him recall his own childhood. Bits and pieces of sermons, Biblical stories, esthetic images, sonorous words, incense, rhythmical prose—all these stir the imagination of a child and are linked to innocence, goodness, Christianity. As Zosima says, "There are no memories more precious than those of early childhood in one's first home." And these unconscious memories of childhood, the period when one is most impressionable, can exert a powerful influence in later life precisely because they are unconscious. Thus Mitya Karamazov may have been saved from killing his father by the unconscious memory of that pound of nuts once given him by a pious kindly German doctor who, at the same time, made the little Mitya repeat: *"Gott der Vater, Gott der Sohn, und Gott der heilige Geist."* Father and son are divinely linked. And the good doctor testifies in court that twenty-three years later Mitya remembered those words. Alyosha emphasizes the importance of good childhood impressions to his twelve disciples at the end of the novel.

Thus the indirect refutation of the Grand Inquisitor is contained not only in the subject matter of Zosima's speech and the veneration of the mystery of man's nature but also in something very practical: in the cunning mosaic of Church Slavic and modern Russian in which Zosima's words are inlaid, so that the Russian reader unconsciously responds with what is best in his own childhood, with the most potent memories of religious and esthetic experience. "The Russian Monk" is the literary equivalent of a precious, hallowed old church icon.

This refutation of the Grand Inquisitor is so indirect, however, that Dostoevsky had good reason to worry whether his "artistic picture would be understood" and whether he "had reached even an inch of his goal." He wrote in his notebook a scathing attack on his critics: "The villains teased me for my *uneducated* and reactionary faith in God. These blockheads did not even dream of such a powerful negation of God as was put into the Inquisitor and in the preceding chapter, to which *the whole novel* serves as an answer."

"*The whole novel* serves as an answer." The italics are Dostoevsky's. Here we have the true refutation of the Grand Inquisitor: in the movements made successively by Alyosha, by Mitya, and by Ivan. Christ's silence before the Grand Inquisitor, deepened by Zosima's non-logical "artistic picture," is now to be made psychologically plausible. The frame of "The Russian Monk," with the pale sketch of Zosima erased or to be covered over as in a palimpsest, is now to be filled with a vivid picture: the destinies of the Karamazov brothers.

Let us glance briefly at those destinies.

Zosima's recollections end with his death, a painless and graceful death in which he sinks to the earth and thanks God: the traditional ending in a saint's life. His death releases Alyosha from tutelage. Alyosha now faces in freedom his first crisis. Zosima's body stinks; the miracle has not come to pass. The Karamazov sensuality breaks out in the despairing Alyosha; he goes to Grushenka to be tempted and seduced. But she too faces a crisis. Should she forget her five years of laceration and return to the Polish officer who had ruined her but who now promised to make amends and marry her—or should she revenge herself upon him for her miseries? A mysterious interaction takes place. Learning of the death of Zosima, Grushenka forgets her own problem, her own ego, and feels acutely Alyosha's agony and bewilderment. This is her "onion." And Alyosha gratefully offers her an onion too: he appeals to her higher nature (which no one hitherto had thought she possessed, hence she too had not thought she possessed it): he tells her she will not yield to her egoistic dream of revenge for humiliation. Grushenka has already taken the first step of suppressing her ego in feeling for Alyosha; she now goes further, suppresses her evil longings, and goes in a forgiving mood to her Polish officer. This episode climaxes in the "Cana of Galilee" scene in which Alyosha kisses the earth in acknowledgment of the true miracle—not the false miracle of coercive power, of Zosima's bones not stinking—but the true miracle that arises each day in each person when he freely follows the verdict of his heart and prefers doing good to doing evil. This movement, powerful and plausible, is the first answer to the Grand Inquisitor.

The second answer is provided by Mitya Karamazov. Despite his passionate nature, his deep hatred of his father, his need of money, his vow to kill his father; even given the opportunity and the weapon to commit the murder with, he finds within himself sufficient strength to run away from the temptation of parricide. Psychologically, regarded theoretically, this "self-denial" on his part would seem improbable. Yet no critic has ever questioned the power and plausibility of Mitya's self-denial. It is psychologically plausible and effective: men enslaved by passion—the presumed subjects of the kingdom of the Grand Inquisitor—are shown to have the inner strength to overcome their passion. This is the second answer to the Grand Inquisitor.

The third answer is provided by Ivan Karamazov. From his rational standpoint he did not kill his father. Even if he had killed him there should be no regret, for how can one regret killing a *reptile* (as he called Fyodor)? Nor should he have conscience stings like Raskolnikov since he is an atheist and there is nothing in his background suggesting a religious upbringing or the importance of his mother (which is stressed as motivation for his brother Alyosha). Nevertheless he is mysteriously driven to confess publicly his role in the murder. If Smerdyakov had murdered his father, then Ivan had tacitly approved it. Still more humiliating for a proud person like Ivan is the realization that even when confessing, he will not be believed: he has no evidence, and Smerdyakov has hanged himself. Confessing in such circumstances is an utterly irrational act, senseless and ridiculous. And yet something drives him to confess. It is not surprising that he goes insane. This is the third answer to the Grand Inquisitor.

These three movements of Alyosha, Mitya, and Ivan are just as powerful and persuasive as—or even more powerful than—the intellectual arguments advanced by Ivan to Alyosha in the chapters on "Rebellion" and "The Grand Inquisitor." These "arguments" of all the brothers—their movements—have one common feature: they are not intellectual but are made with the whole of man's being. And for that reason they are all the more powerful and convincing. We may forget the complicated threads of Ivan's arguments but we cannot forget the destinies of the three brothers.

We see now that the two "culminating points" in the novel, the ideological debate between the Grand Inquisitor and the Russian Monk, are not placed haphazardly but just where they would be most effective: as a prelude that ushers in the main action.

We have also seen that the defects of "The Russian Monk" are both deliberate and unavoidable, arising from the very problem of an "indirect" refutation of the Grand Inquisitor. To make "The Russian Monk" as imaginatively powerful as "The Grand Inquisitor" Dostoevsky would have had to make the conversions of Markel, Zosima, and the Mysterious Stranger psychologically plausible. This would have been to duplicate what he would do so effectively in tracing the destinies of the three Karamazov brothers. It would also have destroyed the point of the debate as an ideological *prelude* to the action. "The Russian Monk" is best understood as a two-dimensional icon that has its fourth dimension in the reader's unconscious memories of childhood.

Finally, by transferring our attention from the Grand Inquisitor to the novel as a whole we have restored a necessary balance. No longer is Ivan seen as the hero of the novel (Rozanov, Camus, Rahv). The hero is the spirit of God acting through all the Karamazovs. This is the refutation contained in Christ's silence before the Grand Inquisitor.

ROGER B. ANDERSON

Mythical Implications of Father Zosima's Religious Teachings[†]

One of the most perplexing questions in *The Brothers Karamazov* is the manner in which Father Zosima serves as Dostoevsky's spokesman on matters of spiritual faith. Zosima's teachings emphasize humility, a mystical union of man and the world, and undifferentiated love; the key to faith for him is the individual's own emotion, the wisdom of the heart.[1] In keeping with the deeply personal quality of Zosima's message, he teaches in the form of short homilies and stories from his own past. * * *

Because Zosima's teachings are personal and symbolic, they are at odds with logical formulations and intellectual programs. His mystical love inspires awe in those he meets, but he offers no clear means for following or reproducing his insights. He is as mute before ordinary standards of consistency as Christ is before the Grand Inquisitor. * * *

The most disturbing problem in Zosima's symbolic and fragmentary teachings is the difficulty of labelling them as unambiguously Christian. Zosima's model was a composite of the Orthodox *starets*,[2] but the church was divided in its attitude toward the fictional elder, and many ecclesiastics were less than pleased by the comparison.[3] For one thing, Zosima expresses a disturbing tendency, by Christian standards, to worship the earth and all forms of creation as being endowed with holy meaning. George Gibian refers to the elder's sense of the soil as a mixture of Christianity and animism.[4] The Russian critic, R. Pletnev, goes further, writing that Zosima leads us back to the ancient Russian folk image of "Moist Mother Earth" and its antecedents in anthropomorphism and pantheism. He considers Dostoevsky to be close to the *Strigol'niki* heresy, the old Russian practice of confessing to the soil rather than to Christian priests.[5]

* * *

† From *Slavic Review*, Vol. 38, No. 2 (June 1979), 272–75, 277–83, 286–89. Reprinted by permission of the American Association for the Advancement of Slavic Studies.

1. For a critical review of Zosima's sentimentally based faith, see Nathan Rosen, "Style and Structure in *The Brothers Karamazov*," *Russian Literature Triquarterly*, 1, no. 1 (1971): 252–54. Rosen contends that it is inherently weaker than the Grand Inquisitor's critique against belief. For a discussion of the Grand Inquisitor as victor in his logical attack on Christ and faith for its own sake, see Edward Wasiolek, *Dostoevsky, The Major Fiction* (Cambridge, Mass.: MIT Press, 1964), 164–70.

2. Dostoevsky used as his model Starets Amvrosii of Optina Pustyn', a contemporary of Dostoevsky with whom he had a short acquaintance in 1878, and Bishop Tikhon of Zadonsk, who lived in the eighteenth century.

3. Mochulsky states that "not only liberal criticism, but also those who venerated the 'old monks and prelates,' such as Konstantin Leont'ev, did not acknowledge the Elder Zosima as the ideal of the 'Russian monk.' The image that Dostoevsky created was likewise rejected by the Elders of Optina" (see Konstantin Mochulsky, *Dostoevsky*, trans. M. A. Minihan [Princeton: Princeton University Press, 1967], 589). In 1886, government censors withheld permission to publish a separate edition of Zosima's biography and teachings on the basis of their subversive potential. For a discussion of the question, see V. K. Lebedev, "Otryvok iz romana *Brat'ia Karamazovy* pered sudom tsenzury," *Russkaia literatura*, 1970, no. 2, 124.

4. See George Gibian, "Dostoevskij's Use of Russian Folklore," *Journal of American Folklore*, 69 (July–September 1956): 242.

5. See R. Pletnev, "Zemlia," *O Dostoevskom: Sbornik statei*, 3 vols., ed. A. L. Bem (Prague, 1929), 1:157.

I propose that Zosima's spiritual vision is clearer when we view it from the perspective of myth; that is, his teachings represent a cluster of discernible themes—which refer to questions of nature, the related issues of time and immortality, and the notion of the individual's place within his group (his nation or his people)—that are similar in outline and function to motifs common to myth. Zosima's teachings diverge from the specifics of church doctrine. They refer to an older spiritual impulse in man that is fundamental to mythical thought. * * *

Zosima's ecstatic attachment to nature and the earth distances him from his church. He calls for his listeners to venerate the soil, to water it with tears: "love all God's creation, the whole and every grain of it. Love every leaf, every ray of God's light. Love the animals, love the plants, love everything."[6] In his book on Dostoevsky, L. A. Zander speaks of Zosima's "love for the earth and 'loyality' to it" as allusions to "pagan virtues."[7] Zander uses the compromissary term "panentheism" in order to read a Christian corollary into the elder's adoration of the earth. G. P. Fedotov, in his classic *The Russian Religious Mind*, speaks more bluntly of Dostoevsky as a typically Russian expression of pre-Christian attachment to the soil. Father Zosima seems a fitting example of what Fedotov terms "sensual mysticism," "the greatest religious temptation for a Russian will be theism of a sensual (hylozoistic) kind."[8] And Konstantin Mochulsky candidly calls Dostoevsky's elder pantheistic.[9] The specific goal of A. B. Gibson's posthumously published book on Dostoevsky is a Christian assessment of the author. But Gibson is also openly bemused by Zosima's place in such a scheme, and writes: "Not only nature but supernature is glorified without mention of God." Immediately afterward, however, he states that "Dostoevsky's natural approach to God was through his manifestations; at the end of his life through the joy and gladness of nature."[1]

* * *

Examining Zosima as a representative of the *starets* tradition reveals more specific discrepancies. In 1921, the metropolitan of Volhynia, Antonii Khrapovitskii, suggested that Zosima is an authentic evangelical representative of the Orthodox faith within the *starets* tradition. But Sven Linnér, who has recently discussed Zosima's links to the historical *startsy*, considers this opinion to be oversimplified and a distortion of Zosima's essential teachings. He quotes Konstantin Leontiev's assertion that within the Orthodox tradition, Dostoevsky's religious views, as articulated by Zosima, were "rosy-colored" and inauthentic. Specifically, Leontiev was dissatisfied with Zosima's lack of any "fear of the Lord,"[2] for the elder

6. F. M. Dostoevskii, *Sobranie sochinenii v desiati tomakh* (Moscow, 1958), 9:399. All references will be made in the text following the quoted material; for convenience, the quotes will be in English using the Constance Garnett translation as revised and edited by R. E. Matlaw (F. M. Dostoevsky, *The Brothers Karamazov* [New York: W. W. Norton, 1976]).
7. L. A. Zander, *Dostoevsky* (New York: Haskell House, 1975), 56.
8. See G. P. Fedotov, *The Russian Religious Mind*, 2 vols. (Cambridge: Harvard UP, 1946 and 1966), 1:56, 63, 20.
9. See Mochulsky, *Dostoevsky*, p. 589.
1. A. B. Gibson, *The Religion of Dostoevsky* (Philadelphia: Westminster Press, 1974), 195–96.
2. See Sven Linnér, *Starets Zosima in the Brothers Karamazov: A Study in the Mimesis of Virtue* (Stockholm: Almqvist & Wiksell, 1975), 95–98.

considers our earthly life joyful rather than a vale of tears, as taught by the church. Furthermore, Zosima reflects none of the rigorous regime of the Christian *starets* as represented by Amvrosii of Optina and Tikhon of Zadonsk, the proclaimed models for Dostoevsky's elder. Amvrosii reflects Orthodoxy's view that earthly life for a monk is a constant battle against his passions; the monk hopes for salvation only in the afterlife, and in fear of the Last Judgment. But, as Linnér puts it: "This certainly differs from the bright hope with which Zosima faces eternity."[3] Zosima preaches celebration in this life, because, if the individual but acknowledges it, paradise is already achieved. In the same vein, there are basic differences between Dostoevsky's elder and Tikhon of Zadonsk. Zosima sees life as part of a great chain linking the individual to eternity, a mythical intertwining of life and death: on the other hand, Tikhon, says Linnér, "looked upon death as the borderline between a life of constantly growing uncertainty and eternal bliss or damnation."[4]

* * *

The liberties Zosima takes with traditional Orthodox doctrines are noted and emphasized by other characters in the novel. Several monks are either suspicious of or hostile to the elder's unusual religious views. Father Ferapont and the traveling monk from Obdorsk are clearly presented as examples of perverted and overly formalized asceticism, and their aversion to Zosima elicits the reader's sympathy for the elder's virtues. These two aberrant monks are not alone in their criticism of Zosima, however. Many of the most respected ascetics in the monastery condemn several of Zosima's spiritual practices: "His teaching was false; he taught that life is a great joy and not a vale of tears"; "he did not recognize material fire in hell"; "he was not strict in fasting"; "'he abused the sacrament of confession,' the fiercest opponent of the institution of elders added in a malicious whisper" (415). Earlier in the novel, this charge of improper confession was also brought against Zosima by Fedor Karamazov. The early decomposition of the elder's body, of course, is testimony to many that Zosima had strayed far from the regular teachings of the church, that the rapid corruption of his body revealed his spiritual "corruption" while alive.[5]

Zosima's constant modification and loosening of Christian doctrine, which were discussed above, raise the question of what constitutes the elder's spiritual vision. Christianity teaches man to seek the meaning of his life and his world through specific theological dogmas (such as the Trinity, the virgin birth, grace, salvation, the Resurrection, and so forth), tenets which are instruments of mediation standing between man in his world and a higher order of existence which is called God. In this sense, man's behavior and actions take on meaning and are judged in terms of values that are above and outside his natural world. Myth, as Richard Chase has

3. Ibid., 102–3.
4. Ibid., 110.
5. Maloney attributes to Sorskii "the necessity of weeping for our sins in order to receive forgiveness in this life before the general judgment when tears will be useless to remit our sins." G. A. Maloney, *Russian Hesychasm: The Spirituality of Nil Sorsky* (The Hague: Mouton, 1973), 133.

phrased it, is different from religion, in that it conceives of the sacred as raw "voltage," which is immanent in the natural world.[6] Since myth regards the ordinary world as already filled with preternatural significance, it tends to have a much looser conception of creeds, ecclesiastical categories, and definitions of the spiritual than does developed religion.

Thus, myth weaves the sacred into the texture of ordinary life, into the here and now. This distinguishes it from teachings of the organized church, through which we confront the duality of temporal, as opposed to sacred, planes of life. Surely Zosima similarly mixes the sacred and the temporal in his teachings about heaven and hell as being part of this life, in his adoration of all existence as being holy, and in his admonition to partake in all of life as spiritual practice. Philip Wheelwright, a prominent contemporary critic of myth, speaks of the immanence of the sacred in the natural world as the "transcendental tenor [which] looms darkly behind the scene as something vague, inarticulate, yet somehow of tremendous, even final, importance and consequentiality."[7] Myth predates organized religion in man's cultural evolution, and has remained too elastic to serve as an explanatory instrument in any developed theological or philosophical sense.[8] Similarly, Zosima's homilies seem more suggestive and evocative than the more organized teachings of Orthodoxy.

* * *

The view of Zosima's faith as mythical is necessarily geared to the network of images he provides. There is no developed explanation of his mysteries. As in myth, those images are themselves parts of the divine order and are to be participated in directly, without explanation.[9] The constituent parts of Zosima's message are his emphasis on nature, his understanding of time and immortality, and his enigmatic idea of the group and its organic national identity. Each component contributes to his message of holistic union and simultaneously repeats that union through integrated symbols. Myth provides a framework for treating Zosima's teachings separately, while allowing an appreciation of how those teachings fit into a major principle within the novel.

Zosima develops his vision of faith within the context of nature. He speaks of watering the soil with tears of ecstacy; of venerating birds, rocks, and trees; of blessing the sun each morning and evening. He says life is a garden sown by God, and whatever grows "lives and is alive only through the feeling of its contact with other mysterious worlds. . . . Water it [the soil] and it will bring forth fruit" (401). For him, human participation in nature's harmony is an integral part of religious faith, it is heaven realized on earth. The central symbol linking human life to transcendent harmony is the elder's repeated image of the kernel of wheat. (The key word here is harmony and its implication of continuity and stability.) The wheat kernel decomposes in the earth and, by its dissolution, produces

---

6. See Richard Chase, *Quest for Myth* (Baton Rouge, La.: Louisiana State UP, 1949), 69–70.
7. Philip Wheelwright, "The Semantic Approach to Myth," in T. A. Sebeok, ed., *Myth: A Symposium* (Bloomington: Indiana UP), 167.
8. See Chase, *Quest for Myth*, 78.
9. See Mircea Eliade, *The Myth of the Eternal Return* (London: Routledge and Kegan Paul, 1955), 31.

new life: "Except a grain of wheat fall into the ground and die, it abideth alone; but if it die, it bringeth forth much fruit" (John 12:24). Zosima's focus on the generation of life from death is a fundamental symbol of fertility in world mythology; it is present in the first Egyptian solar myths (which also use the image of the grain of wheat in reference to Osiris), in Slavic myths referred to by Fedotov and Sokolov,[1] as well as in the Christian reference of John 12:24. Decomposition and the apparent death of nature each year intensify man's sense of his own death. Frye speaks of myth as a means of displacing primal psychological preoccupations by symmetrical and archetypal forms (usually vegetative symbols), which can then be worked out in a satisfying manner, one that entails the overcoming of death through life's cyclic repetition.[2] Man's fear that nature's physical death, and his own, might be permanent has been a persistent terror throughout the ages, and it has traditionally been allayed through nature's return to life in the spring—the kernel of wheat.

For Zosima, too, death is not an end but part of a greater repetitive process; life is not lost at death but reemerges in new forms, both in the vegetative cycle and in each human generation. In myth and for Zosima, the kernel of wheat implies the principle of rebirth and continuity of human life, albeit in altered form. As the elder says, once an event occurs, it continues to have an impact on all existence. The death of Markel, for example, was not an end but the humus out of which Zosima's own faith had grown: "I was young then, a child, but a lasting impression, a hidden feeling of it all, remained in my heart, ready to rise up and respond when the time came. So indeed it happened" (363). He considers Markel "alive," not only in his own life, but in Alesha's spiritual development as well: "He appeared first to me in my childhood and here at the end of my pilgrimage, he seems to have come to me again. It is marvelous, fathers and teachers, that Aleksei, who has some, though not a great, resemblance in face, seems to me so like him spiritually, that many times I have taken him for that young man, my brother, mysteriously come back to me at the end of my pilgrimage, as a reminder and an inspiration" (358). The decomposition of Zosima's body upon his death is particularly interesting in this regard, for it re-creates precisely what nature does each autumn (the time of year of the elder's death). He not only decomposes in physical terms but, like Markel, he "fertilizes" the lives of those who follow him, especially Alesha's. What we have, then, is three generations of human life— Markel, Zosima, and Alesha—each of whom is linked to the same spiritual insights. It is clear that there is no end to the spiritual energy that flows through each of them; it does not die any more than nature dies at the end of its cycle. All life, natural and human, reappears in new forms as part of the same generative process. The denial of death in man and nature has always been the essence of the mythology of the sun and fertility, reflected in Persephone, Adonis, Osiris, Moist Mother Earth, and so forth. In regard to the latter, Fedotov writes: "In Mother Earth, who remains the core of Russian religion, converge the most secret and deep

---

1. See Fedotov, *Russian Religious Mind*, 1:18–19; and Ju. M. Sokolov, *Russian Folklore*, trans. C. R. Smith (New York: Macmillan, 1950), 165–69.
2. See Northrop Frye, *Anatomy of Criticism: Four Essays* (Princeton: Princeton UP), 139–40.

religious feelings of the folk. Beneath the beautiful veil of grass and flowers, the people venerate with awe the black moist depths, the source of all fertilizing powers, the nourishing breast of nature, and their own last resting place."[3]

Zosima's exhortation that people unite in spiritual love is an appropriate restatement of what man has always considered a constant in nature—the undifferentiated blending of the seasons, of life within death. The willingness to dissolve as a temporal individual and to join nature's cycle of perpetual regeneration in new forms held great attraction for traditional man as it does for Zosima. Mother Earth, a cliché that Viacheslav Ivanov sees as a guiding principle in Dostoevsky's fiction, has been a common denominator for mankind since the beginning.[4] Zosima's special vision of nature as pertinent to the human sphere holds the key to spiritual release from death. Nature is the womb of life for the elder, not its grave. Nevertheless, there are characters in the novel who cannot or will not accept a mystery that entails their personal dissolution, and Dostoevsky uses them as a counterpoint to Zosima's notion of faith. As a result of the elder's death, the town and monastery alike anticipate miracles. Such predictability, a longstanding *topos* in saints' lives, would be most soothing. For them, miracles are events that alter the natural process (a pleasant odor from the corpse or a halt to putrefaction altogether, for example). They would have nature's rhythm subordinated to their own static measurements of proof. They deem "unseemly" the very heart of Zosima's vision of faith—the decomposition of one life from which new forms might grow. Here again the kernel of wheat is a touchstone for understanding the necessity of dissolution and the question of process and repetition in the vegetative cycle. Even in death, Zosima demonstrates that man gains spiritual faith by yielding his individuality to the whole of nature, not by demanding that nature adjust to his personal system of temporal expectations.

* * *

Zosima's emphasis on the vegetative cycle implies a special relation to time. As he blends life and death within his ideal of faith, he also blends the usual notions of past, present, and future into one repeating entity. For Zosima, each moment can reveal the sacred, and, therefore, ordinary concepts of "past" or "future" lose their meaning. The elder is an example of what Joseph Campbell has described as a primary quality of myth—the special capacity of the mind to perceive a transcendent secret which is timeless and which holds all life together, regardless of its temporal frame.[5] Graphic examples of Zosima's special understanding of time occur as he retells the story of Job: "the greatness of it lies in the very fact that it is a mystery—that the passing show and the eternal verity are brought together in it. In the face of the earthly truth, the eternal truth is accomplished" (365). He speaks of a sacred mystery that, once revealed in time, becomes unchangeable, applicable to all future moments in its original potency: "And Job's praising the Lord serves not only Him but all creation for generations and generations, and forever and forever . . ." (365). The present

---

3. Fedotov, *Russian Religious Mind*, 1:12.
4. See Viacheslav Ivanov, *Freedom and the Tragic Life: A Study in Dostoevsky*, trans. N. Cameron (New York: Noonday Press, 1960), 55, 77.
5. See Joseph Campbell, *The Hero With a Thousand Faces* (Princeton: Princeton UP, 1969), 17.

and future for him, then, repeat a single process of contact between divine revelation and human awareness. We are again reminded of the elder's intriguing remark about the presence of heaven now, all around man if he could only realize it, rather than sealed off in some future condition. Throughout, Zosima insists on a special, undifferentiated union of states (whether it be life and death or temporal categories), whereas logical man seeks to keep those states separate.

Zosima's freedom from linear time is one of the basic preoccupations of myth. As Frank Kermode has succintly phrased it, the notion of cyclical time is a primary vehicle of the human imagination for handling the question of immortality.[6] By associating human action with the mystery of nature's yearly cycle, says Kermode, man overcomes the idea of his own disappearance in time. Mircea Eliade, who has written extensively on the question of the conception of time in myth, considers that time is outside history in mythical thought, it is repetitive, a reflection of some unchanging cosmology.[7] To speak of one's life as a series of events terminated by death is unacceptable and absurd for myth. Thus, for Zosima, the sacred referent of one's temporal life is not diminished by death, but goes on. Speaking of those who might refuse to listen to his homilies he says: "And if they are not saved hereafter, then their sons will be saved, for your light will not die even when you are dead. The righteous man departs but his light remains. Men are always saved after the death of the deliverer. . . . You are working for the whole, you are acting for the future" (403). Berdiaev seemed to have addressed the same issue when he wrote: "The doctrine of fusion with the divine does not mean the immortality of personality but only the immortality of the divine."[8]

The elder contemplates time patiently. He sees each person attaining faith at his own pace: "If, after your kiss, he [the criminal] goes away untouched, mocking at you, do not let that be a stumbling block to you. It shows his time has not yet come, but it will come in due course" (402). Zosima's patience is based on his own past experience: Markel's visions of nature affect him only after several years have passed, during his conversion at the duel. He also, of course, thinks of the past as repeating itself in the future in that Alesha bears the spiritual features he remembers in Markel. In Zosima's mind, time demarcations fade as he dwells on the constant infusion of a single cosmic truth within all time. He feels no haste in reaching a different or improved future; nothing is in danger of being lost. He possesses the knowledge—common in myth—that the present and future will only reveal what has been vouchsafed in the past.

* * *

The question of salvation, of course, resounds throughout the novel. Each of the three legitimate brothers experiences, to some degree, an individualized resurrection. For each, salvation flows from acknowledgment of a common bond with others and from acceptance of broad mutual responsibility as a great mystical truth in life. (Zosima had gone

6. See Frank Kermode, *The Sense of an Ending, Studies in the Theory of Fiction* (New York: Oxford UP, 1967), 77.
7. See Eliade, *Myth of Eternal Return*, 141.
8. Nikolai Berdiaev, *The Divine and Human*, trans. R. M. French (London: G. Bles, 1949), 152.

through a similarly harrowing experience with his orderly before the duel many years earlier.) The individual gains insight into the spiritual composition of life through the acceptance of collectivity itself, the organic union of the family on an extended scale.

Although Dostoevsky believed in actual resurrection after death,[9] he also subscribed to the idea that the ability of the living to love in this life was necessary for the resurrection of their forefathers.[1] We do not have to become overly involved in Dostoevsky's eschatology in order to gain insight into Zosima's notion of a mystical community. The elder's lessons on resurrection revolve around his dead brother, what he has learned because of him, and how Alesha is destined to repeat that same mysterious lesson in his own future. The cyclical quality of influence from the dead upon the living is clear. Zosima can pass on faith in love to Alesha only because he received the gift of love from Markel. It is the living who must, by their free choice, participate in or reject the miracle of the dead's past love. If they choose to participate, they enter into a community that includes the dead along with the living, and, in so doing, the living return the dead's love to life. If they deny love by emphasizing their individuality, they cut themselves off from their forefathers, for denial of love means rejection of the essence of their dead predecessors. The callous individual who so denies his ancestors destroys the chance for their continued life with the living.[2]

To achieve personal spiritual fulfillment, says Zosima, the individual must acknowledge his identity as a member of the Russian collective and the single body of belief it represents as an organic entity. Again, the essential similarity between members of a family and the nation is clear for Dostoevsky. As Fedotov explains, the direct participation of a dead family member in the affairs of the living refers more to the ancient folk beliefs of the *rod* or gens in Russia than to Orthodox teachings of personal resurrection.[3] If Zosima's vision of spiritual collectivity is understood as reflecting age-old Russian practices, some apparent ambiguities in his teachings gain clarity. The *rod* cult was a Slavic form of ancestor worship. One of its chief practices was the veneration of the departed ancestor at a feast at which the respected deceased was thought to join the living in an atmosphere of celebration. At that time, the dead, hopefully, gave advice to the living as to how to meet the future. Sokolov remarks on the

9. For Dostoevsky's specific comments on this topic, see his entry for December 1876 in F. M. Dostoevskii, *Dnevnik pisatelia*, 3 vols. (Paris: YMCA Press, 1946), 2:474–75.
1. See Linnér, *Starets Zosima*, 203.
2. Such theories about the living having a direct responsibility for resurrecting the dead are apparently close to the philosophy of Dostoevsky's contemporary, N. E. Fedorov. N. O. Losskii summarizes Fedorov's main idea: "One must live not for oneself (egoism) and not for the others (altruism), but with everyone and for everyone; this is the union of the living (sons) for the resurrection of the dead (fathers)" (N. O. Losskii, *History of Russian Philosophy* [New York: International Universities Press, 1951], 78). Sven Linnér puts the apparent similarity to Fedorov in clear perspective, when he says that Fedorov had in mind a science fiction scheme by which future man would gain such technological control over life and the physical world that he would be able to call the dead back to actual physical life (Linnér, *Starets Zosima*, 199–203). Such notions were basically alien to Dostoevsky's imagination. His references to Fedorov's "scientific" visions undoubtedly have more to do with the author's curiosity about their coincidental resemblance to his own theme than actual influence by Fedorov.
3. See Fedotov, *Russian Religious Mind*, 1:16.

similarities of certain rituals of the ancestor holidays with those of Russian weddings.[4] Alesha's vision of Zosima during the elder's funeral duplicates these folklore *topoi*: Alesha dreams he is at a wedding feast where he shares wine and food with Zosima (now dead but interacting with the novice during the feast), who advises him about his future: "Begin your work, dear one, begin it, gentle one" (399).

The *rod* cult is itself an extension of Slavic agricultural mythology.[5] Zosima's central image of the kernel of wheat "dying" recapitulates not only his own death, but the postharvest period—nature's "death"—during which Zosima dies. The kernel's renewal of life in the spring is, as Sokolov maintains, connected to the power of ancestors to affect a good crop and offer spiritual advice to the living. This is certainly evidence of Zosima's effect on Alesha who grows enormously in spiritual terms after his vision of the elder. Alesha is, as most critics point out, the spiritual heir in whom the "kernel" of Zosima's wisdom will next flourish.[6]

Zosima weaves the notion of the individual's immortality within a national collective into the Christian doctrine of personal salvation. The significance of community for the elder is visible in Dostoevsky's notebooks for the novel. Notes for book 6, in which the elder's teachings are concentrated, refer even more emphatically than the novel to the same idea: "History consists in the fact that all will be united . . . the family becomes more encompassing; other than relatives enter into it, the beginning of a new organism begins to develop . . . from an individual organism to a general organism."[7] The inference of ancient *rod* beliefs clarifies Dostoevsky's idea. Fedotov suggests that by sharing ancestor holidays at a common time the village (and, by implication, all of Russia) becomes something of an extended family: "In this procedure all social life is shaped as the extension of family life and all moral relations among men are raised to the level of blood kinship."[8] Fedotov similarly describes the pagan Russian emphasis on the idea of the individual's immortality as meaningful only in terms of the greater entity of his people's immortality: "Russian paganism (as well as the primitive Greek) considered the individual only as a transient moment in the eternal life of the rod."[9] In this sense, Zosima's view of heaven as acknowledged union and hell as the

4. See Sokolov, *Russian Folklore*, 165.
5. Ibid., 168–69.
6. The folkloric and mythological implications of the novel are by no means restricted to Zosima. V. E. Vetlovskaia has assessed the structural similarities between Alesha and the third son of Russian folk tales (the wise fool). Moreover, she suggests that the folkloric elements of the third son also correspond to several saints' lives (see V. E. Vetlovskaia, *Poetika romana Brat'ia Karamazovy* [Leningrad, 1977], 194–97). In a related article, she discusses Alesha as a modern literary version of the revered Saint Aleksei Man-of-God. She concentrates on the Russian folk versions of that *zhitie*, in which she finds a combination of the worldly and divine in indiscriminate love (see V. E. Vetlovskaia, "Literaturnye i fol'klornye istochniki Brat'ev Karamazovykh [Zhitie Alekseia cheloveka bozhiia i dukhovnyi stikh o nem]," in V. Ia. Kirpotin, ed., *Dostoevskii i russkie pisateli: Traditsii, novatorstvo, masterstvo* [Moscow, 1971], 345–50). Whereas the typical saint's life emphasizes the separation of daily matters from ascetic devotion, Vetlovskaia says that Alesha, like Aleksei Man-of-God in folk versions of his life, joins the duality into one all-inclusive love. The source of such interpenetration of secular and divine love in the novel itself is, of course, Zosima. Indirectly, then, we have added evidence of a broad folkloric design behind the elder's meaning for the reader.
7. Wasiolek, *Notebooks for "The Brothers Karamazov,"* 93.
8. Fedotov, *Russian Religious Mind*, 1:16.
9. Ibid., 18.

individual's exclusion from his group takes on special significance. The elder clearly states: "Salvation will come from the people, from their faith and their meekness" (291). Zosima's myth, like Russian myth, insists that the individual can gain immortality only by acknowledging the greater spiritual reality of the group. The group is eternal, immutable. The individual, if alone, perishes; but if he becomes part of that group his life goes on as part of the whole, regardless of his own passing. Again we confront Zosima's mystical reference to the kernel of wheat and his special notion of regeneration in life.

The examination of how Zosima's teachings are constituted and the assessment of how they fit together into a coherent whole has shown that, in large measure, unity is clearest when we depart from a traditional Christian focus. The elder most certainly reshapes some Christian doctrine (such as the Hesychast doctrine of tears), ignores other tenets (such as the usual ecclesiastical definitions of heaven and hell), and emphasizes still others with a fervor that exceeds conventional church definitions (such as humility and communal identity of the believing body). Although Zosima's teachings do not deny any Christian reference—for it is clear that they do apply—it is more accurate to say that his Christian vision relies in a basic way on mythical elements of Russian folk culture. As a result, to understand fully Zosima's teachings on the sacred we must appreciate the extent to which mythical sources penetrate and color his teachings.

Dostoevsky's elder and the structural constants of myth both perceive a pervasive unity between sacred and temporal planes throughout creation. That unity integrates man with his fellows (his tribe or *rod*), with his physical world (nature and its marvels of the generative cycle), and with time itself (the sacred force that vitalizes all existence with eternal meaning). Zosima conceives of worship, therefore, as an active acknowledgment of the spiritual meaning of his own world and the people who inhabit it. He considers spiritual truths to be revealed and open everywhere, in all aspects of their daily lives. To see others and the physical world as manifestations of the Divine means that all existence is charged with the sacred. To see all things, events, and people as aspects of the sacred means the extension of the notion of union to include the past and future as well as the present, that is, a broader form of pantheism. Markel teaches this to Zosima, who teaches it again to Alesha, who, at the end of the novel, teaches it yet again to the "society of children." The mythical urge toward integration of all factual life within divine meaning is the center of Zosima's message. As in myth, there is no progress toward unity for Zosima; the interpenetration of sacred and temporal is already there and only needs to be acknowledged.

ROBIN FEUER MILLER

From The Deep Heart's Core[†]

Book V

The Brothers Karamazov, Book V ("Pro and Contra") presented Dostoevsky with special conflicts between his tasks as an artist and as a believing Christian, for it is here that Ivan, through his magnificent poem in prose, *The Legend of the Grand Inquisitor*, puts forth the terms of his rebellion against God and His ordering of the world. It is this section of the novel that has most consistently gripped Dostoevsky's readers and that Dostoevsky himself knew was the heart of the matter. On 10 May 1879 he wrote from Staraya Russa to his editor, N. A. Lyubimov:

> This fifth book is in my view the culminating point of the novel and must be finished with particular care. Its meaning, as you will see from the text I sent, is the depiction of extreme blasphemy and the kernel of the idea of destruction of our time, in Russia. . . . My hero chooses a theme I consider irrefutable: the absurdity of all historical reality. I don't know whether I executed it well but I know the figure of my hero is a real one to the utmost degree. . . . Everything my hero says in the text I sent you is based on reality. All the anecdotes about children took place, existed, were published in the press. . . . I invented nothing. . . . My hero's blasphemy will be triumphantly refuted in the next (June) issue, on which I am now working with fear, trembling, and veneration. (*BK*, 758)

The paradoxes embedded in his letter virtually leap off the page: he considers the argument upon which Ivan bases his rebellion to be irrefutable, yet he sets out to refute it. It is usual, when reading *The Brothers Karamazov*, to discover the indirect means Dostoevsky brings to bear in this monumental task of refuting Ivan's arguments, both in the words of Zosima's last exhortations and in the rapidly ensuing events of the novel. Yet a close reading of Book V suggests yet another way Dostoevsky deviously refutes Ivan's argument: he uses the words and emotions of Ivan himself. By the end of *The Brothers Karamazov* the reader may decide that Ivan has undergone or is at least in the midst of a genuine spiritual conversion.[1] For we can argue that it is Ivan himself who offers up the most compelling counterpoint to his own objections. The dialogic nature of this novel expresses itself powerfully through the competing and conflicting ideas and actions of its characters, but even more compelling are the dialogisms and polyphonies that exist within single characters, and within single thoughts. The words of Xenos Clark, an obscure American philosopher, so aptly quoted by William James, spring to mind—"The

---

† From *The Brothers Karamazov: Worlds of the Novel*, 53–54, 64–77. © 2008. Reprinted by permission of Yale University Press.
1. I explore the question of Ivan's possible conversion at length in "Adventures in Time and Space: Dostoevsky, William James, and the Perilous Journey to Conversion" (manuscript in preparation, to be part of my forthcoming *Dostoevsky: Transformations and Conversions*).

truth is that we travel on a journey that was accomplished before we set out."[2]

*　*　*

Ivan begins his poem of the Grand Inquisitor with a literary preface that shows off his knowledge and functions well within the medieval scholastic tradition of citing numerous sources and models to prepare the way for one's "own word." It is typical of both Dostoevsky and his literary creation, Ivan, that the scholastic habit of citing sources becomes an excuse to concoct a hearty stew containing some unexpected ingredients. Dante, French clerks and monks, the religious plays performed in the court of Peter the Great, Russian monks—all are more or less likely sources for this historical tale. But then we find a contemporary source in Victor Hugo's *Nôtre Dame de Paris* and his rendition of "Le bon jugement de la très sainte et gracieuse Vierge Marie." This recalls to Ivan's mind another important source about the Virgin Mary, "The Wanderings of Our Lady through Hell," a twelfth-century apocryphal tale. Suddenly the roles reverse: we have the specter of a mother who does plead for mercy to be shown "all without distinction." And God here, in Ivan's rendition, echoes Ivan's rebellious words of a few moments earlier. He "points to the hands and feet of her Son, nailed to the Cross, and asks, 'How can I forgive His tormentors?'" (*BK*, 228). But Mary prevails. Under her influence God offers up a kind of limited or conditional forgiveness. Thus Ivan offers a paradoxical counterpoint to his own just uttered words: "Let her forgive the torturer for the immeasurable suffering of her mother's heart. But the sufferings of her tortured child she has no right to forgive; she dare not forgive the torturer, even if the child were to forgive him" (*BK*, 226). In Ivan's rendering of this apocryphal tale, God has, in part, agreed with Ivan, but Mary has gone ahead with her own forgiveness. Ivan's most powerful interlocutor is his own literary sensibility.

Most important, Ivan's preface continues the dominant thematic motifs that have governed all of Book V: the interconnected problems of parent-child (shepherd and flock) relations and suffering—both the imposition and the endurance of it. Ironically, the poem, the most powerful statement of Ivan's rebellion, begins with a preface whose main episode has been about forgiveness. What is even more surprising perhaps is that forgiveness will figure at the close of Ivan's poem as well. Thus, as readers, we would do well to ask ourselves, what is the relationship of the opening and closing frames to the poem itself?

After his preface Ivan offers up a one-sentence summary of his poem: "He comes on the scene in my poem, but He says nothing, only appears and passes on" (*BK*, 228). Key, then, are His arrival, His departure, His silence. According to Ivan's tale, Jesus appears in Seville during the time of the Spanish Inquisition. "He came softly, unobserved, and yet, strange to say, everyone recognized him. That might be one of the best passages in the poem" (*BK*, 229).

Ivan's ongoing literary critique of his own poem as he narrates it to Alyosha sets up a complex interplay, which continues through the rest of

2. Quoted in William James, *The Varieties of Religious Experience: A Study in Human Nature*, intro. by Reinhold Niebuhr (1902; reprint, New York: Collier Books, 1970), 307.

this pivotal chapter, between Alyosha as listener (audience) and some-time critic and Ivan as author and sometime critic as well. This interplay becomes even more complex as the reader begins to discern the similari-ties between Ivan and his Grand Inquisitor and between Alyosha and Jesus. The net result is a blurring of the usual lines of demarcation between subject and object, author and subject, author and critic, author and audi-ence, and audience and subject. Most significant for the model of reading imposed in this novel by Dostoevsky, this crucial blurring may extend even to the boundary between character and reader.

Moreover, given the growing preoccupation in the novel, and particu-larly in Ivan's recent words, with children, it is fitting that Jesus' single act on arriving in Seville is to raise a child from the dead. There is a mother's joy, as well as general weeping, cries, and confusion, at the enactment of this miracle. Ivan's words in the previous two chapters have prepared us to rejoice at this miracle, for he, Alyosha, and we with them have just heartily rejected any edifice, however just, built on the tears of even a single child.

Yet Jesus' miracle still looms as problematic—mysterious—for he has here chosen to save a single child but not any of those "hundred heretics" burned at the stake the day before. Is Ivan indirectly testing his own proposition? Our emotions at this point are operating in a reverse man-ner from the way in which Ivan structured his argument. Just moments earlier Ivan had argued that he would not even concentrate on adults, who have already eaten of the apple, but would instead focus on children. Yet surely in this chapter we *do* find ourselves more engaged with the vivid agonies of the nameless multitude (those dirty sinners who have already eaten of the apple) than we *do* with the possible suffering endured by the little girl, resting in her coffin of flowers, whom Jesus raises? This refocus-ing of emotional energy is paradoxical; it also underscores the axiom in this novel that miracles, when they do occur, are mysterious, unheralded events that do not serve to solve general problems.

Jesus arrives on this dreadful scene of religious massacre, but he solves no problems and does not alleviate the intense sufferings of the people. He saves a single child, not even a beggar child but the daughter of a prominent citizen, a child who had died a natural death. It almost seems a pointless miracle, given the terrible, unjustified sufferings of the dying multitudes. But it is not, for as we shall see, it reflects the ongoing deter-mination of Jesus not to give in, in any way, to those three temptations proposed to him by the devil in the wilderness some 15 centuries earlier.

The Grand Inquisitor comes on the scene, exercises his firm authority over the people, and has Jesus arrested. Late that night he visits Jesus in his cell and "speaks openly of what he has thought in silence for ninety years" (*BK*, 231). A tension begins to emerge between words and silence: the Grand Inquisitor speaks, Jesus is silent; Ivan speaks, Alyosha, for the most part, listens in silence. According to the Grand Inquisitor, the most "stupendous miracle" of all had involved the statement of words and had occurred on the day that "the great spirit talked with Thee in the wilderness. . . . The statement of those three questions was itself the miracle. . . . From those questions alone, from the miracle of their state-ment, we can see that we have here to do not with the fleeting human intel-lect, but with the absolute and the eternal. For in those three questions the whole subsequent history of mankind is, as it were, brought together into one whole, and foretold, and in them are united all the unsolved historical contradictions of human nature" (*BK*, 232–33).

The Grand Inquisitor, the devil, and perhaps Ivan—because it is he who gives the Grand Inquisitor these words—believe that these statements constitute a miracle because they encapsulate and predict the contradictions and the shape of human history. Jesus, God, Alyosha, and, as we shall see, Zosima indicate indirectly that the miracle lies elsewhere. But words remain crucial to it—perhaps the words with which Jesus answers the devil. But where does that leave silence?

Silence becomes part of the mystery, part of the measure of man's freedom of choice, a verbal absence somehow related to that moment when the seed (word) dies and before it brings forth its great fruit. Dostoevsky frequently offers up to us for consideration rich polarities and juxtapositions, but they never operate in a mechanistically binary way. Words are instruments of both God (grace) and the devil (damnation); silence may be a force of divine good (Jesus' silence here) or may work toward the enabling of evil. (Ivan's later moments of silence are a dangerous goad, an acquiescence.)

The Grand Inquisitor then proceeds to restate the events described in the New Testament, especially in the gospels of Matthew and John, in which the devil appears to Jesus and sets before him the three temptations. The devil urges Jesus to turn stones into bread. "Turn them into bread, and mankind will run after Thee like a flock. . . . But Thou wouldst not deprive man of freedom and didst reject the offer, thinking what is that freedom worth, if obedience is bought with bread? Thou didst reply that man lives not by bread alone" (*BK*, 233). The Grand Inquisitor then goes on to make an argument that continues to exert tremendous force on the social and ethical thought of our time: "Feed men, and then ask of them virtue!" The Grand Inquisitor argues that he and his church, by caring for the weak and by lying to them—saying, "We are Thy servants and rule . . . in Thy name"—are showing greater love for mankind than Jesus. "That deception will be our suffering. . . . Didst Thou forget," asks the Grand Inquisitor, "that man prefers peace, and even death, to freedom of choice in the knowledge of good and evil?" (*BK*, 235). Earlier the Grand Inquisitor had asked, "Dost Thou know that the ages will pass, and humanity will proclaim by the lips of their sages that there is no crime, and therefore no sin; there is only hunger?" (*BK*, 233).[3] The Grand Inquisitor repeats the rationale that virtually every totalitarian system has used to justify its rule, but he also, paradoxically, repeats the beliefs of many benevolent social thinkers and philanthropists.

It is well known that Dostoevsky struggled in all his novels against the prevailing liberal notion of his day, and our own, that criminal acts can be explained away, even excused, by the terrible effect on the criminal of an environment of suffering and poverty. Yet this is not to say that Dostoevsky opposed alleviating dreadful conditions. His letters and, above all, his *Diary of a Writer* reflect his compassion and his understanding of

3. Terras notes that this was one of the central ideas of the 1850s and 1860s, and that Dostoevsky may be paraphrasing, through his Grand Inquisitor's words, the section in Aleksandr Herzen's *My Past and Thoughts* (1852–55) (part 6, chap. 9) that is devoted to Robert Owen (Terras, *Karamazov Companion*, 232).

precisely such potentially adverse effects of environment. Nevertheless, he believed that the capacity to choose between good and evil was present in every human being and should be exercised everywhere.

Moreover, the Grand Inquisitor deftly twists the import of Jesus' response to this first temptation by failing to quote it fully. "It is written, Man shall not live by bread alone, but by every word that proceedeth out of the mouth of God" (Matt. 4:4). The full utterance carries a different connotation, an acknowledgment that bread is indeed important, but the words of God are more so. The Grand Inquisitor's silence about the second part of Jesus' answer returns us to that tension between words and silence. The devil, as Fyodor had observed in Part I, is the father of lies, of words twisted and misshapen. Here the Grand Inquisitor reflects his allegiance to the devil by presenting Jesus' own words to Him, and to us, in misshapen, elliptical form.

The Grand Inquisitor then asserts that there are only three powers that can hold captive the consciences of men and make them happy: miracle, mystery, and authority. "We have corrected Thy work and founded it upon miracle, mystery, and authority" (BK, 237). He accuses Jesus of having rejected all three. In Ivan's poem the Grand Inquisitor will repeat these three words until they gain an incantatory force and become lodged in the reader's mind. At the center of his novel, in the "deep heart's core" occupied jointly by the Grand Inquisitor's words, as spoken by Ivan, and by Zosima's words, as transcribed and edited by Alyosha, Dostoevsky states the key ideas of his novel in their most naked, unadorned, vulnerable form. The riddles of miracle, mystery, and authority figure at the heart of both the Grand Inquisitor's diatribe and Zosima's exhortations, and each uses the rhetoric of persuasion to the utmost. The rest of the novel will renew and recast their words.

In the second temptation, which we have already seen extensively parodied through Smerdyakov's verbal antics, the devil tries to persuade Jesus to hurl himself from the pinnacle of the Temple to show His faith that God would not let Him fall. "Thou didst know then that in taking one step . . . Thou wouldst be tempting God and have lost all Thy faith in Him" (BK, 236). But the Grand Inquisitor argues that men, unlike Jesus, need miracles "at the great moments of their life, the moments of their deepest, most agonizing spiritual difficulties" (BK, 236).

And indeed, the force of the Grand Inquisitor's words will shortly be borne out in Alyosha's own spiritual crisis, whose beginnings are already so evident. He will experience that wrenching need for a miracle at his moment of spiritual difficulty, and it will not come. Like the miracle performed by Jesus at the beginning of Ivan's poem, the miracle that does come—if any does—will be oddly gratuitous and will occur only after Alyosha has clung, simply and devotedly, "to the free verdict of the heart."

As Ivan's narrative continues, the doubling between him and his Inquisitor and between Alyosha and Jesus grows more intense. As the Grand Inquisitor says to Jesus, "And why dost Thou look silently and searchingly at me with Thy mild eyes?" it is the image of Alyosha sitting silently before Ivan that comes to mind. It is at this moment that the Grand Inquisitor lays bare his mystery (and Dostoevsky lays bare his ultimate condemnation of the Church of Rome): "We are not working with Thee, but with *him*—that is our mystery" (BK, 238).

The Grand Inquisitor reveals that the Church had also accepted the devil's third temptation, "that last gift." "We took from him Rome and the sword of Caesar, and proclaimed ourselves sole rulers of the earth" (*BK*, 238). Here Dostoevsky welds together his dislike of the Catholic Church and socialist thought, which he believed were both moving toward atheism and the enslavement of man. He has the Grand Inquisitor spout the language of nineteenth-century socialism tempered with Dostoevsky's own journalistic language of political polemic: "We shall plan the universal happiness of man"; we shall find a means of "uniting all in one unanimous and harmonious anthill" (*BK*, 238). The ambiguity of Ivan's article, which the monks had argued about in Part I, now becomes clearer. The Church that becomes the State has, quite simply, succumbed to the temptation of the devil.

Having gone through his explanatory argument, the acceptance of the three temptations, and the incantatory evocations of miracle, mystery, and authority, the Grand Inquisitor's self-justificatory statement takes a new, poignant, yet familiar twist that brings the novel back to its own reality—the impending spiritual crises of the three brothers, and the overarching theme of parents and children. The Grand Inquisitor accuses Jesus of being a poor shepherd to His flock, a poor father to His children. He claims for himself and his church true compassion for humanity. They "will look to us and huddle close to us in fear, as chicks to the hen. . . . Oh, we shall allow them even sin. They are weak and helpless, and they shall love us like children because we allow them sin . . . and the punishment for these sins we take upon ourselves" (*BK*, 240). Are the Grand Inquisitor's compassion and love counterfeit or genuine?

He argues that he will stand at the judgment day before God and justify his lies in the name of "the thousands of millions of happy children who have known no sin" (*BK*, 240). Has the Grand Inquisitor constructed an edifice that is *not* founded on the unexpiated tears of a child? At this moment of the Grand Inquisitor's moving verbal crescendo we may be tempted to believe that he has. Dostoevsky has, once again, duplicated in the experience of reading the philosophical and metaphysical problems with which his novel abounds: he tempts us.

The narrator-chronicler tells us that Alyosha listens in silence, though toward the end he becomes greatly moved and is on the point of interrupting. Do these words also describe Jesus as He listened to the Grand Inquisitor? At any rate, Alyosha's response may come as a surprise: "Your poem is in praise of Jesus, not in blame of Him—as you meant it to be" (*BK*, 241). Has the Grand Inquisitor indirectly defeated his own argument, and has Jesus' silence ultimately been even more rhetorically persuasive than the Grand Inquisitor's words?

Alyosha at last asks Ivan how the poem ends. "Or was it the end?" Ivan replies that the silent Prisoner looked the Grand Inquisitor quietly and gently in the face. Then suddenly "He approached the old man in silence and softly kissed him on his bloodless aged lips. That was all his answer. The old man shuddered. His lips moved." He goes to the door and lets Him go. "'And the old man?' 'The kiss glows in his heart, but the old man adheres to his idea'" (*BK*, 243). A few moments later Alyosha duplicates this kiss, even as the narrator-chronicler echoes Ivan's words: "Alyosha got up, went to him and softly kissed him on the lips." Ivan, ever the author-critic, exclaims, though with delight, "That's plagiarism . . . You stole that from my poem" (*BK*, 244). Ivan is right, of course; we have just witnessed an example of the most fundamental power of literature (the word): it offers up an artistic model that can inspire one in life. Art may imitate life, but as Oscar Wilde's famous aphorism affirms, life imitates art. This is not Alyosha's first act of plagiarism, however; nor will it be his last.

Indeed, Alyosha's greatest gift as a "good man" is his ability to give back to others what they have given him—what they, unknowingly, already possess. At this moment, Alyosha may, through his loving kiss, be sowing in Ivan the seed of his own redemption. But that kiss actually originates in Ivan's sensibility; it is he who has created the parable of a Jesus who kissed the old sinner; it is he who describes how the kiss glowed in the old atheist's heart. We may ask again what we asked at the outset of Book V: who is saving whom? The chapter closes with a crescendo of religious symbolism as Ivan departs to the left and Alyosha to the right. Alyosha also notices that "Ivan swayed as he walked and that his right shoulder looked lower than his left" (*BK*, 245; see also *BK*, 256, 257).

The many correspondences of Ivan's confession with Mitya's suddenly strike Alyosha. "The strange resemblance flashed like an arrow through Alyosha's mind." Moreover, the wind again rose, "as on the previous evening, and the ancient pines murmured gloomily" (*BK*, 243). And once again Alyosha hurries back to his monastery, burdened with the sad knowledge that his two brothers, and perhaps he himself, are on the brink of disaster. But even as he takes note of the resemblance between these two confessional episodes, Alyosha forgets that he has not yet found Mitya, the search for whom has until this moment guided his movements.

Book V closes with nightmarish intimations of Ivan's oncoming madness—"Some person or thing seemed to be standing out somewhere, just as something will sometimes intrude itself upon the eye"—and with his dreadful encounter with Smerdyakov. The atmosphere quickly fills with stifling foreboding. Alyosha has departed for the monastery, and the demonic lackey Smerdyakov enacts his temptations. "'I am a scoundrel,' whispers Ivan to himself" (*BK*, 260).

Book VI

Dostoevsky had originally planned for Book VI, "The Russian Monk," to be part of Book V, but while working on it he realized that they could not fit together into a single book.[4] Taken together, however, these two books form the core of *The Brothers Karamazov*.

Throughout the rest of the novel, and particularly in "The Russian Monk," Dostoevsky seeks, albeit indirectly, to answer the questions raised by Ivan and the Grand Inquisitor. On 19 May 1879, Dostoevsky wrote to the conservative Konstantin Pobedonostev: "Well, I have finished and mailed off the blasphemy but will send the refutation only for the June issue. . . . The refutation (not a direct one, i.e., not in a face-to-face argument) will come as the last words of the dying elder. Many critics have reproached me for generally choosing, as it were, wrong themes for my novels, themes that are not realistic, etc.; but I feel, on the contrary, that

4. *Pis'ma*, 4 vols., ed. A. S. Dolinin (Moscow and Leningrad: Gosizdat, 1928–59), 464–65, 467.

there is nothing more realistic than precisely these themes" (*Letters*, 467). A month later he wrote to Lyubimov: "In the next book there will be the death of Father Zosima and his last conversations with friends. This is not a sermon, but rather a sort of story, an account of an incident in his own life." Dostoevsky then stated what had been an artistic obsession of his since the writing of *The Idiot*—the desire to portray successfully, in an interesting way, a positively good man: "If I can bring it off, I will have accomplished something useful: *I will force them to admit* that a pure and ideal Christian is not an abstraction but a tangible, real possibility that can be contemplated with our own eyes [Dostoevsky's italics]" (*Letters*, 469–70). He then expressed yet another typical concern—his desire to be original, to portray "new types."

* * *

A few days before "The Russian Monk" was due to appear Dostoevsky wrote that he was trembling over whether it would adequately answer the negative ideas expressed in *The Grand Inquisitor* (*Letters*, 465, 467–470). Again he affirmed that his refutation was through indirect means. Yet how indirect are his means? How *does* Dostoevsky refute the negative view with a positive one? If his means, as he maintained, are indirect, what is the nature of this indirection? Was he right to have trembled?

We have already seen how Ivan's Grand Inquisitor claimed that the Catholic Church had accepted from the devil the very temptations—whose statement was the "great miracle"—that Jesus had rejected and had drawn its power over people from miracle, mystery, and authority. Ivan had composed his poem a year earlier and had recited it for the first time to Alyosha.

The form that Zosima's last exhortations take is equally unusual. Alyosha, like Ivan, relies on his memory; he writes down Zosima's last conversations and exhortations "some time after his elder's death." The narrator takes pains to show us that this narrative constitutes an intimate superimposition of Alyosha's editorial decisions on Zosima's actual words. "But whether this was only the conversation that took place then, or whether he added to it his notes of parts of former conversations with his teacher, I cannot determine" (*BK*, 265). The narrator-chronicler concludes Book VI with even more disclaimers about Alyosha's principles of composition and his editorial philosophy: "I repeat, it is incomplete and fragmentary" (*BK*, 303). In fact, Dostoevsky is saying to us behind his narrator's back, "I repeat, it is complete, and there is a whole there for the reader to discern." Moreover, Alyosha hands these conversations down to us as a monologue, in a genre that Dostoevsky's readers would know well, a "saint's life": *Notes of the Life in God of the Deceased Priest and Monk, the Elder Zosima. Taken from his Own Words by Alexey Fyodorovich Karamazov.*

Thus the document the reader encounters is itself a product of indirection, of multiple layers of mediation. Zosima's words are refracted through the prism of Alyosha, who reports them for his own reasons. The narrator-chronicler frames them with his own observations, and, of course, the author Dostoevsky orchestrates all these voices at once. Thus this single document, which contributes to what Bakhtin would call the polyphony of voices in the novel, is *itself* composed of polyphonic units. The smallest phrase from Zosima's *Life* is a polyphonic one, containing at all times the traces of Zosima, Alyosha, the narrator-chronicler, and the author. Book VI, despite its seeming simplicity of design and serenity of event, is the most complex narrative in the novel.

Moreover, this complexity of form, which is, so to speak, encased in an envelope of uniformity (Zosima's life), becomes a kind of metaphor-through-text of the novel's epigraph from John 12:24 about the seed. Indeed, it is here that the epigraph takes its first strong root in the novel and becomes indelibly linked to the theme of memory. Yet this theme of memory takes us back full circle to the question of the narrative texture of Book VI, whose message from Zosima, composed literally out of his memories of his life, is mediated through the later memories—recollections in tranquillity—of Alyosha.

The framework of Ivan's rebellion is his horror at the unjustified suffering of children and his refusal to participate in a non-Euclidean geometry of forgiveness. Zosima takes a similar starting point. He tells us that, as a child of eight, he "consciously received the seed of God's word in my heart" (*BK*, 270) through reading in church the Book of Job.[5] (We also learn that he had read it again "yesterday" with tears, that is, he read it on the day that the peasant woman whose child had died came to him.) Zosima's rendering of the story of Job has brought upon Dostoevsky the charge of subscribing, at least in part—or when it suits his purposes as an artist—to the Manichean heresy, for here in the words Zosima uses to paraphrase the Book of Job the devil seems to be successful in tempting God to action, much in the same way that he later fails in the desert to tempt Jesus. Zosima's account, mediated through Alyosha's pen, continues in a vein that implies God and the devil are engaged in an open-ended contest: "And God boasted to the devil, pointing to his great and holy servant. And the devil laughed at God's words. 'Give him over to me and Thou wilt see that Thy servant will murmur against Thee and curse Thy name.' And God gave up the just man He loved so, to the devil. And the devil smote his children" (*BK*, 270).

It is in this terrible story (the words almost sound like Ivan's) of the unjust suffering of Job's children that Zosima discovers the true mystery of Christian faith. He finds himself able to accept precisely that mystery, that non-Euclidean geometry, which Ivan so passionately rejects. "Many years pass by, and he has other children and loves them. But how could he love those new ones when those first children were no more, when he has lost them? Remembering them, how could he be fully happy with those new ones, however dear the new ones might be? But he could, he could. It's the great mystery of human life that old grief passes gradually into quiet tender joy" (*BK*, 271). Zosima does not counter Ivan's argument through reason or logic, but through the heart, through the emotional repetition, "he could, he could." He gives himself up to an acceptance of what he experiences as a true mystery. Mystery remains a mystery; faith is an unfathomable giving up of oneself, an acceptance of mystery.

---

5. All the main characters of *The Brothers Karamazov* grapple with the problem of evil, and it is the Book of Job that "confuted for all time the claim that the evils men suffer are their just chastisement by God for the sins they have indubitably perpetrated." Instead, this book of the Bible refutes "utterly the theology of guilt that the prophets [had] advocated" (Lewis S. Feuer, "The Book of Job: The Wisdom of Hebraic Stoicism," in *Biblical and Secular Ethics: The Conflict*, ed. R. Joseph Hoffmann and Gerald A. Larue [Buffalo, N.Y.: Prometheus Books, 1988], 79).

* * *

Zosima's narrative, taken as a whole, exemplifies miracle, mystery, and authority in their redeeming rather than their enslaving aspects. Zosima witnesses the mysterious and miraculous spiritual conversion of Markel. Later, as a young officer, he strikes his servant Afanasy just before he is to fight a duel. Suddenly he weeps; he remembers the words of his dying brother, and a conversion descends on him. His authority over his servant changes instantaneously into a relationship of mutuality. "I dropped at his feet and bowed my head to the ground. 'Forgive me,' I said" (*BK*, 277). A moment earlier he had remembered, from so many years before, Markel's words, "Am I worth it?" and had silently applied them to himself. Suddenly his servant, who, of course, has no knowledge of Markel or his words, cries out, "Am I worth it?" and begins to sob. In this mysterious passing on of the emblematic phrase "Am I worth it?" through the agency of both memory (the past) and utterance (the present), we see a literalization of the central metaphor, the seed, and a specific example of how grace (words as seeds) travels through the novel.

Markel's words and the words of the Book of Job plant a seed of grace in the heart of the child Zosima. The seed dies in him; he leads a life of dissipation. It then brings forth fruit; he experiences a conversion. Meanwhile, he begins, through his words to his servant, to precipitate a conversion within him and later within the mysterious visitor as well.

Alyosha too had received a childhood experience of grace, through the love of his mother. He also listens to these words of Zosima, but to some extent the seed will die in him, too. Yet Alyosha's act of transcribing and rendering Zosima's words shows that he has made them his own, in order to pass them on to those who will read them, including, of course, the readers of the novel. Thus Dostoevsky sought to bring his epigraph to bear on the real world outside the boundaries of his novel and to make his readers participate in this process.

* * *

HORST-JÜRGEN GERIGK

Dmitry Karamazov's Crime and Punishment[†]

Everyone knows: in *The Brothers Karamazov* we are told how Fyodor Karamazov is perfidiously murdered by Pavel Smerdyakov. Through a series of circumstances, however, Dmitry Karamazov is convicted of the murder and sentenced to twenty years of hard labor in Siberia. Smerdyakov hangs himself the night before the trial and Dmitry Karamazov accepts punishment for a crime that he did not commit.

In order to understand Dmitry's reaction, let us recall Dostoevsky's presentation of the problem in detail. The core of the outer storyline is comprised of the reasons and background for the murder of Fyodor

† "Zur Psychologie und Metaphysik des Justizirrtums," from *Die Russen in Amerika: Dostojewskij, Tolstoj und Tschechow in ihrer Bedeutung für die Literatur der USA*. Reprinted with permission of the author and Guido Pressler Verlag. Trans. Katherine Bowers and Susan McReynolds.

Karamazov, whose three sons, Dmitry (from his first marriage), Ivan, and Alexey (from his second marriage), reveal their characters and their world in their reactions to their father. That Pavel Smerdyakov, a castrate-like epileptic employed in the Karamazov house as a cook, is Fyodor Karamazov's illegitimate son is only vouched for as a rumor.

The novel begins with the family history of the Karamazovs, which leads into a presentation of the current conflict. Dmitry, the impetuous, fundamentally honorable, but easygoing soldier accuses his father of intentionally withholding his maternal inheritance. As so often happens in Dostoevsky, all the trouble initially involves only a handful of rubles! The pleasure-seeking father's penchant for Agrafena Svetlova, called Grushenka, a "femme fatale" who is adored by Dmitry, brings the situation to the boiling point. Dmitry openly admits hatred for his father. A representative visit to the monastery where the Elder Zosima is to be approached for advice and help in the family conflict is transformed into a downright farce through Fyodor Karamazov's profound but consistently malicious clowning: the three brothers feel helpless before their cynical begetter, and the clairvoyant Zosima already has a presentiment of the result of the looming catastrophe.

Dmitry eventually threatens to kill his father. But the idea of murder has already blossomed and stayed alive in Ivan, the second brother, as well. Ivan, the intellectual brooder, has planted his intention in the soul of Smerdyakov, who has offered himself as a tool to Ivan with abysmal cleverness. Without speaking it aloud, Ivan commissions the lackey Smerdyakov with the father's murder and keeps far away from the paternal house on the designated night, simultaneously hoping for Dmitry to commit the crime. Alexey is meanwhile absorbed with events in the monastery, where he is paying last respects to the Elder Zosima, who had taken on the role of a spiritual father for him. On such a night Dmitry finds himself brought into the most extreme danger: his search for Grushenka has been futile and he suddenly believes that she could only be at his father's. Dmitry climbs over that strong, high fence surrounding the paternal estate from an isolated, deserted alley, sneaks carefully through the quiet, dark garden to the lighted window, and makes the special knock on the window frame that, as he knows, Smerdyakov has arranged with his father as the signal that Grushenka has come. Fyodor Karamazov immediately appears at the window and whispers love words in an excited voice into the dark garden. Dmitry sees from this that Grushenka has indeed not come, but his father's profile, with its protruding Adam's apple, causes unspeakable aversion in him. Dmitry is no longer in control of his senses and lifts the pestle that he incidentally picked up on the way for the fatal blow.

At the last moment, however, he abandons his intention and flees. So Smerdyakov, who has carefully created an alibi for himself through a counterfeit epileptic fit, can use the situation: he bashes in the skull of the unsuspecting Fyodor Karamazov with a cast-iron paperweight and then disappears once more to his sickbed.

Dmitry Karamazov is arrested for this crime, found guilty by the jury, and sentenced to twenty years' hard labor in Siberia. Smerdyakov hangs himself after his confession to Ivan, in full knowledge of the consequences of his action. When Ivan refers to the dead witness before the court, no one believes him. The trial proceedings are the compositional high point of the novel: everything that has happened is recapitulated here, and brought to a fully unexpected conclusion with Dmitry's guilty verdict.

The epilogue confronts us with the most radical provocation conceivable: Dmitry is determined to take upon himself the punishment for a crime that he did not commit. What is the point made here by Dostoevsky?

A satisfactory answer to this question is only possible when we realize that *The Brothers Karamazov* offers two different ways of reading: one "allegorical" and the other "realistic." In order to comprehend Dostoevsky's unique way of presenting the problem, both readings must be carried out and juxtaposed. Dostoevsky's construction strives towards illuminating an allegorical meaning within reality.

On the realistic level *The Brothers Karamazov* is the story of a judicial error, for Smerdyakov, not Dmitry, committed murder. On the allegorical level, however, *The Brothers Karamazov* is the story of an absolutely just verdict because, if Dmitry had not dared to go to the brink of action, Smerdyakov would not have killed. Even Ivan Karamazov's preparation of the actual culprit could not have brought about the completion of the crime. It is exclusively Dmitry's conduct that sets Smerdyakov in motion as the perpetrator. Smerdyakov slips into the role Dmitry provides for him with a diabolical aptitude for empathy.

When we start from the assumption that the trial in *The Brothers Karamazov* illustrates how the court of justice functions inside us, Dmitry's conviction must be acknowledged as just. The accused in this context consists of four components: Alexey (1), Ivan (2), Dmitry (3), and Smerdyakov (4). Each of these components is characterized by a specific attitude to the evil desire for the father's death. Rejected affirmation: Alexey; secret affirmation: Ivan; open affirmation: Dmitry. Smerdyakov is the executor of the open affirmation. Dostoevsky links each of these components to a specific type of role: Alexey is the "monk," Ivan the "intellectual," Dmitry the "soldier," and Smerdyakov the "lackey." Thus, on the allegorical level, a person who has committed murder comes before the court; this person consists of four components, each representing a firm attitude towards the reality of evil. The court's task is to decide which component is responsible for the deed.

With the example of the four brothers, Dostoevsky provides a genealogy and ontology of evil. A theory about the genesis of the reality of evil is set forth. The reality of evil as executed crime can only come about when it is expressly wished beforehand. In order to become reality, the evil wish must pass through various phases of development. It surfaces first only darkly as the foreboding of a possibility and can still be easily repelled in this initial phase. Alexey represents this incipient stage. Evil sprouts in him too, but is immediately subdued and rejected. In its second phase the evil wish is secretly endorsed but never openly articulated. This phase is represented by Ivan. Ivan wishes that someone else would fulfill the task that he himself only dares to think. The potential executor of the crime is prepared through such behavior. In its third developmental phase, the evil wish finally attains open affirmation and thus becomes evil will. Dmitry represents this phase. Having passed through open affirmation, the wish can become reality. The executor of the wish is Smerdyakov. He represents the fourth and final phase of the genesis of evil: its transformation into reality.

In sum: the reprehensible wish has to pass through the phases of sprouting, secret affirmation, and open affirmation in order to become reality. If we express this process through the four roles or types corresponding to the components of evil, then the facts can be formulated this way: the 'lackey' (Smerdyakov) extends the gesture of the 'soldier' (Dmitry) to correspond with the commission of the 'intellectual' (Ivan) and the evil wish comes true. At the same time the "monk" (Alexey) turns away from the bustle of the world. The crime has taken place. Who is guilty? The inner judge says: Dmitry!

That the first component, Alexey, is not sufficient to produce the reality of evil does not require discussion. But the second component, Ivan, is also insufficient. With the secret affirmation of the evil wish the potential executor is indeed prepared, but only the open affirmation of the evil wish transforms him into the actual perpetrator. Smerdyakov's activity is dependent on Dmitry's disposition. In a world that knew only an Alexey, an Ivan, and a Smerdyakov, the evil wish would indeed exist in specific nuances, but the reality of evil would be absent. Smerdyakov, the tool of the devil, can only become active through Dmitry. And so, Dostoevsky argues, Dmitry alone is responsible for the executed crime. Without Dmitry there would be no murder.

Let us now sum up: on the allegorical level there can be no talk of a miscarriage of justice, because Dmitry alone is responsible for the fact of the crime. He is therefore pronounced guilty by the inner judge, represented by the jury, which strictly considers the evidence of his actions and utterances. In this context it also becomes clear why the defense attorney is called a "hired conscience." Fetyukovich cannot offer any truth of his own; instead he has the sole function of destroying the arguments of the prosecution.

What has been called the allegorical reading of *The Brothers Karamazov* is, from the viewpoint of the characters involved, a construct which shines forth "like an allegory" within reality. For a moment, the truth of conscience becomes identical with the state's truth, in a way, however, that the state does not notice this, because its court is of course forever convinced that Dmitry is the real culprit. In Dostoevsky's language this means that divine truth appears in the garb of earthly justice; and that is only made possible by the fact that the official state court does not notice what it is really doing.

One should note that the puzzling prophetic bow of the Elder Zosima before Dmitry Karamazov is already characterized as an "emblem" and "allegory" at the beginning of the novel.[1] Dmitry experiences the reality of a world that obeys such an allegory. Dmitry's sorrow consists not of enduring injustice, but of bearing justice. For Dmitry does not take punishment upon himself for a "sin of thinking," but for the factual implementation of the crime. It has now become clear that the jury's conviction can be simultaneously characterized as "injustice" and as "justice," without there being

---

1. In a conversation with Alexey Karamazov, Rakitin comments on the Elder Zosima's baffling action as follows: "In my opinion the old man really is clear sighted; he sniffed a crime." As this conversation continues Rakitin expresses the ironic conjecture that, if a real crime should take place, people will see an "emblem" or "allegory" in Zosima's bow.

any contradiction in the case itself. This court deserves nothing but sheer scorn for what it knows on its own; but by serving allegory it is beyond the scope of any derision.

Dostoevsky shows us that Dmitry is innocent before the *law*, but guilty before *God*! Only for that reason can Dmitry take upon himself the punishment for a crime that according to the penal law he has not committed. Regarding the reality of conscience as the true reality becomes possible for Dmitry on the basis of Christianity. It is significant that the encouragement of Alexey, upon whom the Elder Zosima's blessing rests, deeply strengthens Dmitry in his newly won insight. In so far as Dmitry secretly recognizes the justice of the judicial error, he finds his identity in morality. Dostoevsky's world does not permit any other identity.

VLADIMIR GOLSTEIN

Accidental Families and Surrogate Fathers: Richard, Grigory, and Smerdyakov[†]

Judge not, that ye be not judged. For with what judgment ye judge, ye shall be judged.
—Matthew 7:1 AV

Woe to him who offends a child.
—Dostoevsky, *The Brothers Karamazov*

In 1876, Dostoevsky wrote in a letter: "One of the most important problems at the present time to me, for example, is that of the younger generations and, along with it, the contemporary Russian family, which I feel is far from what it used to be even as recently as twenty years ago."[1] Indeed, from 1855 on, that is, after the death of Nicholas I and in the subsequent Great Reforms, Russia underwent a series of drastic social and economic changes that transformed beyond recognition the Russian family and the relations between generations. These changes were so momentous that the plight of the Russian family began to be perceived by Dostoevsky as "one of the most important problems" that he wanted to address. Small wonder that the novelist turned the Russian family into the subject of intense scrutiny. Not only his major novels but also *A Writer's Diary* were used by Dostoevsky as a vehicle to highlight and investigate the new reality and its possible ramifications.

In the January 1876 issue of *A Writer's Diary* Dostoevsky confesses:

> For a long time now I have had the goal of writing a novel about children in Russia today, and about their fathers, too, of course, in their mutual relationship of today. . . . I will take fathers and children

---

† From Robert Louis Jackson, ed., *A New Word on* The Brothers Karamazov (Evanston: Northwestern UP, 2004), 99–105. Copyright © 2004 by Northwestern University Press. Reprinted with permission.

1. F. M. Dostoevskii, *Polnoe sobranie sochinenii v tridsati tomakh*, vol. 24-2 (Leningrad: Nauka, 1986), 78. All quotations from Dostoevsky's works, unless otherwise indicated, refer to this edition of *Polnoe sobranie sochinenii v tridsati tomakh*, 30 vols. (1972–88), hereafter cited parenthetically as *Ps* with volume and page number. The translations, unless otherwise indicated, are my own.

from every level of Russian society I can and follow the children from their earliest childhood.

A year and a half ago, When Nikolai Alekseevich Nekrasov asked me to write a novel for *Otechestvennye zapiski*, I almost began my *Fathers and Sons*; but I held back, and thank God I did, for I was not ready. In the meantime I wrote only *A Raw Youth*, this first attempt at my idea.[2]

Of course, Dostoevsky's view of *A Raw Youth* (1875) as the first sample of his idea is somewhat misleading, since *The Demons* (1871) seems to be directly concerned with the relations between "present-day fathers and their Russian children." Yet regardless of the first attempts at the idea, it is Dostoevsky's last novel, *The Brothers Karamazov*, that analyzes the modern-day fathers and children most intensively.

The opening of the novel, the first sentence of the first chapter, announces the centrality of the father-son theme: "Alexei Fyodorovich Karamazov was the third son of a landowner from our district, Fyodor Pavlovich Karamazov, well known in his own day (and still remembered among us) because of his dark and tragic death, which happened exactly thirteen years ago" (*BK*, 7).[3] A son, a father, and a father's tragic death are announced from the start. And so are the ideas of history and memory: the outcome of the conflict is remembered, it leaves a trace and has an impact upon others.

The first line of the next chapter reinforces the centrality of the novel's problem content, while at the same time introducing the issue of a child's upbringing into the picture: "Of course, one can imagine what sort of father and mentor such a man would be" (*BK*, 10). In the opening lines of these two chapters we find the whole of Dostoevsky's novel: fathers, sons, failed upbringing, tragic death, and the repercussions that are remembered through the years.

In fact, the first book of the novel is subtitled "A Nice Little Family." This book consists of five chapters. The first one introduces the old Karamazov, the next three chapters describe his three sons, while the last chapter switches to elders, usually addressed as "fathers" in Russian. The structure of this first book is thus rather transparent: the stories of children that are placed in the middle are surrounded by the stories of various types of fathers, either physical or surrogate, either real or failed. The novel's progression, introduced by the first book, will be later replayed over the expanse of the whole novel. It is not the progression from fathers to sons, however, but rather the movement from false fathers to the true, usually surrogate ones; from selfishness to sacrifice, from neglect and abuse to love and engagement.[4]

* * *

2. Fyodor Dostoevsky, *A Writer's Diary*, vol. 1, p. 302, 1873–1876, ed. and trans. Kenneth Lantz (Evanston: Northwestern UP, 1993), hereafter cited parenthetically as *WD* with page number.
3. Fyodor Dostoevsky, *The Brothers Karamazov*, translated and annotated by Richard Pevear and Larissa Volokhonsky (New York: Vintage Books, 1991). All English quotations from *The Brothers Karamazov* refer to this edition, hereafter cited parenthetically as *BK* with page number. References to this Norton Critical Edition are in parentheses.
4. Cf. Michael Holquist, "How Sons Become Fathers," in *Dostoevsky and the Novel* (Evanston: Northwestern UP, 1986), 173–77; see also Frederick T. Griffiths and Stanley J. Rabinowitz, "Dostoevsky's *The Brothers Karamazov*," in *Novel Epics: Gogol Dostoevsky, and National Narrative* (Evanston: Northwestern UP, 1990), 137–44.

The Brothers Karamazov features, of course, a wide range of fathers, sons, families, and generations. The typical nineteenth-century family novel is transformed beyond recognition in Dostoevsky's literary universe. The family becomes the locus of the most intense social, political, moral, and theological conflicts. It is within the accidental family that the new generation forms not only its views of its biological fathers but also its views of all other father figures: a government official, a czar, and God.

In March 1878, Dostoevsky wrote to one of his female correspondents:

> Imagine that your child, grown up to the age of fifteen or sixteen, comes to you (influenced by bad friends in school, for example) and asks you or his father: "Why should I love you and why should this be my duty?" Believe me, no knowledge of questions will help you there, nor would there be much sense in answering him. *And therefore you must make sure that he never comes to you with such a question.* (Ps, 30-1:17; emphasis added)

What Dostoevsky suggests here is that the only way to prevent children and the czar's subjects from questioning and challenging various authorities is to prevent the very emergence of such questions. Eager as he is to insist on personal responsibility, Dostoevsky is equally eager to underscore the power of environment to shape a person. Dostoevsky merges these two concerns by stressing the parental responsibility for creating the right environment. Better than any Russian radical, Dostoevsky knew that the modern-day fathers had failed. He does not, however, call for the abolition of the institution of the family. Nor does he blindly uphold the family in the manner of conservatives. Instead, he calls for a new type of family, one in which parental love and lifelong dedication result in a dissolution of the conflicts and tensions.

It is clear that the primary responsibility for the creation of such a family lies with the parents. No matter how critical Dostoevsky was of the radical youth, he would emphasize again and again the role and responsibility of the "fathers."

In his drafts to *The Brothers Karamazov*, Dostoevsky is quite explicit about his desire to reconstruct a family as a microcosm of divine love and unity. One entry acknowledges "family as the practical source of love" (Ps, 15:249). Another maintains that "the Elder says that God gave us close kin [*rodnykh*] so that they could teach us to love" (Ps, 15:205).

Utopian as it all sounds, Dostoevsky is aware that the alternatives are quite terrifying. It is these alternatives that Dostoevsky highlights in *The Brothers Karamazov*. If parents fail to turn the family into a school of love, sacrifice, and patient endeavor, the family becomes the place of judgments, violence, and crime.

In his *Writer's Diary*, Dostoevsky writes about the impact of family violence upon children: "This dismal picture will remain in their souls forever and might painfully undermine their youthful pride . . . The result will be an inability to cope with life's problems, early pangs of vanity, a blush of false shame for their past, and a dull, sullen hatred for people, and this, perhaps, may last a lifetime" (WD, 303).

The failure of fathers results in various forms of rebellion in children ranging from social to religious and cosmic. Two characters of the novel whose maturation had been accompanied by their contact with incompetent parental figures fully embody the dynamics of the rebellion of children. While Smerdyakov reveals that there is a small step between rejecting one's father and killing him, Ivan Karamazov clearly shows that there is only a small step between rejecting one's father and rejecting God.

Parricide is, of course, the most vivid and striking form of rebellion against the fathers. In order fully to appreciate Dostoevsky's deep vision of family interaction, one must examine the social and psychological dynamics leading the failed fathers to create the forces that destroy them.

The Orphan Richard and his Failed Fathers

Among the unforgettable examples of cruelty and injustice that Ivan Karamazov collects and then recites in the chapter "Rebellion" (bk. 5, chap. 4), one particular example might strike a reader as rather odd, confusing, and out of place. It does not quite fit into Ivan's usual script of demonic adults torturing angelic children. I refer to the story of a man named Richard, a person who during his short life managed to be a victim, a murderer, and then a victim again.

Richard, a six-year-old illegitimate child, was handed over by his parents to some Swiss shepherds. These peasants exploit and mistreat him. They seem to care more for their pigs than for the orphan boy. The child, however, survives, grows up, and moves to Geneva, where he lives in poverty and dissipation. Eventually he robs and kills an old man. He is caught. Inspired by numerous priests who surround him in prison, he undergoes a religious conversion. Regardless of his conversion, Richard is taken to the execution, while his "brothers," as Ivan puts it, weep in joy at his forthcoming meeting with his Maker (BK, 240).

Ivan informs Alyosha that he read this story in one of the proselytizing publications that were floating around Russia at that time.[5] This story is remarkable for many reasons. It is a bitter mockery of the idea of "the restoration of a fallen man" (Ps, 20:28), an idea that Dostoevsky considers central in nineteenth-century European literature and one that permeates his own works. The story of Richard also recalls Dmitri's fate at the end of the novel. After his various visions and epiphanies, after his readiness to sing his hymn to God, the Russian court hands down a severe sentence.

More important, the story brings to mind Smerdyakov, whose fate, with the exception of the conversion, parallels that of Richard. The similarities between Smerdyakov and Richard are too striking to be coincidental: both are illegitimate, both are raised by foster parents who use them as servants and treat them like wild animals; both turn into untamable and unsociable adults. Even the crimes of Richard and Smerdyakov are similar: each one kills and robs an old man; each one commits his crimes at the same age of twenty-three.[6]

---

5. Nina Budanova found this publication among Dostoevsky's books. She discusses its relevance to Dostoevsky's own views on the subject of crime and punishment (Nina Budanova, "Rishar i Dostoevskii," in *Dostoevskii: Issledovaniia i materialy* 13 [1996]: 106–19). Budanova, however, does not connect Richard's story with the events, characters, or problem content of the novel itself.

6. A story of an orphan adopted by shepherds takes us, of course, to the myth of Oedipus and its theme of parricide. The tale of a baby abandoned in Switzerland and executed in Geneva hints at Rousseau's biography; it contains an obvious warning to fathers who abandon their children. I am grateful to Liza Knapp for drawing my attention to these subtexts.

The story also presents its narrator, Ivan, in a rather curious light. With his rejection of "harmony" resting on the suffering of innocent children, Ivan is outraged that Richard is led to slaughter for the sake of the harmony of Western civilization. Ivan manifests sympathy for Richard and hatred for his self-righteous tormentors; he mocks the hypocrisy of killing one's brother in Christ. Yet Ivan fails to recognize his brotherhood with his own blood brothers, one of whom, Dmitri, he frequently calls "a monster" and the other, Smerdyakov, "a stinking lackey."

Ivan's complete identification with the child victims of his stories is clearly problematic. Ivan is no longer a child. He grew up into a powerful father figure for his own brothers. In other words, Ivan fails to acknowledge fully all the moral implications of Richard's story. He fails to recognize himself in various participants of this story and glosses over the fact that he himself is not only a victim but a victimizer, not only a Richard but also the church that let down its brother and spiritual son. Richard's story clearly implicates Ivan, as it does the readers of *The Brothers Karamazov*. The latter tend to share Ivan's sensitivities and sympathize with Richard, though they ignore Smerdyakov's fate.[7]

There is another crucial difference between the story of Richard and the other stories that involve tortured children. Richard's story has roots. It involves the fate of a child abandoned by one set of parents, abused by another, and then let down by a third group of parents: the priests. In other words, the story places abused children not only within a rather abstract context of morality or theology (the problem of theodicy) but also within a more immediate one of family and generations.

Compared to the cosmic scope of theological justice, the issue of social justice does not appear to be particularly dramatic or profound. Yet in terms of our novel, the ferocious strife that fathers' failure generates is fundamental. Richard's story, at least in the way Ivan constructs it, testifies to the total failure of fathers. Shepherds, both literal and spiritual, prove incapable of carrying out their duty of guiding and saving. In Ivan's story, Richard compares himself to a prodigal son. Yet, as the outcome of the story suggests, Richard's return to his father is greeted by execution. Ivan's story completely discredits the fathers and thus bodes no good for them. Fyodor is absolutely correct to be wary of Ivan.

When in the first serious discussion of Smerdyakov (in the early chapters entitled "The Disputation" and "Over the Cognac" [bk. 3, chaps. 7 and 8]), Ivan calls him "peredovoe miaso" (the one who is leading the attack), he seems to acknowledge that Smerdyakov harbors enough anger to be at the forefront of rebellion against the fathers in power. Typically, however, Ivan does not explore the implications of his own words or actions. Rather than probing into the causes of Smerdyakov's anger, Ivan immediately dismisses Smerdyakov as a "broth-maker" (*bul'onshchik*) and maintains that "so far the people do not much like listening to these broth-makers" (*BK*, 132).

In other words, Ivan prefers to discuss Smerdyakov's potential rebelliousness and his possible influence among the peasants without truly looking into the causes of such a rebellion. Smerdyakov's tortured past, a

---

7. As Olga Meerson has observed, "The injustice done to him [Smerdyakov] somehow eludes Ivan's (and everyone else's) indignation" (Olga Meerson, *Dostoevsky's Taboos* [Dresden: Dresden UP, 1998], 199).

matter Dostoevsky had already introduced in the chapter immediately preceding Ivan's musings on Smerdyakov, somehow eludes Ivan.

Ivan recognizes the impact that the past abuses have upon some distant and romantic Richard, but not upon the unattractive lackey and half brother, Smerdyakov. Ivan is justifiably offended by the fact that a human being, an orphan Richard, is treated like a swine. He is aware that Richard's monstrous attributes were not his essential quality. The story of Richard's conversion suggests quite the opposite. Smerdyakov, like Richard, was never an incorrigible villain, either.[8]

Here an examination of the people and forces that shaped Smerdyakov's character is in order. We know that in the case of Richard, it was his foster parents, the failed shepherds, who turn him into a criminal and then let him die. The failure of Smerdyakov's father, Fyodor, and of his moral and intellectual mentor, Ivan, is evident. Our main focus must be the person who raised Smerdyakov, his foster parent, Grigory Kutuzov, a person who treated him no better than the Swiss shepherds treated Richard. Grigory, the failed surrogate father of Smerdyakov, bears his share of guilt in the murder of Fyodor Karamazov.

Family: The School of Love or the School of Judgment

Throughout his writings, Dostoevsky suggests that the proliferation of judgment, anger, and malice is tied to the absence of family love, to the tendency of grown-ups to judge, criticize, and punish their young. Behind the conflict of generations, behind the sons' eagerness to judge and condemn the old, traditional, and habitual, lies the fathers' failure to turn a family into a school of love. Dostoevsky, as his own musings on the importance of family disclose, was well aware that without love, such important social forces as duty, sacrifice, obedience, continuity, and tradition would be perceived as restrictive and tyrannical, as something that one would want to overturn and trample upon. In Dostoevsky's view, there is only one step from dysfunctional families to the emergence of criminals, murderers, and rebels.

Already his two previous novels suggest such a progression. In the case of Stepan Verkhovensky (*The Demons*), his liberalism is by far less important in the making of his son than his absenteeism; the same can be said about Versilov and his children (*The Raw Youth*). Fyodor Karamazov, who, besides being a cynic, egoist, and a sinner, simply forgets about his children, is one more manifestation of a similar paradigm. Dostoevsky's view of an absentee father becomes explicit in his presentation of Ivan's devil, a character compared to a type of a widower who dumps his children on distant relatives and happily forgets about them (*BK*, 636).

The demonic nature of these absentee fathers, the progenitors of what Dostoevsky calls "an accidental family," hardly needs further elaboration. However, another type of a father deserves mention: the one who is physically present but who acts as if harshness and cruelty were substitutes for love and pity. On one occasion, Dostoevsky calls such a person "a father unaccustomed to fatherhood" (*WD*, 380).

---

8. For a contrary view of Smerdyakov as radically evil, see Gary Saul Morson, "Verbal Pollution in *The Brothers Karamazov*," in *Critical Essays on Dostoevsky*, ed. Robin Feuer Miller (Boston: G. K. Hall, 1986), 236.

The Grand Inquisitor is the ultimate emblem of such a "father." Of course, as failures in the school of love, absentee fathers and tyrannical ones like the Grand Inquisitor are quite similar: both are absent at least on the emotional and spiritual level. Dostoevsky coined the phrase "unaccustomed to fatherhood" in reference to a man named Kronenberg, a sadistic father whose scandalous trial Dostoevsky covered in his *Writer's Diary*.

Kronenberg was first an absentee father who abandoned his daughter in an orphanage in Geneva. (It is very likely that it was the Kronenberg affair, along with the story of Rousseau, that led Dostoevsky to associate Geneva with the plight of abandoned and abused children.) Kronenberg would later become a tyrannical father. After taking his daughter out of an orphanage, he returned to Russia and began to torture the six-year-old girl in order to rid her of some undesirable habits.

Grigory and His Family

The archvillain of *The Brothers Karamazov*, Smerdyakov, was ushered into the world by absentee fathers: by his biological father and, most important, by the person nominally responsible for raising him: Karamazov's servant, Grigory. Grigory is one more example of a father "unaccustomed to fatherhood." His destructive role in the shaping of Smerdyakov has so far eluded the readers of the novel. On those occasions when Grigory is mentioned at all, he is usually described as tender or pious.[9] There is something in Grigory that elicits trust. Not only Fyodor Karamazov trusts him, but the reader does as well. We trust Grigory because he took care of Fyodor's abandoned children, and we trust him because his negative views of Smerdyakov seem to confirm our view of Smerdyakov as an embodiment of evil.

Grigory, obviously, does not lie on purpose, yet he can be spectacularly wrong. None of his testimony given under oath in the court of law is, in fact, correct; it is there that he characterizes Smerdyakov as honest but foolish (how little, indeed, he knows about the person he cared for from birth); and it is there that he affirms that on the night of the murder, he saw open the door that leads into Fyodor's room. Grigory's remarks clearly constitute the most damning testimony against Dmitri.

It was Grigory's tendency to misjudge that in fact contributed to his master's death. When he saw Dmitri running toward the fence, Grigory charged toward him, screaming, "Parricide!" (*otseubivets*). He did not hesitate or seek to find out what happened. Here is how Dostoevsky describes Grigory's actions and thoughts: "Just so, his forebodings had not deceived him; he recognized the man, it was him, the 'monster,' the 'parricide'! 'Parricide!' the old man shouted for all the neighborhood to hear" (*BK*, 371). Dostoevsky rarely reproduces verbatim the thought processes of his characters, especially minor ones. This glimpse into Grigory's mind is therefore extremely important. Dostoevsky clearly felt the need to underscore

9. For a more sympathetic discussion of Grigory, see Robin Feuer Miller, *The Brothers Karamazov: Worlds of the Novel* (New York: Twayne Publishers, 1992), 43; Harriet Murav, *Holy Foolishness: Dostoevsky's Novels and the Poetics of Cultural Critique* (Stanford: Stanford UP, 1993), 129; and Valentin Nedzvetskii, "Misterial'noe nachalo v romane F. M. Dostoevskogo," in *Dostoevskii i mirovaia kul'tura* 9 (1997): 46.

Grigory's compulsive need to formulate and then convince himself of his forebodings.

It did not even occur to Grigory to check on his master's well-being. Had he returned to his master, who was alive and well at the moment, the murder would most likely have been prevented. The murderer Smerdyakov acknowledges that much to Ivan:

> I went to have a look in the corner, and stumbled over Grigory Vasilievich, lying near the wall, all covered with blood, unconscious. "So it's true, Dmitri Fyodorovich was here," jumped into my mind at once, and I at once decided to finish it all right then and there, sir, since even if Grigory Vasilievich was still alive, he wouldn't see anything while he was unconscious. (*BK*, 628)

In other words, not only did Grigory raise the man who was the actual murderer of Fyodor Karamazov, but he also served as an unwitting accomplice in the murder.

Grigory—his name, ironically, means "wide-awake" in its Greek origins—appears at key junctures of the novel. Critics do not usually identify Grigory with those other people in the novel who bear guilt and responsibility for the murder of Fyodor. Yet Grigory has something to feel guilty about: his foster child, Smerdyakov, commits suicide; he plays a fatal role in sending another foster child, Dmitri, to Siberia; and his own child is dead at two weeks old, Grigory might indeed be described as a sort of Chronos figure who devours his own children. The majority of the novel's characters, including Smerdyakov, are tortured by guilt. Grigory, on the other hand, never questions his actions or convictions. In this respect he joins company with the novel's obvious villains: Rakitin, Father Ferapont, and the merchant Samsonov.

When his wife gives birth to a child, Grigory immediately condemns the baby as "a dragon" only because the boy has six fingers. Much later in the novel, the defense attorney Fetyukovich asks Grigory how many fingers he has—a seemingly unrelated and insulting question. On a symbolic level, however, this question points to something else: figuratively speaking, it is Grigory who has dragon fingers. Instead of counting the fingers of newborn babies and dubbing them dragons, Dostoevsky seems to suggest, Grigory might have taken a good look at his own dragonlike behavior.[1]

In fact, the failure to love and pity coupled with the eagerness to judge, despise, and condemn is as pronounced in Grigory as it is in Ivan Karamazov or the Grand Inquisitor. In Grigory's case, however, this combination of attributes is manifested on the concrete level of domestic life. That realm contrasts with the more abstract moral, philosophical, and religious spheres where these attributes are to be found in Ivan and the Grand Inquisitor. In any case, the outlook and conduct of Grigory, Ivan, and the Grand Inquisitor clearly demonstrate that hell is not only the inability to love, as Zosima remarks, but also the ability and craving to judge.

Grigory judged his newborn babe a "dragon." He deliberately refuses to help his wife take care of the baby: for three days he withdraws into the

---

1. Incidentally, Grigory's last name is Kutuzov, that is, the name of the greatest Russian military leader (at least if we trust Tolstoy's judgment of Kutuzov's military abilities). Once again we have a sly suggestion on Dostoevsky's part that Grigory is a leader of the army, an army of dragons whom he brings forth into the world.

garden and wastes his time digging holes there. As a result, the baby dies of thrush, an infectious fungal disease caused by unsanitary conditions. Grigory, as is the case with demons, is frequently associated with dirt and uncleanness. In this context, it is hardly surprising that his foster son, Smerdyakov, is extremely fastidious. When the tyrannical old bene-factress of Fyodor's second wife arrives to collect Fyodor's children from Grigory, she immediately perceives him as the source of uncleanness: "Seeing at a glance that they were unwashed and in the dirty shirts, she gave one more slap to Grigory himself" (*BK*, 14). Even Grigory's imagina-tion is ruled by dirt. Thus he accuses Smerdyakov of "growing from the mildew in the bathhouse" (*BK*, 124).

Grigory's stubbornness, dogmatism, and constantly judgmental nature might have been praiseworthy under some other circumstances, but not within the family. His behavior instills in his foster children the convic-tion that the family is the place of willful, self-righteous, and cruel judg-ments. Once he judges and condemns someone, Grigory, in the language of Ivan's civil court, cuts off the "harmful member" (*BK*, 55). He does not seek to change the situation through patience and love.

In this respect, it is instructive to compare Grigory with another father in the novel, Captain Snegiryov. Encouraged by Smerdyakov, Snegiryov's son Ilyusha commits a series of rather pugnacious misdemeanors. Yet rather than condemning or punishing his son in the manner of Grigory, Snegiryov treats his son with love and compassion. And of course, it is love that survives against all odds in the bitter and mistreated boy.

Grigory's double is Father Ferapont. This half-mad monk who sees dev-ils everywhere approaches the world with an apocalyptic mentality. Like Grigory, Ferapont is forever ready to judge and condemn. When Zosima's corpse begins to stink, one of the monks recalls Ferapont's accusations of Zosima: "Yes, apparently Father Ferapont judged rightly yesterday" ("Vidno, otets-to Ferapont *spravedlivo* vchera *sudil*"; *BK*, 333; *Ps*, 14:301, emphasis added). This remark provides a vivid characterization of both the speaker and Father Ferapont: of all people, Christian monks should not judge. That is why in response to Ferapont's accusations, Zosima's friend Father Paisy replies, "Get thee hence, Father . . . it is not for men to judge, but for God" (*BK*, 335). Zosima, of course, makes a similar point when, in reply to Alyosha's request to mediate between Fyodor and Dmi-tri, he asks, "[W]ho made me a judge over them?" (*BK*, 32).

The belief that judgment can be just contradicts the very spirit of the novel itself. Justice and judgment consistently occupy opposite poles in Dostoevsky's novelistic world. That is apparent not only on the level of the plot, which culminates in the trial and its miscarriage of justice, but also in the lives of numerous characters who are frequently mistaken in their rash judgments of others. In fact, the novel is so pervaded by misjudg-ments and misreadings that had it not been for its tragic content, it might have been viewed as a comedy of errors. As it now stands, it might be called a tragedy of misjudgments.[2]

2. With the exception of Zosima and Alyosha, it appears that everyone calls Dmitri a monster or par-ricide at one time or another. Zosima, of course, kneels in front of Dmitri, an emblematic gesture that points to anything but judgment and condemnation. The refusal to judge moves even such sinners as Fyodor, who confesses to Alyosha: "I feel that you're the only one in the world who hasn't condemned [*osudil*] me, you are, my dear boy, I feel it, how can I not feel it" (*BK*, 19).

Grigory reads only two books, which, according to the narrator, he scarcely comprehends: the Book of Job and the homilies of Isaac the Syrian, in other words, a book of God's mysterious ways and a book of his mysterious power of love. In the transparently clear world of Grigory, however, there is no place for mystery. Once a monster, always a monster; once a stinking lackey, always a stinking lackey; once a rebel, always a rebel: such are the conclusions of his Euclidean mind, conclusions that he shares, of course, with his intellectual superiors Ivan and the Grand Inquisitor.

Like Ivan's devil who does not carry a watch, Grigory does not even know the date and the year, as he reveals during the trial. Grigory's existence outside of time concords with his apocalyptic outlook (when time shall be no more) and with the finality of his judgments. There is no possibility of change or growth in his world. That is why he reads the same two books over and over again. Not surprisingly, Zosima, in his musings on hell, remarks that sinners in hell are tortured by the awareness that "there will be no more time" to rectify their failure of love (*BK*, 322). Even if he is not yet tortured by it, Grigory already inhabits this loveless and timeless hell.

For some reason, we are told, Grigory dislikes one of Fyodor's wives and adores another. And these predilections or prejudices of his are unchanging. His rigorous dogmatism does not even allow him to conceive of Smerdyakov as a helpless child or to imagine that the boy might view Grigory and Marfa as his parents. As far as Grigory is concerned, Smerdyakov is the fruit of "the devil's son" (*BK*, 100). That is why Grigory, with his usual insensitivity, makes sure that everyone in Moscow knows of Smerdyakov's scandalous heritage when the boy is sent there. Even as an adult, Smerdyakov complains about Grigory's betrayal, a fact that discloses how much it must have wounded him. Alyosha happened to eavesdrop on Smerdyakov's complaints:

> I could have done even better, miss . . . if it wasn't for my destiny ever since childhood . . . I came from Stinking Lizaveta without a father, and they were shoving that in my face in Moscow, it spread there thanks to Grigory Vasilievich. Grigory Vasilievich reproaches me for rebelling against my nativity. "You opened her matrix," he says . . . I'd have let them kill me in the womb, so as not to come out into the world at all, miss. (*BK*, 224)

There is a bitter irony in Grigory's reproach to Smerdyakov. The expression *lozhesna razverz* (opened the womb) comes from Exodus: "And the Lord spake unto Moses, saying, Sanctify unto me all the firstborn, whatsoever openeth the womb among the children of Israel, both of man and of beast: it is mine" (Exodus 13:2 AV). Any firstborn, be it man or beast, is sanctified and belongs to God. Yet Grigory treats these very firstborns, these sanctified and Godly creatures, as if they were dragons or accursed anathemas. Grigory does his best to prevent Smerdyakov from growing; the latter appears to be forever tainted and defined by his last name ("a stinking one"). While the boy's first name, Paul, suggests a possibility of a change, those around Smerdyakov made sure that the possibility of such an outcome was slim indeed.

Grigory's verbal abuses underline his simplistic mind-set. He reduces those he attacks to their base, inescapable, frequently nonhuman origins.

This is how he talks to a boy Smerdyakov: "'You think you are a human being?' he would suddenly address Smerdyakov directly. 'You are not a human being, you were begotten of bathhouse slime, that's who you are'" (*BK*, 124). As the narrator reports, Smerdyakov could never forgive Grigory these words. Grigory, of course, is offended when during the trial Dmitri compares his loyalty to that of a dog. "I am not a poodle" (*BK*, 666), he mutters in indignation.

Upon the birth of Smerdyakov and the death of his son, Grigory declares that "God's orphan child is everyone's kin, all the more so for you and me. Our little dead one sent us this one, who was born from the devil's son and a righteous woman. Nurse him and weep no more" (*BK*, 100). Of this complex lineage—an orphan, a God's child, "from the devil's son and a righteous woman"—Grigory would later remember only the most offensive ones and would be forever happy to remind Smerdyakov of his dubious ancestry and otherwise to condemn and denigrate him.

Late in the novel, when Ivan threatens to denounce Smerdyakov, the latter articulates to Ivan his possible court defense: "I will certainly say right out that I never told you any such thing, sir, and that you . . . invented all that against me since you've considered me like a fly all your life anyway, and not like a man" (*BK*, 632). Such an attitude, expressed by the majority of Smerdyakov's superiors, is, of course, infectious. Thus, in turn, Smerdyakov begins to see others as no more than beasts (and we, of course, remember what he did with cats). On one occasion, Smerdyakov remarks of Grigory that "he is not a man [*eto ne chelovek*], let me tell you, but just like a stubborn mule, sir: he didn't see it, but he fancied he saw it—and you'll never be able to shake him sir" (*BK*, 630). This assessment of Grigory's stubbornness parallels Grigory's own sentence: "You are not a human being [*ty ne chelovek*]." Moreover, he seeks to accomplish the same task: to deny another person his humanity. Like father, like son, or in the words of the New Testament, frequently quoted and misquoted in the novel, "with what measure ye mete, it shall be measured to you" (Mark 4:24 AV).

This world of harsh immutable judgments was bound to implode. Discussing parents' cruelty, Dostoevsky once remarked that "when a society ceases to pity its weak and oppressed, it will itself be afflicted; it will grow callous and wither, it will become depraved and sterile" (*WD*, 383). Is it so surprising, then, that the depraved Fyodor and sterile Grigory are despised, beaten, and even murdered by their children? Chickens come home to roost.

Even though on one occasion the narrator notes Grigory's fondness for children (*BK*, 95), neither Grigory's words nor his actions support this assertion. Grigory, in fact, is very quick to abuse the boy Smerdyakov. He hits, whips, and curses him from the boy's earliest childhood. It is Grigory's violence, in fact, that the narrator connects with Smerdyakov's first epileptic attack at the age of twelve; at that time, unhappy about Smerdyakov's theological cynicism and his questioning the logic of Genesis, Grigory gives the boy "a violent blow on the cheek" (*BK*, 124). Even Fyodor is touched by the outcome of this incident and forbids Grigory to punish the boy. In earlier years, Dostoevsky criticized such methods of correction. He wrote in reference to another violent father: "[H]e supposed that one could eradicate at once, with one stroke, all that evil that had been sown and that had taken root in the heart of the child over the years. But that cannot be done; one must act slowly and have patience" (*WD*, 381).

Needless to say, physical abuse of children is a grave sin in the world of Dostoevsky. As the result of such beatings, Smerdyakov usually would retreat to the corner of the room: the quintessential gesture of a child victim in Dostoevsky's world:

> Do you know what it means to abuse a child? Their hearts are full of innocent, almost unconscious love, and blows such as these cause a grievous shock and tears that God sees and will count. For their reason is never capable of grasping their full guilt. Have you ever seen, or heard of little children who were tormented, or of orphans, say, who were raised among wicked strangers? Have you seen a child cowering in a corner, trying to hide, and weeping there . . . not knowing himself what he is doing, not clearly understanding his own guilt or why he is tormented but sensing all too well that he is not loved. (*WD*, 380)

"Sensing all too well that he is not loved": here is a feeling that must have accompanied Smerdyakov throughout his life and that certainly explains, in part, at least, many aspects of his character and behavior, including his cruelty, anger, envy, and tendency to blame others. It is useful, in this respect, to recall Dickens's approach to one of his most repulsive and negative characters, Uriah Heep. While not denying Heep's bad qualities, the narrator of *David Copperfield* stresses also the formative aspects of his upbringing: "I had never doubted his meanness, his craft, and malice; but I fully comprehend now, for the first time, what a base, unrelenting, and revengeful spirit must have been engendered by this early, and this long, suppression" (*David Copperfield* [New York: Airmont Publishing House], 484).

In his essay on the bloodthirsty terrorist Nechaev, entitled "One of Today's Falsehoods" (1873), Dostoevsky claims that he could never have become another Nechaev; this is only because he had been loved as a child, and had remembered this love: "As far back as I can remember I recall my parents' love for me" (*WD*, 289). On another occasion, he asserts: "The family is created by a ceaseless labor of love" (*WD*, 381). In fact, Dostoevsky stresses the same point in his presentation of Zosima, a man whose fond memories of childhood, shaped by the love of his mother and brother, gave him strength to renounce his old ways and change.[3]

In his portrayal of the Grand Inquisitor, Dostoevsky, one surmises, does not condemn him simply for treating his subjects as children but rather for being a bad father, a father "unaccustomed to fatherhood," a person who thinks only the worst of his children and sees them as weak and corrupt creatures, incapable of finding their own way.[4] Paradoxically, such

---

3. It is telling that in the presentation of numerous criminals in his *House of the Dead*, Dostoevsky never mentions their families, unless he talks about criminals who clearly do not belong in prison. Dostoevsky's favorite person in prison is a young man, Alei, whose description, in fact, bears a striking resemblance to that of Alyosha Karamazov. He is presented as the most loving and devoted son and brother. Alei stresses his mother's love for him at the very first conversation with the narrator (*Ps*, 4:53).

4. The Grand Inquisitor, of course, is the parody and perversion of the true Father, Christ, hence their confrontation over the fate of their "children" or their flock. Dostoevsky's portrayal of the Grand Inquisitor contains a profound insight, one that has been known since the Antichrist of Revelation. The relevance of this insight became especially clear in the twentieth century: any

fathers seem to care about their children, yet because they interpret any sign of independence as ingratitude or rebellion, they are prone to immediate violence.[5]

Both Grigory and Smerdyakov, father and son, embody the vicious circle of harsh judgments and harsh sentences. It is thus hardly surprising that Smerdyakov so resembles Grigory. Grigory is a loner, pompous and taciturn. He never bothers to talk to people around him, including his wife, and presumes an air of superiority. Of Smerdyakov we learn that "he had an arrogant nature and seemed to despise everyone" (*BK*, 124).

The name of Grigory's obedient wife is Mara Ignatievna. Smerdyakov's pomposity impresses a woman named Maria Kondratievna, who views him as her groom and tries to accommodate him in a manner reminiscent of Grigory's wife. Both Grigory and Smerdyakov use glasses for reading, a fact that Dostoevsky finds relevant enough to stress, especially when Ivan with his usual benevolence muses on the bespectacled Smerdyakov: "Such a creature and in spectacles to boot!" ("Ekaia tvar', da esche v ochkakh"; *BK*, 613; *Ps*, 15:50). It is noteworthy that besides Grigory and Smerdyakov, the novel features one more character in obvious need of glasses: Ivan's devil. He appears to Ivan carrying a "lorgnette" (*BK*, 636). Smerdyakov, in fact, needed his glasses to read Isaac the Syrian, that is, the favorite book of Grigory. Both, obviously, hardly have any understanding of the content. The reason seems quite plain: both prefer to judge and condemn instead of yielding to Christian love and forgiveness.

Smerdyakov

In one of his rare monologues, Smerdyakov expresses the Job-like wish never to have been born. This comment alerts us (though not Alyosha, who overhears this complaint) to the harsh reality of his life. During another of his rebellious moments described in the chapter "The Disputation" (bk. 3, chap. 7), Smerdyakov, like Job, proceeds publicly to question God in the presence of his senior friends, such as Fyodor, Grigory, Ivan, and Alyosha. Like Job's friends, these people prefer to blame the victim, accusing Smerdyakov of apostasy or monstrosity or pontificating about the Russianness of his beliefs.

Rather than concentrating on the Joban subtext, however, the narrator gives the story a twist when he characterizes this unexpected rebellion with the following words: "but Balaam's ass suddenly spoke" (*BK*, 127). This reference casts the events of the chapter in a totally different light. We remember from the Book of Numbers that Balaam's ass, after she balks upon seeing an angel blocking her way, gets a sound beating from Balaam. After the beating has been repeated three times, and after the

---

figure with a claim to a surrogate fatherhood has to assume a religious aura, to utilize, or rather abuse, "miracle, mystery, and authority." The great tyrants of the twentieth century, of course, did so rather successfully.

5. Dostoevsky argues that only he who observes, encourages, and participates in the spiritual growth of his children embodies a true fatherhood: "These little creatures only enter into our souls and attach themselves to our hearts when we, having begotten them, watch over them from childhood, without leaving them from the time of their first smile; and then we continue to grow into one another's souls every day, every hour, all through our lives. Now that is the family, that is something sacred" (*WD*, 380–81).

ass addresses Balaam in a human voice, Balaam finally begins to see what she has been seeing all along.

By calling Smerdyakov a Balaam's ass, yet by treating him as if he is just an ass, his "fathers" show the blindness of the Geneva citizens who call Richard "a brother" and then chop his head off, or the blindness of Ivan, who self-righteously condemns them without being aware that he himself is committing a similar moral blunder.

This refusal to recognize the message of Balaam's ass, the message of the ever-present power of miracles and faith which can be revealed to anyone, including an ass, informs the whole scene. Even though Smerdyakov undergoes a barrage of insults, as does Balaam's ass, he, as opposed to this she-ass, denies the plausibility and relevance of both miracles and faith. While God is ever present in the story of Balaam, it is relegated to the useless beyond in the exchange that takes place between Smerdyakov and his listeners, Ivan and Fyodor. The ground is cleared for the world of "two vipers eating each other up" (BK, 143).

Small wonder that Fyodor Karamazov gets very upset with Smerdyakov's performance, especially after Ivan explains to him that the suppression of religion would result in the suppression of him, Fyodor Karamazov. Following Ivan's explanation, Fyodor exclaims, "Ah, what an ass I am [kakaia zhe ia oslitsa]" (BK, 143). Fyodor's exclamation not only underscores Fyodor's kinship to Smerdyakov but also reminds us of the difference that separates the world of Balaam from the world of Karamazov's Skotoprigonievsk. In the Bible, the ass speaks in the language of humans and sees angels; in the novel, humans persistently reject God's relevance to their life and act like beasts. The scene, in fact, is dominated by the persistent comparison of human beings to roaches, pigs, and vipers.

Of course, the reference to Balaam's ass takes on a different meaning at the end of the novel. While the earlier scene suggests that the world of the novel reverses the biblical situation, some later events indicate the presence of visions and miracles. In the long run, Smerdyakov himself begins to be aware of God's presence. During his final interview with Ivan, Smerdyakov indeed speaks like Balaam's ass, as he accuses Ivan of being blind: "There's no ghost, sir, besides the two of us, and some third one. . . . That third one is God, sir, Providence itself, sir, it's right here with us now, sir, only don't look for it, you won't find it" (BK, 623).

Cruelty within the family—the desecration of the divine ideals of love, pity, and forgiveness—becomes for Dostoevsky one of the most disturbing and pervasive offenses. To underscore it, Dostoevsky has the main family offender, Fyodor, spit on an icon. In a similar vein, another failed father, Versilov in The Raw Youth, breaks an icon. These sacrilegious acts highlight the fact that instead of being fathers, these men have become, as it were, anti-fathers. The neglect and abuse of children, these images of God, as well as the desecration of icons constitute the most direct and immediate subversion of the divine. They are presented as truly demonic. It is hardly surprising, then, that cosmic religious imagery pervades Dostoevsky's portrayal of the family. It is also no surprise that the description of a failed family that opens The Brothers Karamazov is juxtaposed with the image of a new kind of family in the novel's conclusion, that is, the family of an ideal foster parent, Alyosha, and his twelve boys. To paraphrase Dostoevsky,

"God and devil are fighting with each other, and the battlefield is a human family." The outcome of the battle will depend on what kind of family will prevail.

ROBERT L. BELKNAP

From The Rhetoric of an Ideological Novel[†]

* * *

* * *Ivan's greatness generates a rhetorical and a genetic argument. First, one may ask why an author would select such an attractive mouthpiece for ideas he hopes to crush. Second, one can deny the possibility of creating a truly great character without real sympathy at some level.* * *

* * *

Indeed, it has been said that Ivan's fate in the novel is designed to show what happens to an atheist and a socialist. He is desperately unhappy; he is rejected in love; and he becomes diseased in the part of him on which he depends excessively, the brain. His suffering and his incapacity at the end of the novel are taken as Dostoevsky's vision of the just punishment of unbelief.

A more sophisticated way of refuting Ivan's position involves not what happens to him but what he does and is. Valentina Vetlovskaia has catalogued enough unpleasant actions and features of Ivan's to make a convincing case that Dostoevsky intended to discredit Ivan's argument by discrediting its spokesman.[1] Her study underlines the problem this novel presents. She shows Dostoevsky using one of the classical rhetorical techniques, the *argumentum ad hominem*, and leaves us with the evidence of Lawrence and scores of other able readers that the technique did not work. * * *

* * *

Zosima offers a rhetorical answer to the problem of children's suffering, which Dostoevsky in his letter had considered unanswerable. Zosima does not justify such suffering; he simply calls on the reader to share the blame. But even this did not seem to satisfy Dostoevsky. He had still another resource for the destruction of Ivan, the reductio ad absurdum, the carrying of Ivan's nature and doctrines to the logical conclusion that would discredit them. This involves the introduction into the novel of a body of characters whose analogy to Ivan is made distinct, and whose ridiculousness is made more distinct.

* * *

The finest parody of Ivan and his Inquisitor is Kolya Krasotkin, the thirteen-year-old schoolboy who can strike terror into the hearts of his

---

† From William Todd Mills III, *Literature and Society in Imperial Russia, 1800–1914.* Copyright © 1978 by the Board of Trustees of the Leland Stanford Jr. University. Reprinted with permission.
1. V. E. Vetlovskaya, "Ritorika i poetika" in *Isseledovaniia po poezii i stilistike* (Leningrad, 1972), 163–84.

mother, his teachers, and his classmates. Like Ivan, Kolya is very intelligent, is incessantly tortured by self-consciousness, quotes Voltaire, and has a breadth of reading that astonishes those around him. But his intelligence is a schoolboy's smartness, amusing to watch, and his self-doubt and self-consciousness involve his appearance and his wits, not his moral position. He quotes Voltaire but does not understand him, and his reading is in trivial school compendiums.

When Ivan meets Alyosha, he says he wants to see him very much: "I want to get acquainted with you once and for all, and to get you to know me . . . I've finally learned to respect you; it's plain this man stands firm. . . . I love these firm ones, whatever they may stand on, even if they're little galoots like you." (IX, 287)[2] The intensity of the affection overrides the patronizing words, and Alyosha responds in kind: "You're just the same sort of young man as all the other 23-year-olds, the same young, youthful, fresh, and wondrous boy, a weanling, and to sum it up, a boy. Tell me, did I hurt your feelings badly?" When Kolya summons Alyosha, he also "very, very much wanted to get acquainted." (X, 39) Later he says, "I'm glad to know you, Karamazov. I've wanted to know you for a long time. . . . I learned long ago to respect you as a rare being. . . . I have heard that you are a mystic and were in the monastery. I know you are a mystic, but—that didn't stop me. Contact with reality will cure you." (X, 57) Kolya here constitutes the realization of Ivan's metaphors. He is a real, not a figurative, boy, and at the simplest level he believes the patronizing words he is using. At the same time, his respect and affection for Alyosha emerge in close parallel to Ivan's.

One puzzling moment in the novel is Kolya's long account of the goose, a lame story of a piece of boyish cruelty (X, 51–52). He had asked a stupid peasant whether a cartwheel would decapitate a goose that was pecking under it. Watching from the side where the goose was pecking, Kolya winked at the right moment, and the peasant made the cart move, cutting the goose's neck in two. "You did that on purpose," people cry. "No, not on purpose," Kolya answers; but the stupid peasant says, "It wasn't me, that's the one who got me to do it." Kolya's answer has the hauteur of his intellectual superiority: "I hadn't taught him at all; I had simply expressed the basic idea and only spoke hypothetically." This guiltily rationalized account seems overly expanded in the novel, until it takes its place with Ivan's struggle to avoid admitting that his basic idea has seduced Smerdyakov into killing, and with Smerdyakov's teaching of little Ilyusha to torture dogs by feeding them bread with pins in it. The vicarious assaults on the animals remind readers of Ivan's place in the murder, and rob him of much of the sympathy that might attach to him as a misunderstood manipulator.

Kolya's behavior trivializes the ideas of the Grand Inquisitor and the Devil, as well as those Ivan expresses himself. Kolya trains the dog Zhuchka to play dead and resurrect itself, and then stages the reappearance of the dog as a miracle for Ilyusha. He exploits the mysterious secret about the founding of Troy, and crushes the boy who divulges it. He performs an exploit that is the modern child's equivalent of Christ's second temptation in the wilderness, casting himself between the tracks of an oncoming train. And he uses authority, deception, and force for the good

2. Fyodor Mikhailovich Dostoevsky, *Sobranie Sochinenii* (Moscow, 1956–58).

of the little group of schoolboys, whom he treats as the Grand Inquisitor treats all humanity. The Inquisitor said:

> Oh we shall finally persuade them not to be proud; . . . we shall show them that though they are feeble, though they are only pitiable children, childish happiness is the sweetest of all. They will grow timid and will start to look up to us and press against us in fear, like fledglings to their mother. They will feel wonder and terror at us. . . . Yes, we will make them work, but in the hours free from work, we will arrange their life like children's play . . . and they will worship us as their benefactors. (IX, 325)

Kolya realizes some of these metaphors. He actually arranges childish games and commands the obedience of the boys "like a god." He even says:

> And, generally, I love the small fry. I have two fledglings on my hands at home right now; even today they delayed me. So [the boys] stopped beating Ilyusha, and I took him under my protection. I can see that he's a proud boy. I tell you that: he's proud, but in the end he has entrusted himself to me like a slave, fulfills my slightest commands, obeys me like a god, and tries to imitate me. . . . So now you too, Karamazov, have gotten together with all these fledglings? (X, 32)

Everything here echoes Ivan and cheapens Ivan. The pride of sinful humanity becomes the stubbornness of a pathetic child. The children or fledglings shrink, from the whole of humanity whom the Inquisitor loves and serves, to a couple of groups of children who reinforce Kolya's ego. The Inquisitor's godlike dominion becomes a child's bossiness. And Kolya's resurrection of the dog becomes a comment on Ivan's dreams of resurrecting the dead and all the talk of miracles, because we can see the effect of this miracle: "If the unsuspecting Krasotkin had understood how torturingly and murderously such a moment could influence the health of the sick boy, he would not have thought of playing a trick like the one he played." (X, 46) The word "murderously" here removes Kolya from the world of real mockery and makes him an involuntary killer in his blind superiority.

Radicalism in Dostoevsky's day was almost a club, and membership required certain attitudes. Various novels and journalistic pieces, friendly, hostile, and ambivalent, ranging from Turgenev's *Fathers and Sons* to Chernyshevsky's *What Is to Be Done?*, had canonized the list: materialism, scientism, positivism, atheism, socialism, internationalism, realism, feminism, and in the 1870's populism, all coupled with hostility to sentiment, tradition, prejudice, manners, the aesthetic, the establishment, and the government. Except for feminism and internationalism Kolya manages to take every pose demanded of a radical. In the chapter "A Schoolboy," he begins: "They're scum . . . doctors and the whole medical filth, speaking in general and, of course, in detail. I reject medicine. It's a useless establishment." (X, 22) This remark might not seem scientistic, but in the tradition of Russia radicalism the deliverers of medical care received none of the honor accorded to the investigators of medical truth.

Kolya goes on to attack Alyosha and the boys for sentimentalizing in their visits to Ilyusha, and later, after an "impressive silence," he makes an excursion into scientism and utopian political positivism (X, 23):

"I love to observe realism, Smurov. Have you observed how dogs meet and sniff each other. They obey some common law of nature there."

"Yes, it's sort of funny."

"No, it's not funny. You're wrong about that. In nature there's nothing funny, however, it might seem to a man with his prejudices. . . . That's a thought of Rakitin's, a remarkable thought. I'm a socialist, Smurov."

"And what's a socialist?" . . .

"That's if all are equal and own common property, and there are no marriages, and religion and all the laws are the way each person wants, and, well, and so on. You're still young for that; it's early for you. It's chilly, though." . . .

"Have you noticed, Smurov, the way in the middle of winter, if it's fifteen or even eighteen degrees, it doesn't seem so cold as now, for example, at the beginning of winter. . . . With people everything's a matter of habit, even in governmental and political relationships."

Kolya then pauses to tease a benign peasant he passes, concluding, "I love to talk with the people, and am always prepared to give it its due. . . . With the people, you have to know how to talk." (X, 24)

The picture of the young radical pontificating to a devotedly receptive follower had become ironic at least as early as *Fathers and Sons* and savage in Leskov's *An Enigmatic Man*. The catalogue of shibboleths recurs two chapters later in another setting, also as old as Turgenev, with the young man patronizingly enlightening the older about radical doctrine. The indoctrination of Alyosha also starts with the statement that medicine is villainy. After an interruption by concerns involving Ilyusha, Kolya expounds on his schoolboy cynicism toward history, which parodies Ivan's sense of the meaninglessness of history as described by Dostoevsky to Liubimov. Kolya says:

I don't ascribe much importance to all those old wives' tales, and in general haven't too much respect for world history. . . . It's the study of the series of human stupidities, and that's all. I respect only mathematics and natural science. . . . Again, these classical languages . . . classical languages, if you want my opinion about them, are a police measure. . . . They're introduced because they're tiresome and because they dull our capacities. . . . It was pointless, so how could it be made more pointless? And that's when they thought up the classical languages. (X, 54)

At this point, one boy in the group shouts out, "And he's the top student in Latin." In enunciating one of the standard doctrines of the practical and scientistic radicals, Kolya displays his disinterestedness. This rejection of what he labels "baseness" (*podlost'*) offers a child's equivalent of the nobility with which the Grand Inquisitor rejects the salvation he has the ability to earn, or with which Ivan returns his ticket. The gesture is the same, and the love for the oppressed is the same, but the schoolboy's showing off infects the reader's recollection of the Inquisitor's magnificent self-sacrifice.

Dostoevsky's central quarrel with the radicals may well have involved their attitude toward religion. Kolya follows his splendid thirteen-year-old statement that contact with reality would cure Alyosha's mysticism with this definition of mysticism: "Well, God and all." He elaborates his ideas about God, which turn out to be a travesty of Ivan's ambivalent abstention from denial.

> "I don't have anything against God. Of course, God is only a hypothesis— but—I admit that He is necessary for order—for the order of the world and so on—and if He did not exist, it would be necessary to invent Him," added Kolya, starting to blush. . . . "Even without believing in God, it's possible to love mankind. . . . I've read *Candide*, in Russian translation. . . . I'm a socialist, Karamazov, an incorrigible socialist. . . . The Christian faith has served only the rich and noble, to hold the lower class in slavery, isn't that true? . . . I am not against Christ. That was a really humane person, and if He had lived in our time, He would have joined the revolutionists right away and maybe played a prominent role—that's certain, even." (X, 57)

The talk about hypotheses, the order of things, the necessity for God, and the possibility of love without God all plainly reminds the reader of Ivan. The talk about socialism, the sins of Christianity, and Christ's need to join the revolutionists recalls the Grand Inquisitor. Ivan has observed, "Everything that in Europe is a hypothesis is immediately an axiom for the Russian boy." His frequent use of the word "boy" (*mal'chik*) prepares the reader for the repetition of these doctrines by a real boy, culminating in the word-for-word repetition of Voltaire's aphorism about the invention of God. But this aphorism is the highest reach of Kolya's sophistication, whereas for Ivan it is the starting point for two passionate statements about a single vision of humanity. We have already noted the first: "I think that if the Devil does not exist, and man in fact created him, then he created him in his own image and likeness" (IX, 299). The second is so powerful that it needed Kolya's parody:

> And indeed, man did invent God. It would be nothing strange and nothing wondrous for God to really exist, but the wondrous thing is that such a thought, the thought of the necessity of God, could creep into the head of such a savage and evil animal as man; it is so holy, so touching, so wise, and does such honor to man. (IX, 294)

Through this entire catalogue of shibboleths, Ivan's doctrines become associated with the conceit and embarrassed self-consciousness that are Kolya's most visible traits. The rhetorical function of Kolya's conceit is curiously related to the best-known source for Kolya. George Chulkov has shown that many of Kolya's doctrines coincide closely with statements made by Belinsky. And we know that in the early seventies Dostoevsky found conceit to be a central feature of Belinsky's character. Arkady Dolinin has summed up Dostoevsky's attitude toward Belinsky at that time by using a series of quotations from Dostoevsky's letters:

> "Belinsky, that most rotten, dull, and shameful phenomenon of Russian life." "A stinkbug, Belinsky was just an impotent and feeble little talent." "Belinsky cursed Russia and knowingly brought upon her so much woe." "In Belinsky there was so much petty conceit, viciousness, impatience, exacerbation, baseness, but most of all conceit. It never occurred to him that he himself was disgusting. He was pleased with

himself in the highest degree, and that was already a stinking, shameful, personal stupidity." "He related to Gogol's characters superficially to the point of meaninglessness. . . . He scolded Pushkin when Pushkin casts off his false pose. . . . He rejected the end of *Eugene Onegin*. . . ." "He didn't even understand his own people. He didn't even understand Turgenev."[3]

Perhaps here, in this vision of Belinsky, is a source for some of the conceit in Kolya, for some of the littleness and incomprehension. Of course, the nastiness that is such a conspicuous part of these letters has disappeared. Kolya can be cruel, arrogant, conceited, but there is no stinking, shameful talentlessness in him. These qualities seem to survive in two places. One is Kolya's vision of himself: "Tell me, Karamazov," he asks, "do you despise me terribly?" And the other repository for these unpleasant qualities is Rakitin, who embodies them superbly.

Dolinin argues, however, that Dostoevsky's view of Belinsky and his political attitude as a whole underwent a revolution in 1876, and that by the time *The Brothers Karamazov* began to emerge, he was expressing some of the old ardor he had felt for the Belinsky who had honored and befriended him in 1846. He refers to him as "the most honorable and noble Belinsky," and echoes Apollon Grigor'ev's claim that "if he had lived longer, Belinsky would necessarily have joined the Slavophiles." The chronological lines may not be so neat as Dolinin makes them, but the ambivalence is certainly there. If the vile and nasty traits Dostoevsky saw in Belinsky went to make Rakitin, we should look in a novel of the 1870's for some expression of the magnificent eloquence and true self-sacrifice Dostoevsky also attributed to him. Here most obvious repository is Ivan himself. Indeed, an excellent critic of Dostoevsky, Alfred Rammelmeyer, considers Belinsky a chief source for the Grand Inquisitor, documenting his case primarily with Belinsky's letters to Botkin, which Pypin had published not long before the writing of *The Brothers Karamazov*.

If Kolya and Ivan both derive from Belinsky, one from the noble vision and one from the little, conceited vision, with Rakitin as the repository for all the vilest traits, at first glance it might seem that Chulkov had oversimplified the pattern, and that Kolya resembles Belinsky because Ivan does and Kolya is a parody of Ivan. On the basis of the notebooks for *The Brothers Karamazov*, I would suggest another pattern of development. For years Dostoevsky had been working on two projects, the life of a great sinner and a book about children. Earlier he had planned two other great novels, "Atheism" and the Russian Candide. The great sinner, whose life was to be traced from childhood, was to fall into radicalism and eventually to be saved. This career coincides not with Ivan's, not with Alyosha's, both of which have been connected with the plan, but with Kolya's. If this formulation is right, in the mid-1870's the plans for the Russian Candide, for "Atheism," for the life of the great sinner, and for the novel about children all became focused on the figure of little Kolya Krasotkin. The earliest surviving notes we have for *The Brothers Karamazov* relate to him. The figure of Ivan the radical emerges only later. Ivan then, like Rakitin, would have come into existence as a repository for traits Dostoevsky

---

3. Fyodor Mikhailovich Dostoevsky, *Pis'ma 1878–81*, ed. A. S. Dolinin, quote at IV, 26.

could not incorporate into a child when he merged the heroes of these four unwritten novels into a single youthful figure.

Once the character of Ivan had been spun off, it assumed the residual loveliness of Belinsky and of Aleksandr Herzen. Indeed, it might perhaps be argued that the ideological revolution in Dostoevsky's thinking which Dolinin dates to the mid-1870's was the result and not the cause of the emergence of Ivan from the mass of materials that were to become the novel. About the figure of Ivan would gather the noble doubts, the mighty pity, the love of life, of humanity, of family that were later to make him so dangerous to the ideological intentions Dostoevsky described in his letter to Liubimov. In this case, I would suggest that the child is father of the man.

*   *   *

ULRICH SCHMID

Split Consciousness and Characterization in *The Brothers Karamazov*†

It has often been observed that Dostoevsky's novels are essentially constructed as dramas. The narrative voice retreats behind the dialogues, which are conveyed primarily as direct speech. In such a scenic narrative, direct contact among individual characters is an indispensable prerequisite for the construction of the plot.[1] Mikhail Bakhtin therefore described Dostoevsky's works as polyphonic novels and indicated that there is no hierarchy among the participating voices:

> A plurality of independent and unmerged voices and consciousnesses, a genuine polyphony of fully valid voices is in fact the chief characteristic of Dostoevsky's novels. What unfolds in his works is not a multitude of characters and fates in a single objective world illuminated by a single authorial consciousness; rather a plurality of consciousnesses, with equal rights and each with its own world, combine but are not merged in the unity of the event.[2]

Bakhtin makes this point even more clearly in a lecture from 1925. He emphasizes the absolute dominance of the characters, which has considerable stylistic consequences for the poetics of Dostoevsky's novels.

> In Dostoevsky there are many heroes, and each of them commands an individual voice. They have stolen the voice of the author. Descriptions are given in the voice of this or that hero, they are stylized after the heroes. There is therefore no space for us in Dostoevsky's works. We must either remain inside the heroes or close the book.[3]

Bakhtin's notion bears a serious disadvantage, however. He assumes that every character appearing in the text is at the same time necessarily

† Reprinted by permission of the author. Trans. Katherine Bowers and Susan McReynolds.
1. This point is made by T. M. Rodina in *Dostoevsky: Povestvovanie i drama* (Moscow: Nauka, 1984).
2. M. M. Bakhtin, *Problems of Dostoevsky's Poetics* (Minneapolis: U of Minnesota P, 1984) 6.
3. *Dostoevskii*, in Mikhail Bakhtin, *Sobranie sochinenii* vol 2 (Moscow: Russkie slovari, 2000), 266–87, quotation at p. 266.

an individual consciousness. Bakhtin views each hero as an autonomous personality that can enter into free contact with other individuals. When reading Dostoevsky, however, one must take into account that character and consciousness do not always coincide. Dostoevsky's artistic intelligence sometimes splits a complex consciousness into multiple characters. A one-to-one correspondence of character and consciousness represents only one and not even the most common case in Dostoevsky's novels. There is a whole spectrum of possible forms of characterization. The problematic consciousness, which lies at the heart of the dramatic plot, can be either much narrower or much broader than an individual fictional character.

The integral representation of one clearly delimited consciousness in a single individual is rather an exception in Dostoevsky. More frequently, we find that a fictional character may be composed out of several consciousnesses; or, conversely, certain aspects of a split consciousness may be attributed to several seemingly individual characters. In the latter case one group of individuals makes up a complex consciousness. The reasons for adopting such a compositional strategy are evident: it is much simpler to present a mental conflict as a dialogue between individuals than to depict this struggle within a single consciousness.

From this perspective, it becomes clear that dialogue in Dostoevsky is frequently the functional equivalent of inner monologue. Whether a specific ideological dilemma is handled artistically as a dramatic dialogue or an inner monologue primarily depends on the structuring of the consciousness and characters. Each analysis of Dostoevsky's fiction has to address this crucial question: What is the status of an individual character—is it part of a complex consciousness on a higher, metanarratological level, or is it, conversely, a composition of contradictory psychic elements?

Bakhtin does not acknowledge this distinction, and therefore remains interested exclusively in the phenomena of polyphony and dialogism in Dostoevsky. Dialogue among characters who, taken together, constitute a complex consciousness corresponds technically to the inner monologue of one contradictory consciousness; yet this essential equivalence remains outside Bakhtin's purview. His blindness to the division of a complex consciousness into multiple characters in Dostoevsky results in a biased assortment of textual examples. Dostoevsky's novel *The Adolescent* (1875), for example, figures very little in Bakhtin's argument, probably because the complex consciousness of the title character dominates the novel. More relevant for Bakhtin's argument are dialogue-intensive works such as *Bobok* or *The Idiot*. Those texts in which Dostoevsky shifts the main conflict of the plot from the interpersonal domain into the interior of one contradictory consciousness are not conducive to Bakhtinian analysis.

Before we can analyze dialogism, the interrelation between the complex dramatic consciousness and the artistic device of characterization must be defined. In his narrative representation of the complex consciousness, Dostoevsky performs a kind of chemical experiment: he brings contradictory elements of consciousness into contact and observes the ensuing reactions. In Dostoevsky's works, the poetological primacy lies therefore not in the action, but, rather, in the characters. Mathematically stated: the course of the plot is a function of the character combination. This thesis can be corroborated by documentary evidence. As a rule, Dostoevsky begins work on a new text with the delineation of the most important characters.

For example, Alexander Dolinin has analyzed the artistic composition of *The Adolescent* and highlighted the dependence of the action on the profiling, composition, and interaction of the protagonists.[4]

Dostoevsky's literary output after his Siberian exile shows a high degree of coherency. The different forms of representation of a complex consciousness in the fictional characters of the five large novels from *Crime and Punishment* (1866) to *The Brothers Karamazov* (1880) are *in nuce* already extant in the experimental novel *The Insulted and the Injured* (1861). At the center of this commonly neglected text stands a moral conflict, which arises from the confrontation of various ideological positions. Dostoevsky tries to distill the reactive elements as purely as possible before he brings them in contact: naked egoism pounces on perfect self-sacrifice, sexual exploitation contrasts with pure love, radical atheism strikes against holy belief. The individual characters which represent these positions are so exaggerated in *The Insulted and the Injured* that they can hardly fulfill expectations of psychological realism. The sharpening of the conflict through an extreme profiling of the characters, however, creates the hysterical atmosphere that is so typical for Dostoevsky's *œuvre*.

The collective body of Dostoevsky's novels can essentially be read as a macrotext addressing a single topic. The main theme is the diagnosis of the crisis of Russian society.[5] Dostoevsky presents his topic, the frustrated expectation of salvation in and for Russia, in ever new combinations. He believes that Russia has a historic mission, that it will redeem the world and bring about a golden age. However, this messianic vision is threatened by what he perceives to be competing messianic ideologies (Catholicism, socialism, Protestantism, Judaism, capitalism). The tension between the radiant utopia he envisions for Russia and the miserable reality he and his readers confront is precisely what forms the dramatic conflict of Dostoevsky's novels. Each novel creates a new artistic solution for the representation of this conflict.

In his study of Dostoevsky, Bakhtin implicitly assumes that all novelistic characters occupy equal positions. According to Bakhtin, the truth constitutes itself in Dostoevsky's works not as the conqueror of one position or another, but, rather, as a concert of various voices. It can be argued, however, that Dostoevsky in fact operates with a distinct hierarchy of values and expresses his own ideological preferences quite clearly. The action of the novel is propelled by the incongruence between the value preferences of the protagonists on one side and of the author on the other side. This discrepancy is resolved either positively or negatively: the protagonist can acquire the author's truth, or tragically fail.

An overview of the most important novels from Dostoevsky's last fifteen productive years shows that the complex consciousness of the protagonists undergoes a process of increasing differentiation into distinct characters. Dostoevsky provides the protagonist of his first major novel, Raskolnikov from *Crime and Punishment*, with a very complex consciousness, one that ultimately proves too broad for an individual character. He

4. A. S. Dolinin, *V tvorcheskoi laboratorii Dostoevskogo (Istoriia sozdaniia romana Podrostok)*. Moscow: Sovetskii pisatel', 1947.
5. See Horst-Jürgen Gerigk, "Das Russland-Bild in den fünf grossen Romanen Dostojewskijs," in *Zeitperspektiven. Studien zu Kultur und Gesellschaft. Beiträge aus der Geschichte, Soziologie, Philosophie und Literaturwissenschaft*, ed. Uta Gerhardt (Stuttgart: Franz Steiner, 2003), 49–79.

then divides the complex consciousness among two complementary characters in *The Idiot*, distributes it among three in *The Devils*, and ultimately arrives at a still more differentiated solution in *The Brothers Karamazov*: here the four brothers and, as the case may be, half-brothers represent components of a superior consciousness.

Crime and Punishment (1866) presents a world that almost entirely coincides with the complex consciousness of the protagonist. The contradictory main character bears the name Raskolnikov, which means "the split one." The novel shows how Raskolnikov is torn between the "Napoleonic idea," the notion that all is permitted to a strong person, and the "Russian idea" of selfless devotion to humanity. Raskolnikov thus is no individual, but rather a "composite": in his consciousness various voices, which belong either to other characters (Sonya) or representatives of a specific ideology (Napoleon), conflict. With this dramatic construction, Dostoevsky is able to switch between internal monologue and external dialogue. The consequent typographical markings of this artistic device are noteworthy: Dostoevsky shows direct speech through a dash, while Raskolnikov's thoughts stand in double quotations. The conflict in *Crime and Punishment* is narrated in two modes: as inner monologue in Raskolnikov's consciousness, and as dramatic dialogue between the protagonist and the characters who come in contact with him (his beloved, family, friends, the police).

In his next novel, *The Idiot* (1868), Dostoevsky adopts a different approach. Dostoevsky initially conceived of his protagonist, the saintly and innocent Prince Myshkin, completely differently, namely as a further continuation of the complex hero from *Crime and Punishment*. In his early notes towards the novel Dostoevsky defines the strong willed character of the idiot in terms that make the similarity to Raskolnikov unmistakable; Dostoevsky definitely wants him to embody primarily "demonic self-empowerment." In these early notes the split nature of the idiot is clearly expressed. Two opposing life goals, which have only hyperbolic self-aggrandizement in common, are under consideration for this protagonist: "Either to rule as a tyrant or to die for all on the cross."[6]

Indeed, Dostoevsky seems to have pursued his original plan with a Raskolnikov-Idiot fairly extensively; on December 4, 1867, however, he throws—as he reports in a letter—everything "to the devil" and begins on December 18, 1867 with the transcript of a "new novel."[7] The innerly-divided character initially intended as the protagonist is now split between two characters: into the light Prince Myshkin and the dark Rogozhin. This opposition is already constructed in the opening scene. Myshkin is "a young fellow [. . .] very fair, with a thin, pointed and very light colored beard; his eyes were large and blue, and had an intent look about them [. . .]. His face was [. . .] quite colorless, except for the circumstance that at this moment it was blue with cold." Rogozhin, on the contrary, has "black curling hair, and small, grey, fiery eyes."[8]

Dostoevsky organizes the appearance of the two characters in the novel very carefully. The beginning as well as the ending scenes present Myshkin and Rogozhin together. This close connection is deepened by a further peculiarity: Rogozhin never appears in the novel unless Myshkin

6. Fyodor Dostoevsky, *Polnoe sobranie sochinenii* 11:180. All quotations from Dostoevsky are the author's translation from this edition unless otherwise noted.
7. Ibid. 28.2:239–40.
8. Ibid. 8:5–6.

is physically present in the scene. This demonstrates that Rogozhin is not an independent character, but is rather conceptualized as a complement to Myshkin. Within his fiction Dostoevsky even allows for the possibility that Rogozhin is an incarnation of a demon that haunts Myshkin.[9]

The intimate familiarity of Myshkin and Rogozhin is also emphasized by the ease of communication between these characters. Myshkin's dialogues with the other characters are marked throughout by misunderstandings, yet Myshkin and his counterpart Rogozhin understand each other even in the absence of words. Rogozhin's attempt to assassinate Myshkin and his murder of Nastasya Filippovna themselves give hardly any cause for discussion—Myshkin intuitively understands Rogozhin's course of action. The intimate relationship between Myshkin and Rogozhin finds pictorial expression in the final scene: Myshkin's tears flow over Rogozhin's cheeks.[1]

The complementary construction of these characters is supported on both sides through verbal cues: Myshkin exclusively uses the informal address (*ty*) exclusively with Rogozhin; similarly, Rogozhin is the only character who never calls Myshkin "Idiot."[2] This last point, especially, merits attention: for all the other characters Myshkin is one who exists for himself alone, isolated from society (this is the meaning of the Greek word *idiotes*), whereas for Rogozhin he is a complementary character, who is not perceived as strange. The parallel fates of Myshkin and Rogozhin follow an authorial logic, which divides specific aspects of a complex consciousness among different characters. The intimate bond of Myshkin and Rogozhin thus constitutes the central axis around which life principles originally attributed to the idiot are distributed among additional characters.

In the axiology of the novel, Rogozhin signifies the dark shadow side of Prince Myshkin, who appears as a Christ figure in Russia, but is not recognized. The novel explains that Russia remains in misery because it has fallen for alternative belief systems: the gentle redeemer relapses into idiocy because the Russians blindly lust after money, power or love without caring for their salvation.[3] Even the omniscient narrator who knows the biographies of all the characters down to the smallest detail does not recognize the salvific-historical relevance of his story.

In the novel *The Demons* (1871), Dostoevsky pushes the splintering of the complex consciousness still further. He unites, to some extent, the previously applied artistic devices: the highly ambivalent protagonist Stavrogin represents, like Raskolnikov, a complex consciousness, but at the same time, as in the novel *The Idiot*, certain aspects of his personality are displayed in complementary characters. The reader can therefore observe Dostoevsky's narrative treatment of his main ideological problem in a synthetic and in an analytic clue: Stavrogin is certainly an autonomous personality, but at the same time his inner conflict is staged as the interaction of three other characters.

The light side of Stavrogin's personality is represented through the student Shatov, who bases his religious program on past statements of the young Stavrogin. Admittedly, the structure of the novel emphasizes the

9. Ibid. 8:192–93.
1. Ibid. 8:507.
2. Ibid. 8:171.
3. Ulrich Schmid, "Rogozhins Hochzeitsnacht. Representationale Spaltung als künstlerisches Verfahren," in *Dostoevsky Studies* NS 3 (1999), 5–18.

temporal non-identity of Stavrogin: Stavrogin himself nowhere expresses the positive Christian ideology of his youth; Shatov appears as a type of "stand in" for this epoch from Stavrogin's biography. The terrorist Peter Verkhovensky is established as the dark polar opposite to Shatov, who, in order to reach his goals, does not shrink from murder. Verkhovensky signals the extreme moral depravity that also appears in Stavrogin's character. The character of the engineer Kirillov is located between Shatov and Verkhovensky. As a person who has lost his faith in God through ratiocination he is open to manipulation from all sides. Stavrogin's complex character is mirrored in these three counter figures: like Shatov he hopes for a Christian rebirth of Russia; like Vekhovensky he believes that the goal or end justifies all means; and, like Kirillov, he commits suicide as an act of final despair. Dostoevsky illuminates the complex nature of Stavrogin's consciousness by developing its constituent elements in the biographies of other characters.

Dostoevsky's records and notes are also revealing of the compositional process through which *Demons* emerged. Work on the novel begins prominently with the note: "NB: Everything lies in the characters."[4] The further conceptualization of the novel shows that Dostoevsky constantly shuffles the central traits back and forth between the various characters. The actual plot of the novel arises from the definitive attribution of specific psychic elements to specific characters.[5]

In *The Demons*, Dostoevsky chooses a new approach for the presentation of his ideological problem. The action of the novel is narrated by Anton Lavrentievich G-v, a character who is not directly entangled in the events related, but who functions primarily as an eyewitness. From the perspective of this chronicler, Stavrogin can only be represented externally; as a rule, his complex consciousness never appears directly. Stavrogin's inner struggle is expressed through the conflict between Verkhovensky, Shatov and Kirillov. The naïve narrator stands admittedly at a loss in the face of the tragic development of events, and can only uncomprehendingly document Stavrogin's downfall in the epilogue. Thus Dostoevsky recycles the artistic device that he had already established in *The Idiot*: the reader's understanding should transcend the incomprehension of the narrator, who is unable to see that these various characters manifest elements of a single complex consciousness or perceive their hidden ideological unity.

Dostoevsky achieved the most precise differentiation of a complex consciousness into distinct characters in the novel *The Brothers Karamazov* (1880). Sigmund Freud, in his famous essay "Dostoevsky and Parricide" (1928), already called attention to the fact that the four brothers must be interpreted as complements of a higher unity. Freud characterizes the four brothers as follows: the effeminate and religious Alyosha, the pleasure driven, impulsive Dmitri, the skeptical cynic Ivan, and the epileptic criminal Smerdyakov.[6]

4. *Pss* 11:58.
5. Jens Herlth, "Maske, Usurpation, Allegorie: Erzählstrategien und Deutungsmodelle in Fedor Dostojewskijs *Besy* (*Die Dämonen*)," in *Die Lust an der Maske. Festschrift für Bodo Zelinsky*, ed. Birgit Harress, Jens Herlth, and Angelika Lauhus (Frankfurt am Main: Peter Lang, 2007) 75–105; see p. 79.
6. Sigmund Freud, "Dostojewski und die Vatertötung," in *Bildende Kunst und Literatur* (Frankfurt am Main: Fischer, 1982) 267–86, 282 (Studienausgabe X).

The novel begins with the family history of the Karamazovs. The fact that the brothers have three different mothers provides the genealogical basis to their differentiation. The uneven distribution of dialogues between the brothers in the novel reveals the ideological structure which hides behind the complicated family tree. A simplified chart of the dialogues between the brothers reveals that Alyosha functions as the discursive fulcrum of the novel.

Book 2	Book 3	Book 5	Book 7	Book 8	Book 11
Chapters VI–VIII: A–I–D	Chapters III–V: A–D	Chapter II: A-S	Chapter I–IV: A	Chapters I–VIII: D	Chapter V: A–I
	Chapter VI: A–S	Chapters III–V: A–I			Chapter VI–VIII: I–S
	Chapters VIII–IX: A–I–D	Chapter VI: I–S			

The chart enables us to see that the brothers stand at various distances from each other. Alyosha is more present than his brothers, he leads lengthy confidential conversations with all of them. There is no tête-à-tête between Dmitri and Ivan, nor is there one between Smerdyakov and Dmitri. A further peculiarity lies in the fact that each of the three legitimate brothers has a book dedicated to him: Alyosha has Book 7, Dmitri has Book 8, and Ivan has Book 11. Only Alyosha and Dmitri can act as the protagonist of "their" respective books entirely; Ivan shares "his" book with Smerdyakov, who assumes a prominent position.

The four brothers represent one complex consciousness which "uses" Alyosha as a broker. Two lengthy, intimate conversation scenes form the dramatic core of the complex consciousness. Dmitri's "Confession of an Ardent Heart" to Alyosha in Book 3 ranges over three chapters, the same amount of space occupied by Ivan's long dialogue with Alyosha in Book 5—this is also the context in which Ivan tells the "Legend of the Grand Inquisitor." Alyosha as passive central point is thus surrounded by two active poles: the impulsive Dmitri and the rational Ivan.

The structure of this complex consciousness is strongly evocative of the conception of the soul in Plato's *Phaedrus* dialogue. Plato compares the soul with a harnessed team comprised of a chariot, a wild horse, and a noble horse. The two horses force the soul forward, but the charioteer must mediate between the two opposing forces. Dostoevsky himself studied Plato in preparation for *The Demons*. His library contained a book on this subject with the title *Plato in the Layout of Clifton Collins* (1876) from the series *Collected Volumes of Ancient Classicists for the Russian Reader*. He undoubtedly knew the *Phaedrus* dialogue, which he also explicitly referred to in his journalism.[7]

---

7. N. F. Budanova, ed., *Biblioteka F. M. Dostoevskogo. Opyt rekonstruktsii. Nauchnoe opisanie* (Sankt-Peterburg: Nauka, 2005); see p. 59.

The constellation of the brothers can be interpreted as a creative transformation of Plato's simile of the soul-horse. Alyosha becomes the charioteer, who seeks to mediate between the two differing instances of
passion and reason. In this light, the relative passivity of Alyosha compared to his brothers can be plausibly explained. The quite astonishing
announcement of the first person narrator, who in the preface purports
to describe the life history of his "hero, Aleksey Fyodorovich Karamazov,"
acquires a special meaning in this context.[8] Alyosha, who in the course of
the action seems to play only a minor role, becomes recognizable as the
spiritual center of a complex consciousness, which, torn between passion
and reason, is propelled back and forth.

Dostoevsky's original contribution to the Platonic concept lies in the fact
that he adds a demonic component to the rational pole. This component
is embodied in the novel through the bastard Smerdyakov. The three key
dialogues between Ivan and Smerdyakov clearly show that Smerdyakov
only radicalizes Ivan's ideas, and discerns their practical consequences.
Ivan loses his belief in God; Smerdyakov seizes Ivan's dictum that "If there
is no God, then everything is allowed," and kills the Karamazov father.

The Karamazov brothers thus stand for different dimensions of the
soul, which together create a complex consciousness. By splitting the
complex consciousness into individual characters, Dostoevsky provides a
literary explanation for illogical, sometimes even absurd human behavior: each dimension of the soul—or, in the context of the novel, each
brother—behaves coherently within its own framework. From the total-
ity, however, there arises an inscrutable, even contradictory mishmash of
ideas, motivations, and vindications. In this sense *The Brothers Karamazov* represents an example of character differentiation that contrasts
to the single consciousness in *Notes from Underground*, in which a protagonist who reasons with himself vindicates his own absurd conduct.

Ivan Karamazov's conversation with the devil offers perhaps the most
famous example of the literary splitting of a character's consciousness.
Dostoevsky here uses an artistic method that the Russian Formalists call
"the baring of the device." This means that a text not only makes use of a
specific representational technique, but also contains explicit discussion
of the technique. More concretely: in *The Brothers Karamazov* it not only
becomes clear that the devil is a part of Ivan's soul; this affiliation is also
reflected in the text itself. The chapter heading "The Devil. Ivan Fyodorovich's Nightmare" already makes it apparent that the devil is an incarnation of a part of Ivan's consciousness. Dostoevsky constantly alludes in
this chapter to the fact that the devil comes directly from Ivan's imagination. Even the entrance of the devil points to this circumstance:

> And so he was sitting almost conscious himself of his delirium and,
> as I have said already, looking persistently at some object on the sofa
> against the opposite wall. Someone appeared to be sitting there.[9]

Ivan obstinately insists on the thought that the devil is his own projection.
He says to the devil: "I sometimes don't see you and don't even hear your
voice as I did last time, but I always guess what you are prating, for *it's I,
I myself speaking, not you*."[1] Ivan repeats the same declaration twice: "No,

8. *Pss* 14:5.
9. See p. 533.
1. See p. 535.

you are not someone apart, you are myself, you are I and nothing more! You are rubbish, you are my fancy!" [. . .] "You are that dream! You are a dream, not a living creature!"[2] The obsessive repetition of this motif is perplexing. It at least poses the question, why did Dostoevsky not leave the ontological status of the devil in limbo? It would have been easy to make it impossible for the reader to decide whether the devil really appeared or if he was a creation of Ivan's imagination. That Dostoevsky possessed the artistic craft to create such a solution stands without question. Even early works such as *The Double* (1846) or *The Landlady* (1847) derive their literary impact from the reader's doubt as to whether the events portrayed are real or only in the imagination of the protagonist, and thus provide exemplary cases for Tsvetan Todorov's *Theory of Fantastic Literature*.

Yet in *The Brothers Karamazov* Dostoevsky abstained from creating this fantastic uncertainty, which was very enticing for him. There were probably two reasons for his decision. First of all, he wanted to give a hermeneutic hint as to how the family relationship of the brothers is to be interpreted. In other words: what Dostoevsky makes explicit in the relationship between Ivan and the Devil implicitly applies to the complex consciousness that is created from the combination of the four brothers. Each of the brothers is an autonomous aspect of a higher consciousness, just as the devil is a dimension of Ivan's consciousness. Ultimately, the interview with the Devil scene is a hermeneutic key, with which the composition of the entire novel can be unlocked.

Secondly, the devil's autonomous status points to his role in the overall axiology of the novel. The novel constantly alludes to the possibility that the devil is guilty of the parricide. The fundamental problem of the novel— the origin of evil—is thus also manifested in the representational distinction of the protagonists: the Satanic is a potentiality that sits in each individual consciousness and can make itself independent under specific circumstances. The devil can appear as a unique character when evil, namely parricide, is either contemplated (Alyosha), vindicated through atheistic rationalism (Ivan), or willed in blind rage (Dmitri).[3]

Dostoevsky's anthropological conception of evil gains depth against the backdrop of this character constellation: the demonic is hidden in human consciousness; it can take autonomous action when it is no longer controlled. The reader's perception of the threat of such an ethical malfunction was so important to Dostoevsky that he sacrificed the possibility of the real existence of the devil, and with it the fantastic effect.

In his analysis of Dostoevsky's novels, Mikhail Bakhtin focused exclusively on polyphony, failing to consider the possibility that elements of a complex consciousness might be distributed among different characters. He likewise paid too little attention to the different levels of insight into the hidden sense of the plot: The characters know less than the narrator, the narrator knows less than the reader. This neglect is all the more astonishing since Bakhtin, in his early work *Author and Hero in the Aes-*

2. See pp. 535 and 542.
3. Horst-Jüergen Gerigk, "Der Mord als Faszinosum: Dostojewskij," in Gerigk, *Die Russen in Amerika. Dostojewskij, Tolstoj, Turgenjew und Tschechow in ihrer Bedeutung für die Literatur der USA* (Hürtgenwald: Guido Pressler, 1995), 103–238; see p. 205.

thetic Activity, already engaged with the complicated relationships that obtain between different narratological levels.

Bakhtin's blindness towards the various forms consciousness can acquire in Dostoevsky's writings may be ascribed to his interest in ethical questions and his polemic against Russian Formalism.[4] Bakhtin analyzes Dostoevsky's novels in the first place as literary representations of people who are viewed from an external position. He is thus interested above all in the interaction of the characters with other human beings, their moral responsibility and their behavior in extreme situations. In focusing on these elements, however, Bakhtin works from an unstated premise: he assumes as self-evident that each character simultaneously represents an autonomous consciousness. Only when one transcends the individual ethical dimension does it become apparent that in Dostoevsky's texts character and consciousness are congruent only in the rarest of cases. Dostoevsky's characters are either conglomerates of consciousness or parts of a complex consciousness.

Bakhtin is concerned with the connection between response and responsibility (*otvet* and *otvetstvennost'*). He therefore must emphasize the free dialogue between autonomous subjects. However, when the specific artistic organization of Dostoevsky's novels is investigated, the hypothesis must also be allowed that individual characters do not always correspond to one single consciousness; instead they are sometimes linked as elements of one overarching complex consciousness. From this point of view, Bakhtin's favoring of dialogue in Dostoevsky over monologue in other authors such as Tolstoy can be challenged: Dostoevsky's dialogues may be only artistically transformed monologues; the partners in the conversation may turn out to be the same person.

GARY SAUL MORSON

The God of Onions: *The Brothers Karamazov* and the Mythic Prosaic[†]

Prosaics and Eschatology

Dostoevsky renders with remarkably consistent power the ideas he opposes, but his alternative often remains vague. The wrong view is almost always the idea that intellectuals possess some theory—utilitarianism, socialism, nihilism, or any other—that can account for all of human existence and ensure salvation if properly applied. For Dostoevsky, the idea that any set of abstract ideas could specify what we do would necessarily reduce us to "piano keys" or "organ stops." And a guarantee of salvation would make all our efforts meaningless.

Salvation and a meaningful life must both by their very nature be uncertain. In *A Writer's Diary,* Dostoevsky observes that if some demon

---

4. See Bakhtin's essay "Art and Answerability" (1919), in which he implicitly criticizes Formalism for its blindness towards moral questions.

† From Robert Louis Jackson, ed., *A New Word on* The Brothers Karamazov (Evanston: Northwestern UP, 2004), 107–22. Copyright © 2004 by Northwestern University Press. Reprinted with permission.

should grant our every wish, the result might at first look like utopia but would soon turn into hell precisely because it is *certain*. People in such a world would soon realize that "their lives had been taken away for . . . 'stones turned into bread' . . . that it is not possible to love one's neighbor without sacrificing something to him of one's own labor . . . and that *happiness lies not in happiness but only in the attempt to achieve it*."[1] With its image of a demon, this passage looks forward to the devil chapter in *The Brothers Karamazov*, and the reference to stones turned into bread—to the temptations of Christ—of course anticipates the Grand Inquisitor legend.

In *The Idiot*, Prince Myshkin ascribes the true horror of capital punishment to its certainty. A man whose throat has been cut by brigands may still hope, he observes: why, there have been cases when a man begged for mercy even *after* his throat had been cut! But a death sentence offers no hope at all because only one outcome is possible. Time is closed, and we are human only insofar as time is open. Scientific determinism also allows for only one outcome at every moment, and so it constitutes a sort of philosophical capital punishment. It deprives us of our capacity to choose, to surprise, to make ourselves unexpectedly different, and so we lose our humanness. In yet another way, socialism removes uncertainty and surprise by taking away risk.

Dostoevsky hesitated between two very different, if not contradictory, alternatives to the theoretical mind-set of the intelligentsia, and he found a way to reconcile them only in *The Brothers Karamazov*. One alternative is pure faith, to which one clings in spite of all "opposite proofs." It leads to ecstatic visions and eschatological hopes. The other alternative that appears repeatedly in Dostoevsky's novels and essays is eschatology's temperamental opposite: the belief in small acts of prosaic goodness, in ordinary decency guided by neither theory nor religious visions but by practical reason. From this perspective, a better world is to be achieved not by a sudden leap or a grand act, which both are almost sure to lead to disaster, but by what Dostoevsky calls "microscopic actions," one small step at a time.[2] In *Crime and Punishment*, Sonya represents faith and Razumikhin prosaic, practical goodness. I think that the key reason so many readers have found that novel's epilogue to be an artistic failure is that while most of the novel leans toward the Razumikhin idea, the epilogue is cast wholly in Sonya's terms: and so it does not seem to follow from the novel as a whole.

Both ideas remain present and active in each of Dostoevsky's great works. Yet it is hard to reconcile them. The problem may be stated as follows: practical reason and small acts of goodness clearly seem to be what really work, but they do not seem terribly Christian or spiritual. Razumikhin is not especially pious. On the other hand, dramatic actions and

---

1. Fyodor Dostoevsky, *A Writer's Diary*, vol. 1, *1873–1876*, ed. and trans. Kenneth Lantz (Evanston: Northwestern UP, 1993), 335 (January 1876, chap. 3, article 3, emphasis in the original) [hereafter cited as *WD* with page number]. All citations from this and other works of Dostoevsky are occasionally modified for accuracy by comparison with F. M. Dostoevskii, *Polnoe sobranie sochinenii v tridsati tomakh* (Leningrad: Nauka, 1972–90).

2. I discuss "microscopic actions" in the "Introductory Study" to Dostoevsky (*WD*, 1–117). This idea represents Dostoevsky's rethinking of an idea usually associated with Tolstoy, and he alludes to Tolstoy in this connection in *Crime and Punishment* when Porfiry Petrovich mentions General Mack (a scene in *War and Peace*). See also Robin Feuer Miller's comments on connections of Tolstoy with *The Idiot* in Miller, *Dostoevsky and "The Idiot": Author, Narrator, and Reader* (Cambridge: Harvard UP, 1981), 59–60.

eschatological strivings seem to reflect deep religious faith but risk making things much worse, as extremism of all types usually does. Basic decency, concern for the person before you, is sacrificed to a grand vision of the whole. Is Father Ferapont not the madman of *The Brothers Karamazov*? In *The Demons*, Kirillov, Shatov, Pyotr Stepanovich, the insane "prophet" Semyon Yakovlevich—all the madmen, whether believers or atheists—are possessed by one or another eschatological vision leading to horror or disaster.

Eschatology resembles gambling fever: both intoxicate with the promise of a sudden transformation, a metaphysical jolt out of the ordinary world, but in fact make us and our neighbors much worse off. Like epilepsy, they leave us with a horrible disorientation and, like a drinking spree, with destruction and one or another kind of hangover, as we see from Smerdyakov and Dmitri in *The Brothers Karamazov*. For all the ecstasy of his epileptic visions, Prince Myshkin cannot forget that idiocy faces him as the direct consequence of those "higher moments"; and Dostoevsky, we know, suffered massive loss of memory and feared death from his own epileptic seizures.[3]

Readers of *The Brothers Karamazov* will remember how often the apocalypse is mentioned. Most notably, it forms the basis for the discussion of Ivan's article in Father Zosima's cell, and the chapter title "So Be It! So Be It!" (bk. 2, chap. 5) cites a call for the Second Coming. The end of the world, the reign of the Antichrist, or the Last Judgment: one or another eschatological motif is envisaged in "Rebellion" (bk. 5, chap. 4), anticipated in "The Grand Inquisitor" (bk. 5, chap. 5), made fun of by Ivan's devil, and suggested countless other times. What readers generally do not know is that only a few years before writing *The Brothers Karamazov*, Dostoevsky, in *The Diary of a Writer*, had himself openly proclaimed that the apocalypse was literally imminent and that the Kingdom of God would at last be realized when Russian troops should occupy Constantinople. These ideas surely will seem quixotic, Dostoevsky asserts, but will be proven literally correct: soon people will have to admit that Don Quixote is now more realistic than Metternich! Realism is changing because the world itself is becoming rapidly and radically different: "Behold, I make all things new!" In 1876, Dostoevsky was specific enough to predict the Kingdom of God for 1877. When his prediction rather obviously failed to be vindicated, he suspended the *Diary* and set to work on *The Brothers Karamazov*. It is therefore not surprising that this novel should have reconsidered the apocalyptic interpretation of Christianity and experimented with the alternate, prosaic view.[4]

But could prosaics be Christianized? In *The Brothers Karamazov*, Dostoevsky found a way to do so. He arrived at a paradoxical set of formulations I like to think of rather oxymoronically as "the mythic prosaic." In fact, the theology of *The Brothers Karamazov* has been little understood. It represents a fundamental departure for Dostoevsky and is much

---

3. See the discussion of Dostoevsky's epilepsy in the years he prepared for and wrote *The Brothers Karamazov* in Joseph Frank, *Dostoevsky: The Mantle of the Prophet, 1871–1881* (Princeton: Princeton UP, 2002).
4. I discuss Dostoevsky's apocalypticism in the "Introductory Study" (*WD*, 1–117); and see Frank's discussion of Dostoevsky's religious and political views (Frank, *Dostoevsky*).

stranger than it at first seems. It centers around Alyosha and it directs
our attention to the third person of the Trinity.

How Love Becomes Hatred

Alyosha begins the novel with the wrong sort of faith. How he finds the
right faith is his story in this novel.

As *The Brothers Karamazov* begins, the narrator describes Alyosha as
sharing the same uncompromising, extremist sense of life and human
action as the socialists and revolutionaries, only turned to God. He is a
revolutionary of the spirit, a utopian seeking sudden, absolute perfection.
Alyosha believed in God and immortality, but

> in the same way, if he had decided that God and immortality did not
> exist, he would at once have become an atheist and a socialist. For
> socialism is not merely the labor question, it is before all things the
> atheistic question, the question of the form taken by atheism today,
> the question of the tower of Babel built without God, not to mount
> to Heaven from earth but to set up Heaven on earth. Alyosha would
> have found it strange and impossible to go on living as before. It is
> written: "Give all thou hast to the poor and follow me, if thou wouldst
> be perfect." Alyosha said to himself: "I can't give two rubles instead
> of 'all,' and only go to mass instead of 'following Him.' "[5]

What the atheists and revolutionaries share with such Christians is belief
in paradise and assurance that it is to be achieved by a sudden transformation. Revolution or Revelation: either would save all humanity at a stroke.
Revolutionaries and Christians of this sort share another characteristic:
they are extremists. They will not compromise on "two rubles" or, for that
matter, on two thousand rubles. Dostoevsky was quite taken with the idealism of the radicals with whom he disagreed. He understood their psychology of selfless devotion because, after all, he had himself been almost
executed as a result of just such idealism. And yet this whole complex of
beliefs—in imminent paradise, sudden transformation, extremist action,
and absolute certainty—turns out to be fundamentally mistaken.

One does not have to have lived through the twentieth century, which
realized the totalitarianism predicted with astonishing accuracy in *The
Demons*, to grasp that nothing causes more evil than the attempt to eliminate it entirely and that no one is more cruel to particular people than
those who love Humanity. One need only think of the French Revolution
or the Spanish Inquisition, both of which are, of course, mentioned in *The
Brothers Karamazov*. In each, love of humanity turned to hatred because
of a special law of human psychology that Dostoevsky calls the "law of
reflection of ideas" and illustrates with a striking example:

> [I]t more than once has been noted how, in a family dying of starva-
> tion the father or mother, toward the end when the sufferings of the
> children have become unbearable, will begin to hate those same chil-
> dren whom they had previously loved so much precisely because their
> suffering has become *unbearable*. Moreover, I assert that the aware-
> ness of one's utter inability to help suffering humanity, coupled with

---

5. Fyodor Dostoevsky, *The Brothers Karamazov*, trans. Constance Garnett (New York: Random
House, 1950), 26, hereafter cited parenthetically as *BK* with page number.

one's complete conviction of the existence of that suffering, can even *transform the love of humanity in your heart to hatred for humanity.*[6]

This process of transformation has clearly progressed rather far in Ivan, moved so much by the suffering of children whom he cannot help that he has begun to hate humanity. Out of compassion he becomes the most profound misanthrope in world literature. In "Rebellion," Ivan maintains that one simply cannot love one's neighbors (much less one's enemies) and asks "whether that's due to men's bad qualities or whether it's inherent in their nature" (*BK*, 281). Ivan means that if evil were only a matter of "bad qualities," then it might be eliminated by education or a different social milieu; but in fact, our very nature is to blame and we are rotten to the core. Theologically, Ivan accepts original sin without the possibility of grace; he correctly sees the propensity for evil as fundamental but mistakenly denies that the potential for goodness goes just as deep. Ivan's creation, the Inquisitor, has also begun to hate people as pitiful empirical beings created in jest and to despise them as so many sheep. His attempt to save them by depriving them of freedom reflects precisely the peculiar form of hatred that is born from heartfelt helpless love.

At some point in the career of everyone who expects a sudden transformation of the world, of humanity, and of himself, the failure of the miraculous change to happen becomes apparent. In a realist novel, as opposed to a saint's life, such a disappointment is presupposed in the story's very genre. Miracles do not arrive on time, as Alyosha learns when Father Zosima's corpse begins to stink. In fact, this miracle not only fails but almost seems to come in reverse. Far from remaining free from the taint of corruption, the elder's corpse stinks in "excess of nature"—much as a revolution may not only fail to establish heaven on earth but may actually create hell. Whether by divine will or (more likely) by its own internal logic, the "law of reflection of ideas" shows what is wrong with eschatological hopes, be they secular or religious. They beget the opposite of what they strive for. Antichrist triumphs in the church itself.

Immediate Exploits

When such hopes fail, one experiences hatred of both humanity and one's self, as we see when Alyosha goes to Grushenka intent on his own fall. Alyosha's expectation of a miracle, now disappointed, grew out of the very dedication that led him to Zosima and the monastery in the first place. Just before the passage about the tower of Babel and "two rubles," the narrator describes the importance Alyosha places on the *suddenness* of the expected transformation:

> He was to some extent a youth of our time—that is, honest by nature, demanding the truth [*pravda*], seeking it and believing in it, and, having once believed, demanding *rapid* participation in it with all his soul, demanding an *immediate exploit*, and with an absolute desire even to sacrifice everything for this exploit, even life itself. . . . Alyosha only chose the opposite path from all others, but with the

6. *WD*, 735 (December 1876, chap. 1, article 3; emphasis in the original). Frank interprets this passage as Dostoevsky's attempt to demonstrate to the populists the danger of accepting Christian values without actually believing in Christ. See Frank, *Dostoevsky*, 235.

same thirst for an *immediate exploit*. (*BK*, 25; emphasis added, translation modified)

The repeated phrase "immediate exploit" (*skoryi podvig*) links Alyosha
first of all to terrorists, who also are prepared to sacrifice life to make a
sudden change. As has often been pointed out, the name Karamazov
recalls Karakozov, the terrorist who made an attempt on the life of the
czar, and this novel repeatedly takes glances at the revolutionary movement. Just as important, the phrase also connects Alyosha to the heroes
of other literary genres. "Exploits" are performed in folktales, in epics,
and in saints' lives, but the term cannot be used without irony in a realistic novel, where it necessarily comes under the shadow of the quixotic.

In introducing Alyosha, Dostoevsky therefore makes him what I have
elsewhere called a "generic refugee," someone who enters the realist novel
from another genre.[7] The prologue to *Middlemarch* compares its heroine
to Saint Theresa, whose nature "demanded an epic life"; but "later-born
Theresas" unfortunately live in a time, and a genre, that makes epic or
saintly action impossible. Dorothea's story thus becomes the story of a
heroine from one genre forced to live in another. In much the same way,
the hero of Tolstoy's *War and Peace*, Prince Andrei, thirsts for "glory hovering over me in the mist" as he tries to live an epic life in a novelistic world.
Like these two displaced figures, Alyosha thirsts for epic and saintly
"exploits." He wants to be a hero of the spirit, to witness and participate
in the evident triumph of the Christian idea.

For Alyosha such exploits must be "immediate": sudden, dramatic, visible, and unmistakable. And so he expects a miracle to honor Zosima osten-
tatiously, to silence all the doubters. In this expectation, Alyosha runs
counter to the very teachings of Zosima himself.

For Zosima emphasizes *prosaic* Christianity. He seeks the slow internal
improvement of each soul, change that happens almost invisibly and whose
beneficent results must be taken largely on faith. He alludes repeatedly to
the Gospel command not to make a show of piety or goodness. And he
does not seem to think "two rubles" a pitiable sum. At the end of the chapter "Peasant Women Who Have Faith" (bk. 3, chap. 3), he is gladdened by
a donation of sixty kopecks.

Exhorting clergymen, Zosima tells them not to sacrifice all their time
but just another hour a week to reading Gospel stories to the illiterate. In
passages that remind us of what he has already said to Madame Khokhlakova, he stresses not grand tests, dramatic struggles, and heroic deeds
but small acts of love and kindness "every day and every hour, every minute." What matters is what we do at every ordinary moment.

> You pass by a little child, you pass by, spiteful with ugly words, with
> wrathful heart; you may not have noticed the child, but he has seen
> you, and your image, unseemly and ignoble, may remain in his
> defenseless heart. You don't know it, but you may have sown an evil
> seed in him. (*BK*, 383)

---

7. I coined the term "generic refugee" in "Genre and Hero/*Fathers and Sons*: Intergeneric Dialogues, Generic Refugees, and the Hidden Prosaic," in *Literature, Culture, and Society in the
Modern Age*, ed. Edward J. Brown, Lazar Fleishman, Gregory Freidin, and Richard Schup-
bach, *Stanford Slavic Studies* 4:1 (1991): 336–81.

As for ordinary evil, so for ordinary good actions: each may inspire others in endless ramifications. The Kingdom of God will come, Zosima explains, only if and when such prosaic acts of kindness change us, bit by bit, from within. What happens at every moment matters. Cast a little bread upon the waters.

Therefore, we help "humanity" most by *not* worrying about it. We must, instead, perform the much harder task of being kind to the person before us at every moment. Zosima tells Madame Khokhlakova about a doctor he once knew:

> "I love humanity," he said, "but I wonder at myself. The more I love humanity in general, the less I love man in particular. In my dreams . . . I have often come to making enthusiastic schemes for the service of humanity, and perhaps I might actually have faced crucifixion if it had been suddenly necessary; and yet I am incapable of living in the same room with anyone for two days together, as I know by experience. . . . In twenty-four hours I begin to hate the best of men: one because he's too long over his dinner; another because he has a cold and keeps on blowing his nose. . . . But it has always happened that the more I detest men individually the more ardent becomes my love for humanity." (*BK*, 64)

Crucifixion would be an "immediate exploit," sudden, dramatic, and visible to all but, if Zosima is to be understood, not what Alyosha should be seeking.

The Gospel According to Luk

The failure of the expected miracle provides the catalyst for Alyosha's change from apocalyptic to prosaic Christianity, which he experiences as intensely as a conversion from atheism to faith:

> [W]ith every instant he felt clearly and, as it were tangibly, that something firm and unshakable as that vault of heaven had entered into his soul. It was as though some idea had seized the sovereignty of his mind—and it was for all his life and for ever and ever. He had fallen on the earth a weak boy, but he rose up a resolute fighter. . . . "Someone visited my soul in that hour," he would afterwards say, with firm faith in his words. (*BK*, 437)

At this moment, he realizes that he has found his new and renewed faith, but the renewal itself has taken place earlier that evening, when he visited Grushenka and heard Father Paissy read the story of Jesus' first miracle. These two chapters, "An Onion" and "Cana of Galilee" (bk. 7, chaps. 3 and 4), clarify the novel's interpretation of Christianity, the beliefs that have inspired Zosima, and the sense of the world that will shape Alyosha's future life.

The remarkable story of the onion (*luk*) falls into two parts, each teaching an important lesson. As Grushenka has heard this tale from her old cook, a wicked woman dies and is cast into the burning lake. Her guardian angel recalls that the woman once carelessly gave an onion to a beggar and informs God of this solitary good deed. You take that onion, God replies, and pull her out of hell with it. Grushenka comments that she is herself just such a wicked woman but has given an onion; and at the end of the chapter, Alyosha also claims to have given her an onion. What have they done for each other?

Grushenka wickedly bribed Rakitin to bring Alyosha to her so that she could accomplish his ruin, not because Alyosha has done her any harm but precisely because she resents his holiness. Her motives are the perverse ones we associate with Dostoevsky characters. They testify to a source of evil that he comprehended better than anyone else who ever lived. The very existence of goodness offends the sinner personally; it is just this kind of offense that, in *The Idiot*, defeats Prince Myshkin's efforts and turns his very beneficence into a source of evil. Alyosha does not know of Prince Myshkin, of course, but the author seems to be posing the Myshkin question anew: How can Christian goodness actually produce good? The answer is: by concentrating on small acts, by giving onions.

Grushenka tells Alyosha that he has been her "conscience" and so has unwittingly insulted her very dignity. This is the same logic that motivates Fyodor Pavlovich:

> He longed to revenge himself on every one for his own unseemliness. He suddenly recalled how he had once in the past been asked, "Why do you hate so and so, so much?" And he had answered them with his shameless impudence: "I'll tell you. He has done me no harm. But I once played a dirty trick on him, and ever since I have hated him." (*BK*, 98–99)

We hate those who are better than ourselves and we hate even more those who do not resent our injuries precisely because their goodness reminds us of our own baseness. Dostoevsky was the first to articulate in detail this objection to Christianity and to answer it. Innocence begets crime, pacifism leads to war, and turning the other cheek invites bloodshed: or at least such perverse effects may result. But they do not when Alyosha visits Grushenka.

Alyosha comes to her not as a saint but as an ordinary sinner. He is in "rebellion," the same state of soul in which she has wallowed for five years. He treats her as someone better than he is, as unexpectedly kind to him; and that unwitting kindness of hers, performed as carelessly as the woman in the folktale gave the onion, turns out to make a significant difference. She hardly knows what has happened but feels their roles unexpectedly reversed. Allowing her to think of herself as the one who is superior, who has helped him, constitutes Alyosha's unexpected gift to her. She gives him an onion, and allowing her to do so is the onion that he gives her.

These onions, small things in themselves, overcome the spiteful logic of offense and resentment as no grand act of goodness ever could, for a grand act of kindness would only make the recipient resent it the more. Sometimes an onion surpasses a banquet.

The Choice and the Seed

In the second part of Grushenka's story, when the angel has almost pulled the wicked woman out of hell, the other sinners grab on to her so they may be saved, too, but the woman kicks them off: "[I]t's my onion, not yours!" she says spitefully. At that moment, of course, the onion breaks. What has happened here is that the woman has been given a *choice* to redefine her life. She may make it resemble all her myriad deeds but one, or she can make it resemble the single act of giving an onion; and she makes the wrong choice. If the first part of the story stressed the importance of ordinary acts of goodness, the second emphasizes our power of choice.

Our lives consist of good acts and bad, and we may make them like either. As we reflect on our lives, we repeatedly face the wicked woman's choice. That is another reason that good memories are so important. Even a single one, even the smallest part of a life, can be the basis for our redefinition if we act to make it so.

Grushenka's initial act of kindness to Alyosha was performed carelessly; but truly to choose goodness, she must do so deliberately. The Pythagoreans held that the first number is really two, for no one counts up to one; and it is in repeating a good act that we make it truly our own. We see this point almost immediately when Grushenka asks Alyosha whether she should forgive her old lover or act spitefully. At this point, she may make the onion she has given Alyosha the principle of her life, or it may remain an isolated incident, as it did for the wicked woman. Alyosha tells her, "but you have forgiven him already" (*BK*, 428). And will she continue to forgive? What she will do remains open, but she understands what her choice entails.

Small things may have great consequences; that is also the logic of the novel's epigraph. To produce much fruit, it takes only a grain of wheat, a mere seed. The seed, as we have seen, is how Zosima describes each good and evil act we do every day ("you have planted a seed"). But not all seeds sprout. It is up to us whether the seed will abide alone or bring forth much fruit.

The lesson of the onion recurs through this novel. Doctor Herzenstube gave the boy Mitya a small gift, a pound of nuts, and he remembered it all his life. This unspectacular deed really mattered, and it forms the basis of a good memory, which, as the novel repeatedly teaches, may save one at a crucial moment. A good memory is itself a sort of onion, a small thing with potentially great consequences, as the novel's ending emphasizes.

The Dream and the Pillow

Every reader of this novel remembers Mitya's dream of "the babe": how, driving past the burned-out peasants, he sees the suffering babe and demands to know not just why this child and these peasants are poor, but why anyone is poor or suffers.

> And he felt that, though his questions were unreasonable and senseless, yet he wanted to ask just that, and he had to ask it just in that way. . . . and he wanted to do something for them all, so that the babe should weep no more . . . that no one should shed tears again from that moment, and he wanted to do it all at once [seichas zhe, seichas zhe], regardless of all obstacles, with all the recklessness of the Karamazovs. (*BK*, 616)

Dostoevsky evokes Ivan when Mitya identifies evil with a suffering child and Alyosha when he desires to eliminate all suffering "at once, at once." Mitya, too, wants an immediate exploit. But such problems are not solved at once, and the recklessness of the Karamazov brothers makes matters worse, as Mitya's life and disastrous decisions demonstrate.

As if to show him what the right answer to his question is, Mitya's dream receives a very different answer when he awakes and

> is suddenly struck by the fact that there was a pillow under his head, which hadn't been there when he had leant back, exhausted on the chest.
>
> "Who put that pillow under my head? Who was so kind?" he cried, with a sort of ecstatic gratitude, and tears in his voice, as though some great kindness had been shown him.
>
> He never found out who this kind man was, perhaps one of the peasant witnesses, or Nikolay Parfenovich's little secretary had compassionately thought to put a pillow under his head, but his whole soul was quivering with tears. (*BK*, 616)

Taken together, the dream and the incident with the pillow that immediately follows form a question and its answer. How shall we solve the problem of evil and suffering? By one small good deed at a time, by acts too small for anyone to remember or reward: placing a pillow under a tired person's head, buying a boy a pound of nuts, or giving an onion to a beggar.

The Everyday Miracle

When Alyosha returns from Grushenka's to the monastery, he feels joy, and joy itself reminds him of Father Zosima, who preached the small joys of life. Alyosha thinks, "'He who loves men loves their gladness, too.' . . . *He* was always repeating that, it was one of his leading ideas" (*BK*, 433). These everyday joys are onions, God's onions to us. Every smile, every ray of sunshine, every onion is an onion. Zosima's Christianity, as all the monks have commented, contrasts with the grim kind that seeks only terrible sacrifice, despises joys, wears chains, as Ferapont does. The story Father Paissy is now reading over the body, "Cana of Galilee," emphasizes the peculiar theology that regards Jesus as the bringer of small prosaic delights.

Pause for a moment to consider what a strange text Dostoevsky has chosen to exemplify Christianity. This miracle appears in only one of the four Gospels, and it lies entirely outside Jesus' mission ("Mine hour has not yet come"). Even in this scene, Jesus' act is not so much as noticed by others: the governor of the feast remarks that the married couple have saved their best wine for last, not that their guest has performed a miracle. This miracle is unspectacular because it is the unspectacular that is truly miraculous.

In all respects, this passage could not differ more strongly from the one that fills the analogous role in *Crime and Punishment*, the raising of Lazarus from the dead. Everyone witnesses that dramatic act, and afterwards, people come to see Lazarus, who was raised. That was the most and the marriage of Cana the least dramatic of Jesus' miracles.

Meditating on "Cana of Galilee," Alyosha remembers that Zosima found holiness in the appreciation of life itself:

> Gladness, the gladness of some poor, very poor people. . . . Of course, they were poor, since they hadn't wine enough even at a wedding. . . . and another great heart, that other great being, His Mother, knew that He had come not only to make His great and terrible sacrifice.

She knew that His heart was open even to the simple, artless merrymaking of some obscure and unlearned people, who had warmly bidden Him to their poor wedding. "Mine hour is not yet come," He said
with a soft smile (He must have smiled gently to her). And indeed was
it to make wine abundant at poor weddings that He had come down
to earth? (BK, 434)

In a very real sense, that *was* why he came down to earth, and it is why
the earth itself is sacred. He came not only for his great sacrifice but also
to teach us the importance of ordinary joys, ordinary gladness, ordinary
kindness and hospitality. "Ah, that miracle! Ah, that sweet miracle! It was
not men's grief, but their joy Christ visited, He worked His first miracle to
help men's gladness," Alyosha thinks (BK, 433).

As Alyosha muses, he dreams he attends the marriage at Cana, for it is
always going on, and Jesus is always bidding new guests to that wedding.
Father Zosima is there, too, and he explains that anyone who gives an
onion can come:

Why do you wonder at me [being here]? I gave an onion to a beggar,
so I, too, am here. And many here have given only an onion each—
only one little onion. . . . What are all our deeds? And you, my gentle
one, you, my kind boy, you too have known how to give a famished
woman an onion today. (BK, 435)

Here the two sanctifications of the prosaic, the folktale of the onion and
the Gospel account of Cana, join in a celebration of the God of wine and
onions.

Prolegomenon to Any Future Theodicy

This conception of God shapes not only the novel's portrait of Jesus but
also its entire conception of the Trinity.[8] *The Brothers Karamazov* develops not only a Christology but also a pneumatology—a theology of the
Holy Spirit, the third person of the Trinity. Dostoevsky extends the traditional association of the Spirit with Life, with the Creation (brooding
over the abyss, the Spirit "mad'st it pregnant"), and with Inspiration.[9] In
this novel, these associations identify the Spirit with the life force, with
the sheer love of existence and with the joys always available to us. If we
love the earth, we love the Spirit.

As if to signal the Trinity's importance to the novel's theology, Dostoevsky repeatedly has it mentioned even when nothing in the plot
demands it. Recall that in giving the boy Dmitri a pound of nuts, Herzenstube teaches him to say, in German, "God the Father, God the Son, God
the Holy Spirit"; Dmitri gets the phrase wrong, so Herzenstube (and Dostoevsky) must repeat it; and when Dmitri, remembering the kindness,
strides into Herzenstube's study twenty years later, he again repeats the
German words for the Trinity. In several passages, we learn that the

8. For more on the Trinity in *The Brothers Karamazov*, see Gary Saul Morson, "Dostoevsky and
   the Holy Spirit," *Modern Greek Studies Yearbook: A Publication of Mediterranean Slavic and
   Eastern Orthodox Studies* 16 (2000): 1–17.
9. "And Chiefly Thou, O Spirit . . . Instruct me, for Thou know'st; Thou from the first / Was present, and with mighty wings outspread / Dovelike satst brooding on the vast Abyss / And mad'st
   it pregnant." John Milton, *Paradise Lost: A Poem in Twelve Books*, ed. Merritt Y. Hughes (New
   York: Odyssey Press, 1962), p. 6 (bk. 1, ll. 17–22).

insane Father Ferapont believes that the Holy Spirit comes down to talk personally with him. Less explicitly, when Alyosha says that "someone visited me at that hour," he presumably means the Holy Spirit, for such inspiring visions and moments are traditionally the gifts of the Spirit. And it may well be that the many memories that turn one to good at crucial moments and the power that restrains Dmitri from killing his father are also the gifts of the Spirit.

The Brothers Karamazov has often been described as a novel of enigmas, and Ivan, who is always posing them, is himself several times described as a riddle incarnate. And yet, he does not guess the novel's central riddle, even though his own speeches contain both it and its answer. For this is a riddle about the nature of God and, if Ivan guessed it, he would be on the road to salvation.

The riddle appears encoded in the three chapters in which Ivan and Alyosha discuss the ultimate questions, "The Brothers Make Friends," "Rebellion," and "The Grand Inquisitor" (bk. 5, chaps. 3, 4, and 5). In "Rebellion," Ivan offers his diatribe against God the Father, as Creator of the world in which children suffer. This attack demonstrates the futility not only of all existing theodicies but also of any conceivable attempt to "justify the ways of God to men." No theory, no ultimate reward, no punishment, could ever make up for, cancel, or otherwise erase the suffering of that little girl in the outhouse or the boy torn to pieces by the dogs. For this is not a question of a mistake made by some theologian but of a flaw in the very project of theology itself. Ivan refutes the very *possibility* of justifying the Creator.

Here is how Ivan summarizes his reasons for rejecting "the higher Harmony":

> It's not worth the tears of that one tortured child who beat itself on the breast with its little fist and prayed in its stinking outhouse, with its unexpiated tears to "dear, kind God!" It's not worth it, because those tears are unatoned for. . . . But how can they be atoned for? . . . By their being avenged? . . . What good can hell do, since those children have already been tortured. . . . I want to forgive. . . . And if the sufferings of children go to swell the sum of sufferings which was necessary to pay for truth, then I protest that the truth is not worth such a price. I don't want the mother to embrace the oppressor who threw her son to the dogs! She dare not forgive him! Let her forgive him for herself, if she will, let her forgive the torturer for the immeasurable suffering of her mother's heart. But the sufferings of her tortured child she has no right to forgive; she dare not forgive the torturer even if the child were to forgive him! And if that is so, if they dare not forgive, what becomes of harmony? Is there in the whole world a being who would have the right to forgive and could forgive? I don't want harmony. . . . I would rather remain with my unavenged suffering and unsatisfied indignation, *even if I were wrong.* (BK, 290–91; emphasis in the original)

Ivan's point is unassailable, and Dostoevsky means it to be so. The mother cannot forgive the torturer for the child's suffering, even if the child should do so, and vice versa. The compass of our love extends far beyond our right to forgive. Some suffering cannot be redeemed.

When, at the end of the world, we see not as through a glass darkly but face-to-face, even then there could not be an answer because "the fact" of the child's suffering would remain. On the one hand, we might have some abstract and utterly correct justification of the suffering of children; on the other, the fact that they have suffered: Which should we choose? Ivan's point is that greater love lies with sticking with "the fact" rather than with any theory, even a true theory, for the suffering of innocents outweighs theory. That is what Ivan means in maintaining his position "even if I were wrong," and he is paradoxically right to do so. It is passages like these that make us see why *The Brothers Karamazov* retains the power to move and persuade us as *Paradise Lost* no longer can. When Milton's God explains that our responsibility is not diminished by God's foreknowledge and that everyone, even the children, receive their proper reward or punishment since evil is our own fault, then we can hear Ivan's moral outrage and "catalogue of facts" subjecting this tissue of theological quibbles to the mockery it deserves.

The Spirit

Alyosha at last replies that all Ivan has shown is why the question of suffering cannot be answered with only God the Father. But we are not Jews or Muslims, we have God the Son, Alyosha adds, and so your argument actually strengthens Christian, as opposed to merely theist, belief: "You said just now, is there a being in the whole world who would have the right to forgive and could forgive? But there is a Being and He can forgive everything, all and for all, because He gave his Innocent blood for all and everything. You have forgotten Him" (*BK*, 292).

But Ivan has not forgotten him. In fact, as it turns out, Ivan's question about whether there is a being who could forgive was a prompt, a reminder to Alyosha to mention Jesus, whom Alyosha should have remembered even sooner. "Ah! The One without sin and His blood!" replies Ivan ironically. "No, I have not forgotten Him; on the contrary, I've been wondering all the time how it was you did not bring Him in before, for usually all arguments on your side put Him in the foreground" (*BK*, 292).

It is at this point that Ivan offers to recite his "poem" about the Grand Inquisitor. He presents this legend as a continuation of the argument in "Rebellion." As that chapter attacks God the Father, this one shows what is wrong with God the Son. Ivan has set up the discussion in just this way, and when Alyosha remembers the second person of the Trinity, he has fallen into Ivan's trap.

Now, for any Christian who recognizes the structure of Ivan's argument, an obvious question arises—so obvious that I am at a loss to explain why it does not dominate discussion of this novel but instead remains unasked. There are *three* persons to the Trinity: If the first two have been refuted, where is the third? In fact, the Holy Spirit, mentioned so often in the novel, *is* present in the dialogue of Ivan and Alyosha and it provides the tacit solution to Ivan's questions.

In *The Brothers Karamazov*, the Holy Spirit appears as sheer force of life and love of life. It inspires Zosima's dying brother to bless all of life, even the birds of the air, who sow not, neither do they reap, yet the heavenly father feedeth them; and the lily, for even Solomon is not clothed in such raiment. Thinking of his brother, Zosima implores: "Love every leaf, every ray of God's light. Love the animals, love the plants, love everything. If you love everything, you will perceive the divine mystery in things" (*BK*, 382–83). The poem Dmitri cites from Schiller thus becomes a hymn not only to joy but also to the Spirit, for the two are the same, as we see in the marriage at Cana and in Zosima's insistence that the joy of life is itself holy. In the lines Dmitri cites, joy inspires all creation, turns the flower to the sun and the soul to God. It echoes and is echoed by Zosima's words.[1]

Ivan has in fact experienced this joy, though he does not recognize its theological significance. He describes it in "The Brothers Make Friends," just before his attack on God the Father in "Rebellion" and God the Son in "The Grand Inquisitor." If I were struck with every horror of disillusionment, he tells Alyosha, I should still want to live. At least until he is thirty, Ivan expects that the "frantic and unseemly thirst for life," which he considers "a feature of the Karamazovs," will triumph over everything.

> The centripetal force on our planet is still fearfully strong, Alyosha. I have a longing for life, and I go on living in spite of logic. Though I may not believe in the order of the universe, yet I love the sticky little leaves as they open in spring. . . . I love the sticky leaves in spring, the blue sky—that's all it is. It's not a matter of intellect or logic, it's loving with one's inside, with one's stomach. (*BK*, 273–74)

Ivan begins ironically by using a materialist metaphor—centripetal force—to describe his longing for the earth. He experiences the joy but remains ironic about it precisely because it is unexplained, inexplicable, "non-Euclidian." But that's the whole point, as Alyosha tells him. One must first love life for it to make sense; one cannot love it because one has made sense of it.

> "Do you understand anything of my tirade, Alyosha?" Ivan laughed suddenly.
> "I understand too well, Ivan. One longs to love with one's inside, with one's stomach. You said that so well and I am awfully glad that you have such a longing for life," cried Alyosha. "I think one should love life above everything in the world."
> "Love life more than the meaning of it?"
> "Certainly, love it, regardless of logic, as you say, it must be regardless of logic, and it's only then one will understand the meaning of it." (*BK*, 274)

Ivan is not at all convinced that one must love life more than the meaning of it, love it in spite of logic, and he bans all such "non-Euclidian" considerations from his conversation in the next two chapters. Ivan tries to find justice and meaning by theory, and he shows, more clearly than anyone ever has, that theory cannot answer such questions.

---

1. I think Robert Louis Jackson is correct to observe in regard to Ivan's arguments for atheism: "Atheism for Dostoevsky is not so much an ideology as a state of behavior and consciousness. When the hero of *A Raw Youth* declares that he is not a believer, his father remarks, 'No, you are not an atheist, you are a cheerful person.' . . . One may declare oneself an atheist and yet not be one because of one's love of, or longing for, life." Robert Louis Jackson, "Last Stop: Virtue and Immortality in *The Brothers Karamazov*," *Dialogues with Dostoevsky: The Overwhelming Questions* (Stanford: Stanford UP, 1993), 299–300.

Ivan therefore concludes that meaning cannot be found, but his conclusion does not follow. Meaning can be found, but not by theory. It
comes not from the top down but from the bottom up, not by argument
but by experience—the experience of active love, of sharing people's joy
and exchanging onions with them.

Earlier in the novel, Madame Khokhlakova has asked Zosima to prove
the soul's immortality. She demands a theoretical proof, an answer to the
atheist doctrines she has heard, which tell her, as Turgenev's Bazarov says,
that only "burdocks" will grow on the grave. Zosima replies not by citing
the cosmological or the ontological arguments for the existence of God
and immortality but by denying there can ever be a theoretical proof. But
that hardly matters, for faith does not come from proof or theory anyway;
it comes from experience, from the bottom up:

> "There's no proving it, though you can be convinced of it."
> "How?"
> "By the experience of active love. Strive to love your neighbor
> actively and indefatigably. In as far as you advance in love you will
> grow surer of the reality of God and of the immortality of your soul."
> (BK, 63)

Indeed, if there were a proof of God, then there would be no room for
faith, for "the free choice of the heart." If God and immortality could be
proven, we would be in the world of the Inquisitor. The essence of faith
depends on uncertainty, for only then can we be freely choosing God.
Proof of God comes from the devil. That is why in the stories of the temptations, the devil precisely demands of Jesus that he prove his divinity
by a miracle: but "Thou wouldst not enslave man by a miracle, and didst
crave faith freely given, not based on miracle" (BK, 304).

We become convinced of God by practicing love. Live in the Spirit and
discover life's meaning. There is no other way. Zosima emphasizes that
such love must be performed untheatrically, without any public acknowledgment; love is given as something ordinary, as one gives an onion to a
beggar.

Love life and love others, and faith may follow. That is what Alyosha
means when he tells Ivan that in loving the sticky green leaves, in loving
life more than the meaning of it, he is halfway to salvation. For the Spirit
is there for him. Ivan dismisses the love of life as the mere force of the
Karamazovs, but in the context of this novel, Karamazovism itself is in
reality the perversion of the Spirit. It is the love of life turned in the wrong
direction, but at its core is the love of sticky leaves. Karamazovism interprets the love of life as mere sensuality, much as the Inquisitor understands love of humanity as perversely eliminating human freedom. Both
perversions reflect how the "law of reflection of ideas" can turn the sacred
into its opposite. But the sacred is nevertheless there.[2]

The answer to Ivan's riddle, then, is already present in its preface,
though he does not see it, much as his diatribe against two persons of the

---

2. Robert L. Belknap stresses "love of life" as part of Karamazovism and its connection with its
   opposite, the tendency to suicide, in Belknap, *The Structure of* The Brothers Karamazov (The
   Hague: Mouton, 1967; reprint, Evanston: Northwestern UP, 1989), 22–24 (page citations are
   to the reprint edition).

Trinity evokes a tacit answer in the third. Dmitri does learn that the answer to "the babe" is the pillow and Alyosha that one must seek not a public miracle to astonish the unbelievers but the small gift of an onion. We may anticipate that those two brothers, in spite of all the suffering they may still undergo, will be saved, but Ivan may be destined to miss the meaning that lies right before his eyes. He does not see an answer as simple as a leaf: it remains cloaked in its ordinariness, and so a very ordinary demon comes to taunt him.

This devil specializes in "witty anecdotes about the other world" and in paradoxes of theology. But the Spirit who gives faith precedes all theology. The God we seek is always before us, in every seed, in the active love we may always practice, and in the onions we may ever give and receive.

Fyodor Dostoevsky: A Chronology

Dates are given "old style," according to the Julian calendar. Implemented by Julius Caesar in 46 B.C.E., the Julian calendar was replaced in most of Europe by the Gregorian calendar in 1582. By the nineteenth century, the Julian calendar was twelve days behind. Russia did not adopt the Gregorian calendar until 1918.

1821   Fyodor Mikhailovich Dostoevsky born at the Mariinsky Hospital for the Poor in Moscow on October 30. He is the second child of Mikhail Dostoevsky, a doctor at the hospital, and his wife, Maria Fyodorovna (née Nechaeva).

1837   Deaths of Maria Fyodorovna and the poet Alexander Pushkin. Dostoevsky wears mourning for both.

1838   Enrolls in the Academy of Military Engineering in Saint Petersburg, in accordance with his father's wishes. Dostoevsky nourishes hopes of becoming a writer and reads avidly.

1839   Dostoevsky's father dies in June at Darovoe, the family estate near Moscow. Persistent rumors suggest that he was murdered by his serfs, who were driven to violence by his cruelty. Dostoevsky says very little about his father's death in his correspondence. Although the manner of Dr. Dostoevsky's death has never been conclusively resolved, recent scholarship suggests that it was due to natural causes.

1843   Graduates from the Academy of Military Engineering and enters government service. Continues to read and write when free from official duties. Translates Balzac's 1833 novel *Eugénie Grandet*.

1844   Publishes his translation of *Eugénie Grandet*.
        Resigns from government duty immediately upon fulfilling the minimum period of service required from graduates of the Academy of Military Engineering. Pursues literary career.

1846   Publishes the short epistolary novel *Poor Folk* in Nikolay Nekrasov's journal *Petersburg Anthology*. Vissarion Belinsky hails the author as a new star in Russian letters, and Dostoevsky enjoys a brief but exhilarating period of acclaim in literary circles.
        Publishes *The Double* in the journal *Notes of the Fatherland*. Belinsky faults this work in a critical review, and Dostoevsky's star wanes.
        Publishes "Mr. Prokharchin" in *Notes of the Fatherland*.

1847   Publishes "The Landlady" and "Petersburg Chronicle" in the *Saint Petersburg News*.
        Begins visiting the Petrashevsky circle, a group of intellectuals who meet to discuss literature and politics.

1848   Publishes "A Faint Heart," "An Honest Thief," "Another Man's Wife and the Husband under the Bed," "The Christmas Party and the Wedding," and *White Nights* in *Notes of the Fatherland*.

1849   Joins what is now known as the Palm-Durov circle, a secret inner society within the Petrashevsky circle. Members of the Palm-Durov circle plan to acquire an illegal printing press and publish pamphlets inciting revolution.

    First parts of novella *Netochka Nezvanova* are published in *Notes of the Fatherland*.

    Arrested for his participation in the Petrashevsky circle in April and incarcerated in the Sts. Peter and Paul Fortress. While in solitary confinement, writes "A Little Hero" (not published until 1857).

    Dostoevsky's trial, April 29–November 16; he is convicted of treason and sentenced to death.

    Faces the firing squad on December 22 on Semenevsky Square in Petersburg, but is reprieved at the last minute. His sentence is commuted to four years of hard labor, to be followed by an indefinite period of military service in Siberian exile; he is put in chains and taken to Siberia by sled on December 24.

1850   Arrives at Tobolsk prison in Siberia in early January. After several weeks, Dostoevsky is transferred to a hard labor camp in Omsk, where he remains incarcerated for four years.

1854   On release from prison, Dostoevsky performs compulsory military service in Semipalatinsk (Siberia). He begins as a soldier and is eventually promoted to the rank of officer in October 1856.

1856   While in exile, writes *Uncle's Dream* and *The Village of Stepanchiko* (not published until 1859, in the journals *Russian Word* and *Notes of the Fatherland*).

1857   Marries Marya Dmitryevna Isayeva, the widow of an acquaintance, in February.

1859   Receives permission to resign from the military and move to Tver', a provincial city 120 miles from Moscow.

    Receives permission to return to Petersburg in December.

1860   Publishes a two-volume collection of his writings, including a revised but still fragmentary version of *Netochka Nezvanova*.

1861   Begins publishing the journal *Time* with his brother Mikhail.

    Publishes *The Insulted and Injured* in *Time*.

    For the next three years, Dostoevsky plays an active role in Russian intellectual life as the author of essays on art, current events, and history that appear in *Time*.

    Begins serial publication of *Notes from the House of the Dead* in the journal *Russian World*.

1862   Transfers publication of *Notes from the House of the Dead* to *Time* in April.

    The government grants Dostoevsky permission to travel abroad in June. Visits the exiled Russian radical Alexander Herzen in London and consults Parisian doctors about his epilepsy.

    Publishes "A Nasty Anecdote" in *Time* in November.

1863   Publishes *Winter Notes on Summer Impressions*, a critical description of French and British society with scathing analysis of the bourgeoisie, in *Time*.

Government censors construe Strakhov's *Time* article "A Fatal Question" (*Rokovoi vopros*) as sympathetic to Poland in the aftermath of a failed Polish uprising against the Russian Empire and force the journal to close in May.

Dostoevsky travels to Europe, where he is drawn to the roulette tables of gambling towns such as Baden-Baden. Joins his mistress, Apollinaria Suslova, in Paris.

1864   The government grants Mikhail Dostoevsky permission to publish a new journal, *Epoch*.

Dostoevsky publishes *Notes from Underground* in two installments in *Epoch*.

Marya Dmitryevna dies of tuberculosis in April after prolonged illness. Dostoevsky assumes responsibility for her son, Pavel Isayev (Pasha).

Mikhail dies suddenly in July, leaving Dostoevsky to manage *Epoch* alone. Dostoevsky voluntarily assumes responsibility for Mikhail's considerable debts and large family.

1865   *Epoch*, never as successful as *Time*, is forced to close in June due to insufficient subscriptions.

In desperate need of money, in July Dostoevsky signs with the publisher Fyodor Stellovsky a contract that provides an advance of 3,000 rubles in exchange for the right to publish a three-volume edition of Dostoevsky's works, plus one new novel. The contract stipulates that if the novel is not submitted on time, Stellovsky will gain the right to publish all of Dostoevsky's writings for nine years without paying royalties to the author.

Dostoevsky uses his advance to support Pasha Isayev, Mikhail's family, manage the many debts for which he is responsible, and travel to Europe, where he frequently plays roulette.

1866   First installment of *Crime and Punishment* appears in *The Russian Messenger* in January.

Hires a young stenographer, Anna Grigoryevna Snitkina (1846–1918), in October to meet Stellovsky's deadline for his new novel, *The Gambler*. Work on *Crime and Punishment* and *The Gambler* proceeds simultaneously.

1867   Marries Anna Grigoryevna in February. All his future works are composed through dictation to her.

Dostoevsky and Anna Grigoryevna leave for Europe in April to escape his creditors, who could have him placed in debtors' prison. The couple plans on a brief sojourn abroad, but are compelled to lead a semi-nomadic life in Europe until 1871.

1868   Anna Grigoryevna gives birth to their first child, Sofya (Sonya), in February, while they are living in Geneva. The baby dies three months later. Anna Grigoryevna and Dostoevsky suffer intensely after her death.

Publishes *The Idiot* in the *Russian Messenger*, January–December.

1869   A second daughter, Lyubov', is born in Dresden in September.

1870   Publishes *The Eternal Husband* in the journal *Dawn*.

1871   Begins publishing *Demons* in *The Russian Messenger*.

Dostoevsky and Anna Grigoryevna return to Petersburg in July. On July 16, shortly after their arrival, Anna Grigoryevna gives birth to a son, Fyodor.

—Dostoevsky meets Konstantin Pobedonostsev, Procurator of the Holy Synod, in late 1871 or early 1872. He will consult with Pobedonostsev regularly while composing *The Brothers Karamazov*.

1872   To save money and to escape the pressures of the capital, Dostoevsky and his family begin spending summers in Staraya Russa, a small town near Petersburg that will serve as a prototype for Skotoprigonevsk.

1873   Dostoevsky becomes editor of *The Citizen*, in which he publishes a column, "The Diary of a Writer." He frequently clashes with the journal's conservative publisher, Prince Meshchersky.

1874   Serves two days in jail for an 1873 "violation of censorship regulations."

Friction with Meshchersky combines with his desire to devote himself full-time to writing a novel; Dostoevsky resigns from editorship of *The Citizen* in April in order to compose *The Adolescent*.

Seeks help for his epilepsy and emphysema from doctors and mineral springs in Bad Ems, Germany, and Geneva in June.

1875   Serial publication of *The Adolescent* begins in *Notes from the Fatherland* in January.

A second son, Alexey, is born in August.

Travels to Bad Ems for his health.

1876   Realizes his long-held ambition to publish a one-man monthly journal, and begins serving as editor and sole contributor to *The Diary of a Writer*, which begins publication in January. Some of his best-known short works will be published in the *Diary*: "The Boy at Christ's Christmas Tree" (1876), "The Peasant Marey" (1876), "The Meek One" (1876), and "The Dream of a Ridiculous Man" (1877).

Tsar Alexander II subscribes to the *Diary* on Pobedonostsev's recommendation.

1877   Suspends publication of the *Diary* after the December issue in order to write *The Brothers Karamazov*.

1878   Works on *The Brothers Karamazov* in late spring/early summer.

Son Alexey dies of a massive epileptic seizure in May. Devastated, Dostoevsky travels to the monastery Optina Pustyn' in June, where the elder Amvrosy offers spiritual comfort and contributes to the portrait of Zosima.

1879   Begins publishing *The Brothers Karamazov* in the *Russian Messenger* in January.

1880   Delivers what becomes known as his Pushkin Speech at a celebration honoring the poet in Moscow in June. Dostoevsky and the Russian public consider the speech to be one of his greatest triumphs.

Publishes the Pushkin Speech, plus commentary, in a special issue of *The Diary of a Writer* in August.

1881   Resumes publication of the *Diary* in January.

Dies of a lung hemorrhage, a consequence of his emphysema, at 8:38 P.M. on January 28. Pobedonostsev arranges a state funeral for Dostoevsky, which elicits a massive outpouring of grief and participation from Russian society. Dostoevsky is buried in the Tikhvin Cemetery of the Alexander Nevsky Monastery in Petersburg. Through Pobedonostsev's influence, Anna Grigoryevna receives an annual pension from the tsar.

The Brothers Karamazov published as a complete novel.

Selected Bibliography

• indicates works included or excerpted in this Norton Critical Edition.

Editions

Dostoevsky, Fyodor. *Polnoe sobranie sochinenii v tridtsati tomakh*. Ed. G. M. Fridlender et al. (Leningrad: Nauka, 1972–90).
———. *A Writer's Diary*. Trans. and annotated by Kenneth Lantz, with an introductory study by Gary Saul Morson. Evanston, IL: Northwestern UP, 1994.
• ———. *The Brothers Karamazov*: A Norton Critical Edition. Trans. Constance Garnett. Ed. Ralph E. Matlaw. New York: Norton, 1976.
The Notebooks for The Brothers Karamazov. Ed. and trans. Edward Wasiolek. Chicago: U of Chicago P, 1971.
Lowe, David A., and Ronald Meyer, ed. and trans. *Fyodor Dostoevsky: Complete Letters*. 5 vols. Ann Arbor, MI: Ardis, 1988–91.

Biographies

Berdyaev, Nikolay. *Dostoevsky*. Trans. Donald Attwater. New York: Meridian Books, 1957.
Carr, Edward Hallett. *Dostoevsky: A New Biography, 1821–1881*. New York: Houghton Mifflin, 1931 (1973).
Coulson, Jessie Senior. *Dostoevsky: A Self-Portrait*. New York: Oxford UP, 1962.
Frank, Joseph. *Dostoevsky: The Seeds of Revolt, 1821–1849*. Princeton: Princeton UP, 1976.
———. *Dostoevsky: The Years of Ordeal, 1850–1859*. Princeton: Princeton UP, 1983.
———. *Dostoevsky: The Stir of Liberation, 1860–1865*. Princeton: Princeton UP, 1986.
———. *Dostoevsky: The Miraculous Years, 1865–1871*. Princeton: Princeton UP, 1995.
———. *Dostoevsky: The Mantle of the Prophet, 1871–1881*. Princeton: Princeton UP, 2002.
———. *Dostoevsky: A Writer in His Time*. Ed. Mary Petrusewicz. Princeton: Princeton UP, 2010.
Lavrin, Janko. *Dostoevsky: A Study*. 1947. Rpt. Whitefish, MT: Kessinger Publishing, LLC, 2005.
Magarshack, David. *Dostoevsky*. New York: Harcourt, Brace, and World, Inc., 1963; Westport, CT: Greenwood Press, 1975.
Mikhailovsky, N. K. *Dostoevsky—A Cruel Talent*. Ann Arbor, MI: Ardis, 1978.
Mochulsky, Konstantin. *Dostoevsky: His Life and Work*. Trans. Michael A. Minihan. Princeton: Princeton UP, 1967.
Simmons, Ernest J. *Dostoevsky: The Making of a Novelist*. New York: Vintage Books, 1950.
Troyat, Henri. *Firebrand: The Life of Dostoevsky*. New York: Roy Publishers, 1946.
Yarmolinsky, Avrahm. *Dostoevsky: His Life and Art*. New York: Criterion Books, 1957.

Reference Aids

Lantz, Kenneth A. *The Dostoevsky Encyclopedia*. Westport, CT: Greenwood Press, 2004.
Leatherbarrow, William J. *Fedor Dostoevsky: A Reference Guide*. Boston: G. K. Hall, 1990.

Serial Publications

Bulletin. The International Dostoevsky Society. Pittsburgh, PA. Vols. 1–9, 1971–79.
Dostoevsky Studies: The Journal of the International Dostoevsky Society. Klagenfurt. Vols. 1–9, 1980–88.
Dostoevsky Studies: The Journal of the International Dostoevsky Society. Salt Lake City, UT; Idyllwild, CA; Dresden; Tübingen. New Series, vols. 1–12, 1993–2008.

General Studies of Dostoevsky

Anderson, Roger B. *Dostoevsky: Myths of Duality*. Gainesville: U of Florida P, 1986.
Bakhtin, Mikhail. *Problems of Dostoevsky's Poetics*. Ed. and trans. Caryl Emerson. Minneapolis: U of Minnesota P, 1984.
Barnhart, Joe E., ed. *Dostoevsky's Polyphonic Talent*. Lanham, MD: UP of America, 2005.
Burnett, Leon, ed. *F. M. Dostoevsky: A Centenary Collection*. Oxford: Holdan Books, 1981.
Cassedy, Steven. *Dostoevsky's Religion*. Stanford, CA: Stanford UP, 2005.
Catteau, Jacques. *Dostoevsky and the Process of Literary Creation*. Trans. Audrey Littlewood. Cambridge: Cambridge UP, 1989.
Fanger, Donald. *Dostoevsky and Romantic Realism: A Study of Dostoevsky in Relation to Balzac, Dickens, and Gogol*. Foreword by Caryl Emerson. Evanston, IL: Northwestern UP, 1998. Orig. pub. Harvard UP, 1965.
Flath, Carol A. *Dostoevsky's Secrets: Reading against the Grain*. Evanston, IL: Northwestern UP, 2009.
Gibson, Alexander Boyce. *The Religion of Dostoevsky*. London: S.C.M.P., 1973.
Holquist, Michael. *Dostoevsky and the Novel*. Princeton: Princeton UP, 1977.
Ivanits, Linda. *Dostoevsky and the Russian People*. New York: Cambridge UP, 2008.
Ivanov, Vyacheslav. *Freedom and the Tragic Life: A Study in Dostoevsky*. Trans. Norman Cameron. 1960; rpt. Wolfeboro, NH: Longwood Academic, 1989.
Jackson, Robert Louis. *The Art of Dostoevsky: Deliriums and Nocturnes*. Princeton: Princeton UP, 1981.
———. *Dialogues with Dostoevsky: The Overwhelming Questions*. Stanford, CA: Stanford UP, 1993.
———. ed. and intro. *Dostoevsky: New Perspectives*. Englewood Cliffs, NJ: Prentice-Hall, 1984.
• ———. ed. *A New Word on* The Brothers Karamazov. Evanston, IL: Northwestern UP, 2004.
Jones, John. *Dostoevsky*. Oxford: Oxford UP, 1983.
Jones, Malcolm V. *Dostoevsky After Bakhtin: Readings in Dostoevsky's Fantastic Realism*. Cambridge: Cambridge UP, 1990.
———. *Dostoevsky and the Dynamics of Religious Experience*. London: Anthem Press, 2005.
——— and Garth M. Terry, eds. *New Essays on Dostoevsky*. Cambridge: Cambridge UP, 1983.
Knapp, Liza. *The Annihilation of Inertia: Dostoevsky and Metaphysics*. Evanston, IL: Northwestern UP, 1996.
Kroeker, P. Travis and Bruce Kinsey Ward. *Remembering the End: Dostoevsky as Prophet to Modernity*. Boulder, CO: Westview Press, 2001.
Leatherbarrow, William J., ed. *The Cambridge Companion to Dostoevskii*. New York: Cambridge UP, 2002.
———. *A Devil's Vaudeville: The Demonic in Dostoevsky's Major Fiction*. Evanston, IL: Northwestern UP, 2005.
Lyngstad, Alexandra H. *Dostoevsky and Schiller*. The Hague and Paris: Mouton, 1975.
Martinsen, Deborah A. *Surprised by Shame: Dostoevsky's Liars and Narrative Exposure*. Columbus: Ohio State UP, 2003.
McReynolds, Susan. *Redemption and the Merchant God: Dostoevsky's Economy of Salvation and Antisemitism*. Evanston, IL: Northwestern UP, 2008.
Meerson, Olga. *Dostoevsky's Taboos*. Dresden: Dresden UP, 1998.
Miller, Robin Feuer, ed. *Critical Essays on Dostoevsky*. Boston: G. K. Hall, 1986.
———. *Dostoevsky's Unfinished Journey*. New Haven, CT: Yale UP, 2007.
Murav, Harriet. *Holy Foolishness: Dostoevsky's Novels & the Poetics of Cultural Critique*. Stanford, CA: Stanford UP, 1992.
• Pattison, George and Diane Oenning Thompson, eds. *Dostoevsky and the Christian Tradition*. New York: Cambridge UP, 2001.

Peace, Richard A. *Dostoyevsky: An Examination of the Major Novels*. Cambridge: Cambridge UP, 1971.

Rosenshield, Gary. *Western Law, Russian Justice: Dostoevsky, the Jury Trial, and the Law*. Madison: U of Wisconsin P, 2005.

Rowe, William Woodin. *Dostoevsky: Child and Man in His Works*. New York: New York UP, 1968.

Scanlan, James P. "Dostoevsky's Arguments for Immortality." *Russian Review* 59 (2000): 1–20.

———. *Dostoevsky the Thinker*. Ithaca, NY: Cornell UP, 2002.

Shestov, Lev. *Dostoevsky, Tolstoy, and Nietzsche*. Athens: Ohio UP, 1969.

Studies in East European Thought, special issue: Dostoevskij's Significance for Philosophy and Theology. Ed. Robert Bird. The Netherlands: Springer. 59.1–2, June 2007.

Terras, Victor. *Reading Dostoevsky*. Madison: U of Wisconsin P, 1998.

· Wasiolek, Edward. *Dostoevsky: The Major Fiction*. Cambridge: M.I.T. Press, 1964.

Wellek, René, ed. *Dostoevsky: A Collection of Critical Essays*. Englewood Cliffs, NJ: Prentice-Hall, 1962.

Williams, Rowan. *Dostoevsky: Language, Faith and Fiction*. Waco, TX: Baylor UP, 2008.

Young, Sarah and Lesley Milne, eds. *Dostoevsky on the Threshold of Other Worlds: Essays in Honour of Malcolm V. Jones*. Ilkeston, UK: Bramcot Press, 2006.

Studies of The Brothers Karamazov

Anderson, Roger B. "The Meaning of Carnival in *The Brothers Karamazov*." *Slavic and East European Journal* 23 (1979): 458–78.

Barineau, R. Maurice. "The Triumph of Ethics Over Doubt: Dostoevsky's *The Brothers Karamazov*." *Christianity and Literature* 43.3–4 (1994): 375–92.

Belknap, Robert L. *The Genesis of* The Brothers Karamazov: *The Aesthetics, Ideology, and Psychology of Text Making*. Evanston, IL: Northwestern UP, 1990.

———. *The Structure of* The Brothers Karamazov. The Hague: Mouton, 1967.

Bloom, Harold. ed. *Fyodor Dostoevsky's* The Brothers Karamazov (Bloom's Modern Critical Interpretations). New York: Chelsea House Publishing, 1988.

Browning, Gary L. "Zosima's 'Secret of Renewal' in *The Brothers Karamazov*." *The Slavic and East European Journal* 33.4 (1989): 516–29.

Camus, Albert. "The Rejection of Salvation." *The Rebel*. Trans. Anthony Bower. New York: Knopf, 1956: 55–61.

Carter, Geoffrey. "Freud and *The Brothers Karamazov*." *Literature and Psychology*. 31.3 (1981): 15–32.

Contino, Paul J. "Zosima, Mikhail, and Prosaic Confessional Dialogue in Dostoevsky's *The Brothers Karamazov*." *Studies in the Novel* 27.1 (Spring 1995): 63–86.

Danow, David. "Subtexts of *The Brothers Karamazov*." *Russian Literature* 11.2 (1982): 173–208.

Eng, Jan van der and J. M. Meijer. The Brothers Karamazov *by F. M. Dostoevskij*. The Hague: Mouton, 1971.

Flath, Carol A. "The Passion of Dmitrii Karamazov." *Slavic Review* 58 (1999): 584–99.

Freud, Sigmund. "Dostoevsky and Parricide." *Collected Works*, vol. 21. New York, 1976.

Friedrich, Paul. "Grushenka." *Dostoevsky Studies* n.s. II (2007): 38–55.

Holland, Kate. "Novelizing Religious Experience: The Generic Landscape of *The Brothers Karamazov*," *Slavic Review* 66.1 (Spring 2007): 63–81.

Hruska, Anne. "The Sins of Children in *The Brothers Karamazov*: Serfdom, Hierarchy, and Transcendence." *Christianity and Literature* 54.4 (Summer 2005): 471–95.

Ivanits, Linda J. "Hagiography in Brat'ja Karamazovy: Zosima, Ferapont, and the Russian Monastic Saint." *Russian Language Journal* 34 (1980): 109–26.

· Jackson, Robert Louis. Ed. *A New Word on* The Brothers Karamozov. Evanston, IL: Northwestern UP, 2003.

Kaladiouk, Anna Schur. "On 'Sticking to the Fact' and 'Understanding Nothing': Dostoevsky and the Scientific Method." *Russian Review* 65.3 (July 2006): 417–38.

Katz, Michael R. "Dostoevsky and Natural Science." *Dostoevsky Studies* 9 (1988): 63–76.

———. "The Theme of Maternity in Alesa Karamazov's Four-Year-Old Memory." *The Slavic and East European Journal* 34 (1990): 506–10.

Knapp, Liza. "The Fourth Dimension of the Non-Euclidean Mind: Time in *The Brothers Karamazov*, or Why Ivan Karamazov's Devil Does Not Carry a Watch." *Dostoevsky Studies* 8 (1987): 105–20.

Lawrence, D. H. "The Grand Inquisitor." *Selected Literary Criticism*. Ed. Anthony Beal. New York: Viking, 1961: 233–41.

Leatherbarrow, William J. *Fyodor Dostoevsky:* The Brothers Karamazov. Cambridge: Cambridge UP, 1992.

Lesic-Thomas, Andrea. "The Answer Job Did Not Give: Dostoevsky's Brat'ia Karamazovy and Camus's *La Peste. Modern Language Review,* 101. 3 (July 2006): 774–88.

Linnér, Sven. *Starets Zosima in* The Brothers Karamazov: *A Study in the Mimesis of Virtue.* Stockholm: Almqvist & Wiksell International, 1975.

Matlaw, Ralph E. The Brothers Karamazov: *Novelistic Technique.* 'S-Gravenhage: Mouton, 1957.

McReynolds, Susan. "'You Can Buy the Whole World:' The Problem of Redemption in *The Brothers Karamazov." Slavic and East European Journal* 52.1 (Spring 2008): 87–111.

• Miller, Robin Feuer. The Brothers Karamazov: *Worlds of the Novel.* New Haven, CT: Yale UP, 2008.

Morson, Gary Saul. "Verbal Pollution in The Brothers Karamazov." *PTL: A Journal for Descriptive Poetics and Theory* 3 (1978): 223–33.

Murav, Harriet. "From Skandalon to Scandal: Ivan's Rebellion Reconsidered." *Slavic Review* 63.4 (Winter 2004): 756–70.

Natov, Nadine. "Dostoevskii and the Theatre: Stage Adaptations of *The Brothers Karamazov." Canadian-American Slavic Studies* 8 (1974): 434–53.

———. "The Ethical and Structural Significance of the Three Temptations in *The Brothers Karamazov." Dostoevsky Studies: Journal of the International Dostoevsky Society* 8 (1987): 3–44.

Neuhäuser, Rudolf. "*The Brothers Karamazov*: A Contemporary Reading of Book VI, 'A Russian Monk.'" *Dostoevsky Studies* 7 (1986): 135–51.

Oates, Joyce C. "The Double Vision of *The Brothers Karamazov." Journal of Aesthetics and Art Criticism* 27 (1968): 203–13.

Perlina, Nina. *Varieties of Poetic Utterance: Quotation in* The Brothers Karamazov. Lanham, MD: UP of America, 1985.

Prestel, David K. "Father Zosima and the Eastern Orthodox Hesychast Tradition." *Dostoevsky Studies* n.s. 2 (1998): 41–59.

Rahv, Philip. "The Legend of the Grand Inquisitor." *Partisan Review* 21 (1954).

Rosenshield, Gary. "Mystery and Commandment in *The Brothers Karamazov*: Leo Baeck and Fedor Dostoevsky." *Journal of the American Academy of Religion* 62.2 (1994): 483–508.

Rozanov, V. V. *Dostoevsky and the Legend of the Grand Inquisitor.* Ithaca, NY: Cornell UP, 1972.

Sewall, R. B. "The Tragic World of the Karamazovs." *Tragic Themes in Western Literature.* Ed. Cleanth Brooks. New Haven, CT: Yale UP, 1955.

Shrayer, Maxim D. "Dostoevsky, the Jewish Question, and *The Brothers Karamazov." Slavic Review* 61 (2002): 273–91.

Silbajoris, Rimvydas. "The Children in *The Brothers Karamazov." Slavic and East European Journal* 7 (1963).

Slochower, Harry. "Incest in *The Brothers Karamazov." American Imago: Studies in Psychoanalysis and Culture* 16 (1959): 127–45.

Smyth, Sarah. "The 'Lukovka' Legend in *The Brothers Karamazov." Irish Slavonic Studies* 7 (1986): 41–51.

Stanton, Leonard J. "Zedergolm's *Life of Elder Leonid of Optina* as a Source of Dostoevsky's *The Brothers Karamazov." The Russian Review* 49.4 (1990): 443–55.

Stoeber, Michael. "Dostoevsky's Devil: The Will to Power." *The Journal of Religion* 74 (1994): 26–44.

Sutherland, Stewart R. *Atheism and the Rejection of God: Contemporary Philosophy and* The Brothers Karamazov. Oxford: Blackwell, 1977.

Terras, Victor. *A Karamazov Companion: Commentary on the Genesis, Language, and Style of Dostoevsky's Novel.* Madison: U of Wisconsin P, 1981.

Thompson, Diane Oenning. The Brothers Karamazov *and the Poetics of Memory.* New York: Cambridge UP, 1991.

———. "Poetic Transformations of Scientific Facts in *Brat'ja Karamazovy." Dostoevsky Studies* 8 (1987): 73–85.

Todd, William Mills. "Storied Selves: Constructing Characters in *The Brothers Karamazov." Self and Story in Russian History.* Ed. and Intro. Laura Engelstein and Stephanie Sandler. Ithaca, NY: Cornell UP, 2000.

Vinokur, Val. "Facing the Devil in Dostoevsky's *The Brothers Karamazov." Stanford Slavic Studies* 29–30: *Word, Music, History: A Festschrift for Caryl Emerson.* Ed. Lazar Fleishman, Gabriella Safran, Michael Wachtel (2005): 464–76. (2005).

Vladiv-Glover, Slobodanka. "Dostoevsky, Freud, and Parricide: Deconstructive Notes on *The Brothers Karamazov.*" *New Zealand Slavonic Journal* (1993): 7–34.

Wasiolek, Edward, ed. *The Brothers Karamazov and the Critics.* Belmont, CA: Wadsworth, 1967.

Whitcomb, Curt M. "The Temptation of Miracle in *Brat'ja Karamazovy.*" *Slavic and East European Journal* 36 (1992): 189–201.

Internet Resources

www.dostoevsky-na.org: Website of the North American Dostoevsky Society.

www.dostoevsky.org: Website of the International Dostoevsky Society.

http://eng.md.spb.ru: Website of the Dostoevsky Museum in Saint Petersburg, Russia.